COMPUTER GRAPHICS

Annual Conference Series 1996

SIGGRAPH 96
Conference Proceedings
August 4 – 9, 1996
Papers Chair: Holly Rushmeier
Panels Chair: Theresa-Marie Rhyne

A publication of ACM SIGGRAPH

Sponsored by the ACM's Special Interest Group on Computer Graphics

PROCEEDINGS

The Association for Computing Machinery, Inc.
1515 Broadway
New York, New York 10036

Sample Citation Information:
...Proceedings of SIGGRAPH 96 (New Orleans, LA, August 4-9, 1996). In *Computer Graphics* Proceedings, Annual Conference Series, 1996, ACM SIGGRAPH, pp. xx - yy.

Orders from ACM Members:

Additional copies may be ordered:

U.S.A. and Canada:
ACM Order Department
P.O. Box 12114
Church Street Station
New York, NY 10257
Telephone: +1-800-342-6626
Telephone: +1-212-626-0500
Fax: +1-212-944-1318
E-mail: `orders@acm.org`
URL: `http://www.acm.org/`

All other countries:
ACM European Service Center
108 Cowley Road
Oxford OX4 1JF
United Kingdom
Telephone: +44-1-865-382338
Fax: +44-1-865-381338
E-mail: `acm_europe@acm.org`

ACM Order Number: 428960
ACM ISBN: 0-89791-746-4
ACM ISSN: 1069-529X

Orders from nonmembers of ACM:

Addison-Wesley will pay postage and handling on orders accompanied by check. Credit card orders may be placed by mail or by calling the Addison-Wesley Order Department at the number above. Followup inquiries should be directed at the same number. Please include the Addison-Wesley ISBN with your order:
A-W Softcover Proceedings and CD-ROM Package ISBN: 0-201-94800-1

United States:
Addison-Wesley Publishing Company
Order Department
Jacob Way
Reading, MA 01867
Telephone: +1-800-447-2226

Europe/Middle East:
Addison-Wesley Publishing Group
Concertgebouwplein 25
1071 LM Amsterdam
The Netherlands
Telephone: +31-20-6717296
Fax: +31-20-6645334

Germany/Austria/Switzerland:
Addison-Wesley Verlag Deutschland GmbH
Hildachstraße 15d
Wachsbleiche 7-12
53111 Bonn
Germany
Telephone: +49-228-98-515-0
Fax: +49-228-98-515-99

United Kingdom/Africa:
Addison-Wesley Publishers Ltd.
Finchampstead Road
Wokingham, Berkshire RG11 2NZ
United Kingdom
Telephone: +44-734-794000
Fax: +44-734-794035

Asia:
Addison-Wesley Singapore Pte. Ltd.
15 Beach Road
#05-02/09/10 Beach Centre
Singapore 0718
Telephone: +65-339-7503
Fax: +65-339-9709

Japan:
Addison-Wesley Publishers Japan Ltd.
Nichibo Building
1-2-2 Sarugakucho
Chiyoda-ku, Tokyo 101
Japan
Telephone: +81-33-2914581
Fax: +81-33-2914592

Australia/New Zealand:
Addison-Wesley Publishers Pty. Ltd.
6 Byfield Street
North Ryde, N.S.W. 2113
Australia
Telephone: +61-2-878-5411
Fax: +61-2-878-5830

Latin America:
Addison-Wesley Iberoamericana S.A.
Boulevard de las Cataratas #3
Colonia Jardines del Pedregal
Delegacion Alvaro Obregon
01900 Mexico D.F.
Telephone: +52-5-660-2695
Fax: +52-5-660-4930

Canada:
Addison-Wesley Publishing (Canada) Ltd.
26 Prince Andrew Place
Don Mills, Ontario M3C 2T8 Canada
Telephone: +1-416-447-5101
Fax: +1-416-443-0948

Contents

Papers Sessions, Thursday, 08 August 1996

8:15 - 10:00 **Animation**
Chair: Jessica Hodgins

10:15 - 12:00 **Geometry**
Chair: Jules Bloomenthal

1:30 - 3:15 **Storytelling**
Chair: Richard Parent

3:30 - 5:15 **Reproduction/Postproduction**
Chair: Gary Meyer

Papers Sessions, Friday, 09 August 1996

Panels Sessions, Wednesday, 07 August 1996

Panels Sessions, Thursday, 08 August 1996

Panels Sessions, Friday, 09 August 1996

Papers Preface

This volume documents the presentations made at SIGGRAPH 96. The 52 papers printed here are the end result of a tremendous amount of creative work and a highly selective review process. They represent the state of the art in computer graphics and interactive techniques. The panels sessions are highlighted in the Preface to the Panels section of this volume.

Several years ago there was concern that the subject matter represented in SIGGRAPH papers was tending to become too narrow, and divorced from the mainstream computer graphics community. Thanks to the efforts of previous papers chairs, and many other dedicated, imaginative people, this has not happened. This year excellent papers were submitted in a rich variety of subject areas. The diversity was so great that one of the challenges was to group sets of papers into sessions that made sense.

Credit for the quality of these proceedings goes first and foremost to the authors. They contributed a great deal of effort and creativity to produce this work, and I am very thankful that they chose SIGGRAPH as the place to present it. All of the authors who submitted papers, both accepted and rejected, are responsible for keeping the SIGGRAPH papers program vital.

Credit also goes to the 24 papers committee members, who donated enormous blocks of time from busy schedules to carefully read and evaluate the 247 submissions. Each submission received 5 reviews, two by committee members and three by appointed reviewers. As a result, each committee member had to review approximately 20 papers, and find an additional 3 reviewers each for 10 of those papers. Committee members were chosen for their leadership in the field, their reputation for honesty and good judgement, and their capacity to enjoy and appreciate other people's work. They all scrupulously avoided any involvement with decisions on papers they were connected with in any way.

The over 400 appointed reviewers selected by the committee members also deserve a lot of credit. Appointed reviewers write lengthy, thoughtful reviews, with nothing in return except the satisfaction of serving the computer graphics community. The papers program could not exist without these contributions.

Credit for the coordination of the printing of this volume and the production of the corresponding CD-ROM goes to Stephen Spencer, SIGGRAPH Director for Publications.

Politics and weather made the administration of the papers program unusually challenging. All papers were to be delivered to my place of employment, the National Institute of Standards and Technology (NIST), an agency of the United States Department of Commerce, located in Gaithersburg, Maryland. On December 18, 1995, NIST was shut down since the government had not appropriated money for the operation of the Department. During a shutdown, facilities are not only closed, but it is against the law for employees to work voluntarily or use government equipment. Historically shutdowns had never lasted more than a few days. As the weeks wore on during this time though, panic set in as submissions accumulated out of reach in the NIST mail room, along with the mountains of other mail for the 3000-employee agency.

Legislation was eventually passed to reopen government January 8, two days before the North American papers deadline. Unfortunately, on January 7, the East Coast was hit by one of the biggest blizzards of the century. I was on the phone and e-mail almost continuously for three days reassuring concerned authors from all over the world that their submission would not be counted late because of the weather.

On January 10, the roads began to clear, but NIST remained closed. Despite the policy that submissions would be accepted as long as they were sent by a courier that would have reached NIST on time under normal circumstances, some people tried to deliver papers the 10th. One individual arrived at NIST after flying across the country and driving through the Washington region in the snow. When the guard wouldn't let him into NIST he made numerous phone calls and drove around Gaithersburg until he located my house. We had finally been able to get out, so he found no one home. Our front door was standing wide open, so he left the paper in our entry way and left.

On January 11, NIST finally reopened, and 190 papers were delivered to my office. I loaded up several carfuls and took them home. Another blizzard came on January 12, the due date for papers from outside North America. The city was closed again. My administrative assistant could not come to help open, log and sort the papers. My husband was pressed into service instead.

Turner Whitted, the 1997 papers chair, had been scheduled to come up from North Carolina and help sort the papers out for distribution to the committee. The weather made this impossible. Fortunately, we had required electronic abstracts for all papers. Instead of meeting together we used ftp, e-mail and the telephone to sort out all of the papers.

January 14 was a Sunday, and Monday January 15 was a Federal holiday. Finally on January 16, the rest of the papers sent by means of express services were delivered. Thanks to the electronic abstracts, we knew what papers to expect. On the 16th we were also able to rescue the rest of the submissions from the still overwhelmed NIST mail room. We worked frantically, and by the end of the week all of the papers and electronic abstracts were logged in, acknowledged and delivered to the committee members.

The rest of the process had its ups and downs, but settled down to being a more "normal" paper review process. The committee members worked hard, and we met to make the final decisions in a very chilly Washington, DC on March 8 – 10. As the result of a lot of preparation by and discussions between committee members beforehand, the meeting went very smoothly. As in past years, committee members left the room any time a paper they were connected with was discussed. There was no quota for the number of papers to be accepted. Each paper was judged individually on the basis of its content and clarity of exposition. On March 11, the notifications of the results were sent to all submitters.

I would like to thank my husband Russell and my administrative assistant Amy Struble for their help processing papers. Our work was made much easier by following the procedures developed and passed along by the SIGGRAPH 95 Papers Chair, Rob Cook. I would also like to thank my NIST co-workers for helping me through everything – Christine Piatko, Bob Lipman, John Hagedorn, Tere Griffin, Jim Sims, Darcy Barnett, Bob Raybold, Lina DeLeonibus, Joan Murphy and Arlene Carlton. Finally, I would like to thank the whole SIGGRAPH 96 conference committee for their support – in particular Theresa-Marie Rhyne (Panels Chair), John Fujii (Conference Chair), and Molly Morgan (Conference Coordinator).

It was difficult, but the 1996 papers saga has a happy ending. You have the book of exciting ideas you are starting to read now. And yes, the paper that was delivered to my house January 10 is in here.

Holly Rushmeier
SIGGRAPH 96 Papers Chair

Panels Preface

Panels are the forum for discussing emerging technologies, debating technical and creative controversies, and sharing diverse viewpoints. This year, the Panels Committee selected seventeen panels and one special session for presentation at SIGGRAPH 96. The expanded descriptions of these sessions are published here. These writeups summarize the content of the panels, and provide an archival reference for the panel topics.

The panels selection process began at SIGGRAPH 95 in Los Angeles. There, the SIGGRAPH 96 Panels Committee began actively encouraging the submission of timely proposals for SIGGRAPH 96. The panels effort also joined a cross-functional early concept submission process with the courses, technical sketches, applications, Digital Bayou, and art show (known as The Bridge) programs. The deadline for early concept proposals was October 4, 1995. Twenty- five early concepts were received electronically and reviewed by the Panels Committee. The intent of early concept proposals was to provide review and comment for final proposal submissions. Twelve of the early concepts became final panel proposal submissions, with eight being selected for presentation at SIGGRAPH 96. In addition to assisting the concept proposal submitters, the early concept deadline also highlighted gaps in the content of the panels program. The Panels Committee then began to seek final proposal submissions to fill these holes.

In January 1996, we received thirty final panel submissions that reflected the wide range of interests in the computer graphics community. The Panels Committee met in February 1996 to determine the final selections for SIGGRAPH 96. Our goal was to select a combination of panels that cover important and developing topics, represent new insights, and illuminate differing viewpoints in computer graphics. After the jury process was completed, each panels committee member selected two or three panels to mentor until the final presentation of the panels at SIGGRAPH 96.

Many of the panels presented at SIGGRAPH 96 will highlight the role of networking and telecommunications in computer graphics. A number of the sessions ponder the World Wide Web and its implications for developing and presenting content. The hardware community is represented by two panels which should stimulate discussion. Virtual Reality, Visualization, Advanced Television, and Animation are also topics covered in the SIGGRAPH 96 Panels Program. Finally, we address public policy and social issues impacting the computer graphics community. We hope you find as much joy in attending this program as we experienced in creating it!

The SIGGRAPH 96 Panels Committee developed and shaped this program. The committee members were: Wes Bethel; Leo Hourvitz; Dorothy Simpson Krause; Bill Kroyer; Barbara Mones-Hattal; and Mary Whitton. We were ably assisted and kept in line by the SIGGRAPH 96 Panels Administrator, Dave Taylor. We are also genuinely indebted to the panel organizers for submitting great panel proposals, and the panelists for their contributions. The University of North Carolina at Chapel Hill's Computer Sciences Department graciously provided a computer account to run the SIGGRAPH 96 Panels Program during the December 1995 and January 1996 historic government shutdown. Finally, I would like to express gratitude to Holly Rushmeier (SIGGRAPH 96 Papers Chair) and Stephen Spencer (SIGGRAPH Director for Publications) for making the development of the technical program and the creation of the conference proceedings a memorable experience.

Theresa Marie Rhyne
SIGGRAPH 96 Panels Chair

1996 ACM SIGGRAPH Awards

Computer Graphics Achievement Award

Marc Levoy

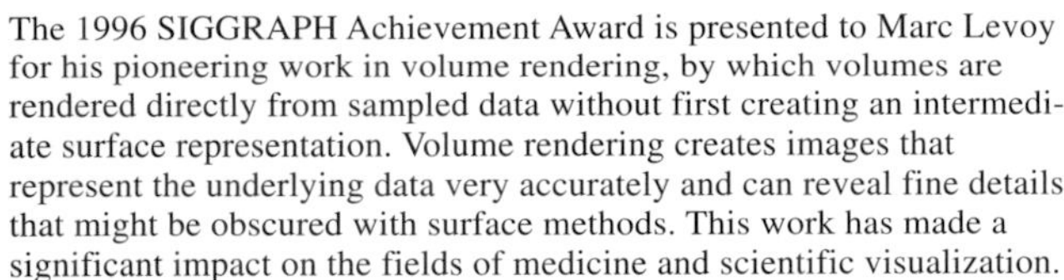

The 1996 SIGGRAPH Achievement Award is presented to Marc Levoy for his pioneering work in volume rendering, by which volumes are rendered directly from sampled data without first creating an intermediate surface representation. Volume rendering creates images that represent the underlying data very accurately and can reveal fine details that might be obscured with surface methods. This work has made a significant impact on the fields of medicine and scientific visualization.

Dr. Levoy began his work in volume rendering at the University of North Carolina, where he published many of the major papers in the field. He continued to advance the field by developing new algorithmic approaches, finding ways to improve efficiency, and demonstrating practical applications for the technique. Following his initial paper where he described the classic volume ray tracing algorithm, Dr. Levoy has published a number of papers that have continued to break new ground. These include a hybrid polygon/volume ray tracer and a volumetric morphing algorithm. He has also developed several algorithms for increasing the efficiency of volume rendering, including taking advantage of spatial coherence, adaptively refining the image, accounting for the observer's gaze, rendering in the frequency domain, and using a shear-warp factorization. More recently Dr. Levoy has begun to use volumetric techniques to aid in the acquisition of 3D models by using a volume representation to integrate multiple range images.

Marc Levoy began his computer graphics career as a freshman at Cornell University in 1971, received a Bachelor of Architecture degree in 1976, and a M.S. of Architecture in 1978. He was the principal developer of the Hanna-Barbera Computer Animation System and served as director of the Hanna-Barbera Animation Laboratory from 1980 through 1983. He then pursued studies in Computer Science and received a Ph. D. in 1989 from the University of North Carolina at Chapel Hill. Today he is a member of the faculty of Computer Science and Electrical Engineering at Stanford University. Professor Levoy received the NSF Young Investigator Award in 1991. He has published over 40 papers on computer animation, volume rendering, and machine vision.

Volume rendering has made a major impact on the many scientific, engineering and medical disciplines that create and display large multi-dimensional datasets. Marc Levoy has been instrumental in opening up this important area of research and is continuing to advance it. The quality of his work reflects both his creativity and his high level of academic professionalism. SIGGRAPH is pleased to present the SIGGRAPH Achievement Award to Marc Levoy.

Publications

Levoy, M., "Display of Surfaces from Volume Data," *IEEE Computer Graphics and Applications*, Vol. 8, No. 3, May 1988, pp. 29-37.

Levoy, M., "Volume Rendering by Adaptive Refinement," *The Visual Computer*, Vol. 6, No. 1, February 1990, pp. 2-7.

Levoy, M., "A Hybrid Ray Tracer for Rendering Polygon and Volume Data," *IEEE Computer Graphics and Applications*, Vol. 10, No. 2, March 1990, pp. 33-40.

Levoy, M. and Whitaker, R., "Gaze-Directed Volume Rendering," *Computer Graphics* (Proc. 1990 Symposium on Interactive 3D Graphics), Vol. 24, No. 2, Snowbird, Utah, March 1990, pp. 217-223.

Levoy, M., "Efficient Ray Tracing of Volume Data," *ACM Transactions on Graphics*, Vol. 9, No. 3, July 1990, pp. 245-261.

Totsuka, T. and Levoy, M., "Frequency Domain Volume Rendering," Proceedings of SIGGRAPH 93 (Anaheim, California, August 1-6, 1993). In *Computer Graphics* Proceedings, Annual Conference Series, 1993, ACM SIGGRAPH, pp. 271-278.

Lacroute, P. and Levoy, M., "Fast Volume Rendering Using a Shear-Warp Factorization of the Viewing Transformation," Proceedings of SIGGRAPH 94 (Orlando, Florida, July 24-29, 1994). In *Computer Graphics* Proceedings, Annual Conference Series, 1994, ACM SIGGRAPH, pp. 451-458.

Lerios, A., Garfinkle, C., Levoy, M., "Feature-Based Volume Metamorphosis," Proceedings of SIGGRAPH 95 (Los Angeles, CA, August 6-11, 1995). In *Computer Graphics* Proceedings, Annual Conference Series, 1995, ACM SIGGRAPH, pp. 449-456.

Curless, B. and Levoy, M., "A Volumetric Method for Building Complex Models from Range Images," Proceedings of SIGGRAPH 96 (New Orleans, LA, August 4–9, 1996). In *Computer Graphics* Proceedings, Annual Conference Series, 1996, ACM SIGGRAPH, pp. 303-312.

Previous Award Recipients

1995 Kurt Akeley
1994 Kenneth E. Torrance
1993 Pat Hanrahan
1992 Henry Fuchs
1991 James T. Kajiya
1990 Richard Shoup and Alvy Ray Smith
1989 John Warnock
1988 Alan H. Barr
1987 Robert Cook
1986 Turner Whitted
1985 Loren Carpenter
1984 James H. Clark
1983 James F. Blinn

Modeling and Rendering Architecture from Photographs: A hybrid geometry- and image-based approach

Paul E. Debevec Camillo J. Taylor Jitendra Malik

University of California at Berkeley[1]

ABSTRACT

We present a new approach for modeling and rendering existing architectural scenes from a sparse set of still photographs. Our modeling approach, which combines both geometry-based and image-based techniques, has two components. The first component is a *photogrammetric modeling* method which facilitates the recovery of the basic geometry of the photographed scene. Our photogrammetric modeling approach is effective, convenient, and robust because it exploits the constraints that are characteristic of architectural scenes. The second component is a *model-based* stereo algorithm, which recovers how the real scene deviates from the basic model. By making use of the model, our stereo technique robustly recovers accurate depth from widely-spaced image pairs. Consequently, our approach can model large architectural environments with far fewer photographs than current image-based modeling approaches. For producing renderings, we present *view-dependent texture mapping*, a method of compositing multiple views of a scene that better simulates geometric detail on basic models. Our approach can be used to recover models for use in either geometry-based or image-based rendering systems. We present results that demonstrate our approach's ability to create realistic renderings of architectural scenes from viewpoints far from the original photographs.

CR Descriptors: I.2.10 [**Artificial Intelligence**]: Vision and Scene Understanding - *Modeling and recovery of physical attributes*; I.3.7 [**Computer Graphics**]: Three-Dimensional Graphics and Realism - *Color, shading, shadowing, and texture* I.4.8 [**Image Processing**]: Scene Analysis - *Stereo*; J.6 [**Computer-Aided Engineering**]: Computer-aided design (CAD).

1 INTRODUCTION

Efforts to model the appearance and dynamics of the real world have produced some of the most compelling imagery in computer graphics. In particular, efforts to model architectural scenes, from the Amiens Cathedral to the Giza Pyramids to Berkeley's Soda Hall, have produced impressive walk-throughs and inspiring fly-bys. Clearly, it is an attractive application to be able to explore the world's architecture unencumbered by fences, gravity, customs, or jetlag.

Unfortunately, current geometry-based methods (Fig. 1a) of modeling existing architecture, in which a modeling program is used to manually position the elements of the scene, have several drawbacks. First, the process is extremely labor-intensive, typically involving surveying the site, locating and digitizing architectural plans (if available), or converting existing CAD data (again, if available). Second, it is difficult to verify whether the resulting model is accurate. Most disappointing, though, is that the renderings of the resulting models are noticeably computer-generated; even those that employ liberal texture-mapping generally fail to resemble real photographs.

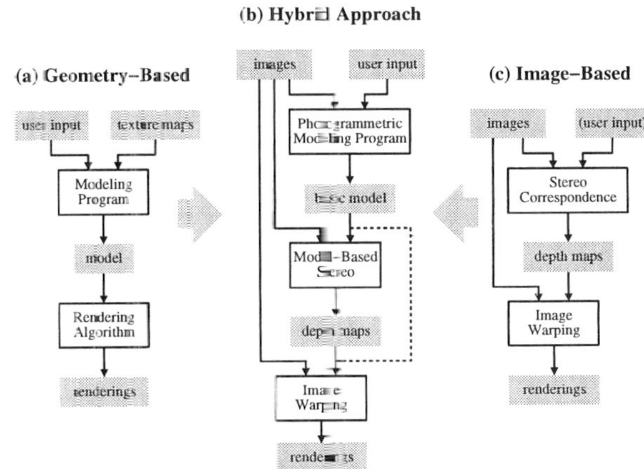

Figure 1: *Schematic of how our hybrid approach combines geometry-based and image-based approaches to modeling and rendering architecture from photographs.*

Recently, creating models directly from photographs has received increased interest in computer graphics. Since real images are used as input, such an image-based system (Fig. 1c) has an advantage in producing photorealistic renderings as output. Some of the most promising of these systems [16, 13] rely on the computer vision technique of computational stereopsis to automatically determine the structure of the scene from the multiple photographs available. As a consequence, however, these systems are only as strong as the underlying stereo algorithms. This has caused problems because state-of-the-art stereo algorithms have a number of significant weaknesses; in particular, the photographs need to appear very similar for reliable results to be obtained. Because of this, current image-based techniques must use many closely spaced images, and in some cases employ significant amounts of user input for each image pair to supervise the stereo algorithm. In this framework, capturing the data for a realistically renderable model would require an impractical number of closely spaced photographs, and deriving the depth from the photographs could require an impractical amount of user input. These concessions to the weakness of stereo algorithms bode poorly for creating large-scale, freely navigable virtual environments from photographs.

Our research aims to make the process of modeling architect-

[1]Computer Science Division, University of California at Berkeley, Berkeley, CA 94720-1776. {debevec,camillo,malik}@cs.berkeley.edu. See also http://www.cs.berkeley.edu/~debevec/Research

scenes more convenient, more accurate, and more photorealistic than the methods currently available. To do this, we have developed a new approach that draws on the strengths of both geometry-based and image-based methods, as illustrated in Fig. 1b. The result is that our approach to modeling and rendering architecture requires only a sparse set of photographs and can produce realistic renderings from arbitrary viewpoints. In our approach, a basic geometric model of the architecture is recovered interactively with an easy-to-use photogrammetric modeling system, novel views are created using view-dependent texture mapping, and additional geometric detail can be recovered automatically through stereo correspondence. The final images can be rendered with current image-based rendering techniques. Because only photographs are required, our approach to modeling architecture is neither invasive nor does it require architectural plans, CAD models, or specialized instrumentation such as surveying equipment, GPS sensors or range scanners.

1.1 Background and Related Work

The process of recovering 3D structure from 2D images has been a central endeavor within computer vision, and the process of rendering such recovered structures is a subject receiving increased interest in computer graphics. Although no general technique exists to derive models from images, four particular areas of research have provided results that are applicable to the problem of modeling and rendering architectural scenes. They are: Camera Calibration, Structure from Motion, Stereo Correspondence, and Image-Based Rendering.

1.1.1 Camera Calibration

Recovering 3D structure from images becomes a simpler problem when the cameras used are *calibrated*, that is, the mapping between image coordinates and directions relative to each camera is known. This mapping is determined by, among other parameters, the camera's focal length and its pattern of radial distortion. Camera calibration is a well-studied problem both in photogrammetry and computer vision; some successful methods include [20] and [5]. While there has been recent progress in the use of uncalibrated views for 3D reconstruction [7], we have found camera calibration to be a straightforward process that considerably simplifies the problem.

1.1.2 Structure from Motion

Given the 2D projection of a point in the world, its position in 3D space could be anywhere on a ray extending out in a particular direction from the camera's optical center. However, when the projections of a sufficient number of points in the world are observed in multiple images from different positions, it is theoretically possible to deduce the 3D locations of the points as well as the positions of the original cameras, up to an unknown factor of scale.

This problem has been studied in the area of photogrammetry for the principal purpose of producing topographic maps. In 1913, Kruppa [10] proved the fundamental result that given two views of five distinct points, one could recover the rotation and translation between the two camera positions as well as the 3D locations of the points (up to a scale factor). Since then, the problem's mathematical and algorithmic aspects have been explored starting from the fundamental work of Ullman [21] and Longuet-Higgins [11], in the early 1980s. Faugeras's book [6] overviews the state of the art as of 1992. So far, a key realization has been that the recovery of structure is very sensitive to noise in image measurements when the translation between the available camera positions is small.

Attention has turned to using more than two views with image stream methods such as [19] or recursive approaches (e.g. [1]). [19] shows excellent results for the case of orthographic cameras, but direct solutions for the perspective case remain elusive. In general, linear algorithms for the problem fail to make use of all available information while nonlinear minimization methods are prone to difficulties arising from local minima in the parameter space. An alternative formulation of the problem [17] uses lines rather than points as image measurements, but the previously stated concerns were shown to remain largely valid. For purposes of computer graphics, there is yet another problem: the models recovered by these algorithms consist of sparse point fields or individual line segments, which are not directly renderable as solid 3D models.

In our approach, we exploit the fact that we are trying to recover geometric models of architectural scenes, not arbitrary three-dimensional point sets. This enables us to include additional constraints not typically available to structure from motion algorithms and to overcome the problems of numerical instability that plague such approaches. Our approach is demonstrated in a useful interactive system for building architectural models from photographs.

1.1.3 Stereo Correspondence

The geometrical theory of structure from motion assumes that one is able to solve the *correspondence* problem, which is to identify the points in two or more images that are projections of the same point in the world. In humans, corresponding points in the two slightly differing images on the retinas are determined by the visual cortex in the process called binocular stereopsis.

Years of research (e.g. [2, 4, 8, 9, 12, 15]) have shown that determining stereo correspondences by computer is difficult problem. In general, current methods are successful only when the images are similar in appearance, as in the case of human vision, which is usually obtained by using cameras that are closely spaced relative to the objects in the scene. When the distance between the cameras (often called the *baseline*) becomes large, surfaces in the images exhibit different degrees of foreshortening, different patterns of occlusion, and large disparities in their locations in the two images, all of which makes it much more difficult for the computer to determine correct stereo correspondences. Unfortunately, the alternative of improving stereo correspondence by using images taken from nearby locations has the disadvantage that computing depth becomes very sensitive to noise in image measurements.

In this paper, we show that having an approximate model of the photographed scene makes it possible to robustly determine stereo correspondences from images taken from widely varying viewpoints. Specifically, the model enables us to warp the images to eliminate unequal foreshortening and to predict major instances of occlusion *before* trying to find correspondences.

1.1.4 Image-Based Rendering

In an image-based rendering system, the model consists of a set of images of a scene and their corresponding depth maps. When the depth of every point in an image is known, the image can be re-rendered from any nearby point of view by projecting the pixels of the image to their proper 3D locations and reprojecting them onto a new image plane. Thus, a new image of the scene is created by warping the images according to their depth maps. A principal attraction of image-based rendering is that it offers a method of rendering arbitrarily complex scenes with a constant amount of computation required per pixel. Using this property, [23] demonstrated how regularly spaced synthetic images (with their computed depth maps) could be warped and composited in real time to produce a virtual environment.

More recently, [13] presented a real-time image-based rendering system that used panoramic photographs with depth computed, in part, from stereo correspondence. One finding of the paper was that extracting reliable depth estimates from stereo is "very difficult". The method was nonetheless able to obtain acceptable results for nearby views using user input to aid the stereo depth recovery: the correspondence map for each image pair was seeded with 100 to 500 user-supplied point correspondences and also post-processed. Even with user assistance, the images used still had to be closely spaced; the largest baseline described in the paper was five feet.

The requirement that samples be close together is a serious limitation to generating a freely navigable virtual environment. Covering the size of just one city block would require thousands of panoramic images spaced five feet apart. Clearly, acquiring so many photographs is impractical. Moreover, even a dense lattice of ground-based photographs would only allow renderings to be generated from within a few feet of the original camera level, precluding any virtual fly-bys of the scene. Extending the dense lattice of photographs into three dimensions would clearly make the acquisition process even more difficult. The approach described in this paper takes advantage of the structure in architectural scenes so that it requires only a sparse set of photographs. For example, our approach has yielded a virtual fly-around of a building from just twelve standard photographs.

1.2 Overview

In this paper we present three new modeling and rendering techniques: photogrammetric modeling, view-dependent texture mapping, and model-based stereo. We show how these techniques can be used in conjunction to yield a convenient, accurate, and photorealistic method of modeling and rendering architecture from photographs. In our approach, the photogrammetric modeling program is used to create a basic volumetric model of the scene, which is then used to constrain stereo matching. Our rendering method composites information from multiple images with view-dependent texture-mapping. Our approach is successful because it splits the task of modeling from images into tasks which are easily accomplished by a person (but not a computer algorithm), and tasks which are easily performed by a computer algorithm (but not a person).

In Section 2, we present our **photogrammetric modeling** method. In essence, we have recast the structure from motion problem not as the recovery of individual point coordinates, but as the recovery of the parameters of a constrained hierarchy of parametric primitives. The result is that accurate architectural models can be recovered robustly from just a few photographs and with a minimal number of user-supplied correspondences.

In Section 3, we present **view-dependent texture mapping**, and show how it can be used to realistically render the recovered model. Unlike traditional texture-mapping, in which a single static image is used to color in each face of the model, view-dependent texture mapping interpolates between the available photographs of the scene depending on the user's point of view. This results in more lifelike animations that better capture surface specularities and unmodeled geometric detail.

Lastly, in Section 4, we present **model-based stereo**, which is used to automatically refine a basic model of a photographed scene. This technique can be used to recover the structure of architectural ornamentation that would be difficult to recover with photogrammetric modeling. In particular, we show that projecting pairs of images onto an initial approximate model allows conventional stereo techniques to robustly recover very accurate depth measurements from images with widely varying viewpoints.

2 Photogrammetric Modeling

In this section we present our method for photogrammetric modeling, in which the computer determines the parameters of a hierarchical model of parametric polyhedral primitives to reconstruct the architectural scene. We have implemented this method in *Façade*, an easy-to-use interactive modeling program that allows the user to construct a geometric model of a scene from digitized photographs. We first overview Façade from the point of view of the user, then we describe our model representation, and then we explain our reconstruction algorithm. Lastly, we present results from using Façade to reconstruct several architectural scenes.

2.1 The User's View

Constructing a geometric model of an architectural scene using Façade is an incremental and straightforward process. Typically, the user selects a small number of photographs to begin with, and models the scene one piece at a time. The user may refine the model and include more images in the project until the model meets the desired level of detail.

Fig. 2(a) and (b) shows the two types of windows used in Façade: image viewers and model viewers. The user instantiates the components of the model, marks edges in the images, and corresponds the edges in the images to the edges in the model. When instructed, Façade computes the sizes and relative positions of the model components that best fit the edges marked in the photographs.

Components of the model, called *blocks*, are parameterized geometric primitives such as boxes, prisms, and surfaces of revolution. A box, for example, is parameterized by its length, width, and height. The user models the scene as a collection of such blocks, creating new block classes as desired. Of course, the user does not need to specify numerical values for the blocks' parameters, since these are recovered by the program.

The user may choose to constrain the sizes and positions of any of the blocks. In Fig. 2(b), most of the blocks have been constrained to have equal length and width. Additionally, the four pinnacles have been constrained to have the same shape. Blocks may also be placed in constrained relations to one other. For example, many of the blocks in Fig. 2(b) have been constrained to sit centered and on top of the block below. Such constraints are specified using a graphical 3D interface. When such constraints are provided, they are used to simplify the reconstruction problem.

The user marks edge features in the images using a point-and-click interface; a gradient-based technique as in [14] can be used to align the edges with sub-pixel accuracy. We use edge rather than point features since they are easier to localize and less likely to be completely obscured. Only a section of each edge needs to be marked, making it possible to use partially visible edges. For each marked edge, the user also indicates the corresponding edge in the model. Generally, accurate reconstructions are obtained if there are as many correspondences in the images as there are free camera and model parameters. Thus, Façade reconstructs scenes accurately even when just a portion of the visible edges and marked in the images, and when just a portion of the model edges are given correspondences.

At any time, the user may instruct the computer to reconstruct the scene. The computer then solves for the parameters of the model that cause it to align with the marked features in the images. During the reconstruction, the computer computes and displays the locations from which the photographs were taken. For simple models consisting of just a few blocks, a full reconstruction takes only a few seconds; for more complex models, it can take a few minutes. For this reason, the user can instruct the computer to employ faster but less precise reconstruction algorithms (see Sec. 2.4) during the intermediate stages of modeling.

To verify the the accuracy of the recovered model and camera positions, Façade can project the model into the original photographs. Typically, the projected model deviates from the photographs by less than a pixel. Fig. 2(c) shows the results of projecting the edges of the model in Fig. 2(b) into the original photograph.

Lastly, the user may generate novel views of the model by positioning a virtual camera at any desired location. Façade will then use the view-dependent texture-mapping method of Section 3 to render a novel view of the scene from the desired location. Fig. 2(d) shows an aerial rendering of the tower model.

2.2 Model Representation

The purpose of our choice of model representation is to represent th[e] scene as a surface model with as few parameters as possible: w[…]

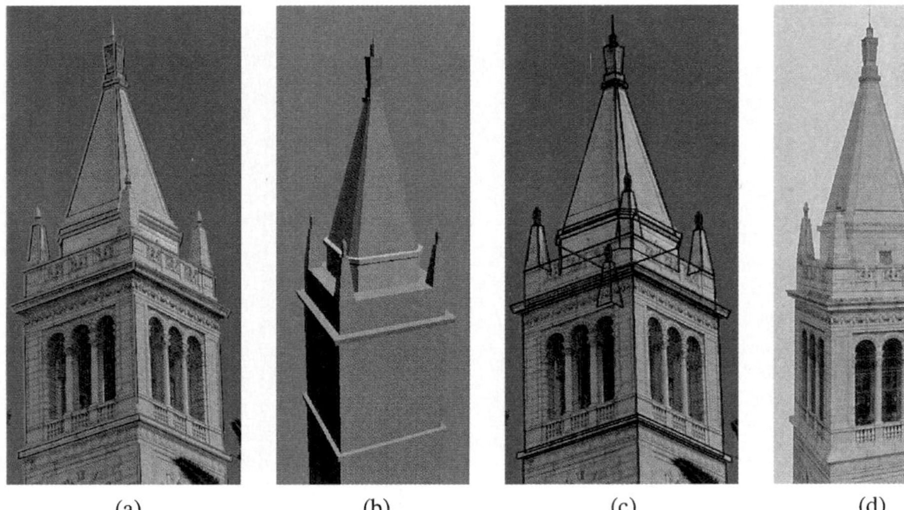

(a) (b) (c) (d)

Figure 2: **(a)** *A photograph of the Campanile, Berkeley's clock tower, with marked edges shown in green.* **(b)** *The model recovered by our photogrammetric modeling method. Although only the left pinnacle was marked, the remaining three (including one not visible) were recovered from symmetrical constraints in the model. Our method allows any number of images to be used, but in this case constraints of symmetry made it possible to recover an accurate 3D model from a single photograph.* **(c)** *The accuracy of the model is verified by reprojecting it into the original photograph through the recovered camera position.* **(d)** *A synthetic view of the Campanile generated using the view-dependent texture-mapping method described in Section 3. A real photograph from this position would be difficult to take since the camera position is 250 feet above the ground.*

the model has fewer parameters, the user needs to specify fewer correspondences, and the computer can reconstruct the model more efficiently. In Façade, the scene is represented as a constrained hierarchical model of parametric polyhedral primitives, called *blocks*. Each block has a small set of parameters which serve to define its size and shape. Each coordinate of each vertex of the block is then expressed as linear combination of the block's parameters, relative to an internal coordinate frame. For example, for the wedge block in Fig. 3, the coordinates of the vertex P_o are written in terms of the block parameters $width$, $height$, and $length$ as $P_o = (-width, -height, length)^T$. Each block is also given an associated bounding box.

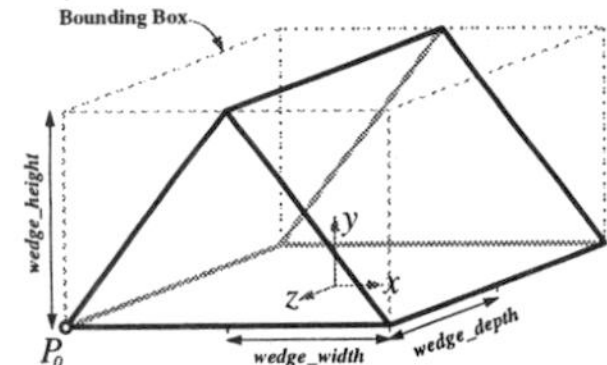

Figure 3: *A wedge block with its parameters and bounding box.*

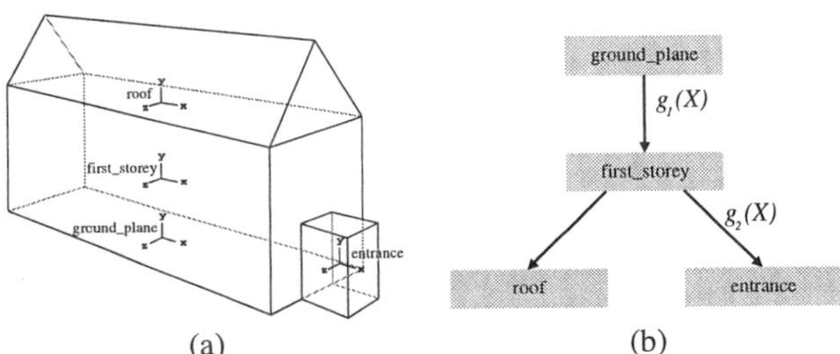

(a) (b)

Figure 4: **(a)** *A geometric model of a simple building.* **(b)** *The model's hierarchical representation. The nodes in the tree represent parametric primitives (called* blocks*) while the links contain the spatial relationships between the blocks.*

The blocks in Façade are organized in a hierarchical tree structure as shown in Fig. 4(b). Each node of the tree represents an individual block, while the links in the tree contain the spatial relationships between blocks, called *relations*. Such hierarchical structures are also used in traditional modeling systems.

The relation between a block and its parent is most generally represented as a rotation matrix R and a translation vector t. This representation requires six parameters: three each for R and t. In architectural scenes, however, the relationship between two blocks usually has a simple form that can be represented with fewer parameters, and Façade allows the user to build such constraints on R and t into the model. The rotation R between a block and its parent can be specified in one of three ways: first, as an unconstrained rotation, requiring three parameters; second, as a rotation about a particular coordinate axis, requiring just one parameter; or third, as a fixed or null rotation, requiring no parameters.

Likewise, Façade allows for constraints to be placed on each component of the translation vector t. Specifically, the user can constrain the bounding boxes of two blocks to align themselves in some manner along each dimension. For example, in order to ensure that the roof block in Fig. 4 lies on top of the first story block, the user can require that the maximum y extent of the first story block be equal to the minimum y extent of the roof block. With this constraint, the translation along the y axis is computed ($t_y = (first\_story_y^{MAX} - roof_y^{MIN})$) rather than represented as a parameter of the model.

Each parameter of each instantiated block is actually a reference to a named symbolic variable, as illustrated in Fig. 5. As a result, two parameters of different blocks (or of the same block) can be equated by having each parameter reference the same symbol. This facility allows the user to equate two or more of the dimensions in a model, which makes modeling symmetrical blocks and repeated structure more convenient. Importantly, these constraints reduce the number of degrees of freedom in the model, which, as we will show, simplifies the structure recovery problem.

Once the blocks and their relations have been parameterized, it is straightforward to derive expressions for the world coordinates of the block vertices. Consider the set of edges which link a specific block in the model to the ground plane as shown in Fig. 4.

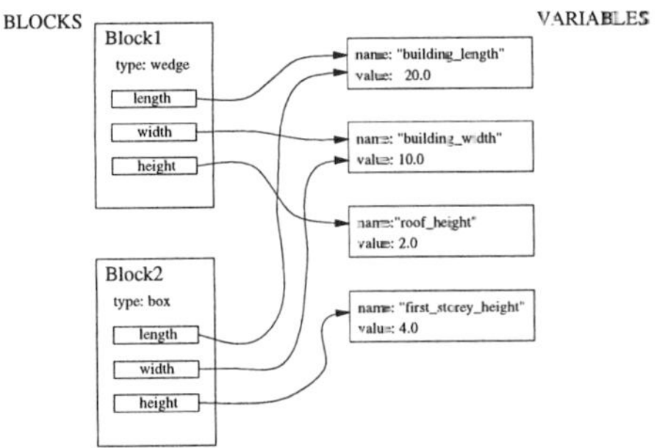

Figure 5: *Representation of block parameters as symbol references. A single variable can be referenced by the model in multiple places, allowing constraints of symmetry to be embedded in the model.*

Let $g_1(X), ..., g_n(X)$ represent the rigid transformations associated with each of these links, where X represents the vector of all the model parameters. The world coordinates $P_w(X)$ of a particular block vertex $P(X)$ is then:

$$P_w(X) = g_1(X)...g_n(X)P(X) \tag{1}$$

Similarly, the world orientation $v_w(X)$ of a particular line segment $v(X)$ is:

$$v_w(X) = g_1(X)...g_n(X)v(X) \tag{2}$$

In these equations, the point vectors P and P_w and the orientation vectors v and v_w are represented in homogeneous coordinates.

Modeling the scene with polyhedral blocks, as opposed to points, line segments, surface patches, or polygons, is advantageous for a number of reasons:

- Most architectural scenes are well modeled by an arrangement of geometric primitives.
- Blocks implicitly contain common architectural elements such as parallel lines and right angles.
- Manipulating block primitives is convenient since they are at a suitably high level of abstraction; individual features such as points and lines are less manageable.
- A surface model of the scene is readily obtained from the blocks, so there is no need to infer surfaces from discrete features.
- Modeling in terms of blocks and relationships greatly reduces the number of parameters that the reconstruction algorithm needs to recover.

The last point is crucial to the robustness of our reconstruction algorithm and the viability of our modeling system, and is illustrated best with an example. The model in Fig. 2 is parameterized by just 33 variables (the unknown camera position adds six more). If each block in the scene were unconstrained (in its dimensions and position), the model would have 240 parameters; if each line segment in the scene were treated independently, the model would have 2,896 parameters. This reduction in the number of parameters greatly enhances the robustness and efficiency of the method as compared to traditional structure from motion algorithms. Lastly, since the number of correspondences needed to suitably overconstrain the minimization is roughly proportional to the number of parameters in the model, this reduction means that the number of correspondences required of the user is manageable.

2.3 Reconstruction Algorithm

Our reconstruction algorithm works by minimizing an objective function $\mathcal{O}$ that sums the disparity between the projected edges of the model and the edges marked in the images, i.e. $\mathcal{O} = \sum Err_i$ where Err_i represents the disparity computed for edge feature i. Thus, the unknown model parameters and camera positions are computed by minimizing $\mathcal{O}$ with respect to these variables. Our system uses the the error function Err_i from [17], described below.

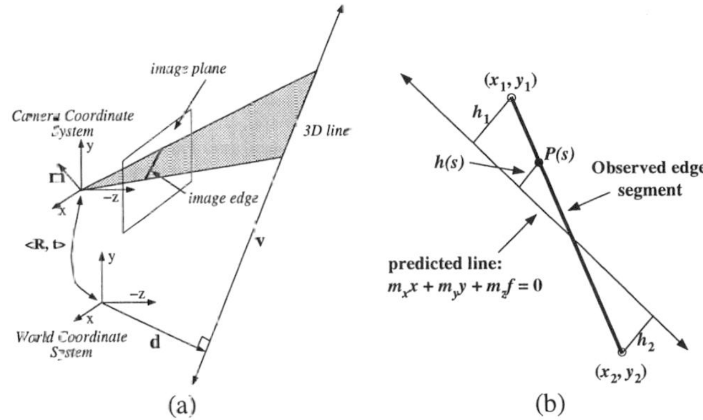

Figure 6: **(a)** *Projection of a straight line onto a camera's image plane.* **(b)** *The error function used in the reconstruction algorithm. The heavy line represents the observed edge segment (marked by the user) and the lighter line represents the model edge predicted by the current camera and model parameters.*

Fig. 6(a) shows how a straight line in the model projects onto the image plane of a camera. The straight line can be defined by a pair of vectors $\langle v, d\rangle$ where v represents the direction of the line and d represents a point on the line. These vectors can be computed from equations 2 and 1 respectively. The position of the camera with respect to world coordinates is given in terms of a rotation matrix R_j and a translation vector t_j. The normal vector denoted by $\mathbf{m}$ in the figure is computed from the following expression:

$$\mathbf{m} = R_j(\mathbf{v} \times (\mathbf{d} - t_j)) \tag{3}$$

The projection of the line onto the image plane is simply the intersection of the plane defined by m with the image plane, located at $z = -f$ where f is the focal length of the camera. Thus, the image edge is defined by the equation $m_x x + m_y y - m_z f = 0$.

Fig 6(b) shows how the error between the observed image edge $\{(x_1, y_1), (x_2, y_2)\}$ and the predicted image line is calculated for each correspondence. Points on the observed edge segment can be parameterized by a single scalar variable $s \in [0, l]$ where l is the length of the edge. We let $h(s)$ be the function that returns the shortest distance from a point on the segment, $p(s)$, to the predicted edge.

With these definitions, the total error between the observed edge segment and the predicted edge is calculated as:

$$Err_i = \int_0^l h^2(s)ds = \frac{l}{3}(h_1^2 + h_1 h_2 + h_2^2) = \mathbf{m}^T(A^T BA)\mathbf{m} \tag{4}$$

where:

$$\mathbf{m} = (m_x, m_y, m_z)^T$$
$$A = \begin{pmatrix} x_1 & y_1 & 1 \\ x_2 & y_2 & 1 \end{pmatrix}$$
$$B = \frac{l}{3(m_x^2 + m_y^2)} \begin{pmatrix} 1 & 0.5 \\ 0.5 & 1 \end{pmatrix}$$

The final objective function $\mathcal{O}$ is the sum of the error terms resulting from each correspondence. We minimize $\mathcal{O}$ using a variant of the Newton-Raphson method, which involves calculating the gradient and Hessian of $\mathcal{O}$ with respect to the parameters of the cam-

and the model. As we have shown, it is simple to construct symbolic expressions for m in terms of the unknown model parameters. The minimization algorithm differentiates these expressions symbolically to evaluate the gradient and Hessian after each iteration. The procedure is inexpensive since the expressions for d and v in Equations 2 and 1 have a particularly simple form.

2.4 Computing an Initial Estimate

The objective function described in Section 2.3 section is non-linear with respect to the model and camera parameters and consequently can have local minima. If the algorithm begins at a random location in the parameter space, it stands little chance of converging to the correct solution. To overcome this problem we have developed a method to directly compute a good initial estimate for the model parameters and camera positions that is near the correct solution. In practice, our initial estimate method consistently enables the non-linear minimization algorithm to converge to the correct solution.

Our initial estimate method consists of two procedures performed in sequence. The first procedure estimates the camera rotations while the second estimates the camera translations and the parameters of the model. Both initial estimate procedures are based upon an examination of Equation 3. From this equation the following constraints can be deduced:

$$m^T R_j \mathbf{v} = 0 \qquad (5)$$

$$m^T R_j(\mathbf{d} - t_j) = 0 \qquad (6)$$

Given an observed edge $\mathbf{u}_{ij}$ the measured normal $\mathbf{m}'$ to the plane passing through the camera center is:

$$\mathbf{m}' = \begin{pmatrix} x_1 \\ y_1 \\ -f \end{pmatrix} \times \begin{pmatrix} x_2 \\ y_2 \\ -f \end{pmatrix} \qquad (7)$$

From these equations, we see that any model edges of known orientation constrain the possible values for R_j. Since most architectural models contain many such edges (e.g. horizontal and vertical lines), each camera rotation can be usually be estimated from the model independent of the model parameters and independent of the camera's location in space. Our method does this by minimizing the following objective function $\mathcal{O}_1$ that sums the extents to which the rotations R_j violate the constraints arising from Equation 5:

$$\mathcal{O}_1 = \sum_i (m^T R_j \mathbf{v}_i)^2, \quad \mathbf{v}_i \in \{\hat{x}, \hat{y}, \hat{z}\} \qquad (8)$$

Once initial estimates for the camera rotations are computed, Equation 6 is used to obtain initial estimates of the model parameters and camera locations. Equation 6 reflects the constraint that all of the points on the line defined by the tuple $\langle \mathbf{v}, \mathbf{d} \rangle$ should lie on the plane with normal vector $\mathbf{m}$ passing through the camera center. This constraint is expressed in the following objective function $\mathcal{O}_2$ where $P_i(X)$ and $Q_i(X)$ are expressions for the vertices of an edge of the model.

$$\mathcal{O}_2 = \sum_i (m^T R_j(P_i(X) - t_j))^2 + (m^T R_j(Q_i(X) - t_j))^2 \quad (9)$$

In the special case where all of the block relations in the model have a known rotation, this objective function becomes a simple quadratic form which is easily minimized by solving a set of linear equations.

Once the initial estimate is obtained, the non-linear minimization over the entire parameter space is applied to produce the best possible reconstruction. Typically, the minimization requires fewer than ten iterations and adjusts the parameters of the model by at most a few percent from the initial estimates. The edges of the recovered models typically conform to the original photographs to within a pixel.

Figure 7: *Three of twelve photographs used to reconstruct the entire exterior of University High School in Urbana, Illinois. The superimposed lines indicate the edges the user has marked.*

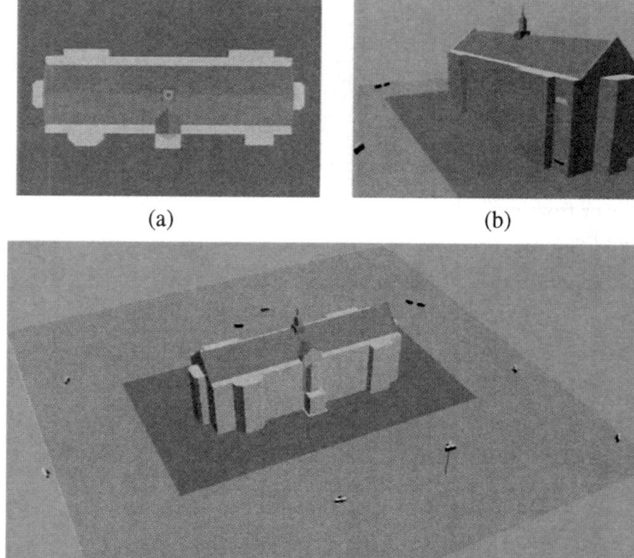

Figure 8: *The high school model, reconstructed from twelve photographs.* **(a)** *Overhead view.* **(b)** *Rear view.* **(c)** *Aerial view showing the recovered camera positions. Two nearly coincident cameras can be observed in front of the building; their photographs were taken from the second story of a building across the street.*

Figure 9: *A synthetic view of University High School. This is a frame from an animation of flying around the entire building.*

(a)

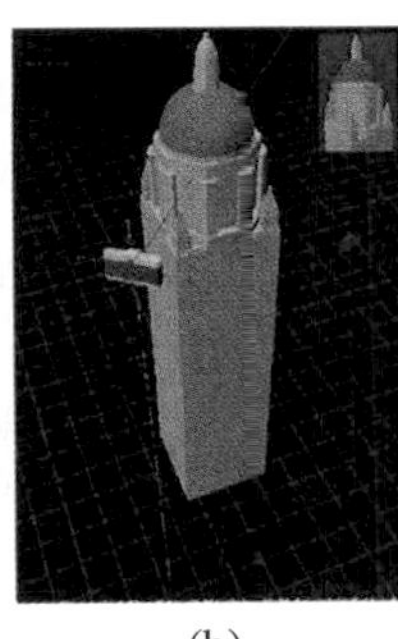

(b)

(c)

Figure 10: *Reconstruction of Hoover Tower, Stanford, CA* **(a)** *Original photograph, with marked edges indicated.* **(b)** *Model recovered from the single photograph shown in (a).* **(c)** *Texture-mapped aerial view from the virtual camera position indicated in (b). Regions not seen in (a) are indicated in blue.*

2.5 Results

Fig. 2 showed the results of using Façade to reconstruct a clock tower from a single image. Figs. 7 and 8 show the results of using Façade to reconstruct a high school building from twelve photographs. (The model was originally constructed from just five images; the remaining images were added to the project for purposes of generating renderings using the techniques of Section 3.) The photographs were taken with a calibrated 35mm still camera with a standard 50mm lens and digitized with the PhotoCD process. Images at the 1536 × 1024 pixel resolution were processed to correct for lens distortion, then filtered down to 768 × 512 pixels for use in the modeling system. Fig. 8 shows some views of the recovered model and camera positions, and Fig. 9 shows a synthetic view of the building generated by the technique in Sec. 3.

Fig. 10 shows the reconstruction of another tower from a single photograph. The dome was modeled specially since the reconstruction algorithm does not recover curved surfaces. The user constrained a two-parameter hemisphere block to sit centered on top of the tower, and manually adjusted its height and width to align with the photograph. Each of the models presented took approximately four hours to create.

3 View-Dependent Texture-Mapping

In this section we present view-dependent texture-mapping, an effective method of rendering the scene that involves projecting the original photographs onto the model. This form of texture-mapping is most effective when the model conforms closely to the actual structure of the scene, and when the original photographs show the scene in similar lighting conditions. In Section 4 we will show how view-dependent texture-mapping can be used in conjunction with model-based stereo to produce realistic renderings when the recovered model only approximately models the structure of the scene.

Since the camera positions of the original photographs are recovered during the modeling phase, projecting the images onto the model is straightforward. In this section we first describe how we project a single image onto the model, and then how we merge several image projections to render the entire model. Unlike traditional texture-mapping, our method projects different images onto the model depending on the user's viewpoint. As a result, our view-dependent texture mapping can give a better illusion of additional geometric detail in the model.

3.1 Projecting a Single Image

The process of texture-mapping a single image onto the model can be thought of as replacing each camera with a slide projector that projects the original image onto the model. When the model is not convex, it is possible that some parts of the model will shadow others with respect to the camera. While such shadowed regions could be determined using an object-space visible surface algorithm, or an image-space ray casting algorithm, we use an image-space shadow map algorithm based on [22] since it is efficiently implemented using z-buffer hardware.

Fig. 11, upper left, shows the results of mapping a single image onto the high school building model. The recovered camera position for the projected image is indicated in the lower left corner of the image. Because of self-shadowing, not every point on the model within the camera's viewing frustum is mapped.

3.2 Compositing Multiple Images

In general, each photograph will view only a piece of the model. Thus, it is usually necessary to use multiple images in order to render the entire model from a novel point of view. The top images of Fig. 11 show two different images mapped onto the model and rendered from a novel viewpoint. Some pixels are colored in just one of the renderings, while some are colored in both. These two renderings can be merged into a composite rendering by considering the corresponding pixels in the rendered views. If a pixel is mapped in only one rendering, its value from that rendering is used in the composite. If it is mapped in more than one rendering, the renderer has to decide which image (or combination of images) to use.

It would be convenient, of course, if the projected images would agree perfectly where they overlap. However, the images will not necessarily agree if there is unmodeled geometric detail in the building, or if the surfaces of the building exhibit non-Lambertian reflection. In this case, the best image to use is clearly the one with the viewing angle closest to that of the rendered view. However, using the image closest in angle at every pixel means that neighboring rendered pixels may be sampled from different original images. When this happens, specularity and unmodeled geometric detail can cause visible seams in the rendering. To avoid this problem, we smooth these transitions through weighted averaging as in Fig. 12.

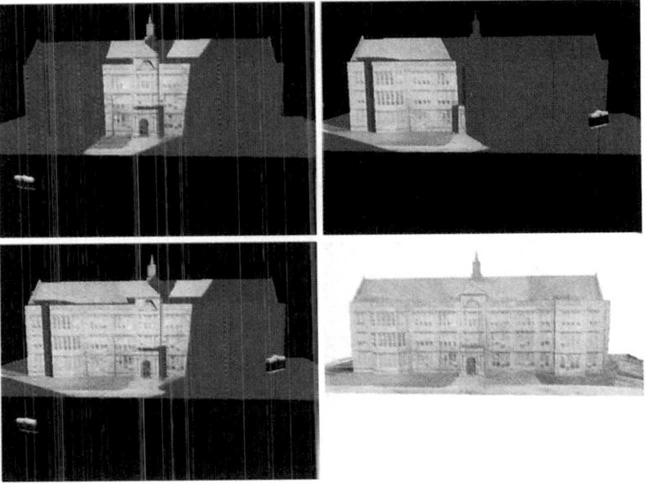

Figure 11: *The process of assembling projected images to form a composite rendering. The top two pictures show two images projected onto the model from their respective recovered camera positions. The lower left picture shows the results of compositing these two renderings using our view-dependent weighting function. The lower right picture shows the results of compositing renderings of all twelve original images. Some pixels near the front edge of the roof not seen in any image have been filled in with the hole-filling algorithm from [23].*

Even with this weighting, neighboring pixels can still be sampled from different views at the boundary of a projected image, since the contribution of an image must be zero outside its boundary.

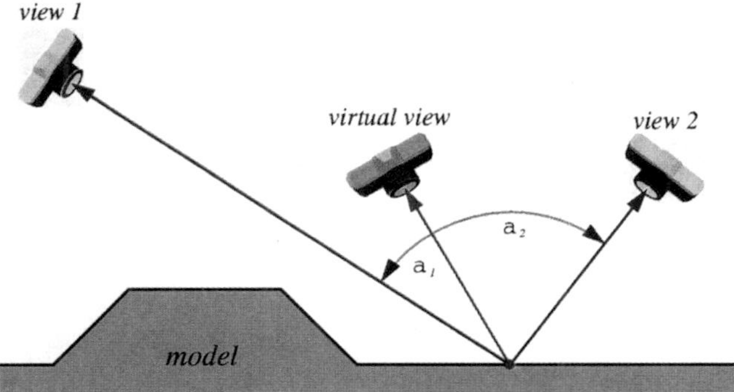

Figure 12: *The weighting function used in view-dependent texture mapping. The pixel in the virtual view corresponding to the point on the model is assigned a weighted average of the corresponding pixels in actual views 1 and 2. The weights w_1 and w_2 are inversely inversely proportional to the magnitude of angles a_1 and a_2. Alternately, more sophisticated weighting functions based on expected foreshortening and image resampling can be used.*

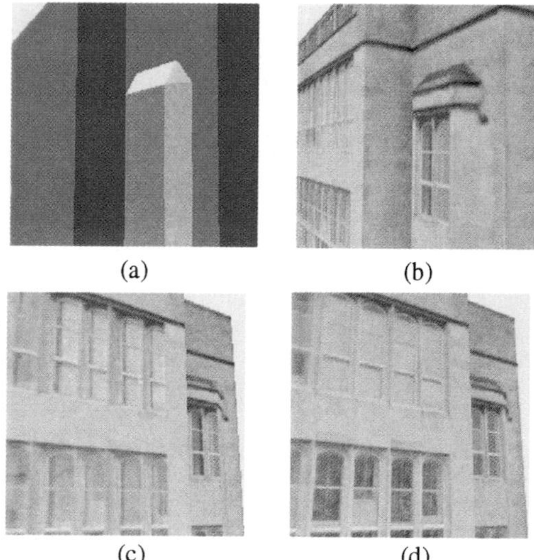

Figure 13: *View-dependent texture mapping.* **(a)** *A detail view of the high school model.* **(b)** *A rendering of the model from the same position using view-dependent texture mapping. Note that although the model does not capture the slightly recessed windows, the windows appear properly recessed because the texture map is sampled primarily from a photograph which viewed the windows from approximately the same direction.* **(c)** *The same piece of the model viewed from a different angle, using the same texture map as in (b). Since the texture is not selected from an image that viewed the model from approximately the same angle, the recessed windows appear unnatural.* **(d)** *A more natural result obtained by using view-dependent texture mapping. Since the angle of view in (d) is different than in (b), a different composition of original images is used to texture-map the model.*

address this, the pixel weights are ramped down near the boundary of the projected images. Although this method does not guarantee smooth transitions in all cases, we have found that it eliminates most artifacts in renderings and animations arising from such seams.

If an original photograph features an unwanted car, tourist, or other object in front of the architecture of interest, the unwanted object will be projected onto the surface of the model. To prevent this from happening, the user may mask out the object by painting over the obstruction with a reserved color. The rendering algorithm will then set the weights for any pixels corresponding to the masked regions to zero, and decrease the weights of the pixels near the boundary as before to minimize seams. Any regions in the composite image which are occluded in every projected image are filled in using the hole-filling method from [23].

In the discussion so far, projected image weights are computed at every pixel of every projected rendering. Since the weighting function is smooth (though not constant) across flat surfaces, it is not generally not necessary to compute it for every pixel of every face of the model. For example, using a single weight for each face of the model, computed at the face's center, produces acceptable results. By coarsely subdividing large faces, the results are visually indistinguishable from the case where a unique weight is computed for every pixel. Importantly, this technique suggests a real-time implementation of view-dependent texture mapping using a texture-mapping graphics pipeline to render the projected views, and α-channel blending to composite them.

For complex models where most images are entirely occluded for the typical view, it can be very inefficient to project every original photograph to the novel viewpoint. Some efficient techniques to determine such visibility *a priori* in architectural scenes through spatial partitioning are presented in [18].

4 Model-Based Stereopsis

The modeling system described in Section 2 allows the user to create a basic model of a scene, but in general the scene will have additional geometric detail (such as friezes and cornices) not captured in the model. In this section we present a new method of recovering such additional geometric detail automatically through stereo correspondence, which we call *model-based* stereo. Model-based stereo differs from traditional stereo in that it measures how the actual scene deviates from the approximate model, rather than trying to measure the structure of the scene without any prior information. The model serves to place the images into a common frame of reference that makes the stereo correspondence possible even for images taken from relatively far apart. The stereo correspondence information can then be used to render novel views of the scene using image-based rendering techniques.

As in traditional stereo, given two images (which we call the *key* and *offset*), model-based stereo computes the associated depth map for the key image by determining corresponding points in the key and offset images. Like many stereo algorithms, our method is *correlation-based*, in that it attempts to determine the corresponding point in the offset image by comparing small pixel neighborhoods around the points. As such, correlation-based stereo algorithms generally require the neighborhood of each point in the key image to resemble the neighborhood of its corresponding point in the offset image.

The problem we face is that when the key and offset images are taken from relatively far apart, as is the case for our modeling method, corresponding pixel neighborhoods can be foreshortened very differently. In Figs. 14(a) and (c), pixel neighborhoods toward the right of the key image are foreshortened horizontally by nearly a factor of four in the offset image.

The key observation in model-based stereo is that even though two images of the same scene may appear very different, they appear similar after being projected onto an approximate model of the scene. In particular, projecting the offset image onto the model and viewing it from the position of the key image produces what we call the *warped offset* image, which appears very similar to the key image. The geometrically detailed scene in Fig. 14 was modeled as two flat surfaces with our modeling program, which also determined the relative camera positions. As expected, the warped offset image (Fig. 14(b)) exhibits the same pattern of foreshortening as the key image.

In model-based stereo, pixel neighborhoods are compared between the key and warped offset images rather than the key and off-

(a) *Key Image*

(b) *Warped Offset Image*

(c) *Offset Image*

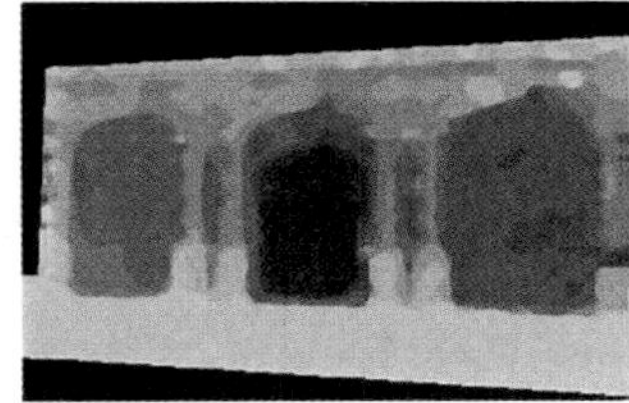

(d) *Computed Disparity Map*

Figure 14: **(a)** *and* **(c)** *Two images of the entrance to Peterhouse chapel in Cambridge, UK. The Façade program was used to model the façade and ground as a flat surfaces and to recover the relative camera positions.* **(b)** *The warped offset image, produced by projecting the offset image onto the approximate model and viewing it from the position of the key camera. This projection eliminates most of the disparity and foreshortening with respect to the key image, greatly simplifying stereo correspondence.* **(d)** *An unedited disparity map produced by our model-based stereo algorithm.*

set images. When a correspondence is found, it is simple to convert its disparity to the corresponding disparity between the key and offset images, from which the point's depth is easily calculated. Fig. 14(d) shows a disparity map computed for the key image in (a).

The reduction of differences in foreshortening is just one of several ways that the warped offset image simplifies stereo correspondence. Some other desirable properties of the warped offset image are:

- Any point in the scene which lies on the approximate model will have zero disparity between the key image and the warped offset image.
- Disparities between the key and warped offset images are easily converted to a depth map for the key image.
- Depth estimates are far less sensitive to noise in image measurements since images taken from relatively far apart can be compared.
- Places where the model occludes itself relative to the key image can be detected and indicated in the warped offset image.
- A linear epipolar geometry (Sec. 4.1) exists between the key and warped offset images, despite the warping. In fact, the epipolar lines of the warped offset image coincide with the epipolar lines of the key image.

4.1 Model-Based Epipolar Geometry

In traditional stereo, the *epipolar constraint* (see [6]) is often used to constrain the search for corresponding points in the offset image to searching along an epipolar line. This constraint simplifies stereo not only by reducing the search for each correspondence to one dimension, but also by reducing the chance of selecting a false matches. In this section we show that taking advantage of the epipolar constraint is no more difficult in model-based stereo case, despite the fact that the offset image is non-uniformly warped.

Fig. 15 shows the epipolar geometry for model-based stereo. If we consider a point P in the scene, there is a unique *epipolar plane* which passes through P and the centers of the key and offset cameras. This epipolar plane intersects the key and offset image planes in *epipolar lines* e_k and e_o. If we consider the projection p_k of P onto the key image plane, the epipolar constraint states that the corresponding point in the offset image must lie somewhere along the offset image's epipolar line.

In model-based stereo, neighborhoods in the key image are compared to the warped offset image rather than the offset image. Thus, to make use of the epipolar constraint, it is necessary to determine where the pixels on the offset image's epipolar line project to in the warped offset image. The warped offset image is formed by projecting the offset image onto the model, and then reprojecting the model onto the image plane of the key camera. Thus, the projection p_o of P in the offset image projects onto the model at Q, and then reprojects to q_k in the warped offset image. Since each of these projections occurs within the epipolar plane, any possible correspondence

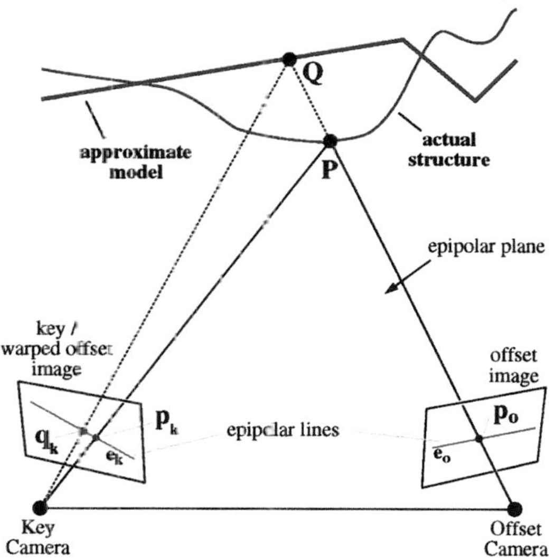

Figure 15: *Epipolar geometry for model-based stereo.*

for p_k in the key image must lie on the *key* image's epipolar line in the warped offset image. In the case where the actual structure and the model coincide at P, p_o is projected to P and then reprojected to p_k, yielding a correspondence with zero disparity.

The fact that the epipolar geometry remains linear after the warping step also facilitates the use of the ordering constraint [2, 6] through a dynamic programming technique.

4.2 Stereo Results and Rerendering

While the warping step makes it dramatically easier to determine stereo correspondences, a stereo algorithm is still necessary to actually determine them. The algorithm we developed to produce the images in this paper is described in [3].

Once a depth map has been computed for a particular image, we can rerender the scene from novel viewpoints using the methods described in [23, 16, 13]. Furthermore, when several images and their corresponding depth maps are available, we can use the view-dependent texture-mapping method of Section 3 to composite the multiple renderings. The novel views of the chapel façade in Fig. 16 were produced through such compositing of four images.

5 Conclusion and Future Work

To conclude, we have presented a new, photograph-based approach to modeling and rendering architectural scenes. Our modeling approach, which combines both geometry-based and image-based modeling techniques, is built from two components that we have developed. The first component is an easy-to-use photogramm-

Figure 16: *Novel views of the scene generated from four original photographs. These are frames from an animated movie in which the façade rotates continuously. The depth is computed from model-based stereo and the frames are made by compositing image-based renderings with view-dependent texture-mapping.*

ric modeling system which facilitates the recovery of a basic geometric model of the photographed scene. The second component is a model-based stereo algorithm, which recovers precisely how the real scene differs from the basic model. For rendering, we have presented view-dependent texture-mapping, which produces images by warping and compositing multiple views of the scene. Through judicious use of images, models, and human assistance, our approach is more convenient, more accurate, and more photorealistic than current geometry-based or image-based approaches for modeling and rendering real-world architectural scenes.

There are several improvements and extensions that can be made to our approach. First, surfaces of revolution represent an important component of architecture (e.g. domes, columns, and minarets) that are not recovered in our photogrammetric modeling approach. (As noted, the dome in Fig. 10 was manually sized by the user.) Fortunately, there has been much work (e.g. [24]) that presents methods of recovering such structures from image contours. Curved model geometry is also entirely consistent with our approach to recovering additional detail with model-based stereo.

Second, our techniques should be extended to recognize and model the photometric properties of the materials in the scene. The system should be able to make better use of photographs taken in varying lighting conditions, and it should be able to render images of the scene as it would appear at any time of day, in any weather, and with any configuration of artificial light. Already, the recovered model can be used to predict shadowing in the scene with respect to an arbitrary light source. However, a full treatment of the problem will require estimating the photometric properties (i.e. the bidirectional reflectance distribution functions) of the surfaces in the scene.

Third, it is clear that further investigation should be made into the problem of selecting which original images to use when rendering a novel view of the scene. This problem is especially difficult when the available images are taken at arbitrary locations. Our current solution to this problem, the weighting function presented in Section 3, still allows seams to appear in renderings and does not consider issues arising from image resampling. Another form of view selection is required to choose which pairs of images should be matched to recover depth in the model-based stereo algorithm.

Lastly, it will clearly be an attractive application to integrate the models created with the techniques presented in this paper into forthcoming real-time image-based rendering systems.

Acknowledgments

This research was supported by a National Science Foundation Graduate Research Fellowship and grants from Interval Research Corporation, the California MICRO program, and JSEP contract F49620-93-C-0014. The authors also wish to thank Tim Hawkins, Carlo Sequin, David Forsyth, and Jianbo Shi for their valuable help in revising this paper.

References

[1] Ali Azarbayejani and Alex Pentland. Recursive estimation of motion, structure, and focal length. *IEEE Trans. Pattern Anal. Machine Intell.*, 17(6):562–575, June 1995.

[2] H. H. Baker and T. O. Binford. Depth from edge and intensity based stereo. In *Proceedings of the Seventh IJCAI, Vancouver, BC*, pages 631–636, 1981.

[3] Paul E. Debevec, Camillo J. Taylor, and Jitendra Malik. Modeling and rendering architecture from photographs: A hybrid geometry- and image-based approach. Technical Report UCB//CSD-96-893, U.C. Berkeley, CS Division, January 1996.

[4] D.J.Fleet, A.D.Jepson, and M.R.M. Jenkin. Phase-based disparity measurement. *CVGIP: Image Understanding*, 53(2):198–210, 1991.

[5] Oliver Faugeras and Giorgio Toscani. The calibration problem for stereo. In *Proceedings IEEE CVPR 86*, pages 15–20, 1986.

[6] Olivier Faugeras. *Three-Dimensional Computer Vision.* MIT Press, 1993.

[7] Olivier Faugeras, Stephane Laveau, Luc Robert, Gabriella Csurka, and Cyril Zeller. 3-d reconstruction of urban scenes from sequences of images. Technical Report 2572, INRIA, June 1995.

[8] W. E. L. Grimson. *From Images to Surface.* MIT Press, 1981.

[9] D. Jones and J. Malik. Computational framework for determining stereo correspondence from a set of linear spatial filters. *Image and Vision Computing*, 10(10):699–708, December 1992.

[10] E. Kruppa. Zur ermittlung eines objectes aus zwei perspektiven mit innerer orientierung. *Sitz.-Ber. Akad. Wiss., Wien, Math. Naturw. Kl., Abt. Ila.*, 122:1939–1948, 1913.

[11] H.C. Longuet-Higgins. A computer algorithm for reconstructing a scene from two projections. *Nature*, 293:133–135, September 1981.

[12] D. Marr and T. Poggio. A computational theory of human stereo vision. *Proceedings of the Royal Society of London*, 204:301–328, 1979.

[13] Leonard McMillan and Gary Bishop. Plenoptic modeling: An image-based rendering system. In *SIGGRAPH '95*, 1995.

[14] Eric N. Mortensen and William A. Barrett. Intelligent scissors for image composition. In *SIGGRAPH '95*, 1995.

[15] S. B. Pollard, J. E. W. Mayhew, and J. P. Frisby. A stereo correspondence algorithm using a disparity gradient limit. *Perception*, 14:449–470, 1985.

[16] R. Szeliski. Image mosaicing for tele-reality applications. In *IEEE Computer Graphics and Applications*, 1996.

[17] Camillo J. Taylor and David J. Kriegman. Structure and motion from line segments in multiple images. *IEEE Trans. Pattern Anal. Machine Intell.*, 17(11), November 1995.

[18] S. J. Teller, Celeste Fowler, Thomas Funkhouser, and Pat Hanrahan. Partitioning and ordering large radiosity computations. In *SIGGRAPH '94*, pages 443–450, 1994.

[19] Carlo Tomasi and Takeo Kanade. Shape and motion from image streams under orthography: a factorization method. *International Journal of Computer Vision*, 9(2):137–154, November 1992.

[20] Roger Tsai. A versatile camera calibration technique for high accuracy 3d machine vision metrology using off-the-shelf tv cameras and lenses. *IEEE Journal of Robotics and Automation*, 3(4):323–344, August 1987.

[21] S. Ullman. *The Interpretation of Visual Motion.* The MIT Press, Cambridge, MA, 1979.

[22] L Williams. Casting curved shadows on curved surfaces. In *SIGGRAPH '78*, pages 270–274, 1978.

[23] Lance Williams and Eric Chen. View interpolation for image synthesis. In *SIGGRAPH '93*, 1993.

[24] Mourad Zerroug and Ramakant Nevatia. Segmentation and recovery of shgcs from a real intensity image. In *European Conference on Computer Vision*, pages 319–330, 1994.

View Morphing

Steven M. Seitz Charles R. Dyer

Department of Computer Sciences
University of Wisconsin—Madison[1]

ABSTRACT

Image morphing techniques can generate compelling 2D transitions between images. However, differences in object pose or viewpoint often cause unnatural distortions in image morphs that are difficult to correct manually. Using basic principles of projective geometry, this paper introduces a simple extension to image morphing that correctly handles 3D projective camera and scene transformations. The technique, called *view morphing*, works by prewarping two images prior to computing a morph and then postwarping the interpolated images. Because no knowledge of 3D shape is required, the technique may be applied to photographs and drawings, as well as rendered scenes. The ability to synthesize changes both in viewpoint and image structure affords a wide variety of interesting 3D effects via simple image transformations.

CR Categories and Subject Descriptors: I.3.3 [Computer Graphics]: Picture/Image Generation– viewing algorithms; I.3.7 [Computer Graphics]: Three-Dimensional Graphics and Realism– animation; I.4.3 [Image Processing]: Enhancement– geometric correction, registration.

Additional Keywords: Morphing, image metamorphosis, view interpolation, view synthesis, image warping.

1 INTRODUCTION

Recently there has been a great deal of interest in *morphing* techniques for producing smooth transitions between images. These techniques combine 2D interpolations of shape and color to create dramatic special effects. Part of the appeal of morphing is that the images produced can appear strikingly lifelike and visually convincing. Despite being computed by 2D image transformations, effective morphs can suggest a natural transformation between objects in the 3D world. The fact that realistic 3D shape transformations can arise from 2D image morphs is rather surprising, but extremely useful, in that 3D shape modeling can be avoided.

[1] 1210 W. Dayton St., Madison WI 53706
Email: {seitz | dyer}@cs.wisc.edu
Web: http://www.cs.wisc.edu/~dyer/vision.html

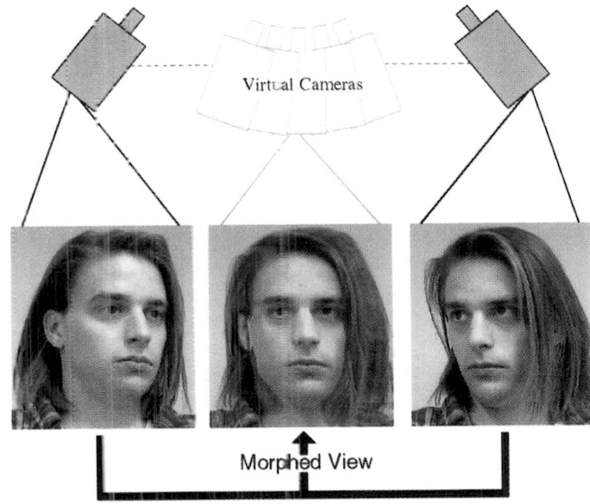

Figure 1: View morphing between two images of an object taken from two different viewpoints produces the illusion of physically moving a virtual camera.

Although current techniques enable the creation of effective image transitions, they do not *ensure* that the resulting transitions appear natural. It is entirely up to the user to evaluate a morph transition and to design the interpolation to achieve the best results. Part of the problem is that existing image morphing methods do not account for changes in viewpoint or object pose. As a result, simple 3D transformations (e.g., translations, rotations) become surprisingly difficult to convey convincingly using existing methods.

In this paper, we describe a simple extension called *view morphing* that allows current image morphing methods to easily synthesize changes in viewpoint and other 3D effects. When morphing between different views of an object or scene, the technique produces new views of the same scene, ensuring a realistic image transition. The effect can be described by what you would see if you physically moved the object (or the camera) between its configurations in the two images and filmed the transition, as shown in Fig. 1. More generally, the approach can synthesize 3D *projective transformations* of objects, a class including 3D rotations, translations, shears, and tapering deformations, by operating entirely on images (no 3D shape information is required). Because view morphing employs existing image morphing techniques as an intermediate step, it may also be used to interpolate between different views of *different* 3D objects, combining image morphing's capacity for dramatic shape transformations with view morphing's ability to achieve changes in viewpoint. The result is a simultaneous interpolation of shape, color, and pose, giving rise to image transitions that appear strikingly 3D.

View morphing works by prewarping two images, comput-

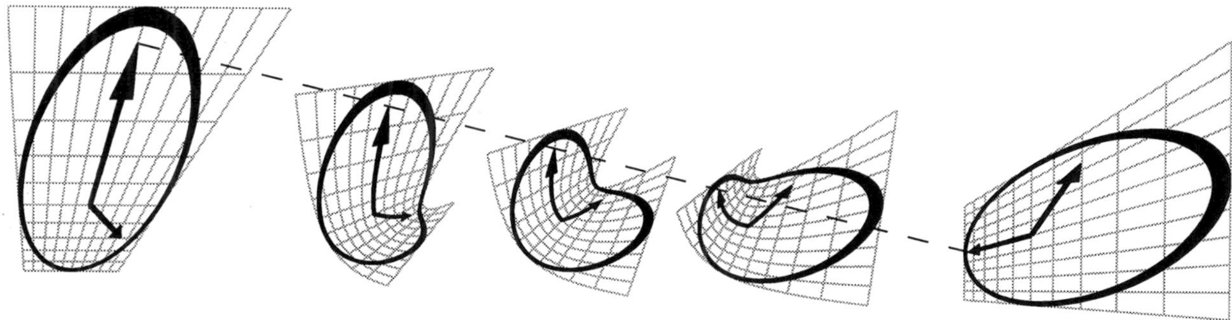

Figure 2: A Shape-Distorting Morph. Linearly interpolating two perspective views of a clock (far left and far right) causes a geometric bending effect in the in-between images. The dashed line shows the linear path of one feature during the course of the transformation. This example is indicative of the types of distortions that can arise with image morphing techniques.

ing a morph (image warp and cross-dissolve) between the prewarped images, and then postwarping each in-between image produced by the morph. The prewarping step is performed automatically, while the postwarping procedure may be interactively controlled by means of a small number of user-specified control points. Any of several image morphing techniques, for instance [15, 1, 8], may be used to compute the intermediate image interpolation. View morphing does not require knowledge of 3D shape, thereby allowing virtual manipulations of unknown objects or scenes given only as drawings or photographs.

In terms of its ability to achieve changes in viewpoint, view morphing is related to previous view-based techniques such as view synthesis [3, 7, 11, 12] and mosaics [10, 2, 14, 6]. However, this paper focuses on creating natural *transitions* between images rather than on synthesizing arbitrary views of an object or scene. This distinction has a number of important consequences. First, in computing the transition between two perspective views, we are free to choose a natural camera path. By choosing this path along the line connecting the two optical centers, we show that the formulation and implementation is greatly simplified. Second, our approach is general in that it can be used to compute transitions between any two images, thereby encompassing both rigid and nonrigid transformations. In contrast, previous view-based techniques have focused on rigid scenes. Finally, view morphing takes advantage of existing image morphing techniques, already in widespread use, for part of the computation. Existing image morphing tools may be easily extended to produce view morphs by adding the image prewarping and postwarping steps described in this paper.

The remainder of this paper is structured as follows: In Section 2 we review image morphing and argue that existing techniques may produce unnatural results when morphing between images of the same or similar shapes. Section 3 describes how to convert image morphing techniques into view morphing techniques by adding prewarping and postwarping steps. Section 4 extends the method to enable interpolations between views of arbitrary projective transformations of the same 3D object. In addition, interactive techniques for controlling the image transformations are introduced. We conclude with some examples in Section 5.

2 IMAGE MORPHING

Image morphing, or *metamorphosis*, is a popular class of techniques for producing transitions between images. There are a variety of morphing methods in the literature, all based on interpolating the positions and colors of pixels in two images. At present, there appears to be no universal criterion for evaluating the quality or realism of a morph, let alone of a morphing method. A natural question to ask, however, is does the method preserve 3D shape. That is, does a morph between two different views of an object produce new views of the same object? Our investigation indicates that unless special care is taken, morphing between images of similar 3D shapes often results in shapes that are mathematically quite different, leading to surprisingly complex and unnatural image transitions. These observations motivate *view morphing*, introduced in the next section, which preserves 3D shape under interpolation.

We write vectors and matrices in bold face and scalars in roman. Scene and image quantities are written in capitals and lowercase respectively. When possible, we also write corresponding image and scene quantities using the same letter. Images, $\mathcal{I}$, and 3D shapes or scenes, $\mathcal{S}$, are expressed as point sets. For example, an image point $(x, y) = \mathbf{p} \in \mathcal{I}$ is the projection of a scene point $(X, Y, Z) = \mathbf{P} \in \mathcal{S}$.

A morph is determined from two images $\mathcal{I}_0$ and $\mathcal{I}_1$ and maps $C_0 : \mathcal{I}_0 \Rightarrow \mathcal{I}_1$ and $C_1 : \mathcal{I}_1 \Rightarrow \mathcal{I}_0$ specifying a complete correspondence between points in the two images. Two maps are required because the correspondence may not be one-to-one. In practice, C_0 and C_1 are partially specified by having the user provide a sparse set of matching features or regions in the two images. The remaining correspondences are determined automatically by interpolation [15, 1, 8]. A warp function for each image is computed from the correspondence maps, usually based on linear interpolation:

$$W_0(\mathbf{p}_0, s) = (1-s)\mathbf{p}_0 + sC_0(\mathbf{p}_0) \qquad (1)$$

$$W_1(\mathbf{p}_1, s) = (1-s)C_1(\mathbf{p}_1) + s\mathbf{p}_1 \qquad (2)$$

W_0 and W_1 give the displacement of each point $\mathbf{p}_0 \in \mathcal{I}_0$ and $\mathbf{p}_1 \in \mathcal{I}_1$ as a function of $s \in [0, 1]$. The in-between images $\mathcal{I}_s$ are computed by warping the two original images and averaging the pixel colors of the warped images. Existing morphing methods vary principally in how the correspondence maps are computed. In addition, some techniques allow finer control over interpolation rates and methods. For instance, Beier et al. [1] suggested two different methods of interpolating line features, using linear interpolation of endpoints, per Eqs. (1) and (2), or of position and angle. In this paper, the term *image morphing* refers specifically to methods that use linear interpolation to compute feature positions in in-between images, including [15, 1, 8].

To illustrate the potentially severe 3D distortions incurred by image morphing, it is useful to consider interpolating between two different views of a planar shape. Any two such images are related by a 2D projective mapping of the form:

$$H(x,y) = (\frac{ax+by+c}{gx+hy+i}, \frac{dx+ey+f}{gx+hy+i})$$

Projective mappings are not preserved under 2D linear interpolation since the sum of two such expressions is in general a ratio of quadratics and therefore not a projective mapping. Consequently, morphing is a *shape-distorting* transformation, as in-between images may not correspond to new views of the same shape. A particularly disturbing effect of image morphing is its tendency to bend straight lines, yielding quite unintuitive image transitions. Fig. 2 shows a Dali-esque morph between two views of a clock in which it appears to bend in half and then straighten out again during the course of the transition. The in-between shapes were computed by linearly interpolating points in the two views that correspond to the same point on the clock.

3 VIEW MORPHING

In the previous section we argued that unless special care is taken, image interpolations do not convey 3D rigid shape transformations. We say that an image transformation is *shape-preserving* if from two images of a particular object, it produces a new image representing a view of the same object. In this section we describe an interpolation-based image morphing procedure that is shape-preserving. Morphs generated by this technique create the illusion that the object moves rigidly (rotating and translating in 3D) between its positions in the two images.

Computing the morph requires the following: (1) two images $\mathcal{I}_0$ and $\mathcal{I}_1$, representing views of the same 3D object or scene, (2) their respective projection matrices $\mathbf{\Pi}_0$ and $\mathbf{\Pi}_1$, and (3) a correspondence between pixels in the two images. Note that no a priori knowledge of 3D shape information is needed. The requirement that projection matrices be known differentiates this technique from previous morphing methods. However, there exist a variety of techniques for obtaining the projection matrices from the images themselves and knowledge of either the internal camera parameters or the 3D positions of a small number of image points. For an overview of both types of techniques, consult [4]. In Section 4 we introduce a variant that does not require knowledge of the projection matrices and also allows interpolations between views of *different* 3D objects or scenes.

The pixel correspondences are derived by a combination of user-interaction and automatic interpolation provided by existing morphing techniques. When the correspondence is correct, the methods described in this section guarantee shape-preserving morphs. In practice, we have found that an approximate correspondence is often sufficient to produce transitions that are visually convincing. Major errors in correspondence may result in visible artifacts such as "ghosting" and shape distortions. Some examples of these effects are shown in Section 5. Other errors may occur as a result of changes in visibility. In order to completely infer the appearance of a surface from a new viewpoint, that surface must be visible in both $\mathcal{I}_0$ and $\mathcal{I}_1$. Changes in visibility may result in *folds* or *holes*, as discussed in Section 3.4.

Following convention, we represent image and scene quantities using homogeneous coordinates: a scene point with Euclidean coordinates (X, Y, Z) is expressed by the column vector $\mathbf{P} = [X\ Y\ Z\ 1]^T$ and a Euclidean image point (x, y) by $\mathbf{p} = [x\ y\ 1]^T$. We reserve the notation $\mathbf{P}$ and $\mathbf{p}$ for points

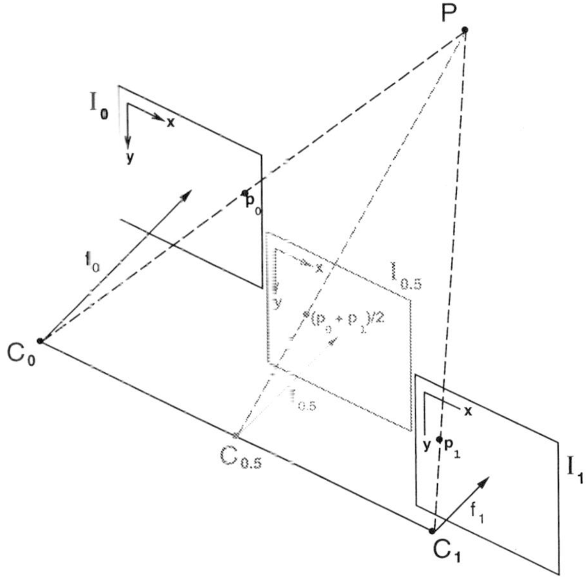

Figure 3: Morphing Parallel Views. Linear interpolation of corresponding pixels in parallel views with image planes $\mathcal{I}_0$ and $\mathcal{I}_1$ creates image $\mathcal{I}_{0.5}$, representing another parallel view of the same scene.

expressed in Euclidean coordinates, i.e., whose last coordinate is 1. Scalar multiples of these points will be written with a tilde, as $\tilde{\mathbf{P}}$ and $\tilde{\mathbf{p}}$. A camera is represented by a 3×4 homogeneous projection matrix of the form $\mathbf{\Pi} = [\mathbf{H} \mid -\mathbf{HC}]$. The vector $\mathbf{C}$ gives the Euclidean position of the camera's optical center and the 3×3 matrix $\mathbf{H}$ specifies the position and orientation of its image plane with respect to the world coordinate system. The perspective projection equation is

$$\tilde{\mathbf{p}} = \mathbf{\Pi P} \tag{3}$$

The term *view* will henceforth refer to the tuple $\langle \mathcal{I}, \mathbf{\Pi} \rangle$ comprised of an image and its associated projection matrix.

3.1 Parallel Views

We begin by considering situations in which linear interpolation of images is shape-preserving. Suppose we take a photograph $\mathcal{I}_0$ of an object, move the object in a direction parallel to the image plane of the camera, zoom out, and take a second picture $\mathcal{I}_1$, as shown in Fig. 3. Alternatively, we could produce the same two images by moving the camera instead of the object. Chen and Williams [3] previously considered this special case, arguing that linear image interpolation should produce new perspective views when the camera moves parallel to the image plane. Indeed, suppose that the camera is moved from the world origin to position $(C_X, C_Y, 0)$ and the focal length changes from f_0 to f_1. We write the respective projection matrices, $\mathbf{\Pi}_0$ and $\mathbf{\Pi}_1$, as:

$$\mathbf{\Pi}_0 = \begin{bmatrix} f_0 & 0 & 0 & 0 \\ 0 & f_0 & 0 & 0 \\ 0 & 0 & 1 & 0 \end{bmatrix}$$

$$\mathbf{\Pi}_1 = \begin{bmatrix} f_1 & 0 & 0 & -f_1 C_X \\ 0 & f_1 & 0 & -f_1 C_Y \\ 0 & 0 & 1 & 0 \end{bmatrix}$$

We refer to cameras or views with projection matrices in this form as *parallel cameras* or *parallel views*, respectively.

Let $\mathbf{p}_0 \in \mathcal{I}_0$ and $\mathbf{p}_1 \in \mathcal{I}_1$ be projections of a scene point $\mathbf{P} = [X\ Y\ Z\ 1]^T$. Linear interpolation of $\mathbf{p}_0$ and $\mathbf{p}_1$ yields

$$\begin{aligned}(1-s)\mathbf{p}_0 + s\mathbf{p}_1 &= (1-s)\frac{1}{Z}\mathbf{\Pi}_0\mathbf{P} + s\frac{1}{Z}\mathbf{\Pi}_1\mathbf{P} \\ &= \frac{1}{Z}\mathbf{\Pi}_s\mathbf{P} \qquad (4)\end{aligned}$$

where

$$\mathbf{\Pi}_s = (1-s)\mathbf{\Pi}_0 + s\mathbf{\Pi}_1 \qquad (5)$$

Image interpolation therefore produces a new view whose projection matrix, $\mathbf{\Pi}_s$, is a linear interpolation of $\mathbf{\Pi}_0$ and $\mathbf{\Pi}_1$, representing a camera with center $\mathbf{C}_s$ and focal length f_s given by:

$$\begin{aligned}\mathbf{C}_s &= (sC_X, sC_Y, 0) \qquad (6) \\ f_s &= (1-s)f_0 + sf_1 \qquad (7)\end{aligned}$$

Consequently, interpolating images produced from parallel cameras produces the illusion of simultaneously moving the camera on the line $\overline{\mathbf{C}_0\mathbf{C}_1}$ between the two optical centers and zooming continuously. Because the image interpolation produces new views of the same object, it is shape-preserving.

In fact, the above derivation relies only on the equality of the third rows of $\mathbf{\Pi}_0$ and $\mathbf{\Pi}_1$. Views satisfying this more general criterion represent a broader class of parallel views for which linear image interpolation is shape preserving. An interesting special case is the class of orthographic projections, i.e., projections $\mathbf{\Pi}_0$ and $\mathbf{\Pi}_1$ whose last row is $[0\ 0\ 0\ 1]$. Linear interpolation of any two orthographic views of a scene therefore produces a new orthographic view of the same scene.

3.2 Non-Parallel Views

In this section we describe how to generate a sequence of in-between views from two non-parallel perspective images of the same 3D object or scene. For convenience, we choose to model the transformation as a change in viewpoint, as opposed to a rotation and translation of the object or scene. The only tools used are image reprojection and linear interpolation, both of which may be performed using efficient scanline methods.

3.2.1 Image Reprojection

Any two views that share the same optical center are related by a planar projective transformation. Let $\mathcal{I}$ and $\hat{\mathcal{I}}$ be two images with projection matrices $\mathbf{\Pi} = [\mathbf{H} \mid -\mathbf{HC}]$ and $\hat{\mathbf{\Pi}} = [\hat{\mathbf{H}} \mid -\hat{\mathbf{H}}\mathbf{C}]$. The projections $\tilde{\mathbf{p}} \in \mathcal{I}$ and $\tilde{\hat{\mathbf{p}}} \in \hat{\mathcal{I}}$ of any scene point $\mathbf{P}$ are related by the following transformation:

$$\begin{aligned}\hat{\mathbf{H}}\mathbf{H}^{-1}\tilde{\mathbf{p}} &= \hat{\mathbf{H}}\mathbf{H}^{-1}\mathbf{\Pi}\mathbf{P} \\ &= \hat{\mathbf{\Pi}}\mathbf{P} \\ &= \tilde{\hat{\mathbf{p}}}\end{aligned}$$

The 3×3 matrix $\hat{\mathbf{H}}\mathbf{H}^{-1}$ is a projective transformation that reprojects the image plane of $\mathcal{I}$ onto that of $\hat{\mathcal{I}}$. More generally, any invertible 3×3 matrix represents a planar projective transformation, a one-to-one map of the plane that transforms points to points and lines to lines. The operation of reprojection is very powerful because it allows the gaze direction to be modified *after* a photograph is taken, or a scene rendered. Our use of projective transforms to compute reprojections takes advantage of an efficient scanline

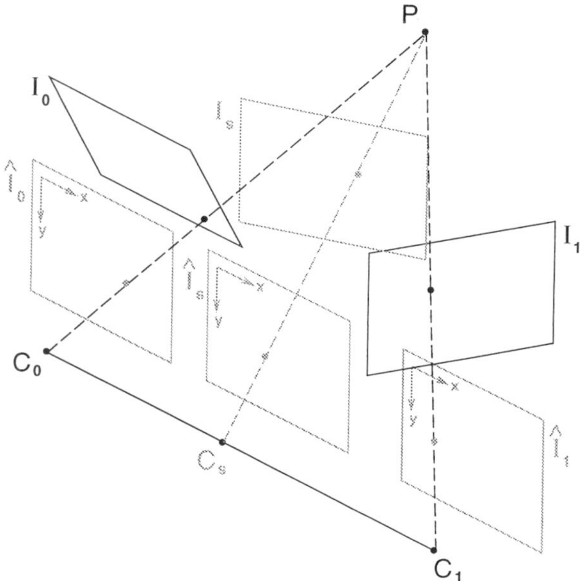

Figure 4: View Morphing in Three Steps. (1) Original images $\mathcal{I}_0$ and $\mathcal{I}_1$ are prewarped to form parallel views $\hat{\mathcal{I}}_0$ and $\hat{\mathcal{I}}_1$. (2) $\hat{\mathcal{I}}_s$ is produced by morphing (interpolating) the prewarped images. (3) $\hat{\mathcal{I}}_s$ is postwarped to form $\mathcal{I}_s$.

algorithm [15]. Reprojection can also be performed through texture-mapping and can therefore exploit current graphics hardware.

Image reprojection has been used previously in a number of applications [15]. Our use of reprojection is most closely related to the techniques used for rectifying stereo views to simplify 3D shape reconstruction [4]. Image mosaic techniques [10, 2, 14, 6] also rely heavily on reprojection methods to project images onto a planar, cylindrical, or spherical manifold. In the next section we describe how reprojection may be used to improve image morphs.

3.2.2 A Three Step Algorithm

Using reprojection, the problem of computing a shape-preserving morph from two non-parallel perspective views can be reduced to the case treated in Section 3.1. To this end, let $\mathcal{I}_0$ and $\mathcal{I}_1$ be two perspective views with projection matrices $\mathbf{\Pi}_0 = [\mathbf{H}_0 \mid -\mathbf{H}_0\mathbf{C}_0]$ and $\mathbf{\Pi}_1 = [\mathbf{H}_1 \mid -\mathbf{H}_1\mathbf{C}_1]$. It is convenient to choose the world coordinate system so that both $\mathbf{C}_0$ and $\mathbf{C}_1$ lie on the world X-axis, i.e., $\mathbf{C}_0 = [X_0\ 0\ 0]^T$ and $\mathbf{C}_1 = [X_1\ 0\ 0]^T$. The two remaining axes should be chosen in a way that reduces the distortion incurred by image reprojection. A simple choice that works well in practice is to choose the Y axis in the direction of the cross product of the two image plane normals.

In between perspective views on the line $\overline{\mathbf{C}_0\mathbf{C}_1}$ may be synthesized by a combination of image reprojections and interpolations, depicted in Fig. 4. Given a projection matrix $\mathbf{\Pi}_s = [\mathbf{H}_s \mid -\mathbf{H}_s\mathbf{C}_s]$, with $\mathbf{C}_s$ fixed by Eq. (6), the following sequence of operations produces an image $\mathcal{I}_s$ corresponding to a view with projection matrix $\mathbf{\Pi}_s$:

1. **Prewarp:** apply projective transforms $\mathbf{H}_0^{-1}$ to $\mathcal{I}_0$ and $\mathbf{H}_1^{-1}$ to $\mathcal{I}_1$, producing prewarped images $\hat{\mathcal{I}}_0$ and $\hat{\mathcal{I}}_1$

2. **Morph:** form $\hat{\mathcal{I}}_s$ by linearly interpolating positions and colors of corresponding points in $\hat{\mathcal{I}}_0$ and $\hat{\mathcal{I}}_1$, using Eq. (4) or any image morphing technique that approximates it

3. **Postwarp:** apply $\mathbf{H}_s$ to $\hat{\mathcal{I}}_s$, yielding image $\mathcal{I}_s$

Prewarping brings the image planes into alignment without changing the optical centers of the two cameras. Morphing the prewarped images moves the optical center to $\mathbf{C}_s$. Postwarping transforms the image plane of the new view to its desired position and orientation.

Notice that the prewarped images $\hat{\mathcal{I}}_0$ and $\hat{\mathcal{I}}_1$ represent views with projection matrices $\hat{\mathbf{\Pi}}_0 = [\mathbf{I} \mid -\mathbf{C}_0]$ and $\hat{\mathbf{\Pi}}_1 = [\mathbf{I} \mid -\mathbf{C}_1]$, where $\mathbf{I}$ is the 3×3 identity matrix. Due to the special form of these projection matrices, $\hat{\mathcal{I}}_0$ and $\hat{\mathcal{I}}_1$ have the property that corresponding points in the two images appear in the same scanline. Therefore, the interpolation $\hat{\mathcal{I}}_s$ may be computed one scanline at a time using only 1D warping and resampling operations.

The prewarping and postwarping operations, combined with the intermediate morph, require multiple image resampling operations that may contribute to a noticeable blurring in the in-between images. Resampling effects can be reduced by supersampling the input images [15] or by composing the image transformations into one aggregate warp for each image. The latter approach is especially compatible with image morphing techniques that employ inverse mapping, such as the Beier and Neely method [1], since the inverse postwarp, morph, and prewarp can be directly concatenated into a single inverse map. Composing the warps has disadvantages however, including loss of both the scanline property and the ability to use off-the-shelf image morphing tools to compute the intermediate interpolation.

3.3 Singular View Configurations

Certain configurations of views cannot be made parallel through reprojection operations. For parallel cameras, (Fig. 5, top) the optical center of neither camera is within the field of view of the other. Note that reprojection does not change a camera's field of view, only its viewing direction. Therefore any pair of views for which the optical center of one camera is within the field of view of the other cannot be made parallel through prewarping[1]. Fig. 5 (bottom) depicts such a pair of *singular* views, for which the prewarping procedure fails. Singular configurations arise when the camera motion is roughly parallel to the viewing direction, a condition detectable from the images themselves (see the Appendix). Singular views are not a problem when the prewarp, morph, and postwarp are composed into a single aggregate warp, since prewarped images are never explicitly constructed. With aggregate warps, view morphing may be applied to arbitrary pairs of views including singular views.

3.4 Changes in Visibility

So far, we have described how to correct for distortions in image morphs by manipulating the projection equations. Eq. (3), however, does not model the effects that changes in *visibility* have on image content. From the standpoint of morphing, changes in visibility result in two types of conditions: *folds* and *holes*. A fold occurs in an in-between image $\mathcal{I}_s$ when a visible surface in $\mathcal{I}_0$ (or $\mathcal{I}_1$) becomes occluded in $\mathcal{I}_s$. In this situation, multiple pixels of $\mathcal{I}_0$ map to the same point in $\mathcal{I}_s$, causing an ambiguity. The opposite case, of an occluded surface suddenly becoming visible, gives rise to a hole; a region of $\mathcal{I}_s$ having no correspondence in $\mathcal{I}_0$.

[1]Prewarping is possible if the images are first cropped to exclude the epipoles (see the Appendix).

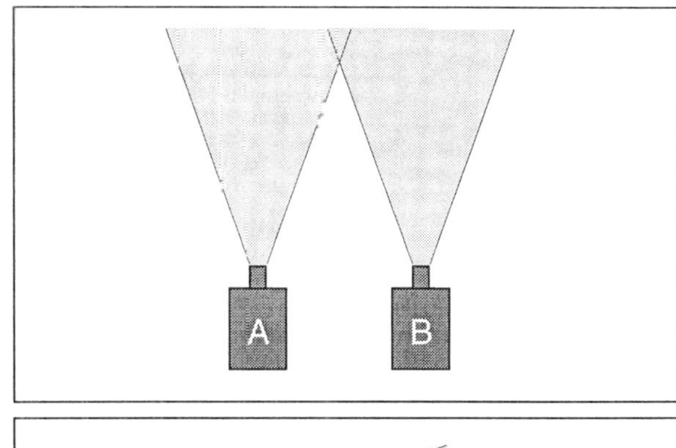

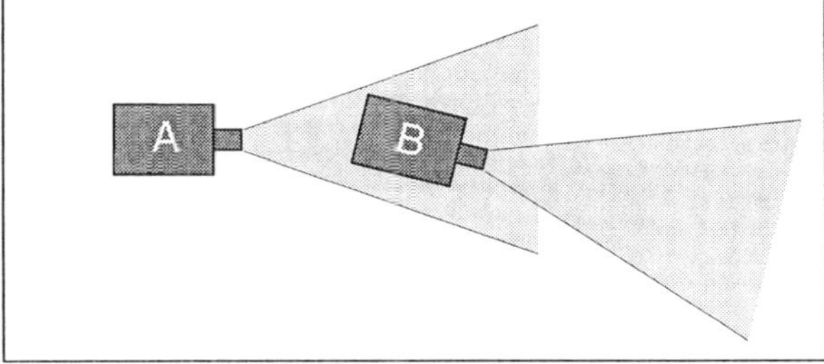

Figure 5: Singular Views. In the parallel configuration (top), each camera's optical center is out of the field of view of the other. A singular configuration (bottom) arises when the optical center of camera B is in the field of view of camera A. Because prewarping does not change the field of view, singular views cannot be reprojected to form parallel views.

Folds can be resolved using Z-buffer techniques [3], provided depth information is available. In the absence of 3D shape information, we use point *disparity* instead. The disparity of corresponding points $\mathbf{p}_0$ and $\mathbf{p}_1$ in two parallel views is defined to be the difference of their x-coordinates. For parallel views, point disparity is inversely proportional to depth so that Z-buffer techniques may be directly applied, with inverse disparity substituted for depth. Because our technique makes images parallel prior to interpolation, this simple strategy suffices in general. Furthermore, since the interpolation is computed one scanline at a time, Z-buffering may be performed at the scanline level, thereby avoiding the large memory requirements commonly associated with Z-buffering algorithms. An alternative method using a Painter's method instead of Z-buffering is presented in [10].

Unlike folds, holes cannot always be eliminated using image information alone. Chen and Williams [3] suggested different methods for filling holes, using a designated background color, interpolation with neighboring pixels, or additional images for better surface coverage. The neighborhood interpolation approach is prevalent in existing image morphing methods and was used implicitly in our experiments.

3.4.1 Producing the Morph

Producing a shape-preserving morph between two images requires choosing a sequence of projection matrices $\mathbf{\Pi}_s = [\mathbf{H}_s \mid -\mathbf{H}_s\mathbf{C}_s]$, beginning with $\mathbf{\Pi}_0$ and ending with $\mathbf{\Pi}_1$. Since $\mathbf{C}_s$ is determined by Eq. (6), this task reduces to choosing $\mathbf{H}_s$ for each value of $s \in (0, 1)$, specifying a continuous transformation of the image plane from the first view to the second.

There are many ways to specify this transformation. A natural one is to interpolate the orientations of the image planes by a single axis rotation. If the image plane normals are denoted by 3D unit vectors $\mathbf{N}_0$ and $\mathbf{N}_1$, the axis $\mathbf{D}$ and angle of rotation θ are given by

$$\begin{aligned} \mathbf{D} &= \mathbf{N}_0 \times \mathbf{N}_1 \\ \theta &= cos^{-1}(\mathbf{N}_0 \cdot \mathbf{N}_1) \end{aligned}$$

Alternatively, if the orientations are expressed using quaternions, the interpolation is computed by spherical linear interpolation [13]. In either case, camera parameters such as focal length and aspect ratio should be interpolated separately.

4 PROJECTIVE TRANSFORMATIONS

By generalizing what we mean by a "view", the technique described in the previous section can be extended to accommodate a range of 3D shape deformations. In particular, view morphing can be used to interpolate between images of different 3D *projective* transformations of the same object, generating new images of the same object, projectively transformed. The advantage of using view morphing in this context is that salient features such as lines and conics are preserved during the course of the transformation from the first image to the second. In contrast, straightforward image morphing can cause severe geometric distortions, as seen in Fig. 2.

As described in Section 3.1, a 2D projective transformation may be expressed as a 3×3 homogeneous matrix transformation. Similarly, a 3D projective transformation is given by a 4×4 matrix $\mathbf{T}$. This class of transformations encompasses 3D rotations, translations, scales, shears, and tapering deformations. Applying $\mathbf{T}$ to a homogeneous scene point produces the point $\tilde{\mathbf{Q}} = \mathbf{TP}$. The corresponding point $\mathbf{Q}$ in 3D Euclidean coordinates is obtained by dividing $\tilde{\mathbf{Q}}$ by its fourth component. 3D projective transformations are notable in that they may be "absorbed" by the camera transformation. Specifically, consider rendering an image of a scene that has been transformed by a 3D projective transformation $\mathbf{T}$. If the projection matrix is given by $\mathbf{\Pi}$, a point $\mathbf{P}$ in the scene appears at position $\mathbf{p}$ in the image, where $\tilde{\mathbf{p}} = \mathbf{\Pi}(\mathbf{TP})$. If we define the 3×4 matrix $\tilde{\mathbf{\Pi}} = \mathbf{\Pi T}$, the combined transformation may be expressed as a single projection, representing a view with projection matrix $\tilde{\mathbf{\Pi}}$.

By allowing arbitrary 3×4 projections, we can model the changes in shape induced by projective transformations by changes in *viewpoint*. In doing so, the problem of interpolating images of projective transformations of an unknown shape is reduced to a form to which the three-step algorithm of Section 3.2.2 may be applied. However, recall that the three-step algorithm requires that the camera viewpoints be known. In order to morph between two different faces, this would require *a priori* knowledge of the 3D projective transformation that best relates them. Since this knowledge may be difficult to obtain, we describe here a modification that doesn't require knowing the projection matrices.

Suppose we wish to smoothly interpolate two images $\mathcal{I}_0$ and $\mathcal{I}_1$ of objects related by a 3D projective transformation. Suppose further that only the images themselves and pixel correspondences are provided. In order to ensure that in-between images depict the same 3D shape (projectively transformed), $\mathcal{I}_0$ and $\mathcal{I}_1$ must first be transformed so as to represent parallel views. As explained in Section 3.2.2, the transformed images, $\hat{\mathcal{I}}_0$ and $\hat{\mathcal{I}}_1$, have the property that corresponding points appear in the same scanline of each image, i.e., two points $\mathbf{p}_0 \in \hat{\mathcal{I}}_0$ and $\mathbf{p}_1 \in \hat{\mathcal{I}}_1$ are projections of the same scene point only if their y-coordinates are equal. In fact, this condition is sufficient to ensure that two views are parallel. Consequently $\mathcal{I}_0$ and $\mathcal{I}_1$ may be made parallel by finding any pair of 2D projective transformations $\mathbf{H}_0$ and $\mathbf{H}_1$ that send corresponding points to the same scanline. One approach for determining $\mathbf{H}_0$ and $\mathbf{H}_1$ using 8 or more image point correspondences is given in the Appendix.

4.1 Controlling the Morph

To fully determine a view morph, $\mathbf{H}_s$ must be provided for each in-between image. Rather than specifying the 3×3 matrix explicitly, it is convenient to provide $\mathbf{H}_s$ indirectly by establishing constraints on the in-between images. A simple yet powerful way of doing this is to interactively specify the paths of four image points through the entire morph transition. These control points can represent the positions of four point features, the endpoints of two lines, or the bounding quadrilateral of an arbitrary image region[2]. Fig. 6 illustrates the process: first, four control points bounding a quadrilateral region of $\hat{\mathcal{I}}_{0.5}$ are selected, determining corresponding quadrilaterals in $\mathcal{I}_0$ and $\mathcal{I}_1$. Second, the control points are interactively moved to their desired positions in $\mathcal{I}_{0.5}$, implicitly specifying the postwarp transformation and thus determining the entire image $\mathcal{I}_{0.5}$. The postwarps of other in-between images are then determined by interpolating the control points. The positions of the control points in $\mathcal{I}_s$ and $\hat{\mathcal{I}}_s$ specify a linear system of equations whose solution yields $\mathbf{H}_s$ [15]. The four curves traced out by the control points may also be manually edited for finer control of the interpolation parameters.

The use of image control points bears resemblance to the view synthesis work of Laveau and Faugeras [7], who used five pairs of corresponding image points to specify projection parameters. However, in their case, the points represented the projection of a new image plane and optical center and were specified only in the original images. In our approach, the control points are specified in the *in-between* image(s), providing more direct control over image appearance.

4.2 View Morphing Without Prewarping

Prewarping is less effective for morphs between different objects not closely related by a 3D projective transform. With objects that are considerably different, it is advisable to leave out the prewarp entirely, since its automatic computation becomes less stable [9]. The postwarp step should not be omitted, however, since it can be used to reduce image plane distortions for more natural morphs. For instance, a large change in orientation results in a noticable 2D image contraction, as seen in Fig. 10.

[2]Care should be taken to ensure that no three of the control points are colinear in any image.

Prewarping is not strictly necessary for images that are approximately orthographic, as noted in Section 3.1. Images taken with a telephoto lens often fall into this category, as do images of objects whose variation in depth is small relative to their distance from the camera. In either case, the images may be morphed directly, yielding new orthographic views. However, the prewarping step does influence the camera motion which, in the orthographic case, cannot be controlled solely by postwarping. The camera transformation determined by Eq. (5) may introduce unnatural skews and twists of the image plane due to the fact that linear matrix interpolation does not preserve row orthogonality. Prewarping the images ensures that the view plane undergoes a single axis rotation. More details on the orthographic case are given in [12].

5 RESULTS

Fig. 6 illustrates the view morphing procedure applied to two images of a bus. We manually selected a set of about 50 corresponding line features in the two images. These features were used to automatically prewarp the images to achieve parallelism using the method described in the Appendix. Inspection of the prewarped images confirms that corresponding features do in fact occupy the same scanlines. An implementation of the Beier-Neely field-morphing algorithm [1] was used to compute the intermediate images, based on the same set of features used to prewarp the images. The resulting images were postwarped by selecting a quadrilateral region delimited by four control points in $\hat{\mathcal{I}}_{0.5}$ and moving the control points to their desired positions in $\mathcal{I}_{0.5}$. The final positions of the control points for the image in the center of Fig. 6 were computed automatically by roughly calibrating the two images based on their known focal lengths and interpolating the changes in orientation [4]. Different images obtained by other settings of the control points are shown in Fig. 8. As these images indicate, a broad range of 3D projective effects may be achieved through the postwarping procedure. For instance, the rectangular shape of the bus can be skewed in different directions and tapered to depict different 3D shapes.

Fig. 7 shows some results on interpolating human faces in varying poses. The first example shows selected frames from a morph computed by interpolating views of the same person facing in two different directions. The resulting animation depicts the subject continuously turning his head from right to left. Because the subject's right ear is visible in only one of the original images, it appears "ghosted" in intermediate frames due to the interpolation of intensity values. In addition, the subject's nose appears slightly distorted as a result of similar changes in visibility. The second sequence shows a morph between different views of two *different faces*. Interpolating different faces is one of the most popular applications of image morphing. Here, we combine image morphing's capacity for dramatic facial interpolations with view morphing's ability to achieve changes in viewpoint. The result is a simultaneous interpolation of facial structure, color, and pose, giving rise to an image transition conveying a metamorphosis that appears strikingly 3D.

When an object has bilateral symmetry, view morphs can be computed from a single image. Fig. 9 depicts a view morph between an image of Leonardo da Vinci's *Mona Lisa* and its mirror reflection. Although the two sides of the face and torso are not perfectly symmetric, the morph conveys a convincing facial rotation.

Fig. 10 compares image morphing with view morphing using two ray-traced images of a helicopter toy. The image morph was computed by linearly interpolating corresponding pixels in the two original images. The change in orientation between the original images caused the in-between images to contract. In addition, the bending effects seen in Fig. 2 are also present. Image morphing techniques such as [1] that preserve lines can reduce bending effects, but only when line features are present. An interesting side-effect is that a large hole appears in the image morph, between the stick and propeller, but not in the view morph, since the eye-level is constant throughout the transition. To be sure, view morphs may also produce holes, but only as a result of a change in visibility.

6 CONCLUSIONS

Achieving realistic image transitions is possible but often difficult with existing image morphing techniques due to the lack of available 3D information. In this paper, we demonstrated how to accurately convey a range of 3D transformations based on a simple yet powerful extension to the image morphing paradigm called *view morphing*. In addition to changes in viewpoint view morphing accommodates changes in projective shape. By integrating these capabilities with those already afforded by existing image morphing methods, view morphing enables transitions between images of different objects that give a strong sense of metamorphosis in 3D. Because no knowledge of 3D shape is required, the technique may be applied to photographs and drawings, as well as to artificially rendered scenes. Two different methods for controlling the image transition were described, using either automatic interpolation of camera parameters or interactive user-manipulation of image control points, based on whether or not the camera viewpoints are known.

Because view morphing relies exclusively on image information, it is sensitive to changes in visibility. In our experiments, the best morphs resulted when visibility was nearly constant, i.e., most surfaces were visible in both images. The visible effects of occlusions may often be minimized by experimenting with different feature correspondences. Additional user input could be used to reduce ghosting effects by specifying the paths of image regions visible in only one of the original images. A topic of future work will be to investigate ways of extending view morphing to handle extreme changes in visibility, enabling 180 or 360 degree rotations in depth.

ACKNOWLEDGEMENTS

The authors would like to thank Paul Heckbert for providing the image morphing code used to interpolate prewarped images in this paper. The original helicopter images in Fig. 10 were rendered using Rayshade with a Z-buffer output extension written by Mark Maimone. The support of the National Science Foundation under Grant Nos. IRI–9220782 and CDA–9222948 is gratefully acknowledged.

REFERENCES

[1] BEIER, T., AND NEELY, S. Feature-based image metamorphosis. Proc. SIGGRAPH 92. In *Computer Graphics* (1992), pp. 35–42.

[2] CHEN, S. E. Quicktime VR — An image-based approach to virtual environment navigation. Proc. SIGGRAPH 95. In *Computer Graphics* (1995), pp. 29–38.

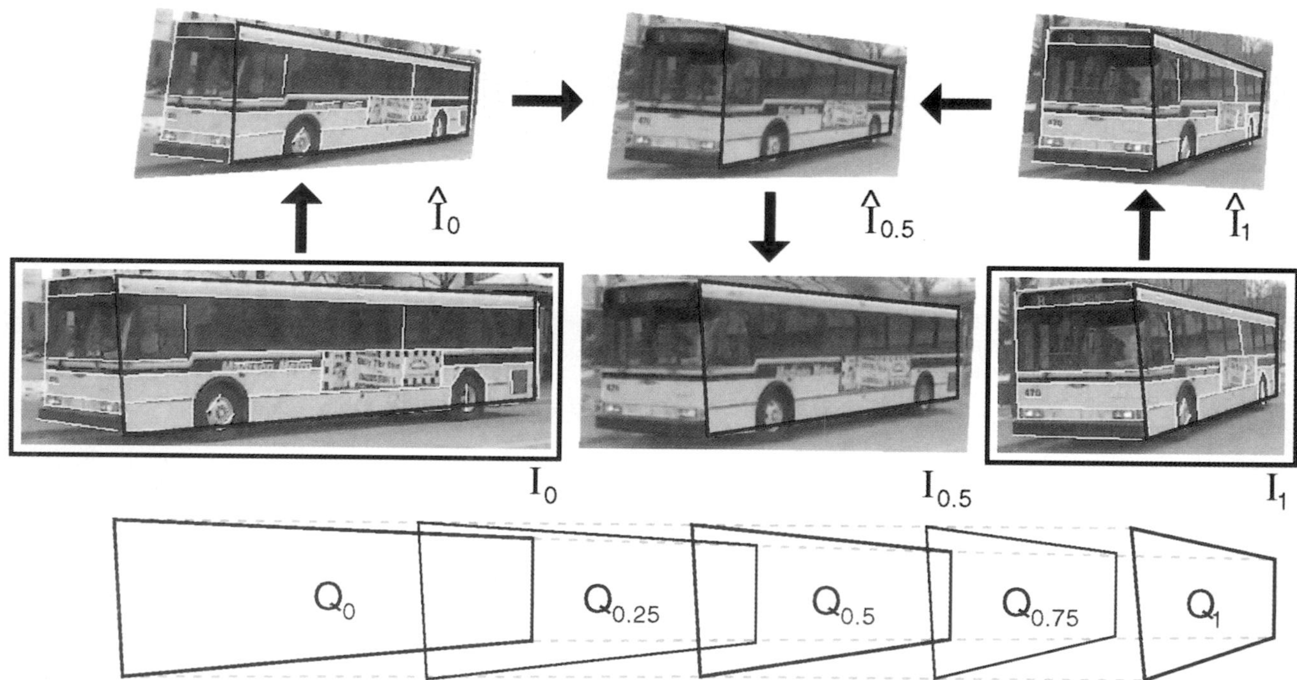

Figure 6: View Morphing Procedure: A set of features (yellow lines) is selected in original images $\mathcal{I}_0$ and $\mathcal{I}_1$. Using these features, the images are automatically prewarped to produce $\hat{\mathcal{I}}_0$ and $\hat{\mathcal{I}}_1$. The prewarped images are morphed to create a sequence of in-between images, the middle of which, $\hat{\mathcal{I}}_{0.5}$, is shown at top-center. $\hat{\mathcal{I}}_{0.5}$ is interactively postwarped by selecting a quadrilateral region (marked red) and specifying its desired configuration, $Q_{0.5}$, in $\mathcal{I}_{0.5}$. The postwarps for other in-between images are determined by interpolating the quadrilaterals (bottom).

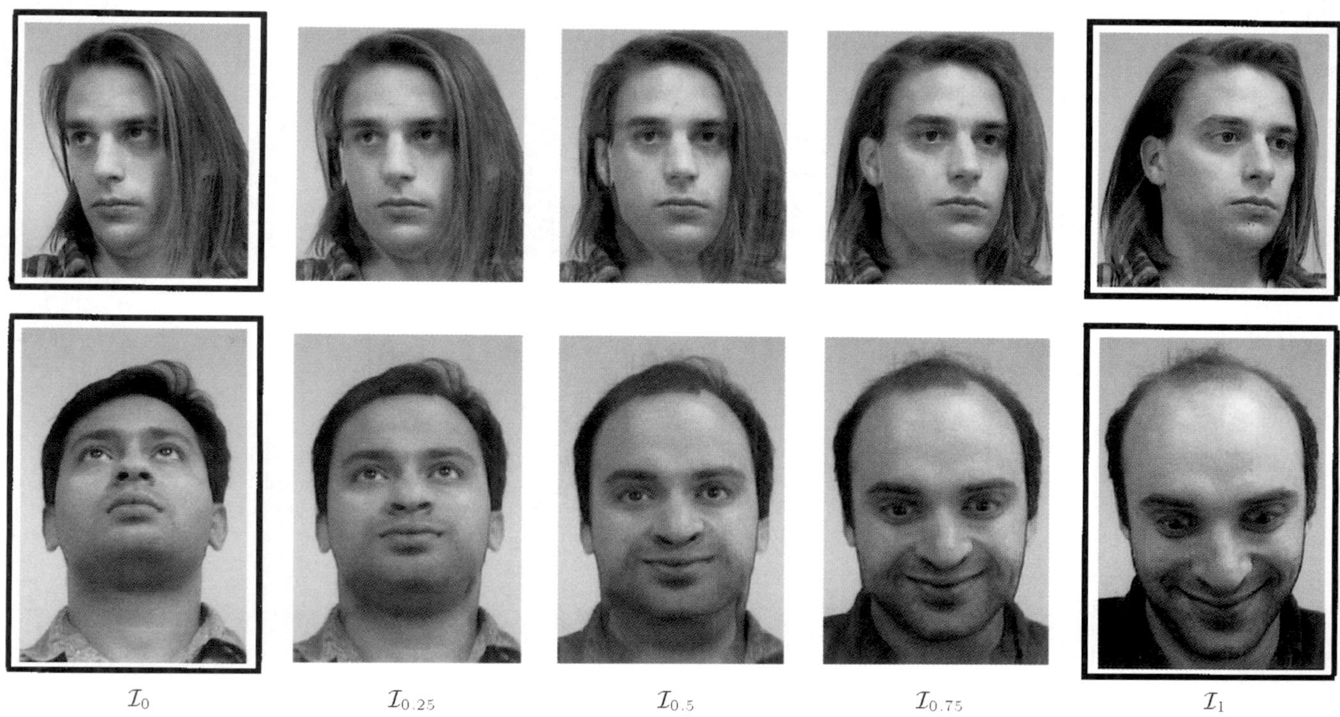

Figure 7: Facial View Morphs. Top: morph between two views of the same person. Bottom: morph between views of two different people. In each case, view morphing captures the change in facial pose between original images I_0 and I_1, conveying a natural 3D rotation.

Figure 8: Postwarping deformations obtained by different settings of the control quadrilateral.

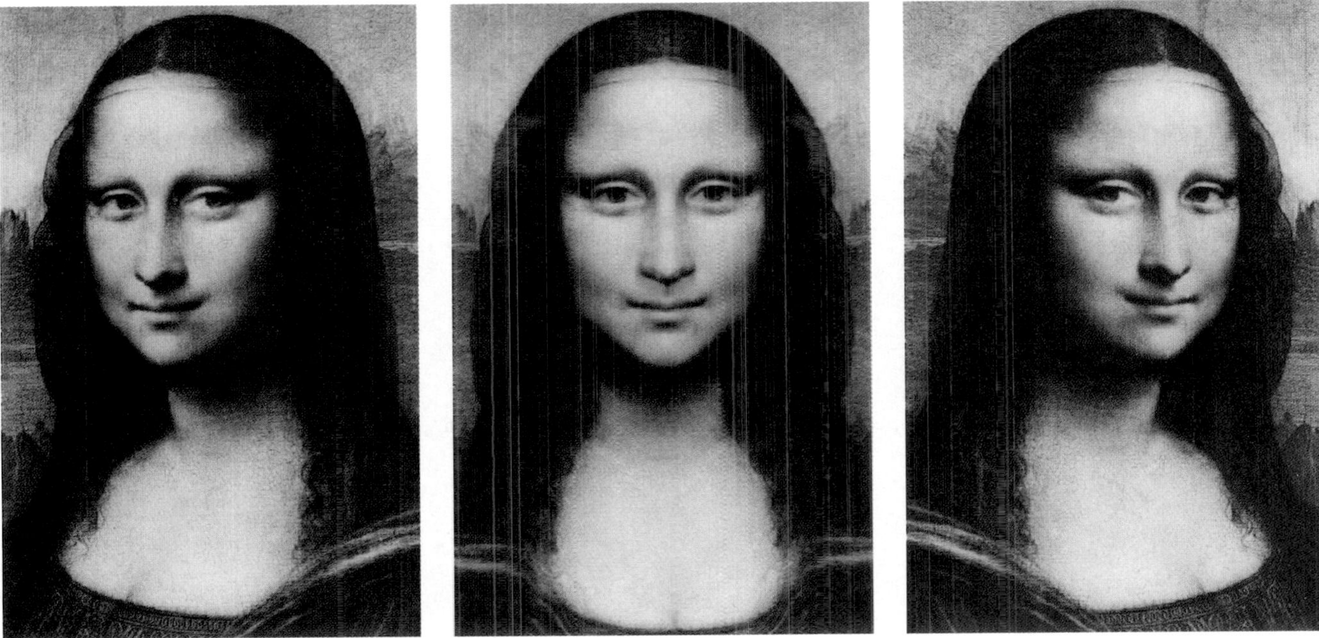

Figure 9: Mona Lisa View Morph. Morphed view (center) is halfway between original image (left) and it's reflection (right).

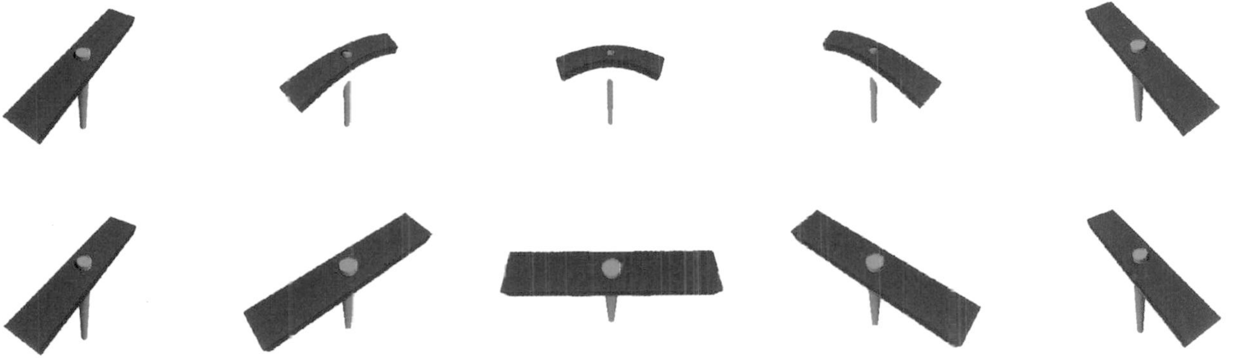

Figure 10: Image Morphing Versus View Morphing. Top: image morph between two views of a helicopter toy causes the in-between images to contract and bend. Bottom: view morph between the same two views results in a physically consistent morph. In this example the image morph also results in an extraneous hole between the blade and the stick. Holes can appear in view morphs as well.

[3] CHEN, S. E., AND WILLIAMS, L. View interpolation for image synthesis. Proc. SIGGRAPH 93. In *Computer Graphics* (1993), pp. 279–288.

[4] FAUGERAS, O. *Three-Dimensional Computer Vision, A Geometric Viewpoint.* MIT Press, Cambridge, MA, 1993.

[5] HARTLEY, R. I. In defence of the 8-point algorithm. In *Proc. Fifth Intl. Conference on Computer Vision* (1995), pp. 1064–1070.

[6] KUMAR, R., ANANDAN, P., IRANI, M., BERGEN, J., AND HANNA, K. Representation of scenes from collections of images. In *Proc. IEEE Workshop on Representations of Visual Scenes* (1995), pp. 10–17.

[7] LAVEAU, S., AND FAUGERAS, O. 3-D scene representation as a collection of images. In *Proc. International Conference on Pattern Recognition* (1994), pp. 689–691.

[8] LEE, S.-Y., CHWA, K.-Y., SHIN, S. Y., AND WOLBERG, G. Image metamorphosis using snakes and free-form deformations. Proc. SIGGRAPH 92. In *Computer Graphics* (1992), pp. 439–448.

[9] LUONG, Q.-T., AND FAUGERAS, O. The fundamental matrix: Theory, algorithms, and stability analysis. *Intl. Journal of Computer Vision 17*, 1 (1996), 43–75.

[10] MCMILLAN, L., AND BISHOP, G. Plenoptic modeling. Proc. SIGGRAPH 95. In *Computer Graphics* (1995), pp. 39–46.

[11] POGGIO, T., AND BEYMER, D. Learning networks for face analysis and synthesis. In *Proc. Intl. Workshop on Automatic Face- and Gesture-Recognition* (Zurich, 1995), pp. 160–165.

[12] SEITZ, S. M., AND DYER, C. R. Physically-valid view synthesis by image interpolation. In *Proc. IEEE Workshop on Representations of Visual Scenes* (1995), pp. 18–25.

[13] SHOEMAKE, K. Animating rotation with quaternion curves. Proc. SIGGRAPH 85. In *Computer Graphics* (1985), pp. 245–254.

[14] SZELISKI, R. Video mosaics for virtual environments. *IEEE Computer Graphics and Applications 16*, 2 (1996), 22–30.

[15] WOLBERG, G. *Digital Image Warping.* IEEE Computer Society Press, Los Alamitos, CA, 1990.

APPENDIX

This appendix describes how to automatically compute the image prewarping transforms $\mathbf{H}_0$ and $\mathbf{H}_1$ from the images themselves. We assume that the 2D positions of 8 or more corresponding points are given in each image. The fundamental matrix of two views is defined to be the 3×3, rank-two matrix $\mathbf{F}$ such that for every pair of corresponding image points $\mathbf{p}_0 \in \mathcal{I}_0$ and $\mathbf{p}_1 \in \mathcal{I}_1$,

$$\mathbf{p}_1^T \mathbf{F} \mathbf{p}_0 = 0$$

$\mathbf{F}$ is defined up to a scale factor and can be computed from 8 or more such points using linear [5] or non-linear [9] methods.

A sufficient condition for two views to be parallel is that their fundamental matrix have the form:

$$\hat{\mathbf{F}} = \begin{bmatrix} 0 & 0 & 0 \\ 0 & 0 & -1 \\ 0 & 1 & 0 \end{bmatrix} \tag{8}$$

Consequently, any two images with fundamental matrix $\mathbf{F}$ may be prewarped (i.e., made parallel) by choosing any two projective transforms $\mathbf{H}_0$ and $\mathbf{H}_1$ such that $(\mathbf{H}_1^{-1})^T \mathbf{F} \mathbf{H}_0^{-1} = \hat{\mathbf{F}}$. Here we describe one method that applies a rotation in depth to make the images planes parallel, followed by an affine transformation to align corresponding scanlines. The procedure is determined by choosing an (arbitrary) axis of rotation $\mathbf{d}_0 = [d_0^x \; d_0^y \; 0]^T \in \mathcal{I}_0$. Given $[x \; y \; z]^T = \mathbf{F}\mathbf{d}_0$, the corresponding axis in $\mathcal{I}_1$ is determined according to $\mathbf{d}_1 = [-y \; x \; 0]^T$. To compute the angles of depth rotation we need the *epipoles*, also known as *vanishing points*, $\mathbf{e}_0 \in \mathcal{I}_0$ and $\mathbf{e}_1 \in \mathcal{I}_1$. $\mathbf{e}_0 = [e_0^x \; e_0^y \; e_0^z]^T$ and $\mathbf{e}_1 = [e_1^x \; e_1^y \; e_1^z]^T$ are the unit eigenvectors of $\mathbf{F}$ and $\mathbf{F}^T$ respectively, corresponding to eigenvalues of 0. A view's epipole represents the projection of the optical center of the other view. The following procedure will work provided the views are not *singular*, i.e., the epipoles are outside the image borders and therefore not within the field of view. The angles of rotation in depth about $\mathbf{d}_i$ are given by

$$\theta_i = -\frac{\pi}{2} - tan^{-1}\left(\frac{d_i^y e_i^x - d_i^x e_i^y}{e_i^z}\right)$$

We denote as $\mathbf{R}_{\theta_i}^{\mathbf{d}_i}$ the 3×3 matrix corresponding to a rotation of angle θ_i about axis $\mathbf{d}_i$. Applying $\mathbf{R}_{\theta_0}^{\mathbf{d}_0}$ to $\mathcal{I}_0$ and $\mathbf{R}_{\theta_1}^{\mathbf{d}_1}$ to $\mathcal{I}_1$ makes the two image planes parallel. Although this is technically sufficient for prewarping, it is useful to add an additional affine warp to align the scanlines. This simplifies the morph step to a scanline interpolation and also avoids bottleneck problems that arise as a result of image plane rotations [15].

The next step is to rotate the images so that epipolar lines are horizontal. The new epipoles are $[\tilde{e}_i^x \; \tilde{e}_i^y \; 0]^T = \mathbf{R}_{\theta_i}^{\mathbf{d}_i} \mathbf{e}_i$. The angles of rotation ϕ_0 and ϕ_1 are given by $\phi_i = -tan^{-1}(\tilde{e}_i^y / \tilde{e}_i^x)$. After applying these image plane rotations, the fundamental matrix has the form

$$\tilde{\mathbf{F}} = \mathbf{R}_{\phi_1} \mathbf{R}_{\theta_1}^{\mathbf{d}_1} \mathbf{F} \mathbf{R}_{-\theta_0}^{\mathbf{d}_0} \mathbf{R}_{-\phi_0} = \begin{bmatrix} 0 & 0 & 0 \\ 0 & 0 & a \\ 0 & b & c \end{bmatrix}$$

The 3×3 matrix $\mathbf{R}_\theta$ denotes an image plane (z axis) rotation of angle θ. Finally, to get $\mathbf{F}$ into the form of Eq. (8), the second image is translated and vertically scaled by the matrix

$$\mathbf{T} = \begin{bmatrix} 1 & 0 & 0 \\ 0 & -a & -c \\ 0 & 0 & b \end{bmatrix}$$

In summary, the prewarping transforms $\mathbf{H}_0$ and $\mathbf{H}_1$ are

$$\begin{aligned} \mathbf{H}_0 &= \mathbf{R}_{\phi_0} \mathbf{R}_{\theta_0}^{\mathbf{d}_0} \\ \mathbf{H}_1 &= \mathbf{T} \mathbf{R}_{\phi_1} \mathbf{R}_{\theta_1}^{\mathbf{d}_1} \end{aligned}$$

The entire procedure is determined by selecting $\mathbf{d}_0$. A suitable choice is to select $\mathbf{d}_0$ orthogonal to $\mathbf{e}_0$, i.e., $\mathbf{d}_0 = [-e_0^y \; e_0^x \; 0]^T$.

Light Field Rendering

Marc Levoy and Pat Hanrahan
Computer Science Department
Stanford University

Abstract

A number of techniques have been proposed for flying through scenes by redisplaying previously rendered or digitized views. Techniques have also been proposed for interpolating between views by warping input images, using depth information or correspondences between multiple images. In this paper, we describe a simple and robust method for generating new views from arbitrary camera positions without depth information or feature matching, simply by combining and resampling the available images. The key to this technique lies in interpreting the input images as 2D slices of a 4D function - the light field. This function completely characterizes the flow of light through unobstructed space in a static scene with fixed illumination.

We describe a sampled representation for light fields that allows for both efficient creation and display of inward and outward looking views. We have created light fields from large arrays of both rendered and digitized images. The latter are acquired using a video camera mounted on a computer-controlled gantry. Once a light field has been created, new views may be constructed in real time by extracting slices in appropriate directions. Since the success of the method depends on having a high sample rate, we describe a compression system that is able to compress the light fields we have generated by more than a factor of 100:1 with very little loss of fidelity. We also address the issues of antialiasing during creation, and resampling during slice extraction.

CR Categories: I.3.2 [Computer Graphics]: Picture/Image Generation — *Digitizing and scanning*, *Viewing algorithms*; I.4.2 [Computer Graphics]: Compression — *Approximate methods*

Additional keywords: image-based rendering, light field, holographic stereogram, vector quantization, epipolar analysis

1. Introduction

Traditionally the input to a 3D graphics system is a scene consisting of geometric primitives composed of different materials and a set of lights. Based on this input specification, the rendering system computes and outputs an image. Recently a new approach to rendering has emerged: *image-based rendering*. Image-based rendering systems generate different views of an environment from a set of pre-acquired imagery. There are several advantages to this approach:

Address: Gates Computer Science Building 3B
Stanford University
Stanford, CA 94305
levoy@cs.stanford.edu
hanrahan@cs.stanford.edu
http://www-graphics.stanford.edu

- The display algorithms for image-based rendering require modest computational resources and are thus suitable for real-time implementation on workstations and personal computers.
- The cost of interactively viewing the scene is independent of scene complexity.
- The source of the pre-acquired images can be from a real or virtual environment, i.e. from digitized photographs or from rendered models. In fact, the two can be mixed together.

The forerunner to these techniques is the use of environment maps to capture the incoming light in a texture map [Blinn76, Greene86]. An environment map records the incident light arriving from all directions at a point. The original use of environment maps was to efficiently approximate reflections of the environment on a surface. However, environment maps also may be used to quickly display any outward looking view of the environment from a fixed location but at a variable orientation. This is the basis of the Apple QuickTimeVR system [Chen95]. In this system environment maps are created at key locations in the scene. The user is able to navigate discretely from location to location, and while at each location continuously change the viewing direction.

The major limitation of rendering systems based on environment maps is that the viewpoint is fixed. One way to relax this fixed position constraint is to use view interpolation [Chen93, Greene94, Fuchs94, McMillan95a, McMillan95b, Narayanan95]. Most of these methods require a depth value for each pixel in the environment map, which is easily provided if the environment maps are synthetic images. Given the depth value it is possible to reproject points in the environment map from different vantage points to warp between multiple images. The key challenge in this warping approach is to "fill in the gaps" when previously occluded areas become visible.

Another approach to interpolating between acquired images is to find corresponding points in the two [Laveau94, McMillan95b, Seitz95]. If the positions of the cameras are known, this is equivalent to finding the depth values of the corresponding points. Automatically finding correspondences between pairs of images is the classic problem of stereo vision, and unfortunately although many algorithms exist, these algorithms are fairly fragile and may not always find the correct correspondences.

In this paper we propose a new technique that is robust and allows much more freedom in the range of possible views. The major idea behind the technique is a representation of the *light field*, the radiance as a function of position and direction, in regions of space free of occluders (free space). In free space, the light field is a 4D, not a 5D function. An image is a two dimensional slice of the 4D light field. Creating a light field from a set of images corresponds to inserting each 2D slice into the 4D light field representation. Similarly, generating new views corresponds to extracting and resampling a slice.

Generating a new image from a light field is quite different than previous view interpolation approaches. First, the new image is generally formed from many different pieces of the original input images, and need not look like any of them. Second, no model information, such as depth values or image correspondences, is needed to extract the image values. Third, image generation involves only resampling, a simple linear process.

This representation of the light field is similar to the epipolar volumes used in computer vision [Bolles87] and to horizontal-parallax-only holographic stereograms [Benton83]. An epipolar volume is formed from an array of images created by translating a camera in equal increments in a single direction. Such a representation has recently been used to perform view interpolation [Katayama95]. A holographic stereogram is formed by exposing a piece of film to an array of images captured by a camera moving sideways. Halle has discussed how to set the camera aperture to properly acquire images for holographic stereograms [Halle94], and that theory is applicable to this work. Gavin Miller has also recognized the potential synergy between true 3D display technologies and computer graphics algorithms [Miller95].

There are several major challenges to using the light field approach to view 3D scenes on a graphics workstation. First, there is the choice of parameterization and representation of the light field. Related to this is the choice of sampling pattern for the field. Second, there is the issue of how to generate or acquire the light field. Third, there is the problem of fast generation of different views. This requires that the slice representing rays through a point be easily extracted, and that the slice be properly resampled to avoid artifacts in the final image. Fourth, the obvious disadvantage of this approach is the large amount of data that may be required. Intuitively one suspects that the light field is coherent and that it may be compressed greatly. In the remaining sections we discuss these issues and our proposed solutions.

2. Representation

We define the light field as the radiance at a point in a given direction. Note that our definition is equivalent to the *plenoptic function* introduced by Adelson and Bergen [Adelson91]. The phrase light field was coined by A. Gershun in his classic paper describing the radiometric properties of light in a space [Gershun36]. [1] McMillan and Bishop [McMillan95b] discuss the representation of 5D light fields as a set of panoramic images at different 3D locations.

However, the 5D representation may be reduced to 4D in free space (regions free of occluders). This is a consequence of the fact that the radiance does not change along a line unless blocked. 4D light fields may be interpreted as functions on the space of oriented lines. The redundancy of the 5D representation is undesirable for two reasons: first, redundancy increases the size of the total dataset, and second, redundancy complicates the reconstruction of the radiance function from its samples. This reduction in dimension has been used to simplify the representation of radiance emitted by luminaires [Levin71, Ashdown93]. For the remainder of this paper we will be only concerned with 4D light fields.

[1] For those familiar with Gershun's paper, he actually uses the term light field to mean the irradiance vector as a function of position. For this reason P. Moon in a later book [Moon81] uses the term photic field to denote what we call the light field.

Although restricting the validity of the representation to free space may seem like a limitation, there are two common situations where this assumption is useful. First, most geometric models are bounded. In this case free space is the region outside the convex hull of the object, and hence all views of an object from outside its convex hull may be generated from a 4D light field. Second, if we are moving through an architectural model or an outdoor scene we are usually moving through a region of free space; therefore, any view from inside this region, of objects outside the region, may be generated.

The major issue in choosing a representation of the 4D light field is how to parameterize the space of oriented lines. There are several issues in choosing the parameterization:

Efficient calculation. The computation of the position of a line from its parameters should be fast. More importantly, for the purposes of calculating new views, it should be easy to compute the line parameters given the viewing transformation and a pixel location.

Control over the set of lines. The space of all lines is infinite, but only a finite subset of line space is ever needed. For example, in the case of viewing an object we need only lines intersecting the convex hull of the object. Thus, there should be an intuitive connection between the actual lines in 3-space and line parameters.

Uniform sampling. Given equally spaced samples in line parameter space, the pattern of lines in 3-space should also be uniform. In this sense, a uniform sampling pattern is one where the *number of lines* in intervals between samples is constant everywhere. Note that the correct measure for number of lines is related to the form factor kernel [Sbert93].

The solution we propose is to parameterize lines by their intersections with two planes in arbitrary position (see figure 1). By convention, the coordinate system on the first plane is (u, v) and on the second plane is (s, t). An oriented line is defined by connecting a point on the uv plane to a point on the st plane. In practice we restrict u, v, s, and t to lie between 0 and 1, and thus points on each plane are restricted to lie within a convex quadrilateral. We call this representation a *light slab*. Intuitively, a light slab represents the beam of light entering one quadrilateral and exiting another quadrilateral.

A nice feature of this representation is that one of the planes may be placed at infinity. This is convenient since then lines may be parameterized by a point and a direction. The latter will prove useful for constructing light fields either from orthographic images or images with a fixed field of view. Furthermore, if all calculations are performed using homogeneous coordinates, the two cases may be handled at no additional cost.

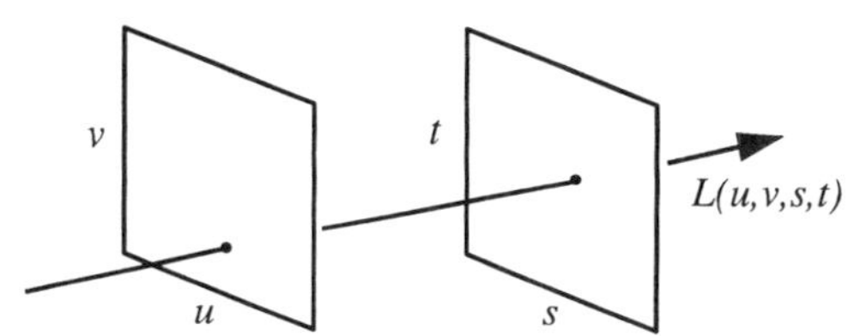

Figure 1: The light slab representation.

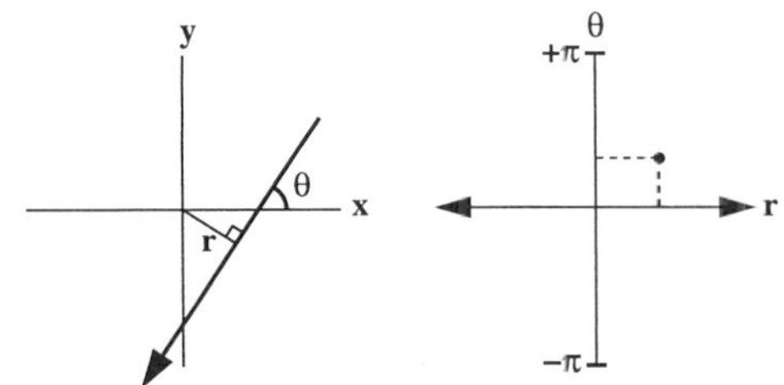

Figure 2: Definition of the line space we use to visualize sets of light rays. Each oriented line in Cartesian space (at left) is represented in line space (at right) by a point. To simplify the visualizations, we show only lines in 2D; the extension to 3D is straightforward.

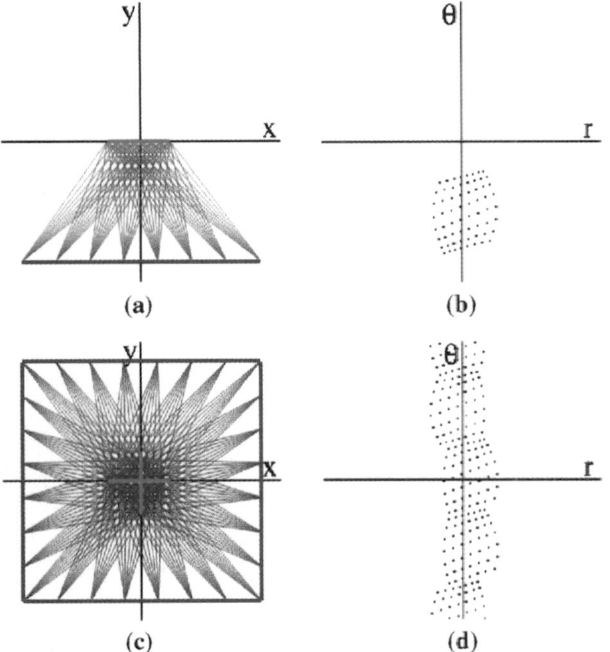

Figure 3: Using line space to visualize ray coverage. (a) shows a single light slab. Light rays (drawn in gray) connect points on two defining lines (drawn in red and green). (c) shows an arrangement of four rotated copies of (a). (b) and (d) show the corresponding line space visualizations. For any set of lines in Cartesian space, the envelope formed by the corresponding points in line space indicates our coverage of position and direction; ideally the coverage should be complete in θ and as wide as possible in r. As these figures show, the single slab in (a) does not provide full coverage in θ, but the four-slab arrangement in (c) does. (c) is, however, narrow in r. Such an arrangement is suitable for inward-looking views of a small object placed at the origin. It was used to generate the lion light field in figure 14d.

A big advantage of this representation is the efficiency of geometric calculations. Mapping from (u, v) to points on the plane is a projective map and involves only linear algebra (multiplying by a 3x3 matrix). More importantly, as will be discussed in section 5, the inverse mapping from an image pixel (x, y) to (u, v, s, t) is also a projective map. Methods using spherical or cylindrical coordinates require substantially more computation.

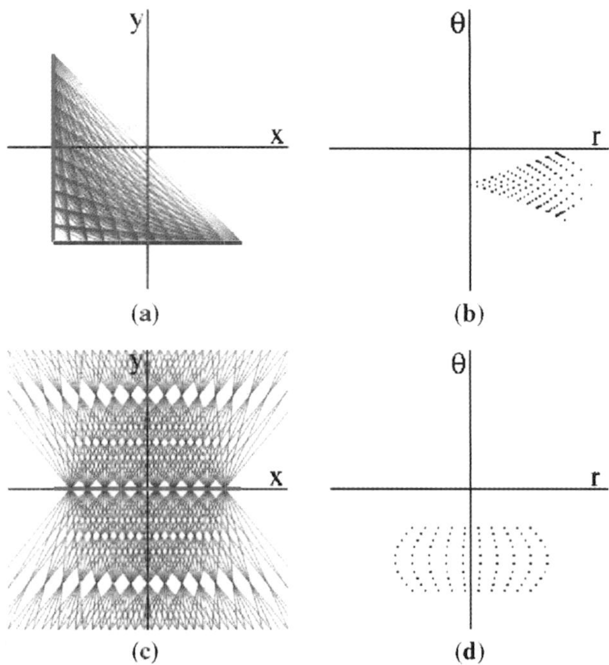

Figure 4: Using line space to visualize sampling uniformity. (a) shows a light slab defined by two lines at right angles. (c) shows a light slab where one defining line is at infinity. This arrangement generates rays passing through the other defining line with an angle between -45° and +45°. (b) and (d) show the corresponding line space visualizations. Our use of (r, θ) to parameterize line space has the property that equal areas in line space correspond to equally dense sampling of position and orientation in Cartesian space; ideally the density of points in line space should be uniform. As these figures show, the singularity at the corner in (a) leads to a highly nonuniform and therefore inefficient sampling pattern, indicated by dark areas in (b) at angles of 0 and $-\pi/2$. (c) generates a more uniform set of lines. Although (c) does not provide full coverage of θ, four rotated copies do. Such an arrangement is suitable for outward-looking views by an observer standing near the origin. It was used to generate the hallway light field in figure 14c.

Many properties of light fields are easier to understand in line space (figures 2 through 4). In line space, each oriented line is represented by a point and each set of lines by a region. In particular, the set of lines represented by a light slab and the set of lines intersecting the convex hull of an object are both regions in line space. All views of an object could be generated from one light slab if its set of lines include all lines intersecting the convex hull of the object. Unfortunately, this is not possible. Therefore, it takes multiple light slabs to represent all possible views of an object. We therefore tile line space with a collection of light slabs, as shown in figure 3.

An important issue related to the parameterization is the sampling pattern. Assuming that all views are equally likely to be generated, then any line is equally likely to be needed. Thus all regions of line space should have an equal density of samples. Figure 4 shows the density of samples in line space for different arrangements of slabs. Note that no slab arrangement is perfect: arrangements with a singularity such as two polygons joined at a corner (4a) are bad and should be avoided, whereas slabs formed from parallel planes (3a) generate fairly uniform patterns. In addition, arrangements where one plane is at infinity (4c) are better than those with two finite planes (3a). Finally, because of symmetry the spacing of samples in uv should in general be the same as st. However, if the observer is likely to stand near the uv plane, then it may be acceptable to sample uv less frequently than st.

3. Creation of light fields

In this section we discuss the creation of both virtual light fields (from rendered images) and real light fields (from digitized images). One method to create a light field would be to choose a 4D sampling pattern, and for each line sample, find the radiance. This is easily done directly for virtual environments by a ray tracer. This could also be done in a real environment with a spot radiometer, but it would be very tedious. A more practical way to generate light fields is to assemble a collection of images.

3.1. From rendered images

For a virtual environment, a light slab is easily generated simply by rendering a 2D array of images. Each image represents a slice of the 4D light slab at a fixed uv value and is formed by placing the center of projection of the virtual camera at the sample location on the uv plane. The only issue is that the xy samples of each image must correspond exactly with the st samples. This is easily done by performing a sheared perspective projection (figure 5) similar to that used to generate a stereo pair of images. Figure 6 shows the resulting 4D light field, which can be visualized either as a uv array of st images or as an st array of uv images.

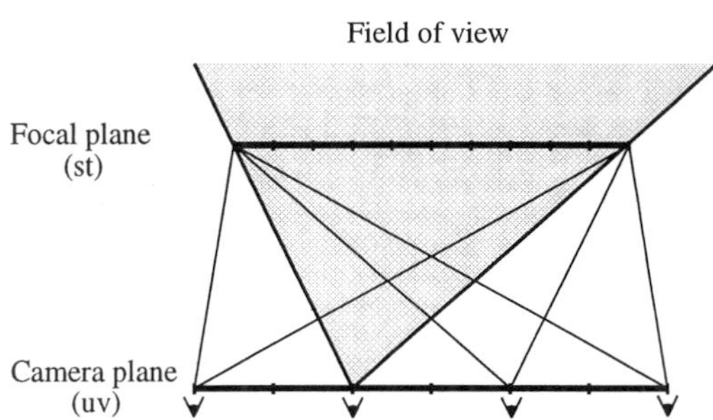

Figure 5: The viewing geometry used to create a light slab from an array of perspective images.

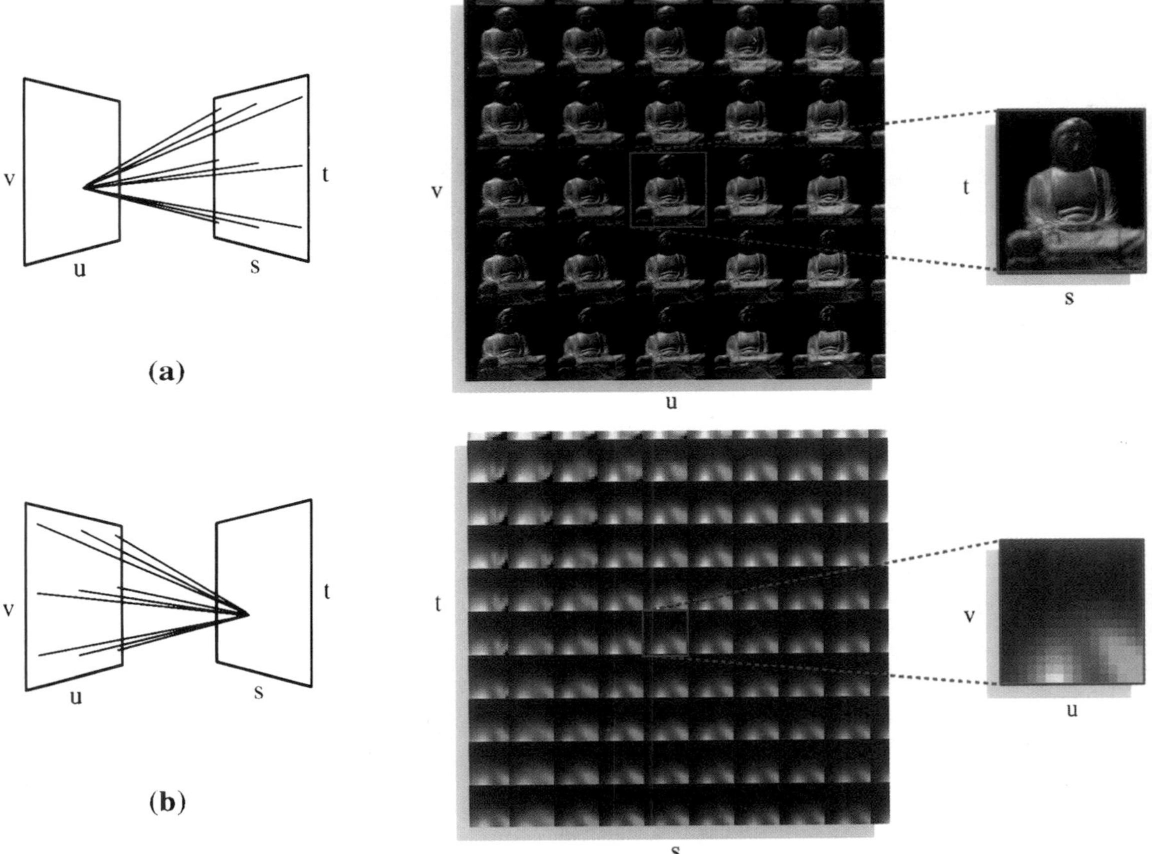

Figure 6: Two visualizations of a light field. (a) Each image in the array represents the rays arriving at one point on the uv plane from all points on the st plane, as shown at left. (b) Each image represents the rays leaving one point on the st plane bound for all points on the uv plane. The images in (a) are off-axis (i.e. sheared) perspective views of the scene, while the images in (b) look like reflectance maps. The latter occurs because the object has been placed astride the focal plane, making sets of rays leaving points on the focal plane similar in character to sets of rays leaving points on the object.

Two other viewing geometries are useful. A light slab may be formed from a 2D array of orthographic views. This can be modeled by placing the uv plane at infinity, as shown in figure 4c. In this case, each uv sample corresponds to the direction of a parallel projection. Again, the only issue is to align the xy and st samples of the image with the st quadrilateral. The other useful geometry consists of a 2D array of outward looking (non-sheared) perspective views with fixed field of view. In this case, each image is a slice of the light slab with the st plane at infinity. The fact that all these cases are equally easy to handle with light slabs attests to the elegance of projective geometry. Light fields using each arrangement are presented in section 6 and illustrated in figure 14.

As with any sampling process, sampling a light field may lead to aliasing since typical light fields contain high frequencies. Fortunately, the effects of aliasing may be alleviated by filtering before sampling. In the case of a light field, a 4D filter in the space of lines must be employed (see figure 7). Assuming a box filter, a weighted average of the radiances on all lines connecting sample squares in the uv and st planes must be computed. If a camera is placed on the uv plane and focussed on the st plane, then the filtering process corresponds to integrating both over a pixel corresponding to an st sample, and an aperture equal in size to a uv sample, as shown in figure 8. The theory behind this filtering process has been discussed in the context of holographic stereograms by Halle [Halle94].

Note that although prefiltering has the desired effect of antialiasing the light field, it has what at first seems like an undesirable side effect — introducing blurriness due to depth of field. However, this blurriness is precisely correct for the situation. Recall what happens when creating a pair of images from two adjacent camera locations on the uv plane: a given object point will project to different locations, potentially several pixels apart, in these two images. The distance between the two projected locations is called the stereo disparity. Extending this idea to multiple camera locations produces a sequence of images in which the object appears to jump by a distance equal to the disparity. This jumping is aliasing. Recall now that taking an image with a finite aperture causes points out of focus to be blurred on the film plane by a circle of confusion. Setting the diameter of the aperture to the spacing between camera locations causes the circle of confusion for each object point to be equal in size to its stereo disparity. This replaces the jumping with a sequence of blurred images. Thus, we are removing aliasing by employing finite depth of field.

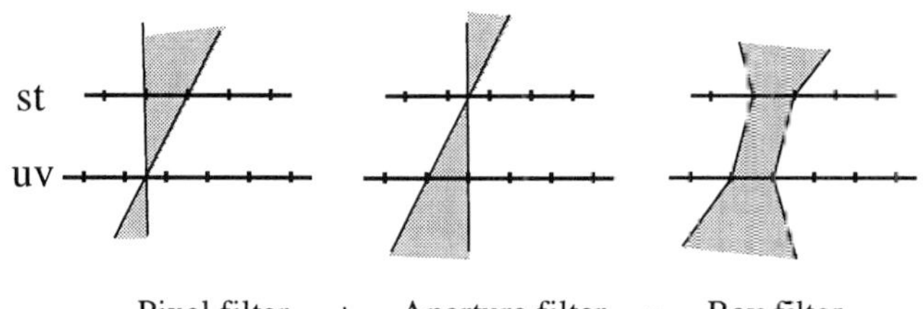

Figure 7: Prefiltering a light field. To avoid aliasing, a 4D low pass filter must be applied to the radiance function.

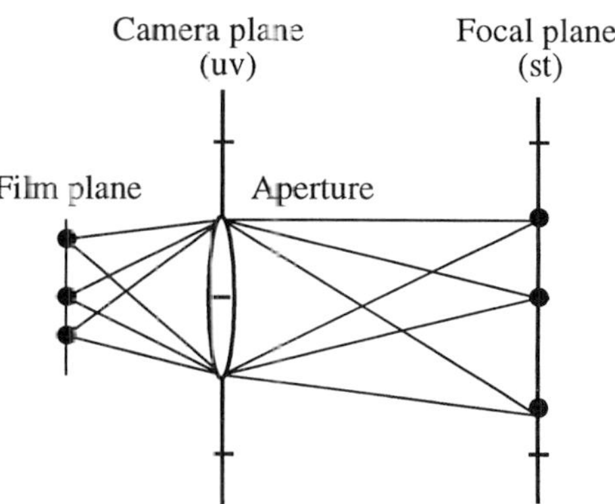

Figure 8: Prefiltering using an aperture. This figure shows a camera focused on the st plane with an aperture on the uv plane whose size is equal to the uv sample spacing. A hypothetical film plane is drawn behind the aperture. Ignore the aperture for a moment (consider a pinhole camera that precisely images the st plane onto the film plane). Then integrating over a pixel on the film plane is equivalent to integrating over an st region bounded by the pixel. Now consider fixing a point on the film plane while using a finite sized aperture (recall that all rays from a point on the film through the aperture are focussed on a single point on the focal plane). Then integrating over the aperture corresponds to integrating all rays through the uv region bounded by the aperture. Therefore, by simultaneously integrating over both the pixel and the aperture, the proper 4D integral is computed.

The necessity for prefiltering can also be understood in line space. Recall from our earlier discussion that samples of the light field correspond to points in line space. Having a finite depth of field with an aperture equal in size to the uv sample spacing insures that each sample adequately covers the interval between these line space points. Too small or too large an aperture yields gaps or overlaps in line space coverage, resulting in views that are either aliased or excessively blurry, respectively.

3.2. From digitized images

Digitizing the imagery required to build a light field of a physical scene is a formidable engineering problem. The number of images required is large (hundreds or thousands), so the process must be automated or at least computer-assisted. Moreover, the lighting must be controlled to insure a static light field, yet flexible enough to properly illuminate the scene, all the while staying clear of the camera to avoid unwanted shadows. Finally, real optical systems impose constraints on angle of view, focal distance, depth of field, and aperture, all of which must be managed. Similar issues have been faced in the construction of devices for performing near-field photometric measurements of luminaires [Ashdown93]. In the following paragraphs, we enumerate the major design decisions we faced in this endeavor and the solutions we adopted.

Inward versus outward looking. The first decision to be made was between a flyaround of a small object and a flythrough of a large-scale scene. We judged flyarounds to be the simpler case, so we attacked them first.

Figure 9: Our prototype camera gantry. A modified Cyberware MS motion platform with additional stepping motors from Lin-Tech and Parker provide four degrees of freedom: horizontal and vertical translation, pan, and tilt. The camera is a Panasonic WV-F300 3-CCD video camera with a Canon f/1.7 10-120mm zoom lens. We keep it locked off at its widest setting (10mm) and mounted so that the pitch and yaw axes pass through the center of projection. While digitizing, the camera is kept pointed at the center of the focal plane. Calibrations and alignments are verified with the aid of a Faro digitizing arm, which is accurate to 0.3 mm.

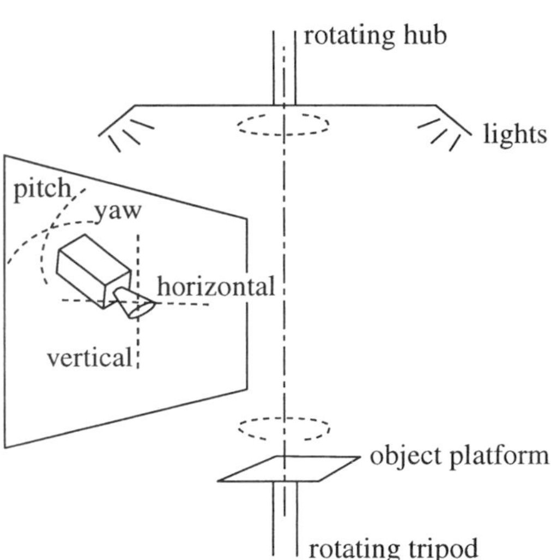

Figure 10: Object and lighting support. Objects are mounted on a Bogen fluid-head tripod, which we manually rotate to four orientations spaced 90 degrees apart. Illumination is provided by two 600W Lowell Omni spotlights attached to a ceiling-mounted rotating hub that is aligned with the rotation axis of the tripod. A stationary 6' x 6' diffuser panel is hung between the spotlights and the gantry, and the entire apparatus is enclosed in black velvet to eliminate stray light.

Human versus computer-controlled. An inexpensive approach to digitizing light fields is to move a handheld camera through the scene, populating the field from the resulting images [Gortler96]. This approach necessitates estimating camera pose at each frame and interpolating the light field from scattered data - two challenging problems. To simplify the situation, we chose instead to build a computer-controlled camera gantry and to digitize images on a regular grid.

Spherical versus planar camera motion. For flyarounds of small objects, an obvious gantry design consists of two concentric hemicycles, similar to a gyroscope mounting. The camera in such a gantry moves along a spherical surface, always pointing at the center of the sphere. Apple Computer has constructed such a gantry to acquire imagery for Quick-Time VR flyarounds [Chen95]. Unfortunately, the lighting in their system is attached to the moving camera, so it is unsuitable for acquiring static light fields. In general, a spherical gantry has three advantages over a planar gantry: (a) it is easier to cover the entire range of viewing directions, (b) the sampling rate in direction space is more uniform, and (c) the distance between the camera and the object is fixed, providing sharper focus throughout the range of camera motion. A planar gantry has two advantages over a spherical gantry: (a) it is easier to build; the entire structure can be assembled from linear motion stages, and (b) it is closer to our light slab representation. For our first prototype gantry, we chose to build a planar gantry, as shown in figure 9.

Field of view. Our goal was to build a light field that allowed 360 degrees of azimuthal viewing. To accomplish this using a planar gantry meant acquiring four slabs each providing 90 degrees. This can be achieved with a camera that translates but does not pan or tilt by employing a wide-angle lens. This solution has two disadvantages: (a) wide-angle lenses exhibit significant distortion, which must be corrected after acquisition, and (b) this solution trades off angle of view against sensor resolution. Another solution is to employ a view camera in which the sensor and optical system translate in parallel planes, the former moving faster than the latter. Horizontal parallax holographic stereograms are constructed using such a camera [Halle94]. Incorporating this solution into a gantry that moves both horizontally and vertically is difficult. We instead chose to equip our camera with pan and tilt motors, enabling us to use a narrow-angle lens. The use of a rotating camera means that, in order to transfer the acquired image to the light slab representation, it must be reprojected to lie on a common plane. This reprojection is equivalent to keystone correction in architectural photography.

Standoff distance. A disadvantage of planar gantries is that the distance from the camera to the object changes as the camera translates across the plane, making it difficult to keep the object in focus. The view camera described above does not suffer from this problem, because the ratio of object distance to image distance stays constant as the camera translates. For a rotating camera, servo-controlled focusing is an option, but changing the focus of a camera shifts its center of projection and changes the image magnification, complicating acquisition. We instead mitigate this problem by using strong lighting and a small aperture to maximize depth of field.

Sensor rotation. Each sample in a light slab should ideally represent the integral over a pixel, and these pixels should lie on a common focal plane. A view camera satisfies this constraint because its sensor translates in a plane. Our use of a rotating camera means that the focal plane also rotates. Assuming that we resample the images carefully during reprojection, the presence of a rotated focal plane will introduce no additional error into the light field. In practice, we have not seen artifacts due to this resampling process.

Aperture size. Each sample in a light slab should also represent the integral over an aperture equal in size to a uv sample. Our use of a small aperture produces a light field with little or no uv antialiasing. Even fully open, the apertures of commercial video cameras are small. We can approximate the required antialiasing by averaging together some number of adjacent views, thereby creating a *synthetic aperture*. However, this technique requires a very dense spacing of views, which in turn requires rapid acquisition. We do not currently do this.

Object support. In order to acquire a 360-degree light field in four 90-degree segments using a planar gantry, either the gantry or the object must be rotated to each of four orientations spaced 90 degrees apart. Given the massiveness of our gantry, the latter was clearly easier. For these experiments, we mounted our objects on a tripod, which we manually rotate to the four positions as shown in figure 10.

Lighting. Given our decision to rotate the object, satisfying the requirement for fixed illumination means that either the lighting must exhibit fourfold symmetry or it must rotate with the object. We chose the latter solution, attaching a lighting system to a rotating hub as shown in figure 10. Designing a lighting system that stays clear of the gantry, yet provides enough light to evenly illuminate an object, is a challenging problem.

Using this gantry, our procedure for acquiring a light field is as follows. For each of the four orientations, the camera is translated through a regular grid of camera positions. At each position, the camera is panned and tilted to point at the center of the object, which lies along the axis of rotation of the tripod. We then acquire an image, and, using standard texture mapping algorithms, reproject it to lie on a common plane as described earlier. Table II gives a typical set of acquisition parameters. Note that the distance between camera positions (3.125 cm) exceeds the diameter of the aperture (1.25 mm), underscoring the need for denser spacing and a synthetic aperture.

4. Compression

Light field arrays are large — the largest example in this paper is 1.6 GB. To make creation, transmission, and display of light fields practical, they must be compressed. In choosing from among many available compression techniques, we were guided by several unique characteristics of light fields:

Data redundancy. A good compression technique removes redundancy from a signal without affecting its content. Light fields exhibit redundancy in all four dimensions. For example, the smooth regions in figure 6a tell us that this light field contains redundancy in s and t, and the smooth regions in figure 6b tell us that the light field contains redundancy in u and v. The former corresponds to our usual notion of interpixel coherence in a perspective view. The latter can be interpreted either as the interframe coherence one expects in a motion sequence or as the smoothness one expects in the bidirectional reflectance distribution function (BRDF) for a diffuse or moderately specular surface. Occlusions introduce discontinuities in both cases, of course.

Random access. Most compression techniques place some constraint on random access to data. For example, variable-bitrate coders may require scanlines, tiles, or frames to be decoded at once. Examples in this class are variable-bitrate vector quantization and the Huffman or arithmetic coders used in JPEG or MPEG. Predictive coding schemes further complicate random-access because pixels depend on previously decoded pixels, scanlines, or frames. This poses a problem for light fields since the set of samples referenced when extracting an image from a light field are dispersed in memory. As the observer moves, the access patterns change in complex ways. We therefore seek a compression technique that supports low-cost random access to individual samples.

Asymmetry. Applications of compression can be classified as symmetric or asymmetric depending on the relative time spent encoding versus decoding. We assume that light fields are assembled and compressed ahead of time, making this an asymmetric application.

Computational expense. We seek a compression scheme that can be decoded without hardware assistance. Although software decoders have been demonstrated for standards like JPEG and MPEG, these implementations consume the full power of a modern microprocessor. In addition to decompression, the display algorithm has additional work to perform, as will be described in section 5. We therefore seek a compression scheme that can be decoded quickly.

The compression scheme we chose was a two-stage pipeline consisting of fixed-rate vector quantization followed by entropy coding (Lempel-Ziv), as shown in figure 11. Following similar motivations, Beers et al. use vector quantization to compress textures for use in rendering pipelines [Beers96].

4.1. Vector quantization

The first stage of our compression pipeline is vector quantization (VQ) [Gersho92], a lossy compression technique wherein a vector of samples is quantized to one of a number of predetermined reproduction vectors. A reproduction vector is called a codeword, and the set of codewords available to encode a source is called the codebook. Codebooks are constructed during a training phase in which the quantizer is asked to find a set of codewords that best approximates a set of sample vectors, called the training set. The quality of a codeword is typically characterized

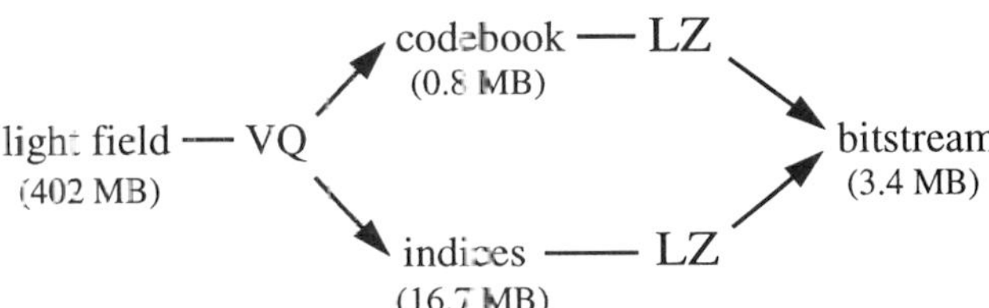

Figure 11 Two-stage compression pipeline. The light field is partitioned into tiles, which are encoded using vector quantization to form an array of codebook indices. The codebook and the array of indices are further compressed using Lempel-Ziv coding. Decompression also occurs in two stages: entropy decoding as the file is loaded into memory, and dequantization on demand during interactive viewing. Typical file sizes are shown beside each stage.

using mean-squared error (MSE), i.e. the sum over all samples in the vector of the squared difference between the source sample and the codeword sample. Once a codebook has been constructed, encoding consists of partitioning the source into vectors and finding for each vector the closest approximating codeword from the codebook. Decoding consists of looking up indices in the codebook and outputting the codewords found there — a very fast operation. Indeed, decoding speed is one of the primary advantages of vector quantization.

In our application, we typically use 2D or 4D tiles of the light field, yielding 12-dimensional or 48-dimensional vectors, respectively. The former takes advantage of coherence in s and t only, while the latter takes advantage of coherence in all four dimensions. To maximize image quality, we train on a representative subset of each light field to be compressed, then transmit the resulting codebook along with the codeword index array. Since light fields are large, even after compression, the additional overhead of transmitting a codebook is small, typically less than 20%. We train on a subset rather than the entire light field to reduce the expense of training.

The output of vector quantization is a sequence of fixed-rate codebook indices. Each index is log N bits where N is the number of codewords in the codebook, so the compression rate of the quantizer is (kl) / $(log\ N)$ where k is the number of elements per vector (i.e. the dimension), and l is the number of bits per element, usually 8. In our application, we typically use 16384-word codebooks, leading to a compression rate for this stage of the pipeline of (48 x 8) / (log 16384) = 384 bits / 14 bits = 27:1. To simplify decoding, we represent each index using an integral number of bytes, 2 in our case, which reduces our compression slightly, to 24:1.

4.2. Entropy coding

The second stage of our compression pipeline is an entropy coder designed to decrease the cost of representing high-probability code indices. Since our objects are typically rendered or photographed against a constant-color background, the array contains many tiles that occur with high probability. For the examples in this paper, we employed gzip, an implementation of Lempel-Ziv coding [Ziv77]. In this algorithm, the input stream is partitioned into nonoverlapping blocks while constructing a dictionary of blocks seen thus far. Applying gzip to our array of code indices typically gives us an additional 5:1 compression. Huffman coding would probably yield slightly higher compression, but encoding and decoding would be more expensive. Our total compression is therefore 24 x 5 = 120:1. See section 6 and table III for more detail on our compression results.

4.3. Decompression

Decompression occurs in two stages. The first stage — gzip decoding — is performed as the file is loaded into memory. The output of this stage is a codebook and an array of code indices packed in 16-bit words. Although some efficiency has been lost by this decoding, the light field is still compressed 24:1, and it is now represented in a way that supports random access.

The second stage — dequantization — proceeds as follows. As the observer moves through the scene, the display engine requests samples of the light field. Each request consists of a (u, v, s, t) coordinate tuple. For each request, a subscripting calculation is performed to determine which sample tile is being addressed. Each tile corresponds to one quantization vector and is thus represented in the index array by a single entry. Looking this index up in the codebook, we find a vector of sample values. A second subscripting calculation is then performed, giving us the offset of the requested sample within the vector. With the aid of precomputed subscripting tables, dequantization can be implemented very efficiently. In our tests, decompression consumes about 25% of the CPU cycles.

5. Display

The final part of the system is a real time viewer that constructs and displays an image from the light slab given the imaging geometry. The viewer must resample a 2D slice of lines from the 4D light field; each line represents a ray through the eye point and a pixel center as shown in figure 12. There are two steps to this process: step 1 consists of computing the (u, v, s, t) line parameters for each image ray, and step 2 consists of resampling the radiance at those line parameters.

As mentioned previously, a big advantage of the light slab representation is the efficiency of the inverse calculation of the line parameters. Conceptually the (u, v) and (s, t) parameters may be calculated by determining the point of intersection of an image ray with each plane. Thus, any ray tracer could easily be adapted to use light slabs. However, a polygonal rendering system also may be used to view a light slab. The transformation from image coordinates (x, y) to both the (u, v) and the (s, t) coordinates is a projective map. Therefore, computing the line coordinates can be done using texture mapping. The uv quadrilateral is drawn using the current viewing transformation, and during scan conversion the (uw, vw, w) coordinates at the corners of the quadrilateral are interpolated. The resulting $u = uw/w$ and $v = vw/w$ coordinates at each pixel represent the ray intersection with the uv quadrilateral. A similar procedure can be used to generate the (s, t) coordinates by drawing the st quadrilateral. Thus, the inverse transformation from (x, y) to (u, v, s, t) reduces essentially to two texture coordinate calculations per ray. This is cheap and can be done in real time, and is supported in many rendering systems, both hardware and software.

Only lines with (u, v) and (s, t) coordinates inside both quadrilaterals are represented in the light slab. Thus, if the texture coordinates for each plane are computed by drawing each quadrilaterial one after the other, then only those pixels that have both valid uv and st coordinates should be looked up in the light slab array. Alternatively, the two quadrilaterals may be simultaneously scan converted in their region of overlap to cut down on unnecessary calculations; this is the technique that we use in our software implementation.

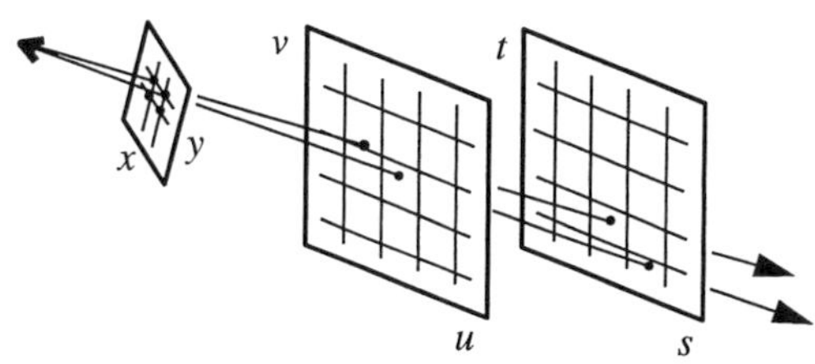

Figure 12: The process of resampling a light slab during display.

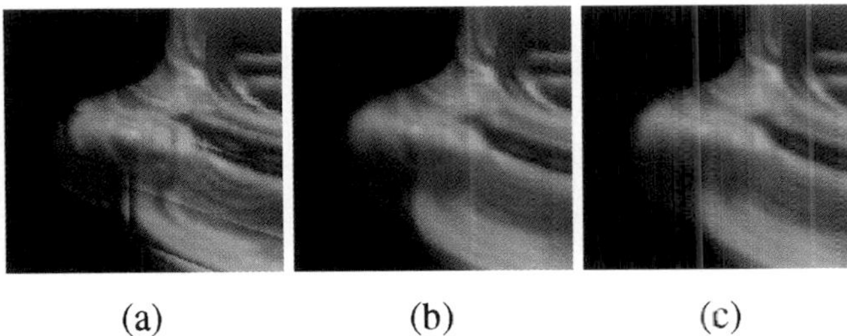

(a) (b) (c)

Figure 13: The effects of interpolation during slice extraction. (a) No interpolation. (b) Linear interpolation in uv only. (c) Quadralinear interpolation in uvst.

To draw an image of a collection of light slabs, we draw them sequentially. If the sets of lines in the collection of light slabs do not overlap, then each pixel is drawn only once and so this is quite efficient. To further increase efficiency, "back-facing" light slabs may be culled.

The second step involves resampling the radiance. The ideal resampling process first reconstructs the function from the original samples, and then applies a bandpass filter to the reconstructed function to remove high frequencies that may cause aliasing. In our system, we approximate the resampling process by simply interpolating the 4D function from the nearest samples. This is correct only if the new sampling rate is greater than the original sampling rate, which is usually the case when displaying light fields. However, if the image of the light field is very small, then some form of prefiltering should be applied. This could easily be done with a 4D variation of the standard mipmapping algorithm [Williams83].

Figure 13 shows the effect of nearest neighbor versus bilinear interpolation on the uv plane versus quadrilinear interpolation of the full 4D function. Quadralinear interpolation coupled with the proper prefiltering generates images with few aliasing artifacts. The improvement is particularly dramatic when the object or camera is moving. However, quadralinear filtering is more expensive and can sometimes be avoided. For example, if the sampling rates in the uv and st planes are different, and then the benefits of filtering one plane may be greater than the other plane.

6. Results

Figure 14 shows images extracted from four light fields. The first is a buddha constructed from rendered images. The model is an irregular polygon mesh constructed from range data. The input images were generated using RenderMan, which also provided the machinery for computing pixel and aperture antialiasing. The light field configuration was a single slab similar to that shown in figure 3a.

Our second light field is a human abdomen constructed from volume renderings. The two tan-colored organs on either side of the spine are the kidneys. In this case, the input images were orthographic views, so we employed a slab with one plane at infinity as shown in figure 4c. Because an orthographic image contains rays of constant direction, we generated more input images than in the first example in order to provide the angular range needed for creating perspective views. The images include pixel antialiasing but no aperture antialiasing. However, the dense spacing of input images reduces aperture aliasing artifacts to a minimum.

Our third example is an outward-looking light field depicting a hallway in Berkeley's Soda Hall, rendered using a radiosity program. To allow a full range of observer motion while optimizing sampling uniformity, we used four slabs with one plane at infinity, a four-slab version of figure 4c. The input images were rendered on an SGI RealityEngine, using the accumulation buffer to provide both pixel and aperture antialiasing.

Our last example is a light field constructed from digitized images. The scene is of a toy lion, and the light field consists of four slabs as shown in figure 3c, allowing the observer to walk completely around the object. The sensor and optical system provide pixel antialiasing, but the aperture diameter was too small to provide correct aperture antialiasing. As a result, the light field exhibits some aliasing, which appears as double images. These artifacts are worst near the head and tail of the lion because of their greater distance from the axis around which the camera rotated.

Table I summarizes the statistics of each light field. Table II gives additional information on the lion dataset. Table III gives the performance of our compression pipeline on two representative datasets. The buddha was compressed using a 2D tiling of the

	buddha	kidney	hallway	lion
Number of slabs	1	1	4	4
Images per slab	16x16	64x64	64x32	32x16
Total images	256	4096	8192	2048
Pixels per image	256^2	128^2	256^2	256^2
Raw size (MB)	50	201	1608	402
Prefiltering	uvst	st only	uvst	st only

Table I: Statistics of the light fields shown in figure 14.

Camera motion	
translation per slab	100 cm x 50 cm
pan and tilt per slab	90° x 45°
number of slabs	4 slabs 90° apart
total pan and tilt	360° x 45°
Sampling density	
distance to object	50 cm
camera pan per sample	3.6°
camera translation per sample	3.125 cm
Aperture	
focal distance of lens	10mm
F-number	f/8
aperture diameter	1.25 mm
Acquisition time	
time per image	3 seconds
total acquisition time	4 hours

Table II: Acquisition parameters for the lion light field. Distance to object and camera pan per sample are given at the center of the plane of camera motion. Total acquisition time includes longer gantry movements at the end of each row and manual setup time for each of the four orientations. The aperture diameter is the focal length divided by the F-number.

	buddha	lion
Vector quantization		
raw size (MB)	50.3	402.7
fraction in training set	5%	3%
samples per tile	2x2x1x1	2x2x2x2
bytes per sample	3	3
vector dimension	12	48
number of codewords	8192	16384
codebook size (MB)	0.1	0.8
bytes per codeword index	2	2
index array size (MB)	8.4	16.8
total size (MB)	8.5	17.6
compression rate	6:1	23:1
Entropy coding		
gzipped codebook (MB)	0.1	0.6
gzipped index array (MB)	1.0	2.8
total size (MB)	1.1	3.4
compression due to gzip	8:1	5:1
total compression	45:1	118:1
Compression performance		
training time	15 mins	4 hrs
encoding time	1 mins	8 mins
original entropy (bits/pixel)	4.2	2.9
image quality (PSNR)	36	27

Table III: Compression statistics for two light fields. The buddha was compressed using 2D tiles of RGB pixels, forming 12-dimensional vectors, and the lion was compressed using 4D tiles (2D tiles of RGB pixels from each of 2 x 2 adjacent camera positions), forming 48-dimensional vectors. Bytes per codeword index include padding as described in section 4. Peak signal-to-noise ratio (PSNR) is computed as $10\log_{10}(255^2/MSE)$.

light field, yielding a total compression rate of 45:1. The lion was compressed using a 4D tiling, yielding a higher compression rate of 118:1. During interactive viewing, the compressed buddha is indistinguishable from the original; the compressed lion exhibits some artifacts, but only at high magnifications. Representative images are shown in figure 15. We have also experimented with higher rates. As a general rule, the artifacts become objectionable only above 200:1.

Finally, table IV summarizes the performance of our interactive viewer operating on the lion light field. As the table shows, we achieve interactive playback rates for reasonable image sizes. Note that the size of the light field has no effect on playback rate; only the image size matters. Memory size is not an issue because the compressed fields are small.

7. Discussion and future work

We have described a new light field representation, the light slab, for storing all the radiance values in free space. Both inserting images into the field and extracting new views from the field involve resampling, a simple and robust procedure. The resulting system is easily implemented on workstations and personal computers, requiring modest amounts of memory and cycles. Thus, this technique is useful for many applications requiring interaction with 3D scenes.

Display times (ms)	no bilerp	uv lerp	uvst lerp
coordinate calculation	13	13	13
sample extraction	14	59	214
overhead	3	3	3
total	30	75	230

Table IV: Display performance for the lion light field. Displayed images are 192 x 192 pixels. Sample extraction includes VQ decoding and sample interpolation. Display overhead includes reading the mouse, computing the observer position, and copying the image to the frame buffer. Timings are for a software-only implementation on a 250 MHz MIPS 4400 processor.

There are three major limitation of our method. First, the sampling density must be high to avoid excessive blurriness. This requires rendering or acquiring a large number of images, which may take a long time and consume a lot of memory. However, denser sample spacing leads to greater inter-sample coherence, so the size of the light field is usually manageable after compression. Second, the observer is restricted to regions of space free of occluders. This limitation can be addressed by stitching together multiple light fields based on a partition of the scene geometry into convex regions. If we augment light fields to include Z-depth, the regions need not even be convex. Third, the illumination must be fixed. If we ignore interreflections, this limitation can be addressed by augmenting light fields to include surface normals and optical properties. To handle interreflections, we might try representing illumination as a superposition of basis functions [Nimeroff94]. This would correspond in our case to computing a sum of light fields each lit with a different illumination function.

It is useful to compare this approach with depth-based or correspondence-based view interpolation. In these systems, a 3D model is created to improve quality of the interpolation and hence decrease the number of pre-acquired images. In our approach, a much larger number of images is acquired, and at first this seems like a disadvantage. However, because of the 3D structure of the light field, simple compression schemes are able to find and exploit this same 3D structure. In our case, simple 4D block coding leads to compression rates of over 100:1. Given the success of the compression, a high density compressed light field has an advantage over other approaches because the resampling process is simpler, and no explicit 3D structure must be found or stored.

There are many representations for light used in computer graphics and computer vision, for example, images, shadow and environment maps, light sources, radiosity and radiance basis functions, and ray tracing procedures. However, abstract light representations have not been systematically studied in the same way as modeling and display primitives. A fruitful line of future research would be to reexamine these representations from first principles. Such reexaminations may in turn lead to new methods for the central problems in these fields.

Another area of future research is the design of instrumentation for acquisition. A large parallel array of cameras connected to a parallel computer could be built to acquire and compress a light field in real time. In the short term, there are many interesting engineering issues in designing and building gantries to move a small number of cameras and lights to sequentially acquire both inward- and outward-looking light fields. This same instrumentation could lead to breakthroughs in both 3D shape acquisition and reflection measurements. In fact, the interaction of light with any object can be represented as a higher-dimensional interaction matrix; acquiring, compressing, and manipulating such representations are a fruitful area for investigation.

8. Acknowledgements

We would like to thank David Addleman and George Dabrowski of Cyberware for helping us design and build the camera gantry, Craig Kolb and James Davis for helping us calibrate it, Brian Curless for scanning the buddha, Julie Dorsey for shading it and allowing us to use it, Carlo Sequin for the Soda Hall model, Seth Teller, Celeste Fowler, and Thomas Funkhauser for its radiosity solution, Lucas Pereira for rendering it, Benjamin Zhu for reimplementing our hardware-accelerated viewer in software, and Navin Chaddha for his vector quantization code. We also wish to thank Eric Chen and Michael Chen for allowing us to examine the Apple ObjectMaker, and Alain Fournier and Bob Lewis for showing us their wavelet light field work. Finally, we wish to thank Nina Amenta for sparking our interest in two-plane parameterizations of lines, Michael Cohen for reinforcing our interest in image-based representations, and Gavin Miller for inspiring us with his grail of volumetric hyperreality. This work was supported by the NSF under contracts CCR-9157767 and CCR-9508579.

9. References

[Adelson91] Adelson, E.H., Bergen, J.R., "The Plenoptic Function and the Elements of Early Vision," In *Computation Models of Visual Processing*, M. Landy and J.A. Movshon, eds., MIT Press, Cambridge, 1991.

[Ashdown93] Ashdown, I., "Near-Field Photometry: A New Approach," *Journal of the Illuminating Engineering Society*, Vol. 22, No. 1, Winter, 1993, pp. 163-180.

[Beers96] Beers, A., Agrawala, M., Chaddha, N., "Rendering from Compressed Textures." In these proceedings.

[Benton83] Benton, S., "Survey of Holographic Stereograms," *Processing and Display of Three-Dimensional Data*, Proc. SPIE, Vol. 367, 1983.

[Blinn76] Blinn, J.F., Newell, M.E., "Texture and Reflection in Computer Generated Images," *CACM*, Vol. 19, No. 10, October, 1976, pp. 542-547.

[Bolles87] Bolles, R., Baker, H., Marimont, D., "Epipolar-Plane Image Analysis: An Approach to Determining Structure from Motion," *International Journal of Computer Vision*, Vol. 1, No. 1, 1987, pp. 7-55.

[Chen93] Chen, S.E., Williams, L., "View Interpolation for Image Synthesis," Proc. SIGGRAPH '93 (Anaheim, California, August 1-6, 1993). In *Computer Graphics Proceedings*, Annual Conference Series, 1993, ACM SIGGRAPH, pp. 279-288.

[Chen95] Chen, S.E., "QuickTime VR — An Image-Based Approach to Virtual Environment Navigation," Proc. SIGGRAPH '95 (Los Angeles, CA, August 6-11, 1995). In *Computer Graphics* Proceedings, Annual Conference Series, 1995, ACM SIGGRAPH, pp. 29-38.

[Fuchs94] Fuchs, H., Bishop, G., Arthur, K., McMillan, L., Bajcsy, R., Lee, S.W., Farid, H., Kanade, T., "Virtual Space Teleconferencing Using a Sea of Cameras," *Proc. First International Conference on Medical Robotics and Computer Assisted Surgery*, 1994, pp. 161-167.

[Gersho92] Gersho, A., Gray, R.M., *Vector Quantization and Signal Compression*, Kluwer Academic Publishers, 1992.

[Gershun36] Gershun, A., "The Light Field," Moscow, 1936. Translated by P. Moon and G. Timoshenko in *Journal of Mathematics and Physics*, Vol. XVIII, MIT, 1939, pp. 51-151.

[Gortler96] Gortler, S.J., Grzeszczuk, R., Szeliski, R., Cohen, M., "The Lumigraph." In these proceedings.

[Greene86] Greene, N., "Environment Mapping and Other Applications of World Projections," *IEEE Computer Graphics and Applications*, Vol. 6, No. 11, November, 1986, pp. 21-29.

[Greene94] Greene, N. and Kass, M., "Approximating Visibility with Environment Maps," Apple Technical Report No. 41, November, 1994.

[Halle94] Halle, M., "Holographic Stereograms as Discrete Imaging Systems." *Practical Holography*, Proc. SPIE, Vol. 2176, February, 1994.

[Katayama95] Katayama, A., Tanaka, K., Oshino, T., Tamura, H., "Viewpoint-Dependent Stereoscopic Display Using Interpolation of Multiviewpoint Images," *Stereoscopic Displays and Virtual Reality Systems II*, Proc. SPIE, Vol. 2409, S. Fisher, J. Merritt, B. Bolas eds. 1995, pp. 11-20.

[Laveau94] Laveau, S., Faugeras, O.D., "3-D Scene Representation as a Collection of Images and Fundamental Matrices," INRIA Technical Report No. 2205, 1994.

[Levin71] Levin, R., "Photometric Characteristics of Light Controlling Apparatus," *Illuminating Engineering*, Vol. 66, No. 4, 1971, pp. 205-215.

[McMillan95a] McMillan, L., Bishop, G., "Head-Tracked Stereoscopic Display Using Image Warping," *Stereoscopic Displays and Virtual Reality Systems II*, Proc. SPIE, Vol. 2409, S. Fisher, J. Merritt, B. Bolas eds. 1995, pp. 21-30.

[McMillan95b] McMillan, L., Bishop, G., Plenoptic Modeling: An Image-Based Rendering System, Proc. SIGGRAPH '95 (Los Angeles, CA, August 6-11, 1995) In *Computer Graphics* Proceedings, Annual Conference Series, 1995, ACM SIGGRAPH, pp. 39-46.

[Miller95] Miller, G., "Volumetric Hyper-Reality: A Computer Graphics Holy Grail for the 21st Century?," *Proc. Graphics Interface '95*, W. Davis and P. Prusinkiewicz eds., Canadian Information Processing Society, 1995, pp. 56-64.

[Moon81] Moon, P., Spencer, D.E., *The Photic Field*, MIT Press, 1981.

[Narayanan95] Narayanan, P.J., "Virtualized Reality: Concepts and Early Results," *Proc. IEEE Workshop on the Representation of Visual Scenes*, IEEE, 1995.

[Nimeroff94] Nimeroff, J., Simoncelli, E., Dorsey, J., "Efficient Rerendering of Naturally Illuminated Scenes," *Proc. Fifth Eurographics Rendering Workshop*, 1994, pp. 359-373.

[Sbert93] Sbert, A.M., "An Integral Geometry Based Method for Form-Factor Computation," *Computer Graphics Forum*, Vol. 13, No. 3, 1993, pp. 409-420.

[Seitz95] Seitz, S., Dyer, C., "Physically-Valid View Synthesis by Image Interpolation," *Proc. IEEE Workshop on the Representation of Visual Scenes*, IEEE, 1995.

[Williams83] Williams, L., "Pyramidal Parametrics," *Computer Graphics (Proc. Siggraph '83)*, Vol. 17, No. 3, July, 1983, pp. 1-11.

[Ziv77] Ziv, J., Lempel, A., "A universal algorithm for sequential data compression," *IEEE Transactions on Information Theory*, IT-23:337-343, 1977.

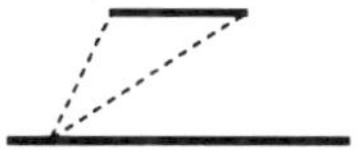

(a) Buddha.

Input images: RenderMan renderings from an irregular polygon mesh model.

Light field: one slab, shown above in plan view. See also figure 3a.

(b) Kidney.

Input images: volume renderings from computed tomography data.

Light field: one slab, shown above. See also figure 4c.

(c) Hallway.

Input images: SGI RealityEngine renderings from a polygon model.

Light field: four slabs like figure 4c, arranged in a cross.

(d) Lion.

Input images: digitized video from a computer–controlled camera

Light field: four slabs arranged in a box. See also figure 3c.

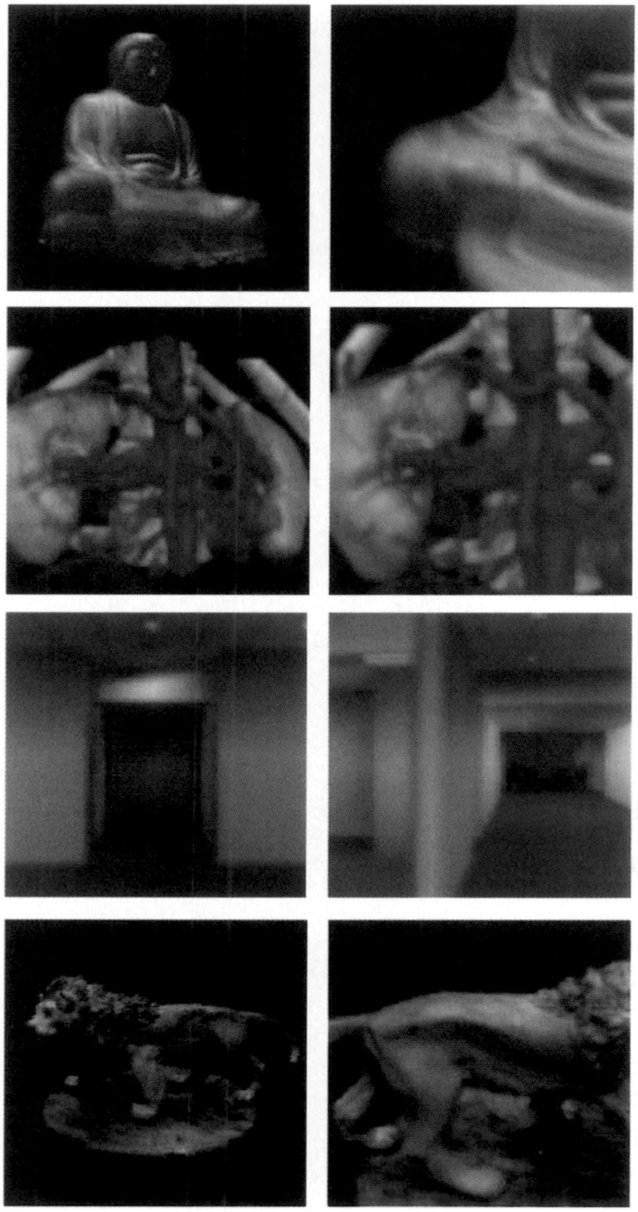

Figure 14: Example images from four light fields, extracted during a typical interactive viewing session.

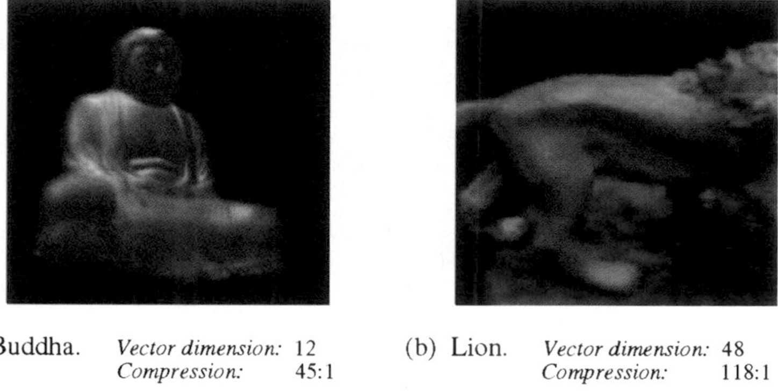

(a) Buddha. *Vector dimension:* 12 *Compression:* 45:1

(b) Lion. *Vector dimension:* 48 *Compression:* 118:1

Figure 15: Images extracted from compressed light fields.

The Lumigraph

Steven J. Gortler Radek Grzeszczuk Richard Szeliski Michael F. Cohen

Microsoft Research

Abstract

This paper discusses a new method for capturing the complete appearance of both synthetic and real world objects and scenes, representing this information, and then using this representation to render images of the object from new camera positions. Unlike the shape capture process traditionally used in computer vision and the rendering process traditionally used in computer graphics, our approach does not rely on geometric representations. Instead we sample and reconstruct a 4D function, which we call a Lumigraph. The Lumigraph is a subset of the complete plenoptic function that describes the flow of light at all positions in all directions. With the Lumigraph, new images of the object can be generated very quickly, independent of the geometric or illumination complexity of the scene or object. The paper discusses a complete working system including the capture of samples, the construction of the Lumigraph, and the subsequent rendering of images from this new representation.

1 Introduction

The process of creating a virtual environment or object in computer graphics begins with modeling the geometric and surface attributes of the objects in the environment along with any lights. An image of the environment is subsequently rendered from the vantage point of a virtual camera. Great effort has been expended to develop computer aided design systems that allow the specification of complex geometry and material attributes. Similarly, a great deal of work has been undertaken to produce systems that simulate the propagation of light through virtual environments to create realistic images.

Despite these efforts, it has remained difficult or impossible to recreate much of the complex geometry and subtle lighting effects found in the real world. The modeling problem can potentially be bypassed by capturing the geometry and material properties of objects directly from the real world. This approach typically involves some combination of cameras, structured light, range finders, and mechanical sensing devices such as 3D digitizers. When successful, the results can be fed into a rendering program to create images of real objects and scenes. Unfortunately, these systems are still unable to completely capture small details in geometry and material properties. Existing rendering methods also continue to be limited in their capability to faithfully reproduce real world illumination, even if given accurate geometric models.

Quicktime VR [6] was one of the first systems to suggest that the traditional modeling/rendering process can be skipped. Instead, a series of captured environment maps allow a user to *look around* a scene from fixed points in space. One can also flip through different views of an object to create the illusion of a 3D model. Chen and Williams [7] and Werner et al [30] have investigated smooth interpolation between images by modeling the motion of pixels (i.e., the *optical flow*) as one moves from one camera position to another. In Plenoptic Modeling [19], McMillan and Bishop discuss finding the disparity of each pixel in stereo pairs of cylindrical images. Given the disparity (roughly equivalent to depth information), they can then move pixels to create images from new vantage points. Similar work using stereo pairs of planar images is discussed in [14].

This paper extends the work begun with Quicktime VR and Plenoptic Modeling by further developing the idea of capturing the complete flow of light in a region of the environment. Such a flow is described by a *plenoptic function*[1]. The plenoptic function is a five dimensional quantity describing the flow of light at every 3D spatial position (x, y, z) for every 2D direction (θ, ϕ). In this paper, we discuss computational methods for capturing and representing a plenoptic function, and for using such a representation to render images of the environment from any arbitrary viewpoint.

Unlike Chen and Williams' view interpolation [7] and McMillan and Bishop's plenoptic modeling [19], our approach does not rely explicitly on any optical flow information. Such information is often difficult to obtain in practice, particularly in environments with complex visibility relationships or specular surfaces. We do, however, use approximate geometric information to improve the quality of the reconstruction at lower sampling densities. Previous flow based methods implicitly rely on diffuse surface reflectance, allowing them to use a pixel from a single image to represent the appearance of a single geometric location from a variety of viewpoints. In contrast, our approach regularly samples the full plenoptic function and thus makes no assumptions about reflectance properties.

If we consider only the subset of light leaving a bounded object (or equivalently entering a bounded empty region of space), the fact that radiance along any ray remains constant[1] allows us to reduce the domain of interest of the plenoptic function to four dimensions. This paper first discusses the representation of this 4D function which we call a Lumigraph. We then discuss a system for sampling the plenoptic function with an inexpensive hand-held camera, and "developing" the captured light into a Lumigraph. Finally this paper describes how to use texture mapping hardware to quickly reconstruct images from any viewpoint with a virtual camera model. The Lumigraph representation is applicable to synthetic objects as well, allowing us to encode the complete appearance of a complex model and to rerender the object at speeds independent of the model complexity. We provide results on synthetic and real sequences and discuss work that is currently underway to make the system more efficient.

[1] We are assuming the medium (i.e., the air) to be transparent.

2 Representation

2.1 From 5D to 4D

The plenoptic function is a function of 5 variables representing position and direction [2]. If we assume the air to be transparent then the radiance along a ray through empty space remains constant. If we furthermore limit our interest to the light leaving the convex hull of a bounded object, then we only need to represent the value of the plenoptic function along some surface that surrounds the object. A cube was chosen for its computational simplicity (see Figure 1). At any point in space, one can determine the radiance along any ray in any direction, by tracing backwards along that ray through empty space to the surface of the cube. Thus, the plenoptic function due to the object can be reduced to 4 dimensions [3].

The idea of restricting the plenoptic function to some surrounding surface has been used before. In full-parallax holographic stereograms [3], the appearance of an object is captured by moving a camera along some surface (usually a plane) capturing a 2D array of photographs. This array is then transferred to a single holographic image, which can display the appearance of the 3D object. The work reported in this paper takes many of its concepts from holographic stereograms.

Global illumination researchers have used the "surface restricted plenoptic function" to efficiently simulate light-transfer between regions of an environment containing complicated geometric objects. The plenoptic function is represented on the surface of a cube surrounding some region; that information is all that is needed to simulate the light transfer from that region of space to all other regions [17]. In the context of illumination engineering, this idea has been used to model and represent the illumination due to physical luminaires. Ashdown [2] describes a gantry for moving a camera along a sphere surrounding a luminaire of interest. The captured information can then be used to represent the light source in global illumination simulations. Ashdown traces this idea of the surface-restricted plenoptic function back to Levin [15].

A limited version of the work reported here has been described by Katayama et al. [11]. In their system, a camera is moved along a track, capturing a 1D array of images of some object. This information is then used to generate new images of the object from other points in space. Because they only capture the plenoptic function along a line, they only obtain horizontal parallax, and distortion is introduced as soon as the new virtual camera leaves the line. Finally, in work concurrent to our own, Levoy and Hanrahan [16] represent a 4D function that allows for undistorted, full parallax views of the object from anywhere in space.

2.2 Parameterization of the 4D Lumigraph

There are many potential ways to parameterize the four dimensions of the Lumigraph. We adopt a parameterization similar to that used in digital holographic stereograms [9] and also used by Levoy and Hanrahan [16]. We begin with a cube to organize a Lumigraph and, without loss of generality, only consider for discussion a single square face of the cube (the full Lumigraph is constructed from six such faces).

[2] We only consider a snapshot of the function, thus time is eliminated. Without loss of generality, we also consider only a monochromatic function (in practice 3 discrete color channels), eliminating the need to consider wavelength. We furthermore ignore issues of dynamic range and thus limit ourselves to scalar values lying in some finite range.

[3] In an analogous fashion one can reconstruct the complete plenoptic function inside an empty convex region by representing it only on the surface bounding the empty region. At any point inside the region, one can find the light entering from any direction by finding that direction's intersection with the region boundary.

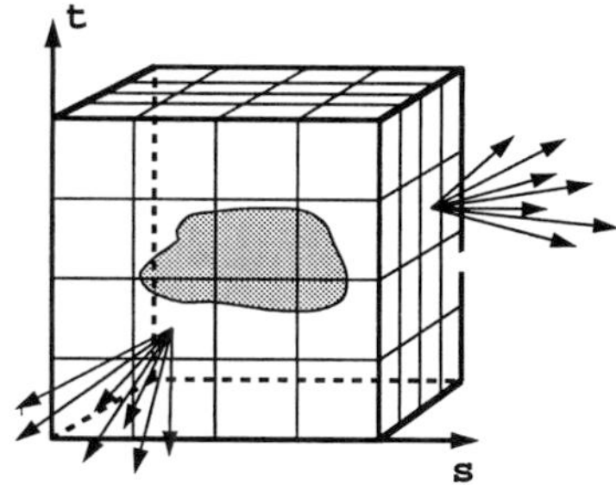

Figure 1: The surface of a cube holds all the radiance information due to the enclosed object.

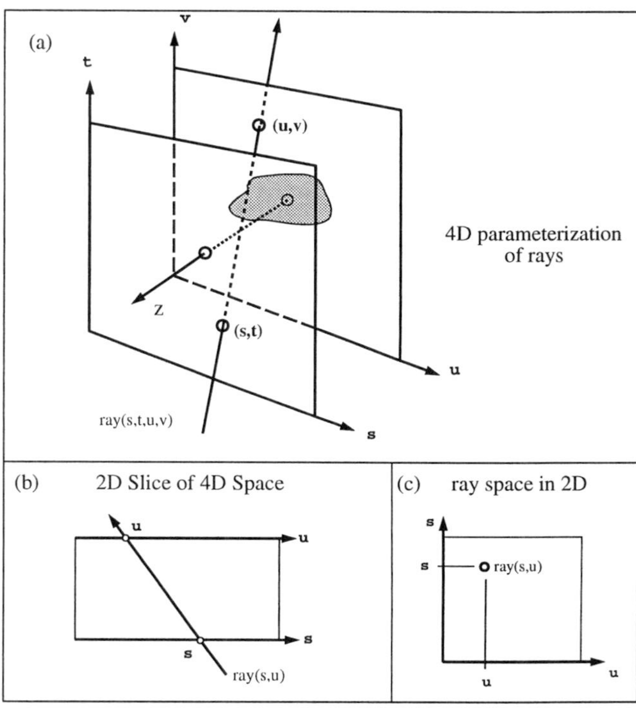

Figure 2: Parameterization of the Lumigraph

We choose a simple parameterization of the cube face with orthogonal axes running parallel to the sides labeled s and t (see Figure 1). Direction is parameterized using a second plane parallel to the st plane with axes labeled u and v (Figure 2). Any point in the 4D Lumigraph is thus identified by its four coordinates (s, t, u, v), the coordinates of a ray piercing the first plane at (s, t) and intersecting the second plane at (u, v) (see Ray(s, t, u, v) in Figure 2). We place the origin at the center of the uv plane, with the z axis normal to the plane. The st plane is located at $z = 1$. The full Lumigraph consists of six such pairs of planes with normals along the x, $-x$, y, $-y$, z, and $-z$ directions.

It will be instructive at times to consider two 2D analogs to the 4D Lumigraph. Figure 2(b) shows a 2D slice of the 4D Lumigraph that indicates the u and s axes. Figure 2(c) shows the same arrangement in *2D ray coordinates* in which rays are mapped to points (e.g., ray(s, u)) and points are mapped to lines.[4]

Figure 3 shows the relationship between this parameterization of the Lumigraph and a pixel in some arbitrary image. Given a Lu-

[4] More precisely, a line in ray space represents the set of rays through a point in space.

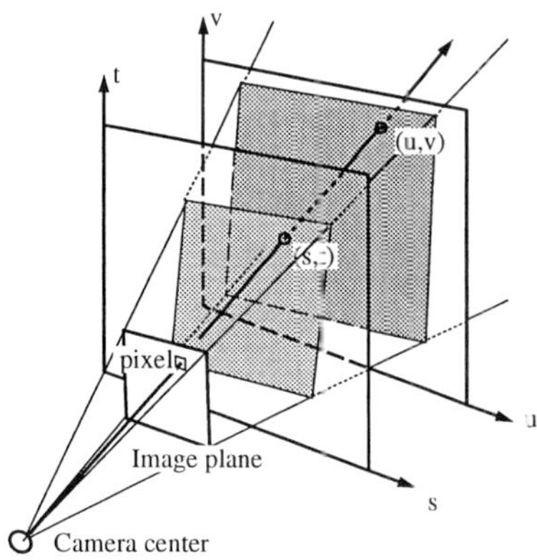

Figure 3: Relationship between Lumigraph and a pixel in an arbitrary image

migraph, L, one can generate an arbitrary new image coloring each pixel with the appropriate value $L(s,t,u,v)$. Conversely given some arbitrary image and the position and orientation of the camera, each pixel can be considered a sample of the Lumigraph value at (s,t,u,v) to be used to construct the Lumigraph.

There are many advantages of the two parallel plane parameterization. Given the geometric description of a ray, it is computationally simple to compute its coordinates; one merely finds its intersection with two planes. Moreover, reconstruction from this parameterization can be done rapidly using the texture mapping operations built into hardware on modern workstations (see section 3.6.2). Finally, in this parameterization, as one moves an eyepoint along the st plane in a straight line, the projection on the uv plane of points on the geometric object track along parallel straight lines. This makes it computationally efficient to compute the apparent motion of a geometric point (i.e., the *optical flow*), and to apply depth correction to the Lumigraph.

2.3 Discretization of the 4D Parameterization

So far, the Lumigraph has been discussed as an unknown, continuous, four dimensional function within a hypercubical domain in s,t,u,v and scalar range. To map such an object into a computational framework requires a discrete representation. In other words, we must choose some finite dimensional function space within which the function resides. To do so, we choose a discrete subdivision in each of the (s,t,u,v) dimensions and associate a coefficient and a basis function (reconstruction kernel) with each 4D grid point.

Choosing M subdivisions in the s and t dimensions and N subdivisions in u and v results in a grid of points on the st and uv planes (Figure 4). An st grid point is indexed with (i,j) and is located at (s_i,t_j). A uv grid point is indexed with (p,q) and is located at (u_p,v_q). A 4D grid point is indexed (i,j,p,q). The data value (in fact an RGB triple) at this grid point is referred to as $x_{i,j,p,q}$

2.3.1 Choice of Basis

We associate with each grid point a basis function $B_{i,j,p,q}$ so that the continuous Lumigraph is reconstructed as the linear sum

$$\tilde{L}(s,t,u,v) = \sum_{i=0}^{M}\sum_{j=0}^{M}\sum_{p=0}^{N}\sum_{q=0}^{N} x_{i,j,p,q}B_{i,j,p,q}(s,t,u,v)$$

where $\tilde{L}$ is a finite dimensional Lumigraph that exists in the space defined by the choice of basis.

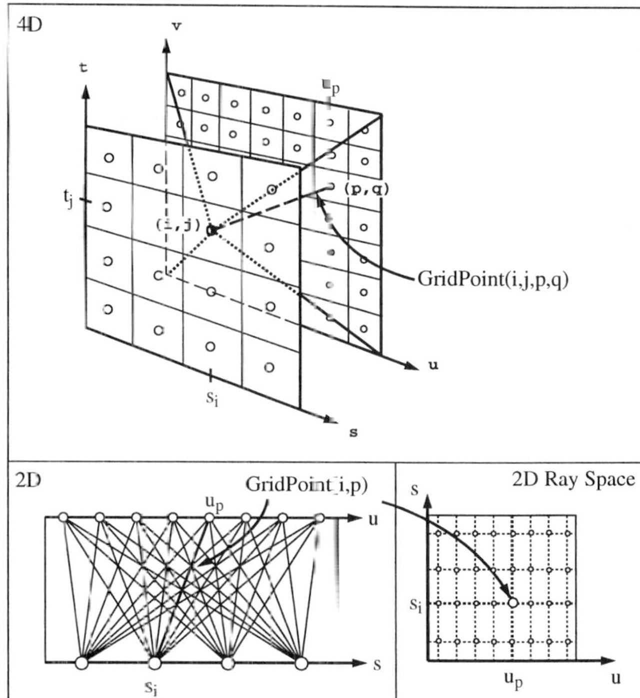

Figure 4: Discretization of the Lumigraph

For example, if we select constant basis functions (i.e., a 4D *box* with value 1 in the 4D region closest to the associated grid point and zero elsewhere), then the Lumigraph is piecewise constant, and takes on the value of the coefficient of the nearest grid point.

Similarly, a quadralinear basis function has a value of 1 at the grid point and drops off to 0 at all neighboring grid points. The value of $\tilde{L}(s,t,u,v)$ is thus interpolated from the 16 grid points forming the hypercube in which the point resides.

We have chosen to use the quadralinear basis for its computational simplicity and the C^0 continuity it imposes on $\tilde{L}$. However, because this basis is not band limited by the Nyquist frequency, and thus the corresponding finite dimensional function space is not shift invariant [24], the grid structure will be slightly noticeable in our results.

2.3.2 Projection into the Chosen Basis

Given a continuous Lumigraph, L, and a choice of basis for the finite dimensional Lumigraph, $\tilde{L}$, we still need to define a *projection* of L into $\tilde{L}$ (i.e., we need to find the coefficients x that result in an $\tilde{L}$ which is by some metric *closest* to L). If we choose the L^2 distance metric, then the projection is defined by integrating L against the *duals* of the basis functions [8], given by the inner products,

$$x_{i,j,p,q} = < L, \tilde{B}_{i,j,p,q} > \qquad (1)$$

In the case of the box basis, $B = \tilde{B}$. The duals of the quadralinear basis functions are more complex, but these basis functions sufficiently approximate their own duals for our purposes.

One can interpret this projection as point sampling L after it has been low pass filtered with the kernel $\tilde{B}$. This interpretation is pursued in the context of holographic stereograms by Halle [9]. One can also interpret this projection as the result of placing a physical or synthetic "skewed" camera at grid point (s_i,t_j) with an aperture corresponding to the bilinear basis and with a pixel centered at

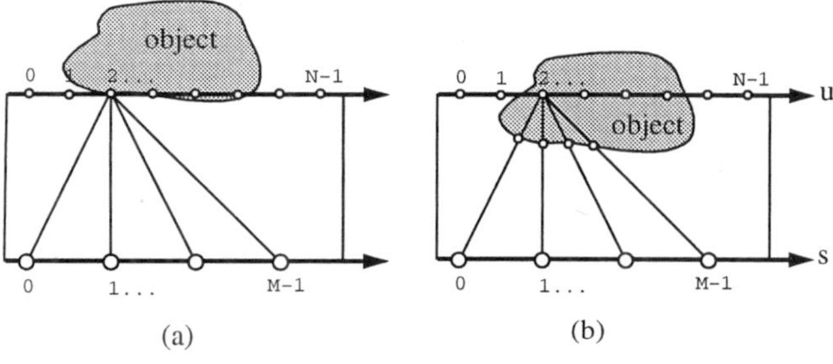

Figure 5: Choice of resolution on the uv plane

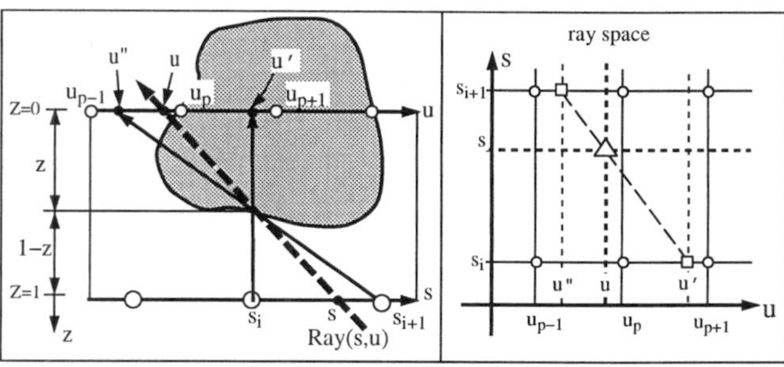

Figure 6: Depth correction of rays

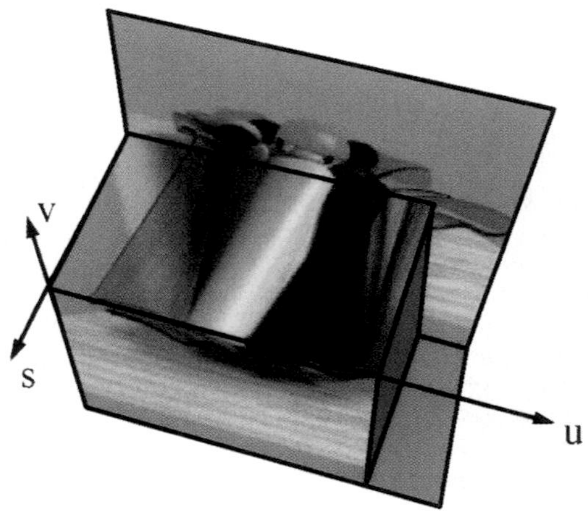

Figure 7: An (s, u, v) slice of a Lumigraph

(u_p, v_q) antialiased with a bilinear filter. This analogy is pursued in [16].

In Figure 16 we show images generated from Lumigraphs. The geometric scene consisted of a partial cube with the pink face in front, yellow face in back, and the brown face on the floor. These Lumigraphs were generated using two different quadrature methods to approximate equation 1, and using two different sets of basis functions, constant and quadralinear. In (a) and (c) only one sample was used to compute each Lumigraph coefficient. In these examples severe ghosting artifacts can be seen. In (b) and (d) numerical integration over the support of $\tilde{B}$ in st was computed for each coefficient. It is clear that best results are obtained using quadralinear basis function, with a full quadrature method.

2.3.3 Resolution

An important decision is how to set the resolutions, M and N, that best balance efficiency and the quality of the images reconstructed from the Lumigraph. The choices for M and N are influenced by the fact that we expect the visible surfaces of the object to lie closer to the uv plane than the st plane. In this case, N, the resolution of the uv plane, is closely related to the final image resolution and thus a choice for N close to final image resolution works best (we consider a range of resolutions from 128 to 512).

One can gain some intuition for the choice of M by observing the 2D subset of the Lumigraph from a single grid point on the uv plane (see $u = 2$ in Figure 5(a)). If the surface of the object lies exactly on the uv plane at a gridpoint, then all rays leaving that point represent samples of the radiance function at a single position on the object's surface. Even when the object's surface deviates from the uv plane as in Figure 5(b), we can still expect the function across the st plane to remain smooth and thus a low resolution is sufficient. Thus a significantly lower resolution for M than N can be expected to yield good results. In our implementation we use values of M ranging from 16 to 64.

2.3.4 Use of Geometric Information

Assuming the radiance function of the object is well behaved, knowledge about the geometry of the object gives us information about the coherence of the associated Lumigraph function, and can be used to help define the shape of our basis functions.

Consider the ray (s, u) in a two-dimensional Lumigraph (Figure 6). The closest grid point to this ray is (s_{i+1}, u_p). However, gridpoints (s_{i+1}, u_{p-1}) and (s_i, u_{p+1}) are likely to contain values closer to the true value at (s, u) since these grid points represent rays that intersect the object nearby the intersection with (s, u). This suggests adapting the shape of the basis functions.

Suppose we know the depth value z at which ray (s, u) first intersects a surface of the object. Then for a given s_i, one can compute a corresponding u' for a ray (s_i, u') that intersects the same geometric location on the object as the original ray $(s, u)^5$. Let the depth z be 0 at the uv plane and 1 at the st plane. The intersections can then be found by examining the similar triangles in Figure 6,

$$u' = u + (s - s_i)\frac{z}{1-z} \tag{2}$$

It is instructive to view the same situation as in Figure 6(a), plotted in *ray space* (Figure 6(b)). In this figure, the triangle is the ray (s, u), and the circles indicate the nearby gridpoints in the discrete Lumigraph. The diagonal line passing through (s, u) indicates the *optical flow* (in this case, horizontal motion in 2D) of the intersection point on the object as one moves back and forth in s. The intersection of this line with s_i and s_{i+1} occurs at u' and u'' respectively.

Figure 7 shows an (s, u) slice through a three-dimensional (s, u, v) subspace of the Lumigraph for the ray-traced fruitbowl used in Figure 19. The flow of pixel motion is along straight lines in this space, but more than one motion may be present if the scene includes transparency. The slope of the flow lines corresponds to the depth of the point on the object tracing out the line. Notice how the function is coherent along these flow lines [4].

We expect the Lumigraph to be smooth along the optical flow lines, and thus it would be beneficial to have the basis functions adapt their shape correspondingly. The remapping of u and v values to u' and v' performs this reshaping. The idea of shaping the support of basis functions to closely match the structure of the function being approximated is used extensively in finite element methods. For example, in the Radiosity method for image synthesis, the mesh of elements is adapted to fit knowledge about the illumination function.

[5] Assuming there has been no change in visibility.

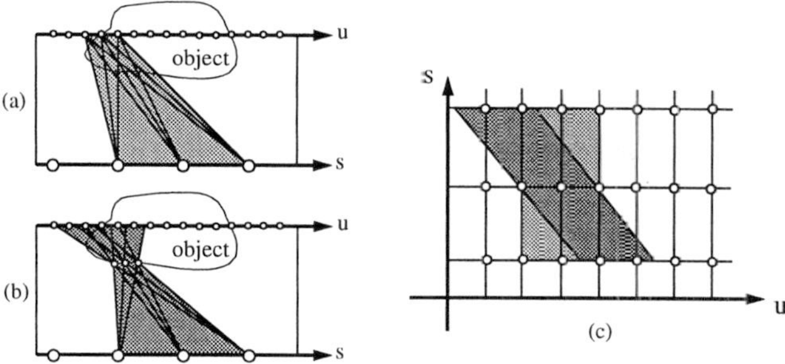

Figure 8: (a) Support of an uncorrected basis function. (b) Support of a depth corrected basis function. (c) Support of both basis functions in ray space.

The new basis function $B'_{i,j,p,q}(s,t,u,v)$ is defined by first finding u' and v' using equation 2 and then evaluating B, that is

$$B'_{i,j,p,q}(s,t,u,v) = B_{i,j,p,q}(s,t,u',v')$$

Although the shape of the new *depth corrected* basis is complicated, $\tilde{L}(s,t,u,v)$ is still a linear sum of coefficients and the weights of the contributing basis functions still sum to unity. However, the basis is no longer representable as a tensor product of simple boxes or hats as before. Figure 8 shows the support of an uncorrected (light gray) and a depth corrected (dark gray) basis function in 2D geometric space and in 2D ray space. Notice how the support of the depth corrected basis intersects the surface of the object across a narrower area compared to the uncorrected basis.

We use depth corrected quadralinear basis functions in our system. The value of $\tilde{L}(s,t,u,v)$ in the corrected quadralinear basis is computed using the following calculation:

```
QuadralinearDepthCorrect(s,t,u,v,z)
  Result = 0
  h_st = s_1 − s_0 /* grid spacing */
  h_uv = u_1 − u_0
  for each of the four (s_i, t_j) surrounding (s, t)
    u' = u + (s − s_i) * z/(1 − z)
    v' = v + (t − t_j) * z/(1 − z)
    temp = 0
    for each of the four (u_p, v_q) surrounding (u', v')
      iterpWeight_uv =
        (h_uv − | u_p − u' |) * (h_uv − | v_q − v' |)/h_uv^2
      temp += interpWeight_uv * L(s_i, t_j, u_p, v_q)
    interpWeight_st =
      (h_st − | s_i − s |) * (h_st − | t_j − t |)/h_st^2
    Result += interpWeight_st * temp
  return Result
```

Figure 17 shows images generated from a Lumigraph using uncorrected and depth corrected basis functions. The depth correction was done using a 162 polygon model to approximate the original 70,000 polygons. The approximation was generated using a mesh simplification program [10]. These images show how depth correction reduces the artifacts present in the images.

3 The Lumigraph System

This section discusses many of the practical implementation issues related to creating a Lumigraph and generating images from it. Figure 9 shows a block diagram of the system. The process begins with capturing images with a hand-held camera. From known markers

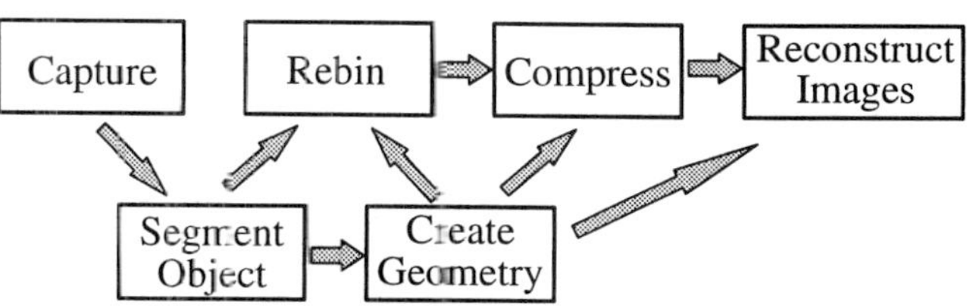

Figure 9: The Lumigraph system

in the image, the camera's position and orientation (its *pose*) is estimated. This provides enough information to create an approximate geometric object for use in the depth correction of (u, v) values. More importantly, each pixel in each image acts as a sample of the plenoptic function and is used to estimate the coefficients of the discrete Lumigraph (i.e., to *develop* the Lumigraph). Alternatively, the Lumigraph of a synthetic object can be generated directly by integrating a set of rays cast in a rendering system. We only briefly touch on compression issues. Finally, given an arbitrary virtual camera, new images of the object are quickly rendered.

3.1 Capture for Synthetic Scenes

Creating a Lumigraph of a synthetic scene is straightforward. A single sample per Lumigraph coefficient can be captured for each gridpoint (i, j) by placing the center of a virtual pin hole camera at (s_i, t_j) looking down the z axis, and defining the imaging frustum using the uv square as the film location. Rendering an image using this skewed perspective camera produces the Lumigraph coefficients. The pixel values in this image, indexed (p, q), are used as the Lumingraph coefficients $x_{i,j,p,q}$. To perform the integration against the kernel $\tilde{B}$, multiple rays per coefficient can be averaged by jittering the camera and pixel locations, weighting each image using $\tilde{B}$. For ray traced renderings, we have used the ray tracing program provided with the Generative Modeling package[25].

3.2 Capture for Real Scenes

Computing the Lumigraph for a real object requires the acquisition of object images from a large number of viewpoints. One way in which this can be accomplished is to use a special motion control platform to place the real camera at positions and orientations coincident with the (s_i, t_j) gridpoints [16]. While this is a reasonable solution, we are interested in acquiring the images with a regular hand-held camera. This results in a simpler and cheaper system, and may extend the range of applicability to larger scenes and objects.

To achieve this goal, we must first calibrate the camera to determine the mapping between directions and image coordinates. Next, we must identify special calibration markers in each image and compute the camera's pose from these markers. To enable depth-corrected interpolation of the Lumigraph, we also wish to recover a rough geometric model of the object. To do this, we convert each input image into a silhouette using a blue-screen technique, and then build a volumetric model from these binary images.

3.2.1 Camera Calibration and Pose Estimation

Camera calibration and pose estimation can be thought of as two parts of a single process: determining a mapping between screen pixels and rays in the world. The parameters associated with this process naturally divide into two sets: extrinsic parameters, which define the camera's pose (a rigid rotation and translation), and intrinsic parameters, which define a mapping of 3D camera coordinates onto the screen. This latter mapping not only includes a perspective (pinhole) projection from the 3D coordinates to undistorted

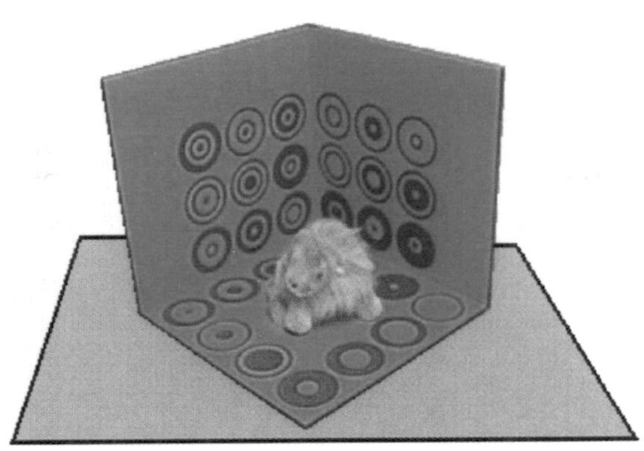

Figure 10: The capture stage

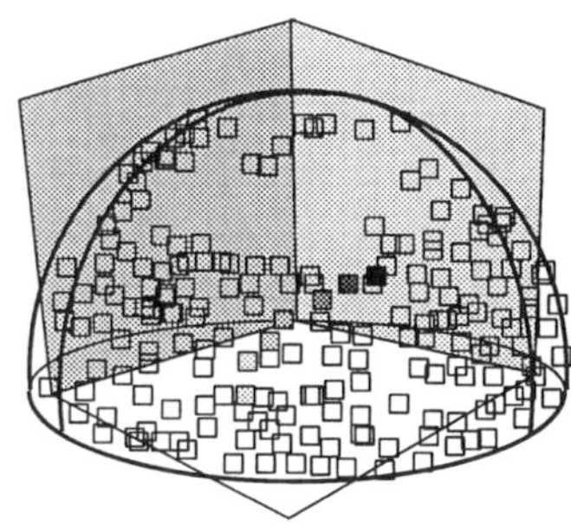

Figure 11: The user interface for the image capture stage displays the current and previous camera positions on a viewing sphere. The goal of the user is to "paint" the sphere.

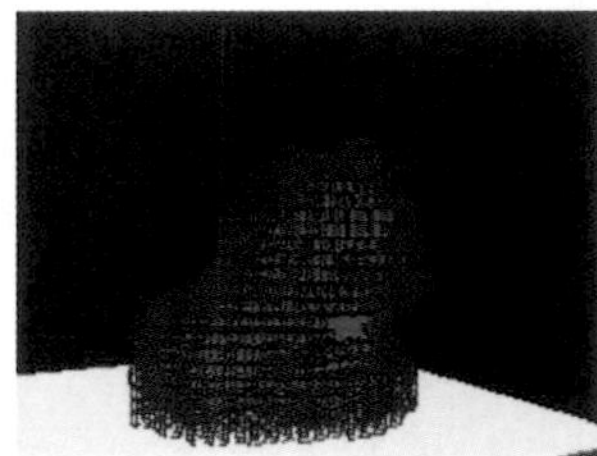

Figure 12: Segmented image plus volume construction

image coordinates, but also a radial distortion transformation and a final translation and scaling into screen coordinates [29, 31].

We use a camera with a fixed lens, thus the intrinsic parameters remain constant throughout the process and need to be estimated only once, before the data acquisition begins. Extrinsic parameters, however, change constantly and need to be recomputed for each new video frame. Fortunately, given the intrinsic parameters, this can be done efficiently and accurately with many fewer calibration points. To compute the intrinsic and extrinsic parameters, we employ an algorithm originally developed by Tsai [29] and extended by Willson [31].

A specially designed stage provides the source of calibration data (see Figure 10). The stage has two walls fixed together at a right angle and a base that can be detached from the walls and rotated in 90 degree increments. An object placed on such a movable base can be viewed from all directions in the upper hemisphere. The stage background is painted cyan for later blue-screen processing. Thirty markers, each of which consists of several concentric rings in a darker shade of cyan, are distributed along the sides and base. This number is sufficiently high to allow for a very precise intrinsic camera calibration. During the extrinsic camera calibration, only 8 or more markers need be visible to reliably compute a pose.

Locating markers in each image is accomplished by first converting the image into a binary (i.e., black or white) image. A *double thresholding* operator divides all image pixels into three groups separated by intensity thresholds T_1 and T_2. Pixels with an intensity below T_1 are considered black, pixels with an intensity above T_2 are considered white. Pixels with an intensity between T_1 and T_2 are considered black only if they have a black neighbor, otherwise they are considered white. The binary thresholded image is then searched for *connected components* [23]. Sets of connected components with similar centers of gravity are the likely candidates for the markers. Finally, the ratio of radii in each marker is used to uniquely identify the marker. To help the user correctly sample the viewing space, a real-time visual feedback displays the current and past locations of the camera in the view space (Figure 11). Marker tracking, pose estimation, feedback display, and frame recording takes approximately 1/2 second per frame on an SGI Indy.

3.3 3D Shape Approximation

The recovery of 3D shape information from natural imagery has long been a focus of computer vision research. Many of these techniques assume a particularly simple shape model, for example, a polyhedral scene where all edges are visible. Other techniques, such as stereo matching, produce sparse or incomplete depth estimates. To produce complete, closed 3D models, several approaches have been tried. One family of techniques builds 3D volumetric models directly from silhouettes of the object being viewed [21]. Another approach is to fit a deformable 3D model to sparse stereo data. Despite over 20 years of research, the reliable extraction of accurate 3D geometric information from imagery (without the use of active illumination and positioning hardware) remains elusive.

Fortunately, a rough estimate of the shape of the object is enough to greatly aid in the capture and reconstruction of images from a Lumigraph. We employ the octree construction algorithm described in [26] for this process. Each input image is first segmented into a binary object/background image using a blue-screen technique [12] (Figure 12). An octree representation of a cube that completely encloses the object is initialized. Then for each segmented image, each voxel at a coarse level of the octree is projected onto the image plane and tested against the silhouette of the object. If a voxel falls outside of the silhouette, it is removed from the tree. If it falls on the boundary, it is marked for subdivision into eight smaller cubes. After a small number of images are processed, all marked cubes subdivide. The algorithm proceeds for a preset number of subdivisions, typically 4. The resulting 3D model consists of a collection of voxels describing a volume which is known to contain the object[6] (Figure 12). The external polygons are collected and the resulting polyhedron is then smoothed using Taubin's polyhedral smoothing algorithm [27].

3.4 Rebinning

As described in Equation 1, the coefficient associated with the basis function $B_{i,j,p,q}$ is defined as the integral of the continuous Lumigraph function multiplied by some kernel function $\tilde{B}$. This can be written as

$$x_{i,j,p,q} = \int L(s,t,u,v)\, \tilde{B}_{i,j,p,q}(s,t,u,v)\, ds\, dt\, du\, dv \quad (3)$$

In practice this integral must be evaluated using a finite number of samples of the function L. Each pixel in the input video stream coming from the hand-held camera represents a single sample

[6] Technically, the volume is a superset of the *visual hull* of the object [13].

$L(s_k, t_k, u_k, v_k)$, of the Lumigraph function. As a result, the sample points in the domain cannot be pre-specified or controlled. In addition, there is no guarantee that the incoming samples are evenly spaced.

Constructing a Lumigraph from these samples is similar to the problem of multidimensional scattered data approximation. In the Lumigraph setting, the problem is difficult for many reasons. Because the samples are not evenly spaced, one cannot apply standard Fourier-based sampling theory. Because the number of sample points may be large ($\approx 10^8$) and because we are working in a 4 dimensional space, it is too expensive to solve systems of equations (as is done when solving thin-plate problems [28, 18]) or to build spatial data structures (such as Delauny triangulations).

In addition to the number of sample points, the distribution of the data samples have two qualities that make the problem particularly difficult. First, the sampling density can be quite sparse, with large gaps in many regions. Second, the sampling density is typically very non-uniform.

The first of these problems has been addressed in a two dimensional scattered data approximation algorithm described by Burt [5]. In his algorithm, a hierarchical set of lower resolution data sets is created using an image pyramid. Each of these lower resolutions represents a "blurred" version of the input data; at lower resolutions, the gaps in the data become smaller. This low resolution data is then used to fill in the gaps at higher resolutions.

The second of these problems, the non-uniformity of the sampling density, has been addressed by Mitchell [20]. He solves the problem of obtaining the value of a pixel that has been super-sampled with a non-uniform density. In this problem, when averaging the sample values, one does not want the result to be overly influenced by the regions sampled most densely. His algorithm avoids this by computing average values in a number of smaller regions. The final value of the pixel is then computed by averaging together the values of these strata. This average is not weighted by the number of samples falling in each of the strata. Thus, the non-uniformity of the samples does not bias the answer.

For our problem, we have developed a new hierarchical algorithm that combines concepts from both of these algorithms. Like Burt, our method uses a pyramid algorithm to fill in gaps, and like Mitchell, we ensure that the non-uniformity of the data does not bias the "blurring" step.

For ease of notation, the algorithm is described in 1D, and will use only one index i. A hierarchical set of basis functions is used, with the highest resolution labeled 0 and with lower resolutions having higher indices. Associated with each coefficient x_i^r at resolution r is a weight w_i^r. These weights determine how the coefficients at different resolution levels are eventually combined. The use of these weights is the distinguishing feature of our algorithm.

The algorithm proceeds in three phases. In the first phase, called *splat*, the sample data is used to approximate the integral of Equation 3, obtaining coefficients x_i^0 and weights w_i^0. In regions where there is little or no nearby sample data, the weights are small or zero. In the second phase, called *pull*, coefficients are computed for basis functions at a hierarchical set of lower resolution grids by combining the coefficient values from the higher resolution grids. In the lower resolution grids, the gaps (regions where the weights are low) become smaller (see figure 13). In the third phase, called *push*, information from the each lower resolution grid is combined with the next higher resolution grid, filling in the gaps while not unduly blurring the higher resolution information already computed.

3.4.1 Splatting

In the splatting phase, coefficients are computed by performing Monte-Carlo integration using the following weighted average estimator:

$$\begin{aligned} w_i^0 &= \sum_k \tilde{B}_i(s_k) \\ x_i^0 &= \frac{1}{w_i^0} \sum_k \tilde{B}_i(s_k)\, L(s_k) \end{aligned} \qquad (4)$$

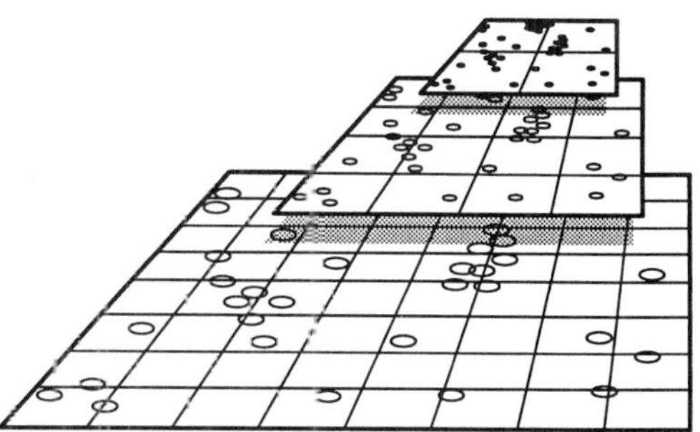

Figure 13: 2D pull-push. At lower resolutions the gaps are smaller.

where s_k denotes the domain location of sample k. If w_i^0 is 0, then the x_i^0 is undefined. If the $\tilde{B}_i$ have compact support, then each sample influences only a constant number of coefficients. Therefore, this step runs in time linear in the number of samples.

If the sample points s_k are chosen from a uniform distribution, this estimator converges to the correct value of the integral in Equation (3), and for n sample points has a variance of approximately $\frac{1}{n}\int \left(\tilde{B}_i(s)\, L(s) - x_i\, \tilde{B}_i(s)\right)^2 ds$. This variance is similar to that obtained using importance sampling, which is often much smaller than the crude Monte Carlo estimator. For a full analysis of this estimator, see [22].

3.4.2 Pull

In the *pull* phase, lower resolution approximations of the function are derived using a set of wider kernels. These wider kernels are defined by linearly summing together the higher resolution kernels ($\tilde{B}_i^{r+1} = \sum_k \tilde{h}_{k-2i} \tilde{B}_k^r$) using some discrete sequence $\tilde{h}$. For linear "hat" functions, $\tilde{h}[-1..1]$ is $\{\frac{1}{2}, 1, \frac{1}{2}\}$

The lower resolution coefficients are computed by combining the higher resolution coefficients using $\tilde{h}$. One way to do this would be to compute

$$\begin{aligned} w_i^{r+1} &= \sum_k \tilde{h}_{k-2i}\, w_k^r \\ x_i^{r+1} &= \frac{1}{w_i^{r+1}} \sum_k \tilde{h}_{k-2i}\, w_k^r\, x_k^r \end{aligned} \qquad (5)$$

It is easy to see that this formula, which corresponds to the method used by Burt, computes the same result as would the original estimator (Equation (4)) applied to the wider kernels. Once again, this estimator works if the sampling density is uniform. Unfortunately, when looking on a gross scale, it is imprudent to assume that the data is sampled uniformly. For example, the user may have held the camera in some particular region for a long time. This non-uniformity can greatly bias the estimator.

Our solution to this problem is to apply Mitchell's reasoning to this context, replacing Equation (5) with:

$$\begin{aligned} w_i^{r+1} &= \sum_k \tilde{h}_{k-2i}\, \min(w_k^r, 1) \\ x_i^{r+1} &= \frac{1}{w_i^{r+1}} \sum_k \tilde{h}_{k-2i}\, \min(w_k^r, 1)\, x_k^r \end{aligned}$$

The value 1 represents full saturation[7], and the min operator is used to place an upper bound on the degree that one coefficient in a highly

[7] Using the value 1 introduces no loss of generality if the normalization of $\tilde{h}$ is not fixed.

sampled region, can influence the total sum [8].

The pull stage runs in time linear in the number of basis function summed over all of the resolutions. Because each lower resolution has half the density of basis functions, this stage runs in time linear in the number of basis functions at resolution 0.

3.4.3 Push

During the push stage, the lower resolution approximation is used to fill in the regions in the higher resolution that have low weight [9]. If a higher resolution coefficient has a high associated confidence (i.e., has weight greater than one), we fully disregard the lower resolution information there. If the higher resolution coefficient does not have sufficient weight, we blend in the information from the lower resolution.

To blend this information, the low resolution approximation of the function must be expressed in the higher resolution basis. This is done by upsampling and convolving with a sequence h, that satisfies $B_i^{r+1} = \sum_k h_{k-2i} B_k^r$.

We first compute temporary values

$$\begin{aligned} tw_i^r &= \sum_k h_{i-2k} \min(w_k^{r+1}, 1) \\ tx_i^r &= \frac{1}{tw_i^r} \sum_k h_{i-2k} \min(w_k^{r+1}, 1)\, x_k^{r+1} \end{aligned}$$

These temporary values are now ready to be blended with the values x and w values already at level r.

$$\begin{aligned} x_i^r &= tx_i^r (1 - w_i^r) + w_i^r x_i^r \\ w_i^r &= tw_i^r (1 - w_i^r) + w_i^r \end{aligned}$$

This is analogous to the blending performed in image compositing.

3.4.4 Use of Geometric Information

This three phase algorithm must be adapted slightly when using the depth corrected basis functions B'. During the splat phase, each sample ray $L(s_k, t_k, u_k, v_k)$ must have its u and v values remapped as explained in Section 2.3.4. Also, during the push and pull phases, instead of simply combining coefficients using basis functions with neighboring indices, depth corrected indices are used.

3.4.5 2D Results

The validity of the algorithm was tested by first applying it to a 2D image. Figure 18 (a) shows a set of scattered samples from the well known mandrill image. The samples were chosen by picking 256 random line segments and sampling the mandrill very densely along these lines [10]. Image (b) shows the resulting image after the *pull/push* algorithm has been applied. Image (c) and (d) show the same process but with only 100 sample lines. The success of our algorithm on both 2D image functions and 4D Lumigraph functions leads us to believe that it may have many other uses.

3.5 Compression

A straightforward sampling of the Lumigraph requires a large amount of storage. For the examples shown in section 4, we use, for a single face, a 32×32 sampling in (s, t) space and 256×256 (u, v) images. To store the six faces of our viewing cube with 24-bits per pixel requires $32^2 \cdot 256^2 \cdot 6 \cdot 3 = 1.125\text{GB}$ of storage.

Fortunately, there is a large amount of coherence between (s, t, u, v) samples. One could apply a transform code to the 4D array, such as a wavelet transform or block DCT. Given geometric information, we can expect to do even better by considering the 4D array as a 2D array of images. We can then *predict* new (u, v) images from adjacent images, (i.e., images at adjacent (s, t) locations). Intraframe compression issues are identical to compressing single images (a simple JPEG compression yields about a 20:1 savings). Interframe compression can take advantage of increased information over other compression methods such as MPEG. Since we know that the object is static and know the camera motion between adjacent images, we can predict the motion of pixels. In addition, we can leverage the fact that we have a 2D array of images rather than a single linear video stream.

Although we have not completed a full analysis of compression issues, our preliminary experiments suggest that a 200:1 compression ratio should be achievable with almost no degradation. This reduces the storage requirements to under 6MB. Obviously, further improvements can be expected using a more sophisticated prediction and encoding scheme.

3.6 Reconstruction of Images

Given a desired camera (position, orientation, resolution), the reconstruction phase colors each pixel of the output image with the color that this camera would create if it were pointed at the real object.

3.6.1 Ray Tracing

Given a Lumigraph, one may generate a new image from an arbitrary camera pixel by pixel, ray by ray. For each ray, the corresponding (s, t, u, v) coordinates are computed, the nearby grid points are located, and their values are properly interpolated using the chosen basis functions (see Figure 3).

In order to use the depth corrected basis functions given an approximate object, we transform the (u, v) coordinates to the depth corrected (u', v') before interpolation. This depth correction of the (u, v) values can be carried out with the aid of graphics hardware. The polygonal approximation of the object is drawn from the point of view and with the same resolution as the desired image. Each vertex is assigned a *red, green, blue* value corresponding to its (x, y, z) coordinate resulting in a "depth" image. The corrected depth value is found by examining the blue value in the corresponding pixel of the depth image for the $\pm z$-faces of the Lumigraph cube (or the red or green values for other faces). This information is used to find u' and v' with Equation 2.

3.6.2 Texture mapping

The expense of tracing a ray for each pixel can be avoided by reconstructing images using texture mapping operations. The st plane itself is tiled with texture mapped polygons with the textures defined by slices of the Lumigraph: $\text{tex}_{i,j}(u_p, v_q) = x_{i,j,p,q}$. In other words, we have one texture associated with each st gridpoint.

Constant Basis

Consider the case of constant basis functions. Suppose we wish to render an image from the desired camera shown in Figure 14. The set of rays passing through the shaded square on the st plane have (s, t) coordinates closest to the grid point (i, j). Suppose that the uv plane is filled with $\text{tex}_{i,j}$. Then, when using constant basis functions, the shaded region in the desired camera's film plane should be filled with the corresponding pixels in the shaded region of the uv plane. This computation can be accomplished by placing a virtual camera at the desired location, drawing a square polygon on the

[8] This is actually less extreme that Mitchell's original algorithm. In this context, his algorithm would set all non-zero weights to 1.

[9] Variance measures could be used instead of weight as a measure of confidence in this phase.

[10] We chose this type of sampling pattern because it mimics in many ways the structure of the Lumigraph samples taken from a hand-held camera. In that case each input video image is a dense sampling of the 4D Lumigraph along a 2D plane.

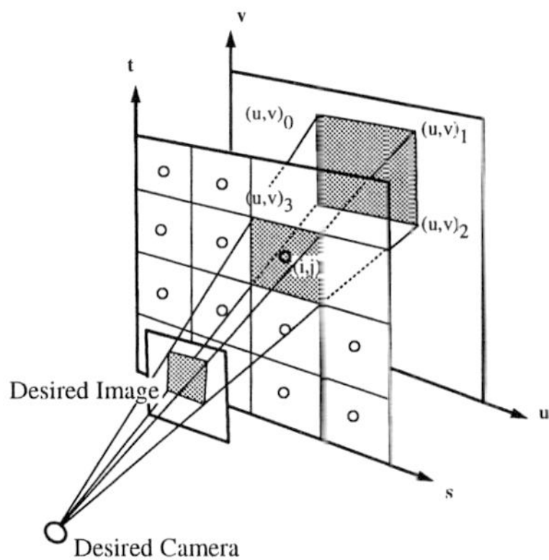

Figure 14: Texture mapping a portion of the st plane

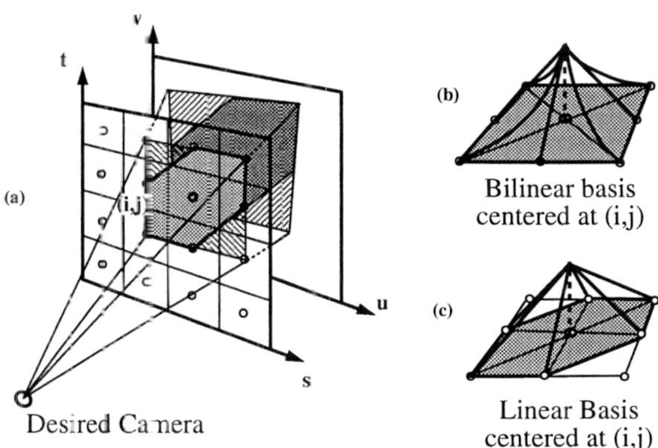

Figure 15: Quadralinear vs. linear-bilinear

st plane, and texture mapping it using the four texture coordinates $(u,v)_0$, $(u,v)_1$, $(u,v)_2$, and $(u,v)_3$ to index into $\text{tex}_{i,j}$.

Repeating this process for each grid point on the st plane and viewing the result from the desired camera results in a complete reconstruction of the desired image. Thus, if one has an $M \times M$ resolution for the st plane, one needs to draw at most M^2 texture mapped squares, requiring on average, only one ray intersection for each square since the vertices are shared. Since many of the M^2 squares on the st plane are invisible from the desired camera, typically only a small fraction of these squares need to be rendered. The rendering cost is independent of the resolution of the final image.

Intuitively, you can think of the st plane as a piece of holographic film. As your eye moves back and forth you see different things at the same point in st since each point holds a complete image.

Quadralinear Basis

The reconstruction of images from a quadralinear basis Lumigraph can also be performed using a combination of texture mapping and alpha blending. In the quadralinear basis, the support of the basis function at i, j covers a larger square on the st plane than does the box basis (see Figure 15(a)). Although the regions do not overlap in the constant basis, they do in the quadralinear basis. For a given pixel in the desired image, values from 16 4D grid points contribute to the final value.

The quadralinear interpolation of these 16 values can be carried out as a sequence of bilinear interpolations, first in uv and then in st. A bilinear basis function is shown in Figure 15(b) centered at grid point (i,j). A similar basis would lie over each grid point in uv and every grid point in st.

Texture mapping hardware on an SGI workstation can automatically carry out the bilinear interpolation of the texture in uv. Unfortunately, there is no hardware support for the st bilinear interpolation. We could approximate the bilinear pyramid with a linear pyramid by drawing the four triangles shown on the floor of the basis function in Figure 15(b). By assigning α values to each vertex ($\alpha = 1$ at the center, and $\alpha = 0$ at the outer four vertices) and using alpha blending, the final image approximates the full quadralinear interpolation with a linear-bilinear one. Unfortunately, such a set of basis functions do not sum to unity which causes serious artifacts.

A different pyramid of triangles can be built that does sum to unity and thus avoids these artifacts. Figure 15(c) shows a hexagonal region associated with grid point (i,j) and an associated linear basis function. We draw the six triangles of the hexagon with $\alpha = 1$ at the center and $\alpha = 0$ at the outside six vertices[11]. The linear interpolation of α values together with the bilinear interpolation of the texture map results in a linear-bilinear interpolation. In practice we have found it to be indistinguishable from the full quadralinear interpolation. This process requires at most 6 M^2 texture mapped, α-blended triangles to be drawn.

Depth Correction

As before, the (u,v) coordinates of the vertices of the texture mapped triangles can be depth corrected. At interior pixels, the depth correction is only approximate. This is not valid when there are large depth changes within the bounds of the triangle. Therefore, we adaptively subdivide the triangles into four smaller ones by connecting the midpoints of the sides until they are (a) smaller than a minimum screen size or (b) have a sufficiently small variation in depth at the three corners and center. The α values at intermediate vertices are the average of the vertices of the parent triangles.

4 Results

We have implemented the complete system described in this paper and have created Lumigraphs of both synthetic and actual objects. For synthetic objects, Lumigraphs can be created either from polygon rendered or ray traced images. Computing all of the necessary images is a lengthy process often taking weeks of processing time.

For real objects, the capture is performed with an inexpensive, single chip Panasonic analog video camera. The capture phase takes less than one hour. The captured data is then "developed" into a Lumigraph. This off-line processing, which includes segmenting the image from its background, creating an approximate volumetric representation, and rebinning the samples, takes less than one day of processing on an SGI Indy workstation.

Once the Lumigraph has been created, arbitrary new images of the object or scene can be generated. One may generate these new images on a ray by ray basis, which takes a few seconds per frame at 450×450 resolution. If one has hardware texture mapping available, then one may use the acceleration algorithm described in Section 3.6.2. This texture mapping algorithm is able to create multiple frames per second from the Lumigraph on an SGI Reality Engine. The rendering speed is almost independent of the desired resolution of the output images. The computational bottleneck is moving the data from main memory to the smaller texture cache.

Figure 19 shows images of a synthetic fruit bowl, an actual fruit bowl, and a stuffed lion, generated from Lumigraphs. No geometric information was used in the Lumigraph of the synthetic fruit bowl. For the actual fruit bowl and the stuffed lion, we have used the approximate geometry that was computed using the silhouette information. These images can be generated in a fraction of a second, independent of scene complexity. The complexity of both the geometry and the lighting effects present in these images would be difficult to achieve using traditional computer graphics techniques.

[11] The alpha blending mode is set to perform a simple summation.

5 Conclusion

In this paper we have described a rendering framework based on the plenoptic function emanating from a static object or scene. Our method makes no assumptions about the reflective properties of the surfaces in the scene. Moreover, this representation does not require us to derive any geometric knowledge about the scene such as depth. However, this method does allow us to include any geometric knowledge we may compute, to improve the efficiency of the representation and improve the quality of the results. We compute the approximate geometry using silhouette information.

We have developed a system for capturing plenoptic data using a hand-held camera, and converting this data into a Lumigraph using a novel rebinning algorithm. Finally, we have developed an algorithm for generating new images from the Lumigraph quickly using the power of texture mapping hardware.

In the examples shown in this paper, we have not captured the complete plenoptic function surrounding an object. We have limited ourselves to only one face of a surrounding cube. There should be no conceptual obstacles to extending this work to complete captures using all six cube faces.

There is much future work to be done on this topic. It will be important to develop powerful compression methods so that Lumigraphs can be efficiently stored and transmitted. We believe that the large degree of coherence in the Lumigraph will make a high rate of compression achievable. Future research also includes improving the accuracy of our system to reduce the amount of artifacts in the images created by the Lumigraph. With these extensions we believe the Lumigraph will be an attractive alternative to traditional methods for efficiently storing and rendering realistic 3D objects and scenes.

Acknowledgments

The authors would like to acknowledge the help and advice we received in the conception, implementation and writing of this paper. Thanks to Marc Levoy and Pat Hanrahan for discussions on issues related to the 5D to 4D simplification, the two-plane parameterization and the camera based aperture analog. Jim Kajiya and Tony DeRose provided a terrific sounding board throughout this project. The ray tracer used for the synthetic fruit bowl was written by John Snyder. The mesh simplification code used for the bunny was written by Hugues Hoppe. Portions of the camera capture code were implemented by Matthew Turk. Jim Blinn, Hugues Hoppe, Andrew Glassner and Jutta Joesch provided excellent editing suggestions. Erynn Ryan is deeply thanked for her creative crisis management. Finally, we wish to thank the anonymous reviewers who pointed us toward a number of significant references we had missed.

References

[1] ADELSON, E. H., AND BERGEN, J. R. The plenoptic function and the elements of early vision. In *Computational Models of Visual Processing*, Landy and Movshon, Eds. MIT Press, Cambridge, Massachusetts, 1991, ch. 1.

[2] ASHDOWN, I. Near-field photometry: A new approach. *Journal of the Illumination Engineering Society 22*, 1 (1993), 163–180.

[3] BENTON, S. A. Survey of holographic stereograms. *Proceedings of the SPIE 391* (1982), 15–22.

[4] BOLLES, R. C., BAKER, H. H., AND MARIMONT, D. H. Epipolar-plane image analysis: An approach to determining structure from motion. *International Journal of Computer Vision 1* (1987), 7–55.

[5] BURT, P. J. Moment images, polynomial fit filters, and the problem of surface interpolation. In *Proceedings of Computer Vision and Pattern Recognition* (June 1988), IEEE Computer Society Press, pp. 144–152.

[6] CHEN, S. E. Quicktime VR - an image-based approach to virtual environment navigation. In *Computer Graphics, Annual Conference Series, 1995*, pp. 29–38.

[7] CHEN, S. E., AND WILLIAMS, L. View interpolation for image synthesis. In *Computer Graphics, Annual Conference Series, 1993*, pp. 279–288.

[8] CHUI, C. K. *An Introduction to Wavelets*. Academic Press Inc., 1992.

[9] HALLE, M. W. Holographic stereograms as discrete imaging systems. *Practical Holography VIII (SPIE) 2176* (1994), 73–84.

[10] HOPPE, H. Progressive meshes. In *Computer Graphics, Annual Conference Series, 1996*.

[11] KATAYAMA, A., TANAKA, K., OSHINO, T., AND TAMURA, H. A viewpoint independent stereoscopic display using interpolation of multi-viewpoint images. *Steroscopic displays and virtal reality sytems II (SPIE) 2409* (1995), 11–20.

[12] KLINKER, G. J. *A Physical Approach to Color Image Understanding*. A K Peters, Wellesley, Massachusetts, 1993.

[13] LAURENTINI, A. The visual hull concept for silhouette-based image understanding. *IEEE Transactions on Pattern Analysis and Machine Intelligence 16*, 2 (February 1994), 150–162.

[14] LAVEAU, S., AND FAUGERAS, O. 3-D scene representation as a collection of images and fundamental matrices. Tech. Rep. 2205, INRIA-Sophia Antipolis, February 1994.

[15] LEVIN, R. E. Photometric characteristics of light-controlling apparatus. *Illuminating Engineering 66*, 4 (1971), 205–215.

[16] LEVOY, M., AND HANRAHAN, P. Light-field rendering. In *Computer Graphics, Annual Conference Series, 1996*.

[17] LEWIS, R. R., AND FOURNIER, A. Light-driven global illumination with a wavelet representation of light transport. UBC CS Technical Reports 95-28, University of British Columbia, 1995.

[18] LITWINOWICZ, P., AND WILLIAMS, L. Animating images with drawings. In *Computer Graphics, Annual Conference Series, 1994*, pp. 409–412.

[19] MCMILLAN, L., AND BISHOP, G. Plenoptic modeling: An image-based rendering system. In *Computer Graphics, Annual Conference Series, 1995*, pp. 39–46.

[20] MITCHELL, D. P. Generating antialiased images at low sampling densities. *Computer Graphics 21*, 4 (1987), 65–72.

[21] POTMESIL, M. Generating octree models of 3D objects from their silhouettes in a sequence of images. *Computer Vision, Graphics, and Image Processing 40* (1987), 1–29.

[22] POWELL, M. J. D., AND SWANN, J. Weighted uniform sampling - a monte carlo technique for reducing variance. *J. Inst. Maths Applics 2* (1966), 228–236.

[23] ROSENFELD, A., AND KAK, A. C. *Digital Picture Processing*. Academic Press, New York, New York, 1976.

[24] SIMONCELLI, E. P., FREEMAN, W. T., ADELSON, E. H., AND HEEGER, D. J. Shiftable multiscale transforms. *IEEE Transactions on Information Theory 38* (1992), 587–607.

[25] SNYDER, J. M., AND KAJIYA, J. T. Generative modeling: A symbolic system for geometric modeling. *Computer Graphics 26*, 2 (1992), 369–379.

[26] SZELISKI, R. Rapid octree construction from image sequences. *CVGIP: Image Understanding 58*, 1 (July 1993), 23–32.

[27] TAUBIN, G. A signal processing approach to fair surface design. In *Computer Graphics, Annual Conference Series, 1995*, pp. 351–358.

[28] TERZOPOULOS, D. Regularization of inverse visual problems involving discontinuities. *IEEE PAMI 8*, 4 (July 1986), 413–424.

[29] TSAI, R. Y. A versatile camera calibration technique for high-accuracy 3D machine vision metrology using off-the-shelf TV cameras and lenses. *IEEE Journal of Robotics and Automation RA-3*, 4 (August 1987), 323–344.

[30] WERNER, T., HERSCH, R. D., AND HLAVAC, V. Rendering real-world objects using view interpolation. In *Fifth International Conference on Computer Vision (ICCV'95)* (Cambridge, Massachusetts, June 1995), pp. 957–962.

[31] WILLSON, R. G. *Modeling and Calibration of Automated Zoom Lenses*. PhD thesis, Carnegie Mellon University, 1994.

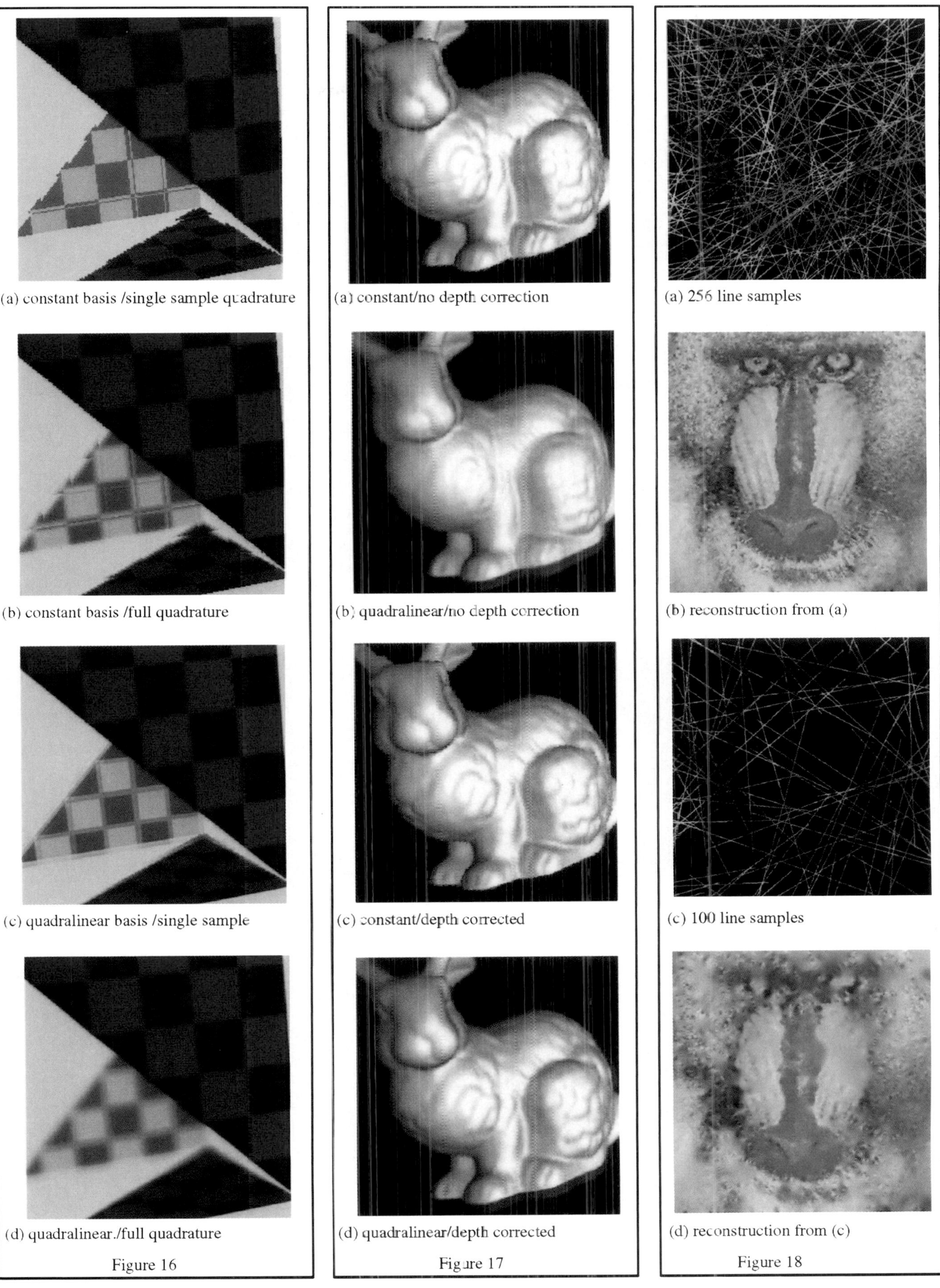

(a) constant basis /single sample quadrature

(b) constant basis /full quadrature

(c) quadralinear basis /single sample

(d) quadralinear./full quadrature

Figure 16

(a) constant/no depth correction

(b) quadralinear/no depth correction

(c) constant/depth corrected

(d) quadralinear/depth corrected

Figure 17

(a) 256 line samples

(b) reconstruction from (a)

(c) 100 line samples

(d) reconstruction from (c)

Figure 18

Figure 19: stereo pairs generated from Lumigraphs. (cross eyed style)

The Feudal Priority Algorithm on Hidden-Surface Removal

Han-Ming Chen
Wen-Teng Wang
Department of Mechanical Engineering
National Taiwan University

ABSTRACT

Development of a real-time shaded rendering approach for a frequently changing viewpoint or view vector is very important in the simulation of 3-D objects in Computer-Aided Design. A new approach is proposed in this paper to meet this demand in a very efficient manner.

A pre-processing phase, in which a feudal priority tree is established for all polygons of an object, and a post-processing phase, in which a rendering priority list is searched for from the feudal priority tree for a new viewpoint or view vector, are included in our approach. The most time-consuming work is finished in the pre-processing phase which only has to be executed once for an object, and the relatively simple task is left to the post-processing phase, which is repeated when the viewpoint or view vector is changed.

For the pre-processing phase, a static version and a dynamic version are proposed in this paper. The one-way priority relations of all polygons are computed in the former part of the dynamic pre-processing in a more efficient way than that in the static pre-processing, but the latter part of the dynamic pre-processing is still based on the static pre-processing.

A new concept of "absolute priority" is introduced to systematically reduce the polygons in which a separating plane is to be searched for so the probability of finding the separating plane is much increased. This is the basis to implement another important concept of "separating before splitting" by which the polygon splittings are much reduced. Hence the efficiency in the pre-processing and the post-processing phases is highly increased.

CR Categories and Subject Descriptors: I.3 [COMPUTER GRAPHICS]: I.3.7 [Three-Dimensional Graphics and Realism] - Hidden line/surface removal, Visible line/surface algorithms.
Additional Key Words and Phrases: The Binary Space-Partitioning Tree Algorithm.

Taipei, Taiwan 107, R.O.C. e-mail: hmchen@ccms.ntu.edu.tw

INTRODUCTION

In 1969, Schumacker first presented some very important notions on the subject of visual simulation [10]. Schumacker [10, 11, 12, 15] observed that within a cluster the face priority is a property of the topology of the cluster and can be calculated independently of the viewpoint if the environment, i.e., objects, can be divided into several adequate clusters. The cluster priority is determined by isolating clusters with separating planes and is dependent on the location of the viewpoint relative to the separating planes.

A subsequent development in this field was the Binary Space-Partitioning (BSP) Tree Algorithm. It was developed by Fuchs, Kedem, and Naylor [5, 7, 6] in 1980. The BSP tree algorithm is based on the work of Schumacker [5, 4]. Its most fundamental notion is to separate the space into two subspaces by a properly selected plane such that no polygon in the subspace on the viewpoint side is obstructed by any polygon in the subspace on the other side. This algorithm pushes much of its work into a pre-processing phase in which a BSP tree is computed and established. Once the BSP tree is established, the post-processing work becomes very simple to each new viewpoint.

Newell, Newell, and Sancha [8] developed an ordering test and a face-splitting routine in their algorithm to find the priority list for 3-D polygons. In their algorithm, it is still necessary to repeat the whole procedure for a new viewpoint, but its basic ideas are very helpful for establishing the "one-way priority" table used in our research [1, 2].

Computer-Aided Design and Manufacturing has become more and more important in modern industry. To render 3-D objects on the computer screen is an important step in CAD/CAM. But the efficiency of this rendering step completely relies upon a good Hidden-Surface Removal algorithm which can handle objects in any shape at a fast speed.

One of the possible disadvantage of the BSP tree algorithm is that the output polygons in the tree would be significantly more than the input polygons so the number of splittings is very large [5]. Another weakness of this algorithm is that the appropriate partitioning hyperplane selection is quite complicated and difficult. Therefore, we have developed a new method which we have named "Feudal Priority Algorithm" which also includes pre-processing and post-processing phases and can compute the rendering priority of polygons in any shape. In the "dynamic pre-processing" of our approach the number of splittings and the number of output polygons is much fewer than those in the pre-processing of the BSP tree algorithm, and even the number of one-way priority relations to be computed is fewer than that in the pre-processing of the BSP tree algorithm. Hence the dynamic pre-processing has a faster speed than the pre-processing of the

BSP tree algorithm. The efficiency of the post-processing is only affected by the number of the output polygons in the feudal priority tree or the BSP tree so our approach has a much higher speed than the BSP tree algorithm in the post-processing work.

FUNDAMENTAL CONCEPTS

If there exits any face(polygon) of an object and you can reach both sides of this face without penetrating any other face, this object is "open-volume". If you can just reach at most one side of each face of an object without penetrating other faces, this object is "closed-volume". All real world objects are constructed with closed-volume objects which are the most interesting objects in the fields of CAD and CAM. But many theoretical applications in the areas of Graphics, Mathematics, etc. make use of examples which contain open-volume objects. A polygon is a typical example of an open-volume object.

The objects discussed in this paper only consist of polygons, i.e., flat faces, which are either convex or concave. The term polygon is used to denote the union of the boundary and the interior of a plane region which is bounded by several successive line segments [9]. The following concepts are valid for both closed-volume and open-volume objects.

[Definition 1] One-way Priority

The "one-way priority" of a polygon P relative to a polygon Q is represented by the symbol "P -> Q" and is divided into the following four categories by substituting the x, y, and z coordinates of all vertices of the polygon P into the plane equation of the polygon Q:

(1) P is on the front side of Q if at least one vertex of P makes the plane equation of Q greater than 0 and all other vertices of P make the plane equation of Q not less than 0. This category is represented by the symbols "P <| Q" or "Q |> P".

(2) P is on the back side of Q if at least one vertex of P makes the plane equation of Q less than 0 and all other vertices of P make the plane equation of Q not greater than 0. This category is represented by the symbols "P >| Q" or "Q |< P".

(3) P is cut by Q if at least one vertex of P makes the plane equation of Q greater than 0 and at least one vertex of P makes the plane equation of Q less than 0. This category is represented by the symbol "P \- Q".

(4) P and Q are coplanar if all vertices of P make the plane equation of Q equal to 0. This category is represented by the symbol "P -- Q". Coplanar polygons have equal rendering priority.

The one-way priority is the most important basis in our approach.

The "absolute priority" is divided into the "absolute front priority" and the "absolute back priority" which are defined as the following:

[Definition 2] Absolute Front Priority

If no other polygons are on the front side of a polygon P, P has the "absolute front priority" to those polygons which are on the back side of P. Polygons which are coplanar and have the same normal direction with P have the same priority as P. All these polygons with the absolute front priority have the same priority. In Figure 1, polygons 1, 2, 3, 4, and 7 have the same priority in which polygons 2 and 3 are coplanar. The arrows in Figure 1 represent the normal vectors of polygons.

All the polygons with the absolute front priority are put in a bunch Fj and all other remaining polygons are put in a group G. In this paper, the term "bunch" is used to put the polygons which have the same priority, but the polygons in the term "group" may not have the same priority.

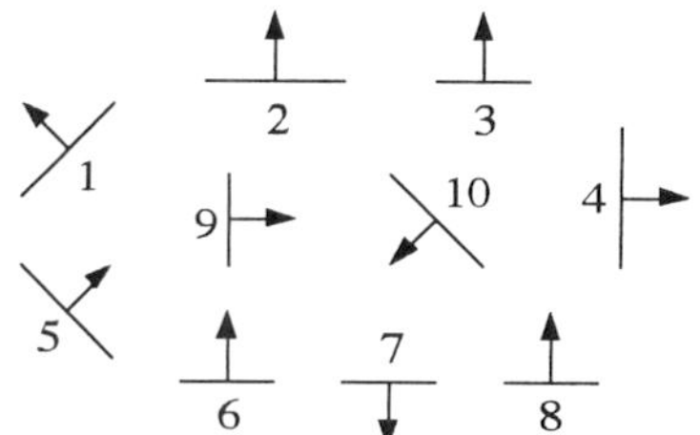

Figure 1. Absolute front priority and absolute back priority.

[Definition 3] Absolute Back Priority

If no other polygons are on the back side of a polygon P, P has the "absolute back priority" to those polygons which are on the front side of P. A polygon has the same priority as P if it is coplanar and has the same normal direction with P. All these polygons with the absolute back priority have the same priority. In Figure 1, polygons 5, 6, and 8 have the same priority in which polygons 6 and 8 are coplanar.

All the polygons with the absolute back priority are put in a bunch Bj and all other remaining polygons are put in a group G. The polygons in Fj and the polygons in Bj have the same priority so they are put in the same level in a "feudal priority tree".

The notion of the separating plane in [10] is extremely helpful in reducing polygon splittings. From the definition of linear separability, a separating plane for a group of polygons is easily found from their one-way priority relations.

[Definition 4] Linear Separability

Two sets of points S1 and S2 in E3(3-dimensional Euclidean space) are said to be linearly separable if there exists a plane P such that S1 and S2 lie on the opposite sides of P [9].

[Definition 5] Separating Planes

Polygons P and Q are said to be separated by a plane S or a plane S is said to be the separating plane of polygons P and Q, if either (1) or (2) is true.

(1) P <| S and Q >| S

(2) Q <| S and P >| S

The "relative priority" of two groups of polygons is determined by the "switch plane". If a separating plane can be found as the switch plane, it is much better than a splitting plane being selected as this switch plane because polygons are divided into two groups by the separating plane without any splitting.

[Definition 6] Relative Priority with A Separating Plane

After all polygons with absolute front priority or absolute back priority have been removed, there is no polygon which has absolute priority. In the remaining polygons, if a polygon S is found which can be a separating plane to all other polygons, separate all other polygons except the coplanar polygons of S into groups C and D. If the group C is on the front side of S and the group D is on the back side of S, this case can be represented by the symbols "C <| S |< D" or "D >| S |> C". In Figure 2, (polygons 4 and 5) <| polygon 3 |< (polygons 1 and 2).

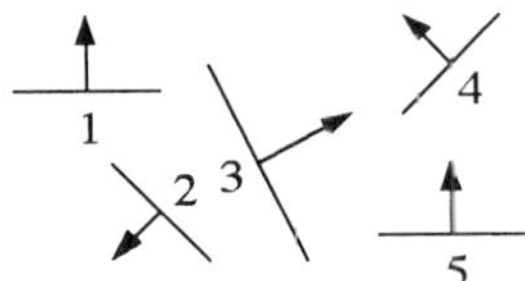

Figure 2. Relative priority with a separating plane.

[Definition 7] Relative Priority with A Splitting Plane

If a separating plane can not be found in the above case, a splitting plane S is selected. From the one-way priority relation of S, the polygons cut by this splitting plane can be easily found and split into smaller polygons. Then all output polygons except S and its coplanar polygons are separated into groups C and D. If C is on the front side of S and D is on the back side of S, this case can be represented by the symbols "C <| S |< D" or "D >| S |> C". In Figure 3, (polygons 1 and 2a) <| polygon 3 |< (polygons 2b, 4, and 5). The polygon 2 is split into polygons 2a and 2b by the splitting plane 3.

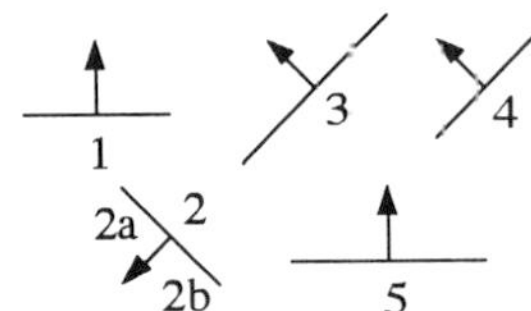

Figure 3. Relative priority with a splitting plane.

PROCEDURE

For each polygon, list all vertices in a sequence which makes the first three vertices be in clockwise direction on the outside surface in order to match the convention of the left-handed coordinate system. This is very important for closed-volume objects because the normal vector of each polygon is set to point outward for doing the back-face culling work. Then compute the plane equation of each polygon with the coordinates of the first three vertices of the polygon and store the coefficients for the plane equation.

The procedure developed in our approach for rendering 3-D objects involves a preprocessing phase and a postprocessing phase which are described next, starting with closed-volume objects. In the preprocessing phase both a static version and a dynamic version are proposed in this paper.

Now, a "feudal priority tree" is to be established step by step and a simple closed-volume object shown in Figure 4 is used to demonstrate the whole procedure.

The Static Preprocessing Phase

1. Establishing One-way Priority Tables

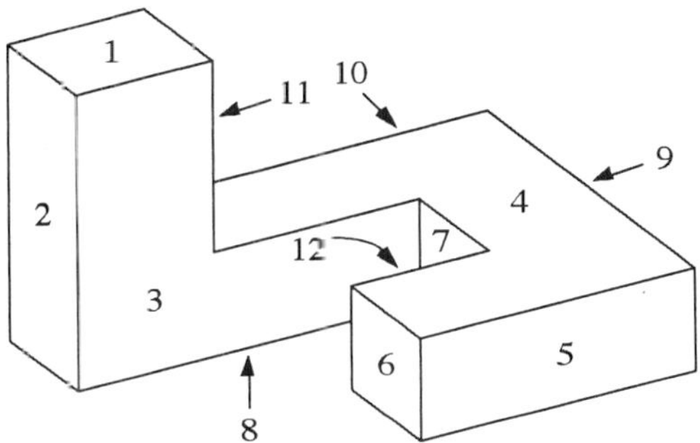

Figure 4. A closed-volume object.

For the i-th polygon of a closed-volume object, substitute the coordinates of all vertices of every other polygon sequentially into the plane equation of the i-th polygon, and then compute and decide the one-way priority relation of every other polygon to the i-th polygon. According to Definition 1, the one-way priority relation of all other polygons to the i-th polygon are divided into four categories: (1) front side, (2) back side, (3) cutting, and (4) coplanar. List every other polygon under its appropriate category in the i-th row in a one-way priority table.

In the i-th row, if there are polygons under the category "coplanar", it is not necessary to compute the one-way priority relation for these coplanar polygons. Just copy the i-th row into the rows of all these coplanar polygons, and then only exchange the polygons under categories "front side" and "back side" for those coplanar polygons with the reverse normal direction with the i-th polygon.

Table 1. A part of the one-way priority table for the object in Figure 4.

Q	P -> Q			
	P <| Q	P > Q	P \- Q	P -- Q
1		2,3,4,5,6,7,8,9,10,11,12		
2		1,3,4,5,6,7,8,9,10,11,12		
3	5,6,7,12	1,2,10,11	4,8,9	
4	1,11	5,6,7,8,9,12	2,3,10	

2. Adding Absolute Priority Polygons to The Feudal Priority Tree and Deleting Them from One-way Priority Tables

(1) In the i-th row, if no polygon is under the categories "back side" and "cutting", the i-th polygon is an absolute back priority polygon and can be added into the bunch Bj on the right side of the current connecting node as shown in Figure 5. Then the i-th row is deleted from the one-way priority table.

(2) In the i-th row, if no polygon is under the categories "front side" and "cutting", the i-th polygon is an absolute front priority polygon and can be added into the bunch Fj on the left side of the current connecting node. Then the i-th row is deleted from the one-way priority table.

(3) After all absolute priority polygons in the above steps (1) and (2) have been found, delete these polygons from all the rows remaining in the one-way priority table.

(4) Repeat steps (1) through (3) again. If there are polygons found in step (1), add them into the bunch Bj+1 linked on the right side of the last bunch Bj. If there are polygons found in

step (2), add them into the bunch F_{j+1} linked on the left side of the last bunch F_j. If there are no polygons found in steps (1) and (2), stop here and execute the next procedure.

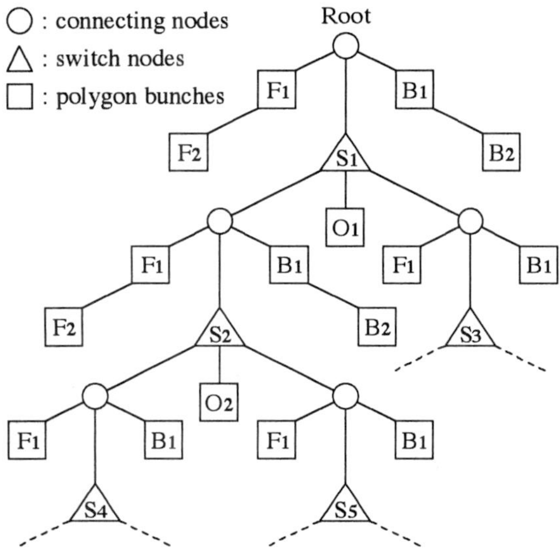

Figure 5. A feudal priority tree.

The polygons in the bunches F_{j+1} and B_{j+1} and all the polygons below F_{j+1} and B_{j+1} in the feudal priority tree are surrounded by the polygons in the bunches F_j and B_j such that this relation is not changed while the viewpoint or the view vector is moved. Hence this relation is called the "absolute priority".

After removing absolute front priority polygons 1, 2, 5, 8, 9, and 10, the one-way priority table of the object in Figure 4 becomes Table 2 in which no absolute priority polygon can be found.

Table 2. The one-way priority table for the object in Figure 4 after all absolute priority polygons are removed.

Q	P -> Q			
	P<|Q	P>|Q	P\\-Q	P -- Q
3	6,7,12	11	4	
4	11	6,7,12	3	
6	11	7,12	3,4	
7	3,6,11,12		4	
11	4,6,7,12		3	
12	3,7,11	6	4	

3. Separating The Remaining Polygons with A Separating Plane

In the i-th row of the current one-way priority table, if no polygon is under the category "cutting", the polygon Q_i can be a separating plane to all other polygons except those polygons coplanar with Q_i. If more than one separating plane can be found, the separating plane with the most balanced polygons on the front and back sides is selected. Setting this separating plane S_k as a switch node in Figure 5, those polygons on the front side of S_k are put in a group G_f as the left branch, those polygons on the back side of S_k are put in a group G_b as the right branch, and those polygons coplanar with S_k are put in a bunch O_k under the switch node S_k. Revise the current one-way priority table into two smaller ones for G_f and G_b separately. Because the rendering order of G_f and G_b is determined by the angle between the normal vector of S_k and the view vector it is called "relative priority".

Then go back to do procedure 2 for G_f and G_b individually. If there is no polygon by which all other polygons can be separated into two groups, do the next procedure to select a splitting plane.

4. Splitting The Remaining Polygons with A Splitting Plane

In the current one-way priority table, a polygon Q_i with (1) the least polygons under the category "cutting" and (2) the most balanced polygons under the categories "front side" and "back side" is selected as the splitting plane S_k. Those polygons under the category "cutting" are split by S_k into smaller polygons. Those split smaller polygons on the front side of S_k and the polygons under the category "front side" are put in a group G_f as the left branch of a switch node S_k in Figure 5. The other split smaller polygons on the back side of S_k and the polygons under the category "back side" are put in a group G_b as the right branch of the switch node S_k. Those polygons coplanar with S_k are put in a bunch O_k under the node S_k. Two smaller one-way priority tables are modified from the current one based on the groups G_f and G_b. The rendering order of G_f and G_b is also determined by the switch plane S_k as in the above procedure.

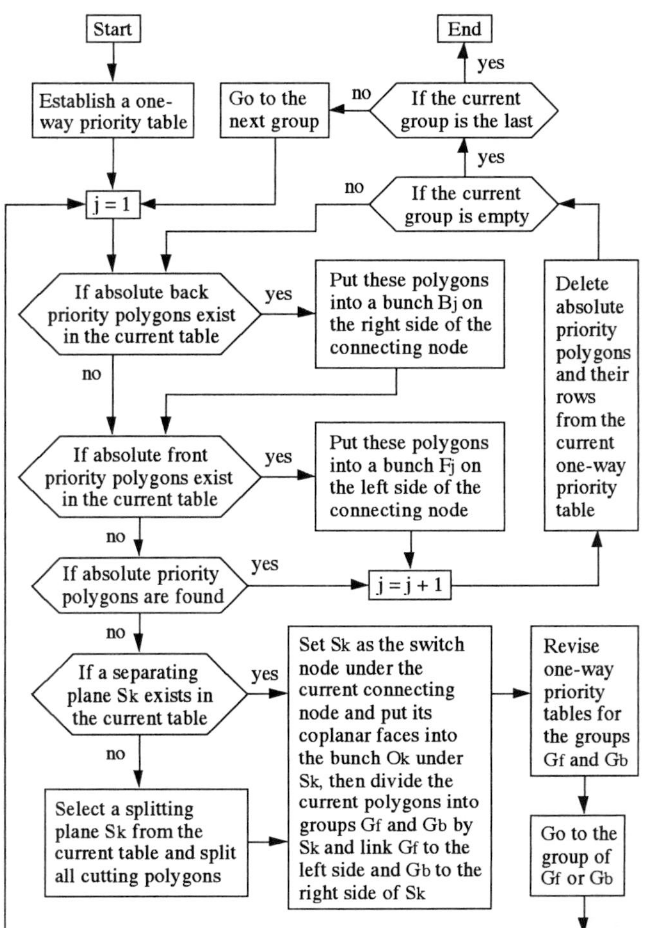

Figure 6. The procedure of the static preprocessing.

Return to do procedure 2 for Gf and Gb individually. In procedure 2, after all absolute priority polygons were removed from Gf and Gb, the separating planes or splitting planes chosen from the remaining polygons in Gf and Gb are set as the switch nodes S_{k+1} and S_{k+2} separately in the feudal priority tree in Figure 5.

The whole procedure for the static preprocessing phase of our approach is illustrated as shown in Figure 6.

In the "static preprocessing phase", all absolute priority polygons and all separating planes are searched for after their corresponding one-way priority tables have been completely built. But the "dynamic preprocessing phase" is developed to find the absolute priority polygons and the separating planes after each row of the one-way priority tables has been just set up.

In Table 2, there is no separating plane that can be found. Polygons 3, 4, and 12 are good candidates as the splitting plane. Polygon 3 is selected to be the splitting plane and split polygon 4 into polygons 13 and 14 as in Figure 7. Polygons 6, 7, 12, and 14 are in the group Gf and polygons 11 and 13 are in the group Gb. The two one-way priority tables of these two groups are shown in Table 3. In the group Gf of Table 3, two absolute front priority polygons 6 and 14 can be removed and put in a bunch F_1 under the left connecting node of the switch node 3, and then its one-way priority table becomes Table 4. Absolute back priority polygons 7 and 12 in Table 4 are put in a bunch B_2. Absolute back priority polygons 11 and 13 in the group Gb are put in a bunch B_1 under the right connecting node of the switch node 3. The feudal priority tree for the object in Figure 7 is shown in Figure 8.

The Dynamic Preprocessing Phase

1. Establishing One-way Priority Tables and Searching Absolute Priority Polygons or Separating Planes

As the one-way priority relation of the polygon Q_i has been computed, go through the following criteria step by step and then execute the appropriate procedure:

(1) If no polygon is under the categories "back side" and "cutting", do procedures 2(1) and 2(3).
(2) If no polygon is under the categories "front side" and "cutting", do procedures 2(2) and 2(3).
(3) If no polygon is under the category "cutting", do procedure 3.
(4) If Q_i is not the last polygon in the current group, go to the next polygon Q_i in this group. If the one-way priority relation of Q_i has not been computed, compute it. Then do procedure 1 for Q_i.
(5) If the current group is not the last group, go to the first polygon Q_i of the next group. If the one-way priority relation of Q_i has not been computed, compute it. Then do procedure 1 for Q_i.
(6) Start to do the static preprocessing for all the one-way priority tables in the feudal priority tree.

While doing the static preprocessing in the latter part of the dynamic preprocessing phase, do procedure 2 of the static preprocessing directly because the one-way priority relations of all the polygons have been built. In order to prevent the building of the feudal priority tree from being affected by the order of the input polygons in the data file, the input polygon is randomly selected in procedure 1 of the dynamic preprocessing phase. In contrast with the dynamic preprocessing, the order of the input polygons in the data file in the static preprocessing is not important because the feudal priority tree is built after the whole one-way priority table has been built.

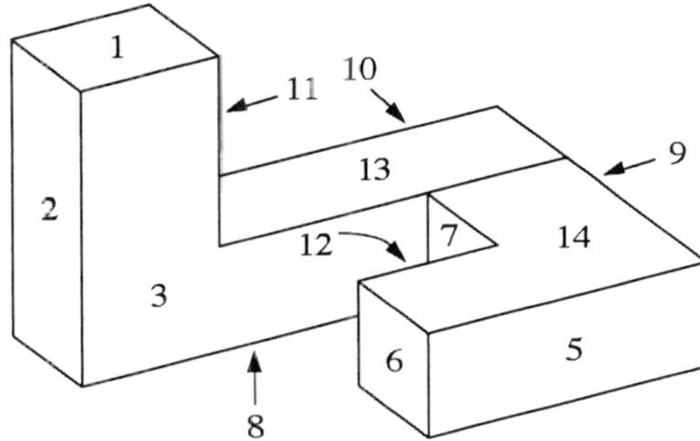

Figure 7. The closed-volume object in Figure 4 after splitting.

Table 3. Two one-way priority tables split from Table 2 by polygon 3.

Q	P -> Q		
	P<l Q	P>l Q	P\- Q
6		7,12,14	
7	6,12		14
12	7	6	14
14		6,7,12	

Q	P -> Q
	P<l Q
11	13
13	11

Table 4. The one-way priority table for the left one in Table 3 after absolute front priority polygons 6 and 14 are removed.

Q	P -> Q		
	P<l Q	P>l Q	P\- Q
7	12		
12	7		

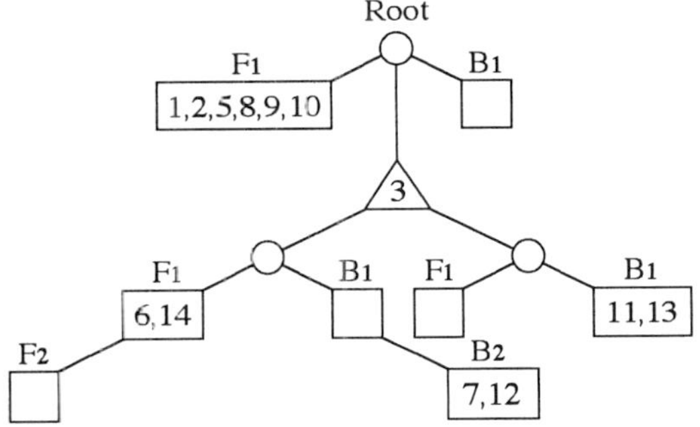

Figure 8. The feudal priority tree built by the static preprocessing for the object in Figure 7.

2. Adding Absolute Priority Polygons to The Feudal Priority Tree and Deleting Them from One-way Priority Tables

(1) Q_i which is an absolute back priority polygon is added into the bunch B_{j+1} connected to the last bunch B_j on the right side of the current connecting node in Figure 5. The coplanar polygons of Q_i having the same normal direction with Q_i are also put into B_{j+1}. The other coplanar polygons of Q_i having

the reverse normal direction with Q_i are put into the bunch F_{j+1} connected to the last bunch F_j on the left side of the current connecting node.

(2) Q_i which is an absolute front priority polygon is added into the bunch F_{j+1} connected to the last bunch F_j on the left side of the current connecting node in Figure 5. The coplanar polygons of Q_i having the same normal direction with Q_i are also put into F_{j+1}. The other coplanar polygons of Q_i having the reverse normal direction with Q_i are put into the bunch B_{j+1} connected to the last bunch B_j on the right side of the current connecting node.

(3) The row of Q_i is deleted from the one-way priority table. Q_i and its coplanar polygons are removed from the previous rows of the one-way priority table. Then search the previous rows of the current table with procedure 1 to find if absolute priority polygons or separating planes exist.

The following polygons in this group are not necessary in computing the one-way priority relations to Q_i and its coplanar polygons so the one-way priority relations to be computed can be reduced.

A random order 2, 8, 7, 11, 1, 5, 6, 3, 10, 4, 12, 9 is used to select the input polygons of the object in Figure 4. After the one-way priority row of polygon 2 has been computed, this row is removed for polygon 2 as an absolute front priority polygon. Then the absolute front priority polygon 8 is also removed. The polygons 7 and 11 are not necessary to compute the one-way priority relations to the polygons 2 and 8 in Table 5. The polygons 2 and 8 also do not appear in the row of polygon 1 which is found to be an absolute front priority polygon and will be removed from Table 5.

Table 5. Computing the one-way priority relation of polygon 1 of the object in Figure 4 after absolute priority polygons 2 and 8 are removed.

Q	P -> Q			
	P<|Q	P>|Q	P\\-Q	P -- Q
7	3,6,11,12	9	4,5,10	
11	4,5,6,7,9,12		3,10	
1		3,4,5,6,7,9,10,11,12		

3. Separating The Remaining Polygons with A Separating Plane

The polygon Q_i can be a separating plane S_k to all other polygons in the current group except its coplanar polygons. Set S_k as the switch node under the current connecting node in Figure 5 and put its coplanar polygons into the bunch O_k under S_k, and then the polygons on the front side of S_k are put in a group G_f as the left branch and the polygons on the back side of S_k are put in a group G_b as the right branch of the switch node S_k. Revise the current one-way priority table into two one-way priority tables for G_f and G_b. Then search the previous rows of the group G_f or G_b with procedure 1 to find if absolute priority polygons or separating planes exist. While searching the previous rows in a table, only those Q_i in which there is no polygon under the category "cutting" can be an absolute priority polygon or a separating plane.

The following polygons in one group are not necessary in computing the one-way priority relations to the polygons in other groups so the one-way priority relations to be computed can be much reduced. The whole procedure for the dynamic preprocessing phase of our approach is illustrated as shown in Figure 9.

The feudal priority tree built by the dynamic preprocessing for the object in Figure 4 with the input polygons being selected in the order 2, 8, 7, 11, 1, 5, 6, 3, 10, 4, 12, 9 is shown in Figure 10. The part below the switch node of the polygon 3 is built by the static preprocessing.

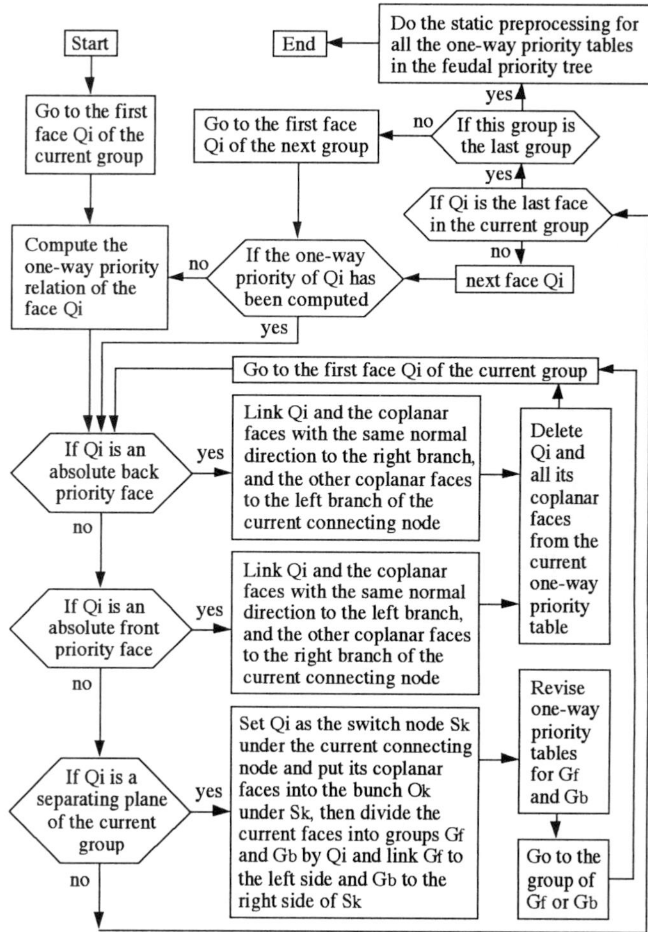

Figure 9. The procedure of the dynamic preprocessing.

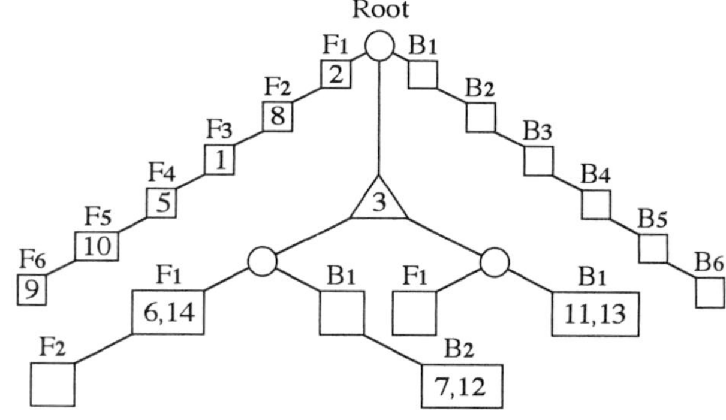

Figure 10. A feudal priority tree built by the dynamic preprocessing for the object in Figure 7.

The Postprocessing Phase

First, the "forward face" and the "backward face" are defined as the following:

(1) A forward face is a polygon whose normal vector forming an angle with the view vector is not greater than 90°.
(2) A backward face is a polygon whose normal vector forming an angle with the view vector is greater than 90°.

Instead of the viewpoint, the view vector is used in this paper to compute and decide if one face is forward or backward. The operations to compute the dot product of the view vector with the normal vector of one face involves 3 multiplications and 2 additions, but the operations to substitute the viewpoint into the plane equation of one face includes 3 multiplications and 3 additions. The forward and backward directions are also defined consistently with the direction of the view vector.

For a new view vector, all forward faces in the bunch F_j in Figure 5 are put into the sub-bunch F_{jf} and all backward faces are put into the sub-bunch F_{jb} as shown in Figure 11. Similarly, each bunch B_j is divided into the sub-bunches B_{jf} and B_{jb} for forward faces and backward faces respectively. For closed-volume objects, all the forward faces are fully obstructed by the backward faces and are invisible so all the faces in the sub-bunches, F_{jf} and B_{jf}, can be discarded before drawing. This procedure is known as "back-face culling".

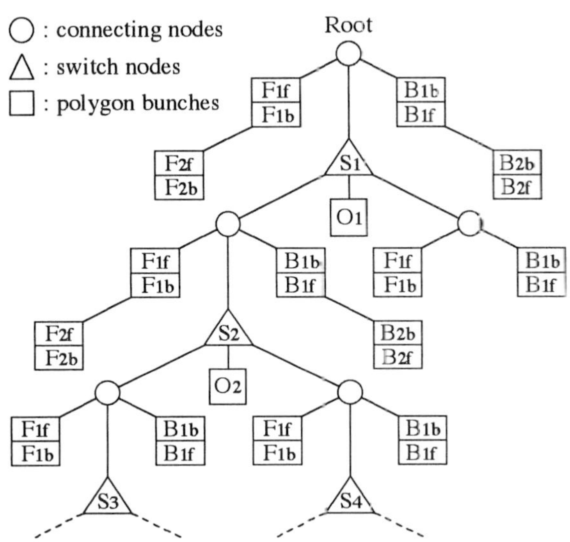

Figure 11. A feudal priority tree for the postprocessing.

Because the faces in F_j and B_j have the same priority, the feudal priority tree is searched level by level. The searching procedure starts from the root which is the first connecting node in the feudal priority tree:

(1) From the head of this connecting node, put the faces of B_{jb} into the next class element of the rendering priority linked list, and then put the faces of $B_{(j+1)b}$ into the next class element to the previous one, until the tail of this connecting node is reached. (a) Under this connecting node, if a switch node S_k exists and S_k is a forward face, do the connecting node which is on the front side of S_k by procedure (1). (b) Under this connecting node, if a switch node S_k exists and S_k is a backward face, do the connecting node which is on the back side of S_k by procedure (1). (c) If no switch node is under this connecting node, call procedure (2).
(2) From the tail of this connecting node, put the faces of F_{jb} into the next class element of the priority list, and then put the faces of $F_{(j-1)b}$ into the next class element to the previous one, until the head of this connecting node is reached. (a) If a switch node S_k is above this connecting node, and the other connecting node under S_k has not been done with procedure (1), put the face S_k and its coplanar faces in O_k into the next class, and then go to the other connecting node under S_k and do procedure (1). (b) If a switch node S_k is above this connecting node, and the other connecting node under S_k has been done with procedure (1), go to the upper connecting node and do procedure (2). (c) If no switch node is above this connecting node, the postprocessing has been finished.

The faces (or polygons) within a "class" element in the rendering priority linked list have the same rendering priority. Therefore, no matter what the drawing order for these faces is, the same picture is obtained . The whole procedure for the postprocessing phase of our approach is illustrated as shown in Figure 12.

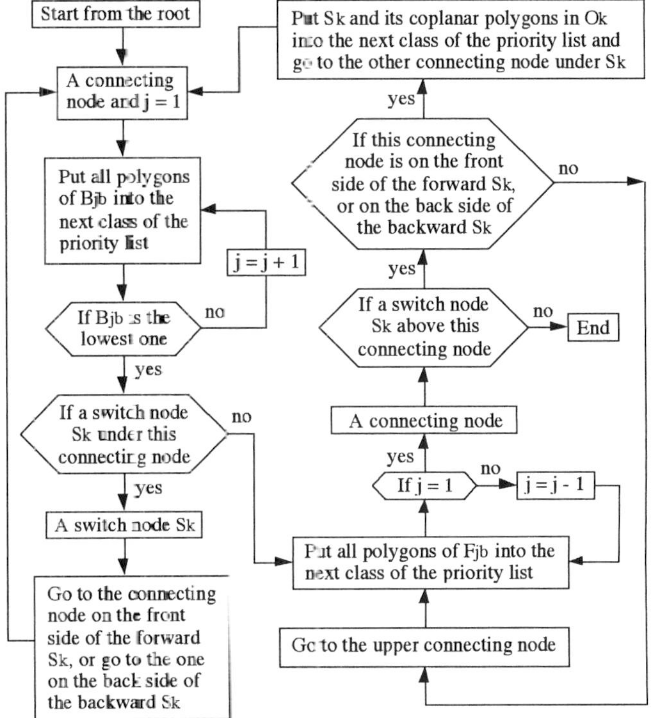

Figure 12. The procedure of the postprocessing for closed-volume objects.

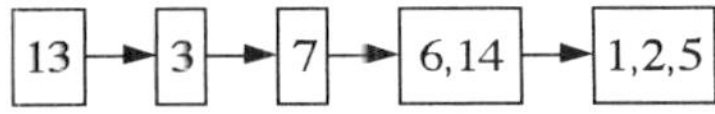

Figure 13. The priority list searched from the feudal priority tree in Figure 8.

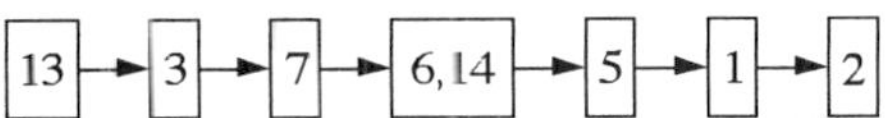

Figure 14. The priority list searched from the feudal priority tree in Figure 10.

For the object in Figure 4, the priority lists searched from the feudal priority trees in the Figures 8 and 10 are shown in Figures 13 and 14 respectively. The priority list obtained from the static preprocessing is always shorter than or at most equal to that obtained from the dynamic preprocessing.

The Procedure for Open-Volume Objects

The procedure of the static preprocessing or the dynamic preprocessing is the same for both closed-volume objects and open-volume objects because the feudal priority tree is constructed for both forward faces and backward faces. Within the postprocessing phase, the forward faces of closed-volume objects are invisible to the viewer so the faces of F_{jf} and B_{jf} are discarded in Figure 12. But all the faces of open-volume objects might be visible to the viewer, forward faces can not be culled so the faces of F_{jf} must be put together with the faces of B_{jb} into the same class element in the priority list. The class of the faces for F_{jb} also includes the faces of B_{jf}.

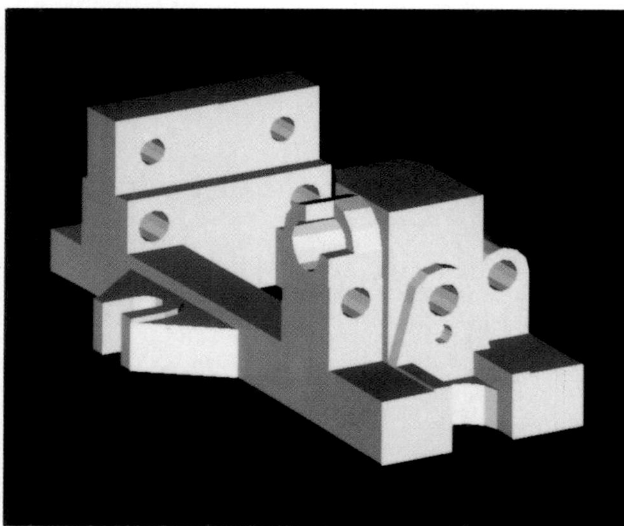

Figure 15. A gray shading display of the base of a machinist's vise which is a closed-volume object.

Figure 16. A color display of a house which is a closed-volume object.

IMPLEMENTATION

The static preprocessing and the dynamic preprocessing respectively with the postprocessing have been successfully implemented as two programs in the C language and tested on personal computers to do real-time rendering for both closed-volume and open-volume 3-D objects.

Two examples are displayed in Figures 15 and 16 which are the orthographic projection.

The data of polygons and running time in Tables 6 and 7 are the average values on executing 20 times the corresponding programs for the closed-volume objects in the Figures 15 and 16 respectively. A polygon is assumed to be split into just two smaller polygons so the difference between output polygons and input polygons is the number of splittings. The numbers in the row of "One-way priority relations" are the times of the execution to substitute all the vertices of a polygon into the plane equation of another polygon.

Table 6. Comparing our approach with the BSP tree algorithm for the example in Figure 15.

304 input polygons	FP alg. with static pre-processing	FP alg. with dynamic pre-processing	BSP tree algorithm
Output polygons	324	324	579
Splittings	20	20	275
One-way priority relations	63162	14234	28636
Connecting nodes	71	106	
Switch nodes	35	70	441
Time of pre-processing (ms)	444	113	125
Time of post-processing (ms)	0.603	0.767	7.55

Table 7. Comparing our approach with the BSP tree algorithm for the example in Figure 16.

736 input polygons	FP alg. with static pre-processing	FP alg. with dynamic pre-processing	BSP tree algorithm
Output polygons	741	741	1290
Splittings	5	5	554
One-way priority relations	141942	45744	84596
Connecting nodes	111	221	
Switch nodes	55	135	1013
Time of pre-processing (ms)	1430	406	356
Time of post-processing (ms)	1.23	1.37	17.8

All the nodes in a BSP tree are switch nodes because the searching order depends on the dot product of the view vector and the normal vector of the faces in the nodes.

EVALUATION AND DISCUSSION

The BSP tree algorithm is an extremely efficient method for calculating the visibility relationships among a static group of 3-D polygons as seen from a frequently moving viewpoint [4]. The most time-consuming tasks in the computer for our approach and the BSP tree algorithm are (1) computing the one-way priority relation between each pair of polygons, and (2) splitting polygons. Hence our approach is proposed to compare with the BSP tree algorithm on these two tasks in the preprocessing phase and the postprocessing phase.

The Preprocessing Phase

1. Computing One-way Priority Relations

Usually, establishing a BSP tree with fewer nodes can save time in preprocessing calculation. While establishing this tree at each node, in order to select a polygon as the splitting plane which intersects the fewest polygons n(n-1) one-way priority relations between any two polygons must be computed, but this procedure can not always lead to a BSP tree with the fewest nodes. Therefore, it is necessary to compute one-way priority relations much more than N(N-1) to build a BSP tree, where N is the number of input polygons and n is the number of polygons in a sub-space in the BSP tree. If the splitting plane is selected randomly, it may significantly increase splittings and output polygons. An alternative method is to select five candidate polygons randomly in each sub-space, and then one of the five candidates with the fewest splittings is chosen as the splitting plane [6, 14]. In this paper, the data for the BSP tree algorithm in the Tables 6 and 7 are based on this alternative method. Consequently, the procedure for establishing an optimal BSP tree is uncertain, difficult, and complicated.

In the static preprocessing of our approach, the one-way priority table is established on N(N-1) one-way priority relations. After computing the one-way priority relation of the polygon Qi in the dynamic preprocessing, if Qi is an absolute priority polygon, it is removed before the one-way priority relation of the next input polygon is computed so the following polygons are not necessary in computing one-way priority relations to these removed polygons. As the current polygons are divided into two groups with a separating plane Qi, the polygons in one group are not necessary to compute the one-way priority relations to the polygons in the other group. Therefore, the one-way priority relations to be computed in the dynamic preprocessing are much fewer than that in the static preprocessing and even fewer than that in the preprocessing of the BSP tree algorithm.

2. Splitting Polygons

In this paper, a polygon is assumed to be split by a splitting plane into two smaller polygons. In fact, a concave polygon may be split into more than two simply-connected polygons [13, 3]. To separate simply-connected polygons from the split polygons is complicated and time-consuming work. Hence more polygons to be split will definitely lower the efficiency in the preprocessing and will produce much more output polygons to decrease the efficiency in the postprocessing.

The dynamic preprocessing has much fewer polygon splittings and fewer one-way priority relations to be computed than those in the preprocessing of the BSP tree algorithm. Hence the dynamic preprocessing is faster than the preprocessing of the BSP tree algorithm. If the separation for simply-connected polygons is also involved, the dynamic preprocessing is definitely the best one among these three preprocessing methods. Because the static preprocessing has to compute the fixed N(N-1) one-way priority relations, it is slower than the dynamic preprocessing.

The Postprocessing Phase

In our approach and the BSP tree algorithm, the preprocessing phase which does the most time-consuming work is just run one time for an object to establish a feudal priority tree or a BSP tree respectively. For any new view vector or viewpoint, only the postprocessing phase, which is much faster than the preprocessing phase, is executed again.

In either the feudal priority tree or the BSP tree for both closed-volume and open-volume objects, almost each output polygon has to be decided if it is forward or backward in the postprocessing so the inner product of its normal vector with the view vector must be computed. This is the most time-consuming work in the postprocessing so more output polygons will slow down the efficiency of the postprocessing. The output polygons for an object in a feudal priority tree built by either the static preprocessing or the dynamic preprocessing is much fewer than that in a BSP tree so the postprocessing efficiency of the feudal priority algorithm is greatly better than that of the BSP tree algorithm.

CONCLUSIONS

Our approach introduces a new concept of "absolute priority" to remove several outward polygons by which the other polygons are surrounded before searching for a separating plane in the current polygon group so the possibility of finding the separating plane is highly enhanced. Hence the splittings are greatly reduced. This is the important concept of "separating before splitting" because if there are more splittings, then it is necessary to spend much more time in preprocessing and this produces much more output polygons which greatly decrease the efficiency both in the preprocessing and the postprocessing [1, 2]. Therefore, if separating is possible, to separate polygons is always better than to split polygons. If there are several planes with the least cutting polygons, select the one with the most balanced polygons on its front side and back side as the splitting plane.

The approach proposed in this paper has been compared with the well known BSP tree algorithm in both the preprocessing and the postprocessing:

(1) In the dynamic preprocessing, an absolute priority polygon is removed at once as it is found and the current polygons are immediately separated into two groups while a separating plane is searched for; therefore, the one-way priority relations to be computed are much fewer than that in the static preprocessing and even fewer than that in the preprocessing of the BSP tree algorithm. The efficiency of the dynamic preprocessing is better than that of the preprocessing of the BSP tree algorithm. If all split polygons are separated into simply-connected polygons, the dynamic preprocessing is much faster than the preprocessing of the BSP tree algorithm.

(2) Polygon splittings either in the dynamic preprocessing or in the static preprocessing are much fewer than that in the preprocessing of the BSP tree algorithm. Consequently, the output polygons in the feudal priority tree is much fewer than that in the BSP tree so the efficiency of the postprocessing of our approach is much better than that of the BSP tree algorithm.

The dynamic preprocessing is very efficient in both the preprocessing and the postprocessing. One drawback of the dynamic preprocessing is that its feudal priority tree is not as brief and uncomplicated as that built by the static preprocessing so the rendering priority list obtained by the dynamic preprocessing is longer than that obtained by the static preprocessing.

A topological property in our approach is that the polygons in the two bunches with the same level linked to a connecting node have the equal priority while searching the priority list. Among the polygons in the same class of a priority list, no one can be obstructed by the other polygons; hence these polygons have the same rendering priority that is another topological property in our approach.

Our approach keeps most output polygons without splitting so this maintains their completeness. But most input polygons are split by the BSP tree algorithm into smaller polygons. The information of the input polygons in our approach is kept more complete than that in the BSP tree algorithm so this is a great advantage for our approach in the CAM application.

ACKNOWLEDGMENTS

We gratefully acknowledge the support of the National Science Council of The Republic of China under the grant NSC82-0115-E-002-396, and specially thank Jenn-Tsuen Wu for his help in creating the data file of the example house.

REFERENCES

[1] CHEN, HAN-MING. *A Real-Time Rendering System for 3-D Objects in Computer-Aided Design and Manufacturing*, Ph.D. Dissertation, University of California at Berkeley, May 1991.

[2] CHEN, HAN-MING, and ADIGA, S. An Ingenious Algorithm for Hidden-Surface Removal. *The Proceedings of The Second International Conference on CAD & CG.* September 1991, Hangzhou, China, pp.159-164.

[3] CHEN, HAN-MING, and JIANG, L. S. Partitioning A Concave Polygon into Simply-Connected Polygons. *The Proceedings of The Twenty-third Midwestern Mechanics Conference*, October 1993, Lincoln, U.S.A., pp.75-77.

[4] FOLEY, J. D., VAN DAM, A., FEINER, S. K., and HUGHES, J. F. *Computer Graphics: Principles and Practice*, second ed. Addison-Wesley, Reading, MA, 1990.

[5] FUCHS, H., KEDEM, Z. M., and NAYLOR, B. F. On Visible Surface Generation by A Priori Tree Structures. *Computer Graphics*, Vol.14(3), July 1980, pp.124-133.

[6] FUCHS, H., ABRAM, G. D., and GRANT, E. D. Near Real-Time Shaded Display of Rigid Objects. *Computer Graphics*, Vol.17(3), July 1983, pp.65-72.

[7] NAYLOR, B. F. *A Priori Based Techniques for Determining Visibility Priority for 3-D Scenes*, Ph.D. Dissertation, University of Texas at Dallas, May 1981.

[8] NEWELL, M. E., NEWELL, R. G., and SANCHA, T. L. A Solution to the Hidden Surface Problem. *The Proceedings of the ACM National Conference*, 1972, pp.443-450.

[9] PREPARATA, F. P., and SHAMOS, M. I. *Computational Geometry: An Introduction*, Springer-Verlag, New York, 1985.

[10] SCHUMACKER, R. A., BRAND, B., GILLILAND, M. G., and SHARP, W. H. Study for Applying Computer-Generated Images to Visual Simulation. *Technical Report AFHRL-TR-69-14*, NTIS AD700375fR, U.S. Air Force Human Resources Lab., Air Force Systems Command, Brooks AFB, TX, September 1969.

[11] SUTHERLAND, I. E., SPROULL, R. F., and SCHUMACKER R. A. Sorting and the Hidden-Surface Problem. *The Proceedings of the National Computer Conference*, 1973, pp.685-693.

[12] SUTHERLAND, I. E., SPROULL, R. F., and SCHUMACKER, R. A. A Characterization of Ten Hidden-Surface Algorithms. *ACM Computing Surveys*, Vol.6(1), March 1974, pp.1-55.

[13] SUTHERLAND, I. E., and HODGMAN, G. W. Reentrant Polygon Clipping. *Communications of the ACM*, Vol.17(1), January 1974, pp.32-42.

[14] THIBAULT, W. C., and NAYLOR, B. F. Set Operations on Polyhedra Using Binary Space Partitioning Trees. *Computer Graphics*, Vol.21(4), July 1987, pp.153-162.

[15] YAO, F. F. On the Priority Approach to Hidden-Surface Algorithms. *The Proceedings of the IEEE Symposium on the Foundations of Computer Science*, 21st Annual, 1980, pp.301-307.

Hierarchical Polygon Tiling with Coverage Masks

Ned Greene

Apple Computer

Abstract

We present a novel polygon tiling algorithm in which recursive subdivision of image space is driven by coverage masks that classify a convex polygon as inside, outside, or intersecting cells in an image hierarchy. This approach permits Warnock-style subdivision with its logarithmic search properties to be driven very efficiently by bit-mask operations. The resulting hierarchical polygon tiling algorithm performs subdivision and visibility computations very rapidly while only visiting cells in the image hierarchy that are crossed by visible edges in the output image. Visible samples are never overwritten. At 512×512 resolution, the algorithm tiles as rapidly as traditional incremental scan conversion, and at high resolution (e.g. 4096×4096) it is much faster, making it well suited to antialiasing by oversampling and filtering. For densely occluded scenes, we combine hierarchical tiling with the hierarchical visibility algorithm to enable hierarchical object-space culling. When we tested this combination on a densely occluded model, it computed visibility on a 4096×4096 grid as rapidly as hierarchical z-buffering [Greene-Kass-Miller93] tiled a 512×512 grid, and it effectively antialiased scenes containing hundreds of thousands of visible polygons. The algorithm requires strict front-to-back traversal of polygons, so we represent a scene as a BSP tree or as an octree of BSP trees. When maintaining depth order of polygons is not convenient, we combine hierarchical tiling with hierarchical z-buffering, resorting to z-buffering only in regions of the screen where the closest object is not encountered first.

CR Categories: I.3.7 [Computer Graphics]: Three-Dimensional Graphics and Realism - Hidden line/surface removal; I.3.3 [Computer Graphics]: Picture/Image Generation.

Keywords: tiling, coverage mask, antialiasing, visibility, BSP tree, octree, recursive subdivision.

1 INTRODUCTION

Polygon tiling algorithms have been an important topic in computer image synthesis since the advent of raster graphics some two decades ago. Their purpose is to determine which point samples on an image raster are covered by the visible portion of each of the polygons composing a scene. Currently, polygon tiling software running on inexpensive computers can render point-sampled images of simple scenes at interactive rates. The fastest tiling algorithms have been carefully tuned to exploit image-space coherence by using incremental methods wherever possible. However, they fail to exploit opportunities for precomputation and they waste time tiling hidden geometry. There is a need for more efficient tiling algorithms that effectively exploit coherence and precomputation to enable efficient culling of hidden geometry and efficient tiling of visible geometry.

The dominant polygon tiling algorithm in use today is incremental scan conversion. Typically, raster samples on a polygon's perimeter are traversed with an incremental line-tiling algorithm. Edge samples on each intersected scanline define spans within a polygon, which are then traversed pixel-by-pixel, permitting incremental update of shading parameters and, in the case of z-buffering, depth values. Visibility of samples can be determined by a) maintaining a z-buffer and performing depth comparisons [Catmull74], b) traversing primitives back to front and writing every pixel tiled [Foley-et-al90], or c) traversing primitives front to back and overwriting only vacant pixels [Foley-et-al90]. With incremental scan conversion, the cost per pixel tiled is very low because incremental edge and span traversal effectively exploits image-space coherence.

One problem with traditional incremental scan conversion is that it must tile every sample on every primitive, whether or not it is visible, and so it wastes time tiling hidden geometry. This is not a big problem for simple scenes, but for densely occluded scenes it severely impairs efficiency. Ideally, a tiling algorithm should cull hidden geometry efficiently so that running time is proportional to the visible complexity of the scene and independent of the complexity of hidden geometry.

The Warnock subdivision algorithm [Warnock69] approaches this goal, performing logarithmic search for visible tiles in the quadtree subdivision of a polygon. If scene primitives are processed front to back, only visible tiles and their children in the quadtree are visited. Although Warnock subdivision satisfies our desire to work only on visible regions of primitives, the traditional subdivision procedure is relatively slow and consequently, this approach is slower than incremental scan conversion, except for densely occluded scenes. Neither traditional incremental scan conversion nor Warnock subdivision is well suited to tiling scenes of moderate depth complexity.

A second shortcoming of incremental scan conversion is that it spends most of its time tiling edges and spans, traversing these features pixel by pixel, even though all possible tiling patterns for an edge crossing a block of samples can be precomputed and stored as bit masks called *coverage masks*. Then the samples that a convex polygon covers within a block can be quickly found by compositing the coverage masks of its edges. Previously, this technique has been

Contact author at greene@apple.com,
Apple Computer, 1 Infinite Loop, Cupertino, CA 95014

used to estimate coverage of polygonal fragments within a pixel to accelerate filtering [Carpenter84, Sabella-Wozny83, Fiume-et-al83, Fiume91].

Here we present a polygon tiling algorithm that combines the best features of traditional algorithms. The key innovation that makes this integration possible is the generalization of coverage masks to permit their application to image hierarchies. The generalized masks, which we call *triage coverage masks*, classify cells in the image hierarchy as *inside*, *outside*, or *intersecting* an edge. This enables them to drive Warnock-style subdivision of image space. The result is a hierarchical tiling algorithm that finds visible geometry by logarithmic search, as with the Warnock algorithm, that exploits precomputation of tiling patterns, as with filtering with coverage masks, and that also uses incremental methods to exploit image-space coherence, as with incremental scan conversion. The algorithm efficiently performs high-resolution tiling (e.g. 4096×4096), so it naturally supports high-quality antialiasing by oversampling and filtering. A-buffer-style antialiasing with coverage masks [Carpenter84] is particularly convenient.

For densely occluded scenes we combine hierarchical tiling with the hierarchical visibility algorithm [Greene-Kass-Miller93, Greene-Kass94, Greene95] to permit hierarchical culling of hidden regions of object space. This combination of algorithms enables very rapid rendering of complex polygonal scenes with high-quality antialiasing. The method has been tested and shown to work effectively on densely occluded scenes. On a test scene containing upwards of 167 million replicated polygons, the algorithm computed visibility on a 4096×4096 grid as rapidly as hierarchical z-buffering [Greene-Kass-Miller93] tiled a 512×512 grid.

In §2, we survey previous work on efficient polygon tiling. In §3, we introduce triage coverage masks, and in §4 we present the rendering algorithm in which they are applied. In §5, we discuss how rendering of densely occluded scenes can be accelerated with object-space culling methods. In §6, we discuss strategies for efficiently processing dynamic scenes. In §7, we compare the hierarchical tiling algorithm to hierarchical z-buffering. In §8, we describe hierarchical tiling of polyhedra. In §9, we describe our implementation and show results for both simple and densely occluded scenes. Finally, we present our conclusions in §10.

2 PREVIOUS WORK

2.1 Warnock Subdivision

Our tiling algorithm is loosely based on the Warnock algorithm [Warnock69], a recursive subdivision procedure that finds the quadtree subdivision of visible edges in a scene by logarithmic search. Scene primitives are inserted into a quadtree data structure beginning at the root cell, which represents the whole screen. At each level of subdivision, the algorithm classifies the quadrants of the current quadtree cell as inside, outside, or intersecting the primitive being processed, and only intersected quadrants are subdivided. Quadrants which are entirely covered by one or more primitives are identified, permitting hidden geometry within them to be culled. The Warnock algorithm is actually a family of algorithms based on a common subdivision procedure, and the control structure varies from implementation to implementation [Rogers85]. A typical implementation processes primitives in no particular order, maintains lists of potentially visible primitives at quadtree cells, and expends considerable work performing depth comparisons in order to cull hidden geometry.

When circumstances permit convenient front-to-back traversal of primitives, as with a presorted static polygonal scene, a simpler and more efficient variation of the Warnock algorithm can be employed. In this case, we insert primitives into the quadtree one at a time in front-to-back order. As subdivision proceeds, we mark cells that primitives completely cover as *occupied* and ignore cells that are already occupied, since any geometry that projects to them is known to be hidden. We complete subdivision of one primitive down to the finest level of the quadtree before processing the next. This version of the Warnock algorithm is simpler because it need not maintain lists of primitives or perform depth comparisons. It is more efficient because, unlike the traditional algorithm, it only subdivides cells crossed by edges that are visible in the output image. Our tiling algorithm is based on this variation of the Warnock algorithm, which we will refer to as the *depth-priority Warnock algorithm.* Although Meagher's volume rendering algorithm uses this procedure to tile faces of octree cubes [Meagher82], to the best of our knowledge this variation of the Warnock algorithm has not been applied previously to rendering geometric models. Incidentally, front-to-back traversal of primitives would accelerate Warnock-style subdivision in the error-bounded rendering algorithm described in [Greene-Kass94].

2.2 Coverage Masks

We turn now to reviewing how filtering algorithms exploit precomputation with coverage masks [Carpenter84, Sabella-Wozny83, Fiume-et-al83, Fiume91]. The underlying idea is that all possible tiling patterns for a single edge crossing a grid of raster samples within a pixel can be precomputed and later retrieved, indexed by the points where the edge intersects the pixel's border [Fiume-et-al83, Sabella-Wozny83]. These tiling patterns can be stored as bit masks, permitting samples inside a convex polygon to be determined by ANDING together the coverage masks for its edges. Moreover, if polygons are processed front to back or back to front, visible-surface determination within a pixel can also be performed with bit-mask operations. For example, Carpenter's A-buffer algorithm [Carpenter84] clips polygons to pixel borders, sorts the polygonal fragments front to back, and determines the visible samples on each fragment on a 4×8 grid by compositing coverage masks. The A-buffer algorithm also uses coverage masks to accelerate filtering. For each visible fragment, a single shading value is computed, weighted by the bit count of its mask, and added to pixel color. This shading method efficiently approximates *area sampling* [Catmull78] and it effectively antialiases edges. Abram, Westover, and Whitted advance similar methods that permit jitter, convolution with arbitrary filter kernels, and evaluation of simple shading functions to be performed by table lookup [Abram-et-al85].

3 TRIAGE COVERAGE MASKS

To accelerate polygon tiling, the hierarchical tiling algorithm generalizes coverage masks to operate on image hierarchies, thereby enabling Warnock-style subdivision of image space to be driven by bit-mask operations. A conventional coverage mask for an edge classifies each grid point within a square region of the screen as inside or outside the edge, as shown in figure 1a. In the context of Warnock subdivision, the analogous operation is classifying subcells of an image hierarchy as inside, outside, or intersecting an edge, as shown in figure 1b for an edge crossing a square containing a 4×4 grid of subcells. We call such masks *triage coverage masks* because the three states that they distinguish correspond to trivial rejection, trivial acceptance, and "do further work." We represent each triage mask as a pair of bit masks, one indicating inside subcells, the other indicating outside subcells, as shown in figures 1c and 1d. We will refer to the bit mask for inside subcells as the "C" mask (for *covered*) and the bit mask for outside subcells as the "V" mask (for *vacant*). We call the intersected subcells the *active* region of the mask, because the corresponding regions of the screen require further work and will later be subdivided. The bit mask for the active region is $A = \tilde{}(C \mid V)$, as shown in figure 1e.[1] In practice, we use 8×8 masks rather than the illustrated 4×4 masks.

The basic tiling and visibility operations performed by conventional coverage masks are (1) finding the mask of a convex polygon from the masks of its edges, and (2) finding the visible samples on a polygon within a pixel by compositing the polygon's mask with the pixel's mask, which represents previously tiled samples. In the context of the hierarchical tiling algorithm, tiling and visibility operations performed by triage masks are entirely analogous, except that compositing is performed recursively on an image hierarchy rather than a single square region of the screen. The image hierarchy is a "coverage pyramid" constructed from both conventional and triage coverage masks, as schematically illustrated in figure 2 (see caption). Operations (1) and (2) for triage masks are easily understood by analogy with conventional coverage masks, as outlined below. See [Greene95] for derivations of the formulas for triage masks and examples illustrating compositing of triage masks.

```
Tiling a convex polygon into a square region of the
screen using coverage masks.  The existing coverage mask
for a screen cell represents previously tiled polygons,
which are in front of the polygon being tiled.

Conventional Coverage Masks
Existing pixel mask: C
(1)  Find intercepts of edges with pixel border and look
       up edge masks (call them E1, E2, ... , EN).
     Find mask P of convex polygon from edge masks:
     P = E1 & E2 & ... & EN
(2)  Find mask W of visible samples on polygon within C:
     W = P & ~C
     Update C:
     C' = C | P.

Triage Coverage Masks
Existing triage mask for cell in the coverage pyramid:
  (Cc,Cv) - covered and vacant bit masks
(1)  Find intercepts of edges with cell border and look
       up edge masks ((E1c,E1v), ... ,(ENc,ENv)).
     Find mask (Pc,Pv) of polygon from edge masks:
     Pc = E1c & E2c & ... & ENc
     Pv = E1v | E2v | ... | ENv
(2)  Find mask W of entirely visible cells on polygon
       within (Cc,Cv):
     W = Cv & Pc
     Find mask A of active cells on polygon in (Cc,Cv):
     A = ~(W | Pv | Cc)
     Update (Cc,Cv):
     Cc' = Cc | W
     Cv' = Cv & ~W
     (Note: (Cc,Cv) may also be modified by propagation
       from finer levels.)
```

[1] We use standard notation for bit-mask operations: & for bitwise AND, | for bitwise OR, and ~ for bitwise complement.

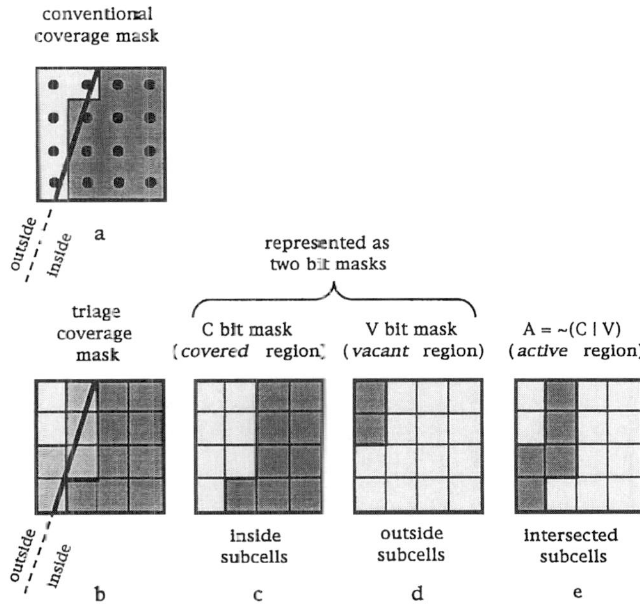

Figure 1: A conventional coverage mask classifies grid points as inside or outside an edge (panel a). A *triage* coverage mask classifies subcells as inside, outside, or intersecting an edge (panel b). We refer to these regions as *covered* (panel c), *vacant* (panel d), and *active* (panel e), respectively. We represent triage masks as the pair of bit masks (C,V) indicating the covered and vacant regions. In practice, we use 8×8 masks rather than 4×4 masks.

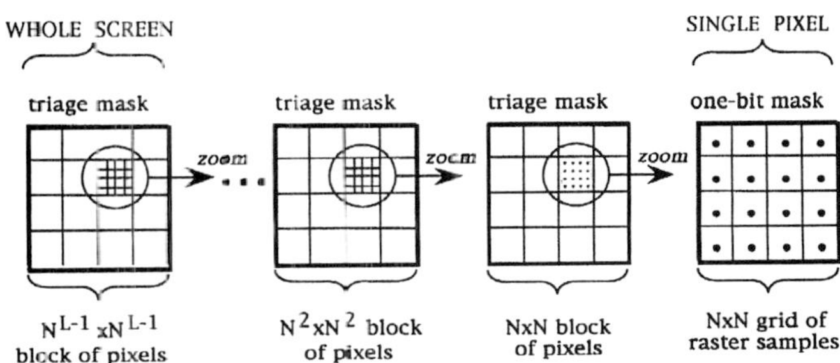

Figure 2: Schematic diagram of a pyramid of $N \times N$ masks with L levels for an image with $N \times N$ oversampling at each pixel. This *coverage pyramid* is built from triage masks, except at the finest level where a conventional one-bit coverage mask is associated with each pixel. In this hierarchical representation of the screen, the C and V bits for each subcell in triage masks indicate whether a square region of the screen is *covered*, *vacant*, or *active*. At the coarsest level, a single triage mask represents the whole screen (left), and at the finest level, a single one-bit mask represents the raster samples within a pixel (right). A four-level pyramid of 8×8 masks corresponds to a 512×512 image with 8×8 oversampling at each pixel. The corresponding diagram for a point-sampled image is the same, except that the masks represent an $N \times N$ block of pixels, an $N^2 \times N^2$ block of pixels, and so forth.

3.1 Tiling by Recursive Subdivision

Now that the primitive tiling and visibility operations have been described, we are ready to outline the recursive procedure for tiling a convex polygon into the coverage pyramid. Initially, the masks in the coverage pyramid are a hierarchical representation of regions of the image raster that are already occupied by previously tiled polygons. To make the discussion more concrete, the following outline assumes 8×8 oversampling and filtering.

To tile polygon P, we begin by finding the triage mask for each of its edges that crosses the screen by finding its intercepts on the screen border and looking up the corresponding mask in a precomputed table. Then we composite the edge masks according to operation (1) above in order to construct P's triage mask. Next, beginning at the root cell of the coverage pyramid, we composite P's mask with cells in the pyramid, using triage mask operations to distinguish three classes of cells: where P is entirely hidden, where P is entirely visible, and where P's visibility is uncertain, i.e. "active" cells (operation (2)). We ignore cells where P is entirely hidden, we display (or tag) cells where P is entirely visible (mask W), and we recursively subdivide active cells (mask A). During subdivision, edge intercepts used to look up edge masks are computed incrementally. In regions of the screen where P's edges cross vacant or active cells, subdivision continues, ultimately down to all vacant and active pixels crossed by P's edges. At the pixel level, coverage masks in the pyramid are conventional one-bit masks. If we are box filtering, operations may follow the traditional A-buffer algorithm: we find P's visible samples, compute their contribution to pixel value and add it to the accumulation buffer, and then update the pixel's coverage mask. If the status of a pixel changes from vacant or active to active or covered, the status of masks in coarser levels of the pyramid may also change, so whenever this occurs, we propagate coverage information to coarser levels by performing simple bit-mask operations during recursive traversal of the pyramid. When this recursive tiling procedure finishes, all visible samples on P have been tiled and the coverage pyramid has been updated. This procedure is outlined in LISTING 1.

4 RENDERING A SCENE

Now that the procedure for tiling a polygon has been described, we are ready to place it in the context of rendering a frame. But first we describe the underlying data structures: the coverage pyramid, the image array, and the model tree.

4.1 Data Structures

To permit Warnock subdivision to be driven by bit-mask operations, we maintain visibility information about previously tiled polygons in an image-space pyramid of coverage masks. As schematically illustrated in figure 2, a single triage mask represents the whole screen, triage masks at the next level of the pyramid correspond to subcells in the root mask, and so forth. Thus, this *coverage pyramid* is a hierarchical representation of the screen with the C and V bits for each subcell in the triage masks indicating whether a square region of the screen is *covered*, *vacant*, or *active*. Within a covered region, all corresponding samples in the underlying image raster are covered, within a vacant region, all corresponding raster samples are vacant, and within an active region, at least one but not all corresponding raster samples are covered. At the finest level of the pyramid only, we use

---

```
LISTING 1  (pseudocode)

/*
Recursive subdivision procedure for tiling a convex
polygon P.

After clipping P to the near clipping plane in object
space, if necessary, and projecting P's vertices into
the image plane, we call tile_poly with the root mask of
the mask pyramid, P's edge list, and "level" set to 1.

arguments:
(Cc,Cv): pyramid mask (input and output)
edge_list: P's edges that intersect pyramid mask
level: pyramid level: 1 is root, 2 is next coarsest, etc.
*/

tile_poly((Cc,Cv), edge_list, level)
{
   set active_edge_list to nil

   /* build P's mask (Pc,Pv) */
   Pc = all_ones
   Pv = all_zeros
   for each edge on edge_list {
      find intercepts on square perimeter of mask
      if square is outside edge
      then return /* polygon doesn't intersect mask */
      if edge intersects square, then {
         append edge to active_edge_list
         /* Note: at the pixel level, Ec is a conventional
            coverage mask and Ev = ~Ec */
         look up edge mask (Ec,Ev)
         Pc = Pc & Ec
         Pv = Pv | Ev
      }
   }

   /* make "write" bit mask and update pyramid mask */
   W = Cv & Pc
   Cc = Cc | W
   Cv = Cv & ~W

   if level is the pixel level, then {
      /* filter pixel using coverage mask W */
      /* to perform A-buffer box filtering:
         add bitcount*color to accumulation buffer */
      evaluate shading and update accumulation buffer
      return
   }

   for each TRUE bit in W {
      for each pixel in this square region of screen {
         /* to perform A-buffer box filtering:
            add 64*(polygon color) to accumulation buffer */
         evaluate shading and update accumulation buffer
      }
   }


   /* Recursive Subdivision */

   /* make "active" bit mask */
   A = ~(W | Pv | Cc)
   /* subdivide active subcells */
   for each TRUE bit in A {
      /* call corresponding subcell S
         call its pyramid mask (Sc,Sv) */
      copy all edges on active_edge_list that intersect
        S to S_edge_list
      tile_poly((Sc,Sv), S_edge_list, level+1)
      /* propagate coverage status to coarser levels of
         mask pyramid */
      if Sc is all_ones
      then Cc = Cc | active_bit   /* set covered status  */
      if Sv is not all_ones
      then Cv = Cv & ~active_bit /* clear vacant status */
   }
}
```

---

conventional one-bit coverage masks to indicate whether or not point samples in the image raster have been covered. If we are oversampling and filtering, each of these one-bit masks corresponds to the 8×8 grid of raster samples within a pixel. The appropriate pyramid for a 512×512 image with 8×8 oversampling at each pixel has four levels, three arrays of triage masks with dimensions 1×1, 8×8, and 64×64, and one 512×512 array of one-bit masks. Alternatively, if we are point sampling rather than filtering, each one-bit mask corresponds to an 8×8 block of pixels. In this case, the pyramid for a 512×512 image would have two arrays of triage masks with dimensions 1×1 and 8×8, and one 64×64 array of one-bit masks.

Memory requirements for the coverage pyramid are very modest. Since the finest level requires only one bit per raster sample and the vast majority of cells in the pyramid are in the finest level, total memory requirements are only slightly more than one bit per raster sample. The actual number of bits per raster sample required for an n-level pyramid lies in the range [1 1/32 1 2/63) for n>1. Note that a z-buffer requires a great deal more memory because it stores a depth value for each raster sample.

The other image-space data structure that our algorithm requires is an image array with an element for each color component at each pixel. If we perform A-buffer-style filtering [Carpenter84], shading contributions from 64 subpixel samples accumulate in each array element. Thus, elements in this *accumulation buffer* require considerable depth. We use 16 bits per pixel per color channel. When filtering with a convolution kernel that overlaps multiple pixels, we store color components as floating-point values in the accumulation buffer. If no filtering is performed, pixel values do not accumulate, so a conventional image array is employed.

Now for representing the model. Our algorithm requires front-to-back traversal of polygons in the scene, so we represent the scene as a binary space partitioning tree (BSP tree) [Fuchs-Kedem-Naylor80], which permits very efficient traversal in depth order. Strategies for handling dynamic scenes are discussed in §6.

4.2 Precomputation Step

In a precomputation step, we build a BSP tree for the model. We also build lookup tables for both conventional and triage coverage masks. In building mask tables, we divide the perimeter of a canonical square into some number of equal intervals (e.g. 64) and create an entry in a two-dimensional table for each pair of intervals not lying on a common edge. Once this table has been constructed, to obtain the mask for an arbitrary edge we determine which two intervals it crosses and look up the corresponding table entry. To conserve storage, we can use the same table entry for edges with opposite directions, because complementing the (C,V) bit masks in a triage mask corresponds to reversing an edge. Hierarchical tiling depends on accurate classification of *vacant* and *covered* regions in triage masks, so we construct them with the following conservative procedure. The endpoints of the pair of intervals used to index a coverage mask define a quadrilateral. Any subcells intersected by the quadrilateral are classified *active*, guaranteeing that cells classified *covered* are completely covered and cells classified *vacant* are completely vacant.

4.3 Generating a Frame

We begin a frame by clearing the accumulation buffer and the coverage pyramid. We traverse polygons in the model's BSP tree in front-to-back order. We clip each polygon to the front clipping plane, if necessary, and project its vertices into the image plane. There is no need to preserve depth information. Before tiling a polygon, we first determine whether its bounding box is visible. If this procedure fails to prove that the polygon is hidden, we then tile it into the smallest enclosing cell in the coverage pyramid using the procedure outlined in LISTING 1. In regions of the screen where the polygon is visible, this procedure updates pixel values in the image buffer and updates coverage status in the coverage pyramid. After all polygons have been processed, the scene is complete and we display the image buffer.

4.4 Other Filtering Methods

We have already discussed A-buffer-style filtering by *area sampling*, a term used to describe convolution of visible samples with a pixel-sized box filter [Catmull78]. Abram, Westover, and Whitted extended coverage-mask techniques to include jitter, table-driven convolution with arbitrary filter kernels, and evaluation of simple shading functions by table lookup [Abram-et-al85]. All of these methods are compatible with hierarchical tiling. To perform table-driven convolution, the contribution of each subpixel sample to neighboring pixels is precomputed and stored in a table of filtering coefficients. For some simple shading functions, the contribution of arbitrary collections of samples can be stored as precomputed coefficients which enables, for example, efficient byte-by-byte processing of coverage masks. We use this method when filtering 3×3 pixel neighborhoods with a one-pixel radius cosine-hump kernel.

4.5 Point Sampling

Modifying the algorithm to produce point-sampled rather than filtered images is straightforward. In this case, each mask at the finest level of the pyramid corresponds to an 8×8 block of pixels. So for each TRUE subcell in the "W" mask (see pseudocode), we evaluate the shading function at the corresponding pixel and write the result to the image buffer. Since pixel values correspond to point samples, color values do not accumulate, so we use a conventional image array rather than an accumulation buffer. Note that it is not necessary to clear the image array at the beginning of a frame. Instead, after tiling all scene polygons, we composite a screen-sized polygon of the desired background color (or texture) with the root mask, thereby tiling all remaining vacant pixels in the image.

5 HIERARCHICAL OBJECT-SPACE CULLING

Because of its ability to cull hierarchically in image space, the hierarchical tiling algorithm processes densely occluded scenes much more efficiently than conventional tiling methods, which must traverse all hidden geometry pixel by pixel. Nonetheless, it must still consider every polygon in a scene, doing some work even on those that are entirely hidden. To avoid this behavior, we integrate our algorithm with the hierarchical visibility algorithm [Greene-Kass-Miller93, Greene-Kass94, Greene95] to enable hierarchical object-space culling of hidden regions of the model. This can be done by substituting hierarchical tiling for z-buffering in the hierarchical z-buffer algorithm of [Greene-Kass-Miller93], although this requires some changes in both the object-space and image-space hierarchies. In image space, instead of using a z-pyramid of depth samples to maintain visibility information, we use a coverage pyramid. In object space, we modify the octree to permit strict front-to-back traversal of polygons. Note that the z-buffer algorithm traverses octree cubes in front-to-back order, but not the primitives contained within them. And since octree cubes are nested, it is not sufficient to simply organize the primitives inside each cube into a BSP tree. Instead we use the following algorithm for building an *octree of BSP trees* that permits strict front-to-back traversal.

5.1 Building an Octree of BSP Trees

Starting with a root cube which bounds model space, we insert polygons one at a time into the cube. If the polygon count in the cube reaches a specified threshold (e.g. 30), we subdivide the cube into eight octants and insert each of its polygons into each octant that it intersects, clipping to the cube's three median planes. When all polygons in the scene have been inserted into the root cube and propagated through the tree, we have an octree where all polygons are associated only with leaf nodes, thereby circumventing the ordering problem caused by nesting. The last step is to organize the polygons in each leaf node of the octree into a BSP tree [Foley-et-al90]. Now scene polygons can be traversed in strict front-to-back order by traversing octree cubes front to back and traversing their BSP trees front to back.

5.2 Combining Hierarchical Tiling with Hierarchical Visibility

Now that we have established how to traverse scene polygons in front-to-back order, combining hierarchical tiling with the basic hierarchical visibility algorithm is straightforward. As with hierarchical z-buffering, we traverse octree cubes in front-to-back order, testing them for visibility and culling those that are hidden. As with hierarchical z-buffering, we determine whether a cube is visible by tiling it, stopping if a visible sample is found. Note that it is only necessary to tile a cube's polygonal silhouette (unless it intersects the front clipping plane), rather than tiling its front faces. By comparison, z-buffering often needs to tile three faces of a cube to establish its visibility. To test cube silhouettes for visibility, we modify the tiling procedure of LISTING 1 to report visibility status, returning TRUE whenever a polygon's mask indicates that it covers a vacant subcell or a vacant grid point in the image raster. Once we have established that an octree cube is visible, we traverse the polygons in its BSP tree in front-to-back order, tiling them into the coverage pyramid. When we finish traversing the octree, all visible polygons have been tiled and the image is complete.

This version of the hierarchical visibility algorithm has very efficient traversal properties in both object-space and image-space. Like the hierarchical z-buffer algorithm, in object space the algorithm only visits visible octree nodes and their children, and it only renders polygons that are in visible octree nodes. In image space, when tiling polygons into the coverage pyramid, hierarchical tiling only visits cells that are crossed by visible edges in the output image. Visible samples are never overwritten. As a result of these properties, this variation of the hierarchical visibility algorithm is very efficient at both culling hidden geometry and tiling visible geometry.

If a hardware graphics accelerator is available to perform shading operations such as texture mapping, we can perform visibility operations with software and shading with hardware. We would use the usual hierarchical tiling algorithm to maintain the coverage pyramid and perform object-space culling, and we would render visible polygons with the graphics accelerator, using an accumulation buffer, if available, to perform antialiasing [Haeberli-Akeley90]. This would be a fast way to produce texture-mapped images of densely occluded scenes.

6 HANDLING DYNAMIC SCENES

One weakness of the hierarchical tiling algorithm is that it requires strict front-to-back traversal of polygons. This does not present a problem for a static model, since it may be represented as a BSP tree [Fuchs-Kedem-Naylor80], and if only a relatively small number of polygons are moving, the tree can be efficiently maintained [Naylor92a]. However, in scenes with numerous moving polygons, maintaining depth order can impose a severe computational burden. Here we consider two different methods that address this problem.

6.1 Lazy Z-Buffering

The following "lazy z-buffering" algorithm is an attractive alternative whenever at least part of the model can be conveniently traversed in approximate front-to-back order. For convenience, the following discussion assumes that we are oversampling and box-filtering. With this variation of hierarchical tiling, we make the following changes to the basic algorithm. For every cell in the coverage pyramid, we maintain *znear* and *zfar* depth values for all potentially visible polygons thus far encountered that intersect the cell. Instead of automatically culling a portion of a polygon that intersects a covered cell, it is culled only if it lies behind the cell's zfar value. At a pixel, we assume that fragments arrive in an order that permits tiling with coverage masks, i.e., one or more non-overlapping fragments cover all of the pixel's samples before any other fragments arrive. These conditions are easily monitored using the pixel's coverage mask and znear/zfar values. Unless and until a fragment violating the conditions arrives, we perform filtering like the usual algorithm, adding shading contributions to the accumulation buffer and updating the pixel's coverage mask. We also cache information about each fragment in case we need it later. If and when the conditions are violated, we discard the current accumulated color value for the pixel and revert to ordinary z-buffering, allocating the memory required for storing color and depth at each subpixel sample, and then tiling the cached fragments. This produces the same image samples as if we had been maintaining an oversampled z-buffer all along. The last step after all polygons in the scene have been tiled is to filter the z-buffered pixels. This procedure produces the same image as hierarchical tiling would have produced if polygons had been traversed in depth order.

This simple strategy exploits whatever depth coherence is in the scene being processed. If polygons are mostly in front-to-back order, lazy z-buffering will not do much more work than the usual hierarchical tiling algorithm. This would occur, for example, if a few small dynamic objects were positioned in front of a static background model that was traversed in depth order. In the worst case, when frontmost objects are never processed first, lazy z-buffering does only slightly more work than hierarchical z-buffering.

Thing Being Compared	Hierarchical Tiling	Hierarchical Z-Buffering
object-space hierarchy	BSP tree / octree of BSP trees	octree
image-space hierarchy	pyramid of coverage masks	z-pyramid
front-to-back polygon traversal required?	yes	no
visibility information per raster sample	$<$ 1 2/63 coverage-mask bits	Z (usu. 24-32 bits)
color information per raster sample	none	RGB (usu. 24-36 bits)
type of output-image buffer	accumulation (deep)	standard
need to store coverage-mask LUTs?	yes	no
pixel overwrite?	no	yes
mask support for filtering built-in?	yes	no
identifies *covered* image-pyramid cells?	yes	no

Table 1: Some points of comparison between hierarchical polygon tiling and hierarchical z-buffering.

6.2 Merging Octrees

For polygonal scenes consisting of independently moving rigid bodies, another strategy can be employed that guarantees front-to-back traversal of polygons, permitting us to render polygons with the standard hierarchical tiling procedure. According to this method, each rigid body is represented as an octree of BSP trees. To render a frame, we simultaneously traverse all octrees front to back, culling any octree cubes which are hidden by the coverage pyramid, and using the following strategy to synchronize traversal of octrees. For each octree, we determine the current frontmost leaf cube and then determine the frontmost leaf cube of all octrees. If this single frontmost cube does not intersect a leaf cube in any other octree, we can safely render its BSP tree. If this cube does intersect other leaf cubes, we clip their polygons to the frontmost cube, insert the clipped fragments into the frontmost cube's BSP tree, and then render that BSP tree. This procedure ultimately will cull or render all octree leaf nodes, whereupon rendering of the scene is finished. This procedure for rendering dynamic scenes is nearly as fast as the standard hierarchical tiling algorithm, except for the time spent merging octree leaf nodes. Although merging operations can require considerable computation, for many scenes merging will only rarely be required, and in such cases this algorithm will run efficiently.

7 HIERARCHICAL TILING VERSUS HIERARCHICAL Z-BUFFERING

Table 1 summarizes some points of comparison between hierarchical polygon tiling and hierarchical z-buffering. As the table points out, hierarchical tiling requires strict front-to-back traversal of polygons, which complicates the object-space hierarchy, assuming that we are maintaining an octree of BSP trees to enable object-space culling. Another point in favor of hierarchical z-buffering is that it does not need to build or store lookup tables for coverage masks. The other points of comparison strongly favor hierarchical tiling. One big advantage is that its memory requirements are much less. Whereas hierarchical z-buffering needs to store depth and color information for each raster sample, hierarchical tiling only needs to store slightly more than one bit of coverage information for each raster sample. The resulting memory savings can be very substantial. In fact, if we are rendering a 512×512 image with 8×8 oversampling at each pixel, hierarchical tiling requires only about 3 7% of the image memory required for z-buffering. Other points in favor of hierarchical tiling are that it never overwrites visible samples, it has built-in support for filtering with coverage masks, and it facilitates exploiting image-space coherence by identifying regions of the image-space pyramid that are completely covered by individual polygons.

8 TILING POLYHEDRA

Hierarchical tiling with coverage masks can also be applied to Warnock subdivision in three dimensions to tile convex polyhedra into a voxel grid. In this case, 64-bit triage masks would classify cells within a 4×4×4 subdivision of a cube as inside, outside, or intersecting a plane. The triage mask for a convex polyhedron within a cube would be obtained by compositing the triage masks of its face planes. The recursive subdivision procedure for tiling a polyhedron into a 3D pyramid of coverage masks would be analogous to hierarchical polygon tiling, and it would only visit cells in the pyramid that are intersected by the polyhedron's faces. The speed and modest memory requirements of this volume tiling algorithm make it an attractive alternative to traditional methods [Kaufman86].

9 IMPLEMENTATION AND RESULTS

Our implementation of hierarchical polygon tiling is programmed in C and renders either point-sampled or filtered images of scenes composed of flat-shaded convex polygons. Our polygon tiling program follows the pseudocode outline, except that we tile a polygon into the smallest enclosing cell in the coverage pyramid after first testing its bounding box for visibility, as described in §4.3. As described in §3 and §4, filtering is performed by box filtering according to the A-buffer method, or by table-driven convolution with a one-pixel radius cosine-hump kernel. In the latter case, kernel coefficients are precomputed for all byte patterns and accessed by table lookup for each non-zero byte within a polygon's coverage mask at a pixel. Color components in the accumulation buffer are represented as 16-bit integer values when box filtering, and as 32-bit floating-point values when filtering with a cosine-hump kernel. Tables of coverage masks are constructed with 64 intervals along each edge of the bounding square. One-bit coverage masks for filtering pixels are constructed with jitter, using random placement of raster samples within the corresponding sub-pixel square [Dippé-Wold85, Cook86]. All of the following tests were performed on a SGI Indigo2 with a 75 megahertz R8000 processor, which performs atomic 64-bit mask operations.

To compare the efficiency of hierarchical tiling to traditional incremental scan conversion for tiling simple polygonal scenes, we employed the color-cube model of figure 5, composed of 192 presorted front-facing squares. We rendered this model with hierarchical tiling and with a back-to-front "painter's" algorithm [Foley-et-al90]. The painter's algorithm maintained a color triplet for each point in the image raster and performed tiling by incremental scan conversion, overwriting the image at every pixel encountered. On a 512×512 grid, hierarchical tiling tiled the color-cube model approximately ten percent faster than the painter's algorithm (.087 seconds versus .097 seconds). At higher resolution, the speed advantage of hierarchical tiling was much more pronounced. For example, hierarchical tiling took .357 seconds to tile the model on a 4096×4096 grid and produce the 512×512 box-filtered image of figure 5. By comparison, the painter's algorithm took 5.3 times longer (1.91 seconds) to tile this scene on a 2048×2048 grid without filtering (our Indigo didn't have enough memory to render a 4096×4096 RGB image). By timing the painter's algorithm at various resolutions, we found that it was only able to tile a 910×910 grid in the .357 seconds it took hierarchical tiling to tile and filter the image of figure 5. This example illustrates that for software tiling at sufficient resolution to enable high-quality antialiasing by oversampling and filtering, hierarchical tiling is much more efficient than traditional incremental scan conversion, even for simple scenes.

To test the effectiveness of hierarchical tiling on densely occluded scenes we integrated hierarchical tiling with hierarchical visibility as described in §5, performing tiling of both model polygons and octree-cube silhouettes with the hierarchical tiling method. For a test model, we used a version of the modular office building described in [Greene-Kass-Miller93]. We built an octree of BSP trees for the repeating module using the method described in §5.1, each BSP tree containing approximately 16,000 quadrilaterals. We replicated this octree within the shell of a 408-story building resembling the Empire State Building to create a model consisting of approximately 167 million replicated quadrilaterals. Figures 4, 6, and 7 show various views of this model.

To compare the relative speed of hierarchical tiling and hierarchical z-buffering, we rendered animation of a building walk-through. We found that hierarchical tiling was able to perform tiling on a 4096×4096 grid and produce box-filtered 512×512 frames as fast as hierarchical z-buffering produced 512×512 point-sampled frames. On viewing the animation produced with the z-buffer algorithm, we observed considerable aliasing as expected. By comparison, we observed high-quality antialiasing with the box-filtered animation generated with hierarchical tiling.

Next, we compared the speed of various rendering options. Hierarchical tiling took 3.21 seconds to tile the scene of figure 4 on a 4096×4096 grid and produce the pictured box-filtered image. When we rendered this same box-filtered image without using the bounding-box culling method of §4.3 and instead tiled all polygons into the root cell of the coverage pyramid, rendering took 1.28 seconds longer, indicating that the bounding-box culling strategy provides significant acceleration. Next we rendered the scene of figure 4 with higher-quality antialiasing using cosine-hump filtering within a 3×3-pixel neighborhood. With this filtering method, it took 4.42 seconds to tile the scene on a 4096×4096 grid and produce the filtered image. Finally, we used the point-sampling variation of hierarchical tiling to render a 512×512 image of the scene, which took 1.71 seconds.

To compare the algorithmic efficiency of hierarchical tiling to hierarchical z-buffering, we constructed "work images" that show the number of times during frame generation that each cell in the coverage pyramid is visited (not counting subpixel samples), with an access to a coarser-than-pixel cell being amortized over the corresponding window of the screen.[2] Work images show the "depth complexity" of the visibility computation and indicate where the algorithm is working hardest [Greene95, Greene-Kass94, Greene-Kass-Miller93]. An average intensity of one in a work image means that, an average, only a single pyramid cell is accessed in the coverage pyramid during visibility operations for each pixel in the output image. With hierarchical tiling, except for very complex scenes or finely tessellated models, average intensity is usually less than one because visibility at most pixels is established at a coarser level in the hierarchy. For example, for the simple model of figure 5, an average of only .123 cells in the coverage pyramid are traversed per pixel in the output image.

Figure 3 shows log-scale work images corresponding to figure 4. Left to right, the images show work tiling cube silhouettes during visibility tests (.09 cells visited per pixel, on average), work tiling model polygons into the coverage pyramid (1.01 cells visited per pixel, on average), and the sum of these two images, showing total work performed on tiling (1.10 cells visited per pixel, on average). In other words, hierarchical tiling visited an average of only 1.10 cells in the coverage pyramid for each pixel in the 512×512 output image, even though tiling and filtering were performed on a 4096×4096 grid. Far fewer cells in the image pyramid are visited with hierarchical tiling than with hierarchical z-buffering [Greene95] because it only visits cells in the image pyramid that are crossed by visible edges in the output image. When we performed a motion test on the scene of figure 4, we found that the number of pyramid cells visited was approximately one for frames rendered with hierarchical tiling and approximately three for frames rendered with hierarchical z-buffering. The lower figure for hierarchical tiling is particularly impressive considering that it resolves visibility at 64 times as many raster samples and many more polygons are visible. Of course the depth complexity of visibility computations for the scene of figure 4 is far lower for both hierarchical tiling and hierarchical z-buffering than for naive z-buffering, which visits each pixel dozens of times on average [Greene95].

To explore the limits of hierarchical tiling to effectively filter images of very complex scenes, we rendered a motion sequence in which the camera flies around and through the 408-story model of the Empire State Building [Greene96]. Figures 6 and 7 are 512×512 frames from this animation, which was produced by tiling on a jittered 4096×4096 grid and filtering with a cosine-hump kernel as previously described. From the viewpoint of figure 6, this scene poses a formidable challenge to effective filtering, since approximately 765,000 polygons are visible, and dozens of polygons are visible within some pixels. Nonetheless, we observed high-quality antialiasing in the motion sequence. Jittering of sub-pixel samples effectively converted aliasing to noise [Dippé-Wold85, Cook86], which was noticeable only in frames having hundreds of thousands of visible polygons. For this motion sequence, we observed subtle patterned aliasing artifacts when the same jitter pattern was employed at all pixels, a problem that was overcome by using several different jitter patterns. To reduce temporal aliasing we rendered each video field separately and to reduce flicker we

[2] Our accounting of work done on visibility does not include clearing of the coverage pyramid. Clearing the pyramid at the beginning of a frame visits each pyramid cell once, but this is not necessary if a "lazy clearing" strategy is employed.

applied a 1-4-6-4-1 filter to every other scanline (not applied to figure 6 or 7). With cosine-hump filtering and multiple jitter patterns, rendering times were 5.15 minutes for figure 6 and 34 seconds for figure 7, which has approximately 81,300 visible polygons. We also recorded the motion sequence with box filtering, but observed noticeably worse image quality, particularly the characteristic "ropyness" of area sampling. When box filtering with a single jitter pattern, rendering time for the scene of figure 6 was 4.28 minutes. We also rendered the version of this model shown in figure 1 of [Greene-Kass94], which took the error-bounded rendering algorithm described in that article one hour to produce on a 50-megahertz workstation. By comparison, this same scene took hierarchical tiling 34 seconds to render. These examples illustrate that hierarchical tiling with object-space culling can produce high-quality animation of very complex scenes in reasonable frame times. Adding a level to the coverage pyramid would permit the algorithm to accurately filter even more complex scenes.

10 CONCLUSION

Warnock subdivision with its elegant simplicity and logarithmic search properties endures as one of the great computer-graphics algorithms. Although polygon tiling by Warnock subdivision is well known, it has rarely been used in practice due to the inefficiency of the traditional subdivision procedure. Here we have shown that Warnock-style subdivision can be driven very efficiently with *triage coverage masks.* The resulting hierarchical polygon tiling algorithm is very efficient, visiting only cells in the image hierarchy that are crossed by visible edges in the output image and never overwriting a visible image sample. At high resolution, hierarchical tiling is much faster than traditional incremental scan conversion, so it is well suited to antialiasing by oversampling and filtering. Moreover, hierarchical tiling with object-space culling can process densely occluded scenes extremely efficiently, considerably faster than hierarchical z-buffering, while facilitating high-quality filtering. Although the practicality of the basic algorithm for dynamic scenes is constrained by the requirement that polygons be traversed front to back, whenever at least part of the model can be traversed in approximate front-to-back order, "lazy z-buffering" helps to overcome this shortcoming. The algorithm is compact, straightforward to implement, and has very modest memory requirements. In short, hierarchical tiling offers the prospect of generating high-quality animation at reasonable frame rates with modest computing resources.

11 Acknowledgments

Gavin Miller suggested the method of combining hardware and software tiling discussed in §5.2. Gavin also contributed to making the test model of figure 4, as did Eric Chen and Steve Rubin. A discussion with Piter van Zee was my impetus for working out the algorithm for merging octrees presented in §6.2. Finally, I gratefully acknowledge Siggraph reviewer #4 for a thoughtful critique of this article.

References

[Abram-et-al85] G. Abram, L. Westover, and T. Whitted, "Efficient Alias-Free Rendering using Bit-Masks and Look-Up Tables," *Proceedings of SIGGRAPH '85*, July 1985, 53–59.

[Carpenter84] L. Carpenter, "The A-buffer, an Antialiased Hidden Surface Method," *Proceedings of SIGGRAPH '84*, July 1984, 103–108.

[Catmull74] E. Catmull, "A Subdivision Algorithm for Computer Display of Curved Surfaces," PhD Thesis, Report UTEC-CSc-74-133, Computer Science Dept., University of Utah, Salt Lake City, Utah, Dec. 1974.

[Catmull78] E. Catmull, "A Hidden-Surface Algorithm with Anti-Aliasing," *Proceedings of SIGGRAPH '78*, Aug. 1978, 6–11.

[Cook86] R. Cook, "Stochastic Sampling in Computer Graphics," *ACM Transactions on Graphics*, Jan. 1986, 51–72.

[Dippé-Wold85] M. A. Z. Dippé and E. H. Wold, "Antialiasing through Stochastic Sampling," *Proceedings of SIGGRAPH '85*, July 1985, 69–78.

[Fiume-et-al83] E. Fiume, A. Fournier, and L. Rudolph, "A Parallel Scan Conversion Algorithm with Anti-Aliasing for a General-Purpose Ultracomputer," *Proceedings of SIGGRAPH '83*, July 1983, 141–150.

[Fiume91] E. Fiume, "Coverage Masks and Convolution Tables for Fast Area Sampling," *Graphical Models and Image Processing*, 53(1), Jan. 1991, 25–30.

[Foley-et-al90] J. Foley, A. van Dam, S. Feiner, and J. Hughes, *Computer Graphics, Principles and Practice*, 2nd edition, Addison-Wesley, Reading, MA, 1990.

[Fuchs-Kedem-Naylor80] H. Fuchs, J. Kedem, and B. Naylor, "On Visible Surface Generation by a Priori Tree Structures," *Proceedings of SIGGRAPH '80*, June 1980, 124–133.

[Greene-Kass-Miller93] N. Greene, M. Kass, and G. Miller, "Hierarchical Z-Buffer Visibility," *Proceedings of SIGGRAPH '93*, July 1993, 231–238.

[Greene-Kass94] N. Greene and M. Kass, "Error-Bounded Antialiased Rendering of Complex Environments," *Proceedings of SIGGRAPH '94*, July 1994, 59–66.

[Greene95] N. Greene, "Hierarchical Rendering of Complex Environments," PhD Thesis, Univ. of California at Santa Cruz, Report No. UCSC-CRL-95-27, June 1995.

[Greene96] N. Greene, "Naked Empire," ACM Siggraph Video Review Issue 115: The Siggraph '96 Electronic Theater, August 1996.

[Haeberli-Akeley90] P. Haeberli and K. Akeley, "The Accumulation Buffer: Hardware Support for High-Quality Rendering," *Proceedings of SIGGRAPH '90*, Aug. 1990, 309–318.

[Kaufman86] A. Kaufman, "3D Scan Conversion Algorithms for Voxel-Based Graphics," *Proceedings of the 1986 Workshop on Interactive 3D Graphics*, Oct. 1986, 45–75.

[Meagher82] D. Meagher, "The Octree Encoding Method for Efficient Solid Modeling," PhD Thesis, Electrical Engineering Dept., Rensselaer Polytechnic Institute, Troy, New York, Aug. 1982.

[Naylor92a] B. Naylor, "Interactive Solid Geometry Via Partitioning Trees," *Proceedings of Graphics Interface '92*, May 1992, 11–18.

[Naylor92b] B. Naylor, "Partitioning Tree Image Representation and Generation from 3D Geometric Models," *Proceedings of Graphics Interface '92*, May 1992, 201–212.

[Rogers85] D. Rogers, *Procedural Elements for Computer Graphics*, McGraw-Hill, New York, 1985.

[Sabella-Wozny83] P. Sabella and M. Wozny, "Toward Fast Color-Shaded Images of CAD/CAM Geometry," *IEEE Computer Graphics and Applications*, 3(8), Nov. 1983, 60–71.

[Teller92] S. Teller, "Visibility Computations in Densely Occluded Polyhedral Environments," PhD Thesis, Univ. of California at Berkeley, Report No. UCB/CSD 92/708, Oct. 1992.

[Warnock69] J. Warnock, "A Hidden Surface Algorithm for Computer Generated Halftone Pictures," PhD Thesis, Computer Science Dept., University of Utah, TR 4-15, June 1969.

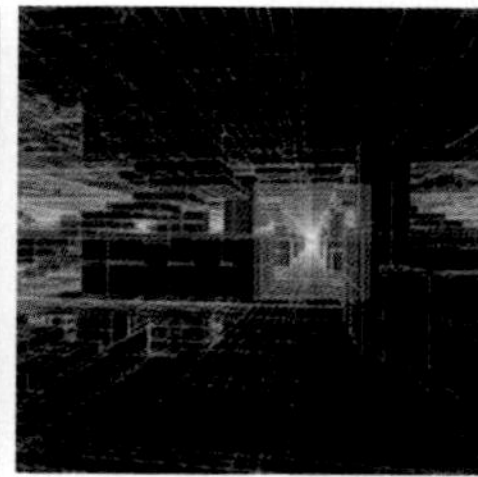
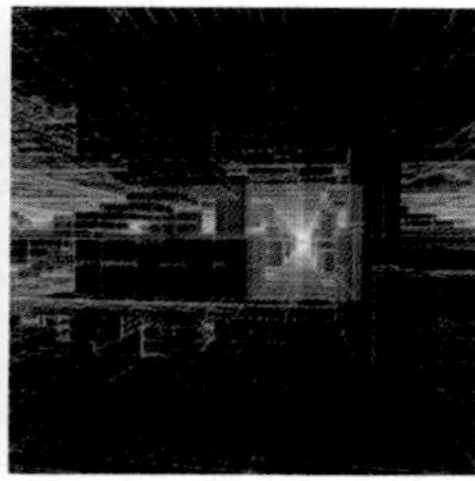

Figure 3. Log-scale work images showing the number of times that cells in the coverage pyramid were visited while tiling the frame of figure 4. These images depict the "depth complexity" of the visibility computation, showing where the algorithm is working hardest.
Left: work tiling cubes: .09 cells visited per pixel (avg)
Middle: work tiling polygons: 1.01 cells visited per pixel (avg)
Right: total work on tiling: 1.10 cells visited per pixel (avg)

Figure 4. Interior view of the Empire State Building model.. Hierarchical tiling took 3.21 seconds to tile this scene on a 4096x4096 grid and produce this 512x512 box-filtered image (75 Mhz processor).

Figure 5. Hierarchical tiling took .36 seconds to tile this simple model on a 4096x4096 grid and produce this 512x512 box-filtered image (75 Mhz processor).

Figure 6. A frame from "Naked Empire," animation produced for the Siggraph '96 Electronic Theater [Greene96]. The model of this 408-story building consists of approximately 167 million quadrilaterals, 765,000 of which are visible in this frame. This 512x512 frame was produced by tiling and filtering on a jittered 4096x4096 grid. Jitter converted aliasing to noise, which is evident in complex regions of the image. Rendering took 5.15 minutes on a 75 Mhz processor.

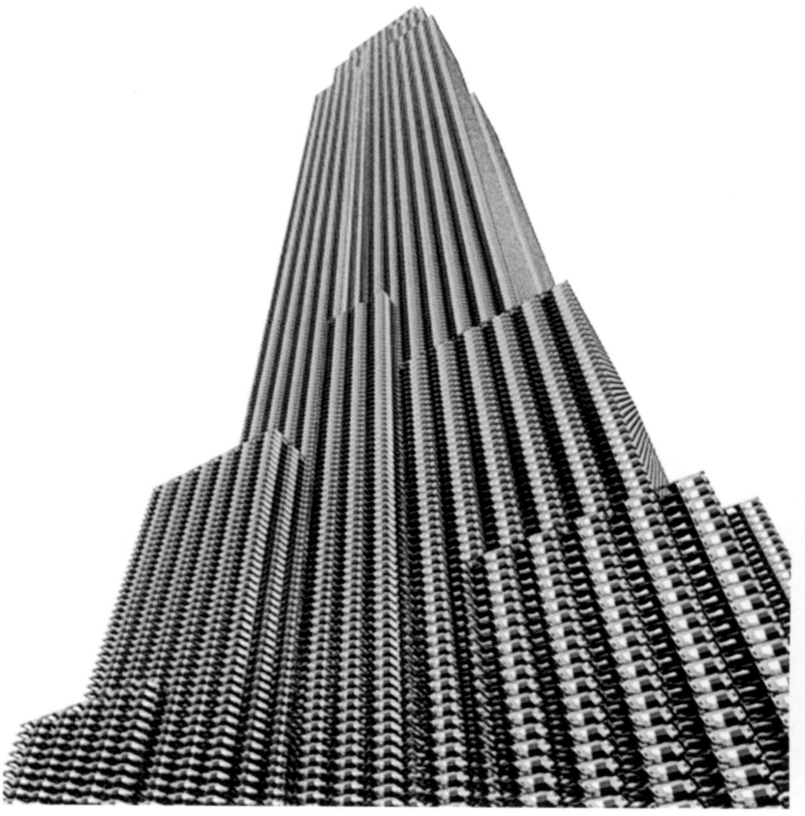

Figure 7. Another frame from "Naked Empire." Note that the building model has no outer shell, making it possible to see deep inside. Rendering time for this frame was 34 seconds (75 Mhz processor).

Hierarchical Image Caching for Accelerated Walkthroughs of Complex Environments

Jonathan Shade *Dani Lischinski* *David H. Salesin* *Tony DeRose* *John Snyder*[†]

University of Washington [†]Microsoft Research

Abstract

We present a new method that utilizes path coherence to accelerate walkthroughs of geometrically complex static scenes. As a preprocessing step, our method constructs a BSP-tree that hierarchically partitions the geometric primitives in the scene. In the course of a walkthrough, images of nodes at various levels of the hierarchy are cached for reuse in subsequent frames. A cached image is reused by texture-mapping it onto a single quadrilateral that is drawn instead of the geometry contained in the corresponding node. Visual artifacts are kept under control by using an error metric that quantifies the discrepancy between the appearance of the geometry contained in a node and the cached image. The new method is shown to achieve speedups of an order of magnitude for walkthroughs of a complex outdoor scene, with little or no loss in rendering quality.

CR Categories and Subject Descriptors: I.3.3 [Computer Graphics]: Picture/Image Generation — Display algorithms; I.3.7 [Computer Graphics]: Three-Dimensional Graphics and Realism.

Additional Key Words: BSP-tree, image-based rendering, level-of-detail (LOD), path coherence, spatial hierarchy, texture mapping.

1 Introduction

Interactive visualization of extremely complex geometric environments is becoming an increasingly important application of computer graphics. Though the throughput of graphics hardware over the past decade has improved dramatically, the demand for performance continues to outpace the supply, as virtual scenes containing many millions of polygons become increasingly common. In order to rapidly visualize truly complex scenes, rendering algorithms must intelligently limit the number of geometric primitives rendered in each frame.

This paper presents a new method for accelerating walkthroughs of geometrically complex and largely unoccluded static scenes by hierarchically caching images of scene portions. As a viewer navigates through a virtual environment, the appearance of distant parts of the scene changes little from frame to frame. We exploit this *path coherence* by caching images created in one frame for possible reuse in many subsequent frames.

{shade | danix | salesin}@cs.washington.edu
derose@pixar.com, johnsny@microsoft.com

Our method starts with a preprocessing stage. Given an unstructured set of objects comprising a scene, we construct a BSP-tree [6] by placing splitting planes inside gaps between objects. This construction produces a hierarchical spatial partitioning of the scene with geometry stored only at the leaves of the hierarchy. During a walkthrough of the scene, our method traverses the hierarchy and caches images of nodes at various levels to be reused in subsequent frames. An error metric that quantifies the discrepancy between the appearance of the actual geometry contained in a node and its cached image is used to estimate the number of frames for which the cached image is likely to provide an adequate approximation of the node's contents. A simple cost-benefit analysis is performed at each node in order to decide whether or not an image should be cached.

The main contribution of our approach is the successful combination of two powerful paradigms: hierarchical methods and image-based rendering. Image-based rendering is capable of drawing arbitrarily complex objects in constant time, once the image is created. Using a hierarchy of images leverages the power of image-based rendering by significantly reducing the number of images that must be drawn. Another contribution is the introduction of a new simple error metric that provides automatic quality control.

1.1 Previous work

Previous work on accelerating the rendering of complex environments can be classified into three major categories: visibility culling, level-of-detail modeling, and image-based rendering.

Visibility culling

Visibility culling algorithms attempt to avoid drawing objects that are not visible in the image. This approach was first investigated by Clark [4], who used an object hierarchy to rapidly cull surfaces that lie outside the viewing frustum. Garlick *et al.* [8] applied this idea to spatial subdivisions of scenes. View-frustum culling techniques are most effective when only a small part of the scene's geometry is inside the view frustum at any single frame. In a complex environment enough geometry remains inside the view frustum to overload the graphics pipeline, and additional acceleration techniques are required.

Airey *et al.* [1] and Teller [19] described methods for interactive walkthroughs of complex buildings that compute the potentially visible set of polygons for each room in a building. Only the potentially visible set of polygons for the room currently containing the viewer needs to be rendered at each frame. Both of these methods require a lengthy preprocessing step for large models. More recently, Luebke and Georges [11] developed a dynamic version of this algorithm that eliminates the preprocessing. Such methods can be very effective for densely occluded polyhedral environments, such as building interiors, but they are not suited for mostly unoccluded outdoor scenes.

The hierarchical Z-buffer [9] is another approach to fast visibility culling that allows a region of the scene to be culled whenever its closest depth value is greater than those of the pixels that have already been drawn at its projected screen location. Like previous approaches, this method can achieve dramatic speed-ups for environments with significant occlusion but is less effective for largely unoccluded environments with high visible complexity, such as a landscape containing thousands of trees.

Level-of-detail modeling

Another approach for accelerating rendering is the use of multiresolution or *level-of-detail* (LOD) modeling. The idea is to render progressively coarser representations of a model as it moves further from the viewer. Such an approach has been used since the early days of flight simulators, and has more recently been incorporated in walkthrough systems for complex environments by Funkhouser and Séquin [7], Maciel and Shirley [12], and Chamberlain *et al.* [2].

One of the chief difficulties with the LOD approach is the problem of generating the various coarse-level representations of a model. Funkhouser and Séquin [7] created the different LOD models manually. Eck *et al.* [5] described methods based on wavelet analysis that can be used to automatically create reasonably accurate low-detail models of surfaces. Maciel and Shirley [12] used a number of LOD representations, including geometric simplifications created by hand, texture maps, and colored bounding boxes. Chamberlain *et al.* [2] partitioned the scene into a spatial hierarchy of cells and associated with each cell a colored box representing its contents. Another approach to creating LOD models is described by Rossignac and Borrel [16], in which objects of arbitrary topology are simplified by collapsing groups of nearby vertices into a single representative vertex, regardless of whether they belong to the same logical part.

Another problem with geometric LOD approaches is that the shading function becomes undersampled, as geometry is decimated. This undersampling causes shading artifacts, especially with Gouraud shading hardware, which evaluates the shading function only a the (decreasing number of) polygon vertices.

Our approach can be thought of as a technique for automatically and dynamically creating view-dependent image-based LOD models. Among the above LOD approaches, ours is closest to that of Maciel and Shirley. However, there are several important differences. First, our approach computes LOD models on demand in a view-dependent fashion, rather than precomputing a fixed set of LOD models and using them throughout the walkthrough. Thus, we incur neither the preprocessing nor the storage costs associated with precomputed LOD models. Second, we use a spatial hierarchy rather than an object hierarchy, and our LOD models represent regions of the scene rather than individual objects. Spatial partitioning allows us to correctly depth-sort the LOD models chosen for rendering at each frame, whereas an object hierarchy can suffer from occlusion artifacts where objects overlap.

Image-based rendering

A different approach for interactive scene display is based on the idea of *view interpolation*, in which different views of a scene are rendered as a pre-processing step, and intermediate views are generated by morphing between the precomputed images in real time. Chen and Williams [3] and McMillan and Bishop [13] have demonstrated two variants of this approach for restricted movement in three-dimensional environments. Although not general purpose, these algorithms provide a viable method of rendering complex environments on machines that do not have fast graphics hardware. Images provide a method of rendering arbitrarily complex scenes in a constant amount of time. This idea is central to both of these papers and to the method we present here.

Another image-based approach, described by Regan and Pose [15], renders the scene onto the faces of a cube centered around the viewer location. Their method allows the display to be updated very rapidly when the viewer is standing in place and looking about. They also use multiple display memories and image compositing with depth to allow different parts of an environment to be updated at different rates. Only parts of the environment that change or move significantly are re-rendered from one frame to the next, resulting in the majority of objects being rendered infrequently.

Our method can be thought of as a hierarchical extension to the method of Regan and Pose, but with more flexibility: instead of using a fixed number of possible update rates, our method updates each object at its own rate. Another important difference is that instead of simply reusing an object's image over several consecutive frames, we use texture-mapping hardware to compensate for motion parallax.

Schaufler and Stürzlinger [17, 18] have concurrently and independently investigated ideas similar to our own. Our approach differs from theirs mostly in the formulation of the error metric and in the cost-benefit analysis that we perform in order to decide whether or not to cache an image.

1.2 Overview

The remainder of the paper is organized as follows. In the next section, we describe our algorithm in detail. In Section 3, we present the error metric used to control the updating of cached images. In Section 4, we describe the preprocessing stage that constructs a hierarchical spatial partitioning of the environment. In Section 5, we report on the performance of our algorithm for a walkthrough of a complex outdoor scene. Section 6 closes with conclusions and future work.

2 Algorithm

As a viewer follows a continuous path through a virtual environment, there is typically considerable coherence between successive frames. The basic idea behind our algorithm is to exploit this coherence by caching images of objects rendered in one frame for possible reuse in many subsequent frames. However, instead of simply reusing the same image, we apply the image as a texture map to a fixed quadrilateral placed at the center of the object. This textured quadrilateral is then rendered instead of the original object during several successive frames, using the current viewing transformation at each frame. In this way, at each frame, the image of the object is slightly warped, approximately correcting for the slight changes in the perspective projection of the original object as the viewer moves through the scene. Compensating for motion parallax in this manner results in fewer "snapping" artifacts when the cached image is updated and increases the number of frames for which the cache yields an acceptable approximation to the object's appearance.

To gain the most from image caching, it is not enough to cache images for individual objects. If too many objects are visible, the sheer number of textured polygons that must be rendered at each frame may overwhelm the hardware. However, distant objects that require infrequent updates can be grouped into clusters, and a single image can be cached and rendered in place of the entire cluster. Thus, our algorithm operates on a hierarchical representation of the entire scene, rather than on a collection of individual objects. An image can be computed and cached for any node in the hierarchy; hence the name "hierarchical image caching".

We construct the hierarchy as a preprocessing step by computing a BSP-tree [6] partitioning of the environment, as described in Section 4. We chose to use a BSP-tree since it allows us to traverse the scene in back-to-front order, which is necessary to ensure that the partially-transparent textured quadrilaterals are composited correctly in the frame-buffer. In addition, BSP-trees are more flexible than other spatial partitioning data structures, making it is easier to avoid splitting objects.

The leaf nodes of the BSP-tree correspond to convex regions of space and have associated with them a set of geometric primitives. This set consists of all the geometric primitives contained inside the node. In addition, it also contains nearby primitives from the neighboring nodes, as will be explained in Section 4. Any node in the tree may also contain a cached image.

At each frame we traverse the BSP-tree twice. The first traversal culls nodes that are outside the view frustum and updates the image caches of the visible nodes:

```
UpdateCaches(node, viewpoint)
if node is outside the view frustum then
    node.status ← CULL
else if node.cache is valid for viewpoint then
    node.status ← DRAWCACHE
else if node is a leaf then
    UpdateNode(node, viewpoint)
else
    UpdateCaches(node.back, viewpoint)
    UpdateCaches(node.front, viewpoint)
    UpdateNode(node, viewpoint)
```

For a leaf node, the routine *UpdateNode* decides whether, for the current viewpoint, it is more cost-effective to draw the geometry stored with the node, or to compute and cache an image:

```
UpdateNode(node, viewpoint)
if viewpoint ∈ node then
    if node is a leaf then
        node.status ← DRAWGEOM
    else
        node.status ← RECURSE
    return
k ← EstimateCacheLifeSpan(node, viewpoint)
amortizedCost ← ⟨cost to create cache⟩/k + ⟨cost to draw cache⟩
if amortizedCost < ⟨cost to draw contents⟩ then
    CreateCache(node, viewpoint)
    node.status ← DRAWCACHE
    node.drawingCost ← ⟨cost to draw cache⟩
else
    if node is a leaf then
        node.status ← DRAWGEOM
        node.drawingCost ← ⟨cost to draw geometry⟩
    else
        node.status ← RECURSE
        node.drawingCost ←
            node.back.drawingCost + node.front.drawingCost
```

Geometry is always drawn if the viewpoint is inside the node. Otherwise, the routine *EstimateCacheLifeSpan* computes an estimate of the number of frames k for which we expect the cached image to remain valid, as will be described in Section 3. This estimate is used to compute an amortized cost-per-frame for this node for each of the next k frames. We compute and cache an image only if the amortized cost is smaller than the cost of simply drawing the node's contents. For a leaf node, this cost is simply the cost of drawing the contained geometry, while for an interior node, this cost is the cost of drawing the node's children. The costs to draw geometric primitives and to create a cached image are established experimentally on each platform and are given as input to our system.

The routine *CreateCache* starts by computing an axis-aligned rectangle that is guaranteed to contain the image of the node's contents on the screen. This rectangle is obtained by transforming the corners of the node's bounding box from world coordinates to screen coordinates and taking the minima and maxima along each axis. If the dimensions of the rectangle exceed those of the viewport, no image is cached. Otherwise, we redefine the viewing frustum so that it contains the entire node without changing the viewpoint or the view direction, and render the node. For a leaf node we draw all of its geometry, while for an interior node we draw its children. In many cases, the children are drawn using their cached images, if any exist. Thus, caching an image typically does not involve drawing all the geometry contained in the corresponding subtree. After drawing the contents of the node, we copy the corresponding rectangular block of pixels into the node's image cache. As mentioned earlier, we use the cached image as a texture map that is applied to a quadrilateral representing the entire node. In order to define an appropriate quadrilateral in world space, we project the corners of the image rectangle onto a plane of constant depth with respect to the viewpoint that goes through the center of the node's bounding box.

Once the cached images have been updated, we can proceed to render the scene into the frame-buffer, during a second traversal of the BSP-tree from back to front:

```
Render(node, viewpoint)
if node.status == CULL then
    return
else if node.status ∈ {DRAWCACHE, DRAWGEOM} then
    Draw(node)
else if viewpoint is in front of node.splittingPlane then
    Render(node.back, viewpoint)
    Render(node.front, viewpoint)
else
    Render(node.front, viewpoint)
    Render(node.back, viewpoint)
```

To complete the description of our algorithm, the next section describes the error metric we use to determine whether a cached image is valid with respect to a given viewpoint and to estimate the life-span of a cached image. Section 4 describes in more detail our BSP-tree construction algorithm.

3 Error metric

The algorithm described in the previous section requires answers to the following two closely-related questions:

1. Given a node with a cached image computed for some previous view, is the cached image valid for the current view?
2. Given a node in the hierarchy and the current view, if we were to compute and cache an image of this node, for how many frames is the cached image likely to remain valid?

In order to answer these questions efficiently we need to define an error metric, which, given a node in the hierarchy, its cache, and the current viewpoint, quantifies the difference between the appearance of the cached image and that of the actual geometry. If this difference is smaller than some user-specified threshold ϵ, the approximation is deemed acceptable, and the cache is considered valid. An important requirement for an acceptable error metric is that it must be fast to compute. For example, we cannot afford to analyze the geometric contents of the node, as the number of primitives contained in a node can be very large.

Our algorithm employs an error metric that measures the maximum angular discrepancy between a point inside a node and the point that represents it in the cached image. We shall use the 2D diagram shown in Figure 1 to define our error metric more precisely. The rectangle in this diagram represents the bounding box of a node in the hierarchy. The thick line segment crossing the bounding box represents the quadrilateral onto which the cached image is texture-mapped, as described in Section 2. The viewpoint for which the

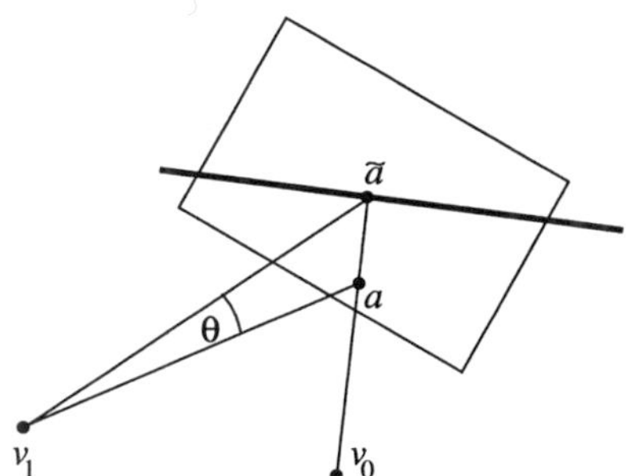

Figure 1 Angular discrepancy.

cache was computed is v_0. Let a be a point inside the node. The point that corresponds to a on the quadrilateral is $\tilde{a}$. By construction, a and $\tilde{a}$ coincide when viewed from v_0; however, for most other views, the two points subtend some angle $\theta > 0$, as illustrated by viewpoint v_1 in the diagram. Our error metric measures the maximum angular discrepancy over all points a inside the node:

$$Error(v, v_0) = \max_a \theta(a, v, \tilde{a}) \tag{1}$$

For a given view direction and field of view, the smaller the maximum angular discrepancy is allowed to be, the closer the projections of points a and $\tilde{a}$ are in the image. Thus, using a smaller error threshold results in fewer visual artifacts caused by using the cached images instead of rendering the geometry.

The right-hand side of equation (1) may be approximated by computing the angular discrepancy for each of the eight corners of a node's bounding box. This is not a conservative estimate, but it is fast to compute, and has been found to work well in practice.

In order to predict the life span of a cached image before creating it for some view v_0, we must estimate how far from v_0 we can travel while keeping the error under ϵ. If the view trajectory is known to us in advance, we can simply search along the trajectory for the farthest point for which the error is within tolerance. This is probably the best course of action for recording a walkthrough or fly-by offline. For an interactive walkthrough, the path of the viewer is not known in advance; however, the current velocity and acceleration are known at any frame, and an upper bound on the acceleration is typically available. In this situation, for each node in the hierarchy we can attempt to find a *safety zone* around v_0, that is, a set of viewpoints v such that for each viewpoint in this set the error is less than ϵ:

$$SafetyZone(v_0) \subseteq \{v \mid Error(v, v_0) \leq \epsilon\}\,, \tag{2}$$

Given the safety zone and using bounds on velocity and acceleration, we can compute a lower bound on the number of frames for which the cache will remain valid. Alternatively, we can obtain a non-conservative estimate by extrapolating the viewer's path and intersecting it with the safety zone. Our implementation uses non-conservative estimates. Next we describe how safety zones are computed in our algorithm.

Consider the 2D diagram in Figure 2. Let v_0 be the current viewpoint, a a point inside a node, and $\tilde{a}$ its projection onto the textured quadrilateral, as in Figure 1. Note that all viewpoints v from which the angle subtended by a and $\tilde{a}$ is equal to ϵ must lie on one of the two circles of radius

$$r = \frac{\|a - \tilde{a}\|}{2 \sin \epsilon} \tag{3}$$

passing through a and $\tilde{a}$. Thus, we can conservatively define a circular safety zone around v_0 (a sphere in 3D), whose radius d is given by the shortest distance between these circles and v_0:

$$d = \sqrt{h^2 + r^2 + 2hr \sin \epsilon} - r \tag{4}$$

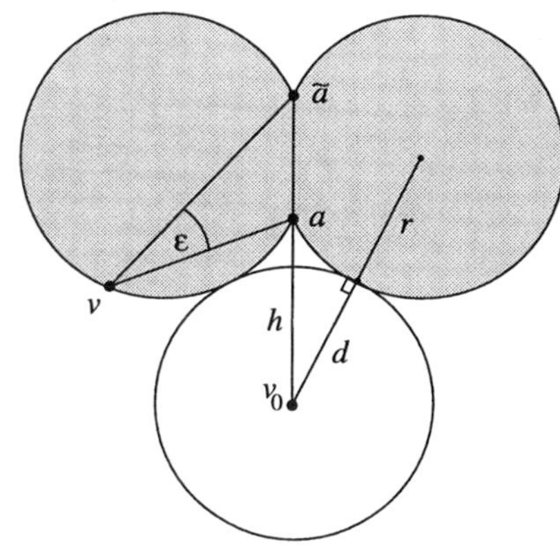

Figure 2 The shaded region contains all the viewpoints v from which a and $\tilde{a}$ subtend an angle greater than or equal to ϵ. The lower circle is a conservative safety zone.

where h is the distance between v_0 and a.

In order to approximate the safety zone for a leaf node in the hierarchy, we evaluate d for each corner of the node's bounding volume and take the smallest of these distances. We then set the safety zone to be the axis-aligned cube inscribed inside a sphere of radius d around v_0. The safety zone of an interior node is computed by first computing the safety zone using the bounding box of the node, and then taking the intersection of this safety zone with the safety zones of the children.

In our implementation, the user specifies the error threshold in pixels. This threshold is converted to an angular error threshold using the current resolution and field-of-view angle. If either the resolution or the field-of-view change in the course of a walkthrough, the angular error threshold must be adjusted accordingly.

4 Partitioning

As a preprocessing step, we construct a BSP-tree [6] partitioning of the scene. The goals of the partitioning algorithm are as follows:

1. split as few objects as possible;
2. make the hierarchy as balanced as possible (in terms of the number of geometric primitives contained in each subtree);
3. make the aspect ratio of each node's bounding volume as close to 1 as possible.

The first goal aims to reduce visual artifacts. The second and third goals help improve performance: balanced trees facilitate hierarchical view-frustum culling, and cached images of nodes with good aspect ratios tend to remain valid longer. Computing the optimal BSP-tree that satisfies these potentially contradictory goals appears difficult. Therefore, our partitioning algorithm employs a simple greedy approach that is not optimal, but seems to work well in practice.

Given a list of objects to partition, we look for gaps between objects, place a splitting plane in the "best" gap we can find, and then recurse on the lists of objects on each side of that plane. To facilitate finding the gaps between objects, we compute their extents with a method similar to the parallelepiped bounding volumes of Kay and Kajiya [10]. For each object, we compute its extent along each of N different directions on the unit sphere. Each splitting plane in the BSP-tree is constrained to be perpendicular to one of the N vectors. For example, if we chose the three coordinate axes as our direction vectors, our partitioning algorithm would yield a binary tree of axis-aligned boxes.

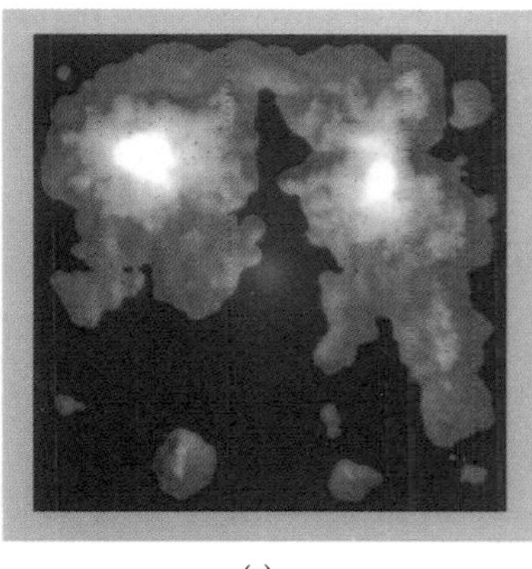
(a)

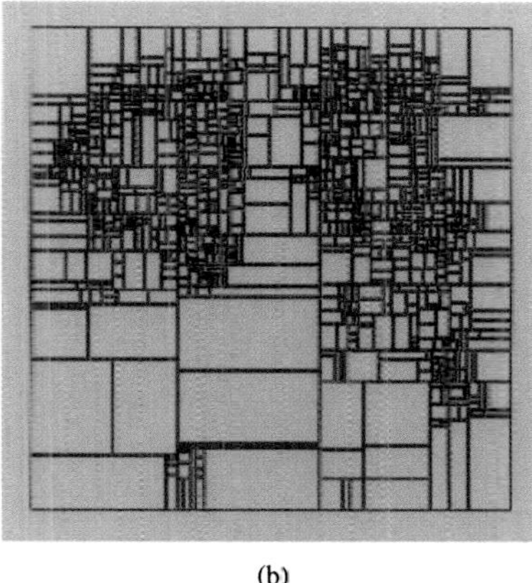
(b)

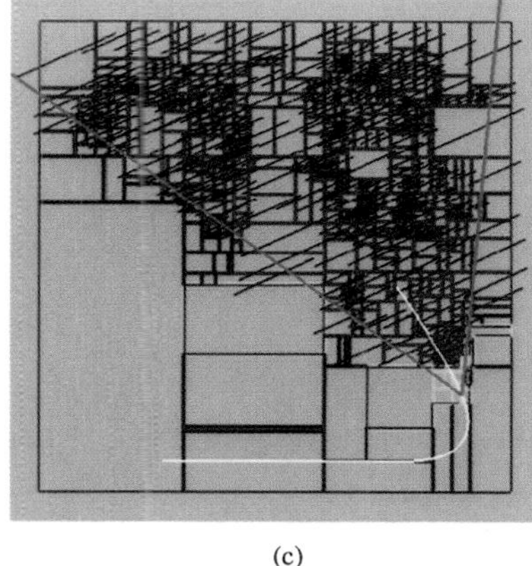
(c)

Figure 3 (a) A bird's eye view of the island scene. (b) The partitioning of the scene. (c) A viewpoint on the walkthrough path.

For each of the N directions, we create two sorted lists of objects: one, according to the lower bound of each object's extent; the other, according to the upper bound. We then scan these lists, while keeping track of the number of "active" objects (i.e., objects whose extents we are currently in). Intervals where the number of active objects is a local minimum are the gaps that we are looking for. Ideally, we are looking for a gap with zero active objects, such that the number of geometric primitives on each side of the gap is roughly equal. Such a gap does not always exist, so we compute a cost for each gap that is a function of the number of its active objects and the ratio of the number of primitives on either side of the gap. For each of the N directions, we choose the gap with the smallest cost. To create good aspect ratios, we tend to choose the best gap from the direction along which the combined extent of all the objects on the list is greatest.

The current implementation of our system is geared towards visualization of complex landscapes. Such scenes have a special structure: they essentially consist of a height-field representing land and water, and of objects such as trees and houses scattered on that height-field. Thus, assuming that the positive Y axis points up, all of the objects are spread above the XZ plane. Our partitioning algorithm takes advantage of this structure by using N direction vectors that evenly divide the unit circle perpendicular to the Y axis. As a result, all of the splitting planes of the BSP-tree are perpendicular to the XZ plane. In all of the experiments reported in Section 5, two direction vectors were used, resulting in axis-aligned boundaries between regions.

When objects are split between two or more leaf nodes, visual artifacts that look like gaps or cracks sometimes appear in the split surfaces. This problem results from approximating a single object by multiple images, with no constraint that the images match along the split boundary. Such artifacts can occur even with small error thresholds because of the discrete sampling involved in creating the caches and rendering the textured quadrilaterals. For small error thresholds, it is possible to overcome these artifacts by ensuring a small amount of overlap in the geometry contained in neighboring leaf nodes. To achieve this overlap, we construct a slightly "inflated" version of each leaf region, and associate with each leaf node the extra geometry that is contained in its inflated region, in addition to the geometry contained in the original region. In our current implementation, the amount by which regions are inflated is a user-specified parameter (typically 10 to 20 percent).

5 Results

This section demonstrates the performance of our method using a walkthrough of a complex outdoor scene. All tests were performed on a Silicon Graphics Indigo2 workstation with a 250MHz R4400 processor, 320 megabytes of RAM, and a Maximum Impact graphics board with 4 megabytes of texture memory.

The outdoor scene used in these tests is a terrain of an island populated with 1117 willow trees. The terrain consists of 131,072 triangles, and each tree consists of 36,230 triangles. The total number of triangles in the database is 40,599,982. To keep the storage requirements down the trees were instanced, and the total amount of storage for the database before any processing by our method is 20 megabytes. The amount of storage required for this scene without instancing is 3.5 gigabytes. Figure 3(a) shows a bird's eye view of the island.

Constructing the BSP-tree for this database took 46 seconds. The resulting partitioning (shown in Figure 3(b)) has 13 levels, 1072 leaf nodes, and is fairly balanced in terms of the geometric primitives contained in each subtree. Most leaf nodes contain a single tree and a portion of the terrain. The partitioning algorithm managed to avoid splitting any of the trees, and the only object split was the terrain.

Partitioning the database causes an increase in the required storage. This increase is primarily due to the need to "inflate" the leaf regions, as described in Section 4. For this database, we used an inflation factor of 17 percent, increasing the storage to 150 megabytes. Note that the increase is only 4 percent relative to the storage the original database would have required if we did not use instancing on the trees.

We recorded timings for several walkthroughs of the island. Each of the walkthroughs was along the same path, defined by a B-spline space curve shown in white in Figure 3(c). This path was designed to help us study the relative performance of image caching over a range of visible scene complexities: the camera first tracks along the edge of the model, then flies in toward the center of the island at tree-top level. Although the path was known in advance, we did not take advantage of this information, in order to get a better sense of how the algorithm would behave under interactive control.

Figure 3(c) provides a snapshot illustrating our algorithm for a particular viewpoint on the path. The view frustum for that viewpoint is indicated by green lines. Nodes outlined in purple are culled, as they lie outside the view frustum. Nodes outlined in yellow are rendered using their geometry. Nodes outlined in red are rendered using their cached images. The quadrilaterals onto which these images are mapped are shown in black.

To assess the relative performance of our algorithm, we first computed two 1200-frame walkthroughs. Each frame was rendered at a resolution of 640×480. The first walkthrough was performed

Figure 4 Frames from walkthroughs of the island. The top row shows two frames rendered using the original geometry. The second row shows the same frames rendered with image caching using an error threshold of two pixels. The third row illustrates the visual artifacts resulting from a larger error threshold (eight pixels).

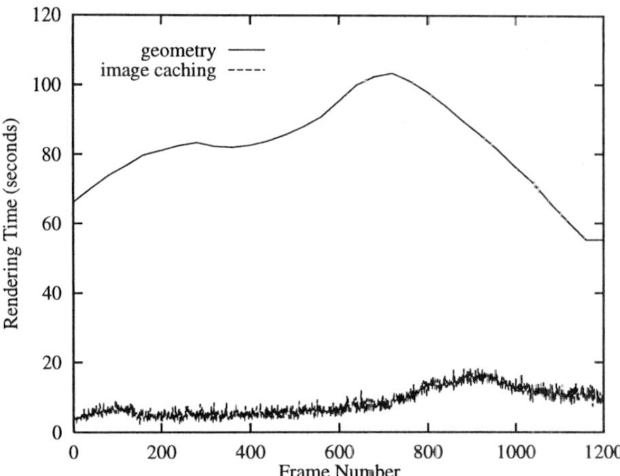

Figure 5 Image caching versus rendering geometry.

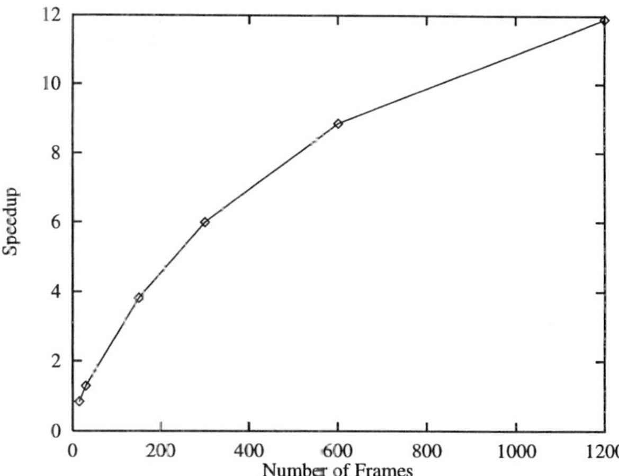

Figure 6 Speedup as a function of frame rate.

using an algorithm that employs hierarchical view frustum culling (using the same BSP-tree), but renders all of the original geometry contained in leaf nodes that are inside the view frustum. The second walkthrough was performed using our method with an error threshold of two pixels.

The top row of images in Figure 4 shows two different frames from the walkthrough rendered using the original geometry. The second row shows the same frames rendered by our method. The images are not identical to those in the top row, but it is very hard to tell them apart, except for the distant trees that appear slightly softer and less blocky when rendered with our method, because of the linear filtering used when rendering texture-mapped primitives.

The plot in Figure 5 shows the rendering times for the two walkthroughs. For each frame, we plot the rendering time spent by each of the two methods. It takes our method 134 seconds to compute the very first frame of the walkthrough, which is two times longer than the time required when rendering the geometry. However, once the initial image caches have been computed, subsequent frames can be rendered 4.1 to 25.2 times faster with our method, with an overall speedup factor of 11.9 for the entire sequence.

In the experiment above, our method used a fairly small error threshold: an angle subtended by roughly two pixels on the image plane. As a result, there are almost no perceptible visual artifacts in the walkthrough, as compared to rendering the geometry. If the error threshold is relaxed, more visual artifacts start to appear, but the rendering becomes faster, as cached images have longer life spans. For instance, with the error threshold set to eight pixels, the overall speedup increases to 14.1. Frames that were rendered with this error threshold are shown in the bottom row of Figure 4. Comparing these images with the ones rendered using geometry (in the top row) reveals increased "ruggedness" along the silhouette of the mountains, as well as some "cracks" in the terrain, through which the blue background shows through.

Since our method utilizes path coherence, it is interesting to examine how different frame rates along the same path affect performance. Therefore, we rendered the same walkthrough using different numbers of frames, equally spaced along the path. For example, when using two frames, the first frame is computed at the beginning of the path and the second in the middle of the path. Thus, for very small numbers of frames there is not much frame-to-frame coherence at all. For each walkthrough the overall speedup factor was computed, and the results are plotted in Figure 6. As expected, the speedup factor becomes larger, as more frames are rendered along the same path. Note that our method is faster than geometry with as

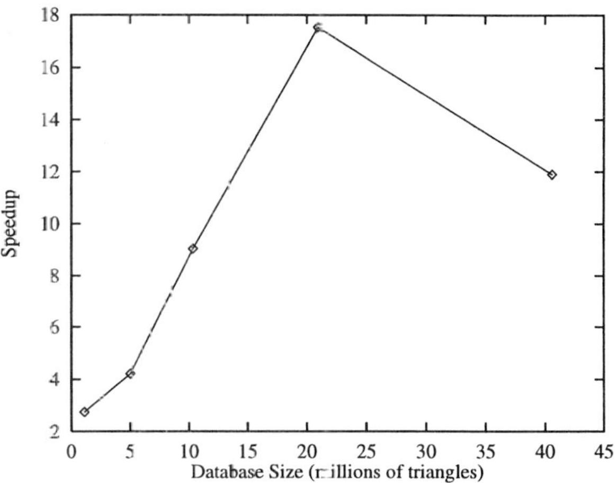

Figure 7 Speedup as a function of scene complexity.

few as 30 frames along the path.

Another interesting statistic is the behavior of our method as a function of overall scene complexity. The same walkthrough path was computed for several versions of the scene, each containing a different number of trees. Except for the number of trees, all of the scenes were identical. The overall speedup factors for these scenes (for a 1200-frame walkthrough with a two-pixel error threshold) are plotted in Figure 7. The speedup factor introduced by our algorithm first rapidly increases with the geometrical complexity of the scene, but there is a drop in the speedup when the number of triangles increases from 20 million (574 trees) to 40 million (1117 trees). The reason for this behavior is that increasing the tree density on the island causes significantly more extra geometry to be added to each leaf node when its region is inflated. This extra geometry makes the overhead of creating a cached image for the node substantially larger.

An important limiting factor on the performance of image caching is the constraint imposed by OpenGL [14] that texture maps have dimensions in powers of 2. Because of these limitations on texture size, almost half of the pixels in the textures defined by our method go unused. The handling of so many unused pixels results in a performance penalty for our image caching method.

6 Conclusions

There are many ways to extend the work presented in this paper:

- *Animation.* Although our method is currently applicable only to static scenes, it should be easy to extend it to handle a few small moving objects or animated sprites. A more challenging problem for further research is to allow scenes where many objects are capable of moving and/or deforming their geometry.
- *Pre-caching.* Our algorithm should be extended to caching images not only for nodes already in the view frustum, but also for nodes that should come into view in the next few frames. This extension would help alleviate temporary degradations in rendering performance that occur as a user travels into an area of the scene that is more complex. Pre-caching could be particularly effective if the caching computations are done in parallel by a separate thread.
- *Geometric LOD modeling.* Many of the objects drawn while creating cached images occupy only a small number of pixels in the image. Thus, instead of drawing such objects in full detail, we could draw a coarser model of the same object, using a multi-resolution representation such as the one by Eck *et al.* [5] or Chamberlain *et al.* [2]. Using a multi-resolution representation could also accelerate rendering of objects for which no cached images were created.
- *Persistent caches.* As regions of the scene pass out of the view frustum, the images cached for the newly culled nodes are invalidated, and the memory is released. In the case that the viewer is simply looking around, these culled caches are still valid representations of their regions. Suspending invalidation of image caches in this case could potentially save a great deal of computation, in much the same way as the method of Regan and Pose [15].
- *Talisman.* Image caching should prove even more effective in an architecture that optimizes the reuse of rendered images as texture maps or sprites, such as the Tasliman architecture [20]. To make the best use of Talisman's capabilities, an affine warp of the cached image should be computed rather than the more general perspective warp resulting from texture-map the cached image onto a quadrilateral in 3D.

In summary, we have presented a new method for accelerating walkthroughs of complex environments by utilizing path coherence. We have demonstrated speedups of an order of magnitude on a current graphics architecture, the Indigo2 Maximum Impact. The speedups increase with the frame rate. While these speedups are significant, we believe they could be made still more dramatic through further optimizations in the underlying graphics hardware and libraries, such as improving the pixel transfer rate from the frame buffer to texture memory, relaxing the existing restrictions on texture map sizes, and providing applications with better control over texture memory management.

Acknowledgments

We would like to thank Eric Brechner, Ka Chai, Brad Chamberlain, Michael Cohen, Hugues Hoppe, and Jack Tumblin for many useful discussions during the early stages of this project.

This work was supported by an Alfred P. Sloan Research Fellowship (BR-3495), an NSF Postdoctoral Research Associates in Experimental Sciences award (CDA-9404959), an NSF Presidential Faculty Fellow award (CCR-9553199), an ONR Young Investigator award (N00014-95-1-0728), a grant from the Washington Technology Center, and industrial gifts from Interval, Microsoft, and Xerox.

References

[1] John M. Airey, John H. Rohlf, and Frederick P. Brooks, Jr. Towards image realism with interactive update rates in complex virtual building environments. *Computer Graphics (1990 Symposium on Interactive 3D Graphics)*, 24(2):41–50, March 1990.

[2] Bradford Chamberlain, Tony DeRose, Dani Lischinski, David Salesin, and John Snyder. Fast rendering of complex environments using a spatial hierarchy. In *Proceedings of Graphics Interface '96*, May 1996.

[3] Shenchang Eric Chen and Lance Williams. View interpolation for image synthesis. In *Computer Graphics* Proceedings, Annual Conference Series, pp. 279–288, August 1993.

[4] James H. Clark. Hierarchical geometric models for visible surface algorithms. *Communications of the ACM*, 19(10):547–554, October 1976.

[5] Matthias Eck, Tony DeRose, Tom Duchamp, Hugues Hoppe, Michael Lounsbery, and Werner Stuetzle. Multiresolution analysis for arbitrary meshes. In *Computer Graphics* Proceedings, Annual Conference Series, pp. 173–182, August 1995.

[6] Henry Fuchs, Zvi M. Kedem, and Bruce Naylor. On visible surface generation by a priori tree structures. *Computer Graphics*, 14(3):175–181, June 1980.

[7] Thomas A. Funkhouser and Carlo H. Séquin. Adaptive display algorithm for interactive frame rates during visualization of complex virtual environments. In *Computer Graphics* Proceedings, Annual Conference Series, pp. 247–254, August 1993.

[8] B. Garlick, D. Baum, and J. Winget. Interactive viewing of large geometric databases using multiprocessor graphics workstations. SIGGRAPH '90 Course Nores: Parallel Algorithms and Architectures for 3D Image Generation, 1990.

[9] Ned Greene, Michael Kass, and Gavin Miller. Hierarchical z-buffer visibility. In *Computer Graphics* Proceedings, Annual Conference Series, pp. 231–238, August 1993.

[10] Timothy L. Kay and James T. Kajiya. Ray tracing complex scenes. *Computer Graphics*, 20(4):269–278, August 1986.

[11] Daivid Luebke and Chris Georges. Portals and mirrors: Simple, fast evaluation of potentially visible sets. In *1995 Symposium on Interactive 3D Graphics*, pp. 105–106, April 1995.

[12] Paulo W. C. Maciel and Peter Shirley. Visual navigation of large environments using textured clusters. In *1995 Symposium on Interactive 3D Graphics*, pp. 95–102, April 1995.

[13] Leonard McMillan and Gary Bishop. Plenoptic modeling: An image-based rendering system. In *Computer Graphics* Proceedings, Annual Conference Series, pp. 39–46, August 1995.

[14] Jackie Neider, Tom Davis, and Mason Woo. *OpengGL Programming Guide.* Addison Wesley, 1993.

[15] Matthew Regan and Ronald Pose. Priority rendering with a virtual reality address recalculation pipeline. In *Computer Graphics* Proceedings, Annual Conference Series, pp. 155–162, July 1994.

[16] Jarek Rossignac and Paul Borrel. Multi-resolution 3D approximations for rendering complex scenes. Research Report RC 17697 (#77951), IBM, Yorktown Heights, New York 10598, 1992. Also appeared in the *IFIP TC 5.WG 5.10.*

[17] Gernot Schaufler. Exploiting frame to frame coherence in a virtual reality system. In *Proceedings of VRAIS '96*, pp. 95–102, April 1996.

[18] Gernot Schaufler and Wolfgang Stürzlinger. A three dimensional image cache for virtual reality. In *Proceedings of Eurographics '96*, 1996. To appear.

[19] Seth J. Teller. *Visibility Computations in Densely Occluded Polyhedral Environments.* PhD thesis, Computer Science Division (EECS), UC Berkeley, Berkeley, California 94720, October 1992. Available as Report No. UCB/CSD-92-708.

[20] Jay Torborg and Jim Kajiya. Talisman: Commodity realtime 3D graphics for the PC. In *Computer Graphics* Proceedings, Annual Conference Series, August 1996.

Hierarchical View-dependent Structures for Interactive Scene Manipulation

Normand Brière and Pierre Poulin

Département d'Informatique et de Recherche Opérationnelle *
Université de Montréal

Abstract

The result of a scene manipulation is usually displayed by re-rendering the entire image even if the change has affected only a small portion of it. This paper presents a system that efficiently detects and recomputes the exact portion of the image that has changed after an arbitrary manipulation of a scene viewed from a fixed camera. The incremental rendering allows for all visual effects produced by ray tracing, including shadows, reflections, refractions, textures, and bump maps.

Two structures are maintained to achieve this. A *ray tree* is associated with each pixel and is used to detect and rebuild only the modified rays after an optical or geometrical change. A *color tree* represents the complete color expression of a pixel. All changes affecting the color of a pixel without changing the corresponding ray tree require only re-evaluation of the affected portions of the color tree.

Optimizations are presented to efficiently detect the modified structures by the use of strategies such as grouping similar information and building hierarchies. Pruning and weighted re-evaluation of information are also considered to manage the memory requirements.

The incremental rendering is done efficiently and accurately and is suitable in an interactive context.

CR Categories and Subject Descriptors: I.3.7 [Computer Graphics]: Three-Dimensional Graphics and Realism.
Additional Key Words and Phrases: scene editing, interactive system, rendering, image quadtree, color tree, ray tree

1 Introduction

Computing the image of a 3D synthetic scene is a complex process, especially when shadows, textures, bump maps, reflections, and refractions are desired. A simple yet powerful algorithm producing such effects is ray tracing [17]. Unfortunately, its computational requirements are generally too high to be considered suitable to calculate intermediate images resulting from an interactive scene manipulation. In fact, ray tracing is mostly used for high quality final rendering, ranging from minutes to hours of computing.

One important reason why ray tracing is rarely considered within an interactive tool is that most interactive systems recompute the entire image of the scene without considering any incremental rendering from the previous image. The fastest rendering technique is usually the projection of wireframe models without any line removal. Unfortunately, it can only convey information about shape, and complex objects are difficult to interpret. The Z-buffer algorithm is quite fast and treats visible-surface determination. It becomes even more competitive by integrating the technique with hierarchical models and treating the image hierarchically [7]. Shading and shadowing for directional and point light sources, as well as textures and filtering can be simulated [3] [18] [14], but with a significant impact on performance and memory usage. However, other important visual phenomena such as reflection and refraction can only be approximated by textures, and this with great effort and potential artifacts [5].

For interaction, one can also benefit from re-ordering the rendering with respect to the phenomena being manipulated, or from choosing between different levels of object complexity [4]. In specific contexts, some manipulations have been optimized by preprocessing. Hanrahan and Haeberli [10] edit material properties on a preprocessed sphere. Interactivity is obtained but the manipulation is done from a different visual context than the scene itself. Litwinowicz and Miller [12] interactively distort a texture directly on a preprocessed projection of the *uv* coordinates of the texture parametrization.

Instead of rendering the entire scene, other researchers have considered updating only the elements affected by a change. For each surface, Cook [2] conserves in a tree structure (shade tree) the symbolic evaluation of the illumination model. If a manipulation does not modify the shape of the tree, then the local illumination may be updated by simply evaluating the shade tree. The evaluation of a tree may not be faster than the calculation itself, but if the tree is replicated at each pixel and compressed according to the parameter currently adjusted, then the evaluation of the smaller tree is faster. By expressing a RenderMan shader by source code instead of a symbolic tree, Guenter *et al.* [8] have defined specialized shaders.

In these techniques, the preprocessing is usually applied on the first visible surface. Séquin and Smyrl [15] preserve in a tree the color expressions of all intersections obtained by ray tracing. The image is updated by traversing these color trees with modified parameters. They only consider changes that do not alter the shape of the trees, which leads to significant time savings because this avoids recomputing visibility. They also propose several compression techniques

*C.P. 6128, succ. Centre-Ville, Montréal (Qc) Canada H3C 3J7
{ briere | poulin }@iro.umontreal.ca

Color Parameters
surface color
ambient, diffuse, specular coefficients
surface roughness
proportion of reflection, refraction, transparency
proportion plastic-metallic
light color and intensity
texture parameter
bump map
surface parametrization
Optical Manipulation
add/delete a reflection, refraction and transparency attribute
change a refraction index
add/delete/change a bump map of a reflective or refractive object
Geometrical Manipulation
add/delete/transform an object
add/delete/transform a light source
add/delete/transform a displacement map

Table 1: Color and ray tree dependent manipulations

to reduce the memory usage and improve on the display time. Systems such as *Atlantis* from Abvent and *IPR* from Wavefront extend these color trees by adding a fixed number of extra ray generations to allow a user, for instance, to make reflective a previously non-reflective object.

Murakami and Hirota [13] extend these previous techniques to handle also changes in visibility for a scene rendered from a static viewpoint. A ray is indexed by the list of regular voxels it traverses. Any change to the scene is associated with its affected voxels, which in turn determine the potentially affected rays. They also use a clever hashing scheme to identify quickly the rays affected by a given voxel. However the visibility determination is performed with respect to the affected voxels rather than the transformed objects. Therefore, all intersections between a ray and the objects in the affected voxels must be precomputed and saved, or recomputed each time a voxel is affected. Increasing the number of voxels reduces this visibility determination, but at the cost of storing many voxels, and also of handling more entries in the hashing table. Jevans [11] removed the previous dependency upon image resolution by storing instead in each voxel the identification of limited regions potentially affected by this voxel. However more unaffected rays can thus be wrongly identified as affected, and the visibility is done with respect to the entire scene.

In this paper, we present a system for the manipulation of a scene viewed from a fixed camera. The visual effects in the images of the scene can include the richness of all those produced by ray tracing, including textures, shadows, reflections, refractions, and bump maps. The central concept behind this system is the ability to efficiently detect and recompute only the modified image portion. Allowed changes are of any kind, whether modifying a surface shading parameter, a texture, making a surface reflective or refractive, or transforming the geometry of any object.

To achieve this, some concepts from the systems described above are unified into two tree-like structures: the *color tree* and the *ray tree*. In the next section, we describe these two structures and how they are used. In section 3, efficiency issues are addressed for the detection and updating of these structures. In section 4, we consider trade-offs between memory requirements and computing efficiency. Finally, we give some typical results from using our system and conclude by summing up our work and by listing potential extensions and applications.

2 Scene Manipulation

Changing some portion of a synthetic scene can affect different properties treated at various stages of the rendering algorithm. To efficiently update the image affected by a specific change may thus require more than one data structure. All possible changes can be divided into two categories. A *color change* may modify the color of at least one pixel without affecting the scene visibility, while a *ray change* (optical or geometrical) may change this visibility.

In an interactive context, the user selects a group of objects (*selection*) and applies a given change to it. In the next subsections, we explain the particularities of each manipulation and describe the two structures used to incrementally render the current image. Please refer to figure 1 for a graphical representation of the concepts described in this section.

2.1 The Color-tree Structure

In ray tracing, the color of a pixel is computed by following a ray through the scene. At each intersection, the color returned depends upon the surface reflection/refraction model which specifies how much of the light reaching this point is sent back along the ray direction. We store the color of a pixel as an expression tree (figure 1 color tree) in which each leaf is a constant or a pointer to a parameter, and each node is an n-ary function. If a color subtree does not contain any parameter, it is replaced by a constant leaf.

One can view our color tree as a union of concepts such as shade trees [2], texture trees [16], and parametrized rays [15]. Indeed, a color tree corresponds to the entire symbolic evaluation of a pixel color without preserving information about the visibility.

A color change is the most simple and efficient change to handle. It corresponds to a change that does not alter the visibility in the image. Re-rendering the modified scene consists of simply re-evaluating the color expression for each pixel. The refresh rate therefore depends upon the number of nodes in each color tree, which is a function of the number of light sources and interreflection/interrefraction combinations. In most cases, the display time is uniform and quite fast. All the shading parameters listed in the top section of table 1 are associated with color changes.

Any shading parameter may be a variable or more generally, a texture function controlling this parameter. At a given intersection point, such a texture function may depend upon that point or upon the surface parametrization at that point. Since a texture function can be expressed as a tree structure, it is integrated as a subtree of our color tree. A change of any texture parameter is thus also resolved by evaluating the color tree.

Finally, if the user manipulates a higher-level property such as changing a procedural texture to another, or changing the illumination model itself, the associated color subtrees are appropriately replaced.

2.2 The Ray-tree Structure

In order to compute visibility changes efficiently, an extended structure is used, namely, the ray tree. It is similar to Murakami and Hirota's ray set [13], but without information related to voxels. The *ray path* of a pixel is the ordered list of objects encountered by a ray originating from the eye position through this pixel. The ray tree of a pixel (figure 1 ray tree) is the geometrically-specific information of the ray path. Each node of the ray tree contains intersection point

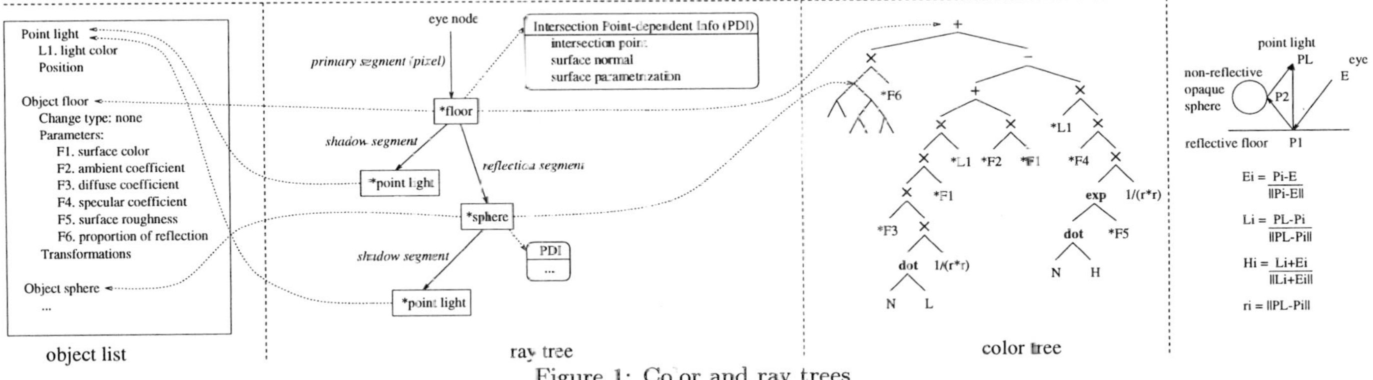

Figure 1: Color and ray trees

dependent information (PDI): the intersection point, its normal, and surface parametrization. Nodes for the eye and for each light are considered global and are not duplicated. A *ray segment* joins two consecutive points of a ray tree. A node of a ray path is only a pointer to an object from the list of objects defining the scene. Rebuilding a portion of a ray tree causes an immediate update of the corresponding color tree.

An *optical change* occurs when a ray tree is modified without changing the scene geometry. The middle section of table 1 lists some optical changes. An optical change is effective at a node when its object pointed to has been modified by an optical change. The intersection point at this node is guaranteed to be valid. However new reflected or refracted rays may have to be re-shot from this point and intersected with respect to the entire scene.

A *geometrical change* occurs when the geometry of the scene has changed. Some of these changes appear in the bottom section of table 1. A general geometrical change is handled in three steps. First the selection is removed from all ray trees. The resulting ray trees will not contain any reference to the selection. Then only the selection is rendered while it is manipulated by the user. Finally when the user releases the selection, the ray trees are updated. A *ray test* is a visibility determination with respect to the selection only. A *ray update* is a visibility determination with respect to the entire scene (except for primary rays which need only a ray test), but only for the affected pixels. This is typically a small fraction of the image.

To remove the selection from the ray trees, all of their nodes are visited. If the corresponding object at a node is contained in the selection, then the entire subtree is no longer valid. It is replaced by a new ray subtree traced from the intersection point of the previous node in the same direction as the incoming ray segment. The intersections are computed with respect to the entire scene, but without the selection itself.

The intermediate rendering does not modify the ray trees in any way since at that time they do not contain any reference to the selection. All ray trees are simply traversed and only intersection tests between the segments and the selection are performed. If a ray segment intersects the selection then the intersection point is computed and all emanating rays (shadow, reflection, refraction) must be re-shot from that point with respect to the entire scene, including the selection.

Adding the selection to the ray trees corresponds to rendering it only once while updating the modified ray trees.

3 Hierarchies and Groups

The color and ray trees allow incremental ray tracing of the scene during manipulation. In most cases, this is already an appreciable gain because a structure test is much faster than its update. Also, the visibility determination is typically the most expensive operation and none are performed for a color change.

Unfortunately, traversing all structures to determine what may be affected quickly becomes a bottleneck. In this section, we propose some optimizations to cull many unnecessary tests. Section 5 will demonstrate the efficiency of these optimizations.

3.1 Selection-dependent Preprocessing

The image represented by its color and ray trees is built as a *quadtree*. Typically, the user adjusts the scene by applying several consecutive color or optical changes to the same selection. The quadtree hierarchical structure can greatly speed up such subsequent changes. Indeed, because the selection does not change, the portion of the image dependent upon the selection remains the same. A flag is kept in each *region* (quadtree element) that indicates if the region is dependent or not upon the current selection. The preprocessing is performed at the first change and the flags are not reset as long as the user applies color or optical changes to the same selection. Because of the hierarchical nature of the quadtree, the rejection of independent regions is very fast.

Figure 2 b) shows with white contours the regions dependent upon the central sphere: the primary ray segments intersecting the central sphere, the interreflections on the floor and the left sphere, and the refraction in the right sphere. Here, only shadows from opaque objects are handled. Note that this preprocessing is also applicable for removing the selection from the ray trees.

3.2 Groups and Atoms

It is also possible to speed up the selection-dependent preprocessing by using the concept of groups. A *group* is a region for which each ray path is identical. As such, their corresponding ray trees only differ by their PDIs, and the subregions of a group are also groups themselves.

A flag in each region indicates if the region is a group by a pointer to its corresponding ray path. If the region is a group, only the ray path needs to be tested. After optical and geometrical changes, ray paths may change and therefore some image groups must be updated. However, because these changes are propagated from the bottom of

a) Original scene

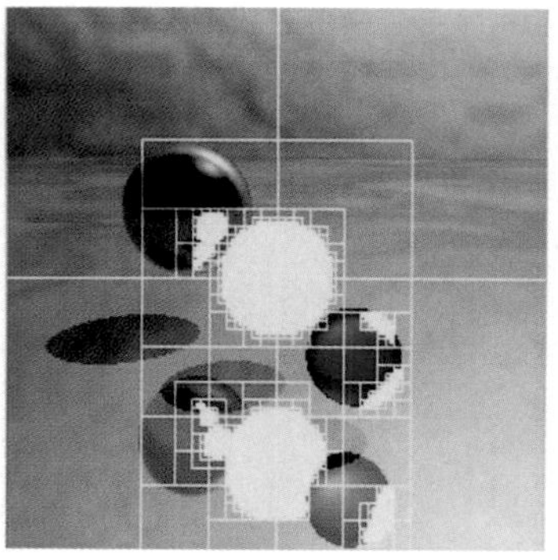

b) Selection-dependent regions

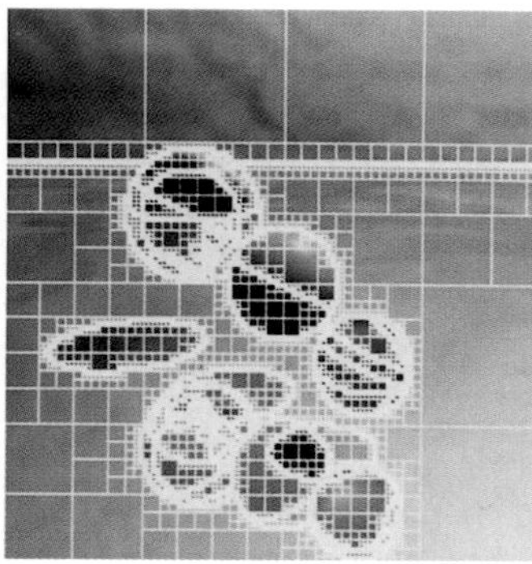

c) Image groups

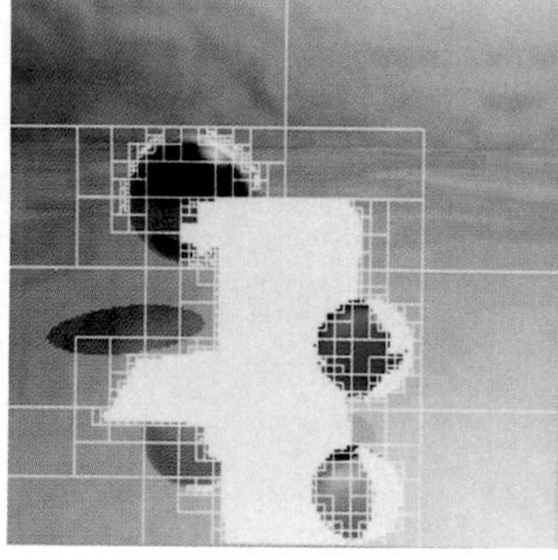

d) Geometrically-dependent regions

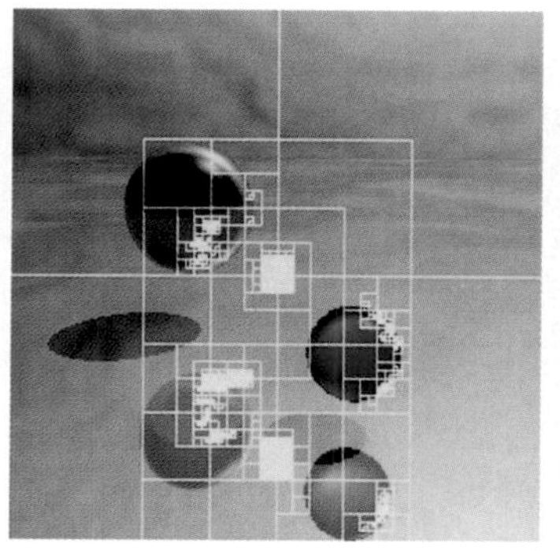

e) Scaling down the selection

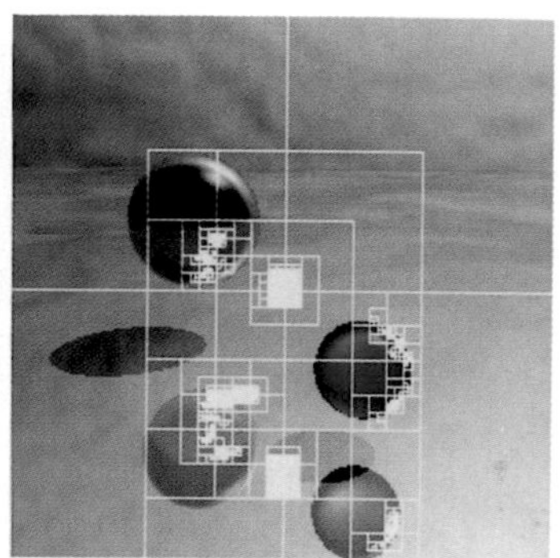

f) Using up to two tunnels per region

Figure 2: A simple scene

the quadtree to its top, the number of regions to be updated is minimal. Figure 2 c) shows with white contours the groups in the image.

In a scene composed of many visible objects, the number of groups can be rather large and their efficiency thus much reduced. If the scene is constructed as a hierarchy of objects, it is possible to consider an *atom* to be at a higher level than the leaves in the model hierarchy. By raising the atom in the hierarchy, the number of groups and ray paths should globally decrease, but if the user tries to modify a subatomic object, the system will have to consider the entire atom as modified. For instance in figure 4, the bust of Beethoven, boat, individual trees, and cows could each be considered an atom.

Many regions contain typically a limited number of ray paths, but because of the distribution of these ray paths within a region, the quadtree subdivision might produce a large number of smaller groups, each in the worst case consisting of a single ray path. To reduce these situations and decrease further the number of groups, the groups are generalized to *path groups*, p-groups, where p indicates the number of different paths in a region. A group is then a 1-group.

Determining if a p-group is dependent upon the selection should be faster as there are no subregions to test, but it may require testing up to p paths. The user can control a maximum value m_p for p so the gains in culling of p-groups are not outweighed by maintaining and testing the list of ray paths.

3.3 Color-tree Evaluation

For a color update, the user typically adjusts the same parameter frequently. In order to speed up the color update, color expression trees can be compressed according to the currently-selected parameter by maintaining at each node the evaluation of its subtree. In particular, the entire color expression of a pixel independent of the current parameter is temporarily replaced by a constant color value. This occurs when the pixel depends upon the selection but not on the selected shading or texture parameter.

This optimization is present in Séquin and Smyrl [15] in which a subtree is simply replaced by its value. The color trees could be also compressed physically, at the cost of rebuilding them each time another parameter is selected. This is also similar to compressing the shaders in Guenter *et al.* [8].

3.4 Bounding Ray Trees

Testing each ray tree for intersection with the selection becomes prohibitive if our goal is interactive manipulation. In order to greatly speed up ray tests, we use a hierarchy of bounding volumes for the ray trees. If the selection does not intersect such a bounding volume, then no ray test has to be performed for the enclosed ray trees.

3.4.1 Tunnels

For each region of the image, a volume that encloses every point of all its ray trees is kept. This region's main volume, called a *tunnel*, is built as a union of convex volumes, each called a *section*. Figure 3 shows a 2D representation of a tunnel and its 3D counterpart for a particular region (a group) and viewpoint from the scene depicted in figure 2. The tunnel encloses the eye (right apex), points on the floor, reflection points on the sphere, and two branching sections going towards the light above.

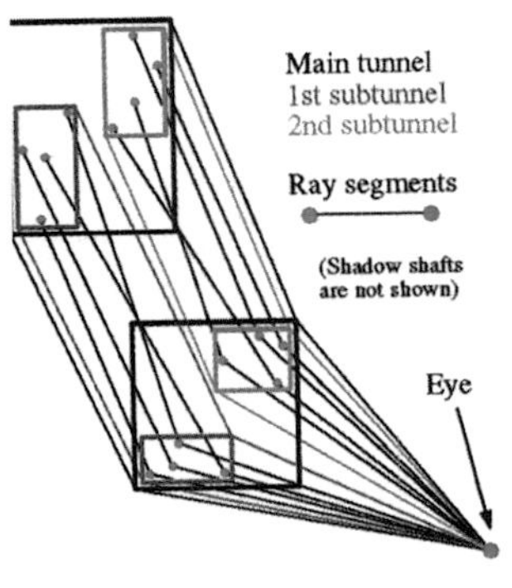

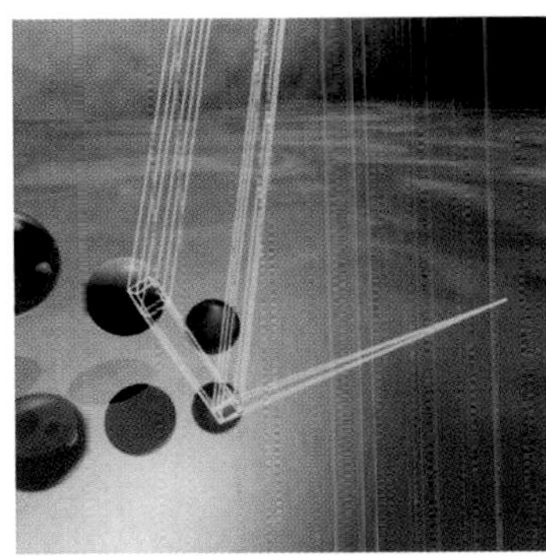

Figure 3: 2D and 3D representations of a tunnel

The first section of a tunnel encloses the eye point and all points directly visible from the eye through this region (first-generation ray segments). For each point light source, there is another section enclosing the same first-generation intersection points and the point light source. All the reflected ray segments of the second generation are enclosed by another section, and similarly for the refracted ray segments of this second generation. The two sets of endpoints of these secondary segments each generate another section respectively with each point light source. This process continues recursively for the next-generation segments.

A special situation occurs when the region is a group. In this case, all n ray trees have the same path and each section always encloses exactly n ray segments. These tunnels are usually thinner as the rays tend to remain closer to each other. However, if the region is not a group, some sections enclose ray segments whose endpoints do not belong to the same objects. Such a section may be much larger than necessary as some ray segments are not correlated. However, if a region forming a p-group consists of p tunnels associated with each p different ray paths, then many of those undesirable sections are eliminated. If the region has more ray paths than the maximum number m_p, the ${m_p}^{th}$ tunnel contains all ray trees belonging to the $p - m_p + 1$ remaining ray paths.

3.4.2 Sections

A section bounds a set of ray segments. We adopted the *shafts* introduced by Haines and Wallace [9]. A shaft is built using two aligned boxes with each bounding plane passing through a face of a box or through a pair of relevant edges, each of them belonging to a different box. This construction has the property that if a shaft is built with two given boxes, then it encloses any subshaft built using two subboxes. A pyramid shaft is a particular shaft where all points at one end are the same. It is used for sections whose apex is the eye or a point light (figure 3).

Rather than testing for an intersection between the shaft and the selection itself, we use a bounding box around the selection. The test is based only on trivial rejections between the vertices of these two bounding volumes and their supporting planes. This is simpler and faster to compute, although if no trivial rejection has occurred, the test proceeds as if there were an intersection. For an exact test between a box and an arbitrary convex polyhedron, see Greene [6].

Figure 2 d) shows with white contours the regions updated when a geometrical change is applied to the selection (the central sphere). The updated portion of the image is larger than the minimal one in figure 2 b) because the bounding volume of the selection is used for the intersection test. This appears first in the projection of the selection in the image, and also in larger shadows and reflections of the selection. Moreover, this test is limited to trivial rejections only. The selection is scaled by $\frac{1}{4}$ in figure 2 e). The corresponding smaller updated regions are displayed with white contours. One can see that some irrelevant regions are located at the silhouette of the reflective sphere because of some incoherently large sections. Allowing up to two tunnels per region eliminates some of these sections (figure 2 f).

3.4.3 Updating the Tunnels

Adding an object to the ray trees may change some tunnels. This is also the case after an optical change. The tunnel of a region with at least one modified ray tree must be recalculated. However, the modification is propagated from bottom to top and no tunnel is rebuilt needlessly.

A region is formed by four subregions (quadtree structure), so a tunnel of this region is formed by its four subtunnels. At the lowest level, the ray segments form the shaft which is built using the two bounding boxes of their endpoints. At a higher level, the bounding boxes used for the shaft bound the respective subboxes of the four subshafts. Each level is thus updated in constant time.

4 Spacetime Considerations

In previous sections, we described the structures and optimizations allowing us to manipulate a scene interactively. However, we did not discuss memory requirements. Memory usage is the major drawback of our scheme as each pixel contains a lot of information.

In order to manipulate a scene at various image resolutions given limited memory, we present various trade-offs between the space required by the full structures and the computing time necessary to rebuild them.

In this section, we discuss strategies to lower the memory requirements, based upon controlling the number of different information pieces. This leads to a more general approach based upon the relative importance of an information. Note that none of these memory strategies affect the resulting images; they only influence what information will need to be recomputed. This makes the system flexible according to the space and time constraints.

4.1 Eliminating Information

All color trees, ray trees, and tunnels represent the largest portion of the memory usage in our system (table 2). Fortunately, we can exploit the locality involved with most changes.

By limiting to m_c the number of color trees, and if a color change does not update more than m_c pixels, then the refresh rate is not affected. However, if the number of updated pixels is larger than m_c, the excess pixels can be updated using the (slower) ray tree evaluation.

Similar to the color and ray tree reduction, a maximum number of tunnels can be specified by the user in order to control their memory usage. The time for reconstructing a tunnel becomes a function of the number of its immediate subtunnels already constructed, and the number of subtunnels to reconstruct. So the worst case of rebuilding a tunnel depends upon its level in the hierarchy.

4.1.1 Color Trees

Another solution specific to color trees prunes color subtrees by replacing them by their corresponding functions rather than their expansion in a tree. A procedural texture is an example of such a function. However when changing one parameter of this texture, the smaller trees thus obtained may be slower to evaluate as the function calculation is usually slower than its subtree evaluation. The user could also select a subset of parameters which are subject to change, and thus replace any subtrees in which no such parameter appears by a constant. Changing another parameter will involve however a ray tree evaluation.

4.1.2 Ray Trees

The ray trees represent another important portion of the storage used. All of this information can be removed in order to reduce the memory usage, requiring any intersection point, normal vector, and surface parametrization to be recalculated on demand. However, these quantities are not usually expensive to recompute, because the object to intersect with is already known. So the visibility calculation for the intersection point is done with respect to that object only. Although it is faster to preserve all this information, another spacetime trade-off is possible by keeping only a certain number of ray trees. A deleted ray tree may be recalculated from a pointer to its ray path, which is stored in a global list.

4.1.3 Tunnels

Because of their hierarchical nature, many lower level subtunnels are rarely accessed. Also the lower we get in the structure, the more such subtunnels there are. By simply eliminating the tunnels at the two lowest levels, one obtains a reduction of a factor of about 16 in the number of tunnels. Moreover, this contributes to improving the global performance, as testing a lowest-level tunnel is more expensive than testing the few enclosed ray trees themselves.

4.2 Shadow Counters

For shadows cast by opaque objects, it is not necessary to know in which order objects are blocking the light, but only if the light is visible or not. Therefore, instead of constructing the list of ray segments starting from a given intersection point up to a point light, we use only a counter to indicate the number of blocking objects.

When an object is removed from the ray trees, the counter for a light at a ray node is decremented if the object was a blocker. If the counter reaches zero, the illumination must be recomputed; otherwise, nothing has to be recomputed. When an object is added to the ray trees, some counters may be incremented. If it is the case for a counter previously at zero, the illumination from that light (now in shadow) must be recalculated.

Still, l such counters must be associated with each intersection point for a scene with l lights. To control the space used by the counters, we set a maximum of $b{+}1$ bits for each counter, hence handling up to $2^b{-}1$ blockers. The *extra* bit represents overflow and it is set only when more than $2^b{-}1$ blockers lie between the light and the intersection point. When removing a blocker, if any shadow counter is decremented to zero and its extra bit is set, we know that the point is still in shadow, but not the number of blockers. It is therefore necessary to re-shoot a ray towards the light with respect to the entire scene to update the counter value. If the value of b is zero, the extra bit becomes a simple flag indicating if the light is visible or not. Because the shadow counters are stored in the ray paths, a small value of b reduces the number of ray paths, but the increased cost of having to re-evaluate more often shadow rays.

If there are semi-transparent blockers among opaque blockers, a counter between two consecutive transparent blockers (along a shadow segment) is used.

Scene	Color trees	Ray paths	1-groups	Ray trees	Tunnels
Figure 2 (simple)	66,000 32.5 MB	125 —	4,500 —	66,000 5.3 MB	10,900 5.4 MB
Figure 4 (complex)	66,000 20.5 MB	5,300 —	12,100 —	66,000 3.7 MB	10,900 4.3 MB

Table 2: Statistics on memory requirements

4.3 Information Weight

A color subtree, a ray tree and a tunnel do not have the same space and time requirements. The specification of a weight with each piece of information, which indicates its relative importance among the others, is a more general approach.

The weight can be a function taking into account (1) the memory size needed by the information, (2) the time needed to recalculate it, and (3) its latest access time. The system will thus give preference to remove information that is more space intensive, that is faster to rebuild, and that has been inactive for a long time. This weight function provides a way to remove the less important information and to preserve the rest.

The memory size of each type of information depends upon the implementation but is simple to estimate. The time to recalculate a piece of information can be measured empirically, or estimated by various means. For instance, due to its hierarchical nature, the time needed to compute a tunnel corresponds to the computing time of its subtunnels plus its own computing time. For tunnels, we can also consider its surface area as a weight factor since the probability of intersecting an object is proportional to this area.

An information's inactive time is not measured in absolute time. Indeed, the wait between two successive manipulations should not influence the inactivity time. We suggest considering instead the number of changes since the latest access to the information.

5 Results

This section provides some statistics on our current implementation. The scene on which the manipulations were applied appears in figure 4, with the original image (a) before any manipulation and the resulting image (b) after all modifications. All times are in seconds and were gathered on a Silicon Graphics Indigo2 Extreme R4400, running at 150 MHz, with 128 MB of RAM.

The original scene consists of about 16,500 objects (13,500 polygons). It takes 1,100 seconds to preprocess the original image at a 256 × 256 resolution, Simply ray tracing the same scene requires 640 seconds. Statistics about the number of different pieces of information as well as their respective memory requirements are provided in table 2. To compare, we also give the same statistics for the simple scene of figure 2. One can notice that although simpler in terms of

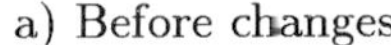

a) Before changes

b) After changes

c) Higher resolution

Figure 4: A more complex scene

geometry, the visibility complexity of figure 2 is higher than the one of figure 4, which is illustrated by larger memory needs for its color trees, ray trees and tunnels.

The top section of table 3 shows statistics on color changes. The modifiable parameters that are integrated in the color tree are all texture parameters defining a constant color, except for the color of the light source. Traversing the image quadtree to identify the pixels dependent upon the selection takes from 1 to 2 seconds. Using groups for this selection-dependent preprocessing (SDP) leads to 20-40% savings of the first color updates. Computing all colors from the ray paths takes less than 10 seconds. If all ray trees are used instead of recomputed from the ray paths, this time goes down by 40-70%. If the color trees themselves are used, this time is reduced by 90-95%. The four color changes in table 3 are all updated under half a second. The savings due to compression of the color trees are less significant (1-20%).

The optical change in the middle section of table 3 displays a similar behavior than first color changes with respect to the use of groups for the selection preprocessing (25%).

Some statistics on geometrical changes are given in the bottom section of table 3. Changes are dependent upon the number of rays that must be shot and how expensive they are to intersect with respect to the entire scene. The use of tunnels greatly reduces all geometrical changes, especially when only a fraction of all ray trees are allowed to reside in memory. This is due to the fact that many ray trees do not need to be recomputed from ray paths because simply culled by the tunnels. Indeed, tunnels culled between 65-90% of the ray tests. The hierarchical nature of the image quadtree and tunnels shows that almost no performance is lost, even when using 10% of all ray trees.

6 Summary and Conclusion

In this paper, we presented two tree structures allowing an incremental recomputation of the image after any modification of a scene viewed from a fixed camera.

The *color tree* preserves the entire expression leading to the final color of a pixel. Any changes affecting the value of parameters in these trees, such as shading and texture parameters, are quickly displayed by re-evaluating only the subtrees dependent upon the modified parameters.

By storing the image in a quadtree of regions, a preprocessing step identifies by a flag each region within which at least one color tree is affected by a given color change. This preprocessing is, in addition, sped up by the notion of groups, where regions are formed by pixels with identical ray paths. So, an entire group can be eliminated by testing a single ray path.

The *ray tree* preserves only the visibility specific information of the rays generated from a pixel. Any changes affecting a ray tree are handled by re-shooting rays from the previous valid intersection point. Any modification in a ray tree is directly updated in its corresponding color tree. All optical and geometrical changes can be handled with this structure.

After a geometrical change, it is possible to avoid testing each individual ray segment with the current selection. To do so, the ray trees are combined into tunnels formed by a union of shafts. The ray segments modified by a geometrical change are therefore quickly detected by intersecting the selection with the hierarchical structure. Any change in the ray trees is updated in a bottom up fashion, from the modified ray trees up only to its bounding tunnels.

As a result, the images are usually updated in less than a second for most color changes. Optical and geometrical update times depend upon the number of rays shot, and upon the complexity of the object (selection or scene) to intersect with these rays. However the number of new rays is usually a small fraction of all rays necessary to render the image.

The question of high memory requirements is addressed by pruning color subtrees and eliminating tunnels and ray trees. This information can be efficiently recomputed on demand by keeping a pointer to its corresponding ray path. Also, an adjustable weight function based on memory size, recomputation time, and age of information, helps to determine the best information to keep within the available memory space.

The main conclusion we can draw from our scheme and its current results is that the entire visibility could be handled efficiently using only ray paths. This information does not require so much memory for the important gains it provides. All remaining memory can be used to speed up specific changes, by building various structures such as color trees, ray trees, and tunnels. Their respective memory spaces can be managed adaptively according to local changes. We expect the benefits of efficient incremental re-rendering to lead to more advanced interactive systems, since processing time can be concentrated on the phenomena the user is interested in, rather than on redundant rendering.

Color Change	SDP without groups	SDP with groups	Only ray paths	1% ray trees	10% ray trees	All ray trees	Color tree	Compression
leaves color left tree	1.5	1.1	4.65	4.45	1.26	1.26	0.28	0.23
highlight left sphere	1.5	1.1	0.94	0.66	0.52	0.52	0.12	0.09
marble color on Beethoven	1.91	1.43	8.36	7.78	5.09	4.91	0.35	0.32
ground color	2.17	1.59	7.60	7.28	4.50	2.49	0.47	0.44
Optical Change								
index of refraction	1.53	1.12	8.55	8.51	8.47	8.47	—	—

Geometrical Change	removing	rendering		
		all ray trees (0 / 1 / 2) tunnels	10% ray trees (0 / 1 / 2) tunnels	1% ray trees (0 / 1 / 2) tunnels
transform central sphere	51.0	37.8/ 8.8/7.8	82.9/11.4/7.8	88.8/16.2/12.4
move left colored cow	111.0	38.4/13.3/12.2	79.2/13.3/12.3	85.0/17.0/14.5
move refractive sphere	12.6	39.4/ 6.0/5.7	85.6/ 6.2/5.7	90.5/ 6.9/6.4
flying furthest tree	10.0	38.5/16.0/13.8	76.0/16.0/13.8	80.5/22.0/19.0

Table 3: Statistics on changes (times in seconds)

7 Future Work

The current system suggests some interesting avenues to investigate. It could be easily extended to render efficiently animated sequences from a fixed camera when a limited number of objects are moving. It should be possible to exploit time coherency from our knowledge of all motions.

The hierarchical structures, ray tracing rendering and weight functions provide essential information about what is changing with respect to all previously computed information. All this knowledge makes the system a potential candidate for well balanced workload distribution in parallel processing, and memory management. For instance, the use of a large storage device provides an alternate solution to the memory usage for higher image resolution. Such a virtual storage has typically slower access time that can however be factored in the information weight when it is removed from the prime memory. So faster access memory acts then as cache which we could manage accordingly.

The structures can also be used for other purposes. The similarity between image formation and light propagation [1] suggests to use the ray paths only for light preprocessing in order to handle the high memory requirements to reduce the aliasing effects. The incremental updating for changing scene geometry should avoid much unnecessary lighting recomputations. Furthermore, the beam-like shape of tunnels suggests a way to estimate the contribution of participating media, coherent ray tracing, and image filtering.

Acknowledgments

We would like to thank Chris Romanzin and Neil Stewart for their help. We acknowledge financial support from NSERC, FCAR, the Université de Montréal, and Taarna Studios.

References

[1] James Arvo. Backward ray tracing. SIGGRAPH 86 Tutorial notes on Developments in Ray Tracing, August 1986.

[2] Robert L. Cook. Shade trees. Proceedings of SIGGRAPH 84. In *Computer Graphics*, 18, 3 (July 1984), pp. 223–231.

[3] Franklin C. Crow. Shadow algorithms for computer graphics. Proceedings of SIGGRAPH 77. In *Computer Graphics*, 11, 2 (July 1977), pp. 242–248.

[4] Thomas A. Funkhouser and Carlo H. Séquin. Adaptive display algorithm for interactive frame rates during visualization of complex virtual environments. Proceedings of SIGGRAPH 93. In *Computer Graphics* Proceedings, Annual Conference Series, August 1993, pp. 247–254.

[5] Ned Greene. Applications of world projections. Proceedings of Graphics Interface 86, (May 1986), pp. 108–114.

[6] Ned Greene. Detecting intersection of a rectangular solid and a convex polyhedron. In Paul Heckbert, editor, *Graphics Gems IV*, pages 74–82. Academic Press, Boston, 1994.

[7] Ned Greene and M. Kass. Hierarchical Z-buffer visibility. Proceedings of SIGGRAPH 93. In *Computer Graphics* Proceedings, Annual Conference Series, August 1993, pp. 231–240.

[8] Brian Guenter, Todd B. Knoblock, and Erik Ruf. Specializing shaders. Proceedings of SIGGRAPH 95. In *Computer Graphics* Proceedings, Annual Conference Series, August 1995, pp. 343–350.

[9] Eric Haines and John Wallace. Shaft culling for efficient ray-traced radiosity. In *Eurographics Workshop on Rendering*, 1991.

[10] Pat Hanrahan and Paul E. Haeberli. Direct WYSIWYG painting and texturing on 3D shapes. Proceedings of SIGGRAPH 90. In *Computer Graphics*, 24, 4 (August 1990), pp. 215–223.

[11] David A. Jevans. Object space temporal coherence for ray tracing. Proceedings of Graphics Interface 92, (May 1992), pp. 176–183.

[12] Peter Litwinowicz and Gavin Miller. Efficient techniques for interactive texture placement. Proceedings of SIGGRAPH 94. In *Computer Graphics* Proceedings, Annual Conference Series, July 1994, pp. 119–122.

[13] K. Murakami and K. Hirota. Incremental ray tracing. In *Eurographics Workshop on Photosimulation, Realism and Physics in Computer Graphics*, June 1989, pp. 17–32.

[14] Mark Segal, Carl Korobkin, Rolf van Widenfelt, Jim Foran, and Paul E. Haeberli. Fast shadows and lighting effects using texture mapping. Proceedings of SIGGRAPH 92. In *Computer Graphics*, 26, 2 (July 1992), pp. 249–252.

[15] Carlo H. Séquin and Eliot K. Smyrl. Parameterized ray tracing. Proceedings of SIGGRAPH 89. In *Computer Graphics*, 23, 3 (July 1989), pp. 307–314.

[16] Alan Watt and Mark Watt. *Advanced Animation and Rendering Techniques: Theory and Practice*. Addison-Wesley Publishing Company, 1992.

[17] Turner Whitted. An improved illumination model for shaded display. *Communications of the ACM*, 23(6):343–349, June 1980.

[18] Lance Williams. Casting curved shadows on curved surfaces. Proceedings of SIGGRAPH 78. In *Computer Graphics*, 12, (August 1978), pp. 270–274.

Interactive Multiresolution Surface Viewing

Andrew Certain[‡] *Jovan Popović* *Tony DeRose* *Tom Duchamp**
David Salesin *Werner Stuetzle*[†]

Department of Computer Science and Engineering
*Department of Mathematics
[†]Department of Statistics
University of Washington

Abstract

Multiresolution analysis has been proposed as a basic tool supporting compression, progressive transmission, and level-of-detail control of complex meshes in a unified and theoretically sound way.

We extend previous work on multiresolution analysis of meshes in two ways. First, we show how to perform multiresolution analysis of colored meshes by separately analyzing shape and color. Second, we describe efficient algorithms and data structures that allow us to incrementally construct lower resolution approximations to colored meshes from the geometry and color wavelet coefficients at interactive rates. We have integrated these algorithms in a prototype mesh viewer that supports progressive transmission, dynamic display at a constant frame rate independent of machine characteristics and load, and interactive choice of tradeoff between the amount of detail in geometry and color. The viewer operates as a helper application to Netscape, and can therefore be used to rapidly browse and display complex geometric models stored on the World Wide Web.

CR Categories and Subject Descriptors: I.3.5 [Computer Graphics]: Computational Geometry and Object Modeling — surfaces and object representations; J.6 [Computer-Aided Engineering]: Computer-Aided Design (CAD).

Additional Keywords: Geometric modeling, wavelets, multiresolution analysis, texture mapping, viewer.

1 Introduction

Three-dimensional meshes of large complexity are rapidly becoming commonplace. Laser scanning systems, for example, routinely produce geometric models with hundreds of thousands of vertices, each of which may contain additional information, such as color.

Working with such complex meshes poses a number of problems. They require a large amount of storage and consequently are slow to transmit. Additionally, they contain more faces than can be interactively displayed on any current hardware.

Existing viewers either do not deal with these problems at all, or do so only in crude ways, for example by showing wireframes or by displaying only a fraction of the faces during dynamic viewing, and then switching back to surfaces once the motion has stopped.

[‡]Department of Computer Science and Engineering,
University of Washington, Box 352350, Seattle, WA 98195-2350

A more sophisticated way of coping with both the transmission and dynamic display problems is to use a precomputed sequence of lower detail approximations to the mesh. Such approximations can be computed, for example, using the method of Rossignac and Borrel [9]. During transmission, a cruder approximation is displayed while the next more detailed approximation is received. For dynamic display, one chooses the highest detail approximation compatible with a desired frame rate.

A major disadvantage of this approach is that the total amount of data that has to be transmitted and stored is larger than the description of the full resolution mesh. In fact, there is a tradeoff between granularity (the difference in resolution between successive models) on the one hand and transmission time and storage requirements on the other hand.

Previous work [1, 5, 6, 10] has demonstrated that, at least in principle, multiresolution analysis offers a unified and theoretically sound way of dealing with these problems. A multiresolution representation of a mesh consists of a simple approximation called the base mesh, together with a sequence of correction terms called wavelet coefficients which supply the missing detail. The key point is that truncated sequences of wavelet coefficients define approximations to the mesh with fewer faces.

Although promising, previous work is lacking in at least two ways. First, either color or geometry were represented in multiresolution form, but not both. Second, algorithms for reconstructing and displaying multiresolution meshes were much too slow for interactive use.

In this paper we address both of these deficiencies. We deal with complex colored meshes using separate multiresolution representations for geometry and color that are combined only at display time. We also describe efficient algorithms and data structures that allow us to incrementally construct and render lower resolution approximations to the mesh from the color and geometry wavelet coefficients at interactive rates.

The separation of color and geometry, together with our incremental algorithms, allows the efficient implementation of the following features:

- ***Progressive transmission:*** We first transmit and display the base mesh and then transmit the wavelet coefficients in decreasing order of magnitude. As wavelets are received, they are incorporated into the approximation, and the approximation is periodically re-rendered. In the examples we have tried the approximation rapidly converges to the original mesh (see Color Plates 1(a–d)). Only a small penalty is incurred for progressive transmission (see Section 5.1).
- ***Performance tuning:*** By truncating the color and geometry expansions we can obtain lower detail approximations of the mesh with essentially any desired number of faces. During dynamic

display, we truncate the expansions at a level of detail that can be rendered with the desired frame rate. We monitor the frame rate and dynamically modify the level of detail in response to changing machine load.

- ***Automatic texture map generation:*** The separation between color and geometry and the way in which they are represented allows us to take advantage of texture-mapping hardware, as described in Section 3.3. Color Plates 1(g) and 1(h) illustrate the gains obtained by exploiting texture mapping. For a given number of polygons, texture mapping allows display of a far better approximation (Color Plate 1(h)), as all the polygons can be dedicated to capturing geometric detail. Color can always be displayed at full resolution because adding color detail does not increase the polygon count.
- ***Adapting to user preferences:*** Color and geometry expansions can be truncated independently. In the absence of texture mapping, the number of faces of the resulting mesh will depend on the truncation thresholds. There will in general be many combinations of color threshold and geometry threshold that result in approximately the same number of faces (see Color Plates 1(e–g)). Automatically finding the combination giving the "best looking" approximation seems to be a hard problem, as it will certainly depend on the model itself. Instead, we allow the user to interactively choose the tradeoff.

To demonstrate our ideas, we have built a prototype viewer running as a helper application for Netscape. As demonstrated in the accompanying videotape, our viewer can be used to rapidly browse and display complex geometric models stored on the World Wide Web.

The rest of the paper is organized as follows. In Section 2 we present a brief summary of multiresolution analysis of colored meshes. In Section 3 we describe the basic data structures and algorithms for efficiently constructing and rendering truncated models. In Section 4 we sketch the architecture of our viewer. In Section 5 we present the results of several numerical experiments. Finally, Section 6 contains a discussion and ideas for future work.

2 Background

In this section we first present a synopsis of multiresolution analysis for piecewise linear functions on triangular meshes. For a more complete exposition, see Stollnitz *et al.* [11]. We then describe how to convert an arbitrary colored mesh to a parametric form amenable to multiresolution analysis.

2.1 Multiresolution analysis

The central idea of multiresolution analysis is to decompose a function into a low resolution ("coarse") part and a sequence of correction ("detail") terms at increasing resolutions. Multiresolution analysis for functions on $\mathbf{R}^n$ was formalized by Meyer [8] and Mallat [7]. Lounsbery [5] and Lounsbery *et al.* [6] extended multiresolution analysis to a class of functions including functions defined on triangular meshes, which we call *level J piecewise linear.* A function f defined on a triangular mesh M^0 is called level J piecewise linear if it is piecewise linear on the mesh M^J obtained by performing J recursive 4-to-1 subdivisions of the faces of M^0 (see Figure 1).

Let $\hat{V}^j$ denote the vector space of level j piecewise linear functions on M^0. Let $\hat{\phi}_i^j$ denote the unique level j piecewise linear function assuming value 1 at vertex i and value 0 at all other vertices of M^j. These *level j hat functions* form a basis of $\hat{V}^j$. In the context of multiresolution analysis they are often referred to as *scaling functions.* The spaces $\hat{V}^0, \hat{V}^1, \ldots$ form a nested sequence, as required by multiresolution analysis.

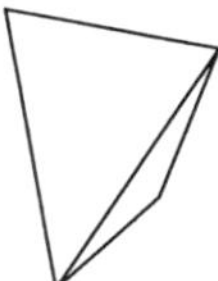 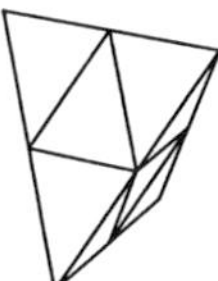 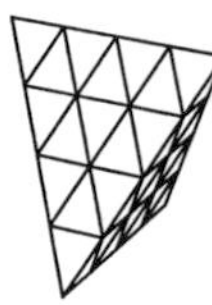

Figure 1 Recursive 4-to-1 splitting of a tetrahedron: (a) M^0, (b) M^1, (c) M^2.

Besides a nested sequence of spaces, the other basic ingredient of multiresolution analysis is an inner product. We use the inner product

$$\langle f \mid g \rangle = \sum_T \int_{\mathbf{x} \in T} f(\mathbf{x})\, g(\mathbf{x})\, d\mathbf{x},$$

where the sum is taken over all faces of M^0 and $d\mathbf{x}$ is the area element, normalized so that all faces of M^0 have unit area.

Given a nested sequence of function spaces and an inner product, we can now define wavelets. The orthogonal complements $\hat{W}^j$ of $\hat{V}^j$ in $\hat{V}^{j+1}$, for $0 \le j < J$, are called orthogonal *wavelet spaces.* A *wavelet basis* for $\hat{V}^J$ consists of the level 0 scaling functions, together with bases for the wavelet spaces $\hat{W}^0, \ldots, \hat{W}^{J-1}$. Given such a wavelet basis, we can express any level J piecewise linear function f on M^0 as a linear combination of scaling functions and wavelets at various levels.

Ideally we would like the wavelets, together with the level 0 scaling functions, to form an orthonormal basis for $\hat{V}^J$. We could then calculate the best k term L^2 approximation to a function $f \in \hat{V}^J$ by keeping the k terms of the expansion with the largest coefficients. On the other hand, we want wavelets to have small support so that the contribution to the approximation from each wavelet term can be rapidly incorporated into the model. Unfortunately, orthogonality of wavelet spaces and small spatial support of wavelets are conflicting goals. As small spatial support is essential for applications, we relax the orthogonality requirement.

Lounsbery *et al.* [6] stipulate *a priori* the size k of the support and then construct *biorthogonal wavelets* $\hat{\psi}_i^j$ that span $\hat{W}^j$ and are as orthogonal as possible to $\hat{V}^j$. The wavelets obtained in this way are called *k-disk wavelets* [11].

More precisely, consider a vertex i of M^{j+1} that is located at the midpoint of an edge e of M^j. The *k-disk wavelet* centered at vertex i is a function of the form

$$\hat{\psi}_i^j = \hat{\phi}_i^{j+1} + \sum_{v \in N_k} s_v^j \hat{\phi}_v^j, \tag{1}$$

where N_k denotes a set of level j vertices in a neighborhood of vertex i. The neighborhoods N_k are defined recursively. The neighborhood N_0 for the 0-disk wavelet consists of the endpoints of e; the neighborhood N_k contains the vertices of all triangles incident on N_{k-1} (see Figure 2). The wavelet consisting of only the level $j+1$ scaling function is called the *lazy wavelet.*

The coefficients s_{iv}^j are chosen to minimize the norm of the orthogonal projection of $\hat{\psi}_i^j$ onto $\hat{V}^j$. They are determined by solving the following system of linear equations:

$$\sum_{v \in N_k} \langle \hat{\phi}_u^j \mid \hat{\phi}_v^j \rangle\, s_{iv}^j = -\langle \hat{\phi}_u^j \mid \hat{\phi}_i^{j+1} \rangle, \quad \text{for all } u \in N_k.$$

Note that the system is local to vertex i. The size of the system for 0-disk wavelets is only 2×2. For larger values of k the size of the system depends on the valence of the parent vertices; in regular regions of the mesh where all vertices have valence 6, the system has size 10×10 for $k = 1$, and size 24×24 for $k = 2$.

The process of expressing a level J piecewise linear function in terms of level 0 scaling functions and wavelets is called *filterbank analysis*. For a description see Stollnitz *et al.* [11].

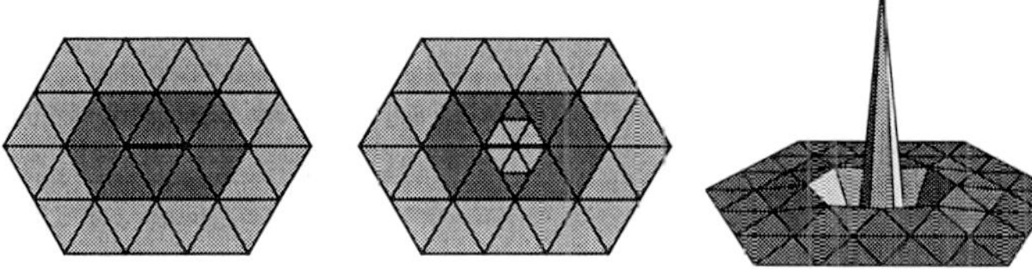

Figure 2 (a) The support of the 1-disk wavelet $\hat{\psi}_i^j$. Dark shaded area: N_0-neighborhood of center edge; light shaded area: faces added to form N_1-neighborhood. (b) The triangles required to introduce $\hat{\psi}_i^j$ during reconstruction. (c) The graph of $\hat{\psi}_i^j$.

2.2 Conversion of colored meshes to multiresolution form

Multiresolution analysis of a colored mesh M is based on the premise that M is defined parametrically by two vector valued level J piecewise linear functions, a *geometry function* f_{geom} and a *color function* f_{color}, each mapping a triangular *base mesh* M^0 into $\mathbf{R}^3$.

Typically, M will not be given in this form, but instead in the form of vertices, edges, and faces, vertex positions, and vertex colors. In order to apply multiresolution analysis, M must be converted to parametric form. We do this by first applying the remeshing algorithm of Eck *et al.* [1]. The output of the remeshing algorithm is a base mesh M^0 with a relatively small number of faces, a parameterization $\rho : M^0 \to M$, and an approximation of ρ by a level J piecewise linear embedding $f_{geom} : M^0 \to \mathbf{R}^3$ of the form $f_{geom} = \sum_i f_i \hat{\phi}_i^J$, where f_i are vectors in $\mathbf{R}^3$ representing the geometric positions of the vertices of M^J.

We next apply the filter bank analysis algorithm of Lounsbery *et al.* [6] to obtain a wavelet expansion of f_{geom}. Note that this analysis will generate a vector of three coefficients for each wavelet, one for each of the three coordinate functions. We sort these coefficient vectors in order of decreasing length and then store them together with identifiers for the wavelets (center vertex and level) in a file called the *geometry-wavelet file*.

We now turn to multiresolution analysis of color. Color is originally given at the vertices of M, and can be extended to all of M by linear interpolation. The parametrization $\rho : M^0 \to M$ obtained during remeshing induces a color function γ on M^0. To construct a level J piecewise linear approximation f_{color} to γ, we sample γ at the vertices of M^J. As in the case of geometry, we then compute the wavelet expansion of f_{color} by filterbank analysis and store the wavelet coefficient vectors in order of decreasing length in a *color-wavelet file*.

The base mesh M^0, its vertex positions (the coefficients of the level 0 scaling functions in the expansion of f_{geom}) and its vertex colors are stored in a *base file*. The geometry-wavelet file, the color-wavelet file, and the base file constitute the input to our multiresolution viewer.

3 Algorithms and data structures

In this section we describe the algorithms and data structures that form the basis of our multiresolution viewer. We assume that the colored mesh is represented in multiresolution form, i.e., by a base mesh and wavelet expansions of the color and geometry functions.

At the full resolution, the number of faces of M^J is 4^J times the number of faces of M^0. The faces of M^J can be naturally organized into a tree Q. The root of Q has as many children as there are faces in the base mesh, while every other internal node has four children. Each leaf of Q corresponds to a face of M^J. This tree organization was also used by Schroeder and Sweldens [10]. The mesh is rendered by traversing the tree Q, evaluating f_{geom} and f_{color} at the vertices, and generating a colored triangle for each leaf.

In the absence of texture-mapping hardware, color and geometry are handled identically, so we will couch the discussion in terms of geometry alone. The use of texture mapping is the topic of Section 3.3.

First some terminology: let f_{geom}^r denote the approximation to f_{geom} obtained by summing the scaling functions and the largest r wavelets, and let Q^r denote the smallest subtree of Q we for which f_{geom}^r is linear on each leaf.

For progressive transmission we first transmit the base mesh M^0 and the coefficients of the level 0 scaling functions. The associated tree Q^0 consists only of the root node and as many leaves as there are faces in the base mesh. As wavelets arrive, we incrementally grow Q^r and update f_{geom}^r, and periodically render the mesh.

Use of the wavelet representation for performance tuned viewing and level-of-detail control is based on the observation that for small r, the tree Q^r will also be small, and therefore rendering Q^r will result in many fewer triangles than rendering Q. In principle we could generate approximations with almost any desired number of faces by growing from the base mesh. For efficiency reasons we cache trees and vertex positions for a sequence of approximations, and then grow the desired tree from the closest approximation with fewer than the desired number of faces.

3.1 Data structures

As previously stated, the primary data structure used to represent the mesh is a tree Q, which has as many descendents from the root as there are faces in the base mesh and is a quadtree for all other levels.

We represent all nodes of Q, except for the root, with the following data structure:

```
type Face = record
    level: Integer
    children[4]: array of pointer to Face
    cornerVertex[3]: array of pointer to Vertex
    edgeVertex[3]: array of pointer to Vertex
end record
```

A face is said to be *of level j* if it is a face of M^j. The array *cornerVertex* has pointers to three vertices of the face, and the array *edgeVertex* has pointers to three vertices that subdivide the edges of this face.

We represent vertices with the following data structure:

```
type Vertex = record
    parentV[2]: array of pointer to Vertex
    parentF[2]: array of pointer to Face
    fGeom: XYZposition
    fColor: RGBcolor
    g: XYZvector
    hGeom[ ]: array of HatFunctionCoefficients
    hColor[ ]: array of HatFunctionCoefficients
end record
```

The array *parentV* contains pointers to the two vertices on either end of the edge that the vertex subdivides — these are called *parent vertices* of the vertex. The array *parentF* contains pointers to the two faces on either side of the edge that the vertex subdivides — these are called the *parent faces* of the vertex. A vertex is said to be *of level j* if it was created at the j-th level of subdivision, i.e., if its parent faces are of level $j-1$. The fields *fGeom* and *fColor* contain the values of f^r_{geom} and f^r_{color} at the vertex. The role of *hGeom* and *hColor* is explained in Section 3.2.

Vertices of level $j > 0$ are indexed by the base face they lie in, together with their barycentric coordinates within the face. As it is often necessary to find the node representing a vertex from its index, we maintain an auxiliary hash table that maps vertex indices to vertex nodes. Whenever a vertex is created, it is added to the table.

3.2 Algorithms

Suppose we have already constructed the face tree Q^r and evaluated f^r_{geom} at all its vertices. Adding a wavelet requires growing Q^r into Q^{r+1} and evaluating f^{r+1}_{geom}. For efficiency reasons we do not re-evaluate f^{r+1}_{geom} for every new wavelet. Instead we *gather* a sequence of s wavelets, then *evaluate* f^{r+s}_{geom} when the new mesh is rendered. We now describe the gather and evaluate stages.

3.2.1 The gather stage

Gathering a wavelet $\hat{\psi}^j_i$ with wavelet coefficient d^j_i involves three steps:

1. Decompose the term $\hat{\psi}^j_i$ into a sum of hat functions at level j and $j+1$ according to Equation (1).
2. For each hat function in the decomposition, grow the current face tree to accommodate it. A face tree is said to *accommodate* a function if the function is linear over each face. This process is described more fully below.
3. For each hat function in the decomposition $\hat{\phi}^{j'}_v$, $j' = j, j+1$, centered at vertex v, update the *hGeom* field of v: $v.hGeom[j'] \mathrel{+}= d^j_i s^{j'}_v$, where $s^{j'}_v$ is the coefficient of $\hat{\phi}^{j'}_v$ in the decomposition of step 1.

The most complicated part of gathering is growing the current face tree Q^r to accommodate a level j hat function $\hat{\phi}^j_v$ centered at a vertex v. We call a level j vertex *complete* if its parent faces have been subdivided. (By definition, all level 0 vertices are complete.) As each vertex has pointers to its two parent faces (nil if a parent face does not exist), it is easy to test a vertex for completeness.

Clearly, Q^r can accommodate a hat function $\hat{\phi}^j_v$ if the level j neighbors of vertex v are complete. Thus, there is a simple recursive procedure to make a vertex complete:

- Make its two parent vertices complete;
- Subdivide the two parent faces of the vertex.

Whenever a new vertex w is created in the completion process, f^r_{geom} is evaluated at the vertex, and the value is recorded in *w.fGeom*. Since f^r_{geom} is linear on the edges of Q^r, this evaluation is accomplished by averaging the *fGeom* values of w's parent vertices.

While this growing process is simple, it can generate more than the minimum number of triangles needed to accommodate a hat function (see Figure 3).

3.2.2 The evaluate stage

Recall that wavelets are added in two stages. In the *gather* stage the face tree is grown so that it contains all the faces necessary to accommodate the new wavelets. At this stage we also compute the values of the *current* approximation f^r_{geom} at the newly introduced vertex positions. The wavelets are decomposed into hat functions, and the coefficient arrays for their center vertices are updated. The new geometry function f^{r+s}_{geom} is not evaluated until the tree is rendered, at which time the contributions from all the hat functions are summed in a single tree traversal. We will now describe this evaluation stage.

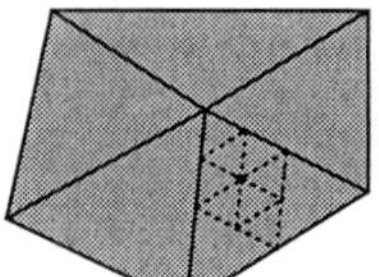
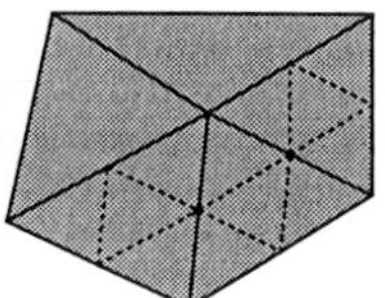
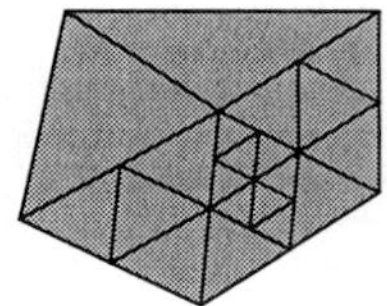

Figure 3 Making a vertex complete: (a) A vertex to be made complete. (The dashed faces are the minimal number that must be added to make the vertex complete.) (b) The parent vertices are created and made complete by subdividing their parent faces. (c) Subdividing the parent faces of the vertex makes it complete.

Let g denote the sum of all the hat functions gathered since the last evaluation stage, and let g_k denote the partial sum obtained by adding all the contributions from hat functions of level k or smaller. By construction $g = g_L$, where L is the maximum level of any leaf of Q^{r+s}. Note that since g_k is linear over the faces of level k and above, it is completely determined by its values at the vertices of Q^{r+s} of level k and less.

We now present an inductive procedure to compute the values of g_L at all of the vertices of Q^{r+s}.

It is easy to compute the values of g_0 at the level 0 vertices — they are the coefficients of the gathered level 0 hat functions.

Next we describe how to compute the values of g_{k+1} at all vertices of Q^{r+s} of level $k+1$ and smaller from the values of g_k at all vertices of level k and smaller. Let h^{k+1}_v denote the coefficient of the level $k+1$ hat function centered at v. If v is a vertex of level k or less, then $g_{k+1}(v) = g_k(v) + h^{k+1}_v$. If v is a level $k+1$ vertex, then it splits an edge connecting its two level k parent vertices, Therefore, $g_k(v)$ is the average of the values of g_k at its parent vertices, and $g_{k+1}(v) = g_k(v) + h^{k+1}_v$.

The calculation of g_L can be performed efficiently during a breadth first traversal of Q^{r+s}, as summarized in the pseudocode given in Figure 4.

3.3 Treatment of color

As mentioned earlier, in the absence of texture-mapping hardware color and geometry are handled identically: both color and geometry wavelets are gathered and evaluated as described in the previous section.

Representing colored meshes in multiresolution form makes it easy to exploit texture mapping hardware. The basic idea is to associate a region of texture memory with each face of the base mesh. If the full resolution model is subdivided to level J, a $2^J \times 2^J$ texture map is allocated, but only the lower diagonal is actually used. (To reduce the wasted texture memory, we pair adjacent base mesh faces whenever possible. We then allocate a square region of texture memory to the pair.)

Since geometry is represented parametrically by a piecewise linear function over M^J, there is a straightforward solution for the normally difficult problem of generating texture coordinates for arbitrary meshes. The texture coordinates for any vertex are simply the pre-image of the vertex under the parametrization. Therefore, the corner vertices of a base mesh face have texture coordinates (0,0), (1,0), and (0,1), and the texture coordinates for every other vertex are the average of its parents' coordinates. The image displayed in

```
procedure Evaluate()
    queue ← Level 0 faces
    do while queue != empty
        currentFace ← GetFirstFace(queue)
        currentLevel ← currentFace.level
        if IsSubdivided(currentFace) then
            for each cornerVertex v of currentFace do
                v.g += v.hGeom[currentLevel]
                v.hGeom[currentLevel] ← 0
            end for
            for each edgeVertex e of currentFace do
                if e has two parent faces then
                    { e will be visited twice, so add 1/2 per visit}
                    e.g += 0.25 (e.parentV[1].g+e.parentV[2].g)
                else
                    e.g += 0.5 (e.parentV[1].g+e.parentV[2].g)
                end if
            end for
            for each i ∈ 0, 1, 2, 3 do
                Append currentFaces.children[i] to queue
        else
            for each cornerVertex v of currentFace
                v.fGeom += v.g + v.hGeom[currentLevel]
                v.g ← v.hGeom[currentLevel] ← 0
            end for
            AddToDisplayList(currentFace)
        end if
    end while
end procedure
```

Figure 4

Figure 5 illustrates texture mapping. The base mesh has been rendered with only the scaling functions of f_{geom}, but with all of the terms of f_{color}.

The texture map associated with a face of the base mesh is initialized by linearly interpolating between the colors at the vertices of the face (i.e., the level 0 color scaling function coefficients). The texture map is updated as soon as color wavelets are received, essentially by "painting" the wavelet into the texture map. Since the addition of color wavelets does not increase the triangle count, systems with texture-mapping hardware color can always display color at its highest resolution.

4 Viewer Architecture

Our viewer, written in OpenGL and Motif for Silicon Graphics Iris workstations, is configured as a helper application for Netscape. When a multiresolution-surface link is followed, the viewer application opens an HTTP connection for the base mesh file. After receiving the base mesh, the viewer displays it in a graphics window (see Figure 5) and opens two parallel HTTP connections, one for the color wavelets file and one for the geometry wavelets file. As wavelet coefficients are received they are incorporated as described in Section 3, and the model is periodically redisplayed. Color Plates 1(a–d) illustrate a model at various stages of transmission. Assuming a 64Kbs link (ISDN speeds), the images shown represent, from top to bottom, the model after 3 seconds, 17 seconds, 59 seconds, and 180 seconds (the full model).

In standard operation, the quality of the model displayed in the viewer is controlled by the slider labeled *Frame Time*. When the user is rotating or translating the model, the viewer attempts to maintain that frame rate by measuring the polygon performance for the previous frames and predicting the desired model size for the upcoming frame. When there is no interaction, a more refined model is rendered, allowing the user to see more detail. If the refined model takes a significant time to render, the rendering is performed in stages, so that the viewer can check for user events during the rendering. If the user decides to interact with the model while the viewer is drawing a refined model, rendering is aborted, and the system returns to interactivity.

Plate	wavelet type	# geom wavelets	# color wavelets	# polys	L^2 error	L^∞ error
(a)	0-disk	770	830	4701	.0961	.3217
(b)	0-disk	4166	4445	22725	.0375	.0949
(c)	0-disk	14350	14605	56418	.0076	.0136
(d)	0-disk	49530	49530	98304	2.3e-6	1.92e-6
(e)	0-disk	114	811	3006	.2555	.5246
(f)	0-disk	371	567	3033	.1607	.3461
(g)	0-disk	743	324	3015	.1225	.2777
(h)	0-disk	774	49530	2994	.1203	.2777
(i)	Lazy	16380	16380	32760	6.7e-8	4.7e-7
(j)	Lazy	1254	1350	5561	.0099	.0503
(k)	0-disk	1129	1084	5510	.0075	.0459
(l)	2-disk	735	883	5573	.0092	.0676

Table 1 Statistics for Color Plate 1

The quality of the model can also be controlled in two other ways: the user can explicitly set either the number of geometry and color wavelets to be added to the base mesh, or the number of polygons to be used in creating the approximation.

If either the frame time or the number of polygons is specified, the tradeoff between color and geometry is controlled with the slider labeled *Color to Geom*. Moving the slider to the left indicates a preference for geometry detail, whereas moving it to the right indicates a preference for color detail. The tradeoff is shown in Color Plates 1(e–g), where (e) corresponds to a strong preference for color, (g) corresponds to a strong preference for geometry, and (f) corresponds to a balance between the two. Each of these model consists of the same number of Gouraud shaded polygons.

The color/geometry slider is only active on machines without texture-mapping hardware. If the machine has texture-mapping hardware, color wavelets do not increase the polygon count, so they are always included. Color Plate 1(h) shows the model that can be displayed for the same polygon budget used in Plates 1(e–g).

5 Results

In this section we present various statistics for the color plates, and we describe a number of numerical experiments we have performed.

Statistics for the color plates are summarized in Table 1. Three different types of wavelets were used as indicated by the second column. All examples were computed using the same type of wavelet for both color and geometry, although in principle different types of wavelets could be used. The other columns should be self-explanatory. The errors reported in the last two columns are normalized so that the crudest model has error 1.

In addition to using the viewer to create the color plates, we conducted a set of numerical experiments to compare the performance of four types of wavelets: lazy, 0-, 1-, and 2-disk wavelets. The experiments focused on the following factors:

- ***Convergence as a function of number of wavelet coefficients:*** For fixed network bandwidth, the rate at which the transmitted model approaches the original depends on how quickly the error decreases as a function of the number of wavelet coefficients.

  Figure 6 is a plot of L^2 error in geometry vs. number of coefficients for the various types of wavelets for the head model shown in Color Plates 1(e–h). The plot of L^∞ error is qualitatively similar. Similar results were obtained for the other two models.

  Our conclusion is that lazy wavelets perform slightly worse than

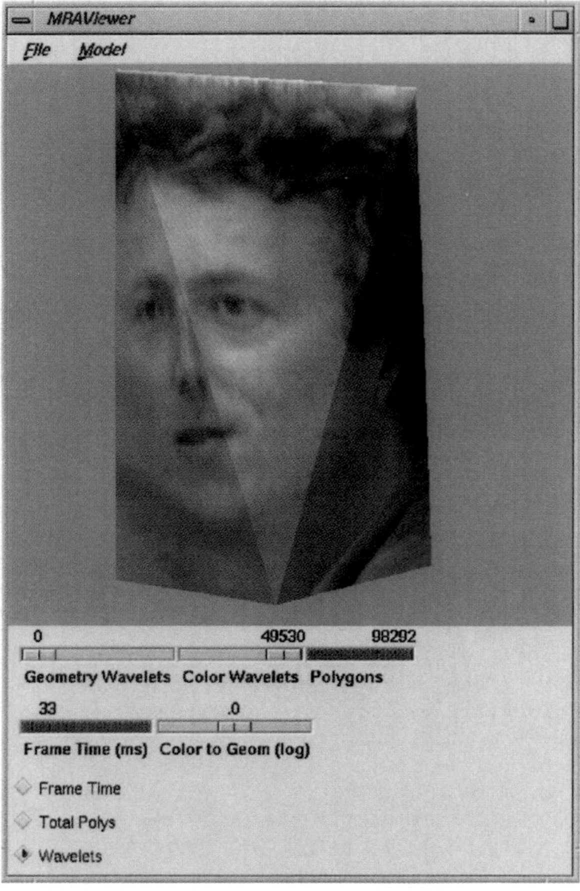

Figure 5 The multiresolution viewer.

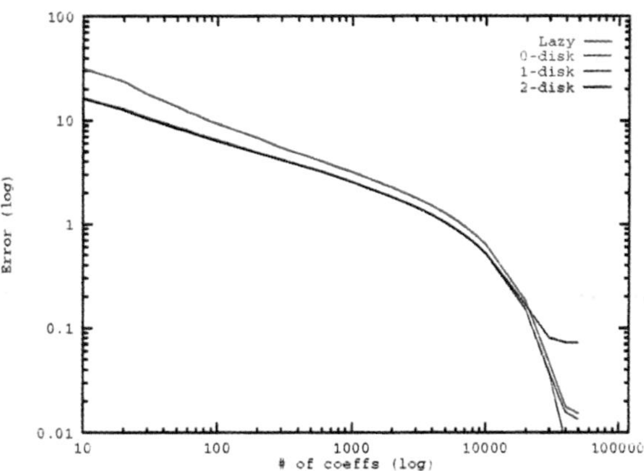

Figure 6 L^2 **error vs. number of wavelet coefficients.**

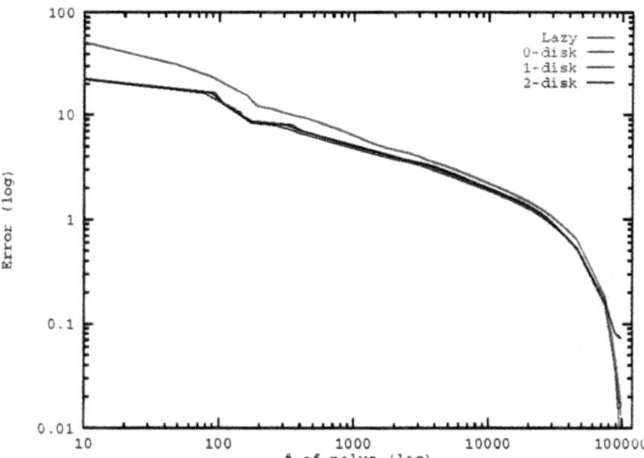

Figure 7 L^2 error vs. number of polygons.

k-disk wavelets, but there seems to be no significant difference between various values of k.

- ***Convergence as a function of number of polygons:*** For fixed polygon display rate and update frequency, the visual appearance of the model depends on how quickly the error decreases as a function of the number of polygons in the model.

  Figure 7 is a plot of the L^2 error vs. number of polygons for the same head model. Again, the corresponding plot for the L^∞ error is qualitatively similar.

  Color Plates 1(i–l) illustrate the visual fidelity for the earth model when different types of wavelets are used to produce a model with a fixed polygon count. Table 5 indicates that the error for this number of polygons is actually less for lazy wavelets than for 2-disk wavelets, due to the large number of polygons that a 2-disk wavelet may introduce. Color plate 1(i) is the full-resolution earth model, subdivided to level-6. The next three color plates, 1(j–l), depict the earth reconstructed to approximately 5500 polygons using lazy wavelets, 1(j), 0-disk wavelets, 1(k), and 2-disk wavelets, 1(l). Although there are visual differences between the images, it is not clear which is preferable.

  Our conclusion is again that lazy wavelets perform slightly worse than k-disk wavelets numerically, but there apparently is no significant difference between various values of k. Visually, there is no clear preference.

- ***Numerical stability:*** In the conversions to and from multiresolution form some numerical error is inevitable. While the numerical stability properties of orthogonal wavelet constructions are relatively well understood, stability of biorthogonal schemes like ours is less clear.

  Lacking theory to guide us, we ran the following experiment on the earth model. For each of the four types of wavelets we performed wavelet analysis followed by wavelet synthesis on a level $J = 6$ version of the model. For lazy wavelets, the relative error in the vertex positions was on the order of the machine precision. For 0-, 1-, and 2-disk wavelets, the relative errors were on the order of 0.00005, 0.001, and 0.002. When we reran the experiment using a level 3 version of the earth, the relative error for 2-disk wavelets was reduced to 1 in 10^6.

  Our conclusion is that wavelets with smaller supports are likely to be more stable numerically than those with larger ones, and that stability becomes increasingly important as the number of levels increases.

- ***Speed:*** Wavelets with larger support clearly take longer to add. There are potentially more new faces to introduce, and there are always a greater number of vertices whose hat function coefficients need to be updated. We ran a series of timing experiments and found that on average each type of wavelet could be added (the gather stage) at the following rate: lazy, 2700 coefficients per second; 0-disk, 2300; 1-disk, 1200; 2-disk, 600. The time for the evaluate stage was unchanged relative to wavelet size, which was expected.

Overall, we conclude that 0-disk wavelets combine good visual fidelity for a given number of coefficients and for a given number of polygons, with good numerical stability and computation time. These findings, however, are preliminary, and require further confirmation.

5.1 Data encoding

As mentioned in the introduction, there is a small penalty for representing a mesh in multiresolution form. Since the wavelet coefficients are sorted in magnitude order for progressive transmission, we need to transmit with each coefficient the vertex identifier for the center of the wavelet. This information could be made implicit if the complete model was transmitted before any processing or display took place.

We use a simple encoding which represents the coefficient for a color or geometry wavelet with three floating point numbers, together with a word of information for the vertex identifier. This represents a 33% penalty for the benefit of progressive transmission. A suggestion for reducing this penalty is described below.

6 Discussion and future work

We have extended previous work on multiresolution analysis of meshes in two ways. First, we have shown how to perform multiresolution analysis of colored meshes by separately analyzing shape and color. Second, we have developed efficient algorithms and data structures that allow us to incrementally construct lower resolution approximations to colored meshes at interactive rates.

We have integrated these algorithms in a prototype mesh viewer that supports progressive transmission, dynamic display at a constant frame rate independent of machine performance and load, and the ability to interactively trade off the amount of detail in geometry and color. The separation of geometry and color also allows us to make efficient use of texture-mapping hardware.

In future work we intend to investigate:

- ***Multiresolution editing:*** In analogy to Finkelstein and Salesin's work on multiresolution curves [2] we plan to extend our multiresolution viewer to allow editing of meshes at different levels of detail.
- ***Other wavelets:*** We currently use piecewise linear wavelets to represent geometry and color. When modeling smooth objects or objects without sharp color transitions, use of smooth wavelets may result in better compression.
- ***Automatic tradeoff between color and geometry:*** If there is no texture-mapping hardware, adding wavelets for either color or geometry will increase the number of polygons that have to be rendered. When there is an upper bound on the number of polygons, for example during dynamic viewing, one has to choose between color detail and geometry detail. Currently the tradeoff is left to the user. Heuristics for automatically choosing a tradeoff that results in a visually close approximation would be useful.
- ***Comparison to progressive meshes:*** In simultaneous work Hoppe [3] has introduced the notion of *progressive meshes* to address the difficulties of storage, transmission, and display of complex meshes. The basic idea is to record the changes a mesh optimizer [4] makes as it simplifies a mesh. Since the original mesh can be recovered by running the record of changes in reverse, the progressive mesh representation is the simplest mesh together with the record of changes in reverse order. The relative advantages and disadvantages of such an approach need further study.
- ***Better encoding:*** The wavelet coefficients for a particular model typically span a large dynamic range, making floating point an obvious choice for encoding their values. Better use of bandwidth and storage could be made, however, by taking advantage of the wavelets being sorted in magnitude order. Fixed point numbers could be transmitted for each coefficient, with the scale information being transmitted only as it changes. This improvement could potentially eliminate the overhead incurred for progressive transmission.

Acknowledgments

This work was supported in part by the National Science Foundation under grants CCR-8957323, DMS-9103002, and DMS-9402734, by an Alfred P. Sloan Research Fellowship (BR-3495), an NSF Presidential Faculty Fellow award (CCR-9553199), an ONR Young Investigator award (N00014-95-1-0728), and industrial gifts from Interval, Microsoft, and Xerox. Head models courtesy of Cyberware.

References

[1] Matthias Eck, Tony DeRose, Tom Duchamp, Hugues Hoppe, Michael Lounsbery, and Werner Stuetzle. Multiresolution analysis of arbitrary meshes. In Robert Cook, editor, *SIGGRAPH 95 Conference Proceedings*, Annual Conference Series, pages 173–182. ACM SIGGRAPH, Addison Wesley, August 1995. held in Los Angeles, California, 06-11 August 1995.

[2] Adam Finkelstein and David Salesin. Multiresolution curves. *Computer Graphics (SIGGRAPH '94 Proceedings)*, 28(3):261–268, July 1994.

[3] H. Hoppe. Progressive meshes. In *SIGGRAPH 96 Conference Proceedings*, Annual Conference Series. ACM SIGGRAPH, Addison Wesley, August 1996. held in New Orleans, Louisiana, 04-09 August 1996.

[4] H. Hoppe, T. DeRose, T. Duchamp, J. McDonald, and W. Stuetzle. Mesh optimization. In J.T. Kajiya, editor, *SIGGRAPH 93 Conference Proceedings*, Annual Conference Series, pages 19–26. ACM SIGGRAPH, Addison Wesley, August 1993. held in Anaheim, California, 01-06 August 1993.

[5] J. Michael Lounsbery. *Multiresolution Analysis for Surfaces of Arbitrary Topological Type*. PhD thesis, Department of Computer Science and Engineering, University of Washington, September 1994. Available as ftp://cs.washington.edu/pub/graphics/LounsPhd.ps.Z.

[6] Michael Lounsbery, Tony DeRose, and Joe Warren. Multiresolution analysis for surfaces of arbitrary topological type. *Submitted for publication*, 1994. Preliminary version available as Technical Report 93-10-05b, Department of Computer Science and Engineering, University of Washington, January, 1994. Also available as ftp://cs.washington.edu/pub/graphics/TR931005b.ps.Z.

[7] Stephane Mallat. A theory for multiresolution signal decomposition: The wavelet representation. *IEEE Transactions on Pattern Analysis and Machine Intelligence*, 11(7):674–693, July 1989.

[8] Yves Meyer. Ondelettes et fonctions splines. Technical report, *Séminaire EDP*, École Polytechnique, Paris, 1986.

[9] J. Rossignac and P. Borrel. Multi-resolution 3D approximations for rendering. In B. Falcidieno and T.L. Kunii, editors, *Modeling in Computer Graphics*, pages 455–465. Springer-Verlag, June-July 1993.

[10] Peter Schröder and Wim Sweldens. Spherical wavelets: Efficiently representing functions on the sphere. In Robert Cook, editor, *SIGGRAPH 95 Conference Proceedings*, Annual Conference Series, pages 161–172. ACM SIGGRAPH, Addison Wesley, August 1995. held in Los Angeles, California, 06-11 August 1995.

[11] Eric Stollnitz, Tony DeRose, and David Salesin. *Wavelets for Computer Graphics: Theory and Applications*. Morgan–Kaufmann, 1996.

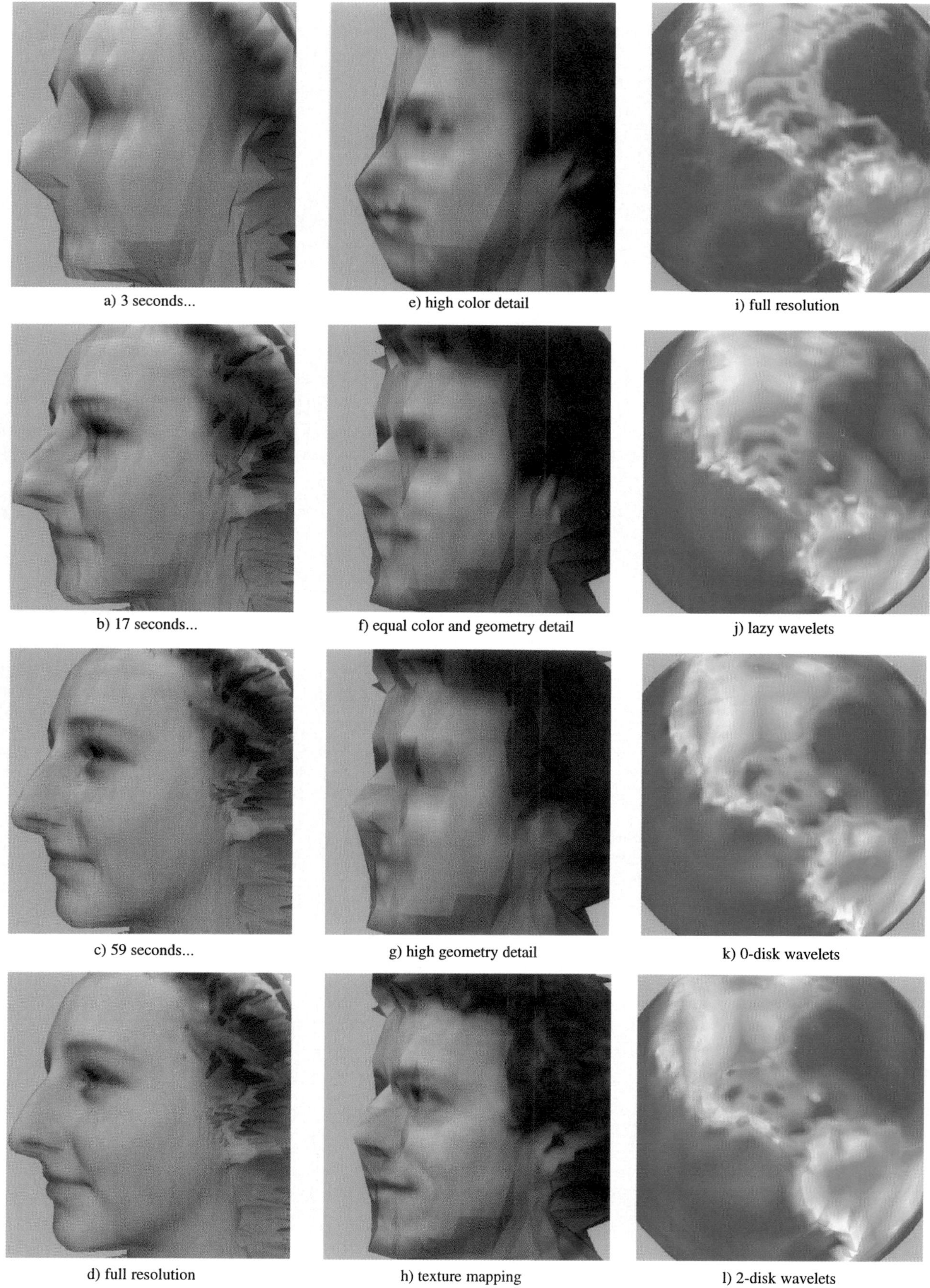

a) 3 seconds...

e) high color detail

i) full resolution

b) 17 seconds...

f) equal color and geometry detail

j) lazy wavelets

c) 59 seconds...

g) high geometry detail

k) 0-disk wavelets

d) full resolution

h) texture mapping

l) 2-disk wavelets

Color Plate 1

Progressive Meshes

Hugues Hoppe
Microsoft Research

ABSTRACT

Highly detailed geometric models are rapidly becoming commonplace in computer graphics. These models, often represented as complex triangle meshes, challenge rendering performance, transmission bandwidth, and storage capacities. This paper introduces the *progressive mesh* (PM) representation, a new scheme for storing and transmitting arbitrary triangle meshes. This efficient, lossless, continuous-resolution representation addresses several practical problems in graphics: smooth geomorphing of level-of-detail approximations, progressive transmission, mesh compression, and selective refinement.

In addition, we present a new mesh simplification procedure for constructing a PM representation from an arbitrary mesh. The goal of this optimization procedure is to preserve not just the geometry of the original mesh, but more importantly its overall appearance as defined by its discrete and scalar appearance attributes such as material identifiers, color values, normals, and texture coordinates. We demonstrate construction of the PM representation and its applications using several practical models.

CR Categories and Subject Descriptors: I.3.5 [Computer Graphics]: Computational Geometry and Object Modeling - surfaces and object representations.

Additional Keywords: mesh simplification, level of detail, shape interpolation, progressive transmission, geometry compression.

1 INTRODUCTION

Highly detailed geometric models are necessary to satisfy a growing expectation for realism in computer graphics. Within traditional modeling systems, detailed models are created by applying versatile modeling operations (such as extrusion, constructive solid geometry, and freeform deformations) to a vast array of geometric primitives. For efficient display, these models must usually be tessellated into polygonal approximations—meshes. Detailed meshes are also obtained by scanning physical objects using range scanning systems [5]. In either case, the resulting complex meshes are expensive to store, transmit, and render, thus motivating a number of practical problems:

Email: hhoppe@microsoft.com
Web: http://www.research.microsoft.com/research/graphics/hoppe/

- *Mesh simplification*: The meshes created by modeling and scanning systems are seldom optimized for rendering efficiency, and can frequently be replaced by nearly indistinguishable approximations with far fewer faces. At present, this process often requires significant user intervention. Mesh simplification tools can hope to automate this painstaking task, and permit the porting of a single model to platforms of varying performance.
- *Level-of-detail (LOD) approximation*: To further improve rendering performance, it is common to define several versions of a model at various levels of detail [3, 8]. A detailed mesh is used when the object is close to the viewer, and coarser approximations are substituted as the object recedes. Since instantaneous switching between LOD meshes may lead to perceptible "popping", one would like to construct smooth visual transitions, *geomorphs*, between meshes at different resolutions.
- *Progressive transmission*: When a mesh is transmitted over a communication line, one would like to show progressively better approximations to the model as data is incrementally received. One approach is to transmit successive LOD approximations, but this requires additional transmission time.
- *Mesh compression*: The problem of minimizing the storage space for a model can be addressed in two orthogonal ways. One is to use mesh simplification to reduce the number of faces. The other is mesh compression: minimizing the space taken to store a particular mesh.
- *Selective refinement*: Each mesh in a LOD representation captures the model at a uniform (view-independent) level of detail. Sometimes it is desirable to adapt the level of refinement in selected regions. For instance, as a user flies over a terrain, the terrain mesh need be fully detailed only near the viewer, and only within the field of view.

In addressing these problems, this paper makes two major contributions. First, it introduces the *progressive mesh* (PM) representation. In PM form, an arbitrary mesh $\hat{M}$ is stored as a much coarser mesh M^0 together with a sequence of n detail records that indicate how to incrementally refine M^0 exactly back into the original mesh $\hat{M} = M^n$. Each of these records stores the information associated with a *vertex split*, an elementary mesh transformation that adds an additional vertex to the mesh. The PM representation of $\hat{M}$ thus defines a continuous sequence of meshes $M^0, M^1, \ldots, M^n$ of increasing accuracy, from which LOD approximations of any desired complexity can be efficiently retrieved. Moreover, geomorphs can be efficiently constructed between any two such meshes. In addition, we show that the PM representation naturally supports progressive transmission, offers a concise encoding of $\hat{M}$ itself, and permits selective refinement. In short, progressive meshes offer an efficient, lossless, continuous-resolution representation.

The other contribution of this paper is a new simplification procedure for constructing a PM representation from a given mesh $\hat{M}$. Unlike previous simplification methods, our procedure seeks to preserve not just the geometry of the mesh surface, but more importantly its overall appearance, as defined by the discrete and scalar attributes associated with its surface.

2 MESHES IN COMPUTER GRAPHICS

Models in computer graphics are often represented using triangle meshes.[1] Geometrically, a triangle mesh is a piecewise linear surface consisting of triangular faces pasted together along their edges. As described in [9], the mesh geometry can be denoted by a tuple (K, V), where K is a *simplicial complex* specifying the connectivity of the mesh simplices (the adjacency of the vertices, edges, and faces), and $V = \{\mathbf{v}_1, \ldots, \mathbf{v}_m\}$ is the set of vertex positions defining the shape of the mesh in $\mathbf{R}^3$. More precisely (cf. [9]), we construct a parametric domain $|K| \subset \mathbf{R}^m$ by identifying each vertex of K with a canonical basis vector of $\mathbf{R}^m$, and define the mesh as the image $\phi_V(|K|)$ where $\phi_V : \mathbf{R}^m \to \mathbf{R}^3$ is a linear map.

Often, surface appearance attributes other than geometry are also associated with the mesh. These attributes can be categorized into two types: *discrete* attributes and *scalar* attributes.

Discrete attributes are usually associated with faces of the mesh. A common discrete attribute, the *material identifier*, determines the shader function used in rendering a face of the mesh [18]. For instance, a trivial shader function may involve simple look-up within a specified texture map.

Many scalar attributes are often associated with a mesh, including diffuse color (r, g, b), normal (n_x, n_y, n_z), and texture coordinates (u, v). More generally, these attributes specify the local parameters of shader functions defined on the mesh faces. In simple cases, these scalar attributes are associated with vertices of the mesh. However, to represent discontinuities in the scalar fields, and because adjacent faces may have different shading functions, it is common to associate scalar attributes not with vertices, but with corners of the mesh [1]. A *corner* is defined as a (vertex,face) tuple. Scalar attributes at a corner (v,f) specify the shading parameters for face f at vertex v. For example, along a *crease* (a curve on the surface across which the normal field is not continuous), each vertex has two distinct normals, one associated with the corners on each side of the crease.

We express a mesh as a tuple $M = (K, V, D, S)$ where V specifies its geometry, D is the set of discrete attributes d_f associated with the faces $f = \{j, k, l\} \in K$, and S is the set of scalar attributes $s_{(v,f)}$ associated with the corners (v,f) of K.

The attributes D and S give rise to discontinuities in the visual appearance of the mesh. An edge $\{v_j, v_k\}$ of the mesh is said to be *sharp* if either (1) it is a boundary edge, or (2) its two adjacent faces f_l and f_r have different discrete attributes (i.e. $d_{f_l} \neq d_{f_r}$), or (3) its adjacent corners have different scalar attributes (i.e. $s_{(v_j,f_l)} \neq s_{(v_j,f_r)}$ or $s_{(v_k,f_l)} \neq s_{(v_k,f_r)}$). Together, the set of sharp edges define a set of *discontinuity curves* over the mesh (e.g. the yellow curves in Figure 12).

3 PROGRESSIVE MESH REPRESENTATION

3.1 Overview

Hoppe et al. [9] describe a method, *mesh optimization*, that can be used to approximate an initial mesh $\hat{M}$ by a much simpler one. Their optimization algorithm, reviewed in Section 4.1, traverses the space of possible meshes by successively applying a set of 3 mesh transformations: edge collapse, edge split, and edge swap.

We have discovered that in fact a single one of those transformations, *edge collapse*, is sufficient for effectively simplifying meshes. As shown in Figure 1, an edge collapse transformation $ecol(\{v_s, v_t\})$ unifies 2 adjacent vertices v_s and v_t into a single vertex v_s. The vertex v_t and the two adjacent faces $\{v_s, v_t, v_l\}$ and $\{v_t, v_s, v_r\}$ vanish in the process. A position $\mathbf{v}_s$ is specified for the new unified vertex.

[1] We assume in this paper that more general meshes, such as those containing n-sided faces and faces with holes, are first converted into triangle meshes by triangulation. The PM representation could be generalized to handle the more general meshes directly, at the expense of more complex data structures.

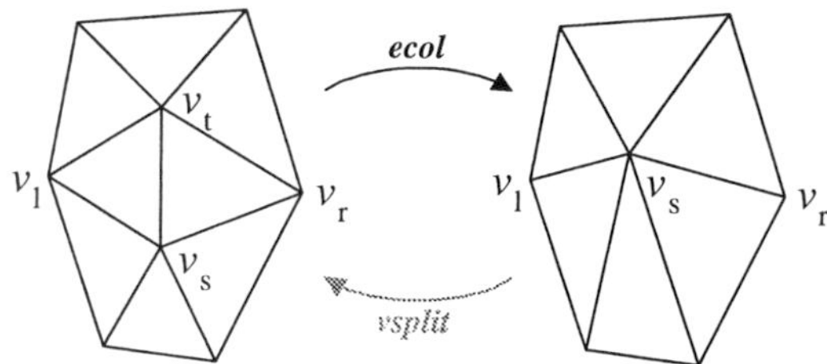

Figure 1: Illustration of the edge collapse transformation.

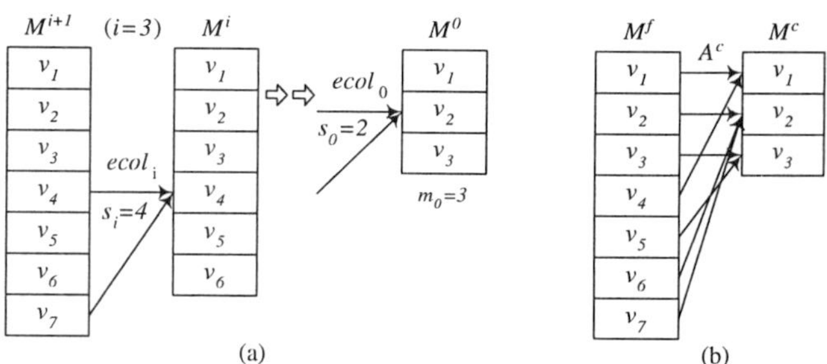

Figure 2: (a) Sequence of edge collapses; (b) Resulting vertex correspondence.

Thus, an initial mesh $\hat{M} = M^n$ can be simplified into a coarser mesh M^0 by applying a sequence of n successive edge collapse transformations:

$$(\hat{M}=M^n) \overset{ecol_{n-1}}{\longrightarrow} \ldots \overset{ecol_1}{\longrightarrow} M^1 \overset{ecol_0}{\longrightarrow} M^0 .$$

The particular sequence of edge collapse transformations must be chosen carefully, since it determines the quality of the approximating meshes $M^i, i < n$. A scheme for choosing these edge collapses is presented in Section 4.

Let m_0 be the number of vertices in M^0, and let us label the vertices of mesh M^i as $V^i = \{v_1, \ldots, v_{m_0+i}\}$, so that edge $\{v_{s_i}, v_{m_0+i+1}\}$ is collapsed by $ecol_i$ as shown in Figure 2a. As vertices may have different positions in the different meshes, we denote the position of v_j in M^i as $\mathbf{v}_j^i$.

A key observation is that an edge collapse transformation is invertible. Let us call that inverse transformation a *vertex split*, shown as *vsplit* in Figure 1. A vertex split transformation $vsplit(s, l, r, t, A)$ adds near vertex v_s a new vertex v_t and two new faces $\{v_s, v_t, v_l\}$ and $\{v_t, v_s, v_r\}$. (If the edge $\{v_s, v_t\}$ is a boundary edge, we let $v_r = 0$ and only one face is added.) The transformation also updates the attributes of the mesh in the neighborhood of the transformation. This attribute information, denoted by A, includes the positions $\mathbf{v}_s$ and $\mathbf{v}_t$ of the two affected vertices, the discrete attributes $d_{\{v_s,v_t,v_l\}}$ and $d_{\{v_t,v_s,v_r\}}$ of the two new faces, and the scalar attributes of the affected corners ($s_{(v_s,\cdot)}$, $s_{(v_t,\cdot)}$, $s_{(v_l,\{v_s,v_t,v_l\})}$, and $s_{(v_r,\{v_t,v_s,v_r\})}$).

Because edge collapse transformations are invertible, we can therefore represent an arbitrary triangle mesh $\hat{M}$ as a simple mesh M^0 together with a sequence of n *vsplit* records:

$$M^0 \overset{vsplit_0}{\longrightarrow} M^1 \overset{vsplit_1}{\longrightarrow} \ldots \overset{vsplit_{n-1}}{\longrightarrow} (M^n = \hat{M})$$

where each record is parametrized as $vsplit_i(s_i, l_i, r_i, A_i)$. We call $(M^0, \{vsplit_0, \ldots, vsplit_{n-1}\})$ a *progressive mesh* (PM) representation of $\hat{M}$.

As an example, the mesh $\hat{M}$ of Figure 5d (13,546 faces) was simplified down to the coarse mesh M^0 of Figure 5a (150 faces) using

6,698 edge collapse transformations. Thus its PM representation consists of M^0 together with a sequence of $n=6698$ *vsplit* records. From this PM representation, one can extract approximating meshes with any desired number of faces (actually, within ± 1) by applying to M^0 a prefix of the *vsplit* sequence. For example, Figure 5 shows approximating meshes with 150, 500, and 1000 faces.

3.2 Geomorphs

A nice property of the vertex split transformation (and its inverse, edge collapse) is that a smooth visual transition (a *geomorph*) can be created between the two meshes M^i and M^{i+1} in $M^i \xrightarrow{vsplit_i} M^{i+1}$. For the moment let us assume that the meshes contain no attributes other than vertex positions. With this assumption the vertex split record is encoded as $vsplit_i(s_i, l_i, r_i, A_i) = (\mathbf{v}_{s_i}^{i+1}, \mathbf{v}_{m_0+i+1}^{i+1})$. We construct a geomorph $M^G(\alpha)$ with blend parameter $0 \le \alpha \le 1$ such that $M^G(0)$ looks like M^i and $M^G(1)$ looks like M^{i+1}—in fact $M^G(1)=M^{i+1}$—by defining a mesh

$$M^G(\alpha) = (K^{i+1}, V^G(\alpha))$$

whose connectivity is that of M^{i+1} and whose vertex positions linearly interpolate from $v_{s_i} \in M^i$ to the split vertices $v_{s_i}, v_{m_0+i+1} \in M^{i+1}$:

$$\mathbf{v}_j^G(\alpha) = \begin{cases} (\alpha)\mathbf{v}_j^{i+1} + (1-\alpha)\mathbf{v}_{s_i}^i & , j \in \{s_i, m_0+i+1\} \\ \mathbf{v}_j^{i+1} = \mathbf{v}_j^i & , j \notin \{s_i, m_0+i+1\} \end{cases}$$

Using such geomorphs, an application can smoothly transition from a mesh M^i to meshes M^{i+1} or M^{i-1} without any visible "snapping" of the meshes.

Moreover, since individual *ecol* transformations can be transitioned smoothly, so can the composition of any sequence of them. Geomorphs can therefore be constructed between *any* two meshes of a PM representation. Indeed, given a finer mesh M^f and a coarser mesh M^c, $0 \le c < f \le n$, there exists a natural correspondence between their vertices: each vertex of M^f is related to a unique ancestor vertex of M^c by a surjective map A^c obtained by composing a sequence of *ecol* transformations (Figure 2b). More precisely, each vertex v_j of M^f corresponds with the vertex $v_{A^c(j)}$ in M^c where

$$A^c(j) = \begin{cases} j & , j \le m_0 + c \\ A^c(s_{j-m_0-1}) & , j > m_0 + c \end{cases}.$$

(In practice, this ancestor information A^c is gathered in a forward fashion as the mesh is refined.) This correspondence allows us to define a geomorph $M^G(\alpha)$ such that $M^G(0)$ looks like M^c and $M^G(1)$ equals M^f. We simply define $M^G(\alpha) = (K^f, V^G(\alpha))$ to have the connectivity of M^f and the vertex positions

$$\mathbf{v}_j^G(\alpha) = (\alpha)\mathbf{v}_j^f + (1-\alpha)\mathbf{v}_{A^c(j)}^c .$$

So far we have outlined the construction of geomorphs between PM meshes containing only position attributes. We can in fact construct geomorphs for meshes containing both discrete and scalar attributes.

Discrete attributes by their nature cannot be smoothly interpolated. Fortunately, these discrete attributes are associated with faces of the mesh, and the "geometric" geomorphs described above smoothly introduce faces. In particular, observe that the faces of M^c are a proper subset of the faces of M^f, and that those faces of M^f missing from M^c are invisible in $M^G(0)$ because they have been collapsed to degenerate (zero area) triangles. Other geomorphing schemes [10, 11, 17] define well-behaved (invertible) parametrizations between meshes at different levels of detail, but these do not permit the construction of geomorphs between meshes with different discrete attributes.

Scalar attributes defined on corners can be smoothly interpolated much like the vertex positions. There is a slight complication in that a corner (v,f) in a mesh M is not naturally associated with any "ancestor corner" in a coarser mesh M^c if f is not a face of M^c. We can still attempt to infer what attribute value (v,f) would have in M^c as follows. We examine the mesh M^{i+1} in which f is first introduced, locate a neighboring corner (v,f') in M^{i+1} whose attribute value is the same, and recursively backtrack from it to a corner in M^c. If there is no neighboring corner in M^{i+1} with an identical attribute value, then the corner (v,f) has no equivalent in M^c and we therefore keep its attribute value constant through the geomorph.

The interpolating function on the scalar attributes need not be linear; for instance, normals are best interpolated over the unit sphere, and colors may be interpolated in a color space other than RGB.

Figure 6 demonstrates a geomorph between two meshes M^{175} (500 faces) and M^{425} (1000 faces) retrieved from the PM representation of the mesh in Figure 5d.

3.3 Progressive transmission

Progressive meshes are a natural representation for progressive transmission. The compact mesh M^0 is transmitted first (using a conventional uni-resolution format), followed by the stream of $vsplit_i$ records. The receiving process incrementally rebuilds $\hat{M}$ as the records arrive, and animates the changing mesh. The changes to the mesh can be geomorphed to avoid visual discontinuities. The original mesh $\hat{M}$ is recovered exactly after all n records are received, since PM is a lossless representation.

The computation of the receiving process should be balanced between the reconstruction of $\hat{M}$ and interactive display. With a slow communication line, a simple strategy is to display the current mesh whenever the input buffer is found to be empty. With a fast communication line, we find that a good strategy is to display meshes whose complexities increase exponentially. (Similar issues arise in the display of images transmitted using progressive JPEG.)

3.4 Mesh compression

Even though the PM representation encodes both $\hat{M}$ and a continuous family of approximations, it is surprisingly space-efficient, for two reasons. First, the locations of the vertex split transformations can be encoded concisely. Instead of storing all three vertex indices (s_i, l_i, r_i) of $vsplit_i$, one need only store s_i and approximately 5 bits to select the remaining two vertices among those adjacent to v_{s_i}.[2] Second, because a vertex split has local effect, one can expect significant coherence in mesh attributes through each transformation. For instance, when vertex $v_{s_i}^i$ is split into $v_{s_i}^{i+1}$ and $v_{m_0+i+1}^{i+1}$, we can predict the positions $\mathbf{v}_{s_i}^{i+1}$ and $\mathbf{v}_{m_0+i+1}^{i+1}$ from $\mathbf{v}_{s_i}^i$, and use delta-encoding to reduce storage. Scalar attributes of corners in M^{i+1} can similarly be predicted from those in M^i. Finally, the material identifiers $d_{\{v_s,v_t,v_l\}}$ and $d_{\{v_t,v_s,v_r\}}$ of the new faces in mesh M^{i+1} can often be predicted from those of adjacent faces in M^i using only a few control bits.

As a result, the size of a carefully designed PM representation should be competitive with that obtained from methods for compressing uni-resolution meshes. Our current prototype implementation was not designed with this goal in mind. However, we analyze the compression of the connectivity K, and report results on the compression of the geometry V. In the following analysis, we assume for simplicity that $m_0 = 0$ since typically $m_0 \ll n$.

A common representation for the mesh connectivity K is to list the three vertex indices for each face. Since the number of vertices is n and the number of faces approximately $2n$, such a list requires $6\lceil \log_2(n) \rceil n$ bits of storage. Using a buffer of 2 vertices, *generalized triangle strip* representations reduce this number to about

[2] On average, v_{s_i} has 6 neighbors, and the number of permutations $P_2^6=30$ can be encoded in $\lceil \log_2(P_2^6) \rceil = 5$ bits.

$(\lceil \log_2(n) \rceil + 2k)n$ bits, where vertices are back-referenced once on average and $k \simeq 2$ bits capture the vertex replacement codes [6]. By increasing the vertex buffer size to 16, Deering's *generalized triangle mesh* representation [6] further reduces storage to about $(\frac{1}{8}\lceil \log_2(n) \rceil + 8)n$ bits. Turan [16] shows that planar graphs (and hence the connectivity of closed genus 0 meshes) can be encoded in $12n$ bits. Recent work by Taubin and Rossignac [15] addresses more general meshes. With the PM representation, each $vsplit_i$ requires specification of s_i and its two neighbors, for a total storage of about $(\lceil \log_2(n) \rceil + 5)n$ bits. Although not as concise as [6, 15], this is comparable to generalized triangle strips.

A traditional representation of the mesh geometry V requires storage of $3n$ coordinates, or $96n$ bits with IEEE single-precision floating point. Like Deering [6], we assume that these coordinates can be quantized to 16-bit fixed precision values without significant loss of visual quality, thus reducing storage to $48n$ bits. Deering is able to further compress this storage by delta-encoding the quantized coordinates and Huffman compressing the variable-length deltas. For 16-bit quantization, he reports storage of $35.8n$ bits, which includes both the deltas and the Huffman codes. Using a similar approach with the PM representation, we encode V in $31n$ to $50n$ bits as shown in Table 1. To obtain these results, we exploit a property of our optimization algorithm (Section 4.3): when considering the collapse of an edge $\{v_s, v_t\}$, it considers three starting points for the resulting vertex position $\mathbf{v}_n$: $\{\mathbf{v}_s, \mathbf{v}_t, \frac{\mathbf{v}_s + \mathbf{v}_t}{2}\}$. Depending on the starting point chosen, we delta-encode either $\{\mathbf{v}_s - \mathbf{v}_n, \mathbf{v}_t - \mathbf{v}_n\}$ or $\{\frac{\mathbf{v}_s + \mathbf{v}_t}{2} - \mathbf{v}_n, \frac{\mathbf{v}_t - \mathbf{v}_s}{2}\}$, and use separate Huffman tables for all four quantities.

To further improve compression, we could alter the construction algorithm to forego optimization and let $\mathbf{v}_n \in \{\mathbf{v}_s, \mathbf{v}_t, \frac{\mathbf{v}_s + \mathbf{v}_t}{2}\}$. This would degrade the accuracy of the approximating meshes somewhat, but allows encoding of V in $30n$ to $37n$ bits in our examples. Arithmetic coding [19] of delta lengths does not improve results significantly, reflecting the fact that the Huffman trees are well balanced. Further compression improvements may be achievable by adapting both the quantization level and the delta length models as functions of the *vsplit* record index i, since the magnitude of successive changes tends to decrease.

3.5 Selective refinement

The PM representation also supports selective refinement, whereby detail is added to the model only in desired areas. Let the application supply a callback function REFINE(v) that returns a Boolean value indicating whether the neighborhood of the mesh about v should be further refined. An initial mesh M^c is selectively refined by iterating through the list $\{vsplit_c, \ldots, vsplit_{n-1}\}$ as before, but only performing $vsplit_i(s_i, l_i, r_i, A_i)$ if

(1) all three vertices $\{v_{s_i}, v_{l_i}, v_{r_i}\}$ are present in the mesh, and

(2) REFINE(v_{s_i}) evaluates to TRUE.

(A vertex v_j is absent from the mesh if the prior vertex split that would have introduced it, $vsplit_{j-m_0-1}$, was not performed due to the above conditions.)

As an example, to obtain selective refinement of the model within a view frustum, REFINE(v) is defined to be TRUE if either v or any of its neighbors lies within the frustum. As seen in Figure 7a, condition (1) described above is suboptimal. The problem is that a vertex v_{s_i} within the frustum may fail to be split because its expected neighbor v_{l_i} lies just outside the frustum and was not previously created. The problem is remedied by using a less stringent version of condition (1). Let us define the *closest living ancestor* of a vertex v_j to be the vertex with index

$$A'(j) = \begin{cases} j & \text{, if } v_j \text{ exists in the mesh} \\ A'(s_{j-m_0-1}) & \text{, otherwise} \end{cases}$$

The new condition becomes:

(1') v_{s_i} is present in the mesh (i.e. $A'(s_i) = s_i$) and the vertices $v_{A'(l_i)}$ and $v_{A'(r_i)}$ are both adjacent to v_{s_i}.

As when constructing the geomorphs, the ancestor information A' is carried efficiently as the *vsplit* records are parsed. If conditions (1') and (2) are satisfied, $vsplit(s_i, A'(l_i), A'(r_i), A_i)$ is applied to the mesh. A mesh selectively refined with this new strategy is shown in Figure 7b. This same strategy was also used for Figure 10. Note that it is still possible to create geomorphs between M^c and selectively refined meshes thus created.

An interesting application of selective refinement is the transmission of view-dependent models over low-bandwidth communication lines. As the receiver's view changes over time, the sending process need only transmit those *vsplit* records for which REFINE evaluates to TRUE, and of those only the ones not previously transmitted.

4 PROGRESSIVE MESH CONSTRUCTION

The PM representation of an arbitrary mesh $\hat{M}$ requires a sequence of edge collapses transforming $\hat{M} = M^n$ into a base mesh M^0. The quality of the intermediate approximations $M^i, i < n$ depends largely on the algorithm for selecting which edges to collapse and what attributes to assign to the affected neighborhoods, for instance the positions $\mathbf{v}^i_{s_i}$.

There are many possible PM construction algorithms with varying trade-offs of speed and accuracy. At one extreme, a crude and fast scheme for selecting edge collapses is to choose them completely at random. (Some local conditions must be satisfied for an edge collapse to be legal, i.e. manifold preserving [9].) More sophisticated schemes can use heuristics to improve the edge selection strategy, for example the "distance to plane" metric of Schroeder et al. [14]. At the other extreme, one can attempt to find approximating meshes that are optimal with respect to some appearance metric, for instance the E_{dist} geometric metric of Hoppe et al. [9].

Since PM construction is a preprocess that can be performed offline, we chose to design a simplification procedure that invests some time in the selection of edge collapses. Our procedure is similar to the mesh optimization method introduced by Hoppe et al. [9], which is outlined briefly in Section 4.1. Section 4.2 presents an overview of our procedure, and Sections 4.3–4.6 present the details of our optimization scheme for preserving both the shape of the mesh and the scalar and discrete attributes which define its appearance.

4.1 Background: mesh optimization

The goal of mesh optimization [9] is to find a mesh $M = (K, V)$ that both accurately fits a set X of points $\mathbf{x}_i \in \mathbf{R}^3$ and has a small number of vertices. This problem is cast as minimization of an energy function

$$E(M) = E_{dist}(M) + E_{rep}(M) + E_{spring}(M) \ .$$

The first two terms correspond to the two goals of accuracy and conciseness: the *distance energy* term

$$E_{dist}(M) = \sum_i d^2(\mathbf{x}_i, \phi_V(|K|))$$

measures the total squared distance of the points from the mesh, and the *representation energy* term $E_{rep}(M) = c_{rep} m$ penalizes the number m of vertices in M. The third term, the *spring energy* $E_{spring}(M)$ is introduced to regularize the optimization problem. It corresponds to placing on each edge of the mesh a spring of rest length zero and tension κ:

$$E_{spring}(M) = \sum_{\{j,k\} \in K} \kappa \|\mathbf{v}_j - \mathbf{v}_k\|^2 \ .$$

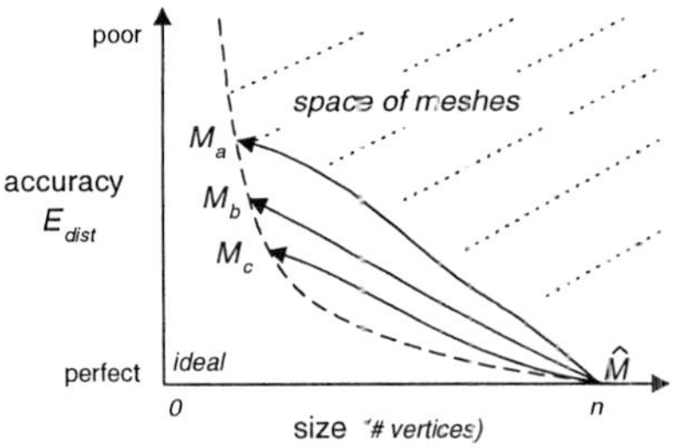

Figure 3: Illustration of the paths taken by mesh optimization using three different settings of c_{rep}.

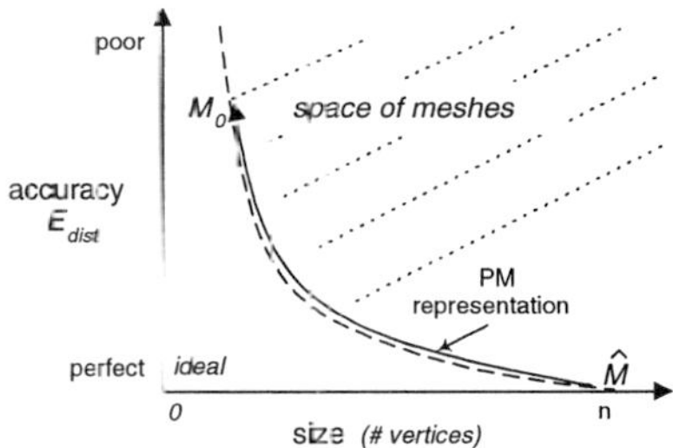

Figure 4: Illustration of the path taken by the new mesh simplification procedure in a graph plotting accuracy vs. mesh size.

The energy function $E(M)$ is minimized using a nested optimization method:

- *Outer loop*: The algorithm optimizes over K, the connectivity of the mesh, by randomly attempting a set of three possible mesh transformations: edge collapse, edge split, and edge swap. This set of transformations is complete, in the sense that any simplicial complex K of the same topological type as $\hat{K}$ can be reached through a sequence of these transformations. For each candidate mesh transformation, $K \rightarrow K'$, the continuous optimization described below computes $E_{K'}$, the minimum of E subject to the new connectivity K'. If $\Delta E = E_{K'} - E_K$ is found to be negative, the mesh transformation is applied (akin to a zero-temperature simulated annealing method).
- *Inner loop*: For each candidate mesh transformation, the algorithm computes $E_{K'} = \min_V E_{dist}(V) + E_{spring}(V)$ by optimizing over the vertex positions V. For the sake of efficiency, the algorithm in fact optimizes only one vertex position $\mathbf{v}_s$, and considers only the subset of points X that project onto the neighborhood affected by $K \rightarrow K'$. To avoid surface self-intersections, the edge collapse is disallowed if the maximum dihedral angle of edges in the resulting neighborhood exceeds some threshold.

Hoppe et al. [9] find that the regularizing spring energy term $E_{spring}(M)$ is most important in the early stages of the optimization, and achieve best results by repeatedly invoking the nested optimization method described above with a schedule of decreasing spring constants κ.

Mesh optimization is demonstrated to be an effective tool for mesh simplification. Given an initial mesh $\hat{M}$ to approximate, a dense set of points X is sampled both at the vertices of $\hat{M}$ and randomly over its faces. The optimization algorithm is then invoked with $\hat{M}$ as the starting mesh. Varying the setting of the representation constant c_{rep} results in optimized meshes with different trade-offs of accuracy and size. The paths taken by these optimizations are shown illustratively in Figure 3.

4.2 Overview of the simplification algorithm

As in mesh optimization [9], we also define an explicit energy metric $E(M)$ to measure the accuracy of simplified meshes $M = (K, V, D, S)$ with respect to the original $\hat{M}$, and we also modify the mesh M starting from $\hat{M}$ while minimizing $E(M)$.

Our energy metric has the following form:

$$E(M) = E_{dist}(M) + E_{spring}(M) + E_{scalar}(M) + E_{disc}(M) .$$

The first two terms, $E_{dist}(M)$ and $E_{spring}(M)$ are identical to those in [9]. The next two terms of $E(M)$ are added to preserve attributes associated with M: $E_{scalar}(M)$ measures the accuracy of its scalar attributes (Section 4.4), and $E_{disc}(M)$ measures the geometric accuracy of its discontinuity curves (Section 4.5). (To achieve scale invariance of the terms, the mesh is uniformly scaled to fit in a unit cube.)

Our scheme for optimizing over the connectivity K of the mesh is rather different from [9]. We have discovered that a mesh can be effectively simplified using edge collapse transformations alone. The edge swap and edge split transformations, useful in the context of surface reconstruction (which motivated [9]), are not essential for simplification. Although in principle our simplification algorithm can no longer traverse the entire space of meshes considered by mesh optimization, we find that the meshes generated by our algorithm are just as good. In fact, because of the priority queue approach described below, our meshes are usually better. Moreover, considering only edge collapses simplifies the implementation, improves performance, and most importantly, gives rise to the PM representation (Section 3).

Rather than randomly attempting mesh transformations as in [9], we place all (legal) candidate edge collapse transformations into a priority queue, where the priority of each transformation is its estimated energy cost ΔE. In each iteration, we perform the transformation at the front of the priority queue (with lowest ΔE), and recompute the priorities of edges in the neighborhood of this transformation. As a consequence, we eliminate the need for the awkward parameter c_{rep} as well as the energy term $E_{rep}(M)$. Instead, we can explicitly specify the number of faces desired in an optimized mesh. Also, a single run of the optimization can generate several such meshes. Indeed, it generates a continuous-resolution family of meshes, namely the PM representation of $\hat{M}$ (Figure 4).

For each edge collapse $K \rightarrow K'$, we compute its cost $\Delta E = E_{K'} - E_K$ by solving a continuous optimization

$$E_{K'} = \min_{V,S} E_{dist}(V) + E_{spring}(V) + E_{scalar}(V, S) + E_{disc}(V)$$

over both the vertex positions V and the scalar attributes S of the mesh with connectivity K'. This minimization is discussed in the next three sections.

4.3 Preserving surface geometry ($E_{dist}+E_{spring}$)

As in [9], we "record" the geometry of the original mesh $\hat{M}$ by sampling from it a set of points X. At a minimum, we sample a point at each vertex of $\hat{M}$. If requested by the user, additional points are sampled randomly over the surface of $\hat{M}$. The energy terms $E_{dist}(M)$ and $E_{spring}(M)$ are defined as in Section 4.1.

For a mesh of fixed connectivity, our method for optimizing the vertex positions to minimize $E_{dist}(V)+E_{spring}(V)$ closely follows that of [9]. Evaluating $E_{dist}(V)$ involves computing the distance of each point $\mathbf{x}_i$ to the mesh. Each of these distances is itself a minimization problem

$$d^2(\mathbf{x}_i, \phi_V(|K|)) = \min_{\mathbf{b}_i \in |K|} \|\mathbf{x}_i - \phi_V(\mathbf{b}_i)\|^2 \quad (1)$$

where the unknown $\mathbf{b}_i$ is the parametrization of the projection of $\mathbf{x}_i$ on the mesh. The nonlinear minimization of $E_{dist}(V) + E_{spring}(V)$ is performed using an iterative procedure alternating between two steps:

1. For fixed vertex positions V, compute the optimal parametrizations $B = \{\mathbf{b}_1, \ldots, \mathbf{b}_{|X|}\}$ by projecting the points X onto the mesh.
2. For fixed parametrizations B, compute the optimal vertex positions V by solving a sparse linear least-squares problem.

As in [9], when considering $ecol(\{v_s, v_t\})$, we optimize only one vertex position, $\mathbf{v}^i_s$. We perform three different optimizations with different starting points, $\mathbf{v}^i_s = (1-\alpha)\mathbf{v}^{i+1}_s + (\alpha)\mathbf{v}^{i+1}_t$ for $\alpha = \{0, \frac{1}{2}, 1\}$, and accept the best one.

Instead of defining a global spring constant κ for E_{spring} as in [9], we adapt κ each time an edge collapse transformation is considered. Intuitively, the spring energy is most important when few points project onto a neighborhood of faces, since in this case finding the vertex positions minimizing $E_{dist}(V)$ may be an under-constrained problem. Thus, for each edge collapse transformation considered, we set κ as a function of the ratio of the number of points to the number of faces in the neighborhood.[3] With this adaptive scheme, the influence of $E_{spring}(M)$ decreases gradually and adaptively as the mesh is simplified, and we no longer require the expensive schedule of decreasing spring constants.

4.4 Preserving scalar attributes (E_{scalar})

As described in Section 2, we represent piecewise continuous scalar fields by defining scalar attributes S at the mesh corners. We now present our scheme for preserving these scalar fields through the simplification process. For exposition, we find it easier to first present the case of continuous scalar fields, in which the corner attributes at a vertex are identical. The generalization to piecewise continuous fields is discussed shortly.

Optimizing scalar attributes at vertices Let the original mesh $\hat{M}$ have at each vertex v_j not only a position $\mathbf{v}_j \in \mathbf{R}^3$ but also a scalar attribute $\underline{\mathbf{v}}_j \in \mathbf{R}^d$. To capture scalar attributes, we sample at each point $\mathbf{x}_i \in X$ the attribute value $\underline{\mathbf{x}}_i \in \mathbf{R}^d$. We would then like to generalize the distance metric E_{dist} to also measure the deviation of the sampled attribute values $\underline{X}$ from those of M.

One natural way to achieve this is to redefine the distance metric to measure distance in $\mathbf{R}^{3+d}$:

$$d^2((\mathbf{x}_i\ \underline{\mathbf{x}}_i), M(K,V,\underline{V})) = \min_{\mathbf{b}_i\in|K|} \|(\mathbf{x}_i\ \underline{\mathbf{x}}_i) - (\phi_V(\mathbf{b}_i)\ \phi_{\underline{V}}(\mathbf{b}_i))\|^2 .$$

This new distance functional could be minimized using the iterative approach of Section 4.3. However, it would be expensive since finding the optimal parametrization $\mathbf{b}_i$ of each point $\mathbf{x}_i$ would require projection in $\mathbf{R}^{3+d}$, and would be non-intuitive since these parametrizations would not be geometrically based.

Instead we opted to determine the parametrizations $\mathbf{b}_i$ using only geometry with equation (1), and to introduce a separate energy term E_{scalar} to measure attribute deviation based on these parametrizations:

$$E_{scalar}(\underline{V}) = (c_{scalar})^2 \sum_i \|\underline{\mathbf{x}}_i - \phi_{\underline{V}}(\mathbf{b}_i)\|^2$$

where the constant c_{scalar} assigns a relative weight between the scalar attribute errors (E_{scalar}) and the geometric errors (E_{dist}).

Thus, to minimize $E(V,\underline{V}) = E_{dist}(V) + E_{spring}(V) + E_{scalar}(\underline{V})$, our algorithm first finds the vertex position $\mathbf{v}_s$ minimizing $E_{dist}(V) + E_{spring}(V)$ by alternately projecting the points onto the mesh (obtaining the parametrizations $\mathbf{b}_i$) and solving a linear least-squares problem (Section 4.1). Then, using those same parametrizations $\mathbf{b}_i$, it finds the vertex attribute $\underline{\mathbf{v}}_s$ minimizing E_{scalar} by solving a single linear least-squares problem. Hence introducing E_{scalar} into the optimization causes negligible performance overhead.

Since ΔE_{scalar} contributes to the estimated cost ΔE of an edge collapse, we obtain simplified meshes whose faces naturally adapt to the attribute fields, as shown in Figures 8 and 11.

Optimizing scalar attributes at corners Our scheme for optimizing the scalar corner attributes S is a straightforward generalization of the scheme just described. Instead of solving for a single unknown attribute value $\underline{\mathbf{v}}_s$, the algorithm partitions the corners around v_s into continuous sets (based on equivalence of corner attributes) and for each continuous set solves independently for its optimal attribute value.

Range constraints Some scalar attributes have constrained ranges. For instance, the components (r, g, b) of color are typically constrained to lie between 0 and 1. Least-squares optimization may yield color values outside this range. In these cases we clip the optimized values to the given range. For least-squares minimization of a Euclidean norm at a single vertex, this is in fact optimal.

Normals Surface normals (n_x, n_y, n_z) are typically constrained to have unit length, and thus their domain is non-Cartesian. Optimizing over normals would therefore require minimization of a nonlinear functional with nonlinear constraints. We decided to instead simply carry the normals through the simplification process. Specifically, we compute the new normals at vertex $v^i_{s_i}$ by interpolating between the normals at vertices $v^{i+1}_{s_i}$ and $v^{i+1}_{m_0+i+1}$ using the α value that resulted in the best vertex position $\mathbf{v}^i_{s_i}$ in Section 4.3. Fortunately, the absolute directions of normals are less visually important than their discontinuities, and we have a scheme for preserving such discontinuities, as described in the next section.

4.5 Preserving discontinuity curves (E_{disc})

Appearance attributes give rise to a set of discontinuity curves on the mesh, both from differences between discrete face attributes (e.g. material boundaries), and from differences between scalar corner attributes (e.g. creases and shadow boundaries). As these discontinuity curves form noticeable features, we have found it useful to preserve them both topologically and geometrically.

We can detect when a candidate edge collapse would modify the topology of the discontinuity curves using some simple tests on the presence of sharp edges in its neighborhood. Let $sharp(v_j, v_k)$ denote that an edge $\{v_j, v_k\}$ is sharp, and let $\#sharp(v_j)$ be the number of sharp edges adjacent to a vertex v_j. Then, referring to Figure 1, $ecol(\{v_s, v_t\})$ modifies the topology of discontinuity curves if either:

- $sharp(v_s, v_l)$ and $sharp(v_t, v_l)$, or
- $sharp(v_s, v_r)$ and $sharp(v_t, v_r)$, or
- $\#sharp(v_s) \geq 1$ and $\#sharp(v_t) \geq 1$ and not $sharp(v_s, v_t)$, or
- $\#sharp(v_s) \geq 3$ and $\#sharp(v_t) \geq 3$ and $sharp(v_s, v_t)$, or
- $sharp(v_s, v_t)$ and $\#sharp(v_s) = 1$ and $\#sharp(v_t) \neq 2$, or
- $sharp(v_s, v_t)$ and $\#sharp(v_t) = 1$ and $\#sharp(v_s) \neq 2$.

If an edge collapse would modify the topology of discontinuity curves, we either disallow it, or penalize it as discussed in Section 4.6.

To preserve the geometry of the discontinuity curves, we sample an additional set of points X_{disc} from the sharp edges of $\hat{M}$, and define an additional energy term E_{disc} equal to the total squared distances of each of these points to the discontinuity curve from which it was sampled. Thus E_{disc} is defined just like E_{dist}, except that the points X_{disc} are constrained to project onto a set of sharp edges in the mesh. In effect, we are solving a curve fitting problem embedded within the surface fitting problem. Since all boundaries of the surface are defined to be discontinuity curves, our procedure preserves bound-

[3] The neighborhood of an edge collapse transformation is the set of faces shown in Figure 1. Using C notation, we set $\kappa = r < 4\ ?\ 10^{-2} : r < 8\ ?\ 10^{-4} : 10^{-8}$ where r is the ratio of the number of points to faces in the neighborhood.

ary geometry more accurately than [9]. Figure 9 demonstrates the importance of using the E_{disc} energy term in preserving the material boundaries of a mesh with discrete face attributes.

4.6 Permitting changes to topology of discontinuity curves

Some meshes contain numerous discontinuity curves, and these curves may delimit features that are too small to be visible when viewed from a distance. In such cases we have found that strictly preserving the topology of the discontinuity curves unnecessarily curtails simplification. We have therefore adopted a hybrid strategy, which is to permit changes to the topology of the discontinuity curves, but to penalize such changes. When a candidate edge collapse $ecol(\{v_s, v_t\})$ changes the topology of the discontinuity curves, we add to its cost ΔE the value $|X_{disc,\{v_s,v_t\}}| \cdot \|\mathbf{v}_s - \mathbf{v}_t\|^2$ where $|X_{disc,\{v_s,v_t\}}|$ is the number of points of X_{disc} projecting onto $\{v_s, v_t\}$. That simple strategy, although ad hoc, has proven very effective. For example, it allows the dark gray window frames of the "cessna" (visible in Figure 9) to vanish in the simplified meshes (Figures 5a–c).

Table 1: Parameter settings and quantitative results.

Object	Original $\hat{M}$		Base M^0		User param.		$\|X_{disc}\|$	V	Time
	m_0+n	#faces	m_0	#faces	$\|X\|-(m_0+n)$	c_{color}		$\frac{bits}{n}$	mins
cessna	6,795	13,546	97	150	100,000	-	46,811	46	23
terrain	33,847	66,960	3	1	0	-	3,796	46	16
mandrill	40,000	79,202	3	1	0	0.1	4,776	31	19
radiosity	78,923	150,983	1,192	1,191	200,000	0.01	74,316	37	106
fandisk	6,475	12,946	27	50	10,000	-	5,924	50	19

5 RESULTS

Table 1 shows, for the meshes in Figures 5–12, the number of vertices and faces in both $\hat{M}$ and M^0. In general, we let the simplification proceed until no more legal edge collapse transformations are possible. For the "cessna", we stopped at 150 faces to obtain a visually aesthetic base mesh. As indicated, the only user-specified parameters are the number of additional points (besides the $m_0 + n$ vertices of $\hat{M}$) sampled to increase fidelity, and the c_{scalar} constants relating the scalar attribute accuracies to the geometric accuracy. The only scalar attribute we optimized is color, and its c_{scalar} constant is denoted as c_{color}. The number $|X_{disc}|$ of points sampled from sharp edges is set automatically so that the densities of X and X_{disc} are proportional.[4] Execution times were obtained on a 150MHz Indigo2 with 128MB of memory.

Construction of the PM representation proceeds in three steps. First, as the simplification algorithm applies a sequence $ecol_{n-1} \ldots ecol_0$ of transformations to the original mesh, it writes to a file the sequence $vsplit_{n-1} \ldots vsplit_0$ of corresponding inverse transformations. When finished, the algorithm also writes the resulting base mesh M^0. Next, we reverse the order of the $vsplit$ records. Finally, we renumber the vertices and faces of $(M^0, vsplit_0 \ldots vsplit_{n-1})$ to match the indexing scheme of Section 3.1 in order to obtain a concise format.

Figure 6 shows a single geomorph between two meshes M^{175} and M^{425} of a PM representation. For interactive LOD, it is useful to select a sequence of meshes from the PM representation, and to construct successive geomorphs between them. We have obtained good results by selecting meshes whose complexities grow exponentially, as in Figure 5. During execution, an application can adjust the granularity of these geomorphs by sampling additional meshes from the PM representation, or freeing some up.

In Figure 10, we selectively refined a terrain (grid of 181×187 vertices) using a new REFINE(v) function that keeps more detail near silhouette edges and near the viewer. More precisely, for the faces F_v adjacent to v, we compute the signed projected screen areas $\{a_f : f \in F_v\}$. We let REFINE(v) return TRUE if

(1) any face $f \in F_v$ lies within the view frustum, and either

(2a) the signs of a_f are not all equal (i.e. v lies near a silhouette edge) or

(2b) $\sum_{f \in F_v} a_f > thresh$ for a screen area threshold $thresh = 0.16^2$ (where total screen area is 1).

6 RELATED WORK

Mesh simplification methods A number of schemes construct a discrete sequence of approximating meshes by repeated application of a simplification procedure. Turk [17] sprinkles a set of points on a mesh, with density weighted by estimates of local curvature, and then retriangulates based on those points. Both Schroeder et al. [14] and Cohen et al. [4] iteratively remove vertices from the mesh and retriangulate the resulting holes. Cohen et al. are able to bound the maximum error of the approximation by restricting it to lie between two offset surfaces. Hoppe et al. [9] find accurate approximations through a general mesh optimization process (Section 4.1). Rossignac and Borrel [12] merge vertices of a model using spatial binning. A unique aspect of their approach is that the topological type of the model may change in the process. Their method is extremely fast, but since it ignores geometric qualities like curvature, the resulting approximations can be far from optimal. Some of the above methods [12, 17] permit the construction of geomorphs between successive simplified meshes.

Multiresolution analysis (MRA) Lounsbery et al. [10, 11] generalize the concept of multiresolution analysis to surfaces of arbitrary topological type. Eck et al. [7] describe how MRA can be applied to the approximation of an arbitrary mesh. Certain et al. [2] extend MRA to capture color, and present a multiresolution Web viewer supporting progressive transmission. MRA has many similarities with the PM scheme, since both store a simple base mesh together with a stream of detail records, and both produce a continuous-resolution representation. It is therefore worthwhile to highlight their differences:

Advantages of PM over MRA:

- MRA requires that the detail terms (wavelets) lie on a domain with subdivision connectivity, and as a result an arbitrary initial mesh $\hat{M}$ can only be recovered to within an ϵ tolerance. In contrast, the PM representation is lossless since $M^n = \hat{M}$.
- Because the approximating meshes $M^i, i < n$ in a PM may have arbitrary connectivity, they can be much better approximations than their MRA counterparts (Figure 12).
- The MRA representation cannot deal effectively with surface creases, unless those creases lie parametrically along edges of the base mesh (Figure 12). PM's can introduce surface creases anywhere and at any level of detail.
- PM's capture continuous, piecewise-continuous, and discrete appearance attributes. MRA schemes can represent discontinuous functions using a piecewise-constant basis (such as the Haar basis as used in [2, 13]), but the resulting approximations have too many discontinuities since none of the basis functions meet continuously. Also, it is not clear how MRA could be extended to capture discrete attributes.

[4] We set $|X_{disc}|$ such that $|X_{disc}|/perim = c(|X|/area)^{\frac{1}{2}}$ where $perim$ is the total length of all sharp edges in $\hat{M}$, $area$ is total area of all faces, and the constant $c = 4.0$ is chosen empirically.

Advantages of MRA over PM:

- The MRA framework provides a parametrization between meshes at various levels of detail, thus making possible multiresolution surface editing. PM's also offer such a parametrization, but it is not smooth, and therefore multiresolution editing may be non-intuitive.
- Eck et al. [7] construct MRA approximations with guaranteed maximum error bounds to $\hat{M}$. Our PM construction algorithm does not provide such bounds, although one could envision using simplification envelopes [4] to achieve this.
- MRA allows geometry and color to be compressed independently [2].

Other related work There has been relatively little work in simplifying arbitrary surfaces with functions defined over them. One special instance is image compression, since an image can be thought of as a set of scalar color functions defined on a quadrilateral surface. Another instance is the framework of Schröder and Sweldens [13] for simplifying functions defined over the sphere. The PM representation, like the MRA representation, is a generalization in that it supports surfaces of arbitrary topological type.

7 SUMMARY AND FUTURE WORK

We have introduced the progressive mesh representation and shown that it naturally supports geomorphs, progressive transmission, compression, and selective refinement. In addition, as a PM construction method, we have presented a new mesh simplification procedure designed to preserve not just the geometry of the original mesh, but also its overall appearance.

There are a number of avenues for future work, including:

- Development of an explicit metric and optimization scheme for preserving surface normals.
- Experimentation with PM editing.
- Application of the work to progressive subdivision surfaces.
- Representation of articulated or animated models.
- Progressive representation of more general simplicial complexes (not just 2-d manifolds).
- Addition of spatial data structures to permit efficient selective refinement.

We envision many practical applications for the PM representation, including streaming of 3D geometry over the Web, efficient storage formats, and continuous LOD in computer graphics applications. The representation may also have applications in finite element methods, as it can be used to generate coarse meshes for multigrid analysis.

ACKNOWLEDGMENTS

I wish to thank Viewpoint Datalabs for providing the "cessna" mesh, Pratt & Whitney for the gas turbine engine component ("fandisk"), Softimage for the "terrain" mesh, and especially Steve Drucker for creating several radiosity models using Lightscape. Thanks also to Michael Cohen, Steven "Shlomo" Gortler, and Jim Kajiya for their enthusiastic support, and to Rick Szeliski for helpful comments on the paper. Mark Kenworthy first coined the term "geomorph" in '92 to distinguish them from image morphs.

REFERENCES

[1] APPLE COMPUTER, INC. *3D graphics programming with QuickDraw 3D*. Addison Wesley, 1995.

[2] CERTAIN, A., POPOVIC, J., DUCHAMP, T., SALESIN, D., STUETZLE, W., AND DEROSE, T. Interactive multiresolution surface viewing. *Computer Graphics (SIGGRAPH '96 Proceedings)* (1996).

[3] CLARK, J. Hierarchical geometric models for visible surface algorithms. *Communications of the ACM 19*, 10 (Oct. 1976), 547–554.

[4] COHEN, J., VARSHNEY, A., MANOCHA, D., TURK, G., WEBER, H., AGARWAL, P., BROOKS, F., AND WRIGHT, W. Simplification envelopes. *Computer Graphics (SIGGRAPH '96 Proceedings)* (1996).

[5] CURLESS, B., AND LEVOY, M. A volumetric method for building complex models from range images. *Computer Graphics (SIGGRAPH '96 Proceedings)* (1996).

[6] DEERING, M. Geometry compression. *Computer Graphics (SIGGRAPH '95 Proceedings)* (1995), 13–20.

[7] ECK, M., DEROSE, T., DUCHAMP, T., HOPPE, H., LOUNSBERY, M., AND STUETZLE, W. Multiresolution analysis of arbitrary meshes. *Computer Graphics (SIGGRAPH '95 Proceedings)* (1995), 173–182.

[8] FUNKHOUSER, T., AND SÉQUIN, C. Adaptive display algorithm for interactive frame rates during visualization of complex virtual environments. *Computer Graphics (SIGGRAPH '93 Proceedings)* (1995), 247–254.

[9] HOPPE, H., DEROSE, T., DUCHAMP, T., MCDONALD, J., AND STUETZLE, W. Mesh optimization. *Computer Graphics (SIGGRAPH '93 Proceedings)* (1993), 19–26.

[10] LOUNSBERY, J. M. *Multiresolution analysis for surfaces of arbitrary topological type*. PhD thesis, Dept. of Computer Science and Engineering, U. of Washington, 1994.

[11] LOUNSBERY, M., DEROSE, T., AND WARREN, J. Multiresolution analysis for surfaces of arbitrary topological type. Submitted for publication. (TR 93-10-05b, Dept. of Computer Science and Engineering, U. of Washington, January 1994.).

[12] ROSSIGNAC, J., AND BORREL, P. Multi-resolution 3D approximations for rendering complex scenes. In *Modeling in Computer Graphics*, B. Falcidieno and T. L. Kunii, Eds. Springer-Verlag, 1993, pp. 455–465.

[13] SCHRÖDER, P., AND SWELDENS, W. Spherical wavelets: Efficiently representing functions on the sphere. *Computer Graphics (SIGGRAPH '95 Proceedings)* (1995), 161–172.

[14] SCHROEDER, W., ZARGE, J., AND LORENSEN, W. Decimation of triangle meshes. *Computer Graphics (SIGGRAPH '92 Proceedings) 26*, 2 (1992), 65–70.

[15] TAUBIN, G., AND ROSSIGNAC, J. Geometry compression through topological surgery. Research Report RC-20340, IBM, January 1996.

[16] TURAN, G. Succinct representations of graphs. *Discrete Applied Mathematics 8* (1984), 289–294.

[17] TURK, G. Re-tiling polygonal surfaces. *Computer Graphics (SIGGRAPH '92 Proceedings) 26*, 2 (1992), 55–64.

[18] UPSTILL, S. *The RenderMan Companion*. Addison-Wesley, 1990.

[19] WITTEN, I., NEAL, R., AND CLEARY, J. Arithmetic coding for data compression. *Communications of the ACM 30*, 6 (June 1987), 520–540.

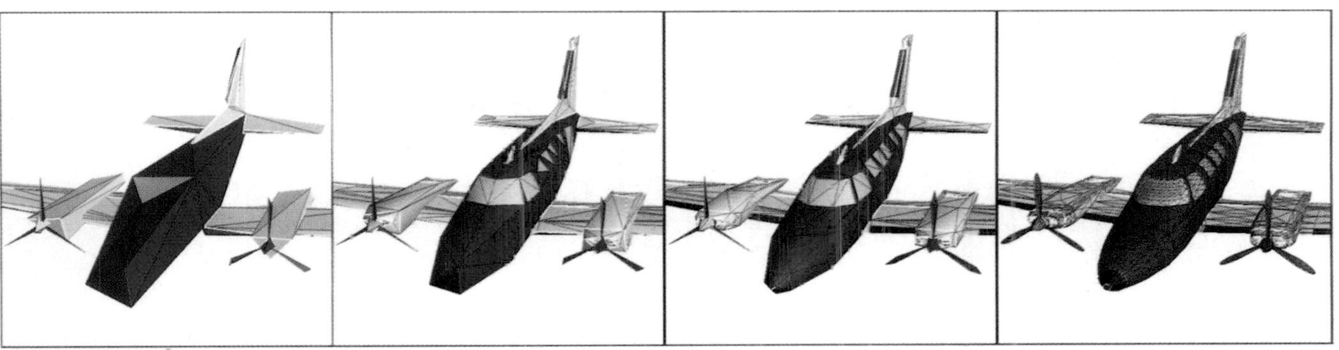

(a) Base mesh M^0 (150 faces) (b) Mesh M^{175} (500 faces) (c) Mesh M^{425} (1,000 faces) (d) Original $\hat{M} = M^n$ (13,546 faces)

Figure 5: The PM representation of an arbitrary mesh $\hat{M}$ captures a continuous-resolution family of approximating meshes $M^0 \ldots M^n = \hat{M}$.

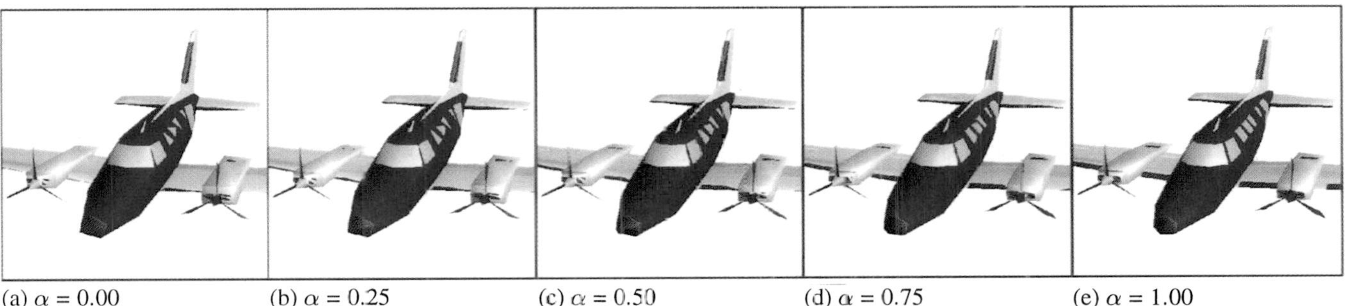

(a) $\alpha = 0.00$ (b) $\alpha = 0.25$ (c) $\alpha = 0.50$ (d) $\alpha = 0.75$ (e) $\alpha = 1.00$

Figure 6: Example of a geomorph $M^G(\alpha)$ defined between $M^G(0) \doteq M^{175}$ (with 500 faces) and $M^G(1) = M^{425}$ (with 1,000 faces).

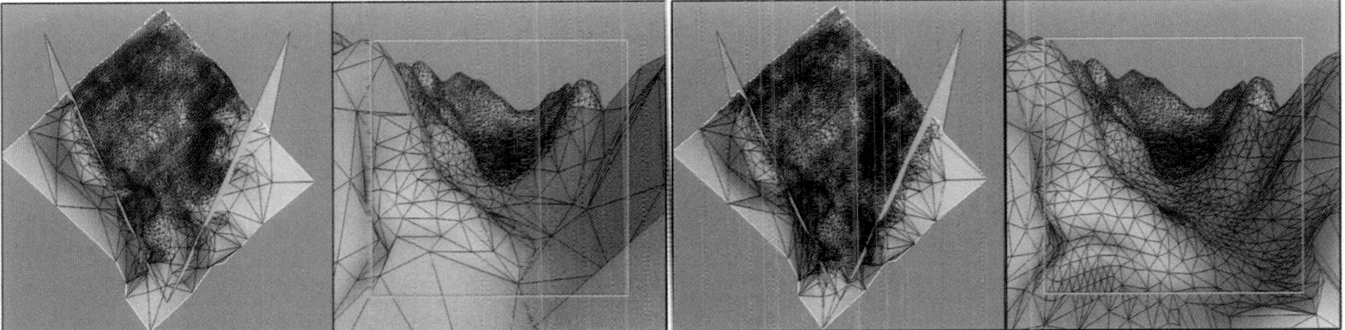

(a) Using conditions (1) and (2); 9,462 faces (b) Using conditions (1') and (2); 12,169 faces

Figure 7: Example of selective refinement within the view frustum (indicated in orange).

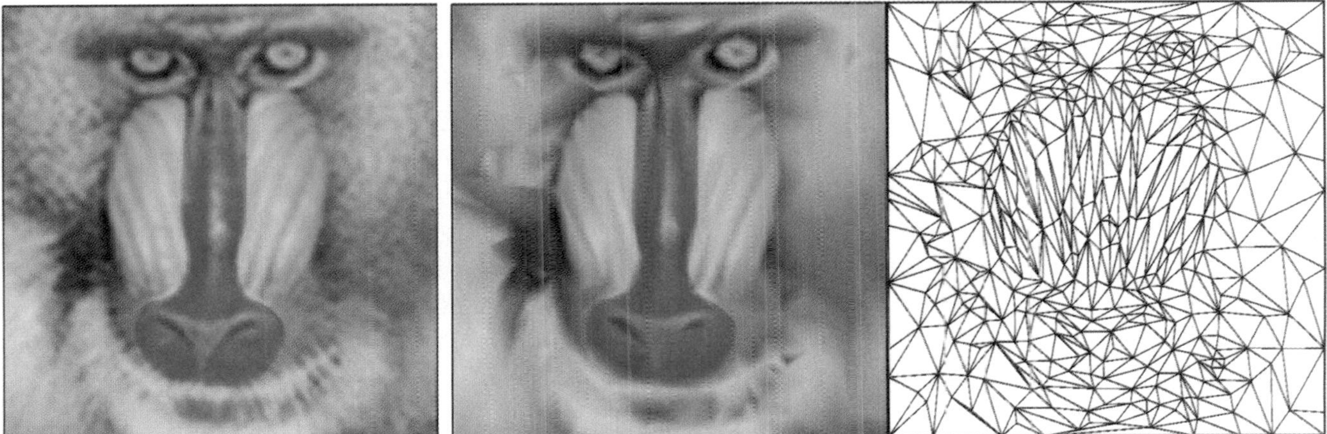

(a) M (200×200 vertices) (b) Simplified mesh (400 vertices)

Figure 8: Demonstration of minimizing E_{scalar}: simplification of a mesh with trivial geometry (a square) but complex scalar attribute field. ($\hat{M}$ is a mesh with regular connectivity whose vertex colors correspond to the pixels of an image.)

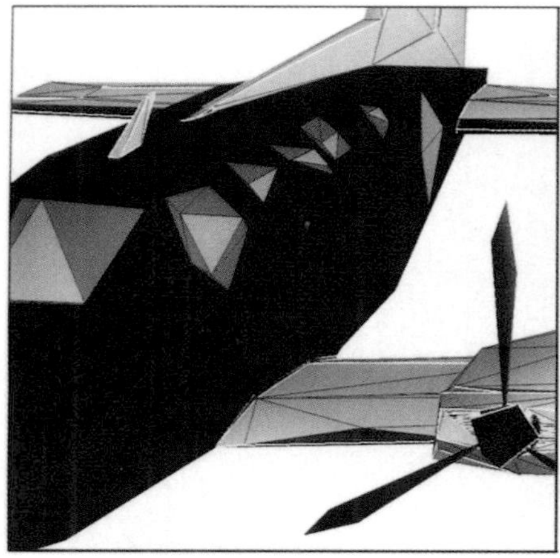

Figure 9: (a) Simplification without E_{disc}

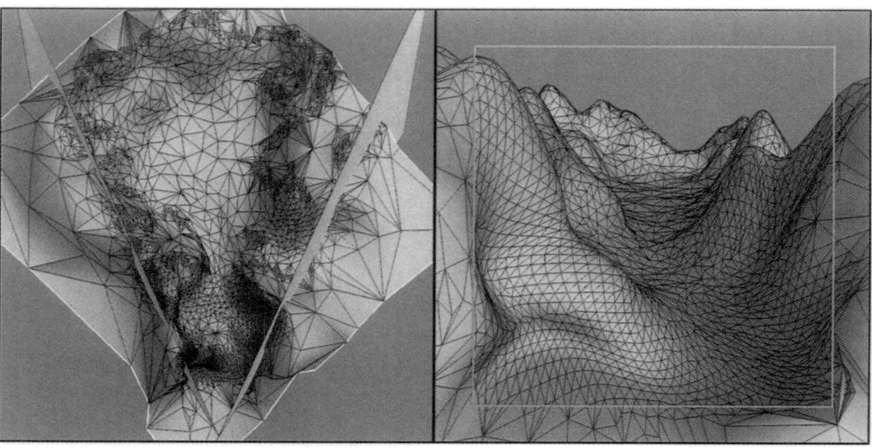

Figure 10: Selective refinement of a terrain mesh taking into account view frustum, silhouette regions, and projected screen size of faces (7,438 faces).

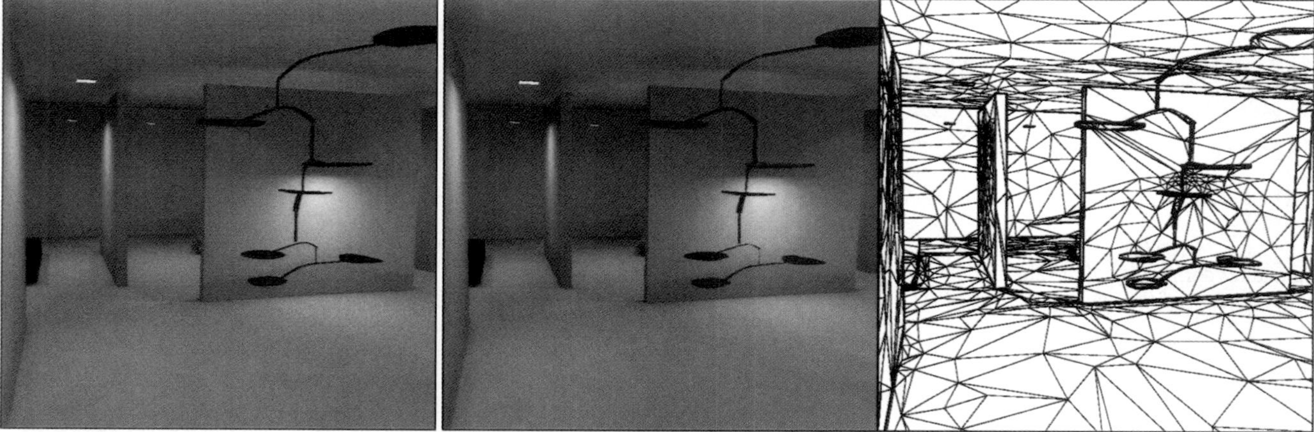

Figure 11: Simplification of a radiosity solution; left: original mesh (150,983 faces); right: simplified mesh (10,000 faces).

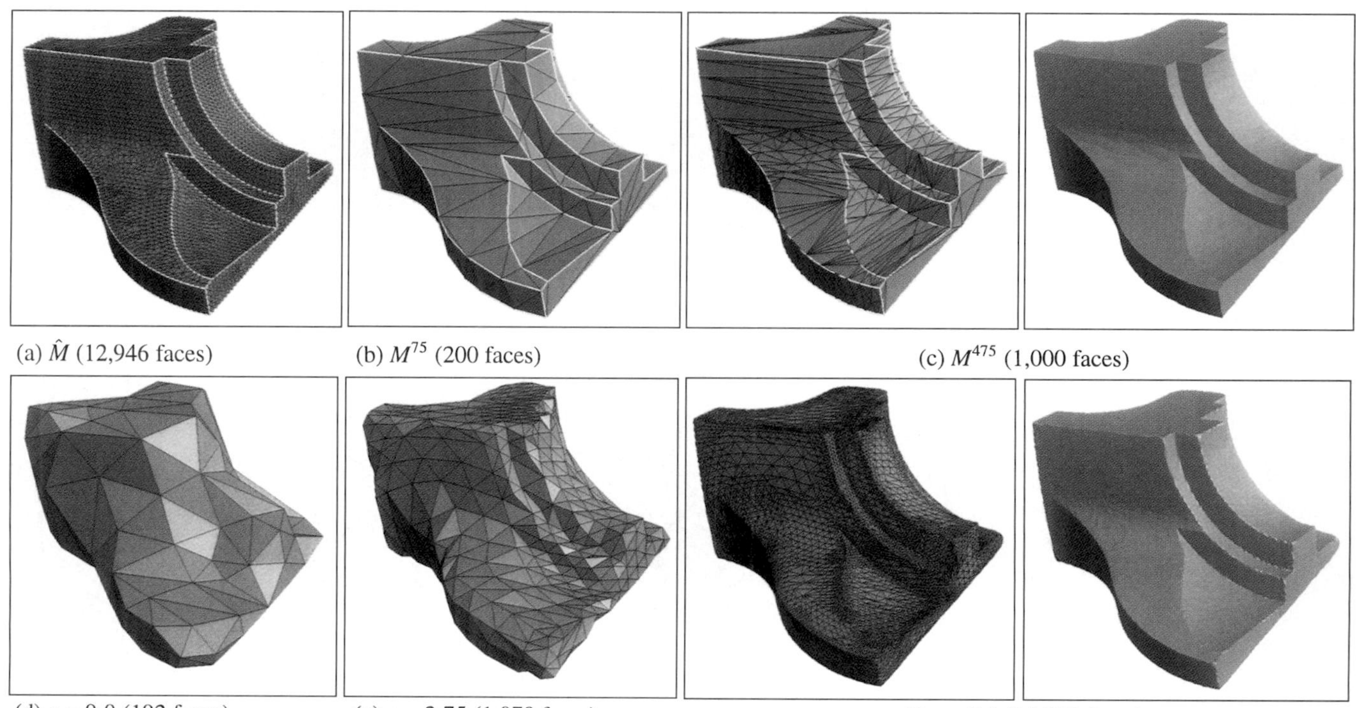

(a) $\hat{M}$ (12,946 faces) (b) M^{75} (200 faces) (c) M^{475} (1,000 faces)

(d) $\epsilon = 9.0$ (192 faces) (e) $\epsilon = 2.75$ (1,070 faces) (f) $\epsilon = 0.1$ (15,842 faces)

Figure 12: Approximations of a mesh $\hat{M}$ using (b–c) the PM representation, and (d–f) the MRA scheme of Eck et al. [7]. As demonstrated, MRA cannot recover $\hat{M}$ exactly, cannot deal effectively with surface creases, and produces approximating meshes of inferior quality.

Real-Time, Continuous Level of Detail Rendering of Height Fields

Peter Lindstrom* David Koller* William Ribarsky*
Larry F. Hodges* Nick Faust† Gregory A. Turner‡

*† Georgia Institute of Technology
‡ SAIC

Abstract

We present an algorithm for real-time level of detail reduction and display of high-complexity polygonal surface data. The algorithm uses a compact and efficient regular grid representation, and employs a variable screen-space threshold to bound the maximum error of the projected image. A coarse level of simplification is performed to select discrete levels of detail for blocks of the surface mesh, followed by further simplification through repolygonalization in which individual mesh vertices are considered for removal. These steps compute and generate the appropriate level of detail dynamically in real-time, minimizing the number of rendered polygons and allowing for smooth changes in resolution across areas of the surface. The algorithm has been implemented for approximating and rendering digital terrain models and other height fields, and consistently performs at interactive frame rates with high image quality.

1 INTRODUCTION

Modern graphics workstations allow the display of thousands of shaded or textured polygons at interactive rates. However, many applications contain graphical models with geometric complexity still greatly exceeding the capabilities of typical graphics hardware. This problem is particularly prevalent in applications dealing with large polygonal surface models, such as digital terrain modeling and visual simulation.

In order to accommodate complex surface models while still maintaining real-time display rates, methods for approximating the polygonal surfaces and using multiresolution models have been proposed [13]. Simplification algorithms can be used to generate multiple surface models at varying levels of detail, and techniques are employed by the display system to select and render the appropriate level of detail model.

*Graphics, Visualization, & Usability Center, College of Computing, Georgia Institute of Technology, Atlanta, GA 30332–0280. {lindstro, koller, ribarsky, hodges}@cc.gatech.edu.

†Center for GIS and Spatial Analysis Technologies, Georgia Tech Research Institute. nick.faust@gtri.gatech.edu.

‡Simulation Technology Division. gturner@std.saic.com.

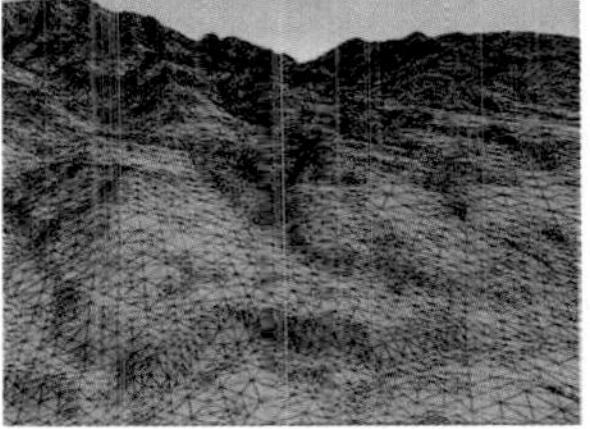

Figure 1: Terrain surface tessellations corresponding to projected geometric error thresholds of one (left) and four (right) pixels.

In this paper we present a new level of detail display algorithm that is applicable to surfaces that are represented as uniformly-gridded polygonal height fields. By extending the regular grid representation to allow polygons to be recursively combined where appropriate, a mesh with fewer polygons can be used to represent the height field (Figure 1). Such small, incremental changes to the mesh polygonalization provide for continuous levels of detail and a near optimal tessellation for any given viewpoint. The algorithm is characterized by the following set of features:

- **Large reduction in the number of polygons to be rendered.** Typically, the surface grid is decimated by several orders of magnitude with no or little loss in image quality, accommodating interactive frames rates for smooth animation.
- **Smooth, continuous changes between different surface levels of detail.** The number and distribution of rendered polygons change smoothly between successive frames, affording maintenance of consistent frame rates.
- **Dynamic generation of levels of detail in real-time.** The need for expensive generation of multiresolution models ahead of time is eliminated, allowing dynamic changes to the surface geometry to be made with little computational cost.
- **Support for a user-specified image quality metric.** The algorithm is easily controlled to meet an image accuracy level within a specified number of pixels. This parameterization allows for easy variation of the balance between rendering time and rendered image quality.

Related approaches to polygonal surface approximation and multiresolution rendering are discussed in the next section. The following sections of the paper describe the theory and procedures necessary for implementing the real-time continuous rendering algorithm. We conclude the paper by empirically evaluating the algorithm with results from its use in a typical application.

2 RELATED WORK

A large number of researchers have developed algorithms for approximating terrains and other height fields using polygonal meshes. These algorithms attempt to represent surfaces with a given number of vertices, or within a given geometric error metric, or in a manner that preserves application specific critical features of the surface. Uniform grid methods or irregular triangulations are employed to represent the surfaces, and techniques including hierarchical subdivisions and decimations of the mesh are used for simplification and creation of multiresolution representations.

Much of the previous work on polygonalization of terrain-like surfaces has concentrated on triangulated irregular networks (TINs). A number of different approaches have been developed to create TINs from height fields using Delaunay and other triangulations [9, 10, 19], and hierarchical triangulation representations have been proposed that lend themselves to usage in level of detail algorithms [3, 4, 18]. TINs allow variable spacing between vertices of the triangular mesh, approximating a surface at any desired level of accuracy with fewer polygons than other representations. However, the algorithms required to create TIN models are generally computationally expensive, prohibiting use of dynamically created TINs at interactive rates.

Regular grid surface polygonalizations have also been implemented as terrain and general surface approximations [2, 7]. Such uniform polygonalizations generally produce many more polygons than TINs for a given level of approximation, but grid representations are typically more compact. Regular grid representations also have the advantage of allowing for easier construction of a multiple level of detail hierarchy. Simply subsampling grid elevation values produces a coarser level of detail model, whereas TIN models generally require complete retriangulation in order to generate multiple levels of detail.

Other surface approximation representations include hybrids of these techniques, and methods that meet application specific criteria. Fowler and Little [9] construct TINs characterized by certain "surface specific" points and critical lines, allowing the TIN representation to closely match important terrain features. Douglas [5] locates specific terrain features such as ridges and channels in a terrain model database, and represents the surface with line segments from these "information rich" features. This method generates only a single surface approximation, however, and is not easily adapted to produce multiresolution models. Gross et al. [12] use a wavelet transform to produce adaptive surface meshing from uniform grid data, allowing for local control of the surface level of detail. This technique, however, has not yet proven to yield interactive frame rates. The general problem of surface simplification has been addressed with methods for mesh decimation and optimization [14, 20], although these techniques are not suitable for on-the-fly generation of multiple levels of detail.

The issue of "continuous" level of detail representations for models has been addressed both for surfaces and more general modeling. Taylor and Barret [22] give an algorithm for surface polygonalization at multiple levels of detail, and use "TIN morphing" to provide for visually continuous change from one resolution to another. Many visual simulation systems handle transitions between multiple levels of detail by alpha blending two models during the transition period. Ferguson [8] claims that such blending techniques between levels of detail may be visually distracting, and discusses a method of Delaunay triangulation and triangle subdivision which smoothly matches edges across areas of different resolution.

3 MOTIVATION

The algorithm presented in this paper has been designed to meet a number of criteria desirable for a real-time level of detail (LOD) algorithm for height fields. These characteristics include:

(i) At any instant, the mesh geometry and the components that describe it should be directly and efficiently queryable, allowing for surface following and fast spatial indexing of both polygons and vertices.

(ii) Dynamic changes to the geometry of the mesh, leading to recomputation of surface parameters or geometry, should not significantly impact the performance of the system.

(iii) High frequency data such as localized convexities and concavities, and/or local changes to the geometry, should not have a widespread global effect on the complexity of the model.

(iv) Small changes to the view parameters (e.g. viewpoint, view direction, field of view) should lead only to small changes in complexity in order to minimize uncertainties in prediction and allow maintenance of (near) constant frame rates.

(v) The algorithm should provide a means of bounding the loss in image quality incurred by the approximated geometry of the mesh. That is, there should exist a consistent and direct relationship between the input parameters to the LOD algorithm and the resulting image quality.

Note that some applications do not require the satisfaction of all of these criteria. However, a polygon-based level of detail algorithm that supports all of these features is clearly of great importance in areas such as terrain rendering, which often requires both high frame rates and high visual fidelity, as well as fast and frequent queries of a possibly deformable terrain surface. Our algorithm successfully achieves all of the goals listed above.

Most contemporary approaches to level of detail management fail to meet at least one of these five criteria. TIN models, for example, do not in general meet the first two criteria. Generation of even modest size TINs requires extensive computational effort. Because TINs are non-uniform in nature, surface following (e.g. for animation of objects on the surface) and intersection (e.g. for collision detection, selection, and queries) are hard to handle efficiently due to the lack of a spatial organization of the mesh polygons. The importance of (ii) is relevant in many applications, such as games and military applications, where dynamic deformations of the mesh occur, e.g. in the form of explosions.

The most common drawback of regular grid representations is that the polygonalization is seldom optimal, or even near optimal. Large, flat surfaces may require the same polygon density as small, rough areas do. This is due to the sensitivity to localized, high frequency data within large, uniform resolution areas of lower complexity. (Most level of detail algorithms require that the mesh is subdivided into rectangular blocks of polygons to allow for fast view culling and coarse level of detail selection.) Hence, (iii) is violated as a small bump in the mesh may force higher resolution data than is needed to describe the remaining area of a block. This problem may be alleviated by reducing the overall complexity and applying temporal blending, or morphing, between different levels of detail to avoid "popping" in the mesh [16, 22].

Common to typical TIN and regular grid LOD algorithms is the discreteness of the levels of detail. Often, only a relatively small number of models for a given area are defined, and the difference in the number of polygons in successive levels of detail may be quite large. When switching between two levels of detail, the net change in the number of rendered polygons may amount to a substantial fraction of the given rendering capacity, and may cause rapid fluctuations in the frame rate.

Many LOD algorithms fail to recognize the need for an error bound in the rendered image. While many simplification methods are mathematically viable, the level of detail generation and selection are often not directly coupled with the screen-space error resulting from the simplification. Rather, these algorithms characterize the data with a small set of parameters that are used in conjunction with viewpoint distance and view angle to select what could be considered "appropriate" levels of detail. Examples of such algorithms include TIN simplification [9], feature (e.g. peaks, ridges, and valleys) identification and preservation [5, 21], and frequency analysis/transforms such as wavelet simplification [6, 12]. These algorithms often do not provide enough information to derive a tight bound on the maximum error in the projected image. If image quality is important and "popping" effects need to be minimized in animations, the level of detail selection should be based on a user-specified error tolerance measured in screen-space, and should preferably be done on a per polygon/vertex basis.

The algorithm presented in this paper satisfies all of the above criteria. Some key features of the algorithm include: flexibility and efficiency afforded by a regular grid representation; localized polygon densities due to variable resolution within each block; screen-space error-driven LOD selection determined by a single threshold; and continuous level of detail, which will be discussed in the following section.

3.1 Continuous Level of Detail

Continuous level of detail has recently been used to describe a variety of properties [8, 18, 22], some of which are discussed below. As mentioned in (iii) and (iv) above, it is important that the complexity of the surface geometry changes smoothly between consecutive frames, and that the simplified geometry doesn't lead to gaps or popping in the mesh. In a more precise description of the term *continuity* in the context of multiresolution height fields, the continuous function, its domain, and its range must be clearly defined. This function may be one of the following:

(i) The elevation function $z(x,y,t)$, where $x,y,t \in \mathbf{R}$. The parameter t may denote time, distance, or some other scalar quantity. This function morphs (blends) the geometries of two discrete levels of detail defined on the same area, resulting in a virtually continuous change in level of detail over time, or over distance from the viewpoint to the mesh.

(ii) The elevation function $z(x,y)$ with domain $\mathbf{R}^2$. The function z is defined piecewise on a per block basis. When discrete levels of detail are used to represent the mesh, two adjacent blocks of different resolution may not align properly, and gaps along the boundaries of the blocks may be seen. The elevation z on these borders will not be continuous unless precautions are taken to ensure that such gaps are smoothed out.

(iii) The polygon distribution function $n(\mathbf{v},A)$. For any given area $A \subseteq \mathbf{R}^2$, the number of polygons used to describe the area is continuous with respect to the viewpoint $\mathbf{v}$.[1] Note that A does not necessarily have to be a connected set. Since the image of n is discrete, we define continuity in terms of the *modulus of continuity* $\omega(\delta,n)$. We say that n is continuous iff $\omega(\delta,n) \to \varepsilon$, for some $\varepsilon \leq 1$, as $\delta \to 0$. That is, for sufficiently small changes in the viewpoint, the change in the number of polygons over A is at most one. As a consequence of a continuous polygon distribution, the number of rendered polygons (after clipping), $n(\mathbf{v})$, is continuous with respect to the viewpoint.

Note that a continuous level of detail algorithm may possess one or more of these independent properties (e.g. (i) does not in general imply (iii), and vice versa). Depending on the constraints inherent in the tessellation method, criterion (iii) may or may not be satisfiable, but a small upper bound ε_{max} on ε may exist. Our algorithm, as presented here, primarily addresses definition (iii), but has been designed to be easily extensible to cover the other two definitions (the color plates included in this paper reflect an implementation satisfying (ii)).

[1]This vector may be generalized to describe other view dependent parameters, such as view direction and field of view.

4 SIMPLIFICATION CRITERIA

The surface simplification process presented here is best described as a sequence of two steps: a coarse-grained simplification of the height field mesh geometry that is done to determine which discrete level of detail models are needed, followed by a fine-grained retriangulation of each LOD model in which individual vertices are considered for removal. The algorithm ensures that no errors are introduced in the coarse simplification beyond those that would be introduced if the fine-grained simplification were applied to the entire mesh. Both steps are executed for each rendered frame, and all evaluations involved in the simplification are done dynamically in real-time, based on the location of the viewpoint and the geometry of the height field.

The height field is described by a rectilinear grid of points elevated above the x-y plane, with discrete sampling intervals of x_{res} and y_{res}. The surface corresponding to the height field (before simplification) is represented as a symmetric triangle mesh. The smallest mesh representable using this triangulation, the *primitive mesh*, has dimensions 3×3 vertices, and successively larger meshes are formed by grouping smaller meshes in a 2×2 array configuration (see Figure 2). For any level l in this recursive construction of the mesh, the vertex dimensions x_{dim} and y_{dim} are $2^l + 1$. For a certain level n, the resulting mesh is said to form a *block*, or a discrete level of detail model. A set of such blocks of fixed dimensions $2^n + 1$ vertices squared, describes the height field dataset, where the boundary rows and columns between adjacent blocks are shared. While the dimensions of all blocks are fixed, the spatial extent of the blocks may vary by multiples of powers of two of the height field sampling resolution, i.e. the area of a block is $2^{m+n}x_{res} \times 2^{m+n}y_{res}$ where m is some non-negative integer. Thus, lower resolution blocks can be obtained by discarding every other row and column of four higher resolution blocks. We term these decimated vertices the *lowest level vertices* of a block (see Figure 2c). A *quadtree* data structure [17] naturally lends itself to the block partitioning of the height field dataset described above.

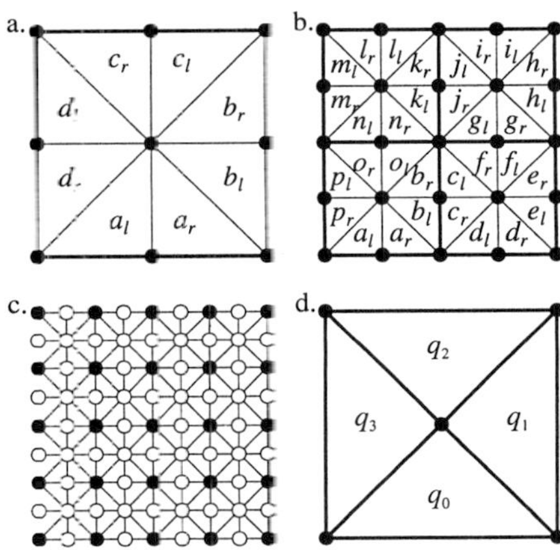

Figure 2: (a, b) Triangulation of uniform height fields of dimensions 3×3 and 5×5 vertices, respectively. (c) Lowest level vertices (unfilled). (d) Block quadrants.

In the following sections, we describe the different simplification steps. We begin by deriving a criterion for the fine-grained (vertex-based) simplification. The coarse-grained (block-based) level of detail selection is then described in terms of the former.

4.1 Vertex-Based Simplification

In the fine-grained simplification step, many smaller triangles are removed and replaced with fewer larger triangles. Conceptually, at the beginning of each rendered frame, the entire height field dataset at its highest resolution is considered. Wherever certain conditions are met, a *triangle/co-triangle pair* $(\triangle_{a_l}, \triangle_{a_r})$ is reduced to one single triangle $\triangle_{a_l} \oplus \triangle_{a_r}$, and the resulting triangle and its co-triangle (if one exists) are considered for further simplification in a recursive manner. In the *x-y* plane with $x_{res} = y_{res}$, a triangle/co-triangle pair is defined by the two congruent right triangles obtained by bisecting a larger isosceles right triangle. Recursive bisection of the resulting two triangles yields lower level triangle/co-triangle pairs. Triangle/co-triangle pairs within a block are descended from the four triangular quadrants of the block, defined by the block boundary and its diagonals (see Figure 2d). For arbitrary height field resolutions, the square mesh is simply stretched in either dimension while retaining the vertex connections. Figure 2a and 2b illustrate the lowest level pairs, where each pair has been assigned a unique letter.

The conditions under which a triangle pair can be combined into a single triangle are primarily described by the amount of change in slope between the two triangles. For triangles $\triangle ABE$ and $\triangle BCE$, with *A*, *B*, and *C* in a plane perpendicular to the *x-y* plane, the slope change is measured by the vertical (*z* axis) distance $\delta_B = |B_z - \frac{A_z + C_z}{2}|$, i.e. the maximum vertical distance between $\triangle ACE = \triangle ABE \oplus \triangle BCE$ and the triangles $\triangle ABE$ and $\triangle BCE$ (see Figure 3). This distance is referred to as vertex *B*'s *delta value*. As the delta value increases, the chance of triangle fusion decreases. By projecting the *delta segment*, defined by *B* and the midpoint of $\overline{AC}$, onto the projection plane, one can determine the maximum perceived geometric (linear) error between the merged triangle and its corresponding sub-triangles. If this error is smaller than a given threshold, τ, the triangles may be fused. If the resulting triangle has a co-triangle with error smaller than the threshold, this pair is considered for further simplification. This process is applied recursively until no further simplification of the mesh can be made. Note that this scheme typically involves a reduction of an already simplified mesh, and the resulting errors (i.e. the projected delta segments) are not defined with respect to the highest resolution mesh, but rather relative to the result of the previous iteration in the simplification process. However, empirical data indicates that the effects of this approximation are negligible (see Section 7).

We now derive a formula for the length of the projected delta segment. Let $\mathbf{v}$ be the midpoint of the delta segment,[2] and define $\mathbf{v}^+ = \mathbf{v} + [\ 0\ \ 0\ \ \frac{\delta}{2}\ ]$, $\mathbf{v}^- = \mathbf{v} - [\ 0\ \ 0\ \ \frac{\delta}{2}\ ]$. Let $\mathbf{e}$ be the viewpoint and $\hat{\mathbf{x}}$, $\hat{\mathbf{y}}$, $\hat{\mathbf{z}}$ be the orthonormal eye coordinate axes expressed in world coordinates. Furthermore, let d be the distance from $\mathbf{e}$ to the projection plane, and define λ to be the number of pixels per world coordinate unit in the screen *x-y* coordinate system. (We assume that the pixel aspect ratio is 1:1.) The subscripts *eye* and *screen* are used to denote vectors represented in *eye coordinates* (after the view transformation) and *screen coordinates* (after the perspective projection), respectively. Using these definitions, the following approximations are made:

- When projecting the vectors $\mathbf{v}^+$ and $\mathbf{v}^-$, their midpoint $\mathbf{v}$ is always assumed to be in the center of view, i.e. along $-\hat{\mathbf{z}}$. This approximation is reasonable as long as the field of view is relatively small, and its effect is that the projected delta segments that represent the errors in the triangle simplification become relatively smaller at the periphery of the screen, where less detail is then used—an artifact that is often acceptable as human visual perception degrades toward the periphery.
- We assume $v^+_{eye_z} \simeq v^-_{eye_z} \simeq v_{eye_z}$ in the perspective division $\frac{1}{-v_{eye_z}}$. This is a fair assumption because, in general, $\delta \ll ||\mathbf{e} - \mathbf{v}|| = -v_{eye_z}$.

[2] One may safely substitute the vertex associated with the delta segment for its midpoint.

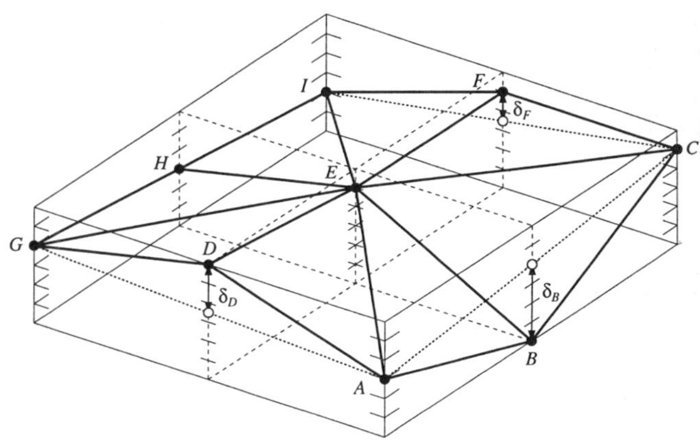

Figure 3: Geometric representation of delta values. $\delta_B = 4$, $\delta_D = 2.5$, $\delta_F = 1.5$, $\delta_H = 0$.

According to the first approximation, the viewing matrix is then:

$$\mathbf{M} = \begin{bmatrix} \hat{x}_x & \hat{y}_x & \frac{e_x - v_x}{||\mathbf{e}-\mathbf{v}||} & 0 \\ \hat{x}_y & \hat{y}_y & \frac{e_y - v_y}{||\mathbf{e}-\mathbf{v}||} & 0 \\ \hat{x}_z & \hat{y}_z & \frac{e_z - v_z}{||\mathbf{e}-\mathbf{v}||} & 0 \\ -\mathbf{e}\cdot\hat{\mathbf{x}} & -\mathbf{e}\cdot\hat{\mathbf{y}} & -\mathbf{e}\cdot\frac{\mathbf{e}-\mathbf{v}}{||\mathbf{e}-\mathbf{v}||} & 1 \end{bmatrix}$$

with $\hat{\mathbf{x}}$ and $\hat{\mathbf{y}}$ perpendicular to $\mathbf{e} - \mathbf{v}$ at all times. This definition of $\mathbf{M}$ leads to the following equalities:

$$\begin{aligned} \mathbf{v}^+_{eye} - \mathbf{v}^-_{eye} &= \mathbf{v}^+\mathbf{M} - \mathbf{v}^-\mathbf{M} \\ &= \delta \left[\ \hat{x}_z \ \ \hat{y}_z \ \ \frac{e_z - v_z}{||\mathbf{e}-\mathbf{v}||} \ \ 0\ \right] \\ \hat{x}_z^2 + \hat{y}_z^2 &= 1 - \left(\frac{e_z - v_z}{||\mathbf{e}-\mathbf{v}||}\right)^2 \end{aligned}$$

The length of the projected delta segment is then described by the following set of equations:

$$\begin{aligned} \delta_{screen} &= ||\mathbf{v}^+_{screen} - \mathbf{v}^-_{screen}|| \\ &= \frac{d\lambda\sqrt{(v^+_{eye_x} - v^-_{eye_x})^2 + (v^+_{eye_y} - v^-_{eye_y})^2}}{-v_{eye_z}} \\ &= \frac{d\lambda\sqrt{(\delta\hat{x}_z)^2 + (\delta\hat{y}_z)^2}}{||\mathbf{e}-\mathbf{v}||} \\ &= \frac{d\lambda\delta\sqrt{1 - \left(\frac{e_z - v_z}{||\mathbf{e}-\mathbf{v}||}\right)^2}}{||\mathbf{e}-\mathbf{v}||} \\ &= \frac{d\lambda\delta\sqrt{(e_x - v_x)^2 + (e_y - v_y)^2}}{(e_x - v_x)^2 + (e_y - v_y)^2 + (e_z - v_z)^2} \end{aligned} \qquad (1)$$

For performance reasons, δ^2_{screen} is compared to τ^2 so that the square root can be avoided:

$$\frac{d^2\lambda^2\delta^2\left((e_x-v_x)^2+(e_y-v_y)^2\right)}{\left((e_x-v_x)^2+(e_y-v_y)^2+(e_z-v_z)^2\right)^2}\leq\tau^2$$

An equivalent inequality that defines the simplification condition reduces to a few additions and multiplications:

$$\delta^2\left((e_x-v_x)^2+(e_y-v_y)^2\right)\leq$$
$$\kappa^2\left((e_x-v_x)^2+(e_y-v_y)^2+(e_z-v_z)^2\right)^2 \qquad (2)$$

where $\kappa=\frac{\tau}{d\lambda}$ is a constant. Whenever $e_x=v_x$ and $e_y=v_y$, i.e. when the viewpoint is directly above or below the delta segment, the projection is zero, and the triangles are coalesced. The probability of satisfying the inequality decreases as e_z approaches v_z, or when the delta segment is viewed from the side. This makes sense, intuitively, as less detail is required for a top-down view of the mesh (assuming a monoscopic view), while more detail is necessary to accurately retain contours and silhouettes in side views. The geometric interpretation of the complement of Equation 2 is a "bialy"—a solid circular torus with no center hole—centered at $\mathbf{v}$, with radius $r=\frac{d\lambda\delta}{2\tau}$ (see Figure 4). The triangles associated with $\mathbf{v}$ can be combined provided that the viewpoint is not contained in the bialy.

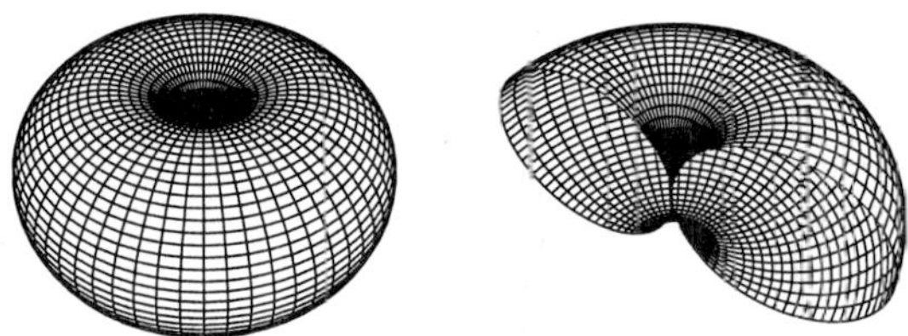

Figure 4: Geometric representation (and its cross-section) of the boundary of Equation 2.

4.2 Block-Based Simplification

Complex datasets may consist of millions of polygons, and it is clearly too computationally expensive to run the simplification process described in the previous section on all polygon vertices for each individual frame. By obtaining a conservative estimate of whether certain groups of vertices can be eliminated in a block, the mesh can often be decimated by several factors with little computational cost. If it is known that the maximum delta projection of all lowest level vertices in a block falls within τ, those vertices can immediately be discarded, and the block can be replaced with a lower resolution block, which in turn is considered for further simplification. Accordingly, a large fraction of the delta projections can be avoided.

The discrete level of detail selection is done by computing the maximum delta value, δ_{max}, of the lowest level vertices for each block. Given the axis-aligned bounding box of a block and δ_{max}, one can determine, for a given viewpoint, whether any of these vertices have delta values large enough to exceed the threshold τ. If none of them do, a lower resolution model may be used. We can expand on this idea to obtain a more efficient simplification algorithm. By using τ, the view parameters, and the constraints provided by the bounding box, one can compute the smallest delta value δ_l that, when projected, can exceed τ, as well as the largest delta value δ_h that may project smaller than τ. Delta values between these extremes fall in an *uncertainty interval*, which we denote by $I_u=(\delta_l,\delta_h]$, for which Equation 2 has to be evaluated. Vertices with delta values less than δ_l can readily be discarded without further evaluation, and conversely, vertices with delta values larger than δ_h cannot be removed. It would obviously be very costly to compute I_u by reversing the projection to get the delta value whose projection equals τ for every single vertex within the block, but one can approximate I_u by assuming that the vertices are dense in the bounding box of the block, and thus obtain a slightly larger superset of I_u. From this point on, we will use I_u to denote this superset.

To find the lower bound δ_l of I_u, the point in the bounding box that maximizes the delta projection must be found. From Equation 1, define $r=\sqrt{(e_x-v_x)^2+(e_y-v_y)^2}$ and $h=e_z-v_z$. We seek to maximize the function $f(r,h)=\frac{r}{r^2+h^2}$ subject to the constraints $r^2+h^2\geq d^2$ and $\mathbf{v}\in B$, where d is the distance from the viewpoint to the projection plane and B is the set of points contained in the bounding box, described by the two vectors

$$\begin{aligned}\mathbf{b}_{min} &= \begin{bmatrix} b_{min_x} & b_{min_y} & b_{min_z}\end{bmatrix}\\ \mathbf{b}_{max} &= \begin{bmatrix} b_{max_x} & b_{max_y} & b_{max_z}\end{bmatrix}\end{aligned}$$

We solve this optimization problem by constraining r, such that $d^2-h^2\leq r^2_{min}\leq r^2\leq r^2_{max}$ (r and h are otherwise independent). Clearly, then, h^2 has to be minimized which is accomplished by setting $h=h_{min}=|e_z-\text{clamp}(b_{min_z},e_z,b_{max_z})|$, where

$$\text{clamp}(x_{min},x,x_{max})=\begin{cases} x_{min} & \text{if } x<x_{min}\\ x_{max} & \text{if } x>x_{max}\\ x & \text{otherwise}\end{cases}$$

In the x-y plane, define r_{min} to be the smallest distance from $\begin{bmatrix} e_x & e_y\end{bmatrix}$ to the rectangular slice (including the interior) of the bounding box defined by $\begin{bmatrix} b_{min_x} & b_{min_y}\end{bmatrix}$ and $\begin{bmatrix} b_{max_x} & b_{max_y}\end{bmatrix}$, and define r_{max} to be the largest such distance. Via partial differentiation with respect to r, the maximum f_{max} of $f(r,h)$ is found at $r=h$. If no $\mathbf{v}$ exists under the given constraints that satisfies $r=h$, r is increased/decreased until $\mathbf{v}\in B$, i.e. $r=\text{clamp}(r_{min},h,r_{max})$.

The upper bound, δ_h, is similarly found by minimizing $f(r,h)$. This is done by setting $h=h_{max}=\max\{|e_z-b_{min_z}|,|e_z-b_{max_z}|\}$. f_{min} is then found when either $r=r_{min}$ or $r=r_{max}$, whichever yields a smaller $f(r,h)$.

The bounds on I_u can now be found using the following equations:

$$\delta_l = \frac{\tau}{d\lambda f_{max}} \qquad (3)$$

$$\delta_h = \begin{cases} 0 & \text{if } \tau=0\\ \frac{\tau}{d\lambda f_{min}} & \text{if } \tau>0 \text{ and } f_{min}>0\\ \infty & \text{otherwise}\end{cases} \qquad (4)$$

After computation of I_u, δ_{max} is compared to δ_l, and if smaller, a lower resolution level of detail block is substituted, and the process is repeated for this block. If $\delta_{max}>\delta_l$, it may be that a higher resolution block is needed. By maintaining $\delta^*_{max}=\max_i\{\delta_{max_i}\}$, the largest δ_{max} of all higher resolution blocks (or *block descendants*) for the given area, δ^*_{max} is compared to δ_l for the current block, and if greater, four higher resolution blocks replace the current block. As mentioned earlier, this implicit hierarchical organization of blocks is best represented by a quadtree, where each block corresponds to a quadnode.

4.3 Vertex Dependencies

As pointed out in Section 4.1, triangle fusion can occur only when the triangles in the triangle pair appear on the same level in the triangle subdivision. For example, in Figure 2b, $\triangle_{e_l}\oplus\triangle_{e_r}$ and

$\triangle_{f_l} \oplus \triangle_{f_r}$ cannot be coalesced unless the triangles in both pairs $(\triangle_{e_l}, \triangle_{e_r})$ and $(\triangle_{f_l}, \triangle_{f_r})$ have been fused. The triangles can be represented by nodes in a binary expression tree, where the smallest triangles correspond to terminal nodes, and coalesced triangles correspond to higher level, nonterminal nodes formed by recursive application of the $\oplus$ operator (hence the subscripts l and r for "left" and "right"). Conceptually, this tree spans the entire height field dataset, but can be limited to each block.

Another way of looking at triangle fusion is as vertex removal, i.e. when two triangles are fused, one vertex is removed. We call this vertex the *base vertex* of the triangle pair. Each triangle pair has a *co-pair* associated with it,[3] and the pair/co-pair share the same base vertex. The mapping of vertices to triangle pairs, or the nodes associated with the operators that act on the triangle pairs, results in a *vertex tree*, wherein each vertex occurs exactly twice; once for each triangle pair (Figures 5g and 5h). Hence, each vertex has two distinct parents (or dependents)—one in each of two binary subtrees T_0 and T_1—as well as four distinct children. If any of the descendants of a vertex v are included in the rendered mesh, so is v, and we say that v is *enabled*. If the projected delta segment associated with v exceeds the threshold τ, v is said to be *activated*, which also implies that v is *enabled*. Thus, the *enabled* attribute of v is determined by

$$\begin{aligned} & activated(v) \vee \\ & \quad enabled(left_{T_0}(v)) \vee \\ & \quad enabled(right_{T_0}(v)) \vee \\ & \quad enabled(left_{T_1}(v)) \vee \\ & \quad enabled(right_{T_1}(v)) \Rightarrow enabled(v) \end{aligned}$$

An additional vertex attribute, *locked*, allows the *enabled* flag to be hardwired to either **true** or **false**, overriding the relationship above. This may be necessary, for example, when eliminating gaps between adjacent blocks if compatible levels of detail do not exist, i.e. some vertices on the boundaries of the higher resolution block may have to be permanently disabled. Figures 5a–e show the dependency relations between vertices level by level. Figure 5f shows the influence of an enabled vertex over other vertices that directly or indirectly depend on it. Figures 5g and 5h depict the two possible vertex tree structures within a block, where intersections have been separated for clarity.

To satisfy continuity condition (ii) (see Section 3.1), the algorithm must consider dependencies that cross block boundaries. Since the vertices on block boundaries are shared between adjacent blocks, these vertices must be referenced uniquely, so that the dependencies may propagate across the boundaries. In most implementations, such shared vertices are simply duplicated, and these redundancies must be resolved before or during the simplification stage. One way of approaching this is to access each vertex via a pointer, and discard the redundant copies of the vertex before the block is first accessed. Another approach is to ensure that the attributes of all copies of a vertex are kept consistent when updates (e.g. *enabled* and *activated* transitions) occur. This can be achieved by maintaining a circular linked list of copies for each vertex.

5 ALGORITHM OUTLINE

The algorithm presented here describes the steps necessary to select which vertices should be included for rendering of the mesh. In Section 5.1, we describe how the mesh is rendered once the vertex selection is done. A discussion of appropriate data structures is presented in Section 6. Using the equations presented in previous sections, the algorithm is summarized by the pseudocode below. Unless qualified with superscripts, all variables are assumed to belong to the current frame and block.

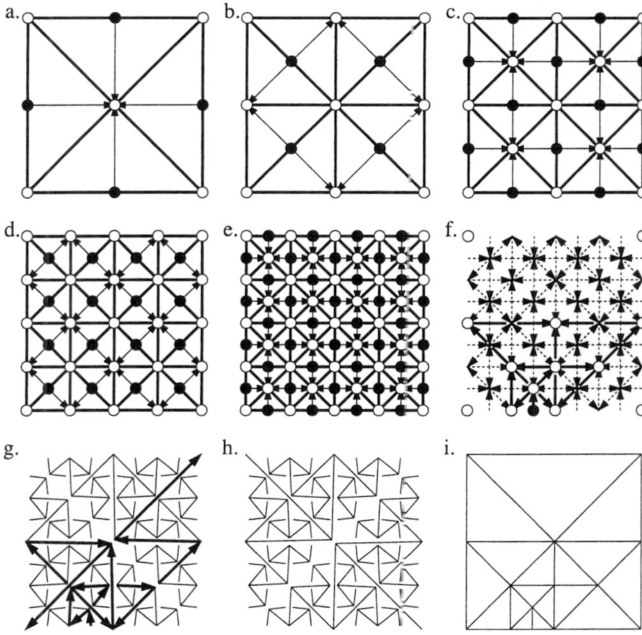

Figure 5: (a–e) Vertex dependencies by descending levels (left to right, top to bottom). An arc from A to B indicates that B depends on A. (f) Chain of dependencies originating from the solid vertex. (g, h) Symmetric binary vertex trees (the arcs in (g) correspond to (f)). (i) Triangulation corresponding to (f).

```
MAIN()
for each frame n
    for each active block b
        compute I_u (Equations 3 and 4)
        if δ_max ≤ δ_l
            replace b with lower resolution block
        else if δ*_max > δ_l
            replace b with higher resolution blocks
    for each active block b
        determine if b intersects the view frustum
    for each visible block b
        I_0 ← (δ_l^{n-1}, δ_l^n]
        I_1 ← (δ_h^n, δ_h^{n-1}]
        for each vertex v with δ(v) ∈ I_0
            activated(v) ← false
            UPDATE-VERTEX(v)
        for each vertex v with δ(v) ∈ I_1
            activated(v) ← true
            UPDATE-VERTEX(v)
        for each vertex v with δ(v) ∈ I_u
            EVALUATE-VERTEX(v)
    for each visible block b
        RENDER-BLOCK(b)
```

```
UPDATE-VERTEX(v)
if ¬locked(v)
    if ¬dependency_i(v) ∀i
        if enabled(v) ≠ activated(v)
            enabled(v) ← ¬enabled(v)
            NOTIFY(parent_T0(v), branch_T0(v), enabled(v))
            NOTIFY(parent_T1(v), branch_T1(v), enabled(v))
```

[3] Triangle pairs with base vertices on the edges of the finite dataset are an exception.

```
EVALUATE-VERTEX(v)
1  if ¬locked(v)
2      if ¬dependency_i(v) ∀i
3          activated(v) ← ¬Equation 2
4          if enabled(v) ≠ activated(v)
5              enabled(v) ← ¬enabled(v)
6              NOTIFY(parent_{T_0}(v), branch_{T_0}(v), enabled(v))
7              NOTIFY(parent_{T_1}(v), branch_{T_1}(v), enabled(v))
```

```
NOTIFY(v, child, state)
1  if v is a valid vertex
2      dependency_child(v) ← state
3      if ¬locked(v)
4          if ¬dependency_i(v) ∀i
5              if ¬activated(v)
6                  enabled(v) ← false
7                  NOTIFY(parent_{T_0}(v), branch_{T_0}(v), false)
8                  NOTIFY(parent_{T_1}(v), branch_{T_1}(v), false)
9          else
10             if ¬enabled(v)
11                 enabled(v) ← true
12                 NOTIFY(parent_{T_0}(v), branch_{T_0}(v), true)
13                 NOTIFY(parent_{T_1}(v), branch_{T_1}(v), true)
```

The term *active block* refers to whether the block is currently the chosen level of detail for the area it covers. All blocks initially have I_u set to $[0,\infty)$, and so do blocks that previously were inactive. When deactivating vertices with delta values smaller than δ_l, the interval $I_0 \subseteq [0,\delta_l]$ is traversed. By inductive reasoning, vertices with deltas smaller than the lower bound of I_0 must have been deactivated in previous frames. Similarly, I_1 is used for vertex activation. In quadtree implementations, the condition on line 4 in MAIN may have to be supplemented; the condition $\delta_{max} \leq \delta_l$ should also hold for the three neighboring siblings of b before b can be replaced.

If a vertex's *enabled* attribute changes, all dependent vertices must be notified of this change so that their corresponding *dependency* flags are kept consistent with this change. The procedure UPDATE-VERTEX checks if $enabled(v)$ has changed, and if so, notifies v's dependents by calling NOTIFY. If the *enabled* flag of a dependent in turn is modified, NOTIFY is called recursively. Since line 2 in NOTIFY necessarily involves a change of a *dependency* bit, there may be a transition in $enabled(v)$ from **true** to **false** on line 6 provided $activated(v)$ is **false** as the vertex is no longer dependent. The evaluation of Equation 2 on line 3 in EVALUATE-VERTEX can be deferred if any of the vertex's *dependency* flags are set, which is of significant importance as this evaluation is one of the most computationally expensive parts of the algorithm. Note that there may be a one-frame delay before the *activated* attribute is corrected due to this deferral if the child vertices are evaluated after the dependent vertex (line 2 of EVALUATE-VERTEX and lines 4–5 of NOTIFY). The function $branch_T(v)$ refers to the field of the parent in tree T that reflects the *enabled* field of vertex v. Note that a check has to be made (line 1 in NOTIFY) whether a vertex is "valid" as some vertices have fewer than two dependents (e.g. boundary vertices).

5.1 Mesh Rendering

Once the vertex selection is made, a triangle mesh must be formed that connects the selected vertices. This mesh is defined by specifying the vertices encountered in a pre-order descent of the binary vertex trees. The recursive stopping condition is a **false** *enabled* attribute. To efficiently render the mesh, a triangle mesh graphics primitive, such as the one supported by IRIS GL and OpenGL [11, 15], may be used. For each specified vertex v, the previous two vertices and v form the next triangle in the mesh. At certain points, the previous two vertices must be swapped via a `swaptmesh()` call (IRIS GL), or a `glVertex()` call (OpenGL). A copy of the two-entry graphics vertex buffer, *my-buffer*, is maintained explicitly to allow the decision as to when to swap the entries to be made. The most recent vertex in this buffer is indexed by *ptr*.

The following pseudocode describes the mesh rendering algorithm. Each of the four triangular quadrants q_i are rendered in counterclockwise order, with the first vertex in each quadrant coincident with the last vertex in the previous quadrant (see Figure 2d). Hence, a single triangle mesh can be used to render the entire block. The indices q_{i_l}, q_{i_t}, and q_{i_r} correspond to the left, top, and right vertex indices of quadrant q_i, respectively, with the "top" index being the center of the block. The block dimensions are 2^n+1 squared.

```
RENDER-BLOCK(b)
1  enter triangle mesh mode
2  render vertex v_{q_{0_l}}
3  my-buffer_ptr ← q_{0_l}
4  previous-level ← 0
5  for each quadrant q_i in block b
6      if previous-level is even
7          toggle ptr
8      else
9          swap vertices in graphics buffer
10     render vertex v_{q_{i_l}}
11     my-buffer_ptr ← q_{i_l}
12     previous-level ← 2n + 1
13     RENDER-QUADRANT(q_{i_l}, q_{i_t}, q_{i_r}, 2n)
14 render vertex v_{q_{0_l}}
15 exit triangle mesh mode
```

```
RENDER-QUADRANT(i_l, i_t, i_r, level)
1  if level > 0
2      if enabled(v_{i_t})
3          RENDER-QUADRANT(i_l, (i_l+i_r)/2, i_t, level − 1)
4          if i_t ∉ my-buffer
5              if level + previous-level is odd
6                  toggle ptr
7              else
8                  swap vertices in graphics buffer
9              render vertex v_{i_t}
10             my-buffer_ptr ← i_t
11             previous-level ← level
12         RENDER-QUADRANT(i_t, (i_l+i_r)/2, i_r, level − 1)
```

The index $\frac{i_l+i_r}{2}$ corresponds to the (base) vertex that in the x-y plane is the midpoint of the edge $\overline{v_{i_l} v_{i_r}}$. Since *my-buffer* reflects what vertices are currently in the graphics buffer, line 9 in RENDER-BLOCK and line 8 in RENDER-QUADRANT could be implemented with a `glVertex()` call, passing the second most recent vertex in *my-buffer*.

6 DATA STRUCTURES

Many of the issues related to the data structures used with this algorithm have purposely been left open, as different needs may demand totally different approaches to their representations. In one implementation—the one presented here—as few as six bytes per vertex were used, and as many as 28 bytes per vertex were needed in another. In this section, we describe data structures that will be useful in many implementations.

For a compact representation, the vertex elevation is discretized and stored as a 16-bit integer. A minimum of six additional bits per vertex are required for the various flags, including the *enabled*, *activated*, and four *dependency* attributes. Optionally, the *locked* attribute can be added to these flags. The theoretical range of delta values becomes $[0, 2^{16}-1]$ in steps of $\frac{1}{2}$. We elect to store each δ in "compressed" form as an 8-bit integer $\hat{\delta}$ in order to conserve space by encapsulating the vertex structure in a 32-bit aligned word. We define the decompression function as $\delta = \frac{1}{2}\lfloor(1+\hat{\delta})^{1+\hat{\delta}^2/(2^8-1)^2} - 1\rfloor$.[4] This exponential mapping preserves the accuracy needed for the more frequent small deltas, while allowing large delta values to be represented, albeit with less accuracy. The compression function is defined as the inverse of the decompression function. Both functions are implemented as lookup tables.

To accommodate tasks such as rendering and surface following, the vertices must be organized spatially for fast indexing. In Section 4.2, however, we implied that vertices within ranges of delta values could be immediately accessed. This is accomplished by creating an auxiliary array of indices, in which the entries are sorted on the corresponding vertices' delta values. Each entry uniquely references the corresponding vertex (i, j) via an index into the array of vertex structures. For each possible compressed delta value within a block, there is a pointer (index) $p_{\hat{\delta}}$ to a bin that contains the vertex indices corresponding to that delta value. The 2^8 bins are stored in ascending order in a contiguous, one-dimensional array. The entries in bin i are then indexed by $p_i, p_i+1, \ldots, p_{i+1}-1$ ($p_i = p_{i+1}$ implies that bin i is empty). For block dimensions up to 2^7+1, the indices can be represented with 16 bits to save space, which in addition to the 32-bit structure described above, results in a total of six bytes storage per vertex.

7 RESULTS

To show the effectiveness of the polygon reduction and display algorithm, we here present the results of a quantitative analysis of the number of polygons and delta projections, frame rates, computation and rendering time, and errors in the approximated geometry. A set of color plates show the resulting wireframe triangulations and textured terrain surfaces at different stages of the simplification and for different choices of τ. Two height field datasets were used in generating images and collecting data: a 64 km^2 area digital elevation model of the Hunter-Liggett military base in California, sampled at 2×2 meter resolution, and 1 meter height (z) resolution (Color Plates 1a–c and 2a–c); and a 1×1 meter resolution, 14 km^2 area of 29 Palms, California, with a z resolution of one tenth of a meter (Color Plates 3a–d). The vertical field of view is 60° in all images, which were generated on a two-processor, 150 MHz SGI Onyx RealityEngine^2 [1], and have dimensions 1024×768 pixels unless otherwise specified.

We first examine the amount of polygon reduction as a function of the threshold τ. A typical view of the Hunter-Liggett terrain was chosen for this purpose, which includes a variety of features such as ridges, valleys, bumps, and relatively flat areas. Figure 6 shows four curves drawn on a logarithmic scale (vertical axis). The top horizontal line, $n_0(\tau) = 13 \cdot 10^6$, shows the total number of polygons in the view frustum before any reduction method is applied. The curve second from the top, $n_1(\tau)$, represents the number of polygons remaining after the block-based level of detail selection is done. The number of polygons rendered, $n_2(\tau)$, i.e. the remaining polygons after the vertex-based simplification, is shown by the lowest solid curve. As expected, these two curves flatten out as τ is increased. The ratio $n_0(\tau)/n_2(\tau)$ ranges from about 2 ($\tau = 0$) to over 6,000 ($\tau = 8$). Of course, at $\tau = 0$, only coplanar triangles are fused. The ratio $n_1(\tau)/n_2(\tau)$ varies between 1.85 and 160 over the same interval, which clearly demonstrates the advantage of refining each uniform level of detail block.

We pay special attention to the data obtained at $\tau = 1$, as this threshold is small enough that virtually no popping can be seen in animated sequences, and the resulting surfaces, when textured, are seemingly identical to the ones obtained with no mesh simplification. Color Plates 1a–c illustrate the three stages of simplification at $\tau = 1$. In Color Plate 1c, note how many polygons are required for the high frequency data, while only a few, large polygons are used for the flatter areas. For this particular threshold, $n_0(1)/n_2(1)$ is slightly above 200, while $n_1(1)/n_2(1)$ is 18. The bottommost, dashed curve in Figure 6 represents the total number of delta values that fall in the uncertainty interval per frame (Section 4.2). Note that this quantity is generally an order of magnitude smaller than the number of rendered polygons. This is significant as the evaluations associated with these delta values constitute the bulk of the computation in terms of CPU time. This also shows the advantage of computing the uncertainty interval, as out of the eight million vertices contained in the view frustum, only 14,000 evaluations of Equation 2 need to be made when $\tau = 1$.

[4] This results in an upper bound $\frac{2^{16}-1}{2}$ for the delta values.

τ	displacement				
	mean	median	max	std. dev.	$> \tau$ (%)
0.000	0.00	0.00	0.00	0.00	0.00
0.125	0.03	0.00	0.52	0.05	6.41
0.250	0.06	0.00	0.85	0.09	4.52
0.500	0.11	0.04	1.56	0.15	3.14
1.000	0.21	0.07	2.88	0.29	2.61
2.000	0.42	0.13	5.37	0.59	2.84
4.000	0.88	0.23	10.41	1.24	3.27
8.000	1.38	0.19	16.69	2.08	1.38

Table 1: Screen-space error in simplified geometry.

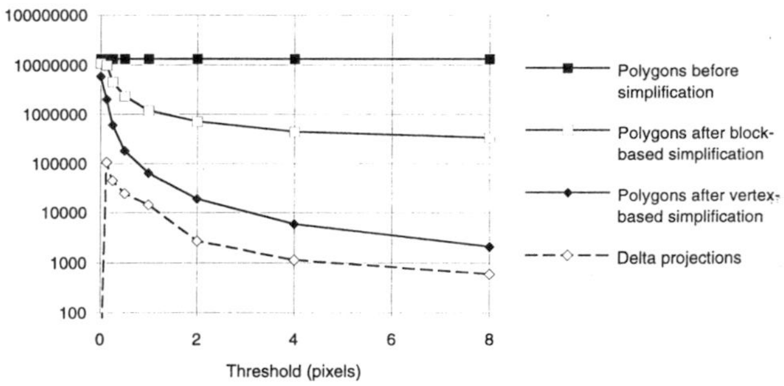

Figure 6: The number of polygons (n_0, n_1, n_2, from top to bottom) as a function of τ. The bottom curve shows the number of times Equation 2 was evaluated per frame.

In order to evaluate the errors due to the simplification, the points on the polygonal surface of the simplified mesh that have been displaced vertically, as well as the remaining triangle vertices, are perspective projected to screen-space and compared to the projections of the original set of vertices. Optimally, each such screen coordinate displacement should fall within the threshold distance τ. However, this constraint may in certain cases be violated due to the approximations discussed in Section 4.1. Table 1 was compiled for each mesh after vertex-based simplification was applied, and the surface points were correlated with the original eight million vertices shown in Color Plate 1a. The table summarizes the mean, median, maximum, and standard deviation of the displacements in number of pixels, as well as the fraction of displacements that exceed τ. In all cases, the average pixel error is well below τ. It can be seen that the approximations presented in Section 4.1 do not significantly impact the accuracy, as the fraction of displacements that exceed τ is typically less than five percent.

Color Plates 2a–c illustrate a checkerboard pattern draped over the polygonal meshes from Color Plates 1a–c. Qualitatively, these images suggest little or no perceivable loss in image quality for a threshold of one pixel, even when the surface complexity is reduced by a factor of 200.

Figure 7 demonstrates the efficiency of the algorithm. The computation time associated with the delta projections (lines 10–20 in MAIN, Section 5) is typically only a small fraction of the rendering time. This data was gathered for the views shown in Color Plates 3a–d.

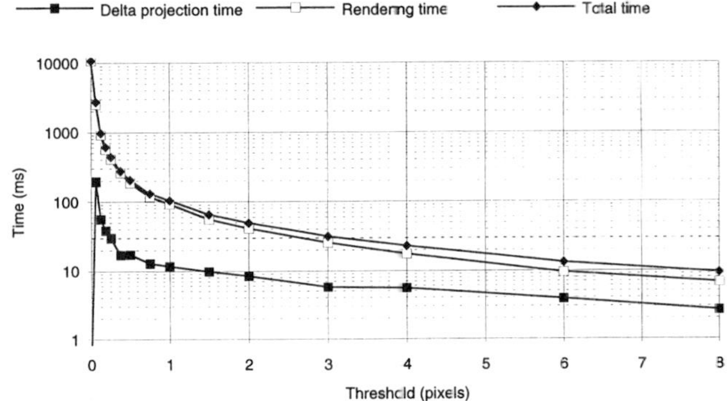

Figure 7: Rendering and evaluation times and their sum as functions of τ.

Figure 8 shows how the quantities in Figure 6, as well as the frame rate vary with time. The data collection for 3,230 frames was done over a time period of 120 seconds, with the viewpoint following a circular path of radius 1 km over the Hunter-Liggett dataset. The terrain was rendered as a wireframe mesh in a 640×480 window, with $\tau = 2$ pixels. It can be seen that the number of rendered polygons does not depend on the total number of polygons in the view frustum, but rather on the complexity of the terrain intersected by the view frustum. As evidenced by the graph, a frame rate of at least 20 frames per second was sustained throughout the two minutes of fly-through.

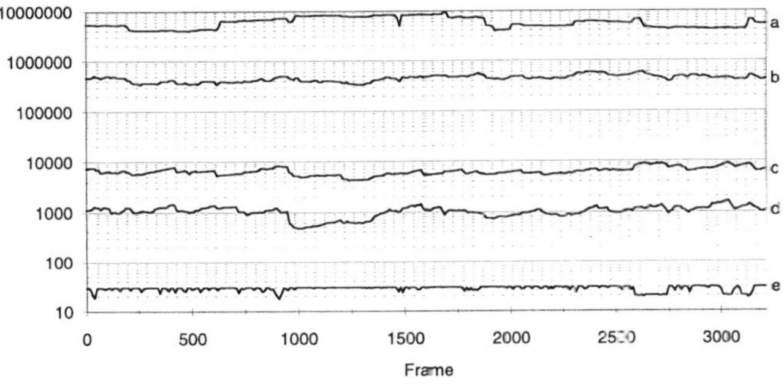

Figure 8: Time graph of (a) total number of polygons in view frustum, (b) number of polygons after block-based simplification, (c) number of polygons after vertex-based simplification, (d) number of delta projections, and (e) frames per second.

8 CONCLUSION

We have presented a height-field display algorithm based on real-time, per vertex level of detail evaluation, that achieves interactive and consistent frame rates exceeding twenty frames per second, with only a minor loss in image quality. Attractive features attributed to regular grid surface representations, such as fast geometric queries, compact representation, and fast mesh rendering are retained. The concept of continuous level of detail allows a polygon distribution that is near optimal for any given viewpoint and frame, and also yields smooth changes in the number of rendered polygons. A single parameter that can easily be changed interactively, with no incurred cost, determines the resulting image quality, and a direct relationship between this parameter and the number of rendered polygons exists, providing capabilities for maintaining consistent frame rates. The algorithm can easily be extended to handle the problem of gaps between blocks of different levels of detail, as well as temporal geometry morphing to further minimize popping effects.

Acknowledgement

This work was performed in part under contract DAKF11-91-D-0004-0034 from the U.S. Army Research Laboratory.

References

[1] AKELEY, K. RealityEngine Graphics. Proceedings of SIGGRAPH 93. In *Computer Graphics* Proceedings, Annual Conference Series, 1993, ACM SIGGRAPH, pp. 109–116.

[2] COSMAN, M. A., MATHISEN, A. E., and ROBINSON, J. A. A New Visual System to Support Advanced Requirements. In *Proceedings, IMAGE V Conference*, June 1990, pp. 370–380.

[3] DE BERG, M. and DOBRINDT, K. T. G. On Levels of Detail in Terrains. In *11th ACM Symposium on Computational Geometry*, June 1995.

[4] DE FLORIANI, L. and PUPPO, E. Hierarchical Triangulation for Multiresolution Surface Description. *ACM Transactions on Graphics* 14(4), October 1995, pp. 363–411.

[5] DOUGLAS, D. H. Experiments to Locate Ridges and Channels to Create a New Type of Digital Elevation Model. *Cartographica* 23(4), 1986, pp. 29–61.

[6] ECK, M., DEROSE, T., DUCHAMP, T., HOPPE, H., LOUNSBERY, M., and STUETZLE, W. Multiresolution Analysis of Arbitrary Meshes. Proceedings of SIGGRAPH 95. In *Computer Graphics* Proceedings, Annual Conference Series, 1995, ACM SIGGRAPH, pp. 173–182.

[7] FALBY, J. S., ZYDA, M. J., PRATT, D. R., and MACKEY, R. L. NPSNET: Hierarchical Data Structures for Real-Time Three-Dimensional Visual Simulation. *Computers & Graphics* 17(1), 1993, pp. 65–69.

[8] FERGUSON, R. L., ECONOMY, R., KELLY, W. A., and RAMOS, P. P. Continuous Terrain Level of Detail for Visual Simulation. In *Proceedings, IMAGE V Conference*, June 1990, pp. 144–151.

[9] FOWLER, R. J. and LITTLE, J. J. Automatic Extraction of Irregular Network Digital Terrain Models. Proceedings of SIGGRAPH 79. In *Computer Graphics* 13(2) (August 1979), pp. 199–207.

[10] GARLAND, M. and HECKBERT, P. S. Fast Polygonal Approximation of Terrains and Height Fields. Technical Report CMU-CS-95-181, CS Dept., Carnegie Mellon U., 1995.

[11] *Graphics Library Programming Guide*. Silicon Graphics Computer Systems, 1991.

[12] GROSS, M. H., GATTI, R., and STAADT, O. Fast Multiresolution Surface Meshing. In *Proceedings of Visualization '95*, October 1995, pp. 135–142.

[13] HECKBERT, P. S. and GARLAND, M. Multiresolution Modeling for Fast Rendering. In *Proceedings of Graphics Interface '94*, 1994, pp. 1–8.

[14] HOPPE, H., DEROSE, T., DUCHAMP, T., MCDONALD, J., and STUETZLE, W. Mesh Optimization. Proceedings of SIGGRAPH 93. In *Computer Graphics* Proceedings, Annual Conference Series, 1993, ACM SIGGRAPH, pp. 19–26.

[15] NEIDER, J., DAVIS, T., and WOO, M. *OpenGL Programming Guide*. Addison-Wesley, 1993.

[16] ROHLF, J. and HELMAN, J. IRIS Performer: A High Performance Multiprocessing Toolkit for Real-Time 3D Graphics. Proceedings of SIGGRAPH 94. In *Computer Graphics* Proceedings, Annual Conference Series, 1993, ACM SIGGRAPH, pp. 381–394.

[17] SAMET, H. The Quadtree and Related Hierarchical Data Structures. *ACM Computing Surveys* 16(2), June 1984, pp. 187–260.

[18] SCARLATOS, L. L. A Refined Triangulation Hierarchy for Multiple Levels of Terrain Detail. In *Proceedings, IMAGE V Conference*, June 1990, pp. 114–122.

[19] SCHRÖDER, F. and ROSSBACH, P. Managing the Complexity of Digital Terrain Models. *Computers & Graphics* 18(6), 1994, pp. 775–783.

[20] SCHROEDER, W. J., ZARGE, J. A., and LORENSON, W. E. Decimation of Triangle Meshes. Proceedings of SIGGRAPH 92. In *Computer Graphics* 26(2) (July 1992), pp. 65–70.

[21] SOUTHARD, D. A. Piecewise Planar Surface Models from Sampled Data. *Scientific Visualization of Physical Phenomena*, June 1991, pp. 667–680.

[22] TAYLOR, D. C. and BARRET, W. A. An Algorithm for Continuous Resolution Polygonalizations of a Discrete Surface. In *Proceedings of Graphics Interface '94*, 1994, pp. 33–42.

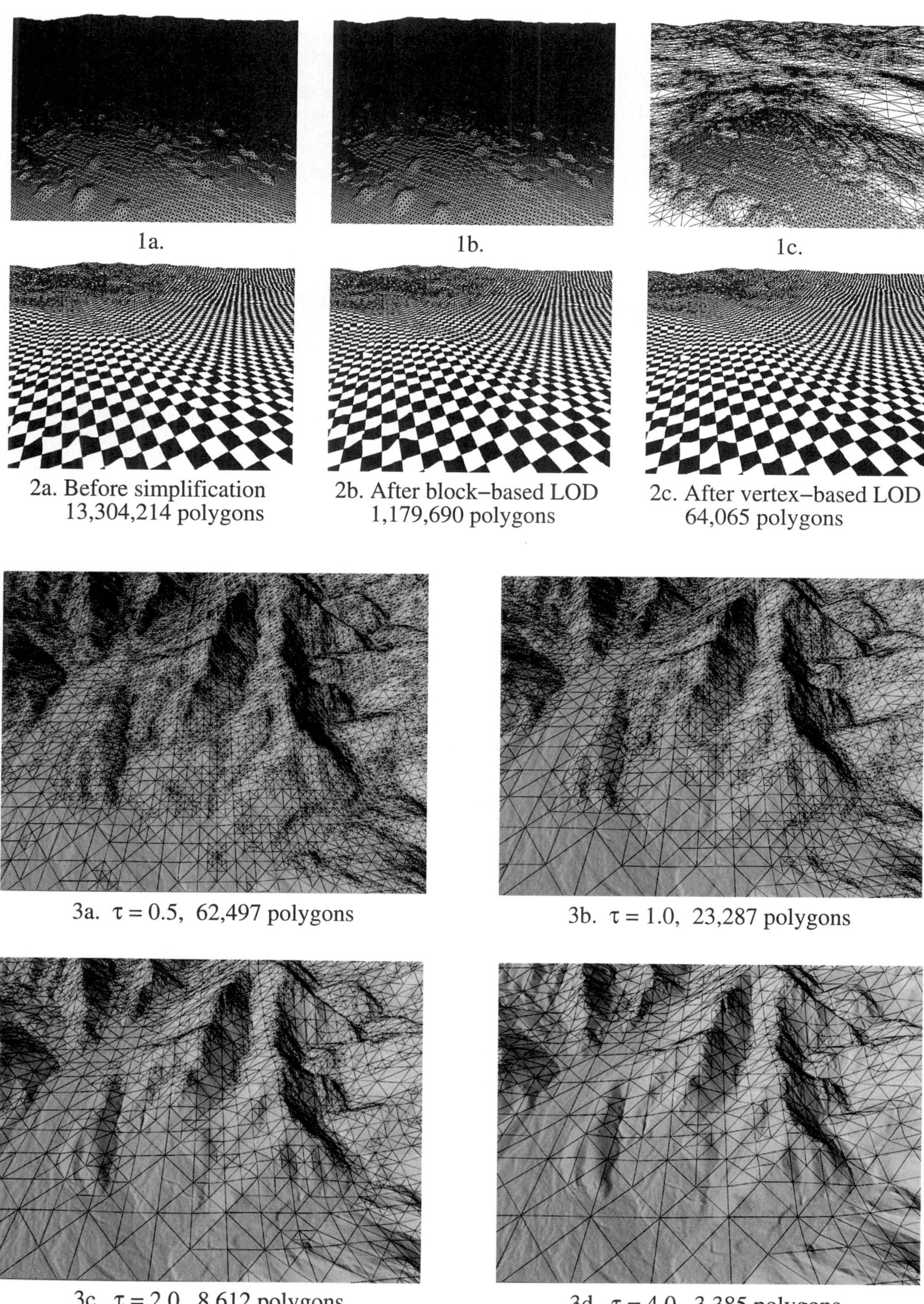

1a.

1b.

1c.

2a. Before simplification
13,304,214 polygons

2b. After block–based LOD
1,179,690 polygons

2c. After vertex–based LOD
64,065 polygons

3a. $\tau = 0.5$, 62,497 polygons

3b. $\tau = 1.0$, 23,287 polygons

3c. $\tau = 2.0$, 8,612 polygons

3d. $\tau = 4.0$, 3,385 polygons

Simplification Envelopes

Jonathan Cohen* Amitabh Varshney† Dinesh Manocha* Greg Turk* Hans Weber*
Pankaj Agarwal‡ Frederick Brooks* William Wright*
http://www.cs.unc.edu/~geom/envelope.html

Abstract

We propose the idea of *simplification envelopes* for generating a hierarchy of level-of-detail approximations for a given polygonal model. Our approach guarantees that all points of an approximation are within a user-specifiable distance ϵ from the original model and that all points of the original model are within a distance ϵ from the approximation. Simplification envelopes provide a general framework within which a large collection of existing simplification algorithms can run. We demonstrate this technique in conjunction with two algorithms, one local, the other global. The local algorithm provides a fast method for generating approximations to large input meshes (at least hundreds of thousands of triangles). The global algorithm provides the opportunity to avoid local "minima" and possibly achieve better simplifications as a result.

Each approximation attempts to minimize the total number of polygons required to satisfy the above ϵ constraint. The key advantages of our approach are:

- General technique providing guaranteed error bounds for genus-preserving simplification
- Automation of both the simplification process and the selection of appropriate viewing distances
- Prevention of self-intersection
- Preservation of sharp features
- Allows variation of approximation distance across different portions of a model

CR Categories and Subject Descriptors: I.3.3 [**Computer Graphics**]: Picture/Image Generation — Display algorithms; I.3.5 [**Computer Graphics**]: Computational Geometry and Object Modeling — Curve, surface, solid, and object representations.

Additional Key Words and Phrases: hierarchical approximation, model simplification, levels-of-detail generation, shape approximation, geometric modeling, offsets.

*Department of Computer Science, University of North Carolina, Chapel Hill, NC 27599-3175. {cohenj,weberh,manocha,turk,brooks,wright}@cs.unc.edu

†Department of Computer Science, State University of New York, Stony Brook, NY 11794-4400. varshney@cs.sunysb.edu

‡Department of Computer Science, Duke University, Durham, NC 27708-0129. pankaj@cs.duke.edu

1 Introduction

We present the framework of *simplification envelopes* for computing various levels of detail of a given polygonal model. These hierarchical representations of an object can be used in several ways in computer graphics. Some of these are:

- Use in a level-of-detail-based rendering algorithm for providing desired frame update rates [4, 10].
- Simplifying traditionally over-sampled models such as those generated from volume datasets, laser scanners, and satellites for storage and reducing CPU cycles during processing, with relatively few or no disadvantages [12, 13, 15, 17, 24, 26].
- Using low-detail approximations of objects for illumination algorithms, especially radiosity [22].

Simplification envelopes are a generalization of *offset surfaces*. Given a polygonal representation of an object, they allow the generation of minimal approximations that are guaranteed not to deviate from the original by more than a user-specifiable amount while preserving global topology. We surround the original polygonal surface with two envelopes, then perform simplification within this volume. A sample application of the algorithms we describe can be seen in Figure 1.

Figure 1: *A level-of-detail hierarchy for the rotor from a brake assembly.*

Such an approach has several benefits in computer graphics. First, one can very precisely quantify the amount of approximation that is tolerable under given circumstances. Given a user-specified error in number of pixels of deviation of an object's silhouette, it is possible to choose which level of detail to view from a particular distance to maintain that pixel error bound. Second, this approach allows one a fine control over which regions of an object should be approximated more and which ones less. This could be used for selectively preserving those features of an object that are *perceptually* important. Third, the user-specifiable tolerance for approximation is the only parameter required to obtain the approximations; fine tweaking of several parameters depending upon the object to be approximated is not required. Thus, this approach is quite useful for *automating the process* of topology-preserving simplifications of a large number of objects. This problem of *scalability* is important for any simplification algorithm. One of our main goals is to create a method for simplification which is not only automatic for large datasets, but tends to preserve the shapes of the original models.

The rest of the paper is organized in the following manner: we survey the related work in Section 2, explain our assumptions and terminology in Section 3, describe the envelope and approximation computations in Sections 4 and 5, present some useful extentions to and properties of the approximation algorithms in Section 6, and explain our implementation and results in Section 7.

2 Background

Approximation algorithms for polygonal models can be classified into two broad categories:

- **Min-# Approximations**: For this version of the approximation problem, given some error bound ϵ, the objective is to minimize the number of vertices such that no point of the approximation $\mathcal{A}$ is farther than ϵ distance away from the input model $\mathcal{I}$.
- **Min-ϵ Approximations**: Here we are given the number of vertices of the approximation $\mathcal{A}$ and the objective is to minimize the error, or the difference, between $\mathcal{A}$ and $\mathcal{I}$.

Previous work in the area of min-# approximations has been done by [6, 23] where they adaptively subdivide a series of bicubic patches and polygons over a surface until they fit the data within the tolerance levels.

In the second category, work has been done by several groups. Turk [26] first distributes a given number of vertices over the surface depending on the curvature and then re-triangulates them to obtain the final mesh. Schroeder et al. [24] and Hinker and Hansen [15] operate on a set of local rules — such as deleting edges or vertices from almost coplanar adjacent faces, followed by local re-triangulation. These rules are applied iteratively till they are no longer applicable. A somewhat different local approach is taken in [21] where vertices that are close to each other are clustered and a new vertex is generated to represent them. The mesh is suitably updated to reflect this.

Hoppe et al. [16] proceed by iteratively optimizing an energy function over a mesh to minimize both the distance of the approximating mesh from the original, as well as the number of approximating vertices. An interesting and elegant solution to the problem of polygonal simplification by using wavelets has been presented in [7, 8] where arbitrary polygonal meshes are first subdivided into patches with *subdivision connectivity* and then multiresolution wavelet analysis is used over each patch. This wavelet approach preserves global topology.

In computational geometry, it has been shown that computing the minimal-facet ϵ-approximation is NP-hard for both convex polytopes [5] and polyhedral terrains [1]. Thus, algorithms to solve these problems have evolved around finding polynomial-time approximations that are *close* to the optimal.

Let k_o be the size of a min-# approximation. An algorithm has been given in [19] for computing an ϵ-approximation of size $O(k_o \log n)$ for convex polytopes. This has recently been improved by Clarkson in [3]; he proposes a randomized algorithm for computing an approximation of size $O(k_o \log k_o)$ in expected time $O(k_o n^{1+\delta})$ for any $\delta > 0$ (the constant of proportionality depends on δ, and tends to $+\infty$ as δ tends to 0). In [2] Brönnimann and Goodrich observed that a variant of Clarkson's algorithm yields a polynomial-time deterministic algorithm that computes an approximation of size $O(k_0)$. Working with polyhedral terrains, [1] present a polynomial-time algorithm that computes an ϵ-approximation of size $O(k_o \log k_o)$ to a polyhedral terrain.

Our work is different from the above in that it allows adaptive, genus-preserving, ϵ-approximation of arbitrary polygonal objects. Additionally, we can simplify bordered meshes and meshes with holes. In terms of direct comparison with the global topology preserving approach presented in [7, 8], for a given ϵ our algorithm has been *empirically* able to obtain "reduced" simplifications, which are much smaller in output size (as demonstrated in Section 7). The algorithm in [21] also guarantees a bound in terms of the Hausdorff metric. However, it is not guaranteed to preserve the genus of the original model.

3 Terminology and Assumptions

Let us assume that $\mathcal{I}$ is a three-dimensional compact and orientable object whose polygonal representation $\mathcal{P}$ has been given to us. Our objective is to compute a piecewise-linear approximation $\mathcal{A}$ of $\mathcal{P}$. Given two piecewise linear objects $\mathcal{P}$ and $\mathcal{Q}$, we say that $\mathcal{P}$ and $\mathcal{Q}$ are *ϵ-approximations* of each other iff every point on $\mathcal{P}$ is within a distance ϵ of some point of $\mathcal{Q}$ and every point on $\mathcal{Q}$ is within a distance ϵ of some point of $\mathcal{P}$. Our goal is to outline a method to generate two envelope surfaces surrounding $\mathcal{P}$ and demonstrate how the envelopes can be used to solve the following polygonal approximation problem. Given a polygonal representation $\mathcal{P}$ of an object and an approximation parameter ϵ, generate a genus-preserving ϵ-approximation $\mathcal{A}$ with minimal number of polygons such that the vertices of $\mathcal{A}$ are a subset of vertices of $\mathcal{P}$.

We assume that all polygons in $\mathcal{P}$ are triangles and that $\mathcal{P}$ is a well-behaved polygonal model, i.e., every edge has either one or two adjacent triangles, no two triangles interpenetrate, there are no unintentional "cracks" in the model, no T-junctions, etc.

We also assume that each vertex of $\mathcal{P}$ has a single normal vector, which must lie within 90° of the normal of each of its surrounding triangles. For the purpose of rendering, each vertex may have either a single normal or multiple normals. For the purpose of generating envelope surfaces, we shall compute a single vertex normal as a combination of the normals of the surrounding triangles.

The three-dimensional ϵ-offset surface for a parametric surface

$$\mathbf{f}(s,t) = (f_1(s,t), f_2(s,t), f_3(s,t)),$$

whose unit normal to $\mathbf{f}$ is

$$\mathbf{n}(s,t) = (n_1(s,t), n_2(s,t), n_3(s,t)),$$

is defined as $\mathbf{f}^\epsilon(s,t) = (f_1^\epsilon(s,t), f_2^\epsilon(s,t), f_3^\epsilon(s,t))$, where

$$f_i^\epsilon(s,t) = f_i(s,t) + \epsilon n_i(s,t).$$

Note that offset surfaces for a polygonal object can self-intersect and may contain non-linear elements. We define a simplification envelope $\mathcal{P}(+\epsilon)$ (respectively $\mathcal{P}(-\epsilon)$) for an object $\mathcal{I}$ to be a *polygonal* surface that lies *within* a distance of ϵ from every point p on $\mathcal{I}$ in the same (respectively opposite) direction as the normal to $\mathcal{I}$ at p. Thus, the simplification envelopes can be thought of as an approximation to offset surfaces. Henceforth we shall refer to simplification envelope by simply envelope.

Let us refer to the triangles of the given polygonal representation $\mathcal{P}$ as the *fundamental triangles*. Let $e = (v_1, v_2)$ be an edge of $\mathcal{P}$. If the normals $\mathbf{n}_1, \mathbf{n}_2$ to $\mathcal{I}$ at both v_1 and v_2, respectively, are identical, then we can construct a plane π_e that passes through the edge e and has a normal that is perpendicular to that of v_1. Thus v_1, v_2 and their normals all lie along π_e. Such a plane defines two half-spaces for edge e, say π_e^+ and π_e^- (see Fig 2(a)). However, in general the normals $\mathbf{n}_1$ and $\mathbf{n}_2$ at the vertices v_1 and v_2 need not be identical, in which case it is not clear how to define the two half-spaces for an edge. One choice is to use a *bilinear patch* that passes through v_1 and v_2 and has a tangent $\mathbf{n}_1$ at v_1 and $\mathbf{n}_2$ at v_2. Let us call such a bilinear patch for e as the *edge half-space* β_e. Let the two half-spaces for the edge e in this case be β_e^+ and β_e^-. This is shown in Fig 2(b).

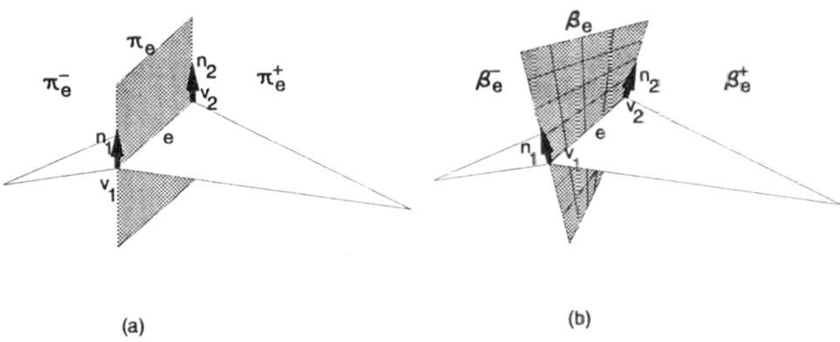

Figure 2: *Edge Half-spaces*

Let the vertices of a fundamental triangle be v_1, v_2, and v_3. Let the coordinates and the normal of each vertex v be represented as $\mathbf{c}(v)$ and $\mathbf{n}(v)$, respectively. The coordinates and the normal of a $(+\epsilon)$-offset vertex v_i^+ for a vertex v_i are: $\mathbf{c}(v_i^+) = \mathbf{c}(v_i) + \epsilon\mathbf{n}(v_i)$, and $\mathbf{n}(v_i^+) = \mathbf{n}(v_i)$. The $(-\epsilon)$-offset vertex can be similarly defined in the opposite direction. These offset vertices for a fundamental triangle are shown in Figure 3.

Now consider the closed object defined by v_i^+ and v_i^-, $i = 1, 2, 3$. It is defined by two triangles, at the top and bottom, and three edge half-spaces. This object contains the fundamental triangle (shown shaded in Figure 3) and we will henceforth refer to it as the *fundamental prism*.

4 Envelope Computation

In order to preserve the input topology of $\mathcal{P}$, we desire that the simplification envelopes do not self-intersect. To meet this criterion we reduce our level of approximation at certain places. In other words, to guarantee that no intersections amongst the envelopes occur, we have to be

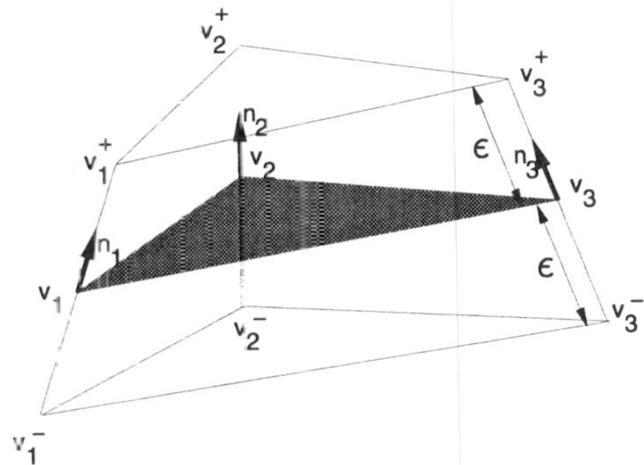

Figure 3: *The Fundamental Prism*

content at certain places with the distance between $\mathcal{P}$ and the envelope being smaller than ϵ. This is how simplification envelopes differ from offset surfaces.

We construct our envelope such that each of its triangles corresponds to a fundamental triangle. We offset each vertex of the original surface in the direction of its normal vector to transform the fundamental triangles into those of the envelope.

If we offset each vertex v_i by the same amount ϵ, to get the offset vertices v_i^+ and v_i^-, the resulting envelopes, $\mathcal{P}(+\epsilon)$ and $\mathcal{P}(-\epsilon)$, may contain self-intersections because one or more offset vertices are closer to some non-adjacent fundamental triangle. In other words, if we define a Voronoi diagram over the fundamental triangles of the model, the condition for the envelopes to intersect is that there be at least one offset vertex lying in the Voronoi region of some non-adjacent fundamental triangle. This is shown in Figure 4 by means of a two-dimensional example. In the figure, the offset vertices b^+ and c^+ are in the Voronoi regions of edges other than their own, thus causing self-intersection of the envelope.

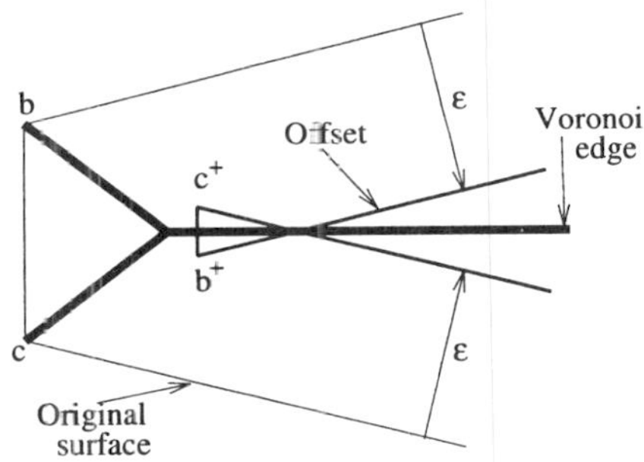

Figure 4: *Offset Surfaces*

Once we make this observation, the solution to avoid self-intersections becomes quite simple — just do not allow an offset vertex to go beyond the Voronoi regions of its adjacent fundamental triangles. In other words, determine the positive and negative ϵ for each vertex v_i such that the vertices v_i^+ and v_i^- determined with this new ϵ do not lie in the Voronoi regions of the non-adjacent fundamental triangles.

While this works in theory, efficient and robust computation of the three-dimensional Voronoi diagram of the fundamental triangles is non-trivial. We now present two methods for computing the reduced ϵ for each vertex, the first method analytical, and the second numerical.

4.1 Analytical ϵ Computation

We adopt a conservative approach for recomputing the ϵ at each vertex. This approach underestimates the values for the positive and negative ϵ. In other words, it guarantees the envelope surfaces not to intersect, but it does not guarantee that the ϵ at each vertex is the largest permissible ϵ. We next discuss this approach for the case of computing the positive ϵ for each vertex. Computation of negative ϵ follows similarly.

Consider a fundamental triangle t. We define a prism t_p for t, which is conceptually the same as its fundamental prism, but uses a value of 2ϵ instead of ϵ for defining the envelope vertices. Next, consider all triangles Δ_i that do not share a vertex with t. If Δ_i intersects t_p above t (the directions above and below t are determined by the direction of the normal to t, above is in the same direction as the normal to t), we find the point on Δ_i that lies within t_p and is closest to t. This point would be either a vertex of Δ_i, or the intersection point of one of its edges with the three sides of the prism t_p. Once we find the point of closest approach, we compute the distance δ_i of this point from t. This is shown in Figure 5.

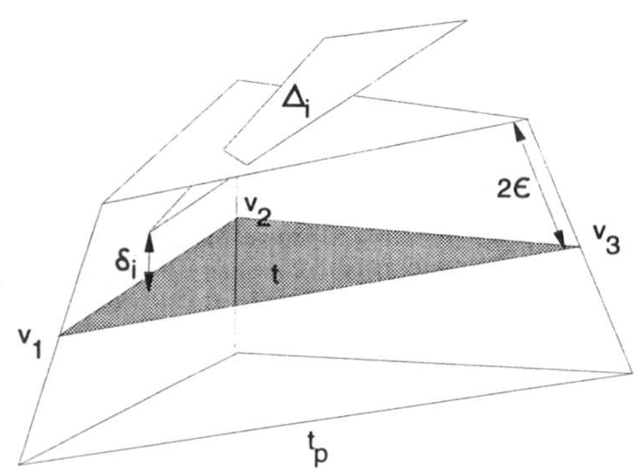

Figure 5: *Computation of δ_i*

Once we have done this for all Δ_i, we compute the new value of the positive ϵ for the triangle t as $\epsilon_{new} = \frac{1}{2}\min_i \delta_i$. If the vertices for this triangle t have this value of positive ϵ, their positive envelope surface will not self-intersect. Once the $\epsilon_{new}(t)$ values for all the triangles t have been computed, the $\epsilon_{new}(v)$ for each vertex v is set to be the minimum of the $\epsilon_{new}(t)$ values for all its adjacent triangles.

We use an octree in our implementation to speed up the identification of triangles Δ_i that intersect a given prism.

4.2 Numerical ϵ Computation

To compute an envelope surface numerically, we take an iterative approach. Our envelope surface is initially identical to the input model surface. In each iteration, we sequentially attempt to move each envelope vertex a fraction of the ϵ distance in the direction of its normal vector (or the opposite direction, for the inner envelope). This effectively stretches or contracts all the triangles adjacent to the vertex. We test each of these adjacent triangles for intersection with each other and the rest of the model. If no such intersections are found, we accept the step, leaving the vertex in this new position. Otherwise we reject it, moving the vertex back to its previous position. The iteration terminates when all vertices have either moved ϵ or can no longer move.

In an attempt to guarantee that each vertex gets to move a reasonable amount of its potential distance, we use an adaptive step size. We encourage a vertex to move at least K (an arbitrary constant which is scaled with respect to ϵ and the size of the object) steps by allowing it to reduce its step size. If a vertex has moved less than K steps and its move is been rejected, it divides its step size in half and tries again (with some maximum number of divides allowed on any particular step). Notice that if a vertex moves i steps and is rejected on the $(i+1)$st step, we know it has moved at least $i/(i+1)$ % of its potential distance, so $K/(K+1)$ which is a lower bound of sorts. It is possible, though rare, for a vertex to move less than K steps, if its current position is already quite close to another triangle.

Each vertex also has its own initial step size. We first choose a global, maximum step size based on a global property: either some small percentage of the object's bounding box diagonal length or ϵ/K, whichever is smaller. Now for each vertex, we calculate a local step size. This local step size is some percentage of the vertex's shortest incident edge (only those edges within 90° of the offset direction are considered). We set the vertex's step size to the minimum of the global step size and its local step size. This makes it likely that each vertex's step size is appropriate for a step given the initial mesh configuration.

This approach to computing an envelope surface is robust, simple to implement (if difficult to explain), and fair to all the vertices. It tends to maximize the minimum offset distance amongst the envelope vertices. It works fairly well in practice, though there may still be some room for improvement in generating maximal offsets for thin objects. Figure 6 shows internal and external envelopes computed for three values of ϵ using this approach.

As in the analytical approach, a simple octree data structure makes these intersection tests reasonably efficient, especially for models with evenly sized triangles.

5 Generation of Approximation

Generating a surface approximation typically involves starting with the input surface and iteratively making modifications to ultimately reduce its complexity. This process may be broken into two main stages: *hole creation*, and *hole filling*. We first create a hole by removing some connected set of triangles from the surface mesh. Then we fill the hole with a smaller set of triangles, resulting in some reduction of the mesh complexity.

We demonstrate the generality of the simplification envelope approach by designing two algorithms. The hole filling stages of these algorithms are quite similar, but their hole creation stages are quite different. The first algorithm makes only local choices, creating relatively small holes, while the second algorithm uses global information about the surface to create maximally-sized holes. These design choices produce algorithms with very different properties.

We begin by describing the envelope validity test used to determine whether a *candidate triangle* is valid for inclusion in the approximation surface. We then proceed to the two example simplification algorithms and a description of their relative merits.

5.1 Validity Test

A *candidate triangle* is one which we are considering for inclusion in an approximation to the input surface. Valid candidate triangles must lie between the two envelopes. Because we construct candidate triangles from the vertices of the original model, we know its vertices lie between the two envelopes. Therefore, it is sufficient to test the candidate triangle for intersections with the two envelope

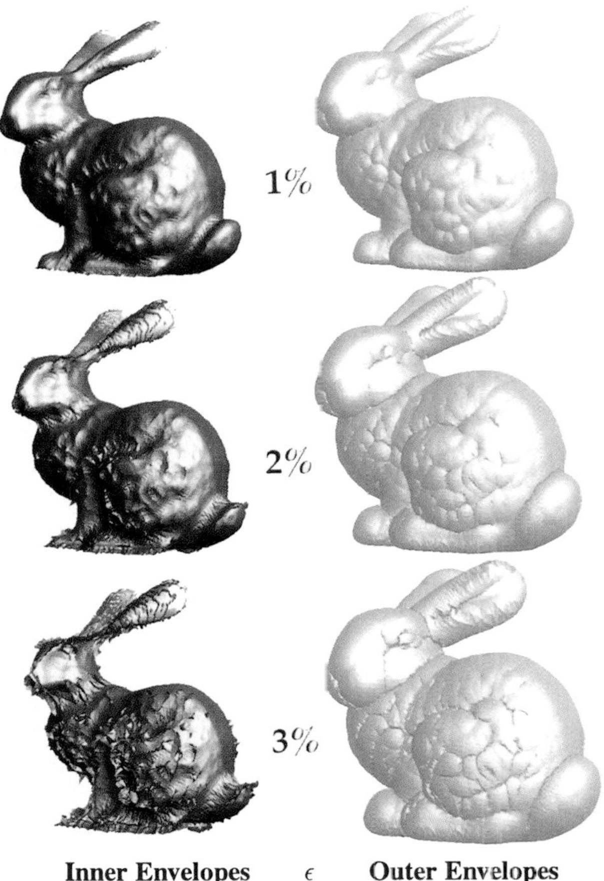

Figure 6: *Simplification envelopes for various* ϵ

surfaces. We can perform such tests efficiently using a space-partitioning data structure such as an octree.

A valid candidate triangle must also not cause a self-intersection in our surface, Therefore, it must not intersect any triangle of the current approximation surface.

5.2 Local Algorithm

To handle large models efficiently within the framework of simplification envelopes we construct a vertex-removal-based local algorithm. This algorithm draws heavily on the work of [24], [26], and [16]. Its main contributions are the use of envelopes to provide global error bounds as well as topology preservation and non-self-intersection. We have also explored the use of a more exhaustive hole-filling approach than any previous work we have seen.

The local algorithm begins by placing all vertices in a queue for removal processing. For each vertex in the queue, we attempt to remove it by creating a hole (removing the vertex's adjacent triangles) and attempting to fill it. If we can successfully fill the hole, the mesh modification is accepted, the vertex is removed from the queue, and its neighbors are placed back in the queue. If not, the vertex is removed from the queue and the mesh remains unchanged. This process terminates when the global error bounds eventually prevent the removal of any more vertices. Once the vertex queue is empty we have our simplified mesh.

For a given vertex, we first create a hole by removing all adjacent triangles. We begin the hole-filling process by generating all possible triangles formed by combinations of the vertices on the hole boundary. This is not strictly necessary, but it allows us to use a greedy strategy to favor triangles with nice aspect ratios. We fill the hole by choosing a triangle, testing its validity, and recursively filling the three (or fewer) smaller holes created by adding that triangle into the hole (see figure 7). If a hole cannot be filled at any level of the recursion, the entire hole filling attempt is considered a failure. Note that this is a single-pass hole filling strategy; we do not backtrack or undo selection of a triangle chosen for filling a hole. Thus, this approach does not guarantee that if a triangulation of a hole exists we will find it. However, it is quite fast and works very well in practice.

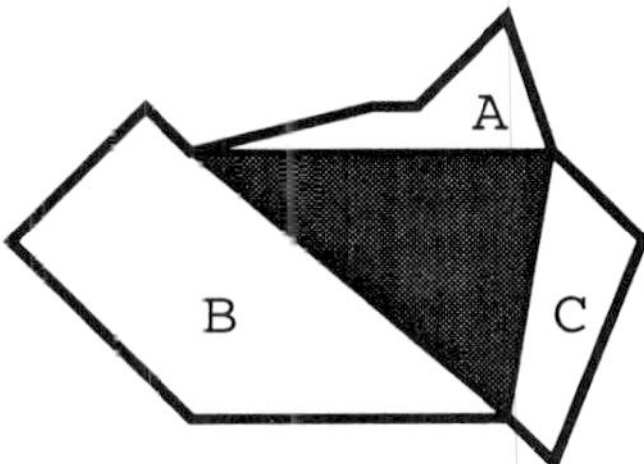

Figure 7: *Hole filling: adding a triangle into a hole creates up to three smaller holes*

We have compared the above approach with an exhaustive approach in which we tried all possible hole-filling triangulations. For simplifications resulting in the removal of hundreds of vertices (like highly oversampled laser-scanned models), the exhaustive pass yielded only a small improvement over the single-pass heuristic. This sort of confirmation reassures us that the single-pass heuristic works well in practice.

5.3 Global Algorithm

This algorithm extends the algorithm presented in [3] to non-convex surfaces. Our major contribution is the use of simplification envelopes to bound the error on a non-convex polygonal surface and the use of fundamental prisms to provide a generalized projection mechanism for testing for regions of multiple covering (overlaps). We present only a sketch of the algorithm here ; see [27] for the full details.

We begin by generating all possible candidate triangles for our approximation surface. These triangles are all 3-tuples of the input vertices which do not intersect either of the offset surfaces. Next we determine how many vertices each triangle *covers*. We rank the candidate triangles in order of decreasing covering.

We then choose from this list of candidate triangles in a greedy fashion. For each triangle we choose, we create a large hole in the current approximation surface, removing all triangles which *overlap* this candidate triangle. Now we begin the recursive hole-filling process by placing this candidate triangle into the hole and filling all the subholes with other triangles, if possible. One further restriction in this process is that the candidate triangle we are testing should not overlap any of the candidate triangles we have previously accepted.

5.4 Algorithm Comparison

The local simplification algorithm is fast and robust enough to be applied to large models. The global strategy is theoretically elegant. While the global algorithm works well for small models, its complexity rises at least quadratically,

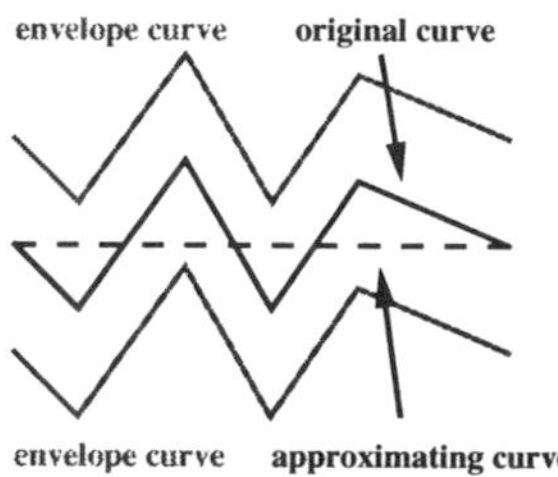

Figure 8: *Curve at local minimum of approximation*

making it prohibitive for larger models. We can think of the simplification problem as an optimization problem as well. A purely local algorithm may get trapped in a local "minimum" of simplification, while an ideal global algorithm will avoid all such minima.

Figure 8 shows a two-dimensional example of a curve for which a local vertex removal algorithm might fail, but an algorithm that globally searches the solution space will succeed in finding a valid approximation. Any of the interior vertices we remove would cause a new edge to penetrate an envelope curve. But if we remove all of the interior vertices, the resulting edge is perfectly acceptable.

This observation motivates a wide range of algorithms of which our local and global examples are the two extremes. We can easily imagine an algorithm that chooses nearby groups of vertices to remove simultaneously rather than sequentially. This could potentially lead to increased speed and simplification performance. However, choosing such sets of vertices remains a challenging problem.

6 Additional Features

Envelope surfaces used in conjunction with simplification algorithms are powerful, general-purpose tools. As we will now describe, they implicitly preserve sharp edges and can be extended to deal with bordered surfaces and perform adaptive approximations.

6.1 Preserving Sharp Edges

One of the important properties in any approximation scheme is the way it preserves any sharp edges or normal discontinuities present in the input model. Simplification envelopes deal gracefully with sharp edges (those with a small angle between their adjacent faces). When the ϵ tolerance is small, there is not enough room to simplify across these sharp edges, so they are automatically preserved. As the tolerance is increased, it will eventually be possible to simplify across the edges (which should no longer be visible from the appropriate distance). Notice that it is not necessary to explicitly recognize these sharp edges.

6.2 Bordered Surfaces

A bordered surface is one containing points that are homeomorphic to a half-disc. For polygonal models, this corresponds to edges that are adjacent to a single face rather than two faces. Depending on the context, we may naturally think of this as the boundary of some plane-like piece of a surface, or a hole in an otherwise closed surface.

The algorithms described in 5 are sufficient for closed triangle meshes, but they will not guarantee our global error bound for meshes with borders. While the envelopes constrain our error with respect to the normal direction of the surface, bordered surfaces require some additional constraints to hold the approximation border close to the original border. Without such constraints, the border of the approximation surface may "creep in," possibly shrinking the surface out of existence.

In many cases, the complexity of a surface's border curves may become a limiting factor in how much we can simplify the surface, so it is unacceptable to forgo simplifying these borders.

We construct a set of border tubes to constrain the error in deviation of the border curves. Each border is actually a cyclic polyline. Intuitively speaking, a border tube is a smooth, non-self-intersecting surface around one of these polylines. Removing a border vertex causes a pair of border edges to be replaced by a single border edge. If this new border edge does not intersect the relevant border tube, we may safely attempt to remove the border vertex.

To construct a tube we define a plane passing through each vertex of the polyline. We choose a coordinate system on this plane and use that to define a circular set of vertices. We connect these vertices for consecutive planes to construct our tube. Our initial tubes have a very narrow radius to minimize the likelihood of self-intersections. We then expand these narrow tubes using the same technique we used previously to construct our simplification envelopes.

The difficult task is to define a coordinate system at each polyline vertex which encourages smooth, non-self-intersecting tubes. The most obvious approach might be to use the idea of Frenet frames from differential geometry to define a set of coordinate systems for the polyline vertices. However, Frenet frames are meant for smooth curves. For a jagged polyline, a tube so constructed often has many self-intersections.

Instead, we use a projection method to minimize the twist between consecutive frames. Like the Frenet frame method, we place the plane at each vertex so that the normal to the plane approximates the tangent to the polyline. This is called the *normal plane*.

At the first vertex, we choose an arbitrary orthogonal pair of axes for our coordinate system in the normal plane. For subsequent vertices, we project the coordinate system from the previous normal plane onto the current normal frame. We then orthogonalize this projected coordinate system in the plane. For the normal plane of the final polyline vertex, we average the projected coordinate systems of the previous normal plane and the initial normal plane to minimize any twist in the final tube segment.

6.3 Adaptive Approximation

For certain classes of objects it is desirable to perform an adaptive approximation. For instance, consider large terrain datasets, models of spaceships, or submarines. One would like to have more detail near the observer and less detail further away. A possible solution could be to subdivide the model into various spatial cells and use a different ϵ-approximation for each cell. However, problems would arise at the boundaries of such cells where the ϵ-approximation for one cell, say at a value ϵ_1 need not necessarily be continuous with the ϵ-approximation for the neighboring cell, say at a different value ϵ_2.

Since all candidate triangles generated are constrained to lie within the two envelopes, manipulation of these envelopes provides one way to smoothly control the level of approximation. Thus, one could specify the ϵ at a given vertex to be a function of its distance from the observer — the larger the distance, the greater is the ϵ.

As another possibility, consider the case where certain

features of a model are very important and are not to be approximated beyond a certain level. Such features might have human perception as a basis for their definition or they might have mathematical descriptions such as regions of high curvature. In either case, a user can vary the ϵ associated with a region to increase or decrease the level of approximation. The bunny in Figure 9 illustrates such an approximation.

Figure 9: *An adaptive simplification for the bunny model. ϵ varies from 1/64% at the nose to 1% at the tail.*

7 Implementation and Results

We have implemented both algorithms and tried out the local algorithm on several thousand objects. We will first discuss some of the implementation issues and then present some results.

7.1 Implementation Issues

The first important implementation issue is what sort of input model to accept. We chose to accept only manifold triangle meshes (or bordered manifolds). This means that each edge is adjacent to two (one in the case of a border) triangles and that each vertex is surrounded by a single ring of triangles.

We also do not accept other forms of degenerate meshes. Many mesh degeneracies are not apparent on casual inspection, so we have implemented an automatic degeneracy detection program. This program detects non-manifold vertices, non-manifold edges, sliver triangles, coincident triangles, T-junctions, and intersecting triangles in a proposed input mesh. Note that correcting these degeneracies is more difficult than detecting them.

Robustness issues are important for implementations of any geometric algorithms. For instance, the analytical method for envelope computation involves the use of bilinear patches and the computation of intersection points. The computation of intersection points, even for linear elements, is difficult to perform robustly. The numerical method for envelope computation is much more robust because it involves only linear elements. Furthermore, it requires an intersection test but not the calculation of intersection points. We perform all such intersection tests in a conservative manner, using fuzzy intersection tests that may report intersections even for some close but non-intersecting elements.

Another important issue is the use of a space-partitioning scheme to speed up intersection tests. We chose to use an octree because of its simplicity. Our current octree implementation deals only with the bounding boxes of the elements stored. This works well for models with triangles that are evenly sized and shaped. For CAD models, which may contain long, skinny, non-axis-aligned triangles, a simple octree does not always provide enough of a speed-up, and it may be necessary to choose a more appropriate space-partitioning scheme.

7.2 Results

We have simplified a total of 2636 objects from the auxiliary machine room (AMR) of a submarine dataset, pictured in Figure 10 to test and validate our algorithm. We reproduce the timings and simplifications achieved by our implementation for the AMR and a few other models in Table 1. All simplifications were performed on a Hewlett-Packard 735/125 with 80 MB of main memory. Images of these simplifications appear in Figures 11 and 12. It is interesting to compare the results on the bunny and phone models with those of [7, 8]. For the same error bound, we are able to obtain much improved solutions.

We have automated the process which sets the ϵ value for each object by assigning it to be a percentage of the diagonal of its bounding box. We obtained the reductions presented in Table 1 for the AMR and Figures 11 and 12 by using this heuristic.

For the rotor and AMR models in the above results, the ith level of detail was obtained by simplifying the $i-1^{th}$ level of detail. This causes to total ϵ to be the sum of all previous ϵ's, so choosing $\epsilon's$ of 1, 2, 4, and 8 percent results in total $\epsilon's$ of 1, 3, 7, and 15 percent. There are two advantages to this scheme:

(a) It allows one to proceed incrementally, taking advantage of the work done in previous simplifications.

(b) It builds a hierarchy of detail in which the vertices at the ith level of detail are a subset of the vertices at the $i-1^{th}$ level of detail.

One of the advantages of the setting ϵ to a percent of the object size is that it provides an a way to automate the selection of switching points used to transition between the various representations. To eliminate visual artifacts, we switch to a more faithful representation of an object when ϵ projects to more than some user-specified number of pixels on the screen. This is a function of the ϵ for that approximation, the output display resolution, and the corresponding maximum tolerable visible error in pixels.

8 Future Work

There are still several areas to be explored in this research. We believe the most important of these to be the generation of correspondences between levels of detail and the moving of vertices within the envelope volume.

Bunny			Phone			Rotor			AMR		
ϵ %	# Polys	Time	ϵ %	# Polys	Time	ϵ %	# Polys	Time	ϵ %	# Polys	Time
0	69,451	N/A	0	165,936	N/A	0	4,735	N/A	0	436,402	N/A
1/64	44,621	9	1/64	43,537	31	1/8	2,146	3	1	195,446	171
1/32	23,581	10	1/32	12,364	35	1/4	1,514	2	3	143,728	61
1/16	10,793	11	1/16	4,891	38	3/4	1,266	2	7	110,090	61
1/8	4,838	11	1/8	2,201	32	1 3/4	850	1	15	87,476	68
1/4	2,204	11	1/4	1,032	35	3 3/4	716	1	31	75,434	84
1/2	1,004	11	1/2	544	33	7 3/4	688	1			
1	575	11	1	412	30	15 3/4	674	1			

Table 1: *Simplification ϵ's and run times in minutes*

8.1 Generating Correspondences

A true geometric hierarchy should contain not only representations of an object at various levels of detail, but also some correspondence information about the relationship between adjacent levels. These relationships are necessary for propagating local information from one level to the next. For instance, this information would be helpful for using the hierarchical geometric representation to perform radiosity calculations. It is also necessary for performing geometric interpolation between the models when using the levels of detail for rendering. Note that the envelope technique preserves silhouettes when rendering, so it is also a good candidate for alpha blending rather than geometric interpolation to smooth out transitions between levels of detail.

We can determine which elements of a higher level of detail surface are covered by an element of a lower level of detail representation by noting which fundamental prisms this element intersects. This is non-trivial only because of the bilinear patches that are the sides of a fundamental prism. We can approximate these patches by two or more triangles and then tetrahedralize each prism. Given this tetrahedralization of the envelope volume, it is possible to stab each edge of the lower level-of-detail model through the tetrahedrons to determine which ones they intersect, and thus which triangles are covered by each lower level-of-detail triangle.

8.2 Moving Vertices

The output mesh generated by either of the algorithms we have presented has the property that its set of vertices is a subset of the set of vertices of the original mesh. If we can afford to relax this constraint somewhat, we may be able to reduce the output size even further. If we allow the vertices to slide along their normal vectors, we should be able to simplify parts of the surface that might otherwise be impossible to simplify for some choices of epsilon. We are currently working on a goal-based approach to moving vertices within the envelope volume. For each vertex we want to remove, we slide its neighboring vertices along their normals to make them lie as closely as possible to a tangent plane of the original vertex. Intuitively, this should increase the likelihood of successfully removing the vertex. During this whole process, we must ensure that none of the neighboring triangles ever violates the envelopes. This approach should make it possible to simplify surfaces using smaller epsilons than previously possible. In fact, it may even enable us to use the original surface and a single envelope as our constraint surfaces rather than two envelopes. This is important for objects with areas of high maximal curvature, like thin cylinders.

9 Conclusion

We have outlined the notion of simplification envelopes and how they can be used for generation of multiresolution hierarchies for polygonal objects. Our approach guarantees non-self-intersecting approximations and allows the user to do adaptive approximations by simply editing the simplification envelopes (either manually or automatically) in the regions of interest. It allows for a global error tolerance, preservation of the input genus of the object, and preservation of sharp edges. Our approach requires only one user-specifiable parameter, allowing it to work on large collections of objects with no manual intervention if so desired. It is rotationally and translationally invariant, and can elegantly handle holes and bordered surfaces through the use of cylindrical tubes. Simplification envelopes are general enough to permit both simplification algorithms with good theoretical properties such as our global algorithm, as well as fast, practical, and robust implementations like our local algorithm. Additionally, envelopes permit easy generation of correspondences across several levels of detail.

10 Acknowledgements

Thanks to Greg Angelini, Jim Boudreaux, and Ken Fast at Electric Boat for the submarine model, Rich Riesenfeld and Elaine Cohen of the Alpha_1 group at the University of Utah for the rotor model, and the Stanford Computer Graphics Laboratory for the bunny and telephone models.Thanks to Carl Mueller, Marc Olano, and Bill Yakowenko for many useful suggestions, and to the rest of the UNC Simplification Group (Rui Bastos, Carl Erikson, Merlin Hughes, and David Luebke) for providing a great forum for discussing ideas. The funding for this work was provide by a Link Foundation Fellowship, Alfred P. Sloan Foundation Fellowship, ARO Contract P-34982-MA, ARO MURI grant DAAH04-96-1-0013, NSF Grant CCR-9319957, NSF Grant CCR-9301259, NSF Career Award CCR-9502239, ONR Contract N00014-94-1-0738, ARPA Contract DABT63-93-C-0048, NSF/ARPA Center for Computer Graphics and Scientific Visualization, NIH Grant RR02170, an NYI award with matching funds from Xerox Corp, and a U.S.-Israeli Binational Science Foundation grant.

References

[1] P. Agarwal and S. Suri. Surface approximation and geometric partitions. In *Proceedings Fifth Symposium on Discrete Algorithms*, pages 24–33, 1994.

[2] H. Brönnimann and M. Goodrich. Almost optimal set covers in finite VC-dimension. In *Proceedings Tenth ACM Symposium on Computational Geometry*, pages 293–302, 1994.

[3] K. L. Clarkson. Algorithms for polytope covering and approximation. In *Proc. 3rd Workshop Algorithms Data Struct.*, Lecture Notes in Computer Science, 1993.

[4] M. Cosman and R. Schumacker. System strategies to optimize CIG image content. In *Proceedings of the Image II Conference*, Scottsdale, Arizona, June 10–12 1981.

[5] G. Das and D. Joseph. The complexity of minimum convex nested polyhedra. In *Proc. 2nd Canad. Conf. Comput. Geom.*, pages 296–301, 1990.

[6] M. J. DeHaemer, Jr. and M. J. Zyda. Simplification of objects rendered by polygonal approximations. *Computers & Graphics*, 15(2):175–184, 1991.

[7] T. D. DeRose, M. Lounsbery, and J. Warren. Multiresolution analysis for surface of arbitrary topological type. Report 93-10-05, Department of Computer Science, University of Washington, Seattle, WA, 1993.

[8] M. Eck, T. DeRose, T. Duchamp, H. Hoppe, M. Lounsbery, and W. Stuetzle. Multiresolution analysis of arbitrary meshes. *Computer Graphics: Proceedings of SIGGRAPH'95*, pages 173–182, 1995.

[9] D. Eppstein, G. Barequet, and M. Dickerson. On triangulating three-dimensional polygons. manuscript, 1995.

[10] T. A. Funkhouser and C. H. Séquin. Adaptive display algorithm for interactive frame rates during visualization of complex virtual environments. In *Computer Graphics (SIGGRAPH '93 Proceedings)*, volume 27, pages 247–254, August 1993.

[11] M. R. Garey and D. S. Johnson. *Computers and Intractability: A Guide to the Theory of NP-Completeness*. W. H. Freeman, New York, NY, 1979.

[12] N. Greene, M. Kass, and G. Miller. Hierarchical z-buffer visibility. In *Computer Graphics: Proceedings of SIGGRAPH 1993*, pages 231–238. ACM SIGGRAPH, 1993.

[13] T. He, L. Hong, A. Kaufman, A. Varshney, and S. Wang. Voxel-based object simplification. In G. M. Nielson and D. Silver, editors, *IEEE Visualization '95 Proceedings*, pages 296–303, 1995.

[14] P. Heckbert and M. Garland. Multiresolution modeling for fast rendering. *Proceedings of Graphics Interface*, 1994.

[15] P. Hinker and C. Hansen. Geometric optimization. In Gregory M. Nielson and Dan Bergeron, editors, *Proceedings Visualization '93*, pages 189–195, October 1993.

[16] H. Hoppe, T. DeRose, T. Duchamp, J. McDonald, and W. Stuetzle. Mesh optimization. In James T. Kajiya, editor, *Computer Graphics (SIGGRAPH '93 Proceedings)*, volume 27, pages 19–26, August 1993.

[17] A. D. Kalvin and R. H. Taylor. Superfaces: Polyhedral approximation with bounded error. Technical Report RC 19135 (#82286), IBM Research Division, T. J. Watson Research Center, Yorktown Heights, NY 10958, 1993.

[18] L. Lovász. On the ratio of optimal integral and fractional covers. *Discrete Mathematics*, 13:383–390, 1975.

[19] J. Mitchell and S. Suri. Separation and approximation of polyhedral surfaces. In *Proceedings of 3rd ACM-SIAM Symposium on Discrete Algorithms*, pages 296–306, 1992.

[20] Kevin J. Renze and J. H. Oliver. Generalized surface and volume decimation for unstructured tessellated domains. In *Proceedings of SIVE'95*, 1995.

[21] J. Rossignac and P. Borrel. Multi-resolution 3D approximations for rendering. In *Modeling in Computer Graphics*, pages 455–465. Springer-Verlag, June–July 1993.

[22] H. E. Rushmeier, C. Patterson, and A. Veerasamy. Geometric simplification for indirect illumination calculations. In *Proceedings Graphics Interface '93*, pages 227–236, 1993.

[23] F. J. Schmitt, B. A. Barsky, and W. Du. An adaptive subdivision method for surface-fitting from sampled data. *Computer Graphics (SIGGRAPH '86 Proceedings)*, 20(4):179–188, 1986.

[24] W. J. Schroeder, J. A. Zarge, and W. E. Lorensen. Decimation of triangle meshes. In Edwin E. Catmull, editor, *Computer Graphics (SIGGRAPH '92 Proceedings)*, volume 26, pages 65–70, July 1992.

[25] G. Taubin. A signal processing approach to fair surface design. In *Proc. of ACM Siggraph*, pages 351–358, 1995.

[26] G. Turk. Re-tiling polygonal surfaces. In *Computer Graphics (SIGGRAPH '92 Proceedings)*, volume 26, pages 55–64, July 1992.

[27] A. Varshney. Hierarchical geometric approximations. Ph.D. Thesis TR-050-1994, Department of Computer Science, University of North Carolina, Chapel Hill, NC 27599-3175, 1994.

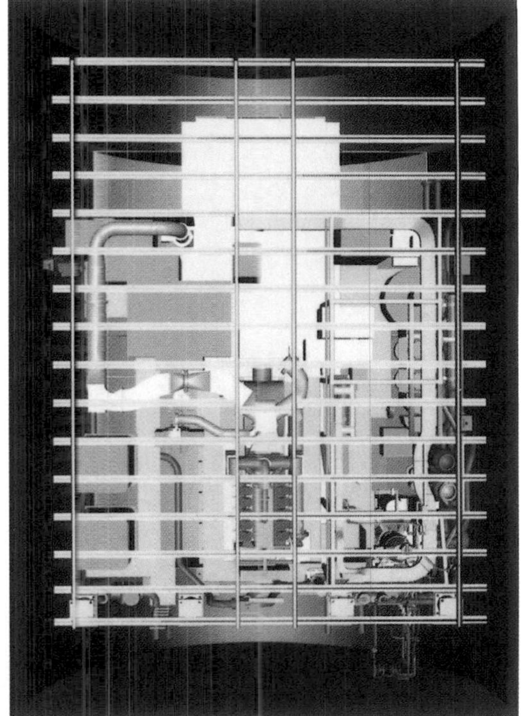

Figure 10: *Looking down into the auxiliary machine room (AMR) of a submarine model. This model contains nearly 3,000 objects, for a total of over half a million triangles. We have simplified over 2,600 of these objects, for a total of over 430,000 triangles.*

Figure 11: *An array of batteries from the AMR. All parts but the red are simplified representations. At full resolution, this array requires 87,000 triangles. At this distance, allowing 4 pixels of error in screen space, we have reduced it to 45,000 triangles.*

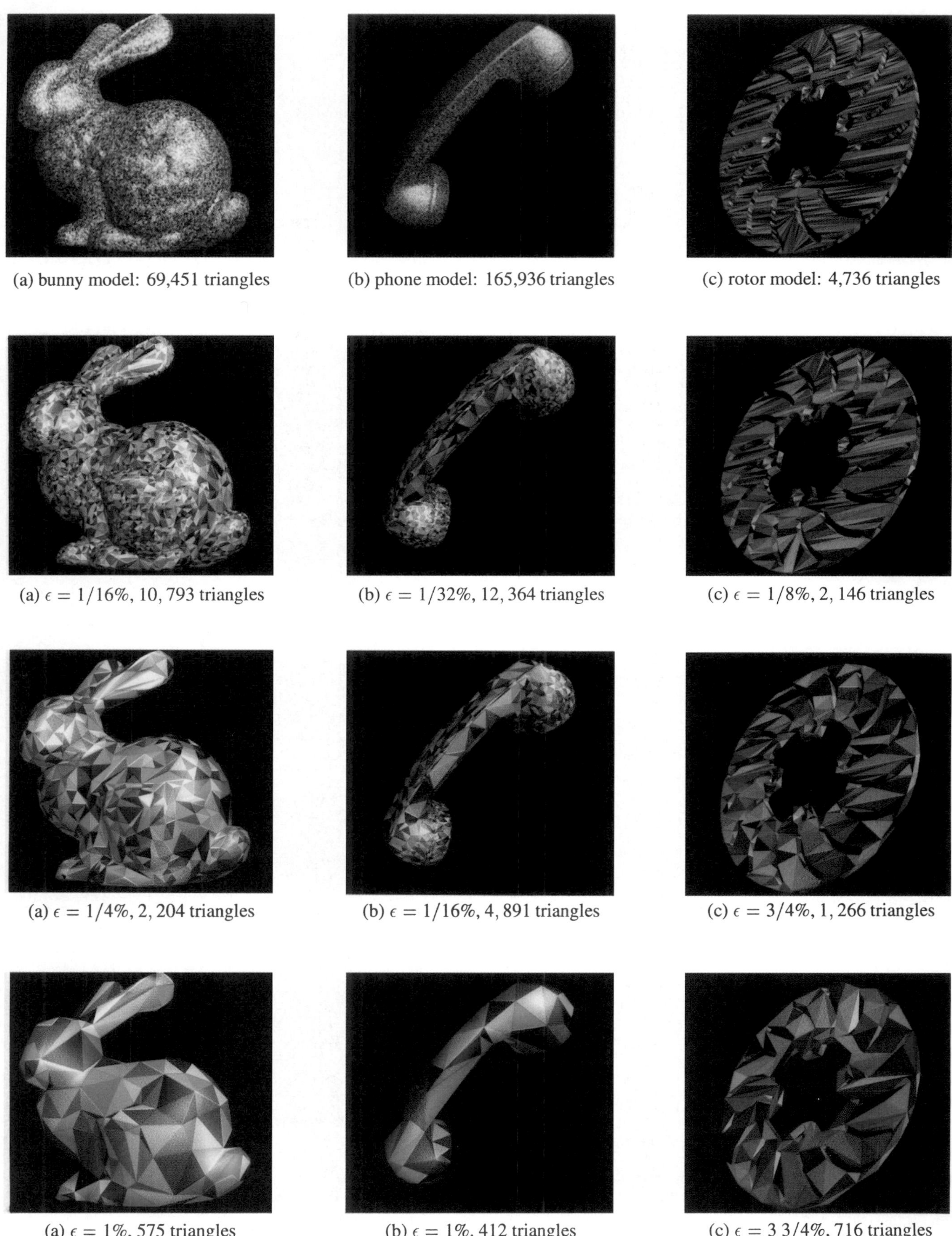

(a) bunny model: 69,451 triangles
(b) phone model: 165,936 triangles
(c) rotor model: 4,736 triangles

(a) $\epsilon = 1/16\%$, 10,793 triangles
(b) $\epsilon = 1/32\%$, 12,364 triangles
(c) $\epsilon = 1/8\%$, 2,146 triangles

(a) $\epsilon = 1/4\%$, 2,204 triangles
(b) $\epsilon = 1/16\%$, 4,891 triangles
(c) $\epsilon = 3/4\%$, 1,266 triangles

(a) $\epsilon = 1\%$, 575 triangles
(b) $\epsilon = 1\%$, 412 triangles
(c) $\epsilon = 3\ 3/4\%$, 716 triangles

Figure 12: *Level-of-detail hierarchies for three models. The approximation distance, ϵ, is taken as a percentage of the bounding box diagonal.*

Position-Based Physics: Simulating the Motion of Many Highly Interacting Spheres and Polyhedra

Victor J. Milenkovic*

University of Miami

Abstract

This paper proposes a simplified *position-based* physics that allows us to rapidly generate "piles" or "clumps" of many objects: local energy minima under a variety of potential energy functions. We can also generate plausible motions for many highly interacting objects from arbitrary starting positions to a local energy minimum. We present an efficient and numerically stable algorithm for carrying out position-based physics on spheres and non-rotating polyhedra through the use of linear programming. This algorithm is a generalization of an algorithm for finding tight packings of (non-rotating) polygons in two dimensions. This work introduces linear programming as a useful tool for graphics animation. As its name implies, position-based physics does not contain a notion of velocity, and thus it is not suitable for simulating the motion of free-flying, unencumbered objects. However, it generates realistic motions of "crowded" sets of objects in confined spaces, and it does so at least two orders of magnitude faster than other techniques for simulating the physical motions of objects. Even for unconfined objects, the new algorithm can rapidly generate realistic "piles" and "clumps."

CR Descriptors: G.1.6 [**Numerical Analysis**]: Optimization - *Linear Programming*; I.3.5 [**Computer Graphics**]: Computational Geometry and Object Modeling - *Physically based modeling*; I.3.7 [**Computer Graphics**]: Three-Dimensional Graphics and Realism - *Animation*; I.6.8 [**Simulation and Modeling**]: Types of Simulation - *Continuous*.

1 Introduction

To generate realistic animation, recent work in computer graphics has focused on methods to simulate the motion of objects under the laws of physics. Suppose one wants to create an animated dancer. Instead of laboriously choosing a sequence of poses, one creates a model of a dancer with masses, joints, and forces, and lets the laws of physics do the dancing. The laws of physics are well understood (for this domain), and current computers can simulate physics for these types of models in near to real time. The main difficulty of this approach is choosing a set of forces (parameters for the model) that allow the dancer to dance and not fall on its face. However, there are other domains for which the forces are easily determined but the physics is very difficult to simulate. Consider the problem of generating a "pile" or "clump" of many objects under gravity or mutually attractive forces. Creating or even verifying an equilibrium state of the physical system is a complex problem. Consider further the problems of animating the sand in an hourglass or the sand on the beach as someone sets foot on it. Consider even the problem of animating the molecules of fluid in a lava lamp. These models involve many highly interacting three-dimensional objects. For even a modest number of grains of sand or molecules, the simulation outstrips our computational resources.[1]

This paper proposes a simplified *position-based* physics that allows us to rapidly generate "piles" or "clumps" of many objects: local energy minima under a variety of potential energy functions. Position-based physics allows us to rapidly generate plausible motions for sets of many highly interacting objects. We present an efficient and numerically stable algorithm, based on linear programming, for carrying out position-based physics on spheres and non-rotating polyhedra. This algorithm is a generalization of an algorithm for finding tight packings of (non-rotating) polygons in two dimensions. This work introduces linear programming as a useful tool for graphics animation. As its name implies, position-based physics does not contain a notion of velocity, and thus it is not suitable for simulating the motion of free-flying, unencumbered objects. However, it generates realistic motions of "crowded" sets of objects in confined spaces, and it does so at least two orders of magnitude faster than other techniques for simulating the physical motions of objects. Even for unconfined objects, the new algorithm can rapidly generate realistic "piles" and "clumps."

Section 2 compares position-based physics to other methods of physical simulation such as velocity-based contact force methods. It describes two problems which severely slow down velocity-based methods: local and global "rattling." Section 3 gives the formal definition of position-based physics and gives an algorithm to carry it out. For a system of translating objects that involves only sphere-sphere and sphere-polyhedron contacts, it is proved that the linear programming based algorithm converges to an equilibrium of the potential energy function: the algorithm cannot "stick" at a non-equilibrium configuration. Section 4 describes how to implement the algorithm using linear programming to simulate position-based physics on a set of spheres inside a polyhedron, in particular, a set of 1000 spheres inside an "hourglass". Section 5 shows how to handle non-gravitational potential functions such as attraction among the spheres. Section 6 presents results and running times, and Section 7 discusses the implication of this work and directions of future research.

[1]Department of Mathematics and Computer Science, University of Miami, P.O. Box 249085, Coral Gables, FL 33124. The research of Victor J. Milenkovic was funded by the Textile/Clothing Technology Corporation from funds awarded to them by the Alfred P. Sloan Foundation and by NSF grants CCR-91-157993 and CCR-90-09272.

[1]Also, numerical instability, which is a minor problem for the simulation of robots or dancers, becomes a serious impediment when the number of interacting objects rises into the hundreds, thousands, or beyond.

2 Techniques for Physical Simulation

We categorize physical simulation techniques as acceleration-based, velocity-based, or position-based. Acceleration-based methods come closest to simulating true physics, and they are the most expensive to carry out in computation. Velocity-based methods are farther divorced from "reality" but are faster. Position-based methods are the farthest from reality and the fastest.

Spring model methods (also called *penalty methods*) [25] [26] are typical acceleration-based methods. They allow the objects to overlap. For each pair of overlapping objects, there is a repulsive force proportional to the amount of overlap. The resulting repulsive forces cause the objects to accelerate. Numerical integration converts acceleration to velocity and then to position. These methods require many small time-steps when the acceleration is high. The large number of steps results in a high computational cost. Also, it is often difficult to determine the correct step size. Incorrect discretization of time can cause unusual numerical results such as non-conservation of energy or momentum.

Contact force model methods (also called *analytical methods*) [14] [1] [8] are examples of velocity-based methods. See [4] for a discussion of the many issues involved in contact force models. Rigid bodies are allowed to contact but not overlap. Given the current set of contacts, the method computes a set of consistent velocities such that no two contacting objects penetrate each other. The objects move with these velocities until a new contact occurs. The velocity-based method is much more stable and faster than the acceleration-based method for two reasons: 1) it can exactly compute the time of the next contact, and 2) the resulting time-step tends to be much larger than that needed to accurately carry out numerical integration. Even though these methods do not simulate acceleration, they can handle increasingly sophisticated types of objects and forces: curved surfaces [2], friction [3], and flexible bodies [7]. Unfortunately, the velocity-based method is subject to two problems which cause small time-steps and thus high computational cost. *Local rattle* occurs when one object bounces between two others (such as the rapid bouncing that occurs when you bring a paddle down on a bouncing ping-pong ball). *Global rattle* occurs when there are many interacting objects. Since there are so many, it is inevitable that *some* pair will make contact in a short amount of time. Even systems which can rapidly detect the next collision [16] cannot reduce the number of collisions. Each new contact forces us to recalculate the velocities.

Just as a velocity-based method eliminates accelerations, a position-based method eliminates velocities (and also time, momentum, and kinetic energy). The model only needs to have a potential energy function. Under position-based physics, the objects are allowed to move from their current configuration (positions) to a lower energy configuration along any valid (non-overlapping) energy-diminishing path. Under a linear programming based algorithm for position-based physics, the motion consists of a sequence of steps yielding a piecewise linear path. Each step diminishes the energy as much as possible within some maximal valid convex set of configurations surrounding the current configuration. This convex set depends both on contacts that are occurring and on all contacts that might occur. Therefore the algorithm does not have to stop prematurely to handle a new contact, and there is no local "rattle". Position-based physics also avoids global "rattle" since each object moves a maximal amount. Even if two objects in the model require only a small motion to come into contact, this does not prevent other objects in the model from moving farther, if they are able to.

In his Ph.D. thesis [19] and in joint work with this author [22, 23], Li introduced the concept of position-based modeling. His application is *compaction*: finding tight packings of polygonal objects in the plane. As he and others have noted [29, 30], for most layout applications the motion of the objects is immaterial, and only the final configuration matters. He attempted to carry out compaction using a velocity-based method similar to Baraff's [1], but he found this to be very expensive computationally and also numerically unstable. He formulated a position-based model and algorithm. This algorithm uses Minkowski sums [27, 13] and a *locality heuristic* to calculate a maximum convex region of the configuration space visible to the current configuration. Linear programming finds the lowest energy configuration in this region, and the model jumps to this configuration. According to his experiments, the method typically reaches a local energy minimum in five or fewer jumps even for a layout of more than 100 polygons with up to 75 vertices per polygon. For the examples which were simple enough for him to carry out the velocity-based minimization, the position-based method was at least two orders of magnitude faster.

The algorithms presented in this paper also use position-based physics. For sphere-sphere and sphere-polyhedron interactions, they do not require explicit calculation of the Minkowski sum (unlike Li's method for polygons). For polyhedron-polyhedron interactions, they do require calculation of the Minkowski sum, but unlike Li's *locality heuristic*, they do not require that the polyhedra be decomposed into star-shaped[2] components. The new algorithms can solve for the motions of spheres and polyhedra, whereas Li's algorithm is restricted to two-dimensional polygons.

Interestingly enough, some recent work has moved *away* from the use of large complex optimization systems [5]. Position-based physics reduces motion planning to linear programming. Instead of dealing with implementing optimization code ourselves, we simply use a commercial linear programming library. Goldsmith *et al.* [12] discuss a number of ways optimization is applied in the field of graphics. Most of these involve "either starting or finishing problems." Furthermore, most are non-linear. We believe that position-based physics is unique in the way it uses linear programming to generate a complex motion from start to finish.

Position-based physics yields realistic motion for crowded sets of objects. For free-flying objects, the motion can be less reasonable. However, even in situations for which position-based methods give an unrealistic motion, there may be other applications. Recent work on manipulation of models makes use of non-physical motion [6] [15].

Finally, it is important to note the difference between position-based physics and particle-based systems. Examples of particle-based systems are too numerous to note all of them. See [32] [17] [31] [33] [10] [9] [21] for recent work. In general, particle-based systems model moving particles with forces between them, not rigid colliding objects. Simulating rigid objects using particles requires a very steep repulsive energy gradient, and hence particle-based systems are subject to the same difficulties as other acceleration-based methods: small time-steps and long running times.

3 Position-Based Physics

The philosophy behind position-based physics is to dispense with acceleration, force, velocity, and time. The state of the system is the current configuration (position). The system has a potential energy that depends only on the configuration. There is no notion of kinetic energy.

Section 3.1 defines position-based physics and describes how it can be used for modeling and animation. Section 3.2 gives an algorithm for simulating position-based physics on models with a *smoothly convex decomposable* overlap space: the set of forbidden configurations is a union of convex regions with smooth boundaries.

[2] A region is *star-shaped* if it contains at least one point which can "see" the entire boundary.

This algorithm uses linear programming. Section 3.3 proves that several types of models have smoothly convex decomposable overlap spaces. Among these are models involving translating spheres inside a fixed polyhedron. We describe what modifications are necessary to handle multiple translating polyhedra.

3.1 Definitions

As per typical usage, *configuration space* denotes the concatenation of the degrees of freedom of the model. For a set of n spheres, the configuration space has $3n$ dimensions. The *free space* is the set of configurations for which no pair of objects overlap.[3] These *free* configurations are also referred to as *valid* or *non-overlapping*. The complement of the free space is the set of *overlapping*, *invalid*, or *forbidden* configurations. We denote the free space by $\mathcal{F}$.

We assume that the model has a potential energy which is a continuous and differentiable real-valued function on the configuration space. For configuration c, the energy is denoted $E(c)$.

A valid motion under position-based physics is an energy-diminishing path in $\mathcal{F}$. Given a starting configuration $c \in \mathcal{F}$, the goal is to generate a continuous and piecewise differentiable curve $\gamma(t)$ such that 1) $\gamma(0) = c$, 2) $\gamma(t) \in \mathcal{F}$ for $t \geq 0$, 3) $E(\gamma(t))$ is monotonically decreasing for $t \geq 0$, 3) $\lim_{t\to\infty} \gamma(t) = c_\infty$ is an *equilibrium configuration.* A configuration c_{equil} is an *equilibrium configuration* if every valid curve $\sigma(t)$ out of c_{equil} ($\sigma(0) = c_{\text{equil}}$ and $\sigma(t) \in \mathcal{F}$ for $t \geq 0$) is non-energy-decreasing: $\frac{\mathrm{d}}{\mathrm{d}t}E(\sigma(t)) \geq 0$.

Note that t is not time and c_∞ may not be the equilibrium state reached by a velocity-based or acceleration-based physics with the same potential energy function. However, a limiting value of $\gamma(t)$ is a valid resting position: a "pile" or "clump". To generate a decent looking animation, we can sample $\gamma(t)$ in a way that makes it appear that the objects in the model are moving with constant or varying velocity, as desired. Also, as shown in Section 4.4, it is possible to add additional constraints on the path to make it appear more natural.

3.2 Linear Programming Based Algorithm

This section gives an algorithm for performing position-based physics on models with a particular type of free/forbidden space. The algorithm is proved to have an equilibrium position as a limit point. If the energy function is linear, then the algorithm can be implemented using linear programming.

3.2.1 Smooth Convex Decompositions

A set S of $\mathbb{R}^n$ is defined to be *convex decomposable* if it is the union of a finite number of convex sets. It is *smoothly convex decomposable* if it is the union of a finite number of convex sets with smooth boundaries. We use a standard definition of smooth: a convex set C is smooth if each point on the boundary has a unique tangent plane and outward unit normal vector and if this plane/normal is a continuous function on the boundary. Actually, it is easy to show that if C is convex and if each point on the boundary of C has a unique outward unit normal, then the normal vector varies continuously on the boundary.

3.2.2 Algorithm

The following is an algorithm for position-based physics when the overlap (forbidden) space $\mathcal{O} = \overline{\mathcal{F}}$ is smoothly convex decomposable. Region $\mathcal{O}$ is the union of m smooth convex regions $\mathcal{O}_1, \mathcal{O}_2, \mathcal{O}_3, \ldots, \mathcal{O}_m$.

[3] We consider the *exterior* of the container to be a fixed object, and hence the definition of free space includes the container constraint.

Let $c = c_0$ be the initial configuration. The algorithm sets $\gamma(0) = c$. The algorithm proceeds in a sequence of steps. During the ith step, it constructs the portion of the curve from $\gamma(i-1)$ to $\gamma(i)$. Let us suppose the algorithm has constructed the curve up to configuration $\gamma(i) = c_i$. Here is how it performs the next step.

- For each convex region $\mathcal{O}_j$, it constructs the half-space $H(c_i, \mathcal{O}_j)$ as follows. First it projects c_i onto the nearest point PROJ$(c_i, \mathcal{O}_j)$ on $\mathcal{O}_j$. It computes the tangent plane to $\mathcal{O}_j$ at PROJ$(c_i, \mathcal{O}_j)$. This tangent plane bounds two half-spaces, and $H(c_i, \mathcal{O}_j)$ is the one which does *not* contain the interior of $\mathcal{O}_j$.
- The algorithm computes the convex region
$$I(c_i, \mathcal{F}) = \bigcap_{j=1}^{m} H(c_i, \mathcal{O}_j).$$
Assuming $\mathcal{F}$ is closed (objects are allowed to touch), it follows that $I(c_i, \mathcal{F}) \subseteq \mathcal{F}$.
- The algorithm computes the minimum energy configuration $c_{i+1} \in I(c_i, \mathcal{F})$ which is reachable by an energy-diminishing path from $\gamma(i) = c_i$ to $\gamma(i+1) = c_{i+1}$ within $I(c_i, \mathcal{F})$.

In general, the last step requires some sort of numerical integration. However, if the energy function is linear, it can be accomplished using linear programming. Linear programming can easily compute the point $c_{i+1} \in I(c_i, \mathcal{F})$ which minimizes the energy. The algorithm can set $\gamma(t)$, $i \leq t \leq i+1$ equal to the line segment from c_i to c_{i+1}. Since $I(c_i, \mathcal{F})$ is convex, this segment is valid.

3.2.3 Correctness and Convergence

The following theorem states that the limit points of the algorithm are equilibrium points. This does not mean that the algorithm has a unique limit. If we have a room full of falling objects, some objects might already be on the floor. Any arbitrary motion of an object along the floor does not change the gravitational energy. For odd i, configuration c_i could have a particular object at one end of the room. For even i, it could be at the other end of the room. Thus, as the rest of the objects settled into a "pile", this one object may never come to rest. Nothing in the definition of position-based physics prevents it from bouncing from one wall to the other forever. In this case, the system will have two limit points.

Any particular linear programming library will "break ties" consistently. Therefore, it will not allow an object to bounce from wall to wall forever. It is also possible to introduce a *conservative* energy term: each object is attracted to its current location. Both of these facts can be used to ensure that the algorithm converges to a unique limit. Section 4 illustrates both of these for spheres inside a polyhedron. It is probably possible to modify the definition of position-based physics and the algorithm to disallow "bouncing". However, there may be cases in which we *want* this behavior. Note that "bouncing" is not like rattling. Bouncing does not affect the amount by which the energy is reduced in one step, and therefore it does not increase the number of steps required to reach an energy minimum. For velocity-based methods, frequent collisions diminish the time-step and greatly increase the time required to reach a minimum.

We remind the reader that the definition of an equilibrium point depends only on $\mathcal{F}$ and the energy function $E()$. An equilibrium point for position-based physics is the same as an equilibrium point for any other type of physics. Therefore, the following theorem asserts that the algorithm converges to physically correct "piles" and "clumps". It does not get stuck at a non-equilibrium configuration. However, most models have very many equilibrium configurations.

The algorithm does not necessarily converge to the same equilibrium as a "true" simulation of physics.

Theorem 3.1 *For compact (closed and bounded) $\mathcal{F}$, the sequence $c_0, c_1, c_2, c_3, \ldots$ generated by the algorithm has at least one limit point. Each limit point is an equilibrium point.*

Proof: The existence of a limit point is a property of any sequence in a compact set. Let $c_{\rm lim}$ be a limit point. Suppose $c_{\rm lim}$ is not an equilibrium point. Therefore, there is a curve $\sigma(t)$ out of $c_{\rm lim}$ which diminishes the energy. It follows that the energy decreases out of $c_{\rm lim}$ in the direction $v = \sigma'(0)$ (the tangent vector to $\sigma(t)$ at $t = 0$). For each j, $c_{\rm lim}$ either lies outside or on the boundary of $\mathcal{O}_j$. If it lies outside, then there exists $\epsilon > 0$ such that $c_{\rm lim} + tv \notin \mathcal{O}_j$ for $0 \leq t < \epsilon$. If $c_{\rm lim}$ lies on the boundary of $\mathcal{O}_j$, then v must lie in the tangent plane to $\mathcal{O}_j$ at $c_{\rm lim}$ or it must point into $H(c_{\rm lim}, \mathcal{O}_j)$. Hence, there exists $\epsilon > 0$ such that $c_{\rm lim} + tv \in I(c_{\rm lim}, \mathcal{F})$ for $0 \leq t < \epsilon$. Also, $E(c_{\rm lim} + tv)$ has the same derivative at $t = 0$ as $E(\sigma(t))$. The conclusion is that *if* the algorithm reached $c_{\rm lim}$, the next step would be able to diminish the energy. Let $\delta_{\rm lim}$ be the amount of decrease.

The algorithm has $c_{\rm lim}$ as a limit point. The construction of $I(c_i, \mathcal{F})$ uses only continuous functions. For c_i sufficiently close to $c_{\rm lim}$, the energy decrease $\delta_i = E(c_i) - E(c_{i+1})$ can be arbitrarily close to $\delta_{\rm lim}$. Since $E()$ is also continuous, there must exist some i such that

$$E(c_i) - E(c_{\rm lim}) < \frac{\delta_{\rm lim}}{2} \quad \text{and} \quad E(c_i) - E(c_{i+1}) = \delta_i > \frac{\delta_{\rm lim}}{2}.$$

It follows that $E(c_{i+1}) < E(c_{\rm lim})$. Since the algorithm always decreases the energy, $c_{\rm lim}$ cannot be a limit point. This contradicts the assumption that $c_{\rm lim}$ is not an equilibrium point. ■

3.3 Models with Convex Decompositions

This section examines some models with smoothly convex decomposable overlap spaces. It is shown how to apply the algorithm of Section 3.2.2 to the problems of animating and generating "piles" of spheres and polyhedra under translation.

3.3.1 Minkowski Sum.

The *Minkowski sum* [24, 13, 27, 28] of two point-sets (of $\mathbf{R}^3$ in the case of this paper) is defined

$$A \oplus B = \{a + b \mid a \in A,\, b \in B\}.$$

For a point-set A, let $\overline{A}$ denote the set complement of A and define $-A = \{-a \mid a \in A\}$. For a vector v, define $A + v = \{a + v \mid a \in A\}$. Note that $A + v = A \oplus \{v\}$.

Suppose we have n translating objects $A_1, A_2, A_3, \ldots, A_n$. It can easily be shown that $A_i + v_i$ and $A_j + v_j$ overlap if and only if $v_j - v_i \in A_i \oplus -A_j$.

Lemma 3.2 *If C is convex and S is smoothly convex, then $C \oplus S$ is smoothly convex.*

Proof: It is easy to show that $C \oplus S$ is convex. Suppose p is a point on the boundary of $C \oplus S$ such that p has two distinct unit normal vectors u and u'. Since u is a normal at p, p maximizes the dot product $u \cdot p$ over all points in $C \oplus S$. Since $p = c + s$ where $c \in C$ and $s \in S$ can be chosen independently, s must maximize $u \cdot s$ over all points of S. Yet, $p = c' + s'$ where $c' \in C$ and $s' \in S$ have maximum dot products with u'. Since s has a unique normal, u' is not a normal at s, and $u' \cdot s < u' \cdot s'$. Therefore $u' \cdot (c + s) < u' \cdot (c + s')$. Therefore, $p = c + s$ does not maximize the dot product with u'. This contradicts the assumption that p has two unit normals. Therefore, p has a unique unit normal vector. It is easily shown that if a convex region with unique unit normal vectors has continuous unit normal vectors: it is smooth. ■

Corollary 3.3 *If C is convex decomposable and if S is smoothly convex decomposable, then $C \oplus S$ is smoothly convex decomposable.*

Proof: Let the decompositions be,

$$C = C_1 \cup C_2 \cup \cdots \cup C_l \quad \text{and} \quad S = S_1 \cup S_2 \cup \cdots \cup S_m.$$

It can easily be shown that,

$$C \oplus S = \bigcup_{g=1}^{l} \bigcup_{h=1}^{m} C_g \oplus S_h.$$

In other words, the Minkowski sum is the union of the Minkowski sum of each possible pair. By Lemma 3.2, each of these sums is smoothly convex. ■

3.3.2 "Good" Models

The following theorem describes the type of problem to which we can apply the algorithm of Section 3.2.

Theorem 3.4 *If 1) only translation is allowed, 2) all objects are convex decomposable, and 3) at most one object is not smoothly convex decomposable, then the overlap space is smoothly convex decomposable.*

Proof: For each pair of objects, A_i and A_j, at least one is smoothly convex decomposable. Corollary 3.3 implies that the pairwise overlap space

$$\{\langle v_i, v_j \rangle \mid v_j - v_i \in A_i \oplus -A_j\}$$

is smoothly convex decomposable. This transforms to a cylinder

$$\{\langle v_1, v_2, \ldots, v_n \rangle \mid v_j - v_i \in A_i \oplus -A_j\}$$

in the configuration space for the entire model which is decomposable into a union of smooth convex cylinders. ■

3.3.3 Applications

The main application of this paper is a collection of translating spheres in a polyhedral container. Clearly each sphere is smoothly convex decomposable. The remaining object, the complement of the container, is polyhedral and therefore convex decomposable: simply cut it along every plane of every face.

We can not directly apply Theorem 3.4 to the problem of multiple translating polyhedra since a polyhedron is convex decomposable but not smoothly convex decomposable. However, we can "smooth" a polyhedral region P by adding a small spherical region S. By Corollary 3.3, $P \oplus S$ is smoothly convex decomposable. Of course, when we render the motion, we will display the original polyhedra, not the smoothed polyhedra. They will have small gaps between them equal to the diameter of S. For moving objects, this will not be noticeable. Once, the objects form a "pile" or "clump", we can run the algorithm with smaller and smaller S, perhaps halving the radius each time, until the desired accuracy is attained.

Li and Milenkovic's algorithm (for translating polygons in the plane) uses a somewhat different framework than that of the algorithm in Section 3.2.2. In essence, it chooses an arbitrary tangent line/unit normal when the normal is not unique. This means, for instance, that our compaction algorithm for polygons in the plane might get "stuck" at a non-equilibrium configuration. We have never seen it get stuck in practice (but we really have no independent way to verify an equilibrium other than visual inspection). It is likely that one could safely animate multiple translating polyhedra without getting stuck. However, we have not yet run any experiments. Baraff [1] indicates that correctly choosing a set of tangents at each non-unique contact is NP-complete.

4 Simulating an Hourglass using Position-Based Physics

The first section of the accompanying video tape demonstrates the simulation of an "hourglass" or "egg-timer" using position-based physics. The main body of the hourglass is shaded as a curved surface, but it is actually a polyhedron Each horizontal cross section is a 32-gon, and thus the sides of the hourglass have 160 faces. Initially, 1000 spheres are arranged in a 10 by 10 by 10 grid in the upper part of the hourglass. Position-based physics calculates a (local) gravitational energy minimum for the spheres in the base. As a side-effect, it simulates the flow through the narrow "waist" of the hourglass. The video presents two hourglass simulations. Both are shown at 30 frames per second. Each frame is an actual energy minimization step. Rendering was done with *rendrib*.[4] The first video has 750 frames, and the second has 812 frames.

Sections 4.1 through 4.3 describe how the first video was generated. Section 4.4 shows how extra constraints where added to generate a more realistic motion in the second video. The modified algorithm has acceleration and conservative forces. This video illustrates how the path generated by position-based physics can be controlled to increase the realism.

4.1 Pairwise Constraints

Instead of working in $3n$-dimensional space, we choose a convex subset of the pairwise free spaces. We must do this for each pair of spheres and each sphere with respect to the hourglass polyhedron. Taken together, these constraints are equivalent to $I(c, \mathcal{F})$ of Section 3.2.2.

For a pair of spheres S_i and S_j with radii r_i and r_j and current positions (centers) p_i^{cur} and p_j^{cur}, define

$$u_{ij}^{\mathrm{cur}} = \frac{p_j^{\mathrm{cur}} - p_i^{\mathrm{cur}}}{|p_j^{\mathrm{cur}} - p_i^{\mathrm{cur}}|}$$

to be the unit vector pointing from S_i to S_j. The convex region $\mathcal{R}_{ij}$ is the set of configurations satisfying

$$(p_j - p_i) \cdot u_{ij}^{\mathrm{cur}} \geq r_i + r_j, \quad \text{for } 1 \leq i < j \leq n. \tag{1}$$

The half-space constraint $p_j - p_i \in \mathcal{R}_{ij}$ prevents the spheres from overlapping, and it is exactly equivalent to one of the half-spaces in the first step of the algorithm in Section 3.2.2.

For a sphere S_i and the hourglass polyhedron G, we do the following. Set $h = 1$. Let q_h be the point on the boundary of G closest to p_i^{cur}. Let,

$$v_{hi}^{\mathrm{cur}} = \frac{p_i^{\mathrm{cur}} - q_h}{|p_i^{\mathrm{cur}} - q_h|}$$

be the unit vector from q_h to p_i^{cur}. We create the constraint,

$$(p_i - q_h) \cdot v_{hi}^{\mathrm{cur}} \geq r_i, \tag{2}$$

and we throw away all points p of the boundary of G which do not satisfy

$$(p - q_h) \cdot v_{hi}^{\mathrm{cur}} > 0.$$

[4] The Blue Moon Rendering Tools by Larry I. Gritz.

(Intersecting a half-space with a polyhedron is easy if the faces are all convex: the intersection of each face with the half-space is also convex.) If some part of the boundary remains, then we increment h and repeat this process. We stop when no point on the boundary of the polyhedron remains. The resulting set of linear constraints on p_i given by all instances of Equation 2 defines a convex region $\mathcal{R}_i$ which is a projection of $I(c_i, \mathcal{F})$ of Section 3.2.2 (actually, it can be a superset, but that can only improve the convergence).

4.2 Minimizing the Potential Energy

For the hourglass example, the potential energy is the sum of the z-coordinates of the spheres. This corresponds to the gravitational energy of a set of spheres with equal mass.

How do we find the next configuration? We need to solve for the configuration that minimizes the gravitational energy under the linear constraints of Equations 1 and 2. This is linear programming. We simply pass this problem to a commercial linear programming package, CPLEX.[5]

Theorem 3.4 implies that the hourglass algorithm cannot "stick" unless the actually physical system would also. Hence, the spheres flow down the hourglass without "clogging" in the middle.

4.3 Box Constraints

We also bound each sphere to lie in a rotated cube centered at the current position of the sphere. The cube has width two times the sphere radius, and it is oriented to have a vertex at minimum z-coordinate. This constraint serves to put an upper bound on the maximum distance a sphere can move in any one step.

This extra constraint serves two purposes. First, it keeps the spheres from falling too fast. In the absence of this constraint, a solitary sphere could fall to rest on the ground from an arbitrary height in a single step. Second, by limiting the motion of the spheres, we limit the pairs of spheres which can collide in the current step. That permits us to reduce the size of the linear program. We do not add a pairwise constraint for two spheres that are too far apart to collide in the next step. We can use bucketing to detect nearby pairs of spheres in nearly linear time.

4.4 Acceleration and Conservative Forces

The reader will notice that the spheres do not accelerate as they fall. We could fix this by detecting if a sphere has fallen the maximum amount, and if so, increasing the height of its bounding box by a fixed amount To make this work properly, we must use unrotated boxes, unlike the rotated cubes of the previous section.

The reader will also notice that the spheres roll to the back of the hourglass Using unrotated boxes makes this effect worse: the spheres fall to the lower-left-rear corner of the box, making them fall at an angle. This is an artifact of the simplex method used to solve the linear program. We can add a "conservative" energy term that penalizes each sphere for changing any of its coordinates. In particular, we express each variable x_i as $x_i = x_i^+ - x_i^-$, where both x_i^+ and x_i^- are constrained to be positive (x_i could represent the x, y, or z coordinate of a sphere). To the objective function, we add

$$c_{\mathrm{conserve}} \sum_i (x_i^+ + x_i^-),$$

where c_{conserve} is small compared to the "gravitational constant". In our system, the gravitational constant is 1 and $c_{\mathrm{conserve}} = 0.001$. The second hourglass video illustrates the addition of acceleration and "conservative forces".

[5] Version 3.0. CPLEX Optimization Inc. Suite 279. 930 Tahoe Boulevard, Building 802. Incline Village, Nevada 89451-9436.

4.5 Polyhedron-Polyhedron Constraints

The hourglass example does not require polyhedron-polyhedron constraints. For the record, we describe how one could add them to the model.

Li's method for constructing a convex subset of the free space, the *locality heuristic*, requires that the interacting polygons be star-shaped. If they are not, they must be decomposed into star-shaped components. Extra constraints must be added to ensure that the components move as one object.

We describe here a method for selecting a convex free region $\mathcal{R}_{ij}$ for a pair of polyhedra P_i and P_j under translation. As in the case of modeling spheres, we can construct these regions for each pair of polyhedra instead of having to work in $\mathbf{R}^{3n}$ as implied by the algorithm of Section 3.2.2. Note that this method does not require that P_i and P_j be star-shaped, which is an improvement of Li's result. Let P_i represent the "resting" position of P_i, and let $P_i + p_i$ represent P_i translated by p_i from its resting position. As stated in Section 3.3.1 $P_i + p_i$ and $P_j + p_j$ do not overlap if and only if $p_j - p_i$ lies in $F = \overline{P_i \oplus -P_j}$. This is all following theory developed by Li to handle the two-dimensional case.

For a given pairwise configuration $c_{ij}^{\text{cur}} = \langle p_i^{\text{cur}}, p_j^{\text{cur}} \rangle$, we construct convex region $\mathcal{R}_{ij}$ as follows. Set $h = 1$ and let q_h be the point on the boundary of F which is closest to $p_j^{\text{cur}} - p_i^{\text{cur}}$. Define

$$w_{hij}^{\text{cur}} = \frac{p_j^{\text{cur}} - p_i^{\text{cur}} - q_h}{|p_j^{\text{cur}} - p_i^{\text{cur}} - q_h|}$$

to be the unit vector from q_h to to $p_j^{\text{cur}} - p_i^{\text{cur}}$. Add the constraint,

$$(p_j - p_i - q_h) \cdot w_{hij}^{\text{cur}} \geq 0. \quad (3)$$

Throw away all points q of the boundary of F that do not satisfy

$$(q - q_h) \cdot w_{hij}^{\text{cur}} \geq 0.$$

Increment h and repeat until no points of the boundary of F remain. The set of constraints given by all instances of Equation 3 define a convex region $\mathcal{R}_{ij}$ which is a subset of the free space for these two polyhedra. This region is the projection of $I(c_i, \mathcal{F})$ of Section 3.2.2 into the configuration space of these two polyhedra (actually, it can be a superset). For this reason, it is sufficient to use these pairwise constraints.

5 Non-gravitational Potential Functions

For some applications, it may be necessary to simulate a constant force, a "spring" force, or an inverse-square law force between spheres. In this section, we describe how this can be done, and give some examples.

5.1 Attraction between Spheres.

To define an attractive force between spheres, we must first define the distance between spheres in a way that can be represented in a linear program. In the following, $1 \leq i < j \leq n$, where n is the number of spheres. Let S_i and S_j be spheres which are to attract each other.

Create a new variable d_{ij} which represents an approximation to the distance from p_i to p_j. The value of d_{ij} will always be a lower bound on the Euclidean distance. Select a set U of unit vectors. The set U should at least include u_{ij}^{cur} (the unit vector from p_i to p_j) and the six axis-parallel vectors $(\pm 1, 0, 0)$, $(0, \pm 1, 0)$, $(0, 0, \pm 1)$. Apply the following constraints on p_i, p_j, and d_{ij}:

$$u \cdot (p_j - p_i) \leq d_{ij}, \quad \text{for } u \in U. \quad (4)$$

Adding more vectors to U makes d_{ij} a better approximation to the Euclidean distance $|p_j - p_i|$. However, the given U is sufficient for realistic motion, and the presence of u_{ij}^{cur} ensures correct convergence.

For a constant force f_{ij} of attraction between S_i and S_j (independent of distance), we can add the term $f_{ij} d_{ij}$ to the potential function for the model. Often, however, one desires a force which "dies off" with distance, such as the inverse-square law. The corresponding potential function $-f_{ij}/d_{ij}$ is nonlinear. In this case, we use a linear approximation,

$$E_{\text{approx}}(d_{ij}) = f_{ij}\left(-\frac{1}{d_{ij}^{\text{cur}}} + \frac{d_{ij} - d_{ij}^{\text{cur}}}{(d_{ij}^{\text{cur}})^2}\right).$$

For any convex potential function, such as the inverse-square law, the linear approximation is an upper bound on the actual potential energy. The configuration to which the system "jumps" will therefore have *lower* energy than expected, and thus the system will converge even if it uses this approximation.

5.2 Spring Force

It is possible to model forces which *increase* with distance such as a spring force. In this case, the potential function is $E(d_{ij}) = f_{ij} d_{ij}^2$. This type of function is concave (upwards), and thus the method in the previous paragraph does not work. To solve such a model using linear programming, we replace the function by a piecewise linear approximation. First, define l variables $0 \leq d_{ij1}, d_{ij2}, \ldots, d_{ijl} \leq 1$ and add the constraint $d_{ij} = d_{ij1} + d_{ij2} + \cdots + d_{ijl}$. The piecewise linear approximation to the energy function is

$$E_{\text{approx}}(d_{ij}) = f_{ij} \sum_{k=1}^{l} (2k - 1) d_{ijk}.$$

For $k \leq d_{ij} < k + 1$, this energy is minimized when $d_{ij1} = d_{ij2} = \cdots = d_{ijk} = 1$ and $d_{ij(k+1)} = d_{ij} - k$. The value of the approximate function is $f_{ij}(k^2 + (2k + 1)(d_{ij} - k))$ which is a good approximation to $f_{ij} d_{ij}^2$.

5.3 Examples.

The video illustrates the application of the constant force, inverse-square law force, and spring force.

In the "trampoline" example, the border of the 30 by 30 grid of spheres is fixed. Each internal grid sphere is attracted to its four immediate neighbors under the constant force. The large sphere falls into this grid and comes to rest. We fake the "bouncing" by playing the sequence forwards and backwards.

5.4 Other Possible Applications.

The examples we have implemented only scratch the surface of what one could do with the current formulation. For example, we could apply these new potential functions to two animations: a pearl falling in "shampoo" and a "lava lamp". The shampoo or "lamp fluid" is a grid-like "gas" of spheres. A constant force attracts sphere S_i to a fixed grid point g_i. The algorithm for modeling attraction of a moving point p_i to a fixed point q_i is straightforward from the math given above.

The pearl is a single sphere in a gravitational potential falling through a "shampoo." The lava lamp fluid uses the same model. We also add a rising "blob" of lava fluid subject to an upwards gravitational field. The beads in the "blob" fluid are subject to a mutually attractive force. For this we choose a potential function which rises linearly to a particular value and then stops increasing. This potential corresponds to a constant, short-range force. This potential function is convex, and thus linear programming can minimize it.

6 Implementation and Results

All examples in the video are a simple mapping of optimization steps to frames. We believe that these demonstrate a variety of realistic looking motions. If necessary, we could modulate the velocity by interpolating between frames. Since consecutive frames correspond to motion from c to c' in the same convex region, every interpolated configuration would also be valid.

6.1 Running Times and Scalability

As usual, our program is always in flux, and it is difficult to generate meaningful timings. The running time depends greatly on the settings of the parameters to the linear programming library. Currently, we use the simplex method. We find that reaching 80-90% of optimum requires only about one-quarter the time as reaching the optimum objective value. Hence, each step can be accomplished in one-quarter the time using only $1/0.8 = 1.25$ times as many steps. This is clearly a good trade-off. At present, we run each linear program for 5000 simplex steps, and this always brings us to within 80% of optimal.

Using these particular methods, we can compute each frame of the second hourglass video in about 1.1 minutes on a DEC Alpha 3000/700 (tm). The entire video can be generated in about 19 hours.

We ran the program with only 500 spheres, and each frame was computed 2.4 times faster than with 1000 spheres. Some of the cost is a naive $O(n^2)$ geometric algorithm, and the cost of this can be improved. In essence, the cost per step appears to be roughly linear in the number of spheres. Of course, about half as many steps are required to simulate the hourglass. Therefore, the cost appears to be roughly quadratic in the number of spheres. As we discuss in Section 7, this is not necessarily the last work. It is unlikely that distant spheres interact over small numbers of steps. Therefore it should be possible to decompose the problem and/or apply multi-scale methods.

6.2 Number of Iterations

If we are simply generating a "pile" or "clump", we usually do not have an obstruction like the neck of the hourglass through which the spheres must pass more or less sequentially. The following table gives the number of iterations for a k by k by k grid of spheres falling to rest in a box. The number iterations rises surprisingly slowly. This compares very favorably with acceleration or velocity-based methods. For these methods "time until next collision" appears to be inversely proportional to the number of spheres and the number of steps to be at least linear in the number of spheres.

Number of Spheres	27	64	125	216
Number of Iterations	21	25	39	54

6.3 Comparison with Velocity-Based Methods

We attempted to simulate the hourglass with a velocity-based method. As expected, collisions caused the time steps to be very small (around 10^{-5}). It takes about 150 steps to reduce the energy by one unit. For this example, it would require 2 or 3 million steps to reach minimum energy. Each step is faster, but only by a factor of two. We estimate it would take about 1000 times as long to reach an energy minimum than it does using the position-based method of this paper.

7 Conclusion and Future Work

Position-based physics and the linear programming algorithms we use to simulate it are very good ways to rapidly find local energy minima for many interacting objects. They are much faster than other physical simulation techniques, and they are certainly useful for CAD/CAM applications for which only the final configuration matters. The current techniques do not allow rotation in three dimensions (a moot issue for spheres but not for moving polyhedra), but Li [19] has found ways to allow rotation in two dimensions, and it may be possible to generalize this work to three dimensions or devise other methods. The algorithms presented here do not simulate true physical motion: 1) the physics is only semi-Newtonian, and 2) the algorithms use a number of approximations to allow us to apply linear programming. However, in graphics appearance and speed are really all that matters, and these methods rapidly generate motions which appear realistic. Since no other method can currently generate such motions with so little computation, position-based physics and linear programming based simulations warrant consideration as useful tools of computer graphics.

Even for 1000 spheres in a polyhedron, the simulation time is faster than the rendering time. For even larger number of spheres, one would have to break the set of spheres into "zones" and simulate within each zone. By switching between overlapping zones, one could still generate a good animation. Multi-scale techniques might also be applicable [20].

The issue of non-convex sets of valid directions arises for sets of translating polyhedra. However, we believe that this potential difficulty will not have a practical impact. A difficult practical problem is that of explicitly computing configuration spaces (Minkowski sums) for pairs of translating non-convex polyhedra. Dealing with rotations will be even more difficult. However, we believe these difficulties can be overcome. Position-based physics may one day simulate many highly interacting, translating and rotating polyhedra, with links and attractive and repulsive forces.

Another direction of future work is to handle the transition from crowding to freedom. Position-based physics does not do a good job on freely moving objects. Section 4.4 describes how to make the falling spheres appear to accelerate. We use another "trick" to make the ball appear to bounce in the trampoline video. A more general solution would somehow switch between the position-based method and an acceleration/velocity-based method in a way that is low-cost yet realistic.

Acknowledgements: Thanks to Kevin Duffy for implementing many of the algorithms as a summer job. Thanks to Lisa Ventry Milenkovic for proofreading and literature search. Thanks to Karen Daniels for proofreading and suggestions.

References

[1] D. Baraff. Analytical methods for dynamic simulation of non-penetrating rigid bodies. *Computer Graphics (Proceedings of SIGGRAPH)*, 23(3):223–232, 1989.

[2] David Baraff. Curved surfaces and coherence for non-penetrating rigid body simulation. In Forest Baskett, editor, *Computer Graphics (SIGGRAPH '90 Proceedings)*, volume 24, pages 19–28, August 1990.

[3] David Baraff. Coping with friction for non-penetrating rigid body simulation. In Thomas W. Sederberg, editor, *Computer Graphics (SIGGRAPH '91 Proceedings)*, volume 25, pages 31–40, July 1991.

[4] David Baraff. Issues in computing contact forces for nonpenetrating rigid bodies. *Algorithmica*, 10(2–4):292–352, 1993.

[5] David Baraff. Fast contact force computation for nonpenetrating rigid bodies. In Andrew Glassner, editor, *Proceedings of*

SIGGRAPH '94 (Orlando, Florida, July 24-29, 1994), Computer Graphics Proceedings, Annual Conference Series, pages 23–34. ACM SIGGRAPH, ACM Press, July 1994.

[6] David Baraff. Interactive simulation of solid rigid bodies. *IEEE Computer Graphics and Applications*, 15(3):63–75, May 1995.

[7] David Baraff and Andrew Witkin. Dynamic simulation of non-penetrating flexible bodies. In Edwin E. Catmull, editor, *Computer Graphics (SIGRAPH '92 Proceedings)*, volume 26, pages 303–308, July 1992.

[8] R. Barzel and A. H. Barr. A modeling system based on dynamics constraints. *Computer Graphics (Proceedings of SIGGRAPH)*, 22(4):179–187, 1988.

[9] Jim X. Chen and Niels Da Vitoria Lobo. Toward interactive-rate simulation of fluids with moving obstacles using navier-stokes equations. *Graphical Models and Image Processing*, 57(2):107–116, March 1995.

[10] N. Chiba, S. Sanakanishi, K. Yokoyama, I. Ootawara, K. Muraoka, and N. Saito. Visual simulation of water currents using a particle-based behavioural model. *Journal of Visualization and Computer Animation*, 6(3):155–172, July 1995.

[11] D. Dobkin, J. Hershberger, D. Kirkpatrik, and S. Suri. Implicitly searching convolutions and computing depth of collision. In *Proceedings of the Second SIGAL*, pages 165–180, 1990.

[12] Jeff Goldsmith and Alan H. Barr. Applying constrained optimization to computer graphics. *SMPTE Journal - Society of Motion Picture and Television Engineers*, 102(10):910–912, October 1993.

[13] L. Guibas, L. Ramshaw, and J. Stolfi. A Kinetic Framework for Computational Geometry. In *Proceedings of the 24th Annual IEEE Symposium on Foundations of Computer Science*, pages 100–111. IEEE, 1983.

[14] James K. Hahn. Realistic animation of rigid bodies. In John Dill, editor, *Computer Graphics (SIGGRAPH '88 Proceedings)*, volume 22, pages 299–308, August 1988.

[15] Mikako Harada, Andrew Witkin, and David Baraff. Interactive physically-based manipulation of discrete/continuous models. In Robert Cook, editor, *Proceedings of SIGGRAPH '95*, Computer Graphics Proceedings, Annual Conference Series, pages 199–208. ACM SIGGRAPH, ACM Press, August 1995.

[16] Vincent Hayward, Stephane Aubry, Andre Foisy, and Yasmine Ghallab. Efficient collision prediction among many moving objects. *The International Journal of Robotics Research*, 14(2):129–143, April 1995.

[17] Michael Kass and Gavin Miller. Rapid, stable fluid dynamics for computer graphics. In Forest Baskett, editor, *Computer Graphics (SIGGRAPH '90 Proceedings)*, volume 24, pages 49–57, August 1990.

[18] A. Kaul, M.A. O'Connor, and V. Srinivasan. Computing Minkowski Sums of Regular Polygons. In Thomas Shermer, editor, *Proceedings of the Third Canadian Conference on Computational Geometry*, pages 74–77, Vancouver, British Columbia, 1991. Simon Frasier University.

[19] Z. Li. *Compaction Algorithms for Non-Convex Polygons and Their Applications*. PhD thesis, Harvard University, Division of Applied Sciences, 1994.

[20] A. Luciani, A. Habibi, and E. Manzotti. A multi scale physical model of granular materials. In *Proceedings of Graphics Interface '95*, pages 136–145, May 1995.

[21] H. Mallinder. The modelling of large waterfalls using string texture. *Journal of Visualization and Computer Animation*, 6(1):3–10, January 1995.

[22] V. Milenkovic, K. Daniels, and Z. Li. Placement and Compaction of Nonconvex Polygons for Clothing Manufacture. In *Proceedings of the Fourth Canadian Conference on Computational Geometry*, pages 236–243, St. Johns, Newfoundland, August 1992. Department of Computer Science, Memorial University of Newfoundland.

[23] V. J. Milenkovic and Z. Li. A Compaction Algorithm for Nonconvex Polygons and Its Application. *European Journal of Operations Research*, 84:539–560, 1995.

[24] H. Minkowski. Volumen und Oberfläche. *Mathematische Annalen*, 57:447–495, 1903.

[25] M. Moore and J. Wilhelms. Collision detection and response for computer animation. *Computer Graphics (Proceedings of SIGGRAPH)*, 22(4):289–298, 1988.

[26] J. C. Platt and A. H. Barr. Constraint methods for flexible models. *Computer Graphics (Proceedings of SIGGRAPH)*, 22(4):279–287, 1988.

[27] J. Serra. *Image Analysis and Mathematical Morphology*, volume 1. Academic Press, New York, 1982.

[28] J. Serra, editor. *Image Analysis and Mathematical Morphology*, volume 2: Theoretical Advances. Academic Press, New York, 1988.

[29] Mikio Shinya and Marie-Claire Forgue. Layout out objects with geometric and pysical constraints. *Visual Computer*, 11:188–201, August 1995.

[30] John Snyder. An interactive tool for placing curved surfaces with interpenetration. In Robert Cook, editor, *Proceedings of SIGGRAPH '95*, Computer Graphics Proceedings, Annual Conference Series, pages 209–218. ACM SIGGRAPH, ACM Press, August 1995.

[31] Richard Szeliski and David Tonnesen. Surface modeling with oriented particle systems. In Edwin E. Catmull, editor, *Computer Graphics (SIGGRAPH '92 Proceedings)*, volume 26, pages 185–194, July 1992.

[32] Demitri Terzopoulos, John Platt, and Kurt Fleischer. Heating and melting deformable models (from goop to glop). In *Proceedings of Graphics Interface '89*, pages 219–226, June 1989.

[33] Andrew P. Witkin and Paul S. Heckbert. Using particles to sample and control implicit surfaces. In Andrew Glassner, editor, *Proceedings of SIGGRAPH '94 (Orlando, Florida, July 24-29, 1994)*, Computer Graphics Proceedings, Annual Conference Series, pages 269–278. ACM SIGGRAPH, ACM Press, July 1994.

Linear-Time Dynamics using Lagrange Multipliers

David Baraff

Robotics Institute
Carnegie Mellon University

Abstract

Current linear-time simulation methods for articulated figures are based exclusively on reduced-coordinate formulations. This paper describes a general, non-iterative linear-time simulation method based instead on Lagrange multipliers. Lagrange multiplier methods are important for computer graphics applications because they bypass the difficult (and often intractable) problem of parameterizing a system's degrees of freedom. Given a loop-free set of n equality constraints acting between pairs of bodies, the method takes $O(n)$ time to compute the system's dynamics. The method does not rely on matrix bandwidth, so no assumptions about the constraints' topology are needed. Bodies need not be rigid, constraints can be of various dimensions, and unlike reduced-coordinate approaches, nonholonomic (e.g. velocity-dependent) constraints are allowed. An additional set of k one-dimensional constraints which induce loops and/or handle inequalities can be accommodated with cost $O(kn)$. This makes it practical to simulate complicated, closed-loop articulated figures with joint-limits and contact at interactive rates. A complete description of a sample implementation is provided in pseudocode.

1 Introduction

Forward simulation with constraints is a key problem in computer graphics. Typically, a system's constraints are *sparse*: each constraint directly affects only one or two bodies (for example, geometric connection constraints) and for a system with n bodies, there are only $O(n)$ constraints. In particular, the simulation of articulated figures and mechanisms falls into this category. Sparse constraint systems are also either nearly or completely acyclic: for example, robot arms are usually open-loop structures, as are animation models for humans and animals. Considerable effort has been directed toward efficiently simulating these types of systems.

Reading through the dynamics literature, a large variety of dynamics formulation can be found (Newton-Euler, Gibbs-Appel, D'Alembert, Gauss' Least Constraint Principle, etc.) but the details of these variations matter little; ultimately, we are faced with a basic choice. Either we model constraints by reducing the number of coordinates needed to describe the system's state, or we introduce additional forces into the system to maintain the constraints.

A *reduced-coordinate* formulation takes a system with m degrees of freedom (d.o.f.'s), a set of constraints that removes c of those d.o.f.'s, and parameterizes the remaining $n = m - c$ d.o.f.'s using a reduced set of n coordinates. Reduced coordinates are usually known as *generalized* coordinates; coordinates describing the original m-d.o.f. system are called *maximal* coordinates. For an arbitrary set of constraints, finding a parameterization for m maximal coordinates in terms of n generalized coordinates is arbitrarily hard; if such a parameterization can be found, $O(n^3)$ time is required to compute the acceleration of the n generalized coordinates at any instant. However, loop-free articulated rigid bodies are trivially parameterized, and methods for computing the n generalized coordinate accelerations in $O(n)$ time are well known [7].

In contrast, Lagrange multiplier methods express the system's state using the simpler set of m maximal coordinates. Constraints are enforced by introducing *constraint forces* into the system. At each instant, a basis for the constraint forces is known *a priori*; the Lagrange multipliers (which we must compute) are a vector of c scalar coordinates that describe the constraint force in terms of the basis. Lagrange multiplier approaches are extremely important for interactive computer graphics applications, because they allow an arbitrary set of constraints to be combined. This is difficult (often impossible) to achieve with a reduced-coordinate formulation. Additionally, Lagrange multiplier formulations allow (and frankly encourage) a highly modular knowledge/software design, in which bodies, constraints, and geometry regard each other as black-box entities (section 2 develops this further). Lagrange multipliers also allow us to handle nonholonomic constraints, such as velocity-dependent constraints; reduced-coordinate approaches inherently lack this capability.

For a system whose constraints remove c d.o.f.'s, the Lagrange multipliers are the c unknown variables of a set of c linear equations. If c is much greater than n, so that the constrained system possesses only a few d.o.f.'s, clearly the reduced-coordinate approach is preferred. However, for the case of open-loop articulated three-dimensional rigid bodies, $c = O(n)$, since c is at least $1/5n$ and at most $5n$. Even though n and c are linearly related for articulated figures, the current prevailing view is that articulated figures can be simulated in linear time *only* by using a reduced-coordinate formulation. The possibility of achieving $O(n)$ performance for Lagrange multiplier methods has been largely discounted, because the prospects for easily solving the resulting $O(n) \times O(n)$ matrix system in $O(n)$ time have seemed dismal, at best.

We show in this paper that a very simple direct (that is, non-iterative) $O(n)$ solution method exists for computing Lagrange multipliers for sparse acyclic constraint systems. We would like to emphasize that the matrix equation equation (8) presented in section 6 is well-known to the robotics and mechanical engineering communities, as is the fact that this linear system is sparse. As a result, there is the feeling (again, well-known) that linear-time performance can be achieved by applying general sparse-matrix techniques to the problem. What is not well-known, and is thus the focus of this paper, is that general, complicated sparse-matrix techniques are not needed at all, and that a tight, $O(n)$ running-time is easily demonstrated. An analysis of equation (8)'s structure will show that a very simple (and, we again emphasisize, well-known) sparse-matrix technique can easily be applied to compute the Lagrange multipliers in linear time.

1.1 Specific Contributions

The results of this paper are the following. Consider a set of n bodies (not necessarily rigid) and a set of $n-1$ constraints, with each constraint enforcing a relationship of some dimension between two of the bodies. Assuming the constraint connectivity is acyclic (for example, a system with constraints between body 1 and 2, between body 2 and 3, and between body 3 and 1 would *not* be acyclic) we describe a simple, direct $O(n)$ method for computing the Lagrange multipliers for these constraints. We will call this acyclic set of constraints the *primary constraints*. The primary constraints need not be holonomic, though they must be equality constraints. Nonholonomic velocity-based constraints—such as a relationship between rotational speeds of bodies—fit into this framework and are handled as primary constraints. Reduced-coordinates approaches are restricted to holonomic constraints.

In addition, a set of *auxiliary* constraints can also be accommodated. Closed loops are handled by designating constraints which cause cycles as auxiliary, rather than primary constraints. Similarly, constraints that act on only a single body, or on more than two bodies are designated as auxiliary constraints, as are inequality constraints, such as joint-angle limits or contact constraints. If the primary constraints partition the bodies into separate components (for example, two separate chains), then an inequality might involve only one of the primary constraint components (a chain colliding with itself); however, a constraint involving two or more components (two different chains colliding with each other) is handled just as easily. In addition to the $O(n)$ time required to deal with the primary constraints, k one-dimensional auxiliary constraints cost $O(nk)$ time to formulate a $k \times k$ matrix system and $O(k^3)$ time to solve the system. When k is small compared to n, the added cost is essentially just an additional $O(nk)$. The auxiliary constraint method described is particularly efficient in conjunction with our $O(n)$ primary constraint method and is easily adapted for use with linear-time reduced-coordinate formulations.[1]

In our (biased) view, linear-time performance is achieved far more easily for Lagrange multiplier methods than for reduced-coordinate formulations. While $O(n)$ *inverse* reduced-coordinate approaches are easily understood, *forward* reduced-coordinate formulations with linear time complexity have an extremely steep learning curve, and make use of a formidable array of notational tools. The author admits (as do many practitioners the author has queried) to lacking a solid, intuitive understanding of these methods. We believe that a reader who already understands the standard $O(n^3)$ method for formulating and computing Lagrange multipliers should have no difficulty in implementing the $O(n)$ method presented in this paper. To back this point up, appendix A contains a complete (yet extremely short) pseudocode implementation. Given an existing $O(n^3)$ Lagrange multiplier based simulation system, converting to the required $O(n)$ datastructures is simply and easily accomplished.

2 Motivation

It is probably as important for us to stress what this paper does *not* say as to stress what this paper does say. The existence of a linear-time Lagrange multiplier method shows that the Lagrange multiplier approach can achieve the same asymptotic complexity results as reduced-coordinate formulations; this is of theoretical interest. However, in presenting a linear-time method for computing multipliers we are *not* asserting that such a method is faster on articulated figures than, say, Featherstone's $O(n)$ method. On the other hand, we are also not asserting it is necessarily slower. It used to be that one could attempt to discuss the running times of algorithms based on the number of multiplications and additions; today, when a memory access may be as costly as a multiplication, such analysis no longer holds true. In section 9, we will discuss and relate actual running times of our algorithm to the few published results with which we are familiar.

[1] We imagine that a similar approach is used by some systems that combine Lagrange multipliers for loop-closing/contact with reduced-coordinate formulations for primary constraints (for example, Symbolic Dynamic's SD/FAST system).

2.1 Why Reduced Coordinates?

There are certainly valid reasons for preferring a reduced-coordinate approach over a multiplier approach. In particular, if the n d.o.f.'s left to the system is very much smaller than the c d.o.f.'s removed by the constraints, a reduced-coordinate approach is clearly called for. Even if c and n are linearly related the use of generalized coordinates eliminates the "drifting" problem that multiplier methods have. (For example, two links which are supposed to remain connected will have a tendency to drift apart somewhat when a multiplier approach is used.) Such drift is partly a consequence of numerical errors in computing the multipliers, but stems mostly from the inevitable errors of numerical integration during the simulation. Constraint stabilization techniques [4, 3] are used to help combat this problem.[2] The use of generalized coordinates eliminates this worry completely, since generalized coordinates only express configurations which exactly satisfy the constraints. There is anecdotal evidence that the use of generalized coordinates thus allows simulations to proceed faster, not because evaluation of the generalized coordinate accelerations is faster, but because larger timesteps can be taken by the integrator. This may well be true. More importantly, for the case of articulated figures, we know that with a reduced-coordinate approach, linear-time performance is achievable.

2.2 Why Lagrange Multipliers?

On the other hand, there are also strong motivations for preferring a multiplier approach. Work by Witkin *et al.* [17], Barzel and Barr [3], Baraff [1], and most recently and comprehensively Gleicher [8], present a variety of arguments in favor of multiplier methods. In particular, multiplier methods neatly compartmentalize knowledge, enabling strongly modular systems. For general-purpose, extensible simulation systems, this is vital. Consider two bodies and a constraint that the world-space location of two points (each point having a fixed body-space location) be coincident. Parameterizing the system's degrees of freedom using generalized coordinates requires us to have symbolic knowledge of the body-space to world-space mapping for each body. This is obviously not a problem if we limit ourselves to rigid bodies, but suppose that one or both of the bodies can rotate, translate, and scale (possibly among one or more axes). We must know the freedoms of the bodies, in order to form the generalized coordinates. Similarly, a constraint that depends upon surface geometry requires symbolic knowledge of the surface equation. From a software modularity standpoint, every combination of constraint, body, and geometry yields a new type of parameterization. This results in a quadratic explosion in the amount of code that must be generated.

In some cases it may be either too difficult, or even impossible, to derive the necessary generalized coordinate parameterizations. Once we move past rigid bodies to globally deformable frames, parameterization of the constraints becomes totally impractical. Even

[2] A significantly more complicated but also more powerful approach is to perform the simulation using *differential-algebraric equation* (DAE) solution techniques [5]. In the author's experience, constraint stabilization works so well for the simulation problems encountered within the computer graphics domain that the DAE approach is not warranted. Clearly, this is not true for all simulation domains.

for rigid bodies, parameterization can be hard: imagine a tangency constraint between two rigid smooth surfaces, that requires that the bodies remain in tangential contact (thus allowing sliding motions). This constraint removes exactly one degree of freedom from the bodies' motions. For all but the simplest shapes, the required parameterization is extremely complicated (and closed-form solutions will not in general exist).

Finally, nonholonomic constraints cannot be expressed in terms of generalized coordinates. Consider a mechanical simulation, with an abstraction of a complicated gearing mechanism. We may have a simple constraint—for example, that the rotational speed of one three-dimensional object be twice the speed of another—but be completely unable to express it in a reduced-coordinate formulation. In contrast, such velocity-based constraints are trivially handled using multiplier methods.

Suppose however that we are interested only in simulating articulated rigid bodies, so that none of the above issues apply. If the implementation of one of the $O(n)$ reduced-coordinate algorithms described in the literature is seen as manageable, quite possibly there is no gain to be realized from the algorithm described in this paper. If generalized coordinates are desired but the effort to implement a linear-time reduced-coordinate approach is prohibitive, a middle ground exists: at each step of the simulation, translate the generalized coordinates and velocities to maximal coordinates and velocities, compute the Lagrange multipliers and thus the maximal coordinate accelerations, and translate these accelerations back into generalized coordinates. For all other cases (when a reduced-coordinate approach is infeasible because of the demands it places on software architecture, or because the necessary parameterization simply cannot be realized) the algorithm described in this paper yields a practical, simple linear-time alternative to traditional reduced-coordinate techniques.

3 Background

In this paper, the term simulation does not merely refer to dynamic, physical simulation: the use of constrained differential kinematic manipulation, as pioneered by Witkin *et al.* [17] and Gleicher [8] is also considered simulation. For dynamic, or "second-order" simulation, we relate acceleration to force according to Newton's law $f = ma$, while for kinematic manipulation we instantaneously relate velocity and "force" according to the first-order law $f = mv$. Similarly, in a dynamics simulation with collisions, the velocity discontinuity Δv caused by a collision is related to an impulsive force j according to the law $\Delta v = mj$. In all of the above cases, the problem is to compute the correct acceleration, velocity, or velocity change that satisfies the constraints of the system. We will not distinguish between any of these problems further; this paper deals with $f = ma$ problems, with the understanding that the results obtained obviously transfer to the other two problems.

Lagrange multipliers are usually computed by solving a matrix equation (which we describe in greater detail later)

$$\mathbf{J}\mathbf{M}^{-1}\mathbf{J}^T\boldsymbol{\lambda} = \mathbf{c}.$$

The elements of the vector $\boldsymbol{\lambda}$ are the multipliers we wish to solve for, while $\mathbf{M}$ is a block-diagonal matrix. The vector $\mathbf{c}$ expresses the forces being applied to the bodies. The rows of $\mathbf{J}$ encode the constraints' connectivity in block-form: if the ith constraint affects only bodies p and q, then only the pth and qth blocks of $\mathbf{J}$'s ith row are nonzero. (We discuss the block structure of $\mathbf{J}$ and $\mathbf{M}$ more carefully in the next section.) Because of $\mathbf{J}$'s and $\mathbf{M}$'s structure, for some special cases it is obvious that $\boldsymbol{\lambda}$ can be computed in linear time.

For example, consider a serial chain (an unbranching sequence of links). The dynamics of serial chain robot arms were not generally known to be solvable in linear time until very recently, with the advent of Featherstone's [7] recursive articulated-body method.[3] This is a curious oversight, when one considers that linear-time simulation of serial chains with Lagrange multiplier methods is obvious and trivial, because $\mathbf{J}\mathbf{M}^{-1}\mathbf{J}^T$ is tightly banded (assuming an ordering so that body p is connected to body $p+1$ for all bodies).

Once we move past simple chains, the problem becomes more complicated. Depending on the structure of the constraints, exploiting bandedness is still a possibility. For example, Surles [15] exploited bandedness (by symmetrically permuting rows and columns of $\mathbf{J}\mathbf{M}^{-1}\mathbf{J}^T$) to achieve a direct, linear-time solution for the multipliers on systems that are very chain-like in their connectivity, but have some limited branching. As structures become less chainlike however, the bandwidth of the system increases, and his method reduces to a regular $O(n^3)$ dense solution method. Negrut *et al.* [12] describe a similar method. The method described in this paper does not attempt to exploit bandwidth because for many structures there is *no* permutation that yields a matrix system with reasonable bandwidth.

While sparse (but not necessarily acyclic) constraint systems always yield sparse matrices $\mathbf{J}$ and $\mathbf{M}^{-1}$, in more general problems the product $\mathbf{J}\mathbf{M}^{-1}\mathbf{J}^T$ (although usually sparse) need not be. One well-known approach to dealing with this kind of sparsity is the use of iterative methods, with time-complexity $O(n^2)$ (or lower, depending on convergence properties). Despite impressive recent results by Gleicher [8] in applying conjugate-gradient methods to compute multipliers, the prospect of computing multipliers in less than $O(n^3)$ still seems to be largely viewed by the computer graphics community as a theoretical result, but not a practical actuality. Similarly, many papers in computer graphics, robotics, and mechanical engineering in have pointed out that, in theory, the sparsity of $\mathbf{J}\mathbf{M}^{-1}\mathbf{J}^T$ can be exploited by direct, non-iterative methods in linear time by applying general sparse-matrix solvers to the problem. (The same observation is also made about equation (8) of section 6.) However, this first supposes that $\mathbf{J}\mathbf{M}^{-1}\mathbf{J}^T$ is sparse which is generally but not always true. Even if sparsity exists, solving such problems by employing a general-purpose sparse-matrix solver is, practically speaking, not something that most computer graphicists would approach with much enthusiasm.

To the best of our knowledge though, no one has made the observation that *any* pairwise, acyclic set of constraints results in a system that (when formulated correctly) is easily solved in linear time using rudimentary sparse-matrix principles. The next few sections simply elaborate on this basic observation. In section 8, we describe a practical method for dealing with loop-closing and inequality constraints that are not handled by the simpler sparse formulation we are about to describe.

4 The Lagrange Multiplier Formulation

Our goal is to treat bodies, forces, and constraints as "anonymously" as possible: we wish to assume the minimum possible structure. For example, we may have a mix of body types (e.g. rigid, rigid plus scalable, etc.) and constraints of various dimensions (e.g. a pin-joint of dimension three, a point-to-surface constraint with dimension one). This leads us to a formulation where matrices are composed of smaller, dense matrices; this is known as a *block-matrix* formulation [9]. The dimensions of an individual block are dictated by the dimensions of bodies and constraints. A body's dimension is the number of d.o.f.'s the body has when unconstrained, while a constraint's dimension is the number of d.o.f.'s the constraint removes

[3] Featherstone made this discovery independently of earlier work by Vereshchagin, in 1974. Vereshchagin [16] described a solution algorithm for serial chains which turned out to have linear time complexity, although the algorithm was not advertised as such.

from the system. If no body has a dimension greater than p, then no constraint will have a dimension greater than p. As a result, all blocks will be of size $p \times p$ or smaller. Regarding p as a constant for the simulation, an operation on a single block or pair of blocks (inversion, multiplication, addition) takes constant time.

Our assumptions about the constraints are made as weak as possible. At any instant, each constraint is specified as a linear condition on the acceleration of a pair of bodies. The mechanics of expressing various geometric and velocity-based constraints as conditions on bodies' accelerations has been extensively considered in past work [3, 1, 8, 13]; we therefore omit the details of particular constraints. Hopefully, this rather aggressive retreat into anonymous notation will both simplify the resulting discussion, and explicitly define the modular relationship between bodies, constraints, and the computation of the Lagrange multipliers. (A more basic introduction, including information on reduced-cordinate methods, multiplier approaches, and various numerical methods can be found in Shabana [14].)

4.1 Notation

With the above in mind, we introduce a small amount of notation. The dimension of the ith body is denoted $\dim(i)$ and is the number of d.o.f.'s the body has when unconstrained. We describe the ith body's velocity as a vector $\mathbf{v}_i \in \mathbb{R}^{\dim(i)}$; a force $\mathbf{F}_i$ acting on the ith body is also a vector in $\mathbb{R}^{\dim(i)}$. The acceleration $\dot{\mathbf{v}}_i$ of the ith body in response to the force $\mathbf{F}_i$ is

$$\mathbf{M}_i\dot{\mathbf{v}}_i = \mathbf{F}_i$$

where $\mathbf{M}_i$ is a $\dim(i) \times \dim(i)$ symmetric positive definite matrix which describes the mass properties of body i. The matrix $\mathbf{M}_i$ may vary over time according to the body's geometric state; however, $\mathbf{M}_i$ is independent of $\mathbf{v}_i$. For a system of n bodies, the vector $\mathbf{v} = (\mathbf{v}_1, \mathbf{v}_2, \dots, \mathbf{v}_n)$ denotes the velocity of the entire system, and similarly for $\dot{\mathbf{v}}$. (Note that $\mathbf{v}$ is described in block-fashion; $\mathbf{v}$'s ith element $\mathbf{v}_i$ is itself a vector, with dimension $\dim(i)$.) Similarly, a force $\mathbf{F} = (\mathbf{F}_1, \mathbf{F}_2, \dots, \mathbf{F}_n)$ acting on the system means that a force $\mathbf{F}_1$ act on body 1, and so on. Given such a force $\mathbf{F}$, the system's evolution over time is

$$\mathbf{M}\dot{\mathbf{v}} = \mathbf{F} \tag{1}$$

where $\mathbf{M}$ is the block-diagonal matrix

$$\mathbf{M} = \begin{pmatrix} \mathbf{M}_1 & \mathbf{0} & \cdots & \mathbf{0} \\ \mathbf{0} & \mathbf{M}_2 & \cdots & \mathbf{0} \\ \vdots & \vdots & \ddots & \vdots \\ \mathbf{0} & \mathbf{0} & \cdots & \mathbf{M}_n \end{pmatrix}.$$

The dimension of a constraint is the number of d.o.f.'s the constraint removes from the system. As we said earlier, a constraint is expressed as a linear condition on bodies' accelerations. If the ith constraint has dimension m, then an expression for the constraint is an m-dimensional acceleration condition of the form

$$\mathbf{j}_{i1}\dot{\mathbf{v}}_1 + \cdots + \mathbf{j}_{ik}\dot{\mathbf{v}}_k + \cdots + \mathbf{j}_{in}\dot{\mathbf{v}}_n + \mathbf{c}_i = \mathbf{0}. \tag{2}$$

Each matrix $\mathbf{j}_{ik}$ has dimension $m \times \dim(k)$, $\mathbf{c}_i$ is an m-length column vector, and $\mathbf{0}$ is the zero vector of length m. The coefficients of this equation (the $\mathbf{j}_{ik}$ matrices and the vector $\mathbf{c}_i$) depend on the specifics of the bodies and the exact constraint being enforced, as well as the position and velocities of the bodies at the current instant. In the next section, we will require that each primary constraint affect only a pair of bodies; this means that for each value of i, all but two of the $\mathbf{j}_{ik}$ matrices will be zero. For now, this restriction is not important.

4.2 Constraint Forces

In order to enforce the acceleration conditions of the constraints, a constraint force must be added to the system. For the primary constraints of the system, we deal only with constraints that are maintained by *workless* constraint forces. A rigorously physical definition of workless constraints is difficult, because explicitly time-varying constraint functions (such as those in Barzel and Barr [3], which cause gradual assemblages of structures) can add energy into the system.[4] The most direct way to attack the problem is to say that by workless constraint forces, we really mean "constraint forces that are as lazy as possible." Fortunately, this intuitive notion has a simple mathematical translation: the constraint force $\mathbf{F}_i^c$ that maintains the ith constraint is workless only if the force it exerts on the bodies is of the form

$$\mathbf{F}_i^c = \begin{pmatrix} \mathbf{j}_{i1}^T \\ \vdots \\ \mathbf{j}_{in}^T \end{pmatrix} \boldsymbol{\lambda}_i \tag{3}$$

where $\boldsymbol{\lambda}_i$ is a column vector of dimension m (the dimension of the ith constraint). We call the vector $\boldsymbol{\lambda}_i$ the Lagrange multiplier of the ith constraint. (If the ith constraint is not maintained by such a force, it must be treated as an auxiliary constraint.)

To talk about a total of q constraints, we switch to matrix notation. We can express these q multi-dimensional acceleration conditions in the form

$$\begin{aligned} \mathbf{j}_{11}\dot{\mathbf{v}}_1 + \cdots + \mathbf{j}_{1n}\dot{\mathbf{v}}_n + \mathbf{c}_1 &= \mathbf{0} \\ \mathbf{j}_{21}\dot{\mathbf{v}}_1 + \cdots + \mathbf{j}_{2n}\dot{\mathbf{v}}_n + \mathbf{c}_2 &= \mathbf{0} \\ &\vdots \\ \mathbf{j}_{q1}\dot{\mathbf{v}}_1 + \cdots + \mathbf{j}_{qn}\dot{\mathbf{v}}_n + \mathbf{c}_q &= \mathbf{0}. \end{aligned} \tag{4}$$

If we define

$$\mathbf{J} = \begin{pmatrix} \mathbf{j}_{11} & \mathbf{j}_{12} & \cdots & \mathbf{j}_{1n} \\ \vdots & \vdots & & \vdots \\ \mathbf{j}_{q1} & \mathbf{j}_{q2} & \cdots & \mathbf{j}_{qn} \end{pmatrix} \quad \text{and} \quad \mathbf{c} = \begin{pmatrix} \mathbf{c}_1 \\ \vdots \\ \mathbf{c}_q \end{pmatrix}$$

then we can replace equation (4) with simply

$$\mathbf{J}\dot{\mathbf{v}} + \mathbf{c} = \mathbf{0}. \tag{5}$$

In a similar fashion, we group the individual vectors $\boldsymbol{\lambda}_1$ through $\boldsymbol{\lambda}_n$ into one large vector $\boldsymbol{\lambda} = (\boldsymbol{\lambda}_1, \dots, \boldsymbol{\lambda}_n)$.

From equation (3), we see that the vector being multiplied by $\boldsymbol{\lambda}_i$ forms the ith block-column of $\mathbf{J}^T$; accordingly, the sum of all the individual constraint forces $\mathbf{F}_i^c$ has the form $\mathbf{J}^T\boldsymbol{\lambda}$. The problem now is to find a vector $\boldsymbol{\lambda}$ so that the constraint force $\mathbf{J}^T\boldsymbol{\lambda}$, combined with any external forces (such as gravity), produces a motion of the system that satisfies the constraints; that is, $\mathbf{J}\dot{\mathbf{v}} + \mathbf{c} = \mathbf{0}$.

5 The $\mathbf{JM}^{-1}\mathbf{J}^T$ Approach

The formulation most commonly used by the graphics community to compute $\boldsymbol{\lambda}$ is as follows. Given that an unknown constraint force $\mathbf{J}^T\boldsymbol{\lambda}$ acts upon the bodies, and letting $\mathbf{F}^{\text{ext}}$ represent the known net

[4] A lengthy discussion on the topic of rheonomic, scleronomic, monogenic and polygenic constraints and forces, as in Lanczos [10], can pin down an exact definition, but offers little insight. We forego such a discussion here. A precise, but nonconstructive mathematical definition would be to say that workless constraint forces are those which maintain the system according to Gauss' "principle of least constraint."

external force acting on the system (including all inertial velocity-dependent forces), from equation (1) we know that

$$\mathbf{M}\dot{\mathbf{v}} = \mathbf{J}^T\boldsymbol{\lambda} + \mathbf{F}^{\text{ext}}.$$

Solving for $\dot{\mathbf{v}}$, this yields

$$\dot{\mathbf{v}} = \mathbf{M}^{-1}\mathbf{J}^T\boldsymbol{\lambda} + \mathbf{M}^{-1}\mathbf{F}^{\text{ext}}. \tag{6}$$

Thus, once we compute $\boldsymbol{\lambda}$, we will be able to easily compute $\dot{\mathbf{v}}$. Since $\mathbf{M}$ is block diagonal, $\mathbf{M}^{-1}$ is as well. Substituting equation (6) into equation (5), we obtain

$$\mathbf{J}(\mathbf{M}^{-1}\mathbf{J}^T\boldsymbol{\lambda} + \mathbf{M}^{-1}\mathbf{F}^{\text{ext}}) + \mathbf{c} = \mathbf{0}.$$

If the matrix $\mathbf{A}$ and vector $\mathbf{b}$ are defined by

$$\mathbf{A} = \mathbf{J}\mathbf{M}^{-1}\mathbf{J}^T \qquad \text{and} \qquad \mathbf{b} = -(\mathbf{J}\mathbf{M}^{-1}\mathbf{F}^{\text{ext}} + \mathbf{c})$$

then we can express $\boldsymbol{\lambda}$ as the solution of the equation

$$\mathbf{A}\boldsymbol{\lambda} = \mathbf{b}. \tag{7}$$

This formulation has a number of desirable properties. First, assuming that $\mathbf{J}$ has full rank (equivalently, none of the imposed constraints are conflicting or redundant) then since $\mathbf{M}^{-1}$ is symmetric positive definite, $\mathbf{A}$ is as well. Note that for an articulated structure, $\mathbf{J}$ automatically has full rank, independent of the structure's current geometric configuration.[5]

As long as $\mathbf{A}$ is not too large, we can use direct methods to compute $\boldsymbol{\lambda}$. In particular, when $\mathbf{A}$ is nonsingular, the Cholesky decomposition is an excellent method for computing $\boldsymbol{\lambda}$. As $\mathbf{A}$ becomes larger, iterative methods can be used to solve equation (7), either by explicitly forming the matrix $\mathbf{A}$ when it is sparse, or by using methods that work in terms of the (always) sparse factors $\mathbf{J}$ and $\mathbf{M}^{-1}$. In discussing the sparsity of $\mathbf{A}$, we regard $\mathbf{A}$ as a block matrix, with the blocks defined by the blocks of $\mathbf{M}$ and $\mathbf{J}$.

At this point, we restrict ourselves to constraints that act between a pair of bodies. Referring to equation (2), this means that for a given value i, only two elements of the ith block-row of $\mathbf{J}$ are nonzero. If constraint i acts on bodies r and s, then only $\mathbf{j}_{ir}$ and $\mathbf{j}_{is}$ will be nonzero. How does this translate to sparsity on the matrix $\mathbf{A}$? From the definition of $\mathbf{A}$, the ijth block of $\mathbf{A}$ is

$$\mathbf{A}_{ij} = \sum_{k=1}^{n} (\mathbf{j}_{ik})(\mathbf{M}_k)(\mathbf{j}_{jk}^T).$$

When is $\mathbf{A}_{ij}$ nonzero? Since each $\mathbf{M}_k$ is nonzero, $\mathbf{A}_{ij}$ is nonzero only if there exists k such that $\mathbf{j}_{ik}\mathbf{j}_{jk}^T \neq \mathbf{0}$. From equation (2), this means that there must exist a body k that both the ith and jth constraint affect.

As was previously pointed out, serial chains yield tightly banded matrix system. Assuming a chain of n links ordered so that body i connects to body $i+1$ (figure 1a) we see that $\mathbf{A}_{ij}$ is zero if $|i-j| > 1$. Thus, we can trivially solve $\mathbf{A}\boldsymbol{\lambda} = \mathbf{b}$ in $O(n)$ time using a banded solution method (e.g. banded Cholesky decomposition). However, if we have instead a branching structure, so that neither $\mathbf{A}$ (nor any permutation of $\mathbf{A}$) is banded, can we find some general way to exploit the sparsity of $\mathbf{A}$? The answer to this is "no," because $\mathbf{A}$ is not necessarily sparse at all!

Consider a structure where constraint 1 acts between body 1 and 2, constraint 2 acts between body 1 and 3, and so on (figure 1b).

[5] The *inverse dynamics* of a straight chain are singular; however, the forward dynamics are always well defined. Contrary to popular belief, $\mathbf{A}$ remains nonsingular for articulated figures unless one accidentally repeats some of the articulation constraints in forming $\mathbf{J}$. However, a perfectly straight chain that has *both* its endpoints constrained does result in a singular matrix $\mathbf{A}$.

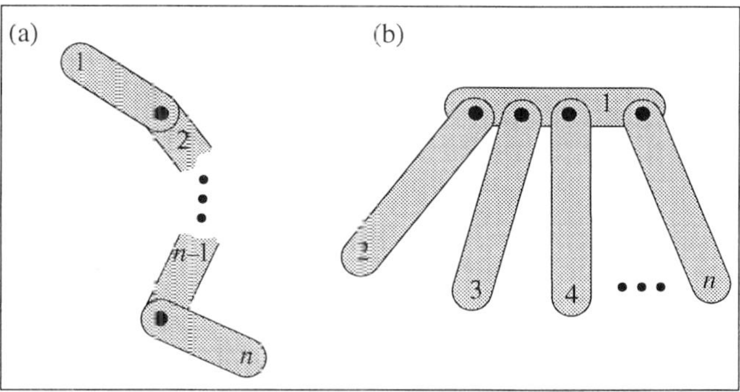

Figure 1: (a) A serial chain. (b) A branched object yielding a completely dense matrix $\mathbf{A} = \mathbf{J}\mathbf{M}^{-1}\mathbf{J}^T$.

The matrix $\mathbf{A}$ for this structure is not sparse at all: in fact, $\mathbf{A}$ is completely dense, because every constraint has body 1 in common (i.e. the product $(\mathbf{j}_{i1})\mathbf{M}_1(\mathbf{j}_{j1}^T)$ is nonzero for all pairs i and j). To exploit sparsity we must abandon the approach of computing $\boldsymbol{\lambda}$ in terms of the matrix $\mathbf{J}\mathbf{M}^{-1}\mathbf{J}^T$.

6 An (Always) Sparse Formulation

The matrix $\mathbf{A}$ is square and has dimension $N_c \times N_c$ where N_c is the sum of all the constraint's dimensions. Instead of computing $\boldsymbol{\lambda}$ in terms of $\mathbf{A}$, consider the matrix equation

$$\begin{pmatrix} \mathbf{M} & -\mathbf{J}^T \\ -\mathbf{J} & \mathbf{0} \end{pmatrix} \begin{pmatrix} \mathbf{y} \\ \boldsymbol{\lambda} \end{pmatrix} = \begin{pmatrix} \mathbf{0} \\ -\mathbf{b} \end{pmatrix}. \tag{8}$$

The top row yields $\mathbf{M}\mathbf{y} - \mathbf{J}^T\boldsymbol{\lambda} = \mathbf{0}$, or equivalently, $\mathbf{y} = \mathbf{M}^{-1}\mathbf{J}^T\boldsymbol{\lambda}$. Substituting this into the bottom row and multiplying by -1 yields

$$\mathbf{J}\mathbf{y} = \mathbf{J}(\mathbf{M}^{-1}\mathbf{J}^T\boldsymbol{\lambda}) = \mathbf{b}$$

which is equation (7). Thus, we can compute $\boldsymbol{\lambda}$ by solving equation (8) for $\boldsymbol{\lambda}$ and $\mathbf{y}$ (although $\mathbf{y}$ is an unneeded byproduct).

Let us define the matrix of equation (8) by writing

$$\mathbf{H} = \begin{pmatrix} \mathbf{M} & -\mathbf{J}^T \\ -\mathbf{J} & \mathbf{0} \end{pmatrix}.$$

This formulation is commonly seen in the robotics and mechanical-engineering literature. While some see the use of $\mathbf{H}$ as helping to explicitly separate the equations of motion (the top row of the matrix) from the constraint conditions (the bottom row of the matrix), it is clear that actually computing $\boldsymbol{\lambda}$ directly from equation (8) is a very foolish thing to do, *using dense matrix methods*. Using an $O(n^3)$ technique, equation (7) is easier to solve because $\mathbf{A}$ is much smaller than $\mathbf{H}$ and also because $\mathbf{A}$ is positive definite, while $\mathbf{H}$ is not. However, when we consider the problem from a sparse viewpoint, it becomes apparent that equation (8) is superior to equation (7), because $\mathbf{H}$ is *always* sparse. In the next section, we describe a simple $O(n)$ solution procedure for solving equation (8).

7 A Sparse Solution Method

Our $O(n)$ algorithm is based solely on the properties of the graph of $\mathbf{H}$. The *graph* of a square symmetric s block by s block matrix $\mathbf{H}$ is an undirected graph with s nodes. For $i \neq j$, there is an edge between nodes i and j if $\mathbf{H}_{ij}$ is nonzero. (The diagonal elements of $\mathbf{H}$ are always regarded as nonzero elements, but they do not contribute

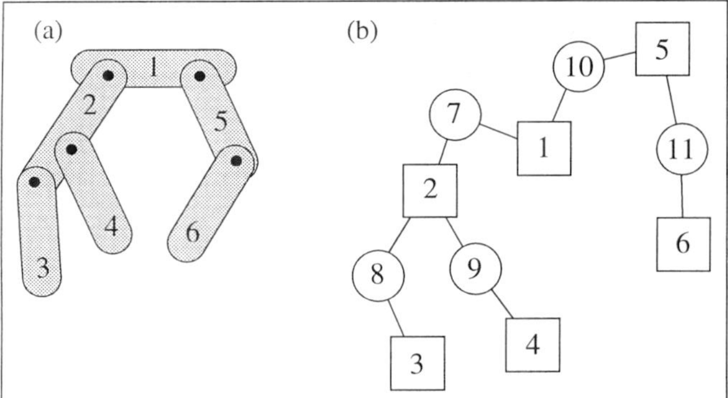

Figure 2: (a) An articulated object. (b) The graph of the matrix H corresponding to the object. Nodes corresponding to bodies are squares; circles indicate constraint nodes. For clarity, constraints are numbered beginning with 7.

edges to the graph.) Because the connectivity of the primary constraint is acyclic, the graph of $\mathbf{H}$ is also acyclic; hence, $\mathbf{H}$'s graph is a tree.[6] For example, consider the structure shown in figure 2a: the matrix $\mathbf{J}$ associated with this set of constraints has the form

$$\mathbf{J} = \begin{pmatrix} \mathbf{j}_{11} & \mathbf{j}_{12} & \mathbf{0} & \mathbf{0} & \mathbf{0} & \mathbf{0} \\ \mathbf{0} & \mathbf{j}_{22} & \mathbf{j}_{23} & \mathbf{0} & \mathbf{0} & \mathbf{0} \\ \mathbf{0} & \mathbf{j}_{32} & \mathbf{0} & \mathbf{j}_{34} & \mathbf{0} & \mathbf{0} \\ \mathbf{j}_{41} & \mathbf{0} & \mathbf{0} & \mathbf{0} & \mathbf{j}_{45} & \mathbf{0} \\ \mathbf{0} & \mathbf{0} & \mathbf{0} & \mathbf{0} & \mathbf{j}_{55} & \mathbf{j}_{56} \end{pmatrix}$$

and thus yields the matrix

$$\mathbf{H} = \begin{pmatrix} \mathbf{M}_1 & \mathbf{0} & \mathbf{0} & \mathbf{0} & \mathbf{0} & \mathbf{0} & \mathbf{j}_{11}^T & \mathbf{0} & \mathbf{0} & \mathbf{j}_{41}^T & \mathbf{0} \\ \mathbf{0} & \mathbf{M}_2 & \mathbf{0} & \mathbf{0} & \mathbf{0} & \mathbf{0} & \mathbf{j}_{12}^T & \mathbf{j}_{22}^T & \mathbf{j}_{32}^T & \mathbf{0} & \mathbf{0} \\ \mathbf{0} & \mathbf{0} & \mathbf{M}_3 & \mathbf{0} & \mathbf{0} & \mathbf{0} & \mathbf{0} & \mathbf{j}_{23}^T & \mathbf{0} & \mathbf{0} & \mathbf{0} \\ \mathbf{0} & \mathbf{0} & \mathbf{0} & \mathbf{M}_4 & \mathbf{0} & \mathbf{0} & \mathbf{0} & \mathbf{0} & \mathbf{j}_{34}^T & \mathbf{0} & \mathbf{0} \\ \mathbf{0} & \mathbf{0} & \mathbf{0} & \mathbf{0} & \mathbf{M}_5 & \mathbf{0} & \mathbf{0} & \mathbf{0} & \mathbf{0} & \mathbf{j}_{45}^T & \mathbf{j}_{55}^T \\ \mathbf{0} & \mathbf{0} & \mathbf{0} & \mathbf{0} & \mathbf{0} & \mathbf{M}_6 & \mathbf{0} & \mathbf{0} & \mathbf{0} & \mathbf{0} & \mathbf{j}_{56}^T \\ \mathbf{j}_{11} & \mathbf{j}_{12} & \mathbf{0} & \mathbf{0} & \mathbf{0} & \mathbf{0} & \mathbf{0} & \mathbf{0} & \mathbf{0} & \mathbf{0} & \mathbf{0} \\ \mathbf{0} & \mathbf{j}_{22} & \mathbf{j}_{23} & \mathbf{0} & \mathbf{0} & \mathbf{0} & \mathbf{0} & \mathbf{0} & \mathbf{0} & \mathbf{0} & \mathbf{0} \\ \mathbf{0} & \mathbf{j}_{32} & \mathbf{0} & \mathbf{j}_{34} & \mathbf{0} & \mathbf{0} & \mathbf{0} & \mathbf{0} & \mathbf{0} & \mathbf{0} & \mathbf{0} \\ \mathbf{j}_{41} & \mathbf{0} & \mathbf{0} & \mathbf{0} & \mathbf{j}_{45} & \mathbf{0} & \mathbf{0} & \mathbf{0} & \mathbf{0} & \mathbf{0} & \mathbf{0} \\ \mathbf{0} & \mathbf{0} & \mathbf{0} & \mathbf{0} & \mathbf{j}_{55} & \mathbf{j}_{56} & \mathbf{0} & \mathbf{0} & \mathbf{0} & \mathbf{0} & \mathbf{0} \end{pmatrix} \quad (9)$$

The graph defined by $\mathbf{H}$ is shown in figure 2b.

Our first thought was to solve equation (8) by computing the Cholesky decomposition $\mathbf{H} = \mathbf{L}\mathbf{L}^T$ where $\mathbf{L}$ is lower triangular. Unfortunately, this does not work because the lower-right corner of $\mathbf{H}$ is zero, making $\mathbf{H}$ indefinite. Instead, we factor $\mathbf{H}$ as $\mathbf{H} = \mathbf{L}\mathbf{D}\mathbf{L}^T$ where $\mathbf{L}$ is a lower-triangular block matrix whose diagonal entries are identity matrices, and $\mathbf{D}$ is a block-diagonal matrix. We then solve the system $\mathbf{L}\mathbf{D}\mathbf{L}^T\mathbf{x} = \left(\begin{smallmatrix}\mathbf{0}\\ -\mathbf{b}\end{smallmatrix}\right)$ and extract the portion of $\mathbf{x}$ which corresponds to $\boldsymbol{\lambda}$. Although $\mathbf{H}$ is always sparse, we must permute $\mathbf{H}$ to exploit this sparsity.

7.1 Elimination Order

A fundamental fact of sparse-matrix theory is that a matrix whose graph is acyclic possesses a *perfect elimination order* [6, chapter 7]; this means that $\mathbf{H}$ can be reordered so that when factored, the matrix factor $\mathbf{L}$ will be *just as sparse as* $\mathbf{H}$. As a result $\mathbf{L}$ can be computed in $O(n)$ time (and stored in $O(n)$ space) and then $\mathbf{L}\mathbf{D}\mathbf{L}^T\mathbf{x} = \left(\begin{smallmatrix}\mathbf{0}\\ -\mathbf{b}\end{smallmatrix}\right)$ can be solved in $O(n)$ time.

The matrix $\mathbf{H}$ is correctly ordered if it satisfies the following property. Let us view $\mathbf{H}$'s graph as a rooted tree, with node n being the root. This defines a parent/child relationship between every pair of nodes connected by an edge. The matrix $\mathbf{H}$ must be ordered so that every node's index is greater than its children's indices. When $\mathbf{H}$ is ordered so that the tree has this property, then the factor $\mathbf{L}$ will have its nonzero entries only where $\mathbf{H}$ has nonzero entries. An ordering with this property is trivially found by perfoming a depth-first search on the original $\mathbf{H}$'s graph (see appendix A). The reordered matrix $\mathbf{H}$, when factored, is said to have no "fill-in"; in other words, factoring methods such as Gaussian elimination (or the $\mathbf{L}\mathbf{D}\mathbf{L}^T$ decomposition we will use) do not introduce new nonzero elements during the factoring process.

As an example, a proper reordering of the matrix in equation (9) would be

$$\mathbf{H} = \begin{pmatrix} \mathbf{M}_3 & \mathbf{j}_{23}^T & \mathbf{0} & \mathbf{0} & \mathbf{0} & \mathbf{0} & \mathbf{0} & \mathbf{0} & \mathbf{0} & \mathbf{0} & \mathbf{0} \\ \mathbf{j}_{23} & \mathbf{0} & \mathbf{0} & \mathbf{0} & \mathbf{j}_{22} & \mathbf{0} & \mathbf{0} & \mathbf{0} & \mathbf{0} & \mathbf{0} & \mathbf{0} \\ \mathbf{0} & \mathbf{0} & \mathbf{M}_4 & \mathbf{j}_{34}^T & \mathbf{0} & \mathbf{0} & \mathbf{0} & \mathbf{0} & \mathbf{0} & \mathbf{0} & \mathbf{0} \\ \mathbf{0} & \mathbf{0} & \mathbf{j}_{34} & \mathbf{0} & \mathbf{j}_{32} & \mathbf{0} & \mathbf{0} & \mathbf{0} & \mathbf{0} & \mathbf{0} & \mathbf{0} \\ \mathbf{0} & \mathbf{j}_{22}^T & \mathbf{0} & \mathbf{j}_{32}^T & \mathbf{M}_2 & \mathbf{j}_{12}^T & \mathbf{0} & \mathbf{0} & \mathbf{0} & \mathbf{0} & \mathbf{0} \\ \mathbf{0} & \mathbf{0} & \mathbf{0} & \mathbf{0} & \mathbf{j}_{12} & \mathbf{0} & \mathbf{j}_{11} & \mathbf{0} & \mathbf{0} & \mathbf{0} & \mathbf{0} \\ \mathbf{0} & \mathbf{0} & \mathbf{0} & \mathbf{0} & \mathbf{0} & \mathbf{j}_{11}^T & \mathbf{M}_1 & \mathbf{j}_{41}^T & \mathbf{0} & \mathbf{0} & \mathbf{0} \\ \mathbf{0} & \mathbf{0} & \mathbf{0} & \mathbf{0} & \mathbf{0} & \mathbf{0} & \mathbf{j}_{41} & \mathbf{0} & \mathbf{j}_{45} & \mathbf{0} & \mathbf{0} \\ \mathbf{0} & \mathbf{0} & \mathbf{0} & \mathbf{0} & \mathbf{0} & \mathbf{0} & \mathbf{0} & \mathbf{j}_{45}^T & \mathbf{M}_5 & \mathbf{0} & \mathbf{j}_{55}^T \\ \mathbf{0} & \mathbf{0} & \mathbf{0} & \mathbf{0} & \mathbf{0} & \mathbf{0} & \mathbf{0} & \mathbf{0} & \mathbf{0} & \mathbf{M}_6 & \mathbf{j}_{56}^T \\ \mathbf{0} & \mathbf{0} & \mathbf{0} & \mathbf{0} & \mathbf{0} & \mathbf{0} & \mathbf{0} & \mathbf{0} & \mathbf{j}_{55} & \mathbf{j}_{56} & \mathbf{0} \end{pmatrix}.$$

In practice, $\mathbf{H}$ is not actually changed; rather the rows and columns are processed in a particular order. The bookkeeping associated with this is very simple and is given in appendix A.

7.2 An $O(n^3)$ Factorization Method

If we treat $\mathbf{H}$ as dense, then an $O(n^3)$ solution method is as follows. First, the upper triangular portion of $\mathbf{H}$ is overwritten with the entries of $\mathbf{L}^T$, and the diagonal of $\mathbf{H}$ is overwritten with the entries of $\mathbf{D}$. (The diagonal entries of $\mathbf{L}$ are identity matrices so there is no reason to keep track of them.) The code for this is short, and requires $O(n^3)$ time:

```
procedure densefactor
for i = 1 to n
    for k = i − 1 to 1
        H_ii = H_ii − H_ki^T H_kk H_ki
    for j = i + 1 to n
        for k = i − 1 to 1
            H_ij = H_ij − H_ki^T H_kk H_kj
        H_ij = H_ii^{-1} H_ij
```

Then, defining $\mathbf{z} = \left(\begin{smallmatrix}\mathbf{0}\\ -\mathbf{b}\end{smallmatrix}\right)$, we solve $\mathbf{L}\mathbf{x}^{(1)} = \mathbf{z}$, followed by $\mathbf{D}\mathbf{x}^{(2)} = \mathbf{x}^{(1)}$ and finally $\mathbf{L}^T\mathbf{x} = \mathbf{x}^{(2)}$, which yields a solution to $\mathbf{H}\mathbf{x} = \mathbf{z}$, with the lower portion of $\mathbf{x}$ containing $\boldsymbol{\lambda}$. This can be done (successively overwriting $\mathbf{x}$ at each step) in $O(n^2)$ time:

```
procedure densesolve
for i = 1 to n
    x_i = z_i
    for j = 1 to i − 1
        x_i = x_i − H_ij^T x_j
for i = n to 1
    x_i = H_ii^{-1} x_i
    for j = i + 1 to n
        x_i = x_i − H_ij x_j
```

7.3 An $O(n)$ Factorization Method

Now let us treat $\mathbf{H}$ as sparse. To simplify our discussion of the solution procedure below, assume we are dealing with a matrix $\mathbf{H}$ which has been reordered as described in section 7.1. To make the two previous procedures run in linear time, we need a small amount of

[6] If the primary constraints partition the bodies into discrete components, $\mathbf{H}$'s graph is a forest (i.e. a set of trees). For simplicity, assume the primary constraints do not partition the bodies into more than one component.

bookkeeping. Let us define $\text{par}(i) = j$ to denote that in $\mathbf{H}$'s graph, node j is the parent of node i. Conversely, let us define $\text{child}(j) = \{i \mid \text{par}(i) = j\}$ and note that

- if $i < j$ then $\mathbf{H}_{ij}$ is nonzero only if $\text{par}(i) = j$, which means that $i \in \text{child}(j)$ and
- if $i > j$ then $\mathbf{H}_{ij}$ is nonzero only if $\text{par}(j) = i$, which means that $j \in \text{child}(i)$.

Since every node in the graph has at most one parent, $\mathbf{H}$ has the property that in each row, only *one* nonzero block ever occurs to the *right* of the diagonal. We can store the upper triangular portion of $\mathbf{H}$ by row, with each row having only two entries (one entry for the diagonal, and one entry for the single nonzero element to the right of the diagonal). As we overwrite $\mathbf{H}$ with $\mathbf{L}^T$, this structure is preserved. The pseudocode in appendix A gives specific implementation details.

Given these relations, we can simplify the $O(n^3)$ method as follows. In lines 3 and 4 of **densefactor**, k is less than i, which means $\mathbf{H}_{ki}$ is nonzero only for $k \in \text{child}(i)$. Lines 6 and 7 can be omitted entirely, because $k < i < j$, so that the product $\mathbf{H}_{ki}^T\mathbf{H}_{kk}\mathbf{H}_{kj}$ is always zero (since k cannot be i's child *and* j's child). Finally, since $i < j$ in line 8 and $\mathbf{H}_{ij}$ is nonzero only when $j = \text{par}(i)$, the factoring step reduces to simply

```
procedure sparsefactor
for i = 1 to n
    for k ∈ child(i)
        H_ii = H_ii − H_ki^T H_kk H_ki
    if i ≠ n
        H_i,par(i) = H_ii^{-1} H_i,par(i)
```

Note that assignment to $\mathbf{H}_{ii}$ is executed once for each child node of another node, which means that **sparsefactor** takes time $O(n)$. Employing a similar strategy, we solve $\mathbf{Hx} = \begin{pmatrix} \mathbf{0} \\ -\mathbf{b} \end{pmatrix} = \mathbf{z}$ in $O(n)$ time:

```
procedure sparsesolve
for i = 1 to n
    x_i = z_i
    for j ∈ child(i)
        x_i = x_i − H_ij^T x_j
for i = n to 1
    x_i = H_ii^{-1} x_i
    if i ≠ n
        x_i = x_i − H_i,par(i) x_par(i)
```

After computing $\mathbf{x}$, we extract the appropriate elements to form the vector $\boldsymbol{\lambda}$, and then perform two (sparse!) multiplications to compute

$$\dot{\mathbf{v}} = \mathbf{M}^{-1}(\mathbf{J}^T\boldsymbol{\lambda} + \mathbf{F}^{\text{ext}}).$$

Thus, we can compute an acceleration $\dot{\mathbf{v}}$ that satisfies the primary constraints in only $O(n)$ time. A complete (yet surprisingly short) pseudocode implementation of both **sparsefactor** and **sparsesolve**, using sparse datastructures, is presented in appendix A.

8 Auxiliary Constraints

Now that we know how to quickly compute the multipliers for the primary constraints, we can turn our attention to handling the auxiliary constraints (such as loop-closure or contact) which cannot be formulated as part of the primary constraints. In this section, it is best to internalize the results of the last few sections as the statement "we can quickly determine the primary constraint force $\mathbf{J}^T\boldsymbol{\lambda}$ that would arise in response to an external force $\mathbf{F}^{\text{ext}}$."

8.1 Constraint Anticipation

Our approach to computing the multipliers for the secondary constraints is as follows. We will begin by first computing the multipliers for the *auxiliary* constraints; however, in doing so, we will anticipate the response of the primary constraints due to the auxiliary constraint forces. Once we have computed the auxiliary constraint forces, we then go back and compute the primary constraint forces; but since we have already anticipated their effects, adding the primary constraint forces into the system will not violate the conditions of the auxiliary constraints.

This "anticipation" of the primary constraints effects is as follows. Consider a force $\mathbf{F}$ acting on the system. If not for the primary constraints, the accelerational response of the system in reaction to the force $\mathbf{F}$ would be $\dot{\mathbf{v}} = \mathbf{M}^{-1}\mathbf{F}$. However, because of the primary constraints, the response is quite different. What we would like to do is compute a new mass matrix $\widehat{\mathbf{M}}$ which reflects how the system behaves as a result of the primary constraints. That is, we would like to be able to write that the response of the system due to a force $\mathbf{F}$ is, taking into account the primary constraints, $\widehat{\mathbf{M}}^{-1}\mathbf{F}$. We will not compute either the actual matrix $\widehat{\mathbf{M}}$ or its inverse $\widehat{\mathbf{M}}^{-1}$; we will use the $O(n)$ method of section 7.3 to compute vectors $\widehat{\mathbf{M}}^{-1}\mathbf{F}$ for a variety of forces $\mathbf{F}$.

In describing the k auxiliary constraints, we will regard each constraint as a separate, one-dimensional constraint. This means the matrix system we build will not have any block structure: this is appropriate, because the matrix system will be in general completely dense. For each constraint, we will produce a scalar expression a_i which is a measure of acceleration; each a_i will have an associated scalar multiplier μ_i. The relation between the vector of a's and the vector of μ's is, as always, a linear relation. Our goal here is to show how we can efficiently compute the $k \times k$ coefficient matrix that relates the a_is to the μ_is in $O(kn) + O(k^2)$ time, where n is the number of primary constraints to be maintained by the system.[7] Once we have computed this coefficient matrix, we can use known techniques to compute the μ_i multipliers. For an equality constraint, a_i is forced to be zero, and μ_i can have any sign. If all the constraints are equality constraints, we can solve for the μ_i using standard matrix techniques in time $O(k^3)$. Going beyond this, simple workless inequality constraints, such as contact or joint-angle limits require that $a_i \geq 0$ and $a_i\mu_i = 0$. Methods for handling a mix of equality, inequality and frictional conditions are described by Baraff [2] and have time complexity $O(k^3)$ for a system of k constraints. As long as k is small compared to n, it is the computation of the $k \times k$ matrix of coefficients which dominates the running time, and not the computation of the μ_i multipliers. Thus, our focus here is on computing the coefficient matrix as opposed to the multipliers themselves.

The auxiliary constraints are described in a form similar to that of equation (2). Let the vector $\mathbf{a}$ of the k auxiliary a_i variables be expressed in the form

$$\mathbf{a} = \begin{pmatrix} a_i \\ \vdots \\ a_k \end{pmatrix} = \mathbf{J}^a\dot{\mathbf{v}} + \mathbf{c}^a \qquad (10)$$

where $\mathbf{J}^a$ has k rows and $\mathbf{c}^a \in \mathbb{R}^k$. Since the auxiliary constraint forces do not have to be workless, let the constraint force acting on the system due to the ith constraint have the form

$$\mathbf{k}_i\mu_i$$

[7] If each auxiliary constraint acts on only one or two bodies, the time required to formulate the system is $O(kn) + O(k^2)$. If auxiliary constraints constrain n bodies at a time, (which is rare), the time becomes $O(kn) + O(nk^2)$ In either case, it is the $O(kn)$ term which dominates; the constant in front of the $O(k^2)$ term or $O(nk^2)$ term is small.

where $\mathbf{k}_i$ is a column vector of the same dimension as $\mathbf{v}$ (that is, $\mathbf{k}$'s dimension is the sum of all the bodies' dimensions). Defining $\mathbf{K}$ as the k-column matrix

$$\mathbf{K} = [\mathbf{k}_1 \quad \mathbf{k}_2 \quad \dots \quad \mathbf{k}_k] \tag{11}$$

the constraint force due to all k constraints has the form

$$\mathbf{k}_1\mu_i + \dots + \mathbf{k}_k\mu_k = \mathbf{K}\boldsymbol{\mu}.$$

The process of computing both the primary and auxiliary multipliers is as follows. First, we compute what $\dot{\mathbf{v}}$ would be *without* the auxiliary constraints. That is, given an external force $\mathbf{F}^{\text{ext}}$, we solve equation (7) for $\boldsymbol{\lambda}$ (using **sparsefactor** and **sparsesolve**). We then define

$$\widehat{\mathbf{F}}^{\text{ext}} = \mathbf{J}^T\boldsymbol{\lambda} + \mathbf{F}^{\text{ext}}.$$

The force $\widehat{\mathbf{F}}^{\text{ext}}$ is the external force *as seen by the auxiliary constraints.* (Remember, the auxiliary constraints are formulated so as to anticipate the response of the primary constraints. The first step in this anticipation is to know what the primary constraint force would have been in the absence of any auxiliary constraint forces.) Having computed $\widehat{\mathbf{F}}^{\text{ext}}$, we know that the system's acceleration without the auxiliary constraints is $\mathbf{M}^{-1}\widehat{\mathbf{F}}^{\text{ext}}$. Let us write

$$\dot{\mathbf{v}}^{\text{aux}} = \mathbf{M}^{-1}\widehat{\mathbf{F}}^{\text{ext}}$$

to express this. The auxiliary constraint forces must now "kick in" to the extent that the acceleration $\dot{\mathbf{v}}^{\text{aux}}$ violates the auxiliary constraints.

Using the anticipated response matrix $\widehat{\mathbf{M}}^{-1}$, the acceleration $\dot{\mathbf{v}}$ of the system in response to an auxiliary constraint force $\mathbf{K}\boldsymbol{\mu}$ is the system's acceleration without the auxiliary constraint force, $\dot{\mathbf{v}}^{\text{aux}}$, plus the response to $\mathbf{K}\boldsymbol{\mu}$:

$$\dot{\mathbf{v}} = \widehat{\mathbf{M}}^{-1}\mathbf{K}\boldsymbol{\mu} + \dot{\mathbf{v}}^{\text{aux}}.$$

If we actually had access to the matrix $\widehat{\mathbf{M}}^{-1}$, we could stop at this point: from equation (10), we obtain

$$\mathbf{a} = \mathbf{J}^a\dot{\mathbf{v}} + \mathbf{c}^a = \mathbf{J}^a\widehat{\mathbf{M}}^{-1}\mathbf{K}\boldsymbol{\mu} + (\mathbf{J}^a\dot{\mathbf{v}}^{\text{aux}} + \mathbf{c}^a) \tag{12}$$

which gives the desired relation between $\mathbf{a}$ and $\boldsymbol{\mu}$. (At this point, we can easily evaluate $\mathbf{J}^a\dot{\mathbf{v}}^{\text{aux}} + \mathbf{c}^a$, since we have actually computed $\dot{\mathbf{v}}^{\text{aux}}$.) The real trick then is to compute the coefficient matrix $\widehat{\mathbf{M}}^{-1}\mathbf{K}$.

Remember that equation (11) defines $\mathbf{K}$ in terms of columns $\mathbf{k}_i$, and that $\mathbf{k}_i$ is the direction that the ith auxiliary constraint force acts in. We cannot (nor do we wish to) formulate $\widehat{\mathbf{M}}^{-1}$ directly; instead, we wish to compute $\widehat{\mathbf{M}}^{-1}\mathbf{K}$ column by column. Since $\widehat{\mathbf{M}}^{-1}$ encapsulates the response of the system to a force, given a vector $\mathbf{k}_i$, we compute $\widehat{\mathbf{M}}^{-1}\mathbf{k}_i$ as follows. The primary constraints, in reaction to a force $\mathbf{k}_i$, generate a response force $\mathbf{F}^{\text{resp}} = \mathbf{J}^T\boldsymbol{\lambda}$ where $\mathbf{A}\boldsymbol{\lambda} = \mathbf{J}\mathbf{M}^{-1}\mathbf{k}_i$. As a result, the system's response to a force $\mathbf{k}_i$, is not $\mathbf{M}^{-1}\mathbf{k}_i$, but rather

$$\mathbf{M}^{-1}(\mathbf{F}^{\text{resp}} + \mathbf{k}_i).$$

This gives us a computational definition of $\widehat{\mathbf{M}}^{-1}$: we can now write that the system's response to the force $\mathbf{k}_i$ is

$$\widehat{\mathbf{M}}^{-1}\mathbf{k}_i = \mathbf{M}^{-1}(\mathbf{F}^{\text{resp}} + \mathbf{k}_i)$$

where $\mathbf{F}^{\text{resp}} = \mathbf{J}^T\boldsymbol{\lambda}$ and $\boldsymbol{\lambda}$ is computed by solving $\mathbf{A}\boldsymbol{\lambda} = \mathbf{J}\mathbf{M}^{-1}\mathbf{k}_i$. The cost to compute $\widehat{\mathbf{M}}^{-1}\mathbf{k}_i$ is thus $O(n)$. Given equation (11), we can express $\widehat{\mathbf{M}}^{-1}\mathbf{K}$ column-wise as

$$\widehat{\mathbf{M}}^{-1}\mathbf{K} = [\widehat{\mathbf{M}}^{-1}\mathbf{k}_1 \quad \widehat{\mathbf{M}}^{-1}\mathbf{k}_2 \quad \dots \quad \widehat{\mathbf{M}}^{-1}\mathbf{k}_k]$$

where each column $\widehat{\mathbf{M}}^{-1}\mathbf{k}_i$ is computed according to the above procedure. The cost to do this $O(nk)$, since we have k columns, and each column requires $O(n)$ work. Having computed $\widehat{\mathbf{M}}^{-1}\mathbf{K}$, we can easily compute the coefficient matrix $\mathbf{J}^a\widehat{\mathbf{M}}^{-1}\mathbf{K}$ of equation (12). If $\mathbf{J}^a$ is sparse, the $k \times k$ matrix $\mathbf{J}^a\widehat{\mathbf{M}}^{-1}\mathbf{K}$ is computed in $O(k^2)$ time while a dense matrix $\mathbf{J}^a$ takes $O(nk^2)$ time.

8.2 Computing the Net Constraint Force

It is extremely important to note that although we must compute a total of $k+2$ different $\boldsymbol{\lambda}$'s during the solution process (see below), each $\boldsymbol{\lambda}$ is actually computed by solving a system of the form $\mathbf{H}\mathbf{x} = \binom{0}{-\mathbf{b}}$ and then extracting $\boldsymbol{\lambda}$ from $\mathbf{x}$. The significance of this is that what is changing each time is *not* the matrix $\mathbf{H}$, but $\mathbf{b}$. This means that we call the procedure **sparsefactor** of section 7.3 only once during the entire constraint force computation described below; for each different vector $\mathbf{b}$, we only need to perform the second step **sparsesolve**. Although both steps take $O(n)$ time, **sparsefactor** is approximately four times as expensive as **sparsesolve**. Thus, refactoring each time would still yield an $O(n)$ algorithm, but would needlessly repeat computation.

At this point, the entire sequence of steps required may sound complicated, but again, the implementation is straightforward. In the description below, whenever we solve an equation $\mathbf{A}\boldsymbol{\lambda} = \mathbf{b}$ we do so in terms of the associated equation $\mathbf{H}\mathbf{x} = \binom{0}{-\mathbf{b}}$ of the previous section. The steps for the entire solution process are as follows.

1. Formulate the sparse matrix $\mathbf{H}$ for the primary constraints, and run **sparsefactor** to factor $\mathbf{H}$.

2. Given the external force $\mathbf{F}^{\text{ext}}$, compute the primary constraint force $\mathbf{J}^T\boldsymbol{\lambda}$ due to $\mathbf{F}^{\text{ext}}$ by solving $\mathbf{A}\boldsymbol{\lambda} = -(\mathbf{J}\mathbf{M}^{-1}\mathbf{F}^{\text{ext}} + \mathbf{c})$. This requires one call to **sparsesolve**. Once $\boldsymbol{\lambda}$ has been computed, set $\dot{\mathbf{v}}^{\text{aux}} = \mathbf{M}^{-1}(\mathbf{J}^T\boldsymbol{\lambda} + \mathbf{F}^{\text{ext}})$.

3. For j from 1 to k, compute the response force $\mathbf{F}^{\text{resp}} = \mathbf{J}^T\boldsymbol{\lambda}$ by solving $\mathbf{A}\boldsymbol{\lambda} = -\mathbf{J}\mathbf{M}^{-1}\mathbf{k}_j$. This requires k calls to **sparsesolve**. Forming the product $\mathbf{M}^{-1}(\mathbf{F}^{\text{resp}} + \mathbf{k}_j)$ yields the jth column of $\widehat{\mathbf{M}}^{-1}\mathbf{K}$. Multiplying the ith row of $\mathbf{J}^a$ with this jth column yields the ijth entry in the coefficient matrix $\mathbf{J}^a\widehat{\mathbf{M}}^{-1}\mathbf{K}$. Computing these k^2 different products takes either $O(k^2)$ or $O(nk^2)$ time, depending on the sparsity of $\mathbf{J}^a$.

4. Now that the coefficients of equation (12) have been determined, compute the multipliers $\boldsymbol{\mu}$, employing either a standard linear solution method (for example, Gaussian elimination) or the method for contact constraints and friction described by Baraff [2]. This takes approximately $O(k^3)$ time.

5. Given the auxiliary constraint force $\mathbf{K}\boldsymbol{\mu}$, compute the primary constraint's response to the force $\mathbf{F}^{\text{ext}} + \mathbf{K}\boldsymbol{\mu}$; that is, solve $\mathbf{A}\boldsymbol{\lambda} = -\mathbf{J}\mathbf{M}^{-1}(\mathbf{K}\boldsymbol{\mu} + \mathbf{F}^{\text{ext}} + \mathbf{c})$. The final constraint force due to both the primary and auxiliary constraints is $\mathbf{K}\boldsymbol{\mu} + \mathbf{J}^T\boldsymbol{\lambda}$; adding to this the external force $\mathbf{F}^{\text{ext}}$ yields the net force acting on the system.

6. Compute the net acceleration of the system and move on to the next timestep.

9 Results

We have implemented the described system, and used it for a number of simulations. Simulations were run on an SGI Indigo[2] workstation, with a 250 Mhz R4400 processor. The 108 multipliers for a system of 2D rigid bodies with 54 two-dimensional primary constraints required 7.75 milliseconds to compute. Approximately 2.75 milliseconds of that time was spent computing the entries of **J**. When the connectivity was changed so that there were 96 primary multipliers and 12 auxiliary multipliers, the computation time increased by about 17 milliseconds. Virtually all of this increase was due to the $O(nk)$ computation of the auxiliary constraint coefficient matrix $\widehat{\mathbf{M}}^{-1}\mathbf{K}$. The $O(k^3)$ time spent actually computing the 12 auxiliary constraint multipliers was too small to notice.

A 3D rigid body system with 96 primary multipliers and 3 auxiliary multipliers due to 3 frictionless contacts required 18 milliseconds. Approximately 4.4 milliseconds of that time was spent computing the entries of **J**. A larger 3D system with 127 constraints resulting in 381 primary multipliers (figure 3) required 44.6 milliseconds, with approximately 4 milliseconds spent evaluating **J**. It is worth pointing out that on the first problem, with 99 multipliers, the $O(n)$ method yields only a factor of two speedup over Baraff [2]'s $O(n^3)$ method for equality and inequality constraints. However, for the larger problem, the speedup is close to a factor of forty.

Schröder [13] discusses an implementation of a linear-time reduced-coordinate scheme due to Lathrop [11], and reports some running times. Adjusting for machine speeds, our results appear to be competitive with the figures reported by Schröder (but we had to guess about a number of parameters, so it is hard to say for sure). We do note that Schröder discusses a number of numerical difficulties with the algorithm; in fact, the use of a singular-value decomposition is required, which is always a sign of ill-conditioning. We were pleasantly surprised to find that the sparse methods described in this paper required *no* numerical adjustments, even on large examples—glancing at the pseudocode in appendix A, there are no numerical tolerance values to be found.[8]

We were able to run Gleicher's "Bramble" system on our 2D example. Bramble uses a Lagrange multiplier formulation, and exploits sparsity to compute multipliers by using a conjugate gradient method [8]. Comparing relative performance is still difficult, since the performance of any iterative method can vary greatly based on the desired accuracy of the answer; on the other hand, the ability to compute results to a lower (but acceptable) precision is one of the great strengths of iterative methods. For the 2D problem with 108 primary multipliers and no auxiliary multipliers, our method was about three times faster than Bramble at computing the multipliers; however, when we induced loops, changing 12 of the primary multipliers to auxiliary multipliers, both simulation systems ran at approximately the same same speed. Thus, for problems of this size, an $O(n^2)$ conjugate gradient method is competitive with the presented method. As problems grow larger (for example, the 3D example with 381 multipliers) our $O(n)$ method enjoys a significant advantage. On today's machines, examples fast enough to run at interactive speeds enjoy modest speed gains using our linear-time algorithm; however, as machine speeds increase, allowing larger interactive-rate simulations, the difference between $O(n)$, (n^2), and $O(n^3)$ methods will only become more pronounced.

[8]The algorithm as described requires the inversion of small matrices (for rigid bodies, these matrices are of size 6×6 or smaller). Since the matrices are always either positive or negative definite, a Cholesky decomposition can be used to simply and stably perform the inversion. The Cholesky decomposition has no numerical tolerance values in it either.

10 Acknowledgments

This research was supported in part by an ONR Young Investigator award, an NSF CAREER award, and NSF grants MIP-9420396, IRI-9420869 and CCR-9308353. Many thanks to Nathan Loofbourrow for pointing out numerous errors in the program listings.

I would also like to thank Dan Rosenthal of Symbolic Dynamics, Inc. for pointing out that if the auxiliary constraints are workless, one third of the back-solves in **sparsesolve** are unnecessary. (The results given in this paper are for an implementation where it is assumed auxiliary constraints are not necessarily workless.) The key point of his observation is that for workless auxiliary constraints, $\mathbf{K}^T = \mathbf{J}^a$. As a result, the matrix computed in step 3 of section 8.2 can be expressed as $\mathbf{K}^T\mathbf{M}^{-1}\mathbf{J}^T\mathbf{A}^{-1}\mathbf{J}\mathbf{M}^{-1}\mathbf{K} + \mathbf{K}^T\mathbf{M}^{-1}\mathbf{K}$. Note that the first matrix of this sum has the form $\mathbf{Z}^T\mathbf{A}^{-1}\mathbf{Z}$ with $\mathbf{Z} = \mathbf{J}\mathbf{M}^{-1}\mathbf{K}$. Because of this symmetry and the $\mathbf{LDL}^T$ factorization employed in this paper, computing the matrix as described in step 3 results in repeating each computation $\mathbf{Lx} = \mathbf{y}$ (where $\mathbf{x}$ is the unknown being solved for) twice. By slightly restructuring the algorithm, the repeated computation can be avoided.

References

[1] D. Baraff. Issues in computing contact forces for non-penetrating rigid bodies. *Algorithmica*, 10:292–352, 1993.

[2] D. Baraff. Fast contact force computation for nonpenetrating rigid bodies. *Computer Graphics (Proc. SIGGRAPH)*, 28:23–34, 1994

[3] R. Barzel and A.H. Barr. A modeling system based on dynamic constraints. In *Computer Graphics (Proc. SIGGRAPH)*, volume 22, pages 179–188. ACM, July 1988.

[4] J. Baumgarte. Stabilization of constraints and integrals of motion in dynamical systems. *Computer Methods in Applied Mechanics*, pages 1–36, 1972.

[5] K.E. Brenan, S.L. Campbell, and L.R. Petzold. *Numerical Solution of Initial-value Problems in Differential-algebraic Equations*. North-Holland, 1989.

[6] I.S. Duff, A.M. Erisman, and J.K. Reid. *Direct Methods for Sparse Matrices*. Clarendon Press, 1986.

[7] R. Featherstone. *Robot Dynamics Algorithms*. Kluwer, 1987.

[8] M. Gleicher. *A Differential Approach to Graphical Manipulation*. PhD thesis, Carnegie Mellon University, 1994.

[9] G. Golub and C. Van Loan. *Matrix Computations*. John Hopkins University Press, 1983

[10] C. Lanczos. *The Variational Principles of Mechanics*. Dover Publications, Inc., 1970.

[11] R.H. Lathrop. Constrained (closed-loop) robot simulation by local constraint propagation. In *International Conference on Robotics and Automation*, pages 689–694. IEEE, 1986.

[12] D. Negrut, R. Serban, and F.A. Potra. A topology based approach for exploiting the sparsity of multibody dynamics. Technical Report 84, Department of Mathematics, University of Iowa, December 1995.

[13] P. Schröder and D. Zeltzer. The virtual erector set: Dynamic simulation with linear recursive constraint propagation. In *Proceedings 1990 Symposium on Interactive 3d Graphics*, volume 24, pages 23–31, March 1990.

[14] A. Shabana. *Dynamics of Multibody Systems.* Wiley, 1989.

[15] M.C. Surles. An algorithm with linear complexity for interactive, physically-based modeling of large proteins. *Computer Graphics (Proc. SIGGRAPH)*, 26:221–230, 1992.

[16] A.F. Vereshchagin. Computer simulation of the dynamics of complicated mechansisms of robot manipulators. *Engineering Cybernetics*, 6:65–70, 1974.

[17] A. Witkin, M. Gleicher, and W. Welch. Interactive dynamics. In *Proceedings 1990 Symposium on Interactive 3d Graphics*, volume 24, pages 11–21, March 1990.

A Pseudocode

This appendix gives a complete implementation of the bookkeeping and datastructures needed to perform the computations described by procedures **sparsefactor** and **sparsesolve** in section 7.3. As you can see, the code is extremely short, and thus easily implementable. Each body and constraint is represented by a node structure; a node also stores a row of the upper triangular portion of **H**. Recall that rows of the upper triangular portion of the (properly ordered) matrix **H** only have two nonzero elements: the diagonal element itself (denoted D below), and one off-diagonal element (denoted J below). Each node also stores space for a portion of the solution vector **x**.

```
struct node {
    boolean    isconstraint;
    int        i;
    matrix     D, Dinv, J;
    vector     x;
}
```

A node corresponding to a body has isconstraint set false, and the index field i set to the index of the body the node represents. Both D and Dinv are square matrices of size dim(i). If a node corresponds to a constraint, then D and Dinv are square with size equal to the dimension of the constraint, and isconstraint is set true. The variable i is the index of the constraint; constraints are numbered starting from 1, because λ_1 is the multiplier for the first constraint. We assume that for a node n, the function **parent**(n) yields n's parent, or **NULL** if n is the root. Similarly, **children**(n) yields the set of nodes that are children of n, or the empty set if n is a leaf. (Obviously, this can be done in terms of extra pointers stored within a **node** structure.)

The global variables Forward and Backward are lists of nodes, with Forward ordered so that parent nodes occur later in the list than their children, and Backward being the reverse of Forward. Thus, the notation "**for** n ∈ Forward" indicates processing nodes from the leaves up, while "**for** n ∈ Backward" indicates processing nodes from the root down. The following routine, called once with the root of the tree, initializes the two lists (assuming that Forward and Backward are initially empty):

```
procedure ordermatrix(n)
for c ∈ children(n)
    ordermatrix(c)
Forward = [Forward  n]
Backward = [n  Backward]
```

Assuming that we have procedures which compute the blocks $\mathbf{M}_i$ and $\mathbf{j}_{pq}$ (with $\mathbf{j}_{pq}$ defined as in section 4), we store and factor **H** as follows:

```
procedure factor
for n ∈ Forward
    if n.isconstraint
        n.D = 0
    else
        n.D = M_n.i
    if parent(n) ≠ NULL
        int p = n.i, q = parent(n).i
        n.J = n.isconstraint ? J_pq : J^T_pq
for n ∈ Forward
    for c ∈ children(n)
        n.D −= (c.J^T)(c.D)(c.J)
    n.Dinv = n.D^-1
    if parent(n) ≠ NULL
        n.J = (n.Dinv)(n.J)
```

As previously mentioned, after we have called **factor**, we can solve the system $\mathbf{Hx} = \binom{0}{-\mathbf{b}}$ (extracting $\boldsymbol{\lambda}$ from **x**) as many times as we wish. The solution process computes $\boldsymbol{\lambda}$ as follows:

```
procedure solve(b)
for n ∈ Forward
    n.soln = n.isconstraint ? b_n.i : 0
    for c ∈ children(n)
        n.soln −= c.J^T c.soln
for n ∈ Backward
    n.soln = (n.Dinv)(n.soln)
    if parent(n) ≠ NULL
        n.soln −= (n.J)(parent(n).soln)
    if n.isconstraint
        λ_n.i = n.soln
```

Figure 3: A structure with 127 constraints. Each sphere represents a 3 d.o.f. constraint between two rigid bodies, for a total of 381 primary multipliers.

Efficient Generation of Motion Transitions using Spacetime Constraints

Charles Rose
Princeton University
(currently at Microsoft Research)

Brian Guenter
Microsoft Research

Bobby Bodenheimer
Microsoft Research

Michael F. Cohen
Microsoft Research

Abstract

This paper describes the application of space time constraints to creating transitions between segments of human body motion. The motion transition generation uses a combination of spacetime constraints and inverse kinematic constraints to generate seamless and dynamically plausible transitions between motion segments. We use a fast recursive dynamics formulation which makes it possible to use spacetime constraints on systems with many degrees of freedom, such as human figures. The system uses an interpreter of a motion expression language to allow the user to manipulate motion data, break it into pieces, and reassemble it into new, more complex, motions. We have successfully used the system to create basis motions, cyclic data, and seamless motion transitions on a human body model with 44 degrees of freedom.

Additional Keywords and Phrases: computer animation, inverse kinematics, motion capture, motion control, human figure animation, cyclification.

CR Categories and Subject Descriptions: I.3.7 [Computer Graphics]: Three Dimensional Graphics and Realism: Animation; I.6.3 [Simulation and Modeling]: Applications; G.1.6 [Constrained Optimization]; I.3.5 [Physically-Based Modeling].

1 Introduction

Existing 3D animation tools primarily provide support for creating a single linear stream of animation where the entire motion is planned in advance and computed off-line. Interactive 3D character animation, however, is characterized by a degree of uncertainty that is not present in animation for film or television. Characters are under the control of the user and must be able to change the way they move at any time. Crafting animation for an interactive application presents a new set of problems and requires a different set of specialized tools.

One solution for these problems is to generate a set of high quality motions, called basis motions in the remainder of the paper, and then create transitions between these motions so they can be strung together into animations of unlimited length and great variety. Basis motions are typically short and can be combined into motions representative of the type of actions that the body has to perform. For example, basis motions might be walk cycles, arm waves, karate kicks, and so forth. Basis motions need not specify all the degrees of freedom in the body; they can specify just those of one limb or even a part of a limb. Using motion capture techniques, it is relatively easy to make high quality basis motions, but generating high-quality transitions among those basis motions is still difficult and involves significant manual labor. The techniques presented work well with motion capture data, but would work equally well with hand-animated basis motions.

We have developed an algorithm for generating these transitions semi-automatically, greatly reducing the time spent and the number of parameters an animator must specify. The system provides two semi-automatic mechanisms for generating motion: motion transition generation and cyclification. Motion transition generation uses a combination of spacetime constraints [10] and inverse kinematic constraints [12] to generate transitions between basis motions. A fast dynamics formulation makes it practical to use spacetime transition generation on high degree of freedom systems. With this dynamics formulation, the algorithm achieves the lower bound time complexity for spacetime algorithms that use gradient based optimization techniques.

The motion transitions satisfy both dynamic and kinematic constraints. This differs from the work described in [2, 11, 9]. These papers described various mechanisms, such as dynamic time warping, Fourier interpolation, and multi-resolution signal processing, for transforming existing motion data. Transitions between motion clips were achieved using linear combinations of the two motions being transitioned. This can result in motion which does not have realistic dynamic qualities and which may not necessarily satisfy kinematic or anthropomorphic constraints. The transition mechanism described here generates motion which minimizes the torque required to transition from one motion to another while maintaining joint angle constraints. Inverse kinematics are used to ensure that kinematic constraints are satisfied.

Additionally, we have defined a motion expression language to allow the user to manipulate motion data, break it into pieces, and reassemble it into new, more complex motions. We have successfully used the system to create basis motions, cyclic data, and motion transitions on our human body model which has 44 degrees of freedom.

Section 2 of the paper describes the human body model and how motion capture data is processed before it gets into the system. Section 3 describes the semi-automatic spacetime and inverse kinematic transition mechanism. This section also explains the fast dynamic formulation which allows spacetime constraint optimization to run quickly on systems with many degrees of freedom. Section 3 also describes our method of motion cyclification. Section 4 explains how body motion is internally represented and describes the motion expression language. Section 5 presents results of transitions generated with the system. Section 6 concludes the paper. Appendix A contains an explanation of the notation used in the dynamics formulation, the dynamics equations, and their partial derivatives as they are used in the spacetime optimization.

Email: {t-chuckr, briangu, bobbyb, mcohen}@microsoft.com

2 Human Body Model

Before motion data can be edited by the system it usually needs to be preprocessed to remove degrees of freedom which are not actually present in humans. Most motion capture data, for example, has three rotational degrees of freedom at each joint. A handful of human joints actually have three degrees of freedom but most have one or two. Anatomically extraneous degrees of freedom cause trouble when generating motion transitions since the synthetic body may move in ways that are impossible for a real human. We use an optimization procedure [12] which minimizes the angular and positional deviation between our internal model of a human and the motion capture data. Limb lengths are automatically extracted from the motion data and used to scale the internal model appropriately. Our human body model has 38 joint degrees of freedom and six degrees of freedom at the root, located between the hips, for positioning and orienting the entire body. As with most other animation work on human body models we assume that human joints can be accurately modeled as revolute joints. While this is not precisely the case, especially for the knee and the shoulder, for most joints the errors introduced by making this assumption are typically small.

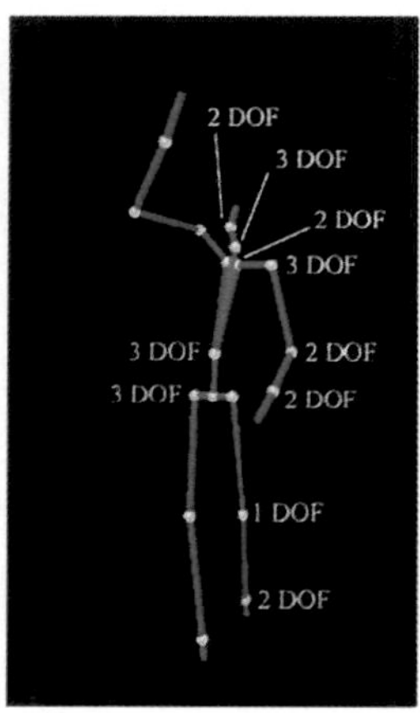

Figure 1: Human body model illustrating degrees of freedom.

3 Semi-Automatic Motion Generation

Two primary semi-automatic motion generation capabilities are provided. The first is motion transition generation and the second is motion cyclification. Motion transition generation creates new motion to span undefined regions between two basis motions. Motion cyclification transforms a motion which may not be perfectly cyclic into one which is.

3.1 Function Representation

Representations used in the past for the joint angle function,

$$\mathbf{q}(t) = (q_1(t), \ldots, q_n(t))$$

where $q_i(t)$ is the angle of joint i at time t, include piecewise constant [10], B-splines [4], and B-spline wavelets [8]. B-spline wavelets show good convergence properties for spacetime optimization when the number of basis functions in a single degree of freedom is large, e.g., more than 20 or 30. Since the transitions we are generating are generally short, on the order of 1 second or less, good paths can be represented with 5 to 10 B-spline coefficients. Our experience has been that very few iterations are required to achieve convergence with a B-spline basis, so the extra complexity and computation of the B-spline wavelet basis was not justified. For these reasons we use cubic B-splines as the basis functions for $\mathbf{q}(t)$.

3.2 Motion Transitions

Motion transitions are generated using a combination of kinematics and dynamics. The motion of the root of the body is determined kinematically while the motion of all the limbs which are not supporting the body is determined using spacetime constraints. Limbs which support the body during the transition are controlled using an optimization procedure to solve the inverse kinematics problem over the entire transition time interval instead of just at one point in time. A support limb is defined as the kinematic chain from the support point (e.g., a foot on the floor) back up the kinematic tree to the root.

3.2.1 Root Motion

The x-z plane is defined to be coincident with the floor with the y axis pointing upward. The x and z components of the root position are interpolated based on either the velocities or accelerations available at the beginning and end of the transition. The y component of the root translation is linearly interpolated from the end of the first motion (at time t_1) to the beginning of the second motion (at time t_2). The root position in the x-z plane, $\mathbf{p}(t)$, during the transition time is

$$\mathbf{p}(t) = \mathbf{p}(t_1) + \int_{t_1}^{t} \left\{ \mathbf{v}_1 \left(1 - \frac{\alpha - t_1}{t_2 - t_1}\right) + \mathbf{v}_2 \frac{\alpha - t_1}{t_2 - t_1} \right\} d\alpha$$

where $\mathbf{v}_1$ and $\mathbf{v}_2$ are the vector velocities in the x-z plane of the root at time t_1 and t_2. This expression can be easily evaluated analytically and provides a C^1 path for the root. A C^2 path is more desirable and could be achieved by double integration of the accelerations of the root. However due to limitations in the motion capture process estimates of the acceleration are poor especially at the beginning and end of a motion capture data stream.

3.2.2 Inverse Kinematics

Support limbs are controlled kinematically. The system attempts to locate support points automatically by finding coordinate frames with motion that remains within a small bounding box over an extended period of time. The animator has the option of overriding the system's guess, manually specifying a joint coordinate frame as being a support frame. During the transition this coordinate frame will be held fixed using inverse kinematics constraints. Enforcing kinematic constraints is done using an extension of the techniques presented in [12], optimizing for coefficients influencing a range of time. The inverse kinematics constraint is enforced by minimizing the deviation

$$r_k(t) = \|\mathbf{p}_k(t) - \hat{\mathbf{p}}_k(t)\|_2$$

of the constrained joint coordinate frame k from its desired position, where $\mathbf{p}_k$ is the actual position of the constrained coordinate frame and $\hat{\mathbf{p}}_k$ is the desired position. The total error, R, is given by the sum over all K constrained frames and integrated across the constrained time interval

$$R = \int_{t_1}^{t_2} \sum_{k=1}^{K} r_k(t)\, dt$$

Since a finite and usually small number of B-spline coefficients are used to represent the motion curves, minimizing this objective does not result in rapid oscillations. These can occur when inverse kinematic constraints are maintained independently at each frame time.

R is a function of the joint angles in the body

$$R = f(q_1(t), \ldots, q_n(t))$$

which are themselves functions of the B-spline control points defining each joint angle function

$$q_i(t) = g(b_{i,1}, \ldots, b_{i,m})$$

where the $b_{i,j}$ are the control points of the B-spline curve for joint angle function $q_i(t)$. We minimize R using the BFGS optimization algorithm described in more detail in Section 3.2.3. For the purposes of the present discussion the only relevant part of the BFGS algorithm is that it requires the gradient of R at each iteration in the optimization

$$\nabla R = \left[\frac{\partial R}{\partial b_{i,1}}, \ldots, \frac{\partial R}{\partial b_{n,m}} \right]$$

$$\frac{\partial R}{\partial b_{i,j}} = \int_{t_1}^{t_2} \sum_{k=1}^{K} \frac{\partial r_k}{\partial b_{i,j}} dt$$

$$\frac{\partial r_k}{\partial b_{i,j}} = 2\left(\mathrm{p}_k(t) - \hat{\mathrm{p}}_k(t)\right)(\mathrm{u}_i \times \mathrm{d}_{ki}) \frac{\partial q_i}{\partial b_{i,j}}$$

where u_i is the axis of rotation of joint i and d_{ki} is the vector from joint i to the constrained frame k. Figure 2 shows the effect using the inverse kinematic constraint to fix the feet of the body on the ground during a motion transition period. The left leg is constrained to be on the ground during the entire transition interval while the right leg is constrained to be on the ground only at the end of the interval. In the image on the left the inverse kinematic constraints were turned off; the left leg drifts from its desired position and the right leg fails to meet its desired position. In the image on the right the inverse kinematic constraints are satisfied. The left leg remains fixed during the transition period and the right leg touches down at the end of the interval.

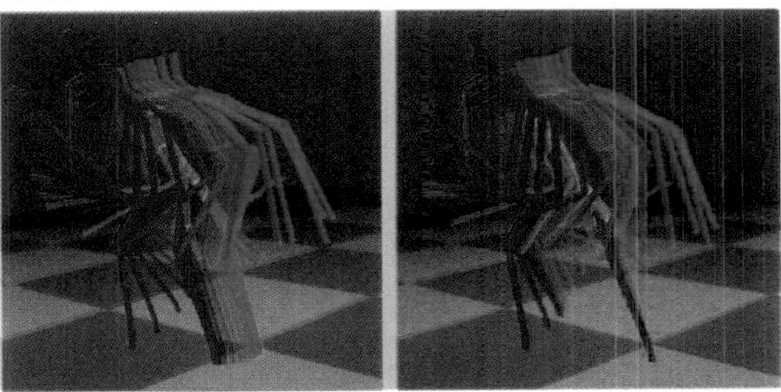

Figure 2: Effect of inverse kinematics constraint on placement of feet.

3.2.3 Spacetime Dynamics Formulation

The energy required for a human to move along a path is actually a complex non-linear function of the body motion since energy can be stored in muscle and tendon in one part of the motion and released later on. As shown in [3], joint torques are a reasonable predictor of metabolic energy, so minimizing torque over time should be a reasonable approximation to minimizing metabolic energy. Experience has shown that motion that minimizes energy looks natural. This leads to the minimization problem:

$$\text{minimize } e = \int_{t_1}^{t_2} \sum_i \tau_i^2(t)\, dt.$$

We use the BFGS optimization algorithm [5] to find a minimum of this integral equation. BFGS belongs to the class of quasi-Newton algorithms which progress toward a solution by using the gradient of the objective function

$$\mathrm{g} = \nabla e.$$

The gradient is used to incrementally update a matrix decomposition of a pseudo-Hessian matrix, H, and to compute a new step direction

$$\mathrm{d} = -\mathrm{H}^{-1}\mathrm{g}.$$

The relative amount of computation for each subtask required at every iteration of the algorithm is common to several quasi-Newton algorithms: gradient computation, pseudo-Hessian update, and computation of the step direction.

Since each of the τ_i is potentially a function of all the $q_i, \dot{q}_i, \ddot{q}_i$ the gradient requires the evaluation of $O(n^2)$ partial derivatives where n is the number of degrees of freedom of the body. This is in fact a lower bound for the asymptotic time complexity of space time algorithms which use gradient-based optimization techniques.

If m is the number of B-spline coefficients used to define the time function of each degree of freedom then the pseudo-Hessian is of size nm by nm. The update of the pseudo-Hessian and computation of the step direction are both $O((nm)^2)$. For m small, less than 20, and n large, more than 30, the time required to compute g dominates all other computation thus an efficient formulation for g will pay the greatest dividends in reducing computation.

Computing g requires finding the joint torques and a variety of subsidiary quantities, such as angular velocity and acceleration. This is the inverse dynamics problem which has been extensively studied in the robotics literature. See [1] for a good overview of many of these algorithms. Many inverse dynamics formulations have been proposed in the robotics literature ranging from $O(n^4)$ non-recursive to $O(n)$ recursive algorithms. The inverse dynamics formulation we use is due to Balafoutis [1]. This is an $O(n)$ recursive formulation which requires $96n - 77$ multiplications and $84n - 77$ additions to solve the inverse dynamics problem for a robot manipulator with n joints. This is faster than the $O(n)$ Lagrangian recursive formulation developed by Hollerbach [6] and used in [7], which requires $412n - 277$ multiplications and $320n - 201$ additions.

The efficiency of the Balafoutis algorithm derives from the computational efficiency of Cartesian tensors and from the recursive nature of the computations. These efficiencies carry over to the computation of the gradient terms.

The Balafoutis algorithm proceeds in two steps. In the first step velocities, accelerations, net torques, and forces at each joint are computed starting from the root node and working out to the tips of all the chains in the tree. In the second step the joint torques are computed starting from the tips of the chains back to the root node. See the appendix for details. These recursive equations can be differentiated directly to compute g or one can use Cartesian tensor identities to compute the derivatives. Since the differentiation is tedious and somewhat involved we have included some of the partial derivatives of the recursive equations in the appendix as an aid to those attempting to reproduce our results.

3.3 Motion Cyclification

If cyclic motions, such as walking and running, come from motion capture data they will not be precisely cyclic due to measurement errors and normal human variation in movement. The discontinuities in motion will likely be small enough that the full power of a spacetime transition will not be necessary in order to splice a motion back onto itself smoothly. In this case we use a much simpler and faster algorithm for generating seamless cycles.

The cyclification algorithm proceeds in two steps. First the user marks the approximate beginning and end of a cycle. We create two time regions I_s and I_f centered about the markers the user has chosen. The time regions are set to be one-fifth the length of the time between markers. The system then finds one time point in each interval that minimizes the difference between position, velocity, and acceleration of the body:

$$\min_{t_1 \in I_s,\, t_2 \in I_f} \|\mathbf{a} - \mathbf{b}\|_2$$

where $\mathbf{a} = [q(t_1), \dot{q}(t_1), \ddot{q}(t_1)]^T$ and $\mathbf{b} = [q(t_2), \dot{q}(t_2), \ddot{q}(t_2)]^T$.

For most motions there will still be a discontinuity at the time where the motion cycles. We distribute this discontinuity error over the entire time interval so that the end points of the cycle match exactly by adding a linear offset to the entire time interval. We then construct a C^2 motion curve by fitting a least squares cyclic B-spline approximation to the modified motion.

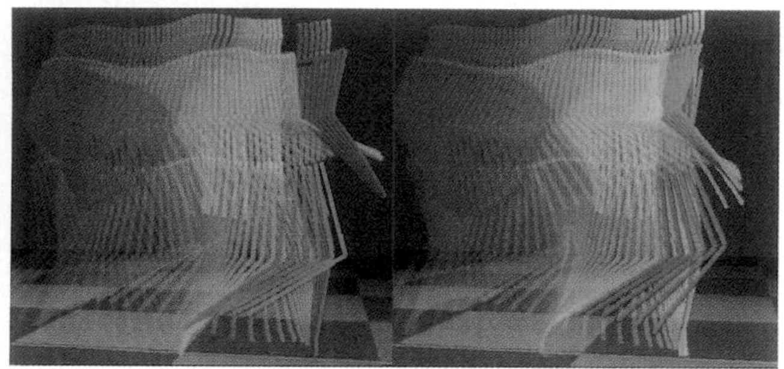

Figure 3: Results of cyclification on a walk

4 Motion Representation

To minimize the complexity of working with motions which involve many degrees of freedom we have developed a flexible functional expression language, and an interactive interpreter for the language, for representing and manipulating motions. Using this language it is a simple matter to interactively type in or procedurally generate complex composite motions from simpler constituent motions. We include a small example to demonstrate the simplicity of using the language.

Motions are represented as a hierarchy of motion expressions. Motion exressions can be one of three types of objects: intervals; degrees of freedom (DOF); and motion units (MU). These primitives are described in a pseudo-BNF notation below:

$$\begin{aligned} interval &\rightarrow (f_1, \ldots, f_n, t_s, t_f) \,|\, \epsilon \\ DOF &\rightarrow interval \,|\, DOF, interval \,|\, \epsilon \\ \mathrm{MU} &\rightarrow array\, 1 \ldots n\, [DOF] \end{aligned}$$

An interval is a list of scalar functions of time plus a start time t_s and a stop time t_f. A DOF is a list of intervals. A DOF defines the value over time of one of the angular or translational degrees of freedom of a body. An MU is an array of DOFs which defines the value over time of some, but not necessarily all, of the degrees of freedom of the body.

There are three kinds of operations defined on these primitives: set operations, function operations, and insert and delete operations.

The set operations are intersection, undefine, and composition, denoted $\wedge$, $-$, and $+$ respectively. They are defined on intervals as follows (without loss of generality assume $t_3 > t_1$):

$$I_1 = (f_1, \ldots, f_n, t_1, t_2)$$
$$I_2 = (g_1, \ldots, g_n, t_3, t_4)$$

$$I_1 \wedge I_2 = \begin{cases} \epsilon & t_1 \leq t_2 \\ (f_1,\ldots,f_n,g_1,\ldots,g_n,t_3,t_2) & t_3<t_2, t_2<t_4 \\ (f_1,\ldots,f_n,g_1,\ldots,g_n,t_3,t_4) & t_3<t_2, t_4<t_2 \end{cases}$$

$$I_1 - I_2 = \begin{cases} (f_1,\ldots,f_n,t_1,t_2)(g_1,\ldots,g_n,t_1,t_2) & t_2 \leq t_3 \\ (f_1,\ldots,f_n,t_1,t_3)(g_1,\ldots,g_n,t_2,t_4) & t_3<t_2, t_2<t_4 \\ (f_1,\ldots,f_n,t_1,t_3)(f_1,\ldots,f_n,t_4,t_2) & t_3<t_2, t_4<t_2 \end{cases}$$

$$I_1 + I_2 = I_1 - I_2, I_1 \wedge I_2$$

where the comma denotes list concatenation.

The intersection operation takes two intervals as arguments and returns an interval. The undefine operator takes as arguments two intervals I_1 and I_2 and returns a DOF containing two intervals A and B. A diagrammatic representation of this operation is shown in Figure 4. The effect of the undefine operator is to undefine any portions of I_1 which overlap with I_2.

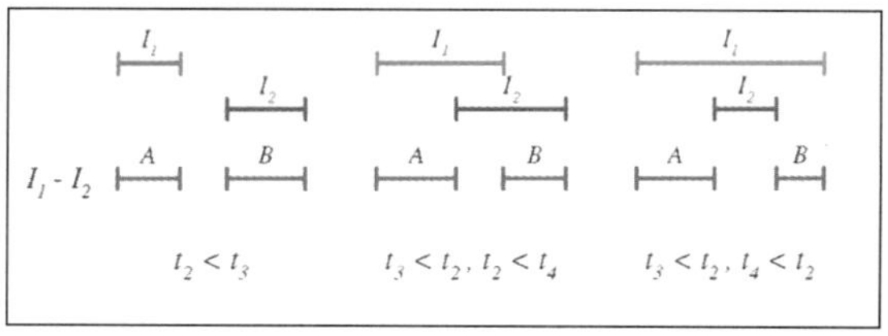

Figure 4: Interval undefine operation.

The set addition operator takes as arguments two intervals I_1 and I_2 and returns a DOF containing two intervals, A and B, if the intersection of I_1 and I_2 is empty, or three intervals, A, B, and C, if the intersection of I_1 and I_2 is not empty. A diagrammatic representation of this operator is shown in Figure 5.

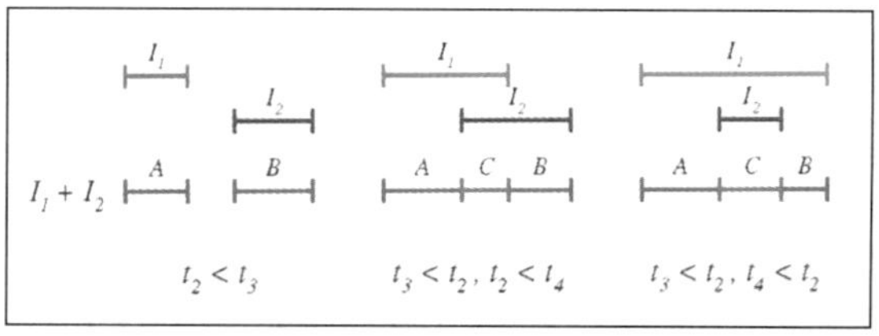

Figure 5: Interval addition operation.

The effect of this operator is to replace the region of I_1 that was removed by the set undefine operator with a new interval C. Set operations are useful for finding all the time regions over which two intervals, DOFs, or MUs are defined or those time regions where they are multiply defined, i.e., where composed motions conflict.

The function operations perform functional composition on the elements of an interval: functions and times. For example, one of the functional operators is *affine*(t_s, d, I). This operator scales and translates the time components of an interval, and implicitly the time value at which the functions in that interval are evaluated. Other functional operations we have implemented include *clip*(t_s, t_f, I) which clips out a portion of an interval and translates the beginning of the clip back to time zero, *clip-in-place*(t_s, t_f, I) which performs the same operation as *clip* except that it leaves the clip time unchanged, and *concatenate*(I_1, I_2) which puts the two intervals in time sequence.

Both the set and function operations can be applied to any interval, DOF, or MU. The operations are pushed down to the level of intervals at which point the primitive interval operations are invoked. For example if we intersect MU_1 and MU_2, first we intersect all the DOFs of MU_1 and MU_2 and then we intersect all the intervals in all the DOFs.

Complex motions can be easily created by functional composition of simple motions using the set and function operations defined above. Figure 6 shows an example of a spacetime transition from a walk arm motion to a wave arm motion and then back to a walk arm motion. The arm wave MU defines only the DOFs of the arm and the walk MU defines all the DOFs of the body. First we perform an affine transformation on the arm wave MU and undefine this from the walk MU. This will undefine the arm degrees of freedom of the walk MU during a time that is slightly longer than the arm wave MU. When we add a time shifted version of the arm wave MU to the resulting MU there will be two undefined regions surrounding it which the spacetime operator will fill in with spacetime transition motion. The result will be a smooth transition from a walking arm motion to an arm wave motion and back to a walking arm motion. This operation is shown in both a time line view and an operator tree view in Figure 6. Letting SP denote the spacetime optimization, the algebraic representation of this motion is

$$SP\left(affine_2(\text{wave}) + (\text{walk} - affine_1(\text{wave}))\right).$$

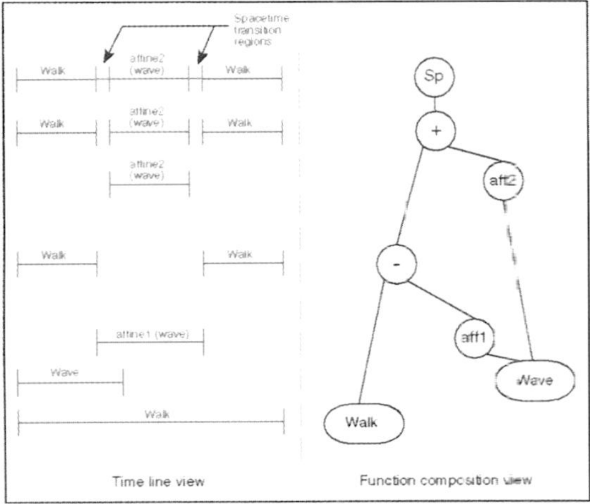

Figure 6: Spacetime composition of motions.

5 Results

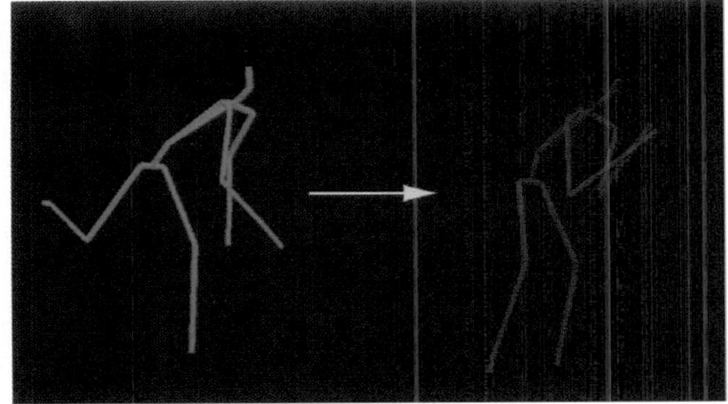

Figure 7: End position of motion 1 and beginning position of motion 2 for a motion transition

We have successfully applied the motion transition algorithm on many motions. For this example the transition time was set to .6, and the number of B-spline coefficients to 5. The resulting transition is shown in Figure 8. Our experience has been that successful transitions are quite short, usually in the range of .3 to .6 seconds. Without a biomechanical model to guide a large motion, our minimal energy model will often prove insufficient.

The beginning of the transition is colored blue and the end is colored red with intermediate times a linear blend of the two colors. This motion is one transition from a longer animation which has 5 transitions between 6 motions.

Figure 8: Multiple time exposure of transition generated from the motions in Figure 7

Figure 9 shows an example of a motion transition which affects only the arm degrees of freedom of the motion. This sequence actually consists of two space time transitions: one from a walking arm motion to the salute motion and another back to the walking arm motion. Each transition motion is .3 seconds long.

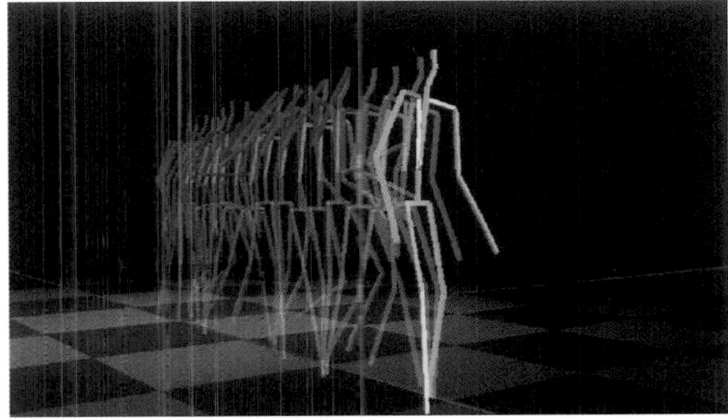

Figure 9: Arm walk motion transitioning to salute motion and back to walk motion. Arm degrees of freedom affected by the transition are colored green.

Computation times for transitions are strongly dependent on the number of degrees of freedom involved since the spacetime formulation we use is $O(n^2)$ in the number of degrees of freedom. For the transition of Figure 8 generating the spacetime transition motion took 72 seconds. This transition involved 44 degrees of freedom. For the transition of Figure 9 generating the spacetime transition took 20 seconds. All timings were performed on a 100 MHz Pentium processor.

Spacetime transitions are more costly to generate than joint angle interpolation techniques, but they often produce more realistic motion. One type of motion that demonstrates this superiority is motion that has identical joint space beginning and ending conditions on some of the degrees of freedom of the figure. An example of this type of motion is shown in Figure 10. This motion begins with the forearm nearly vertical, held close to the shoulder with zero initial velocity. The motion ends with the forearm held horizontal also with zero velocity. Because the upper arm and the wrist have identical

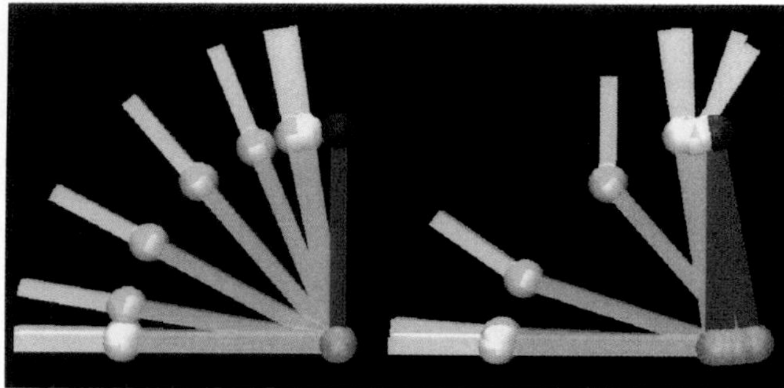

Figure 10: Joint angle interpolation versus spacetime optimization.

joint space starting and ending conditions any simple interpolation technique, which would include linear interpolation, polynomial interpolation, and most other types of interpolation which simply take a weighted sum of the two endpoint conditions will yield a motion such as that shown on the left in Figure 10. This is an unnatural motion since there is no joint space motion at the shoulder or the wrist. The spacetime motion, however, has motion at every joint and looks much more like the kind of motion a person might make.

6 Conclusion

This paper has presented a powerful animation system for manipulating motion data using a motion expression interpreter. Data can be positioned in space and time, and complete control of the degrees of freedom in the system allows motions to be spliced and mixed in arbitrary manners.

The system is capable of generating seamless transitions between segments of animations using spacetime constraints and inverse kinematics. Using a new, fast, dynamics formulation we can apply spacetime constraints to systems having a large number of degrees of freedom and still have reasonable computation time. An additional capability of the system is the generation of arbitrary length periodic motions, such as walking, by cyclifying segments of motion data which are approximately periodic.

The results of using our system to generate animations starting from a base library of soccer motions are quite good. Cyclification of a segment of such motions as a walk produces a quite realistic walk of arbitrary length. The spacetime constraint and inverse kinematic optimization produce transitions between diverse motions which are seamless and invisible to the viewer. While the optimization cannot be done in real time, it is relatively fast, and quite usable by an animator designing motions.

We plan to extend our motion model to more accurately model the dynamics of the human body model. The current approximation used for computing root motion works reasonably well for the class of transitions we have worked with but is not accurate for free body motion.

Acknowledgements

The authors thank Jessica Hodgins, College of Computing, Georgia Institute of Technology, for providing inertia matrices for the human body model. The Microsoft Consumer Division generously shared motion capture data with us for use in this project.

A Appendix: Dynamics Details

A.1 List of Symbols

$\mathbf{o}_i$ origin of the i-th link coordinate frame.

$\mathbf{c}_i$ center of mass of the i-th link.

ω_i^i angular velocity of the i-th link.

$\mathbf{z}_i^i$ joint axis of the i-thlink expressed in the i-thcoordinate frame.

$\mathbf{s}_{i,j}^i$ vector from $\mathbf{o}_i$ to $\mathbf{o}_j$ expressed in the i-th coordinate frame.

$\mathbf{r}_{i,j}^i$ vector from $\mathbf{o}_i$ to $\mathbf{c}_j$ expressed in the i-th coordinate frame.

$\mathbf{A}_i$ 3x3 coordinate (or 4x4 homogeneous) transformation relating the i-th coordinate frame to the $(i-1)$-th frame.

$\mathbf{I}_{c_i}^k$ inertia tensor of the i-th link about $\mathbf{c}_i$ expressed in the k-th coordinate frame.

$\mathbf{J}_{c_i}^k$ Euler's inertia tensor of the i-th frame about $\mathbf{c}_i$ expressed in the k-th coordinate frame.

$\mathbf{\Omega}_i^i$ angular acceleration tensor of the i-th link expressed in the i-th coordinate frame.

$\mathbf{F}_{c_i}^i$ force vector acting on $\mathbf{c}_i$ expressed in the i-th coordinate frame.

$\mathbf{M}_{c_i}^i$ moment vector about $\mathbf{c}_i$ expressed in the i-th coordinate frame.

$\mathbf{f}_i^i$ force vector exerted on link i by link $(i-1)$.

η_i^i moment vector exerted on link i by link $(i-1)$.

τ_i torque at joint i.

$\mathbf{g}$ gravity.

m_i mass of the i-th link.

In the above, the subscript indicates the coordinate frame being represented and superscript the coordinate frame in which it is represented.

We use $+$ and $-$ on index variables to denote relative placement in the joint hierarchy. Thus, $i-$ is the predecessor of i which is the predecessor of $i+$. For example, in the equation $\omega_{i+}^{i+} = \mathbf{A}_{i+}^T \omega_i^i + \mathbf{z}_{i+}^{i+} \dot{q}_{i+}$, the variable ω_i^i is the angular velocity in the coordinate frame which precedes the coordinate frame of ω_{i+}^{i+}. In other words, coordinate frame i is closer to the root coordinate frame than is frame $i+$. Note that there is no guarantee of a uniquely defined successor.

$$\mathbf{g} = [0.0, -9.80655, 0.0]^T$$

$$\mathbf{J}_{c_i}^i = \frac{1}{2}\,\mathrm{trace}\left(\mathbf{I}_{c_i}^i\right) 1 - \mathbf{I}_{c_i}^i$$

$$\mathrm{dual}(\mathbf{v}) = \tilde{\mathbf{v}} = \begin{bmatrix} 0 & -\mathbf{v}_3 & \mathbf{v}_2 \\ \mathbf{v}_3 & 0 & -\mathbf{v}_1 \\ -\mathbf{v}_2 & \mathbf{v}_1 & 0 \end{bmatrix}$$

$$\mathrm{dual}(\tilde{\mathbf{v}}) = \mathbf{v}$$

A.2 Forward Dynamics Equations

Base conditions at the root of the creature:

$$\omega_0^0 = \mathbf{z}_0^0 \dot{q}_0$$

$$\dot{\omega}_0^0 = \mathbf{z}_0^0 \ddot{q}_0$$

$$\ddot{\mathbf{s}}_{0,0}^0 = \mathbf{A}_0^T \mathbf{g}$$

Recursive forward dynamics equations:

$$
\begin{aligned}
\omega_{i+}^{i+} &= \mathbf{A}_{i+}^T \omega_i^i + \mathbf{z}_{i+}^{i+} \dot{q}_{i+} \\
\dot{\omega}_{i+}^{i+} &= \mathbf{A}_{i+}^T \dot{\omega}_i^i + \tilde{\omega}_i^{i-} \mathbf{z}_{i+}^{i+} \dot{q}_{i+} + \mathbf{z}_{i+}^{i+} \ddot{q}_{i+} \\
\boldsymbol{\Omega}_{i+}^{i+} &= \tilde{\dot{\omega}}_{i+}^{i+} + \tilde{\omega}_{i+}^{i+} \tilde{\omega}_{+}^{+} \\
\ddot{\mathbf{s}}_{0,i+}^{i+} &= \mathbf{A}_{i+}^T \left[\ddot{\mathbf{s}}_{0,i}^i + \boldsymbol{\Omega}_i^i \mathbf{s}_{i,i+}^i \right] \\
\ddot{\mathbf{r}}_{0,i+}^{i+} &= \boldsymbol{\Omega}_{i+}^{i+} \mathbf{r}_{i+,i+}^{i+} + \ddot{\mathbf{s}}_{0,i+}^{i+} \\
\mathbf{F}_{c_{i+}}^{i+} &= m_{i+} \ddot{\mathbf{r}}_{0,i+}^{i+} \\
\tilde{\mathbf{M}}_{c_{i+}}^{i+} &= \left(\boldsymbol{\Omega}_{i+}^{i+} \mathbf{J}_{c_{i+}}^{i+} \right) - \left(\boldsymbol{\Omega}_{i+}^{i+} \mathbf{J}_{c_{i+}}^{i+} \right)^T
\end{aligned}
$$

A.3 Backward Recursive Equations (Torque Equations)

At a joint controlling an end-effector:

$$
\begin{aligned}
\mathbf{f}_i^i &= \mathbf{F}_{c_i}^i \\
\eta_i^i &= \tilde{\mathbf{r}}_{i,i}^i \mathbf{F}_{c_i}^i + \mathbf{M}_{c_i}^i \\
\tau_i &= \eta_i^i \cdot \mathbf{z}_i^i
\end{aligned}
$$

At an internal joint:

$$
\begin{aligned}
\mathbf{f}_i^i &= \mathbf{F}_{c_i}^i + \sum_{i+} \left[\mathbf{A}_{i+} \mathbf{f}_{i+}^{i+} \right] \\
\eta_i^i &= \tilde{\mathbf{r}}_{i,i}^i \mathbf{F}_{c_i}^i + \mathbf{M}_{c_i}^i + \sum_{i+} \left[\mathbf{A}_{i+} \eta_{i+}^{i+} + \tilde{\mathbf{s}}_{i,i+}^i \mathbf{f}_{i+}^i \right] \\
\tau_i &= \eta_i^i \cdot \mathbf{z}_i^i
\end{aligned}
$$

A.4 The Energy Function and its Partial

$$
e = \int_t \sum_i \tau_i^2 \, dt
$$

$$
\frac{\partial e}{\partial q_j} = \frac{\partial \int_{t_1}^{t_2} \sum_i \tau_i^2 \, dt}{\partial q_j} = 2 \int_{t_1}^{t_2} \sum \tau_i \frac{\partial \tau_i}{\partial q_j} \, dt
$$

A.5 Forward Partials with Initial Conditions

$$
\begin{aligned}
\frac{\delta \omega_{i+}^{i+}}{\delta q_j} &\underset{i+>j}{=} \mathbf{A}_{i+}^T \frac{\delta \omega_i^i}{\delta q_j} \\
\frac{\delta \omega_{i+}^{i+}}{\delta q_j} &\underset{i+=j}{=} \frac{\delta \mathbf{A}_j^T}{\delta q_j} \omega_{j-}^{j-}
\end{aligned}
$$

$$
\begin{aligned}
\frac{\delta \dot{\omega}_{i+}^{i+}}{\delta q_j} &\underset{i+>j}{=} \mathbf{A}_{i+}^T \frac{\delta \dot{\omega}_i^i}{\delta q_j} + \widetilde{\frac{\delta \omega_i^{i+}}{\delta q_j}} \mathbf{z}_{i+}^{i+} \dot{q}_{i+} \\
\frac{\delta \dot{\omega}_{i+}^{i+}}{\delta q_j} &\underset{i+=j}{=} \frac{\delta \mathbf{A}_j^T}{\delta q_j} \dot{\omega}_{j-}^{j-} + \left(\widetilde{\frac{\delta \mathbf{A}_j^T}{\delta q_j} \dot{\omega}_{j-}^{j-}} \right) \mathbf{z}_j^j \dot{q}_j
\end{aligned}
$$

$$
\frac{\delta \boldsymbol{\Omega}_{i+}^{i+}}{\delta q_j} = \widetilde{\frac{\delta \dot{\omega}_{i+}^{i+}}{\delta q_j}} + \widetilde{\frac{\delta \omega_{i+}^{i+}}{\delta q_j}} \tilde{\omega}_{i+}^{i+} + \left(\widetilde{\frac{\delta \omega_{i+}^{i+}}{\delta q_j}} \tilde{\omega}_{i+}^{i+} \right)^T
$$

$$
\begin{aligned}
\frac{\delta \ddot{\mathbf{s}}_{0\,i+}^{i-}}{\delta q_j} &\underset{i+>j}{=} \mathbf{A}_{i+}^T \left[\frac{\delta \ddot{\mathbf{s}}_{0,i}}{\delta q_j} + \frac{\delta \boldsymbol{\Omega}_i^i}{\delta q_j} \mathbf{s}_{i,i+}^i \right] \\
\frac{\delta \ddot{\mathbf{s}}_{0\,i+}^{i-}}{\delta q_j} &\underset{i+=j}{=} \frac{\delta \mathbf{A}_j^T}{\delta q_j} \left[\ddot{\mathbf{s}}_{0,j-}^{j-} + \boldsymbol{\Omega}_{j-}^{j-} \mathbf{s}_{j-,j}^{j-} \right]
\end{aligned}
$$

$$
\frac{\delta \mathbf{M}_{c_{i+}}^{i+}}{\delta q_j} = \frac{\delta \boldsymbol{\Omega}_{i+}^{i+}}{\delta q_j} \mathbf{J}_{c_{i+}}^{i+} - \left(\frac{\delta \boldsymbol{\Omega}_{i+}^{i+}}{\delta q_j} \mathbf{J}_{c_{i+}}^{i+} \right)^T
$$

$$
\frac{\delta \mathbf{F}_{c_{i+}}^{i+}}{\delta q_j} = m_{i+} \frac{\delta \ddot{\mathbf{r}}_{0,i+}^{i+}}{\delta q_j}
$$

A.6 Reverse Partials with Initial Conditions

$$
\begin{aligned}
\frac{\delta \mathbf{f}_i^i}{\delta q_j} &\underset{\exists i+}{=} \frac{\delta \mathbf{F}_{c_i}^i}{\delta q_j} + \sum_{i+} \left[\frac{\delta \mathbf{A}_{i+}}{\delta q_j} \mathbf{f}_{i+}^{i+} + \mathbf{A}_{i+} \frac{\delta \mathbf{f}_i^i}{\delta q_j} \right] \\
\frac{\delta \mathbf{f}_i^i}{\delta q_j} &\underset{\nexists i+}{=} \frac{\delta \mathbf{F}_{c_i}^i}{\delta q_j}
\end{aligned}
$$

$$
\begin{aligned}
\frac{\delta \eta_i^i}{\delta q_j} &\underset{\exists i+}{=} \widetilde{\mathbf{r}_{i,i+}^i} \frac{\delta \mathbf{F}_{c_i}^i}{\delta q_j} + \widetilde{\frac{\delta \mathbf{M}_{c_i}^i}{\delta q_j}} + \sum_{i+} \left[\frac{\delta \mathbf{A}_{i+}}{\delta q_j} \eta_{i+}^{i+} + \right. \\
&\qquad \left. \mathbf{A}_{i+} \frac{\delta \eta_{i+}^{i+}}{\delta q_j} + \widetilde{\mathbf{s}_{i,i+}^i} \frac{\delta \mathbf{A}_{i+}}{\delta q_j} \mathbf{f}_{i+}^{i+} + \widetilde{\mathbf{s}_{i,i+}^i} \mathbf{A}_{i+} \frac{\delta \mathbf{f}_{i+}^{i+}}{\delta q_j} \right] \\
\frac{\delta \eta_i^i}{\delta q_j} &\underset{\nexists i+}{=} \widetilde{\mathbf{r}_{i,i+}^i} \frac{\delta \mathbf{F}_{c_i}^i}{\delta q_j} + \widetilde{\frac{\delta \mathbf{M}_{c_i}^i}{\delta q_j}}
\end{aligned}
$$

$$
\frac{\delta \tau_i}{\delta q_j} = \frac{\delta \eta_i^i}{\delta q_j} \cdot \mathbf{z}_i^i
$$

References

[1] BALAFOUTIS, C. A., AND PATEL, R. V. *Dynamic Analysis of Robot Manipulators: A Cartesian Tensor Approach.* Kluwer Academic Publishers, 1991.

[2] BRUDERLIN, A., AND WILLIAMS, L. Motion signal processing. In *Computer Graphics* (Aug. 1995), pp. 97–104. Proceedings of SIGGRAPH 95.

[3] BURDETT, R. G., SKRINAR, G. S., AND SIMON, S. R. Comparison of mechanical work and metabolic energy consumption during normal gait. *Journal of Orhopaedic Research 1*, 1 (1983), 63–72.

[4] COHEN, M. F. Interactive spacetime control for animation. In *Computer Graphics* (July 1992), pp. 293–302. Proceedings of SIGGRAPH 92.

[5] GILL, P. E., MURRAY, W., AND WRIGHT, M. H. *Practical Optimization.* Academic Press, 1981.

[6] HOLLERBACH, J. M. A recursive lagrangian formulation of manipulator dynamics and a comparative study of dynamics formulation complexity. *IEEE Transactions on Systems, Man, and Cybernetics SMC-10*, 11 (Nov. 1980).

[7] LIU, Z., AND COHEN, M. F. An efficient symbolic interface to constraint based animation systems. In *Proceedings of the 5th EuroGraphics Workshop on Animation and Simulation* (Sept. 1994).

[8] LIU, Z., GORTLER, S. J., AND COHEN, M. F. Hierarchical spacetime control. In *Computer Graphics* (July 1994), pp. 35–42. Proceedings of SIGGRAPH 94.

[9] UNUMA, M., ANJYO, K., AND TEKEUCHI, R. Fourier principles for emotion-based human figure animation. In *Computer Graphics* (Aug. 1995), pp. 91–96. Proceedings of SIGGRAPH 95.

[10] WITKIN, A., AND KASS, M. Spacetime constraints. In *Computer Graphics* (Aug. 1988), pp. 159–168. Proceedings of SIGGRAPH 88.

[11] WITKIN, A., AND POPOVÍC, Z. Motion warping. In *Computer Graphics* (Aug. 1995), pp. 105–108. Proceedings of SIGGRAPH 95.

[12] ZHAO, J., AND BADLER, N. I. Inverse kinematics positioning using non-linear programming for highly articulated figures. *ACM Transactions on Graphics 13*, 4 (Oct. 1994), 313–336.

Limit Cycle Control And Its Application To The Animation Of Balancing And Walking

Joseph Laszlo† Michiel van de Panne Eugene Fiume

Department of Computer Science and
†Department of Electrical and Computer Engineering
University of Toronto

ABSTRACT

Seemingly simple behaviors such as human walking are difficult to model because of their inherent instability. Kinematic animation techniques can freely ignore such intrinsically dynamic problems, but they therefore also miss modeling important motion characteristics. On the other hand, the effect of balancing can emerge in a physically-based animation, but it requires computing delicate control strategies. We propose an alternative method that adds closed-loop feedback to open-loop periodic motions. We then apply our technique to create robust walking gaits for a fully-dynamic 19 degree-of-freedom human model. Important global characteristics such as direction, speed and stride rate can be controlled by changing the open-loop behavior alone or through simple control parameters, while continuing to employ the same local stabilization technique. Among other features, our dynamic "human" walking character is thus able to follow desired paths specified by the animator.

Keywords: control, limit cycles, physically-based modeling, locomotion, human animation

1. INTRODUCTION

As with any modeling endeavor, Nature has much to tell us about modeling motion. When observing the running motion of a charging bull, before we take cover we can clearly see that motion is a product of both physics and muscular action. Physically based animation mimics Nature by modeling both.

While techniques for simulating the basic physics of motion are well known, less is known about how to provide the necessary control over the muscles or actuators in order to produce a desired motion [1]. By analogy, for most adults, walking is a seemingly effortless task. We know from watching toddlers that the apparent ease of walking, running, and maintaining balance is deceiving. It comes as little surprise, then, that walking has proven to be a difficult motion to model. Indeed the most successful approach has been literally to "watch Nature" by capturing motion data from real walks and mapping this data to computer generated characters. The

{jflaszlo | van | elf}@dgp.utoronto.ca

We gratefully acknowledge the financial support of our research by ITRC (Ontario) and NSERC (Canada). The ongoing benevolence of Alias|Wavefront to our graphics lab is also appreciated.

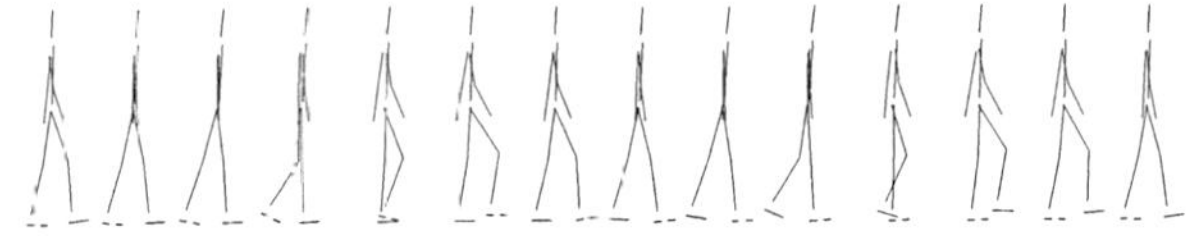

Figure 1. A 3-D dynamic walk using limit cycle control.

work of [16, 5, 30, 35] is a good survey of recent techniques aimed at making the most flexible use of existing motion-capture and keyframe data. The advantages of motion capture are obvious: the immediate generation of realistic human motions. However, motion capture does not provide us with sufficient understanding to create more general walking motions, especially when conditions are unpredictable, when new motions need to be generated, or when dealing with non-human characters. Developing methods to control physical simulations can potentially provide us with a more general tool, and it is therefore the modeling paradigm we adopt.

This paper proposes a solution for the control of periodic, unstable motions. The technique automates the addition of feedback to otherwise unstable motions, such as walking and running (see Figure 1). We also present an application of our technique by demonstrating a human model capable of a variety of walking styles, as well as a second, imaginary creature.

2. BACKGROUND

Many solutions to animation control problems have been proposed in the animation literature and elsewhere. In particular, there is a large body of work focussed on the important problem of locomotion control. What follows is a brief summary of some of these techniques, with an emphasis on algorithms for locomotion, including human walks and runs.

Procedural methods have been popular for generating motion [10], especially for human walking [2, 3, 4]. These methods directly generate walking motions by using a series of constraints, which are based on empirical data or on kinematic relationships. The work of [3] uses a mixed kinematic/dynamic model. A positive feature of such systems is that they give the animator direct control over useful gait characteristics, such as stride length, pelvic list, etc. The motions produced are typically parameterized in a way that is directly meaningful to an animator.

In physical approaches to animation, one must solve for the control actions that will, upon simulation, produce a desired motion. One approach has been to use a type of underconstrained inverse dynamics with automatic addition and removal of constraints which can be hand-tailored to yield stable 3D walks [29]. Several other approaches have treated control directly as a search problem, employing a particular choice of control representation and a choice of search algorithm, including genetic algorithms [24, 28], and simulated annealing [23, 12, 31]. The results indicate that such techniques are surprisingly adept at finding novel modes of locomotion. Unfortunately, it is less clear that such global search techniques are an efficient means of finding control strategies for motions requir-

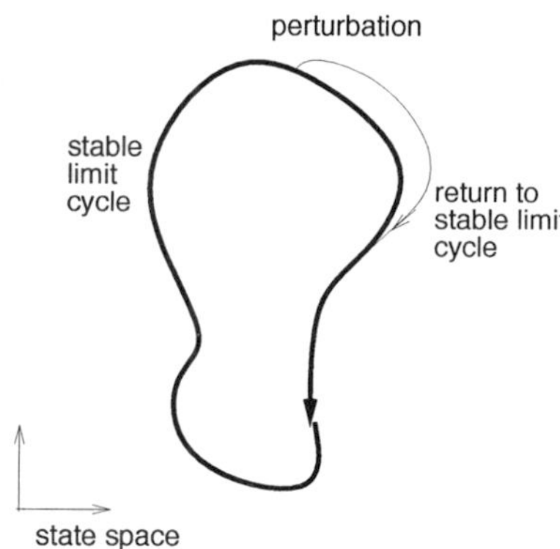

Figure 2. A passively-stable limit cycle.

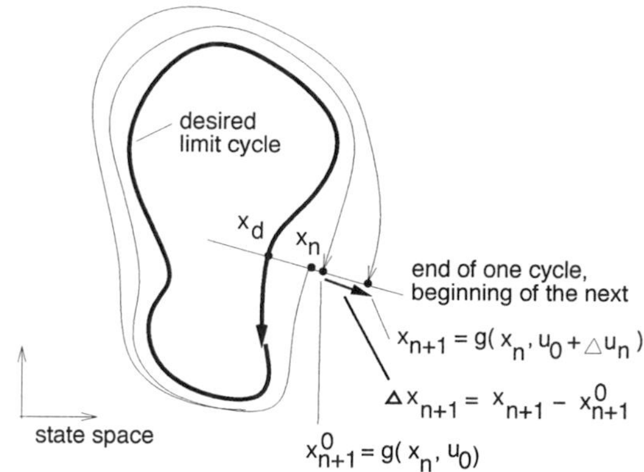

Figure 3. A limit cycle as a discrete dynamical system.

ing fine control and feedback, such as human walking and running. One would think that to create this type of controller, we should be able to do better than to explore a large solution space at random. Toward this end, some methods, including ours, draw upon previous work in robotics and control.

The hopping and running control strategies presented in [14, 26] represent a more methodical approach to arriving at a control strategy. The basic idea stems from earlier robotics work [25] and is a powerful control technique for hopping and running motions, given that certain assumptions are fulfilled. The key is an elegant decomposition of the control problem which arises from assuming the legs are lightweight with respect to the body mass. This assumption can be overcome to some extent as shown in the work of [14]. A more analytical examination of the remarkable robustness of this and a class of related strategies can be found in [17].

Other specific controller designs have also met with success. The simulated cockroach in [22] is a good example. Strategies proposed for walking robots also have possible applications for animation [34, 9, 11, 23]. Demonstrations of passively-powered walking down a slight incline show that active walking may only require small amounts of energy [20, 21].

The point of departure for our work is the concept of *periodic limit cycles*. Consider for a moment the motion of a typical mechanical toy, which drives its joints in a repetitive, periodic fashion and is oblivious to its environment. This type of open-loop control is sufficient for many types of animated motion, as has been pointed out in [32]. However, it is insufficient as a control mechanism for unstable dynamic motions such as walking and running. The control technique we propose provides a general method of turning unstable open-loop motions into stable closed-loop motions. The basis of the technique is a process that perturbs the open-loop control actions slightly in order to yield a desired stable, cyclic motion. A broad range of related work on limit cycles and periodic control can be found in the control systems literature [15, 13, 19, 6, 33]. While this paper provides all the essential information for implementing our technique, more details can be found in [18].

3. LIMIT CYCLE CONTROL

A mechanical toy owes its successful motion to a stable limit cycle that arises naturally from the interaction of the toy with its environment. Typically, the environment acts on the toy in such a way that any disturbance to the motion, such as a small external push, is rapidly damped. Figure 2 illustrates this concept using a phase diagram. The phase diagram is a projection of the path a motion traces through state-space over time.[1] Unfortunately, recalling our wobbly toddler, unstable motions such as walking cannot rely solely on passive damping of disturbances

The goal of limit-cycle (LC) control is to actively drive motions that would otherwise be unstable back to a fixed limit cycle. The key point to implementing LC control is to avoid dealing with the complexities of non-linear dynamics by representing the motion using a well-behaved *discrete* dynamical system.

In general, the continuous equations of motion can be expressed by the non-linear differential equation

$$\dot{\mathbf{x}} = f(\mathbf{x}, \mathbf{u})$$

where $\mathbf{x}$ is the system state, $\dot{\mathbf{x}}$ its time derivative, and $\mathbf{u}$ is the control input. The discrete dynamical system that we shall deal with has the following iterative form:

$$\mathbf{x}_{n+1} = g(\mathbf{x}_n, \mathbf{u}_0 + \Delta\mathbf{u}_n)$$

where $\mathbf{x}_n$ represents the initial state of the nth periodic limit cycle, $\mathbf{x}_{n+1}$ is the state on the next cycle, $\mathbf{u}_0$ is the periodic open-loop control, and $\Delta\mathbf{u}_n$ is an applied control perturbation. The purpose of $\Delta\mathbf{u}_n$ will be to drive the sequence $\mathbf{x}_1, \mathbf{x}_2, \ldots, \mathbf{x}_i$ to a desired value, $\mathbf{x}_d$. Figure 3 depicts an abstraction of the discrete dynamical system.

The advantage of dealing with the discrete dynamical system is that it is relatively smooth and therefore subject to linear approximation. There is no *guarantee* that the discrete system will be smooth, although we have in general found this to be the case for our experiments. For small control perturbations, $\Delta\mathbf{u}_n$, that will be applied on each cycle, the resulting change in state, $\Delta\mathbf{x}_{n+1}$, has a first order approximation of

$$\Delta\mathbf{x}_{n+1} = J\Delta\mathbf{u}_n$$

where J is a Jacobian relating the change in state after one cycle to the control perturbation. A first order approximation of the change of state makes it possible to calculate the control perturbation required to bring a system back onto a desired limit cycle, namely

$$\Delta\mathbf{u}_n = J^{-1}\Delta\mathbf{x}_{n+1}$$

where the desired $\Delta\mathbf{x}_{n+1}$ is calculated as $\Delta\mathbf{x}_{n+1} = \mathbf{x}_d - \mathbf{x}^0_{n+1}$, $\mathbf{x}_d$ being the desired state and $\mathbf{x}^0_{n+1}$ being the state achieved when the nominal control, $\mathbf{u}_0$, is applied.

3.1 Linearity of Control Perturbations

Our evidence for the above linear approximation is empirical, although this type of linearization has been justified more rigorously in the application of control theory to certain types of dynamical systems [8, 13]. Figure 4 provides some experimental evidence that a linear model is a sufficient for modeling the effect of control perturbations over a complete cycle of motion, despite the occurrence of discontinuous events such as foot-falls during the cycle itself.

[1] An object's state is the minimal set of parameters necessary to describe the position and velocity of all points on the object.

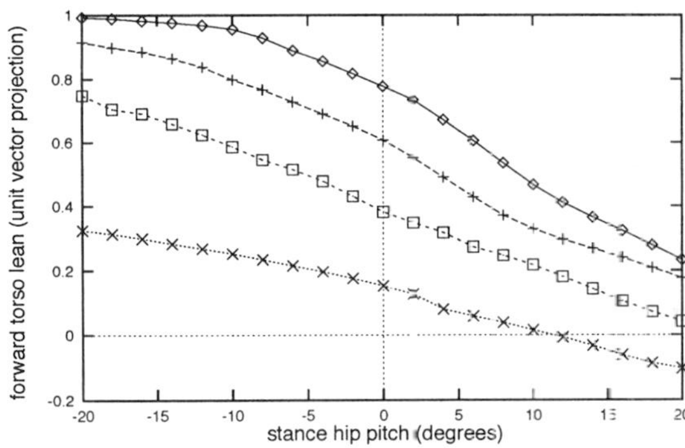

Figure 4. Linearity of perturbation control.

The vertical axis on this graph is a variable we would like to be able to control, namely some aspect of the system state. In this particular example, it is a measure of the forward pitch of the body of a simulated human model performing a walking movement, as measured at the end of a single step. The horizontal axis gives the magnitude of an applied control perturbation, in this case an alteration of the hip pitch angle during a particular part of the step. The graph thus tells us what type of forward pitch our simulated human body will have after having taken one step, using different variations of applied control. Each line shows an example of this relationship for a different step. It is evident in this figure that we can alter the forward pitch of the body as we desire and that a linear approximation is a reasonable model for the effect of a control perturbation.

It is important to note that the effects of control perturbations depend on the initial state, $\mathbf{x}_n$. This is clear from Figure 4, which shows that the relationship between control perturbation and change in state varies for different steps. What this means in practice is that for each cycle of the motion, we need to recompute the Jacobian J, which defines the relationship between applied control perturbations and the resulting changes in state after one cycle.

3.2 Regulation Variables

For many models, it is possible to make further simplifications and still effect proper LC control. It is typically neither necessary nor practical to work with a complete state vector in producing a controlled, stable limit cycle, as has thus far been implied. Instead, it can be sufficient to work with a small number of *regulation variables* (RVs). Ensuring that these regulation variables are controlled to follow a limit cycle is sufficient to stabilize the limit cycle for the motion as a whole. The use of RVs instead of the complete state vector could also be considered advantageous for animation, as it potentially leads to a less-constrained, freer motion. This is loosely related to the use of *reduced-order models* in control theory [8, 13]. Along with choosing the regulation variables, one must provide a choice of desired target values for these variables to take.

So as to make the notion of regulation variables more concrete, we introduce some of the possible choices that we know (through experiments) work well for a human walking model. A well chosen set of regulation variables should give a meaningful projection of the system state over a large range of possible states.

Figure 5 shows two possible choices for sets of regulation variables, each based upon the definition of a particular type of vector. The simplest of the two is the *up-vector*, so we begin by explaining this choice. The up-vector is a fixed vector of unit length, defined in the coordinate frame of the pelvis, which can be used to measure the forward lean and sideways tilt of the pelvis. The regulation variables are the forward and lateral components of the up-vector, i.e., the projection of the up-vector onto a horizontal ground plane. Controlling the values of these two scalar variables using LC control is sufficient to yield a balanced, fully three-dimensional walking motion for our human model.

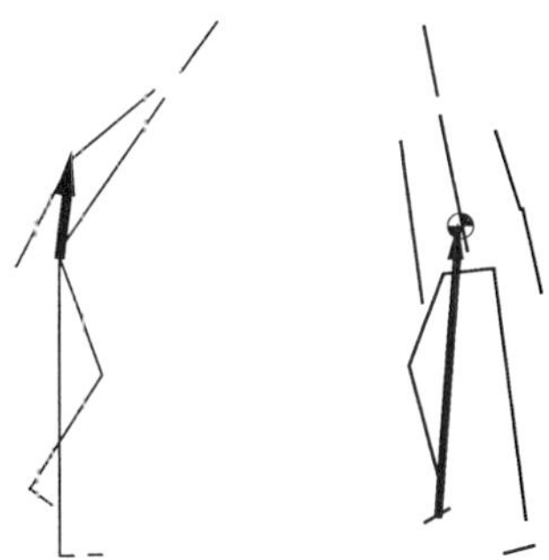

Figure 5. Regulation variables for use in walking. From left to right: (a) Up vector, (b) Swing-COM vector.

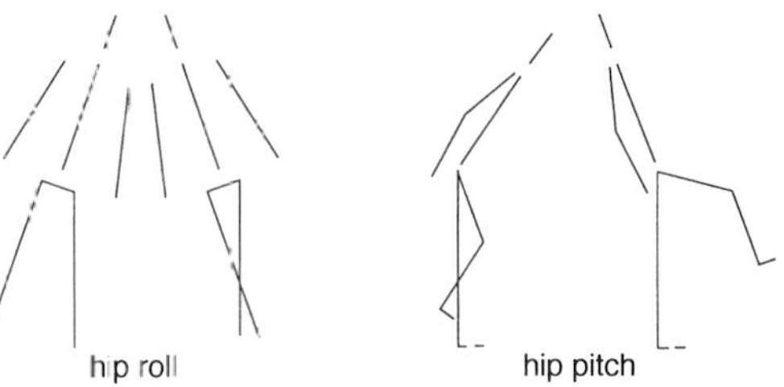

Figure 6. Control perturbations used for walking.

Other choices of regulation variable are also possible. The swing-center-of-mass (swing-COM) defines a vector from the swing foot to the center-of-mass, and thus measures where the center-of-mass will lie with respect to the future point of support. Once again, the two scalar components of the projection of the vector onto the ground plane form the set of regulation variables. In the presentation of the results, we primarily demonstrate the use of the up vector.

3.3 Control Perturbations

Given that it is often sufficient to work with a limited number of regulation variables, we need to determine the type and number of control perturbations to effect the necessary control. For two regulation variables, as is the case for our walking example, we shall require two appropriately-chosen control perturbations in order to yield a well-formed Jacobian J.

The control perturbations we work with for our human model are twofold. First, one can use changes to the stance-hip pitch and roll, effected over a particular portion of the walk cycle. Figure 6 illustrates the effects of these perturbations in an exaggerated fashion. The two figures on the left demonstrate stance-hip roll, while those on the right demonstrate stance-hip pitch. Second, the use of alterations to swing-hip pitch and roll can be similarly used as a suitable pair of control perturbations. In this case, the resulting control can be thought of as a type of foot-placement strategy. As with the choice of regulation variables, the choice of control perturbations is not unique, although they must be chosen to span the space of desired changes to the regulation variables

4. MODEL DESCRIPTIONS

We choose human walking as our primary example to illustrate the limit cycle control technique for two reasons. The first is that it is typical of motions for which the open-loop control actions are relatively easy to construct and can thus benefit immediately from LC control in order to "close the loop." The second reason is that the control of a dynamic human walking model demonstrates the effec-

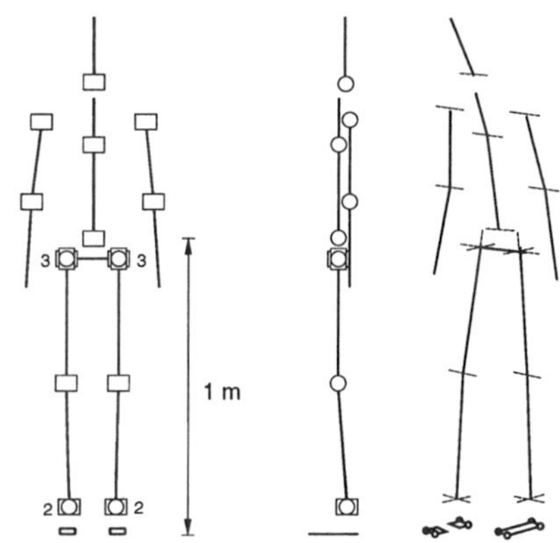

Figure 7. Construction of the human model. Joints are 1 DOF except where indicated.

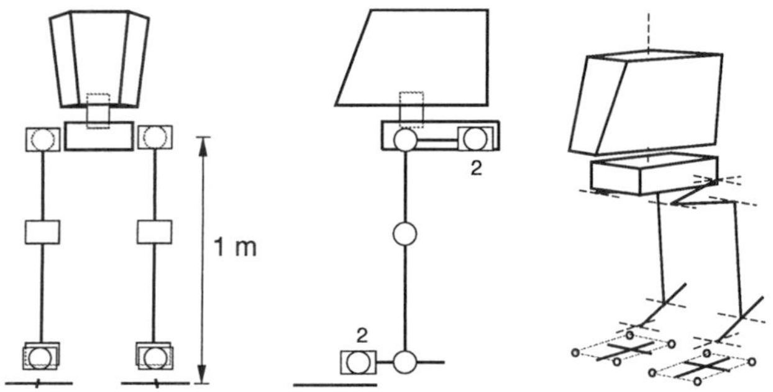

Figure 8. Construction of the robot model. Joints are 1 DOF except where indicated.

tiveness and scalability of this technique. The dynamic control of models with many degrees-of-freedom (DOF) of the type used in animation is problematic for many control techniques.

4.1 The Human Model

The physical model we use has a mass and inertia distribution comparable to those of a real human. The parameters are identical to those used in [36] and were originally obtained from [7]. The model has 13 joints and 19 DOF, as shown in Figure 7. The hip joints have three rotational DOF, while the ankle joints have two rotational DOF. All other joints have one DOF. The equations of motion are calculated and integrated using a commercially-available simulation package [27]. The ground is modelled using a penalty method. Stiff springs and dampers exert forces on a set of four points on the feet whenever they penetrate the ground. Each point is allowed to slip independently when the ratio of its applied horizontal and vertical component forces exceeds a user supplied threshold. The ground model thus uses no artificial constraints to hold the foot in place, which have in the past been used to simplify the simulation (and to some extent the control) of human motion.

4.2 The Robot Model

As a second test case, we consider the robot shown in Figure 8. This figure has 11 joints and 15 rotational DOF. The lateral base of support is much wider than that of the human model, yielding a very different type of motion. Mass and inertia parameters for this model are shown in Table 1.

5. APPLYING LC CONTROL

In the following sections we present the details of the limit cycle control algorithm as applied to our human walking model. The discussion first looks at the open-loop control before proceeding on to examine how the LC-control algorithm can be superimposed on it.

Link	Mass (kg)	Moment of Inertia (x, y, z kgm^2)		
body	14.72	0.47	0.26	0.40
head	20.9	1.11	0.92	0.72
upper leg	1.2	0.001	0.01	0.01
mid-leg	1.6	0.023	0.0013	0.023
lower leg	2.2	0.057	0.0018	0.057
ankle	1.4	0.0012	0.015	0.015
foot	2.52	0.0098	0.024	0.016

Table 1. Robot model mass and inertia parameters. The x, y and z axes are the forward, vertical and lateral axes respectively.

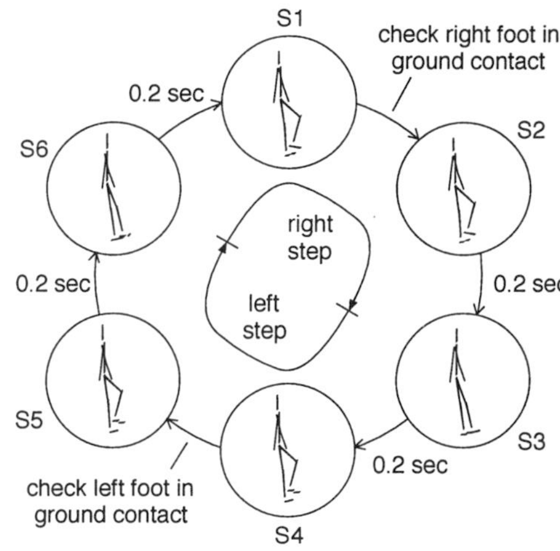

Figure 9. Finite state machine employed for walking.

5.1 Open-Loop Control

Finite state machines (FSMs) combined with proportional-derivative (PD) controllers are a common control mechanism in both physically-based animation [14, 22, 32] and robotics. The finite-state machine used as a basic controller for the walking motions is shown in Figure 9.

Each state in the FSM provides a fixed set of desired angles to the individual PD joint controllers. In our FSM, the desired angles change as a step function when proceeding from one state to the next. The PD controllers calculate a torque according to

$$\tau = k_v(\theta_d - \theta) - k_v\dot{\theta}$$

where θ_d is the desired joint angle, θ is the actual joint angle, $\dot{\theta}$ is the angular velocity of the joint and k_p and k_v are gain constants which serve to define the strength of the joint.

The state transitions in the finite state machine are time-based, with the exception of the transitions exiting states S1 and S4. These latter transitions are sensor-based and perform the simple job of ensuring that the proper stance foot is on the ground before completing the current step.

A basic open-loop motion can be constructed by defining the poses in states S2 and S3, where a pose consists of the set of desired joint angles to be used in a state. The pose for state S1 is identical to the pose for state S2. The poses for states S4, S5, and S6 are the same as the poses for states S1, S2, and S3, respectively, with the left and right sides exchanging roles. In typical operation, state S2 (S5) raises and advances the swing leg and state S3 (S6) straightens it in anticipation of ground contact. Normally, the foot contacts the ground some time after entering state S3 (S6) and the remaining time in the state is spent in double-stance phase[2]. Since the next stance foot is already on the ground, the transition out of state S4 (S1) occurs immediately after entering it, essentially skipping the

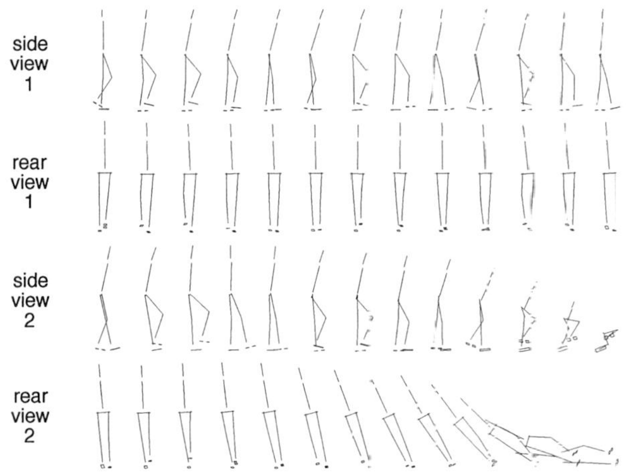

Figure 10. Walking with open-loop control (front/side views).

state. The cycle then repeats for the other leg. The sensor-based transitions serve only to make for a more robust motion. They effectively provide a way for the controlling FSM to remain synchronized with the actual motion and are typically only necessary during startup or when an FSM is dynamically altered to obtain a different motion.

Note that strictly speaking, the FSM does not provide true open-loop control since the desired joint angles are realized using local PD controllers. Nevertheless, the motion is open-loop in the sense that no system-wide feedback is used to drive it towards the desired trajectory. The result of using the "open-loop" FSM of Figure 9 for walking control is shown in Figure 10. It produces a motion which takes several steps and then falls over.

A certain amount of trial-and-error parameter tuning is required to produce open-loop motions which can be balanced successfully. Although tedious, this process is relatively straightforward. Tasks might include ensuring that toes do not stub the ground and that the basic motion can produce movement in the desired directions. Once a good open loop controller has been generated, it can be used to produce a wide variety of motions.

5.2 LC Control for Walking

The first step in implementing LC control is to choose a set of regulation variables and a set of control perturbations. We have experimented with two choices for the former, as shown in Figure 5, and two choices for the latter.

As indicated in Figure 3, the final nature of the limit cycle is defined by the target state to be achieved at the end of the current cycle. It should be noted that LC control is not successful for all choices of target values. Target values should be similar to the values that can be observed during the first few steps of the open-loop motion. This ensures that the generated limit cycle is close to the unstable open-loop limit cycle, thereby limiting the LC control to having to perform relatively small control corrections.

The power of LC control lies in being able to predict the change in values of the regulation variables with respect to the applied control perturbations. Using a linear model for this allows us to easily predict the required perturbation.

The chosen pair of control perturbations for human walking, namely alterations to the desired hip pitch and roll angles, were designed to allow for more-or-less independent control of each of the regulation variables. The hip roll is effectively used to provide balance in the coronal (side-to-side) plane, while the hip pitch provides balance in the sagittal (front-back) plane. In effect, this corresponds to only requiring the use of the diagonal elements of the Jacobian. We have not yet attempted to make use of the full Jacobian.

[2] The double-stance phase is the part of the walking cycle during which both feet are in ground contact.

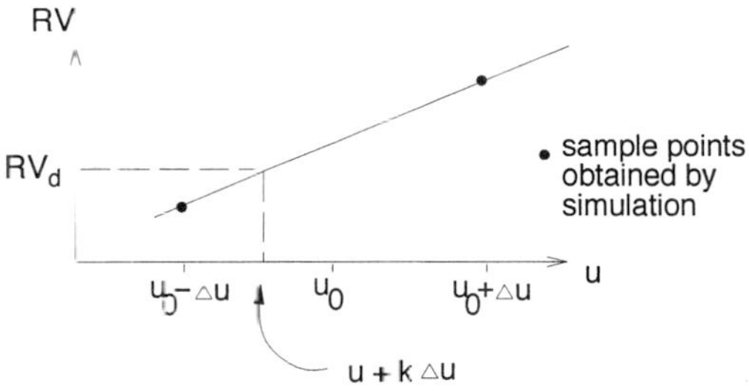

Figure 11. Interpolating for a desired control perturbation.

Figure 12. A falling motion illustrating the torso servo.

Figure 11 illustrates the linear interpolation scheme, which is applied twice, once for sagittal balance, and once for coronal balance.

Carrying out one actual step in a walking motion requires performing five simulations of the step, each slightly different from one another. The first four simulations are used to capture the necessary data to construct a simple model of how control perturbations will affect the state of the body at the end of the step. This model is then used to estimate the necessary control perturbations to achieve the desired target state, and hence the desired limit cycle. The fifth simulation is required to produce the final balanced motion for the current step before proceeding on to the next. The blind reconstruction of the RV-perturbation model each step in this fashion results in a five-fold increase in the required computation time compared to normal forward dynamic simulation. If the local perturbation model can itself be predicted, true closed-loop control can be achieved. We are optimistic that this is possible.

The robot model uses very similar choices to the human model's to achieve a running motion. Stance hip variations provide the control perturbations and the chosen RVs are projections of an up vector attached to the creature's head. The primary difference between the control for the two models is in the open loop FSM. Aside from differences in the particular poses, the robot's transition times are smaller than the human FSM (by about half) since the creature's wide stance makes it difficult to remain on one foot for long.

5.3 Torso Servo

While the limit cycle control mechanism described thus far generates stable walks, the resulting motions exhibit a characteristic bobbing of the torso. This is an artifact of the simple open-loop motion chosen as a point of departure for our walking gait. We implement a simple vertical torso servo which not only smoothes the torso motion (if desired), but also demonstrates the robustness of the limit cycle control in continuing to provide effective balance. For LC control, stabilizing a system which already contains some feedback components such as torso servoing is no different than stabilizing an open-loop motion.

The torso servo consists of a PD controller applied to the one degree-of-freedom waist joint. The applied torque at this joint serves to force the torso to always remain upright with respect to the world coordinate frame. Note that the torso servoing does not prevent the biped from falling because the legs must still ultimately

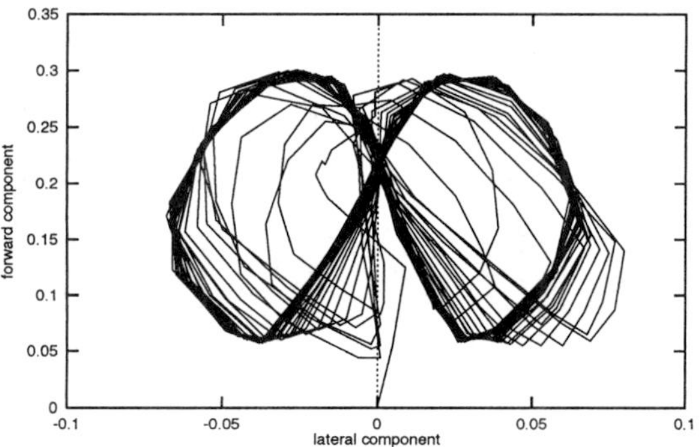

Figure 13. Regulation variable limit cycle (up-vector based).

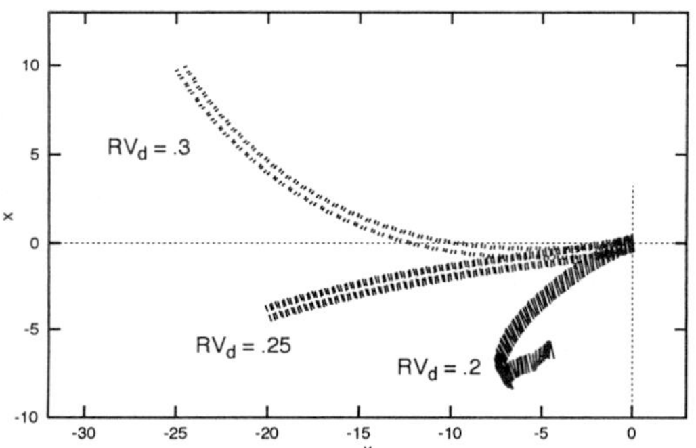

Figure 14. Dynamic walks using the up-vector

provide for balanced support, as illustrated in Figure 12.

6. RESULTS

Limit cycle control has been applied to obtain stable walking gaits for a 19-DOF human model of realistic proportions. As a second example, we control the running motions of a two-legged robot with a bird-like skeleton.

Figure 1 shows a sequence of frames from a typical dynamic walk, resulting from the application of limit cycle control to an open-loop walking motion, with torso servoing enabled.

An illustration of the typical limit cycle which is achieved is shown in Figure 13. The path indicates the continuous-time projection of the unit up vector onto the horizontal plane. This figure is the real analog of the earlier abstraction shown in Figure 3. For walking, the limit cycle consists of two roughly symmetric halves. This occurs because a single cycle consists of a left step and a right step, each forming half of the complete limit cycle for a stride. The desired values for the regulation variables lie at the center of this diagram, at $RV_{forward} = 0.25$, $RV_{lateral} = 0$. Perturbation control is applied on each step, thus forcing the limit cycle towards the desired point twice on each cycle. The startup phase of the motion is also evident from the figure, with the regulation variables eventually being driven onto a stable limit cycle.

While LC control is a general method of adding balance to a walk, it does not by itself ensure a straight walk. Figure 14 illustrates different paths taken for different target values (RV_d) of the regulation variable controlling the desired forward lean. The figure is a top view of the walking motion, showing only the position of the pelvis, enlarged in order to make the orientation of the body clearly visible during the walk. The correct scale for the walk is given by the axes, indicated in metres.

An example of an alternative choice for the set of regulation variables is the use of the swing-center-of-mass (swing-COM) vector. This also leads to stable walks, but not necessarily straight walks. Figure 15 shows how the path can vary as the target value

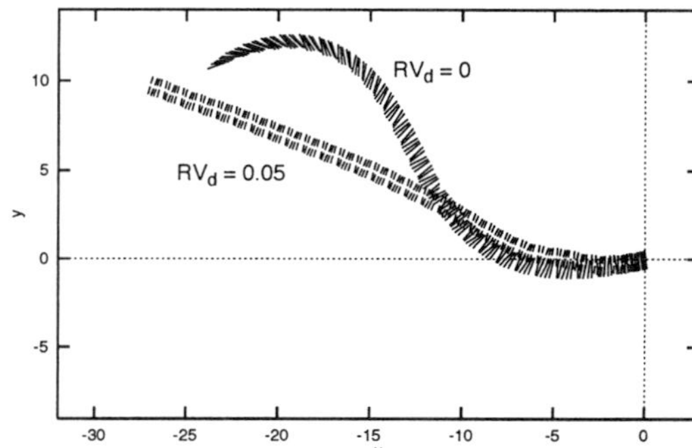

Figure 15. Dynamic walks using the COM-vector.

for the forward component of the vector takes on different values.

The quality of the final motion depends heavily on the open-loop motion on which it is based. The simple four pose FSM used to generate most of the human model walks is quite robust, but produces a motion more akin to a robot marching than to normal human walking. A more human-like walk has been generated by increasing the number of states and changing the timing of the swing leg motions. The use of motion captured data for tuning the open-loop gait for realism presents the possibility of further refining the motion while retaining both the guarantee of realistic motion and the flexible autonomy LC control can provide.

6.1 Additional Animator Control

Control over the speed and direction of a walking gait is of obvious necessity to an animator. Because the stabilization (i.e., balance) of the walk is automated, it is a relatively simple matter to provide the necessary hooks to control these parameters, as well as other possible stylistic variations.

6.2 Speed Control

The speed of the walking gait can be controlled in several ways. One technique we have applied is to alter the underlying open-loop motion to produce particular faster and slower velocity walks and to use interpolations of these *base controllers* to achieve intermediate speeds. Another successful approach makes use the fact that the forward speed is a function of the target values chosen for the regulation variables. As we choose limit cycles for which the pelvis and torso lean forward more, the speed of the gait increases. In this case, a simple form of velocity feedback is used to give consistent, stable steady-state velocities. The RV target value for each step, i, is:

$$RV_d^i = RV_d^* + K(v_d - v)$$

where v and v_d are the actual and desired speeds respectively, K is a proportionality constant, and RV_d^* is a bias term used to relate RV values to speed. Either the bias term or the desired velocity can be used to vary walking speed. Figure 16 illustrates the walking speed for a set of walks obtained using this approach. The startup phase can be recognized during the first several steps and the longest walk demonstrates both positive and negative acceleration phases. All of the motions begin from rest. Only relatively small changes in the final RV target values are required to achieve a reasonable range of speeds. The fastest walk in Figure 16 has $RV_d^i \approx 0.30$ while the slowest walk (nearly stationary) has $RV_d^i \approx 0.25$. These correspond to forward pelvis angles of approximately 17 and 14 degrees from vertical respectively. This technique allows the underlying open loop motion to remain fixed, but tends to reduce motion quality somewhat at higher speeds.

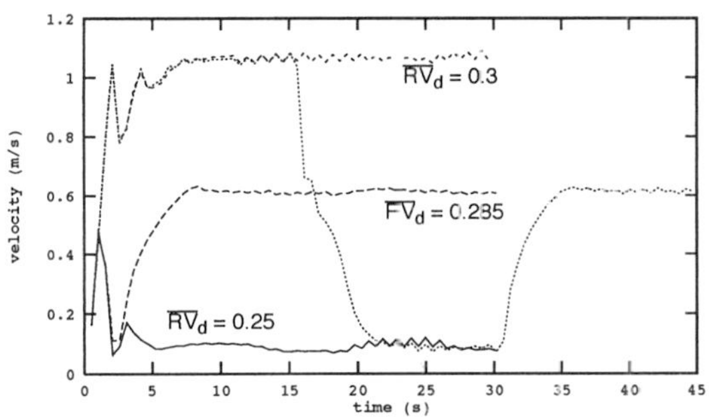

Figure 16. Speed control for a dynamic walk. $\overline{RV}_d$ = steady-state RV_d.

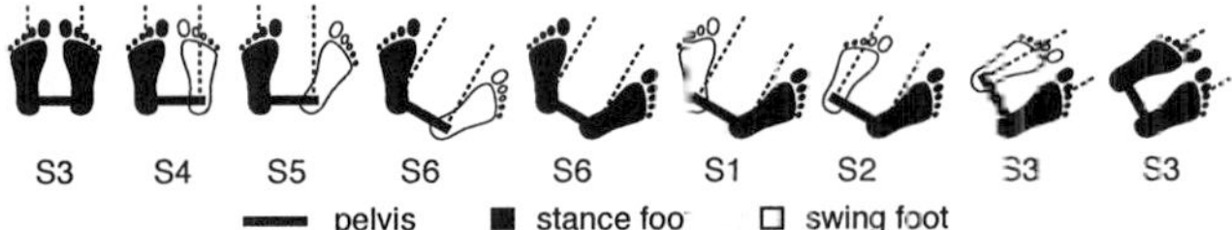

Figure 17. Hip rotations for turning during a walk.

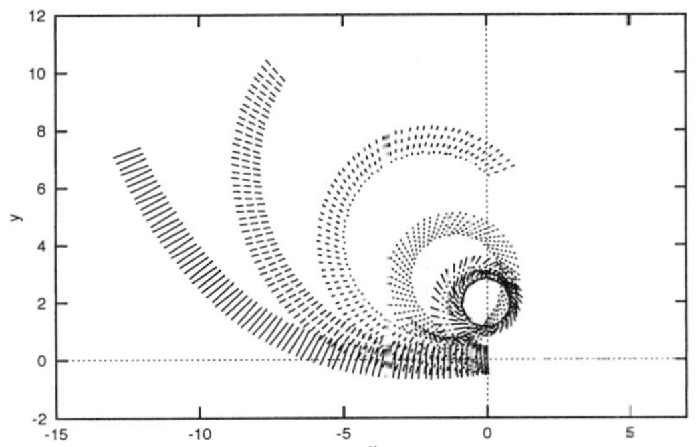

Figure 18. Turning motions for a dynamic walk

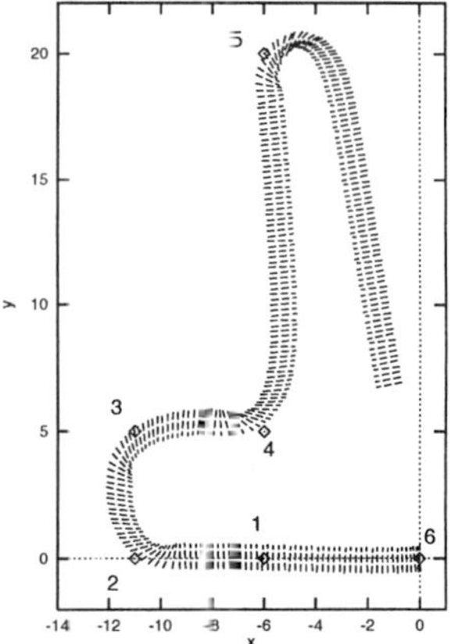

Figure 19. Path following using six target points.

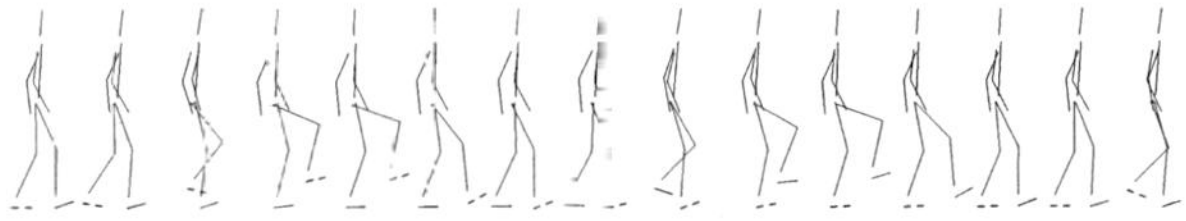

Figure 20. Stylistic variation on a walk.

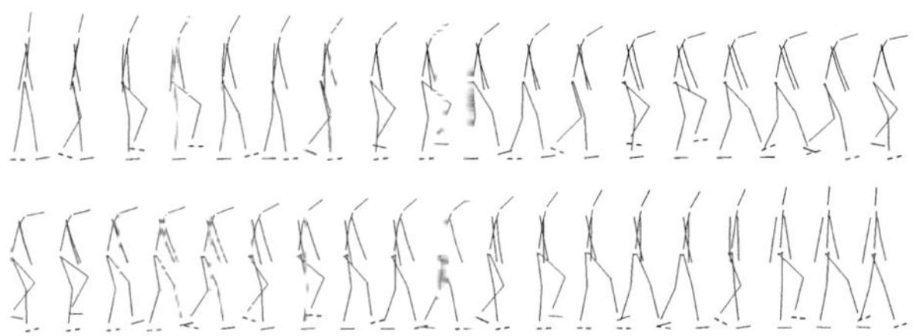

Figure 21. A ducking motion.

6.3 Direction Control

By changing the open-loop motion to include suitable hip twists, controllable turning motions can be achieved. Figure 17 shows a sequence of footprints which illustrate the effect of the hip joint rotations on the orientation of the pelvis for the case of a stationary walk. The figure indicates the hip rotations relative to the pelvis at key points in the walking cycle and the states of the basic FSM (Figure 9) in which they occur. The turning motion works best when torso servoing is applied, in that turns of tighter radius can be performed. Figure 18 shows turns obtained using scaled versions of the twisting motion and stabilized using LC control.

Once the turning radius can be controlled, it can be used to produce a path-following algorithm. Figure 19 shows a dynamic walk following a desired trajectory. The algorithm makes use of a *target point* on the trajectory and chooses a turning rate proportional to the current error in direction. When the target point has almost been reached, its position is updated to be further along the desired path.

6.4 Other Variations

Many other walking styles can be implemented by tailoring the open-loop control as desired. In many cases, transitions between different motions can be performed by simple linear interpolation of the underlying open-loop control over a period of a few steps. In some cases, a more gradual transition or more complex control of the desired RV values is necessary to avoid a fall. In either case, the basic LC control mechanism remains the same. Note that because a dynamic simulation is always being used, ground constraints and other physics constraints are always fulfilled, something that is not necessarily the case with direct kinematic interpolation of motion data, especially for large variations.

Figure 19 illustrates a stylistic variation on a walk with the knees being bent and lifted high on each step. Figure 21 shows a ducking motion obtained by transitioning into and out of a bent-over walk. Stride rate variations can be achieved by changing the duration of time-based state transitions in the open-loop FSM. We have also simulated walking motions into a strong wind, for which the automatic feedback provided by the LC control visibly alters the motion to lean into the wind. In addition to these variations, LC control has proven capable of balancing lateral and backward walking motions obtained using exactly the same open-loop FSM as the forward moving walks. When the human model's initial state has a sufficient backward or lateral velocity component, a balanced walk ensues in the direction of this initial nudge. The application of velocity control to effect transitions into and out of such motions has not yet been attempted but is expected to be relatively straightforward.

As a final example, Figure 22 shows our robot model which can run in a controlled fashion using LC control. This example serves to further illustrate the generality of LC control with respect to significant model and gait variations.

7. CONCLUSIONS

Physically-based animation is difficult because of the lack of general control techniques. Motions such as walking are known to be

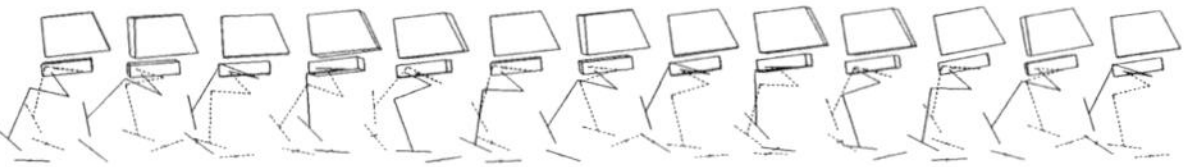

Figure 22. Running motion for the robot.

particularly difficult to control because of their unstable nature. The limit cycle control technique offers an automated way of adding closed-loop control to a basic desired open-loop motion. The open-loop component of the control can be tailored in a variety of ways to produce stylistic variations and useful parameterizations of the motion without any loss of physical realism.

While the human walks obtained are not yet equivalent to motion-capture quality, they are among the first demonstrations that general control techniques can indeed be developed for figures of relatively high complexity performing unstable motions such as walking. For imaginary creatures, physically-based simulation at present provides the best way of ensuring that motions abide by all the laws of physics. Thus, a general method of providing closed-loop control for such simulations is of considerable importance.

In the near future, we foresee integrating the closed-loop motion control developed here with an ever-growing library of other types of skilled motor control in order to produce simulated synthetic actors capable of a truly diverse set of physically-correct behaviors.

8. REFERENCES

[23] J. AUSLANDER ET AL. Further Experience With Controller-based Automatic Motion Synthesis For Articulated Figures. ACM Transactions on Graphics, October 1995.

[1] N. I. BADLER, B. BARSKY and D. ZELTZER. Making them move. Morgan Kaufmann Publishers Inc., 1991.

[2] R. BOULIC, N. M. THALMANN and D. THALMANN. A Global Human Walking Model With Real-time Kinematic Personification. The Visual Computer, 6, 1990, pp. 344-358.

[3] A. BRUDERLIN and T. W. CALVERT. Goal-Directed Animation of Human Walking. Proceedings of SIGGRAPH 89 (1989), In Computer Graphics 23, 4, (1989), pp. 233-242.

[4] A. BRUDERLIN and T. W. CALVERT. Interactive Animation of Personalized Human Locomotion. Proceedings of Graphics Interface (1993), pp. 17-23.

[5] A. BRUDERLIN and L. WILLIAMS. Motion Signal Processing. Proceedings of SIGGRAPH 95 (Los Angeles, August,1995). In Computer Graphics Proceedings, Annual Conference Series, 1994, ACM SIGGRAPH, pp. 97-104.

[6] H. C. CHANG, ET AL. A General Approach For Constructing The Limit Cycle Loci Of Multiple-Nonlinearity Systems. IEEE Transactions on Automatic Control, AC-32, 9, 1987, pp. 845-848.

[7] W. T. DEMPSTER and G. R. L. GAUGHRAN. Properties Of Body Segments Based On Size And Weight. American Journal of Anatomy, 1965, 120, 33-54.

[8] J. FURUSHO and M. MAUBUCHI. A Theoretically Motivated Reduced Order Model for the Control of Dynamic Biped Locomotion. Journal of Dynamic Systems, Measurement, and Control, 109, 1987, pp. 155-163.

[9] J. FURUSHO and A. SANO. Sensor-Based Control of a Nine-Link Robot. The International Journal of Robotics Research, 9, 2, 1990, pp. 83-98.

[10] M. GIRARD. Interactive Design Of Computer-animated Legged Animal Motion. IEEE Computer Graphics and Applications, 7, 6, June, 1987, pp. 39-51.

[11] C. L. GOLLIDAY and H. HEMAMI. An Approach to Analyzing Biped Locomotion Dynamics and Designing Robot Locomotion Controls. IEEE Transactions on Automatic Control, AC-22, 6, 1970, pp. 963-972.

[12] R. GRZESZCZUK and D. TERZOPOULOS. Automated Learning of Muscle-Actuated Locomotion Through Control Abstraction. Proceedings of SIGGRAPH 95 (Los Angeles, California, August 1995). In Computer Graphics Proceedings, Annual Conference Series, 1994, ACM SIGGRAPH, pp. 63-70.

[13] H. M. HMAM and D. A. LAWRENCE. Robustness Analysis of Nonlinear Biped Control Laws Via Singular Perturbation Theory. Proceedings of the 31st IEEE Conference on Decision and Control, 1992, pp. 2656-2661.

[14] J. K. HODGINS ET AL. Animating Human Athletics. Proceedings of SIGGRAPH 95 (Los Angeles, August, 1995). In Computer Graphics Proceedings, Annual Conference Series, 1995, ACM SIGGRAPH, pp. 71-78.

[15] R. KATOH and M. MORI. Control Method of Biped Locomotion Giving Asymptotic Stability Of Trajectory. Automatica, 20, 1984, pp. 405-414.

[16] H. KO and N. I. BADLER. Straight Line Walking Animation Based on Kinematic Generalization that Preserves the Original Characteristics. Proceedings of Graphics Interface '93, 1993, pp. 9-16.

[17] D. E. KODITSCHEK and M. BÜHLER. Analysis Of A Simplified Hopping Robot. The International Journal of Robotics Research, 10, 6, 1991, pp. 587-605.

[18] J. F. LASZLO. Controlling Bipedal Locomotion for Computer Animation, M.A.Sc. thesis, University of Toronto, 1996.
URL: <www.dgp.utoronto.ca/~jflaszlo>

[19] J. M. LIN and K. W. HAN. Reducing The Effects Of Model Reduction On Stability Boundaries And Limit-Cycle Characteristics. IEEE Transactions on Automatic Control, AC-31, 6, 1986, pp. 567-569.

[20] T. MCGEER. Passive Dynamic Walking. The International Journal of Robotics Research, 9, 2, 1990, pp. 62-82.

[21] T. MCGEER. Passive Walking with Knees. Proceedings of IEEE International Conference on Robotics and Automation, 1990, pp. 1640-1645.

[22] M. MCKENNA and D. ZELTZER. Dynamic Simulation of Autonomous Legged Locomotion. Proceedings of SIGGRAPH 90 (1990). In Computer Graphics (1991), pp. 29-38.

[23] H. MIURA and I. SHIMOYAMA. Dynamic Walk Of A Biped. International Journal of Robotics Research, Summer 1984, pp. 60-74.

[24] J. T. NGO and J. MARKS. Spacetime Constraints Revisited. Proceedings of SIGGRAPH 93 (1993). In Computer Graphics Proceedings, Annual Conference Series, 1993, ACM SIGGRAPH, pp. 343-350.

[25] M. H. RAIBERT. Legged Robots that Balance. MIT Press, 1986.

[26] M. H. RAIBERT and J. K. HODGINS. Animation Of Dynamic Legged Locomotion. Proceedings of SIGGRAPH 91 (1991). In Computer Graphics, 1991, pp. 349-358.

[27] SYMBOLIC DYNAMICS INC. SD/Fast User's Manual, 1990.

[28] K. SIMS. Evolving Virtual Creatures. Proceedings of SIGGRAPH 94 (Orlando, Florida, July, 1994). In Computer Graphics Proceedings, Annual Conference Series, 1994, ACM SIGGRAPH, pp. 15-22.

[29] A. J. STEWART and J. F. CREMER. Beyond Keyframing: An Algorithmic Approach to Animation. Proceedings of Graphics Interface '92, 1992, pp. 273-281.

[30] M. UNUMA, K. ANJYO and R. TAKEUCHI. Fourier Principles for Emotion-based Human Figure Animation. Proceedings of SIGGRAPH 95 (Los Angeles, California, August, 1995). In Computer Graphics Proceedings, Annual Conference Series, 1995, ACM SIGGRAPH, pp. 91-96.

[31] M. VAN DE PANNE and E. FIUME. Sensor-Actuator Networks. Proceedings of SIGGRAPH 93, (1993). In Computer Graphics Proceedings, Annual Conference Series, 1993, ACM SIGGRAPH, pp. 335-342.

[32] M. VAN DE PANNE, R. KIM and E. FIUME. Virtual Wind-up Toys for Animation. Proceedings of Graphics Interface '94, 1994, pp. 208-215.

[33] H. G. VISSER and J. SHINAR. First-Order Corrections In Optimal Feedback Control Of Singularly Perturbed Nonlinear Systems. IEEE Transactions on Automatic Control, AC-31, 5, 1986, pp. 387-393.

[34] VUKOBRATOVIC ET AL. Biped Locomotion: Dynamics, Stability, Control and Applications, Springer Verlag, 1990.

[35] A. WITKIN and Z. POPOVI´C. Motion Warping. Proceedings of SIGGRAPH 95 (Los Angeles, California, August, 1995). In Computer Graphics Proceedings, Annual Conference Series, 1995 ACM SIGGRAPH, pp. 105-107.

[36] W. L. WOOTEN and J. K. HODGINS. Simulation Of Human Diving. Proceedings of Graphics Interface '95, 1995, pp. 1-9.

SKETCH: An Interface for Sketching 3D Scenes

Robert C. Zeleznik
Kenneth P. Herndon John F. Hughes
{bcz,kph,jfh}@cs.brown.edu
Brown University site of
the NSF Science and Technology Center
for Computer Graphics and Scientific Visualization
PO Box 1910, Providence, RI 02912

Abstract

Sketching communicates ideas rapidly through approximate visual images with low overhead (pencil and paper), no need for precision or specialized knowledge, and ease of low-level correction and revision. In contrast, most 3D computer modeling systems are good at generating arbitrary views of precise 3D models and support high-level editing and revision. The SKETCH application described in this paper attempts to combine the advantages of each in order to create an environment for *rapidly* conceptualizing and editing *approximate* 3D scenes. To achieve this, SKETCH uses simple non-photorealistic rendering and a purely gestural interface based on simplified line drawings of primitives that allows all operations to be specified *within* the 3D world.

Keywords: Interaction Techniques, 3D Modeling, Gestural Interface, Direct Manipulation, Sketching, Nonphotorealistic Rendering

CR Categories: I.3.8. [Computer Graphics]: Applications; I.3.6. [Computer Graphics]: Methodology and Techniques — Interaction Techniques

1 Introduction

SKETCH targets the exploration and communication of 3D geometric ideas. Traditionally, people have attacked conceptual design with paper and pencil, not with computers, even though computer models offer numerous advantages. The reasons for this include the low overhead of a single-tool interface (pencil), the lack of special knowledge needed to draw, the ease with which many kinds of changes can be made, and the fact that precision is not required to express an idea. Consider Ann sketching a table with an oval top for Joe. Joe gets an immediate sense of the object, without Ann having to indicate the precise locations of the legs, nor the exact shape of the top. By scribbling over what she has sketched, Ann can make the top round or square or freeform without affecting Joe's perception that the legs are attached to the top. (Imagine doing this in a typical CAD or drawing program.) Nevertheless, pencil and paper are still imperfect. After many changes, the paper can become cluttered. Drastic alterations such as showing the model from different viewpoints require new drawings, and collections of drawn objects cannot be transformed as a unit. While computer models do not have these disadvantages, they are typically considerably more difficult to create.

SKETCH is designed to bridge the gap between hand sketches and computer-based modeling programs, combining some of the features of pencil-and-paper sketching and some of the features of CAD systems to provide a lightweight, gesture-based interface to "approximate" 3D polyhedral modeling. Conceptually, our approach is very similar to Landay and Myers' use of sketching to support the early stages of conventional 2D interface design [16]. SKETCH uses a gestural mode of input in which all operations are available directly in the 3D scene through a three-button mouse. The user sketches the salient features of any of a variety of 3D primitives and, following four simple placement rules, SKETCH instantiates the corresponding 3D primitive in the 3D scene. SKETCH allows both geometry and the camera to be gesturally manipulated, and uses an automatic grouping mechanism, similar to that described by Bukowski and Sequin [6], to make it easier to transform aggregates of geometry. Since the set of geometric primitives is more restricted than those in most CAD systems, the user *approximates* complex shapes with aggregates of simpler primitives. Since we know these conceptual models are approximations (often to only partially formed mental images) SKETCH renders them with *non-photorealistic* rendering techniques designed to help viewers see what they want to see.

We also imagine that SKETCH might be used as part of a storyboarding system, for generating a series of scenes and camera views in planning a 3D animation.

The accompanying videotape[1] shows the features of SKETCH and indicates the utility of its simple approach in creating and editing 3D models.

2 Related work

A variety of efforts have been made to simplify the process of generating 3D models, including the "idea sketching" described by Akeo et al. [1]. Akeo allows users to scan real sketches into the computer where they are "marked-up" with perspective vanishing lines and 3D cross sections. The scanned data is then projected onto the 3D mark-up to complete the process.

Nearly all CAD applications employ some form of 2D sketching, although sketching is rarely used in 3D views. A notable exception is Artifice's Design Workshop [2], which allows cubes, walls, and constructive solid geometry (CSG) operations to be constructed directly in the 3D view. However, the overall style of interaction is still menu-oriented and the set of primitives is small.

The considerable work done in the area of drawing interpretation, surveyed by Wang and Grinstein [28], focuses solely on interpreting an entire line drawing at once. In contrast, we attempt to provide a complete interface for progressively conceptualizing 3D scenes using aspects of drawing interpretation to recognize primitives from

[1]The videotape can be obtained upon request from the authors.

a gesture stream. Viking [20] uses a constraint based approach to derive 3D geometry from 2D sketches. In Viking, the user draws line segments, and the system automatically generates a number of constraints which then must be satisfied in order to re-create a 3D shape. The difficulty with these approaches is that even though they are generally restricted to polygonal objects, they are often slow and difficult to implement. In addition, they are often intolerant of noisy input and may either be unable to find a reasonable 3D solution, or may find an unexpected solution. Branco et al. [5] combine drawing interpretation with more traditional 3D modeling tools, like CSG operators in order to simplify the interpretation process; however, their system is limited by a menu-oriented interaction style and does not consider constructing and editing full 3D scenes.

Deering [10], Sachs et al. [22], Galyean and Hughes [11], and Butterworth et al. [7] take a very different approach to constructing 3D models that requires 3D input devices as the primary input mechanism. A variety of systems have incorporated gesture recognition into their user interfaces, including Rubine [21], who uses gesture recognition in a 2D drawing program, but we know of no systems that have extended the use of gesture recognition for 3D modeling.

We also use a variety of direct-manipulation interaction techniques for transforming 3D objects that are related to the work of Snibbe et al. [25], and Strauss and Cary [27]. In addition, we also exploit some very simple flexible constrained manipulation techniques that are similar to those described by Bukowski and Sequin [6]. The latter automatically generates motion constraints for an object directly from that object's semantics. Therefore, for example, when a picture frame is dragged around a room, the frame's back always remains flush with some wall in the room to avoid unnatural situations in which the picture frame might float in mid-air. Also, when a table is manipulated, all of the objects that are on top of the table are automatically moved as well.

In our system, since we have less semantic information than Bukowski, we have less opportunity to automatically generate appropriate constraints, and therefore we occasionally require the user to explicitly sketch constraints in addition to geometry. Our constraint techniques are fast, flexible and almost trivial to implement, but they are not as powerful as the constrained manipulation described by Gleicher [12] or Sistare [24]. Although Gleicher exploits the fact that constraints always start off satisfied, thereby reducing constraint satisfaction to constraint maintenance, he still must solve systems of equations during each manipulation which are often slow and subject to numerical instability. Other approaches like Bier's snap-dragging [4] are also related to our constrained manipulation, although we never present the user with a set of constraint choices from which to select.

Lansdown and Schofield [17] and Salisbury et al. [23] provide interesting techniques for non-photorealistic rendering, although none of these systems specifically targets interactive rendering.

3 The interface

All interaction with SKETCH is via a three-button mouse[2] with occasional use of one modifier key on the keyboard, and a single orthographic window onto the 3D scene. The mouse is used to generate gestures rather than to select operations from menus. Choosing an operation like object creation, transformation or grouping is seamlessly integrated with the natural expression of intent. SKETCH infers intended tools by recognizing gestures — sequences of two types of gestural elements — in its input stream.

Strokes, the first type of gestural element, are pixel-tracks on the film plane[3], made with the first mouse button. There are five classes of strokes shown in Table 1.

Each axis-aligned stroke is aligned with the projection of one the three principal axes of the world. We have also tried aligning strokes with the three principal axes of the surface over which the gesture is drawn. In general, this latter approach seems more effective, although it also presents some difficulties, especially for curved surfaces and for gestures which span over different surfaces. Since we have not yet adequately handled these concerns in our implementation, we will assume for the rest of the paper that all lines are aligned with the world's principal axes except those that are drawn with the "tearing" or freehand strokes.

mouse action	stroke
click and release	dot
click and drag without delaying	axis-aligned line: line follows axis whose screen projection is most nearly parallel to dragged-out segment
click and drag, then "tearing" motion to "rip" line from axis	non-axis-aligned line
click, pause, draw	freehand curve
click with Shift key pressed, draw	freehand curve drawn on *surface* of objects in scene

Table 1: The five stroke classes.

Interactors, the second type of gestural element, are made with the second mouse button. The two classes of interactors, a "click and drag" and a "click," have no visual representation.

In addition to gestural elements, SKETCH supports direct-manipulation of camera parameters with the third mouse button, as outlined in Table 2. Third-button manipulations are not discussed further in this paper.

mouse action	camera manipulation
click and drag	*pan*: point on film plane beneath mouse remains beneath mouse
click, pause, drag	*zoom/vertical pan*: dragging horizontally zoom in/out towards clicked-on point, dragging vertically pan up/down
click near window boundary, drag	*rotate*: performs continuous XY controller rotation about center of screen [8]
click on object	*"focus"*: camera moves so that object is in center of view [18]
shift-click	*change rendering*: cycles through available rendering styles (see Section 5)

Table 2: Gestures for camera manipulation.

4 The implementation

SKETCH processes sequences of *strokes* and *interactors* to perform various modeling functions with a finite-state machine. The mapping between gestural input and modeling functions is easy to remember and gives the user a clear and direct correspondence. However, one of the principal difficulties in developing a good gesture-based interface is managing the delicate tradeoff among gestures that are natural, gestures that are effective, and gestures that are effective within a system that may already use similar gestures for other functions. For superior gestures to evolve, this tradeoff should continue to be explored especially with user studies.

4.1 Creating geometry

We believe gestures can be a natural interface for the fundamentally visual task of creating 3D geometry. The difficulty is choosing the "right" gesture for each geometric primitive. In SKETCH, we define "primary" gestures for instantiating primitives as sequences

[2] We think that a tablet/pen and an active LCD screen implementation might be even better. See Section 6.

[3] A plane perpendicular to the view direction and close enough to the eyepoint not to interfere with the objects in the scene.

of strokes that correspond to important visual features — generally edges — in partial drawings of the primitives. (see Figure 2 for an overview of all such gestures.) For instance, a drawing of three non-collinear line segments which meet at a point imply a corner, based on our visual understanding of drawings [19]; consequently, we interpret similar gestures composed of three line strokes as a cuboid construction operation.

We also provide alternate construction gestures using non-edge strokes. For example, an object of revolution is sketched via its profile and axis, and cuboids can be created by sketching a single edge and two "dimensioning segments" (perpendicular to the edge) that meet at a vertex lying anywhere along this edge. These alternative gestures take their structure from the notions of generative modeling [26].

SKETCH's other primitives — cones, cylinders, spheres, objects of revolution, prisms, extrusions, ducts and superquadrics — have their own gestures. For most, SKETCH forces some aspect of the shapes to be axis-aligned, so that the gestures are easier to both draw and recognize. For example, to create a duct, the user strokes a closed freehand curve for its cross section, and another freehand curve for its path of extrusion. However, an arbitrary 3D curve is not uniquely determined by a single 2D projection, so SKETCH's ducts must have extrusion paths that lie on an axis-aligned plane, specified by a third gesture — an axis-aligned line stroke normal to the plane on which the path of extrusion should be projected.

The small number of primitive objects sometimes requires the user to build up geometry from simpler pieces, and precludes some complex objects — freeform surfaces and true 3D ducts, for example — from being made at all. But in exchange for this, we believe that our small set of primitives minimizes cognitive load on the user and makes gesture recognition and disambiguation easier. Future work, including user studies, should explore this tradeoff.

4.2 Placing geometry

Object creation requires *placement* of the object in the scene. We base object placement on four rules: first, geometry is placed so that its salient features project onto their corresponding gesture strokes in the film plane; second, new objects are instantiated in contact with an existing object when possible; third, certain invariants of junctions in line drawings [9] that indicate the placement or dimension of geometry are exploited; and fourth, CSG subtraction is inferred automatically from the direction of gesture strokes (Figure 2).

These easy-to-understand rules often generate good placement choices; when they do not, users can edit the results. Furthermore, the few users that the system has had so far have rapidly learned to use the simple rules to their advantage, "tricking" the algorithm into doing what they want. (This may be a consequence of their programming background.)

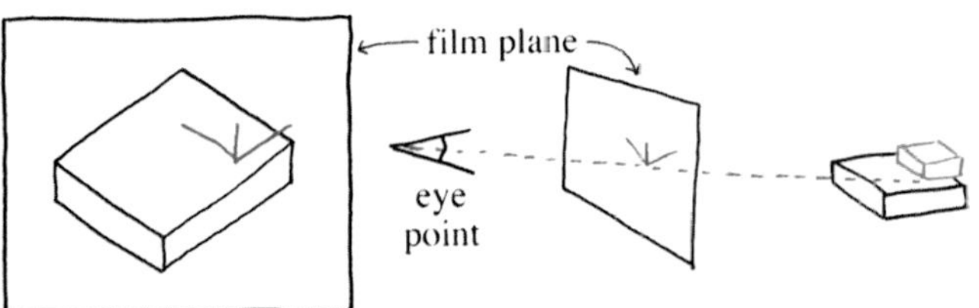

Figure 1: A series of strokes is drawn in the film plane in red (left). The salient vertex is projected into the scene thus defining the placement of new geometry (green). Though this figure suggests a perspective camera, we use a parallel projection in our application.

The first rule determines object placement except for translation along the view direction. This ambiguity is generally resolved by the second rule, implemented as follows: each gesture has a "most salient" vertex (the trivalent vertex for a cuboid, for example, or the first vertex of the two parallel strokes that indicate a cylinder); a ray is traced through this vertex to hit a surface at some point in the scene. The object is then instantiated so that the salient vertex is placed at the intersected surface point (Figure 1).[4]

The third placement rule exploits invariants of vertex junctions in line drawings, as described by Clowes [9]. However, our use of T junctions is related to the treatment given by Lamb and Bandopadhay [15]. In particular, T-shaped junctions arise in line drawings when a line indicating the edge of one surface, *Estem*, ends somewhere along a line segment indicating the edge of another surface, *Ebar*. These junctions generally signify that the surface associated with *Estem* is occluded by the surface associated with *Ebar*, although it does not necessarily indicate that the two surfaces meet. In SKETCH, a similar notion exists when a straight line segment (except for connected polyline segments) of a gesture ends along an edge of an object already in the scene (Figure 3). To uphold the intuition that such T junctions indicate the occlusion of one surface by another, SKETCH first places the gesture line into the 3D scene according to the previous two placement rules. Then, SKETCH sends a ray out along the gesture line (toward the T junction). If this ray intersects the object that defined the bar of the T junction and the normal at the point of intersection is pointed in approximately the opposite direction of the ray, then the gesture edge is extended so that it will meet that surface.

If the ray does not intersect the surface, then the object defined by the surface is translated along the viewing vector toward the viewer until its edge exactly meets the end of the gesture edge. If the end of the gesture edge is never met (because it was farther away from the viewer), then neither the gesture, nor the existing objects are modified. We never translate objects away from the viewer as a result of T junctions; tests of this behavior on a variety of users indicated that it was both unintuitive and undesirable.

The final rule determines whether the new geometry should be CSG-subtracted from the scene when added to it. If one or more of the gesture strokes are drawn *into* an existing surface (i.e., the dot product of a stroke and the normal to the existing surface on which it is drawn is negative), then the new piece of geometry is placed in the scene and subtracted from the existing object (Figure 2). CSG subtraction is recomputed each time the new geometry is manipulated. If the new geometry is moved out of the surface from which it was subtracted, CSG subtraction is no longer recomputed. This makes possible such constructions as the desk drawer in the Editing-Grouping-Copying section of the videotape.

4.3 Editing

SKETCH supports multiple techniques for editing geometry. Some exploit paper and pencil editing techniques by recognizing editing gestures composed of strokes (e.g., oversketching and drawing shadows). Others use gestures that contain an interactor to transform shapes as a whole by translation or rotation.

Resizing. A common way to "resize" a surface with pencil and paper is to sketch back and forth over its bounding lines until they are of the right size. SKETCH recognizes a similar "oversketching" gesture to reshape objects. If two approximately coincident lines are drawn in opposite directions nearly parallel to an existing edge, SKETCH infers a resizing operation (Figure 2). This sketching operation works for all primitives constructed of straight line segments, including cubes, cylinders and extrusions. Additionally, the two endpoints of an extrusion path can be attached to two objects

[4] If the ray intersects no surface (possible because we use a finite ground rectangle instead of an infinite ground plane), the object is placed in the plane perpendicular to the view direction that passes through the origin; this turns out in practice to be a reasonable compromise.

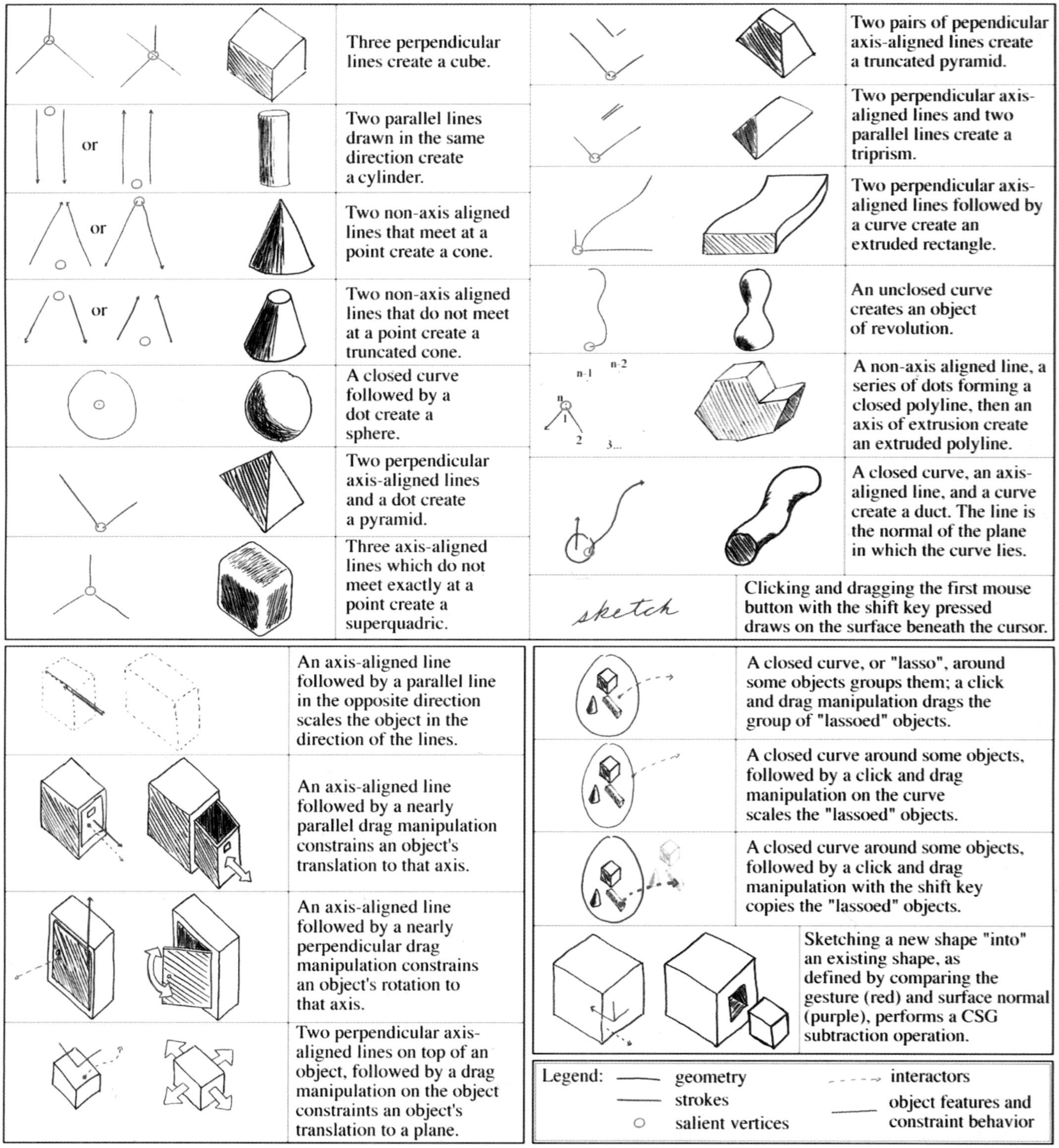

or

Three perpendicular lines create a cube.

Two parallel lines drawn in the same direction create a cylinder.

Two non-axis aligned lines that meet at a point create a cone.

Two non-axis aligned lines that do not meet at a point create a truncated cone.

A closed curve followed by a dot create a sphere.

Two perpendicular axis-aligned lines and a dot create a pyramid.

Three axis-aligned lines which do not meet exactly at a point create a superquadric.

Two pairs of pependicular axis-aligned lines create a truncated pyramid.

Two perpendicular axis-aligned lines and two parallel lines create a triprism.

Two perpendicular axis-aligned lines followed by a curve create an extruded rectangle.

An unclosed curve creates an object of revolution.

n-1 n-2 n 1 2 3...

A non-axis aligned line, a series of dots forming a closed polyline, then an axis of extrusion create an extruded polyline.

A closed curve, an axis-aligned line, and a curve create a duct. The line is the normal of the plane in which the curve lies.

sketch

Clicking and dragging the first mouse button with the shift key pressed draws on the surface beneath the cursor.

An axis-aligned line followed by a parallel line in the opposite direction scales the object in the direction of the lines.

An axis-aligned line followed by a nearly parallel drag manipulation constrains an object's translation to that axis.

An axis-aligned line followed by a nearly perpendicular drag manipulation constrains an object's rotation to that axis.

Two perpendicular axis-aligned lines on top of an object, followed by a drag manipulation on the object constraints an object's translation to a plane.

A closed curve, or "lasso", around some objects groups them; a click and drag manipulation drags the group of "lassoed" objects.

A closed curve around some objects, followed by a click and drag manipulation on the curve scales the "lassoed" objects.

A closed curve around some objects, followed by a click and drag manipulation with the shift key copies the "lassoed" objects.

Sketching a new shape "into" an existing shape, as defined by comparing the gesture (red) and surface normal (purple), performs a CSG subtraction operation.

Legend: geometry; strokes; salient vertices; interactors; object features and constraint behavior

Figure 2: Gestures for creating and manipulating shapes, and for applying constraints.

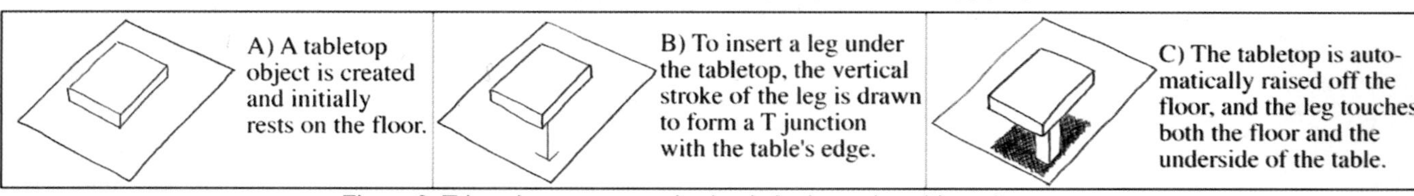

Figure 3: T junctions are recognized to help determine object placement.

in the scene; whenever either object moves, the extrusion will resize to maintain the span. However, general reshaping of objects defined by freehand curves is more difficult and not yet fully implemented. We are currently adapting Baudel's mark-based interaction paradigm [3] for use in reshaping 3D objects.

Sketching shadows. Shadows are an important cue for determining the depth of an object in a scene [29]. In SKETCH, we exploit this relationship by allowing users to edit an object's position by drawing its shadow. The gesture for this is first to stroke a dot over an object, and then to stroke its approximate shadow — a set of impressionistic line strokes — on another surface using the Shift modifier key.[5] The dot indicates which object is being shadowed, and the displacement of the shadow from the object determines the new position for the object (as if there were a directional light source directed opposite to the normal of the surface on which the shadow is drawn). The resulting shadow is also "interactive" and can be manipulated as described by Herndon et al. [13].

Transforming. Objects can be transformed as a unit by using a "click-and-drag" interactor (with the second mouse button): the click determines the object to manipulate, and the drag determines the amount and direction of the manipulation. By default, objects are constrained to translate, while following the cursor, along the locally planar surface on which they were created. However, this motion can be further constrained or can be converted to a rotational motion.

It is important to keep in mind that our interaction constraints are all very simple. In SKETCH, instead of using a constraint solver capable of handling a wide variety of constraints, we associate an interaction handler with each geometric object. This handler contains constraint information including which plane or axis an object is constrained to translate along, or which axis an object is constrained to rotate about. Then when the user manipulates an object, all of the mouse motion data is channeled through that object's handler which converts the 2D mouse data into constrained 3D transformations. To define which of our simple constraints is active, we require that the user explicitly specify the constraint with a gesture. Whenever a new constraint is specified for an object it will persist until another constraint is specified for that object. Each new constraint for an object overwrites any previous constraint on the object.

The advantages of such a simple constraint system are that it is robust, fast, and easy to understand. A more sophisticated constraint engine would allow a greater variety of constrained manipulation, but it would also require that the user be aware of which constraints were active and how each constraint worked. It would also require additional gestures so that the user could specify these other constraints.

Systems such as Kurlander and Feiner's [14] attempt to infer constraints from multiple drawings, but this approach has the drawback that multiple valid configurations of the system need to be made in order to define a constraint. Such approaches may also infer constraints that the user never intended, or may be too limited to be able to infer constraints that a user wants.

Constrained transformation. The gestures for constraining object transformations to single-axis translation or rotation, or to plane-aligned translation are composed of a series of strokes that define the constraint, followed by a "click-and-drag" interactor to perform the actual manipulation (Figure 2). To constrain the motion of an object to an axis-aligned axis, the user first strokes a constraint axis, then translates the object with an interactor by clicking and dragging parallel to the constraint axis. The constraint axis is stroked just as if a new piece of geometry were being constructed; however, since this stroke is followed by an interactor, a translation gesture is recognized and no geometry is created. Similarly, if the user drags perpendicular to the constraint axis instead of parallel to it, the gesture is interpreted as a single axis rotation. (This gesture roughly corresponds to the motion one would use in the real world to rotate an object about an axis.)

To translate in one of the three axis-aligned planes, two perpendicular lines must be stroked on an object. The directions of these two lines determine the plane in which the object is constrained to translate. If the two perpendicular lines are drawn over a different object from the one manipulated, they are interpreted as a *contact* constraint (although non-intuitive, this gesture is effective in practice). This forces the manipulated object to move so that it is always in contact with *some* surface in the scene (but not necessarily the object over which the gesture was drawn) while tracking the cursor. Finally, a dot stroke drawn on an object before using an interactor is interpreted as the viewing vector; the object will be constrained to translate along this vector. This constraint is particularly useful for fine-tuning the placement of an object if SKETCH has placed it at the "wrong" depth; however, since we use an orthographic view that does not automatically generate shadows, feedback for this motion is limited to seeing the object penetrate other objects in the scene. We believe that a rendering mode in which shadows were automatically generated for all objects would be beneficial, although we have not implemented such a mode because of the expected computational overhead. We did, however, mock up a rendering mode in which just the manipulated object automatically cast its shadow on the rest of the scene. People in our group generally found the shadow helpful, but were slightly disturbed that none of the other objects cast shadows.

In each case, the manipulation constraint, once established, is maintained during subsequent interactions until a new constraint is drawn for that object. The only exception is that single axis rotation and single axis translation constraints can both be active at the same time; depending on how the user gestures — either mostly parallel to the translation axis or mostly perpendicular to the rotation axis — a translation or rotation operation, respectively, is chosen.

Finally, objects are removed from the scene by clicking on them with an interactor gesture. In early versions of SKETCH we used an apparently more natural gesture to remove objects: the user "tossed" them away by translating them with a quick throwing motion, as one might brush crumbs from a table. We found, however, that this gesture presented a complication: it was too easy to toss out the wrong object, especially if its screen size were small.

4.4 Grouping and copying

By default, objects are automatically unidirectionally grouped with the surface on which they were created, an idea borrowed from Bukowski and Sequin [6], generally resulting in hierarchical scenes. Each geometric object in SKETCH contains a list of objects that are grouped to it. Whenever an object is transformed, that object will also apply the same transformation to all other objects that are grouped to it; each grouped object will in turn transform all objects grouped to itself. Cycles can occur and are handled by allowing each object to move only once for each mouse motion event.

This kind of hierarchical scene is generally easier to manipulate than a scene without groupings since the grouping behavior typically corresponds to both expected and useful relationships among objects. For example, objects drawn on top of a table move whenever the table is manipulated, but when the objects are manipulated, the table does not follow. Grouping also applies to non-vertical relationships, so a picture frame drawn on a wall is grouped with the wall.

In some cases, grouping is bidirectional. The choice of bidirectional and uni-directional grouping is guided by what we be-

[5]Recall from Table 1 that Shift-modified strokes normally produce lines drawn on the surface of objects without special interpretation.

lieve is an inherent difference in the way people interpret relationships between certain horizontal versus vertical drawing elements. When an object is drawn that extends horizontally between two surfaces, like a rung on a ladder, the two surfaces that are spanned are grouped bidirectionally, so that if one rail of the ladder moves so does the other. Although the rung moves whenever either rail is manipulated, the rails do not move when the rung is manipulated. The grouping relationship for objects that span vertically, however, establishes only one-way relationships: the topmost object is unidirectionally grouped to the bottommost object and the spanning object is similarly grouped to the topmost object. Thus, a table leg that spans between a floor and a table top causes the top to be grouped to the floor and the leg to be grouped to the top, but the floor is *not* grouped to the top. We only exploit the difference between horizontal and vertical elements to distinguish these two grouping relationships. However we believe it is important to study with user tests how effective this automatic grouping approach actually is, and perhaps to determine as well if there are other ways that we might be able to exploit the differences between vertical and horizontal elements.

Unlike Bukowski, object grouping is not automatically recomputed as objects are moved around the scene. Therefore, if an object is moved away from a surface, it will still be grouped with the surface. Grouping relationships are recomputed only when objects are moved using the contact constraint mentioned in Section 4.3 — the moved object is grouped to the surface it now contacts and ungrouped from any surface it no longer contacts. We have found this approach to automatic grouping to be simple and effective, although in some environments, Bukowski's approach may be more appropriate.

Lassoing groups. SKETCH also allows the user to explicitly establish groups by stroking a *lasso* around them (Figure 2).[6] Deciding which objects are considered *inside* the lasso is based on the heuristic that the geometric center and all of the visible corners of the object must be inside the lasso; shapes like spheres must be completely contained in the lasso. SKETCH currently approximates this heuristic by first projecting an object's geometric center and all of its crease vertices (where there is a discontinuity in the derivative of the surface) and silhouette vertices into the film plane, then testing whether all these projected points are contained within the lasso. Currently, no test is made for whether objects are occluded or not; future work should address the ambiguities that arise in using the lasso operation.

All lassoed objects are copied if they are manipulated while the Shift modifier is used. Lassoed objects can be scaled by dragging the lasso itself.

Repeating gestures. A different form of copying is used when a user wants to repeat the last geometry-creation operation. After SKETCH recognizes gesture strokes corresponding to a geometric construction, it creates and places the new geometry in the scene, but *does not erase* the gesture strokes. Thus, the user can click on any of these strokes (using button 1) in order to "drag and drop" (re-execute) them elsewhere. Gesture strokes are erased when a new gesture is started or when any object is manipulated. These techniques are shown in the videotape.

5 Rendering

SKETCH renders orthographic views of 3D scenes using a conventional z-buffer. Color Plates I-VI show some of the rendering techniques that SKETCH supports.

[6]The lasso gesture is similar to the sphere gesture. We differentiate between them by requiring that the sphere gesture be followed by a dot stroke, whereas the lasso is simply a free-hand closed curve stroke followed by a manipulation gesture.

"Sketchy" rendering styles are essential because they often enable users to focus on the essence of a problem rather than unimportant details. Non-photorealistic rendering draws a user's attention away from imperfections in the *approximate* scenes she creates while also increasing the scene's apparent complexity and ambiguity. By making scenes more ambiguous, users can get beyond SKETCH's approximate polygonal models to see what they want to see. This is an important concept: we do not believe that sketchy rendering adds noise to a signal; rather we believe that it conveys the very wide tolerance in the user's initial estimates of shape. The user is saying "I want a box *about* this long by *about* that high and *about* that deep." Showing a picture of a box with *exactly* those dimensions is misleading, because it hides the important information that the dimensions are not yet completely determined.

A line drawing effect is achieved by rendering all polygonal objects completely white, and then rendering the outlines and prominent edges of the scene geometry with multiple deliberately jittered lines; the z-buffer therefore handles hidden-line removal. A charcoal effect is created by mapping colors to grayscale and increasing the ambient light in the scene; a watercolor effect that washes out colors is created by increasing the scene's ambient light. There are a number of other techniques that we would like to explore, including pen and ink style textures, and drawing hidden edges with dashed lines.

Objects are assigned a default random color when they are created to help differentiate them from the scenery. We can also copy colors from one object to another. By just placing the cursor on top of one object and pressing the Shift modifier, we can "pick up" that object's color. Then, we can "drop" this color on another object by placing the cursor over it and releasing the modifier. We can also explicitly specify colors or textures for objects. In our present implementation, we do this by placing the cursor over the object and typing the name of the color or texture. Although this interface requires the keyboard, it is consistent with SKETCH's interface philosophy of not making users search through a 2D interface for tools to create particular effects. In the future, we expect that voice recognition, perhaps in conjunction with gesturing, will be a more effective way to establish surface properties for objects (and perhaps other operations as well).

6 Future Work

We regard SKETCH as a proof-of-concept application, but it has many flaws. Many of the gestures were based on an ad hoc trial and error approach, and some of the gestures still do not satisfy us. For example, the pause in the freehand curve gesture rapidly becomes annoying in practice — the user wants to do something, and is forced to wait. Possible solutions of course include using more modifier keys, although we would rather find a solution that preserves the simplicity of the interface.

SKETCH is based on an interface that is stretched to its limits. We expect that adding just a few more gestures will make the system hard to learn and hard to use. We'd like to perform user studies on ease of use, ease of learning, and expressive power for novice users as a function of the number of gestures. We're also interested in trying to determine to what extent artistic and spatial abilities influence users' preference for sketching over other modeling interfaces.

We have begun to implement a tablet-based version of SKETCH. The current generation of tablet pens include pressure sensitivity in addition to a single finger-controlled button, and one "eraser-like" button. In order to develop an equivalent interface for the tablet, we simply need to treat a specific pressure level as a button click to achieve the equivalent of three buttons. Therefore, the button 1 drawing interactions described for the mouse are done by simply pressing hard enough with the penpoint of the tablet pen. To achieve the button 2 operations of the mouse, the user simply presses the finger controlled button on the tablet pen. Finally, to effect camera motion, the user turns the pen over and uses its "eraser" to manipulate the camera. Our initial efforts with a tablet based interface lead us to believe that a tablet based system could be far more effective than a mouse based system, especially if pressure sensitivity is cleverly exploited.

SKETCH is a tool for initial design — the "doodling" stage, where things are deliberately imprecise. But initial design work should not be cast away, and we are examining ways to export models from SKETCH to modelers that support more precise editing, so that the sketch can be moved towards a final design. Since subsequent analysis and design often requires re-thinking of some initial choices, we are also interested in the far more difficult task of re-importing refined models into SKETCH and then re-editing them, without losing the high-precision information in the models except in the newly-sketched areas.

The scenes shown here and in the video are relatively simple. Will sketching still work in a complex or cluttered environments? We do not yet have enough experience to know. Perhaps gestures to indicate an "area of interest," which cause the remainder of the scene to become muted and un-touchable might help.

The tradeoffs in gesture design described in Section 4 must be further explored, especially with user-studies.

7 Acknowledgments

Thanks to Dan Robbins, Tim Miller, and Lee Markosian for many helpful discussions. Thanks also to Andries van Dam and the Graphics Group, as well as our sponsors: grants from NASA, NSF, Microsoft, Sun and Taco; hardware from SGI, HP and Sun.

References

[1] M. Akeo, H. Hashimoto, T. Kobayashi, and T. Shibusawa. Computer graphics system for reproducing three-dimensional shape from idea sketch. *Eurographics '94 Proceedings*, 13(3):477–488, 1994.

[2] Artifice, Inc. Design Workshop. Macintosh application.

[3] T. Baudel. A mark-based interaction paradigm for free-hand drawing. *UIST '94 Proceedings*, pages 185–192, Nov. 1994.

[4] E.A. Bier. Snap-dragging in three dimensions. *Computer Graphics (1990 Symposium on Interactive 3D Graphics)*, 24(2):193–204, Mar. 1990.

[5] V. Branco, A. Costa, and F.N. Ferriera. Sketching 3D models with 2D interaction devices. *Eurographics '94 Proceedings*, 13(3):489–502, 1994.

[6] R. Bukowski and C. Séquin. Object associations: A simple and practical approach to virtual 3D manipulation. *Computer Graphics (1995 Symposium on Interactive 3D Graphics)*, pages 131–138, Apr. 1995.

[7] J. Butterworth, A. Davidson, S. Hench, and T.M. Olano. 3DM: A three dimensional modeler using a head-mounted display. *Computer Graphics (1992 Symposium on Interactive 3D Graphics)*, 25(2):135–138, Mar. 1992.

[8] M. Chen, S. Joy Mountford, and Abigail Sellen. A study in interactive 3-D rotation using 2-D control devices. *Computer Graphics (SIGGRAPH '88 Proceedings)*, 22(4):121–129, August 1988.

[9] M. Clowes. On seeing things. *Artificial Intelligence*, (2):79–116, 1971. North-Holland.

[10] M. Deering. Holosketch: A virtual reality sketching/animation tool. *ACM Transactions on Computer-Human Interaction*, 2(3):220–238, 1995.

[11] T. Galyean and J. Hughes. Sculpting: An interactive volumetric modeling technique. *Computer Graphics (SIGGRAPH '91 Proceedings)*, 25(4):267–274, July 1991.

[12] M. Gleicher. Integrating constraints and direct manipulation. *Computer Graphics (1992 Symposium on Interactive 3D Graphics)*, 25(2):171–174, March 1992.

[13] K.P. Herndon, R.C. Zeleznik, D.C. Robbins, D.B. Conner, S.S. Snibbe, and A.van Dam. Interactive shadows. *UIST '92 Proceedings*, pages 1–6, Nov. 1992.

[14] D. Kurlander and S. Feiner. Inferring constraints from multiple snapshots. *ACM Transactions on Graphics*, 12(4):277–304, Oct. 1993.

[15] D. Lamb and A. Bandopadhay. Interpreting a 3D object from a rough 2D line drawing. *Visualization '90 Proceedings*, pages 59–66, 1990.

[16] J.A. Landay and B.A. Myers. Interactive sketching for the early stages of user interface design. *Proceedings of CHI'95*, pages 43–50, 1995.

[17] J. Lansdown and S. Schofield. Expressive rendering: A review of nonphotorealistic techniques. *IEEE Computer Graphics & Applications*, pages 29–37, May 1995.

[18] J.D. Mackinlay, S.K. Card, and G.G. Robertson. Rapid controlled movement through a virtual 3d workspace. In *Proceedings of the 1986 Workshop on Interactive 3D Graphics*, pages 171–176, October 1986.

[19] G. Magnan. *Using technical art: An industry guide*. John Wiley and Sons, Inc., 1970.

[20] D. Pugh. Designing solid objects using interactive sketch interpretation. *Computer Graphics (1992 Symposium on Interactive 3D Graphics)*, 25(2):117–126, Mar. 1992.

[21] D. Rubine. Specifying gestures by example. *Computer Graphics (SIGGRAPH '91 Proceedings)*, 25(4):329–337, July 1991.

[22] E. Sachs, A. Roberts, and D. Stoops. 3-draw: A tool for designing 3D shapes. *IEEE Computer Graphics & Applications*, pages 18–25, Nov. 1991.

[23] M. Salisbury, S. Anderson, R. Barzel, and D. Salesin. Interactive pen–and–ink illustration. *Computer Graphics (SIGGRAPH '94 Proceedings)*, pages 101–108, July 1994.

[24] S. Sistare. Graphical interaction techniques in constraint-based geometric modeling. *Proceedings of Graphics Interface '91*, pages 85–92, June 1991.

[25] S.S. Snibbe, K.P. Herndon, D.C. Robbins, D.B. Conner, and A. van Dam. Using deformations to explore 3D widget design. *Computer Graphics (SIGGRAPH '92 Proceedings)*, 26(2):351–352, July 1992.

[26] J.M. Snyder and J.T. Kajiya. Generative modeling: A symbolic system for geometric modeling. *Computer Graphics (SIGGRAPH '92 Proceedings)*, 26(2):369–378, July 1992.

[27] P. Strauss and R. Carey. An object-oriented 3D graphics toolkit. *Computer Graphics (SIGGRAPH '92 Proceedings)*, 26(2):341–349, July 1992.

[28] W. Wang and G. Grinstein. A survey of 3D solid reconstruction from 2D projection line drawings. *Computer Graphics Forum*, 12(2):137–158, June 1993.

[29] L.R. Wanger, J.A. Ferwerda, and D.P. Greenberg. Perceiving spatial relationships in computer-generated images. *IEEE Computer Graphics and Applications*, 12(3):44–58, May 1992.

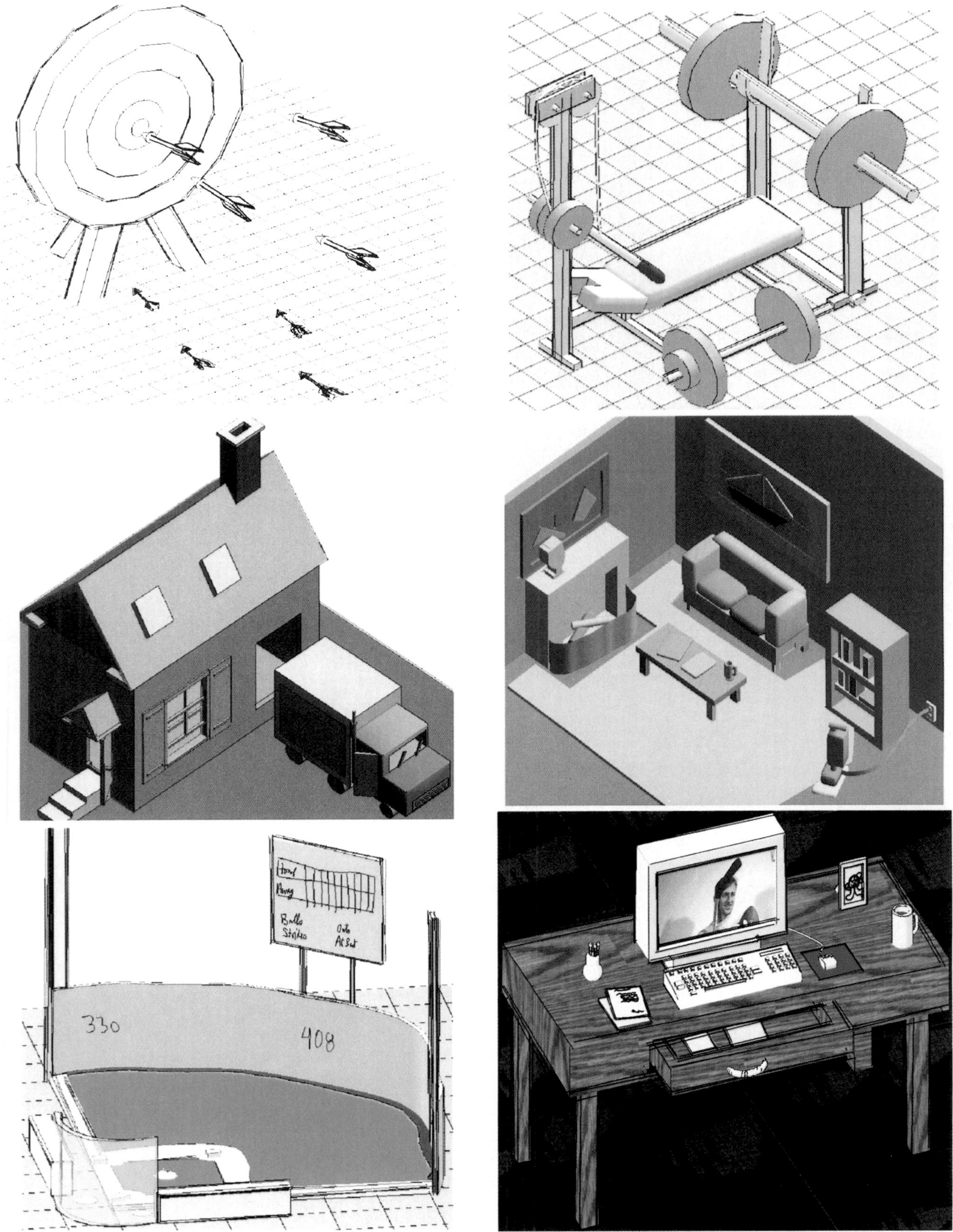

Color Plates I–VI: Sample images

OBBTree: A Hierarchical Structure for Rapid Interference Detection

S. Gottschalk M. C. Lin* D. Manocha
Department of Computer Science
University of North Carolina
Chapel Hill, NC 27599-3175
{gottscha,lin,manocha}@cs.unc.edu
http://www.cs.unc.edu/~geom/OBB/OBBT.html

Abstract: We present a data structure and an algorithm for efficient and exact interference detection amongst complex models undergoing rigid motion. The algorithm is applicable to all general polygonal models. It pre-computes a hierarchical representation of models using tight-fitting oriented bounding box trees (OBBTrees). At runtime, the algorithm traverses two such trees and tests for overlaps between oriented bounding boxes based on a separating axis theorem, which takes less than 200 operations in practice. It has been implemented and we compare its performance with other hierarchical data structures. In particular, it can robustly and accurately detect all the contacts between large complex geometries composed of hundreds of thousands of polygons at interactive rates.

CR Categories and Subject Descriptors: I.3.5 [Computer Graphics]: Computational Geometry and Object Modeling

Additional Key Words and Phrases: hierarchical data structure, collision detection, shape approximation, contacts, physically-based modeling, virtual prototyping.

1 Introduction

The problems of interference detection between two or more geometric models in static and dynamic environments are fundamental in computer graphics. They are also considered important in computational geometry, solid modeling, robotics, molecular modeling, manufacturing and computer-simulated environments. Generally speaking, we are interested in very efficient and, in many cases, real-time algorithms for applications with the following characterizations:

1. **Model Complexity:** The input models are composed of many hundreds of thousands of polygons.

2. **Unstructured Representation:** The input models are represented as collections of polygons with no topology information. Such models are also known as 'polygon soups' and their boundaries may have cracks, T-joints, or may have non-manifold geometry. No robust techniques are known for cleaning such models.

3. **Close Proximity:** In the actual applications, the models can come in close proximity of each other and can have multiple contacts.

4. **Accurate Contact Determination:** The applications need to know accurate contacts between the models (up to the resolution of the models and machine precision).

Many applications, like dynamic simulation, physically-based modeling, tolerance checking for virtual prototyping, and simulation-based design of large CAD models, have all these four characterizations. Currently, fast interference detection for such applications is a major bottleneck.

Main Contribution: We present efficient algorithms for accurate interference detection for such applications. They make no assumptions about model representation or the motion. The algorithms compute a hierarchical representation using *oriented bounding boxes (OBBs)*. An OBB is a rectangular bounding box at an arbitrary orientation in 3-space. The resulting hierarchical structure is referred to as an OBBTree. The idea of using OBBs is not new and many researchers have used them extensively to speed up ray tracing and interference detection computations. Our major contributions are:

1. New efficient algorithms for hierarchical representation of large models using tight-fitting OBBs.

2. Use of a 'separating axis' theorem to check two OBBs in space (with arbitrary orientation) for overlap. Based on this theorem, we can test two OBBs for overlap in about 100 operations on average. This test is about one order of magnitude faster compared to earlier algorithms for checking overlap between boxes.

3. Comparison with other hierarchical representations based on sphere trees and *axis-aligned bounding boxes (AABBs)*. We show that for many close proximity situations, OBBs are asymptotically much faster.

4. Robust and interactive implementation and demonstration. We have applied it to compute all contacts between very complex geometries at interactive rates.

The rest of the paper is organized in the following manner: We provide a comprehensive survey of interference detection methods in Section 2. A brief overview of the algorithm is given in Section 3. We describe algorithms for efficient computation of OBBTrees in Section 4. Section 5 presents the separating-axis theorem and shows how it can be used to compute overlaps between two OBBs very efficiently. We compare its performance with hierarchical representations composed of spheres and AABBs in Section 6. Section 7 discusses the implementation and performance of the algorithms on complex models. In Section 8, we discussion possible future extensions.

*Also with U.S. Army Research Office

2 Previous Work

Interference and collision detection problems have been extensively studied in the literature. The simplest algorithms for collision detection are based on using bounding volumes and spatial decomposition techniques in a hierarchical manner. Typical examples of bounding volumes include axis-aligned boxes (of which cubes are a special case) and spheres, and they are chosen for to the simplicity of finding collision between two such volumes. Hierarchical structures used for collision detection include cone trees, k-d trees and octrees [31], sphere trees [20, 28], R-trees and their variants [5], trees based on S-bounds [7] etc. Other spatial representations are based on BSP's [24] and its extensions to multi-space partitions [34], spatial representations based on space-time bounds or four-dimensional testing [1, 6, 8, 20] and many more. All of these hierarchical methods do very well in performing "rejection tests", whenever two objects are far apart. However, when the two objects are in close proximity and can have multiple contacts, these algorithms either use subdivision techniques or check very large number of bounding volume pairs for potential contacts. In such cases, their performance slows down considerably and they become a major bottleneck in the simulation, as stated in [17].

In computational geometry, many theoretically efficient algorithms have been proposed for polyhedral objects. Most of them are either restricted to static environments, convex objects, or only polyhedral objects undergoing rigid motion [9]. However, their practical utility is not clear as many of them have not been implemented in practice. Other approaches are based on linear programming and computing closest pairs for convex polytopes [3, 10, 14, 21, 23, 33] and based on line-stabbing and convex differences for general polyhedral models [18, 26, 29]. Algorithms utilizing spatial and temporal coherence have been shown to be effective for large environments represented as union of convex polytopes [10, 21]. However, these algorithms and systems are restrictive in terms of application to general polygonal models with unstructured representations. Algorithms based on interval arithmetic and bounds on functions have been described in [12, 13, 19]. They are able to find all the contacts accurately. However, their practical utility is not clear at the moment. They are currently restricted to objects whose motion can be expressed as a closed form function of time, which is rarely the case in most applications. Furthermore, their performance is too slow for interactive applications.

OBBs have been extensively used to speed up ray-tracing and other interference computations [2]. In terms of application to large models, two main issues arise: how can we compute a tight-fitting OBB enclosing a model and how quickly can we test two such boxes for overlap? For polygonal models, the minimal volume enclosing bounding box can be computed in $O(n^3)$ time, where n is the number of vertices [25]. However, it is practical for only small models. Simple incremental algorithms of linear time complexity are known for computing a minimal enclosing ellipsoid for a set of points [36]. The axes of the minimal ellipsoid can be used to compute a tight-fitting OBB. However, the constant factor in front of the linear term for this algorithm is very high (almost 3×10^5) and thereby making it almost impractical to use for large models. As for ray-tracing, algorithms using structure editors [30] and modeling hierarchies [35] have been used to construct hierarchies of OBBs. However, they cannot be directly applied to compute tight-fitting OBBs for large unstructured models.

A simple algorithm for finding the overlap status of two OBBs tests all edges of one box for intersection with any of the faces of the other box, and vice-versa. Since OBBs are convex polytopes, algorithms based on linear programming [27] and closest features computation [14, 21] can be used as well. A general purpose interference detection test between OBBs and convex polyhedron is presented in [16]. Overall, efficient algorithms were not known for computing hierarchies of tight-fitting OBBs for large unstructured models, nor were efficient algorithms known for rapidly checking the overlap status of two such OBBTrees.

3 Hierarchical Methods & Cost Equation

In this section, we present a framework for evaluating hierarchical data structures for interference detection and give a brief overview of OBBTrees. The basic cost function was taken from [35], who used it for analyzing hierarchical methods for ray tracing. Given two large models and their hierarchical representation, the total cost function for interference detection can be formulated as the following cost equation:

$$T = N_v \times C_v + N_p \times C_p, \qquad (1)$$

where

T: total cost function for interference detection,
N_v: number of bounding volume pair overlap tests
C_v: cost of testing a pair of bounding volumes for overlap,
N_p: is the number primitive pairs tested for interference,
C_p: cost of testing a pair of primitives for interference.

Given this cost function, various hierarchical data structures are characterized by:

Choice of Bounding Volume: The choice is governed by two conflicting constraints:

1. It should fit the original model as tightly as possible (to lower N_v and N_p).
2. Testing two such volumes for overlap should be as fast as possible (to lower C_v).

Simple primitives like spheres and AABBs do very well with respect to the second constraint. But they cannot fit some primitives like long-thin oriented polygons tightly. On the other hand, minimal ellipsoids and OBBs provide tight fits, but checking for overlap between them is relatively expensive.

Hierarchical Decomposition: Given a large model, the tree of bounding volumes may be constructed bottom-up or top-down. Furthermore, different techniques are known for decomposing or partitioning a bounding volume into two or more sub-volumes. The leaf-nodes may correspond to different primitives. For general polyhedral models, they may be represented as collection of few triangles or convex polytopes. The decomposition also affects the values of N_v and N_p in (1).

It is clear that no hierarchical representation gives the best performance all the times. Furthermore, given two models, the total cost of interference detection varies considerably with relative placement of the models. In particular, when two models are far apart, hierarchical representations based on spheres and AABBs work well in practice. However, when two models are in close proximity with multiple number of closest features, the number of pair-wise bounding volume tests, N_v increases, sometimes also leading to an increase in the number pair-wise primitive contact tests, N_p.

For a given model, N_v and N_p for OBBTreestend to be smaller as compared to those of trees using spheres or AABBs as bounding volumes. At the same time, the best known earlier algorithms for finding contact status of two OBBs were almost two orders of magnitude slower than checking two spheres or two AABBs for overlap. We present efficient algorithms for computing tight fitting OBBs given a set of polygons, for constructing a hierarchy of OBBs, and for testing two OBBs for contact. Our algorithms are able to compute tight-fitting hierarchies effectively and the overlap test between two OBBs is one order of magnitude faster than best known earlier methods. Given sufficiently large models, our interference detection algorithm based on OBBTrees much faster as compared to using sphere trees or AABBs.

4 Building an OBBTree

In this section we describe algorithms for building an OBB-Tree. The tree construction has two components: first is the placement of a tight fitting OBB around a collection of polygons, and second is the grouping of nested OBB's into a tree hierarchy.

We want to approximate the collection of polygons with an OBB of similar dimensions and orientation. We triangulate all polygons composed of more than three edges. The OBB computation algorithm makes use of first and second order statistics summarizing the vertex coordinates. They are the mean, μ, and the covariance matrix, C, respectively [11]. If the vertices of the i'th triangle are the points $\mathbf{p}^i$, $\mathbf{q}^i$, and $\mathbf{r}^i$, then the mean and covariance matrix can be expressed in vector notation as:

$$\mu = \frac{1}{3n}\sum_{i=0}^{n}(\mathbf{p}^i + \mathbf{q}^i + \mathbf{r}^i),$$

$$\mathbf{C}_{jk} = \frac{1}{3n}\sum_{i=0}^{n}(\overline{\mathbf{p}}^i_j\overline{\mathbf{p}}^i_k + \overline{\mathbf{q}}^i_j\overline{\mathbf{q}}^i_k + \overline{\mathbf{r}}^i_j\overline{\mathbf{r}}^i_k), \qquad 1 \le j,k \le 3$$

where n is the number of triangles, $\overline{\mathbf{p}}^i = \mathbf{p}^i - \mu$, $\overline{\mathbf{q}}^i = \mathbf{q}^i - \mu$, and $\overline{\mathbf{r}}^i = \mathbf{r}^i - \mu$. Each of them is a 3×1 vector, e.g. $\overline{\mathbf{p}}^i = (\overline{\mathbf{p}}^i_1, \overline{\mathbf{p}}^i_2, \overline{\mathbf{p}}^i_3)^T$ and $\mathbf{C}_{jk}$ are the elements of the 3 by 3 covariance matrix.

The eigenvectors of a symmetric matrix, such as C, are mutually orthogonal. After normalizing them, they are used as a basis. We find the extremal vertices along each axis of this basis, and size the bounding box, oriented with the basis vectors, to bound those extremal vertices. Two of the three eigenvectors of the covariance matrix are the axes of maximum and of minimum variance, so they will tend to align the box with the geometry of a tube or a flat surface patch.

The basic failing of the above approach is that vertices on the interior of the model, which ought not influence the selection of a bounding box placement, can have an arbitrary impact on the eigenvectors. For example, a small but very dense planar patch of vertices in the interior of the model can cause the bounding box to align with it.

We improve the algorithm by using the convex hull of the vertices of the triangles. The convex hull is the smallest convex set containing all the points and efficient algorithms of $O(n \lg n)$ complexity and their robust implementations

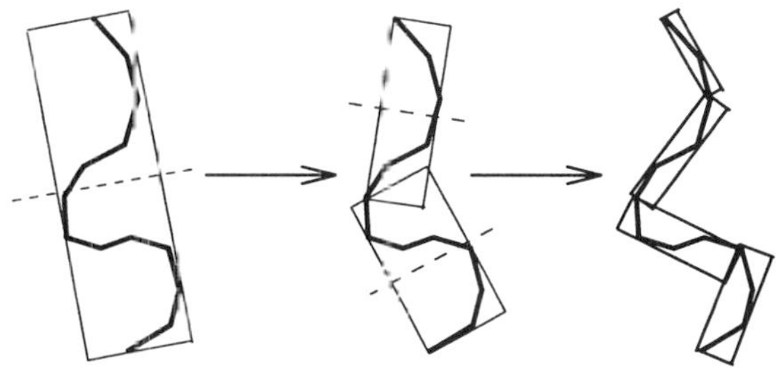

Figure 1: Building the OBBTree: recursively partition the bounded polygons and bound the resulting groups.

are available as public domain packages [4]. This is an improvement, but still suffers from a similar sampling problem: a small but very dense collection of nearly collinear vertices on the convex hull can cause the bounding box to align with that collection.

One solution is to sample the surface of the convex hull densely, taking the mean and covariance of the sample points. The uniform sampling of the convex hull surface normalizes for triangle size and distribution.

One can sample the convex hull "infinitely densely" by integrating over the surface of each triangle, and allowing each differential patch to contribute to the covariance matrix. The resulting integral has a closed form solution. We let a point $\mathbf{x}^i$ in the i'th triangle be parameterized by s and t as in:

$$\mathbf{x}^i = \mathbf{p}^i + s(\mathbf{q}^i - \mathbf{p}^i) + t(\mathbf{r}^i - \mathbf{p}^i), \qquad s,t \in [0,1]$$

The mean point of the convex hull is then

$$\mu = \frac{1}{n}\sum_{i=1}^{n}\left(\frac{1}{m^i}\int_0^1\int_0^{1-t}\mathbf{x}^i\,ds\,dt\right) = \frac{1}{6n}\sum_{i=1}^{n}\frac{1}{m^i}(\mathbf{p}^i+\mathbf{q}^i+\mathbf{r}^i)$$

where m^i = area of i'th triangle $= \frac{1}{2}|(\mathbf{q}^i-\mathbf{p}^i)\times(\mathbf{r}^i-\mathbf{p}^i)|$. The elements of the covariance matrix C have the following closed-form,

$$\mathbf{C}_{jk} = \frac{1}{24n}\sum_{i=1}^{n}m^i[(\overline{\mathbf{p}}^i_j + \overline{\mathbf{q}}^i_j + \overline{\mathbf{r}}^i_j)(\overline{\mathbf{p}}^i_k + \overline{\mathbf{q}}^i_k + \overline{\mathbf{r}}^i_k) + \overline{\mathbf{p}}^i_j\overline{\mathbf{p}}^i_k + \overline{\mathbf{q}}^i_j\overline{\mathbf{q}}^i_k + \overline{\mathbf{r}}^i_j\overline{\mathbf{r}}^i_k], \qquad 1 \le j,k \le 3$$

where $\overline{\mathbf{p}}^i = \mathbf{p}^i - \mu$, $\overline{\mathbf{q}}^i = \mathbf{q}^i - \mu$, and $\overline{\mathbf{r}}^i = \mathbf{r}^i - \mu$.

Given an algorithm to compute tight-fitting OBBs around a group of polygons, we need to represent them hierarchically. Most methods for building hierarchies fall into two categories: bottom-up and top-down. Bottom-up methods begin with a bounding volume for each polygon and merge volumes into larger volumes until the tree is complete. Top-down methods begin with a group of all polygons, and recursively subdivide until all leaf nodes are indivisible. In our current implementation, we have used a simple top-down approach.

Our subdivision rule is to split the longest axis of a box with a plane orthogonal to one of its axes, partitioning the polygons according to which side of the plane their center point lies on (a 2-D analog is shown in Figure 1). The subdivision coordinate along that axis was chosen to be that of the mean point, μ, of the vertices. If the longest axis cannot not be subdivided, the second longest axis is chosen. Otherwise, the shortest one is used. If the group of polygons cannot be partitioned along any axis by this criterion, then the group is considered indivisible.

If we choose the partition coordinate based on where the median center point lies, then we obtain balanced trees. This arguably results in optimal worst-case hierarchies for collision detection. It is, however, extremely difficult to evaluate average-case behavior, as performance of collision detection algorithms is sensitive to specific scenarios, and no single algorithm performs optimally in all cases.

Given a model with n triangles, the overall time to build the tree is $O(n \lg^2 n)$ if we use convex hull, and $O(n \lg n)$ if we don't. The recursion is similar to that of quicksort. Processing fitting a box to a group of n triangles partitioning them into two subgroups takes $O(n \lg n)$ with convex hull and $O(n)$ without it. Applying the process recursively creates a tree with leaf nodes $O(\lg n)$ levels deep.

5 Fast Overlap Test for OBBs

Given OBBTrees of two objects, the interference algorithm typically spends most of its time testing pairs of OBBs for overlap. A simple algorithm for testing the overlap status for two OBB's performs 144 edge-face tests. In practice, it is an expensive test. Other algorithms based on linear programming and closest features computation exist. In this section, we present a new algorithm to test such boxes for overlap.

One trivial test for disjointness is to project the boxes onto some axis (not necessarily a coordinate axis) in space. This is an 'axial projection.' Under this projection, each box forms an interval on the axis. If the intervals don't overlap, then the axis is called a 'separating axis' for the boxes, and the boxes must then be disjoint. If the intervals do overlap, then the boxes may or may not be disjoint – further tests may be required.

How many such tests are sufficient to determine the contact status of two OBBs? We know that two disjoint convex polytopes in 3-space can always be separated by a plane which is parallel to a face of either polytope, or parallel to an edge from each polytope. A consequence of this is that two convex polytopes are disjoint iff there exists a separating axis orthogonal to a face of either polytope or orthogonal to an edge from each polytope. A proof of this basic theorem is given in [15]. Each box has 3 unique face orientations, and 3 unique edge directions. This leads to 15 potential separating axes to test (3 faces from one box, 3 faces from the other box, and 9 pairwise combinations of edges). If the polytopes are disjoint, then a separating axis exists, and one of the 15 axes mentioned above will be a separating axis. If the polytopes are overlapping, then clearly no separating axis exists. So, testing the 15 given axes is a sufficient test for determining overlap status of two OBBs.

To perform the test, our strategy is to project the centers of the boxes onto the axis, and also to compute the radii of the intervals. If the distance between the box centers as projected onto the axis is greater than the sum of the radii, then the intervals (and the boxes as well) are disjoint. This is shown in 2D in Fig. 2.

We assume we are given two OBBs, A and B, with B placed relative to A by rotation $\mathbf{R}$ and translation $\mathbf{T}$. The half-dimensions (or 'radii') of A and B are a_i and b_i, where $i = 1, 2, 3$. We will denote the axes of A and B as the unit

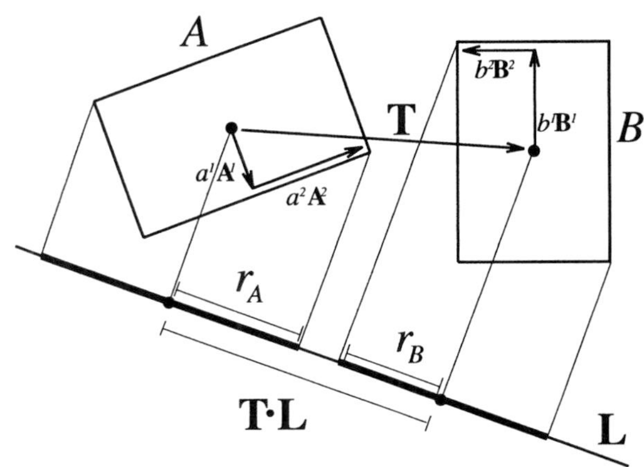

Figure 2: $\mathbf{L}$ is a separating axis for OBBs A and B because A and B become disjoint intervals under projection onto $\mathbf{L}$.

vectors $\mathbf{A}^i$ and $\mathbf{B}^i$, for $i = 1, 2, 3$. These will be referred to as the 6 box axes. Note that if we use the box axes of A as a basis, then the three columns of $\mathbf{R}$ are the same as the three $\mathbf{B}^i$ vectors.

The centers of each box projects onto the midpoint of its interval. By projecting the box radii onto the axis, and summing the length of their images, we obtain the radius of the interval. If the axis is parallel to the unit vector $\mathbf{L}$, then the radius of box A's interval is

$$r_A = \sum_i |a_i \mathbf{A}^i \cdot \mathbf{L}|$$

A similar expression is used for r_B.

The placement of the axis is immaterial, so we assume it passes through the center of box A. The distance between the midpoints of the intervals is $|\mathbf{T} \cdot \mathbf{L}|$. intervals. So, the intervals are disjoint iff

$$|\mathbf{T} \cdot \mathbf{L}| > \sum_i |a_i \mathbf{A}^i \cdot \mathbf{L}| + \sum_i |b_i \mathbf{B}^i \cdot \mathbf{L}|$$

This simplifies when $\mathbf{L}$ is a box axis or cross product of box axes. For example, consider $\mathbf{L} = \mathbf{A}^1 \times \mathbf{B}^2$. The second term in the first summation is

$$\begin{aligned} |a_2 \mathbf{A}^2 \cdot (\mathbf{A}^1 \times \mathbf{B}^2)| &= |a_2 \mathbf{B}^2 \cdot (\mathbf{A}^2 \times \mathbf{A}^1)| \\ &= |a_2 \mathbf{B}^2 \cdot \mathbf{A}^3| \\ &= |a_2 \mathbf{B}^2_3| \\ &= a_2 |\mathbf{R}_{32}| \end{aligned}$$

The last step is due to the fact that the columns of the rotation matrix are also the axes of the frame of B. The original term consisted of a dot product and cross product, but reduced to a multiplication and an absolute value. Some terms reduce to zero and are eliminated. After simplifying all the terms, this axis test looks like:

$$|\mathbf{T}_3 \mathbf{R}_{22} - \mathbf{T}_2 \mathbf{R}_{32}| > a_2 |\mathbf{R}_{32}| + a_3 |\mathbf{R}_{22}| + b_1 |\mathbf{R}_{13}| + b_3 |\mathbf{R}_{11}|$$

All 15 axis tests simplify in similar fashion. Among all the tests, the absolute value of each element of $\mathbf{R}$ is used four times, so those expressions can be computed once before beginning the axis tests. The operation tally for all 15 axis tests are shown in Table 1. If any one of the expressions is satisfied, the boxes are known to be disjoint, and the remainder of the 15 axis tests are unnecessary. This permits early exit from the series of tests, so 200 operations is the absolute *worst case*, but often much fewer are needed.

Degenerate OBBs: When an OBB bounds only a single polygon, it will have zero thickness and become a rectangle. In cases where a box extent is known to be zero, the expressions for the tests can be further simplified. The operation counts for overlap tests are given in Table 1, including when one or both boxes degenerate into a rectangle. Further reductions are possible when a box degenerates to a line segment. Nine multiplies and ten additions are eliminated for every zero thickness.

OBBs with infinite extents: Also, when one or more extents are known to be infinite, as for a fat ray or plane, certain axis tests require a straight-forward modification. For the axis test given above, if a_2 is infinite, then the inequality cannot possibly be satisfied unless $\mathbf{R}_{32}$ is zero, in which case the test proceeds as normal but with the $a_2|\mathbf{R}_{32}|$ term removed. So the test becomes,

$$\begin{aligned} \mathbf{R}_{32} &= 0 \textbf{ and} \\ |\mathbf{T}_3\mathbf{R}_{22} - \mathbf{T}_2\mathbf{R}_{32}| &> a_3|\mathbf{R}_{22}| + b_1|\mathbf{R}_{13}| + b_3|\mathbf{R}_{11}| \end{aligned}$$

In general, we can expect that $\mathbf{R}_{32}$ will not be zero, and using a short-circuit **and** will cause the more expensive inequality test to be skipped.

Operation	Box-Box	Box-Rect	Rect-Rect
compare	15	15	15
add/sub	60	50	40
mult	81	72	63
abs	24	24	24

Table 1: Operation Counts for Overlap Tests

Comparisons: We have implemented the algorithm and compared its performance with other box overlap algorithms. The latter include an efficient implementation of closest features computation between convex polytopes [14] and a fast implementation of linear programming based on Seidel's algorithm [33]. Note that the last two implementations have been optimized for general convex polytopes, but not for boxes. All these algorithms are much faster than performing 144 edge-face intersections. We report the average time for checking overlap between two OBBs in Table 2. All the timings are in microseconds, computed on a HP 735/125.

Sep. Axis Algorithm	Closest Features	Linear Programming
5 – 7 us	45 – 105 us	180 – 230 us

Table 2: Performance of Box Overlap Algorithms

6 OBB's vs. other Volumes

The primary motivation for using OBBs is that, by virtue of their variable orientation, they can bound geometry more tightly than AABBTrees and sphere trees. Therefore, we reason that, all else being the same, fewer levels of an OBBTree need to be be traversed to process a collision query for objects in close proximity. In this section we present an analysis of asymptotic performance of OBBTrees versus AABBTrees and sphere trees, and an experiment which supports our analysis.

In Fig. 9(at the end), we show the different levels of hierarchies for AABBTrees and OBBTrees while approximating a torus. The number of bounding volumes in each tree at each level is the same. The ϵ for OBBTrees is much smaller as compared to ϵ for the AABBTrees.

First, we define *tightness*, *diameter*, and *aspect ratio* of a bounding volume with respect to the geometry it covers. The *tightness*, τ, of a bounding volume, B, with respect to the geometry it covers, G, is B's Hausdorff distance from G. Formally, thinking of B and G as closed point sets, this is

$$\tau = \max_{b \in B} \min_{g \in G} \mathsf{dist}(b, g)$$

The diameter, d, of a bounding volume with respect to the bounded geometry is the maximum distance among all pairs of enclosed points on the bounded geometry,

$$d = \max_{g,h \in G} \mathsf{dist}(g, h)$$

The *aspect ratio*, ρ, of a bounding volume with respect to bounded geometry is $\rho = \tau/d$.

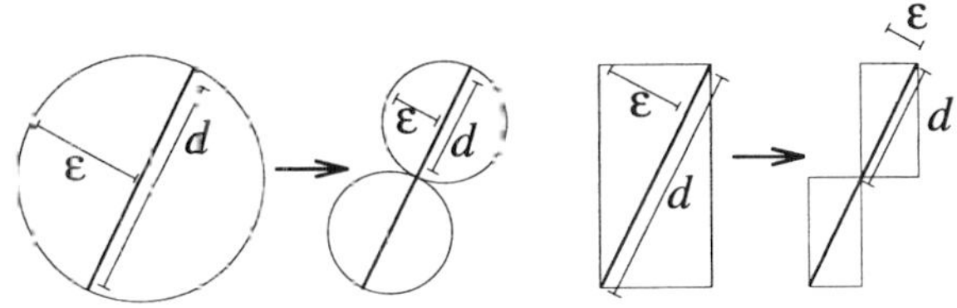

Figure 3: Aspect ratios of parent volumes are similar to those of children when bounding nearly flat geometry.

We argue that when bounded surfaces have low curvature, AABBTrees and sphere trees form fixed aspect ratio hierarchies, in the sense that the aspect ratio of a node in the hierarchy will have an aspect ratio similar to its children. This is illustrated in Fig. 3 for plane curves. If the bounded geometry is nearly flat, then the children will have shapes similar to the parents, but smaller. In Fig 3 for both spheres and AABBs, d and τ are halved as we go from parents to children, so $\rho = d/\tau$ is approximately the same for both parent and child. For fixed aspect ratio hierarchies, τ has linear dependence on d.

Note that the aspect ratio for AABBs is very dependent on the specific orientation of the bounded geometry – if the geometry is conveniently aligned, the aspect ratio can be close to 0, whereas if it is inconveniently aligned, ρ can be close to 1. But whatever the value, an AABB enclosing nearly flat geometry will have approximately the same ρ as its children.

Since an OBB aligns itself with the geometry, the aspect ratio of an OBB does not depend on the geometry's orientation in model space. Rather, it depends more on the local curvature of the geometry. For the sake of analysis, we are assuming nearly flat geometry. Suppose the bounded geometry has low constant curvature, as on the surface of a large sphere. In Fig. 4 we show a plane curve of fixed radius of curvature r and bounded by an OBB. We have $d = 2r \sin\theta$, and $\tau = r - r\cos\theta$. Using the small angle approximation and eliminating θ, we obtain $\tau = d^2/8r$. So

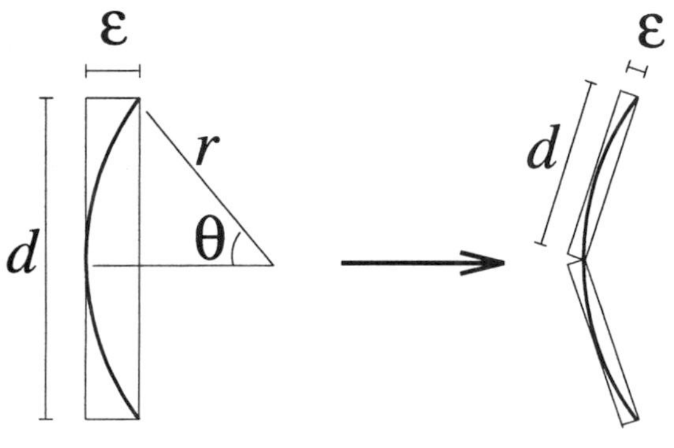

Figure 4: OBBs: Aspect ratio of children are half that of parent when bounding surfaces of low constant curvature when bounding nearly flat geometry.

τ has quadratic dependence on d. When d is halved, τ is quartered, and the aspect ratio is halved.

We conclude that when bounding low curvature surfaces, AABBTrees and spheres trees have τ with linear dependence on d, whereas OBBTrees have τ with quadratic dependence on d. We have illustrated this for plane curves in the figures, but the relationships hold for surfaces in three space as well.

Suppose we use N same-sized bounding volumes to cover a surface patch with area A and require each volume to cover $O(A/N)$ surface area (for simplicity we are ignoring packing inefficiencies). Therefore, for these volumes, $d = O(\sqrt{A/N})$. For AABBs and spheres, τ depends linearly on d, so $\tau = O(\sqrt{A/N})$. For OBBs, quadratic dependence on d gives us OBBs, $\tau = O(A/N)$. So, to cover a surface patch with volumes to a given tightness, if OBBs require $O(m)$ bounding volumes, AABBs and spheres would require $O(m^2)$ bounding volumes.

Most contact scenarios do not require traversing both trees to all nodes of a given depth, but this does happen when two surfaces come into *parallel close proximity* to one another, in which every point on each surface is close to some point on the other surface. This is most common in virtual prototyping and tolerance analysis applications, in which fitted machine parts are tested for mechanical consistency. Also, dynamic simulations often generate paths in which one object comes to rest against another. It should be also be noted that when two smooth, highly tessellated surfaces come into near contact with each other, the region of near contact locally resembles a parallel close proximity scenario in miniature, and, for sufficiently tessellated models, the expense of processing that region can dominate the overall collision query. So, while it may seem like a very special case, parallel close proximity is an abstract situation which deserves consideration when designing collision and evaluating collision detection algorithms.

Experiments: We performed two experiments to support our analysis. For the first, we generated two concentric spheres consisting of 32,000 triangles each. The smaller sphere had radius 1, while the larger had radius $1+\epsilon$. We performed collision queries with both OBBTrees and AABBTrees. The AABBTrees were created using the same process as for OBBTrees, except that instead of using the eigenvectors of the covariance matrix to determine the box orientations, we used the identity matrix.

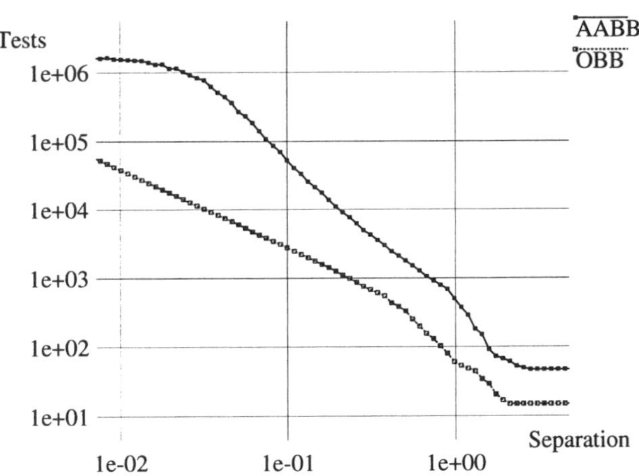

Figure 5: AABBs (upper curve) and OBBs (lower curve) for parallel close proximity (log-log plot)

The number of bounding box overlap tests required to process the collision query are shown in Fig. 5 for both tree types, and for a range of ϵ values. The graph is a log-log plot. The upper curve is for AABBTrees, and the lower, OBBTrees. The slopes of the the linear portions the upper curve and lower curves are approximately -2 and -1, as expected from the analysis. The differing slopes of these curves imply that OBBTrees require asymptotically fewer box tests as a function of ϵ than AABBTrees in our experiment.

Notice that the curve for AABBTrees levels off for the lowest values of ϵ. For sufficiently small values of ϵ, even the lowest levels of the AABBTree hierarchies are inadequate for separating the two surfaces – all nodes of both are visited, and the collision query must resort to testing the triangles. Decreasing ϵ even further cannot result in more work, because the tree does not extend further than the depth previously reached. The curve for the OBBTrees will also level off for some sufficiently small value of ϵ, which is not shown in the graph. Furthermore, since both trees are binary and therefore have the same number of nodes, the OBBTree curve will level off at the same height in the graph as the AABBTree curve.

For the second experiment, two same-size spheres were placed next to each other, separated by a distance of ϵ. We call this scenario *point close proximity*, where two nonparallel surfaces patches come close to touching at a point. We can think of the surfaces in the neighborhood of the closest points as being in parallel close proximity – but this approximation applies only locally. We have not been able to analytically characterize the performance, so we rely instead on empirical evidence to claim that for this scenario OBBTrees require asymptotically fewer bounding box overlap tests as a function of ϵ than AABBTrees. The results are shown in Fig. 6. This is also a log-log plot, and the increasing gap between the upper and lower curves show the asymptotic difference in the number of tests as ϵ decreases. Again, we see the leveling off for small values of ϵ.

Analysis: A general analysis of the performance of collision detection algorithms which use bounding volume hierarchies is extremely difficult because performance is so situation specific. We assumed that the geometry being bounded had locally low curvature and was finely tessel-

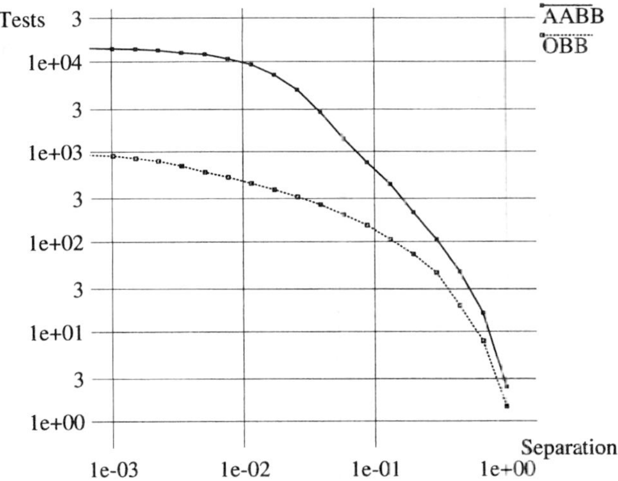

Figure 6: AABBs (upper curve) and OBBs (lower curve) for point close proximity. (log-log plot)

lated. This enabled the formulation of simple relationships between τ and d. We also assumed that the packing efficiency of bounding volumes was perfect so as to formulate the relationships between d and the area of the surface covered. We believe that the inaccuracies of these assumptions account for the deviations from theory exhibited in the graph of Fig. 5.

For surface patches with high curvature everywhere, such as a 3D fractal, we may not expect to see asymptotic performance advantages for OBBs. Similarly, a coarse tessellation of a surface will place a natural limit on the number, N, the number of volumes used to approximate the surface. For a coarse tessellation, OBB-, sphere-, and AABBTrees may have to traverse their entire hierarchies for sufficiently close proximity scenarios, thus requiring approximately the same number of bounding volume overlap tests. Furthermore, for scenarios in which parallel close proximity does not occur, we don't expect the quadratic convergence property of OBBs to be of use, and again don't expect to see superior asymptotic performance.

7 Implementation and Performance

The software for the collision detection library was written in C++. The primary data structure for an OBB is a "box" class whose members contain a rotation matrix and translation vector, defining its placement relative to its parent, pointers to its parent and two children, the three box dimensions, and an object which holds a list of the triangles the box contains. The overall data structure for the box occupies 168 bytes. The tree formed from boxes as nodes, and the triangle list class, are the only compound data structures used.

An OBBTree of n triangles contains n leaf boxes and $n-1$ internal node boxes. In terms of memory requirements, there are approximately two boxes per triangle. The triangle itself requires 9 double precision numbers plus an integer for identification, totaling 76 bytes (based on 64-bit IEEE arithmetic). The memory requirement therefore totals 412 bytes per triangle in the model. This estimate does not include whatever overhead may exist in the dynamic memory allocation mechanism of the runtime environment. Using quaternions instead of rotation matrices (to represent box orientations), results in substantial space savings, but need 13 more operations per OBB overlap test. Single precision arithmetic can also be used to save memory.

7.1 Robustness and Accuracy

The algorithm and the implementations are applicable to all unstructured polygonal models. The polygons are permitted to be degenerate, with two or even one unique vertex, have no connectivity restrictions. The algorithm requires no adjacency information. This degree of robustness gives the system wider applicability. For example, space curves can be approximated by degenerate triangles as line segments – the system will correctly find intersections of those curves with other curves or surfaces.

The OBB overlap test is very robust as compared to other OBB overlap algorithms. It does not need to check for non-generic conditions such as parallel faces or edges; these are not special cases for the test and do not need to be handled separately. As a series of comparisons between linear combinations, the test is numerically stable: there are no divisions, square roots, or other functions to threaten domain errors or create conditioning problems. The use of an error margin, ϵ, guards against missing intersections due to arithmetic error. Its value can be set by the user.

Since the flow of control for the overlap test is simple and the number of operations required is small, the overlap test is a good candidate for microcoding or implemented in assembly. The test could also be easily implemented in hardware. Since most of the collision query time is spent in the overlap tests, any such optimization will significantly improve overall running time.

The Qhull package [4] is optionally used for computing the OBB orientation. It has been found to be quite robust. If we do use Qhull, we have to ensure that the input to Qhull spans 3 dimensions. If the input is rank deficient, our current implementation skips the use of Qhull, and uses all the triangles in the group. A more complete solution would be to project the input onto a lower dimensional space, and compute the convex hull of the projection (Qhull works on input of arbitrary specified dimension, but the input must be full rank).

There is the issue of propagation of errors as we descend the hierarchies, performing overlap tests. When we test two boxes or two triangles, their placement relative to one another is the result of a series of transformations, one for each level of each hierarchy we have traversed. We have not found errors due to the cascading of transformation matrices, but it is a theoretical source of errors we are aware of.

7.2 Performance

Our interference detection algorithm has been applied to two complex synthetic environments to demonstrate its efficiency (as highlighted in Table 3). These figures are for an SGI Reality Engine (90 MHz R8000 CPU, 512 MB).

A simple dynamics engine exercised the collision detection system. At each time step, the contact polygons were found by the collision detection algorithm, an impulse was applied to the object at each contact before advancing the clock.

In the first scenario, the pipes model was used as both the environment and the dynamic object, as shown in Fig. 8. Both object and environment contain 140,000 polygons. The object is 15 times smaller in size than the environment. We simulated a gravitational field directed toward the center of the large cube of pipes, and permitted the smaller cube to fall inward, tumbling and bouncing. Its path contained 4008 discrete positions, and required 16.9

Scenario	Pipes	Torus
Environ Size	143690 pgns	98000 pgns
Object Size	143690 pgns	20000 pgns
Num of Steps	4008	1298
Num of Contacts	23905	2266
Num of Box-Box Tests	1704187	1055559
Num of Tri-Tri Tests	71589	7069
Time	16.9 secs	8.9 secs
Ave. Int. Detec. Time	**4.2 msecs**	**6.9 msecs**
Ave. Time per Box Test	7.9 usecs	7.3 usecs
Ave. Contacts per Step	6.0	1.7

Table 3: *Timings for simulations*

seconds to determine all 23905 contacts along the path. This is a challenging scenario because the smaller object is entirely embedded within the larger model. The models contain long thin triangles in the straight segments of the pipes, which cannot be efficiently approximated by sphere trees, octrees, and AABBTrees, in general. It has no obvious groups or clusters, which are typically used by spatial partitioning algorithms like BSP's.

The other scenario has a complex wrinkled torus encircling a stalagmite in a dimpled, toothed landscape. Different steps from this simulation are shown in Fig. 10. The spikes in the landscape prevent large bounding boxes from touching the floor of the landscape, while the dimples provide numerous shallow concavities into which an object can enter. Likewise, the wrinkles and the twisting of the torus makes it impractical to decompose into convex polytopes, and difficult to efficiently apply bounding volumes. The wrinkled torus and the environment are also smooth enough to come into parallel close proximity, increasing the number of bounding volume overlap tests. Notice that the average number of box tests per step for the torus scenario is almost twice that of the pipes, even though the number of contacts is much lower.

We have also applied our algorithm to detect collision between a moving torpedo on a pivot model (as shown in Fig. 7). These are parts of a torpedo storage and handling room of a submarine. The torpedo model is 4780 triangles. The pivot structure has 44921 triangles. There are multiple contacts along the length of the torpedo as it rests among the rollers. A typical collision query time for the scenario shown in Fig. 7 is 100 ms on a 200MHz R4400 CPU, 2GB SGI Reality Engine.

7.3 Comparison with Other Approaches

A number of hierarchical structures are known in the literature for interference detection. Most of them are based on spheres or AABBs. They have been applied to a number of complex environments. However, there are *no standard benchmarks* available to compare different algorithms and implementations. As a result, it is non-trivial to compare two algorithms and their implementations. More recently, [18] have compared different algorithms (based on line-stabbing and AABBs) on models composed of tens of thousands of polygons. On an SGI $Indigo^2$ Extreme, the algorithms with the best performance are able to compute all the contacts between the models in about $1/7 - 1/5$ of a second. Just based on the model complexity, we are able to handle models composed of hundreds of thousands of polygons (with multiple parallel contacts) in about $1/25 - 1/75$ of a second. We also compared our algorithm with an implementation of sphere tree based on the algorithm presented in [28]. A very preliminary comparison indicates one order of magnitude improvement. More comparisons and experiments are planned in the near future.

7.4 RAPID and benchmarks

Our implementation of our algorithms is available as a software package called RAPID (Rapid and Accurate Polygon Interference Detection). It can be obtained from: **http://www.cs.unc.edu/~geom/OBB/OBBT.html**.

Most of the models shown in this paper are also available, as well as precomputed motion sequences.

Overall, we find that given two large models in close proximity, with C_v, N_v, and N_p from the cost equation (1):

- C_v for OBBTrees is one-order of magnitude slower than that for sphere trees or AABBs.
- N_v for OBBTrees is asymptotically lower than that for sphere trees or AABBs. Likewise, N_p for OBBTrees is asymptotically lower.

Thus, given sufficiently large models in sufficiently close proximity, using OBBTrees require less work to process a collision query than using AABBTrees or sphere trees.

8 Extensions and Future Work

In the previous sections, we described the algorithm for interference detection between two polygonal models undergoing rigid motion. Some of the future work includes its specialization and extension to other applications. These include ray-tracing, interference detection between curved surfaces, view frustum culling and deformable models. As far as curve and surface intersections are concerned, current approaches are based on algebraic methods, subdivision methods and interval arithmetic [32]. Algebraic methods are restricted to low degree intersections. For high degree curve intersections, algorithms based on interval arithmetic have been found to be the fastest [32]. Such algorithms compute a decomposition of the curve in terms of AABBs. It will be worthwhile to try OBBs. This would involve subdividing the curve, computing tight-fitting OBBs for each segment, and checking them for overlaps.

In terms of view frustum culling, most applications use hierarchies based on AABBs. Rather, we may enclose the object using an OBBTree and test for overlap with the view frustum. The overlap test presented in Section 5 can be easily extended to test for overlap between an OBB and a view frustum.

Libraries and Benchmarks: There is great need to develop a set of libraries and benchmarks to compare different algorithms. This would involve different models as well as scenarios.

9 Conclusion

In this paper, we have presented a hierarchical data structure for rapid and exact interference detection between polygonal models. The algorithm is general-purpose and makes no assumptions about the input model. We have presented new algorithms for efficient construction of tight-fitting OBBTrees and overlap detection between two OBBs based on a new separating axis theorem. We have compared its performance with other hierarchies of spheres and AABBs and find it asymptotically faster for close proximity situations. The algorithm has been implemented and is able to detect all contacts between complex geometries (composed of a few hundred thousand polygons) at interactive rates.

10 Acknowledgements

Thanks to Greg Angelini, Jim Boudreaux, and Ken Fast at Electric Boat for the model of torpedo storage and handling room. This work was supported in part by a Sloan foundation fellowship, ARO Contract P-34982-MA, NSF grant CCR-9319957, NSF grant CCR-9625217, ONR contract N00014-94-1-0738, ARPA contract DABT63-93-C-0048, NSF/ARPA Science and Technology Center for Computer Graphics & Scientific Visualization NSF Prime contract No. 8920219 and a grant from Ford Motor company.

References

[1] A.Garica-Alonso, N.Serrano, and J.Flaquer. Solving the collision detection problem. *IEEE Computer Graphics and Applications*, 13(3):36–43, 1994.

[2] J. Arvo and D. Kirk. A survey of ray tracing acceleration techniques. In *An Introduction to Ray Tracing*, pages 201–262, 1989.

[3] D. Baraff. Curved surfaces and coherence for non-penetrating rigid body simulation. *ACM Computer Graphics*, 24(4):19–28, 1990.

[4] B. Barber, D. Dobkin, and H. Huhdanpaa. The quickhull algorithm for convex hull. Technical Report GCG53, The Geometry Center, MN, 1993.

[5] N. Beckmann, H. Kriegel, R. Schneider, and B. Seeger. The r*-tree: An efficient and robust access method for points and rectangles. *Proc. SIGMOD Conf. on Management of Data*, pages 322–331, 1990.

[6] S. Cameron. Collision detection by four-dimensional intersection testing. *Proceedings of International Conference on Robotics and Automation*, pages 291–302, 1990.

[7] S. Cameron. Approximation hierarchies and s-bounds. In *Proceedings. Symposium on Solid Modeling Foundations and CAD/CAM Applications*, pages 129–137, Austin, TX, 1991.

[8] J. F. Canny. Collision detection for moving polyhedra. *IEEE Trans. PAMI*, 8:200–209, 1986.

[9] B. Chazelle and D. P. Dobkin. Intersection of convex objects in two and three dimensions. *J. ACM*, 34:1–27, 1987.

[10] J. Cohen, M. Lin, D. Manocha, and M. Ponamgi. I-collide: An interactive and exact collision detection system for large-scale environments. In *Proc. of ACM Interactive 3D Graphics Conference*, pages 189–196, 1995.

[11] R.O. Duda and P.E. Hart. *Pattern Classification and Scene Analysis*. John Wiley and Sons, 1973.

[12] Tom Duff. Interval arithmetic and recursive subdivision for implicit functions and constructive solid geometry. *ACM Computer Graphics*, 26(2):131–139, 1992.

[13] J. Snyder et. al. Interval methods for multi-point collisions between time dependent curved surfaces. In *Proceedings of ACM Siggraph*, pages 321–334, 1993.

[14] E. G. Gilbert, D. W. Johnson, and S. S. Keerthi. A fast procedure for computing the distance between objects in three-dimensional space. *IEEE J. Robotics and Automation*, vol RA-4:193–203, 1988.

[15] S. Gottschalk. Separating axis theorem. Technical Report TR96-024, Department of Computer Science, UNC Chapel Hill, 1996.

[16] N. Greene. Detecting intersection of a rectangular solid and a convex polyhedron. In *Graphics Gems IV*, pages 74–82. Academic Press, 1994.

[17] J. K. Hahn. Realistic animation of rigid bodies. *Computer Graphics*, 22(4):pp. 299–308, 1988.

[18] M. Held, J.T. Klosowski, and J.S.B. Mitchell. Evaluation of collision detection methods for virtual reality fly-throughs. In *Canadian Conference on Computational Geometry*, 1995.

[19] B. V. Herzen, A. H. Barr, and H. R. Zatz. Geometric collisions for time-dependent parametric surfaces. *Computer Graphics*, 24(4):39–48, 1990.

[20] P. M. Hubbard. Interactive collision detection. In *Proceedings of IEEE Symposium on Research Frontiers in Virtual Reality*, October 1993.

[21] M.C. Lin. *Efficient Collision Detection for Animation and Robotics*. PhD thesis, Department of Electrical Engineering and Computer Science, University of California, Berkeley, December 1993.

[22] M.C. Lin and Dinesh Manocha. Fast interference detection between geometric models. *The Visual Computer*, 11(10):542–561, 1995.

[23] M. Moore and J. Wilhelms. Collision detection and response for computer animation. *Computer Graphics*, 22(4):289–298, 1988.

[24] B. Naylor, J. Amanatides, and W. Thibault. Merging bsp trees yield polyhedral modeling results. In *Proc. of ACM Siggraph*, pages 115–124, 1990.

[25] J. O'Rourke. Finding minimal enclosing boxes. *Internat. J. Comput. Inform. Sci.*, 14:183–199, 1985.

[26] M. Ponamgi, D. Manocha, and M. Lin. Incremental algorithms for collision detection between general solid models. In *Proc. of ACM/Siggraph Symposium on Solid Modeling*, pages 293–304, 1995.

[27] F.P. Preparata and M. I. Shamos. *Computational Geometry*. Springer-Verlag, New York, 1985.

[28] S. Quinlan. Efficient distance computation between non-convex objects. In *Proceedings of International Conference on Robotics and Automation*, pages 3324–3329, 1994.

[29] A. Rappoport. The extended convex differences tree (ecdt) representation for n-dimensional polyhedra. *International Journal of Computational Geometry and Applications*, 1(3):227–41, 1991.

[30] S. Rubin and T. Whitted. A 3-dimensional representation for fast rendering of complex scenes. In *Proc. of ACM Siggraph*, pages 110–116, 1980.

[31] H. Samet. *Spatial Data Structures: Quadtree, Octrees and Other Hierarchical Methods*. Addison Wesley, 1989.

[32] T.W. Sederberg and S.R. Parry. Comparison of three curve intersection algorithms. *Computer-Aided Design*, 18(1):58–63, 1986.

[33] R. Seidel. Linear programming and convex hulls made easy. In *Proc. 6th Ann. ACM Conf. on Computational Geometry*, pages 211–215, Berkeley, California, 1990.

[34] W.Bouma and G.Vanecek. Collision detection and analysis in a physically based simulation. *Proceedings Eurographics workshop on animation and simulation*, pages 191–203, 1991.

[35] H. Weghorst, G. Hooper, and D. Greenberg. Improved computational methods for ray tracing. *ACM Transactions on Graphics*, pages 52–69, 1984.

[36] E. Welzl. Smallest enclosing disks (balls and ellipsoids). Technical Report B 91-09, Fachbereich Mathematik, Freie Universitat, Berlin, 1991.

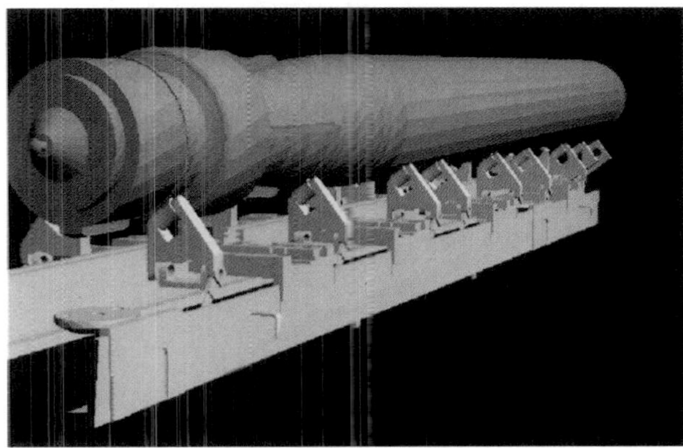

Figure 7: Interactive Interference Detection for a Torpedo (shown in yellow) on a Pivot Structure (shown in green) – Torpedo has 4780 triangles; Pivot has 44921 triangles; Average time to perform collision query: 100 msec on SGI Reality Engine with 200MHz R4400 CPU

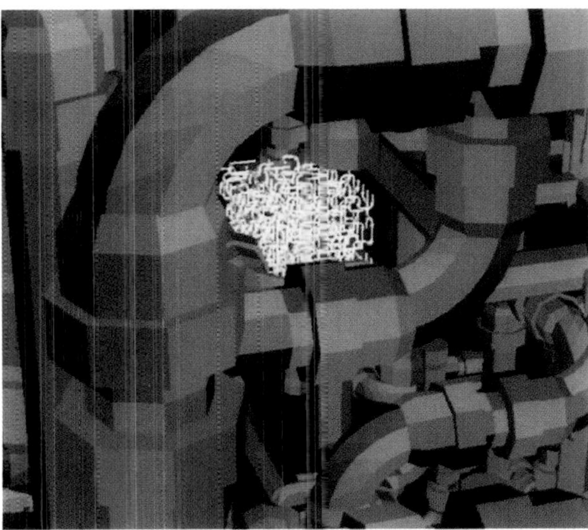

Figure 8: Interactive Interference Detection on Complex Interweaving Pipeline: 140,000 polygons each; Average time to perform collision query: 4.2 msec on SGI Reality Engine with 90MHz R8000 CPU

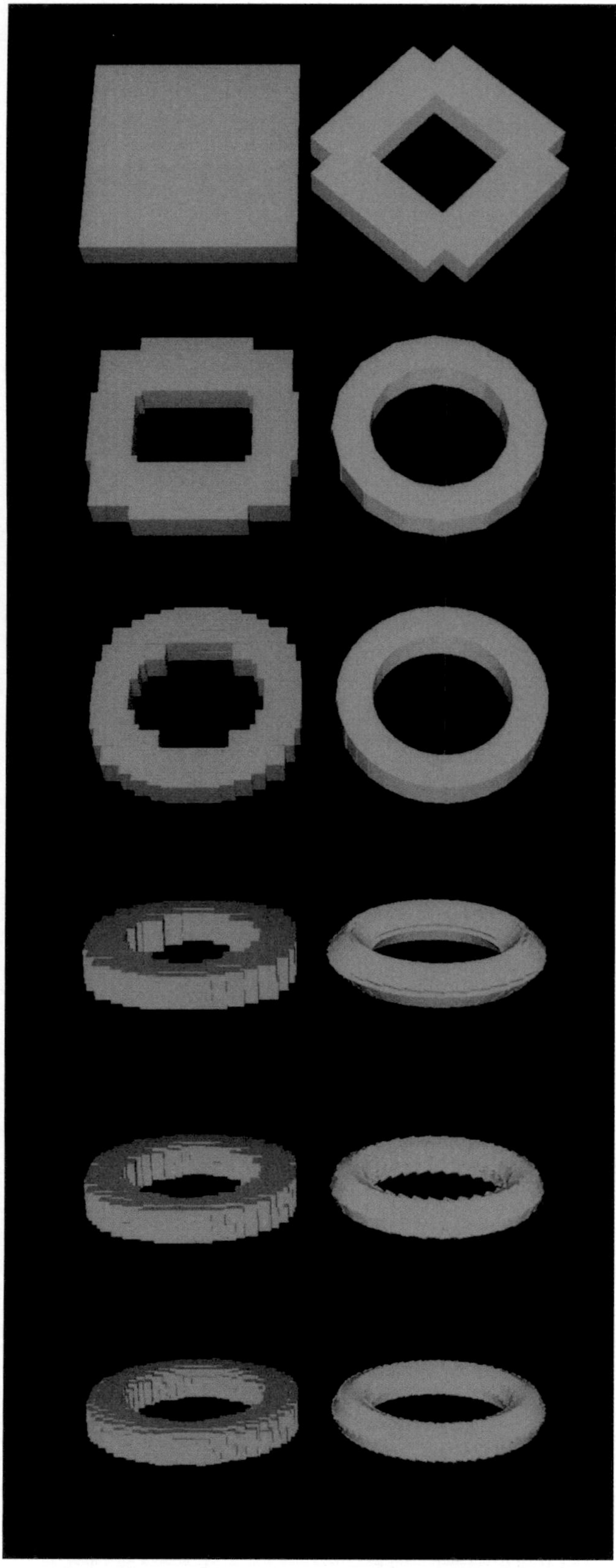

Figure 9: AABBs vs. OBBs: Approximation of a Torus – This shows OBBs converging to the shape of a torus more rapidly than AABBs.

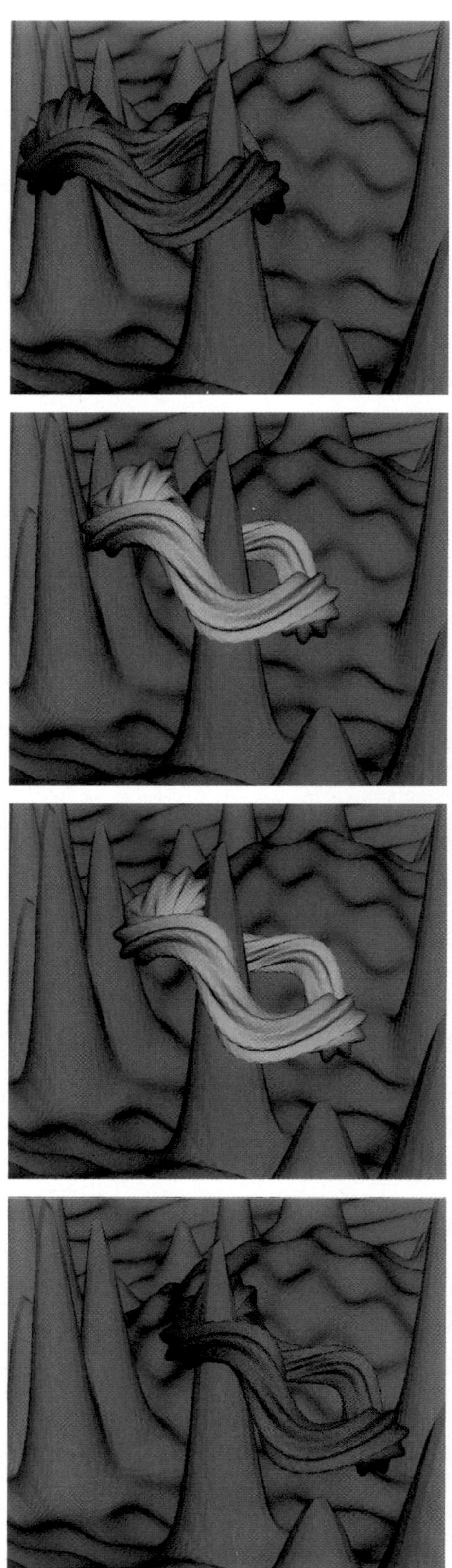

Figure 10: Interactive Interference Detection for a Complex Torus – Torus has 20000 polygons; Environment has 98000 polygons; Average time to perform collision query: 6.9 msec on SGI Reality Engine with 90MHz R8000 CPU

Free-Form Deformations With Lattices of Arbitrary Topology

Ron MacCracken
Kenneth I. Joy

Computer Graphics Research Laboratory
Department of Computer Science
University of California, Davis[1]

Abstract

A new free-form deformation technique is presented that generalizes previous methods by allowing 3-dimensional deformation lattices of arbitrary topology. The technique uses an extension of the Catmull-Clark subdivision methodology that successively refines a 3-dimensional lattice into a sequence of lattices that converge uniformly to a region of 3-dimensional space. Deformation of the lattice then implicitly defines a deformation of the space. An underlying model can be deformed by establishing positions of the points of the model within the converging sequence of lattices and then tracking the new positions of these points within the deformed sequence of lattices. This technique allows a greater variety of deformable regions to be defined, and thus a broader range of shape deformations can be generated.

1 Introduction

Efficient and intuitive methods for three-dimensional shape design, modification, and animation are becoming increasingly important areas in computer graphics. The model-dependent techniques initially used by designers to modify surfaces required each primitive type to have different parameters and/or control points that defined its shape. Model designers had to consider this mathematical model when making the desired modifications, and shape design could be difficult – making simple changes to the surface required the modification of many surface parameters. The process grew more difficult when local changes, such as adding arbitrarily shaped bumps, or global changes, such as bending, twisting, or tapering were necessary.

The free-form deformations [5, 6, 9, 19] were designed to deal with some of these problems. These methods embed an object in a deformable region of space such that each point of the object has a unique parameterization that defines its position in the region. The region is then altered, causing recalculation of the positions based upon their initial parameterization. If a deformable space can be defined with great flexibility and with few control points relative to the number in the surface model, then complex models comprised of thousands of control points can be deformed in many interesting ways with very little user-interaction.

Barr [1] first introduced deformations by creating operations for stretching, twisting, bending and tapering surfaces around a central axis (x, y, or z). Operations that involved moving many control points could now be accomplished with the altering of as little as one parameter. However, this technique limits the possible definitions of the deformable space to that of a single coordinate system about an axis, and restricts the ways in which the space can be altered - the axis can not be modified and the deformable space can only be modified by a few parameters.

Barr's deformations were followed by a more generalized approach to the problem, the Free-Form Deformations (FFDs) of Sederberg and Parry [19]. This method imposes an initial deformation lattice on a parallelepiped, and defines the deformable space as the trivariate Bézier volume defined by the lattice points. The parallelepiped form of the lattice allows points of an embedded object to be quickly parameterized in the space of the lattice, and as the lattice is deformed, the deformed points can be calculated by simple substitution into the defining equations of the trivariate volume. This method is widely used because of its ease of use and power to create many types of deformations with little user-interaction. Griessmair and Purgathofer [9] extended this technique by utilizing a trivariate B-Spline representation. Although both methods give the user many controls to alter the deformable space, both Sederberg and Parry's FFDs and Griessmair and Purgathofer's deformation techniques handle only a specific type of space definition, that defined initially by a parallelepiped lattice.

In order to generate free-form deformations for a more general lattice structure, Coquillart introduced Extended Free-Form Deformations (EFFD) [5, 6]. This method uses the initial lattice points to define an arbitrary trivariate Bézier volume, and allows the combining of many lattices to form arbitrary shaped spaces. Modifying the points of the defining lattice creates a deformation of space where one trivariate volume is deformed into another. This extension allows a greater inventory of deformable spaces, but loses some of the flexibility and stability of Sederberg and Parry's FFDs: While the corner control points of the joined lattices are user-controllable, the internal control points are constrained to preserve continuity; and, calculating the parameterization of a point embedded in the initial trivariate volume requires numerical techniques.

A recent deformation technique developed by Chang and Rockwood [4] generalizes Barr's technique in a different manner. Instead of defining the space in a free-form manner, Chang's approach deals with increasing the flexibility of an axis-based approach by allowing modifications to the axis during the deformation. The technique allows the user to define the axis as a Bézier curve with two user-defined axes at each control point of the curve. Repeated affine transformations using a generalized deCasteljau approach are used to define the deformable space. This technique is very powerful, in-

[1] Department of Computer Science, University of California, Davis CA 95616. Email: {maccrack,joy}@cs.ucdavis.edu

tuitive, and efficient, but again restricts the ways in which the space surrounding the curve can be altered.

This paper introduces a further extension to these techniques by establishing deformation methods defined on lattices of arbitrary topology. In this case, the deformable space is defined by using a volume analogy of subdivision surfaces [2, 7, 8]. In these subdivision methods, the lattice is repeatedly refined, creating a sequence of lattices that converge to a region in three-dimensional space. This refinement procedure is used to define a pseudo-parameterization of an embedded point. As the points of the lattice are modified a deformation of the space is created, and the embedded points can be relocated within the deformed space.

This method has been found to be quite intuitive for the designer and dramatically increases the inventory of lattices that can be considered in a free-form deformation. The twists and bends of Barr [1] and the cylindrical lattices of Coquillart [5] can be easily simulated. By allowing meshes of arbitrary topology, the continuity problems of adjoining lattices virtually disappear.

In section 2, we give an overview of the subdivision methods that are used to define the deformable space from the lattice. In our case these methods are based upon an extension of the Catmull-Clark refinement rules for surfaces [2]. In section 3, we modify the Catmull-Clark procedure to control the boundary surfaces and curves of the deformable region. This produces a deformable region that can be intuitively defined from the lattice. In section 4 we discuss the methods that give a correspondence between a point embedded in the deformable space and the sequence of lattices generated by the refinement procedure. In section 5 we present an overview of the complete deformation procedure. Implementation details of the algorithm are discussed in section 6 and results are given in section 7.

2 Defining the Deformable Space from the Lattice

A *lattice* $\mathcal{L}$ is defined to be a set of vertices $\{\mathbf{P}_0, \mathbf{P}_1, ..., \mathbf{P}_n\}$ and an associated simplicial complex which specifies the connectivity of the vertices[2]. A *subdivision method* applied to a lattice is a function from the set of lattices into itself. A subdivision method is usually implemented as a set of *refinement rules* which define how to generate the vertices of the resulting lattice, and also how to connect these new vertices. A set of refinement rules can be repeatedly applied to a lattice $\mathcal{L}$, creating a sequence of lattices $\{\mathcal{L}_1, \mathcal{L}_2, \mathcal{L}_3, ...\}$. In many cases, this sequence can be made to converge to a region of 3-dimensional space.

To describe the components of a lattice, we will use the following terms:

- An edge of the lattice is defined by two vertices that are connected in the simplicial complex of the lattice.
- A face of the lattice is defined by a minimal connected loop of vertices.
- a cell of the lattice is the region of space bounded by a set of faces.

A control polygon has vertices and edges, a control mesh has vertices, edges and faces, and a control lattice has vertices, edges, faces and cells. In the bivariate B-spline case, each face of the control mesh is defined by four vertices, and each vertex of the mesh has connectivity four (four edges radiating from the vertex). In the trivariate case, each cell of the control lattice is defined by six faces and each face by four vertices. Each vertex has connectivity six.

[2] For consistency, we will refer to a set of points that generates a volume as a *lattice*. The set of points generating a surface will be called a *mesh*. The set of points generating a curve will be called a *control polygon*.

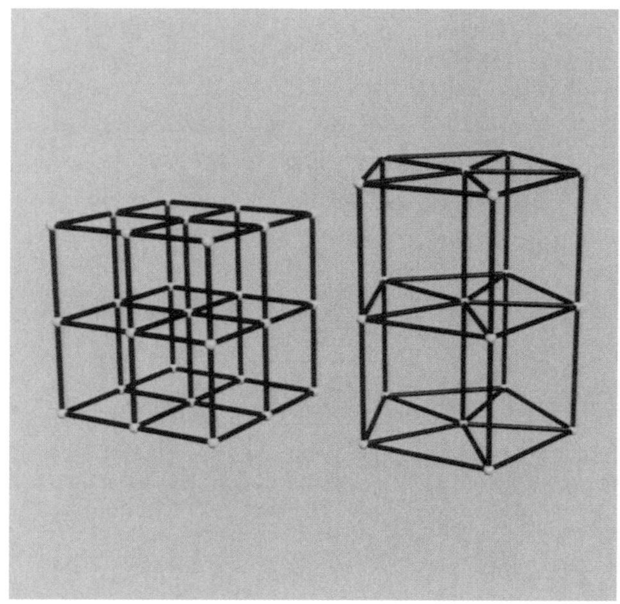

Figure 1: Lattice Structures

We allow lattices of arbitrary topology with the following properties:

- The lattice is well-connected, i.e. no vertex lies on an edge not containing that vertex.
- All cells are closed, meaning the faces comprising the cells do not form any holes. For example, a cube with one face missing is not a valid cell.
- No two cells of the lattice intersect – that is, we will not consider self-intersecting lattices.

Figure 1 illustrates two sample lattices, one based upon a parallelepiped structure and one based upon a cylindrical structure.

The uniform B-spline curves, surfaces and volumes can be defined by subdivision methods. In the curve case, the refinement rules were first presented by George Chaikin [3]. Riesenfeld [18] proceeded to show that Chaikin's curves were uniform quadratic B-spline curves. Doo and Sabin [7, 8] extended Chaikin's method to uniform quadratic B-spline surfaces and then extended the refinement rules for the quadratic case to meshes of an arbitrary topology. Catmull and Clark [2] developed a similar technique for the uniform cubic B-spline case. These methods have now come into widespread use in geometric modeling. They have been used for interpolation and fairing [10], approximation [12], and multiresolution design [16].

In this paper, we consider lattices of arbitrary topology and develop a set of refinement rules that subdivide this lattice to generate a deformable region in three-dimensional space. To generate the deformable regions, we utilize an extension of the Catmull-Clark subdivision method to volumes. In the following sections, we summarize the Catmull-Clark refinement rules for the uniform B-spline volume, along with the extensions of these methods to lattices of arbitrary topology. The complete details of the development of these refinement rules can be found in [13].

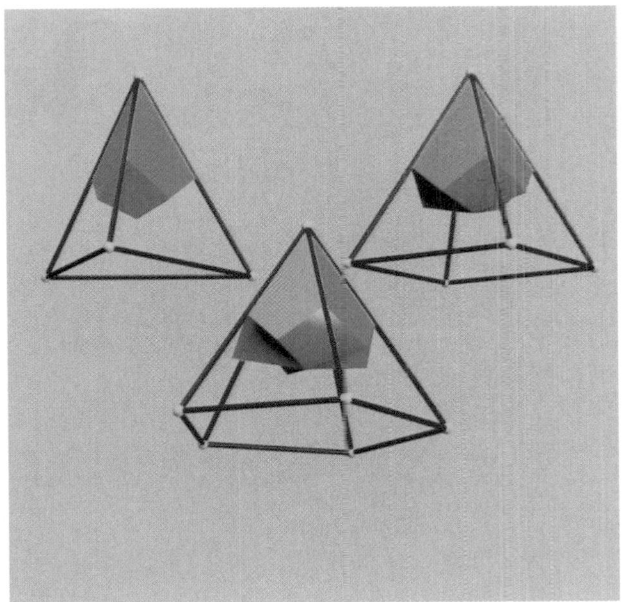

Figure 2: Type-3, 4 and 5 cells generated by the subdivision process.

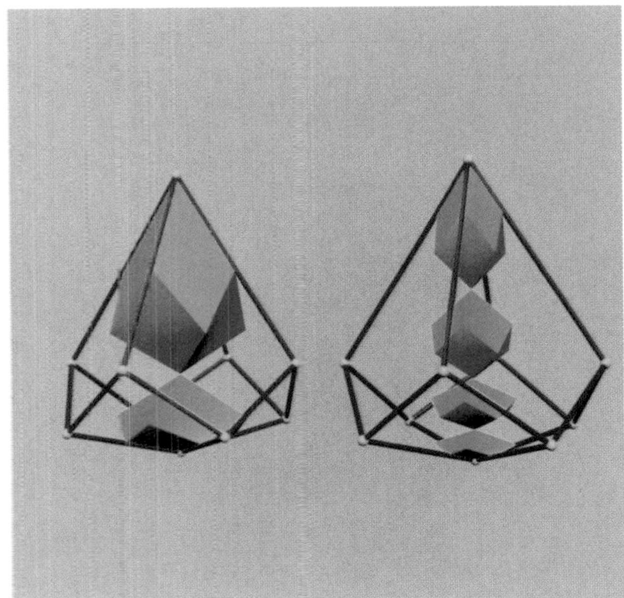

Figure 3: The type-4 cells generated by repeated subdivision.

2.1 Subdivision Methods for Trivariate Cubic Uniform B-Spline Volumes

Given a control lattice $\mathcal{L}$ that defines a trivariate uniform B-spline volume, the subdivision method generates a new control lattice $\mathcal{L}_1$ which consists of the union of all the vertices generated by a binary subdivision of the trivariate volume. These points can be classified into

1. cell points – these points are the average of the vertices in the lattice that make up the cell.

2. face points – these points can be written as

$$\mathbf{F} = \frac{\mathbf{C}_0 + 2\mathbf{A} + \mathbf{C}_1}{4}$$

where $\mathbf{C}_0$ and $\mathbf{C}_1$ are the cell points of the two adjacent hexahedral cells that contain the face and $\mathbf{A}$ is the face centroid (the average of the vertices that surround the face).

3. edge points – these points can be written as

$$\mathbf{E} = \frac{\mathbf{C}_{avg} + 2\mathbf{A}_{avg} + \mathbf{M}}{4}$$

where $\mathbf{C}_{avg}$ is the average of the cell points for those hexahedral cells that contain this edge, $\mathbf{A}_{avg}$ is the average of the face centroids for those faces that contain this edge, and $\mathbf{M}$ is the midpoint of the edge.

4. vertex points – these points can be written as

$$\mathbf{V} = \frac{\mathbf{C}_{avg} + 3\mathbf{A}_{avg} + 3\mathbf{M}_{avg} + \mathbf{P}}{8}$$

where $\mathbf{C}_{avg}$ is the average of the cell points for each of the hexahedral cells that contain this vertex, $\mathbf{A}_{avg}$ is the average of the face centroids for the faces that contain this vertex, $\mathbf{M}_{avg}$ is the average of the midpoints for the edges that radiate from the vertex, and $\mathbf{P}$ is the vertex itself.

At each subdivision step, a cell point is inserted into the lattice for each cell according to the first rule, a face point is inserted for each face according to the second rule, an edge point is inserted for each edge according to the third rule, and each vertex's position is recalculated according to the fourth rule. To reconnect the lattice after these rules have been applied, we first connect each new cell point to the new face points generated for the faces defining the cell. Each new face point is connected to the new edge points of the edges defining the original face. Each new edge point is connected to the two vertex points defining the original edge.

2.2 Catmull-Clark Volumes

Extension of the above rules to lattices of arbitrary topology is straightforward, using an extension of the bivariate Catmull-Clark subdivision strategy[2]. We can classify the points of the refinement into four types:

1. cell points – these points are the average of the vertices of the lattice that bound the cell.

2. face points – these points can be written as

$$\mathbf{F} = \frac{\mathbf{C}_0 + 2\mathbf{A} + \mathbf{C}_1}{4}$$

where $\mathbf{C}_0$ and $\mathbf{C}_1$ are the cell points of the two cells that contain the face and $\mathbf{A}$ is the face centroid.

3. edge points – these points can be written as

$$\mathbf{E} = \frac{\mathbf{C}_{avg} + 2\mathbf{A}_{avg} + (n-3)\mathbf{M}}{n}$$

where $\mathbf{C}_{avg}$ is the average of the cell points for those cells that contain this edge, $\mathbf{A}_{avg}$ is the average of the face centroids for those faces contain this edge, and $\mathbf{M}$ is the midpoint of the edge. n is the number of faces that contain the edge.

4. vertex points – these points can be written as

$$\mathbf{V} = \frac{\mathbf{C}_{avg} + 3\mathbf{A}_{avg} + 3\mathbf{M}_{avg} + \mathbf{P}}{8}$$

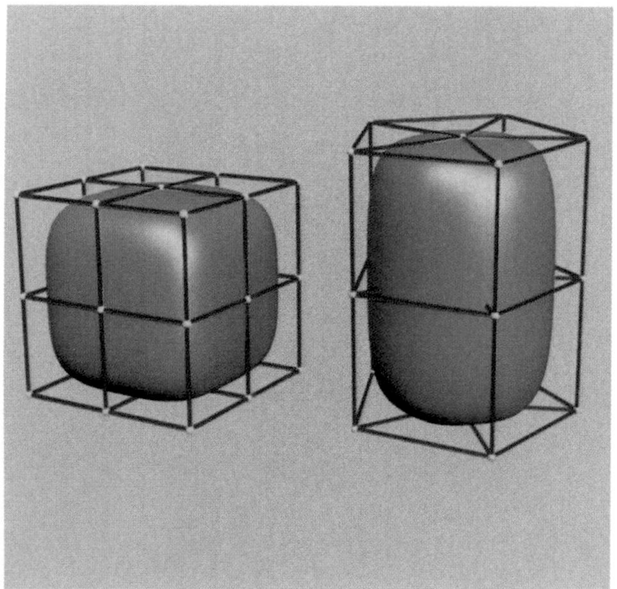

Figure 4: Catmull-Clark Volumes defined by a rectangular and cylindrical lattice.

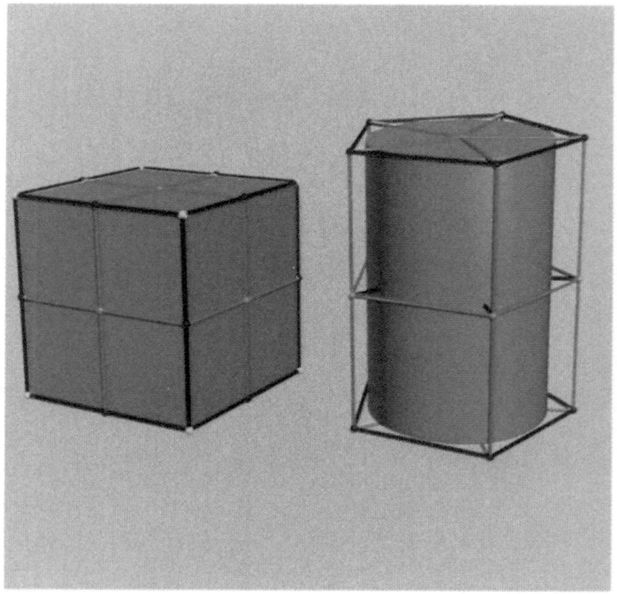

Figure 5: Catmull-Clark volumes with boundary and edge control. The corner vertices are yellow, the sharp edges are red, the boundary edges are green and the internal edges are blue.

where $\mathbf{C}_{avg}$ is the average of the cell points for each of the cells that contain this vertex, $\mathbf{A}_{avg}$ is the average of the face centroids for the faces that contain this vertex, $\mathbf{M}_{avg}$ is the average of the midpoints for the edges that radiate from the vertex, and $\mathbf{P}$ is the vertex itself.

These refinement rules can be applied to a lattice of arbitrary topology creating a new set of vertex points, edge points, face points and cell points. The reconnection strategy is identical to that of the trivariate uniform B-spline lattice: the new cell point are connected to the new face points generated for the faces defining the cell; the new face points are connected to the new edge points from the edges defining the original face; and, each new edge point is connected to the two new vertex points from the original edge.

To describe the cell structure of the subdivided lattice, we define the *valence* of a vertex $\mathbf{V}$ within a cell $\mathbf{C}$ to be the number of edges in $\mathbf{C}$ that contain the vertex $\mathbf{V}$. Given a cell $\mathbf{C}$ of a lattice $\mathcal{L}$, consider a vertex $\mathbf{V}$ of the cell $\mathbf{C}$ of valence n. The refinement process creates a new cell from $\mathbf{V}$ that contains $2n$ 4-sided faces, 2 vertices of valence n and $2n-2$ vertices of valence 3 (see figure 2). We call these characteristic cells type-n cells. After the first subdivision, all cells can be classified as type-n cells.

In the subdivision process, a type-n cell is refined into two type-n cells and $2n-2$ type-3 cells. The type-3 cell is a hexahedral cell with 4-sided faces and 3-valence vertices. After a few subdivisions, the bulk of the lattice will consist of type-3 cells arranged in a regular pattern – that of the trivariate uniform B-spline case – except around a finite number of type-n cells where this regularity is disturbed. For $n > 3$, the number of type-n cells doubles in each application of the subdivision algorithm (see figure 3).

Figure 4 illustrates the Catmull-Clark volumes generated from the lattices shown in figure 1.

3 Boundary Control of the Subdivision Volume

Designing a lattice that represents a particular region of space is a difficult task. The free-form deformations of Sederberg and Parry [19] were based upon an initial lattice that was formed on a parallelepiped, with the deformable space filling the lattice completely. In our case, the region of space resulting from applying the trivariate Catmull-Clark subdivision method to an arbitrary lattice does not conform closely to the general shape of the lattice – shrinking away from the boundary substantially. In figure 4 for example, the cylindrical lattice does not refine into a cylindrical region of space. This feature creates an unusual burden on the designer and limits the usefulness of the technique.

To solve this problem and create a tool that will construct regions of space that are intuitive to the designer, we modify the refinement rules for those areas of the lattice that correspond to boundary surfaces, sharp edges, and corner vertices. These rules are summarized as follows:

- Corner vertices are identified as those incident to only one cell of the lattice. In the refinement procedure, the position of a corner vertex does not change.

- Sharp edges are those edges joining vertices that are incident to only one or two cells of the lattice, including corner vertices. The edge and vertex points along the sharp edges of the lattice are calculated according to subdivision rules for uniform cubic B-spline curves[13].

- All other vertex, edge, and face points on the boundary are generated according to the Catmull-Clark rules for surfaces[2].

- All internal points are calculated using the Catmull-Clark rules for volumes.

Given a lattice based on a cube, these methods will generate a region of space that is the cube. In the case of the lattice approximating a cylinder, the region is flat at either end of the cylinder and rounded along the length of the cylinder as one would expect. These are shown in figure 5. The corner vertices are yellow, the sharp edges are red, the boundary edges are green and the internal edges are blue.

These techniques have been previously used by Nasri [17] for Doo-Sabin surfaces, and are similar to the techniques used by Hoppe et al. [12] in defining edges, creases, corners and darts on Loop Surfaces [15]. When added to the subdivision procedure, these new rules generate deformable regions of space that closely represent their lattice.

4 Calculating the Location of Vertices Embedded in the Deformable Space

Sederberg and Parry [19] impose the initial lattice on a parallelepiped in space and calculate the parameterization of a point within the deformable space by using the local coordinates of a point within the parallelepiped. The location of the point under the deformation is calculated by substituting these local coordinate values into the defining equation for the trivariate Bézier volume. Coquillart [5] uses a similar method, but numerical iteration is required to calculate the local coordinate, as her initial lattices are not formed as parallelepipeds. In both these cases, the cells of the lattice are hexahedral. In the case that the lattice is of an arbitrary topology and the above subdivision procedure is used, a simple trivariate parameterization is not available. Fortunately, the subdivision procedure itself can be used to establish a correspondence between points in the deformable region and points in the deformed region.

Given an initial lattice $\mathcal{L}$, the subdivision procedure generates a sequence of lattices $\{\mathcal{L}_1, \mathcal{L}_2, \mathcal{L}_3, \mathcal{L}_4 ..., \}$ that converge to the deformable region. Each lattice in the sequence induces a partitioning of the deformable space by its cells. We select a lattice, say $\mathcal{L}_i$, that has the property that the maximum volume of the individual cells of $\mathcal{L}_i$ is small. We then identify the cell of $\mathcal{L}_i$ that contains a given point $\mathbf{P}$ and assume that $\mathbf{P}$ is deformed to a position within the corresponding cell of the deformed lattice – in the same relative position in the cell. Whereas this is an approximation, it can be made arbitrarily close to the actual deformation.

To determine the relative position of a point in the cell, we take advantage of the fact that after the first refinement all cells are type-n cells, and most are type-3 (hexahedral). In the type-3 case we can calculate a trilinear approximation of the position of the point in the cell and use this trilinear parameterization to adjust the position of the point in the deformed cell. In the type-n case, we can calculate a piecewise trilinear approximation, by partitioning the cell into tetrahedra, and use this to adjust the position in the deformed cell.

5 The Deformation Process

To deform an object, we follow the 4-step procedure outlined by Coquillart in [5]. First, the user must construct the lattice. This is normally done by utilizing an inventory of lattices and a set of tools to merge and build new lattices from this inventory. A common tool is the extrusion tool that takes a mesh and extrudes it in a specified direction to become a lattice (the cylinder of figure 1 was generated in this manner.) At the lowest level, the user is allowed to to create cells one by one, attaching them face by face to form the lattice. Boundary surfaces, sharp edges and corner vertices can be marked automatically (as in section 3), or a manual marking procedure can determine them. Once the lattice has been constructed, the user must place the lattice around the object, or the part of the object, to be deformed.

When the lattice is oriented properly, it is frozen to the object. At this time, the lattice is refined, and the number of refinement steps n is retained.

Each point embedded in the deformable region can be "tagged" with a pointer to the cell of the refined lattice that contains the point, and a finite number of parameters that defines its position in the cell.

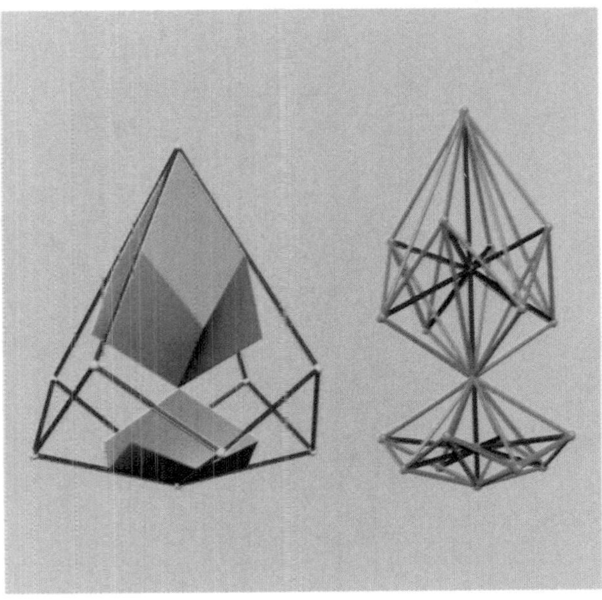

Figure 6: Partitioning of a type-n cell for approximation. The green edges represent the original edges of the cell. The blue edges are generated by the tetrahedral partition.

- For a type-3 hexahedral cell, the parameters consist of a (u, v, w) triple which defines the point's trilinear parameterization within the cell.
- For a type-n cell, a new cell point is calculated and the cell is partitioned into $4n$ tetrahedra about this cell point, each face contributing two tetrahedra to the partition (see figure 6). The parameters consist of an index into the tetrahedra containing the point and a (u, v, w) triple which defines the point's parameterization within the tetrahedra.

Finally, the original lattice is deformed by moving one or more of its vertices. The deformed lattice is then refined n times and the tag on each point is used to obtain the corresponding cell in the deformed lattice. The vertices of this cell are used to calculate a position for the deformed point according to the parameters associated with the original.

6 Implementation Details

The data structure holding the lattice is implemented as an extension of the half-edge data structure for surfaces – much like the radial-edge structure of Weiler [20]. The primary difference between halfedge structure for a mesh representing a surface and a lattice representing a volume is that the lattice structure may have several faces that contain each edge – the mesh structure will have at most two. In addition, a real-time deformation algorithm requires that the sequence of lattices be stored hierarchically. The n subdivision steps are then executed only once during the initialization (or freezing) phase of the deformation. Subsequent deformations of the lattice then require only the recalculation of the refinement rules for the vertices in lattices $\mathcal{L}_i$ to $\mathcal{L}_n$, without recreating the lattice structure. With each subdivision, the size of the data structure nearly triples and so deformations where the user desires a very small cell size can be quite memory intensive.

Many numerical algorithms exist to generate the trilinear approximation of a point in a type-3 cell. We have utilized an adaptation of an algorithm presented by Hamann, et al. [11]. Given a point $\mathbf{P}$ in a cell, we generate a point $\mathbf{P}_0$ as the trilinear point defined by $(\frac{1}{2}, \frac{1}{2}, \frac{1}{2})$. We then obtain

$$(u_0, v_0, w_0) = (\frac{1}{2}, \frac{1}{2}, \frac{1}{2}) + (\mathbf{P} - \mathbf{P}_0)\tilde{J}^{-1}$$

where $\tilde{J}$ is the transpose of a local approximate of the Jacobian at $(\frac{1}{2}, \frac{1}{2}, \frac{1}{2})$ obtained by interpolating the estimates of the Jacobians at the vertices of the cell. In general,

$$(u_i, v_i, w_i) = (u_{i-1}, v_{i-1}, w_{i-1}) + (\mathbf{P} - \mathbf{P}_i)\tilde{J}_i^{-1}$$

where $\tilde{J}_i$ is obtained by performing trilinear interpolation at $(u_{i-1}, v_{i-1}, w_{i-1})$ of the Jacobians at the vertices of the cell.

The procedure is repeated until the distance between $\mathbf{P}_i$ and $\mathbf{P}$ is sufficiently small. We found that few iterations were needed as the algorithm converges quickly and the cells are generally small.

In the case of a type-n cell, we partition the cell into $4n$ tetrahedra by utilizing the cell point (average of the vertices of the cell). A simple interpolation function for tetrahedral cells can be written as

$$\mathbf{P}(u, v, w) = \mathbf{P}_0 + u(\mathbf{P}_1 - \mathbf{P}_0) + v(\mathbf{P}_2 - \mathbf{P}_0) + w(\mathbf{P}_3 - \mathbf{P}_0)$$

where $\mathbf{P}_0$, $\mathbf{P}_1$, $\mathbf{P}_2$, and $\mathbf{P}_3$, are the four vertices of the tetrahedra. This can be put into matrix form and solved directly [14].

With this implementation, we have found that the algorithm executes in real time on an SGI Indigo^2 Extreme.

7 Results

The primary motivation for moving from the hexahedral topological lattices of the trivariate Bézier and B-spline representations of [5, 9, 19] was to increase the inventory of available lattices and thus the number of possible deformations. Figures 7 through 9 show the results of this algorithm with a variety of meshes and shapes.

Figure 7 exhibits a deformation by a cylindrical lattice, resulting in a surface deformation in the form of a star.

Figure 8 illustrates a complex lattice in the shape of a barbell. This lattice was generated by creating a mesh in the shape of a barbell and extruding the shape to form the lattice. The subdivision methodology automatically handles the continuity between the segments of the lattice.

Figure 9 shows a deformation applied to the arm of the "mobster" which causes the arm to lift upward, and the hand to twist toward the viewer. This is an excellent example of our technique, as it was necessary to construct the lattice about the appendage that was to be moved.

8 Conclusions

We have described a new free-form deformation technique that generalizes previous methods by allowing 3-dimensional deformation lattices of arbitrary topology. The technique uses an extension of the Catmull-Clark subdivision methodology to successively refine a 3-dimensional lattice into a sequence of lattices that converge uniformly to a region of 3-dimensional space. Deformation of the lattice then implicitly defines a deformation of this region. An underlying model can be deformed by establishing positions of the points of the model within the converging sequence of lattices, establishing the cell of the lattice that contains the point, establishing an approximation of the position of the point within the cell, and using this information to establish the new positions of these points within the deformed lattice.

This method is very powerful in that it can be applied to virtually any geometric model, as it directly modifies the vertices that define the model. The variety of lattices that can be used with this technique greatly increases the number of deformations that can be accomplished.

We have only discussed positional data of the embedded object in this paper. It is clear that the lattice could hold additional parameters. For example, we could store, in the lattice points the parameters of a solid texture. As the lattice is deformed, the texture would be deformed along with the object.

The careful reader will notice that, for the vertex points of the Catmull-Clark volume, we utilize the form

$$\mathbf{V} = \frac{\mathbf{C}_{avg} + 3\mathbf{A}_{avg} + 3\mathbf{M}_{avg} + \mathbf{P}}{8}$$

which does not contain an adjustment for the number of edges radiating from a vertex. We found that the Catmull-Clark surface methodology directly generalizes to edge points, but not to the vertex points of the refinement rules. It was our purpose to use this refinement to generate a partitioning of the deformable space by its cells, and for this purpose, this calculation appears to work very well. A detailed theoretical analysis of the continuity of the derivatives of these volumes at the extraordinary points [2, 8]. will have to be addressed in a future paper.

9 Acknowledgments

We are very grateful to the anonymous referees for their many helpful comments on the first version of this paper. We would also like to thank Bernd Hamann for pointing us toward the simple trivariate schemes that make this algorithm possible. Special thanks go to Justin Legakis for many useful critiques of the research, and who assisted us in the production of our final images. The data for the "mobster" in figure 9 was contributed via the avalon cite at *www.viewpoint.com*. The research reported here was partially supported by a grant through the University of California MICRO Program.

References

[1] Alan H. Barr. Global and local deformations of solid primitives. In *Computer Graphics (SIGGRAPH '84 Proceedings)*, volume 18, pages 21–30, July 1984.

[2] E. Catmull and J. Clark. Recursively generated B-spline surfaces on arbitrary topological meshes. *Computer-Aided Design*, 10:350–355, September 1978.

[3] G. Chaikin. An algorithm for high speed curve generation. *Computer Graphics and Image Processing*, 3:346–349, 1974.

[4] Yu–Kuang Chang and Alyn P. Rockwood. A generalized de Casteljau approach to 3D free–Form deformation. In *Proceedings of SIGGRAPH '94 (Orlando, Florida, July 24–29, 1994)*, Computer Graphics Proceedings, Annual Conference Series, pages 257–260.

[5] Sabine Coquillart. Extended free-form deformation: A sculpturing tool for 3D geometric modeling. In *Computer Graphics (SIGGRAPH '90 Proceedings)*, volume 24, pages 187–196, August 1990.

[6] Sabine Coquillart and Pierre Jancéne. Animated free-form deformation: An interactive animation technique. In *Computer Graphics (SIGGRAPH '91 Proceedings)*, volume 25, pages 23–26, July 1991.

[7] D. Doo. A subdivision algorithm for smoothing down irregularly shaped polyhedrons. In *Proceedings of the Int'l Conf. Interactive Techniques in Computer Aided Design*, pages 157–165, 1978.

[8] D. Doo and M. Sabin. Behaviour of recursive division surfaces near extraordinary points. *Computer-Aided Design*, 10:356–360, September 1978.

[9] Josef Griessmair and Werner Purgathofer. Deformation of solids with trivariate B-splines. In *Eurographics '89*, pages 137–148. North-Holland, September 1989.

[10] Mark Halstead, Michael Kass, and Tony DeRose. Efficient, fair interpolation using Catmull-Clark surfaces. In *Computer Graphics (SIGGRAPH '93 Proceedings)*, volume 27, pages 35–44, August 1993.

[11] Bernd Hamann, Donhua Wu, and Robert J. Moorhead II. On particle path generation based on quadrilinear interpolation and Bernstein-Bézier polynomials. *IEEE Transactions on Visualization and Computer Graphics*, 1(3):210–217, 1995.

[12] Hugues Hoppe, Tony DeRose, Tom Duchamp, Mark Halstead, Hubert Jin, John McDonald, Jean Schweitzer, and Werner Stuetzle. Piecewise smooth surface reconstruction. In *Proceedings of SIGGRAPH '94 (Orlando, Florida, July 24–29, 1994)*, Computer Graphics Proceedings, Annual Conference Series, pages 295–302.

[13] Kenneth I. Joy and Ron MacCracken. The refinement rules for Catmull-Clark solids. Technical Report CSE-96-1, Department of Computer Science, University of California, Davis, January 1996.

[14] David N. Kenwright and Davis A. Lane. Optimization of time-dependent particle tracing using tetrahedral decomposition. In *Proceedings of Visualization '95*, pages 321–328. IEEE Computer Society, 1985.

[15] Charles Loop. Smooth subdivision surfaces based on triangles. Master's thesis, Department of Mathematics, University of Utah, August 1987.

[16] Mike Lounsbery. *Multiresolution Analysis for Surfaces of Arbitrary Topological Type*. PhD thesis, Department of Computer Science and Engineering, University of Washington, Seattle, WA, June 1994.

[17] A. Nasri. Polyhedral subdivision methods for free-form surfaces. *ACM Transactions on Graphics*, 6:29–73, 1987.

[18] R. Riesenfeld. On Chaikin's algorithm. *Computer Graphics and Image Processing*, 4(3):304–310, 1975.

[19] Thomas W. Sederberg and Scott R. Parry. Free-form deformation of solid geometric models. In *Computer Graphics (SIGGRAPH '86 Proceedings)*, volume 20, pages 151–160, August 1986.

[20] Kevin J. Weiler. *Topological structures for geometric modeling*. PhD thesis, Rensselaer Polytechnic Institute, August 1986.

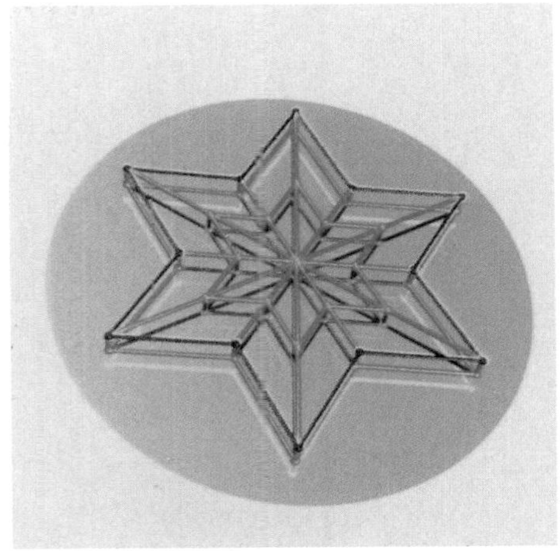

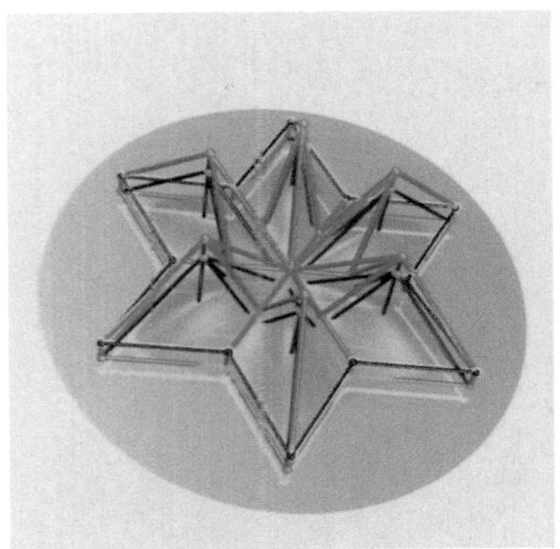

Figure 7: Deforming a disk with a star-shaped lattice.

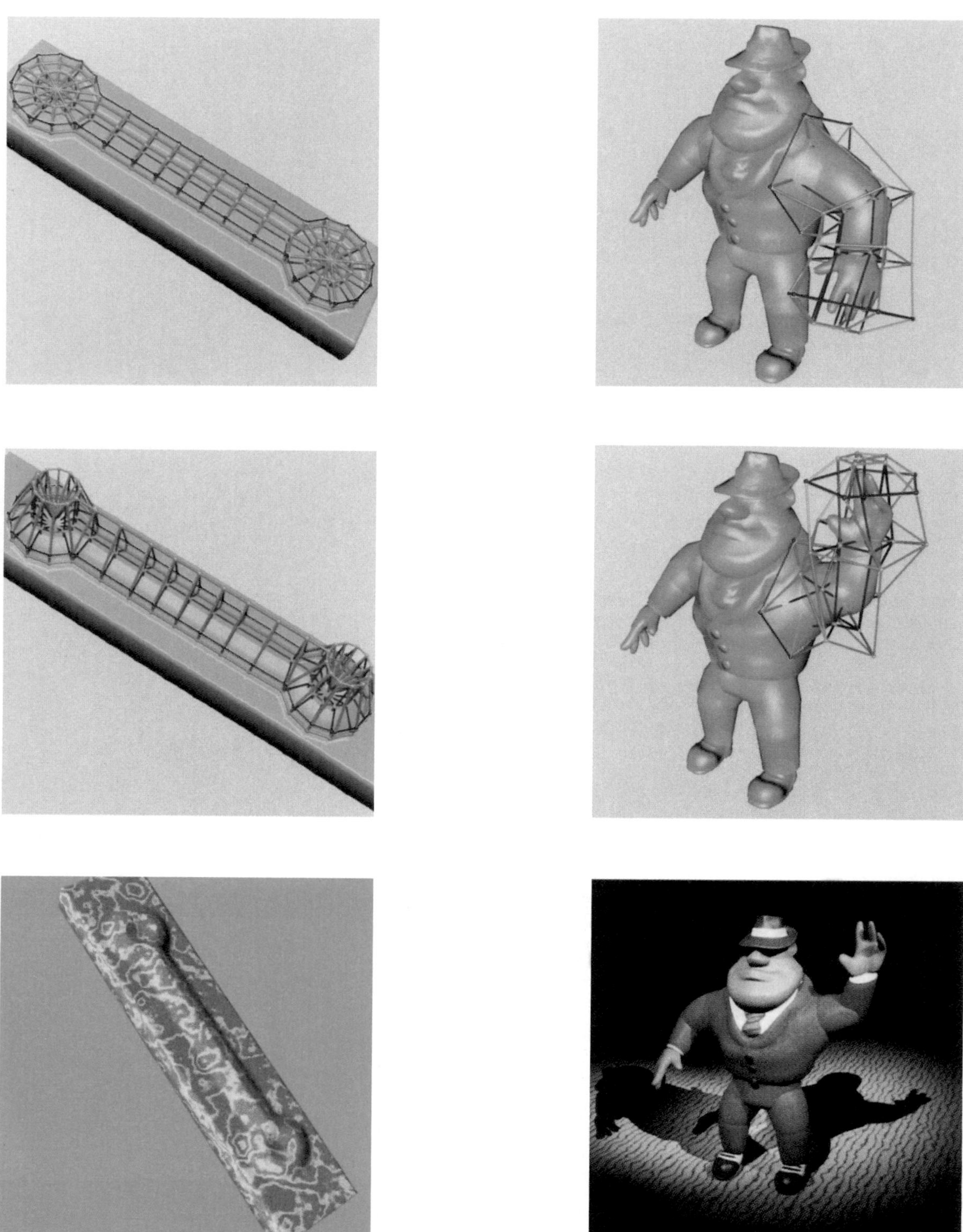

Figure 8: Deforming a block with a barbell-shaped lattice.

Figure 9: Deforming the mobster's arm.

Interpolating Subdivision for Meshes with Arbitrary Topology

Denis Zorin† Peter Schröder† Wim Sweldens*

Abstract

Subdivision is a powerful paradigm for the generation of surfaces of arbitrary topology. Given an initial triangular mesh the goal is to produce a smooth and visually pleasing surface whose shape is controlled by the initial mesh. Of particular interest are interpolating schemes since they match the original data exactly, and play an important role in fast multiresolution and wavelet techniques. Dyn, Gregory, and Levin introduced the Butterfly scheme, which yields C^1 surfaces in the topologically regular setting. Unfortunately it exhibits undesirable artifacts in the case of an irregular topology. We examine these failures and derive an improved scheme, which retains the simplicity of the Butterfly scheme, is interpolating, and results in smoother surfaces.

1 Introduction

Beginning with an initial mesh, subdivision produces a sequence of refinements. New vertices are defined as local affine combinations of nearby vertices. An attractive feature of these schemes is *locality*, i.e., no global system of equations needs to be solved. Examples of subdivision include classical spline constructions which are generally not interpolating. The most common interpolating scheme is based on piecewise linears. Unfortunately this is not smooth enough for many applications. A scheme that achieves C^1 continuity in the topologically regular setting, was pioneered by Dyn, Gregory, and Levin [9, 10] and has been applied to the construction of smooth surfaces[1].

The mathematical analysis of the surfaces resulting from subdivision is not always straightforward (see for example Reif [20]). However, the simplicity of the algorithms and associated data structures makes subdivision attractive for large data sets and interactive applications.

Recently, interpolating subdivision has been used for multiresolution analysis of complex geometries [16]. It provides a powerful tool for the constructions of *finite* analysis and synthesis filters for wavelet algorithms on general manifolds [22] using the *lifting scheme*[23]. Further, *adaptive* subdivision is greatly simplified with interpolating rules. Multiresolution decomposition algorithms are of importance in compression, progressive display and transmission, multiresolution editing, and multigrid/wavelet based numerical methods.

While the Butterfly scheme of Dyn, Gregory and Levin can be used to generate smooth surfaces over regular triangular meshes (all vertices have valence 6), it exhibits degeneracies when applied in a topologically irregular setting: undesirable creases can result at vertices of valence other than 6. Figure 1 demonstrates such a failure for vertices of valence 3. The left picture shows the result of applying the original Butterfly scheme to a tetrahedron, the right picture is obtained using our modified scheme.

Motivated by these observations, we consider the construction of a subdivision scheme under the following constraints:

- **Interpolation:** The original mesh vertices are interpolated and all newly generated vertices are on the limit surface.
- **Locality:** The neighborhood used to define new vertex positions from old ones should be as small as possible to enable fast algorithms.
- **Symmetry:** The scheme should exhibit the same type of symmetries as the local mesh topology.
- **Generality:** The scheme should work for triangulations which are not topologically restricted, including the proper handling of boundaries.
- **Smoothness:** We require the resulting scheme to reproduce polynomials up to some power—a necessary but not sufficient condition for higher order continuity.
- **Simplicity:** The scheme should only require simple data structures.

Since the Butterfly scheme satisfies these requirements except for topological generality, we make it the starting point of our investigation.

The main result of our work is a simple modification of the Butterfly scheme around vertices of valence not equal to 6. It combats the cusp like artifacts exhibited by the unmodified scheme in those circumstances. We use Fourier transform techniques [5, 1], which are typically used for *analysis* of subdivision, for the *synthesis* of our new interpolating subdivision scheme.

In the next section we briefly review related work. Then we describe the construction of our modified scheme and present the results. We conclude with a discussion and outlook.

2 Related Work

We briefly review subdivision algorithms for arbitrary topology control meshes. They come in two flavors: approximating and interpolating.

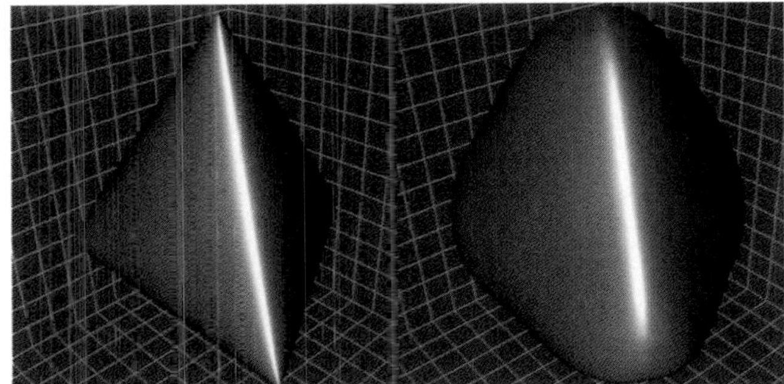

Figure 1 : A tetrahedron is subdivided according to the original Butterfly scheme (on the left) and with our modified Butterfly scheme (right).

† Department of Computer Science, California Institute of Technology, Pasadena CA 91125.
* Lucent Technologies (formerly AT&T), Bell Laboratories, 700 Mountain Avenue, Rm. 2C-175, Murray Hill, NJ 07974; Department of Computer Science, K.U.Leuven, Belgium. (On leave from the NFWO)
dzorin@gg.caltech.edu, ps@cs.caltech.edu, wim@bell-labs.com

[1]An alternative was recently proposed by Kobbelt [13].

2.1 Approximating Subdivision Schemes

Approximating subdivision schemes for arbitrary topology meshes are typically modifications of spline based schemes. The algorithms of Doo and Sabin [4, 5, 21] and Catmull and Clark [2] are generalizations of quadratic and cubic B-splines respectively. The behavior around extraordinary vertices was analyzed by Doo and Sabin [5] using Fourier transforms and an eigen analysis of the subdivision process. More recently Ball and Storry [1], Warren [24], and Reif [20] refined these techniques. A generalization of quartic box splines for arbitrary triangulations was given by Loop [14].

Alternatively one can directly derive a set of spline patches which globally achieve some order of continuity [15, 18, 19, 3]. The output of these algorithms is a set of patches of varying, at times rather high, polynomial order and varying shape.

2.2 Interpolating Subdivision Schemes

Since the ability to control the resulting surface exactly is very important in many applications, modifications of approximating schemes have been proposed to force the limit surface to *interpolate* particular points and normals. Nasri [17] presents such a modification for the Doo-Sabin scheme, while Halstead *et al.* [11] do the same for the Catmull-Clark scheme. Both cases have a number of limitations. For example, it is unclear under what conditions the linear system to be solved for the interpolation constraints is solvable. Additionally, the interpolation conditions are only satisfied in the limit. Among the patch based schemes only Peters [18] recently gave one which can incorporate interpolation constraints without requiring the solution of a global linear system. We choose a more direct route by considering subdivision schemes which are interpolating by design.

The Butterfly scheme is interpolating, local, and simple to implement, but only leads to C^1 surfaces in the regular setting [10] (all vertices of the mesh have valence 6.) Topological regularity is a rather severe restriction: the failure to be smooth for vertices of valence other than six can be quite noticeable (see Figures 1 and 4).

3 Interpolating Subdivision Surfaces

We first discuss surface smoothness, next present the main idea behind our construction and then give the description of the subdivision algorithm. Space limitations do not permit us to go into the details of the mathematical derivation. These are presented in [25].

3.1 Smoothness

One of the advantages of patch based polynomial schemes is that their *analytic* smoothness properties are well understood and closely correlate with what a human observer would call a smooth surface. This property is only partially covered by such notions as C^k continuity, e.g., a C^2 function may be quite "wiggly." Absence of unnecessary undulations is often referred to as "fairness." For example, Halstead, *et al.* [11] observed that enforcing interpolation conditions on Catmull-Clark surfaces resulted in a loss of fairness, an issue they addressed with a global optimization pass.

In the present paper we do not consider the question of globally optimal fairness. Nonetheless we are attempting to build smooth interpolating subdivision schemes which yield surfaces whose shape is as pleasing as possible. Because no vertex is ever moved once it is computed, any distortion in the early stages of the subdivision will persist. This makes particularly the first few subdivision steps very important.

Local smoothness of the surface requires the existence of smooth coordinate functions $(x, y, z)(s, t)$. In the next section we discuss the smoothness of coordinate functions in greater detail.

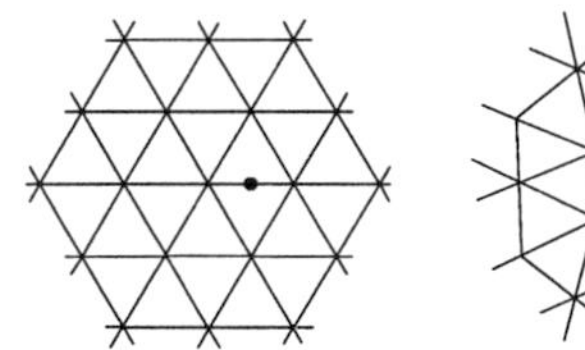

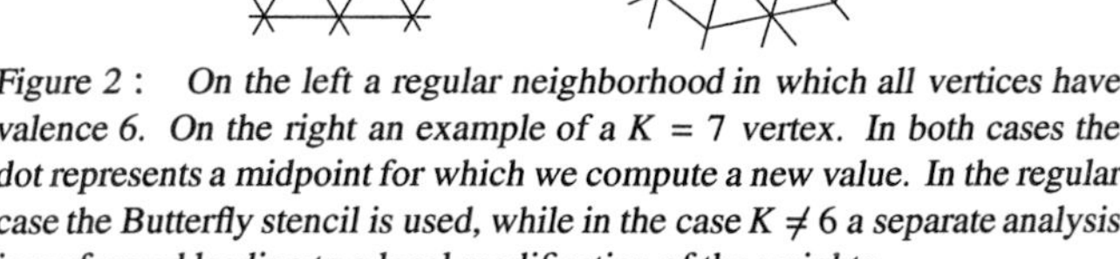

Figure 2 : On the left a regular neighborhood in which all vertices have valence 6. On the right an example of a $K = 7$ vertex. In both cases the dot represents a midpoint for which we compute a new value. In the regular case the Butterfly stencil is used, while in the case $K \neq 6$ a separate analysis is performed leading to a local modification of the weights.

3.2 The Idea of the Construction

Consider a single coordinate function. This function can be visualized as the graph of some function over the real parameter plane (not to be confused with the actual surface). More concretely, instead of thinking about generating new vertices in $\mathbf{R}^3$ by taking local averages of vertices in the control polyhedron, we are now thinking of *scalar values* which are assigned to the vertices of a triangulation in $\mathbf{R}^2$. This triangulation is refined through splitting each edge in two and reconnecting. The interpolating subdivision scheme is used to define a value associated with the new point of the planar triangulation by taking suitable weighted sums of nearby values. Note that all new planar vertices will be of valence 6. The neighbors participating in the computation are part of the subdivision *stencil* and their weights characterize the scheme.

Since we assume that all our schemes will be local, we need to analyze only a small number of possible cases of the relationship between the new vertex and the topology of its graph neighborhood. The two cases of primary importance are the regular sites (all vertices are regular), and the extraordinary sites (adjacent to a non-regular vertex.) After several subdivision steps, at most one vertex in the neighborhood has valence not equal to 6, so it is sufficient to analyze behavior of the scheme only on regular and K-regular triangulations, with only one extraordinary vertex of valence K.

For the regular case, we use the Butterfly scheme which *reproduces polynomials* of degree 3. If initial values at the vertices of a regular triangulation are samples of a polynomial function on the plane, the limit of polynomial-reproducing subdivision will be that function.

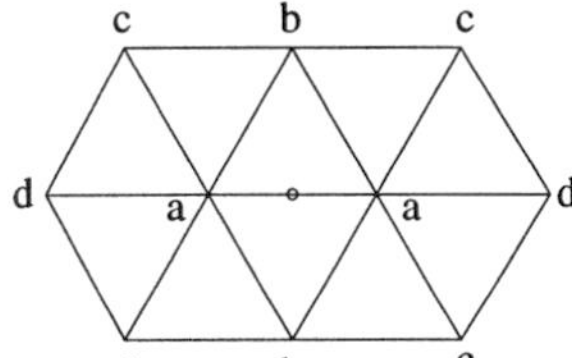

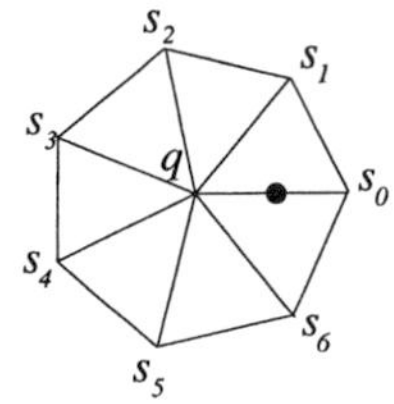

Figure 3 : a: Ten-point stencil. The dot indicates the midpoint of the edge for which a new value is computed. b: Stencil for a vertex in the 1-neighborhood of an extraordinary vertex

For the K-regular case, we try to choose the coefficients in such a way that the behavior of the scheme is similar to the regular case. To keep the support minimal we use only the immediate neighbors of an extraordinary vertex to compute the values at new sites next to it (see Figure 3(b).) We use a limited version of polynomial reproduction for the neighborhood of an extraordinary vertex: the values of a polynomial function of degree less than 3 have to be reproduced only for the immediate neighbors of the extraordinary vertex on each level, except the case $K = 3$, when only some second degree polynomials are reproduced.

The Discrete Fourier Transform and an eigen analysis allow us to to construct subdivision rules with these constraints [25]. The subdivision matrices for extraordinary vertices have the same eigenvalues as the matrices for regular vertices.

3.3 The Modified Subdivision Scheme

The subdivision scheme computes a new scalar value for each edge midpoint of the triangulation. We distinguish between four positions of the edge that we subdivide.

1. *The edge connects two vertices of valence 6.* In that case we use the extension of the Butterfly scheme to the ten point stencil [8] (see Figure 3a). This is the canonical setting and the weights are given by

$$a = 1/2 - w,\ b = 1/8 + 2w,\ c = -1/16 - w,\ d = w$$

   where w can be chosen suitably small [8] (we used $w = 0$).
2. *The edge connects a K-vertex ($K \neq 6$) and a 6-vertex;* the 1-neighbors of the K-vertex are used in the stencil as indicated in Figure 3b. For $K \geq 5$ the weights are given by

$$s_j = (1/4 + \cos(2\pi j/K) + 1/2\cos(4\pi j/K))/K$$

   with $j = 0, \ldots, K-1$. For $K = 3$ we take $s_0 = 5/12$, $s_{1,2} = -1/12$, and for $K = 4$, $s_0 = 3/8$, $s_2 = -1/8$, $s_{1,3} = 0$.
3. *The edge connects two extraordinary vertices;* in this case we take the average of the values computed using the appropriate scheme of the previous paragraph for each endpoint. Since this case can only occur at the topmost level of subdivision the ultimate smoothness of the scheme is not influenced by this choice. However, we have found that the overall *fairness* of the resulting shapes tends to be better with this scheme.
4. *Boundary edges* are subdivided using the 1-dimensional 4 point scheme ($s_{-1} = -1/16, s_0 = 9/16, s_1 = 9/16, s_2 = -1/16$) [7, 6]. In this case only other edge points participate in the stencil. A consequence of this rule is that two separate meshes, whose boundary is identical, will have a matching boundary curve after subdivision. Edges which are not on the boundary but which have a vertex which is on the boundary are subdivided as before while any vertices in the stencil which would be on the other side of the boundary are replaced with "virtual" vertices. These are constructed on the fly by reflecting vertices across the boundary.

4 Results

We built an interactive application supporting general triangular meshes and adaptive subdivision, using restricted triangular quadtrees. All subdivision coefficients are precomputed and stored in a table indexed by the valence K of a given vertex. We present here some results obtained with this application.

In the top half of Figure 4 we show how application of our scheme to an initial polyhedron (on the right) produces a smooth pipe joint.[1] Note that the original control polyhedron contains vertices of valence 7 and 4 next to each other. Six levels of the original Butterfly subdivision lead to the shape that is shown in the middle. In several regions the surface has creases. In contrast on the top right is the shape resulting from applying our modified scheme to the same original control polyhedron. These images also demonstrate the treatment of boundaries. We applied our scheme to a data set of a mannequin head (courtesy University of Washington) and a torso (a dataset from the *Avalon* site maintained by Viewpoint Datalab.) The bottom half of Figure 4 shows the original polyhedron and subdivision surfaces approximated with 3 subdivision levels. The mannequin dataset was obtained from the control mesh for the Loop subdivision scheme by moving each control vertex to its limit position on the surface. Then the surface was interpolated using the modified Butterfly scheme.

It is important to note the difference between averaging schemes like Loop's and interpolating schemes. While averaging schemes are able to produce relatively fair surfaces from highly irregular control polyhedra acting as low-pass filters, interpolating schemes by their nature are much more sensitive to the irregularities in the initial mesh. Our examples demonstrate that if the initial mesh is sampled from a smooth surface, the interpolation scheme performs quite well.

[1]This configuration was inspired by a similar configuration of Jens Albrecht, Erlangen University.

5 Summary and Future Work

We have presented a simple interpolating subdivision scheme for meshes with arbitrary topology. Our scheme is based on the Butterfly scheme, with special rules applied in the neighborhood of the extraordinary vertices. The proposed scheme has a number of properties that make it attractive:

- it is interpolating at all levels of subdivision;
- the support of the scheme is minimal;
- it is easy to implement;
- limit surfaces have adequate smoothness;
- subdivision can be performed adaptively;
- explicit formulas for the normals exists [25].

Our scheme is especially convenient for multiresolution representation of surfaces and wavelet representation of functions on surfaces as in [22].

There are several aspects which we believe to be worth investigating further:

- Currently we perform only a limited adaptation of the scheme at the boundary. A more detailed analysis of K-vertices on or near the boundary is desirable.
- By collapsing vertices and edges, this scheme can immediately accommodate mesh tagging approaches such as in [12]. Furthermore, the degree of smoothness of the surface can be continuously adjusted by manipulating the remaining degrees of freedom of the scheme.
- Preliminary tests show that Hoppe's subdivision surface fitting methodology works well with the scheme proposed in this paper.
- The question of C^1 smoothness will be analyzed based on the work of Reif [20] and Warren [24] in a forthcoming paper.
- We have observed that the "fairness" of the surface is determined by the behavior of the scheme at the first two subdivision steps. A more thorough analysis of the scheme in the first subdivision steps may shed more light on how to maintain fairness under the constraint of interpolation.

Acknowledgements

This work was supported in part by an equipment grant from Hewlett Packard and funds provided to the second author by the Charles Lee Powell Foundation. Additional support was provided by NSF (ASC-89-20219), as part of the NSF/DARPA STC for Computer Graphics and Scientific Visualization. All opinions, findings, conclusions, or recommendations expressed in this document are those of the authors and do not necessarily reflect the views of the sponsoring agencies.

References

[1] Ball, A. A., and Storry, D. J. T. Conditions for tangent plane continuity over recursively generated B-spline surfaces. *ACM Transactions on Graphics 7*, 2 (1988), 83–102.

[2] Catmull, E., and Clark, J. Recursively generated B-spline surfaces on arbitrary topological meshes. *Computer Aided Design 10*, 6 (1978), 350–355.

[3] Dahmen, W., Micchelli, C. A., and Seidel, H.-P. Blossoming begets B-splines bases built better by B-patches. *Mathematics of Computation 59*, 199 (1992), 97–115.

[4] Doo, D. A subdivision algorithm for smoothing down irregularly shaped polyhedrons. In *Proceedings on Interactive Techniques in Computer Aided Design* (Bologna, 1978), pp. 157–165.

[5] Doo, D., and Sabin, M. Analysis of the behaviour of recursive division surfaces near extraordinary points. *Computer Aided Design 10*, 6 (1978), 356–360.

[6] Dubuc, S. Interpolation through an iterative scheme. *J. Math. Anal. Appl. 114* (1986), 185–204.

[7] Dyn, N., Gregory, J. A., and Levin, D. A four-point interpolatory subdivision scheme for curve design. *Computer Aided Geometric Design 4* (1987), 257–268.

[8] Dyn, N., Hed, S., and Levin, D. Subdivision schemes for surface interpolation. In *Workshop in Computational Geometry* (1993), A. C. et al., Ed., World Scientific, pp. 97–118.

Initial Mesh Butterfly scheme interpolation Modified Butterfly interpolation

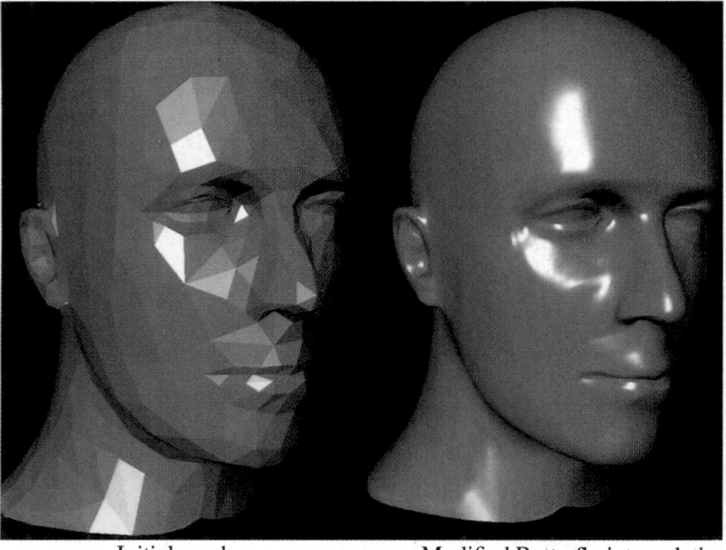

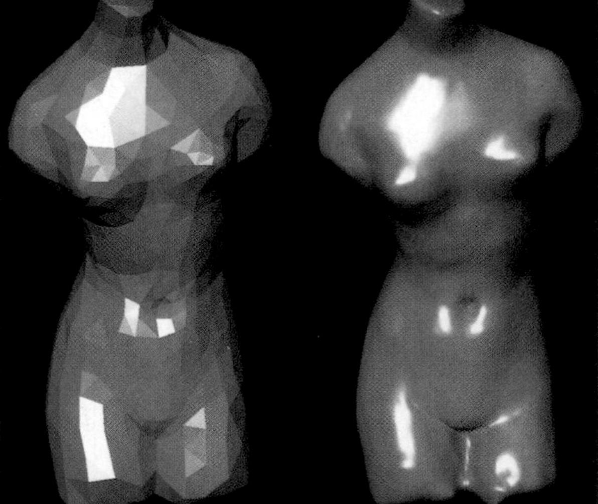

Initial mesh Modified Butterfly interpolation Initial mesh Modified Butterfly interpolation

Figure 4 : Top row: pipe joint. Note the difference between Butterfly and Modified Butterfly. Lower left: mannequin head. Lower right: torso.

[9] Dyn, N., Levin, D., and Gregory, J. A. A butterfly subdivision scheme for surface interpolation with tension control. *ACM Transactions on Graphics 9*, 2 (1990), 160–169.

[10] Dyn, N., Levin, D., and Micchelli, C. A. Using parameters to increase smoothness of curves and surfaces generated by subdivision. *Computer Aided Geometric Design 7* (1990), 129–140.

[11] Halstead, M., Kass, M., and DeRose, T. Efficient, fair interpolation using catmull-clark surfaces. In *Computer Graphics Proceedings* (1993), Annual Conference Series, ACM Siggraph, pp. 35–44.

[12] Hoppe, H., DeRose, T., Duchamp, T., Halstead, M., Jin, H., McDonald, J., Schweitzer, J., and Stuetzle, W. Piecewise smooth surface reconstruction. In *Computer Graphics Proceedings* (1994), Annual Conference Series, ACM Siggraph, pp. 295–302.

[13] Kobbelt, L. Interpolatory subdivision on open quadrilateral nets with arbitrary topology. In *Computer Graphics Forum* (1996), vol. 15, Eurographics, Basil Blackwell Ltd. Eurographics '96 Conference issue.

[14] Loop, C. Smooth subdivision surfaces based on triangles. Master's thesis, University of Utah, Department of Mathematics, 1987.

[15] Loop, C. Smooth spline surfaces over irregular meshes. In *Computer Graphics Proceedings* (1994), Annual Conference Series, ACM Siggraph, pp. 303–310.

[16] Lounsbery, M., DeRose, T. D., and Warren, J. Multiresolution surfaces of arbitrary topological type. Department of Computer Science and Engineering 93-10-05, University of Washington, October 1993. Updated version available as 93-10-05b, January, 1994.

[17] Nasri, A. H. Surface interpolation on irregular networks with normal conditions. *Computer Aided Geometric Design 8* (1991), 89–96.

[18] Peters, J. C^1 surface splines. *SIAM J. Numer. Anal. 32*, 2 (1995), 645–666.

[19] Peters, J. Curvature continuous spline surfaces over irregular meshes. *Computer Aided Geometric Design* (to appear).

[20] Reif, U. A unified approach to subdivision algorithms near extraordinary points. *Computer Aided Geometric Design 12* (1995), 153–174.

[21] Sabin, M. *The use of Piecewise Forms for the Numerical Representation of Shape.* PhD thesis, Hungarian Academy of Sciences, Budapest, 1976.

[22] Schröder, P., and Sweldens, W. Spherical wavelets: Efficiently representing functions on the sphere. In *Computer Graphics Proceedings* (1995), Annual Conference Series, ACM Siggraph, pp. 161–172.

[23] Sweldens, W. The lifting scheme: A construction of second generation wavelets. Tech. Rep. 1995:06, Industrial Mathematics Initiative, Department of Mathematics, University of South Carolina, 1995.

[24] Warren, J. Subdivision methods for geometric design. Unpublished manuscript, November 1995.

[25] Zorin, D., Schröder, P., and Sweldens, W. Interpolating subdivision for meshes of arbitrary topology. Tech. Rep. CS-TR-96-06, Caltech, Department of Computer Science, Caltech, 1996.

Disney's Aladdin: First Steps Toward Storytelling in Virtual Reality

Randy Pausch[1], Jon Snoddy[2], Robert Taylor[2], Scott Watson[2], Eric Haseltine[2]
[1]University of Virginia [2]Walt Disney Imagineering

Figure 1: A Guest's View of the Virtual Environment

ABSTRACT

Disney Imagineering has developed a high-fidelity virtual reality (VR) attraction where guests fly a magic carpet through a virtual world based on the animated film "Aladdin." Unlike most existing work on VR, which has focused on hardware and systems software, we assumed high fidelity and focused on using VR as a new medium to tell stories. We fielded our system at EPCOT Center for a period of fourteen months and conducted controlled experiments, observing the reactions of over 45,000 guests.

Riders filled out an exit survey after the experience, and with select groups we used a number of other data-gathering techniques, including interviews and mechanically logging where guests looked and flew.

Our major finding is that in a high fidelity VR experience, men and women of all ages suspend disbelief and accept the illusion that they are in a different place. We have found that in VR, as in all media, content matters. Novices are unimpressed with the technology for its own sake; they care about what there is to do in the virtual world. We can improve the experience by telling a pre-immersion "background story" and by giving the guest a concrete goal to perform in the virtual environment. Our eventual goal is to develop the lexicon for this new storytelling medium: the set of communication techniques shared between directors and the audience. We conclude with a discussion of our second version of the Aladdin project, which contains a large number of synthetic characters and a narrative story line.

contact author: Randy Pausch, Computer Science Department, Thornton Hall, University of Virginia, Charlottesville, VA 22903. Pausch@virginia.edu, 804/982-2211

INTRODUCTION

Most existing work on virtual reality (VR) has focused on hardware and system software [1, 3, 5, 6, 7, 10, 12, 23, 24]. The price of a high quality system has placed it out of reach for most people interested in content. Building high quality, low cost VR systems is important, but we believe the exciting challenge in VR is learning what to do with the medium.

We believe that the content questions are the really hard ones. The goal of this project has been to allow the content producers, or authors, to assume the existence of satisfactory technology and to focus directly on authoring in the new medium of VR. We produced high-quality content based on flying a magic carpet in the animated film "Aladdin" [2]. Figure 1 shows a screen shot from the system.

We field-tested the system on over 45,000 guests at EPCOT Center. In this paper we report our detailed observations, the guests' exit surveys, and data we recorded during guest experiences. This is not a systems implementation paper; we describe the hardware and software only as context for describing the guest experience. In addition to guest experiences, we also describe industrial design solutions to the problems of high volume usage. In early 1996, we will deploy a second version with a narrative story line and a large number of reactive characters. We conclude with lessons learned from creating virtual environments and characters for our second version, especially controlling the narrative in an interactive medium.

Our underlying premise is that VR is a new medium, as film, radio, and television once were. As motion pictures matured, directors and audiences developed a lexicon including close ups, cross cuts, flash backs, etc. Over time a common language, or lexicon, will evolve for VR; this project is our first step towards that goal.

SYSTEM DESCRIPTION

In each of our field trials, four guests donned head-mounted displays and piloted a flying carpet. Because they were running on separate systems, the pilots could neither see nor interact with each other.

We designed the system for robustness, high volume usage, and high accessibility. Unlike research setups, theme park equipment is used extensively, continuously, and abusively. Failures with a one-in-a-million chance of happening can occur once a week in a typical theme park attraction.

The Head Mounted Display

The system used an internally developed head-mounted display (HMD), shown in Figure 2. The two main design constraints were to provide high image quality and to make it easy to put the HMD on quickly, to support the high throughput of guests in a theme park attraction. In early trials we learned that having adjustments such as a focus knob on the HMD confused guests, since they had no baseline to distinguish between high and low image quality. Therefore, we designed a system that would accommodate a large variation in where a guest's eyes sit with respect to the optics.

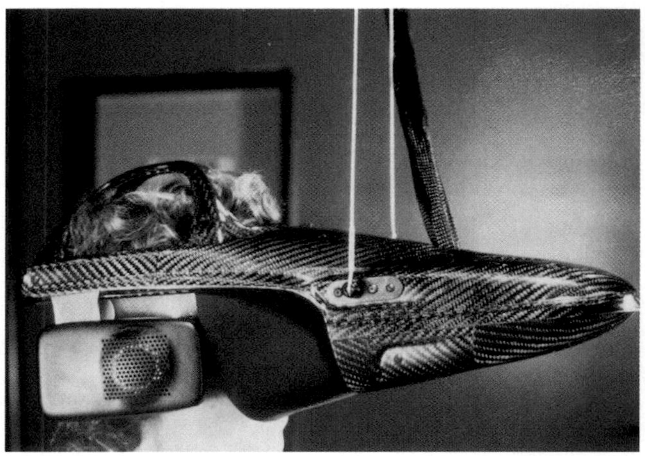

Figure 2: The Head Mounted Display

Image quality considerations drove us to use CRTs instead of LCDs, a tradeoff that increased the HMD's weight and extended its center of mass. We partially compensated for this by providing spring-suspension of the HMD from the ceiling. Major design challenges in the HMD included avoiding visible pixel boundaries, obtaining high contrast, minimizing inter-ocular rivalry, and addressing the weight balance and packaging issues. For head-tracking, we used a magnetic position/orientation tracker.

Unlike many other VR systems, our HMD display was bi-ocular, not stereo. We rendered a single, horizontally wide graphics window and fed partially overlapping view windows to each of the CRTs in the HMD. For applications such as ours, stereoscopy is surprisingly unimportant as a depth cue [8].

We addressed hygiene issues by having the HMD snap onto a per-guest inner "cap" that can be cleaned separately. The inner liner also allowed us to adjust tightness to each guest's head before monopolizing the more expensive HMD and image generator. The HMD fit comfortably over eyeglasses; the only notable issue was guests with hair tied in buns.

Sound

The HMD contained two speakers that rested close to, but not in physical contact with, the guest's ears. We used a combination of stereo ambient sound, binaural recorded sound, and eight channels of localized sound. We recorded the binaural sound track via a high quality binaural head (essentially, microphones placed in a mannequin head). The binaural soundtrack included background voices, animals, and other "clutter" sounds. We recorded multiple binaural tracks, and then mixed those layers to form a composite recording. When the binaural recording was played during the VR experience, even though those sounds "moved with the head," they established a believable background sound field. It is in this context that the eight special channels were convolved to localize in real-time based on head tracking [26]. The localized channels provided main characters and large sound effects. The stereo sound (primarily music) established emotional context, the binaural sound established the believable three-dimensional space, and the localized sounds gave strong, specific cues for orientation. The three levels increasingly traded recording quality for localization, and the binaural and localized sounds worked well together because they employed the same head-related transfer functions [4].

Seating, Controls, and Motion Base

Guests were seated straddling a motorcycle-style seat as shown in Figure 3. A benefit of this design is that the guests were firmly grounded, with weight on their buttocks, knees, and feet. Additionally, this design accommodated a wide range of heights. Guests gripped a steering mechanism representing the front of a magic carpet. Turning left or right controlled yaw of the carpet, and tilting controlled the pitch of the carpet Imagine a car's steering wheel; pulling the top of the wheel toward the driver pitched the carpet up, pushing it pitched the carpet down. Pushing the entire mechanism forward controlled velocity. Figure 4 shows a schematic diagram of the carpet controls.

Figure 3: The Physical Setup

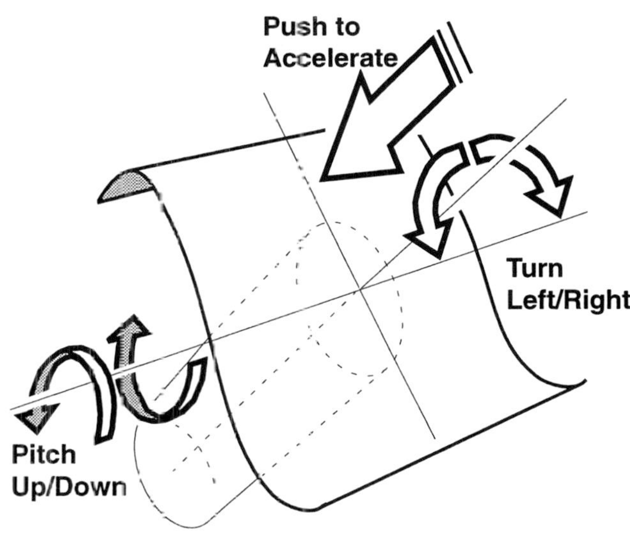

Figure 4: Schematic Diagram of Carpet Controls

We mounted the seat on a movable base that pitched up and down in response to the steering control. Originally, the motion base also tilted side-to-side, but this caused discomfort during early testing so we removed the side-to-side tilt. Surprisingly, the presence or absence of a motion base had no substantial effect on guest satisfaction, or anything else we measured with exit surveys.

An early version of the system simulated wind with a rate-controlled fan blowing air over the guests. Much to our disappointment, most guests wearing the HMD did not notice it.

Image Generation

For each guest, we used a custom Silicon Graphics computer with 512 megabytes of RAM, 16 megabytes of texture memory, eight 150 MHz MIPS R4400 CPUs and three Reality Engine pipelines with four RM5 raster managers each. We rendered 20 frames per second on each pipe, interleaving the frames to achieve a 60 Hz frame rate. Although the frame rates could vary between 15 and 60 during a flight, the overwhelming majority of the time the system rendered at 60 Hz.

Because hardware lighting can draw attention to edges in models with low polygon count, our artists decided to render all polygons with hand-painted textures, with no hardware lighting. This also improves rendering time slightly, but we did it for image quality, not speed.

Model Management And Show Programming

A custom software system, called the *player*, provided scene management and character animation playback. The player provided a Scheme interface on top of a C/C++ layer, all on top of SGI Performer [19].

The player used Performer's support for multiple levels of detail. Unlike a flight simulator, most of our scene was close, so we used only two levels of detail per object. Artists created both models for each object because degrading a model "by hand" still produces better results than automatic means [20]. We sometimes used large texture "flats" for distant objects, and switched to three dimensional models as the guest approached.

Programming of various show elements, such as an object's reaction when hit by the carpet, was performed in the topmost layer of the player, a locally developed "Story Animation Language." This SAL layer implemented cooperative lightweight threads on top of Chez Scheme [9], an incrementally compiled Scheme.

In our second version, the database is much larger, and is partitioned into distinct scenes. The player software pre-fetches geometry and texture maps as guests fly from one scene to another [11]. Between scenes, we include explicit "transition areas," such as hallways and caverns. Transition areas have a smaller number of polygons, which buys us time to pre-fetch textures. Transitions bend and twist, thus ensuring that at no point can the guest quickly look back to the previous scene.

GUEST SELECTION

We deployed the system at EPCOT Center in Orlando, Florida, from July 1, 1994 until September 8, 1995. Every twenty minutes a group of up to 120 guests was given a brief technical lecture about VR followed by a demonstration where four guests were selected to "fly a magic carpet."

The attraction was intentionally hidden in a remote area of the park. Most guests entered not because they had a strong interest in VR, but because our attraction was "the next thing" to do. Guests could not volunteer to fly; they were selected by the ride operators. The operators maintained a strict policy of avoiding guests who showed an active interest in VR. Therefore, rather than pertaining to a small subset of VR enthusiasts, we believe that our results are essentially a fair cross section of the theme park population. Some guests did decline the invitation to fly. Interviews revealed this was primarily due to stage fright, not an aversion to trying VR.

The selected pilots did not hear the technical lecture about VR. We gave them a background story that they would be stepping into the feature film "Aladdin." We instructed them that the main goal was to have fun, but that they were also searching for a character from the film. The marketplace scene was chosen because it 1) contains familiar objects such as doors which establish scale, 2) is a brightly lit daytime scene, and 3) contains wide variety, encouraging exploration. There was typically time for a one-to-three minute practice flight followed by a few minutes of rest before the audience entered and the four minute flight began.

NOVICES' EXPERIENCES

We exposed a large, non-self selected, population of guests to a high-fidelity virtual experience in a controlled environment. At least one other system has exposed large numbers of novices to VR [25]. However, Virtuality's users were self-selected. Their users wanted to try VR, and paid for the experience. Our sample is much more diverse.

Our findings are drawn from a variety of sources, including written post-flight guest surveys, logged flight data, extensive conversations with the day-to-day attraction operators, observations of guests' flights, and interviews of guests before, during and after their flights.

Technologists should be aware that most guests were not impressed by the technology itself; guests assumed VR was possible and had an expectation of extremely high quality. Many had seen the "holodeck" on Star Trek, and expected that level of quality. Once in a virtual environment, guests focused on what there was to do in the virtual world – content matters!

General Observations

We were able to sustain the illusion that the guests were in another place. Men and women of all ages suspended disbelief and a large number reported the sensation that they were "in" the scene. This is hard to conclude from exit surveys, but guests also provided unsolicited cues, such as panicking or ducking their heads as they approached obstacles.

Guests cared about the experience, not the technology. Most guests had no concept of how VR works, nor did they care. They focused on the sensation, which was exhilarating for most guests. Many guests shouted "Wow!" or "Whee!" in their first thirty seconds.

The experience was overwhelming. Between sensory overload and the task of trying to control the carpet's flight, many guests were so cognitively taxed that they had trouble answering questions early in their flights.

Guests needed a goal. If not given a specific goal, guests would ask "What should I be doing?"

Guests needed a background story. We found that giving as much context as possible about the scene helped reduce the severity of the transition from the real to the virtual environment. *Background story* is the set of expectations, goals, major characters, and set of rules that apply to the virtual world. Ironically, in lower fidelity, less believable VR systems, this need for background story may not be as evident. We believe it is the abrupt transition into a *believable* virtual world that is problematic. Performing a good transition from the real to the virtual world is an open challenge.

Guests liked exploring, and seeing new spaces. Most guests did not spend much time studying detail in a given place; they tended to move on quickly to new vistas.

Guests did not turn their heads very much. This could be because they were piloting a vehicle, or because they were not accustomed to being able to turn their heads when looking at displayed images. For many, we believe the latter. Guests often watched characters "walk out of frame," as would happen with television or movies. Our strongest indication came from many pilots where we waited 90 seconds into their flight, then explicitly told them to turn their heads. At that point, they clearly had the "aha" of the head-tracking experience. While we suspect that different content would be more conducive to head turning, head tracking is far enough from most guests' experiences with film and television that we suspect this will be a problem for many systems.

Controlling the carpet was a problem for many guests. This prompted the addition of test flights before the show began. Many guests flew out into the desert or up above the city to find a space where there were fewer obstacles, making flight easier. Although we could have had the magic carpet fly itself, our surveys indicated that the control and freedom are important parts of the experience. Six-axis control is a very difficult problem and an important design challenge is finding appropriate control constraints.

VR must be personally experienced. In addition to the 45,000 guests who piloted carpets, we had over one million audience members who observed the pilots' progress on display monitors. The audience members enjoyed the show and understood that *something* fascinating was going on with the pilots, but it was clear that VR is foreign enough that most people can not fully comprehend it without direct personal experience. Audience members often asked if the pilots could see or interact with each other.

Presence and Immersion

Although it is difficult to formally measure, we believe that most guests suspended disbelief and had the experience of being in a new place. Our choice of an animated world underscored that believability is different from photo-realism. In fact, we reject the term "simulation," as we provide an experience not possible in reality. Our virtual environment was not realistic, but it was consistent with the large number of animated worlds that guests had seen before. Guests flew, but had no fear of heights; guests reacted to the characters, but were not afraid of a guard who brandished a sword. In many ways, this environment was compelling without being disturbing.

A common sight in a 3-D theater is to see large numbers of guests reaching out to grab the projected image. We speculate that they are compelled to conduct this test because their perceptual and cognitive systems are in conflict; their eyes tell them the object is within arm's length, but their brain tells them it is just a projection. In our system, we saw no evidence of the need to test. Guests did not intentionally run into objects to see if the objects really existed. In fact, guests did the opposite, often involuntarily ducking when they felt they could not avoid a collision.

In general, we believe that the need for high fidelity can be reduced by engaging the user in a complex, real-time task. For example, the desktop DOOM game [14] and the SIMNET tank simulator [18] both get users to the point where the interface becomes transparent and the user focuses on task performance, which requires a sense of presence. Our system did so with the mildest of tasks, that of searching for a character. At first, we suspected that the difficult task of piloting the carpet might lower our fidelity requirements. Therefore, we ran experiments where the carpet flew itself. During those tests guests achieved the same suspension of disbelief, with the only task being to look around. Our metric for suspension of disbelief was their reactions to the environment, such as ducking when flying near objects.

What produced the effect of immersion is difficult to know. Even for guests who did not turn their heads much, the HMD physically blocked out the real world. Sound was also very important, as many guests remarked that the sound of wind when they flew high, or the crashing noises when they ran into walls strongly reinforced their sense of being there. In post flight interviews, guests told us that their illusion of presence was destroyed when characters did not react.

Reaction to Virtual Characters

It is more difficult to build a believable character than a believable scene. Although our major focus was on building the environments, we were pleased that a few of our guests did respond to characters. The show began with instructions from a parrot who told the pilots to nod their heads. Some guests actually heeded his command. Another character covered his head and shouted "Don't you have a horn on that thing?!" when guests flew near him. Many guests shouted back at this character. One young girl finished the attraction in tears because she had spent several minutes attempting to apologize to him, but instead continually triggered hostile responses whenever she approached him. (All the characters had a small set of dialog sequences that could be triggered).

The key to a successful character is the suspension of disbelief; one must talk to the puppet, not the puppeteer. Most guests flew at high speed, zooming past the characters. When guests did slow down, they expected the characters to respond and were very disappointed when the characters did not. At the very least, characters should orient their heads and eyes and look at the guest. Our next system is incorporating this feature.

We suspect that the limited believability of our first system's characters is due to low fidelity. All characters in the first show, such as those shown in Figure 5, were animated with motion capture, where sensors recorded an actor's body motions in real time, and those values were used to drive the animation. Our second version uses higher quality key frame animation. While testing of the second version is not yet complete, early indications are that we will cross a fidelity threshold in character animation much as this project crossed one in environment fidelity.

Figure 5: Animated Characters

Men vs. Women

One of our original objectives was to discover whether VR appealed only to the narrow (primarily young male) video game market, or was more like feature films, appealing to males and females of all ages. While *content* will still matter, the technology itself did not turn away any guests. On post flight surveys, the reaction of both genders and all age groups was almost identical on all questions. One major difference was that many women are afraid that they would not be able to operate the equipment properly. This surfaced both as a pre-flight concern and as a post-flight comparison. They often asked how they performed relative to the other pilots. Also, during in-flight interviewing men were more likely to talk about the technology, whereas women were more likely to talk about the experience and emotional impact. Neither men nor women complained about having to wear the HMD.

VR for the Disabled

Everyone involved with the project noted the impact on both the pilots and the audience when motion-impaired guests flew. Accessibility is a fundamental design constraint at Disney parks, and we have a substantial wheelchair population. One of our four stations could be converted for wheelchair access in about ten seconds, and we had several wheelchair fliers per day. The sense of mobility and the joy it brought them was overwhelming.

Motion Sickness

We did not find motion sickness to be as significant an issue as we had feared. During selection, we asked guests if they were prone to motion sickness, and warned that they might feel motion sick during the experience. We also told them they could stop at any time and remove the HMD. Post flight surveys indicated that, as with many theme park attractions, some guests reported discomfort or dizziness, but they mostly described it as a mild sensation. We do not know if guests who felt discomfort or dizziness self-limited their head motion; our logged data showed no such correlation. Reports of discomfort went up when the room was warmer, which is consistent with discomfort reports from platform-based simulator rides. We were careful to limit the duration of the experience. As with any "thrill" experience, discomfort increases with ride length.

GUEST POST-RIDE SURVEYS

After their flights, we asked guests to complete a one page survey with about five multiple choice questions. Guests were identified on the survey only by first name, and over 95 percent of the guests completed a survey. Most who declined did so because of low English skills. We asked many questions and report here a relevant subset. Our sample was 48.5 percent female, and included all ages.

We tried to ask questions that would yield different responses by gender and age. However, we were unable to design questions where the responses were not reasonably consistent across all groups. Thus, we conclude that VR experiences have broad appeal. Responses are presented here by gender (M = male, F = female); breakdown by age is equally similar. The possible responses are listed in the same order as they appeared on the printed survey form. Because we made ongoing changes to the surveys, the number of total responses to any question is variable -- after each question is the total number of responses.

What did you LIKE the most? (N=25,038)

	all	M	F
characters	11%	10%	12%
helmet fit	4%	4%	3%
motion	32%	32%	32%
picture quality	17%	19%	15%
sound	8%	7%	9%
steering control	21%	21%	21%
town	7%	7%	7%

What did you DISLIKE the most? (N=22,479)

	all	M	F
characters	5%	6%	4%
helmet fit	20%	20%	20%
motion	13%	14%	13%
picture quality	13%	13%	13%
sound	6%	6%	6%
steering control	34%	33%	36%
town	8%	8%	7%

Guest rating of the Experience (N=1,903)

	all	M	F
terrible	1%	1%	1%
okay	4%	4%	5%
good	11%	9%	13%
great	54%	49%	57%
best thing at Disney	23%	28%	20%
best thing in my life	7%	9%	5%

As an absolute answer, we take this with a grain of salt. It is unlikely that our system is really the best thing in seven percent of our guests' lives. However, the scale is useful for comparing males and females; again, we found an overwhelming similarity.

Would You Recommend it To a Friend? (N=273)

	all	M	F
yes	99%	100%	98%
no	1%	0%	2%

It Made Me Feel Like I Was... (N=1,336)

	all	M	F
visiting a town	14%	15%	14%
playing a video game	23%	19%	25%
being inside a movie	45%	49%	43%
in the middle of a dream	17%	16%	17%
invisible	1%	1%	2%

Had You Heard About Virtual Reality Before Today? (N=307)

	all	M	F
no	16%	12%	18%
I had read about it	36%	37%	34%
seen on TV or movies	49%	50%	47%

On My Next Ride, I Would Most Like To... (N=324)

	all	M	F
see more characters	35%	32%	40%
see more towns/places	38%	37%	38%
see the other pilots	27%	31%	22%

The Best Thing About it Was... (N=439)

	all	M	F
the characters	5%	3%	6%
flying	42%	41%	43%
exploring/seeing new things	23%	23%	23%
being able to go where I wanted	30%	33%	28%

I would most like to... (N=426)

	all	M	F
have the carpet fly itself	9%	5%	12%
fly the carpet myself	84%	90%	80%
ride while a friend is flying	6%	4%	8%

LOGGED DATA

For over two thousand guests we recorded the position and orientation of the pilot's head and the carpet twenty times each second. Our original hope was that we could see patterns of where guests flew and what they found interesting. In fact, we discovered that guests flew almost indiscriminately; no obvious patterns of travel emerged from the data.

The analysis of head turning data was more interesting. Our first question was "How much do guests turn their heads?" The data confirmed what many researchers describe as the dirty secret of VR. In many scenarios, people in HMDs do not turn their heads very much. Figure 6 shows a top-view polar histogram of head yaw; for a guest facing right, the length of each line shows the proportional amount of time spent at each angle. Figure 7 shows a conventional histogram of guest head yaw; the height of each bar is the portion of total time spent at that angle.

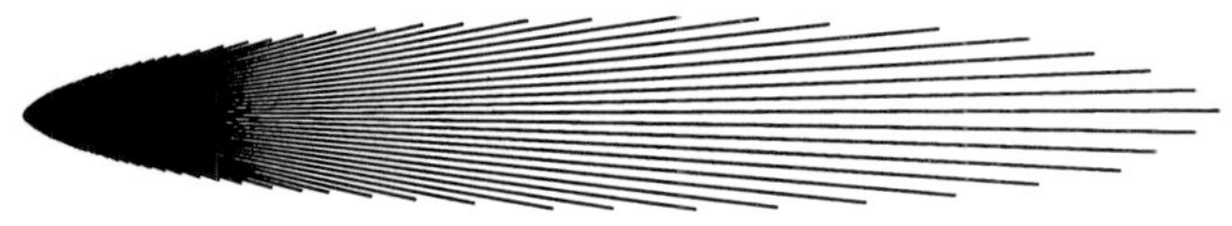

Figure 6: Polar Histogram of Head Yaw

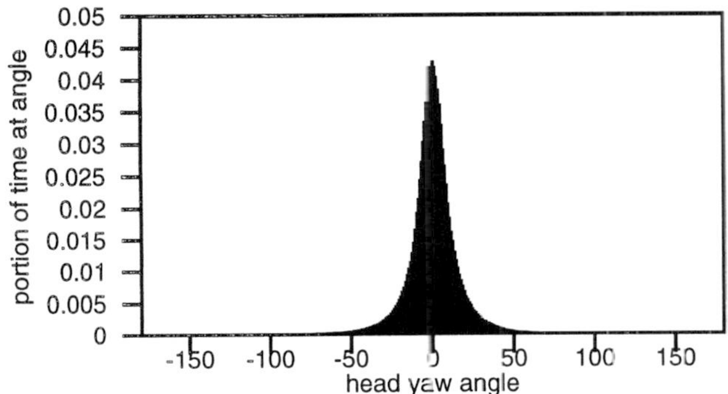

Figure 7: Conventional Histogram of Head Yaw

Figure 8 shows that the difference between male and female head yaw is negligible. In fact, every category that we examined (gender, age, which lab technician instructed them, whether or not they experienced motion discomfort, how much they enjoyed the ride) yielded essentially the same profile.

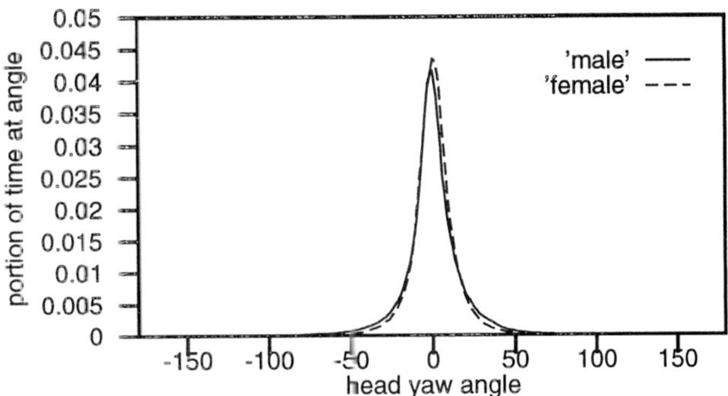

Figure 8: Male vs. Female Head Yaw

Figure 9 shows that head pitch, or up/down tilt, is even more confined than head yaw.

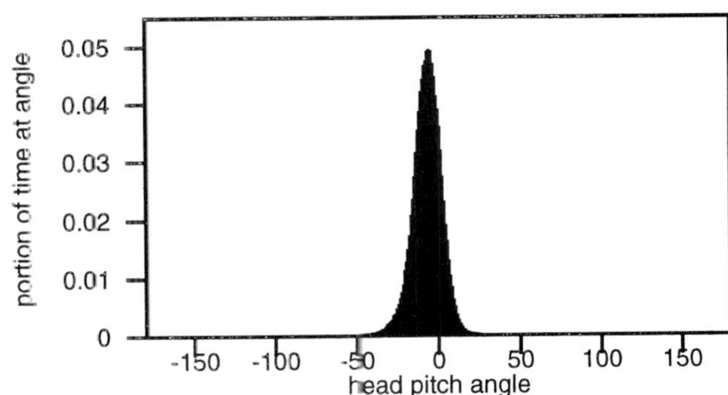

Figure 9: Head Pitch

We were not surprised that guests looked straight ahead most of the time. However, we were surprised by the following: instead of portion of total time, Figure 10 graphs the widest yaw angle guests *ever* experienced. One way to read this graph is that 90% of the guests never looked more than 75 degrees to either side. One could infer that building a 150 degree wide, screen-based display would be as good as an HMD for 90% of the guests. That conclusion would ignore that the HMD field of view must be added to the head yaw, and that the HMD also prevents visual intrusion from the real world.

TELLING STORIES IN VR

Given that VR can present a compelling illusion, researchers can and should pursue its uses for education, training, medical applications, games, and many other purposes. As a storytelling company, we are focusing on using VR as a storytelling medium.

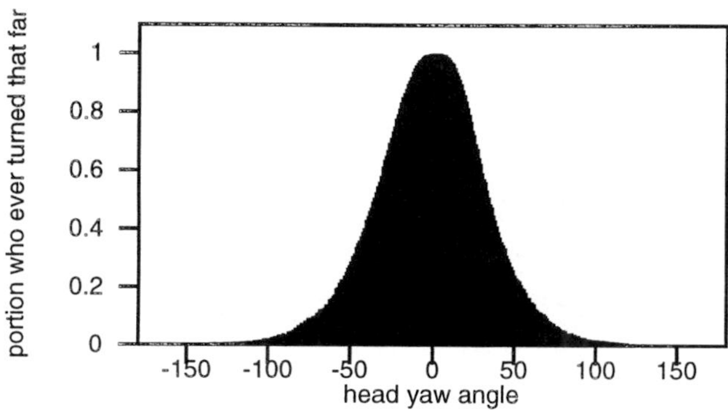

Figure 10: Widest Yaw Angles Seen by Various Guest Percentages

Script vs. Guest Controlled Cameras

Our first system was the first of many steps towards telling stories in VR. Our next show contains over twenty scenes, approximately fifteen high-fidelity characters, and a narrative story line that includes the ability to alter the sequence of events. Our guest assumes a role in an immersive feature film. The major challenge of allowing the guest to become a character is that the director gives up control of the narrative. While this is true of many interactive, non-HMD based games, the problem becomes acute with an HMD.

Because we let the guest control the viewpoint we must build characters and scenes that look good from all vantage points. By establishing entrances to scenes we control the initial view of each scene, a technique used in well-designed theme parks. The inability to cut from scene to scene or view to view is very frustrating for content authors. We have experimented with having characters that are attached to the guest's head, and appear to be hanging off the front of the HMD. This allows us to interject a brief "scene" including that character.

There is an intrinsic conflict between a pre-constructed narrative and a guest-controlled exploration. An interactive system can dynamically re-configure the story to avoid omission of critical portions. As our director said, "It's as if you decide to leave a movie early, and the projectionist edits the film to make sure you see the important ending before you leave."

In other perceptually intensive theme park attractions such as effects-laden stereoscope films or platform simulators, we have learned to keep the story line simple and clear. We must do the same for VR. Our initial experience indicates that VR is good at placing guests in an environment, and we look forward to seeing its storytelling capacities evolve.

All our experiences to date have been with a novice audience. Filmmakers once used devices such as tearing away calendar pages to show flashbacks or passage of time. As the audience became more experienced, these devices became unnecessary.

Controlling the Narrative

We are fairly successful at composing a scene that draws the guest's attention to a desired spot. We have also experimented with using characters to direct attention. In some scenes characters point where we want the guest to look, and in others, we have a character move to be in line with another object we want in view. All these techniques can be quickly tried; the key is to test them on novices.

We have experimented with explicit techniques for controlling the guest's position, such as having a character grab the carpet and drag the guest to a desired location. Another coarse grain technique is to close doors behind guests to keep them from back-tracking. We have also experimented with implicit techniques such as a "water skiing tow rope" metaphor [13], where an invisible boat is controlling the eventual position and the guest is free to fly within a moving envelope.

Sound

In films, the sound track, particularly the musical score, tends to carry the emotional tone for most scenes. Because we no longer control timing we must choose sound tracks that work with wide variation in duration, and we must be able to make the transition smoothly from one ambient sound to the next based on guest actions.

Many VR system architects are concerned with the underlying technology for localizing sound. In our experience, the careful selection/creation of ambient sounds and music, i.e. the content, is much more important than the specific details, or even the use of, sound localization.

AUTHORING

In the process of building our first show we have learned a number of lessons regarding the process of authoring in VR.

Rapid prototyping is essential for authoring. Flight simulator technologies often guarantee rendering frame rates, but require long (many hour) periods to change the show's content. Our SAL/Scheme layer allows code interpretation at run time, similar to MR/OML [22], Alice [16], and World Toolkit [21]. We could not have developed the show without this interpreted layer.

Character animation in our second system approaches the look of traditional animation. This is not surprising, since the principles of animation apply regardless of the medium [15]. The key to achieving this was involving the artists in the development of the underlying technology, rather treating it as a given. We can now generate a new scene or character animation in under a week.

The fidelity trap for VR is that unlike many other media, a low-quality "quick and dirty" mockup is often misleading. Since a partial or low-quality mockup may not yield accurate results when we test guests on it, we often must build systems to completion before we know what works well. This is partially because there are not yet good tools for sketching three dimensional scenes and animations.

Motion capture vs. key frame animation: Our first system used motion capture to animate characters. This allowed us to produce a large amount of animation quickly, but the quality was not as high as the key frame-based animation we are using for the second version. Motion capture is troublesome for non-human characters, often seems too realistic, and requires laborious post-processing of the data.

Branching story: In a linear narrative, a character's behavior is completely pre-planned. When the guest's actions can cause a character to perform different pre-animated sequences, we refer to that as a *branch*. In the original show most characters performed a repose animation until the guest approached, and then branched to perform a reaction animation. While this makes an interesting and active scene, in most cases it does not provide enough different branches to allow the guest to easily suspend disbelief.

Autonomous characters vs. authored branching: Artificially intelligent characters are an interesting concept, but it will be a long time before they are believable in any but the simplest background role. For the next few years, we feel that believable character performances will be made up of branches of pre-animated material rather than computer programs for several reasons: 1) 'thinking" characters are far enough into the future to be off the planning horizon, 2) characters who can construct decent sounding sentences are not much closer, 3) a good animator can achieve a much more believable dramatic performance than a computer program, and 4) even simple branching works when properly done.

In our second version characters have multiple possible behaviors that are triggered by context. Even our simplest characters have a default behavior, a reaction to the guest's presence, and a reaction to the guest's departure. A major technical challenge is to smoothly blend between various pre-defined animations [17].

Rotation of characters to face guests is important to present the illusion that characters are real. We find that first turning a character's head, then his or her body, works best. The technical challenge is to avoid bad interactions between the automatic rotation and the character's key frame animation.

RESEARCH CHALLENGES

Based on our experiences, we present the following as open challenges to the research community:

1) Finding mechanisms that allow guests to self-calibrate the intensity of the experience. Currently we must keep the experience tame enough to be enjoyable for our more sensitive guests.

2) Developing constraints to solve the six-degree-of-freedom problems in controlling flight; i.e. navigation and motion through virtual spaces.

3) Development of software to better support animators, especially in the sketching phase. Animators use onion skin paper to superimpose views from multiple frames; this ability is lacking in most software tools.

4) The automatic generation of mouth animation from sound source. This is currently labor intensive and not particularly creative work.

CONCLUSIONS

This project gave over 45,000 people a first exposure to virtual reality (VR). While we have made what we consider to be substantial advances in HMD and rendering technology, our major advances have been in learning how to create and present compelling virtual environments. We stress that this is an exercise that requires both artistic and engineering talent and creativity.

Our guests completed written surveys, and with subsets we logged head and carpet motions. Based on that data and interviews before, during and after guest flights, we conclude that:

Guests suspend disbelief. The illusion is compelling enough that most guests accept being in a synthetically generated environment and focus on the environment, not the technology.

VR appeals to everyone. Both genders and all ages had similar responses to our attraction. This leads us to conclude that VR is like feature films in that different content may segment the market, but the basic technology does not. We also note that wheelchair guests find mobility within VR extremely exciting.

VR must be personally experienced. VR is foreign enough that most people can not comprehend it without direct personal experience.

Fidelity matters. To get most guests to suspend disbelief requires extremely high fidelity. We provide 60 frames per second (at the expense of stereo), for polygonal models with hand-painted texture maps, and we do not use hardware lighting. Texture quality matters much more than polygon count.

Content matters. People love the experience of VR, but even at high fidelity VR by itself is not enough. The public, unlike the developers, is not impressed with the technology. In fact, the public *assumes* that high fidelity VR exists and immediately focuses on what there is to do in the synthetic environment.

The illusion of presence is fragile. Although guests suspend disbelief, inconsistencies can *instantly* shatter the illusion. For example, objects inter-penetrating, or characters not responding to the guest's presence completely shatter the sense of presence.

Guests need a background story. VR is an overwhelming experience of being thrust into a new environment. A good way to soften this transition is to provide a background story that familiarizes the guest with the new environment before the immersion. This is a standard technique in theme park attractions, typically provided in a pre-show.

Guests need a goal. Guests need to know why they are in the virtual world and what they are supposed to do.

Guests do not turn their heads much. We were surprised at how little people turned their heads in this flight-based experience. We attribute this to the mass of the HMD, the need to look where one is flying, and guests' inexperience with a head-tracked medium.

Input controls are hard. We developed a novel input mechanism for controlling flight. Since no one flies magic carpets in the real world we could not transfer everyday skills. After many design iterations we believe that six axis control is a phenomenally difficult problem and conclude that designers must limit degrees of freedom.

Tell a straightforward story. As we have learned with other intensive media, such as effects laden stereoscopic films and motion-base simulators, when the guest is perceptually overwhelmed it helps to keep the story short and clear.

Aladdin is a beginning, not an end. Our original goal was to move past the technology. Our first system produces a compelling illusion and our next efforts are to examine whether we can tell stories in this new medium. Our second version of the project, scheduled for release in early 1996, contains a large number of characters and a narrative story line.

ACKNOWLEDGMENTS

This work is the effort of many talented people over several years; we mention here only a subset, but express our gratitude to all involved.

Special thanks, in alphabetical order, to: Daniele Colajacomo, for managing the character modeling in the EPCOT show; Dave Fink, for helping start the project; Phillip Freer and Gary Daines, for their art direction and world design; Andy Ogden, for his industrial design on the steering and HMD; George Scribner, for his work on story and character in the EPCOT show; and Dave Spencer, for his management of the EPCOT show installation.

We thank all the other artists and engineers who worked on this project, and we would especially like to express our deepest gratitude to the families and significant others who supported these individuals in their efforts.

We would also like to thank Evans & Sutherland, Silicon Graphics, NASA Ames Research Center, the staff who ran the attraction at EPCOT Center, and Matt Conway.

REFERENCES

[1] Jon Airey, John Rohlf, Frederick Brooks, Towards Image Realism with Interactive Update Rates in Complex Virtual Building Environments, ACM SIGGRAPH Special Issue on 1990 Symposium on Interactive 3D Graphics 24:2, 1990, pages 41-50.

[2] Walt Disney Home Video. Distributed by Buena Vista Home Video, Dept. CS, Burbank, CA, 91521. ISBN 1-55890-663-0. Originally released in 1992 as a motion picture.

[3] Chuck Blanchard, Scott Burgess, Young Harvill, Jaron Lanier, Ann Lasko, Reality Built for Two: A Virtual Reality Tool, ACM SIGGRAPH 1990 Symposium on Interactive 3D Graphics, March 1990.

[4] J. P. Blauert, Spatial Hearing, MIT Press, Cambridge, MA, 1983.

[5] Frederick Brooks, Walkthrough -- A Dynamic Graphics System for Simulating Virtual Buildings, Proceedings of the 1986 Workshop on 3D Graphics, Chapel Hill, NC, October 23-24, 1986, ACM, pages 9-21.

[6] Steve Bryson, Creon Levit, The Virtual Wind Tunnel, IEEE Computer Graphics and Applications, July 1992, pages 25-34.

[7] Christopher Codella et al., Interactive Simulation in a Multi-Person Virtual World, Proceedings of the ACM SIGCHI Human Factors in Computer Systems Conference, May 1992, pages 329-334.

[8] James Cutting and Peter Vishton, Perceiving Layout and Knowing Distances: The Integration, Relative Potency, and Contextual Use of Different Information About Depth, Handbook of Perception and Cognition: Perception of Space and Motion, Vol. 5, Academic Press (to appear).

[9] R. Kent Dybvig. The Scheme Programming Language. Prentice-Hall, 1987.

[10] S. S. Fisher, A M. McGreevy, J. Humphries, W. Robinett, Virtual Environment Display System, Proceedings on the 1986 Workshop on Interactive 3D Graphics, pages 77-87, October 23-24, 1986.

[11] Thomas Funkhouser, Carlo Sequin, Seth Teller, Management of Large Amounts of Data in Interactive Building Walkthroughs, Proceedings of the 1992 ACM Symposium on Interactive Three-Dimensional Graphics, April, 1992, pages 11-20.

[12] Thomas Furness, The Super Cockpit and Human Factors Challenges, Human Interface Technology (HIT) Laboratory of the Washington Technology Center, Tech Report HITL-M-886-1, October, 1986.

[13] Tinsley A. Galyean, Guided Navigation of Virtual Environments, 1995 ACM Symposium on Interactive 3D Graphics, April 1995, pages 103-104, Monterey, CA.

[14] Id Software, Inc.; information available via http://www.idsoftware.com/ .

[15] John Lasseter, Principles of Traditional Animation Applied to 3D Computer Animation, Computer Graphics (SIGGRAPH '87 Proceedings) Volume 21, number 4, pages 35-44, July 1987.

[16] Randy Pausch, et al, A Brief Architectural Overview of Alice, a Rapid Prototyping System for Virtual Reality, IEEE Computer Graphics and Applications, May 1995.

[17] Ken Perlin, Real Time Responsive Animation with Personality, IEEE Transactions on Visualization and Computer Graphics, Vol. 1, No. 1.

[18] A. Pope, BBN Report No 7102. The SIMNET Network and Protocols. BBN Systems and Technologies, Cambridge, Massachusetts, 1989.

[19] John Rohlf and James Helman, IRIS Performer: A High Performance Multiprocessing Toolkit for Real-Time 3D Graphics, SIGGRAPH '94 Conference Proceedings, Computer Graphics, July, 1994.

[20] William J. Schroeder, Jonathan A. Zarge, William E. Lorensen, Decimation of Triangle Meshes, Computer Graphics (SIGGRAPH '92 Proceedings) Volume 26, pages 65-70, July 1992.

[21] Sense8 Corporation, 100 Shoreline Highway, Suite 282, Mill Valley, CA 94941, 415/331-6318, http://www.sense8.com/ , info@sense8.com .

[22] Chris Shaw, Mark Green, Jiandong Liang, Yunqi Sun, Decoupled Simulation in Virtual Reality with the MR Toolkit, ACM Transactions on Information Systems, 11:3, pages 287-317, July 1993.

[23] Ivan Sutherland, The Ultimate Display, Proceedings of IFIP (International Federation of Information Processing) '65, Vol. 2, pages 506-508.

[24] Ivan Sutherland, A Head-mounted Three-dimensional Display, Proceedings of the Fall Joint Computer Conference, AFIPS, Vol. 33, pages 757-764.

[25] Virtuality, http://www.virtuality.com, UK office: Virtuality House, 3 Oswin Road, Brailsford Industrial Park, Leicester LE3 1HR, United Kingdom, Tel: +44(0) 116 233 7000, enquiries@virtuality.com . USA office: 7801-7805 Mesquite End Drive, Suite 105, Irving, Texas 75063, USA 001-214-556-1800, 1-800-ILLUSION, enquiries@tx.viruality.com.

[26] E. Wenzel, F. Wightman, S. Fisher, A Virtual Display System for Conveying Three-dimensional Acoustic Information, Proceedings of the Human Factors Society, 32nd Annual Meeting, 1988, pages 86-90.

Improv: A System for Scripting Interactive Actors in Virtual Worlds

Ken Perlin / Athomas Goldberg †
Media Research Laboratory
Department of Computer Science
New York University

ABSTRACT

Improv is a system for the creation of real-time behavior-based animated actors. There have been several recent efforts to build network distributed autonomous agents. But in general these efforts do not focus on the author's view. To create rich interactive worlds inhabited by believable animated actors, authors need the proper tools. **Improv** provides tools to create actors that respond to users and to each other in real-time, with personalities and moods consistent with the author's goals and intentions.

Improv consists of two subsystems. The first subsystem is an Animation Engine that uses procedural techniques to enable authors to create layered, continuous, non-repetitive motions and smooth transitions between them. The second subsystem is a Behavior Engine that enables authors to create sophisticated rules governing how actors communicate, change, and make decisions. The combined system provides an integrated set of tools for authoring the "minds" and "bodies" of interactive actors. The system uses an english-style scripting language so that creative experts who are not primarily programmers can create powerful interactive applications.

INTRODUCTION

Believability And Interaction

Cinema is a medium that can suspend disbelief; the audience enjoys the psychological illusion that fictional characters have an internal life. When this is done properly, these characters can take the audience on a compelling emotional journey. Yet cinema is a linear medium; for any given film, the audience's journey is always the same. Likewise, the experience is inevitably a passive one as the audience's reactions can have no effect on the course of events.

† NYU-MRL, 719 Broadway 12th Floor, New York, NY 10003
Fax: (212) 995-4122 Web: http://www.mrl.nyu.edu
Email:perlin@nyu.edu | athomas@mrl.nyu.edu

This suspension of disbelief, or believability, does not require realism. For example, millions of people relate to Kermit the Frog and to Bugs Bunny as though they actually exist Likewise, Bunraku puppet characters can create for their audience a deeply profound and moving psychological experience.

All of these media have one thing in common. Every moment of the audience's journey is being guided by talented experts, whether an screenwriter and actor/director, a writer/animator, or a playwright and team of puppeteers. These experts use their judgment to maintain a balance: characters must be consistent and recognizable, and must respond to each other appropriately at all times. Otherwise believability is lost.

In contrast current computer games are non-linear, offering variation and interactivity. While it is possible to create for characters in these games that convey a sense of psychological engagement, it is extremely difficult with existing tools.

One limitation is that there is no expert, no actor, director, animator or puppeteer, actually present during the unfolding drama, and so authors using existing techniques are limited by what they can anticipate and produce in advance.

In this paper, we discuss the problem of building believable characters that respond to users and to each other in real-time, with consistent personalities, properly changing moods and without mechanical repetition, while always maintaining an author's goals and intentions. We describe an approach in which actors follow **scripts**, sets of author-defined rules governing their behavior, which are used to determine the appropriate animated **actions** to perform at any given time. We also describe a behavioral architecture that supports author-directed multi-actor coordination as well as run-time control of actor behavior for the creation of user-directed actors or **avatars**. Next, we describe how the system has been implemented using an "english-style" scripting language and a network distribution model to enable creative experts, who are not primarily programmers, to create powerful interactive applications. Finally, we discuss our experiences with the system and future work.

Related Work

The phrase "Desktop Theater" was coined by Steve Strassman [Strassman91]. His philosophy was quite similar to ours. Yet because his work slightly predated the age of fast graphical workstations, it did not deal with real time visual interaction. But there was already the emphasis on expressive authoring tools for specifying how characters would respond to direction.

The novel *Snow Crash* by Neil Stephenson also influenced this work. That novel posits a "Metaverse", a future version of the Internet which appears to its participants as a quasi-physical world. Participants are represented by fully articulate human figures, or avatars. Body movements of avatars are computed automatically by the system.

Snow Crash specifically touches on the importance of proper authoring tools for avatars, although it does not describe those tools. Our system takes these notions further, in that it supports autonomous figures that do not directly represent any participant.

Most autonomous actor simulation systems follow the parallel layered intelligence model of [Minsky86], which was partially implemented by the subsumption architecture of [Brooks86] as well as in [Bates92] and [Johnson94]. Several systems have been developed which share this layered architecture with **Improv**, yet which solve distinctly different problems. The **Jack** system of [Badler93] focuses on proper task planning and biomechanical simulation, as does [Hodgins95] The general goal is to produce accurate simulations of biomechanical robots. Similarly, the simulations of Terzopoulis et. al [Terzopoulos94] has simulated autonomous animal behaviors that respond to their environment according to biomechanical rules. Autonomous figure animation has been studied by [Badler91], [Girard85], [Morawetz90] and [Sims94].

The **Alive** system of [Maes95] and [Blumberg95] focuses on self-organizing embodied agents, which are capable of making inferences and of learning from their experiences. Instead of maximizing an authors ability to express personality, the **Alive** system use ethological mechanisms to maximize the actor's ability to reorganize its own personality, based on its own perception and accumulated experience.

APPROACH

Improv: An Expert System For Authors

As an authoring system, **Improv** must provide creative experts with tools for constructing the various aspects of an interactive application. These must be intuitive to use, allow for the creation of rich, compelling content, and produce behaviorat run-time which is consistent with the author's vision and intentions. Animated actors must be able to respond to a wide variety of user-interactions, in ways that are both appropriate and non-repetitive. This is complicated by the fact that in applications involving several characters, these actors must be able to work together while faithfully carrying out the author's intentions. The author needs to control the choices an actor makes and how the actors move their bodies.

ARCHITECTURE

The behavior model used by **Improv** is similar to that proposed by [Blumberg95] in that it consists of geometry that is manipulated in real-time, an Animation Engine which utilizes descriptions of atomic animated actions (such as Walk or Wave) to manipulate the geometry, and a Behavior Engine which is responsible for higher-level capabilities, (such as going to the store, or engaging another actor in a conversation), and decisions about which animations to trigger. In addition, the Behavior Engine maintains the internal model of the actor, representing various aspects of an actor's moods, goals and personality. The Behavior Engine constitutes the *mind* of the actor. An run-time, an actor's movements and behavior are computed by iterating an *update cycle* that alternates between the Animation and Behavior Engines.

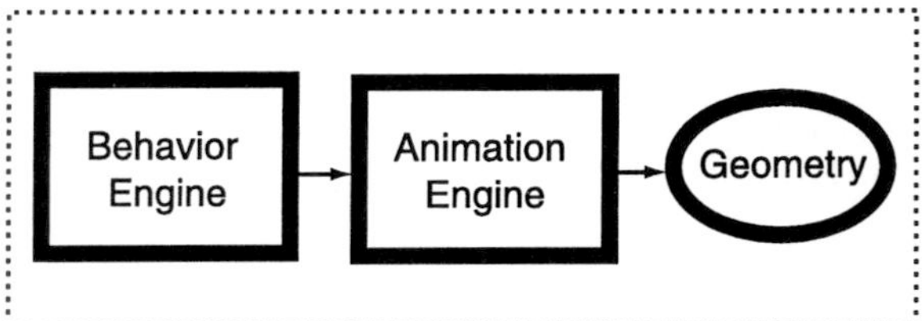

figure 1. The basic architecture for an actor in the run-time system.

ANIMATION ENGINE

The Animation Engine provides tools for generating and interactively blending realistic gestures and motions. This is a generalization of the system presented in [Perlin 95]. Actors are able to move from one animated motion to another in a smooth and natural fashion in real time. Motions can be layered and blended to convey different moods and personalities. The Animation Engine controls the *body* of the actor.

Geometry

An animator can build any variety of articulated character. Actors can be given the form of humans, animals, animate objects, or fantasy creatures. An actor consists parts that are connected by rotational joints. The model can be deformable, which is useful for muscle flexing or facial expressions as illustrating in [Chadwick89].

Degrees Of Freedom

Authors specify individual actions in terms of how those actions cause changes over time to each individual *degree of freedom* (DOF) in the model. The system then combines these DOF values to make smooth transitions and layerings among actions.

There are various types of DOFs that an author can control. The simplest are the three rotational axes between any two connected parts. Examples of this are head turning and knee bending. The author can also simply position a part, such as a hand or a foot. The system automatically does the necessary inverse kinematics to preserve the kinematic chain. From the author's point of view, the x,y,z coordinates of the part are each directly available as a DOF.

The author can also specify part mesh deformations as DOFs. To make a deformation, the author must provide a "deformation target," a version version of the model (or just some parts of the model) in which some vertices have been moved. For each deformation target, the **Improv** system detects which vertices have been moved, and builds a data structure containing the x,y,z displacement for each such vertex. For example, if the author has provided a smiling face as a deformation target, then the (s)he can declare SMILE to be a DOF. The author can then specify various values for SMILE between 0. (no smile) and 1. (full smile). The system handles the necessary interpolation between mesh vertices. In the particular case of smiling, the author can also specify negative values for SMILE, to make the face frown.

figure 2. Flexing a deformable mesh.

Continuous Signal Generation

The author defines an action simply as a list of DOFs, together with a range and a time varying expression for each DOF. Most actions are constructed by varying a few DOFs over time via combinations of sine, cosine and coherent noise. For example, sine and cosine signals are used together within actions to impart elliptical rotations.

One of the key ingredients to realism in **Improv** characters is the ability to apply coherent noise. This mechanism was originally developed for procedural textures [Perlin85][Ebert94]. In the current work it is used in essentially the same way. Using noise in limb movements allows authors to give the impression of naturalistic motions without needing to incorporate complex simulation models.

For example, coherent noise can be used to convey the small motions of a character trying to maintain balance, the controlled randomness of eye blinking, or the way a character's gaze wanders around a room. Although in real life each of these examples has a different underlying mechanism, viewers do not perceive the mechanism itself. Instead they perceive some statistics of the motion it produces. When coherent noise is applied in a way that matches those statistics, the actor's movements are believable.

The author can also import keyframed animation from commercial modeling systems, such as Alias or SoftImage. The **Improv** system internally converts these into actions that specify time varying values for various DOFs. To the rest of the system, these imported actions look identical to any other action.

Defining Actions

The author uses DOF's to build **actions**. Below are three different actions that define how an actor might gesture with his arm while talking. Each one uses several frequencies of noise to modulate arm movement. The first two are general hand waving gestures, while the third shakes the arm more emphatically, as though pointing at the listener.

On each line of an action, the part name is followed first by three angular intervals, and then by three time-varying interpolants in braces. Each interpolant is used to compute a single angle in its corresponding interval. The results are applied to the part as Pitch, Roll and Yaw rotations respectively. The angle intervals are constant over time, whereas the time varying interpolants are reevaluated at each update cycle. For example, in the first line below, if N0 possesses the value 0.5 at some time step then the resulting Pitch rotation at that time step will be 0.5 of the way between 25 degrees and 55 degrees, or 40 degrees.

```
define ACTION "Talk Gesture1"
{
R_UP_ARM     25:55  0    -35:65        { N0 0 N0 }
R_LO_ARM     55:95  0    0             { N1 0 0 }
R_HAND       -40:25 75:-25 120         { N1 N2 0 }
}

define ACTION "Talk Gesture2"
{
R_UP_ARM     10:47  0    -10:45        { N0 0 N0 }
R_LO_ARM     35:77  0    0             { N1 0 0 }
R_HAND       -53:55 -40:15 120         { N1 N2 0 }
}

define ACTION "Talk_Gesture3"
{
R_UP_ARM     45     20:15  0           { 0 N0 N0 }
R_LO_ARM     70:120 0      0           { N1 0 0 }
R_HAND       40:15  0      120         { N2 0 0 }
}
```

The variables N0, N1 and N2 are shorthand that the **Improv** system provides the author to denote time varying coherent noise signals of different frequencies. N1 is one octave higher than N0, and N2 is one octave higher than N1. The value of each signal varies between 0.0 and 1.0.

Note that the upper arm movement is controlled by N0, whereas the lower arm movement is controlled by N1. The result is that the upper arm will, on the average, swing back and forth about the shoulder once per second, whereas the lower arm will, on the average, swing back and forth about the elbow twice per second. Meanwhile, the hand will make small rapid rotations about the wrist. These frequencies were chosen simply because they looked natural. In our tests, frequency ratios that varied significantly from these did not look natural. Presumably this frequency ratio reflects the fact that the lower arm has about half as much mass as the total arm, and therefore tends to swing back and forth about twice as frequently.

Action Compositing

An **Improv** actor can be doing many things at once, and these simultaneous activities can interact in different ways. For example, an author may want an actor who is waving to momentarily scratch his head with the same hand. It would be incorrect for the waving movement to continue during the time the actor is scratching his head. The result could be strange. For example, actor might try to feebly to wave while his arm while making vague scratching motions about his cranium. Clearly in this case we want to decrease the amount of waving activity as we increase the scratching activity. Some sort of ease-in/out transition is called for.

In contrast, suppose we want an actor to scratch his head for a moment while walking downstage. It would be incorrect if the **Improv** system were to force the actor to stop walking every time he scratched his head. In this case, an ease-in/out transition would be inappropriate.

The difference between these two examples is that the former situation involves two actions which cannot coexist, whereas the latter situation involves two actions that can gracefully coexist. The authoring system should provide a mechanism to allow authors to make these distinctions in an easy and unambiguous way. To do this, **Improv** contains a simple set of rules. The approach we take is borrowed from image compositing methods. The **Improv** author thinks of motion as being layered, just as composited images can be layered back to front. The difference is that whereas an image maps pixels to colors, an action maps DOFs to values.

The author can place actions in different groups, and

these groups are organized into a "back-to-front" order. Also the author may "select" any action. Given this structure, the two compositing rules are as follows:

(1) Actions which are in the same group compete with each other. At any moment, every action possesses some weight, or opacity. When an action is selected, its weight transitions smoothly from zero to one. Meanwhile, the weights of all other actions in the same group transition smoothly down to zero.

(2) Actions in groups which are further forward obscure those in groups which are further back.

Using this system, authors place actions which should compete with each other in the same group. Some actions, such as walking, are fairly global in that they involve many DOFs through the body. Others, such as head scratching, are fairly localized and involve relatively few DOFs. The author places more global actions in the rear-most groups. More localized actions are placed in front of these. Also, some actions are relatively persistent. Others are generally done fleetingly. Groups of very fleeting or temporary actions (like scratching or coughing) are placed still further in front.

For the author, this makes it easy to specify intuitively reasonable action relationships. For example, suppose the author specifies the following action grouping:

```
GROUP       Stances
    ACTION          Stand
    ACTION          Walk

GROUP       Gestures
    ACTION          No_waving
    ACTION          Wave_left
    ACTION          Wave_right

GROUP       Momentary
    ACTION          No_scratching
    ACTION          Scratch_head_left
```

Then let's say actions are selected in the following order:

```
Stand
Walk
Wave_left
Scratch_head_left
No_scratching
Wave_right
```

The actor will start to walk. While continuing to walk he will wave with his left hand. Then he will scratch his head with his left hand, and resume waving again. Finally he will switch over to waving with his right hand.

Because of the grouping structure, the author has easily imparted to the actor many convenient rules. For example, the actor knows to wave with either one hand or the other (not both at once), that he doesn't need to stop walking in order to wave or to scratch his head, and that after he's done scratching he can resume whatever else he was doing with that arm.

Applying Actions To The Model

At any animation frame, the run time system must assign a unique value to each DOF for the model, then move the model into place and render it. To compute these DOFs, the algorithm proceeds as follows. Within each group, a weighted sum is taken over the contribution of each action to each DOF. The values for all DOFs in every group are then composited, proceeding from back to front. The result is a single value for each DOF, which is then used to move the model into place.

There are subtleties in this algorithm, such as correctly compositing inverse kinematic DOFs over direct rotational DOFs. But these are beyond the space limitations of this paper. For a full treatment of the DOF compositing algorithm, the reader is referred to [Perlin96].

The author is given tools to easily synchronize movements of the same DOF across actions; transitions between two actions that must have different tempos are handled by a morphing approach: During the time of the transition, speed of a master clock is continuously varied from the first tempo to the second tempo, so that the phases of the two actions are always aligned. This is similar to the approach taken by [Bruderlin95] and [Witkin95].

Action Buffering

Sometimes it would be awkward for an actor to make a direct transition between two particular actions in a group. For example, let's say the actor has his hands behind his back, and then claps his hands. Because DOFs are combined linearly, the result would be that the actor passes his hands through his body!

We allow the author to avoid such situations by declaring that some action in a group can be a buffering action for another. The system implements this by building a finite state machine that forces the actor to pass through this buffering action when entering or leaving the troublesome action.

For example, the author can declare that the action hands-at-the-sides is a buffering action for hands-behind-the-back. Then when the actor transitions between hands-behind-the back and any other action, he will always first move his hands around the sides of his body.

figure 3: Otto demonstrating action buffering.

BEHAVIOR ENGINE

Motivation

Improv authors cannot create deterministic scenarios, because the user is a variable in the run-time system. The user's responses are always implicitly presenting the actor with a choice of what to do next. Because of this variability, the user's experience of an actor's personality and mood must be conveyed largely by that actor's probability of selecting one choice over another.

As a very simple example, suppose the user often goes away for awhile, keeping an actor waiting for various amounts of time. If the actor usually sits down or naps before the user returns, then the actor will appear to the user as a lazy or tired character. The user is forming an impression based on probabilities.

The influence of the author lies in carefully tuning of such probabilities. The goal of the behavior engine is to help the author to do so in the most expressive way possible.

Mechanism

The behavior engine provides tools for the author to guide an actor's behavioral choices. Several tools are provided to the author.

The most basic tool is a simple parallel scripting system. Scripts are sequences of things to do over time. The most basic thing a script does is to choose some action or some other script, in response to events in the actor's environment.

Generally speaking, at any given moment an actor will be executing a number of scripts in parallel. In each of these scripts the most common operation is to select one item from a list of items. These items are usually other scripts or actions for the actor (or for some other actor) to perform.

The real power of the behavior engine comes from tools we provide authors for guiding an actor's choices. These "probability shaping" tools provide the **Improv** author with real power over an actor's appearance of personality and mood. The more expressive are the tools for shaping these probabilities, the more believable actors will be, in the hands of a talented author.

In the following sections we describe the working of the behavior engine. First we describe the basic parallel scripting structure. After that, we will describe the probability shaping tools.

Scripts For an Interactive World

If actions are the mechanism for continuous control of the movements made by an actor's body, then scripts are the mechanism for discrete control of the decisions made by the actor's mind.

The author must assume that the user will be making unexpected responses. For this reason, it is not sufficient to provide the author with a tool for scripting long linear sequences. Rather, the author must be able to create layers of choices, from more global and slowly changing plans, to more localized and rapidly changing activities.

In the next two sections, we first discuss how scripts are organized into layers, and then how an individual script operates.

Grouping Scripts

Like actions, scripts are organized into groups. However unlike actions, when a script within a group is selected, any other script that was running in the same group immediately stops. In any group at any given moment, exactly one script is running.

Generally, the author organizes into the same group those scripts that represent alternative modes that an actor can be in at some level of abstraction. For example, the group of activities that an actor performs during his day might be:

ACTIVITIES	Resting Working Dining Conversing Performing

In general, the author first specifies those groups of scripts that control longer term goals and plans. These tend to change slowly over time, and their effects are generally not immediately felt by the user.

The last scripts are those that are most physical. They tend to choose actual body actions, in response to the user and to the state of higher level scripts. For example, an actor might contain the following groups of scripts, in order, within a larger set of scripts:

...	
DAY_PLANS	Waking Morning Lunch Afternoon Dinner Evening
...	
ACTIVITIES	Resting Working Dining Conversing Performing
...	
BEHAVIOR	Sleeping Eating Talking Joking Arguing Listening Dancing

We can think of the Animation Engine, with its groups of continuous actions, as an extension of this grouping structure to even lower semantic levels.

Individual Scripts

A script is organized as a sequence of clauses. During run-time, the system runs these clauses sequentially for the selected script in each group. At any update cycle, the system may run the same clause that it ran on the previous cycle, or it may move on to the next clause. The author is provided with tools to "hold" clauses in response to events or timeouts.

The two primary functions of a script clause are 1) to trigger other actions or scripts and 2) to check, create or modify the actor's properties

Triggering Actions and Scripts

The simplest thing an author can do within a script clause is trigger a specific action or script, which is useful when the author has a specific sequence of activities (s)he wants the actor to perform. In the following example, the actor walks onstage, turns to the camera, bows, and then walks offstage again.

```
define SCRIPT "Curtain Call"

    { "walk to center" }
    { continue until my location equals center }
    { "turn to camera" }
    { continue until { "turn to camera" is done } }
    { "bow" }
    { continue for 3 seconds }
    { "walk offstage" }
```

In this case, phrases in quotes represent scripts or actions. Each of these scripts might, in turn, call other scripts and/or actions. The other information (continue, etc) is used by **Improv** to control the timing of the scene.

Layered Behavior

Through layering, an author can create complex behaviors from simpler scripts and actions. Take the following example:

```
define SCRIPT "greeting"
```

```
{
        { "enter" }
        { wait 4 seconds }
        { "turn to camera" }
        { wait 1 second }
        { "wave" for 2 seconds
          "talk" for 6 seconds }
        { wait 3 seconds }
        { "sit" }
        { wait 5 seconds }
        { "bow" toward "Camera" }
        { wait 2 seconds }
        { "leave" }
}
```

In this example, the actor first activates the "enter" script (which instructs the actor to walk to center). The "enter" script and "greeting" script are now running in parallel. The "greeting" script waits four seconds before activating the "turn to camera" script. This tells the actor to turn to face the specified target, which in this case is the camera. The script then waits one second, before instructing the actor to begin the "wave" and "talk" actions. The script waits another 3 seconds before activating the "sit" action during which time the "wave" action has ended, returning to the default "No Hand Gesture" action in its group. Meanwhile, the "talk" action continues for another three seconds after the actor sits. Two seconds later the actor bows to the camera, waits another two seconds and then leaves.

Non-Deterministic (Stochastic) Behavior

In addition to commands that explicitly trigger specific actions and scripts, **Improv** provides a number of tools for generating the more non-deterministic behavior required for interactive non-linear applications. An author may specify that an actor choose randomly from a set of actions or scripts. as in the following example:

```
SCRIPT "Rock Paper Scissors"

    { choose from { "Rock" "Paper" "Scissors" } }
```

Once an action or script is chosen it is executed as though it had been explicitly specified.

Alternately, the author can specify weights associated with each item in the choice. These weights are used to affect the probability of each item being chosen, as in the following example:

```
define SCRIPT "Rock Paper Scissors2"

   { choose from { "Rock" .5 "Paper" .3 "Scissors" .1 } }
```

In this case, there is a 5/9 chance the actor executing this script will choose the "Rock" action, 3/9 that the actor will choose "Paper", and a 1/9 chance the actor will pick "Scissors". The decision is still random, but the author has specified a distinct preference for certain behaviors over others.

In order to create believable characters, the author also needs to be able to have these decisions reflect an actor's mental state as well as the state of the actor's environment. An actor's decision about what to do may depend on any number of factors, including mood, time of day, what other actors are around and what they're doing, what the user is doing, etc.

In **Improv**, authors can create **decision rules** which take information about an actor and his environment and use this to determine the actor's tendencies toward certain choices over others. The author specifies what information is relevant to the decision and how this information influences the weight associated with each choice. As this information changes, the actor's tendency to make certain choices over others will change as well.

Decision Rules

Properties

The information about an actor and his relationship to his environment are stored in an actor's properties. These properties may be used to describe aspects of an actor's personality, such as assertiveness, temperament or dexterity, an actor's current mood, such as happiness or alertness, or his relationship to other actors or objects, such as his sympathy toward the user or his attitude toward strained peas. These properties are specified by the author either when the actor is created, or else within a clause of a script, to reflect a change in the actor due to some action or event. The latter case is shown in the following example:

```
define SCRIPT "Eat Dinner"

  { "Eat" }
  { set my "Appetite" to 0 }
  { "Belch" }
```

In this case, the author specifies how an actor's behavior is reflected in his personality by reducing the actor's appetite after eating.

An author can also use properties to provide information about any aspect of an actor's environment, including inanimate props and scenery and even the scripts and actions an actor chooses from. An author can assign properties to actions and scripts describing the various semantic information associated with them, such as aggressiveness, formality, etc

The author can then uses these values in the construction of **decision rules**. **Decision rules** allow actors to make decisions that reflect the state of the world the author has created.

What Decision Rules Do

When a **decision rule** is invoked, a list of objects is passed to it. The system then uses the decision-rule to generate a weight between zero and one for each object. This list can then be used to generate a weighted decision.

Each **decision rule** consists of a list of author-specified **factors**: pieces of information that will influence the actor's decision. Each of these **factors** is assigned a weight which the author uses to control how much influence that piece of information has upon the decision. This information can simply be the value of a property of an object as in the following example:

```
  { choose from { "Steph" "Bob" "Sarah" }
      based on "who's interesting" }

define DECISION-RULE "who's interesting"

factor { his/her "Charisma" }          influence .8
```

```
factor { his/her "Intelligence" }          influence .2
```

In this example, the decision rule will use the "Charisma" and "Intelligence" properties of the three actors to generate a weight for each actor that will used in the decision. In this case, the author has specified that the value of an actor's "Charisma" will have the greatest influence in determining that weight, with "Intelligence" having a lesser role. The influence is optional and defaults to 1.0 if unspecified. The equations for determining these weights can be found in Appendix A: *Decision Rule Equations.*

An author can also use the relationship between the actor and the various choices to influence a decision, by making "fuzzy" comparisons between their properties. For example:

```
{ choose from ("Fight" "Flee") based on "how courageous" }

define DECISION-RULE: "how courageous"
{
    factor { my "Courage"
             equals its "Courage Level" to within .5 }
}
```

Here, the author is comparing the actor's "Courage" property with the "Courage Level" property associated with the scripts "Fight" and "Flee". If the actor's "Courage" equals the script's "Courage Level" the decision rule will assign a weight of 1 to that choice. If the values aren't equal, a weight between 0 and 1 will be assigned based on the difference between them, dropping to 0 when the difference is greater than the "within" range. In this case, .5 . (The equations for this can be found in Appendix B: *Fuzzy Logic Equations)* As the actor's "Courage" increases or decreases, so will the actor's tendency toward one option or the other.

An author may want an actor to choose from a set of options using different **factors** to judge different kinds of items. A list of objects passed to the decision rule may be divided into subsets using author-defined criteria for inclusion. The weights assigned to a given subset may be scaled, reflecting a preference for an entire group of choices over another. For example:

```
{ choose from ("Steph" "Bob" "Sarah")
    based on "who's interesting2" }

define DECISION-RULE: "who's interesting2"
{
    subset "Those I'd be attracted to'                scale 1
    factor { his/her "Intelligence" equals
             my "Confidence" to within .4 }

    subset "Those I wouldn't be attracted to"   scale .8
    factor { his/her "Intelligence" equals
             my "Intelligence" to within .4 }
}

define SUBSET: "Those I'd be attracted to"
  { his/her "Gender" equals my "Preferred Gender" }

define SUBSET: "Those I wouldn't be attracted to"
  { his/her "Gender" does not equal my "Preferred Gender" }
```

Let's assume the actor is considered a heterosexual male (ie his "Gender" is "Male" and his "Preferred Gender" is "Female"). The weight assigned to "Steph" and "Sarah" will depend on how closely their intelligence matches our actor's confidence (being put off by less intelligent women and intimidated by more intelligent ones, perhaps). The factor used to judge "Bob" reflects a sympathy toward men who are his intellectual equal, unaffected by the actor's confidence. The **scale** values reflect a general preference for one gender over the other.

Coordination Of Multiple Actors

Ideally we would prefer to give an author the same control over groups of actors that (s)he has over individual actors. The proper model is that the author is a director who can direct the drama via pre-written behavior rules. To the author, all of the actors constitute a coordinated "cast", which in some sense is a single actor that just happens to have multiple bodies.

For this reason, we allow actors to modify each other's properties with the same freedom with which an actor can modify his own properties. From the author's point of view, this is part of a single larger problem of authoring dramatically responsive group behavior. If one actor tells a joke, the author may want the other actors to respond, favorably or not, to the punchline. By having the joke teller cue the others actors to respond, proper timing is maintained, even if the individual actors make their own decisions about how exactly to react. In this way, an actor can give the impression of always knowing what other actors are doing and respond immediately and appropriately in ways that fulfill the author's goals.

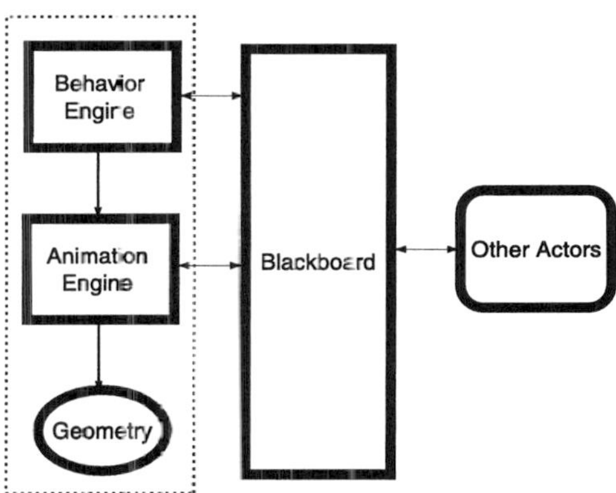

Figure 4: Actors communicate with each other through a shared blackboard.

This communication occurs through the use of a shared blackboard. The blackboard allows actors to be coordinated, even when running on a single processor, on multiple processors or across a network.

USER-INTERACTION

Multi-Level Control Of Actor State

Creating and Modifying User Interface Elements

Authors can create and modify user interface elements at run-time, enabling widgets to be easily generated in response to actor behavior or to serve the needs of the current scene or interaction. The user can employ these widgets to trigger actions and scripts at any level of an actor's behavioral hierarchy. This enables users to enter the virtual environment, by allowing them to direct the actions of one (or more) animated actor(s). By making this interface a scriptable element, **Improv** enables authors to more easily choreograph the interaction between the virtual actors and the human participant.

Controlling An Actor From Multiple Levels of Abstraction

One important feature of **Improv** is ability fo the user to interaction with the system at different semantic levels. The result of the user's actions can cause changes in the system anywhere from high level scripts to low level actions. This means that the author can give the user the right kind of control for every situation. If the user requires a very fine control over actors' motor skills, then the author can provide direct access to the action level. On the other hand, if the user is involved in a conversation, the author might let the user specify a set of gestures for the actor to use, and have the actor decide on the specific gestures from moment to moment. At an even higher level, the author may want to have the user directing large groups of actors, such as an acting company or an army, in which case (s)he might have the user give the entire group directions and leave it to the individual actors to carry out those instructions. Since any level of the actor's behavior can be made accessible to the user, the author is free to vary the level of control, as necessary, at any point in the application.

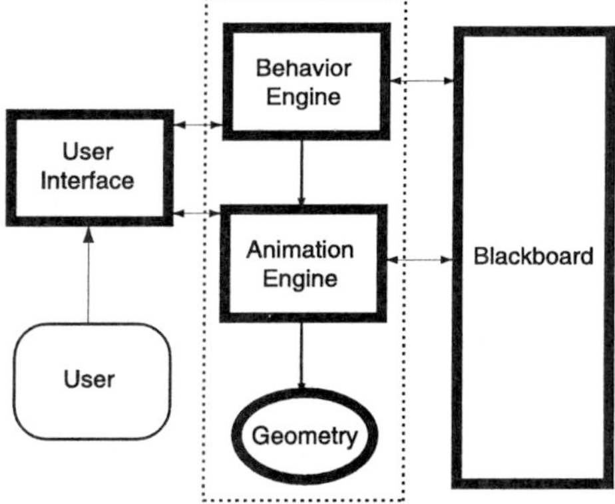

figure 5: Users interact with both the Behavior Engine and the Animation Engine through an author-defined user-interface.

IMPLEMENTATION

English-Style Scripting Language

Many of the authors and artists interested in creating interactive content are not primarily programmers, and therefore we have developed a number of "english-style" scripting language extensions to **Improv** that make it easier for authors and artists to begin scripting interactive scenarios. For example, all of the code examples shown in this paper were written in the current **Improv** syntax.

Because the scripting language is written as an extension of the system language, as users become more experienced they can easily migrate from scripting entirely using the high-level english-style syntax, to extending the system through low-level algorithmic control.

Network Distribution

Improv is implemented as a set of distributed programs in UNIX, connected by TCP/IP socket connections, multicast protocols and UNIX pipes. The participating processes can be running on any UNIX machines. This transport layer is hidden from the author.

All communication between participant processes is done by continually sending and receiving programs around the network. These are immediately parsed into byte code and executed. At the top of the communication structure are routing processes. There must be at least one routing process on every participating Local Area Network. The router relays information among actors and renderer processes. For Wide Area Network communication, the router opens sockets to routers at other LAN's.

In our current implementation, each actor maintains a complete copy of the blackboard information for all actors. If an actor's behavior state changes between the beginning and end of a time step, then these changed are routed to all other actors.

Virtual Simultaneity

Typical Wide Area Network (WAN) latencies can be several seconds. This poses a problem for two virtual actors interacting in a distributed system. From the viewpoint of believability, some latency is acceptable for high level decisions but not for low level physical actions. For example, when one character waves at another, the second character can get away with pausing for a moment before responding. But two characters who are shaking hands cannot allow their respective hands to move through space independently of each other. The hands must be synchronized to at least the animation frame rate.

The blackboard model allows us to deal with this situation gracefully. We can split the Behavior Engine and Animation Engine for an actor across a Wide Area Network, and have these communicate with each other through the blackboard. For the DOFs produced by the Animation Engine, we allow the blackboard to contain different values at each LAN. For the states produced by the Behavioral Engine, the actor maintains a single global blackboard.

Computationally, each actor runs the Behavioral Engine at only a single Local Area Network (LAN), but duplicates Animation Engine calculations at each LAN. When two characters must physically coordinate with each other, then they use the local versions of their DOFs. In this way, an actor is always in a single Behavioral State everywhere on the WAN, even though at each LAN he might appear to be in a slightly different position. In a sense, the actor has one mind, but multiple bodies, each inhabiting a parallel universe. Although these bodies may differ slightly in their position within their own universe, they are all consistent with this one mind.

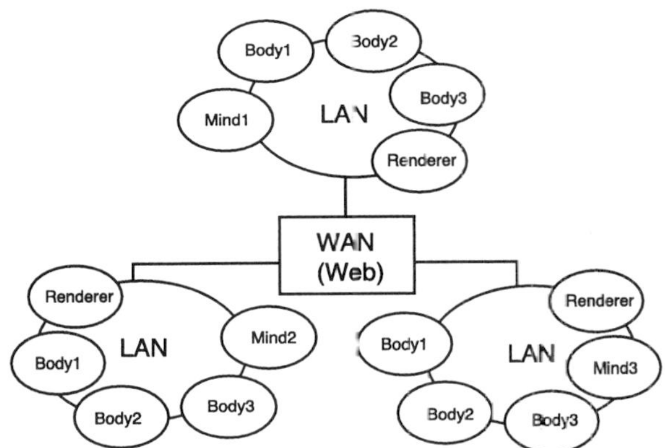

figure 6: Wide Area Network Distribution Model

This leads to an interesting and fundamental property. Let us suppose that our **Improv** actor Gregor is dancing while balancing a tray in an **Improv** scene. Further, suppose that the scene is being watched at the same time by people in Sao Paulo, Brazil, and in Manhattan, New York. Perhaps some of these people are interacting with Gregor. The connection is through the Internet.

In this scene, Gregor's Behavior Engine makes all the choices about whether to dance, whether to keep balancing the tray, how much joy and abandon versus self-conscious restraint he puts into the dance. His Animation Engine must set all the DOFs that determine how he moves when doing these things, so as to be responsive and coordinated.

If the people in NY and those in SP are talking on the telephone, they will report seeing the same thing. Yet, if a high speed dedicated video link were established, and participants could see the two Gregors side by side, they would see two somewhat different animations. In one, Gregor's hand might thrust up to balance the tray half a second sooner, in the other he might have his other arm extended a bit further out. He might be rocking right to left on one screen, while he is rocking from left to right on the other.

Thus, everywhere in the world there is only one social Gregor. He has a single mood, a single personality, he is only engaged in one task. Yet Gregor can have many slightly different physical realities, differing only up to the threshold where they might disrupt the social unity of his Behavioral State.

figure 7: Two versions of Gregor dancing, each on different networked computer.

In fact, if communication lag exceeds several seconds, significant differences may have occurred between the various Gregor instances. This can lead to problems. For example, suppose two actors that are temporarily out of communication each try to pick up some physical object.

This is a standard collaborative work dilemma. The only reliable solution is to make the object itself an actor (albeit a light weight one). As odd as it seems, the object itself must agree to be picked up, since it too must maintain a consistent physical reality. This was also independently observed by [Karaul95].

Communicating with Improv Actors From Outside The System

The blackboard protocol has a great advantage in terms of flexibility. To take full advantage of this flexibility, we provide a C support library that gives access to the blackboard. This allows researchers who know nothing about the **Improv** system, except for the names of actions and scripts, to begin immediately to control **Improv** actors.

For example, a researcher can write a standalone C program that links with the support library. The program can pass string arguments such as "Gregor Sit" or "Otto Walk_To_Door" to an output function. This is all that the program needs to do, in order to modify actors' behavior states.

Since the system treats the standalone program as just another actor, the program can also listen for messages by calling an input routine. These messages contain the information that updates the blackboard, saying where various actors are, what they are doing, what their moods are, etc.

In practice, this allows researchers and students at other institutions who know nothing about **Improv** except its GUI to immediately begin to use the system for their own applications. In our research collaborations we find that this is a highly successful way for our collaborators to bootstrap.

Improv also has several audio subsystems. These subsystems are used for speech generation, music generation, allowing actors to follow musical cues, and generating ambient background noise.

Extended Example

The following is an example of a scene involving multiple actors involved in a social interaction with a user.

```
define SCRIPT "Tell Joke"
{
   { do "Turn to Face" to
        choose from { others except player }
   }
   { cue { others except player } to "Listen To Joke" to me }
   {
      do "No Soap, Radio"
      do "Joke Gestures" }
   { wait until { current "Joke" is "completed" } }
   { do "Laugh" for 3 seconds }
   { cue { others except player } to "React To Joke" }
   { wait 3 seconds }
   {  do "React To Player" }
}
```

In this example, the actor executing the script randomly chooses one of the actors not being controlled by the user, and turns to him or her. The actor then cues the other non-user actors to execute the "Listen To Joke" script, in which the actor chooses the appropriate gestures and body language that will give the appearance of listening attentively.

```
define SCRIPT "Listen To Joke"
{
   {
```

```
      choose from { entire set of "Stances" } based on
         "appropriate listening gestures"
     choose from { entire set of "Gestures" } based on
         "appropriate listening gestures"
   }
   { continue for between 3 and 12 seconds }
   { repeat }
}
```

Here, the actor chooses from the actions in the of "Stances" and "Gestures" using the decision rule "appropriate listening gestures"

```
define DECISION_RULE "appropriate listening gestures"
{
   subset "Listening?"                  scale      1
   factor {
             my "confidence" is greater than
             its "confidence" to within 0.3
          }                           influence          .5

   factor {
          my "self control" is less than
          its "self control" to within 0.3
          }                           influence          .5
}

define SUBSET "Listening?"
   { it is "reactive" and "conversational" or  "generic" }
```

In this rule, the actor narrows the list down to those actions that are reactive and conversational, or generic actions that can be used in any context. The rule than compares the "confidence" and "self control" of the actor those assigned to each action, creating a weighted list favoring actions that match the fuzzy criteria. After choosing from the list the actor will wait from 3 to 12 seconds before repeating the script and choosing another gesture.

Meanwhile, The actor telling the joke then executes the "No Soap, Radio" script which contains a command to an external speech system to generate the text of the joke. At the same time, the actor executes the "Joke Gestures" script which, like the "Listen To Joke" script chooses appropriate gestures based on the actor's personality.

The actor continues until the joke is finished (the speech system sends a command to set the script's "completed" property to true) and then laughs, cuing the other actors to execute the "React To Joke" script.

```
define SCRIPT "React To Joke"
{
   {
    choose from { "Laugh" "Giggle" "Ignore" "Get Upset" }
         based on "feelings toward player"
   }
}

define DECISION_RULE "feelings toward player"
{
    factor { my "sympathy toward" player
                does not equal its "mood"  to within .4 }
}
```

Simply put, the more sympathy actor have for the player, the less likely they are to react positively to the joke.

Finally, the actor executes the "React To Player" script in which the actor chooses an appropriate reaction to the player, depending on whether or not the player tells his actor to laugh. if he does, the joke teller laughs, maliciously if her sympathy for the player is low, playfully if her sympathy for the player is high. If the player's actor doesn't laugh the joke teller executes the "Get It?" script, taunting the player until he gets mad and/or leaves.

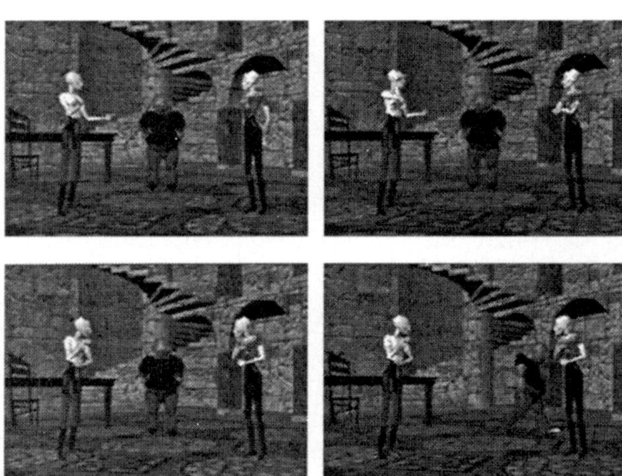

figure 8: Izzy tells Otto (the user) and Elli a joke. Elli is amused, Otto isn't.

EXPERIENCE

SIGGRAPH 95

At SIGGRAPH 95 we demonstrated an interactive embodied actor named Sam who responded to spoken statements and requests. Voice recognition was provided by *DialecTech*, a company that has developed an interface for an IBM continuous speech recognition program. In our demonstration, untrained participants could conduct a game of "Simon Says". Sam would follow requests only if they were preceded by the words "Simon Says". To make it more interesting we programmed Sam so that sometimes he would also follow requests not preceded by "Simon Says", but then he would act embarrassed at having been fooled. Our experience was that the sense of psychological involvement by participants was very great and compelling. Participants appeared to completely "buy into" Sam's presence. We believe that this was due to several factors:

- *(i)* participants could talk with Sam directly,
- *(ii)* participants knew Sam was not being puppeteered (the participant was the only human in the interaction loop), and
- *(iii)* Sam's motions were relatively lifelike and never repeated themselves precisely.

We have also found that allowing the participant to appear as an embodied avatar enhances the participant's sense of fun and play, and therefore involvement. We had positive experience of this at SIGGRAPH 95. We presented the participant with a large rear projection of a room full of embodied conversational agents. The participant's position, as well as simple arm gestures, were tracked by an overhead video camera. The participant appeared in the scene as a flying bat. As the participant walked around, the bat flew around accordingly. The nearest agent would break out of conversing with the other agents, and begin to play with the bat. When the participant flapped his/her arms, the bat would fly higher in the scene, and the camera would follow, which gave the participant a sense of soaring high in the air. We found that participants, and children in particular, enjoyed this experience very much, and would spend long periods of time "being" the bat and flying in turn around the heads of each of the embodied agents.

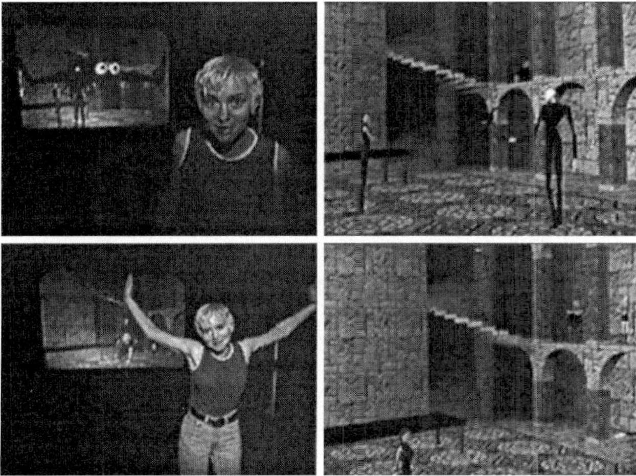

figure 9: Participant interacting with **Improv** actors as a bat. From *SIGGRAPH 95* Interactive Entertainment Exhibit.

Other Users

We have also provided a copy of **Improv** to a number of researchers at other Universities. These researchers are pursuing their own research on top of our actor embodiment substrate. In at least one case, they plan to do comparisons with their own existing agent embodiment system.

Feedback from these collaborators on the use of **Improv** indicates that it is a useful tool for the embodiment of intelligent actors, especially for study of social interaction. In particular, it was suggested as a good tool for building educational VR environments, when used in conjunction with research software for virtual Interactive Theater. The combination can be used to simulate behaviors that would be likely to engage children to respond to, identify with and learn from knowledge agents.

We have added extensions to **Improv** so that animators can use commercial tools, such as Alias and SoftImage, to create small atomic animation components. Trained animators can use these tools to build up content. Such content can include various walk cycles, sitting postures, head scratching, etc. The procedural animation subsystem is designed in such a way that such action styles can be blended. For example, two or three different styles of walks can be separately designed from commercial key frame animation packages, and then blended together, or else blended with various procedural walks, to create continuously variable walk styles that reflect the actor's current mood and attitude, as well as the animator's style.

FUTURE DIRECTIONS

It is well known in traditional animation that human motions are created from combinations of temporarily overlapping gestures and stances. One of our current goals is to use **Improv**'s ability to tie into commercial animation tools to build up a library of component motions, and to classify these motions in a way that makes them most useful as building blocks.

We have begun to embed **Improv** into a client-based application for a Java compatible browser (such as Netscape version 2.0). For use in educational and home settings, we plan to augment the full 3D subsystem with a "nearly 3D" version. This would run on a low end platform, such as a PC with an Intel processor. The user would still be able to see a view into a three dimensional world, but the visual representations of the actors would be simpler and largely two dimensional. For example, two participants to a graphical MUD, one with an SGI Onyx, and one with an Intel/486 based PC, could interact in the same scene. They would both see the same actors at the same locations, actions and personality. The only difference would be that the first participant would see a much more realistic quality of rendering.

We plan to integrate **Improv**'s voice recognition and english-like behavioral sub-systems. This will allow a user to fully exploit the object substrate, giving access to direction of goals, mood changes, attitudes and relationships between actors, all via spoken English sentences.

CONCLUSION

We have described an interactive system that lets authors of various abilities create remarkably lifelike, responsively animated character interactions that run over networks in real time. We believe these techniques have the potential to have a large impact on many areas. These include: computer Role Playing Games, simulated conferences, "clip animation," graphical front ends for MUDs, synthetic performance, shared virtual worlds, interactive fiction, high-level direction for animation, digital puppetry, computer guides and companions, point to point communication interfaces, true non-linear narrative TV, and large scale deployment of bots for the Metaverse.

As **Improv** is a very large system, we could not cover many of its detail in this paper. We refer the reader to [Perlin96] for a more in-depth treatment.

ACKNOWLEDGEMENTS

We gratefully acknowledge the support of Microsoft Corporation (and especially Dan Ling), the National Science Foundation, the New York State Science and Technology Foundation, and Silicon Graphics Incorporated (especially Keith Seto). Daniel Wey and Jon Meyer have both made important contributions to the Improv substrate. Mauricio Oka designed the flexible face model. Many other people have helped with this effort in many ways. In particular, we'd like to thank Cynthia Allen, Clilly Castiglia, Troy Downing, Steve Feiner, Laura Haralyi, Mehmet Karaul, Sabrina Liao, Marcelo Tocci More, Ruggero Ruschioni, Eduardo Toledo Santos, Jack Schwartz, Gerry Seidman, Eric Singer, Michael Wahrman, and Marcelo Zuffo. Also everyone at the, CAT and MRL at NYU, and LSI at USP. E Emi, com beijos.

APPENDICES

A. Decision Rules Equation

When an object is passed through a decision rule, a weighted sum is made of each of the values returned from the associated factors, modified by the scale assigned to the set of choices. This becomes the final weight assigned to the object that is used in making the decision.

The formula for this is as follows:

$$FinalWeight=Scale(factor_1^{influence1} factor_2^{influence2} ... factor_n^{influencen})$$

B. Fuzzy Logic Equations

The function compares how close the *Input Value* comes to the *Target Value* (or *Target Range*); returning a value of 1 at the *Target Value* (or inside the *Target Range*), dropping to 0 at a distance of *Spread* from the *TargetValue*. The fuzzy comparison is implemented as follows:

$$y = w\left(\frac{|InputValue - TargetValue|}{Spread}\right)$$

where:
- y is the Fuzzy Value
- w is a bell curve weighting kernel (we use a raised cos function)

A high and low spread may be specified, in which case input values greater than the target value (or range) will use the high spread in the calculation, while input values lower than the target value (or range) will apply the low spread.

The returned value is then modified based on the type of fuzzy operation as follows:

equals	y Value
not equals	1-y, its complement
greater than	y, high spread defaults to infinity
not greater than	1-y, high spread defaults to infinity
less than	y, low spread defaults to -infinity
not less than	1-y, low spread defaults to -infinity

REFERENCES

N. Badler, B. Barsky, D. Zeltzer, *Making Them Move: Mechanics, Control, and Animation of Articulated Figures* Morgan Kaufmann Publishers, San Mateo, CA, 1991.

N. Badler, C. Phillips, B. Webber, *Simulating Humans: Computer Graphics, Animation, and Control* Oxford University Press, 1993.

J. Bates, A. Loyall, W. Reilly, *Integrating Reactivity, Goals and Emotions in a Broad Agent,* Proceedings of the 14th Annual Conference of the Cognitive Science Society, Indiana, July 1992.

B. Blumberg, T. Galyean, *Multi-Level Direction of Autonomous Creatures for Real-Time Virtual Environments* Computer Graphics (SIGGRAPH '95 Proceedings), 30(3):47--54, 1995.

A. Broderlin, L. Williams, *Motion Signal Processing,* Computer Graphics (SIGGRAPH '95 Proceedings), 30(3):97--104, 1995.

R. Brooks. *A Robust Layered Control for a Mobile Robot*, IEEE Journal of Robotics and Automation, 2(1):14--23, 1986.

J. Chadwick, D. Haumann, R. Parent, *Layered construction for deformable animated characters.* Computer Graphics (SIGGRAPH '89 Proceedings), 23(3):243--252, 1989.

D. Ebert and et. al., *Texturing and Modeling, A Procedural Approach* Academic Press, London, 1994.

M. Girard, A. Maciejewski, *Computational modeling for the computer animation of legged figures.* Computer Graphics (SIGGRAPH '85 Proceedings), 20(3):263--270, 1985.

J. Hodgins, W. Wooten, D. Brogan, J O'Brien, *Animating Human Athletics,* Computer Graphics (SIGGRAPH '95 Proceedings), 30(3):71--78, 1995.

M. Johnson, *WavesWorld:* PhD Thesis, *A Testbed for Three Dimensional Semi-Autonomous Animated Characters*, MIT, 1994.

M. Karaul, *personal communication*

P. Maes, T. Darrell and B. Blumberg, *The Alive System: Full Body Interaction with Autonomous Agents* in Computer Animation'95 Conference, Switzerland, April 1995 .IEEE Press, pages 11-18.

M. Minsky, *Society of Mind*, MIT press, 1986.

C. Morawetz, T. Calvert, *Goal-directed human animation of multiple movements*. Proc. Graphics Interface}, pages 60--67, 1990.

K. Perlin, *An image synthesizer*. Computer Graphics (SIGGRAPH '85 Proceedings)}, 19(3):287--293, 1985.

K. Perlin, *Danse interactif.* SIGGRAPH '94 Electronic Theatre, Orlando.

K. Perlin, *Real Time Responsive Animation with Personality*, IEEE Transactions on Visualization and Computer Graphics, 1(1), 1995.

K. Perlin, A. Goldberg, *The Improv System* Technical Report NYU Department of Computer Science, 1996.
(online at http://www.mrl.nyu.edu/improv)

K. Sims, *Evolving virtual creatures*. Computer Graphics (SIGGRAPH '94 Proceedings)}, 28(3):15--22, 1994.

N. Stephenson, *Snow Crash* Bantam Doubleday, New York, 1992.

S. Strassman, *Desktop Theater: Automatic Generation of Expresssive Animation, PhD thesis,* MIT Media Lab, June 1991
(online at http://www.method.com/straz/straz-phd.pdf)

D. Terzopoulos, X. Tu, and R. Grzesczuk *Artificial Fishes: Autonomous Locomotion, Perception, Behavior, and Learning in a Simulated Physical World,* Artificial Life, 1(4):327-351, 1994.

A. Witkin, Z. Popovic, *Motion Warping* Computer Graphics (SIGGRAPH '95 Proceedings), 30(3):105-108, 1995.

The Virtual Cinematographer: A Paradigm for Automatic Real-Time Camera Control and Directing

Li-wei He * — Microsoft Research
Michael F. Cohen * — Microsoft Research
David H. Salesin † — University of Washington

Abstract

This paper presents a paradigm for automatically generating complete camera specifications for capturing events in virtual 3D environments in real-time. We describe a fully implemented system, called the Virtual Cinematographer, and demonstrate its application in a virtual "party" setting. Cinematographic expertise, in the form of film *idioms*, is encoded as a set of small hierarchically organized finite state machines. Each idiom is responsible for capturing a particular type of scene, such as three virtual actors conversing or one actor moving across the environment. The idiom selects shot types and the timing of transitions between shots to best communicate events as they unfold. A set of *camera modules*, shared by the idioms, is responsible for the low-level geometric placement of specific cameras for each shot. The camera modules are also responsible for making subtle changes in the virtual actors' positions to best frame each shot. In this paper, we discuss some basic heuristics of filmmaking and show how these ideas are encoded in the Virtual Cinematographer.

CR Categories and Subject Descriptors: I.3.3 [Computer Graphics]: Picture/Image Generation—viewing algorithms, I.3.6 [Computer Graphics]: Methodology and Techniques—interaction techniques.

Additional Keywords: cinematography, virtual worlds, virtual environments, screen acting, camera placement, hierarchical finite state machines

1 Introduction

With the explosive growth of the internet, computers are increasingly being used for communication and for play between multiple participants. In particular, applications in which participants control virtual actors that interact in a simulated 3D world are becoming popular. This new form of communication, while holding much promise, also presents a number of difficulties. For example, participants often have problems comprehending and navigating the virtual 3D environment, locating other virtual actors with whom they wish to communicate, and arranging their actors in such a way that they can all see each other.

*Microsoft Research, One Microsoft Way, Seattle, WA 98052. Email: {a-liweih | mcohen}@microsoft.com

†Department of Computer Science and Engineering, University of Washington, Seattle, WA 98195. Email: salesin@cs.washington.edu

In fact, these same types of problems have been faced by cinematographers for over a century. Over the years, filmmakers have developed a set of rules and conventions that allow actions to be communicated comprehensibly and effectively. These visual conventions are now so pervasive that they are essentially taken for granted by audiences.

This paper addresses some of the problems of communicating in 3D virtual environments by applying rules of cinematography. These rules are codified as a hierarchical finite state machine, which is executed in real-time as the action unfolds. The finite state machine controls camera placements and shot transitions automatically. It also exerts subtle influences on the positions and actions of the virtual actors, in much the same way that a director might stage real actors to compose a better shot.

Automatic cinematography faces two difficulties not found in real-world filmmaking. First, while informal descriptions of the rules of cinematography are mentioned in a variety of texts [1, 13, 15], we have not found a description that is explicit enough to be directly encoded as a formal language. Second, most filmmakers work from a script that is agreed upon in advance, and thus they have the opportunity to edit the raw footage as a post-process. In constrast, we must perform the automatic camera control in real time. Thus, live coverage of sporting events is perhaps a better analogy to the problem we address here, in that in neither situation is there any explicit knowledge of the future, nor is there much opportunity for later editing.

In this paper, we discuss an implementation of a real-time camera controller for automatic cinematography, called the Virtual Cinematographer (VC). We demonstrate its operation in the context of a "virtual party," in which actors can walk, look around, converse, get a drink, and so on. The various actors are controlled either by human users over a network, or by a party "simulator," which can control certain actors automatically. Each user runs his or her own VC, which conveys the events at the party from the point of view of that user's actor, or "protagonist."

The Virtual Cinematographer paradigm is applicable to a number of different domains. In particular, a VC could be used in any application in which it is possible to approximately predict the future actions of virtual "actors." For example, in virtual reality games and interactive fiction, the VC could be used to improve upon the fixed point-of-view shots or ceiling-mounted cameras that such applications typically employ.

1.1 Related work

There are a number of areas in which related work has been explored. Karp and Feiner [11, 12] describe an animation-planning system that can customize computer-generated presentations for a particular viewer or situation. Sack and Davis [17] present the IDIC system, which assembles short "trailers" from a library of *Star Trek, The Next Generation* footage. Christianson *et al.* [3] have developed an interactive story-telling system that plans a camera sequence based on a simulated 3D animation script. All of these techniques

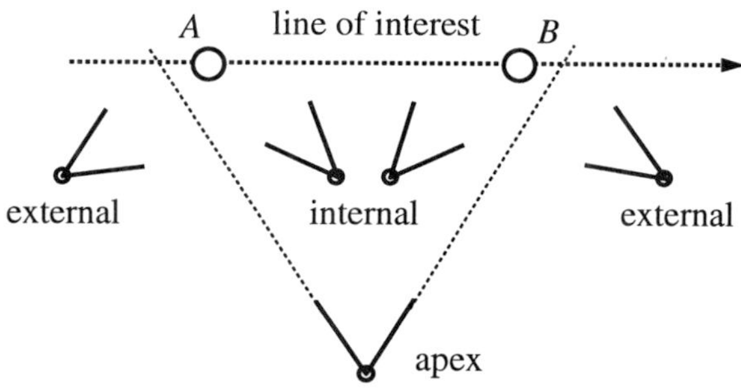

Figure 1 (Adapted from figure 4.11 of [1].) Camera placement is specified relative to "the line of interest."

use an off-line planning approach to choose the sequence of camera positions. In this paper, by contrast, we are concerned with real-time camera placement as the interactively-controlled action proceeds.

A number of other systems concentrate on finding the best camera placement when interactive tasks are performed [8, 14, 16]. In particular, Drucker *et al.* [4, 5, 6] show how to set up the optimal camera positions for individual shots by solving small constrained optimization problems. For efficiency reasons, in the real-time setting we select shots from a small set of possible camera specifications so that camera positions can be computed using closed-form methods. The mathematics for defining low-level camera parameters, given the geometry of the scene and the desired actor placements, is described in a number of texts [7, 10]. We found Blinn's treatment [2] to be the most helpful single source.

2 Principles of cinematography

It is useful to consider a film as a hierarchy. At the highest level, a film is a sequence of scenes, each of which captures a specific situation or action. Each scene, in turn, is composed of one or more shots. A single shot is the interval during which the movie camera is rolling continuously. Most shots generally last a few seconds, although in certain cases they can go on much longer.

2.1 Camera placement

Directors specify camera placements relative to *the line of interest*, an imaginary vector either connecting two actors, directed along the line of an actor's motion, or oriented in the direction that an actor is facing. Common camera placements include *external*, *internal*, and *apex* views, as shown in Figure 1.

Cinematographers have identified that certain *cutting heights* make for pleasing compositions while others yield ugly results (e.g., an image of a man cut off at the ankles). There are approximately five useful camera distances [1]. An *extreme closeup* cuts at the neck; a *closeup* cuts under the chest or at the waist; a *medium view* cuts at the crotch or under the knees; a *full view* shows the entire person; and a *long view* provides a distant perspective.

Individual shots also require subtly different placement of actors to look natural on the screen. For example, the closeup of two actors in Figure 2(a) looks perfectly natural. However, from a distance it is clear that the actors are closer together than expected. Similarly, shots with multiple actors often require shifting the actor positions to properly frame them (Figure 2(b)).

2.2 Cinematographic heuristics and constraints

Filmmakers have articulated numerous heuristics for selecting good shots and have informally specified constraints on successive shots for creating good scenes. We have incorporated many of these heuristics in the design of the Virtual Cinematographer. Some examples are:

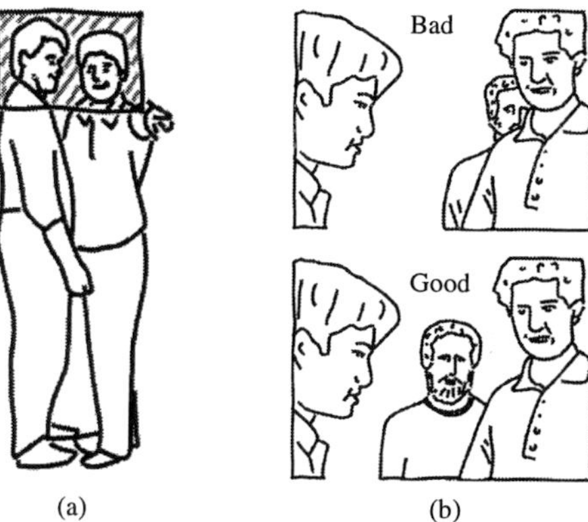

Figure 2 (Adapted from Tucker [18, pp. 33, 157].) Actor positions that look natural for a particular closeup look too close together when viewed from further back (a). Correctly positioning three actors for a shot may require small changes in their positions (b).

- *Don't cross the line*: Once an initial shot is taken from the left or right side of the line of interest, subsequent shots should remain on that side. This rule ensures that successive shots of a moving actor maintain the direction of apparent motion.
- *Avoid jump cuts*: Across the cut there should be a marked difference in the size, view, or number of actors between the two setups. A cut failing to meet these conditions creates a jerky, sloppy effect.
- *Use establishing shots*: Establish a scene before moving to close shots. If there is a new development in the scene, the situation must be re-established.
- *Let the actor lead*: The actor should initiate all movement, with the camera following; conversely, the camera should come to rest a little before the actor.
- *Break movement*: A scene illustrating motion should be broken into at least two shots. Typically, each shot is cut so that the actor appears to move across half the screen area.

A more complete survey of these heuristics can be found in Christianson *et al.* [3].

2.3 Sequences of shots

Perhaps the most significant invention of cinematographers is a collection of stereotypical formulas for capturing specific scenes as sequences of shots. Traditional film books, such as *The Grammar of the Film Language* by Arijon [1], provide an informal compilation of formulas, along with a discussion of the various situations in which the different formulas can be applied.

As an example, Figure 3 presents a four-shot formula that will serve as an extended example throughout the remainder of this paper. The formula provides a method for depicting conversations among three actors. The first shot is an external shot over the shoulder of actor C toward actors A and B. The second and third shots are external shots of actors A and B alone. The fourth shot is an internal reaction shot of actor C. Arijon [1] stipulates that an editing order for a typical sequence using this setup would be to alternate between shots 1 and 4 while actors A and B talk to actor C. When A and B begin to talk to each other, the sequence shifts to an alternation between shots 2 and 3, with an occasional reaction shot 4. Shot 1 should be introduced every now and then to re-establish the whole group.

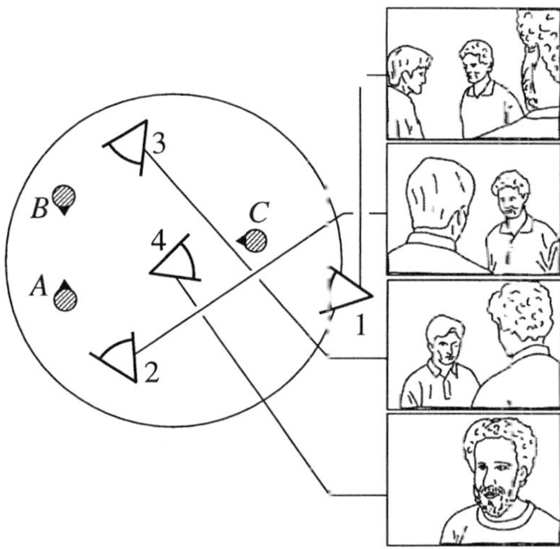

Figure 3 (Adapted from Figure 6.29 of Arijon [1].) A common formula for depicting a conversation among three actors.

The particular formulas prefered by any individual director lend a certain flavor or *style* to that director's films. In the Virtual Cinematographer, the style is dictated by the particular formulas encoded. (In fact, as each of the authors of this paper worked on the VC, a slightly different style emerged for each one.)

3 The Virtual Cinematographer

The Virtual Cinematographer is one part of the overall architecture shown in Figure 4. The other two parts consist of the *real-time application* and the *renderer*. The real-time application supplies the renderer with any static geometry, material properties, and lights. At each time tick (i.e., at each frame of the resulting animation), the following events occur:

1. The real-time application sends the VC a description of *events* that occur in that tick and are significant to the protagonist. Events are of the form (*subject, verb, object*). The subject is always an actor, while the object may be an actor, a current *conversation* (comprising a group of actors), a fixed object (e.g., the bar), or *null*.
2. The VC uses the current events plus the existing state of the animation (e.g., how long the current shot has lasted) to produce an appropriate camera specification that is output to the renderer. The VC may query the application for additional information, such as the specific locations and bounding boxes of various actors. The VC may also make subtle changes in the actors' positions and motion, called *acting hints*. These are also output to the renderer.
3. The scene is rendered using the animation parameters and description of the current environment sent by the application, and the camera specification and acting hints sent by the VC.

3.1 The VC architecture

The cinematography expertise encoded in the Virtual Cinematographer is captured in two main components: *camera modules* and *idioms* (see Figure 5). Camera modules implement the different camera placements described in Section 2.1. Idioms describe the formulas used for combining shots into sequences, as described in Section 2.3. The idioms are organized hierarchically, from more general idioms near the top, to idioms designed to capture increasingly specific situations. This structure allows each idiom to simply return control back to a more general idiom when unforseen events are encountered.

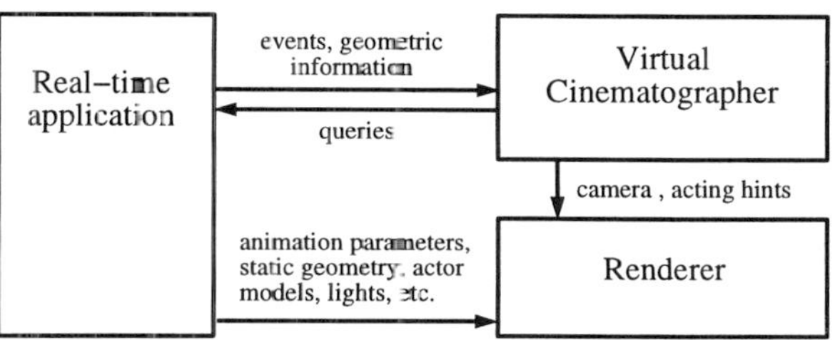

Figure 4 System including the Virtual Cinematographer.

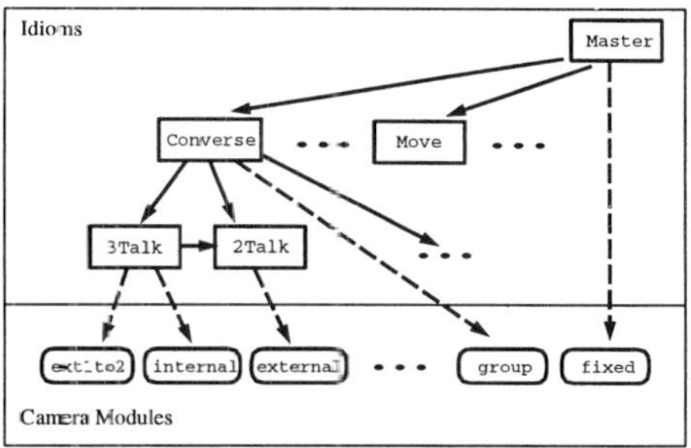

Figure 5 The Virtual Cinematographer structure.

3.2 Camera modules

Each camera module takes as input a number of actors, called *primary actors*; the exact number depends on the particular camera module. Each camera module automatically positions the camera so as to place the actors at particular locations on the screen and allow for pleasing cutting heights. In addition, the camera module may decide to reposition the actors slightly to improve the shot. Finally, the camera placement is automatically chosen so as to not cross the line of interest.

3.2.1 Example camera modules

Sixteen different camera modules have been implemented, several of which are shown in Figure 6. The most heavily used camera modules include:

- `apex`(*actor1*, *actor2*): The `apex` camera module takes two actors as input and places the camera so that the first actor is centered on one side of the screen and the second actor is centered on the other. The camera distance is thus a function of the distance between the two actors.
- `closeapex`(*actor1*, *actor2*): This camera module also implements an apex camera placement. However, it differs from the previous camera module in that it always uses a close-up camera distance. To compose a more pleasing shot, this camera module may move the actors closer together, as discussed in Section 2.1 and illustrated by A' and B' in Figure 6.
- `external`(*actor1*, *actor2*): The `external` camera module takes as input two actors and places the camera so that the first actor is seen over the shoulder of the second actor, with the first actor occupying two-thirds of the screen and the second actor the other third.
- `internal`(*actor1*, [*actor2*]): The `internal` camera module places the camera along the same line of sight as the `external` camera module, but closer in and with a narrower field of view, so that only the first actor is seen. If only one actor is specified,

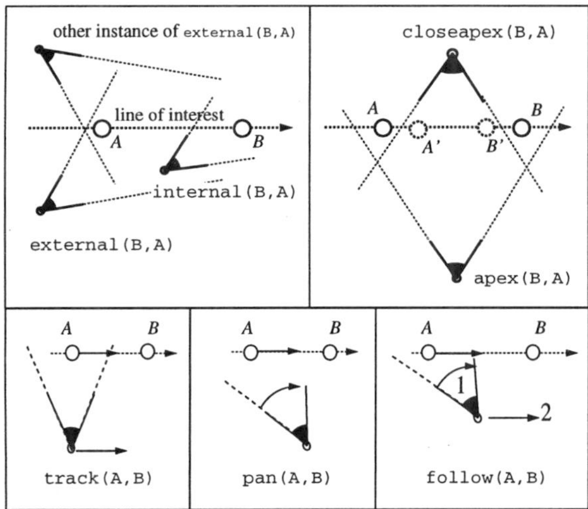

Figure 6 Some camera modules.

then the line of interest is taken to be along the direction the actor is facing.

- `ext1to2`(*actor1*, *actor2*, *actor3*): This camera module implements an external camera placement between one actor and two others. It places the camera so that the first two actors are seen over the shoulder of the third actor, with the first two actors occupying two-thirds of the screen, and the third actor the rest of the screen (see camera 1 in Figure 3). This camera module may also sometimes perturb the actors' positions to compose a better shot.
- {`track` | `pan` | `follow`}(*actor1*, *actor2*, *mindist*, *maxdist*): These three related camera modules are used when *actor1* is moving (Figure 6). They differ from the preceding modules in that they define a moving camera that dynamically changes position and/or orientation to hold the actor's placement near the center of the screen. The `track` camera sets the camera along a perpendicular from the line of interest and then moves with the actor, maintaining the same orientation. The `pan` module sets itself off the line of interest ahead of the actor and then pivots in place to follow the motion of the actor. The `follow` module combines these two operations. It first behaves like a panning camera, but as the actor passes by it begins to "follow" the actor from behind rather than allowing the actor to move off into the distance.
- `fixed`(*cameraspec*): This camera module is used to specify a particular fixed location, orientation, and field of view. We use it in our application to provide an overview shot of the scene.
- `null`(): This camera module leaves the camera in its previous position.

3.2.2 Respecting the line of interest

Recall that the line of interest is defined relative to the two actors in a shot. Most of the camera modules can choose one of two *instances*, corresponding to symmetric positions on opposite sides of the line of interest (Figure 6). The rules of cinematography dictate that when the line of interest remains constant, the camera should remain on the same side of the line. When the line of interest changes, for example, when one of the two actors in the shot changes position, the choice is not as well defined. We have found that a good rule is to choose the instance in which the camera orientation with respect to the new line of interest is closest to the orientation of the previous shot.

3.2.3 Influencing the acting

The camera modules are also able to subtly improve a shot by influencing the positions of the actors in the scene. Since the real-time application is primarily in charge of manipulating the actors, the changes made by the VC must be subtle enough to not disturb the continuity between shots (Figure 10).

For example, the `closeapex` camera module moves the two primary actors closer together if their distance is greater than some minimum, as in Figure 6. The `ext1to2` camera module adjusts the positions of the three primary actors so that no actor is obscured by any other in the shot. Some camera modules remove actors altogether from the scene, to avoid situations in which an actor appears only part-way on screen or occludes another primary actor in the scene. For example, the `internal` camera module removes the second actor from the scene.

3.2.4 Detecting occlusion

Camera modules are also responsible for detecting when one or more of the primary actors becomes occluded in the scene. In the case of occlusion, at each time tick, the camera module increments an occlusion counter, or resets the counter to zero if the occluded actors become unoccluded. This counter can be used by the idioms to decide whether to change to a different shot.

3.3 Idioms

At the core of the Virtual Cinematographer is the film *idiom*. A single idiom encodes the expertise to capture a particular type of situation, such as a conversation between two actors, or the motion of a single actor from one point to another. The idiom is responsible for deciding which shot types are appropriate and under what conditions one shot should transition to another. The idiom also encodes when the situation has moved outside the idiom's domain of expertise — for example, when a third actor joins a two-person conversation.

In the VC, an idiom is implemented as a hierarchical finite state machine (FSM) [9]. Each state invokes a particular camera module. Thus, each state corresponds to a separate shot in the animation being generated. Each state also includes a list of conditions, which, when satisfied, cause it to exit along a particular arc to another state. Thus, a cut is implicitly generated whenever an arc in the FSM is traversed to a state that uses a different camera module. The FSM's are hierarchically arranged through call/return mechanisms.

We will introduce the concepts involved in constructing idioms by way of examples. In the first example, we construct an idiom for depicting a conversation between two actors, called `2Talk`. In the second example, we use this idiom as a primitive in building a more complex idiom, called `3Talk`, for depicting a conversation among three actors.

3.3.1 The 2Talk idiom

The `2Talk` idiom (Figure 7) encodes a simple method for filming two actors as they talk and react to each other. It uses only external shots of the two actors. The `2Talk` procedure takes as parameters the two actors A and B who are conversing. It has four states. The first state uses an `external` camera module, which shows A talking to B. The second state is used for the opposite situation, when B talks to A. The third and fourth states use external camera placements to capture reaction shots of each of the actors.

When the idiom is activated, it follows one of two initial arcs that originate at the small circle in the diagram of Figure 7, called the

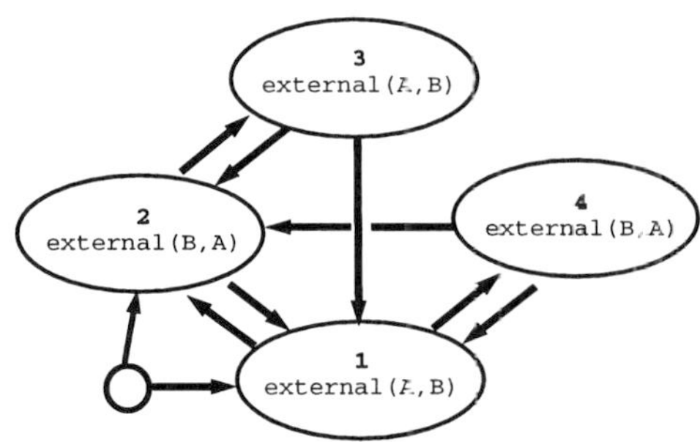

Figure 7 The 2Talk idiom.

entry point. The arc to be used is determined by the following code:

```
DEFINE_IDIOM_IN_ACTION(2Talk)
   WHEN ( talking(A, B) )
      DO ( GOTO (1); )
   WHEN ( talking(B, A) )
      DO ( GOTO (2); )
END_IDIOM_IN_ACTION
```

This code, like the rest of the code in this paper, is actual C++ code, rather than pseudocode. The keywords written in all-caps are macros that are expanded by the C preprocessor. This code tests whether *A* is talking to *B*, or *B* is talking to *A*, and transitions immediately to the appropriate state, in this case, either 1 or 2, respectively.

As a state is entered, it first executes a set of *in-actions*. The in-actions are often null, as is the case for all of the states in the 2Talk idiom. Once the state is entered, the state's camera module is called to position the camera. The state then executes a sequence of *actions* at every clock tick. The actions can be used to affect conditional transitions to other states. Finally, when exiting, the state executes a set of *out-actions*, again, often null.

In the 2Talk idiom, the camera modules are defined as follows:

```
DEFINE_SETUP_CAMERA_MODULES(2Talk)
   MAKE_MODULE(1, external, (A, B))
   MAKE_MODULE(2, external, (B, A))
   LINK_MODULE(1, 1, "A talks")
   LINK_MODULE(2, 2, "B talks")
   LINK_MODULE(3, 1, "A reacts")
   LINK_MODULE(4, 2, "B reacts")
END_SETUP_CAMERA_MODULES
```

MAKE_MODULE(*module_id, type, parameter list*) creates a new camera module of the designated type with the specified parameters and gives it an identifying number. LINK_MODULE(*state_id, module_id, name*) associates the specified camera module with the specified state. Thus for example, whenever state 1 is entered, an external shot of actor *A* over the shoulder of actor *B* will be used.

The first action code to be executed in each state is specified in a block common to all states, called the *common actions*. This is primarily a shorthand mechanism to avoid having to respecify the same *(condition, arc)* pairs in each state of the idiom. The common actions in the 2Talk idiom are:

```
DEFINE_STATE_ACTIONS(COMMON)
   WHEN (T < 10)
      DO ( STAY; )
   WHEN (!talking(A, B) && !talking(B, A))
      DO ( RETURN; )
END_STATE_ACTIONS
```

The first statement checks to see whether the total time T spent so far in this state is less than 10 ticks; if so, the current state remains unchanged. (However, an exception mechanism takes precedence and may in fact pre-empt the shot, as discussed in Section 3.3.2.) If the shot has lasted at least 10 ticks, but *A* and *B* are no longer conversing, then the idiom should return to the idiom that called it. The action statements are evaluated sequentially. Thus, earlier statements take precedence over statements listed later in the code.

The variable T is a global variable, which is accessible to any state. There are several other global variables that can be used in state actions:

- Occluded, the number of consecutive ticks that one or more of the primary actors has been occluded;
- IdiomT, the total number of ticks spent so far in this idiom;
- D[A,B], the distance between the actors (measured in units of "head diameters");
- forwardedge[x], rearedge[x], centerline[x], the edges of the bounding box of actor x, relative to the screen coordinates.

There are also a number of predefined control structures:

- STAY, remain in the same state for another tick;
- GOTO(x), transition to state x;
- RETURN, return to the parent state;
- CALL(*idiom, parameter list*), execute the specified idiom by passing it the specified list of parameters.

Finally, the actions code above makes use of a domain-specific subroutine called talking(A,B), which returns true if and only if the current list of events includes (A,talk,B).

State 1 of the 2Talk idiom is used to depict actor *A* talking to *B*. In addition to the common actions, the list of actions executed at each clock tick when in state 1 are:

```
DEFINE_STATE_ACTIONS(1)
   WHEN ( talking(B, A) )
      DO ( GOTO (2); )
   WHEN ( T > 30 )
      DO ( GOTO (4); )
END_STATE_ACTIONS
```

If *B* is now talking to *A*, then a transition to state 2 is required to capture this situation. Otherwise, if an actor has been in the same shot for more than 30 ticks, there should be a transition to state 4 to get a reaction shot from the other actor.

State 2, which addresses the case of actor *B* talking to actor *A*, is completely symmetric: the code is exactly the same except that *A* and *B* are swapped and states 1 and 3 are used in place of states 2 and 4.

For completeness, the action code for state 3 is shown below:

```
DEFINE_STATE_ACTIONS(3)
   WHEN ( talking(A, B) )
      DO ( GOTO (1); )
   WHEN ( talking(B, A)   T > 15 )
      DO ( GOTO (2); )
END_STATE_ACTIONS
```

Note that this state can make a transition back to state 1, which uses the same camera module as is used here in state 3. In this case, the two shots are really merged into a single shot without any cut. Finally, state 4 is symmetric to state 3 in the same way that state 2 is symmetric to state 1.

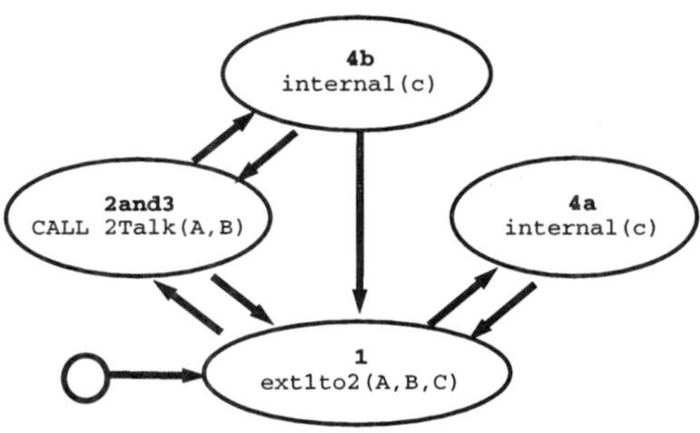

Figure 8 The 3Talk idiom.

Since the out-actions for 2Talk are null, we have now completely described the 2Talk idiom. The next section shows how 2Talk can be used as a subroutine for a higher-level idiom that handles conversations among three actors.

3.3.2 The 3Talk idiom

The finite state machine for 3Talk, which handles conversations among three actors, is shown in Figure 8. This idiom implements the cinematic treatment of three actors sketched in Figure 3 and illustrated in Figure 10. The 3Talk FSM has the same types of components as 2Talk: it has states and arcs representing transitions between states. In addition, this FSM also uses the *exception* mechanism, as discussed below.

The idiom has four states. The first state, labeled 1, is an establishing shot of all three actors, corresponding to the first camera position in Figure 8 and the second shot in Figure 10. The second state, labeled 2and3, is a parent state that calls the 2Talk idiom, corresponding to cameras 2 and 3 in Figure 3. Finally, the last two states, labeled 4a and 4b, capture the reaction shot of the first actor; these two states correspond to camera 4 of Figure 3.

All four states have actions that are similar to the ones described in 2Talk. The two states 4a and 4b have been implemented as separate states because they function differently in the idiom, even though they both shoot the scene from the same camera. State 4a is used in the opening sequence or after a new establishing shot, allowing shots of all three actors to be alternated with reaction shots of actor *C*. By contrast, state 4b is used only after a two-way conversation between actors *A* and *B* has been established, in this case to get an occasional reaction shot of actor *C* and then quickly return to the two-way conversation between *A* and *B*.

The one state that differs significantly from the states considered earlier is the state labeled 2and3. First, unlike the previous states, state 2and3 does have in-actions:

```
DEFINE_STATE_IN_ACTION(2and3)
   REG_EXCEPTION(left_conv, C, LEFT_CONV);
   REG_EXCEPTION(too_long, 100, TOO_LONG);
   REG_EXCEPTION(reacts, C, GET_REACTION);
   CALL( 2Talk, (A, B) );
END_STATE_IN_ACTION
```

These in-actions set up a number of exceptions, which, when raised, will cause a child idiom to exit, returning control to the parent state. Each REG_EXCEPTION command takes three parameters: the name of a function to call to test whether or not the exception should be raised; an arbitrary set of parameters that are passed to that function; and the exception name, which is an enumerated type. The final in-action of state 2and3 calls the 2Talk idiom, passing it actors *A* and *B* as parameters. The 2Talk idiom is then executed at once. All of the exceptions are implicitly tested before the actions in every state of the child idiom are executed.

The 2Talk idiom will return either when it executes a RETURN in one of its actions or when one of the exceptions is raised. In either case, control is returned to the parent state at that point, and its actions are executed. The actions for state 2and3 are:

```
DEFINE_STATE_ACTIONS(2and3)
   WHEN(EXCEPTION_RAISED(LEFT_CONV))
      DO( GOTO(1); )
   WHEN(EXCEPTION_RAISED(TOO_LONG))
      DO( GOTO(1); )
   OTHERWISE
      DO( GOTO(4b); )
END_STATE_ACTION
```

If either the LEFT_CONV or TOO_LONG exception has been raised, then a transition is made back to state 1 to get another establishing shot. Otherwise, a transition is made to get a reaction shot.

The out-actions of state 2and3, evaluated just before the transition to the new state is made, are used to remove the exceptions that were set up by the in-actions:

```
DEFINE_STATE_OUT_ACTION(2and3)
   DELETE_EXCEPTION(LEFT_CONV);
   DELETE_EXCEPTION(TOO_LONG);
   DELETE_EXCEPTION(GET_REACTION);
END_STATE_OUT_ACTION
```

3.3.3 Idioms for movement

Capturing screen motion (Figure 9) presents special problems. In particular, it may be desirable to end a shot not only when an event is triggered by the real-time system, but also when an actor reaches a certain position on the screen (such as the edge of the screen). The global variables forwardedge[x], rearedge[x], centerline[x] are used to facilitate these kinds of tests. These variables are measured in a *screen-coordinate system of the actor*, which is set up relative to the orientation of each actor x. The edge of the screen that the actor is facing is defined to be at $+1$, and the edge to the actor's rear, -1. The center line of the screen is at 0. Thus, for example, a state can see if actor x has just reached the edge of the screen by testing whether forwardedge[x] is greater than 1. It can test whether the actor has walked completely off the screen by testing whether rearedge[x] is greater than 1.

4 The "Party" application

For illustration, the Virtual Cinematographer has been applied to a simulated "party" environment. The party application runs over a network, so that multiple participants can interact in a single virtual environment. Each participant controls a different actor (their *protagonist*) at the party. The actors can walk, look around, converse with each other, or go to the bar where they can drink and talk to the bartender.

The user interface allows the user to invoke *(verb, object)* pairs, which are translated into *(subject, verb, object)* triples in which the protagonist is the subject. Current *verbs* include *talk*, *react*, *goto*, *drink*, *lookat*, and *idle*. Each invocation of a verb causes a change in the action of the protagonist shortly after the corresponding button is pushed.

An additional interface button allows the actors who stand alone or in a conversation to "vote" on whether to accept or reject a new actor *signaling* to join in the conversation. The *signal* verb is implicitly generated when an actor approaches within a short distance of the object of the *goto* verb.

At each time tick, the party application running on each client workstation sends an update of the current actions of that client's protagonist to a server. The server then broadcasts a list of *(subject, verb, object)* triples of interest to each protagonist's private VC. Triples of interest are those involving the protagonist (or others in the same conversation as the protagonist) as subject or object. The party application is responsible for all low-level motion of the actors, including walking, mouth movements, head turning, etc.

5 Results

The party application, renderer, and Virtual Cinematographer run on a Pentium PC. They are implemented in Visual C++, except for the user interface code, which is written in Visual Basic. The renderer uses *Rendermorphics®* to generate each frame. The full system runs at a rate of approximately 5 ticks per second, of which the majority of time is spent in the renderer.

Figures 9 and 10 depict the `Moving` idiom in action and the hierarchy of `Converse`, `3Talk`, and `2Talk`. Individual frames are shown on the left, with a corresponding shot from above on the right (which includes the camera itself circled in black.) In Figure 10, the arcs are labeled with the condition causing a transition to occur between states. (Heavy lines indicate the path taken through the idiom. Dotted lines indicate jumps between idioms caused by the calling and exception mechanisms.)

Figure 10 depicts the use of the hierarchy of film idioms. The sequence begins in the generic `Converse` idiom, which specifies the `group` shot. The converse idiom then calls `3Talk`, which follows an `ext1to2` shot by calling `2Talk`. Eventually `2Talk` is interrupted by an exception and by the `3Talk` idiom. Note the subtle rearrangement of the characters and the removal of extraneous characters in the `3Talk` idiom.

6 Conclusion and future work

This paper has described a Virtual Cinematographer whose architecture is well suited to a number of real-time applications involving virtual actors. The VC has been demonstrated in the context of a networked "virtual party" application. By encoding expertise developed by real filmmakers into a hierarchical finite state machine, the VC automatically generates camera control for individual shots and sequences these shots as the action unfolds.

There are a number of areas for future work. Although the camera modules have proved quite robust, they can fail for a few frames due to unexpected occlusions, or they may miss a critical action due to minimum-length shot constraints. Some of these issues can be resolved by redesigning the idioms in the current structure. We are also looking into incorporating simple constraint solvers, such as the ones proposed by Drucker [4, 5, 6] and Gleicher and Witkin [8]. In addition, we would like to expand the input to the VC to include such ancillary information as the emotional state of the scene or of individual actors. For example, if the situation is tense, faster cuts might be made, or if one actor is scared, the camera might be lowered to give the other actors a looming appearance. We would also like to apply similar rules for automatically lighting the scenes and actors in a cinematographic style.

Acknowledgements

We would like to thank Daniel Weld and Sean Anderson for their significant contributions during an earlier phase of this work. We would also like to thank Jutta M. Joesch for her help in editing the paper.

References

[1] Daniel Arijon. *Grammar of the Film Language*. Communication Arts Books, Hastings House, Publishers, New York, 1976.

[2] James Blinn. Where am I? What am I looking at? *IEEE Computer Graphics and Applications*, pages 76–81, 1988.

[3] David B. Christianson, Sean E. Anderson, Li-wei He, David H. Salesin, Daniel S. Weld, and Michael F. Cohen. Declarative camera control for automatic cinematography. In *Proceedings of the AAAI-96*, August 1996.

[4] Steven M. Drucker, Tinsley A. Galyean, and David Zeltzer. CINEMA: A system for procedural camera movements. In David Zeltzer, editor, *Computer Graphics (1992 Symposium on Interactive 3D Graphics)*, volume 25, pages 67–70, March 1992.

[5] Steven M. Drucker and David Zelter. CamDroid: A system for implementing intelligent camera control. In Michael Zyda, editor, *Computer Graphics (1995 Symposium on Interactive 3D Graphics)*, volume 28, pages 139–144, April 1995.

[6] Steven M. Drucker and David Zeltzer. Intelligent camera control in a virtual environment. In *Proceedings of Graphics Interface '94*, pages 190–199, Banff, Alberta, Canada, May 1994. Canadian Information Processing Society.

[7] James D. Foley, Andries van Dam, Steven K. Feiner, and John F. Hughes. *Computer Graphics, Principles and Practice*. Addison-Wesley Publishing Company, Reading, Massachusetts, second edition, 1990.

[8] Michael Gleicher and Andrew Witkin. Through-the-lens camera control. In Edwin E. Catmull, editor, *Computer Graphics (SIGGRAPH '92 Proceedings)*, volume 26, pages 331–340, July 1992.

[9] David Harel. Statecharts: A visual formalism for complex systems. *Science of Computer Programming*, pages 231–274, 1987.

[10] Donald Hearn and M. Pauline Baker. *Computer Graphics*. Prentice Hall, Englewood Cliffs, New Jersey, second edition, 1994.

[11] Peter Karp and Steven Feiner. Issues in the automated generation of animated presentations. In *Proceedings of Graphics Interface '90*, pages 39–48, May 1990.

[12] Peter Karp and Steven Feiner. Automated presentation planning of animation using task decomposition with heuristic reasoning. In *Proceedings of Graphics Interface '93*, pages 118–127, Toronto, Ontario, Canada, May 1993. Canadian Information Processing Society.

[13] Christopher Lukas. *Directing for Film and Television*. Anchor Press/Doubleday, Garden City, N.Y., 1985.

[14] Jock D. Mackinlay, Stuart K. Card, and George G. Robertson. Rapid controlled movement through a virtual 3D workspace. In Forest Baskett, editor, *Computer Graphics (SIGGRAPH '90 Proceedings)*, volume 24, pages 171–176, August 1990.

[15] Joseph V. Mascelli. *The Five C's of Cinematography*. Cine/Grafic Publications, Hollywood, 1965.

[16] Cary B. Phillips, Norman I. Badler, and John Granieri. Automatic viewing control for 3D direct manipulation. In David Zeltzer, editor, *Computer Graphics (1992 Symposium on Interactive 3D Graphics)*, volume 25, pages 71–74, March 1992.

[17] Warren Sack and Marc Davis. IDIC: Assembling video sequences from story plans and content annotations. In *IEEE International Conference on Multimedia Computing and Systems*, Boston, MA, May 1994.

[18] Patrick Tucker. *Secrets of Screen Acting*. Routledge, New York, 1994.

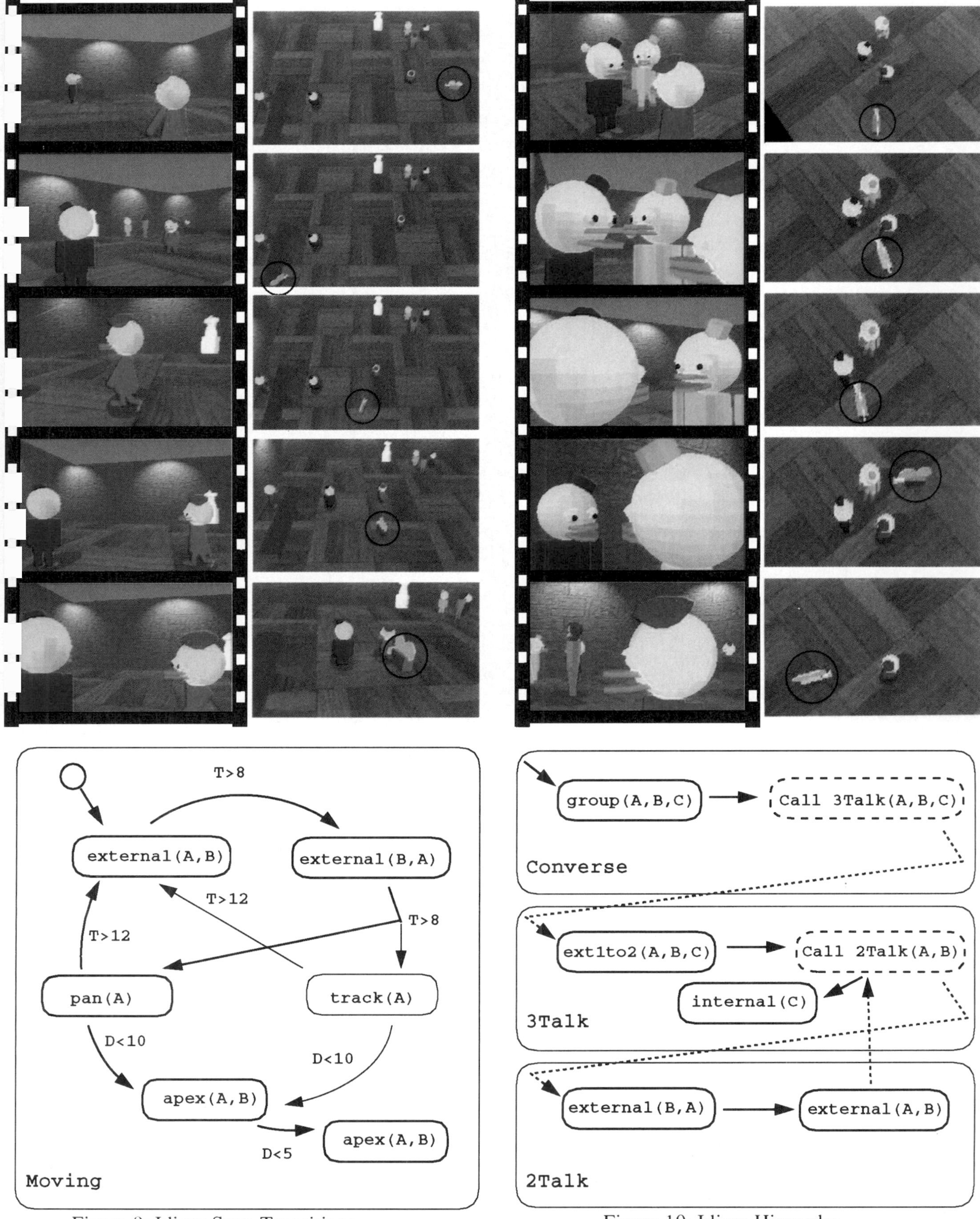

Figure 9: Idiom State Transitions

Figure 10: Idiom Hierarchy

Comic Chat

David Kurlander
Microsoft Research
One Microsoft Way
Redmond, WA 98052
djk@microsoft.com

Tim Skelly
Microsoft Research
One Microsoft Way
Redmond, WA 98052
timsk@microsoft.com

David Salesin
Department of Computer Science
University of Washington
Seattle, WA 98195
salesin@cs.washington.edu

ABSTRACT

Comics have a rich visual vocabulary, and people find them appealing. They are also an effective form of communication. We have built a system, called Comic Chat, that represents on-line communications in the form of comics. Comic Chat automates numerous aspects of comics generation, including balloon construction and layout, the placement and orientation of comic characters, the default selection of character gestures and expressions, the incorporation of semantic panel elements, and the choice of zoom factor for the virtual camera. This paper describes the mechanisms that Comic Chat uses to perform this automation, as well as novel aspects of the program's user interface. Comic Chat is a working program, allowing groups of people to communicate over the Internet. It has several advantages over other graphical chat programs, including the availability of a graphical history, and a dynamic graphical presentation.

CR Categories: I.3.2 [Computer Graphics]: Graphics Systems—distributed /network graphics; K.8.1 [Personal Computing]: Application Packages; D.2.2 [Information Interfaces and Presentation]: Tools and Techniques—user interfaces.

Keywords: Non-photorealistic rendering, comics, chat programs, virtual worlds, graphical histories, automated presentation, illustration, user interfaces, Internet, World Wide Web.

1. INTRODUCTION

Computers are rapidly changing the way that people communicate, as is evidenced by the proliferation of electronic mail and the advent of the World Wide Web. As the Internet and on-line services have grown in popularity, so has another form of computer-assisted communication: electronic chat rooms. Although electronic chat programs originally supported only text-based communications, fast modems and network connections have enabled the authors of these programs to create a richer user experience through the addition of graphics [14, 16, 22]. Participants in these new chat rooms communicate with one another not only by typing text, but also by changing the gesture or facial expression of an *avatar*, which serves as their graphical representation. In these chat rooms, graphics serves as a first-class form of communication—it is essential, not merely ornamental.

Considering the importance of graphics to modern chat rooms, it is a true failing that these programs provide only textual history transcripts. Histories are crucial in chat programs, since participants commonly interleave several tasks while chatting on-line. For example, people often participate in chats while writing documents, taking care of children, compiling programs, or monitoring other chat rooms. Any graphical communication that occurs while a participant is tending to another task is either lost or translated into textual form. Since there is no graphical history of the conversation, it is difficult to share the experience with non-participants, or to review the chat at a later time.

A second problem with current graphical chat programs is the requirement that participants must spend a significant amount of time doing things other than chatting. Most graphical chat programs require that participants navigate the room (or world), looking for an interesting conversation. Gestures must be specified either by hitting memorized function keys, or navigating menus or buttons. Care must be taken not to obstruct the view of other avatars, or to keep them in view. In 2D chat rooms avatars often overlap, and in 3D rooms they can accidently move behind or between other participants in the conversation.

A third aspect of graphical chat programs that can be improved upon is the relatively static nature of the graphical presentation. Although some chat rooms have animated backgrounds, the participants tend to see the same exact scene composition, at the same exact point of view, unless they or others move. Much can be done to make the view and scene composition more dynamic, and to make them reflect and enhance aspects of the conversation.

To address these problems, we have developed a new graphical representation of electronic chat rooms, based on the visual conventions of comics. Comics have a very rich tradition, and a distinctive, compelling, and entertaining visual vocabulary. Nearly everyone is familiar with the comic form, and many of its conventions have become second nature, even to the few that rarely read comics. Many of the same visual conventions are shared by comics throughout the world, which is important when choosing a graphical presentation for chat rooms on worldwide electronic networks.

We have built a system, called "Comic Chat," that automatically generates comics to depict on-line graphical chats. Relying on the rules of comic panel composition, this system chooses which avatars (presented as comic characters) to include in each panel, determines their placement and orientation, constructs word balloons of multiple types, and places these word balloons according to the rules for proper reading order. The system also chooses an appropriate camera zoom factor for each panel, decides when to begin a new panel, and selects default gestures and expressions that the participants can override. To make the chat rooms more lively and fun, Comic Chat can adjust the background or scene elements to reflect the topic of the conversation. All of the comics appearing in this paper were generated automatically by the Comic Chat system. In several instances, we felt it important to show examples of what can go wrong in constructing comics, and in these cases we generated comics by disabling components of the system.

Although the origins of comics are very old, this project was undertaken to coincide with the centennial of the modern comic strip, as commonly measured from the publication of Richard Outcault's "Yellow Kid," first appearing in 1895 in the New York World [10]. This past year, the comic strip centennial has been celebrated in the U. S. with a set of commemorative stamps, the opening of the National Gallery of Caricature and Cartoon Art, and even a series of textual chat room discussions with professional comic artists [11]. We consider it a fitting time to explore how on-line communications might benefit from the comic strip.

The next section describes related work. Section 3 explains the methodology that we used to select the features of comics to automate in our system. Section 4 describes how Comic Chat decides which characters to include in each panel, and how it positions and draws them. Issues related to balloon construction and layout are covered in Section 5. Section 6 addresses other important considerations in constructing panels. Section 7 discusses implementation issues. Several examples of our system's output are provided in Section 8. Finally Section 9 presents our conclusions and describes possible directions for future work.

2. RELATED WORK

Some of the best analyses of the visual language of comics have been written by comic artists. Both McCloud [13] and Eisner [5] authored excellent books on the subject. Several comics have been published electronically, some of which use techniques like color-table animation and staged presentation, to achieve effects beyond the scope of traditional comics [4]. Other commercial software programs allow people to author their own comics [15]. However, these programs are essentially drawing programs that allow users to assemble comics from clip art—they do not attempt to automate the process of comics production.

Several computer graphics researchers have built systems to produce illustrations automatically that satisfy a specified goal. Feiner's APEX system generates 3D illustrations depicting the steps of tasks, such as equipment repair [6]. Mackinlay's APT system determines the form of graph that best represents a given type of quantitative information, selecting which graphical attributes are best suited to represent that information [12]. The IBIS system, developed by Seligmann and Feiner, employs a generate-and-test mechanism with backtracking, to create illustrations that satisfy a given communicative intent [19]. Comic Chat also automates the construction of illustrations, but it is more special purpose, relying on domain-specific techniques.

Cassel et al. developed techniques to automate gestures and facial expressions in the animation of conversations between animated characters [3]. Their system relies on a database of facts, goals, and beliefs, not only to generate aspects of the characters' animations, but also to generate the text spoken by the characters. Comic Chat also generates default gestures and facial expressions for its characters, but because the system receives unconstrained textual input, it is difficult to produce sophisticated inferences about the conversation to control gesture and expression. Instead, Comic Chat uses simple rules, based on comics and on-line chat conventions, to choose default gestures and expressions, which can be overridden by the user.

Research aimed at achieving aesthetic, non-photorealistic images is receiving increasing interest in the graphics community. Haeberli developed techniques to produce artfully painted pictures interactively from image data [8]. Winkenbach and Salesin [21] and Salisbury et al. [18] devised methods for generating pen and ink illustrations from 3D models and images. Today, comics are also gaining recognition as an artform, and although a few comic artists are beginning to use computer-based tools, comics have not previously been targeted for computer graphics research.

A benefit of depicting chat sessions in comics form is that the primary visual representation also serves as a history transcript. Kurlander's editable graphical histories also represent the history of graphical user interaction as a series of panels [9]. However, that history representation adopts no other conventions from the visual language of comics.

Comic Chat was motivated by the appearance of several graphical chat programs in recent years. Habitat, built by members of Lucasfilm's game group [16], is a virtual multi-user world, rather than simply a chat system, although providing a new means for social interaction and communication was one of the project's major goals. Habitat places a very simple word balloon over the head of the last avatar to speak. When the next avatar speaks, the earlier word balloon loses its tail and scrolls upwards. As avatars move about, their balloons do not follow. Balloon construction in Habitat is very coarse, only slightly reminiscent of comics, and no real layout is performed. Yet Habitat was revolutionary in showing that online graphical virtual communities are not only possible but worthwhile, and later incarnations of the system are popular today, including Fujitsu Habitat in Japan, and CompuServe's WorldsAway.

More recently, several companies have deployed three-dimensional graphical chat rooms. In Worlds Inc.'s WorldsChat, participants navigate a virtual space station, and see the environment from either a first-person or third-person perspective [22]. All communication, however, is textual. On the Microsoft Network, V-Chat (for "Virtual Chat") provides several 2D and 3D environments. Participants can gesture and change their avatars' expressions, as well as type text to one another [14].

3. METHODOLOGY

To help us determine how to best represent chat sessions in the comic form, we first gathered numerous chat transcripts from an on-line service. We then read through the transcripts and annotated them with any information that we felt a computer would be able to extract easily, and that might be useful in composing the strips. Jim Woodring, a professional comic artist, took these transcripts, and illustrated a representative session.

Prior to seeing Woodring's illustrations, we were concerned that an effective comic chat representation might need to reflect deep semantics of the conversation, semantics beyond the reach of current natural language understanding technology. After reviewing the prototype illustrations, it became clear that we could produce interesting comics with only very limited semantics, and without any natural language processing.

Comic styles vary so dramatically that a single system capable of producing them all is inconceivable. Instead, we undertook to mimic the style of Woodring's prototype illustrations as precisely as possible in the Comic Chat system, and we designed the architecture so that it could be readily extended to include additional styles.

Carefully reviewing the artist-drawn prototypes, we determined the design elements that require automation. These elements fall under three broad categories: *characters*, *balloons*, and *panels*. The following three sections address each category in turn.

4. CHARACTERS

In our system, comic characters serve as avatars for the chat participants. Participants select their own character from a presupplied list. In composing the panels, several aspects of the characters need to be determined, including their gestures and expressions, which characters to draw, and their positions and orientations.

4.1 Gestures and expressions

We refer to *gesture* as a character's body pose, and *expression* as its facial pose. Most of the characters in Comic Chat have a set of heads that can fit on a set of bodies; hence their expressions can be independent of their gestures. Since one of our design goals is to minimize the amount of user interaction necessary, Comic Chat picks default gestures and expressions, which the user is free to override.

When a participant types in dialogue for his or her character, Comic Chat uses this dialogue to determine a default gesture and expression. An analysis of chat transcripts revealed a number of chat-specific conventions that we could effectively exploit, and our comic artist suggested a few additional indicators:

1. **Emoticons:** for example, :-) and :-(, indicate happy and sad.
2. **Chat acronyms:**
   - **a.** LOL (Laughing Out Loud), ROTFL (Rolling On The Floor Laughing) indicate laughter
   - **b.** IMHO (In My Humble Opinion) results in character pointing to self.
   - **c.** BRB (Be Right Back) results in character waving.
   - **d.** <g> (or <grin>) indicates smiling.
3. **Typesetting:** All caps indicates shouting.
4. **Punctuation:** !!! indicates shouting.
5. **Greetings:** Hi, hello, bye, goodbye, welcome (at beginning of sentence), result in character waving.
6. **Self-references:** I (at beginning of sentence), I'll, I will, I'm, I am, I'd, I would, etc... result in character pointing to self.
7. **Other-references:** You (at beginning of sentence), are you, will you, did you, don't you, etc.. result in character pointing to other.

Initially, we had thought that simple punctuation would be a much better indicator for expressions in comics (for example, a "?" for questioning, or a single "!" for exclaiming). However, typically punctuation is an indicator of fairly subtle expressions, and such subtlety tends to get lost in comics. In contrast, characters pointing and waving, which occur relatively infrequently in real life, come off well in comics.

Note that since gesture and expression can be controlled independently, multiple indicators can be extracted and used from the same input. For example, "I can't make it :-(", results in a character pointing to itself and frowning. Since multiple indicators can be extracted from a single input, they may also conflict. For example, "Hi Sue, how are you?", would suggest that the character both wave and point outward. Since constructing composite gestures from many individual 2D bitmaps of body parts (left arm pose, right arm pose, etc...) makes for a nearly impossible art authoring process, Comic Chat instead uses a prioritization scheme to choose the most important gesture.

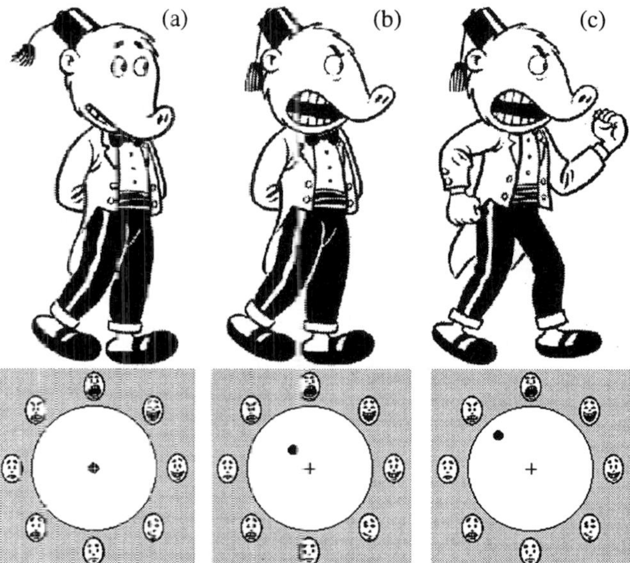

Figure 1. Emotion wheel and three bodies. a) a neutral pose; b) somewhat angry; c) very angry.

When no expression or gesture indicators are found in the utterance, the system chooses a default neutral expression and gesture. The system has multiple neutral expressions and gestures, and cycles through these to increase the visual richness of the comics produced. Often there are multiple versions of other expressions and gestures, too. Participants can see the system-selected expression and gesture for their character as they enter text. If they would prefer to override these, they can do so with a user-interface widget that we call an *emotion wheel.*

The emotion wheel is a circle, with emotions distributed along its perimeter: coy, happy, laughing, shouting[1], angry, sad, scared, and bored. At the center of the circle is neutral, and the further from the center, the greater the intensity of the emotion. The emotion wheel is similar to color choosers that distribute fully-saturated hues along the perimeter and have a shade of gray at the center. A nice aspect of the emotion wheel is that although emotion type and intensity are controlled with a single mouse movement, the results are still very intuitive.

Figure 1 shows the emotion wheel, along with the character feedback pane from Comic Chat's user interface. Initially, in Figure 1a, the control is at the center, and the character is in a neutral pose. In Figure 1b, the character becomes slightly angry, as the control is moved towards the "angry" direction on the perimeter. The character becomes much angrier in Figure 1c, as the control is moved further toward the perimeter. Emotions can affect both expression and gesture, as seen in Figure 1. Having both expression and gesture contribute to the portrayal of an emotion can provide many more shades of an emotion, given a limited supply of art.

In comics as in life, intense emotions can turn to actions, so it may make sense to add actions to the emotion wheel as well. For example, if the character becomes extremely angry, he or she might punch another. While this may be amusing at first, we fear it would become overly disruptive.

Actions that do not correspond to emotions, such as waving and pointing, are not accessible from the wheel. Instead, users can invoke them by mousing on the target character in any panel, and

1. Technically, shouting is not an emotion, but an action. However, we have found that it works best to include it on the wheel.

Figure 2. Three poorly composed panels, and one well-composed panel. a) missing speaker; b) conversational participants face away from each other; c) outer conversational pair is separated; d) well-composed panel.

then choosing the action from a pop-up menu. Since much of communication is non-verbal, Comic Chat allows gestures and expressions to be transmitted with or without accompanying text.

4.2 Characters for inclusion

Only about five characters can fit in one of our panels, and as in television and film, it is best not to show every character in every shot. It is, however, critical to show characters whenever they are speaking. Professional comic artists break this rule extremely rarely, and then typically only to make a stylistic statement. Figure 2a shows an example of breaking this rule.

If a character starts speaking to someone new, it is also important to include the character (or characters) being addressed. Once the addressee has been established, he or she can optionally be omitted from subsequent panels. When a participant reacts to what is said with either a gesture or expression, the system must show this as well.

When new characters enter the chat world, they are shown immediately, whether or not they say something. This makes it clear to the other participants that they have someone new monitoring their conversation, as well as someone new with whom they may wish to speak.

4.3 Position and orientation

Once it is determined which characters should be included in the panel, the next step is to position the characters and determine the direction they should face. In comics, as in life, people talking to each other tend to face one another and be situated together. Hence, the characters in Figures 2b and 2c are poorly arranged, and Figure 2d presents a better configuration. Of course, this rule suggests that it is important to know who is speaking to whom when rendering a conversation as comics.

Since the intended recipient of an utterance is not always apparent, participants in textual chat rooms often follow the convention of addressing each of their statements to particular individuals. Comic Chat looks for the nicknames of each of the chat participants in every utterance and tries to infer who is being addressed. (The nickname of a character appears whenever the cursor is placed over a character.) Alternatively, the user can also make the addressees explicit by selecting them with the mouse. Since there is a great deal of coherence in who is talking to whom in a conversation, this is not a significant hassle for the participants, and it also allows us to provide an option to hide all utterances not explicitly addressed to a specific participant. If someone chooses not to address their comment to specific individuals, it is interpreted as a general statement to the group, and the character is ideally made to face as many participants as possible.

We have constructed an evaluation function that considers these criteria, as well as some additional ones, and returns a lower value for better layouts. Keep in mind that the actual numbers in this function are arbitrary, but the function does capture the criteria we feel are important as well as the relative significance of the criteria. Let C be the set of characters to be included in the panel. Let a and b range over every member of C. We search for an ordering and orientation of the characters that minimizes the sum:

$$\sum_{a,\, b \in C \mid a \neq b} (Facing\,(a, b) + Neighbors\,(a, Left\,(a), Right\,(a)))$$

The *Facing* function penalizes conversational pairs in which the characters do not face one another or are not proximal. It is the sum of the numbers on the left whose predicate on the right is true:

4: if a has not addressed his utterance, and is not facing b.
2: if a has not addressed his utterance, and b is not facing a.
4: if a has addressed his utterance to b, and b is not facing a.
40: if a has addressed his utterance to b, and a is not facing b.
$4n$: if a has addressed his utterance to b, and the number of characters between them is n.

The *Neighbors* function discourages the system from shuffling the positions of characters from panel to panel. For each character in the sequence, we consider the characters to the left and the right, and for each of these that is different from the character last appearing there, a single point penalty is assessed. Note that maintaining consistency of positions from panel to panel is the least important consideration, and some comic artists do not feel this to be important at all.

Now that we have an evaluation function, we try to find the positions and orientations of the characters that minimize it. Instead of trying every combination, we use a greedy algorithm. After placing the first character, we find which of the two possible positions (and two possible orientations in each position) is best for the second. After placing the second, we consider the three possible positions for the third, and so on. Although this technique is not guaranteed to find the best possible arrangement, it tends to do an adequate job and is fast.

4.4 Rendering

The process of rendering a character consists of composing together a head bitmap with a body bitmap at the proper offset, and flipping them if necessary to make the character face the proper direction.

There is however one subtle yet important detail. Comic artists that draw complicated backgrounds often leave a little white space around the character. This makes the character much more visible,

Figure 3. Halos. a) characters without halos; b) characters with halos, improving visibility.

and makes it "pop" out of the background. We call this area around the character, the *halo*. Figure 3a shows two characters drawn without halos, and Figure 3b shows two characters with halos.

For each head and body bitmap, we also save a halo mask. It is important to draw both of the halos before drawing either the head or body, since the head's halo must not overwrite any of the body, and the body's halo must not overwrite any of the head.

5. BALLOONS

Word balloons are one of the most distinctive and readily recognizable elements of the comic medium. Most comic artists represent dialogue in word balloons, and these balloons are clearly critical in Comic Chat, since much of the communications between participants is still textual. This section addresses the various types of word balloons, as well as issues in their layout and construction.

5.1 Types

The appearance of balloons varies dramatically from artist to artist. Some artists draw balloons as ovals, others draw rectangular balloons. Certain artists omit the traditional balloon outline, and draw a dash from the character to the words. Woodring draws balloons that flow around his text. We felt that these balloons would be ideal for Comic Chat, because every balloon is different, and the resulting variety and visual richness assist in hiding the machine-constructed origin of the panels.

Even for a given artistic style, there are several types of balloons within the comic vocabulary. Figure 4 shows three different balloon types in the style that we are emulating. The most basic type is the speech balloon, an example of which appears in Figure 4a. The outline is solid, with the upper part (the *body* of the balloon) surrounding the dialogue. Emanating from the body is the *tail*, which points towards the speaker. Figure 4b illustrates a thought balloon. It is similar to the speech balloon, except instead of having a solid tail, its tail is composed of ovals. In some styles, the body of the thought balloon appears more like a cloud.

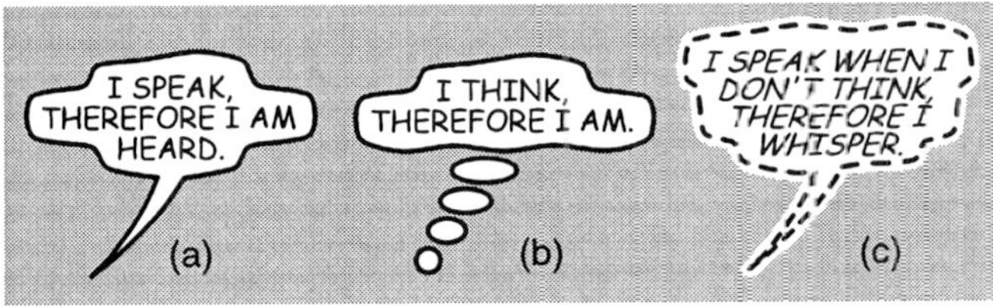

Figure 4. Three types of balloons: a) speech balloon; b) thought balloon; c) whisper balloon.

Figure 4c shows a whisper balloon. It differs from speech balloons in having a dashed outline, which is made more visible by the presence of a halo. The text in whisper balloons is often italicized. In chat terminology, *whispering* means sending a message only to a select subset of the participants, and it is convenient that the comic vocabulary already has a convention for this. A fourth type of balloon is the shout balloon, which has a jagged outline (and is yet to be implemented in Comic Chat). Although other types of balloons do exist, these four are the most prevalent.

5.2 Layout

Before constructing balloons, we run a layout algorithm that determines each balloon's dimensions and placement. In the style that we are emulating, all balloons appear above the tallest character's head. However, additional constraints must be considered as well.

In comics, the relative placement of balloons determines the reading order. Because it is important in Comic Chat to convey the order of the utterances, we strictly follow the appropriate comic conventions. The rule is that balloons are read in a top-down order, and when multiple balloons are at the same height, they are read from left to right. Note that the order in which balloons are read is independent of where characters are placed in the panel.

A third point that helps constrain the placement of the balloons in Comic Chat is the style-specific requirement that some part of each balloon float at least partially over the center of the speaker's face. We have designed a layout algorithm that takes all of these rules into account, while adding a little randomness to each layout to avoid the appearance of machine-generated regularity.

We use a greedy algorithm for placing the bodies of balloons; once the algorithm chooses a body location, it never alters it. However, the tail placement is not greedy; instead, the algorithm defers placing the tails until all the bodies have been placed. Note that using a greedy algorithm is suitable for body placement because it is fast, does a good job, and because there is no real need to pack the maximum amount of text into a panel, as cartoonists do not typically do this either. On the other hand, we originally tried using a greedy algorithm for tail placement, with poor results.

Our layout algorithm makes use of intervals, called *routing channels*, for ensuring that there will be enough room to place the tails once the bodies are positioned. Routing channels are disjoint—they are a partitioning of the space available for routing balloon tails. Each routing channel is associated with a balloon and indicates where that balloon's tail could be placed. For example, in Figure 5a, the darkly shaded area is the original routing channel for the topmost balloon, spoken by the center character. This region spans the width of the balloon; initially, the tail could go anywhere in this region and be guaranteed not to intersect another balloon or tail. When a second character speaks (in this case, the leftmost character), the first routing channel is decreased in size in order to accommodate the second balloon, as shown in Figure 5b. The third balloon, in its original position, completely covers what remains of the first routing channel, leaving no place for the first balloon's tail. Our algorithm recognizes this situation and shifts the third balloon right in order to leave enough space for the first balloon's tail. The final routing channel for all three balloons is shown in Figure 5c.

Now that we have run through this example, let's define the routing algorithm more formally. To describe our algorithm, we will first introduce some notation. Let $B = (B_1,...,B_n)$ be an array of balloons in the order in which they appear, with $T = (T_1,...,T_n)$ representing the text in the balloons. Let $R = (R_1,...,R_n)$ be a corresponding array of routing channels, with each routing channel R_i specified by left and right endpoints $R_i.l$ and $R_i.r$. Each balloon B_i is spoken by a

(a)

(b)

(c)

Figure 5. Routing Channels. (a) Lower left balloon requests channel allocation from top balloon; (b) Lower right balloon requests channel allocation from top balloon; (c) Lower right balloon shifts right, routing regions successfully allocated.

character, and the x coordinate of the center of that character's face is represented by x_i.

The following procedure computes the horizontal placement for an array of n balloons, and sets up the routing channels $R_1,...,R_n$. It returns the number of balloons that is placed successfully.

```
function PlaceBalloons(B, R, x, T)
   for j = 1 to n do
      w_j := FindWidth(B_j);
      R_j := [x_j-w_j, x_j+w_j]
      for i = 1 to j-1 do:
         R_j := MaxAllowable (R_i, x_i, R_j, x_j);
      end for
      if width (R_j) >= w_j then
         R_j := Position (B_j, R_j)
      else
         if not SqueezeBalloon (R_j, T_j) then
            return j-1;
         end if
      end if
      for i=1 to j-1 do
         R_i := ReduceChannel (R_i, x_i, R_j, x_j)
      end for
   end for
   return n
end function
```

The *PlaceBalloons* function loops through each balloon, placing them one at a time. Let us assume that balloons B_1 through B_{j-1} have been placed, and let's look at how to place balloon B_j. The first step is to choose a target width for the balloon (described in detail later), and set the largest possible routing channel that would allow the balloon's horizontal extent to pass above the center of the character's face.

Next, we trim the routing channel R_j just enough to ensure that all of the previous routing channels $R_1,...,R_{j-1}$ remain wide enough to support a tail. If the resulting routing channel R_j is wider than the target width, then we have to choose a horizontal position for the balloon in the routing channel (we do this randomly); we then set the routing channel to be the horizontal extent of the balloon. Otherwise, we attempt to squeeze the balloon into a narrower channel than the original target width. If the amount of text in the balloon is too large to fit, then we give up and return the number of balloons previously placed. Finally, we reduce all of the previous routing channels to accommodate the new one.

This describes the heart of the algorithm. All that is left are the details. To choose the target width, we initially estimate the area that the body will cover, by computing the area of a single typeset line, and scaling it up by a factor of a third to account for linebreaks and leading. If the line is short, it should not be broken into multiple lines, and we assume a height of one text line. Otherwise, we determine a conservative estimate of the allowable height of this balloon by calculating the distance from the bottom of the lowest previously placed balloon to the bottom of the rectangle in which balloons can be placed. The minimum allowable width of the balloon text is the maximum of the widest word, and the balloon area divided by the allowable height. We randomly select a width between this minimum and the width of the panel.

The function below is used to trim the routing channel R_j just enough to ensure that routing channel R_i remains wide enough to support a tail. It ensures that the width of routing region R_i is at least t, and that R_i continues to contain x_i:

```
function MaxAllowable (R_i, x_i, R_j, x_j):
   R := R_j
   if x_i < x_j then
      R.l := max{R_i.l + t, x_i}
   else
      R.r := min{R_i.r - t, x_i}
   end if
   return R
end function
```

Finally, the *ReduceChannel* function reduces the interval R_i so that it no longer overlaps R_j:

```
function ReduceChannel (R_i, x_i, R_j, x_j)
   R := R_i
   if x_i < x_j then
      R_i.r := min{R_i.r, R_j.l}
   else
      R_i.l := max{R_i.l, R_j.r}
   end if
   return R
end function
```

As mentioned earlier, the above algorithm finds the horizontal placement of a set of balloons. Next we calculate the vertical placement. The rules for proper reading order require that the new balloon be no higher than the bottom of any balloons already placed to its right, and no higher than the top of any balloons already placed to its left. We place each balloon as high as possible, such that proper reading order is maintained.

If the function fails, at least one balloon could not be successfully placed in the current panel. We check to see if the balloon can fit in a panel by itself. If it cannot, we break up the text of the balloon into smaller balloons that do fit the panel size constraint, and add ellipses to each of the new balloons to indicate that a split occurred.

5.3 Balloon body construction

Since the bodies of our balloons flow around the text that they contain, the first step of constructing balloons consists of computing the layout of this text. The artist we are emulating typically centers text in word balloons, so we first compute word breaks and then center the text on each line.

Because our goal is to create balloons that wrap smoothly around text, it makes sense to construct the bodies of these balloons with splines. After experimenting with cardinal splines and B-splines, we chose the latter, since they produce the best effect. Our artist draws moderately sharp bends in his balloon outlines, which we were able to mimic using a high B-spline tension of 5.0. When comic artists draw balloons, they always leave a margin between the text and the balloon outline, so we expand the boundaries of the text lines outward before computing the spline.

Our original attempt at balloons appeared amoeba-like, following the text too closely, responding to its every turn. We prefer balloons that flow around the text, but do not draw too much attention to themselves. In studying a set of sample balloons drawn by our artist, we determined that he avoids this problem in two ways. First, he never dips the balloon inwards towards the text on one line, just to move outwards again on the next. Second, he tends not to shift the balloon outline inwards or outwards by very small increments—instead he responds only to larger changes in the text outline.

We implemented these two additional rules, and the resulting balloons were much improved, yet still inferior to balloons that we wished to emulate. The large remaining difference between our balloons and Woodring's was the lack of small-scale perturbation in the outline. Whenever there is a long segment of the outline that does not bend in or outward with the text, Woodring adds small, low frequency waves to give the balloon additional richness. We have been able to mimic this effect by placing additional control points along these large segments, which alternately move towards and away from the text. The resulting balloons produced by Comic Chat faithfully capture Woodring's style, and examples of these balloons appear in figures throughout the paper.

5.4 Balloon tail construction

Now that we have placed and constructed the bodies of the balloons and computed routing channels for the tails, it is time to construct the tails themselves. The tails of speech and whisper balloons are composed of arcs or straight segments, and the tails of thought balloons consist of ovals forming either an arc or a line.

The best looking balloons have tails emanating from under the bottom line of text. Depending upon the placement of the characters and balloons in a panel, it is sometimes necessary to choose a non-optimal tail connection point, as comic artists do from time to time. To choose the connection point of a tail, we first see if a large enough part of the last line of text spans the routing channel. If so, we choose a location further than a specified distance from the edge of the routing channel, to insure that the tail will not be exactly adjacent to other balloon bodies or tails. Failing this, we attach the tail to a piece of the balloon within the routing channel, at a small horizontal distance from the center of the speaking character's head. This allows us to give the tail a definite arc, but not an arc that will span diagonally over a large part of the illustration.

We construct balloon tails so that they come to a point at roughly the same height, (which of course must be below the lowest balloon), and always at least in the lowest third of the region reserved for balloons. Since the best balloon tails head directly and clearly toward the speaker, it is preferable not to have tail arcs cross over the head of the character responsible for the balloon. In our comic style, tails emanating from a part of the balloon to the left of the speaker curve counterclockwise and end above the center of the speaker's face. Tails beginning to the right of the speaker curve clockwise and end at the same point.

5.5 Rendering

Rendering a balloon is simply a matter of filling its interior (to hide a background that was drawn first), scan-converting its outline, and drawing the text. There are two important details worth mentioning. Whisper balloons have halos, and these are easily rendered by initially scan-converting the outline of the balloon with a thick, solid, white pen, before rendering the true outline with a smaller, black, dashed pen. Also, most comic artists draw balloon text in all-caps, with a very distinctive (though varying) comic lettering. We also display the text in all-caps, no matter how it was typed. A wide variety of comic fonts is available commercially and as share-ware.

6. PANELS

Several additional issues should be taken into account when composing and rendering panels. These include choosing when to begin a new panel, adjusting the zoom factor of the virtual camera, and adding semantic elements to the panels.

6.1 Panel breaks

As participants specify new dialogue and body poses, Comic Chat proceeds to redraw the last panel, incorporating this additional information. At some point, however, it is necessary to start a new panel, and Comic Chat has several rules for choosing when to do so.

First, Comic Chat always begins a new panel whenever the balloon layout algorithm cannot successfully fit an additional balloon in the panel.

A second rule is that Comic Chat always starts a new panel whenever the additional input would result in too many characters in the current panel. We limit the number of characters per panel to five, since facial expressions are otherwise difficult to read. In the current implementation, Comic Chat will not draw more than one balloon for a character in a single panel, so multiple utterances from a given character is also reason to start a new panel.

Third, we also start a new panel whenever rendering the new data in the current panel would result in a loss of information. For example, if a participant specifies two different facial expressions for his or her character, then these two expressions cannot be represented in the same panel.

Finally, since we believe it desirable to have the system occasionally draw a single character in a panel, we also will break to a new panel with a given probability (15%) whenever the first utterance of the panel is longer than a few words.

6.2 Camera zoom

If movies and television were always shot with the same camera parameters, they would quickly become visually tedious, and though comics technically do not have cameras, it is still important to add variety by changing the scale at which characters and the back-

(a) 

(b) 

(c) 

Figure 6. Semantic elements. a) map; b) scene object; c) Greek Chorus.

ground appear. Word balloons are unaffected by the virtual zoom factor.

As in the movies, it is often important to have an establishing shot. Whenever a new person enters a chat room, that person sees a panel showing the immediate surroundings. From time to time (about every 15 panels), we remind participants of their surroundings by generating another establishing shot. Other times, we pull in as close as possible, with the following caveats. First, we will not zoom in so far as to cut off a character at the neck; it nearly always looks better to include part of the character's shoulders. Second, we will not let an important character (one that we decided earlier must be included in the panel) be cut by the sides of the panel. Third, it is also best not to cut characters off at the ankles. In such cases it is better to pull back a little, and show the characters in their entirety. Some comic artists also prefer not to cut off characters at their knees either, but this is far from a universal rule, and we currently allow it.

Subject to the above restrictions, we pull in to the tightest shot possible. Since the number of characters selected to be included in the panels varies, as discussed in Section 4.2, the scale chosen for the panels also varies, contributing to the resulting visual richness.

6.3 Semantic elements

The pictures in human-drawn comics often reflect the words and stories that the comics tell. Since it is impossible given the current state of natural language technology to extract the semantics of arbitrary chat text, it is also impossible to automatically represent the meaning of this dialogue in pictures. However, things can still be done in composing the comics panels to reflect very simple semantic elements. In fact, we have already discussed how simple gestures and expressions can be selected automatically. Comic Chat reflects semantics in additional ways.

There is a collection of topics that seem to come up repeatedly in chat sessions. For example, where people are from, what they do for a living, sports teams, pets, and kids are all very popular topics. For each of these common topics, we can define keywords to look for, which when found alter the composition of the scene. Figure 6 shows three different ways that we change the panel composition whenever "Ohio" is mentioned. In Figure 6a, the background is changed to a map of Ohio for the duration of a single panel. Comic artists often use such non-realistic, representational backgrounds [13]. A disadvantage to this approach is that it dramatically increases the amount of art necessary to run the application, but it is still reasonable if the user has a CD-ROM drive. A second approach is shown in Figure 6b, where instead of changing the entire background, a new element is added to an existing background. Here we draw a banner for the soon-to-be-former-Cleveland Browns, which appropriately states, "Go Browns!"

In Figure 6c, we introduce a little meta-character at the bottom of the panel that makes smart-allecky remarks. Our comic artist refers to him as the "Greek Chorus". Here, in response to Ohio being mentioned, he asks "What's round on the ends and hi in the middle?" This character's size and placement and its balloon position distinguish him from human participants.

The beauty of the keyword approach is that it tends to work well, independent of the meaning of the entire sentence. For example, it is fine to show a map of Ohio whether a participant said "I was born in Ohio," "I've never been to Ohio," or "My plane got stuck in Ohio." A problem with this approach is that it requires a large effort to generate enough pictures and clever remarks to have reasonable coverage.

7. IMPLEMENTATION

Comic Chat is implemented in C++ and runs on both the Microsoft Windows 95 and Windows NT operating systems. Currently Comic Chat uses the Internet Relay Chat (IRC) protocol [17], and it interoperates with the many IRC servers already on the Internet. Non-textual information, such as gesture and expression choice, is encoded as a small string at the beginning of each message. Users of existing textual chat programs can communicate with Comic Chat participants, except they receive a text-only view of the proceedings, and are represented by a randomly selected character to Comic Chat participants. An early version of Comic Chat used Microsoft Network Protocols, which allowed text to be transmitted in specially-marked text packets, and all other information to be transmitted in data packets. This enabled Comic Chat to make the non-textual information totally invisible to text clients. Unfortunately, IRC lacks this capability.

Information communicated between clients includes indices of the specific bitmaps used, as well as the symbolic gestures and expressions. When a receiving client has the same character art used by the sender, it can simply consult the bitmap indices to render the exact pose chosen by the sender. However, if the receiver does not have the same character art, the symbolic gesture and expression information is applied to a different character that does reside on the system to yield a pose with the same intent.

Comic Chat has an extensible rule set for inferring a pose from typed text. End users can define their own rules. These rules are only applied to the text that the sender types, and the resulting pose information is communicated to other clients. However, when a message is received from a text-only client, the rules are applied to that message as well to assign a reasonable gesture and pose to the text client's character.

Each Comic Chat client makes its own panel composition decisions, which are not communicated from client to client. Hence, the participants in a single conversation can see different panels representing the same communications. Although on the surface this may seem to be a poor choice, it actually makes panel display more flexible, because each participant sees a custom view of the conversation. Currently, there are several factors that affect this custom view. First, participants can customize their panel size, and since more conversation fits in larger panels, this affects panel composition. Also, because Comic Chat displays an establishing shot for new participants, the panel appearance can differ according to when the participant joined the chat. In addition, individuals can whisper to one another, and these utterances appear only to those involved.

Comic Chat works as a standalone application or in conjunction with Web browsers. People can place pointers to chat rooms on their Web pages, and clicking on such a pointer will automatically launch Comic Chat to the chat room. Because it was written as an ActiveX Document [20], Comic Chat appears as a dynamic Web page within the window frame of browsers that support this interface, such as Microsoft Internet Explorer 3.0.

Performance of Comic Chat meets our original goal of requiring less than a second to compose and draw panels on a Pentium class machine. The background and character art are kept resident on each client machine, so that they need not be transmitted over the network. Artwork for a single character can vary in size according to the size and color depth of the bitmaps, as well as the number of poses provided. We have found 50 KBytes (compressed) to be sufficient for representing a character with ten to fifteen head and body drawings. New characters and backgrounds can be loaded dynamically.

Although we focused much of our efforts on recreating a particular comics style, the system architecture was designed to allow new styles to be plugged in. Comic Chat has an object-oriented structure, and includes classes for comics pages, panels, balloons, characters, character poses, and backgrounds. Elements of our artist's style are encapsulated in sub-classes of these. However, it is important to note that large amounts of effort went into defining these sub-classes, so reproducing additional artists' styles will be easier in the future, yet far from trivial.

8. EXAMPLES

This section shows three different types of chat interactions depicted by Comic Chat. The first, Figure 7, is an ordinary chat exchange between two of the authors. It contains six panels of comics, including a title panel. The title panel lists the most active participants (both of them in this case), and this information is also available interactively. All aspects of these panels, including character placement, gesture and expression choice, balloon construction and layout, panel breaks, and panel zoom, were chosen automatically by the system.

The second example, Figure 8, shows one person's interactions with a *bot*. Bots are simple computer programs, often masquerading as humans on chat channels. In some cases they perform useful functions, in others they exist to irritate other chat participants. One conversational bot is loosely modeled after the Eliza program, originally written by Joseph Weizenbaum at MIT to mimic a human psychoanalyst [2]. By joining an Eliza room, chat users can receive free (and valueless) psychoanalytical help. Figure 8 was generated by a volunteer from a Cub Scout troop, getting a demonstration of Comic Chat. The Cub Scout appears on the left, Eliza appears on the right. We halted the demonstration after the eighth panel.

People often use chat programs for role playing and interactive fiction. Figure 9 is an excerpt from such a gathering on the Internet. The participants were all using textual chat clients, and their dialogue was rendered using Comic Chat. Note that the third panel of Figure 9 also includes a *narration box*, an additional comics element supported by our program. Narration boxes help to describe what is taking place in a panel. Balloons can be placed to the right and below the narration box, according to the algorithm presented earlier. IRC clients typically support a special kind of message to indicate what a participant is doing. Comic Chat looks for such messages, and places them in narration boxes. Other kinds of information could be placed in narration boxes as well, such as who is entering and leaving. The character wearing a tie in this figure is in charge of the role playing game, and is providing narration through dialogue that is rendered in balloons. Much of this could be placed in narration boxes to produce a different effect.

9. CONCLUSIONS AND FUTURE WORK

The panels produced by the methods described in this paper are acceptably composed according to comic conventions. Jim Woodring is very pleased with the results in general, and occasionally points out panels that (he claims) he would be proud to have drawn. However, we feel that reproducing the creativity and variability of a human comic artist, particularly one of Woodring's abilities, is in all practicality an unachievable goal. Nevertheless, people seem to take delight in the output of Comic Chat, and we look forward to performing user studies to compare Comic Chat to other graphical chat systems

There are still numerous additional features that we would like to add to the system. Professional comic book artists (in contrast to most comic strip artists) tend to show a great deal of imagination in how they lay out panels on the page. Currently, Comic Chat places square panels regularly on an infinitely long page. To create more variability, we would like to alter the size and shapes of our panels, and lay them out more creatively. This could either be done algorithmically, or by selection from a pool of template pages.

Although we have distinct locations where characters can enter our comics world (including a room in a house, a pastoral scene, a balcony, a fantasy world, and a pond scene), we should have a mechanism to allow our characters to graphically transition from one scene to another. This could happen when a character decides to join a conversation elsewhere; however, the system itself, to add variety and unpredictability, might choose to move a conversation to a new location. We would also like to make the system capable of showing participants performing various activities, like having tea or swimming in a pond. This need not be under user control, and in fact putting it under user control might be a distraction to the primary chatting activity. Having the system control such activities would add variety and unpredictability, and give the participants even more to chat about.

One of the innovations of Comic Chat is that it provides a graphical transcript of an on-line conversation in which a person has participated. It could also provide a transcript of a conversation that a person *might* want to join. In current chat systems, after entering a chat room, prospective participants wait to see if the conversation interests them. This not only creates a distraction for the other participants, but it is potentially a waste of time if the conversation turns out not to be of interest. Instead we could provide a graphical transcript of conversations for prospective participants to review immediately. We can take this idea further, and intersperse *meanwhile panels* during gaps in a Comic Chat conversation. These panels

SIGGRAPH
DEADLINE
MUSINGS
STARRING

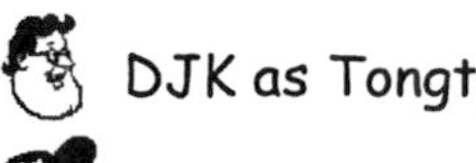

Figure 7. A page from a session with Comic Chat.

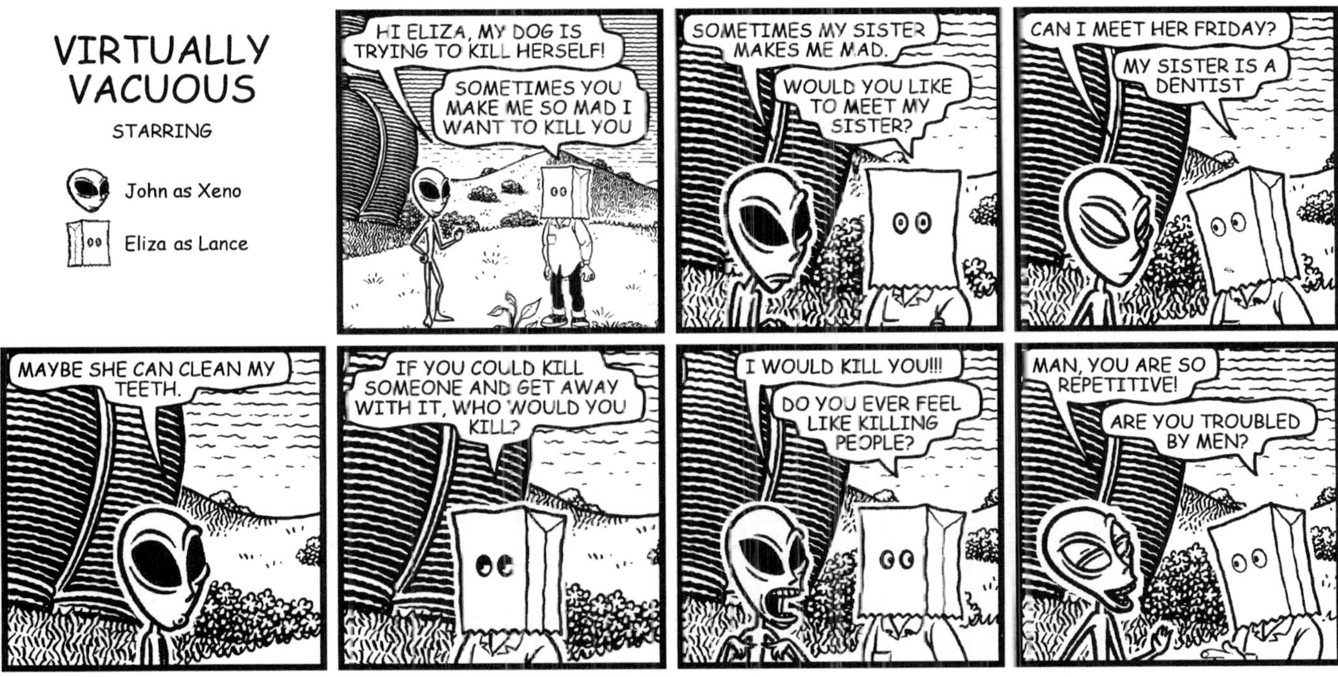

Figure 8. The first panels from a chat session with an Eliza bot.

THE GANG'S ALL HERE
STARRING
Rictor as Dan
MoonGirl as Margaret
Rabid_Dog as Mike
Chyrric as Tiki
FROM SEEMINGLY NOWHERE, A DOG APPEARS ON THE ROAD AHEAD OF YOU, WAGGING HIS TAIL AND CARRYING A STICK IN HIS MOUTH. HE APPROACHES YOU AND DROPS THE STICK AND BARKS.
I'LL PICK UP THE STICK.
RABID_DOG BITES MOONGIRL
OK, I THREW IT TO HIM.
NOT SURPRISINGLY, THE DOG FETCHES THE STICK.
RRRUUUUFFFFF. I LOVE THE STICK!!!
THE DOG PICKS THE STICK BACK UP AND DROPS IT AT MOONGIRL'S FEET, AND BARKS.
WOULD SOMEONE JUST FOLLOW THAT DOG?
I THREW THE STICK. I DON'T FEEL LIKE FOLLOWING SOME OL' DOG AROUND. I DON'T GET DIRTY UNLESS I HAVE TO.
MOONGIRL, BEFORE THROWING THE STICK, NOTICES AN INSCRIPTION THAT THE DOG'S MASTER MUST HAVE PUT ON IT.
WHAT DOES IT SAY?
IT SAYS, "HELP TRAPPED NW ROAD".
WE COULD HAVE PROBABLY FOLLOWED LASSIE THERE!

Figure 9. The beginning of a fantasy role playing quest. Participants are using text IRC clients, monitored by Comic Chat.

would show snippets of conversations occurring elsewhere in the Comic Chat world (and be labeled "MEANWHILE...", following another comics convention). Of course, there is a potential privacy issue here that needs consideration.

Using more powerful technology to identify the semantics of the conversation would certainly allow us to generate better comics. Natural language processing systems would allow us to improve our choice of default expressions and gestures for the characters, and would allow Comic Chat to provide additional types of (and better targeted) semantic feedback beyond that described in Section 6.3. Many comic artists emphasize certain words in their balloons by setting them in bold type, and natural language technology could help select which words to make bold.

Comics are used for a wide variety of purposes other than entertainment, and computer-generated comics can be applied to far more than chat rooms. For example, human-drawn comics have instructed people about history [7] and the repair of military equipment [1]. Computer-generated comics could be used for education as well, but they could also serve as a tool in the production of interactive, collaborative fiction, a visual presentation for MUDs and other virtual worlds, and a graphical history of interactions with social or agent-based interfaces. The examples presented in Figures 8 and 9 hint at these possibilities. Automatically-generated comics could be used in computer-based help and instruction. They could also provide a graphical transcript or serve as the primary visual representation for adventure games. The leader of a large computer-supported cooperative work project tells us that he believes computer-generated comics could help people separated in space and time to collaborate on joint projects.

Comics are a rich form of communication, with a visual vocabulary that most of us have already internalized. They can also be wonderfully entertaining. We have found comics to be ideally suited as a visual representation for on-line chat rooms, but the potential application of comics to other computer-based applications is equally promising. The possibilities are vast, and we look forward to investigating other ways of combining comics and computer graphics.

A free copy of Comic Chat can be downloaded from our Web site, http://www.research.microsoft.com/comicchat.htm.

ACKNOWLEDGMENTS

Foremost, we would like to thank Jim Woodring for sharing his knowledge of comics, and creating such wonderful art for this project. Rick Rashid has been a great advocate (and occasional hacker). Thanks to George Robertson, Maarten Van Dantzich, Ben Slivka, David Thiel, Dan Ling, Jim Kajiya, and Steve Drucker for helpful comments. Comic Chat is publicly available on the Internet, largely due to the efforts of Linda Stone, Ross M. Brown, Diana Murray, Eric George, Mark Mecham, Bob Tabscott, and Albert Tan. Interaction with members of Microsoft Research and Microsoft's Virtual Worlds Group contributed to both the design and deployment of Comic Chat.

REFERENCES

1. Anderson, M. Joe's Dope: If Ya Gotta Do It... Do It Right! *PS: The Preventive Maintenance Monthly.* Issue 279, February 1976. 29-36.
2. Barr, A. and Feigenbaum, E. A. *The Handbook of Artificial Intelligence.* volume 1. William Kaufmann, Inc., Los Altos, CA. 1981. 285-287.
3. Cassell, J., Pelachaud, C., Badler, N., Steedman, M., Achorn, B., Beckett, T., Douville, B., Prevost, S., and Stone, M. Automated Conversation: Rule-based Generation of Spoken Expression, Gesture, and Spoken Intonation for Multiple Conversational Agents. Proceedings of SIGGRAPH '94 (Orlando, FL, July 24-29, 1994). In Computer Graphics Proceedings, Annual Conf. Series, ACM, New York. 413-420.
4. CD-ROMIX! Inc., *FREEX #1.* P. O. Box 2961, Torrance, CA 90509. 1993.
5. Eisner, W. *Comics & Sequential Art.* Poorhouse Press. Tamarac, FL. 1985.
6. Feiner, S. APEX: An Experiment in the Automated Creation of Pictorial Explanations. *IEEE Computer Graphics and Applications, 5,* 11. November 1985. 29-37.
7. Gornick, L. *The Cartoon History of the Universe.* Doubleday. New York. 1990.
8. Haeberli, P. Paint by Numbers: Abstract Image Representations. Proceedings of SIGGRAPH '90 (Dallas, TX, Aug. 6-10). In *Computer Graphics*, 24, 4 (Aug. 1990), ACM, New York. 1990. 207-214.
9. Kurlander, D. and Feiner, S. A History of Editable Graphical Histories. In *Watch What I Do: Programming by Demonstration.* Allen Cypher, ed. MIT Press, Cambridge, MA. 1993. 405-413.
10. Lent, J. Oh, What a Time It Was: The Early Days of the Funnies. Witty World: International Cartoon Magazine. No. 19. Summer/Autumn 1995. 16-22.
11. Lent, J. "Yellow Kid" Celebrates Century with Hectic Schedule in 1995. Witty World: International Cartoon Magazine. No. 19. Summer/Autumn 1995. 18-19.
12. Mackinlay, J. Automating the Design of Graphical Presentations of Relational Information. *ACM Trans. on Graphics, 5*, 2. April 1986. 110-141.
13. McCloud, S. *Understanding Comics.* Kitchen Sink Press. Northampton, MA. 1993.
14. Microsoft Corp., Microsoft Introduces V-Chat Communications for MSN, The Microsoft Network. Nov. 30, 1995. Microsoft Press Release. Redmond, WA 98052.
15. Montgomery R. and Gilligan, S. Comic Creator. Spark Interactive, 112 W. San Francisco St., Sante Fe, NM 87501, 1995.
16. Morningstar, C. and Farmer, F. R. The Lessons of Lucasfilm's Habitat. In *Cyberspace: First Steps.* Benedikt, M., ed. MIT Press, Cambridge, MA. 1991. 273-301.
17. Oikarinen, J. and Reed, D. Internet Relay Chat Protocol. Internet RFC #1459. May 1993.
18. Salisbury, M. P., Anderson, S. E., Barzel, R., and Salesin, D.H. Interactive Pen and Ink Illustration. Proceedings of SIGGRAPH '94 (Orlando, FL, July 24-29). In Computer Graphics Proceedings, Annual Conf. Series, ACM, New York. 1994. 101-108.
19. Seligmann, D. D., and Feiner, S. Automated Generation of Intent-Based 3D Illustrations. Proceedings of SIGGRAPH '91 (Las Vegas, Nevada, July 28 - Aug. 2). In *Computer Graphics, 25,* 4 (July 1991) ACM, New York. 1991, 123-132.
20. Trupin, J. The Visual Programmer Puts ActiveX Documents Through Their Paces. *Microsoft Systems Journal, 11,* 6. June 1996. 55-76.
21. Winkenbach, G., and Salesin, D. Computer Generated Pen and Ink Illustration. Proceedings of SIGGRAPH '94 (Orlando, FL, July 24-29). In Computer Graphics Proceedings, Annual Conf. Series, ACM, New York. 1994, 91-100.
22. Worlds, Inc. Worlds Chat: Meet Your New Cyberfriends. http://www.worlds.net/products/wchat/readme.html.

Reproducing Color Images as Duotones

Joanna L. Power† *Brad S. West* *Eric J. Stollnitz* *David H. Salesin*

University of Washington

Abstract

We investigate a new approach for reproducing color images. Rather than mapping the colors in an image onto the gamut of colors that can be printed with cyan, magenta, yellow, and black inks, we choose the set of printing inks for the particular image being reproduced. In this paper, we look at the special case of selecting inks for duotone printing, a relatively inexpensive process in which just two inks are used. Specifically, the system we describe takes an image as input, and allows a user to select 0, 1, or 2 inks. It then chooses the remaining ink or inks so as to reproduce the image as accurately as possible and produces the appropriate color separations automatically.

CR Categories: I.3.4 [Computer Graphics]: Graphics Utilities

Additional Keywords: color reproduction, color printing, duotone, gamut mapping, Neugebauer model

1 Introduction

Modern color reproduction typically employs a fixed set of *process-color inks*: cyan, magenta, yellow, and sometimes black. Placed on top of one another and in juxtaposition, these inks can be used to reproduce a range of colors, called their *gamut*. Although the standard process colors were carefully chosen to provide a relatively large gamut, this gamut is nevertheless quite limited when compared to the full range of colors visible to the human eye. Thus, color fidelity must generally be compromised when reproducing images with process colors (or any other small, fixed set of inks).

A number of approaches have been suggested for mitigating this problem, including methods for smoothly mapping the original image colors to the process color gamut [21], and, in the case of three-dimensional computer-synthesized imagery, redefining the original object colors so that the rendered image will lie inside the process-color gamut [5]. However, to our knowledge, there has been no research to date on a very different but equally promising approach: allowing the inks used for printing to be selected for the particular image being reproduced.

In this paper, we investigate a first step toward this goal: selecting inks for *duotone* color reproduction, a less expensive printing process in which just two inks are used. In particular, the problem we address can be stated formally as follows:

†Department of Computer Science and Engineering, University of Washington, Box 352350, Seattle, WA 98195-2350

> ***Given:*** A color image C, a paper color, the set of all available printing inks $\mathcal{I}$, and a subset of $k = 0$, 1, or 2 inks in $\mathcal{I}$ chosen by the user.
>
> ***Find:*** The best $2 - k$ additional inks for reproducing C on the selected paper, along with the appropriate color separations.

While duotones obviously have more limited color gamuts than three- and four-ink processes, they can nevertheless be used to reproduce a surprising range of color—especially when the inks are chosen for the particular image being reproduced, as we show in this paper. Indeed, a duotone print is really a combination of four colors: the paper color alone, the colors of each of the inks individually, and the color of the two inks superimposed on each another. These four colors define a bilinear surface in color space that may span a broad range of the full color gamut.

Whereas duotone printing has traditionally been used almost exclusively to enhance monochrome gray-scale images with a tint of color, the kind of duotone color reproduction we explore in this paper has a variety of new applications. First, duotone printing is significantly less expensive than process color, typically about two-thirds the cost. Thus, there is a clear economic advantage in using duotones for images that are adequately reproduced in this way. Second, the general form of the problem expressed above allows a user to select one or both of the two printing inks. This formulation is useful when other requirements of the page design, such as matching the precise colors of a company logo, already constrain the choice of inks. Also, because a large number of printing presses are two-color presses, printed documents are often designed for just two inks, generally black (for text) and one additional color. In these cases, we show how duotone separations can still be computed to match the colors of an image as well as possible with the inks available. Finally, our formulation also allows duotone separations to be computed for a colored paper, which may be useful in a variety of situations. As one example, this form of the problem could be useful for creating duotone separations of full-color images for a "yellow pages" telephone directory.

1.1 Related work

To our knowledge, there has been no previous work that proposes a general approach to reproducing images using duotones. The most closely related work in the field of computer graphics addresses the problem of gamut mapping, or smoothly mapping the colors of an original image to those available on an output device. Fundamentally, a duotone gamut is much more restricted than the gamut of a typical output device. Our duotone mapping differs from the approaches taken by Stone *et al.* [21] and Gentile and Allebach [3] primarily in that we require a mapping from three dimensions to two. Harrington *et al.* [8] describe a technique for creating a "highlight color image," a specialized duotone in which one ink is black.

There are a few articles in the optical engineering literature on calculating halftone separations for inks other than the standard four-color process inks. Marcu and colleagues [11, 14] describe how to compute separations when printing with an arbitrary number of inks.

However, the inks and the order in which they will be printed must be specified by the user. Furthermore, Marcu *et al.* do not specify how to handle a color that is out of gamut (the common case for duotone mapping). Ostromoukhov [16] describes how the traditional process-color printing gamut can be extended by introducing additional basic colors.

In the printing industry, a number of empirical studies have developed improved models for halftone color reproduction [1, 7, 19]. Instead of complicating our duotone mapping with the correction factors described in these works, we adjust the output of the model according to our own empirically determined correction factor. Kang [12] takes a similar approach, though he assumes that each ink can be corrected independently, while we adjust the duotone gamut as a whole.

1.2 Overview of paper

The remainder of the paper is organized as follows: Section 2 provides relevant background information on color, color printing, and the Neugebauer model of halftone printing. Section 3 describes the duotone mapping in detail, and Section 4 discusses the ink-selection process. Section 5 describes some variations on duotone printing that are easily accommodated by our algorithm. Section 6 presents some actual duotones as well as some rough timing results. We conclude in Section 7 with a discussion of possible directions for future work.

2 Background

Before we dive into the details of our duotone mapping, we present some background material on color and color spaces, color halftone printing, and the Neugebauer halftone model.

2.1 Color and color spaces

Color is determined by the intensity of light in the range of visible wavelengths from about 400nm to 700nm. According to the tristimulus theory of color perception [9], all colors can be reproduced using combinations of three primary wavelengths (roughly corresponding to red, green, and blue). Thus, color can be expressed as a function of wavelength, known as a *spectral reflectance*, or as a three-dimensional quantity. More information about color can be found in standard graphics texts [2, 4].

The *XYZ* color space was developed in 1931 by the Commission Internationale de l'Éclairage (CIE) to standardize color specification. The *XYZ* color space is additive, meaning that the color resulting from the superposition of two colored light sources can be calculated by simply adding the coefficients of the two known colors. A spectral reflectance can be converted to *XYZ* coordinates by integrating the spectral information against three functions $\bar{x}$, $\bar{y}$ and $\bar{z}$ [2, pages 579–580]. The computer graphics community is more familiar with the *RGB* color space, an additive color space that is device-dependent. Conversion between *RGB* and *XYZ* coordinates can be accomplished by a linear transform if the *XYZ* coordinates of the device's red, green and blue primaries are known [2, pages 585–587].

In contrast to additive color spaces, perceptually uniform color spaces allow the difference between two colors (as perceived by the human eye) to be measured as the distance between points. For example, two colors c_1 and c_2 separated by some distance d in a perceptually uniform color space appear about as different as two other colors c_3 and c_4 separated by the same distance d. The CIE developed two perceptually uniform spaces: $L^*a^*b^*$ and $L^*u^*v^*$. Both color spaces require the definition of a *reference white*, which is usually taken to be a standard light source defined by the CIE. In both spaces, L^* indicates brightness and has a value of 100 for reference white. Though neither $L^*a^*b^*$ nor $L^*u^*v^*$ is perfectly perceptually uniform, both come close to satisfying the condition that colors separated by the same distance appear equally similar [4, pages 59–66].

2.2 Color halftone printing

In color halftone printing, a continuous-tone image is reproduced by printing a number of versions of the image atop one another. Each version, known as a *halftone separation*, consists of various sized dots of a single ink. Color halftone printing differs from color dithering on monitors in that subtractive effects as well as additive effects play a role. The subtractive effect of superimposing dots of different color produces the set of *printing primaries* for a particular set of inks. For example, for cyan, magenta, and yellow ink printed on white paper, the set of printing primaries is cyan, magenta, yellow, blue (cyan + magenta), green (cyan + yellow), red (magenta + yellow), black (cyan + magenta + yellow), and white (no ink). The additive effect of juxtaposing dots of different sizes produces the entire set, or *gamut*, of colors that can be achieved by printing halftone separations using a particular set of inks. Figure 1 illustrates the reproduction of a color image using cyan, magenta, yellow, and black inks. More information on color reproduction can be found in the classic texts by Hunt [10] and Yule [23].

2.3 Neugebauer halftone model

In 1937, Neugebauer developed a series of equations that, given ink and paper colors, describe the amount of each ink needed to reproduce a given color [15]. Intuitively, the model says that the overall color of a small area is a weighted average of the printing primaries, with each primary weighted by the relative area it covers. For example, in a square printed with cyan, magenta and yellow ink on white paper, the contribution of blue is given by the fraction of the square that is covered by cyan and magenta but not yellow. If α_1, α_2, and α_3 are the amounts of cyan, magenta and yellow ink printed, then the contribution of blue is $\alpha_1\alpha_2(1-\alpha_3)$.

The "Neugebauer equations" express colors in terms of their coordinates in the *XYZ* color space. The model was originally designed to describe three-color printing, though it can be generalized to handle any number of inks. Let $\boldsymbol{g}_0$ be the color of the paper, $\boldsymbol{g}_i$ the color of ink i on the paper, $\boldsymbol{g}_{i,j}$ the color of inks i and j superimposed on the paper, $\boldsymbol{g}_{i,j,k}$ the color of all three inks i, j and k superimposed on the paper, and α_i the amount of ink i (between 0 and 1). For three inks, the Neugebauer model describes $\boldsymbol{c}$, a color in the printing gamut, in terms of the eight printing primaries and the amounts of the three inks required to achieve $\boldsymbol{c}$:

$$\boldsymbol{c} = \begin{bmatrix} \boldsymbol{g}_0 & \boldsymbol{g}_1 & \boldsymbol{g}_2 & \boldsymbol{g}_3 & \boldsymbol{g}_{1,2} & \boldsymbol{g}_{1,3} & \boldsymbol{g}_{2,3} & \boldsymbol{g}_{1,2,3} \end{bmatrix} \begin{bmatrix} (1-\alpha_1)(1-\alpha_2)(1-\alpha_3) \\ \alpha_1(1-\alpha_2)(1-\alpha_3) \\ (1-\alpha_1)\alpha_2(1-\alpha_3) \\ (1-\alpha_1)(1-\alpha_2)\alpha_3 \\ \alpha_1\alpha_2(1-\alpha_3) \\ \alpha_1(1-\alpha_2)\alpha_3 \\ (1-\alpha_1)\alpha_2\alpha_3 \\ \alpha_1\alpha_2\alpha_3 \end{bmatrix}$$

3 Duotone mapping

We are now prepared to tackle the following problem: Given 0, 1, or 2 inks out of a set of available inks, choose the remaining 0, 1, or 2 inks and compute the separations that most accurately reproduce a given image. In this section we present the duotone mapping, our technique for computing the separations for an image once the two inks are known. In Section 4 we will describe the process of choosing inks.

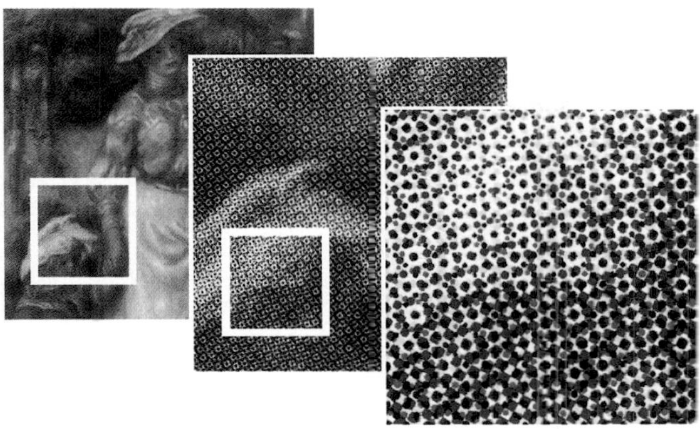

Figure 1 Color halftoning of an image.

3.1 Neugebauer model for duotone printing

For two-color printing, the Neugebauer model describes c, a color in the printing gamut, in terms of the four printing primaries and the amounts of the two inks:

$$c = \begin{bmatrix} g_0 & g_1 & g_2 & g_{1,2} \end{bmatrix} \begin{bmatrix} (1-\alpha_1)(1-\alpha_2) \\ \alpha_1(1-\alpha_2) \\ (1-\alpha_1)\alpha_2 \\ \alpha_1\alpha_2 \end{bmatrix}$$

The gamut described by the above equation is a bilinear surface in an additive color space such as *XYZ* or *RGB*, as shown in Figure 2.

Finding the duotone gamut

The duotone gamut is fully specified by the Neugebauer model given the printing primaries g_0, g_1, g_2 and $g_{1,2}$. We obtained spectral reflectance data for inks and papers using a Colortron™ spectrophotometer. The Colortron™ software also provides data for PANTONE® ink sets. In order to find the printing primaries, we must estimate the color of inks printed on the selected paper. We must also estimate the color of two inks superimposed on the selected paper.

We used a simple model to approximate the effect of printing ink on paper. The data for a layer of ink or paper can be expressed in two parts: an overall reflectance spectrum R and a Fresnel reflectance spectrum F. The overall reflectance spectrum indicates how much light of each wavelength is reflected back by the layer and can be directly measured with a spectrophotometer. The Fresnel information indicates how much light of each wavelength bounces off the surface without entering the layer.

Inks act very much like filters, which are purely subtractive layers A paper acts like an opaque layer. This simple behavior allows us to approximate layer composition by multiplying reflectance spectra and adjusting for Fresnel effects [6]. To approximate the result of superimposing a subtractive layer i on another layer j, we remove the Fresnel component from each layer's overall reflectance, multiply the altered spectra, and add back the Fresnel reflectance of the top layer:

$$\begin{aligned} R_{i,j} &= (R_i - F_i)(R_j - F_j) + F_i \\ F_{i,j} &= F_i \end{aligned}$$

Since we cannot directly measure the Fresnel component of reflectance, we approximate the Fresnel spectrum of an ink by the reflectance spectrum of black ink. The intuition behind this approximation is that black absorbs nearly all incident light; thus, any reflectance from a layer of black ink is primarily due to a Fresnel effect at the surface. For simplicity, we use the same Fresnel spectrum for paper, and we ignore any Fresnel effect between ink and paper.

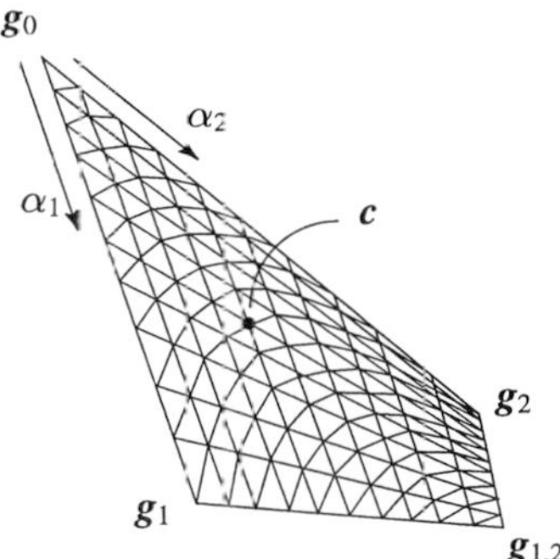

Figure 2 Bilinear surface described by the Neugebauer halftone model.

The layering model described above does not completely solve our problem, as the measured spectral reflectance data for an ink includes information about the stock paper on which the ink was originally printed. To compute the result of removing one layer from another, we simply invert the above equations:

$$\begin{aligned} F_i &= F_{i,j} \\ R_i &= \frac{(R_{i,j} - F_{i,j})}{(R_j - F_j)} + F_i \end{aligned}$$

Division by zero does not arise in practice, as we only remove inks from papers, and the papers have high overall reflectance spectra and low Fresnel components. Once we have the spectral reflectance information for the paper, the individual inks on paper, and the combination of both inks on paper, we can find the printing primaries g_0, g_1, g_2, and $g_{1,2}$ by first converting the appropriate spectral quantities to *XYZ* or *RGB* coordinates [2, pages 579–587].

3.2 Goals of duotone mapping

The core of our algorithm is the mapping that transforms image colors onto the duotone gamut. There are many characteristics of colors and of sets of colors that one could seek to preserve in designing a mapping. The fundamental tradeoff is between mapping colors exactly and maintaining overall relationships between colors. Our approach places more importance on overall relationships than on exact matches, and weighs certain relationships more heavily than others.

The basic idea behind our mapping technique is to define an orthogonal axis system for each duotone gamut, then transform the image colors along two directions and use parallel projection along the third. The choice of directions is clearly critical to the effectiveness of the mapping and corresponds to preserving certain relationships between image colors at the expense of other relationships. Here are the choices we made:

1. ***Preserve relative luminance.*** The eye is more sensitive to light at some wavelengths than others. The *luminance-efficiency curve*, which describes the relationship between wavelength and visual sensitivity, corresponds to a direction in a three-dimensional color space. Preserving separation of image colors along this direction of greatest sensitivity, called the *luminance direction*, is the primary goal of our duotone mapping. The Y axis of the *XYZ* color space corresponds exactly to the luminance direction [2], and therefore we take Y to be the direction of our first transformation. (Stone *et al.* also used preservation of relative luminance in their gamut mapping work [21].)
2. ***Preserve ink-spread separation.*** The second relationship our

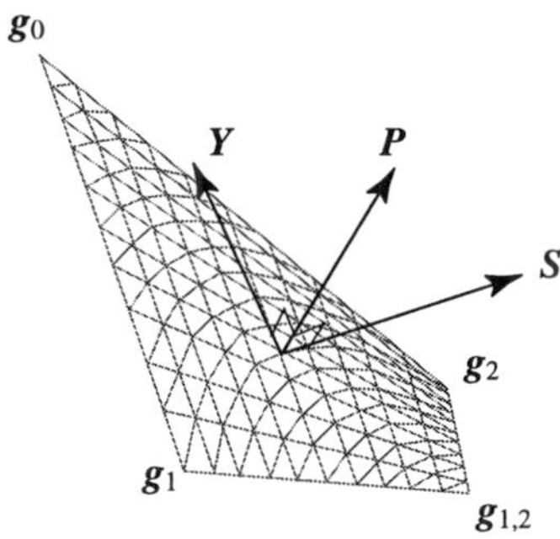

Figure 3 Axes associated with a typical duotone gamut.

mapping preserves is separation in the direction of most color variation on the duotone gamut. The curve on the gamut between the two individual ink primaries describes the widest variation in color achievable with the selected paper and inks. Thus, the vector $\boldsymbol{g}_2 - \boldsymbol{g}_1$ is the ideal direction for the second transformation. However, our duotone mapping requires an orthogonal axis system, and we have already chosen the $\boldsymbol{Y}$ axis. Therefore we orthogonalize $\boldsymbol{g}_2 - \boldsymbol{g}_1$ with respect to $\boldsymbol{Y}$ and use the resulting *ink-spread direction* $\boldsymbol{S}$ as the direction of the second transformation.

3. ***Sacrifice normal separation.*** Separation must be sacrificed in some direction in order to map points from three-dimensional space onto a surface. As we have chosen two axes and require mutual orthogonality, the *projection direction* $\boldsymbol{P}$ is already defined by $\boldsymbol{Y} \times \boldsymbol{S}$. The $\boldsymbol{P}$ axis approximates the average normal of the bilinear surface, which is the direction of least color variation on the gamut. It is therefore a good direction in which to sacrifice separation.

Given a duotone gamut, the constraints listed above completely define the orthogonal axis system we will use for our duotone mapping. A typical example is illustrated in Figure 3.

3.3 Computing the duotone mapping

The duotone mapping takes image colors $\boldsymbol{c}_1, \ldots, \boldsymbol{c}_n$ and maps them to colors $\hat{\boldsymbol{c}}_1, \ldots, \hat{\boldsymbol{c}}_n$ on the duotone gamut. The mapping of image color $\boldsymbol{c}_i$ takes place in three steps, with each step affecting a different orthogonal component of $\boldsymbol{c}_i$. We will denote the components as follows:

$$\begin{aligned} c_i^Y &\equiv \boldsymbol{c}_i \cdot \boldsymbol{Y} \\ c_i^S &\equiv \boldsymbol{c}_i \cdot \boldsymbol{S} \\ c_i^P &\equiv \boldsymbol{c}_i \cdot \boldsymbol{P} \end{aligned}$$

We will use the same superscript notation to indicate the orthogonal components of the printing primaries $\boldsymbol{g}_0, \boldsymbol{g}_1, \boldsymbol{g}_2$ and $\boldsymbol{g}_{1,2}$.

3.3.1 Calculating the luminance transformation

The first transformation applied to the image colors is a mapping along $\boldsymbol{Y}$ to bring all colors within the luminance range of the current duotone gamut. Although this mapping could be any monotonically increasing function, for the sake of simplicity we use a linear function. If we let c_i^Y be the y-value of the original image color $\boldsymbol{c}_i$, and $\hat{c}_i^Y$ the y-value of the transformed color, the luminance transformation can be written as follows:

$$\begin{aligned} y_{\min} &= \min_i\{c_i^Y\} \\ y_{\max} &= \max_i\{c_i^Y\} \\ \hat{y}_{\min} &= \max\{y_{\min},\ \min\{g_0^Y, g_1^Y, g_2^Y, g_{1,2}^Y\}\} \\ \hat{y}_{\max} &= \min\{y_{\max},\ \max\{g_0^Y, g_1^Y, g_2^Y, g_{1,2}^Y\}\} \\ \hat{c}_i^Y &= \hat{y}_{\min} + \left(\frac{c_i^Y - y_{\min}}{y_{\max} - y_{\min}}\right)(\hat{y}_{\max} - \hat{y}_{\min}) \end{aligned}$$

Figure 4 shows a set of image colors before and after their luminance values have been transformed to lie within the range of luminance values available in a typical duotone gamut.

3.3.2 Calculating the ink-spread transformation

The second transformation is along the ink-spread axis $\boldsymbol{S}$. This transformation depends upon luminance, since at some luminance values the duotone gamut is wide and at others it consists of a single point. Consider a particular luminance value $\hat{y}$ between $\hat{y}_{\min}$ and $\hat{y}_{\max}$. We define $\hat{s}_0$ and $\hat{s}_1$ to be the s-values of the points found by intersecting the edges of the duotone gamut with a plane of constant luminance $\hat{y}$. The ink-spread transformation at luminance value $\hat{y}$ brings the s-values of all image colors with luminance value $\hat{y}$ into the range $[\hat{s}_0, \hat{s}_1]$. Figure 5 illustrates the effect of an ink-spread transformation on a set of image colors.

In our current implementation, the non-uniformity along $\boldsymbol{Y}$ is handled by separating colors into bins according to y-value and calculating a different transformation for each bin. The coherence among colors in most natural images prevents this discrete approach from introducing noticeable discontinuities into a duotone.

The ink-spread transformation, like the luminance transformation, can be any monotonically increasing function that maps the s-values of image colors to the s-values available on the gamut. In what follows, we present both a simple linear mapping and a more complex mapping based on Bézier curves.

Linear mapping

The simplest transformation of s-values is a linear mapping, which we can define in a manner similar to the luminance transformation. If we consider only colors within a particular luminance bin, the lin-

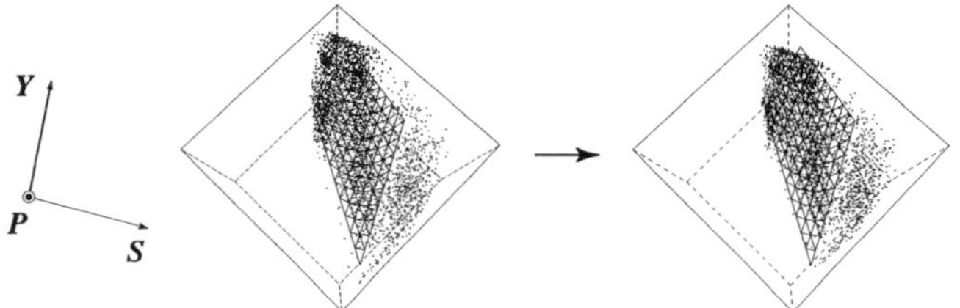

Figure 4 Image colors before and after a uniform transformation in the luminance direction $\boldsymbol{Y}$.

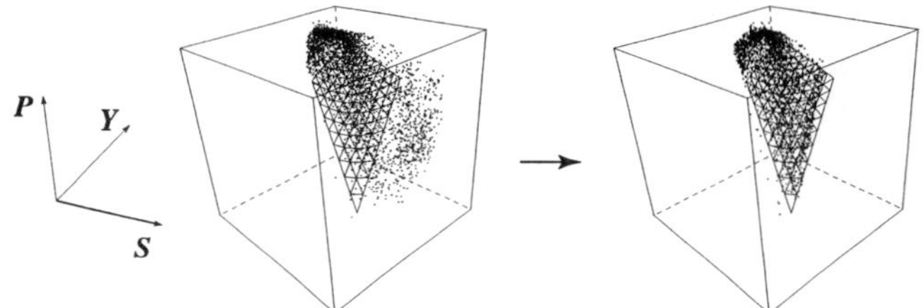

Figure 5 Image colors before and after a non-uniform transformation in the ink-spread direction $\boldsymbol{S}$.

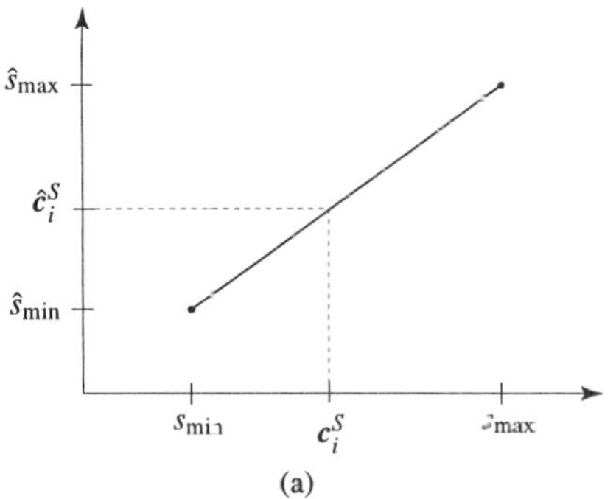

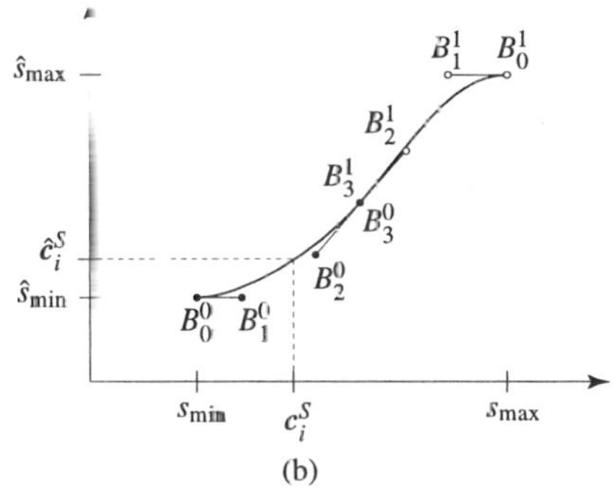

Figure 6 Two possible ink-spread transformations: (a) a linear mapping; (b) a Bézier curve mapping.

ear mapping is given by:

$$
\begin{aligned}
s_{min} &= \min_i\{c_i^S\} \\
s_{max} &= \max_i\{c_i^S\} \\
\hat{s}_{min} &= \max\{s_{min},\ \min\{\hat{s}_0,\ \hat{s}_1\}\} \\
\hat{s}_{max} &= \min\{s_{max},\ \max\{\hat{s}_0,\ \hat{s}_1\}\} \\
\hat{c}_i^S &= \hat{s}_{min} + \left(\frac{c_i^S - s_{min}}{s_{max} - s_{min}}\right)(\hat{s}_{max} - \hat{s}_{min})
\end{aligned}
$$

An example of a linear ink-spread transformation for a single luminance bin is illustrated in Figure 6(a).

Bézier-curve mapping

The linear mapping given above does not attempt to preserve the s-values of image colors, despite the fact that many such values may be available in the duotone gamut. Instead, the linear mapping preserves the relationships between s-values of the image colors. At the other extreme, we could map each s-value to the closest value in the interval of available values $[\hat{s}_0, \hat{s}_1]$, thereby accurately reproducing some colors while clamping others to the interval endpoints.

We are interested in obtaining some of the benefits of both these alternatives. As a compromise, we construct a mapping based on Bézier curves, as illustrated in Figure 6(b) for a typical luminance bin.

In the interest of brevity, we will only describe the Bézier-curve mapping qualitatively here. As with the linear mapping, the two endpoints of the curve are constrained to map s_{min} to $\hat{s}_{min}$ and s_{max} to $\hat{s}_{max}$. However, because we are using two cubic Bézier curves that meet with C^1 continuity, we have five additional control points with which we can alter the behavior of the mapping. These additional degrees of freedom are utilized to meet the constraints that follow.

First, the slope of the Bézier-curve mapping at either end (controlled by B_1^0 and B_1^1) is constrained to be zero, while the tangent at the middle of the curve (controlled by the segment $B_2^1 - B_2^0$) is constrained to be parallel to the line from B_1^0 to B_1^1. Together, these constraints impose a nonlinearity on the mapping that tends to preserve separation of s-values for colors that are in gamut while squeezing together the colors that are out of gamut. This approach strikes a balance between a linear mapping and an approach that clamps values.

Second, the center of the curve is constrained to pass through the point $B_3^0 = B_3^1$, which is chosen to lie on the line $\hat{s} = s$ so as to guarantee that s-values near the center of the mapping are preserved. We determine the precise location of this center constraint by intersecting the line from g_0 to $g_{1,2}$ with a plane of constant luminance $\hat{y}$. As a result, the constraint at the center of the Bézier curves prevents colors that are closer in hue to one ink from mapping to a color on the opposite side of the gamut.

Our implementation of the Bézier-curve mapping relies on a lookup table in order to efficiently transform a value c_i^S to a new value $\hat{c}_i^S$. The table corresponding to each luminance bin is calculated before any colors are transformed. We evaluate a curve at a large number of parameter values, and store the resulting $(s, \hat{s})$ coordinates in a table. Then, to map a value c_i^S we need only find the correct interval of s-values and use linear interpolation to approximate the result $\hat{c}_i^S$.

3.4 Calculating the projection

Image colors transformed by the luminance and ink-spread mappings above are guaranteed to project onto the gamut in the $\boldsymbol{P}$ direction. The projection point corresponding to a color can be calculated analytically by solving for the intersection of a line and the bilinear surface defined by the Neugebauer equation. In the appendix, we derive a solution for α_1 and α_2, the amounts of the two inks required to produce the projected color. Thus, in addition to computing the desired color, the projection step calculates the halftone separations required for the duotone printing process. Figure 7 illustrates the result of projecting a set of image colors onto a duotone gamut.

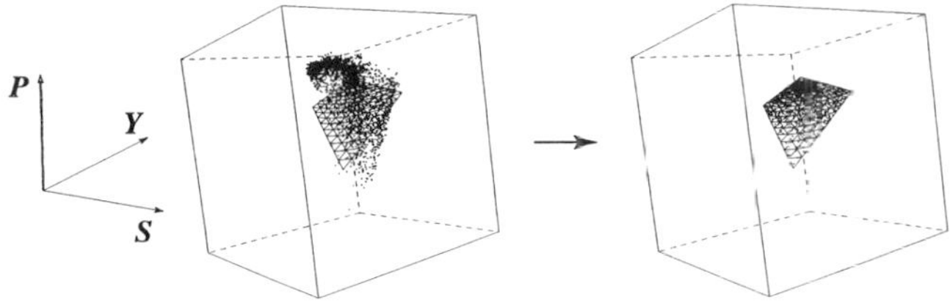

Figure 7 Image colors before and after being projected onto the duotone gamut in the direction $\boldsymbol{P}$.

4 Selecting inks

The duotone mapping described in the previous section assumed that two inks were given. Now we consider more general cases in which neither ink or just one ink is specified by the user. Our goal is to find a few good pairs of inks for a given image, in addition to finding the halftone separations. We define a *good* pair of inks as one for which the duotone mapping algorithm produces an image that is as close as possible to the original full-color image. We define the closeness of two images as the pixel-wise L^2 distance measured in a perceptually uniform color space. Thus, the selection of one or two inks amounts to an optimization problem whose goal (or objective) function is a function of the original image and two inks.

Simulated annealing is a heuristic optimization technique designed to avoid local minima [18]. Transitions from the current state to another state are generated randomly and accepted with some probability. This "acceptance probability" depends both on the relative scores of the two states, as rated by the objective function, and on the value of a control parameter T. Unfavorable moves are likely when T is high but are accepted with decreasing probability as T decreases. The "cooling schedule" describes the rate at which T decreases and the number of moves made at each value of T. In our problem, a state consists of a pair of inks, each of which has a set of neighbor inks. Taken together, the neighbor sets describe a fully connected, symmetric graph. The set of legal moves from a state is the set of all possible combinations of neighbor moves for each ink.

Simulated annealing is an ideal optimization technique for our particular problem. We require a heuristic technique because most interesting ink sets, such as the PANTONE® inks, contain hundreds of inks. In addition, our preliminary experiments indicated that our objective function has many local minima. Finally, the large number of parameters associated with simulated annealing allow us to tune the optimizer to our needs. In particular, by adjusting the cooling schedule and starting conditions, we can cause the optimizer to find several relatively deep local minima instead of a single global minimum. This adjustment is useful because it allows us to present several alternative choices of ink pairs to the user.

Evaluating the objective function tends to be costly because it requires that we transform every pixel color in the original image and compare the resulting color to its original value. In order to solve the optimization problem efficiently, the annealer uses a low-resolution version of the color information present in the original image. Such low-resolution information can be obtained either by quantizing the colors in the original image or by reducing the size of the original image. The low-resolution information is provided to the duotone mapping step instead of the original image colors.

5 Variations

There are several variations on the basic algorithm that lead to improvements in the duotones of certain images.

5.1 Outlying clusters

In our implementation, clustering of image colors is performed as a preprocessing step. Clusters of small size and large average distance from other clusters are marked as outlying clusters. Colors that have been identified as members of outlying clusters are ignored when calculating the ink-spread transformation. The rationale is that such colors matter less to the overall image, and that mapping them well at the expense of more prevalent colors is not justified.

Colors that are ignored in calculating the ink-spread transformation may not project onto the gamut. We transform each such color to a gray of the appropriate luminance, and then project that gray onto the gamut.

5.2 Black enhancement

Full-color printing relies on three colored inks—cyan, magenta, and yellow—that combine to make black. However, a black halftone separation is usually printed in addition to the three color separations. Adding a black separation permits denser blacks than three colors can produce, allows more detail to be expressed in shadowed areas, substitutes inexpensive black ink for more expensive colored inks, and avoids a thick accumulation of ink [23, page 282].

Adding a black separation to duotone printing offers a further benefit: for images with a wide range of luminance values, the two colored inks no longer need to be chosen so that their combination is close to black. Instead, the first two inks can be chosen to reproduce the image's hues, while the black ink permits fine gradations in luminance.

Extending the duotone process to support a black separation is simpler than the general problem of using three arbitrary inks (called a *tritone* process), thanks to the nearly accurate assumption that composing black ink with any other ink results in black. This assumption simplifies the problem in two ways. First, whereas a general tritone gamut is a trilinear volume according to the Neugebauer equations, a black-enhanced duotone is a volume bounded by four triangles, $(g_0, g_1, black)$, $(g_0, g_2, black)$, $(g_1, g_{1,2}, black)$, $(g_2, g_{1,2}, black)$, and one bilinear surface, as illustrated in Figure 8. Second, black enhancement can be implemented as a simple extension to the duotone algorithm using the following steps:

1. Subtract some amount of black from each color in the original image.
2. Apply the optimization and duotone mapping algorithm to produce two color separations.
3. Calculate a black separation that adds back the appropriate amount of black to each color.

These three steps are illustrated in Figure 9.

Removing black from an image in order to create a better duotone is similar to the four-color process of *under-color removal* (UCR), though slightly more complicated. Applying UCR to a color is fairly simple: a fraction of the minimum component of cyan, magenta, and yellow is removed from all three components, and then replaced by an equal amount of black [13]. The success of this technique hinges on the fact that cyan, magenta, and yellow combine to black, a property that is not necessarily true for the two inks used in a duotone.

For duotones, removal of black from an *RGB* color $\boldsymbol{c}$ is performed by moving $\boldsymbol{c}$ in a straight line away from the *RGB* position of black ink to a new position $\boldsymbol{c}'$, as shown in Figure 10(a). The amount of shift depends on the color's saturation: a fully saturated color does not benefit from using any black, while a fully desaturated (gray) color benefits most from using pure black ink. Performing this operation on every color in the original image yields a new target image for the duotone mapping.

Once we have applied the duotone mapping algorithm to obtain new colors, we can compute how much black to use by comparing the duotone colors to the original colors. Because we are primarily concerned with preserving the luminance of image colors, our goal is to match the luminance of the corresponding color in the original image. We cannot reproduce the complete range of original luminance values, though; instead we attempt to match a luminance scaled to lie between that of the paper and that of the black ink. For each color $\hat{\boldsymbol{c}}$ in our duotone, we create a line segment from that color to the position of black ink. We then shift $\hat{\boldsymbol{c}}$ toward black until it achieves the desired luminance at some position $\hat{\boldsymbol{c}}'$, as illustrated in

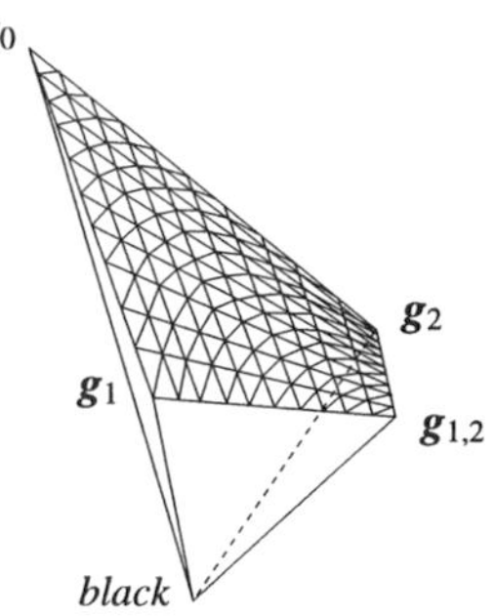

Figure 8 The gamut of two inks and black.

Figure 9 Steps of black enhancement (counterclockwise from top left): original, original with black removed, duotone without black, and duotone with black replaced.

Figure 10(b). The amount of shifting along the line through black determines the amount of black to print.

5.3 Minimized hue difference

For some very colorful images, even the best duotone will not be able to adequately reproduce all colors. Mapping an unachievable original color to gray may produce a more pleasing duotone than mapping it to another color. To achieve this effect we introduced the idea of an optional second pass over the duotone, performed after the desired pair of inks is selected. During the second pass, we perform a pixel-by-pixel comparison of the duotone and the original image, calculating the perceptual hue difference of each pixel. Hues are measured as *hue angles* in a perceptually uniform color space. In both $L^*a^*b^*$ and $L^*u^*v^*$, a plane perpendicular to the L^* axis and passing through a particular brightness value contains a disk of all the hues present at that brightness, ranging from gray at the center to saturated colors on the edge. Thus the hue angle of a color is defined as $h_{uv} = \tan^{-1}(v^*/u^*)$ or $h_{ab} = \tan^{-1}(b^*/a^*)$ [4, page 65]. The perceptual hue difference between two colors is the difference between the hue angles of the colors.

Our algorithm for reducing hue differences proceeds by desaturating (moving toward gray) each pixel in the original image by an amount parameterized by the magnitude of the hue difference computed for that pixel. The duotone mapping is then applied to the grayed-out image. In addition to reducing offensive hue mappings, graying-out parts of the original may improve the ink-spread transformation by bringing s_{min} and s_{max} closer to $\hat{s}_{min}$ and $\hat{s}_{max}$. Effectively, minimizing hue difference treats some potentially significant image colors like outliers, sacrificing them so that other colors will be mapped better.

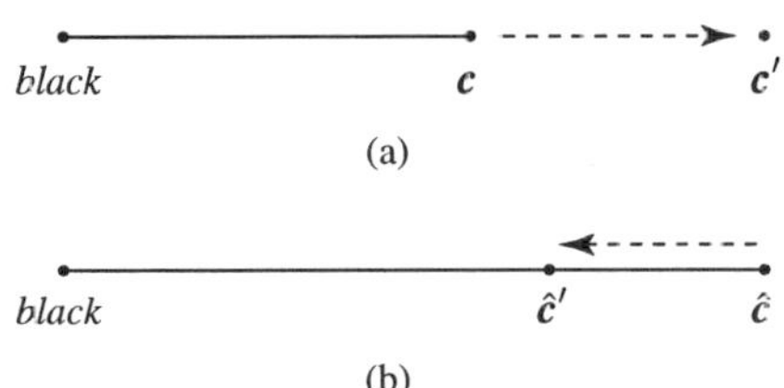

Figure 10 Transformations of black enhancement: (a) reducing black of a color in the original image by moving away from black; (b) replacing black in the duotone by moving toward black.

5.4 Colored paper

The paper used in a duotone need not be white. For an input image without much white, using a colored paper can greatly improve a duotone reproduction by providing an additional color essentially for free. Our implementation allows the user to specify a paper color or leave the choice of paper up to the optimizer. We modified the simulated annealing algorithm to select a paper color by extending the definition of a state to include two inks and a paper.

It is important to note that the colors in a duotone surrounded by an expanse of colored paper (as might occur in a yellow pages directory) appear quite different from the colors in the same duotone printed to cover all of the paper (as in a postcard). The difference is caused by adaptation effects in the visual system, which allow a subtle color to be perceived as white when nothing perceptually closer to white is present [22]. We are currently investigating quantitative models of adaptation that might improve a duotone surrounded by an expanse of colored paper.

6 Results

We have implemented an application that allows a user to create duotone separations. In this section we discuss some details of our implementation, as well as the results we obtained by printing duotones on a two-color press.

6.1 Performance

Our naïve implementation of the optimization loop takes approximately five minutes on a 133 MHz SGI Indy to find three good ink pairs, using the clustered version of an image and an ink set of more than 400 inks. While the optimization process is not interactive, it only needs to be run once for a given image. For a 300×300 image, producing full-size color separations and a preview duotone takes approximately four seconds on the same machine.

6.2 Printing

Testing our method requires that we print duotones on an actual printing press and compare the results to reference prints. While ordinarily a reproduction should look as much as possible like a photograph or an image displayed on a monitor, for the purposes of this paper we chose to compare duotone prints to four-color process prints. As a consequence, when we provide an input image to our duotone mapping algorithm, its colors should be those that are printed by a four-color press.

All of our original images are stored as *RGB* colors; in order to transform those colors to match the colors obtained from a four-color printing process, we use an *RGB correction* function. We generated data for the *RGB* correction by printing (on a four-color press) a square for each color in a regular three-dimensional grid of colors spanning the *RGB* cube. We scanned each printed square using a spectrophotometer and then converted the spectral data to an *RGB* color. For this set of colors, we constructed a mapping from intended *RGB* values to actual printed *RGB* values. Using piecewise-trilinear interpolation between these discrete colors, we can transform any given *RGB* color to the corresponding *RGB* color that process printing would produce.

There is a second aspect of our color printing experiments that also requires color correction. The Neugebauer model is not entirely accurate in its prediction of colors obtained by halftoning two inks. Therefore, in keeping with the empirical spirit of printing, we developed an empirical correction method for adjusting duotone separations. This *duotone correction* is similar to the *RGB* correction, but we need to measure data for only two dimensions. Using the two selected inks, we print a regular grid of values for α_1 and α_2. Once again, we measure the *RGB* color of each square in the grid. Locating each measured *RGB* color on the duotone gamut associates intended percentages with printed percentages of inks. Using bilinear interpolation, we construct a mapping from intended amounts to actual printed amounts. Applying the inverse of this function to a pair of separations before printing compensates for the simplicity of the Neugebauer model.

It should be noted that while the *RGB* transformation is valid for all images, the duotone correction is only accurate for the particular pair of inks that were measured. Since one of our goals is to make printing duotones inexpensive and easy, we do not want to require two trips to the printer. We therefore calculated an average correction function based on the duotone correction functions for three different pairs of inks. This average correction was used for most of the results described below.

6.3 Examples

Example 1 depicts a painting by Cézanne printed with process inks and as three duotones. The first two duotones, both printed with black and gold, demonstrate the difference between the traditional approach to printing duotones and our approach. (The traditional duotone was created using Adobe Photoshop™.) The last image in the series, printed with black and two inks selected by optimization, demonstrates black enhancement.

Some very different images reproduce well using a single pair of inks. Conversely, certain images reproduce well using several remarkably different pairs of inks. Example 3 shows a photograph of a koala printed in process color and as a duotone. Example 4 depicts a painting by Renoir in process color and as two duotones. The first duotone of the Renoir painting uses the same pair of user-selected inks as the duotone of the koala photograph. Choosing an unrelated pair of inks for the second duotone of the Renoir painting results in a very different, but still successful reproduction.

Though skin tones are notoriously difficult to reproduce, photographs of people are not beyond the scope of two-color reproduction. Examples 4, 5, and 6 show three portrait photographs printed in process color and as duotones. All three duotones are printed with blue and orange-brown, inks that were selected by the optimizer for the photograph in Example 4.

Example 7 shows a photograph of a sunset in process color and as a black-enhanced duotone printed with hand-picked inks. Viewed on a monitor, the original image contains colors not present in the process gamut. These colors are better achieved in a duotone that has not undergone the correction described in the previous section. Using the same inks, we printed an uncorrected black-enhanced duotone as the final image in the series.

Example 8 shows a painting by Schiele printed in process color and as a duotone on yellow paper with optimizer-selected inks. Using colored paper allows us to reproduce the three dominant hues (yellow, red, and green) present in the original image.

7 Discussion and future work

We have presented an algorithm for reproducing color images with duotones. Our hope is that our approach will be of interest to the desktop publishing community as a high-quality, economical alternative to full-color printing. While the limited number of examples we have sent to a printing press may not be perfect reproductions of the original images, they are certainly vast improvements over traditional duotones.

The core of our method is the duotone mapping: the transformation of a set of scattered image colors onto a surface in three-dimensional color space. Our mapping preserves relationships between image colors at the expense of matching exact colors. One can imagine many other mappings; below are some of the difficulties we found with two alternate approaches:

- ***Finding the closest color.*** The obvious problem with the approach of mapping an image color to the closest point on the duotone gamut is that out-of-gamut image colors will be clamped. While clamping may be acceptable for certain images and duotone gamuts, in general clamping results in artificial discontinuities and a loss of information.
- ***Using orthogonal projection.*** Using orthogonal rather than parallel projection would complicate the ink-spread transformation, making it a function of three variables rather than two: $\hat{s} = f(y, s, p)$. A more fundamental difficulty with orthogonal projection is the absence of an obvious continuous mapping, since there are colors for which there is no orthogonal projection onto the gamut.

Our research suggests several intriguing directions for future work. Some of the methods presented in this paper might apply to the more general problem of finding the best n inks with which to reproduce an image. Our extension of the optimization algorithm to choose a paper as well as inks suggests that we should adjust our algorithm to take advantage of psychophysical effects such as von Kries adaptation [22] and simultaneous contrast. These effects may allow us to effectively expand the printing gamut by tricking the eye into seeing colors that are not actually achievable.

Another possible extension to our implementation is a system that facilitates the production of two-color brochures by optimizing over images, inks, and papers. The system would take several images as input and choose two inks, one paper, and a specified number of the images that would reproduce well with the selected inks and paper.

Our algorithm has no sense of what parts of images are semantically or aesthetically important. Because the creation of a duotone from an image frequently requires loss of color information, our algorithm would benefit from user input indicating which colors in the original image are most important to preserve. Finally, we are considering combining our duotone mapping algorithm with the artistic screening approach to halftoning presented by Ostromoukhov and Hersch [17].

Acknowledgments

We wish to thank the University of Washington Publications Services for assisting us with our printing experiments. This work was supported by an Alfred P. Sloan Research Fellowship (BR-3495), an NSF Presidential Faculty Fellow award (CCR-9553199), an ONR Young Investigator award (N00014-95-1-0728), a NASA Space Grant, an NSF Graduate Research Fellowship, and industrial gifts from Interval, Microsoft, and Xerox.

Appendix: Parallel projection onto a bilinear surface

Suppose we have a color $\boldsymbol{c}$ that we want to project in the direction $\boldsymbol{P}$ onto a duotone gamut defined by the colors $\boldsymbol{g}_0, \boldsymbol{g}_1, \boldsymbol{g}_2$, and $\boldsymbol{g}_{1,2}$. The solution, which we will denote by $\hat{\boldsymbol{c}}$, must lie on the line that passes through $\boldsymbol{c}$ in the direction $\boldsymbol{P}$, so we know $\hat{\boldsymbol{c}} = \boldsymbol{c} + t\boldsymbol{P}$ for some real number t. The solution must also lie on the bilinear surface defining the duotone gamut:

$$\hat{\boldsymbol{c}} = \boldsymbol{c} + t\boldsymbol{P} = \begin{bmatrix} \boldsymbol{g}_0 & \boldsymbol{g}_1 & \boldsymbol{g}_2 & \boldsymbol{g}_{1,2} \end{bmatrix} \begin{bmatrix} (1-\alpha_1)(1-\alpha_2) \\ \alpha_1(1-\alpha_2) \\ (1-\alpha_1)\alpha_2 \\ \alpha_1\alpha_2 \end{bmatrix} \tag{1}$$

for some values of α_1 and α_2. In what follows, we will solve for the unknown ink amounts α_1 and α_2, rather than the projection point $\hat{\boldsymbol{c}}$.

First, let's rewrite equation (1) by grouping the terms differently:

$$\boldsymbol{g}_0 - \boldsymbol{c} - t\boldsymbol{P} + (\boldsymbol{g}_1 - \boldsymbol{g}_0)\alpha_1 + (\boldsymbol{g}_2 - \boldsymbol{g}_0)\alpha_2 + (\boldsymbol{g}_0 + \boldsymbol{g}_{1,2} - \boldsymbol{g}_1 - \boldsymbol{g}_2)\alpha_1\alpha_2 = 0$$

Notice that if we take the dot product of both sides of this equation with either the $\boldsymbol{S}$ direction or the $\boldsymbol{Y}$ direction, we eliminate t because $\boldsymbol{P}$, $\boldsymbol{S}$, and $\boldsymbol{Y}$ are defined to be mutually orthogonal. We can write the two equations that result from these dot products as follows:

$$u_1 + u_2\alpha_1 + u_3\alpha_2 + u_4\alpha_1\alpha_2 = 0 \tag{2}$$

$$v_1 + v_2\alpha_1 + v_3\alpha_2 + v_4\alpha_1\alpha_2 = 0 \tag{3}$$

where the constants $u_1, \ldots, u_4$ and $v_1, \ldots, v_4$ are given by

$$\begin{aligned} u_1 &= (\boldsymbol{g}_0 - \boldsymbol{c}) \cdot \boldsymbol{S} & v_1 &= (\boldsymbol{g}_0 - \boldsymbol{c}) \cdot \boldsymbol{Y} \\ u_2 &= (\boldsymbol{g}_1 - \boldsymbol{g}_0) \cdot \boldsymbol{S} & v_2 &= (\boldsymbol{g}_1 - \boldsymbol{g}_0) \cdot \boldsymbol{Y} \\ u_3 &= (\boldsymbol{g}_2 - \boldsymbol{g}_0) \cdot \boldsymbol{S} & v_3 &= (\boldsymbol{g}_2 - \boldsymbol{g}_0) \cdot \boldsymbol{Y} \\ u_4 &= (\boldsymbol{g}_0 + \boldsymbol{g}_{1,2} - \boldsymbol{g}_1 - \boldsymbol{g}_2) \cdot \boldsymbol{S} & v_4 &= (\boldsymbol{g}_0 + \boldsymbol{g}_{1,2} - \boldsymbol{g}_1 - \boldsymbol{g}_2) \cdot \boldsymbol{Y} \end{aligned}$$

Next, we can solve equation (2) for α_2 in terms of α_1 to get

$$\alpha_2 = -\frac{u_1 + u_2\alpha_1}{u_3 + u_4\alpha_1} \tag{4}$$

When we substitute this expression for α_2 into equation (3) and simplify, we get a quadratic equation for α_1 alone:

$$w_1\alpha_1^2 + w_2\alpha_1 + w_3 = 0$$

where

$$\begin{aligned} w_1 &= u_4v_2 - u_2v_4 \\ w_2 &= u_4v_1 - u_1v_4 + u_3v_2 - u_2v_3 \\ w_3 &= u_3v_1 - u_1v_3 \end{aligned}$$

Therefore, the solution for α_1 is given by

$$\alpha_1 = \begin{cases} \dfrac{-w_2 \pm \sqrt{w_2^2 - 4w_1w_3}}{2w_1} & \text{if } w_1 \neq 0 \\ -\dfrac{w_3}{w_2} & \text{if } w_1 = 0 \end{cases}$$

When $w_1 \neq 0$, there are two possible projections of $\boldsymbol{c}$ onto the bilinear surface; we choose the solution for α_1 that results in a value between zero and one. Once we obtain α_1, we can compute α_2 from equation (4) and the projection point $\hat{\boldsymbol{c}}$ from equation (1).

References

[1] F. R. Clapper and J. A. C. Yule. The effect of multiple internal reflections on the densities of half-tone prints on paper. *Journal of the Optical Society of America*, 43(7):600–603, July 1953.

[2] James D. Foley, Andries van Dam, Steven K. Feiner, and John F. Hughes. *Computer Graphics: Principles and Practice*. Addison-Wesley, Reading, MA, second edition, 1990.

[3] Ronald S. Gentile and Jan P. Allebach. A comparison of techniques for color gamut mismatch compensation. In *Human Vision, Visual Processing, and Digital Display*, volume 1077 of *Proceedings of the SPIE*, pages 342–354. SPIE, Bellingham, WA, 1989.

[4] Andrew S. Glassner. *Principles of Digital Image Synthesis*, volume 1. Morgan Kaufmann, San Francisco, 1995.

[5] Andrew S. Glassner, Kenneth P. Fishkin, David H. Marimont, and Maureen C. Stone. Device-directed rendering. *ACM Transactions on Graphics*, 14(1):58–76, January 1995.

[6] Ed Granger. Light Source Computer Images, Inc. Personal communication, December 1995.

[7] Arthur C. Hardy and F. L. Wurzburg, Jr. Color correction in color printing. *Journal of the Optical Society of America*, 38(4):300–307, April 1948.

[8] Steven J. Harrington and R. Victor Klassen. Color printing having a highlight color image mapped from a full color image. U.S. Patent 5,237,517, August 17, 1993.

[9] Ewald Hering. *Outlines of a Theory of the Light Sense*. Harvard University Press, Cambridge, MA, 1964.

[10] R. W. G. Hunt. *The Reproduction of Colour*. Fountain Press, Kingston-upon-Thames, England, fifth edition, 1995.

[11] Kansei Iwata and Gabriel Marcu. Computer simulation of printed colors on textile materials. In *Color Hard Copy and Graphic Arts III*, volume 2171 of *Proceedings of the SPIE*, pages 228–238. SPIE, Bellingham, WA, 1994.

[12] Henry R. Kang. Applications of color mixing models to electronic printing. *Journal of Electronic Imaging*, 3(3):276–287, July 1994.

[13] Bruce J. Lindbloom. Accurate color reproduction for computer graphics applications. In *Proceedings of SIGGRAPH '89*, pages 117–126. ACM, New York, 1989.

[14] Gabriel Marcu and Satoshi Abe. Color designing and simulation in non-conventional printing process. In *Applications of Digital Image Processing XVII*, volume 2298 of *Proceedings of the SPIE*, pages 216–223. SPIE, Bellingham, WA, 1994.

[15] H. E. J. Neugebauer. Die Theoretischen Grundlagen des Mehrfarbenedruckes (The theoretical foundation for multicolor printing). *Z. Wiss Photogr.*, pages 73–89, 1937. Reprinted in Sayanai [20], pages 194–202.

[16] Victor Ostromoukhov. Chromaticity gamut enhancement by heptatone multi-color printing. In *Device-Independent Color Imaging and Imaging Systems Integration*, volume 1909 of *Proceedings of the SPIE*, pages 139–151. SPIE, Bellingham, WA, 1989.

[17] Victor Ostromoukhov and Roger D. Hersch. Artistic screening. In *Proceedings of SIGGRAPH 95*, pages 219–228. ACM, New York, 1995.

[18] R. H. J. M. Otten and L. P. P. P. van Ginneken. *The Annealing Algorithm*. Kluwer Academic Publishers, Boston, 1989.

[19] Warren Rhodes. Fifty years of the Neugebauer equations. In Sayanai [20], pages 7–18.

[20] Kazuo Sayanai, editor. *Neugebauer Memorial Seminar on Color Reproduction*, volume 1184 of *Proceedings of the SPIE*. SPIE, Bellingham, WA, 1990.

[21] Maureen C. Stone, William B. Cowan, and John C. Beatty. Color gamut mapping and the printing of digital color images. *ACM Transactions on Graphics*, 7(4):249–292, October 1988.

[22] Johannes von Kries. Chromatic adaptation. In David L. MacAdam, editor, *Sources of Color Science*, pages 109–119. MIT Press, Cambridge, MA, 1970.

[23] John A. C. Yule. *Principles of Color Reproduction*. Wiley, New York, 1967.

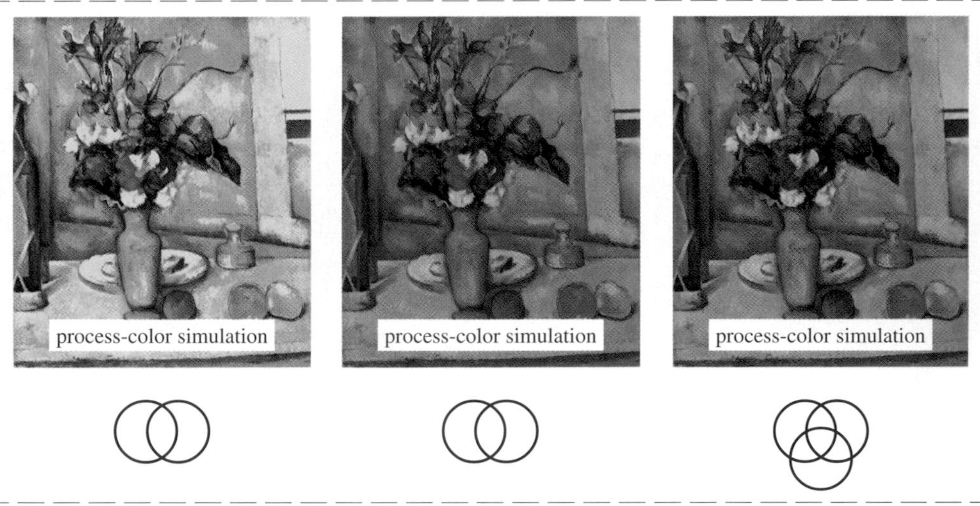

Example 1 Cézanne's *Blue Vase*: (left) process-color print; (center left) traditional duotone using PANTONE 130 and Process Black; (center right) our algorithm's duotone using the same inks; (right) black-enhanced duotone using PANTONE 198, PANTONE 604, and PANTONE Process Black.

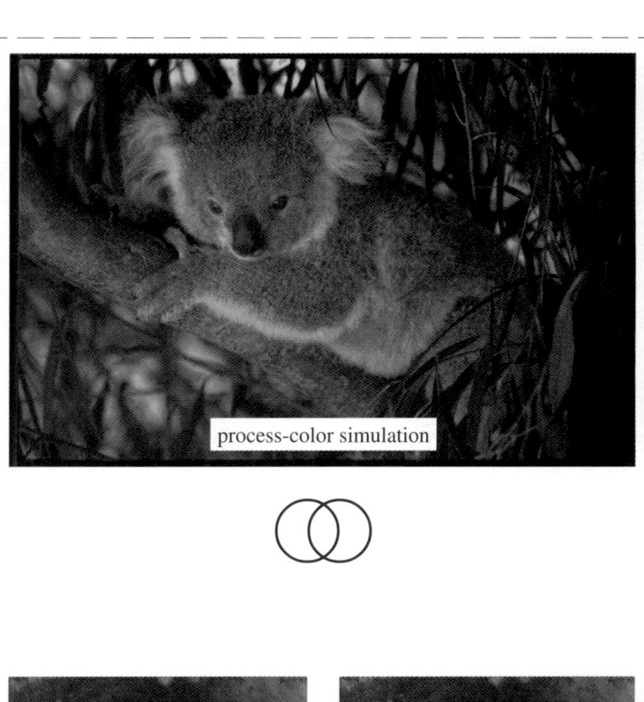

Example 2 Photograph of a koala: (left) process-color print; (right) duotone using PANTONE 144 and PANTONE 546.

Example 3 Renoir's *Women*: (left) process-color print; (center) duotone using PANTONE 144 and PANTONE 546; (right) duotone using PANTONE 172 and PANTONE 354.

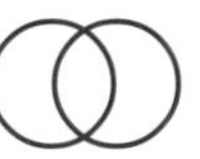

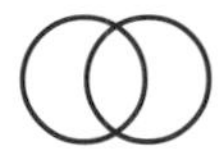

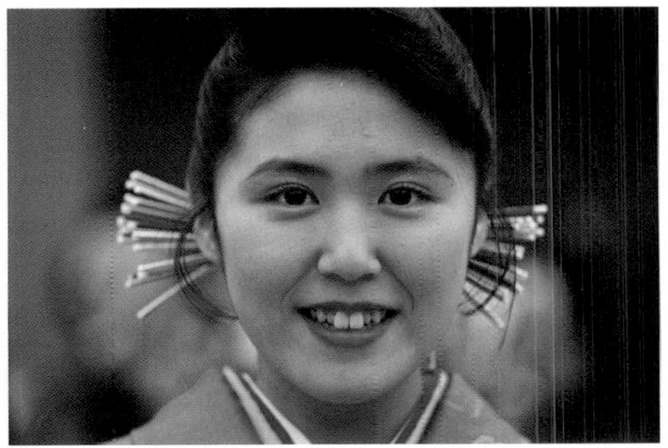

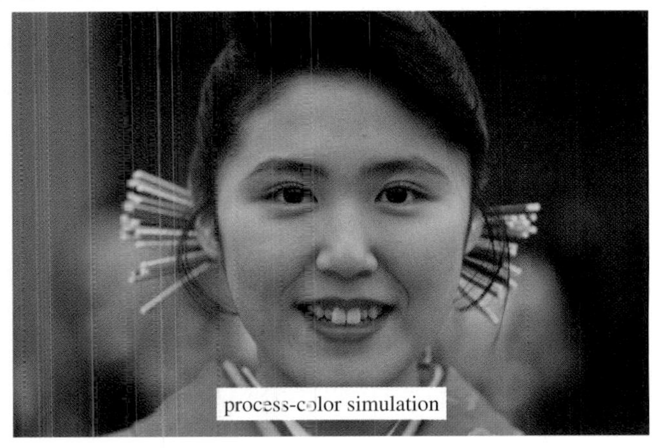

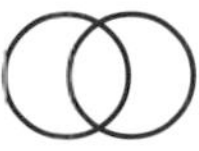

Example 4 Photograph of a woman: (left) process-color print; (right) duotone using PANTONE 152 and PANTONE Process Blue.

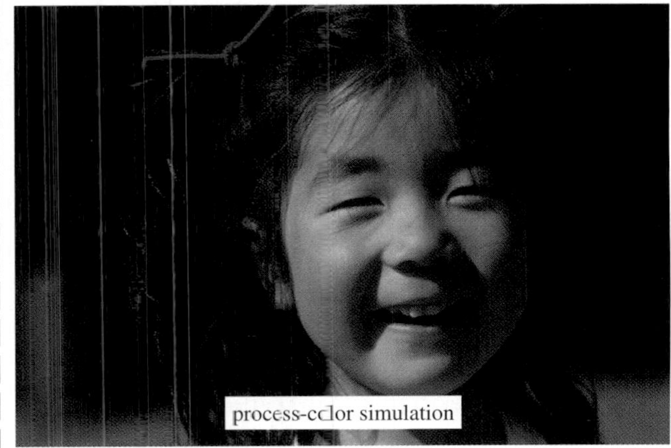

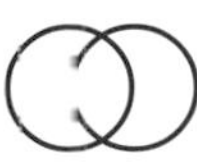

Example 5 Photograph of a girl: (left) process-color print; (right) duotone using PANTONE 152 and PANTONE Process Blue.

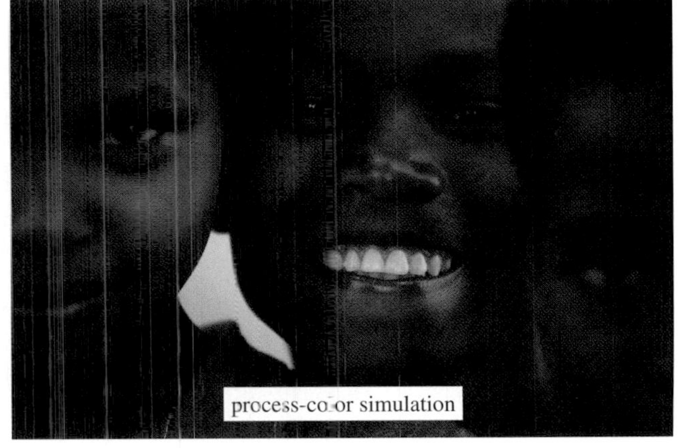

Example 6 Photograph of three boys: (left) process-color print; (right) duotone using PANTONE 152 and PANTONE Process Blue.

Example 7 Photograph of a sunset: (above) process-color print; (top right) duotone using PANTONE 151, PANTONE 246, and PANTONE Process Black, corrected to match the process-color print; (bottom right) duotone using the same inks but without correction in order to obtain colors outside the gamut of process color printing.

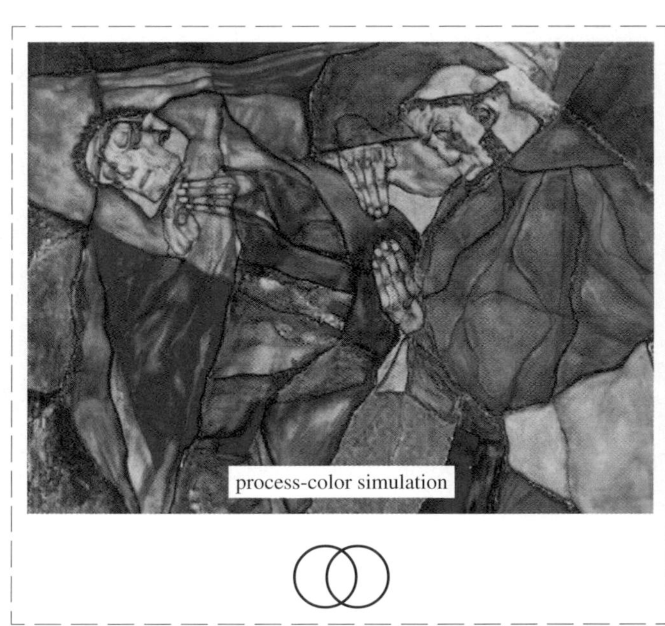

Example 8 Schiele's *Agony*: (left) process-color print; (right) duotone using PANTONE 329 and PANTONE Warm Red on yellow paper.

A Model of Visual Adaptation for Realistic Image Synthesis

James A. Ferwerda Sumanta N. Pattanaik Peter Shirley Donald P. Greenberg

Program of Computer Graphics, Cornell University*

Abstract

In this paper we develop a computational model of visual adaptation for realistic image synthesis based on psychophysical experiments. The model captures the changes in threshold visibility, color appearance, visual acuity, and sensitivity over time that are caused by the visual system's adaptation mechanisms. We use the model to display the results of global illumination simulations illuminated at intensities ranging from daylight down to starlight. The resulting images better capture the visual characteristics of scenes viewed over a wide range of illumination levels. Because the model is based on psychophysical data it can be used to predict the visibility and appearance of scene features. This allows the model to be used as the basis of perceptually-based error metrics for limiting the precision of global illumination computations.

CR Categories and Subject Descriptors: I.3.0 [Computer Graphics]: General; I.3.6 [Computer Graphics]: Methodology and Techniques.

Additional Key Words and Phrases: realistic image synthesis, vision, visual perception, adaptation.

1 Introduction

The goal of realistic image synthesis is to produce images that capture the visual appearance of modeled scenes. Physically-based rendering methods make it possible to accurately simulate the distribution of light energy in scenes, but physical accuracy in rendering does not guarantee that the displayed images will have a realistic visual appearance. There are at least two reasons for this. First, the range of light energy in the scene may be vastly different from the range that can be produced by the display device. Second, the visual states of the scene observer and the display observer may be very different.

To produce realistic images we need to model not only the physical behavior of light propagation, but also the parameters of perceptual response. This is particularly true of the visual system's adaptation to the range of light we encounter in the natural environment since visual function changes dramatically over the range of environmental illumination.

*580 Frank H. T. Rhodes Hall, Ithaca, NY 14853, USA. http://www.graphics.cornell.edu.

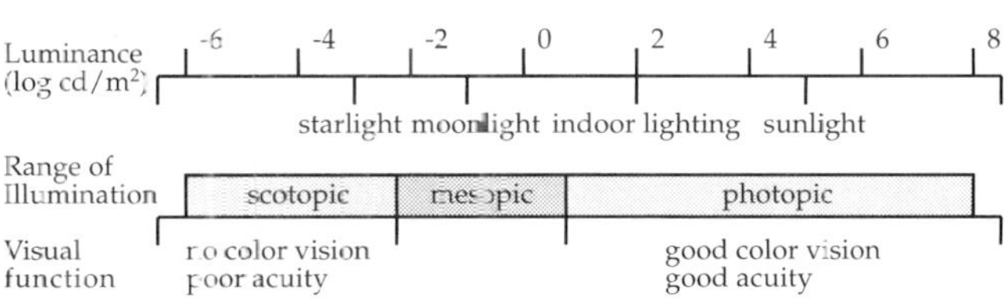

Figure 1: The range of luminances in the natural environment and associated visual parameters. After Hood (1986).

Very little work has been done in computer graphics on adaptation. Earlier work has focused primarily on overcoming the limits of conventional CRT displays and determining how to best display simulated environments within the limited dynamic range available. Tumblin and Rushmeier (1993) introduced the concept of tone reproduction to the computer graphics community and developed a tone reproduction operator that preserves the apparent brightness of scene features. Ward (1994) has taken a somewhat different approach and has developed a tone reproduction operator that preserves apparent contrast and visibility. Spencer (1995) has developed a psychophysical model of glare and has implemented a glare filter that increases the apparent dynamic range of images.

The model of adaptation presented herein deals with many more visual parameters than dynamic range. We develop a model that includes the effects of adaptation on *threshold visibility*, *color appearance*, *visual acuity*, and *changes in visual sensitivity over time*. The algorithm we derive from our model is based on the psychophysics of adaptation measured in experimental studies. Therefore, it can be used predictively for illumination engineering work, and can be used to develop perceptually-based approaches to rendering and display.

1.1 Background

The range of light energy we experience in the course of a day is vast. The light of the noonday sun can be as much as 10 million times more intense than moonlight. Figure 1 shows the range of luminances we encounter in the natural environment and summarizes some visual parameters associated with this luminance range. Our visual system copes with this huge range of luminances by adapting to the prevailing conditions of illumination. Through adaptation the visual system functions over a luminance range of nearly 14 log units.

Adaptation is achieved through the coordinated action of mechanical, photochemical, and neural processes in the visual system. The pupil, the rod and cone systems, bleaching and regeneration of receptor photopigments, and changes in neural processing all play a role in visual adaptation.

Although adaptation provides visual function over a wide range of ambient intensities, this does not mean that we see equally well at all intensity levels. For example, under dim illumination our eyes are very sensitive, and we are able to detect small differences in luminance, however our acuity for pattern details and our ability to distinguish colors are both poor. This is why it is difficult to read a newspaper at twilight or to correctly choose a pair of colored socks while dressing at dawn. Conversely, in daylight we have sharp color vision, but absolute sensitivity is low and luminance differences must be great if we are to detect them. This is why it is impossible to see the stars against the sunlit sky.

Further, adaptation does not happen instantaneously. Nearly everyone has experienced the temporary blindness that occurs when you enter a dark theatre for a matinee. It can sometimes take a few minutes before you can see well enough to find an empty seat. Similarly, once you have dark adapted in the theatre and then go out into the daylight after the show, the brightness is at first dazzling and you need to squint or shield your eyes, but within about a minute, you can see normally again.

To produce realistic synthetic images that capture the appearance of actual scenes, we need to take adaptation-related changes in vision into account. In this paper we develop a computational model of visual adaptation and apply it to the problem of rendering scenes illuminated at vastly different levels. The model predicts the visibility of object features and colors at particular illumination levels, and simulates the changes in visibility and appearance that occur over the time-course of light and dark adaptation.

2 Physiological foundations of adaptation

Through adaptation the visual system functions over a luminance range of nearly 14 log units, despite the fact that the individual neural units that make up the system have a response range of only about 1.5 log units (Spillman 1990). Through four distinct adaptation mechanisms, the visual system moderates the effects of changing levels of illumination on visual response to provide sensitivity over a wide range of ambient light levels.

2.1 The pupil

The most obvious mechanism available to regulate the amount of light stimulating the visual system is the pupil. Over a 10 log unit range of luminance, the pupil changes in diameter from approximately 7 mm down to about 2 mm (Pugh 1988). This range of variation produces a little more than a log unit change in retinal illuminance so pupillary action alone is not sufficient to completely account for visual adaptation (Spillman 1990). In fact, rather than playing a significant role in adaptation it is thought that variation in pupil size serves to mitigate the visual consequences of aberrations in the eye's optical system. At high levels where there is plenty of light to see by, the pupil stops down to limit the effects of the aberrations. At low levels where catching enough light to allow detection is more essential than optimizing the resolution of the retinal image, the pupil opens to allow more light into the eye.

2.2 The rod and cone systems

There are somewhere between 75 and 150 million rod and 6 to 7 million cone photoreceptors in each retina (Riggs 1971). The rods are extremely sensitive to light and provide achromatic vision at *scotopic* levels of illumination ranging from 10^{-6} to 10 cd/m^2. The cones are less sensitive than the rods, but provide color vision at *photopic* levels of illumination in the range of 0.01 to 10^8 cd/m^2. At light levels from 0.01 to 10 cd/m^2 both the rod and cone systems are active. This is known as the *mesopic* range. Relatively little is known about vision in the mesopic range but this is increasingly a topic of interest because computer-based office environments with CRT displays and subdued lighting exercise the visual system's mesopic range.

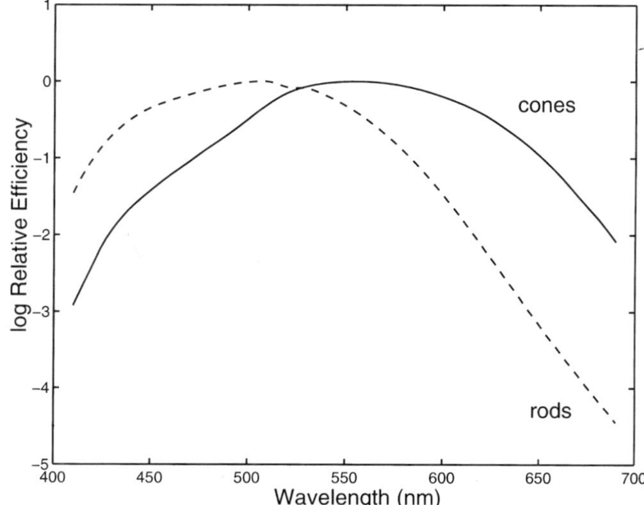

Figure 2: Scotopic V'_λ and photopic V_λ luminous efficiency functions. After Wyszecki (1982).

The rod and cone systems are sensitive to light with wavelengths from about 400nm to 700nm. The rods have their peak sensitivity at approximately 505nm. Spectral sensitivity of the composite cone system peaks at approximately 555 nm. The rod and cone systems are not equally sensitive to light at all wavelengths. *Luminous efficiency functions* show how effective light of a particular wavelength is as a visual stimulus. Differences between the rod and cone systems lead to separate photopic and scotopic luminous efficiency functions that apply to typical daytime and nighttime illumination levels. Figure 2 shows the normalized scotopic and photopic luminous efficiency functions developed by the CIE (Wyszecki 1982).

2.3 Bleaching and regeneration of photopigments

At high light intensities, the action of light depletes the photosensitive pigments in the rods and cones at a faster rate than chemical processes can restore them. This makes the receptors less sensitive to light. This process is known as *pigment bleaching.* Early theories of adaptation were based the idea that light adaptation was produced by pigment bleaching and dark adaptation was produced by pigment restoration (Hecht 1934). However pigment bleaching cannot completely account for adaptation for two reasons: first, a substantial amount of adaptation takes place in both the rod and cone systems at ambient levels where little bleaching occurs (Granit 1939); and second, the time courses of the early phases of dark and light adaptation are too rapid to be explained by photochemical processes alone (Crawford 1947).

2.4 Neural processes

The neural response produced by a photoreceptor cell depends on chemical reactions produced by the action of light on the cell's photopigments. The cell's response to light is limited by the maximum rate and intensity of these chemical reactions. If the reactions are occurring near their maximum levels, and the amount of light striking the photopigments is increased, the cell may not be able to fully signal the increase. This situation is known as *saturation*. The result of saturation is *response compression*: above a certain level incremental increases in light intensity will produce smaller and smaller changes in the cell's response rate.

The rod and cone photoreceptors connect through a network of neurons in the retina to ganglion cells whose axons form the optic nerve. Adaptive processes sited in this neural network adjust the base activity and gain of the early visual system to mitigate the effects of response compression in the photoreceptors. A *multiplicative process* adjusts the gain of the system by effectively scaling the input by a constant related to the background luminance. This process acts very rapidly and accounts for changes in sensitivity over the first few seconds of adaptation. A slower acting *subtractive process* reduces the base level of activity in the system caused by a constant background. This process accounts for the slow improvement in sensitivity measured over minutes of adaptation (Adelson 1982).

3 A psychophysical model of adaptation

The physiological mechanisms described above provide the basis for visual adaptation. The action of these mechanisms is reflected in the changes in visibility, color appearance, visual acuity, and sensitivity over time that can be observed in everyday experience and measured in psychophysical experiments. In this section we will review a series of experiments that measure the changes in visual function that accompany adaptation. The results of these experiments will serve as the basis of our computational model of adaptation.

3.1 Threshold studies

Visual sensitivity is often measured psychophysically in a *detection threshold* experiment. In the typical experimental paradigm, an observer is seated in front of a blank screen that fills their field of view. To determine the absolute threshold the screen is made dark. To determine the contrast threshold a large region of the screen is illuminated to a particular background luminance level. Before testing begins, the observer fixates the center of the screen until they are completely adapted to the background level. On each trial a disk of light is flashed near the center of fixation for a few hundred milliseconds. The observer reports whether they see the disk or not. If the disk is not seen its intensity is increased on the next trial. If it is seen, its intensity is decreased. In this way, the detection threshold for the target disk against the background is measured.

There are many stimulus parameters that affect detection thresholds. Background and target size, color, duration, and position all affect threshold magnitude. To allow comparison of the different experiments in this section we have summarized the experimental parameters in insets on each graph. We have also converted from the diverse range of luminance and illuminance units used in the literature to a standard scale of log cd/m^2 taking into account the changes in retinal illuminance due to changes in pupil size and differences in the luminous efficiency of the rod and cone systems.

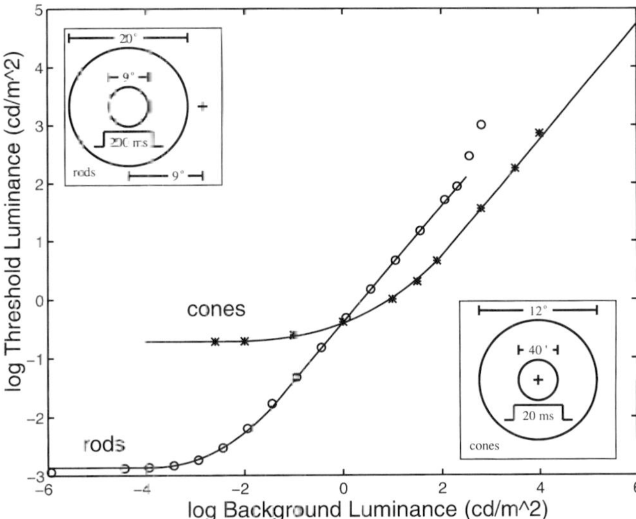

Figure 3: A psychophysical model of detection thresholds over the full range of vision

3.2 Changes in threshold sensitivity

As the luminance of the background in a detection threshold experiment is increased from zero, the luminance difference between target and background required for detection increases in direct proportion to the background luminance. Plotting the detection threshold against the corresponding background luminance gives a *threshold-versus-intensity (t.v.i.)* function. Figure 3 shows the psychophysically measured t.v.i. functions for the rod and cone systems.

At luminance levels below about -4 log cd/m^2, the rod curve flattens to a horizontal asymptote. This indicates that the luminance of the background has little effect on the threshold which approaches the limit for detecting a stimulus in the dark. At levels above 2 log cd/m^2 the curve approaches a vertical asymptote. This indicates that the rod system is being overloaded by the background luminance with the result that no amount of luminance difference between the background and target will allow detection.

Over a wide middle range covering 3.5 log units of background luminance the function is linear, this relationship can be described by the function $\Delta L = kL$. This relationship is known as *Weber's law* (Riggs 1971). Weber's law behavior is indicative of a system that has constant contrast sensitivity, since the proportional increase in threshold with increasing background luminance corresponds to a luminance pattern with constant contrast.

The other curve in Figure 3 shows the t.v.i. function for the cone system. In many ways the rod and cones show similar patterns of response. At levels below -2.6 log cd/m^2, the t.v.i function is essentially flat indicating that the background has no effect on the response threshold. In this region the cones are operating at their absolute levels of sensitivity. At background levels above 2 log cd/m^2 the function is linear, indicating Weber's law behavior and constant contrast sensitivity. One important difference between the rod and cone functions is that the cone system never saturates in the upper reaches of the luminance range. Instead, pigment bleaching gradually lowers sensitivity all the way up

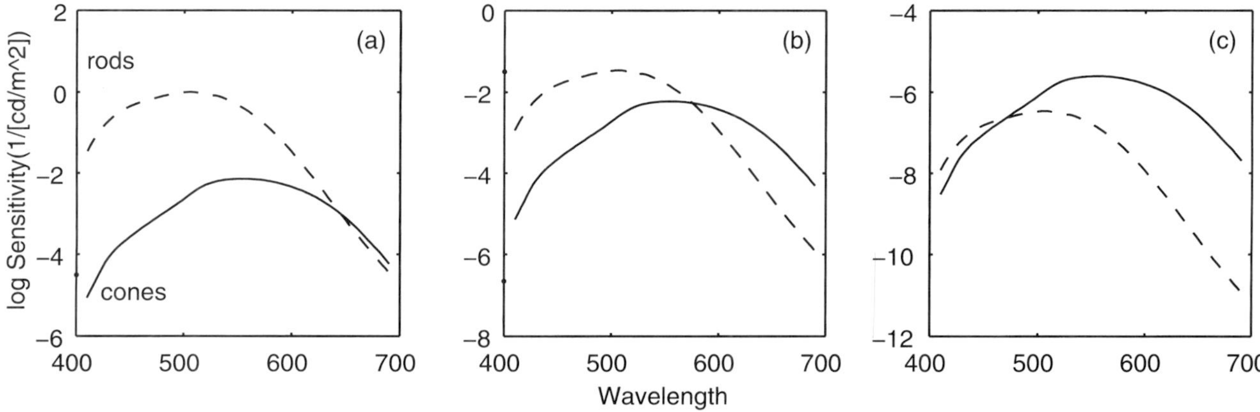

Figure 4: Changes in the spectral sensitivity of the visual system at (a) scotopic, (b) mesopic, and (c) photopic illumination levels. After Hood (1986).

to damaging intensity levels.

We have placed the rod and cone t.v.i. functions on the same graph to show the relative sensitivities of the systems and to show how threshold sensitivity varies over a wide range of scotopic and photopic background luminances. At background luminances from about -6 to 0 log cd/m^2 the rod system is more sensitive than the cone system. In this range the rods account for the magnitude of the detection threshold. As the background luminance is increased, the rod system loses sensitivity and the detection threshold rises. At a background level around 0 log cd/m^2 the rod and cone t.v.i. functions cross. Above this level the cone system is more sensitive than the rod system and it accounts for the detection threshold. Over a wide range of background luminances the visual system's threshold sensitivity can be described by the envelope of the rod and cone t.v.i. curves.

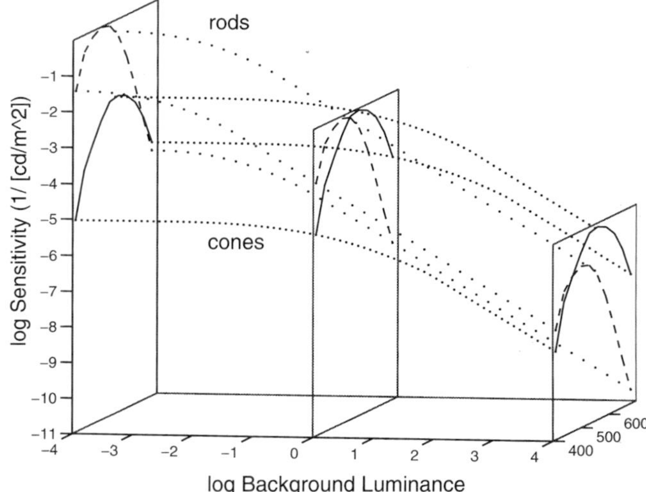

Figure 5: A model of threshold sensitivity as a function of wavelength and background luminance for the rod and cone systems.

3.3 Changes in color appearance

The spectral sensitivities of the rod and cone systems are described by the scotopic and photopic luminous efficiency functions. When presented graphically, the functions are typically normalized which masks the fact that the rod and cone systems differ greatly in sensitivity and operate over different luminance ranges.

Figure 4 (a) shows the visual system's spectral sensitivity at scotopic levels. At these levels detection is dominated by the rod system. Absolute sensitivity is quite high, but since the rod system is achromatic, color will not be apparent.

Figure 4 (b) shows spectral sensitivity at mesopic levels. Here the rod and cone systems are nearly equal in absolute sensitivity. Detection at a particular wavelength will be served by the more sensitive system. The graph shows that the rods will detect wavelengths below about 575 nm and the cones will detect wavelengths above this point.

Figure 4 (c) shows the visual system's spectral sensitivity at photopic levels. At these levels detection is dominated by the cone system. Absolute sensitivity has dropped considerably, but due to the trichromatic nature of the cone system, colors will now be seen.

Figure 5 shows the luminous efficiency functions as surfaces positioned with respect to the rod and cone system threshold sensitivities at different luminance levels. This 3d graph shows how the visual system's spectral sensitivity changes with changing luminance levels and which system is dominant at a particular level. The subfigures show cross sections of these spectral sensitivity vs. luminance surfaces.

This model of the changes in spectral sensitivity with changing luminance levels can account for a number of different color appearance phenomena observed over the scotopic to photopic range. First, at low luminance levels vision will be achromatic since detection at all wavelengths is served by the rod system. As the luminance level is raised into the mesopic range, the cone system will become active and colors will begin to be seen beginning with the long wavelength reds and progressing toward the middle wavelength greens. Only at relatively high luminances will short wavelength blue targets begin to appear colored.

3.4 Changes in visual acuity

Acuity is a measure of the visual system's ability to resolve spatial detail. Acuity is often measured clinically with the Snellen chart. A portion of the Snellen chart is shown in Figure 6. The letters of the chart are constructed such that the strokes of each character subtend precise visual angles when viewed from a distance of 20 feet. The bottom line

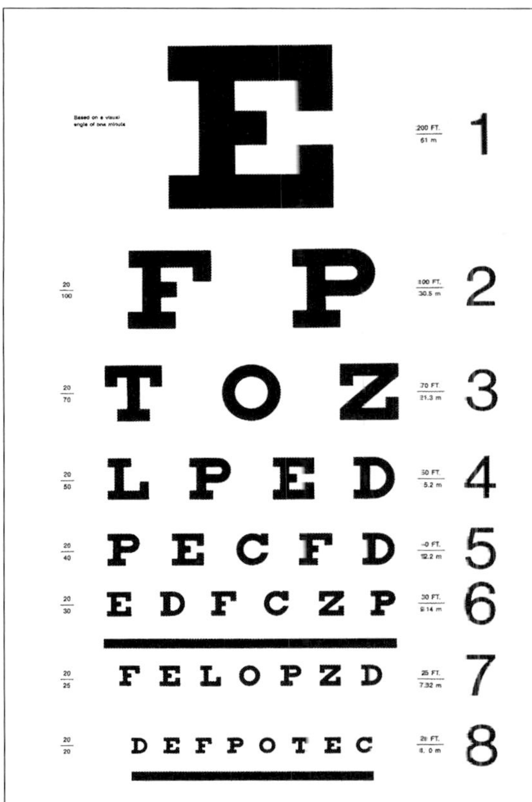

Figure 6: The Snellen acuity chart.

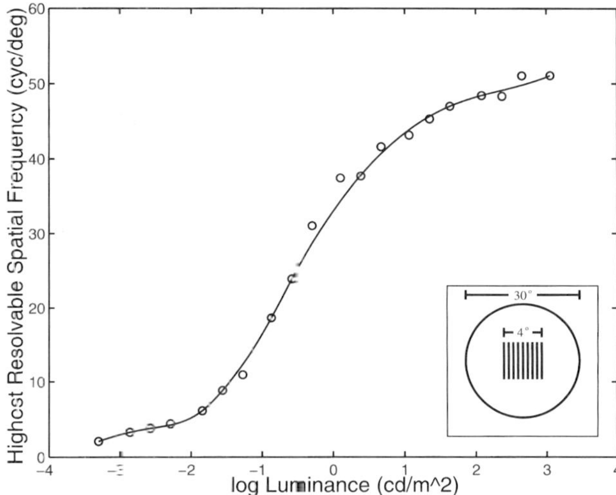

Figure 7: Changes in grating acuity as a function of background luminance. After Shaler (1937).

of the chart is taken as the standard of normal acuity. At 20 feet each character stroke in the bottom line (8) subtends one minute of visual angle. A viewer who can correctly identify the characters on this line is said to have 20/20 vision. The upper lines in the chart have progressively wider stroke widths. These lines are used to assess subnormal acuity. For example each stroke in the characters on line 5 is twice as big as those on line 8. A person with normal acuity can identify the characters in this line from a distance of 40 feet. If you can just identify this line at the standard 20 foot viewing distance then you have 20/40 vision. The large E on line 1 of the chart is equivalent to a visual acuity of 20/200.

Acuity is lower at scotopic levels of illumination than at photopic levels. The curve in Figure 7 shows how visual acuity changes with background luminance. The data cover the range from daylight down to starlight. The experiment measured acuity by testing the detectability of square wave gratings of different spatial frequencies. The graph shows that the highest frequency grating that can be resolved drops from a high of about 50 cycles/degree at 3 log cd/m^2 down to about 2 cycles/degree at -3.3 log cd/m^2. This is equivalent to a change from almost 20/10 vision at daylight levels down to nearly 20/300 under starlight. This curve can be used to predict the visibility of scene details at different levels of illumination. At low levels of illumination it should be difficult to resolve detailed patterns, like the smaller lines on the Snellen chart or fine textures.

3.5 The time-course of adaptation

3.5.1 Light adaptation

Adaptation does not happen instantaneously. If you are seated in a dark room and the lights are suddenly switched on it takes several seconds before you adjust to seeing at the new level of illumination. This process is known as *light adaptation.* Figure 8 shows the results of an experiment on the time course of light adaptation in the rod system (Adelson 1982). Prior to the experiment the observer was dark adapted. At the beginning of the experiment a large background field of 0.5 log cd/m^2 was switched on and from that moment forward the threshold was measured repeatedly. In the instant after the background field was switched on the detection threshold jumped from its dark adapted level to about 0.1 log cd/m^2, but after 2 seconds the threshold has dropped back to about -1.7 log cd/m^2. The graph shows that light adaptation in the scotopic range of the rod system is extremely rapid. More than 80% of sensitivity recovery occurs within the first 2 seconds, and nearly 75% happens within the first 200 ms.

Figure 9 shows the results of a similar experiment on the time-course of light adaptation in the cone system (Baker 1949). As with the rod system, thresholds are highest immediately after the onset of the background field. At a 3.75 log cd/m^2 background level, the instantaneous threshold is about 3.5 log cd/m^2. The threshold decreases over time and reaches a minimum after about 3 minutes of exposure. The threshold drops more than 0.5 log units during this period. After 3 minutes the threshold rises again slightly (due to interactions between neural and photochemical processes in adaptation) and reaches its fully adapted level at about 10 minutes. This experiment also shows that the time course of light adaptation in the cone system is slower than the rod system.

Visually, light adaptation provides a distinctive experience. When we go quickly from low to high levels of illumination, at first everything is painfully glaring and we squint or close one eye to reduce the discomfort. However over time the overall brightness of the visual field diminishes to more comfortable levels and normal vision is restored.

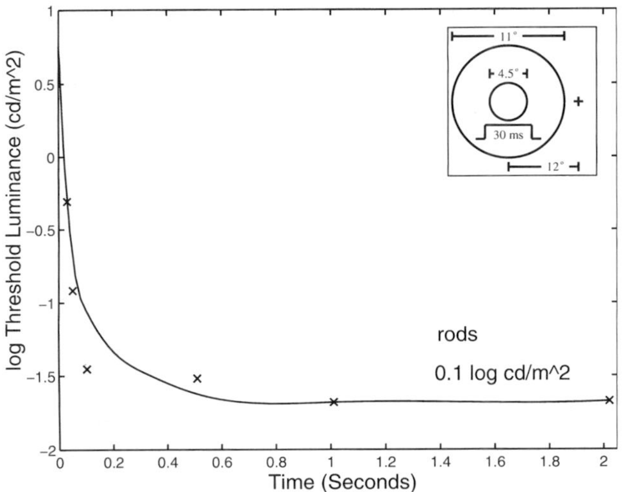

Figure 8: The time course of light adaptation in the rod system. After Adelson (1982).

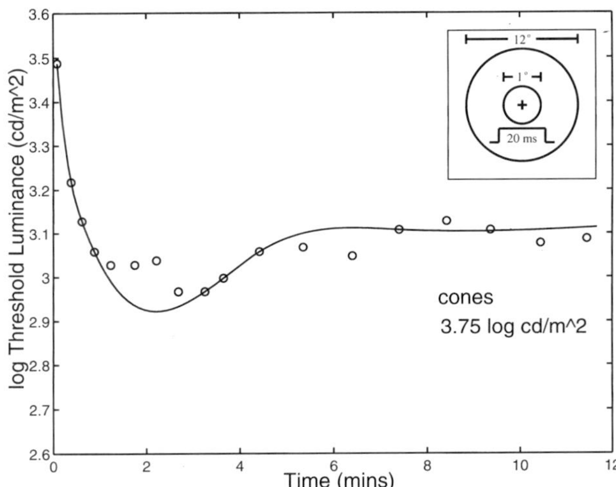

Figure 9: The time course of light adaptation in the cone system. After Baker (1949).

3.5.2 Dark adaptation

Figure 10 shows the time-course of *dark adaptation* as measured by Hecht (1934). In this experiment, the observer was first adapted to a high background luminance and then plunged into darkness. Detection thresholds were measured continuously over more than 30 minutes. The graph shows the detection threshold as a function of time in the dark. The kinked threshold curve is actually the envelope of the curves for the separately tested rod and cone systems. In the first 5 minutes after the adapting field is switched off, the threshold drops rapidly, but then it levels off at a relatively high level because the cone system has reached its greatest sensitivity, but the rod system has still not recovered significantly. After about 7 minutes rod system sensitivity surpasses that of the cone system and the threshold begins to drop again. This point is known as the *Purkinje break* (Riggs 1971) and indicates the transition from detection by the cone system to detection by the rods. Changes in the threshold can be measured out to about 35 minutes, at which point the visual system has reached its absolute levels of sensitivity, and the threshold has dropped nearly 4 log units.

Visually, dark adaptation is experienced as the temporary blindness that occurs when we go rapidly from photopic to scotopic levels of illumination. The relatively slow time-course of dark adaptation means that vision can be impaired for several minutes when we move quickly from high illumination levels to low ones.

3.6 Summary

The cumulative achievement of adaptation is that the visual system is sensitive over a vast range of ambient light levels despite severe limits on the dynamic ranges of the individual neural units that make up the system. However this does not mean that we see equally well at all levels of illumination. The experiments show that threshold visibility, color appearance, and visual acuity are different at different illumination levels, and that these visual parameters change over the time-course of light and dark adaptation.

We will now develop a computational model of the changes in threshold visibility, color appearance, visual acuity, and sensitivity over time that are given by the experiments described above. This computational model will allow us to produce synthetic images that better capture the appearance of scenes illuminated at different levels. Because the computational model is based on psychophysical data, it will allow us to predict the visibility, color appearance, and clarity of scene features at a given level of illumination and to describe the changes in these visual parameters over the time-courses of light and dark adaptation.

4 Implementation

We implement our model in a program that maps image files with photopic luminance (CIE Y), scotopic luminance, and CIE XZ channels to displayable images in a fixed RGB color space. Since this is fundamentally a tone reproduction problem, our algorithm draws on the state-of-the-art in this area.

Tumblin and Rushmeier (1993) introduced the concept of *tone reproduction* to the computer graphics community. Tone reproduction addresses the goal of making an image that is a faithful visual representation of the photometric properties of a scene. Tone reproduction operators describe the mapping from scene to display in terms of physical processes in the display system and psychophysical processes in hypothetical scene and display viewers that affect the fidelity of the displayed image to the scene.

Tumblin and Rushmeier developed a tone reproduction operator that preserves *brightness* relationships. Their operator uses a psychophysical model of brightness perception developed by Stevens and Stevens (1960) to produce a mapping from scene luminances to display luminances such that the perceived brightness of a region on the display will match the perceived brightness of a region in the scene.

A somewhat different approach to tone reproduction has been developed by Ward (1994). Ward's operator differs from Tumblin and Rushmeier's in that it preserves perceived *contrast* rather than perceived brightness. Ward's operator is based on threshold contrast sensitivity data collected by Blackwell (CIE 1981). The operator maps *just noticeable* contrast *differences* (JND's) in the scene to just noticeable differences in the image.

From a psychophysical point of view, Tumblin and

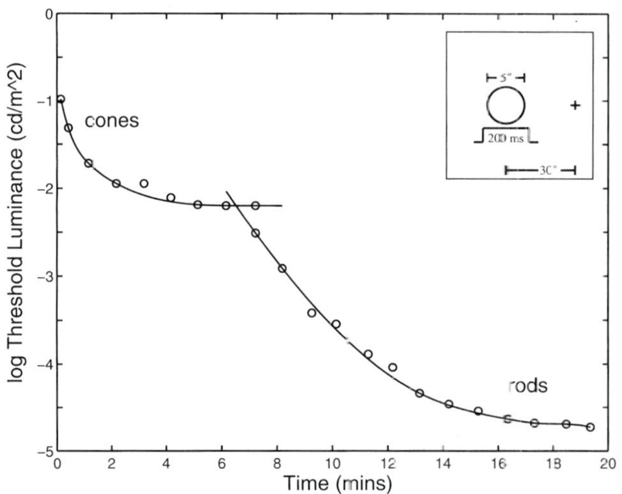

Figure 10: The time course of dark adaptation. After Riggs (1971).

Rushmeier and Ward have taken fundamentally different approaches to the tone reproduction process. Tumblin and Rushmeier's brightness-based operator seeks to match suprathreshold brightness appearance across the range of scene luminances. On the other hand, Ward's contrast-based operator, seeks to match contrast visibility at threshold and scales suprathreshold values relative to the threshold measure. Each approach has its strengths and weaknesses. A brightness-based operator may better capture the subjective appearance of surfaces in a scene, but it may not correctly capture the visibility of surfaces near threshold. Conversely, a contrast-based operator will correctly predict threshold visibility, but may not account well for suprathreshold appearance. A more complete model of tone reproduction for computer graphics may have to combine these two approaches to correctly account for *visibility at threshold* as well as *suprathreshold appearance*.

Because we have based our adaptation model on threshold data, our implementation is based on Ward's concept of matching just noticeable differences for the world and display observers. Ward's tone reproduction operator is:

$$L_d(L_w) = mL_w, \tag{1}$$

where L_w is the luminance seen by the world observer, and L_d is the luminance that L_w is mapped to on the display device. The multiplier m is chosen to achieve matches in visibility for the world and display observers. To achieve this, Ward assumes that we have a t.v.i. function $t(L)$ that gives a threshold luminance that is barely visible for a given adaptation luminance L. He further assumes that we have a way to estimate the adaptation luminance L_{wa} for the world observer and L_{da} for the display observer. This means that his multiplier m is a function of the adaptation levels of world and display observer. So he chooses $m(L_{wa}, L_{da})$ such that:

$$t(L_{da}) = m(L_{wa}, L_{da})t(L_{wa}), \tag{2}$$

so

$$m(L_{wa}, L_{da}) = t(L_{da})/t(L_{wa}). \tag{3}$$

This determines how luminance is mapped. Ward assumes that the chromatic channels follow the same mapping.

To construct our operator we first apply Ward's model without change using our cone t.v.i data from Figure 3, which is approximated by:

$$\log t_p(L_a) = \begin{cases} -0.72 & \text{if } \log L_a \leq -2.6, \\ \log L_a - 1.255 & \text{if } \log L_a \geq 1.9, \\ (0.249 \log L_a + 0.65)^{2.7} - 0.72 & \text{otherwise.} \end{cases} \tag{4}$$

This operator would work much the same as Ward's model, although Equation 4 is slightly different from Ward's because it is derived from different experimental data. We chose this data because we did not have access to the raw data Ward used, and because the differences are small enough that they are probably not significant.

We now extend Ward's model to include the rod t.v.i. function shown in Figure 3. Our approximation to this data is:

$$\log t_s(L_a) = \begin{cases} -2.86 & \text{if } \log L_a \leq -3.94, \\ \log L_a - 0.395 & \text{if } \log L_a \geq -1.44, \\ (0.405 \log L_a + 1.6)^{2.18} - 2.86 & \text{otherwise.} \end{cases} \tag{5}$$

Since we expect an achromatic response from the rod system, we produce only a grayscale mapping. We do this by applying Equation 3 using the t.v.i. curves from Equation 5 for the world observer and Equation 4 for the display observer, because the display observer is in a photopic state of adaptation. This would be a plausible tone reproduction operator to preserve visibility for a coneless observer (a "rod monochromat"). This technique was inspired by Meyer's (1986) model for simulating the visual experience of color-defective viewers.

For photopic conditions we can apply the photopic tone reproduction operator. For scotopic conditions we can apply the scotopic operator. But what do we do for mesopic conditions? Simply adding the results of the photopic and scotopic operators would be a mistake, because for high mesopic levels the rods would produce quite a bright image, when in fact they are shutting down due to saturation. Instead, we generate both a photopic display luminance L_{dp} and a scotopic luminance L_{ds}, and combine them with the formula:

$$L_d = L_{dp} + k(L_a)L_{ds}, \tag{6}$$

where k is a constant that varies from 1 to 0 as the scotopic world adaptation level goes from the bottom to the top of the mesopic range. The rods rather than the cones have a multiplier because the rod system is losing sensitivity as the intensity increases toward the photopic range, while the cones are quiescent and in a ready state. Because the cones are ready to respond, we apply Equation 6 for all scene adaptation levels. This way, a red stoplight in a night scene will be displayed properly.

4.1 Acuity

Just as we want threshold contrast to be mapped between the world and display observers, we would like resolvable detail to be preserved as well. From the data shown in Figure 7, we can determine what spatial frequencies are visible to the world observer. We simply remove all spatial frequencies above this in the image we present to the display observer. Because we don't want ringing in the displayed image, we use a Gaussian convolution filter whose power spectrum amplitude at the cutoff frequency is matched to the observer's threshold. Thus we remove frequencies in the image which would not be discernable to the world observer:

$$f^\star(\omega_c(L_{wa})) = \frac{t(L_{wa})}{L_{wa}}, \qquad (7)$$

where $f^\star$ is the Fourier transform of the convolution filter, and $\omega_c(L_{wa})$ is the threshold frequency for the world adaptation of the viewer. This way a high contrast scene grating at frequency $\omega_c(L_{wa})$ will be displayed at the threshold of visibility for the display viewer.

4.2 Light Adaptation

The detection threshold for an observer who suddenly enters a bright environment, is high relative to the threshold for an observer adapted to the bright environment. The t.v.i. data for this situation is shown in Figures 8 and 9. We can apply Equation 3 to make sure that only high contrasts are visible. Although this would be valid in terms of visibility, it would produce a dim appearance, which is the opposite of qualitative experience. This is because whenever Equation 3 raises the contrast threshold for the world observer, it does this by making m small, thus assuring a dim appearance on the display. To combat this we note that any linear model can be put in place of Equation 3, and visibility can still be preserved, but we gain a free parameter that can increase the qualitative accuracy of appearance. We keep the m multiplier and add an offset, so that contrast can be reduced and screen brightness can be adjusted separately:

$$L_d(L_w) = mL_w + b. \qquad (8)$$

The multiplier m will still be set by the same formulas as above. However, b will be a function of time. Because we have no quantitative data to set b, we do the simplest thing possible: we set b such that

$$L_d(L_{wa}) = \text{constant over time}. \qquad (9)$$

This means the overall luminance of the display will not change during the light adaptation process. We could adjust the value of b in an ad-hoc manner to create a "flash" immediately after the viewer changes viewing conditions. We choose not to do this because we want to preserve a "hands-off" objective model.

4.3 Dark Adaptation

The detection threshold for an observer who suddenly enters a dim environment is high relative to the threshold of an observer adapted to the dim environment. The procedure we used for light adaptation can be applied without change.

4.4 Determining adaptation luminances

When applying display equations such as Equation 3, the result depends on the choices of the adaptation states L_{wa} and L_{da}. In the absence of any obviously correct answer, we opt for the simplest choice. For the world adaptation we choose half the highest visible luminance. For the display observer we use half the maximum screen luminance (typically $80/2 = 40cd/m^2$). We have observed that the appearance of many displayed images can be improved by tuning the adaptation luminances, but we purposely avoid doing this because we want to maintain an automatic process based on psychophysical data.

5 Results

The panels of Figure 11 show the results of applying our model of visual adaptation to a simulated scene. The scene is an office that contains a Snellen chart, and a Macbeth Colorchecker chart used as a standard in color reproduction. The rendered image file was created using Monte Carlo path tracing with a spectral color model, diffuse illumination that is uniform across the visible spectrum, and the standard reflectivities for the Macbeth chart (Wyszecki 1982). Panel (a) shows the image produced by our model for a scene illuminated at 1000 cd/m^2. This image simulates what the scene looks like under photopic conditions that approximate normal daylight levels. Notice that all the colors in Macbeth chart are bright and saturated, and that all the letters in the Snellen chart can be recognized. Panel (b) shows the scene illuminated at 10 cd/m^2. This approximates dim interior lighting and is near the top of the mesopic range. Notice that the scene is darker overall, that some contrast has been lost, and that the colors are less saturated, but acuity is still good since all the lines on the Snellen chart are recognizable. Panel (c) shows the scene illuminated at 0.04 cd/m^2. This is a moonlight level near the the mesopic/scotopic transition. Notice that the saturation of all the colors in the Macbeth chart is greatly reduced, and that the blues and greens have become completely achromatic. Notice also that visual acuity has dropped significantly, and that the smaller letters on the Snellen chart can no longer be identified. Panel (d) shows the scene illuminated at starlight levels of 0.001 cd/m^2 near the lower threshold of vision. At this level detection is the primary function of vision. The ability to distinguish colors and details has been lost. Only the largest and highest contrast forms can be discerned. The differences in contrast, color appearance, and spatial resolution that can be observed across this set of images are a consequence of the adaptation-related changes in visual function that are captured by our model.

One particular visual phenomenon predicted by our model is the *Purkinje shift* in the relative lightness of reds and blues in the mesopic range (Minnaert 1954). The shift is due to the re-ordering of the relative sensitivities of the rod and cone systems at mesopic levels. The effect can be seen in the reversal of the lightnesses of the red and blue squares in the Macbeth chart. In panel (b) the scene is illuminated at 10 cd/m^2 near the top end of the mesopic range. At this level the red square appears lighter than the blue square. In panel (c), illuminated at 0.04 cd/m^2 near the bottom of the mesopic range the blue square now appears lighter than the red.

Figure 12 (a) shows an image sequence that simulates the changes in visual function over the time course of light adaptation. In the first frame of the sequence the scene is illuminated to a level of 0.1 cd/m^2. In the second frame the light level has just been raised to 5623 cd/m^2. Notice that much of the scene is washed out. Apparent contrast is reduced and the colors in the Macbeth chart appear desaturated. The subsequent frames show how the scene appears at intervals following the change in illumination level. Notice that apparent contrast and color gamut increase over time. The final frame shows the scene after 75 seconds of light adaptation. After this time, adaptation is almost complete and visibility, color appearance, and acuity are near their steady state photopic levels.

Figure 12 (b) shows an image sequence that simulates the changes in visual function over the time course of dark adaptation. In the first frame of the sequence the scene is il-

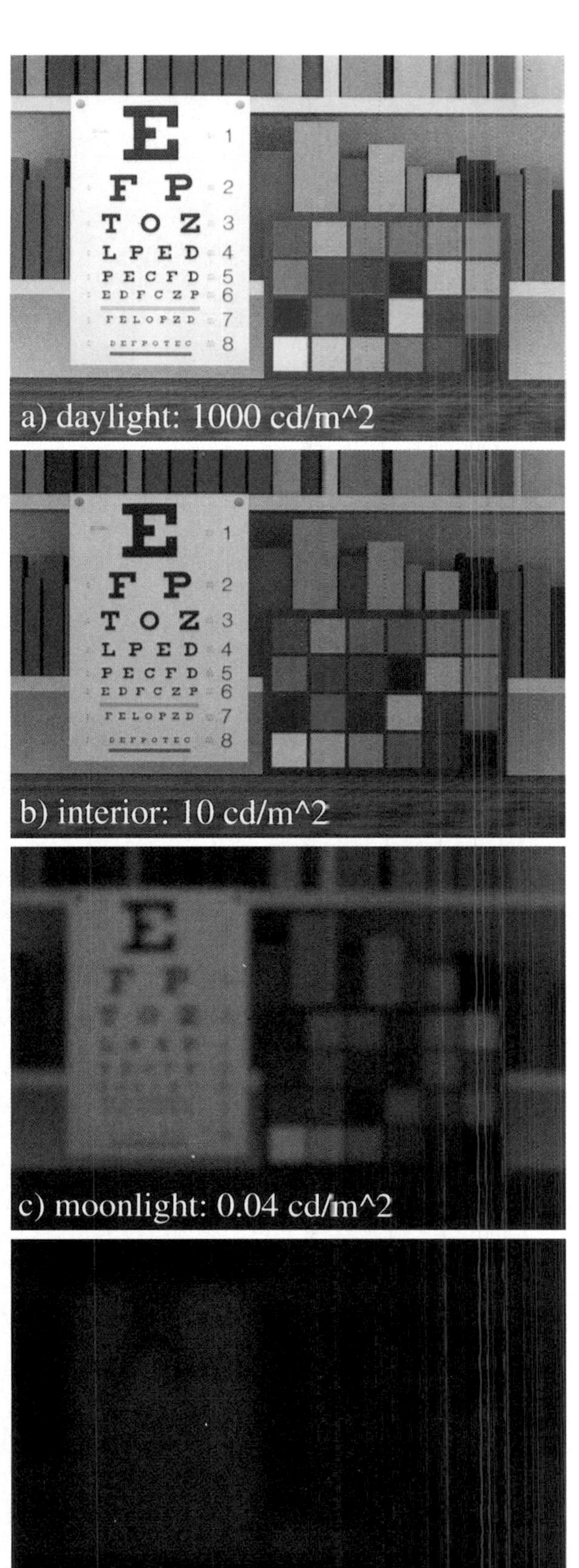

Figure 11: Visual function across the range of light.

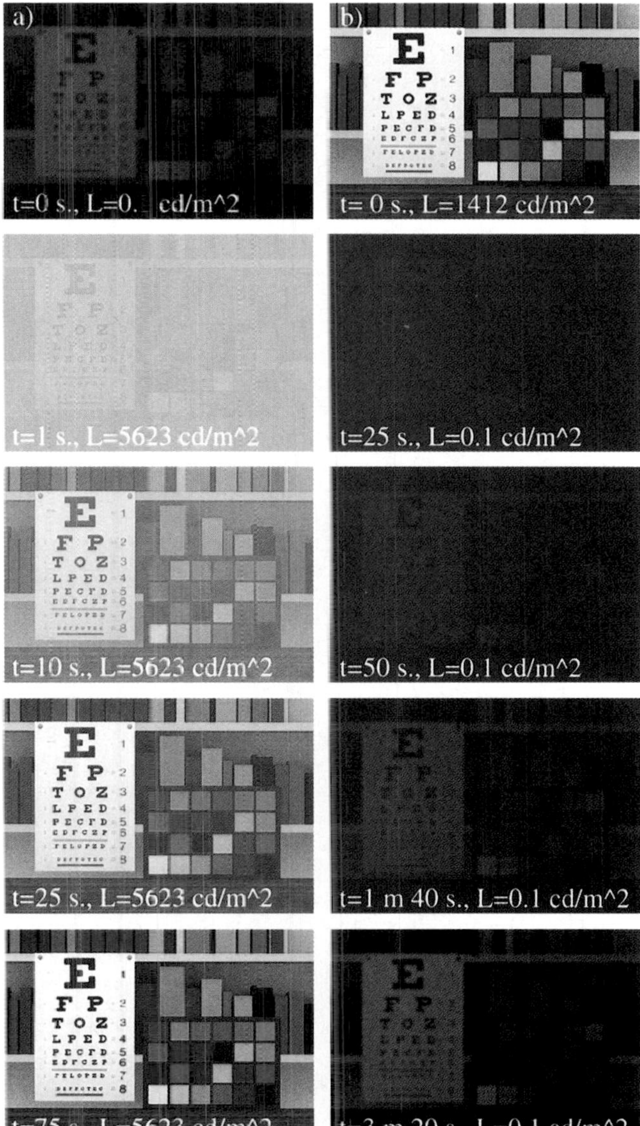

Figure 12: (a) Image sequence showing the time-course of light adaptation. (b) Image sequence showing the time-course of dark adaptation.

luminated to a level of 1412 cd/m^2. In the second frame the light level has just been reduced to 0.1 cd/m^2. Notice that at first the appearance is low contrast and that only the major scene features can be distinguished. The subsequent frames show how the scene appears at intervals during dark adaptation. The final frame shows the appearance after more than 3 minutes of dark adaptation. At this time adaptation is almost complete, and visibility, color appearance and acuity are close to their steady state scotopic levels.

6 Conclusions/Future Work

In this paper we have developed a computational model of the changes in visual function that are produced by adaptation. By applying this model to global illumination solutions we have generated images that better capture the visual appearance of scenes illuminated over a wide range of intensity levels. Because this model is based on psychophysical experiments, the images produced are visually faithful representations and can be used predictively. However we must caution that since our data is derived from experiments conducted under widely varying conditions, none of which are likely to match typical viewing conditions, our images should be taken as approximations to a precisely accurate simulation.

There is still much work to be done in this area. While we have modeled the visual consequences of adaptation we still do not have a good model for a viewer's state of adaptation. This is a complex problem because the retina adapts locally and because eye movements cause the state of adaptation to change continuously.

We are also less than completely satisfied with our simulations of light and dark adaptation. While we believe our model predicts the changes in threshold visibility that occur over the time course of adaptation, we feel that our images do not completely capture the appearance of the early phases of light and dark adaptation. Our algorithm is based on Ward's contrast-threshold tone reproduction operator. Tumblin and Rushmeier have presented an alternative tone reproduction operator based on suprathreshold brightness measurements. Perhaps a more complete solution to the questions of adaptation-related changes in visibility and appearance will come from some combination of these models.

A more complete model of adaptation will be important for advances in realistic image synthesis. The quest for realism in computer graphics is pushing advanced software and hardware technology toward a convergence. On the software side are physically-based global illumination rendering methods that produce accurate simulations of the distribution of light energy in scenes. On the hardware side are high-resolution immersive displays in which computer generated images fill the visual field. True visual realism in image synthesis will eventually occur with the merging of these advanced technologies, but two problems stand in the way. First, current rendering methods are too slow to accommodate the real-time update rates required for immersive environments. Second, we do not know how to correctly display the results of global illumination simulations to produce realistic visual appearance in immersive display systems.

A better model of visual adaptation can help solve both of these problems. In the first case, an adaptation model can be used as the basis of perceptual error metrics to limit the precision of global illumination calculations based on visibility and appearance criteria. This could lead to time-critical global illumination rendering algorithms that achieve real-time rates. In the second case an adaptation model can be used to determine how to properly display images in immersive display systems where the display output fills the visual field and provides all the viewer's visual stimulation. Bringing these two techniques together in algorithms where rendering computations can be tightly constrained because the viewer's visual state is precisely known could lead to even greater computational efficiencies and greater visual realism.

Acknowledgements

Dan Kartch and Steve Marschner helped with the preparation of the paper and color figures. This work was supported by the NSF/ARPA Science and Technology Center for Computer Graphics and Scientific Visualization (ASC-8920219) and by NSF CCR-9401961 and performed on workstations generously provided by the Hewlett-Packard Corporation.

Bibliography

Adelson E.H. (1982). Saturation and adaptation in the rod system. Vision Research, 22, 1299-1312.

Aguilar, M. & Stiles, W.S. (1954). Saturation of the rod mechanism of the retina at high levels of stimulation. Optica Acta, 1, 59-65.

Baker, H.D. (1949). The course of foveal adaptation measured by the threshold intensity increment. Journal of the Optical Society of America, 39, 172-179.

CIE (1981). An analytic model for describing the influence of lighting parameters upon visual performance, vol. 1. Technical foundations. CIE 19/2.1, Technical committee 3.1.

Crawford, B.H. (1947). Visual adaptation in relation to brief conditioning stimuli. Proceedings of the Royal Society of London, Series B, 128, 283-302.

Granit R., Munsterhjelm, A., and Zewi, M. (1939). The relation between concentration of visual purple and retinal sensitivity to light during dark adaptation. Journal of Physiology, 96, 31-44.

Hecht, S. (1934). Vision II: the nature of the photoreceptor process. In C. Murchison (Ed.), A handbook of general experimental psychology. Worchester, Massachusetts: Clark University Press.

Hood, D.C. & Finkelstein M.A. (1986). Visual sensitivity. In K.Boff, L. Kaufman, & J. Thomas (Eds.), Handbook of Perception and Human Performance (Volume 1). 5-1-5-66.

IES (1993). Lighting handbook:reference and application volume, (8th edition). Mark S. Rea (Ed.). New York: Illuminating Engineering Society of North America.

Meyer, G.W. (1986) Color calculation for and perceptual assessment of computer graphic images. Ph.D. thesis, Cornell University.

Mueller, C.G. (1951). Frequency of seeing functions for intensity discrimination at various levels of adapting intensity. Journal of General Physiology, 34, 463-474.

Minnaert, M. (1954) The nature of light and color in the open air. New York: Dover.

Pugh, E.N. (1988). Vision: physics and retinal physiology, In R.C. Atkinson (Ed.), Steven's handbook of experimental psychology, (2nd edition). New York: Wiley.

Riggs, L.A. (1971) Vision. In J.W. Kling & L.A. Riggs (Eds.), Woodworth and Schlosberg's Experimental Psychology , (3rd edition). New York: Holt, Rinehart, and Winston.

Shaler, S. (1937) The relation between visual acuity and illumination. Journal of General Physiology, 21, 165-188.

Spencer, G., Shirley P., Zimmerman, K. & Greenberg, D. (1995). Physically-based glare effects for computer generated images, Proceedings ACM SIGGRAPH '95, 325-334.

Spillman, L., & Werner, J.S. (Eds.) (1990). Visual perception: the neurophysiological foundations. SanDiego: Academic Press.

Stevens, S.S., & Stevens, J.C. (1960). Brightness function: parametric effects of adaptation and contrast, Journal of the Optical Society of America , 53, 1139.

Tumblin, J., and Rushmeier, H. (1993). Tone Reproduction for Realistic Images, IEEE Computer Graphics and Applications, 13(6), 42-48.

Ward, G. (1994). A contrast-based scalefactor for luminance display. In P.S. Heckbert (Ed.), Graphics Gems IV, Boston: Academic Press Professional.

Wyszecki G. & Stiles W.S. (1982). Color science: concepts and methods, quantitative data and formulae (2nd edition). New York: Wiley.

Blue Screen Matting

Alvy Ray Smith and James F. Blinn[1]
Microsoft Corporation

ABSTRACT

A classical problem of imaging—the *matting problem*—is separation of a non-rectangular foreground image from a (usually) rectangular background image—for example, in a film frame, extraction of an actor from a background scene to allow substitution of a different background. Of the several attacks on this difficult and persistent problem, we discuss here only the special case of separating a desired foreground image from a background of a constant, or almost constant, *backing* color. This backing color has often been blue, so the problem, and its solution, have been called *blue screen matting*. However, other backing colors, such as yellow or (increasingly) green, have also been used, so we often generalize to *constant color matting*. The mathematics of constant color matting is presented and proven to be unsolvable as generally practiced. This, of course, flies in the face of the fact that the technique is commonly used in film and video, so we demonstrate constraints on the general problem that lead to solutions, or at least significantly prune the search space of solutions. We shall also demonstrate that an algorithmic solution is possible by allowing the foreground object to be shot against *two* constant backing colors—in fact, against two completely arbitrary backings so long as they differ everywhere.

Key Words: Blue screen matte creation, alpha channel, compositing, chromakey, blue spill, flare, backing shadows, backing impurities, separating surfaces, triangulation matting.

CR Categories: I.3.3, I.4.6, J.5.

DEFINITIONS

A *matte* originally meant a separate strip of monochrome film that is transparent at places, on a corresponding strip of color film, that one wishes to preserve and opaque elsewhere. So when placed together with the strip of color film and projected, light is allowed to pass through and illuminate those parts desired but is blocked everywhere else. A *holdout matte* is the complement: It is opaque in the parts of interest and transparent elsewhere. In both cases, partially dense regions allow some light through. Hence some of the color film image that is being matted is partially illuminated.

The use of an *alpha channel* to form arbitrary compositions of images is well-known in computer graphics [9]. An alpha channel gives shape and transparency to a color image. It is the digital equivalent of a holdout matte—a grayscale channel that has full value pixels (for opaque) at corresponding pixels in the color image that are to be seen, and zero valued pixels (for transparent) at corresponding color pixels not to be seen. We shall use 1 and 0 to represent these two alpha values, respectively, although a typical 8-bit implementation of an alpha channel would use 255 and 0. Fractional alphas represent pixels in the color image with partial transparency.

We shall use "alpha channel" and "matte" interchangeably, it being understood that it is really the holdout matte that is the analog of the alpha channel.

The video industry often uses the terms "key" and "keying"—as in "chromakeying"—rather than the "matte" and "matting" of the film industry. We shall consistently use the film terminology, after first pointing out that "chromakey" has now taken on a more sophisticated meaning (e.g., [8]) than it originally had (e.g., [19]).

We shall assume that the color channels of an image are premultiplied by the corresponding alpha channel and shall refer to this as the *premultiplied alpha* case (see [9], [14], [15], [2], [3]). Derivations with non-premultiplied alpha are not so elegant.

THE PROBLEM

The mixing of several pictures—the *elements*—to form a single resulting picture—the *composite*—is a very general notion. Here we shall limit the discussion to a special type of composite frequently made in film and television, the *matte shot*. This consists of at least two elements, one or more *foreground objects* each shot against a special backing color—typically a bright blue or green—and a *background*. We shall limit ourselves to the case of one foreground element for ease of presentation.

The matting problem can be thought of as a perceptual process: the analysis of a complex visual scene into the objects that comprise it. A matte has been successfully *pulled*, if it in combination with the given scene correctly isolates what most humans would agree to be a separate object in reality from the other objects in the scene, that we can collectively refer to as the background. Note that this analysis problem is the reverse of classic 3D geometry-based computer graphics that synthesizes both the object and its matte simultaneously, and hence for which there is no matting problem.

There is also no matting problem of the type we are considering in the case of several *multi-film* matting techniques such as the sodium, infrared, and ultraviolet processes [6], [16]. These record the foreground element on one strip of film and its matte simultaneously on another strip of film.

[1] One Microsoft Way, Redmond, WA 98052-6399.
alvys@microsoft.com, blinn@microsoft.com.

The problem we address here is that of extracting a matte for a foreground object, given only a composite image containing it. We shall see that, in general, this is an underspecified problem, even in the case where the background consists of a single backing color. Note that a composite image contains no explicit information about what elements comprise it. We use the term "composite" to convey the idea that the given image is in fact a representation of several objects seen simultaneously. The problem, of course, is to determine, the objecthood of one or more of these objects. In the film (or video) world, the problem is to extract a matte in a *single-film* process—that is, one with no special knowledge about the object to be extracted, such as might be contained in a separate piece of film exposed simultaneously in a multi-film process.

Now a formal presentation of the problem: The *color* $C = [R\ \ G\ \ B\ \ \alpha]$ at each point of a desired composite will be some function of the color C_f of the foreground and color C_b of the new background at the corresponding points in the two elements. We have for convenience extended the usual color triple to a quadruple by appending the alpha value. As already mentioned, each of the first three *primary color coordinates* is assumed to have been premultiplied by the alpha coordinate. We shall sometimes refer to just these coordinates with the abbreviation $c = [R\ \ G\ \ B]$, for color C. For any subscript i, $C_i = [R_i\ \ G_i\ \ B_i\ \ \alpha_i]$ and $c_i = [R_i\ \ G_i\ \ B_i]$. Each of the four coordinates is assumed to lie on [0, 1]. We shall always assume that $\alpha_f = \alpha_b = 1$ for C_f and C_b—i.e., the given foreground and new background are opaque rectangular images.

The foreground element C_f can be thought of as a composite of a special background, all points of which have the (almost) constant backing color C_k, and a foreground C_o that is the foreground object in isolation from any background and which is transparent, or partially so, whenever the backing color would show through. We sometimes refer to C_o as the *uncomposited foreground color*. Thus $C_f = f(C_o, C_k)$ expresses the point-by-point foreground color as a given composite f of C_k and C_o. We shall always take $\alpha_k = 1$ for C_k.

We assume that f is the *over* function [9], $C_a + (1 - \alpha_a)\ C_b$, combining C_b with (premultiplied) C_a by amount α_a, $0 \le \alpha_a \le 1$. One of the features of the premultiplied alpha formulation is that the math applied to the three primary color coordinates is the same as that applied to the alpha coordinate. An alpha channel holds the factor α_a at every point in an image, so we will use channel and coordinate synonymously. This facilitates:

The Matting Problem

Given C_f and C_b at corresponding points, and C_k a known backing color, and assuming $C_f = C_o + (1 - \alpha_o)C_k$, determine C_o which then gives composite color $C = C_o + (1 - \alpha_o)C_b$ at the corresponding point, for all points that C_f and C_b share in common.

We shall call C_o—that is, the color, including alpha, of a foreground object—a *solution* to the Matting Problem. Once it is known at each point, we can compute C at each point to obtain the desired result, a composite over a new background presumably more interesting than a single constant color. We shall refer to the equation for C_f above as the Matting Equation. We sometimes refer to an uncomposited foreground object (those pixels with $\alpha_o > 0$) as an *image sprite*, or simply a *sprite*.

PREVIOUS WORK

Blue screen matting has been used in the film and video industries for many years [1], [6], [21] and has been protected under patents [17], [18], [19], [20] until recently. The most recent of these expired July, 1995. Newer patents containing refinements of the process still exist, however. Any commercial use of the blue screen process or extensions should be checked carefully against the extant patents—e.g., [22], [23], [24], [25], [5], [4].

An outstanding inventor in the field is Petro Vlahos, who defined the problem and invented solutions to it in film and then in video. His original film solution is called the *color-difference technique*. His video solution is realized in a piece of equipment, common to the modern video studio, called the Ultimatte®. It is essentially an electronic analog of the earlier color-difference film technique. He was honored in 1995 with an Academy Award for lifetime achievement, shared with his son Paul.

Vlahos makes one observation essential to his work. We shall call it the *Vlahos Assumption*: Blue screen matting is performed on foreground objects for which the blue is related to the green by $B_o \le a_2 G_o$. The usual range allowed by his technique is $.5 \le a_2 \le 1.5$ [20]. That this should work as often as it does is not obvious. We shall try to indicate why in this paper.

The Vlahos formula for α_o, abstracted from the claims of his earliest electronic patent [18] and converted to our notation, is

$$\alpha_o = 1 - a_1(B_f - a_2 G_f),$$

clamped at its extremes to 0 and 1, where the a_i are tuning adjustment constants (typically made available as user controls). We will call this the First Vlahos Form. The preferred embodiment described in the patent replaces B_f above with $\min(B_f, B_k)$, where B_k is the constant backing color (or the minimum such color if its intensity varies, as it often does in practice). In the second step of the Vlahos process, the foreground color is further modified before compositing with a new background by clamping its blue component to $\min(B_f, a_2 G_f)$.

A more general Vlahos electronic patent [20] introduces

$$\alpha_o = 1 - a_1(B_f - a_2(a_5 \max(r, g) + (1 - a_5)\min(r, g))),$$

where $r = a_3 R_f$, $g = a_4 G_f$, and the a_i are adjustment parameters. Clamping again ensures 0 and 1 as limiting values. We shall call this the Second Vlahos Form. Again the blue component of the foreground image is modified before further processing.

A form for α_o from a recent patent [4] (one of several new forms) should suffice to show the continued refinements introduced by Vlahos and his colleagues at Ultimatte Corp.:

$$\alpha_o = 1 - ((B_f - a_1) - a_2 \max(r, g) - \max(a_5(R_f - G_f), a_6(G_f - R_f))),$$

with clamping as before. They have continually extended the number of foreground objects that can be matted successfully.

We believe Vlahos et al. arrived at these forms by many years of experience and experiment and not by an abstract mathematical approach such as presented here. The forms we derive are related to their forms, as we shall show, but more amenable to analysis.

With these patents Vlahos defined and attacked several problems of matting: *blue spill* or *blue flare* (reflection of blue light from the blue screen on the foreground object), *backing shadows* on the blue screen (shadows of the foreground object on the backing, that one wishes to preserve as part of the foreground object), and *backing impurities* (departures of a supposedly pure blue backing screen from pure blue). We shall touch on these issues further in later sections.

Another contribution to matting [8] is based on the following thinking: Find a family of nested surfaces in colorspace that separate the foreground object colors from the backing colors. Each surface, corresponding to a value of α_o, is taken to be the set of colors that are the α_o blend of the foreground and backing colors.

See Fig. 4. The Primatte® device from Photron Ltd., based on this concept, uses a nested family of convex multi-faceted polyhedra (128 faces) as separating surfaces. We shall discuss problems with *separating surface models* in a later section.

THE INTRINSIC DIFFICULTY

We now show that single-film matting, as typically practiced in a film or video effects house, is intrinsically difficult. In fact, we show that there is an infinity of solutions. This implies that there is no algorithmic method for pulling a matte from a given foreground element. There must be a human—or perhaps someday a sufficiently intelligent piece of image processing software—in the loop who "knows" a correct matte when he (she or it) sees one, and he must be provided with a sufficiently rich set of controls that he can successfully "home in" on a good matte when in the neighborhood of one. The success of a matting machine, such as the Ultimatte or Primatte, reduces then to the cleverness of its designers in selecting and providing such a set of controls.

The argument goes as follows: We know that R_f is an interpolation from R_k to R_o with weight α_o, or $R_f = R_o + (1 - \alpha_o)R_k$, and that similar relations hold for G_f and B_f. This is $c_f = c_o + (1 - \alpha_o)c_k$ in our abbreviated notation. (We ignore the relation for α_f because it is trivial.) A complete solution requires R_o, G_o, B_o, and α_o. Thus we have three equations and four unknowns, an incompletely specified problem and hence an infinity of solutions, unsolvable without more information.

There are some special cases where a solution to the matting problem does exist and is simple.

SOLUTION 1: NO BLUE

If c_o is known to contain no blue, $c_o = [R_o \;\; G_o \;\; 0]$, and c_k contains only blue, $c_k = [0 \;\; 0 \;\; B_k]$, then

$$c_f = c_o + (1-\alpha_o)c_k = [R_o \quad G_o \quad (1-\alpha_o)B_k].$$

Thus, solving the $B_f = (1 - \alpha_o) B_k$ equation for α_o gives solution

$$C_o = \left[R_f \quad G_f \quad 0 \quad 1 - \frac{B_f}{B_k} \right], \quad \text{if } B_k \neq 0.$$

This example is exceedingly ideal. The restriction to foreground objects with no blue is quite serious, excluding all grays but black, about two-thirds of all hues, and all pastels or tints of the remaining hues (because white contains blue). Basically, it is only valid for one plane of the 3D RGB colorspace, the RG plane.

The assumption of a perfectly flat and perfectly blue backing color is not realistic. Even very carefully prepared "blue screens" used in cinema special effects as backings have slight spatial brightness variations and also have some red and green impurities (backing impurities). A practical solution for brightness variations, in the case of repeatable shots, is this: Film a pass without the foreground object to produce a record of B_k at each point to be used for computing C_o after a second pass with the object.

We rather arbitrarily chose pure blue to be the backing color. This is an idealization of customary film and video practice (although one sees more and more green screens in video). We shall soon show how to generalize to arbitrary and non-constant backing colors and hence do away with the so-called backing impurities problem in certain circumstances.

SOLUTION 2: GRAY OR FLESH

The matting problem can be solved if c_o is known to be gray. We can loosen this claim to say it can be solved if either R_o or G_o equals B_o. In fact, we can make the following general statement: There is a solution to the matting problem if R_o or $G_o = aB_o + b\alpha_o$, and if c_k is pure blue with $aB_k + b \neq 0$. To show this, we derive the solution C_o for the green case, since the solution for red can be derived similarly.

The conditions, rewritten in color primary coordinates, are:

$$c_f = [R_o \quad aB_o + b\alpha_o \quad B_o + (1-\alpha_o)B_k].$$

Eliminate B_o from the expressions for G_f and B_f to solve for α_o:

$$C_o = \left[R_f \quad G_f \quad B_\Delta + \alpha_o B_k \quad \frac{G_f - aB_\Delta}{aB_k + b} \right], \quad \text{if } aB_k + b \neq 0.$$

Here we have introduced a very useful definition $C_\Delta = C_f - C_k$.

The special case C_o gray clearly satisfies Solution 2, with $a = 1$ and $b = 0$ for both R_o and G_o. Thus it is not surprising that science fiction space movies effectively use the blue screen process (the color-difference technique) since many of the foreground objects are neutrally colored spacecraft. As we know from practice, the technique often works adequately well for desaturated (towards gray) foreground objects, typical of many real-world objects.

A particularly important foreground element in film and video is flesh which typically has color $[d \;\; .5d \;\; .5d]$. Flesh of all races tends to have the same ratio of primaries, so d is the darkening or lightening factor. This is a non-gray example satisfying Solution 2, so it is not surprising that the blue screen process works for flesh.

Notice that the condition $G_o = aB_o + b\alpha_o$, with $^2/_3 \leq a \leq 2$ and $b = 0$, resembles the Vlahos Assumption, $B_o \leq a_2 G_o$. In the special case $b = 0$, our derived expression for α_o can be seen to be of the same form as the First Vlahos Form:

$$\alpha_o = 1 - \frac{1}{B_k}\left(B_f - \frac{1}{a} G_f \right).$$

Thus our B_k is Vlahos' $1/a_1$ and our a is his $1/a_2$. Careful reading shows that $B_k = 1/a_1$ is indeed consistent with [18]. By using these values, it can be seen that Vlahos' replacement of B_f by $\min(B_f, a_2 G_f)$ is just his way of calculating what we call B_o.

The next solution does not bear resemblance to any technique used in the real world. We believe it to be entirely original.

SOLUTION 3: TRIANGULATION

Suppose c_o is known against two different shades of the backing color. Then a complete solution exists as stated formally below. It does not require any special information about c_o. Fig. 1(a-d) demonstrates this *triangulation solution*:

Let B_{k_1} and B_{k_2} be two shades of the backing color—i.e., $B_{k_1} = cB_k$ and $B_{k_2} = dB_k$ for $0 \leq d < c \leq 1$. Assume c_o is known against these two shades. Then there is a solution C_o to the matting problem. N.B., c_{k_2} could be black—i.e., $d = 0$.

The assumption that c_o is known against two shades of B_k is equivalent to the following:

$$\begin{aligned} c_{f_1} &= [R_o \quad G_o \quad B_o + (1-\alpha_o)B_{k_1}] \\ c_{f_2} &= [R_o \quad G_o \quad B_o + (1-\alpha_o)B_{k_2}] \end{aligned}.$$

The expressions for B_{f_1} and B_{f_2} can be combined and B_o eliminated to show $\alpha_o = 1 - \frac{B_{f_1} - B_{f_2}}{B_{k_1} - B_{k_2}}$, where the denominator is not 0 since the two backing shades are different. Then

$$R_o = R_{f_1} = R_{f_2} \qquad G_o = G_{f_1} = G_{f_2} \qquad B_o = \frac{B_{f_2} B_{k_1} - B_{f_1} B_{k_2}}{B_{k_1} - B_{k_2}}$$

completes the solution.

No commonly used matting technique asks that the foreground object be shot against two different backgrounds. For computer controlled shots, it is a possibility but not usually done. If passes of a computer controlled camera are added to solve the problem of nonuniform backing mentioned earlier, then the triangulation solution requires four passes.

Consider the backing shadows problem for cases where the triangulation solution applies. The shadow of a foreground object is part of that object to the extent that its density is independent of the backing color. For a light-emitting backing screen, it would be tricky to perform darkening without changing the shadows of the foreground objects. We will give a better solution shortly.

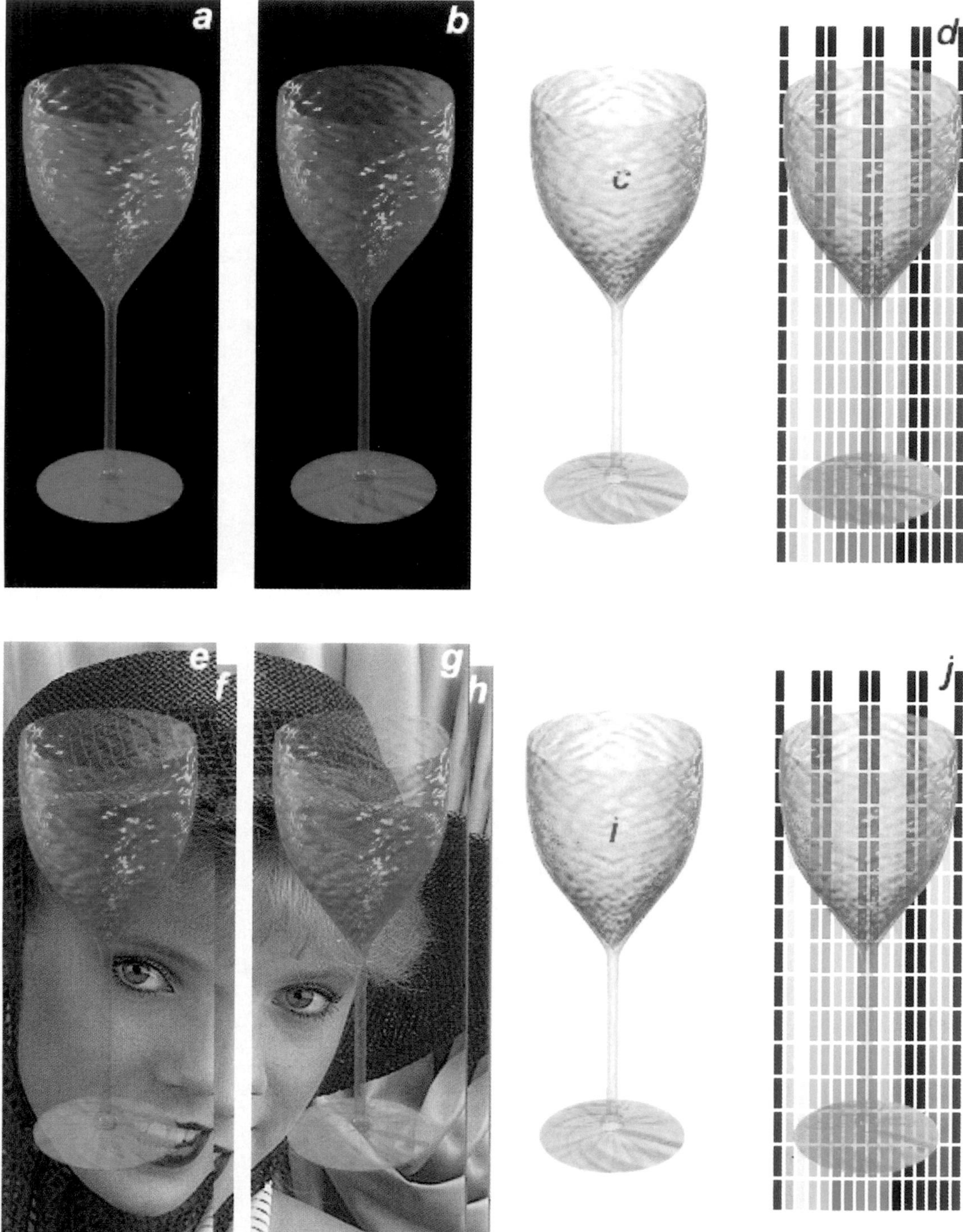

Figure 1. Ideal triangulation matting. (a) Object against known constant blue. (b) Against constant black. (c) Pulled. (d) Composited against new background. (e) Object against a known backing (f). (g) Against a different known backing (h). (i) Pulled. (j) New composite. Note the black pixel near base of (i) where pixels in the two backings are identical and the technique fails.

GENERALIZATIONS

The preceding solutions are all special cases of the generalization obtained by putting the Matting Equation into a matrix form:

$$C_o\begin{bmatrix}1 & 0 & 0 & t_1\\ 0 & 1 & 0 & t_2\\ 0 & 0 & 1 & t_3\\ -R_k & -G_k & -B_k & t_4\end{bmatrix}=\begin{bmatrix}R_\Delta & G_\Delta & B_\Delta & T\end{bmatrix},$$

where a fourth column has been added in two places to convert an underspecified problem into a completely specified problem. Let

$$\bar{t}=\begin{bmatrix}t_1 & t_2 & t_3 & t_4\end{bmatrix}.$$

The matrix equation has a solution C_o if the determinant of the 4x4 matrix is non-0, or

$$t_1R_k+t_2G_k+t_3B_k+t_4=\bar{t}\cdot C_k\neq 0.$$

Standard linear algebra gives, since $\alpha_\Delta=0$ always,

$$\alpha_o=\frac{T-(t_1R_\Delta+t_2G_\Delta+t_3B_\Delta)}{\bar{t}\cdot C_k}=\frac{T-\bar{t}\cdot C_\Delta}{\bar{t}\cdot C_k}=1-\frac{\bar{t}\cdot C_f-T}{\bar{t}\cdot C_k}.$$

Then $c_o=c_\Delta+\alpha_o c_k$ by the Matting Equation.

Thus Solutions 1 and 2 are obtained by the following two choices, respectively, for $\bar{t}$ and T, where the condition on $\bar{t}\cdot C_k$ is given in parentheses:

$$\bar{t}=\begin{bmatrix}0 & 0 & 1 & 0\end{bmatrix};\quad T=0;\quad (B_k\neq 0)$$

$$\bar{t}=\begin{bmatrix}0 & -1 & a & b\end{bmatrix};\quad T=0;\quad (-G_k+aB_k+b\neq 0).$$

The latter condition reduces to that derived for Solution 2 by the choice of pure blue backing color—i.e., $G_k=0$. We state the general result as a theorem of which these solutions are corollaries:

Theorem 1. There is a solution C_o to the Matting Problem if there is a linear condition $\bar{t}\cdot C_o=0$ on the color of the uncomposited foreground object, with $\bar{t}\cdot C_k\neq 0$.

Proof. $T=0$ in the matrix equation above gives $\alpha_o=1-\frac{\bar{t}\cdot C_f}{\bar{t}\cdot C_k}$. ■

The Second Vlahos Form can be shown to be of this form with a_1 proportional to $1/(\bar{t}\cdot C_k)$. Geometrically, Theorem 1 means that all solutions C_o lie on a plane and that C_k does not lie on that plane.

Solution 3 above can also be seen to be a special case of the general matrix formulation with these choices and condition, where by extended definition $C_{\Delta_i}=C_{f_i}-C_{k_i}$, $i=1$ or 2:

$$\bar{t}=\begin{bmatrix}0 & 0 & 1 & -B_{k_2}\end{bmatrix};\quad T=B_{\Delta_2};\quad (B_{k_1}-B_{k_2}\neq 0),$$

with $C_k=\begin{bmatrix}0 & 0 & B_{k_1} & 1\end{bmatrix}$ and right side $\begin{bmatrix}R_{f_1} & G_{f_1} & B_{\Delta_1} & B_{\Delta_2}\end{bmatrix}$. The condition is true by assumption. This solution too is a corollary of a more general one, C_{k_1} not restricted to a shade of blue:

Theorem 2. There is a solution C_o to the Matting Problem if the uncomposited foreground object is known against two distinct backing colors C_{k_1} and C_{k_2}, where C_{k_1} is arbitrary, C_{k_2} is a shade of pure blue, and $B_{k_1}-B_{k_2}\neq 0$.

Proof. This is just the matrix equation above with $\bar{t}$ and T as for Solution 3, but with C_k generalized to $\begin{bmatrix}R_{k_1} & G_{k_1} & B_{k_1} & 1\end{bmatrix}$ and the right side of the matrix equation being $\begin{bmatrix}R_{\Delta_1} & G_{\Delta_1} & B_{\Delta_1} & B_{\Delta_2}\end{bmatrix}$. Thus, as for Solution 3, $\alpha_o=\frac{B_{\Delta_2}-B_{\Delta_1}}{B_{k_1}-B_{k_2}}=1-\frac{B_{f_1}-B_{f_2}}{B_{k_1}-B_{k_2}}$. ■

The following generalization of Theorem 2 utilizes all of the C_{k_2} backing color information. Let the sum of the color coordinates of any color C_a be $\Sigma_a=R_a+G_a+B_a$.

Theorem 3. There is a solution C_o to the Matting Problem if the uncomposited foreground object is known against two distinct backing colors C_{k_1} and C_{k_2}, where both are arbitrary and $\Sigma_{k_1}-\Sigma_{k_2}=(R_{k_1}-R_{k_2})+(G_{k_1}-G_{k_2})+(B_{k_1}-B_{k_2})\neq 0$.

Proof. Change $\bar{t}$ and T in the proof of Theorem 2 to

$$\bar{t}=\begin{bmatrix}1 & 1 & 1 & -\Sigma_{k_2}\end{bmatrix};\quad T=\Sigma_{\Delta_2}.$$

This gives $\bar{t}\cdot C_o=\Sigma_o-\alpha_o\Sigma_{k_2}=\Sigma_{f_2}-\Sigma_{k_2}$, which is exactly what you get by adding together the three primary color equations in the Matting Equation, $C_o-\alpha_oC_{k_2}=C_{\Delta_2}$. The solution is

$$\alpha_o=\frac{\Sigma_{\Delta_1}-\Sigma_{\Delta_2}}{\Sigma_{k_1}-\Sigma_{k_2}}=1-\frac{\Sigma_{f_1}-\Sigma_{f_2}}{\Sigma_{k_1}-\Sigma_{k_2}}$$

$$=1-\frac{(R_{f_1}-R_{f_2})+(G_{f_1}-G_{f_2})+(B_{f_1}-B_{f_2})}{(R_{k_1}-R_{k_2})+(G_{k_1}-G_{k_2})+(B_{k_1}-B_{k_2})},$$

$c_o=c_{\Delta_1}+\alpha_oc_{k_1}=c_{f_1}-(1-\alpha_o)c_{k_1}$, or $c_o=c_{f_2}-(1-\alpha_o)c_{k_2}$. ■

The conditions of Theorem 3 are quite broad—only the *sums* of the primary color coordinates of the two backing colors have to differ. In fact, a constant backing color is not even required. We have successfully used the technique to pull a matte on an object against a backing of randomly colored pixels and then against that same random backing but darkened by 50 percent. Fig. 1(e-j) shows another application of the technique, but Fig. 2 shows more realistic cases. See also Fig. 5.

The triangulation problem, with complete information from the two shots against different backing colors, can be expressed by this non-square matrix equation for an overdetermined system:

$$C_o\begin{bmatrix}1 & 0 & 0 & 1 & 0 & 0\\ 0 & 1 & 0 & 0 & 1 & 0\\ 0 & 0 & 1 & 0 & 0 & 1\\ -R_{k_1} & -G_{k_1} & -B_{k_1} & -R_{k_2} & -G_{k_2} & -B_{k_2}\end{bmatrix}=$$

$$\begin{bmatrix}R_{\Delta_1} & G_{\Delta_1} & B_{\Delta_1} & R_{\Delta_2} & G_{\Delta_2} & B_{\Delta_2}\end{bmatrix}.$$

The Theorem 3 form is obtained by adding the last three columns of the matrix and the last three elements of the vector.

The standard least squares way [7] to solve this is to multiply both sides of the equation by the transpose of the matrix yielding:

$$C_o\begin{bmatrix}2 & 0 & 0 & -(R_{k_1}+R_{k_2})\\ 0 & 2 & 0 & -(G_{k_1}+G_{k_2})\\ 0 & 0 & 2 & -(B_{k_1}+B_{k_2})\\ -(R_{k_1}+R_{k_2}) & -(G_{k_1}+G_{k_2}) & -(B_{k_1}+B_{k_2}) & \Lambda\end{bmatrix}=$$

$$\begin{bmatrix}R_{\Delta_1}+R_{\Delta_2} & G_{\Delta_1}+G_{\Delta_2} & B_{\Delta_1}+B_{\Delta_2} & \Gamma\end{bmatrix}$$

where $\Lambda=R_{k_1}^2+G_{k_1}^2+B_{k_1}^2+R_{k_2}^2+G_{k_2}^2+B_{k_2}^2$ and $\Gamma=-(R_{k_1}R_{\Delta_1}+G_{k_1}G_{\Delta_1}+B_{k_1}B_{\Delta_1}+R_{k_1}R_{\Delta_1}+G_{k_1}G_{\Delta_1}+B_{k_1}B_{\Delta_1})$.

Inverting the symmetric matrix and multiplying both sides by the inverse gives a least squares solution C_o if the determinant of the matrix, $4((R_{k_1} - R_{k_2})^2 + (G_{k_1} - G_{k_2})^2 + (B_{k_1} - B_{k_2})^2)$, is non-0. Thus we obtain our most powerful result:

Theorem 4. There is a solution C_o to the Matting Problem if the uncomposited foreground object is known against two arbitrary backing colors C_{k_1} and C_{k_2} with nonzero distance between them—$(R_{k_1} - R_{k_2})^2 + (G_{k_1} - G_{k_2})^2 + (B_{k_1} - B_{k_2})^2 \neq 0$ (i.e., distinct).

The desired alpha α_o can be shown to be one minus

$$\frac{(R_{f_1} - R_{f_2})(R_{k_1} - R_{k_2}) + (G_{f_1} - G_{f_2})(G_{k_1} - G_{k_2}) + (B_{f_1} - B_{f_2})(B_{k_1} - B_{k_2})}{(R_{k_1} - R_{k_2})^2 + (G_{k_1} - G_{k_2})^2 + (B_{k_1} - B_{k_2})^2}.$$

Figure 2. Practical triangulation matting. (a-b) Two different backings. (c-d) Objects against the backings. (e) Pulled. (f) New composite. (g-i) and (j-l) Same triangulation process applied to two other objects (backing shots not shown). (l) Object composited over another. The table and other extraneous equipment have been "garbage matted" from the shots. See Fig. 5.

The Theorem 3 and 4 expressions for α_o are symmetric with respect to the two backings, reflected in our two expressions for c_o (in the proof of Theorem 3).

Theorems 2 and 3 are really just special cases of Theorem 4. For Theorem 2, the two colors are required to have different blue coordinates. For Theorem 3, they are two arbitrary colors that do not lie on the same plane of constant Σ. In practice we have found that the simpler conditions of Theorem 3 often hold and permit use of computations cheaper than those of Theorem 4.

Theorem 4 allows the use of *very* general backings. In fact, two shots of an object moving across a fixed but varied background can satisfy Theorem 4, as indicated by the lower Fig. 1 example. If the foreground object can be registered frame to frame as it moves from, say, left to right, then the background at two different positions can serve as the two backings.

Notice that the Theorem 3 and 4 techniques lead to a backing shadows solution whereas simple darkening might not work. The additional requirement is that the illumination levels and light-emitting directions be the same for the two backing colors so that the shadows are the same densities and directions.

The overdetermined linear system above summarizes all information about two shots against two different backing colors. A third shot against a third backing color could be included as well, replacing the 4×6 matrix with a 4×9 matrix and the 1×6 right-hand vector with a 1×9 vector. Then the same least squares solution technique would be applied to find a solution for this even more overdetermined problem. Similarly, a fourth, fifth, etc. shot against even more backing colors could be used. An overdetermined system can be subject to numerical instabilities in its solution. We have not experienced any, but should they arise the technique of singular value decomposition [11] might be used.

IMPLEMENTATION NOTES

The Fig. 1(a-d) example fits the criteria of Theorem 2 (actually the Solution 3 special case) perfectly because the given blue and black screen shots were manufactured by compositing the object over perfect blue and black backings. As predicted by the theorem, we were able to extract the original object in its original form, with only small least significant bit errors. Similarly Fig. 1(e-j) illustrates Theorem 3 or 4.

Fig. 2 is a set of real camera shots of real objects in a real studio. Our camera was locked down for the two shots required by Theorem 3 and 4 plus two more required for backing color calibrations as mentioned before. Furthermore, constant exposure was used for the four shots, and a remote-controlled shutter guarded against slight camera movements. The results are good enough to demonstrate the effectiveness of the algorithm but are nevertheless flawed from misregistration introduced during the digitization process—pin registration was not used—and from the foreground objects having different brightnesses relative one another, also believed to be a scanning artifact.

Notice from the Theorem 3 and 4 expressions for α_o that the technique is quite sensitive to brightness and misregistration errors. If the foreground colors differ where they should be equal, then α_o is lowered from its correct value of 1, permitting some object transparency. In general, the technique tends to err towards increased transparency.

Another manifestation of the same error is what we term the "fine line" problem. Consider a thin dark line with bright surroundings in an object shot against one backing, or the complement, a thin bright line in a dark surround. Such a line in slight misregister with itself against the other backing can differ dramatically in brightness at pixels along the line, as seen by our algorithm. The error trend toward transparency will cause the appearance of a fine transparent line in the pulled object.

The conclusion is clear: To effectively use triangulation, pin-registered filming and digitization should be used to ensure positional constancy between the four shots, and very careful monitoring of lighting and exposures during filming must be undertaken to ensure that constant brightnesses of foreground objects are recorded by the film (or other recording medium).

Since triangulation works only for non-moving objects (excluding rigid motions, such as simple translation), it should be possible to reduce brightness variations between steps of the process due to noise by averaging several repeated shots at each step.

A LOWER BOUND

The trouble with the problems solved so far is that the premises are too ideal. It might seem that the problems which have Solutions 1 and 2, and Theorem 1 generalizations, are unrealistically restrictive of foreground object colors. It is surprising that so much real-world work approaches the conditions of these solutions. Situations arising from Solution 3, and Theorems 2-4 generalizations, require a doubling of shots, which is a lot to ask even if the shots are exactly repeatable. Now we return to the general single-background case and derive bounds on α_o that limit the search space for possible solutions.

Any C_o offered as solution must satisfy the physical limits on color. It must be that $0 \le R_o \le \alpha_o$ (since R_o is premultiplied by α_o) and similarly for G_o and B_o. The Matting Equation gives $R_f = R_o + (1 - \alpha_o)R_k$. The inequalities for R_o applied to this expression give

$$(1-\alpha_o)R_k \le R_f \le (1-\alpha_o)R_k + \alpha_o,$$

with the left side being the expression for $R_o = 0$ and the right for $R_o = \alpha_o$. Similar inequalities apply to G_f and B_f. Fig. 3 shows all regions of valid combinations of α_o, R_f, G_f, and B_f using equality in the relationship(s) above as boundaries. The color c_k for this figure is taken to be the slightly impure blue [.1 .2 .98].

The dashed vertical lines in Fig. 3 represent a given c_f—in this figure, [.8 .5 .6]. The dotted horizontal lines represent the minimum α_o for each of R_f, G_f, and B_f which gives a valid R_o, G_o, and B_o, respectively. Let these three α_o's be called α_R, α_G, and α_B. Since only one α_o is generated per color, the following relationship must be true:

$$\alpha_o \ge \max(\alpha_R, \alpha_G, \alpha_B).$$

We shall call the α_o which satisfies this relationship at equality $\alpha_{\min}$, and any $\alpha_o \ge \alpha_{\min}$ will be called a valid one. Notice that although the range of possible α_o's is cut down by this derivation, there are still an infinity of valid ones to choose from, hence an infinity of solutions.

If $R_f > R_k$ as in the Fig. 3 example, then α_R corresponds to $R_o = \alpha_o$, the right side of the inequalities above for R_f and α_o. If $R_f < R_k$ then α_R corresponds to $R_o = 0$, the left side. Thus

$$\alpha_R = \begin{cases} 1-\dfrac{R_f}{R_k}, \text{ if } R_f < R_k \\ \dfrac{R_\Delta}{1-R_k}, \text{ if } R_f > R_k \\ 0, \text{ if } R_f = R_k \end{cases}.$$

In the example of Fig. 3, $\alpha_{\min} \approx .78$. For the special case of pure blue backing, $\alpha_{\min} = \max(R_f, G_f, 1 - B_f)$. So long as a valid α_o

exists, a foreground object color can be derived from the given c_f by $c_o = c_\Delta + \alpha_o c_k$ as before.

AN UPPER BOUND

Tom Porter pointed out (in an unpublished technical memo [10]) that an upper bound could also be established for α_o, by taking lessons from Vlahos.

The Vlahos Assumption, when valid, has $B_o \le a_2 G_o$. The rearrangement of the Matting Equation above for the green channel is

$$G_o = G_f - (1-\alpha_o)G_k\ .$$

Another rearrangement, this time for the blue channel, gives us

$$\alpha_o = 1 + \frac{B_o - B_f}{B_k} \le 1 + \frac{a_2 G_o - B_f}{B_k}\ .$$

Combining these two, by substituting the equation for G_o into the inequality for α_o and solving, gives

$$\alpha_o \le 1 - \frac{B_f - a_2 G_f}{B_k - a_2 G_k}\ ,$$

clamped to [0, 1] if necessary. Recall that $.5 \le a_2 \le 1.5$ typically. Let α_o at equality be α_{max}. Then, in our Fig. 3 example, $a_2 = 1$ yields $\alpha_{max} \approx .87$, which constrains the possible solutions a bit more: $.78 \le \alpha_o \le .87$.

BLUE SPILL

Vlahos tackled the very important blue spill (blue flare) problem of backing light reflecting off the foreground object in [19]. He solved it for an important class of objects, bright whites and flesh tones, by making what we call the Second Vlahos Assumption: Foreground objects have $\max(B_o - G_o, 0) \le \max(G_o - R_o, 0)$. If this is not true, the color is assumed to be either the backing color or flare from it. Object transparency is taken, as before, to be proportional to $B_o - G_o$, and this distinguishes the two cases.

Our statement of the Matting Problem needs to be altered to include the blue spill problem. Our current model says that the foreground color C_f is a linear combination of the uncomposited foreground object color C_o and the backing color C_k, $C_f = C_o + (1 - \alpha_o)C_k$. The Extended Matting Problem would include a term C_s for the backing spill contribution. For example, it might be modeled as a separate foreground object, with its own alpha α_s, in linear combination with the desired foreground object color C_o: $C_f = C_s + (1 - \alpha_s)(C_o + (1 - \alpha_o)C_k)$. Now the problem becomes the more difficult one of determining both C_s and C_o from the given information C_f and C_k.

A simplification is to assume that the spill color is the same as the backing color, $C_s = \alpha_s C_k$. Thus $C_f = (1 - \alpha_s)C_o + (1 - \alpha_o + \alpha_o\alpha_s)C_k$. For brevity, let $C_{\Delta_s} = C_\Delta / (1-\alpha_s)$. Then this spill model can be put into a matrix equation of the same form as before (but notice the $\alpha_s = 1$ singularity):

$$C_o \begin{bmatrix} 1 & 0 & 0 & t_1 \\ 0 & 1 & 0 & t_2 \\ 0 & 0 & 1 & t_3 \\ -R_k & -G_k & -B_k & t_4 \end{bmatrix} = \begin{bmatrix} R_{\Delta_s} & G_{\Delta_s} & B_{\Delta_s} & T \end{bmatrix}.$$

Hence, since $\alpha_{\Delta_s} = 0$ always, the solutions are of the same form as before: $\alpha_o = \dfrac{T - \bar{t}\cdot C_{\Delta_s}}{\bar{t}\cdot C_k}$ and $c_o = c_{\Delta_s} + \alpha_o c_k$. This does not solve the problem since α_s is still unknown. We shall not pursue the spill problem further here but recommend it for future research.

SEPARATING SURFACE PROBLEMS

Fig. 4 illustrates the separating surface approach to the general matting problem. A single plane of colorspace is shown for clarity. A family of three separating surfaces for different values of α_o have been established between the body of backing colors C_k and the body of object colors C_o. A given foreground color C_f is shown at the point of intersection with the $\alpha_o = .5$ locus along the straight line through object colors A and B.

The Vlahos (or Ultimatte) matting solutions can be cast into the separating surface model. In the First Vlahos Form (as well as in our Solutions 1 and 2 and Theorem 1), each dotted line of Fig.

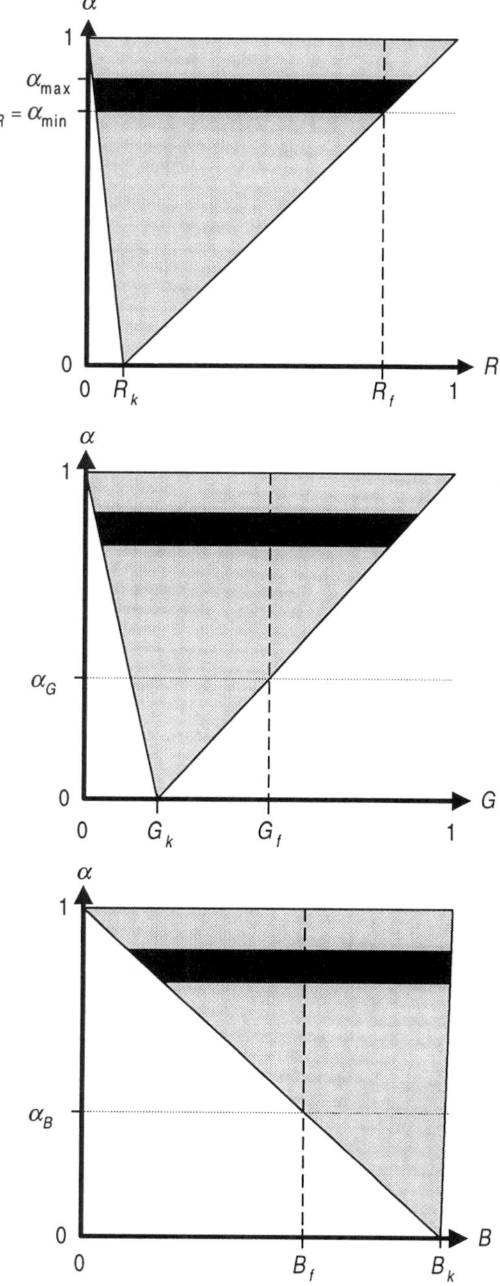

Figure 3. Shaded areas show solution space. Black areas are constrained by upper and lower alpha limits to valid alphas for the given foreground color. Valid alphas for C_o lie along intersection of C_f (dashed lines) with black areas.

4 would simply be a straight line (a plane in RGB). In the Second Vlahos Form it would be a line with two straight segments (two polygons sharing an edge in RGB). The third form simply adds a third segment (polygon) to this shape. The Primatte solution extends this trend to many (up to 128) segments (faces of a convex polyhedron).

Fig. 4 illustrates a general problem with the separating surface model. All mixtures of A with the backing color will be correctly pulled if they indeed exist in the foreground object. However, all mixtures of B with the backing will not be correctly pulled because they have been disguised as mixtures of A.

Another problem is that it is not always possible to have foreground object colors disjoint from backing colors. Another is the assumption that a locus of constant α_o is a surface rather than a volume, connected rather than highly disconnected, and planar or convex.

SUMMARY

The expiration of the fundamental Vlahos patents has inspired us to throw open the very interesting class of constant color matting problems to the computer graphics community. Thus one of our purposes has been to review the problems of the field—the general one of pulling a matte from a constant color shot plus related subproblems such as blue spill, backing impurities, and backing shadows.

The mathematical approach introduced here we believe to be more understandable than the ad hoc approach of the Vlahos patents, the standard reference on blue screen matting. Furthermore, we believe that the treatment here throws light on why the process should work so well as it does in real-world applications (gray, near-gray, and flesh tones), surprising in light of the proof herein that the general problem has an infinity of solutions. Consistent with the lack of a general algorithmic solution is the fact that human interaction is nearly always required in pulling a matte in film or video.

Our principal idea is that an image from which a matte is to be pulled can be represented by a model of two images, an uncomposited foreground object image (a sprite) and a backing color image, linearly combined using the alpha channel of the foreground object. Our main results are deduced from this model. In each case, the expression for the desired alpha channel α_o is a function of the two images in the model, C_f, the given image—a composite by our model—and C_k, the given backing image. This may be compared to the Vlahos expressions for alpha which are functions of the given image C_f only.

We have introduced an algorithmic solution, the triangulation solution, by adding a new step to the blue screen process as usually practiced: Another shot of the foreground object against a second backing color. This *multi-background* technique cannot be used for live actors or other moving foreground objects because of the requirement for repeatability. Whenever it is applicable, however, it is powerful, the only restriction on the two backings being that they be different pixel by pixel. Hence the backing colors do not even have to be constant or pure—the backing impurities problem does not exist. However, to solve the backing shadows problem, illumination level and direction must be the same for both backings, particularly important if they are generated by light emission rather than reflection.

We have bounded the solution space for the general non-algorithmic problem, a new extension to the Vlahos oeuvre. Hopefully, this will inspire further researches into this difficult problem. See the Vlahos patents (including [4] and [5]) for further inspiration.

We have touched on the blue spill (blue flare) problem and suggest that additional research be aimed at this important problem. We have sketched a possible model for this research, generalizing the idea of the given image being a composite of others. In particular, we propose that the idea of modeling blue spill by an additional blue spill image, with its own alpha, might lead to further insight.

Finally, we have briefly reviewed the modeling of the matting problem with separating surface families (cf. [8]), shown how to cast the Vlahos work in this light, and discussed some problems with the general notion. We urge that this class of solutions be further explored and their fundamental problems be elucidated beyond the initial treatment given here.

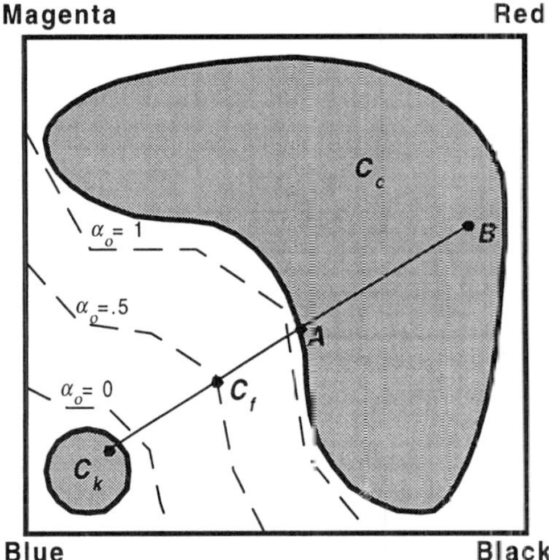

Figure 4. A slice through a (non-convex) polyhedral family of surfaces of constant alpha separating backing colors from foreground object colors. Given color C_f will be interpreted as A with alpha of .5 whereas the object might actually be B with an alpha of .25.

ACKNOWLEDGMENTS

To Tom Porter for his alpha upper limit. To Rob Cook for an early critical reading of [12] and [13] on which much of this paper is based. To Rick Szeliski for use of his automatic image registration software To Jack Orr and Arlo Smith for studio photography and lighting.

REFERENCES

[1] BEYER, W. Traveling Matte Photography and the Blue Screen System. *American Cinematographer*, May 1964, p. 266. The second of a four-part series.

[2] BLINN, J. F. Jim Blinn's Corner: Compositing Part 1: Theory. *IEEE Computer Graphics & Applications*, September 1994, pp. 83-87.

[3] BLINN, J. F. Jim Blinn's Corner: Compositing Part 2: Practice. *IEEE Computer Graphics & Applications*, November 1994, pp. 78-82.

[4] DADOURIAN, A. Method and Apparatus for Compositing Video Images. U. S. Patent 5,343,252, August 30, 1994.

[5] FELLINGER, D. F. Method and Apparatus for Applying Correction to a Signal Used to Modulate a Background Video Signal to be Combined with a Foreground Video Signal. U. S. Patent 5,202,762, April 13, 1993.

[6] FIELDING, R. *The Technique of Special Effects Cinematography*. Focal/Hastings House, London, 3rd edition, 1972, pp. 220-243.

[7] LANCZOS, C. *Applied Analysis*. Prentice Hall, Inc., Englewood Cliffs, NJ, 1964, pp. 156-161.

[8] MISHIMA, Y. A Software Chromakeyer Using Polyhedric Slice. Proceedings of NICOGRAPH 92 (1992), pp. 44-52 (Japanese). See http://206.155.32.1/us/primatte/whitepaper.

[9] PORTER, T. and DUFF, T. Compositing Digital Images. Proceedings of SIGGRAPH 84 (Minneapolis, Minnesota, July 23-27, 1984). In *Computer Graphics* 18, 3 (July 1984), pp. 253-259.

[10] PORTER, T. Matte Box Design. Lucasfilm Technical Memo 63, November 1986. Not built.

[11] PRESS, W. H., TEUKOLSKY, S. A., VETTERLING, W. T., and FLANNERY, B. P. *Numerical Recipes in C*. Cambridge University Press, Cambridge, 1988, p. 59.

[12] SMITH, A. R. Analysis of the Color-Difference Technique. Technical Memo 30, Lucasfilm Ltd., March 1982.

[13] SMITH, A. R. Math of Mattings. Technical Memo 32, Lucasfilm Ltd., April 1982.

[14] SMITH, A. R. Image Compositing Fundamentals. Technical Memo 4, Microsoft Corporation, June 1995.

[15] SMITH, A. R. Alpha and the History of Digital Compositing. Technical Memo 7, Microsoft Corporation, August 1995.

[16] VLAHOS, P. Composite Photography Utilizing Sodium Vapor Illumination. U. S. Patent 3,095,304, May 15, 1958. Expired.

[17] VLAHOS, P. Composite Color Photography. U. S. Patent 3,158,477, November 24, 1964. Expired.

[18] VLAHOS, P. Electronic Composite Photography. U. S. Patent 3,595,987, July 27, 1971. Expired.

[19] VLAHOS, P. Electronic Composite Photography with Color Control. U. S. Patent 4,007,487, February 8, 1977. Expired.

[20] VLAHOS, P. Comprehensive Electronic Compositing System. U. S. Patent 4,100,569, July 11, 1978. Expired.

[21] VLAHOS, P. and TAYLOR, B. Traveling Matte Composite Photography. *American Cinematographer Manual*. American Society of Cinematographers, Hollywood, 7th edition, 1993, pp. 430-445.

[22] VLAHOS, P. Comprehensive Electronic Compositing System. U. S. Patent 4,344,085, August 10, 1982.

[23] VLAHOS, P. Encoded Signal Color Image Compositing. U. S. Patent 4,409,611, October 11, 1983.

[24] VLAHOS, P., VLAHOS, P. and FELLINGER, D. F. Automatic Encoded Signal Color Image Compositing. U. S. Patent 4,589,013, May 13, 1986.

[25] VLAHOS, P. Comprehensive Electronic Compositing System. U. S. Patent 4,625,231, November 25, 1986.

Figure 5. A composite of nine image sprites pulled from studio photographs using the triangulation technique shown in Fig. 2.

Combining Frequency and Spatial Domain Information for Fast Interactive Image Noise Removal

Anil N. Hirani, Takashi Totsuka

Sony Corporation

Abstract

Scratches on old films must be removed since these are more noticeable on higher definition and digital televisions. Wires that suspend actors or cars must be carefully erased during post production of special effects shots. Both of these are time consuming tasks but can be addressed by the following image restoration process: given the locations of noisy pixels to be replaced and a prototype image, restore those noisy pixels in a natural way. We call it image noise removal and this paper describes its fast iterative algorithm. Most existing algorithms for removing image noise use either frequency domain information (e.g low pass filtering) or spatial domain information (e.g median filtering or stochastic texture generation). The few that do combine the two domains place the limitation that the image be band limited and the band limits be known.

Our algorithm works in both spatial and frequency domains without placing the limitations about band limits, making it possible to fully exploit advantages from each domain. While global features and large textures are captured in frequency domain, local continuity and sharpness are maintained in spatial domain. With a judicious choice of operations and domains in which they work, our dual-domain approach can reconstruct many contiguous noisy pixels in areas with large patterns while maintaining continuity of features such as lines. In addition, the image intensity does not have to be uniform. These are significant advantages over existing algorithms. Our algorithm is based on a general framework of projection onto convex sets (POCS). Any image analysis technique that can be described as a closed convex set can be cleanly plugged into the iteration loop of our algorithm. This is another important advantage of our algorithm.

CR Categories: I.3.3 [Computer Graphics]: Picture / Image Generation; Display Algorithms; I.3.6 [Computer Graphics]: Methodology and Techniques – Interaction techniques; I.4.4 [Image Processing]: Restoration; I.4.9 [Image Processing]: Applications.

Additional Keywords: scratch and wire removal, projections onto convex sets, POCS.

{hirani | totsuka}@av.crl.sony.co.jp
Research Center, Sony Corporation
6-7-35 Kitashinagawa Shinagawa-ku, Tokyo 141, Japan

1 INTRODUCTION

The proliferation of television channels and increasing use of multimedia viewing platforms means that older films are likely to see increased use. In addition, higher definition and digital television formats mean that imperfections in old film stock are going to become more noticeable. Removal of scratches from old films and photographs is one motivation for this paper.

Another motivation comes from needs of film and video post production. In some special effects scenes in films, actors or objects are suspended from wires. These wires are later removed in post production either by using an optical process or by processing the digitized film. The digital process is much more commonly used now. As a result, increasing the efficiency of tools for digital wire removal has become important. All these factors indicate the need for efficient and accurate tools for removing scratch, wire and other unwanted noise from images.

All these problems can be addressed by the following image restoration process.

> Given *(i)* the locations of noisy pixels and *(ii)* a prototype (sample) image, restore those noisy pixels in a *natural* way.

By *natural*, we mean that the continuity of intensity and features (e.g., textures, lines) with the surrounding area is maintained. For the scratch removal and the wire removal applications described above, pixels to be restored are those under a scratch or a wire, and the sample image is usually taken from a nearby region. In this paper, we refer to this image restoration process as "image noise removal".

Although image restoration is not a new concept, existing noise removal algorithms have difficulty with noise which *(i)* consists of many contiguous pixels and *(ii)* is in a textured area of image or areas with prominent lines. Note that by *texture* we mean not only small stochastic texture but also small patterns like fabric texture as shown in Fig. 10(b). In addition there can be prominent systematic lines or lines placed randomly in the image. The brick wall in Fig. 10(a) and the stone wall in Fig. 10(c) are examples. Our algorithm for removal of noise is based on the theory of projections onto convex sets. Ours is a fast iterative algorithm that uses the available information from both frequency and spatial domain.

The pixels determined by the algorithm to replace the noise are *(a)* as sharp as the surrounding area *(b)* maintain continuity of prominent lines running across the noise pixels and *(c)* have a texture matching the surrounding texture. While some previous algorithms were able to remove such noise from images with stochastic texture or small regularly patterned textures, ours works on those as well as the more difficult cases of systematic or randomly placed prominent lines. To our knowledge it is the first application of POCS for interactive image noise removal. Ours is also the first image noise removal algorithm that combines frequency and spatial domain information in an extendible way. It does this by using the clean and well understood formalism of POCS and without requiring that the images be band limited. In addition it works even when the noisy pixels are contiguous and numerous. Another key

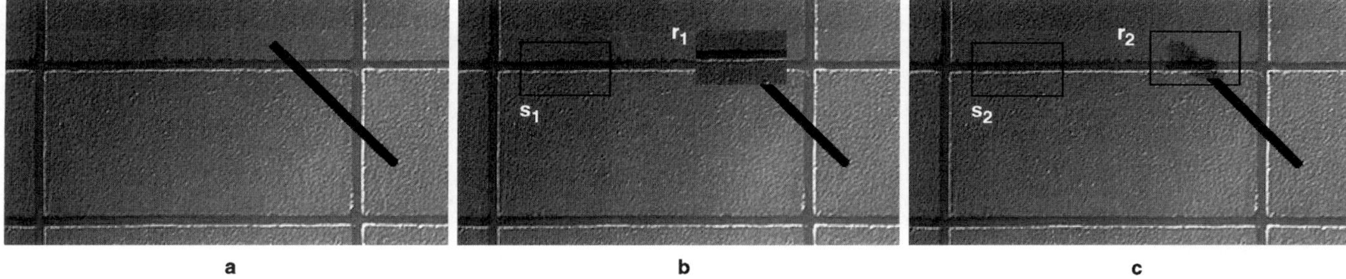

Figure 1: Problems with copying from another area of image. (a) Image with noise (noise is the black diagonal line). (b) The area s_1 has been copied into the area r_1 in an attempt to cover up the noise. Note the alignment and shading mismatch. The horizontal "cement" line appears broken in r_1 now and the area is darker than surrounding. (c) Using a cloning brush the area s_2 has been sampled and copied carefully into r_2 to maintain alignment of the horizontal cement line. But such a tool cannot solve the problems of mismatched intensity. The cloning source is darker than the destination area. Results of order statistics non linear filters like median and results of low pass filters are not shown here. But they do not work on images and types of noise shown here. See text for detail.

advantage of our algorithm is that the image intensity does not have to be uniform across the image.

The rest of the paper is organized as follows. Section 2 summarizes related previous works. Following a brief overview of POCS in section 3, our algorithm is described in section 4. Section 5 shows results of our algorithm and section 6 gives conclusions and possible future directions.

2 PREVIOUS WORK

Previous work on image noise removal can be divided into intra-frame and inter-frame techniques depending on where the information needed for removal comes from. Inter-frame algorithms copy needed pixels from preceding or succeeding frames. They may compensate for motion of object or camera by tracking key points of an image. Inter-frame methods fail when scratches run across many frames (such scratches are common because of the vertical motion of the film through projectors) or when there is too much camera activity. In either of these cases, the needed pixels cannot be found easily in the preceding or succeeding frames.

This paper describes an intra-frame algorithm assuming that other frames do not have the needed pixels. Previous intra-frame methods can be further classified as follows based on which information they use.

1. Use frequency domain information only (e.g low pass filter).
2. Use spatial domain information only
   (a) Median and similar order statistics filters.
   (b) Spatial statistical texture synthesis.
   (c) Cloning by copying pixels.
3. Use spatial and frequency domain information
   (a) Projections onto convex sets for band limited images.
   (b) Matrix algorithms for band limited images.
   (c) Spatial and frequency based statistical texture synthesis.

2.1 Frequency Domain Only

Frequency domain algorithms such as low pass filtering can capture global structure of the image but lose local control (line continuity, sharpness). As a result lines and other details become blurred. Since human visual system is very sensitive to details of an image like those conveyed by the lines, the result is unacceptable for removing noise that consists of many contiguous pixels. We have not shown results of low pass filtering here because such filters perform very poorly for the kind of noise and images shown in Fig. 10 (many contiguous noisy pixels in textured areas or in textured areas with prominent lines).

2.2 Spatial Domain Only

One problem shared by all spatial-only methods is that they have local control and information but do not have any information about the global structure of the image. The limitation to local neighborhood is due to practical computational constraints in some cases. In addition, some of these methods like median filtering etc. are inherently incapable of using the global information meaningfully.

Cloning tools of popular commercial image manipulation programs allow copying from another area of the image using brush like strokes. However, aligning reconstructed lines with existing lines by this method is time consuming and error prone. An even bigger problem is when the image has uneven intensity due to lighting conditions or inter reflections. In such cases, finding the same intensity source area can be difficult.

Fig. 1 demonstrates these problems with copying from another area of the image. Fig. 1(b) shows how the shading as well as the alignment can be different between source (s_1) and destination (r_1) areas. Fig. 1(c) shows how careful use of a manual cloning tool can somewhat ameliorate the alignment problem in this case. But without using the frequency domain information, such a tool can do nothing about shading mismatch as shown in the figure.

A recent survey of median and similar non-linear order statistics filters describes the advantages and shortcomings of these [7]. The problem with order statistics filters is when not enough correct information is available for meaningful order statistics. This is typically the case when numerous contiguous pixels are noisy.

Spatial domain texture synthesis algorithms [5] have shown remarkable results for stochastic type or small regular texture. However, these methods fail when the image has long range structure as in the image of brick wall in Fig. 10(a). The computational cost increases prohibitively for long range image structure because such algorithms use second order statistics.

2.3 Spatial And Frequency Domains

In the case of texture synthesis it is possible to use multi-resolution directional filters and then work with only single order statistics (histograms) as in [4]. This could be considered a spatial and frequency domain algorithm. However this method works only for stochastic texture or small regular texture. In addition [4] is not a noise removal algorithm. It is designed for generating large texture areas from sample images. It cannot be used to generate pixels that maintain continuity of prominent lines crossing noise pixels while retaining the noise free pixels.

Gerchberg-Papoulis and related algorithms [6, 2] are POCS based algorithms that use frequency and spatial domain information. However, they work only for band limited images and the

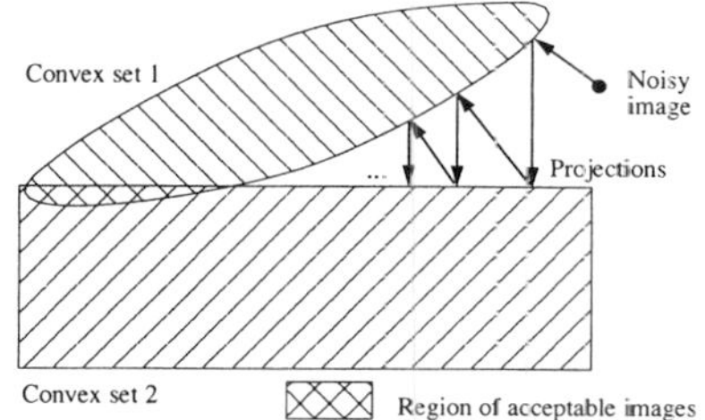

Figure 2: Pictorial representation of POCS. See section 3 for details.

band limits must be known. In addition, recent extensions like [10] require expensive calculations of lines that intersect noise pixels. In other recent work [1] shows how to reduce band-limited interpolation and extrapolation problems for finite-dimensional signals to solution of a set of linear equations. Further, they show that the corresponding matrix is positive-definite with a spectral radius less than 1. The authors then derive properties of convergence of algorithms for different types of noises. Another matrix based method is [9]. These methods require that the image be band limited and the limits be known.

3 PROJECTIONS ONTO CONVEX SETS

Papoulis [6] introduced an algorithm for reconstructing band limited signals by alternating between signal and transform domains and applying the constraints of each domain. The constraints are preservation of known pixel values and enforcement of band limits. This approach was later generalized and given a geometric interpretation. A further generalization [11, 8] has come to be known as the method of projections onto convex sets (POCS). It allows the use of *any* information about the image (or any other signal) as long as the information can be represented as a closed convex set. Although the POCS theory was developed in the context of Hilbert spaces, for digital image restoration, it is convenient to restrict our attention to finite dimensional spaces. This space might be, for example, the space of all $M \times N$ complex matrices where the image has M rows and N columns.

Given a set $\mathcal{C}$ in such a space, $x, y \in \mathcal{C}$, we say the $\mathcal{C}$ is convex iff for any $0 \leq \mu \leq 1, \mu x + (1-\mu)y \in \mathcal{C}$. $\mathcal{C}$ is closed if it contains all its limit points. See [11] for details. We'll use the words *closed convex set* and *constraints* interchangeably since the only constraints we'll be working with will select closed convex sets from a larger set. Projection onto a convex set consists of finding an image satisfying the constraint and "closest" to the image being projected. Intuitively, this can be thought of as making the least possible change to satisfy the constraints. See Fig. 2 for a pictorial representation of POCS.

Repeated projection onto all the convex sets is guaranteed to find an image that satisfies all the constraints if at least one such image exists. See the classic Youla and Webb paper [11] for more details. The advantages of POCS come from the fact that finding a direct projection onto the desired intersection is usually very difficult and expensive, while an efficient projection onto each set is more likely to be found. This is why formulating and solving a problem as POCS can be quite attractive computationally. Note that POCS is a general algorithm, with potential applications in many areas besides image restoration.

4 OUR ALGORITHM

The Fourier transform is an integration over the entire signal. After a transform, many of the essential global features of an image become localized, i.e come closer in the spectrum. These can include repeating patterns, overall image intensity, slow variation in intensity due to inter reflection or shading etc. On the other hand, rapidly varying stochastic texture or sharpness of lines and edges appear scattered in the spectrum. These are features that are localized in the spatial domain.

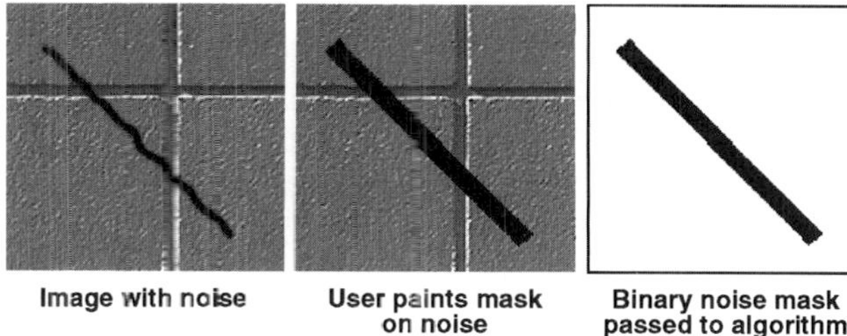

Figure 3: The creation of noise mask for algorithm A1. Left image shows the actual noise (the dark uneven line running diagonally). Middle image shows the image with a binary mask that user has painted over the noise, to cover the noise. This does not have to be a straight line or rectangle, although it happens to be so in this case. The right most image shows the binary mask that will be passed to the algorithm. The middle image will become the r_0 input of the algorithm. See section 4 and Fig. 4 for details.

Clearly there is a need to combine these two for noise removal and texture synthesis. As we will show, POCS is a way of doing this in a clean and extendible fashion. In this section we first describe our basic algorithm A1, which combines the frequency and spatial domains in a POCS framework. Then we show how the use of POCS allows us to easily and cleanly extend A1 to solve important practical problems. The efficiency of the algorithm comes from the fact that each iteration requires fast operations on small subimages, not on the entire image.

4.1 Information Needed

No algorithm can restore an image or generate new texture without information, every algorithm needs some hint. Existing algorithms take a sample subimage (can be the entire image in some cases), which is usually taken from nearby pixels, analyze it, and extract hint information.

Our algorithm is no exception. It also needs some hint. In our case, a neighborhood of the noise (called repair subimage) is selected by the user to provide hint about the local spatial information. A nearby or similar subimage (called sample subimage) is selected by the user to provide a hint for the frequency information. The noise is located by the user creating a binary mask that covers it completely (the mask can be larger than the actual noise). Example of binary noise mask can be seen in Fig. 3. The black line in the noisy images in Fig. 10 can also be thought of as the noise mask covering the actual noise underneath. The algorithm starts with these images as the noisy image input.

This does not necessarily mean we need more information. We use two subimages, one for extracting global features, and one for maintaining local continuity. The algorithm does not place any restriction on choosing the location of the sample subimage. If these pieces of information can be obtained from one place, the sample and the repair subimages can overlap as in several subimages shown in Fig. 5 and 7. Or they can be far apart as in the case of some subimages in the brick wall, the first image in Fig. 6.

4.2 Base Algorithm (A1)

Fig. 4 gives a flowchart of the base algorithm A1. First, the global features are restored. This is best done in frequency domain by cor-

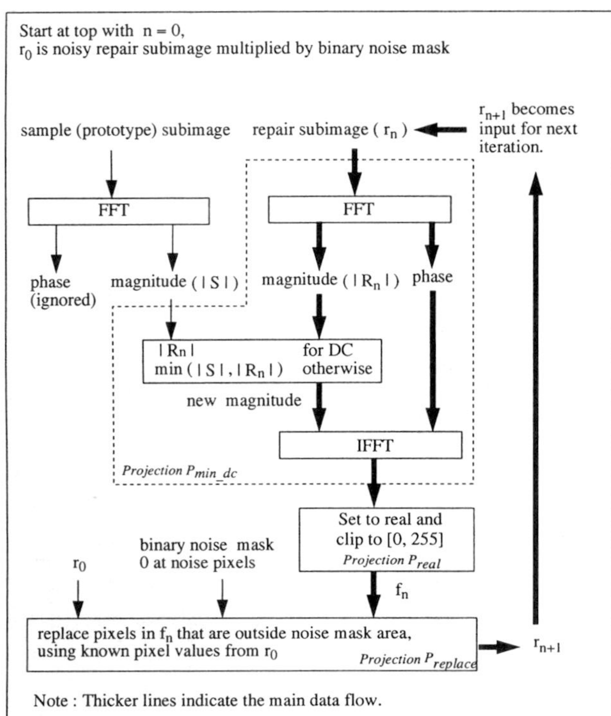

Figure 4: Details of our base algorithm A1. See section 4 for details.

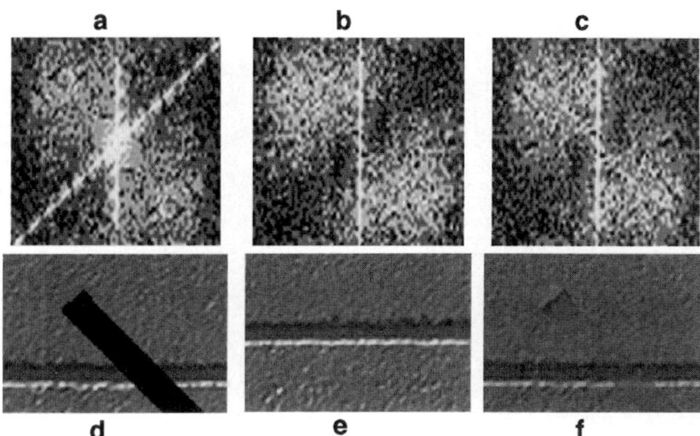

Figure 5: Part of one iteration of A1 in spatial and frequency domains. (a)-(c) in first row show magnitudes of the Fourier transforms; (a) Repair subimage with binary noise mask ; (b) Sample subimage ; (c) Minimum of the first two, except at DC (center of FT) where the value from first one is used. The high energy in (a) due to the noise mask is seen as a diagonal white brightness. This has been considerably reduced in (c). Note that (a) and (b) are similar, except for the high energy due to the noise mask. This is because the repair and sample subimages are approximately translated versions of each other. (d)-(f) in second row show corresponding spatial domain data. See section 4.2.1 for details.

recting the spectrum magnitude. The first step is to Fourier transform the repair and sample subimages. Since the repair-spectrum is corrupted due to noise, the sample-spectrum is used as a template for improving the repair-spectrum. It is very important to use this sample information correctly and this is where the theory of convex projections is important. The information must be represented as a convex set and an orthogonal projection to this set must be used. In addition this must be an efficient projection.

Several "obvious" ways of using the sample-spectrum are actually incorrect, in that they will yield algorithms that diverge because of non convexity. For example, one may think of using the sample spectrum to replace the repair spectrum completely. The practical objection to this is that good information is thrown away along with the bad. Theoretically too, this is unworkable because replacing the spectrum magnitude is not a projection onto a convex set.

Another plausible improvement might be to use a mixture of the two spectra, perhaps weighted by an α and $1-\alpha$ respectively, where α is chosen by the user. This too leads to a diverging algorithm which is incapable of noise removal. Again the reason is non convexity of the underlying set. Other plausible choices like using the high peaks of the sample spectrum etc. are also incorrect due to the same reason.

Before we start the description of our projections and convex sets, a note about notation. In the following equations r_0 is the starting repair subimage multiplied by the binary noise mask and s is the sample subimage (thus these are real matrices). r is an arbitrary complex matrix. r_0, s and r all have the same dimension. R and S are the Fourier transforms of r and s respectively i.e in a typical implementation $R = \text{FFT}(r)$, $S = \text{FFT}(s)$ where FFT stands for the Fast Fourier Transform operation. IFFT is the inverse FFT.

4.2.1 *Using Global Frequency Information*

The first projection operation that we use

$$\mathcal{P}_{\textit{min-dc}}(r) = \text{IFFT}(M_S e^{i \text{ phase}(R)}). \tag{1}$$

involves M_S which is nearly a MIN operation, hence the name $\mathcal{P}_{\textit{min-dc}}$. The M_S in the above equation is

$$M_S(r) = \begin{cases} \min(|R(u,v)|, |S(u,v)|) & \text{if } (u,v) \neq (0,0) \\ |R(0,0)| & \text{if } u = 0, v = 0 \end{cases} \tag{2}$$

Noise in general adds magnitude to the spectrum. Taking MIN effectively reshapes the repair spectrum into the sample spectrum. Our projection, $\mathcal{P}_{\textit{min-dc}}$ has this nice property, and it is a projection onto a closed convex set (see below). M_S defined in Eq.2 is a kind of minimum taking operation on $|R(u,v)|$ and $|S(u,v)|$. The only exception is at DC, $u = 0, v = 0$ where the value of $|R(0,0)|$ is retained. The motivation for not modifying the DC value of the repair-spectrum is that it contains the value of the overall repair subimage intensity.

Also note that the phase is retained in Eq. 1, i.e while reshaping spectrum magnitude we leave the phase of the repair spectrum untouched. It turns out that the phase is reconstructed automatically over several iterations as in the phase reconstruction algorithms used in astronomy and other fields [3]. Phase reconstruction results in the automatic alignment of global features, e.g the alignment of the "cement" line in subimage r_a in Fig. 6. Doing this in frequency domain is easy. In spatial domain, an alignment would have required expensive block matching.

The underlying set

$$\mathcal{C}_{\textit{min-dc}} = \{r : |R(u,v)| \leq |S(u,v)|, (u,v) \neq (0,0)\}. \tag{3}$$

is closed and convex and this can be proved similarly to proof on pp. 86 of [11] after making straightforward adjustments to go to the discrete case. In that proof, set $M(\omega_1, \omega_2) = S$ and $\Delta = \{(\omega_1, \omega_2) \neq (0,0)\}$. Note that $\mathcal{P}_{\textit{min-dc}}$ is a projection because it makes the least change possible to make its input satisfy $\mathcal{C}_{\textit{min-dc}}$.

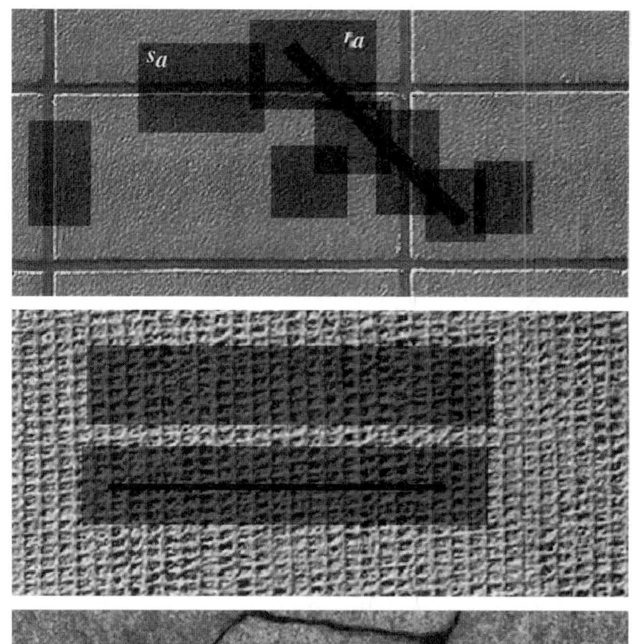

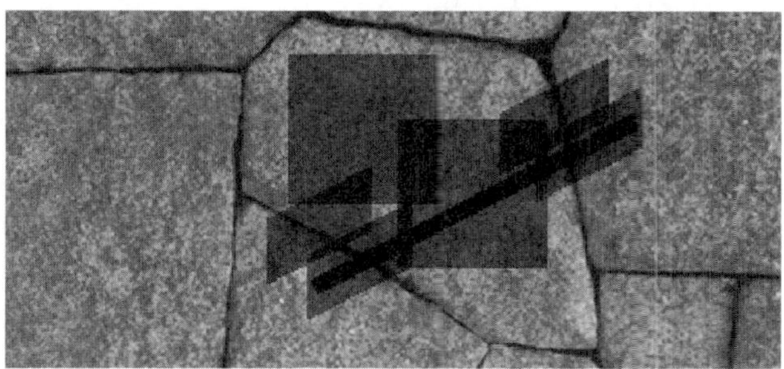

Figure 6: Repair and sample subimages used for examples in Fig. 10(a)-(c) with algorithm A1. Black line is scratch, sample and repair subimages are shown as dark patches. outlines. Prominent lines in sample and repair subimage don't have to be aligned. See e.g the thick horizontal line between bricks in s_a and r_a.

Thus the complete operation $\mathcal{P}_{min\text{-}dc}(r)$ consists of *(i)* taking an FFT of r *(ii)* creating a new spectrum magnitude by taking a minimum of $|R|$ and $|S|$ at all frequencies except DC where $|R(0,0)|$ is retained and and retaining the phase of R and, *(iii)* taking an IFFT using the new magnitude and the phase of R unchanged. See Fig. 4.

As described above, this projection $\mathcal{P}_{min\text{-}dc}$ thus has two purposes – to reshape the spectrum magnitude to match the prototype in order to get the global information correct and to align the prominent global features like prominent lines correctly. See Fig. 5 to see effect of one application of $\mathcal{P}_{min\text{-}dc}$ in frequency and spatial domains (for the purpose of displaying, Fig. 5(f) is actually shown after clipping the output of $\mathcal{P}_{min\text{-}dc}$ to real values between 0 and 255).

4.2.2 *Using Local Spatial Information*

At the end of $\mathcal{P}_{min\text{-}dc}$ (Fig. 4) we are back in spatial domain. The result is now closer to the answer. But since we modified the spectrum magnitude it is possible that after IFFT we now have imaginary component in the image matrix. Some values may also be outside the feasible range of $[0, 255]$. To bring the values back into the feasible range, the values of the spatial domain matrix are made real and clipped to $[0, 255]$. In addition, since the operation $\mathcal{P}_{min\text{-}dc}$ was in frequency domain it affects even the pixels outside of the scratch. These must now be corrected in spatial domain. This is done simply by copying the known pixel values around the noise from the original repair subimage. These two rather simple projections are given below as equations, along with the closed convex sets. Proof of their convexity is simple and can be found in [11].

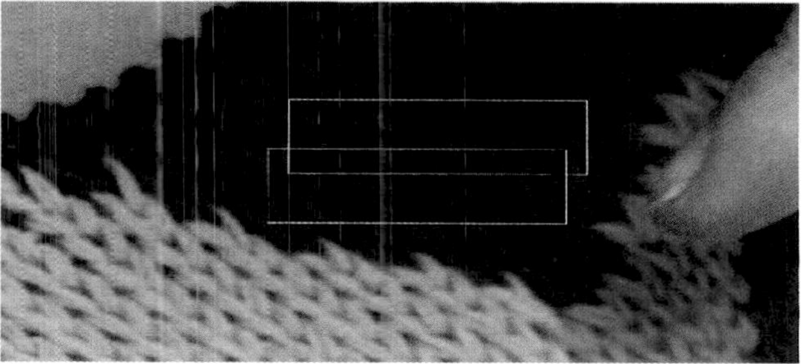

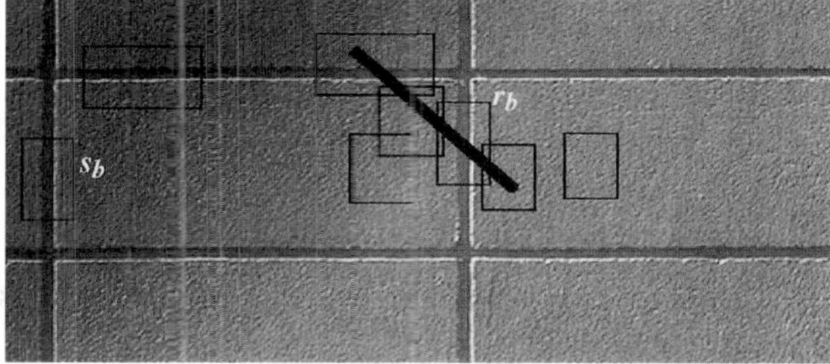

Figure 7: Repair and sample subimages used for examples in Fig. 10 (d) and (e) for algorithm A2 and A3 respectively. Black line is scratch, sample and repair subimages are shown as white or black outlines. For A3 (and to a lesser extent, for all algorithms), the repair and sample subimages can have very different shading. See for example s_b and r_b.

The convex set corresponding to the clipping to real values in $[0, 255]$ is

$$\mathcal{C}_{real} = \{r : r(j,k) \in \Re, 0 \le r(j,k) \le 255\}. \quad (4)$$

The corresponding projection $\mathcal{P}_{real}(q)$ clips the input to a real value between 0 and 255.

Let W be the set of coordinate pairs where the binary noise mask is 0, i.e W is the set of locations under the noise mask pixels. The convex set corresponding to known pixel replacement is

$$\mathcal{C}_{rep} = \{r : r(j,k) = r_0(j,k), (j,k) \notin W\}. \quad (5)$$

Let w be the binary mask which is 0 at noise pixel locations and 1 otherwise. Then the appropriate projection corresponding to the convex set $\mathcal{C}_{rep}$ is

$$\mathcal{P}_{rep}(r) = r(1-w) + r_0 w. \quad (6)$$

4.2.3 *Iterations*

After applying $\mathcal{P}_{min\text{-}dc}$, $\mathcal{P}_{real}$ and $\mathcal{P}_{rep}$ we come to the end of the first iteration of A1. This process is then repeated. Thus the algorithm A1 can be written as

$$\begin{aligned} r_0 &= \text{initial repair subimage} \times \text{noise mask} \quad (7)\\ r_{n+1} &= \mathcal{P}_{rep}\mathcal{P}_{real}\mathcal{P}_{min\text{-}dc}\, r_n. \quad (8)\end{aligned}$$

In the current implementation, the user sets the number of iterations. It is easy to implement other termination criteria. The algorithm is fast because it usually converges in under 10 iterations and each iteration requires 1 FFT, 1 IFFT and copying, all performed on a small neighborhood of the noise and *not* on the entire image. Results of A1 are shown in Fig. 10(a)-(c).

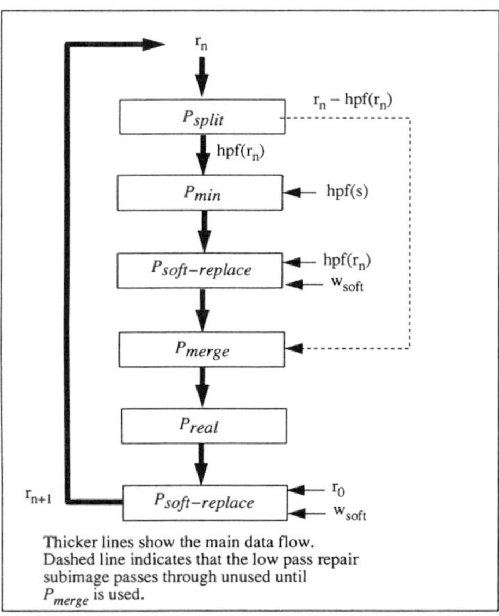

Figure 8: Algorithm A3. See section 4.4 for details.

4.3 Soft Scratch Algorithm (A2)

In this and Sec. 4.4 we present two extensions to the basic algorithm A1. Our purpose in doing this is twofold. First, these two extensions solve some practical shortcomings of algorithm A1. Equally important, we show that by working in a POCS framework and using a dual-domain approach, important and substantial extensions can be made fairly easily. Hopefully, these extensions will also serve as guides for someone trying to extend the basic algorithm A1 in other ways.

The continuity of large prominent lines crossing the binary noise mask is generated by $\mathcal{P}_{min\text{-}dc}$. But a transition in the local high frequency texture near the noise mask edge might be noticeable to human eye since the mask is sharp edged. It would be useful to use a soft edged mask for the noise to fix this potential problem.

This is easy to do with a slight modification in A1. In the final projection $\mathcal{P}_{rep}$ in each iteration of A1, use a soft edged noise mask instead of a binary mask. This new projection that we will call $\mathcal{P}_{soft\text{-}rep}$ can be written as

$$\mathcal{P}_{\text{soft-rep}}(r) = r(1 - w_{\text{soft}}) + r_0 w_{\text{soft}} \quad (9)$$

where w_{soft} is a soft edged noise mask. The underlying convex set $\mathcal{C}_{soft\text{-}rep}$ can be written as

$$\mathcal{C}_{\text{soft-rep}} = \{r(j,k) : r_0(j,k) = p(j,k)w_\alpha + q(j,k)(1 - w_\alpha)\} \quad (10)$$

where q is an arbitrary image and w_α is 1 outside binary noise mask, 0 inside binary noise mask and $\alpha(d)$ in soft noise mask edge region, and $0 <= \alpha(d) <= 1$ is a nice smoothly rising function like 1 - gaussian, depending on the distance d from the binary noise mask edge. Thus the algorithm can be now written similar to A1 using $\mathcal{P}_{soft\text{-}rep}$ instead of $\mathcal{P}_{rep}$. Showing that $\mathcal{C}_{soft\text{-}rep}$ is convex is straightforward using simple algebra. The results of using A2 on a color image by applying it to the r, g, b channels is shown in Fig. 10 (d). More explanation of results is in section 5.

4.4 Split Frequency Algorithm (A3)

Notice that the example images used for A1 and A2 have had nearly uniform shading across the image, as in Fig. 10 (a)-(d). The next extension we describe removes this restriction of uniform shading. The resulting algorithm is A3, shown in Fig. 8. The results of this algorithm A3 are shown in Fig. 10 (e). A comparison between A1 and A3 on a very unevenly shaded image is shown in Fig. 9. Although it may not be visible in the final printed paper, the circled area shows remnants of noise in the left image on which A1 has been applied. This problem is absent in the result of A3 on right in Fig. 9.

Note that overall variation in shading of an image is a global feature and so we choose the frequency domain to attack this problem. The basic idea is very simple – ignore the shading (which is a very large, global feature) by ignoring the low frequency components. Then, to the high frequency image, apply the projections similar to A2 followed by merging the effect of the shading. Now we go through the algorithm step by step. As shown in Fig. 8, the algorithm can be written as

$$r_0 = \text{initial repair subimage} \times \text{noise mask} \quad (11)$$

$$r_{n+1} = \mathcal{P}_{\text{soft-rep}}\mathcal{P}_{\text{real}}\mathcal{P}_{\text{merge}}\mathcal{P}_{\text{soft-rep}}\mathcal{P}_{\text{min}}\mathcal{P}_{\text{split}}\, r_n. \quad (12)$$

The main new projections are $\mathcal{P}_{split}$ and $\mathcal{P}_{merge}$. The first of these splits the input image r into two images, a high pass filtered $\text{hpf}(r)$ and a low pass filtered $r - \text{hpf}(r)$. We use a gaussian filter to create $\text{hpf}(r)$ and $r - \text{hpf}(r)$. $\mathcal{P}_{merge}$ does the reverse of $\mathcal{P}_{split}$ by simply adding the output of previous projections, which is the *processed* high pass filtered component of the repair subimage, with the *unprocessed* low pass filtered repair subimage as shown in Fig. 8.

Note that since the lower frequencies are being ignored during processing we can simplify $\mathcal{P}_{min\text{-}dc}$ to $\mathcal{P}_{min}$ by simplifying M_S (2) of algorithm A1 to $M_S(r) = \min(|R(u,v)|, |S(u,v)|)$. Thus now we are taking MIN across the entire spectrum, including the DC unlike A1.

After this, a replace operation will be performed. Since we are using a high pass filtered repair subimage, the effect of the noise will be seen outside the noise mask after $\mathcal{P}_{split}$. Therefore when we replace the known pixel values, we should use a better estimate in each iteration. This is done by using the latest $\text{hpf}(r_n)$ instead of $\text{hpf}(r_0)$ as input for $\mathcal{P}_{soft\text{-}rep}$. Thus the first $\mathcal{P}_{soft\text{-}rep}$ of A3 is similar to equation 9 of A2 except that $\text{hpf}(r_n)$ is used instead of r_0 in equation 9. After merging the result with the low frequency image using $\mathcal{P}_{merge}$, $\mathcal{P}_{real}$ is applied which is the same as in A1 or A2. Finally the known values are replaced using the original r_0 just as in A1 or A2. It is easy to show convexity of the underlying sets for $\mathcal{P}_{merge}$ and $\mathcal{P}_{split}$ using linearity of the Fourier transform.

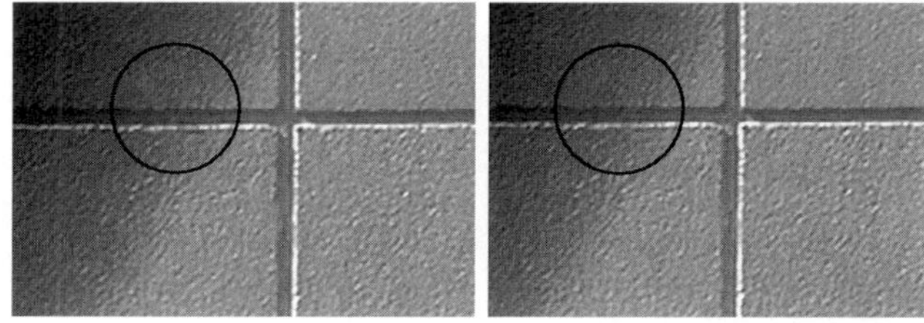

Figure 9: Comparison of A1 and A3 on an image with intensity variation. In the circled area some leftover noise is visible in the A1 result on the left whereas the A3 result on the right is cleaner [the difference may not be obvious in the final printed version]. See section 4.4 for details.

5 RESULTS

Fig. 10 shows noise removal using our algorithms A1, A2 and A3. The images shown have stochastic and regular textures and prominent systematic and random lines. The black line running across the first image of each group of images in Fig. 10 is the noise. (a)-(c) show the result of algorithm A1, (d) shows result of A2 and (e) shows result of A3.

The first four images, shown as group (a) are – clockwise from top left – image with noise, image after 1, 2 and 10 iterations of our algorithm A1. The other groups shown in (b)-(e) show only the noisy image and the image after 10 iterations of our algorithms.

The sample and repair subimages used for (a)-(c) are shown in Fig. 6 as darkened patches. It is important to note that the formulation of the algorithm makes the selection of subimages easy. No manual alignment of features is necessary during subimage selection. This can be seen in the Fig. 6. Note for example that the subimage r_a has the cement line running towards the bottom of it while that horizontal line is nearly in the middle in the corresponding sample subimage s_a.

The next improvement to A1 is the algorithm A2 which uses a soft edged mask instead of a binary mask. Fig. 10 (d) shows noise removal from a color image using our algorithm A2. A2 is applied to r, g and b channels separately. The subimage selection is shown in Fig. 7.

Our last and most powerful algorithm is A3 which is able to handle images with varying intensity which might have been caused by shading or inter-reflection etc. The result is shown in Fig. 10 (e) and the subimage selection is shown in Fig. 7. Note that for example, in Fig. 7, s_b and r_b are two subimages with very different intensity, one is darker than the other. To some extent variation in intensity is tolerated by all three algorithms, though A3 is best able to deal with that.

See sections 4.2, 4.3 and 4.4 for algorithms A1, A2 and A3 respectively. Although not shown here, removing non-straight contiguous noise, or noise removal from synthetic images with precisely repeating patterns (and no stochastic texture) requires no extra work for our algorithm. In fact synthetic images with exactly repeating patterns are reconstructed perfectly.

The limitations of our approach are that the contents of sample and repair subimages must be approximately translated versions of each other. The can be seen in the subimage selections in Fig. 6 and Fig. 7. If the prominent lines and texture in repair and sample subimages are rotated versions of each other or there is perspective or other distortion between the two, then the algorithm will not work. Thus for example, we can't use a vertical feature as in s_b of Fig. 7 to fix the noise in an area which has a horizontal feature.

6 CONCLUSIONS AND FUTURE WORK

A fast iterative algorithm for image noise removal has been described. While most existing algorithms have worked solely in spatial or frequency domain, our algorithm works in both domains, making it possible to fully exploit the advantages from each domain. Although a few previous algorithms combine frequency and spatial domain information [6, 2], they required the image to be band limited, required that the band limits be known. Our algorithm does not place this limitation.

As shown in the results, with a judicious choice of operations (in terms of constraints and projections) and domains in which the operations work, our dual-domain approach can (1) reconstruct many contiguous noisy pixels, (2) reconstruct textures even when they are large featured, (3) maintain sharpness, (4) maintain continuity of features (e.g., lines) across the noisy region. These advantages make the algorithm very useful in many areas.

Important applications of this algorithm are in the field of film and video post production: for removing wires used in special effects scenes and for restoring old films and photographs that have become scratched.

Our algorithm is based on a general framework of POCS and can be extended in a clean way. Besides the constraints and the projections described in this paper, any image analysis and/or feature extraction techniques that are described in a closed convex set can be plugged into the iteration loop. Also, the choice of domain is not limited to the spatial and frequency domains. For example, one could choose the Wavelet transform if multiresolutional analysis is desired.

One of our motivations for presenting this work was to increase awareness about the general and powerful method of Projections Onto Convex Sets in the graphics community. To us, it appears to be an interesting way of thinking about various problems and until now it has been popular only amongst the image processing community. It is possible to imagine other uses for POCS besides image restoration, by using appropriate convex sets. Examples related to our work could be : restoring missing 3D geometry data acquired by range data acquisition systems, filling occluded information during image based rendering etc.

In the context of image restoration there are a few areas that need attention. An interactive brush implementation in which the sample and the repair subimages are automatically selected based on a brush stroke, would be useful. A multi-frame extension which allows better inter-frame continuity is another important extension. We have found that when we restore multiple frames of a still image in which the wire noise is moving some kind of moving noise is visible when the images are observed in sequence. But when the movie is stopped, the restorations seems good and the noise disappears. A straightforward extension by using 3D Fourier transform using a few frames at a time has not worked. Our color image processing is also rather naive and needs more attention. A study of how the variation in binary noise mask size affects the performance would also be desirable. Finally, what to do about rotation of features or perspective distortion between sample and repair subimages are other areas that need attention. We are currently working on these issues.

References

[1] FERREIRA, P.J.S.G. and PINHO, A.J. "Errorless Restoration Algorithms for Band-Limited Images", *Proc. IEEE Intl. Conf. Image Proc. (ICIP)*, III, 157-161, 1994.

[2] FERREIRA, P.J.S.G. "Interpolation and the Discrete Papoulis-Gerchberg Algorithm", *IEEE Trans. Sig. Proc.*, 42, No. 10, 2596-2606, Oct 1994.

[3] FIENUP, J.R. "Phase Retrieval Algorithms: a Comparison", *Appl. Opt.*, 21, No. 15, 2758-2769, 1982.

[4] HEEGER, D.J. and BERGEN, J.R. "Pyramid-Based Texture Analysis/Synthesis", *Proc. SIGGRAPH 95*, 229-238, 1995.

[5] MALZBENDER, T. and SPACH, S. "A Context Sensitive Texture Nib", *Communicating with Virtual Worlds*, Thalmann, N.M. and D. Thalmann (eds.), Springer-Verlag Tokyo, 1993.

[6] PAPOULIS, A. "A New Algorithm in Spectral Analysis and Band-Limited Extrapolation", *IEEE Trans. Cir. & Sys.*, 22, No. 9, 735-742, 1975.

[7] PITAS, I. and VENETSANOPOULOS, A.N. "Order Statistics in Digital Image Processing", *Proc. IEEE*, 80, No. 12, Dec 1992.

[8] SEZAN, M. I. and STARK, H. "Image Restoration by the Method of Convex Projections: Part 2 – Applications and Numerical Results", *IEEE Trans. Med. Imag.*, 1, No. 2, 95-101, 1982.

[9] STROHMER, T. "On Discrete Band-Limited Signal Extrapolation", In *Mathematical Analysis, Wavelets, and Signal Processing*, Ismail, M. et. al. (eds.), AMS Contemporary Mathematics, 190, 323-337, 1995. Also available from *http://tyche.mat.univie.ac.at*, the home page of NUHAG in University of Vienna.

[10] SUN, H. and KWOK, W. "Concealment of Damaged Block Transform Coded Images Using Projections onto Convex Sets", *IEEE Trans. Image Proc.*, 4, No. 4, April 1995.

[11] YOULA D.C. and WEBB, H. "Image Restoration by the Method of Convex Projections: Part 1 – Theory", *IEEE Trans. Med. Imag.*, 1, No. 2, 81-94, 1982.

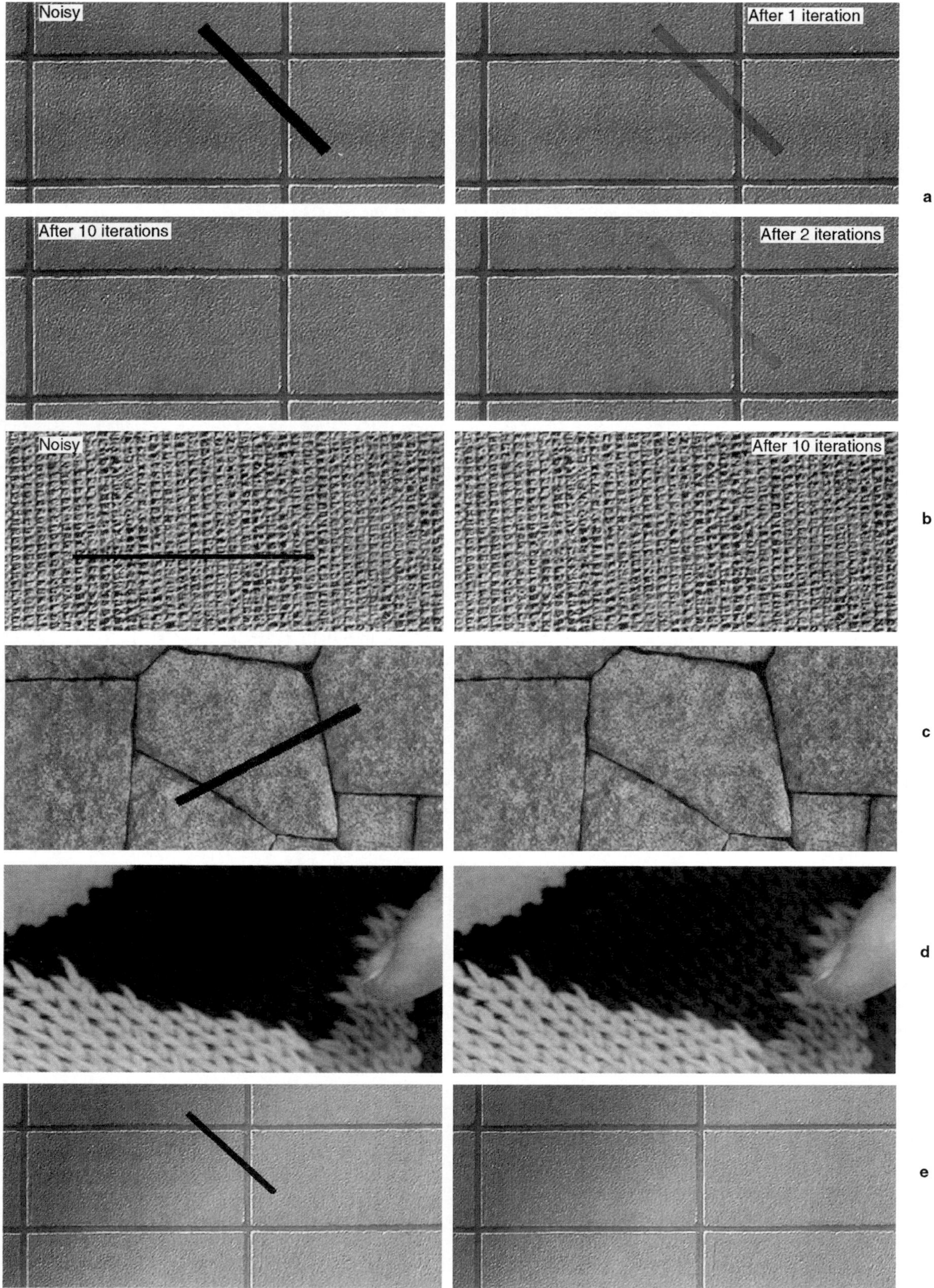

Figure 10: Results of algorithms A1, A2, A3. (a)-(c) Show removal of noise using A1 from textured images with (a) systematic long distance structure (cement lines in brick wall) (b) small regular texture (fabric) and (c) randomly placed prominent lines (stone wall). Images are 377×176, scratches approx. 9, 4 and 8 pixels wide. (d) Shows a simple application of A2 to a color image by applying A2 to each channel. (e) Shows results of A3 on an image with intensity varying across the image. See section 5 for more details and Fig. 6 and Fig. 7 for sample and repair subimages.

Consequences Of Stratified Sampling In Graphics

Don P. Mitchell
Microsoft Corporation

ABSTRACT

Antialiased pixel values are often computed as the mean of N point samples. Using uniformly distributed random samples, the central limit theorem predicts a variance of the mean of $O(N^{-1})$. Stratified sampling can further reduce the variance of the mean. This paper investigates how and why stratification effects the convergence to mean value of image pixels, which are observed to converge from N^{-2} to N^{-1}, with a rate of about $N^{-3/2}$ in pixels containing edges. This is consistent with results from the theory of discrepancy. The result is generalized to higher dimensions, as encountered with distributed ray tracing or form-factor computation.

CR Categories and Descriptors: I.3.3 [**Computer Graphics**]: Picture/Image generation.

Additional Key Words: Sampling, Stratification, Discrepancy, Antialiasing, Variance Reduction.

INTRODUCTION

One of the most general solutions to the aliasing problem in image synthesis is to supersample, compute many sample values within a pixel area and average them to estimate the actual integral of the image over an area. Several different theories have been applied to this sampling problem. Shannon's sampling theorem provides the justification for sampling at a higher density when an image is not sufficiently bandlimited for sampling at the pixel rate. The signal-processing viewpoint is not perfectly suited for treating the sampling of discontinuous signals (i.e., an image with sharp edges) or for understanding nonuniform sampling methods, although nonuniform sampling has been analyzed from this standpoint [Dippe85, Cook86, Mitchell87].

Another point of view is the theory of statistical sampling or Monte Carlo integration [Lee85, Kajiya86, Purgathofer86, Painter89]. The pixel value is estimated by the mean of a number of samples taken within the pixel area. If the pixel area is sampled at uniformly distributed random locations, the central limit theorem implies that the variance of the mean is $O(N^{-1})$. This is true even if the pixel area contains edges or if the domain being sampled has an unusual topology (e.g., sampling a function on the surface of a sphere) – cases where signal processing theory is difficult to apply.

A third viewpoint is the theory of discrepancy, which deals with the ability of a sampling pattern to estimate areas of subregions in a pixel. Quasi Monte Carlo methods [Halton70] are based on deterministic sampling patterns with low discrepancy, typically optimized to estimate the area of arbitrary axis-aligned rectangles within a square pixel area. Shirley introduced this sample-pattern quality measure to computer graphics [Shirley91], and Dobkin *et al.* introduced and analyzed a discrepancy measure based on arbitrary edges through a pixel [Dobkin93].

The most commonly used sampling strategy in ray tracing and distributed ray tracing is stratified sampling (often equivalent to the so-called jittered sampling patterns). This type of sampling has been studied from all three theoretical viewpoints mentioned above. This paper presents some theory and observations about the consequences of stratified sampling in computer graphics.

EXPERIMENTAL OBSERVATIONS

In the statistical viewpoint, a pixel value is the mean value of a small square area in an image. This assumes the use of a box filter, which is not ideal. Using a better filter simply involves computing a weighted mean, so for simplicity we will restrict the discussion to pixel-area averaging. A pixel value is estimated by a sample mean, the average of a number of point samples within the pixel area. The variance of the sample mean is a measure of the accuracy of this pixel estimate.

The variance of the mean can be directly measured by repeatedly estimating the same pixel with M independent trials of N samples x_i:

$$\overline{x_j} = \frac{1}{N}\sum_{i=1}^{N} x_i$$

$$\sigma_{\bar{x}}^2 = \frac{1}{M-1}\sum_{i=1}^{M}(\bar{x} - \overline{x_j})^2$$

Figure 1. *One of several ray-traced images analyzed.*

A simple experiment demonstrates the $O(N^{-1})$ behavior predicted by the central limit theorem. Choose a set of pixels to study in a ray traced image such as the one shown in Figure 1. For progressively increasing values of N, measure the variance of the mean by performing M trials of uniformly distributed random samples. Plotting the log of the variance versus the log of N shows points fitting closely to a line of slope 1, for any pixel area in the image. Figure 2 shows a histogram of the measured slopes (derived from least-square fits) for test pixels.

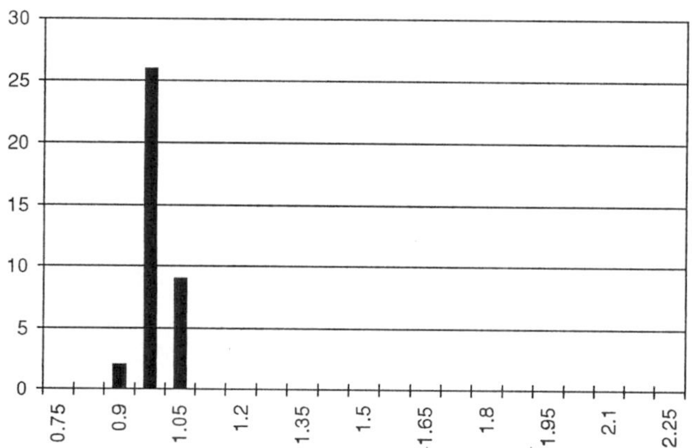

Figure 2. *Convergence of the Mean for Uniformly Distributed Random Sampling of Pixels.*

A standard variance-reducing technique is stratified sampling. Instead of distributing N random samples uniformly within the pixel area, the area can be divided into a grid of $\sqrt{N} \times \sqrt{N}$ cells, with one sample placed randomly within each cell. The literature of Monte Carlo methods contains varying comments about the effectiveness of stratification. Hammersley reports a "general rough working rule" that stratification gives a variance of the mean of $O(N^{-3})$ [Hammersley64]. Hammersley was commenting on the numerical integration of one-dimensional functions. Looking at multi-dimensional radiation transport, Spanier reports that stratification doesn't give much benefit [Spanier69].

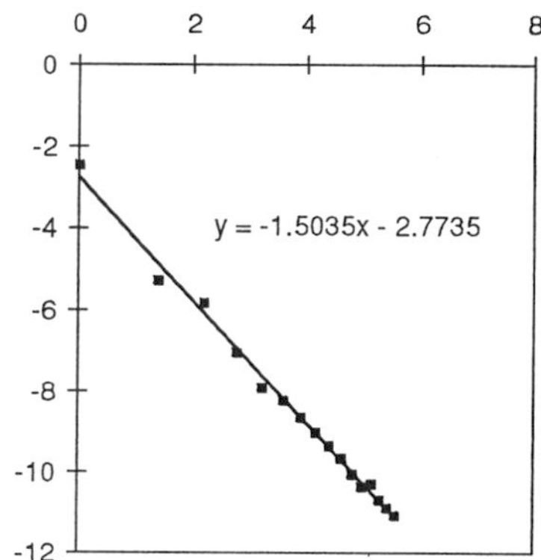

Figure 3. *Measured variance of mean for a pixel versus*

It seems appropriate then to actually measure the variance of the mean in the pixels of an image. Using several ray-traced images, $M = 50$ trials were performed with stratified sampling for N taking on values of 1, 4, 9, 16, ... up to 256, and performed a least-square fit in log space to measure the closest fit to a convergence of the mean of the form $O(N^{-p})$. Figure 3 shows the data from one pixel and the least-square fit. Figure 4 shows the histogram of resulting values of p, using pixels from the image in Figure 1. The result is typical: a range of values from 1.0 to 2.0.

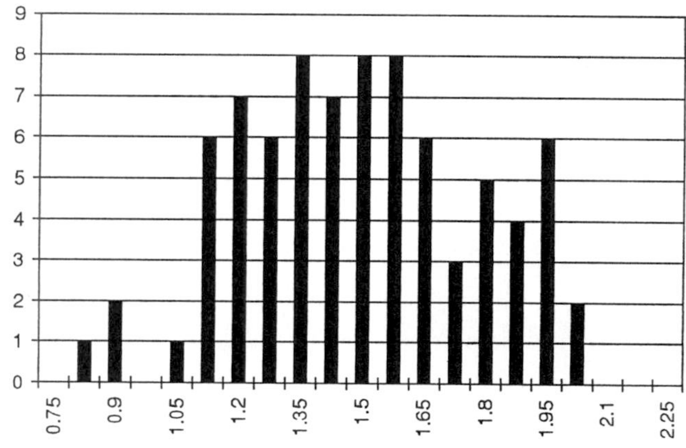

Figure 4. *Convergence of the Mean for Stratified Sampling of Pixels.*

By inspecting various pixels and their associated rates of convergence, three fairly distinct types can be found. Areas containing extremely complex features converge with a variance proportional to N^{-1}. Areas containing smooth regions of the image exhibit a variance of the mean that converges more rapidly, as N^{-2}. Pixels that exhibit $N^{-3/2}$ variance are found to contain smooth areas delimited by a few edges. Figure 5 shows several typical examples:

Figure 5. *Pixels with p = 1.89, 1.45, and 1.12.*

THEORETICAL ANALYSIS

The N^{-1} behavior in highly complex regions of the image is not surprising, since this is what would result from sampling a randomly varying function, according to the central limit theorem. There is no benefit from stratification in this case.

The $N^{-3/2}$ behavior in pixels with edges is consistent with the arbitrary-edge discrepancy of stratified/jittered sample patterns, as proven in Beck and Chen [Beck87]. In their derivation of the discrepancy, they note that edge discontinuities are one-dimensional features. As N (the number of samples and the number of strata) increases, an edge intersects only $O(\sqrt{N})$ strata. In computing the variance of the mean, the samples in the edge-crossing strata will dominate. Each sample x_i is given a weight of $1/N$, and so the total variance of the mean is:

$$\sigma_{\bar{x}}^2 = \frac{1}{N^2}\sum_{i=1}^{\sqrt{N}} \sigma_i^2 \approx \frac{\sigma^2}{N^{1.5}}$$

This is equivalent to a convergence of the standard deviation (square root of variance) proportional to $N^{-3/4}$. This is in line with Beck and Chen's bounds for arbitrary edge discrepancy are $\Omega(N^{-3/4})$ and $O(N^{-3/4}\log N^{1/2})$ [Beck87]. Dobkin *et al.* and Cross have used simulated annealing to generate sampling patterns with nearly half the discrepancy of jittered patterns [Dobkin94, Cross95]. These patterns may yield smaller pixel error, but Beck and Chen's lower bound proves that no pattern will be asymptotically better than jittered samples.

This analysis can be generalized to the case of N strata in d dimensions, with a sharp discontinuity of k dimensions. In this case, we expect $O(N^{k/d})$ strata to be cut by the discontinuity and dominate the variance. In that case, the variance of the mean should converge as $O(N^{k/d-2})$.

The $O(N^{-2})$ convergence in smooth regions of the image can be justified if we make the fairly general assumption that the image obeys a Lipshitz smoothness condition within the pixel area. That is, the range of values of the image function $f(x)$ (where x is a point in d dimensions) is no more than a constant factor times the diameter of the region:

$$\frac{|f(x) - f(y)|}{|x - y|} \le C$$

In d dimensions, the diameter of each strata is proportional to $N^{-1/d}$ and so we expect the standard deviation (root of the variance) of the function to be lower by the same proportion. The variance of the average of samples taken from each strata should therefore be:

$$\frac{1}{N^2}\sum_{i=1}^{N} \sigma_i^2 (N^{-1/d})^2 = O(N^{-1-2/d})$$

For d=2, this agrees with the observed result of $O(N^{-2})$. It may also explain Hammersley's "working rule" for one-dimensional smooth functions, while Sparier was working with radiation transport problems of high dimension and saw less benefit from stratification.

A FOUR-DIMENSIONAL EXPERIMENT

An additional experiment was done to test these results in higher dimensions. The calculation of the form factor between two parallel unit squares (two units apart and aligned) was computed by Monte Carlo integration in four dimensions. Once again, the result was recomputed with $M = 50$ independent trials for values of $N = 1^4, 2^4, \ldots 10^4$, and an estimation of the variance of the mean was found for each value of N. Since this is a smooth function with a four-dimensional domain, we expect a convergence of $O(N^{-3/2})$. The measured least-square fit to the data (in log space) gave $p = 1.430$. Removing the first (least accurate) point from the set gave $p = 1.501$.

The same experiment was then performed, with a smaller occluding square between the two planes. For each point on a given (two-dimensional) plane, the perimeter of the occluding square presents a one-dimensional discontinuity in the differential form factor. Thus, the overall discontinuity in the form factor is three-dimensional. Thus for $d = 4$ and $k = 3$, we expect a convergence of the mean of $O(N^{-5/4})$. The measured result was $p = 1.233$, and with the $N = 1$ point removed we found $p = 1.245$.

CONCLUSIONS

Stratified sampling is commonly used in ray tracing and distributed ray tracing, but its benefit has not been fully analyzed. Pixel accuracy is strictly improved by using stratification. For $N = 1$ samples per pixel, uniformly distributed random sampling and stratified sampling are the same, and as N increases, stratified sampling will often converge to the mean asymptotically faster than uniform random sampling.

The improvement in pixel accuracy depends on the nature of the image within the pixel area. In the worst case, stratification is no better (but no worse) than uniform random sampling, . If a finite number of edges pass through the pixel area, we expect an variance of the mean to be lower by a factor of $N^{1/2}$. If the image is smooth within the pixel area, we expect a variance of the mean to be lower by a factor of N.

The absolute pixel error will actually be proportional to the square root of the variance (i.e., the standard deviation). The asymptotic reduction of error due to stratification is a little less impressive when we take the square root. The benefits of stratification are probably a mix of genuine error reduction and the spectral consequences of jittering as described by Dippe, Cook and Mitchell (i.e., the tendency of these sampling patterns to distribute the error in a high frequency pattern over the image).

ACKNOWLEDGEMENTS

I would like to thank Steve Drucker, Steven Gortler, Mike Marr, and my SIGGRAPH reviewers for their helpful comments. Thanks also to Josef Beck, Bernard Chazelle and David Dobkin for discussions about discrepancy.

REFERENCES

[Beck87] J. Beck and W. W. L. Chen. *Irregularities of Distribution,* Cambridge University Press, 1987.

[Cook86] R. L. Cool, Stochastic sampling in computer graphics. *ACM Trans. Graphics* 5:1 (1986) 51-72.

[Cross95] R. A. Cross. Sampling Patterns Optimized for Uniform Distributed Edges. *Graphics Gems V,* Academic Press, 1995, 359-363.

[Dippe85] M.A.Z. Dippe and E. H. Wold. Antialiasing through stochastic sampling. *Computer Graphics* 19:3 (1985) 69-78.

[Dobkin93] D. P. Dobkin and D. P. Mitchell. Random-edge discrepancy of supersampling patterns. *Graphic Interface,* York, Ontario (1993).

[Dobkin94] D. P. Dobkin, D. Eppstein and D. P. Mitchell. Computing the Discrepancy with Applications to Supersampling Patterns. *Trans. Graphics (to appear).*

[Halton70] J. H. Halton. A retrospective and prospective survey of the Monte Carlo method. *SIAM Review* 12 (1970) 1-63.

[Hammersley64] J. M. Hammersley and D. C. Handscomb. *Monte Carlo Methods.* Methuen & Co., London, 1964.

[Kajiya86] J. T. Kajiya. The Rendering Equation. *Computer Graphics* 20 (1986) 143-150.

[Lee85] M. Lee, R. A. Redner, and S. P. Uselton. Statistically optimized sampling for distributed ray tracing. *Computer Graphics* 19:3 (1985) 61-67.

[Mitchell87] D. P. Mitchell. Generating antialiased images at low sampling densities. *Computer Graphics* 21:4 (1987) 65-72.

[Painter89] J. Painter and K. Sloan. Antialiased ray tracing by adaptive progressive refinement. *Computer Graphics* 23:3 (1989) 281-288.

[Purgathofer86] W. Purgathofer. A statistical model for adaptive stochastic sampling. *Proc. Eurographics* (1986) 145-152.

[Shirley91] P. Shirley. Discrepancy as a quality measure for sample distributions. *Proc. Eurographics* (1991) 183-193.

[Spanier69] J. Spanier and E. M. Gelbard. *Monte Carlo Principles and Neutron Transport Problems.* Addison-Wesley, Reading, MA, 1969.

Multiresolution Video

Adam Finkelstein *Charles E. Jacobs* *David H. Salesin*

Department of Computer Science and Engineering*
University of Washington

Abstract

We present a new representation for time-varying image data that allows for varying—and arbitrarily high—spatial and temporal resolutions in different parts of a video sequence. The representation, called *multiresolution video*, is based on a sparse, hierarchical encoding of the video data. We describe a number of operations for creating, viewing, and editing multiresolution sequences. These operations support a variety of applications: multiresolution playback, including motion-blurred "fast-forward" and "reverse"; constant-speed display; enhanced video scrubbing; and "video clip-art" editing and compositing. The multiresolution representation requires little storage overhead, and the algorithms using the representation are both simple and efficient.

CR Categories and Subject Descriptors:
H.5.1 [Information Interfaces]: Multimedia Information Systems—video
I.3.3 [Computer Graphics]: Picture/Image Generation—display algorithms
I.4.10 [Image Processing]: Image Representation—hierarchical

Additional Keywords: clip-art, compositing, image pyramids, multigrid methods, multimedia, scientific visualization, video editing

1 Introduction

Scientists often run physical simulations of time-varying data in which different parts of the simulation are performed at differing spatial and temporal resolutions. For example, in a simulation of the air flow about an airplane wing, it is useful to run the slowly-varying parts of the simulation—generally, the portion of space further from the wing—at a fairly coarse scale, both spatially and temporally, while running the more complex parts—say, the region of turbulence just aft of the wing—at a much higher resolution. The *multigrid techniques* used frequently for solving large-scale problems in physics [15], astronomy [16], meteorology [1], and applied mathematics [8] are a common example of this kind of computation.

In this paper, we present a new approach for representing the time-varying data produced by such algorithms, called *multiresolution video*. The multiresolution video representation provides a means of capturing time-varying image data produced at multiple scales, both spatially and temporally. In addition, we introduce efficient algorithms for viewing multiresolution video at arbitrary scales and speeds. For example, in a sequence depicting the flow of air about a wing, a user can interactively zoom in on an area of relative turbulence, computed at an enhanced *spatial resolution*. Analogously, fast-changing components in a scene can be represented and viewed at a higher *temporal resolution*, allowing, for example, a propeller blade to be represented and viewed in slow motion.

Moreover, we have found that multiresolution video has applications that are useful even for conventional *uniresolution* video. First, the representation facilitates a variety of viewing applications, such as multiresolution playback, including motion-blurred "fast-forward" and "reverse"; constant-speed viewing of video over a network with varying throughput; and an enhanced form of video "scrubbing." The representation also provides a controlled degree of lossy compression, particularly in areas of the video that change little from frame to frame. Finally, the representation supports the assembly of complex multiresolution videos from either uniresolution or multiresolution "video clip-art" elements.

1.1 Related work

The multiresolution video representation described in this paper generalizes some of the multiresolution representations that have previously been proposed for images, such as "image pyramids" [18] and "MIP maps" [19]. It is also similar in spirit to the wavelet-based representations for images described by Berman *et al.* [2] and Perlin and Velho [11]. In particular, like these latter works, our representation is sparse, and it supports efficient compositing operations [12] for assembling complex frames from simpler elements.

Several commercially available video editing systems support many of the operations described in this paper for uniresolution video. For example, Adobe After Effects allows the user to view video segments at low resolution and to construct an edit list that is later applied to the high-resolution frames off-line. Discrete Logic's Flame and Flint systems also provide digital video compositing and many other digital editing operations on videos of arbitrary resolution. Swartz and Smith [17] describe a language for manipulation of video segments in a resolution-independent fashion. However, the input and output from all of these systems is uniresolution video.

Multiresolution video also allows the user to pan and zoom to explore a flat video environment. This style of interaction is similar in spirit to two image-based environments: Apple Computer's QuickTime® VR [3] and the "plenoptic modeling" system of McMillan and Bishop [9]. These methods provide an image-based representation of an environment that surrounds the viewer. In section Section 4.5, we describe how such methods can be combined with multiresolution video to create a kind of "multiresolution video QuickTime VR," in which a viewer can investigate a panoramic environment by panning and zooming, with the environment changing in time and having different amounts of detail in different locations.

While not the emphasis of this work, we also describe a simple form of lossy compression suitable for multiresolution video. Video compression is a heavily-studied area, with too many papers to adequately survey here. MPEG [5] and QuickTime [13] are two industry standards. Other techniques based on multiscale transforms [7, 10] might be adapted to work for multiresolution video.

* For project updates, addresses, and email see our Web page:
`http://www.cs.washington.edu/research/graphics/mrvideo`

1.2 Overview

The rest of this paper is organized as follows. Section 2 describes our representation for multiresolution video, and Section 3 describes how it is created and displayed. Section 4 describes a variety of applications of the multiresolution video representation, and Section 5 provides some concrete examples. Finally, Section 6 outlines some areas for future work. The appendix provides additional low-level operations useful for editing multiresolution video.

2 Representation

Our goals in designing a multiresolution video representation were fivefold. We wanted it to:

- support varying spatial and temporal resolutions;
- require overall storage proportional only to the detail present (with a small constant of proportionality);
- efficiently support a variety of primitive operations for creating, viewing, and editing the video;
- permit lossy compression; and
- require only a small "working storage" overhead, so that video could be streamed in from disk as it is needed.

The rest of this section describes the multiresolution video format we chose and an analysis of the storage required.

2.1 The basic multiresolution video format

Perhaps the most obvious choice for a multiresolution video format would be a sparse octree [14], whose three dimensions were used to encode the two spatial directions and time. Indeed, such a representation was our first choice, but we found that it did not adequately address a number of the goals enumerated above. Put briefly, the problem with such a representation is that it couples the dimensions of space and time too tightly. In an octree structure, each node would correspond to a "cube" with a fixed extent in space and time. Thus, it would be efficient to rescale a video to, say, twice the spatial resolution only if it were equally rescaled in time—that is, played at half the speed. We therefore needed to develop a representation that, while still making it possible to take advantage of temporal and spatial coherence, could couple space and time more loosely.

The structure we ultimately chose is a sparse binary tree of sparse quadtrees. The binary tree encodes the flow of time, and each quadtree encodes the spatial decomposition of a frame (Figure 1).

In the binary tree, called the *Time Tree*, each node corresponds to a single image, or *frame*, of the video sequence at some temporal resolution. The leaves of the Time Tree correspond to the frames at the highest temporal resolution for which information is present in the video. Internal nodes of the Time Tree correspond to box-filtered averages of their two children frames. Visually, these frames appear as motion-blurred versions of their children. Note that this representation supports video sequences with varying degrees of temporal resolution simply by allowing the Time Tree to grow to different depths in different parts of the sequence. For convenience, we will call the child nodes of the Time Tree *child time nodes* and their parents *parent time nodes*. We will use capitalized names for any time node.

Time Tree nodes are represented by the following data structure:

```
type TimeNode = record
    frame: pointer to ImageNode
    Half1, Half2: pointer to TimeNode
end record
```

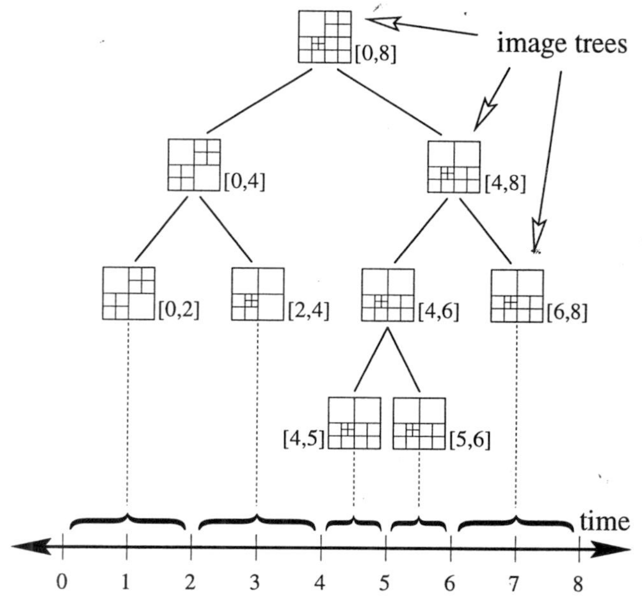

Figure 1 Binary tree of quadtrees.

Each node of the Time Tree points to a sparse quadtree, called an *image tree*, which represents the multiresolution image content of a single frame of the video sequence. In analogy to the Time Tree, leaves of an image tree correspond to pixels at the highest spatial resolution for which information is present in the particular frame being represented. Internal nodes of an image tree correspond, once again, to box-filtered averages of their children—in this case, to a 2×2 block of higher-resolution pixels. Note that the image tree supports varying spatial resolution simply by allowing the quadtree to reach different depths in different parts of the frame. We will call the child nodes of an image tree *child image nodes* and their parents *parent image nodes*. In our pseudocode we will use lower-case names for any image node. Figure 4 shows a frame from a video clip, where leaf nodes of the image tree are boxed in yellow.

Specifically, here is how we encode each node in the image tree:

```
type ImageNode = record
    type: TREE | COLOR
    uplink: UpLinkInfo
    union
        tree: pointer to ImageSubtree
        color: PixelRGBA
    end union
end record

type ImageSubtree = record
    avgcolor: PixelRGBA
    child[0..1, 0..1]: array of ImageNode
end record
```

Each subtree contains both the average color for a region of the image, stored as an RGBA pixel, and also image nodes for the four quadrants of that region. We compute the average of the pixels as if each color channel were premultiplied by alpha—as prescribed by Porter and Duff [12]—but we do not actually represent the pixels that way in our image nodes, in order to preserve color fidelity in highly-transparent regions. Each image node generally contains a pointer to a subtree for each quadrant. However, if a given quadrant only has a single pixel's worth of data, then the color of the pixel is stored in the node directly, in place of the pointer. (This trick works nicely, since an RGBA pixel value is represented in our system with 4 bytes, the same amount of space as a pointer. Packing the pixel in-

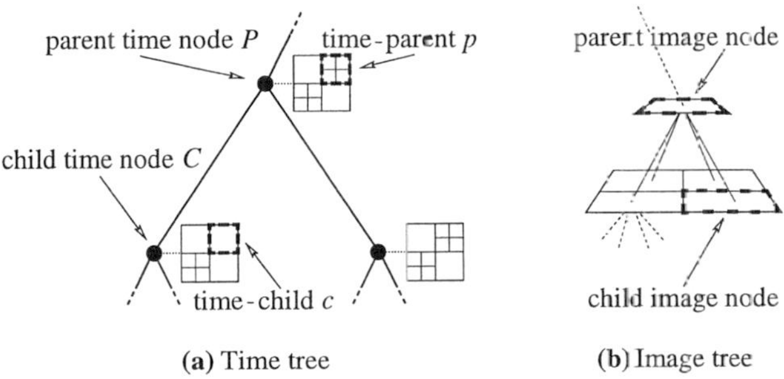

Figure 2 Parent-child relationships in the trees.

formation into the pointer space allows us to save a large amount of memory that we might otherwise waste on null pointers at the leaves.) There is also an *uplink* field, whose use we will discuss in the next section.

There is an additional relationship between image nodes that is not represented explicitly in the structure, but which is nevertheless crucial to our algorithms. As described already, there are many different image nodes that correspond to the same region of space, each hanging from a different time node. We will call any two such image nodes *time-relatives*. In particular, for a given image node c hanging from a time node C, we will call the time-relative p hanging from the parent time node P of C the *time-parent* of c. In this case, the image node c is also called the *time-child* of p. (See Figure 2.) Note that a given node does not necessarily have a time-parent or a time-child, as the quadtree structures hanging from P and C may differ.

2.2 Temporal coherence

Recall that the representation of each frame exploits spatial coherence by pruning the image tree at nodes for which the image content is nearly constant. We can take advantage of temporal coherence in a similar way, even in regions that are spatially complex.

Consider an image node p and its two time-children c_1 and c_2. Whenever the images in c_1 and c_2 are similar to each other, the image in p will be similar to these images as well. Rather than triplicating the pixels in all three places, we can instead just store the image in the time-parent p and allow c_1 and c_2 to point to this image directly. We call such pointers *up-links*. See Figure 3 for a schematic example. Figure 5 shows a frame from a multiresolution video clip in which all up-link regions (which cover most of the frame) are shaded red.

The up-links are described by the following structure:

type *UpLinkInfo* = **record**
  linked: *Boolean*
  type: FIRST | MIDDLE | LAST
end record

The *linked* field tells whether or not there is an up-link. There is also a *type* field, which we will describe in Section 3.2.

2.3 Storage complexity

Now that we have defined the multiresolution video data structure, we can analyze its storage cost. The *type* and *uplink* fields require very few bits, and in practice these two fields for all four children may be bundled together in a single 4-byte field in the *ImageSubtree* structure. Thus, each *ImageSubtree* contains 4 bytes (for the average color), 4×4 bytes (for the children), and 4 bytes (for the flags), yielding a total of 24 bytes. Each leaf node of an image tree comprises 4 pixels, and there are 4/3 as many total nodes in these trees as there are leaves. Assuming P pixels per time node, we get:

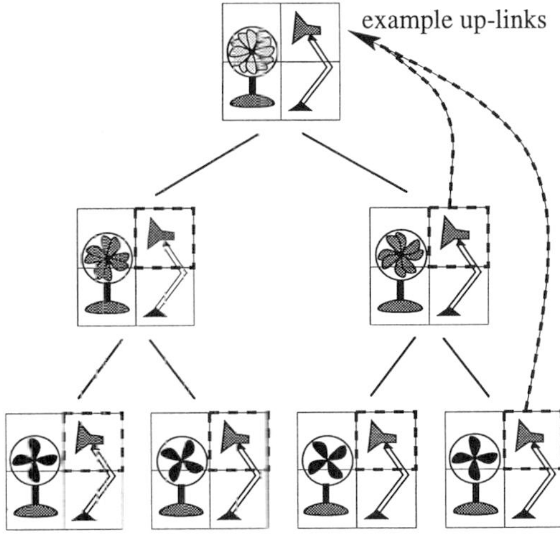

Figure 3 Exploiting temporal coherence. The quadrants containing the Luxo lamp are not duplicated in the lower six frames of the Time Tree. Instead, the right two quadrants in all six frames contain "up-links" to the corresponding quadrants in the Time Tree's root.

$$\frac{24 \text{ bytes}}{\text{node}} \times \frac{4 \text{ nodes}}{3 \text{ leaf}} \times \frac{1 \text{ leaves}}{4 \text{ pixels}} \times \frac{P \text{ pixels}}{\text{time node}} = \frac{8P \text{ bytes}}{\text{time node}}$$

Furthermore, there are twice as many time nodes as there are leaves (or frames) in the Time Tree, so the storage complexity is really $16P$ bytes/frame. In addition, each *TimeNode* contains 3×4 = 12 bytes, and there are twice as many nodes in this tree as there are leaves. Thus, the Time Tree needs an additional 24 bytes/frame. However, since $16P$ is generally much larger than 24, we can ignore the latter term in the analysis. The overall storage is therefore 16 bytes/pixel.

In the worst case—a complete tree with no up-links—we have as many pixels in the tree as in the original image. Thus, the tree takes 4 times as much space as required by just the highest-resolution pixel information alone. It is worthwhile to compare this overhead with the cost of directly storing the same set of time- and space-averaged frames, without allowing any space for pointers or flags. Such a structure would essentially involve storing all powers-of-two time and spatial scales of each image, requiring a storage overhead of 8/3. Thus, our storage overhead of 4 is only slightly larger than the minimum overhead required. However, as will be described in Section 3.1, the very set of pointers that makes our worst-case overhead larger also permits both lossless and lossy compression by taking advantage of coherence in space and time.

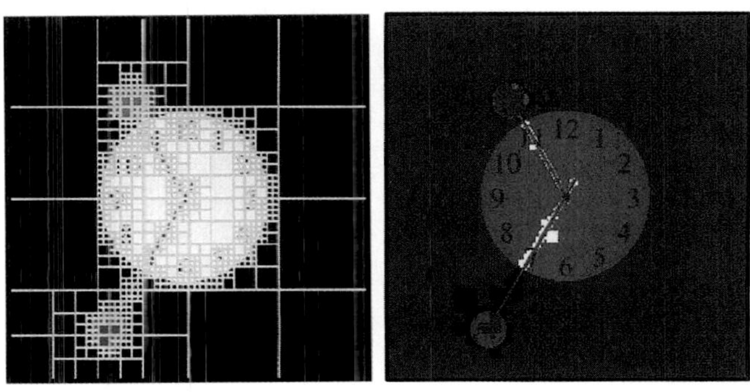

Figure 4 Quadtree. **Figure 5** Up-links.

2.4 Working storage

One of the goals of our representation was to require a small "working storage" overhead, so that video could be streamed in from disk only as it is needed. This feature is crucial for viewing very large sequences, as well as for the editing operations we describe in the appendix. As we will see when we discuss these operations in detail, this goal is easily addressed by keeping resident in memory just the image trees that are currently being displayed or edited, along with all of their time-ancestors. For a video clip with 2^k frames, the number of time-ancestors required is at most k.

2.5 Comparison with wavelets

Wavelets have been successfully used to represent multiresolution functions in a variety of domains. Our first impulse—and, in fact, our first implementation—was to use a 3D wavelet representation for the video. However, we eventually moved to the data structure described in this section for several reasons. First, the box basis functions we use now are simpler, making it faster to render a frame of video. Second, wavelet coefficients require increasing numbers of bits at finer levels of detail, so we had to use floating-point numbers (rather than bytes) to store the color channels—a factor of four expansion. Third, the wavelets we were using (nonstandard tensor-product Haar wavelets) made it difficult to separate the spatial and temporal dimensions; thus, it was expensive to extract a frame in which the time and space dimensions were scaled differently. While it is possible to construct a wavelet basis that avoids this problem, we were not able to find an efficient compositing algorithm for it. Finally, the current representation takes advantage of areas of a video sequence that have temporal coherence but no spatial coherence; the wavelets we used were unable to compress such sequences.

3 Basic algorithms

In this section we describe algorithms for creating and displaying multiresolution video. Algorithms for translating, scaling, and compositing multiresolution video clips appear in the appendix.

3.1 Creating multiresolution video

We begin with the problem of creating multiresolution video from conventional uniresolution video. We break this process into two parts: creating the individual frames, and linking them together into a multiresolution video sequence.

3.1.1 Creating the individual frames

Given a $2^\ell \times 2^\ell$ source frame S we construct an image tree by calling the following function with arguments $(S, 0, 0, \ell)$:

```
function CreateFrame(S, x, y, ℓ): returns ImageNode
    if ℓ = 0 then return ImageNode(COLOR, S[x, y])
    for each i,j ∈ {0, 1} do
        x' ← 2x + i
        y' ← 2y + j
        subtree.child[i,j] ← CreateFrame(S, x', y', ℓ − 1)
    end for
    subtree.avgcolor ← AverageChildren(subtree.child[0..1, 0..1])
    return ImageNode(TREE, subtree)
end function
```

Image trees built from images that are not of dimension $2^\ell \times 2^\ell$ are implicitly padded with transparent, black pixels.

The quadtree constructed by *CreateFrame*() is complete. The next step is to take advantage of spatial coherence by culling redundant information from the tree. The following function recursively traverses the image tree p and prunes any subtree whose colors differ from its average color a by less than a threshold δ:

```
function PruneTree(p, a, δ): returns Boolean
    if p.type = COLOR then return (ColorDiff(p.color, a) ≤ δ)
    prune ← TRUE
    for each i,j ∈ {0, 1} do
        prune ← prune and PruneTree(p.child[i,j], p.avgcolor, δ)
    end for
    if prune = FALSE then return FALSE
    free(p.child[0..1, 0..1])
    p ← ImageNode(COLOR, p.avgcolor)
    return TRUE
end function
```

Choosing $\delta = 0$ yields lossless compression, whereas using $\delta > 0$ permits an arbitrary degree of lossy compression at the expense of image degradation. The function *ColorDiff*() measures the distance between two colors (r_1, g_1, b_1, a_1) and (r_2, g_2, b_2, a_2). We chose to measure the distance as the sum of the distances between color components, weighted by their luminance values:

$$0.299|r_1a_1 - r_2a_2| + 0.587|g_1a_1 - g_2a_2| + 0.114|b_1a_1 - b_2a_2|$$

In practice, the source material may be multiresolution in nature. For example, the results of some of the scientific simulations described in Section 5 were produced via adaptive refinement. It is easy to modify the function *CreateFrame*() to sample source material at different levels of detail in different parts of a frame. In this case, the recursive function descends to varying depths, depending on the amount of detail present in the source material.

3.1.2 Linking the frames together

The next step is to link all the frames together into the Time Tree. We first insert all the image trees at the leaves of the Time Tree, and then compute all of the internal nodes by averaging pairs of frames in a depth-first recursion. Now that the complete Time Tree is built, the following two procedures discover and create all the up-links:

```
procedure MakeMRVideo(Timetree, δ):
    for each Half ∈ {Half1, Half2} of Timetree do
        if Half ≠ NULL then
            MakeUpLinks(Half.frame, Timetree.frame, δ)
            MakeMRVideo(Half, δ)
        end if
    end for
end procedure
```

```
function MakeUpLinks(p, c, δ): returns Boolean
    c.uplink.linked ← FALSE
    if p = NULL or p.type ≠ c.type then
        return FALSE
    else if c.type = COLOR then
        c.uplink.linked ← (ColorDiff(p.color, c.color) ≤ δ)
        return c.uplink.linked
    end if
    link ← TRUE
    for each i,j ∈ {0, 1} do
        link ← (link and MakeUpLinks(p.child[i,j], c.child[i,j]), δ)
    end for
    if link = FALSE then return FALSE
    free(c.tree)
    c.tree ← p.tree
    c.uplink.linked ← TRUE
    return TRUE
end function
```

The *MakeMRVideo*() routine works by finding all of the up-links between the root of the Time Tree and its two child time nodes. The routine then calls itself recursively to find up-links between these children and their descendents in time. Because of the preorder recursion, up-links may actually point to any time-ancestor, not just a time-parent. (See Figure 3.)

The *MakeUpLinks*() function attempts to create an up-link from a time-child c to its time-parent p. An up-link is created if the two nodes are both subtrees with identical structure, and all of their descendent nodes are sufficiently close in color. The function returns TRUE if such an up-link is created. It also returns TRUE if the two nodes are colors and the two colors are sufficiently close; it furthermore sets the child node's *uplink* flag, which is used to optimize the display operation in the following section.

After executing *MakeMRVideo*(), we traverse the entire Time Tree in a separate pass that sets the *type* field of the *uplink* structure, whose use is explained in the following section.

3.2 Display

Drawing a frame at an arbitrary power-of-two spatial or temporal resolution is simple. Displaying at a particular temporal resolution involves drawing frames at the corresponding level in the Time Tree. Displaying at a particular spatial resolution involves drawing the pixels situated at the corresponding level in the image trees.

The up-links that were used in the previous section to optimize storage can also play a role in optimizing the performance of the display routine when playing successive frames. We would like to avoid refreshing any portion of a frame that is not changing in time; the up-links provide exactly the information we need. In particular, if we have just displayed frame t, then we do not need to render portions of frame $t+1$ (at the same time level) that share the same up-links. We will use the *type* field in the *UpLinkInfo* structure to specify the first and last up-links of a sequence of frames that all share the same parent data. When playing video forward, we do not need to render any region that is pointed to by an up-link, unless it is a FIRST up-link. Conversely, if we are playing backward, we only need to render LAST up-links.

To render the image content c of a single multiresolution video frame at a spatial resolution $2^\ell \times 2^\ell$ we can call the following recursive routine, passing it the root c of an image tree and other parameters $(0, 0, \ell)$:

```
procedure DrawImage(c, x, y, ℓ):
   if c.uplink.linked and c.uplink.type ≠ FIRST then return
   if c.type = COLOR then
      DrawSquare(x, y, 2^ℓ, c.color)
   else if ℓ = 0 then
      DrawPixel(x, y, c.avgcolor)
   else
      for each i,j ∈ {0,1} do
         DrawImage(c.child[i,j], 2x + i, 2y + j, ℓ − 1)
      end for
   end if
end procedure
```

The routine *DrawSquare*() renders a square at the given location and size in our application window, while *DrawPixel*() renders a single pixel. Note that *DrawImage*() assumes that the video is being played in the forward direction from beginning to end. A routine to play the video in reverse would have to use LAST in place of FIRST in the first line. A routine to display a single frame that does not immediately follow the previously displayed frame (for example, the first frame to be played) would have to omit the first line of code entirely.

One further optimization is that we actually keep track of the bounding box of non-transparent pixels in each frame. We intersect this bounding box with the rectangle containing the visible portion of the frame on the screen, and only draw this intersection. Thus, if only a small portion of the frame is visible, we only draw that portion.

The *DrawImage*() routine takes time proportional to the number of squares that are drawn, assuming that the time to draw a square is constant.

Fractional-level zoom

The *DrawImage*() routine as described displays multiresolution video at any power-of-two spatial resolution. Berman *et al.* [2] describe a simple method to allow users to view multiresolution images at any arbitrary scale. We have adapted their method to work for multiresolution video. The basic idea is that if we want to display a frame of video at a fractional level between integer levels $\ell-1$ and ℓ, we select pixels from the image tree as though we were drawing a $2^\ell \times 2^\ell$ image, and then display those pixels at locations appropriate to the fractional level. So if a pixel would be drawn at location (x, y) in a $2^\ell \times 2^\ell$ image, then it would be drawn at location (x', y') in an $M \times M$ image, where

$$x' = \lfloor xM/2^\ell \rfloor \qquad y' = \lfloor yM/2^\ell \rfloor$$

Furthermore, as with MIP maps [19], we interpolate between the colors appearing at levels ℓ and $\ell - 1$ in the image tree in order to reduce point-sampling artifacts. Drawing at this fractional level is only slightly more expensive than drawing pixels at level ℓ.

Similarly, even though we are selecting frames from the Time Tree corresponding to power-of-two intervals of time, we can achieve "fractional rates" through the video, as will be described in Section 4.2.

4 Applications

We now describe several applications of the primitive operations presented in the last section. These applications include multiresolution playback, with motion-blurred "fast-forward" and "reverse"; constant perceived-speed playback; enhanced video scrubbing; "video clip-art" editing and compositing; and "multiresolution video QuickTime VR."

These applications of multiresolution video serve as "tools" that can be assembled in various combinations into higher-level applications. We describe our prototype multiresolution video editing and viewing application in Section 5.

4.1 Multiresolution playback

The primary application of multiresolution video is to support playback at different temporal and spatial resolutions. To play a video clip at any temporal resolution 2^k and spatial resolution $2^\ell \times 2^\ell$ we simply make successive calls to the procedure *DrawImage*(), passing it a series of nodes from level k of the Time Tree, as well as the spatial level ℓ. We can zoom in or out of the video by changing the level ℓ.

Similarly, for "motion-blurred" fast-forward and reverse, we use a smaller time level k. In our implementation the motion-blur effect comes from simple box filtering of adjacent frames. Though box-filtering may not be ideal for creating high-quality animations, it does appear to be adequate for searching through video.

Sometimes it may be desirable to have a limited degree of motion blur, which might, for example, blur the action in just the first half of the frame's time interval. This kind of limited motion blur can be implemented by descending one level deeper in the Time Tree, displaying the first child time node rather than the fully motion-blurred frame.

4.2 Constant perceived-speed playback

During video playback, it is useful to be able to maintain a constant perceived speed, despite variations in the network throughput or CPU availability. Multiresolution video provides two ways of adjusting the speed of play, which can be used to compensate for any such variations in load. First, by rendering individual frames at a finer or coarser spatial resolution, the application can adjust the rendering time up or down. Second, by moving to higher or lower levels in the Time Tree, the application can also adjust the perceived rate at which each rendered frame advances through the video.

These two mechanisms can be traded off in order to achieve a constant perceived speed. One possibility is to simply adjust the spatial resolution to maintain a sufficiently high frame rate, say 30 frames/second. If, however, at some point the degradation in spatial resolution becomes too objectionable (for instance, on account of a large reduction in network bandwidth), then the application can drop to a lower frame rate, say, 15 frames/second, and at the same time move to the next higher level of motion-blurred frames in the Time Tree. At this lower frame rate, the application has the liberty to render more spatial detail, albeit at the cost of more blurred temporal detail.

Note that by alternating between the display of frames at two adjacent levels in the Time Tree, we can play at arbitrary speeds, not just those related by powers of two.

4.3 Scrubbing

Conventional broadcast-quality video editing systems allow a user to search through a video interactively by using a slider or a knob, in a process known as "scrubbing." In such systems, frames are simply dropped to achieve faster speeds through the video.

Multiresolution video supports a new kind of scrubbing that shows all of the motion-blurred video as the user searches through it, rather than dropping frames. In our implementation, the user interface provides a slider whose position corresponds to a position in the video sequence. As the user moves the slider, frames from the video are displayed. The temporal resolution of these frames is related to the speed at which the slider is pulled: if the slider moves slowly, frames of high temporal detail are displayed; if the slider moves quickly, blurred frames are displayed.

The benefits of this approach are similar to those of the constant perceived-speed playback mechanism described above. If the slider is pulled quickly, then the application does not have an opportunity to display many frames; instead, it can use the motion-blurred frames, which move faster through the video sequence. In addition, the motion blur may provide a useful visual cue to the speed at which the video is being viewed.

4.4 Clip-art

In our multiresolution video editor, the user may load video fragments, scale them, arrange them spatially with respect to each other, and preview how they will look together. These input fragments may be thought of as "video clip-art" in the sense that the user constructs the final product as a composite of these elements.

Since the final composition can take a long time to construct, our application provides a preview mode, which shows roughly how the final product will appear. The preview may differ from the final composite in that it performs compositing on the images currently being displayed rather than on the underlying video, which is potentially represented at a much higher resolution. (The degree to which the preview differs from the final composite corresponds exactly to the degree to which the "compositing assumption" [12] is violated.) When viewing the motion-blurred result of compositing two video sequences, there is a similar difference between the preview provided in our editor and the actual result of the compositing operation.

Figure 6 The application.

Once the desired effect is achieved, the user can press a button that translates, scales, and composites the various clip-art elements into a single multiresolution video, employing the operations described in the appendix. This video may be saved for subsequent viewing, or it may be combined with other elements as clip-art to form an even more elaborate multiresolution video.

4.5 Multiresolution video QuickTime VR

Apple Computer's QuickTime VR (QTVR) allows a user to explore an environment by looking from a fixed camera position out into a virtual world in any direction. Chen [3] proposes a potential augmentation of QTVR based on quadtrees that would provide two benefits. First, it would allow users to zoom into areas where there is more detail than in other areas. Second, it would reduce aliasing when the user zooms out. We implemented this idea, and extended it in the time dimension as well. Two simple modifications to multiresolution video were all that were required to achieve this "multiresolution video QuickTime VR" (MRVQTVR?!). First, we treat the video frames as panoramic images, periodic in the x direction. Second, we warp the displayed frames into cylindrical projections based on the view direction.

5 Results

We have implemented all of the operations of the previous section as part of a single prototype multiresolution video editing and viewing application, shown in Figure 6. Using the application, a user can zoom in and out of a video either spatially or temporally, pan across a scene, grab different video clips and move them around with respect to each other, play forward or backward, and use several sliders and dials to adjust the zoom factor, the speed of play through the video, the desired frame rate, and the current position in time.

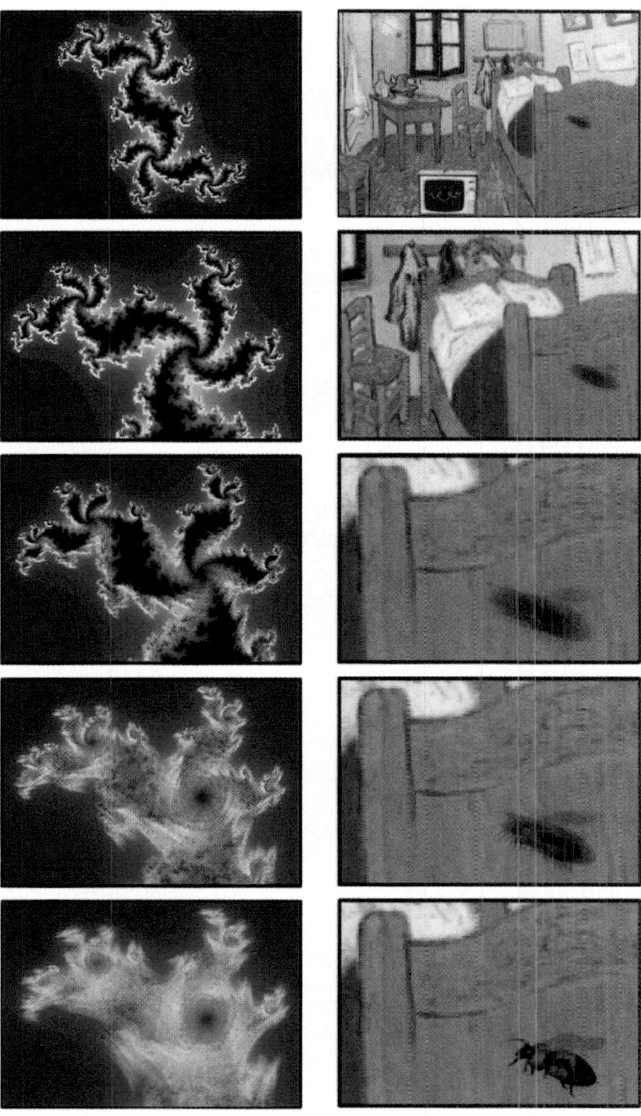

Figure 7 Julia set. **Figure 8** Van Gogh room.

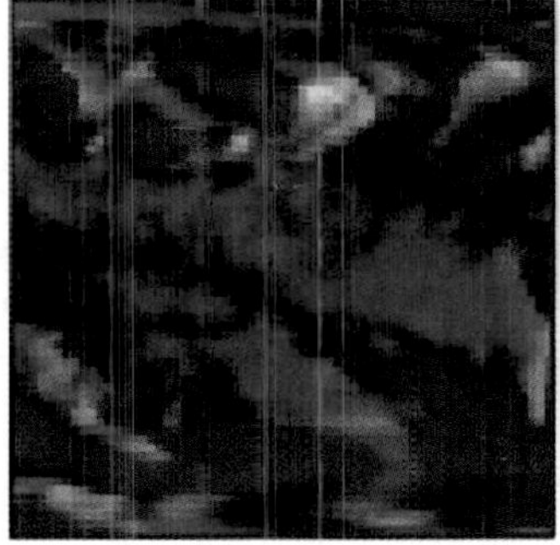

Figure 9 Wind stress over the Pacific Ocean.

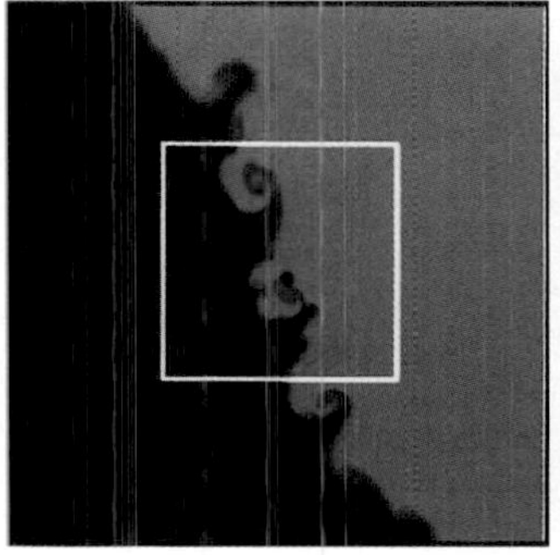
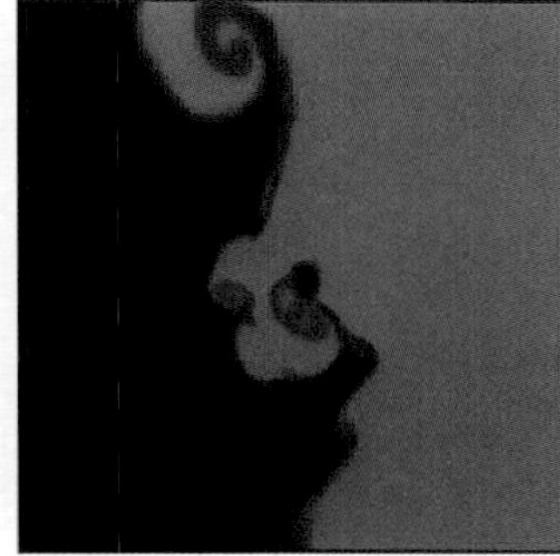

Figure 10 Fluid dynamics simulation.

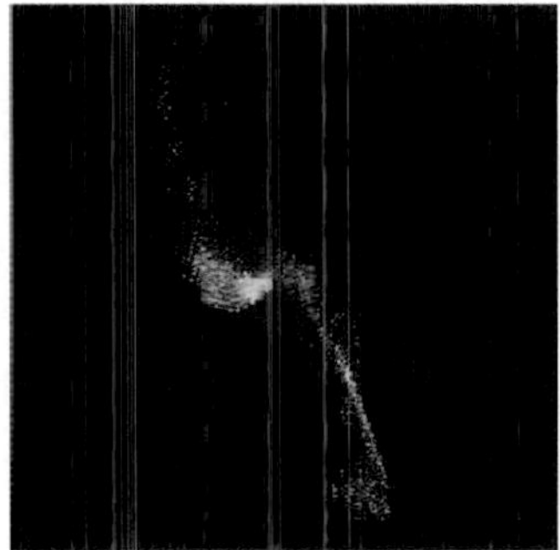
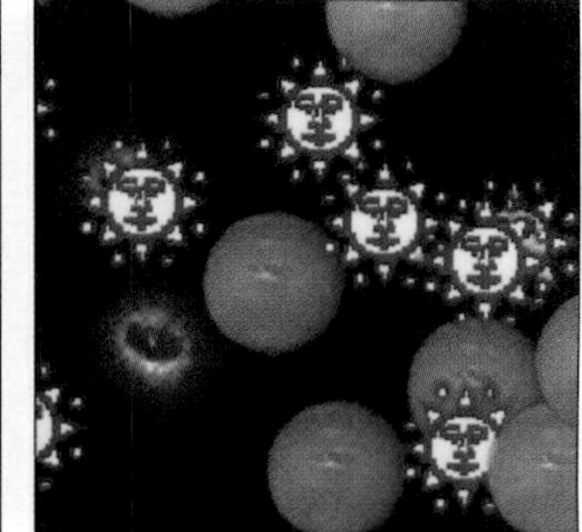

Figure 11 Astrophysical simulation of a galaxy.

Figure 7 illustrates how multiresolution video can be used for visualization of multiresolution data, in this case, an animation of the Julia set [4]. The data were generated procedurally, with higher spatial resolution in places of higher detail, as described in Section 3.1. The top three cells show increasing spatial detail, and the lower two cells show increasing "motion blur."

Figure 8 shows the result of arranging and compositing the many "clip-art" elements from the work area of the application shown in Figure 6 into a single multiresolution video, and then viewing this video at different spatial and temporal resolutions. (Apologies to Vincent Van Gogh.)

Figure 9 shows *wind stress*, the force exerted by wind over the earth's surface, measured for 2000 days over the Pacific Ocean by the National Oceanographic and Atmospheric Administration (NOAA). Wind stress is a vector quantity, which we encoded in multiresolution video using hue for direction and value for magnitude. The left image shows a leaf time node (reflecting a single day's measurements), while the right image shows the root time node (reflecting the average wind stress over the 2000-day period). Note the emergence of the dark continents in the right image, which reveals the generally smaller magnitude of wind stress over land.

The left side of Figure 10 shows a frame from a computational fluid dynamics simulation in which two fluids (one heavy, one light) interact in a closed tank. The simulation method [6] adaptively refines its sample grid in regions where the function is spatially complex, so the resolution of the data is higher at the interface between the two fluids than it is in the large, constant regions containing just one fluid. This refinement also occurs in time, providing higher temporal resolution in areas that are changing rapidly. The right image shows a close-up of the boxed region in the left image.

One more scientific visualization is shown in Figure 11. In this simulation, a galaxy is swept about a cluster of other astronomical bodies and is eventually ripped apart by their gravitational forces. The left image shows a close-up—late in the entire simulation— focused on the galaxy. The right image shows an even closer view of a single frame in which some whimsical high-resolution detail has been added. (However, creating the entire video sequence at this level of detail would be prohibitively expensive.)

Finally, Figure 12 shows a QTVR panoramic image that we have adapted for use with multiresolution video QuickTime VR. Over the picture frame on the wall we have composited the entire Van Gogh room video from Figure 8.

Figure 12 Panoramic image for multiresolution video QuickTime VR, and two views in the scene.

Figure	*Video*	*Disk Size*	*Memory Size*	*Unires Size*
7	Julia set	23,049	58,926	67,109
8	Van Gogh	46,738	98,798	34,359,730
9	Wind stress	68,566	134,201	33,554
10	Fluids	40,091	106,745	536,870
11	Galaxy	37,222	315,098	137,438,953
12	Panorama	47,723	100,804	2,199,023,256

Table 1 Sizes (in Kb) of some example multiresolution video clips.

Table 1 reports information about the storage space for the examples in Figures 7–12. The "Disk Size" column gives the total amount of space required to store the entire structure on disk, with averages and pointers included, after it has been compressed without loss using a Lempel-Ziv compressor [20]. The next column, "Memory Size" gives the total space required in memory, including all averages, pointers, and flags. The "Unires Size" column reports the total space that would be required to store the raw RGBA pixel values, assuming the entire video had been expanded to its highest spatial and temporal resolution present anywhere in the multiresolution video, but not including spatial or temporal averages. With the exception of the wind stress data, all of the video clips were smaller (in several cases much, much smaller) in the multiresolution video format than they would be in a uniresolution format, despite the overhead of the spatial and temporal averages. The wind stress data was difficult to consolidate because it has very little spatial or temporal coherence. The galaxy data compressed very well on disk because all of the colors stored in our structure (most of which were black) were selected from a small palette of very few colors.

6 Future work

This investigation of multiresolution video suggests a number of areas for future work:

User-interface paradigms. As in the multiresolution image work of Berman *et al.* [2], there is an important user-interface issue to be addressed: How does the user know when there is more spatial or temporal detail present in some part of the video? We have considered changing the cursor in areas where there is more spatial detail present than is currently being displayed. Perhaps a timeline showing a graph of the amount of temporal detail present in different parts of the video would address the corresponding temporal problem.

Environment mapping. Multiresolution video could be used for environment maps that change in time, allowing, for example, the rendering of a crystal glass, with animated objects in the environment reflecting in the glass. One benefit of using a multiresolution representation is that as the viewpoint and curvature of the glass surface vary, an accurate rendering may require more or less information from the surrounding environment.

Better compression. We currently require the up-links in our representation to point to a time-ancestor, primarily because coherence is fairly easy to discover this way. However, by relaxing this restriction—that is, by allowing up-links to point to any other place in the structure—we might be able to achieve much better compression, particularly for areas that have spatially repeating patterns. Unfortunately, finding the optimal set of up-links in this more general setting could be very expensive.

Spatial and temporal antialiasing. So far we only have used box-basis functions to represent the colors in multiresolution video. When the user zooms in to view a region at a higher spatial resolution than is present in the frame, large blocky pixels are displayed. Furthermore, if the user zooms in in time to view frames at higher temporal detail than is present in the video sequence, the motion is choppy. It would be interesting to explore the use of higher-order filters to produce smoother interpolations when the user views regions at higher resolution than is represented.

Acknowledgements

We would like to thank David Herbstman and David Simons for useful discussions during the initial phase of the project; Richard Anderson, Ronen Barzel, and Richard Ladner for valuable advice along the way; Neal Katz and Tom Quinn for the astronomical simulation; Randy LeVeque for the computational fluid dynamics; Xuri Yu for the wind stress data; Sean Anderson for the bee model; and Lightscape Technologies for the hotel lobby panorama.

This work was supported by an Alfred P. Sloan Research Fellowship (BR-3495), an NSF Presidential Faculty Fellow award (CCR-9553199), an ONR Young Investigator award (N00014-95-1-0728), an Intel Graduate Research Fellowship, and industrial gifts from Interval, Microsoft, and Xerox.

A Algorithms for combining video clips

This appendix describes a set of linear-time algorithms for translating, scaling and compositing multiresolution video sequences. Such operations are useful, for example, in the video clip-art application described in Section 4.4.

A.1 Translating a video clip

When combining video sequences, the various elements may need to be registered with respect to one another, requiring that they be translated and scaled within their own coordinate frames.

The basic operations of translation and scaling are well-understood for quadtrees [14]. However, as with drawing frames, we want these operations to take advantage of the temporal coherence encoded in the up-links of our data structure. For example, suppose we wanted to translate the fan and lamp video of Figure 3 a bit to the left. The regions of the video that contain the lamp should only be translated in the root node of the Time Tree, and all the time-children must somehow inherit that translation.

The following routine translates a multiresolution video clip, rooted at time node C, by an amount (dx, dy) at level ℓ_{tran} to produce a resulting Time Tree C'. In order to handle up-links, the routine is also passed the parent time node P of C, as well as the result P' of (previously) translating P by the given amount. In the top-level call to the procedure, the parameters P and P' are passed as NULL, and the Time Tree C' initially points to an image node containing just a single clear pixel. As the procedure writes its result into C', the translated image tree is developed (and padded with clear pixels as it is extended).

```
procedure TranslateTimeTree(C, C', P, P', dx, dy, ℓ_tran):
    TranslateFrame(C.frame, C'.frame, P.frame, P'.frame, dx, dy, ℓ_tran, 0, 0, 0)
    ComputeSpatialAverages(C'.frame)
    for each Half ∈ {Half1, Half2} of Timetree do
        if C.Half ≠ NULL then
            TranslateTimeTree(C.Half, C'.Half, C, C', dx, dy, ℓ_tran)
        end if
    end for
end procedure
```

The call to *ComputeSpatialAverages*() in the above procedure calculates average colors in the internal nodes of the image tree, using code similar to the *CreateFrame*() routine from Section 3.

The *TranslateFrame*() routine translates a single image tree c by an amount (dx, dy) at level ℓ_{tran}. In general the translation can cause large regions of constant color (leaves high in c) to be broken up across many nodes in the resulting tree c'. To handle the up-links, we must pass into the procedure the time-parent p of c, as well as the result p' of (previously) translating p. We also pass into the procedure arguments x, y and ℓ (initially all 0), which keep track of the location and level of node c.

```
procedure TranslateFrame(c, c', p, p', dx, dy, ℓ_tran, x, y, ℓ):
    if c.Type = COLOR or c.uplink.linked or ℓ_tran = ℓ then
        w ← 2^(ℓ_tran − ℓ)
        r ← Rectangle(w · x + dx, w · y + dy, w, w, ℓ_tran)
        PutRectInTree(c, c', p', r, 0, 0, 0)
    else
        for each i, j ∈ {0, 1} do
            TranslateFrame(c.child[i, j], c', p.child[i, j], p', dx, dy, ℓ_tran,
                                                    2x + i, 2y + j, ℓ + 1)
        end for
    end if
end procedure
```

The above procedure recursively descends image tree c, pausing to copy any "terminal" squares that it encounters as it goes. There are three kinds of terminal squares: large regions of constant color, subtrees that hang from level ℓ_{tran}, and up-links. In the first two cases, we copy the source from the original tree, whereas in the latter case we copy from the time-parent. A square's size and position are combined in a single structure *Rectangle*$(x, y, width, height, \ell_r)$, the coordinates of which are relative to the level ℓ_r. When the procedure finds one of these squares, it copies it into the resulting tree using the following procedure:

```
procedure PutRectInTree(c, c', p', r, x, y, ℓ):
    coverage ← CoverageType(r, x, y, ℓ)
    if coverage = COMPLETE then
        if c.type = COLOR or not c.uplink.linked then
            c' ← c
        else
            c' ← p'
            c'.uplink.linked ← TRUE
        end if
    else if coverage = PARTIAL then
        for each i, j ∈ {0, 1} do
            PutRectInTree(c, c'.child[i, j], p'.child[i, j], r, 2x + i, 2y + j, ℓ + 1)
        end for
    end if
end procedure
```

The above procedure recursively descends the result tree c' to find those nodes that are completely covered by the given rectangle, an approach reminiscent of Warnock's algorithm [4]. The function *CoverageType*(r, x, y, ℓ) returns a code indicating whether rectangle r completely covers, partially covers, or does not cover pixel (x, y) at level ℓ. For those nodes that are completely covered, *PutRectInTree*() copies either a color or a pointer, depending on the type of node being copied. If the node is a color, then the color is simply copied to its new position. If the node is a pointer but not an up-link, the routine copies the pointer, which essentially moves an entire subtree from the original tree. Finally, if the node is an up-link, the routine copies the corresponding pointer from the (already translated) time-parent p'. Thus, we have to descend the result tree c' and its time-parent p' in lock-step in the recursive call.

As with *DrawImage*(), the complexity of *TranslateFrame*() is related to the number of nodes it copies using *PutRectInTree*(). The latter procedure is dependent on the number of nodes it encounters when copying a rectangle. Since the former call makes a single pass over the source quadtree c, and the collective calls to the latter procedure make a single pass over the resulting image tree c', the overall complexity is proportional to the sum of the complexities of c and c'.

A.2 Scaling a video clip

Here, we consider scaling a Time Tree by some integer factors s_x in the x direction and s_y in y. Note that to shrink a video frame by any power of two in *both* x and y we simply insert more image parent nodes above the existing image root, filling in any new siblings with "clear." Conversely, to magnify a video frame by any power of two, we simply scale all other videos down by that factor, since we are only interested in their *relative* scales. Thus, scaling both x and y by any power of two is essentially free, and we can really think of the scales as being $s_x/2^\ell$ and $s_y/2^\ell$ for any (positive or negative) ℓ. For efficiency, it is best to divide both s_x and s_y by their greatest common power-of-two divisor.

The algorithms for scaling multiresolution video are structurally very similar to those for translation. The two main differences are that they copy scaled (rather than translated) versions of the source tree into the destination tree, and that they must descend down to the leaves of the image trees. We omit the specific pseudocode for scaling a video clip for lack of space. The time complexity of scaling is the same as translation: linear in the size of the input and output.

A.3 Compositing two video clips

The final operation addressed in this appendix is compositing two Time Trees A and B using the compositing operation op [12]:

```
function CompositeTimeTrees(A, B, op): returns TimeTree
    for each Half ∈ {Half1, Half2} do
        if A.Half = NULL and B.Half = NULL then
            Result.Half ← NULL
        else
            Ahalf ← A.Half
            Bhalf ← B.Half
            if Ahalf = NULL then Ahalf ← NewUplinkNode(A) end if
            if Bhalf = NULL then Bhalf ← NewUplinkNode(B) end if
            Result.Half ← CompositeTimeTrees(Ahalf, Bhalf, op)
        end if
    end for
    Result.frame ← CompositeFrames(A.frame, B.frame, FALSE, FALSE,
                                    Result.Half1.frame, Result.Half2.frame, op)
    return Result
end function
```

This function recursively traverses A and B in a bottom-up fashion, compositing child time nodes first, then their parents. If one of A or B has more temporal resolution than the other, then a temporary node is created by the function *NewUplinkNode*(). Invoking this function with the argument A creates a new *TimeNode* containing a single *ImageNode*, each of whose four children is an up-link pointing to its "time-parent" in A.

The following function works on two image trees a and b, taking a pair of arguments *aUp* and *bUp* that are set to FALSE in the top-level call; these flags are used to keep track of whether a and b are really parts of a time-parent. The function also takes a pair of arguments c_1 and c_2 that are the time-children of the resulting tree. In order to pass c_1 and c_2, the *CompositeTimeTrees*() function must have already computed these time-children, which is why it makes a bottom-up traversal of the Time Tree.

```
function CompositeFrames(a, b, aUp, bUp, c1, c2, op): returns ImageNode
    if a.uplink.linked then aUp ← TRUE end if
    if b.uplink.linked then bUp ← TRUE end if
    if aUp and bUp then return NULL end if
    if a.Type = COLOR and b.Type = COLOR then
        if c1 = NULL or c2 = NULL then
            return ImageNode(COLOR, CompositePixels(a, b, op))
        else
            return ImageNode(COLOR, Average(c1.avgcolor, c2.avgcolor))
        end if
    end if
    for each i, j ∈ {0, 1} do
        result.child[i, j] ← CompositeFrames(GC(a, i, j), GC(b, i, j),
                                  aUp, bUp, GC(c1, i, j), GC(c2, i, j), op)
    end for
    result.avgcolor ← AverageChildColors(result)
    return result
end function
```

We composite two image trees by traversing them recursively, in lock-step, compositing any leaf nodes. Child colors are propagated up to parents to construct internal averages. The helper function *GC*() (for "*GetChild*" or "*GetColor*") simply returns its argument node if it is a color, or the requested child if it is a subtree.

There are two subtleties to this algorithm. The first is that when the routine finds some region of the result for which both a and b are up-links (or subtrees of up-links), then it can assume that the result will be an up-link as well; in this case it simply returns NULL. Later, after all of the frames in the Time Tree have been composited, we invoke a simple function that traverses the Time Tree once, replacing all NULL pointers with the appropriate up-link. (This assignment cannot occur in *CompositeFrames*() because the nodes to which the up-links will point have not been computed yet.) The second subtlety is that if time-child c_1 or c_2 is NULL it means that the resulting image node has no time-children: either the node is part of an image tree that hangs from a leaf of the Time Tree, or its children are up-links. In either case we perform the compositing operation. If, on the other hand, c_1 and c_2 exist, then we are working on an internal node in the Time Tree and we can simply average c_1 and c_2.

The compositing operation described in this section creates a new Time Tree that uses up-links to take advantage of any temporal coherence in the resulting video. Since this resulting Time Tree is built using two bottom-up traversals, the complexity of creating it is linear in the size of the input trees.

References

[1] J. Adams, R. Garcia, B. Gross, J. Hack, D. Haidvogel, and V. Pizzo. Applications of multigrid software in the atmospheric sciences. *Monthly Weather Review*, 120(7):1447–1458, July 1992.

[2] Deborah F. Berman, Jason T. Bartell, and David H. Salesin. Multiresolution painting and compositing. In *Proceedings of SIGGRAPH '94*, Computer Graphics Proceedings, Annual Conference Series, pages 85–90, July 1994.

[3] Shenchang Eric Chen. Quicktime VR—an image-based approach to virtual environment navigation. In *Proceedings of SIGGRAPH 95*, Computer Graphics Proceedings, Annual Conference Series, pages 29–38, August 1995.

[4] James D. Foley, Andries van Dam, Steven K. Feiner, and John F. Hughes. *Computer Graphics: Principles and Practice*. Prentice-Hall, 1990.

[5] D. Le Gall. MPEG: A video compression standard for multimedia applications. *CACM*, 34(4):46–58, April 1991.

[6] Randy LeVeque and Marsha Berger. AMRCLAW: adaptive mesh refinement + CLAWPACK. `http://www.amath.washington.edu/~rjl/amrclaw/`

[7] A. S. Lewis and G. Knowles. Video compression using 3D wavelet transforms. *Electronics Letters*, 26(6):396–398, 15 March 1990.

[8] S. McCormick and U. Rude. A finite volume convergence theory for the fast adaptive composite grid methods. *Applied Numerical Mathematics*, 14(1–3):91–103, May 1994.

[9] Leonard McMillan and Gary Bishop. Plenoptic modeling: An image-based rendering system. In *Proceedings of SIGGRAPH 95*, Computer Graphics Proceedings, Annual Conference Series, pages 39–46, August 1995.

[10] Arun N. Netravali and Barry G. Haskell. *Digital Pictures*. Plenum Press, New York, 1988.

[11] Ken Perlin and Luiz Velho. Live paint: Painting with procedural multiscale textures. In *Proceedings of SIGGRAPH 95*, Computer Graphics Proceedings, Annual Conference Series, pages 153–160, August 1995.

[12] Thomas Porter and Tom Duff. Compositing digital images. In Hank Christiansen, editor, *Computer Graphics (SIGGRAPH '84 Proceedings)*, volume 18, pages 253–259, July 1984.

[13] Steven Radecki. *Multimedia With Quicktime*. Academic Press, 1993. ISBN 0-12-574750-0.

[14] Hanan Samet. *Applications of Spatial Data Structures*. Addison-Wesley, Reading, Massachusetts, 1990.

[15] P. S. Sathyamurthy and S. V. Patankar. Block-correction-based multigrid method for fluid flow problems. *Numerical Heat Transfer, Part B (Fundamentals)*, 25(4):375–94, June 1994.

[16] I. Suisalu and E. Saar. An adaptive multigrid solver for high-resolution cosmological simulations. *Monthly Notices of the Royal Astronomical Society*, 274(1):287–299, May 1995.

[17] Jonathan Swartz and Brian C. Smith. A resolution independent video language. In *ACM Multimedia 95*, pages 179–188. ACM, Addison-Wesley, November 1995.

[18] S. L. Tanimoto and Theo Pavlidis. A hierarchical data structure for picture processing. *Computer Graphics and Image Processing*, 4(2):104–119, June 1975.

[19] Lance Williams. Pyramidal parametrics. In *Computer Graphics (SIGGRAPH '83 Proceedings)*, volume 17, pages 1–11, July 1983.

[20] L. Ziv and A. Lempel. A universal algorithm for sequential data compression. *IEEE Trans. Inform.Theory, Vol.IT-23*, (3), May 1977.

A Cellular Texture Basis Function

Steven Worley[1]

ABSTRACT

Solid texturing is a powerful way to add detail to the surface of rendered objects. Perlin's "noise" is a 3D basis function used in some of the most dramatic and useful surface texture algorithms. We present a new basis function which complements Perlin noise, based on a partitioning of space into a random array of cells. We have used this new basis function to produce textured surfaces resembling flagstone-like tiled areas, organic crusty skin, crumpled paper, ice, rock, mountain ranges, and craters. The new basis function can be computed efficiently without the need for precalculation or table storage.

INTRODUCTION

Procedural texturing has proved itself valuable in image synthesis, allowing for complex surfaces to be rendered without requiring image mapping or hand modeling of geometric details. The most useful texturing techniques were introduced by Perlin [7] with his introduction of a fractal noise basis function which has become the primary tool used in procedural texturing. Since the fractal noise basis does not need any storage or precomputation, and returns a value for all locations in $\Re^3$, it is easy to use and applicable to many applications. The scalar value can be directly mapped into a color, but it is often used for spatially perturbing regular patterns. Its derivatives can be used for bump mapping. [1, 3, 5, 6, 7, 8]

Many texture algorithms are not as broadly applicable as noise because of their limited form. For example, the class of *reaction-diffusion* textures, as in [10], provides interesting surfaces, with a character that provides features such as spots and stripes. An algorithm by Miyata [4] generates impressive stone wall patterns. These methods, while powerful, aren't as generally useful as noise since they require extensive precomputation and don't return a scalar value to be used as part of a larger texture.

The simple functional nature of noise makes it an adaptable tool one might call a texture "basis" function. A basis function should be a scalar value, defined over $\Re^3$. This allows it to be used in the same manner noise is applied. Fourier methods [1, 2] produce effective basis functions, but usually similar appearances can be produced more easily using noise. The immense utility of the noise function motivates us to find new texture functions that can also be used as basis functions, so they may be used in the same versatile manner that noise is used.

[1]405 El Camino Real Suite 121, Menlo Park CA 94025 E-mail: steve@worley.com

In this paper, we propose a new set of related texture basis functions. They are based on scattering "feature points" throughout $\Re^3$ and building a scalar function based on the distribution of the local points. The use of distributed points in space for texturing is not new; "bombing" is a technique which places geometric features such as spheres throughout space, which generates patterns on surfaces that cut through the volume of these features, forming polkadots, for example. [9, 5] This technique is not a basis function, and is significantly less useful than noise. Lewis also used points scattered throughout space for texturing. His method forms a basis function, but it is better described as an alternative method of generating a noise basis than a new basis function with a different appearance.[3]

In this paper, we introduce a new texture basis function that has interesting behavior, and can be evaluated efficiently without any precomputation. After defining the function and its implementation, we show some applications demonstrating its utility.

nTH-CLOSEST POINT BASIS FUNCTION

We can define a new basis function based on the idea of random *feature points*. Imagine points randomly distributed through all of $\Re^3$. For any location $\mathbf{x}$, there is some feature point which lies closer to $\mathbf{x}$ than any other feature point. Define $F_1(\mathbf{x})$ as the distance from $\mathbf{x}$ to that closest feature point. As $\mathbf{x}$ is varied, F_1 varies smoothly since the distance between the sample location and the fixed feature point varies smoothly. However, at certain cusp locations, the point $\mathbf{x}$ will be equidistant between two feature points. Here, the value of $F_1(\mathbf{x})$ is still well defined, since the value is the same no matter which feature point is chosen to calculate the distance. Varying the position of $\mathbf{x}$ will return values of F_1 that are still continuous, though the derivative of F_1 will change discontinuously as the distance calculation "switches" from one feature point to its neighbor.

It can be seen that the locations where the function F_1 "switches" from one feature point to the next (where its derivative is discontinuous) are along the equidistance planes that separate two points in $\Re^3$. These planes are exactly the planes that are computed by a Voronoi diagram, which by definition partitions space into cellular regions where all the points within each region are closer to its defining point than any other point.

The function $F_2(\mathbf{x})$ can be defined as the distance between the location $\mathbf{x}$ and the feature point which is the *second* closest to the $\mathbf{x}$. With similar arguments as before, F_2 is continuous everywhere, but its derivative is not at those locations where the second-closest point swaps with either the first-closest or third-closest. Similarly, we can define $F_n(\mathbf{x})$ as the distance between $\mathbf{x}$ and the nth closest feature point.

The functions F have some interesting properties. F_n is always continuous. F_n are nondecreasing; $0 \leq F_1(\mathbf{x}) \leq F_2(\mathbf{x}) \leq F_3(\mathbf{x})$. In general, $F_n(\mathbf{x}) \leq F_{n+1}(\mathbf{x})$ by the definition of F_n. The gradient of F_n is simply the unit direction vector from the nth closest feature point to $\mathbf{x}$.

COMPUTATION OF $F_n(\mathbf{x})$

To evaluate the functions F_n, we must first define how feature points are spread through space. The density and distribution of points will change the character of the basis functions. We want an isotropic distribution of points to avoid artifacts such as an obvious grid-like pattern. This eliminates any regular lattices such as a cubic spacing. Even if the lattice points are jittered, the underlying lattice structure may cause odd patterns.

The simplest distribution is simply a Poisson distribution, which specifies a mean density of points in space, with the location of each point being independent of the other points. The expected number of points in any region is simply the point density times the volume of the region. There may be more or less than this expected number of points in the region; the exact probabilities of any number of points in a region can be computed by using the discrete Poisson distribution function.

Our approach divides space into a grid of uniformly spaced cubes, separated at the integer coordinate locations. Each "cube" in space can be uniquely represented by its integer coordinates, and by simple floor operations we can determine, for example, that a point like (1.2, 3.33, 2.3) lies within the cube indexed by (1, 3, 2).

Each cube in space may contain zero, one, or more feature points. We determine this on-the-fly quite simply by noting that the Poisson random distribution function describes the exact probabilities of each of the possible number of feature points occuring in the cube. For a mean density of λ feature points per unit volume , the probability of m points occuring in a unit cube is $(\lambda^{-m}\, e^{\lambda}\, m!)^{-1}$. Thus we can tabulate the probabilities for $m = 0, 1, 2, 3...$ and index a random number into this table to determine how many feature points fall within this cube. In practice, we use a density of about $m = 4$, but clamp the points in each cell to range between 1 and 9, for efficiency reasons discussed later. This cutoff in theory breaks some of the isotropy of the distribution of feature points, but in practice we see no visual consequence.

The "random" number we use to determine the number of feature points in a cube obviously must be unique to that cube and reproducible at need. There is a similar requirement in the noise function, which also uses a cubic lattice with fixed values associated with each gridpoint. The solution to this problem is to hash the three integer coordinates of a cube into a single 32 bit integer which is used as the seed for a fast random number generator. One simple (but poor) hash function of three variables (i, j, k) is a linear combination like $541i + 79j + 31k \bmod 2^{32}$, but a much better (less correlated) method uses permutation arrays, such as the one described in ([1] pp 198.)

We find the number of points in the cube by using the first value from the seeded random number generator as an index into a list of the precomputed probabilities for different numbers of feature points. This is a binary search needing just couple of comparison tests to identify m.

Next, we compute the locations of the m feature points. Again, these are values that are random, but fixed for each cube. We use the already initialized random number generator to compute the XYZ locations of each of the feature points. These coordinates are relative to the base of the cube, and always range from 0..1 for each coordinate.

As we generate these points, we compute its distance to the original function evaluation location x, and keep a sorted list of the of the n smallest distances we've seen so far. As we test each point in turn, we effectively do an insertion sort to include the new point in the current list. This sounds expensive, but for typical values of n of 1 or 2, these cases are hard-wired tests of only one or two comparisons.

This finds the closest feature points and the values of F_n for the points within the current cube of space. However, the feature points within a neighboring cube could quite possibly contain a feature point even closer than the ones we have found already, so we must iterate among the boundary cubes too. Testing each of 26 boundary cubes would be slow, but by checking the closest distance we've computed so far (our tentative nth closest feature distance) we can throw out whole rows of cubes at once by noting that no point in the cube could possibly contribute to our list. Typically, only 1–3 cubes actually need to be tested.

Note that when we compute F_n we are effectively finding values for $F_1, F_2, ..., F_n$ simultaneously. In practice our routine returns all these values, plus the direction vectors corresponding to each feature point, plus a unique ID integer for each point (equal to the hashed cube ID plus the index of the feature point as it was computed). These tend to be useful when using the function to form solid textures.

In practice, computation is extremely efficient. A fast, linear congruential (LCG) random number generator is effectively just an integer multiply and add. By using fixed point arithmetic, the 32 bit random number can be manipulated directly. We avoid square roots by sorting on squared distance. Testing a point requires generation of its coordinates (three multiplies), computing the squared distance to the sample location (three multiplies), and insertion into the best candidate list (usually one to three compares.) The computation speed is therefore surprisingly fast. In our implementation, simultaneously computing F_1 and F_2 requires about the same amount of time as computing one scale of Perlin's noise.

We also found that by varying the point density λ we were able to tune our algorithm. Low λ requires fewer points to be computed in each cube. Higher λ makes it more likely to find the best points in the initial cube, reducing the number of neighboring cubes that must also be tested. We can choose λ to optimize speed, since the final point density can be manipulated at evaluation by simply scaling x before $F_n(\mathbf{x})$ is evaluated.Our implementation was most efficient at about $\lambda = 3$.

We lost some isotropy with the decision to forbid empty cubes. This was done to solve the problem of having such a sparse set of points in the cubes that huge numbers of neighbors may have to be evaluated to find all potential candidates. This is mainly a problem with low λ, since higher densities quickly reduce the average number of neighbors that need to be visited.

APPLICATION TO TEXTURING

The effort in implementing a function to compute $F_n(\mathbf{x})$ is rewarded by its extreme effectiveness as a solid texturing primitive. As with the Perlin noise function, mapping values of the function into a color and normal-displacement can produce visually interesting and impressive effects. A dense collection of ways to use the noise function can be found in [1]; since this new texturing basis function has the same functional form, it can be used in similar ways (but with different appearances.)

In the simplest case, $F_1(\mathbf{x})$ can be mapped into a color spline and bump. The character of F_1 is very simple, since the function increases radially around each feature point. Thus, mapping a color to small values of F_1 will cause a surface texture to place spots around each feature point; polka dots! Figure 1 shows this radial behavior in the upper left corner.

More interesting behavior begins when we start using the functions F_2 and F_3, shown as grey gradients in the upper right and lower left of Figure 1. These have more rapid changes and internal structure, and are slightly more visually interesting. These can be directly mapped into colors and bumps, but they can also produce even more interesting patterns by forming linear combinations with each other. For example, since $F_2 \geq F_1$ for all $\mathbf{x}$, we can map the function $F_2(\mathbf{x}) - F_1(\mathbf{x})$ to colors and bumps. The bottom right of Figure 1 shows this as a grey scale. This combination has a value of

0 where $F_1 = F_2$, which occurs at the Voronoi boundaries. This allows an interesting way to make a latticework of connected ridges, forming a vein-like tracery.

If the F_1 function returns a unique ID number to represent the closest feature point's identity, this number can be used to form values that are constant over a Voronoi cell; for example to shade the entire cell a single constant color. When combined with bumping based on $F_2 - F_1$, quite interesting surfaces can be easily generated. Figure 2 shows this technique, which also uses fractal noise discoloration in each cell. Note that unlike [4], no precomputation is necessary and the surface can be applied at any 3D object.

Bump mapping of the flagstone-like areas is particularly effective, and it is cheap to add since the gradient of F_n is just the radial unit vector pointing away from the appropriate feature point towards the sample location. Making raised spots or inset channels is done exactly like noise-based textures; ([1], pp105–110) has a useful discussion of applicable bump mapping methods.

We have slightly interesting patterns in the basis functions F_1, F_2, F_3 and now we see that the linear combination $F_2 - F_1$ forms a yet another basis. This leads us to experiment with other linear combinations, such as $2F_3 - F_2 - F_1$ or $F_1 + F_2$. In our first experiments, we generated about 40 different linear combinations to evaluate their appearance. We find that F_4 and other high n start looking similar, but the lower values of n (up to 4) are quite interesting and distinct. More importantly, linear combinations of these F_n have more "character" than the plain F_n, particularly differences of two or more simple bases. Figure 4 shows twenty sample surfaces which are all just examples of combinations of these low n basis functions ($C_1F_1 + C_2F_2 + C_3F_3 + C_4F_4$ for various values of C_n). We found that it was easy to try dozens of combinations simultaneously by mapping the value of each combination into a generic color spline. After empirically determining the range of values that the combination returns (by evaluating it at several thousand locations), we normalized this range to fall approximately between 0 and 1 for easier use as a texturing primitive. This process was only done once for each combination, after which it was simply hard-wired into the primitive basis.

These patterns are interesting and useful, but we can also use the basis functions to make *fractal* versions, much like noise is used to produce fractal noise. By computing multiple "scales" of the function at different weights and scaling factors, a more visually complex appearance can be made. This is a simple loop, computing a function $G_n = \sum 2^{-i} F_n(2^i \mathbf{x})$ for moderate ranges of i ($i = 0-5$), and using G_n as the index for colors and bumps.

The fractal versions of any of the basic basis function combinations become extremely appealing. Figure 5 shows a fractal version of F_1 forming the spotted pattern and bumps on the hide of a creature. Fractal noise is used for the tongue, and a linear gradient is applied to the main body for color variation. Other fractal versions of primitives are shown in the row of cut tori in Figure 6.

The fractal version of F_1 is perhaps the most useful. Applied solely as bump map, the surface becomes crumpled like paper or tinfoil. This surface has been extremely popular with artists as a way to break up a smooth surface, providing a subtle roughening with an appearance unlike fractal noise bumps. A surprising discovery was that a reflective, bumped map plane with this "crumple" appearance bears an excellent resemblance to seawater, as shown in Figure 7.

A variation of the algorithm uses different distance metrics. Using the Manhattan distance metric forms regions that are rigidly rectangular, but still random. These make surfaces like random right angle channels; useful for space ship hulls. Figure 3 shows a non-fractal version of F_1 which uses this Manhattan distance metric. A radial coordinate version can cover spheres, creating a surface similar to the "Death Star."

Other variations of the basic algorithms can produce even more effects. The density of the feature points can be made to vary spatially, allowing for small, dense features in one area and larger features in another. Object geometry might be used to disperse precomputed feature spots (similar to Turk[10]) at the expense of requiring precomputation and table lookup, but gaining object surface dependence similar to the advantages Turk found. The algorithm is normally computed in 3D, but 2D variants are even faster. 4D variants can be used for animated fields, though we find this to become significantly slower to compute by about a factor of 10.

CONCLUSION

We have found that this new texturing basis function is extremely useful in practical texture design. We have been using it in commercial products for several years and it is now an essential part of our texturing toolkit. It complements Perlin fractal noise; in any algorithm that uses noise, the new basis can be substituted. The visual effects are not necessarily similar, but this is desirable since it increases the visual diversity of the possible images.

ACKNOWLEDGEMENTS

Thanks to Richard Payne for his Gator and to Greg Teegarden for his water renderings. Particular thanks go to the referees with their excellent suggestions which made this a significantly better paper.

References

[1] EBERT, D. E. *Texturing and Modeling: A Procedural Approach* Academic Press, 1994.

[2] GARDNER, G. Y. Simulation of natural scenes using textured quadric surfaces. In *Computer Graphics (SIGGRAPH '84 Proceedings)* (July 1984), H. Christiansen, Ed., vol. 18, pp. 11–20.

[3] LEWIS, J.-P. Algorithms for solid noise synthesis. In *Computer Graphics (SIGGRAPH '89 Proceedings)* (July 1989), J. Lane, Ed., vol. 23, pp. 263–270.

[4] MIYATA, K. A method of generating stone wall patterns. In *Computer Graphics (SIGGRAPH '90 Proceedings)* (Aug. 1990), F. Baskett, Ed., vol 24, pp. 387–394.

[5] PEACHEY, D. Solid texturing of complex surfaces. In *Computer Graphics (SIGGRAPH '85 Proceedings)* (July 1985), B. A. Barsky, Ed., vol. 19, pp. 279–286.

[6] PEACHEY, D. Writing renderman shaders. In *1992 Course 21 Notes*. ACM SIGGRAPH, 1992.

[7] PERLIN, K. An image synthesizer. In *Computer Graphics (SIGGRAPH '85 Proceedings)* (July 1985), B. A. Barsky, Ed., vol. 19, pp. 287–296.

[8] PERLIN, K., AND HOFFERT, E. M. Hypertexture. In *Computer Graphics (SIGGRAPH '89 Proceedings)* (July 1989), J. Lane, Ed., vol. 23, pp. 253–262.

[9] SCHACHTER, B. J., AND AHUIA, N. Random pattern generation processes. *Computer Graphics and Image Processing 10* (1979), 95–114.

[10] TURK, G. Generating textures for arbitrary surfaces using reaction-diffusion. In *Computer Graphics (SIGGRAPH '91 Proceedings)* (July 1991), T. W. Sederberg, Ed., vol. 25, pp. 289–298.

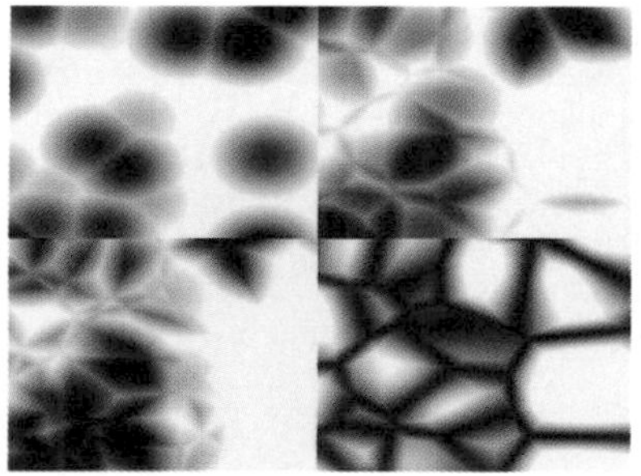
Figure 1: Plain basis functions

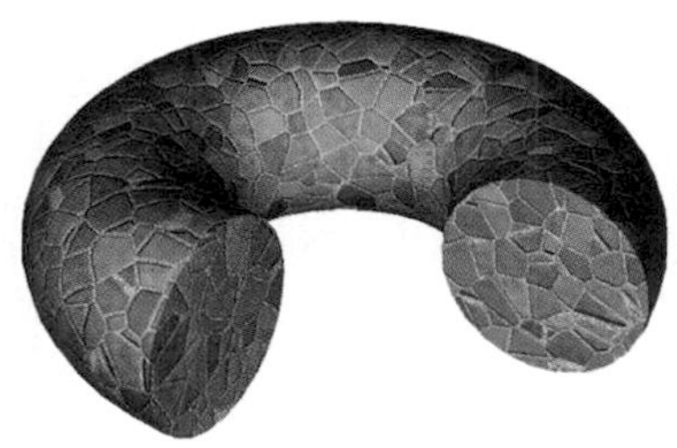
Figure 2: $F_2 - F_1$

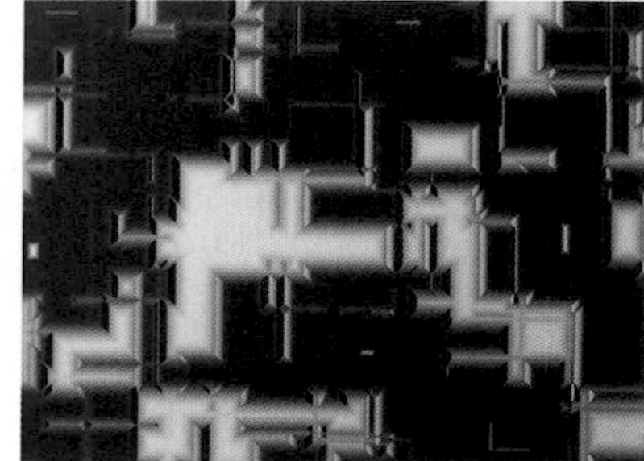
Figure 3: F_1, Manhattan distance metric

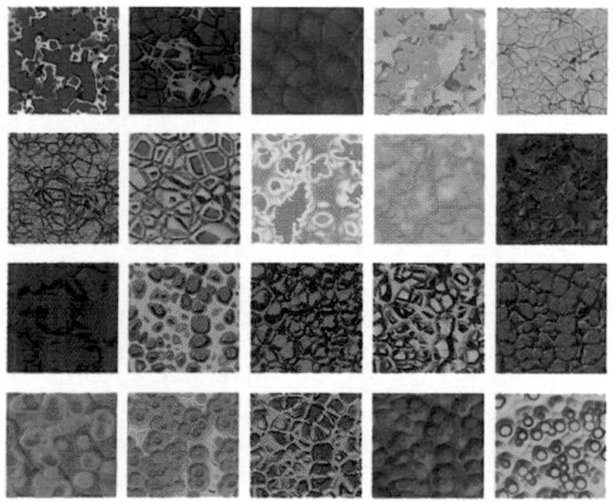
Figure 4: Various linear combinations of F_{1-4}

Figure 5: Fractal F_1 mapped to color and bumps

Figure 6: Fractal versions of F_{1-4} combinations

Figure 7: Fractal F_1 mapped to bump

A Framework for Interactive Texturing on Curved Surfaces

Hans Køhling Pedersen
Computer Science Department
Stanford University*

Abstract

Existing techniques for texturing curved surfaces are either only applicable for a limited subset of surface representations (3d painting of parametric patches or dense polygonal meshes for example), or do not lend themselves naturally to interactive texture editing (e.g. procedural and solid textures). Although such methods have been used to produce stunning effects, there is a lack of flexible and general purpose tools, such as those provided by 2d image processing applications. This work argues that interactive texturing could benefit from a more cohesive paradigm built around a kernel of powerful and general operations. Using an analogy to the evolution of 2d painting algorithms, the paper motivates a framework for interactive texturing operations on curved surfaces and describes an approach for translating, rotating, and warping regions of texture (*patchinos*), on a surface. These ideas have been implemented for parametric and implicit surfaces. As an interesting side effect, this more unified framework also opens the door to a number of new interactive 3d texturing techniques that have no natural counterparts in two dimensions.

1 Introduction

In the past decade, 2d painting systems have revolutionized the field of desktop publishing. The success of these products has stimulated an intense research interest in interactive image processing tools and a diverse range of applications based on highly specialized operations has been absorbed into this thriving market, such as "Adobe PhotoShop", "Fractal Design Painter" and "Kai's Power Tools". However, underneath this diversity is an underlying framework consisting of a few general and powerful algorithms, most prominently the concepts of *digital compositing* [1] and *copy and paste* [2].

The idea behind compositing is to reduce the complexity of rendering by separating the image into a number of layers, generate an image for each layer, and subsequently synthesize the layers into one composite image using *mattes* and *alpha blending* [3]. Copy and paste operations allow portions of an image to be extracted, moved, warped and repositioned interactively. The two ideas supplement each other well as they share the underlying philosophy of looking at an image as a combination of layers that can be combined using high level operators. The two methods will henceforth be referred to under the common term of *image compositing*.

Today, image compositing forms the foundation for all commercial painting packages, a success which can be attributed to a convenient and intuitive user interface, simplicity and elegance of the underlying theoretical model, and computational efficiency that makes the idea practical.

1.1 Interactive 3d texturing

Compared to traditional framebuffer systems, which date back to the early 1970s [4], 3d painting is a new discipline [5]. Recently, however, the market for these products has experienced an explosive growth that rivals that of 2d systems a decade ago. Unfortunately, the literature on 3d painting algorithms exhibits a tendency to focus on one particular type of surface representation, such as parametric patches [5], scanned polygonal meshes [6], parameterized meshes [7], or implicit surfaces [8], thus polarizing the spectrum of painting algorithms rather than moving towards a unifying standard. Although the fundamental differences between the underlying surface representations make certain operations better suited for one particular class of surfaces than another (cubic patches, for example, are ideal for patterns utilizing trim curves, while polygonal meshes often provide a more compact representation for low frequency textures), it would be desirable to identify a nucleus of operations, a lowest common denominator, that could serve as a general framework for all painting systems. In order to design such an architecture, we need to identify a suitable core of generic operations. Fleisher et al. [9] introduced a novel framework for *cellular texturing* compatible with all standard surface representations. However, since our focus is on more general operations supported by an intuitive interface, the proven concept of image compositing forms an even better source of inspiration. Furthermore, Daily and Kiss's [10] recent study of users of painting systems concluded that artists are more likely to embrace a 3d application if its interface resembles that of the well known 2d packages. Motivated by these observations, this paper proposes a framework for interactive texturing of general smooth surfaces that extends the power of the interactive image compositing paradigm to three dimensions.

1.2 Overview

Section 2 presents an architecture for texturing operations on smooth surfaces, followed by a generalization of the basic concepts of image compositing to surfaces in section 3. Section 4 discusses more advanced high level operations, followed by a conclusion and ideas for future work.

* I can be reached at Laboratory for Computer Science, Massachusetts Institute of Technology.

2 Architecture

Before moving on to texture compositing on surfaces, we will start by developing an architecture that will allow such operations to be applied on general smooth models. Pedersen [8] took a step towards this goal with an approach for placing images arbitrarily on implicit surfaces in lieu of extending the method to other types of surfaces. In this section, a more elaborate architecture will be presented.

2.1 Surfaces

For some operations, such as dragging curves smoothly across a surface, it is most convenient to work with a representation that offers continuous derivatives, but for others a polyhedral approximation is more practical (estimating coordinate transformations between a surface and a patch on it, for example). To get the best of both worlds, surfaces are represented by a differentiable function as well as a parameterized polygonal mesh. For our study, we will assume that both representations are readily available. This assumption is reasonable because such techniques exist for widely used surface representations, such as spline patches (the trivial case), implicit surfaces [8], polyhedral surfaces [7, 11] and dense uniform point clouds [12].

```
Class Vector2   Real u,v
Class Vector3   Real x,y,z

Class Surface
  private:
    DifferentiableSurface smooth
            ; Differentiable function
    Mesh mesh   ; Parameterized polygonal mesh
  public:
    ComputeNormal(Sample p) ↦ Vector3
    Slide(Sample p, Vector3 v)
    ComputeCurve(Sample p1,Sample p2) ↦ Curve
    GetTextureCoordinates(Sample p) ↦ (u,v,patch_id)

Class DifferentiableSurface
  virtual Vector3 ComputeNormal(Sample p)
  virtual Slide(Sample p, Vector3 v)

Class Parametric : public DifferentiableSurface
  private:
    Patch patches[MAX_SIZE]
      ; Parameterizations for individual patches
  public:
    ComputeNormal(Sample p) ↦ Vector3
    Slide(Sample p, Vector3 v)

Class Implicit : public Smooth
  private:
    Gradient(Vector3 x) ↦ Vector3
    AttractPoint(Vector3 x) ↦ Vector3
            ; Prevents points from drifting away.
            ; See [13] for details.
  public:
    ComputeNormal(Sample p) ↦ Vector3
    Slide(Sample p, Vector3 v)
```

Figure 1: *Representation of surfaces. See section 2.1 for further comments.*

More specifically, surfaces are represented by the data structure shown in figure 1. *Slide* moves a sample point p with velocity v constrained to the surface[1], *Surface : ComputeCurve* computes a curve between two arbitrary points on the surface, and *GetTextureCoordinates* determines the surface texture coordinates corresponding to a point on the surface. Internally, *ComputeNormal* and *Move* are implemented using only the differentiable function, while the two latter procedures utilize both the smooth and polygonal representations.

Any high level texturing algorithm that can be implemented in terms of these primitives can be applied for any class for surfaces for which the above library is available.

2.2 Differentiable surfaces

Class *DifferentiableSurface* is used for operations that require a continuous derivative. In principle, it could have any number of sub-classes corresponding to subsets of surfaces with different mathematical representations, but we will focus on the important cases of implicit and parametric surfaces. Because different types of surfaces possess inherently different internal representations, surface samples are also represented as derived classes. The corresponding data structures are shown in figure 2.

```
Class Sample
  Vector3 x   ; Position

Class ParametricSample : public Sample
  Real u,v   ; (u,v) coordinates
  Integer patch_id   ; Index of surface patch

Implicit: ComputeNormal(Sample p) ↦ Vector3
  g = Gradient(p.x)
  return g/|g|

Implicit: Slide(Sample p, Vector3 v)
  v_proj = p.ProjectToTangentPlane(v)
  p.x = p.x + v_proj
  p.x = AttractPoint(p.x)

Parametric: ComputeNormal(Sample p) ↦ Vector3
  φ_u = patches[p.patch_id].U_Derivative(p.u, p.v)
  φ_v = patches[p.patch_id].V_Derivative(p.u, p.v)
  return (φ_u × φ_v)/|φ_u × φ_v|

Parametric: Slide(Sample p, Vector3 v)
  v_proj = p.ProjectToTangentPlane(v)
  ⟨⟨ Update (p.u,p.v,p.patch_id) by v_proj ⟩⟩
    ; See section 2.2 for detailed comments
```

Figure 2: *Implementation of smooth surfaces.*

In *Parametric:Slide*, the velocity vector v is projected to the tangent plane and the partial derivatives are used to estimate a uv-offset, which is added to $(p.u,p.v)$. Care must be taken when a sample moves across a patch boundary: first, the point is moved to the boundary of the patch, then $(p.u,p.v,p.patch\_id)$ is set to the corresponding triple in the adjacent patch's coordinates and, finally, a recursive call to *Slide* completes the operation.

Notice that although procedures like *ComputeNormal* and *Slide* may be implemented very differently for para-

[1] For simplicity, it is assumed that $|v|$ is small enough for the differentiable surface to be approximated by its tangent plane within this distance. Larger velocity vectors should be subdivided into a number of smaller steps.

metric and implicit surfaces, we do not have to worry about such low level details when we move on to design higher level operations. Thus, from now on we will no longer distinguish between different types of surfaces but formulate all algorithms in terms of the methods of the *Surface* superclass.

3 Texture compositing

Whereas digital images can be represented by a simple uniform grid of samples, the corresponding problem of sampling a texture on a 3d surface currently has no equally convenient solution. We choose to sample the texture signal in texture maps corresponding to parameterized polygonal patches (see [8] for a motivation of this representation).

Similar to image compositing our approach consists of three simple steps:

1. Copy a region of texture.
2. Move it.
3. Paste it back.

This section will describe how each step can be generalized to surfaces.

3.1 Copying and pasting

2d painting systems offer a variety of interactive and automatic tools for outlining regions of an image. After a region has been selected, a rectangular bounding region is copied along with an alpha channel specifying the opaqueness of each pixel. Whereas computing bounding boxes and copying pixels is uncomplicated for images, the corresponding problems for curved surfaces are a little less straightforward.

In our system, the region to be extracted is outlined by one or more closed polygonal curves on the surface using the *ComputeCurve* operation. Ideally, it would be convenient to compute a bounding box for the region automatically, but we leave this problem to future work and currently draw a rectangular bounding patch interactively. From now on, such a patch will be referred to as a *patchino* to distinguish it from the patches that constitute the polygonal mesh. After the patchino has been parameterized (see section 4 of [8] for details), the closed curves are projected to it ([8], section 5.1) and a matte is computed by performing an inside-outside test for each texel (in practice, we tessellate the closed regions and scan-convert the resulting triangles directly into the alpha channel). Finally, a coordinate transformation between the surface patches and the patchino is computed and used to copy the texels from the surface into the texture space of the latter. In section 5.2.1 of [8], an algorithm for *pasting* textures from a patchino to a surface was outlined (see also figure 9a), and the corresponding *cut* operation can be implemented similarly using the *GetTextureCoordinates* primitive (figure 9b). Although these algorithms are somewhat more time consuming to implement for surface textures than for images, the procedures are completely analogous and the simple and intuitive user interface is preserved.

3.2 Moving textures - overview

In two dimensions, regions of an image can be translated, rotated and scaled using simple affine transformations. Unfortunately, the attractive simplicity of planar geometry does not generalize directly to curved surfaces. In differential geometry, the literature on curves and surfaces in surfaces present various approaches to the problem of describing regions of curved surfaces independently of the surface representation. In some cases, such as cubic spline patches on low degree implicit surfaces [14], it is possible to derive expressions for regions of a surface analytically, but, unfortunately, the range of mathematical tools for analyzing this problem is limited, and existing results are too special case to be practical for our problem: to slide patches freely across general surfaces reliably and at interactive speed.

Due to these shortcomings of existing analytical tools, we choose to make some simplifying assumptions:

1. A patchino is approximated by a mesh of coupled springs connecting a grid of sample points.
2. As the patchino moves across the surface, only the sample points are constrained to remain on the surface.

Given these assumptions, moving a patchino can be formulated as a constrained optimization problem, namely that of minimizing metric distortion relative to some *rest shape* subject to the constraint that all samples in the grid must remain on the surface. Although parts of the patchino thus may not lie exactly on the surface, the accuracy with which it approximates the surface geometry can be chosen arbitrarily by increasing or decreasing the density of the samples in the mesh. Since most smooth surfaces are eventually rendered as a set of polygons instead of a differentiable function, it is not unreasonable to use a polygonal approximation to the patches in the texturing stage as well. We will return with a further discussion of the implications of these assumptions in section 6.

3.3 Moving textures - theory

Let $\phi : U \mapsto S$ be a parameterization of a regular patch, R, on smooth surface, S, that has a normal vector field with continuous derivative (notice that S is not required to have a parameterization).

Finding a reparameterization such that the metric distortion

$$E(U) = \int\int_U Error(\phi_u, \phi_v) du dv$$

is minimal, where ϕ_u and ϕ_v denote the partial derivatives and $Error$ is some objective function measuring the distortion within the patch, is a standard problem in graphics research [15, 7, 16, 11]. Various functionals have been proposed, weighting the preservation of angles and distances in different ways. The Green-Lagrange deformation tensor is a simple example:

$$E_{GL}(U) = \int\int_U ||G_\phi(u, v) - I||^2 du dv$$

$$= \int\int_U (\phi_u{}^2 - 1)^2 + 2(\phi_u \phi_v)^2 + (\phi_v{}^2 - 1)^2 du dv$$

where G_ϕ denotes the metric tensor of ϕ.

Our problem, however, is slightly different: instead of minimizing distortion relative to a plane, it is minimized relative to a curved rest shape parameterization θ:

$$\mathcal{E}(U) = \int\int_U ||G_\phi(u, v) - G_\theta(u, v)||^2 du dv$$

$$= \int\int_U (\phi_u{}^2 - \theta_u{}^2)^2 + 2(\phi_u \phi_v - \theta_u \theta_v)^2 + (\phi_v{}^2 - \theta_v{}^2)^2 du dv,$$

subject to the constraint that $\phi(U) \subseteq S$. Just like E_{GL} penalizes the deviation between the metric tensor to ϕ and the identity matrix, $\mathcal{E}$ measures the difference between the metric tensor of ϕ and that of θ. Naturally, there is a trade-off between minimizing metric distortion and the "stick-to-surface" constraint, and, aside from a few simple surfaces, it is impossible to avoid some degree of distortion.

Although conceptually simple, the problem of implementing these ideas feasibly in an interactive system is challenging. To make the approach practical, we will have to replace $\mathcal{E}$ with a slightly different functional.

3.3.1 Discretization

Given a patch on a surface, its parameterization, θ, is said to be the rest shape of any other patch (with parameterization ϕ) for which $\mathcal{E}(U) = 0$. As patchinos are stored as a discrete grid of samples rather than a continuous function, the rest shape is represented as a list of spring coordinates, (k_u, k_v), for each node, p_i, in the grid:

$$q_{ij}.x_{proj} = p_i.x + k_u^{ij} p_i.\theta_u + k_v^{ij} p_i.\theta_v$$

where $q_{ij}.x_{proj}$ denotes the projection of p_i's j'th neighbor onto the tangent plane at $p_i.x$ (see also *Sample* in figure 7), and (k_u^{ij}, k_v^{ij}) are the rest coordinates of spring j emanating from node i. Each (k_u, k_v) pair thus represents the coordinates of an adjacent node in the tangent plane through $p.x$ and spanned by the basis $p.\theta_u, p.\theta_v$ (see figure 3).

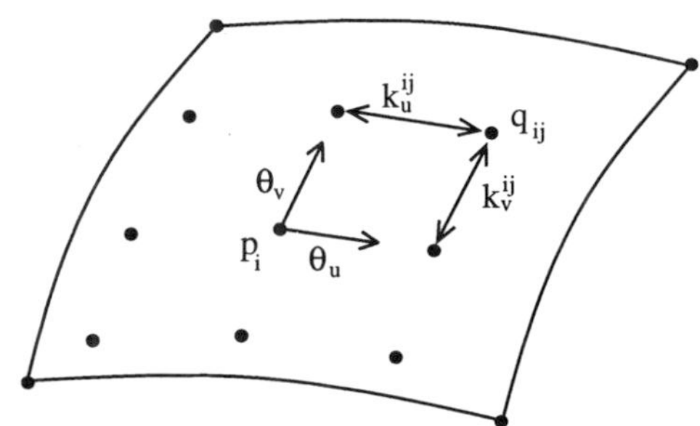

Figure 3: *The local coordinates of the rest lengths of the springs are measured in the (θ_u, θ_v) coordinate frame at p.*

The reason for measuring the rest lengths of the springs in local coordinates rather than in absolute distances is that the partial derivatives inevitably will change as the patchino moves across the surface, and fighting this distortion by trying to keep the metric tensors identical everywhere (see $\mathcal{E}$ above) is a losing battle that will quickly result in the patchino folding onto itself. Our solution to the tradeoff between minimizing $\mathcal{E}$ and preserving the structural integrity of the grid is to assign a priority to each sample point, indicating the relative importance of minimizing distortion in this particular region. Since the base surface was assumed to be relatively smooth, it is reasonable to allow a greater amount of distortion near the edges of a patchino than at its center, and this can be accomplished using local coordinates as described above and controlling the order in which the nodes are updated in each iteration. More specifically, the algorithm, which will be described in detail in section 3.4, proceeds in a spiral pattern emanating from the center as shown in figure 4.

The discretization of the modified $\mathcal{E}$ is

$$\mathcal{E}^*(U) = \sum_i \sum_j (k_{u_\phi}^{ij} - k_{u_\theta}^{ij})^2 + (k_{v_\phi}^{ij} - k_{v_\theta}^{ij})^2$$

where the greek subscript denotes the parameterization for which the derivatives define the basis vectors where the spring coordinates are measured. In essence, the procedure adapts the stiffness of the springs to the geometry of the surface, but still preserves the shape of the patch in the sense that no matter how far it moves from the location where its rest shape was specified, it will reattain its original shape when it returns.

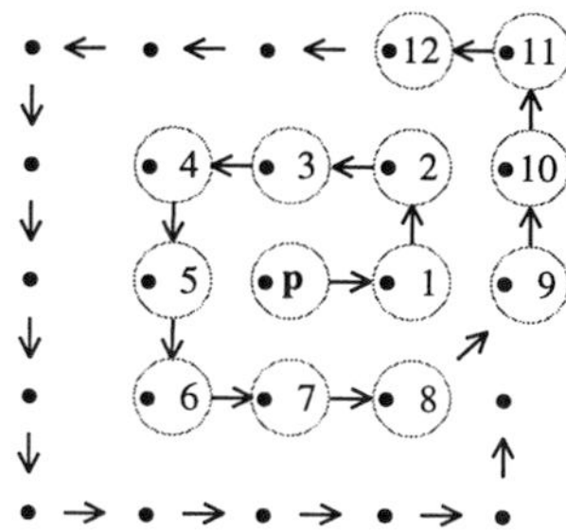

Figure 4: *The order in which the nodes are visited forms a spiral emanating from the center node.*

To summarize, the algorithm works by first estimating the partial derivatives at each sample point using finite differences, then minimizing $\mathcal{E}^*$ by updating the positions of the samples in a specific order subject to the constraint that all the samples must remain on the surface. These two steps are repeated continously, only interrupted by external forces exerted on a patchino by user interaction. We will return with more details on the implementation in a moment.

3.3.2 Moving patchinos

Motion can be integrated into the optimization procedure by repeating two steps. First, each sample point $p_i.x$ is moved with a velocity vector $p_i.v$, perturbing $\mathcal{E}^*$ slightly from a local minimum, and the objective function is then pulled back towards a minimum as described in the previous section.

As with any optimization technique, the robustness depends on the step size, and the trick is to pick the sample velocities so that the updated positions will remain in the proximity of a local minimum for $\mathcal{E}^*$.

3.4 Moving textures - implementation

Figure 7 outlines an implementation of the most basic operations needed for interacting with patchinos. In the following, each step will be described in more detail.

3.4.1 Freezing the rest shape

Before a patchino can be moved, its rest shape must be initialized to the parameterization of a patchino. The algorithm for *freezing* the current shape of a patch to its rest shape is sketched as *Patchino : Freeze* in figure 7. Given the resulting data structure and the partial derivatives at each node, the mesh can be optimized towards the rest shape as shown in procedure *Pathino : ReduceDistortion.*

3.4.2 Translation

In our interface, the user selects a patch by clicking on a control point. As the projection of this point is dragged in screen space, the patch moves constrained to the surface so that the control point on the patch follows the cursor. Per default, the control point is taken to be the center vertex, but it could be any fixed point on the patch. Thus, the input to the translation algorithm is simply a three-dimensional vector.

If this velocity vector only was applied to the center node, it might take many iterations for the operation to propagate to the entire patchino grid, and this lag makes the idea infeasible in an interactive system. A naive alternative would be to add the same velocity vector to every node, but this idea fails because it violates the stick-to-surface constraint in regions of high curvature. Instead, the velocity vector estimates are propagated outwards from

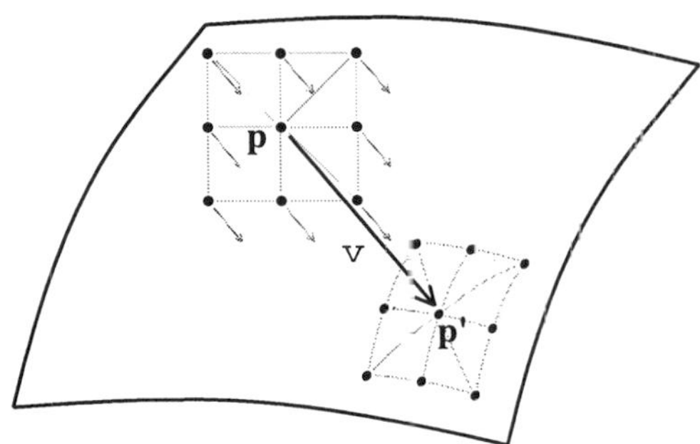

Figure 5: *Propagating transformation velocities through a patch. When a transformation is applied to the center point in the grid, similar transformations are applied to its neighbors.*

the control point in a spiral order (see figure 4): First, the location of the control sample, $p.x$, is moved with velocity v constrained to the surface using *Surface : Slide*, and the tangent plane component of the difference between the new and the old position is stored in $p.v$. Second, for each immediate neighbor, q, to the control point, $p.v$ is projected to the tangent plane at $q.x$ and restored to its original length, and the resulting velocity vector is used to update $q.x$ constrained to the surface. Finally, the velocity vector $q.v$ is computed as described for $p.v$. This spiral continues until every vertex has been visited.

3.4.3 Rotation

Rotations are performed by pulling a *handle vector* (see figure 9c) emanating from the center node and constrained to the tangent plane. As the user moves the cursor, the patchino is updated so that the center node remains fixed in screen space and the projection of the handle vector always points towards the cursor. The input to the rotation operation is thus an angular offset in the tangent plane to the center node.

Guessing a set of velocity vectors for a rotation is a little more tricky than the similar problem for translations, as even a tiny rotation angle could potentially result in large displacements at nodes further from the center, thus causing numerical difficulties. Our solution is to propagate the rotation velocity vectors using the same maximum step size for every node in the grid. This yields a faster angular velocity for nodes near the center of a patchino than for nodes at its border, bounding the maximum step size at the expense of introducing a delay for nodes further away from the center. In practice, this heuristic has performed well, and it provides a sensible solution to the tradeoff between interactive feedback and robustness. The details of the algorithm are outlined as *Patchino : Rotate* on figure 7.

3.4.4 Warping

While scaling and shearing are standard features in traditional painting systems, it appears that these operations may not be as useful on curved surfaces. Instead, more general non-linear warping operations have proven to be convenient.

Patches are not restricted to remain the same shape while they are being translated and rotated on the surface. The user can interactively deform a patch by manipulating control points. This type of warping is simple to implement given the framework described for the above operations:all that needs to be done is to modify the rest shape of the patch as it is being deformed, and the optimization process described in section 3.3.1 will automatically make the patch return to its new rest shape.

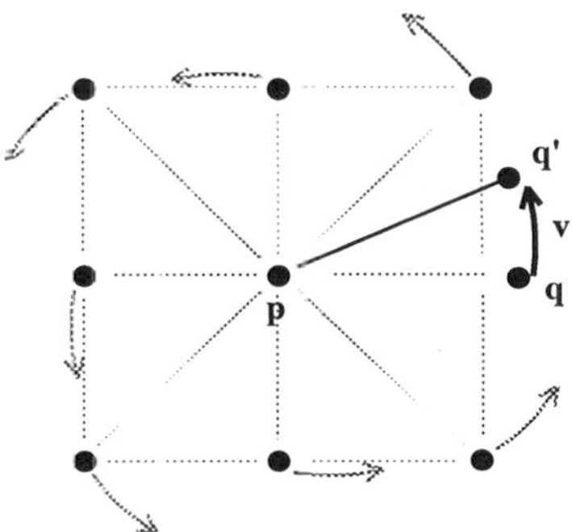

Figure 6: *Propagating rotations to the samples in a patch. Given a rotation angle ω in the tangent plane, the neighbors to p try to "rotate" around this point, while remaining constrained to the surface. For example, sample q moves to q'. The samples are updated in the same order as shown on figure 4.*

It is best to use a separate mesh of *texture springs* to store the warped patch coordinates. The original mesh of *geometry springs* should remain relatively undistorted, as the translation and rotation operations require this mesh to be as regular as possible to assure maximum robustness. Therefore, the warped coordinate system is specified independently of the geometry coordinates (see figure 8) with the exception that geometry nodes at patchino boundaries can be repositioned freely (texture and geometry nodes coincide at the boundaries). At any time, the user can map the warped texture into the texture space of the patch using the *Surface : GetTextureCoordinates* operation.

In our current implementation, the interface lets the user click on a number of feature points inside the patch and move these freely. The key points can be constrained to remain at fixed positions in the patch, allowing detailed feature alignment between texture and geometry (see figure 10). These basic operations could be extended to a more sophisticated library of warping tools, allowing points, curves and regions inside a patch to be dragged and constrained.

In our experience, surface warping is a natural and useful extension of the translation and rotation operations, and it forms the last element in our interactive texturing framework.

4 Higher level operations

Just as there are 2d image processing methods that have no meaning on curved surfaces, there are interactive texturing algorithms unique to surfaces. An interesting aspect of the architecture described in the previous sections is that it has served as inspiration for a number of new texturing operations that have no natural counterparts in traditional 2d painting systems.

4.1 Cylindrical patchinos

As many interesting shapes have parts that are relatively cylindrical, a cylindrical patchino feature has been implemented. Cylindrical patchinos are defined by three boundary curves: two cyclic geodesic curvature minimizing interpolants and one geodesic arranged in the shape of an oldfashioned pair of eye-glasses (see figures 9d and 11) and parameterized using a straightforward extension of the techniques described in [8] and [11]. The optimization procedure from rectangular patchinos generalizes almost directly, except that the order in which the nodes are visited is specified by circular curves, emanating from middle of

```
Class Sample
    Vector3 x, n, v          ; Position, normal and velocity
    Vector3 φu,φv   ; Derivatives
    Sample neighbors[8]   ; Spring coordinates
    Vector2 k[8]

Class Patchino
  private:
    DifferentiableSurface surface          ; Pointer to surface
    Sample grid[DIM_U][DIM_V]  ; Grid of samples
  public:
    Freeze()                    ; Set θ = φ
    Translate( Vector3 v)   ; Slide in direction v
    Rotate(Real ω)   ;Rotate by angle ω around center
    ReduceDistortion()  ; Minimize E*(U)

Patchino : Freeze()
    for p_i ∈ grid
      for q_ij ∈ p_i.neighbors
        ⟨⟨ (p_i.k[j].u, p_i.k[j].v) = coordinates of
          q_ij.x − p_i.x projected to tangent plane at q_ij.x
          as a linear combination as q_ij.φu and q_ij.φu ⟩⟩

Patchino : ReduceDistortion()
    new_p.x.x = new_p.x.y = new_p.x.z = 0
    for p ∈ grid in spiral order
      for q ∈ p.neighbors
        new_p.x = new_p.x + q.x+
            q.k[j].u·q.φu + q.k[j].v·q.φv
                ; Here, q.neighbors[j] = p
    for p ∈ grid
      p.x = new_p.x/#p.neighbors
    ⟨⟨ Recompute n, φ.u and φ.v at each sample ⟩⟩

Patchino : Translate( Vector3 v)
    center = grid[DIM_U/2][DIM_V/2]
    surface.Slide(center,v)
    center.v = ⟨⟨ center.x − center.x_old
      projected to tangent plane at center.x ⟩⟩
    for p ∈ grid/{center} in spiral order   ; See figure 4
      q = p.neighbors["interior"]   ; See section 3.4.2
      surface.Slide(p, q.v)
      p.v = ⟨⟨ p.x − p.x_old projected
              to tangent plane at p.x ⟩⟩
    ⟨⟨ Recompute n, φ.u and φ.v at each sample ⟩⟩

Patchino : Rotate(Real ω)
    center =grid[DIM_U/2][DIM_V/2]
    ⟨⟨ Rotate center.φu and center.φv
      by ω in tangent plane at center.x ⟩⟩
    for p ∈ grid/{center} in spiral order
      q = p.neighbors["interior"]   ; See text
      v = ⟨⟨ p.x rotated by ω around q.x in
        tangent plane at q.x ⟩⟩ - p.x
      surface.Slide(p,v)
      ⟨⟨ Estimate p.φu and p.φv based on p.x and q.x ⟩⟩
    ⟨⟨ Recompute n, φ.u and φ.v at each sample ⟩⟩
```

Figure 7: *Implementation of patchinos.*

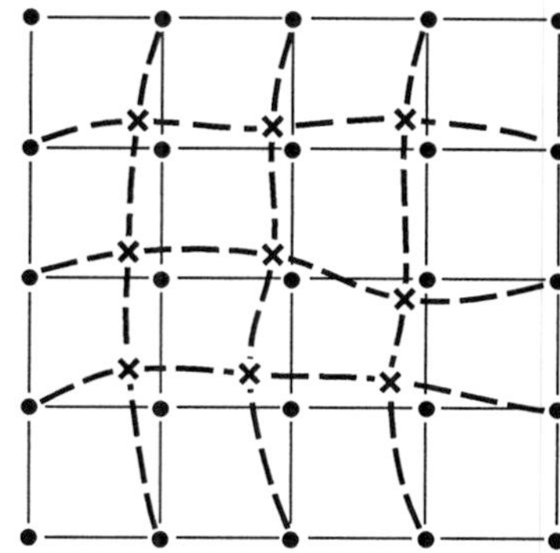

Figure 8: *Texture warping. The regular grid illustrates the geometric coordinates of the patch, which should remain as undistorted as possible at all times. The curved lines shows the separate texture coordinate grid for the patch.*

the cylinder and proceeding up and down, rather than a spiral.

Experiments have shown that compositing using cylindrical patchinos is a highly useful addition to the lower level operations from section 3. Moreover, the general idea of working with patches of different topologies present an interesting new set of sub-problems, such as how to apply transformations between rectangular and cylindrical patches interactively and how to deal with rotations. Potential applications of spherical and Mobius strip patchinos are left as a thought experiment for the interested reader.

4.2 Multi-layered compositing

In our system, any number of texture patches can exist on the surface at any time, and the user is free to translate, rotate, scale and deform these by clicking on them. Motivated by the image compositing paradigm, the patches reside in different layers and can be lowered or raised similar to the way windows can be manipulated on graphically oriented operating systems.

At any time, textures can be copy and pasted between any patch and the surface. Aside from the special case of mappings between a texture patch and the surface as described in section 3.1, textures can also be mapped between arbitrary combinations of patchinos and the surface (see figure 9e). This facilitates general image processing operations between sets of patches equivalent to [3] and thus the entire digital compositing paradigm to be applied on curved surfaces. Current texture mapping hardware supports alpha blending and allows the various textures to be rendered at interactive rates, making the approach practical on widely used high-end graphics workstations.

5 Future work

We will conclude with a few ideas for other new and potentially useful texturing operations.

Geometric patterns. A look at almost any intriguing 3d surface will reveal a correlation between geometry and textures. Tools allowing artists to take advantage of symmetries and constrain the position and extent of patchinos relative to each other would probably be very useful.

Swiss cheese patchinos. Some surfaces have regions that are relatively flat except for a hole or a branch extending outwards. In such cases, it would be convenient to operate with patchinos that would ignore the highly irregular regions. This might be accomplished by drawing feature curves around the base of a branch and constraining a surrounding patchino not to move within these.

Copy and paste of surface geometry. Recent progress in 3d data acquisition and surface fitting techniques ([17] and [11], [12]), present an interesting challenge in how to texture models of a hitherto unseen level of complexity. This problem might be alleviated by a new range of interactive applications between traditional modeling and painting systems. Operations supported by such systems could include features for dragging free-form-deformation lattices constrained to a surface while minimizing volumetric distortion subject to appropriate constraints, and copy and paste of actual geometric features extending from the surface.

6 Limitations

The underlying assumption of this work is that the base surface has to be "smooth". If the user tries to drag a patchino over a sharp spike or across any region containing frequencies that are high compared to the sampling density of the spring mesh, the patchino mesh may start to fold onto itself. In this case, the user currently looses the rest shape and has to reparameterize the interior of the patchino. Although improved robustness would obviously be desirable, the prototype implementation of these ideas is capable of dealing with a sufficiently general range of surfaces to make the approach feasible (see figures 9f, 12 and 13). In a nutshell, the more irregular the surface, the less favorable texture compositing is going to be compared to brush painting, and just like copy and paste has not replaced hand painting in 2d systems, the same is unlikely to happen for 3d surfaces. However, severe distortion is unavoidable on highly irregular surfaces, and as severely distorted texture mappings rarely look attractive, it is questionable whether this capability would even be desirable. Instead, it appears that texture compositing of relatively smooth surfaces could be a much more feasible endeavor.

7 Conclusion

Considering the demand for interactive texturing algorithms for 3d painting applications, there is a need for a more cohesive methodology for texturing of 3d surfaces. This work has proposed a kernel of powerful and general operations in the hope that this will serve as a starting point for a process that could eventually lead to more friendly 3d painting applications. Furthermore, a stronger underlying framework for texturing of general surfaces could potentially help point towards new interesting directions of research and thus accelerate the development of exciting new interactive tools.

8 Acknowledgments

Thanks to Pat Hanrahan for a fun year in California, to Venkat Krishnamurthy for many helpful and enjoyable discussions and for allowing me to use his excellent parameterization package [11], to Julie Dorsey for lots of inspiration and cool ideas, to Tamara Munzner for kindly helping with an important video tape in the last minutes before a challenging deadline, to Brian Curless for allowing me to use his friendly 3d scanning software [17], and to all of the reviewers for their much appreciated advise. Finally, I would like to thank everyone in the Stanford graphics group who helped make my visit as pleasant as it was, i særdeleshed et stort tak til Bill Lorensen for being the best sort-of-Danish officemate I have ever had.

References

[1] E. Catmull. A hidden-surface algorithm with anti-aliasing. In *Computer Graphics (SIGGRAPH '78 Proceedings)*, volume 12, pages 6–11, August 1978.

[2] Richard Shoup. *SuperPaint*. Xerox PARC, 1974.

[3] Thomas Porter and Tom Duff. Compositing digital images. In Hank Christiansen, editor, *Computer Graphics (SIGGRAPH '84 Proceedings)*, volume 18, pages 253–259, July 1984.

[4] 1990 computer graphics achievement award. *Computer Graphics (SIGGRAPH '90 Proceedings)*, 24:17–18, August 1990.

[5] Pat Hanrahan and Paul E. Haeberli. Direct WYSIWYG painting and texturing on 3D shapes. In Forest Baskett, editor, *Computer Graphics (SIGGRAPH '90 Proceedings)*, volume 24, pages 215–223, August 1990.

[6] Maneesh Agrawala, Andrew C. Beers, and Marc Levoy. 3d painting on scanned surfaces. In *Proceedings 1995 Symposium on Interactive 3D Graphics (Monterey, California, April 9–12, 1995)*, pages 145–152.

[7] Jérôme Maillot, Hussein Yahia, and Anne Verroust. Interactive texture mapping. In James T. Kajiya, editor, *Computer Graphics (SIGGRAPH '93 Proceedings)*, volume 27, pages 27–34, August 1993.

[8] Hans K. Pedersen. Decorating implicit surfaces. In Robert Cook, editor, *Proceedings of SIGGRAPH '95 (Los Angeles, California, August 6–11, 1995)*, Computer Graphics Proceedings, Annual Conference Series, pages 291–300. ACM SIGGRAPH, ACM Press, August 1995.

[9] Kurt Fleisher, David H. Laidlaw, Bena L. Currin, and Alan H. Barr. Cellular texture generation. In Robert Cook, editor, *Proceedings of SIGGRAPH '95 (Los Angeles, California, August 6–11, 1995)*, Computer Graphics Proceedings, Annual Conference Series, pages 239–248. ACM SIGGRAPH, ACM Press, August 1995.

[10] Julie Daily and Kenneth Kiss. 3d painting: Paradigms for painting in a new dimension. chi '95 conference proceedings (denver colorado, may 7–11, 1995).

[11] Venkat Krishnamurthy and Marc Levoy. Fitting smooth surfaces to dense polygonal meshes for computer animation. In *Proceedings of SIGGRAPH '96 (New Orleans, Louisiana, August 4–9, 1996)*, august 1996.

[12] Matthias Eck and Hugues Hoppe. Automatic reconstruction of b-spline surfaces of arbitrary topological type. In *Proceedings of SIGGRAPH '96 (New Orleans, Louisiana, August 4–9, 1996)*, august 1996.

[13] Andrew P. Witkin and Paul S. Heckbert. Using particles to sample and control implicit surfaces. In Andrew Glassner, editor, *Proceedings of SIGGRAPH '94 (Orlando, Florida, July 24–29, 1994)*, Computer Graphics Proceedings, Annual Conference Series, pages 269–278. ACM SIGGRAPH, ACM Press, July 1994. ISBN 0-89791-667-0.

[14] R. Dietz, J. Hoschek, and B. Jüttler. An algebraic approach to curves and surfaces on the sphere and on other quadrics. *Computer Aided Geometric Design*, 10(3):211–230, August 1993.

[15] Chakib Bennis, Jean-Marc Vézien, Gérard Iglésias, and André Gagalowicz. Piecewise surface flattening for non-distorted texture mapping. In Thomas W. Sederberg, editor, *Computer Graphics (SIGGRAPH '91 Proceedings)*, volume 25, pages 237–246, July 1991.

[16] Matthias Eck et al. Multiresolution analysis of arbitrary meshes. In Robert Cook, editor, *Proceedings of SIGGRAPH '95 (Los Angeles, California, August 6–11, 1995)*, Computer Graphics Proceedings, Annual Conference Series, pages 173–182. ACM SIGGRAPH, ACM Press, August 1995.

[17] Brian Curless and Marc Levoy. A volumetric method for building complex models from range images. In *Proceedings of SIGGRAPH '96 (New Orleans, Louisiana, August 4–9, 1996)*, august 1996.

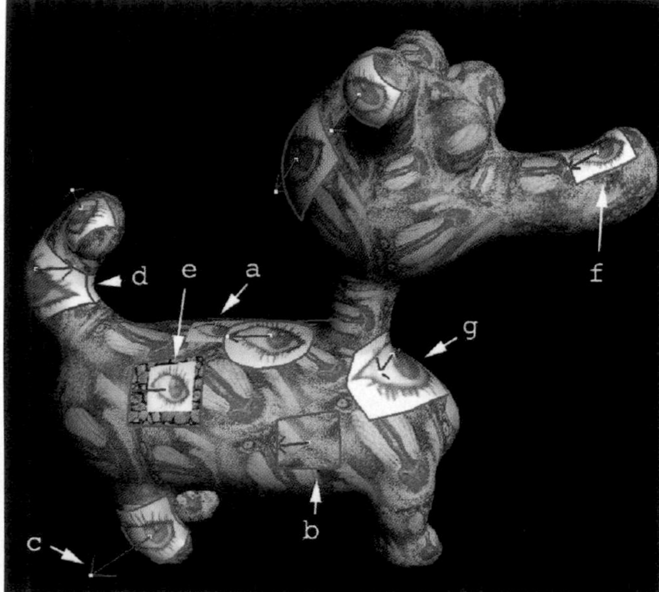

Figure 9: *Patchinos on an implicit surface. a) Pasted texture. b) Copied texture. c) Handle for rotations. d) Cylindrical patchino. e) Layered operations: texture mapped from one patchino to another. f) This and the other patchions were dragged from the back of the dog in less than 10 seconds. g) Warped texture.*

Figure 10: *Copy and paste with cylindrical patchinos.*

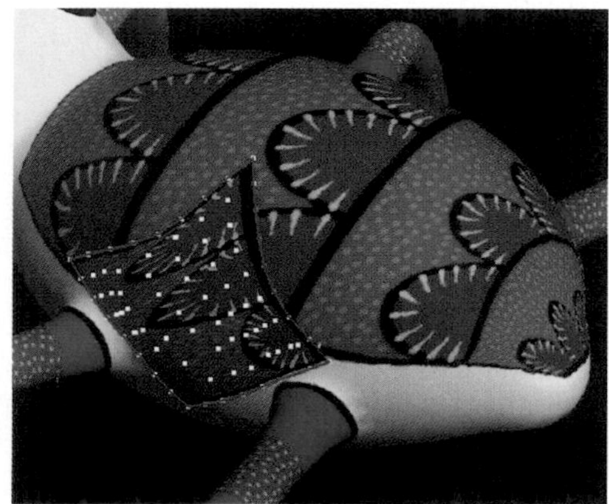

Figure 11: *Warping for feature alignment. The same patchino has been pasted onto the surface at four different locations.*

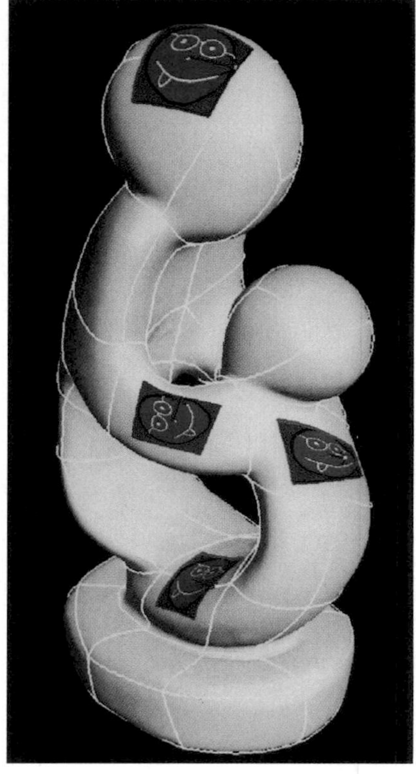

Figure 12: *Patchinos on cubic spline patches.*

Figure 13: *Copy and paste on an implicit insect.*

A Volumetric Method for Building Complex Models from Range Images

Brian Curless and Marc Levoy
Stanford University

Abstract

A number of techniques have been developed for reconstructing surfaces by integrating groups of aligned range images. A desirable set of properties for such algorithms includes: incremental updating, representation of directional uncertainty, the ability to fill gaps in the reconstruction, and robustness in the presence of outliers. Prior algorithms possess subsets of these properties. In this paper, we present a volumetric method for integrating range images that possesses all of these properties.

Our volumetric representation consists of a cumulative weighted signed distance function. Working with one range image at a time, we first scan-convert it to a distance function, then combine this with the data already acquired using a simple additive scheme. To achieve space efficiency, we employ a run-length encoding of the volume. To achieve time efficiency, we resample the range image to align with the voxel grid and traverse the range and voxel scanlines synchronously. We generate the final manifold by extracting an isosurface from the volumetric grid. We show that under certain assumptions, this isosurface is optimal in the least squares sense. To fill gaps in the model, we tessellate over the boundaries between regions seen to be empty and regions never observed.

Using this method, we are able to integrate a large number of range images (as many as 70) yielding seamless, high-detail models of up to 2.6 million triangles.

CR Categories: I.3.5 [Computer Graphics] Computational Geometry and Object Modeling
Additional keywords: Surface fitting, three-dimensional shape recovery, range image integration, isosurface extraction

1 Introduction

Recent years have witnessed a rise in the availability of fast, accurate range scanners. These range scanners have provided data for applications such as medicine, reverse engineering, and digital film-making. Many of these devices generate *range images*; i.e., they produce depth values on a regular sampling lattice. Figure 1 illustrates how an optical triangulation scanner can be used to acquire a range image. By connecting nearest neighbors with triangular elements, one can construct a *range surface* as shown in Figure 1d. Range images are typically formed by sweeping a 1D or 2D sensor linearly across an object or circularly around it, and generally do not contain enough information to reconstruct the entire object being scanned. Accordingly, we require algorithms that can merge multiple range images into a single description of the surface. A set of desirable properties for such a surface reconstruction algorithm includes:

- *Representation of range uncertainty.* The data in range images typically have asymmetric error distributions with primary directions along sensor lines of sight, as illustrated for optical triangulation in Figure 1a. The method of range integration should reflect this fact.
- *Utilization of all range data,* including redundant observations of each object surface. If properly used, this redundancy can reduce sensor noise.
- *Incremental and order independent updating.* Incremental updates allow us to obtain a reconstruction after each scan or small set of scans and allow us to choose the next best orientation for scanning. Order independence is desirable to ensure that results are not biased by earlier scans. Together, they allow for straightforward parallelization.
- *Time and space efficiency.* Complex objects may require many range images in order to build a detailed model. The range images and the model must be represented efficiently and processed quickly to make the algorithm practical.
- *Robustness.* Outliers and systematic range distortions can create challenging situations for reconstruction algorithms. A robust algorithm needs to handle these situations without catastrophic failures such as holes in surfaces and self-intersecting surfaces.
- *No restrictions on topological type.* The algorithm should not assume that the object is of a particular genus. Simplifying assumptions such as "the object is homeomorphic to a sphere" yield useful results in only a restricted class of problems.
- *Ability to fill holes in the reconstruction.* Given a set of range images that do not completely cover the object, the surface reconstruction will necessarily be incomplete. For some objects, no amount of scanning would completely cover the object, because some surfaces may be inaccessible to the sensor. In these cases, we desire an algorithm that can automatically fill these holes with plausible surfaces, yielding a model that is both "watertight" and esthetically pleasing.

In this paper, we present a volumetric method for integrating range images that possesses all of these properties. In the next section, we review some previous work in the area of surface reconstruction. In section 3, we describe the core of our volumetric algorithm. In section 4, we show how this algorithm can be used to fill gaps in the reconstruction using knowledge about the emptiness of space. Next, in section 5, we describe how we implemented our volumetric approach so as to keep time and space costs reasonable. In section 6, we show the results of surface reconstruction from many range images of complex objects. Finally, in section 7 we conclude and discuss limitations and future directions.

2 Previous work

Surface reconstruction from dense range data has been an active area of research for several decades. The strategies have proceeded along two basic directions: reconstruction from unorganized points, and

Authors' Address: Computer Science Department, Stanford University, Stanford, CA 94305
E-mail: {curless,levoy}@cs.stanford.edu
World Wide Web: http://www-graphics.stanford.edu

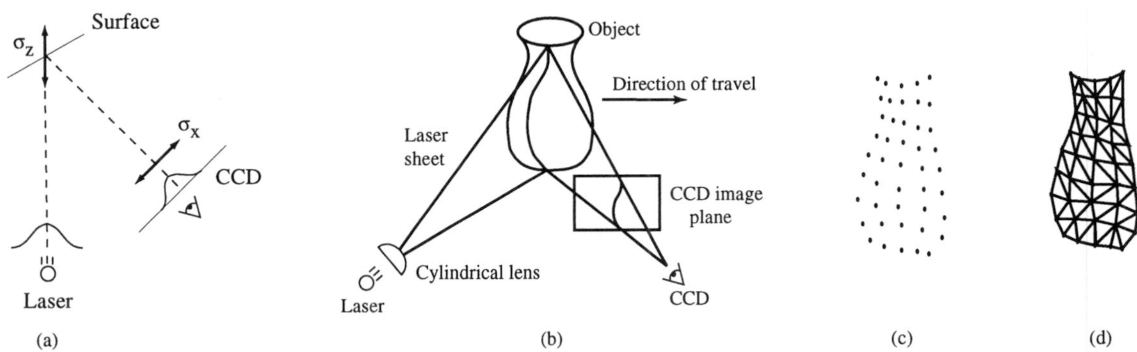

Figure 1. From optical triangulation to a range surface. (a) In 2D, a narrow laser beam illuminates a surface, and a linear sensor images the reflection from an object. The center of the image pulse maps to the center of the laser, yielding a range value. The uncertainty, σ_x, in determining the center of the pulse results in range uncertainty, σ_z along the laser's line of sight. When using the spacetime analysis for optical triangulation [6], the uncertainties run along the lines of sight of the CCD. (b) In 3D, a laser stripe triangulation scanner first spreads the laser beam into a sheet of light with a cylindrical lens. The CCD observes the reflected stripe from which a depth profile is computed. The object sweeps through the field of view, yielding a range image. Other scanner configurations rotate the object to obtain a cylindrical scan or sweep a laser beam or stripe over a stationary object. (c) A range image obtained from the scanner in (b) is a collection of points with regular spacing. (d) By connecting nearest neighbors with triangles, we create a piecewise linear range surface.

reconstruction that exploits the underlying structure of the acquired data. These two strategies can be further subdivided according to whether they operate by reconstructing parametric surfaces or by reconstructing an implicit function.

A major advantage of the unorganized points algorithms is the fact that they do not make any prior assumptions about connectivity of points. In the absence of range images or contours to provide connectivity cues, these algorithms are the only recourse. Among the parametric surface approaches, Boissanat [2] describes a method for Delaunay triangulation of a set of points in 3-space. Edelsbrunner and Mücke [9] generalize the notion of a convex hull to create surfaces called alpha-shapes. Examples of implicit surface reconstruction include the method of Hoppe, et al [16] for generating a signed distance function followed by an isosurface extraction. More recently, Bajaj, et al [1] used alpha-shapes to construct a signed distance function to which they fit implicit polynomials. Although unorganized points algorithms are widely applicable, they discard useful information such as surface normal and reliability estimates. As a result, these algorithms are well-behaved in smooth regions of surfaces, but they are not always robust in regions of high curvature and in the presence of systematic range distortions and outliers.

Among the structured data algorithms, several parametric approaches have been proposed, most of them operating on range images in a polygonal domain. Soucy and Laurendeau [25] describe a method using Venn diagrams to identify overlapping data regions, followed by re-parameterization and merging of regions. Turk and Levoy [30] devised an incremental algorithm that updates a reconstruction by eroding redundant geometry, followed by zippering along the remaining boundaries, and finally a consensus step that reintroduces the original geometry to establish final vertex positions. Rutishauser, et al [24] use errors along the sensor's lines of sight to establish consensus surface positions followed by a re-tessellation that incorporates redundant data. These algorithms typically perform better than unorganized point algorithms, but they can still fail catastrophically in areas of high curvature, as exemplified in Figure 9.

Several algorithms have been proposed for integrating structured data to generate implicit functions. These algorithms can be classified as to whether voxels are assigned one of two (or three) states or are samples of a continuous function. Among the discrete-state volumetric algorithms, Connolly [4] casts rays from a range image accessed as a quad-tree into a voxel grid stored as an octree, and generates results for synthetic data. Chien, et al [3] efficiently generate octree models under the severe assumption that all views are taken from the directions corresponding to the 6 faces of a cube. Li and Crebbin [19] and Tarbox and Gottschlich [28] also describe methods for generating binary voxel grids from range images. None of these methods has been used to generate surfaces. Further, without an underlying continuous function, there are no mechanism for representing range uncertainty or for combining overlapping, noisy range surfaces.

The last category of our taxonomy consists of implicit function methods that use samples of a continuous function to combine structured data. Our method falls into this category. Previous efforts in this area include the work of Grosso, et al [12], who generate depth maps from stereo and average them into a volume with occupancy ramps of varying slopes corresponding to uncertainty measures; they do not, however, perform a final surface extraction. Succi, et al [26] create depth maps from stereo and optical flow and integrate them volumetrically using a straight average. The details of his method are unclear, but they appear to extract an isosurface at an arbitrary threshold. In both the Grosso and Succi papers, the range maps are sparse, the directions of range uncertainty are not characterized, they use no time or space optimizations, and the final models are of low resolution. Recently, Hilton, et al [14] have developed a method similar to ours in that it uses weighted signed distance functions for merging range images, but it does not address directions of sensor uncertainty, incremental updating, space efficiency, and characterization of the whole space for potential hole filling, all of which we believe are crucial for the success of this approach.

Other relevant work includes the method of probabilistic occupancy grids developed by Elfes and Matthies [10]. Their volumetric space is a scalar probability field which they update using a Bayesian formulation. The results have been used for robot navigation, but not for surface extraction. A difficulty with this technique is the fact that the best description of the surface lies at the peak or ridge of the probability function, and the problem of ridge-finding is not one with robust solutions [8]. This is one of our primary motivations for taking an isosurface approach in the next section: it leverages off of well-behaved surface extraction algorithms.

The discrete-state implicit function algorithms described above also have much in common with the methods of extracting volumes from silhouettes [15] [21] [23] [27]. The idea of using backdrops to help carve out the emptiness of space is one we demonstrate in section 4.

3 Volumetric integration

Our algorithm employs a continuous implicit function, $D(\mathbf{x})$, represented by samples. The function we represent is the weighted signed distance of each point $\mathbf{x}$ to the nearest range surface along the line of

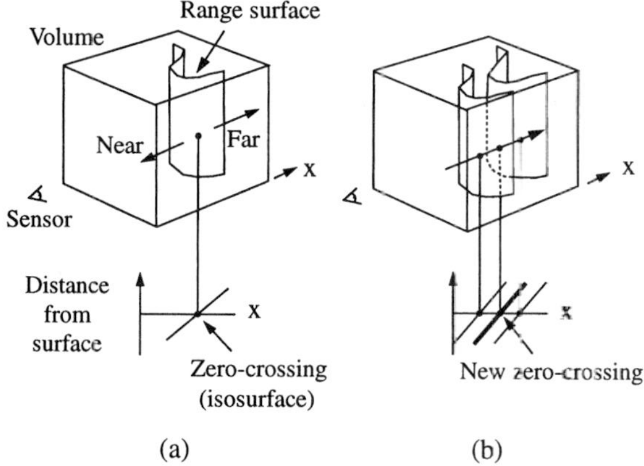

Figure 2. Unweighted signed distance functions in 3D. (a) A range sensor looking down the x-axis observes a range image, shown here as a reconstructed range surface. Following one line of sight down the x-axis, we can generate a signed distance function as shown. The zero crossing of this function is a point on the range surface. (b) The range sensor repeats the measurement, but noise in the range sensing process results in a slightly different range surface. In general, the second surface would interpenetrate the first, but we have shown it as an offset from the first surface for purposes of illustration. Following the same line of sight as before, we obtain another signed distance function. By summing these functions, we arrive at a cumulative function with a new zero crossing positioned midway between the original range measurements.

sight to the sensor. We construct this function by combining signed distance functions $d_1(\mathbf{x})$, $d_2(\mathbf{x})$, ... $d_n(\mathbf{x})$ and weight functions $w_1(\mathbf{x})$, $w_2(\mathbf{x})$, ... $w_n(\mathbf{x})$ obtained from range images 1 ... n. Our combining rules give us for each voxel a cumulative signed distance function, $D(\mathbf{x})$, and a cumulative weight $W(\mathbf{x})$. We represent these functions on a discrete voxel grid and extract an isosurface corresponding to $D(\mathbf{x}) = 0$. Under a certain set of assumptions, this isosurface is optimal in the least squares sense. A full proof of this optimality is beyond the scope of this paper, but a sketch appears in appendix A.

Figure 2 illustrates the principle of combining unweighted signed distances for the simple case of two range surfaces sampled from the same direction. Note that the resulting isosurface would be the surface created by averaging the two range surfaces along the sensor's lines of sight. In general, however, weights are necessary to represent variations in certainty across the range surfaces. The choice of weights should be specific to the range scanning technology. For optical triangulation scanners, for example, Soucy [25] and Turk [30] make the weight depend on the dot product between each vertex normal and the viewing direction, reflecting greater uncertainty when the illumination is at grazing angles to the surface. Turk also argues that the range data at the boundaries of the mesh typically have greater uncertainty, requiring more down-weighting. We adopt these same weighting schemes for our optical triangulation range data.

Figure 3 illustrates the construction and usage of the signed distance and weight functions in 1D. In Figure 3a, the sensor is positioned at the origin looking down the +x axis and has taken two measurements, r_1 and r_2. The signed distance profiles, $d_1(x)$ and $d_2(x)$ may extend indefinitely in either direction, but the weight functions, $w_1(x)$ and $w_2(x)$, taper off behind the range points for reasons discussed below.

Figure 3b is the weighted combination of the two profiles. The combination rules are straightforward:

$$D(\mathbf{x}) = \frac{\Sigma w_i(\mathbf{x}) d_i(\mathbf{x})}{\Sigma w_i(\mathbf{x})} \tag{1}$$

$$W(\mathbf{x}) = \Sigma w_i(\mathbf{x}) \tag{2}$$

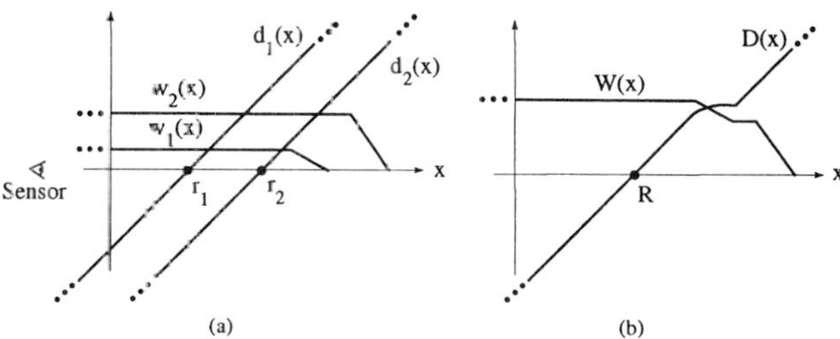

Figure 3. Signed distance and weight functions in one dimension. (a) The sensor looks down the x-axis and takes two measurements, r_1 and r_2. $d_1(x)$ and $d_2(x)$ are the signed distance profiles, and $w_1(x)$ and $w_2(x)$ are the weight functions. In 1D, we might expect two sensor measurements to have the same weight magnitudes, but we have shown them to be of different magnitude here to illustrate how the profiles combine in the general case. (b) $D(x)$ is a weighted combination of $d_1(x)$ and $d_2(x)$, and $W(x)$ is the sum of the weight functions. Given this formulation, the zero-crossing, R, becomes the weighted combination of r_1 and r_2 and represents our best guess of the location of the surface. In practice, we truncate the distance ramps and weights to the vicinity of the range points.

where, $d_i(\mathbf{x})$ and $w_i(\mathbf{x})$ are the signed distance and weight functions from the ith range image.

Expressed as an incremental calculation, the rules are:

$$D_{i+1}(\mathbf{x}) = \frac{W_i(\mathbf{x}) D_i(\mathbf{x}) + w_{i+1}(\mathbf{x}) d_{i+1}(\mathbf{x})}{W_i(\mathbf{x}) + w_{i+1}(\mathbf{x})} \tag{3}$$

$$W_{i+1}(\mathbf{x}) = W_i(\mathbf{x}) + w_{i+1}(\mathbf{x}) \tag{4}$$

where $D_i(\mathbf{x})$ and $W_i(\mathbf{x})$ are the cumulative signed distance and weight functions after integrating the ith range image.

In the special case of one dimension, the zero-crossing of the cumulative function is at a range, R given by:

$$R = \frac{\Sigma w_i r_i}{\Sigma w_i} \tag{5}$$

i.e., a weighted combination of the acquired range values, which is what one would expect for a least squares minimization.

In principle, the distance and weighting functions should extend indefinitely in either direction. However, to prevent surfaces on opposite sides of the object from interfering with each other, we force the weighting function to taper off behind the surface. There is a trade-off involved in choosing where the weight function tapers off. It should persist far enough behind the surface to ensure that all distance ramps will contribute in the vicinity of the final zero crossing, but, it should also be as narrow as possible to avoid influencing surfaces on the other side. To meet these requirements, we force the weights to fall off at a distance equal to half the maximum uncertainty interval of the range measurements. Similarly, the signed distance and weight functions need not extend far in front of the surface. Restricting the functions to the vicinity of the surface yields a more compact representation and reduces the computational expense of updating the volume.

In two and three dimensions, the range measurements correspond to curves or surfaces with weight functions, and the signed distance ramps have directions that are consistent with the primary directions of sensor uncertainty. The uncertainties that apply to range image integration include errors in alignment between meshes as well as errors inherent in the scanning technology. A number of algorithms for aligning sets of range images have been explored and shown to yield excellent results [11][30]. The remaining error lies in the scanner itself. For optical triangulation scanners, for example, this error has been shown to be ellipsoidal about the range points, with the major axis of the ellipse aligned with the lines of sight of the laser [13][24].

Figure 4 illustrates the two-dimensional case for a range curve derived from a single scan containing a row of range samples. In practice, we use a fixed point representation for the signed distance func-

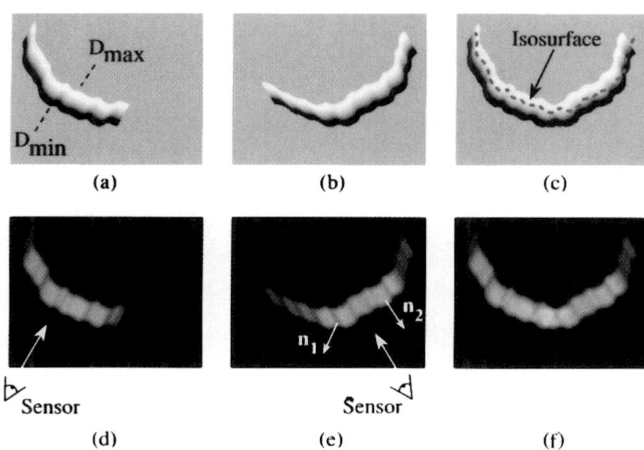

Figure 4. Combination of signed distance and weight functions in two dimensions. (a) and (d) are the signed distance and weight functions, respectively, generated for a range image viewed from the sensor line of sight shown in (d). The signed distance functions are chosen to vary between D_{min} and D_{max}, as shown in (a). The weighting falls off with increasing obliquity to the sensor and at the edges of the meshes as indicated by the darker regions in (e). The normals, $\mathbf{n_1}$ and $\mathbf{n_2}$ shown in (e), are oriented at a grazing angle and facing the sensor, respectively. Note how the weighting is lower (darker) for the grazing normal. (b) and (e) are the signed distance and weight functions for a range image of the same object taken at a 60 degree rotation. (c) is the signed distance function $D(\mathbf{x})$ corresponding to the per voxel weighted combination of (a) and (b) constructed using equations 3 and 4. (f) is the sum of the weights at each voxel, $W(\mathbf{x})$. The dotted green curve in (c) is the isosurface that represents our current estimate of the shape of the object.

tion, which bounds the values to lie between D_{min} and D_{max} as shown in the figure. The values of D_{min} and D_{max} must be negative and positive, respectively, as they are on opposite sides of a signed distance zero-crossing.

For three dimensions, we can summarize the whole algorithm as follows. First, we set all voxel weights to zero, so that new data will overwrite the initial grid values. Next, we tessellate each range image by constructing triangles from nearest neighbors on the sampled lattice. We avoid tessellating over step discontinuities (cliffs in the range map) by discarding triangles with edge lengths that exceed a threshold. We must also compute a weight at each vertex as described above.

Once a range image has been converted to a triangle mesh with a weight at each vertex, we can update the voxel grid. The signed distance contribution is computed by casting a ray from the sensor through each voxel near the range surface and then intersecting it with the triangle mesh, as shown in figure 5. The weight is computed by linearly interpolating the weights stored at the intersection triangle's vertices. Having determined the signed distance and weight we can apply the update formulae described in equations 3 and 4.

At any point during the merging of the range images, we can extract the zero-crossing isosurface from the volumetric grid. We restrict this extraction procedure to skip samples with zero weight, generating triangles only in the regions of observed data. We will relax this restriction in the next section.

4 Hole filling

The algorithm described in the previous section is designed to reconstruct the observed portions of the surface. Unseen portions of the surface will appear as holes in the reconstruction. While this result is an accurate representation of the known surface, the holes are esthetically unsatisfying and can present a stumbling block to follow-on algorithms that expect continuous meshes. In [17], for example, the authors describe a method for parameterizing patches that entails

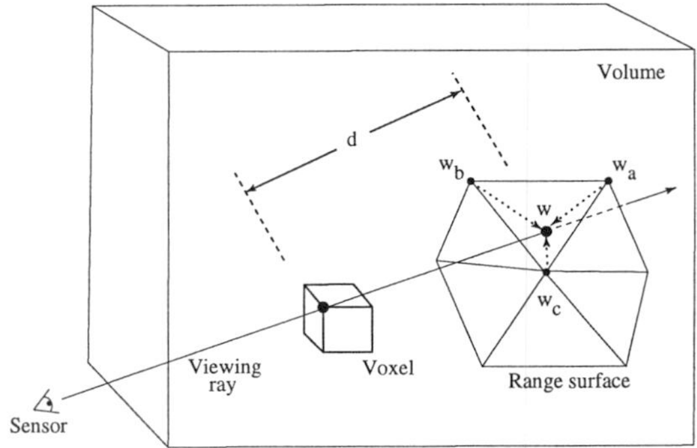

Figure 5. Sampling the range surface to update the volume. We compute the weight, w, and signed distance, d, needed to update the voxel by casting a ray from the sensor, through the voxel onto the range surface. We obtain the weight, w, by linearly interpolating the weights (w_a, w_b, and w_c) stored at neighboring range vertices. Note that for a translating sensor (like our Cyberware scanner), the sensor point is different for each column of range points.

generating evenly spaced grid lines by walking across the edges of a mesh. Gaps in the mesh prevent the algorithm from creating a fair parameterization. As another example, rapid prototyping technologies such as stereolithography typically require a "watertight" model in order to construct a solid replica [7].

One option for filling holes is to operate on the reconstructed mesh. If the regions of the mesh near each hole are very nearly planar, then this approach works well. However, holes in the meshes can be (and frequently are) highly non-planar and may even require connections between unconnected components. Instead, we offer a hole filling approach that operates on our volume, which contains more information than the reconstructed mesh.

The key to our algorithm lies in classifying all points in the volume as being in one of three states: unseen, empty, or near the surface. Holes in the surface are indicated by frontiers between unseen regions and empty regions (see Figure 6). Surfaces placed at these frontiers offer a plausible way to plug these holes (dotted in Figure 6). Obtaining this classification and generating these hole fillers leads to a straightforward extension of the algorithm described in the previous section:

1. Initialize the voxel space to the "unseen" state.
2. Update the voxels near the surface as described in the previous section. As before, these voxels take on continuous signed distance and weight values.
3. Follow the lines of sight back from the observed surface and mark the corresponding voxels as "empty". We refer to this step as *space carving*.
4. Perform an isosurface extraction at the zero-crossing of the signed distance function. Additionally, extract a surface between regions seen to be empty and regions that remain unseen.

In practice, we represent the unseen and empty states using the function and weight fields stored on the voxel lattice. We represent the unseen state with the function values $D(\mathbf{x}) = D_{max}$, $W(\mathbf{x}) = 0$ and the empty state with the function values $D(\mathbf{x}) = D_{min}$, $W(\mathbf{x}) = 0$, as shown in Figure 6b. The key advantage of this representation is that we can use the same isosurface extraction algorithm we used in the previous section without the restriction on interpolating voxels of zero weight. This extraction finds both the signed distance and hole fill isosurfaces and connects them naturally where they meet, i.e., at the corners in Figure 6a where the dotted red line meets the dashed green line. Note that the triangles that arise from interpolations across voxels of zero weight are distinct from the others: they are hole fillers.

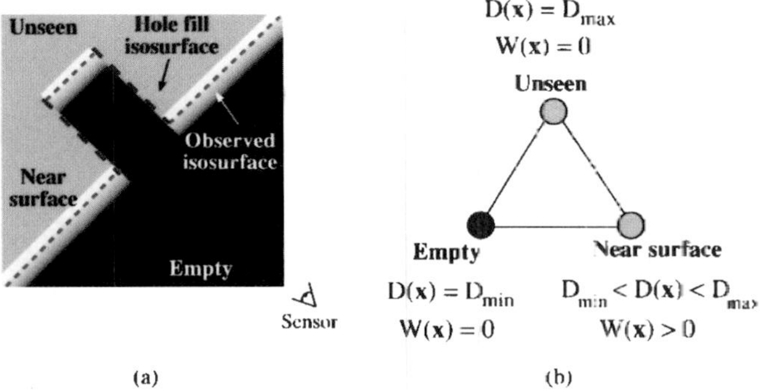

Figure 6. Volumetric grid with space carving and hole filling. (a) The regions in front of the surface are seen as empty, regions in the vicinity of the surface ramp through the zero-crossing, while regions behind remain unseen. The green (dashed) segments are the isosurfaces generated near the observed surface, while the red (dotted) segments are hole fillers, generated by tessellating over the transition from empty to unseen. In (b), we identify the three extremal voxel states with their corresponding function values.

We take advantage of this distinction when smoothing surfaces as described below.

Figure 6 illustrates the method for a single range image, and provides a diagram for the three-state classification scheme. The hole filler isosurfaces are "false" in that they are not representative of the observed surface, but they do derive from observed data. In particular, they correspond to a boundary that confines where the surface could plausibly exist. In practice, we find that many of these hole filler surfaces are generated in crevices that are hard for the sensor to reach.

Because the transition between unseen and empty is discontinuous and hole fill triangles are generated as an isosurface between these binary states, with no smooth transition, we generally observe aliasing artifacts in these areas. These artifacts can be eliminated by prefiltering the transition region before sampling on the voxel lattice using straightforward methods such as analytic filtering or super-sampling and averaging down. In practice, we have obtained satisfactory results by applying another technique: post-filtering the mesh after reconstruction using weighted averages of nearest vertex neighbors as described in [29]. The effect of this filtering step is to blur the hole fill surface. Since we know which triangles correspond to hole fillers, we need only concentrate the surface filtering on the these portions of the mesh. This localized filtering preserves the detail in the observed surface reconstruction. To achieve a smooth blend between filtered hole fill vertices and the neighboring "real" surface, we allow the filter weights to extend beyond and taper off into the vicinity of the hole fill boundaries.

We have just seen how "space carving" is a useful operation: it tells us much about the structure of free space, allowing us to fill holes in an intelligent way. However, our algorithm only carves back from observed surfaces. There are numerous situations where more carving would be useful. For example, the interior walls of a hollow cylinder may elude digitization, but by seeing through the hollow portion of the cylinder to a surface placed behind it, we can better approximate its geometry. We can extend the carving paradigm to cover these situations by placing such a backdrop behind the surfaces being scanned. By placing the backdrop outside of the voxel grid, we utilize it purely for carving space without introducing its geometry into the model.

5 Implementation

5.1 Hardware

The examples in this paper were acquired using a Cyberware 3030 MS laser stripe optical triangulation scanner. Figure 1b illustrates the scanning geometry: an object translates through a plane of laser light while the reflections are triangulated into depth profiles through a CCD camera positioned off axis. To improve the quality of the data, we apply the method of spacetime analysis as described in [6]. The benefits of this analysis include reduced range noise, greater immunity to reflectance changes, and less artifacts near range discontinuities.

When using traditional triangulation analysis implemented in hardware in our Cyberware scanner, the uncertainty in triangulation for our system follows the lines of sight of the expanding laser beam. When using the spacetime analysis, however, the uncertainty follows the lines of sight of the camera. The results described in section 6 of this paper were obtained with one or the other triangulation method. In each case, we adhere to the appropriate lines of sight when laying down signed distance and weight functions.

5.2 Software

The creation of detailed, complex models requires a large amount of input data to be merged into high resolution voxel grids. The examples in the next section include models generated from as many as 70 scans containing up to 12 million input vertices with volumetric grids ranging in size up to 160 million voxels. Clearly, time and space optimizations are critical for merging this data and managing these grids.

5.2.1 Run-length encoding

The core data structure is a run-length encoded (RLE) volume with three run types: empty, unseen, and varying. The varying fields are stored as a stream of varying data, rather than runs of constant value. Typical memory savings vary from 10:1 to 20:1. In fact, the space required to represent one of these voxel grids is usually *less* than the memory required to represent the final mesh as a list of vertices and triangle indices.

5.2.2 Fast volume traversal

Updating the volume from a range image may be likened to inverse volume rendering: instead of reading from a volume and writing to an image, we read from a range image and write to a volume. As a result, we leverage off of a successful idea from the volume rendering community: for best memory system performance, stream through the volume and the image simultaneously in scanline order [18]. In general, however, the scanlines of a range image are not aligned with the scanlines of the voxel grid, as shown in Figure 7a. By suitably resampling the range image, we obtain the desired alignment (Figure 7b). The resampling process consists of a depth rendering of the range surface using the viewing transformation specific to the lines of sight of the range sensor and using an image plane oriented to align with the voxel grid. We assign the weights as vertex "colors" to be linearly interpolated during the rendering step, an approach equivalent to Gouraud shading of triangle colors.

To merge the range data into the voxel grid, we stream through the voxel scanlines in order while stepping through the corresponding scanlines in the resampled range image. We map each voxel scanline to the correct portion of the range scanline as depicted in Figure 7d, and we resample the range data to yield a distance from the range surface. Using the combination rules given by equations 3 and 4, we update the run-length encoded structure. To preserve the linear memory structure of the RLE volume (and thus avoid using linked lists of runs scattered through the memory space), we read the voxel scanlines from the current volume and write the updated scanlines to a second RLE volume; i.e., we double-buffer the voxel grid. Note that depending on the scanner geometry, the mapping from voxels to range image pixels may not be linear, in which case care must be taken to resample appropriately [5].

For the case of merging range data only in the vicinity of the surface, we try to avoid processing voxels distant from the surface. To that end, we construct a binary tree of minimum and maximum depths for every adjacent pair of resampled range image scanlines. Before processing each voxel scanline, we query the binary tree to decide

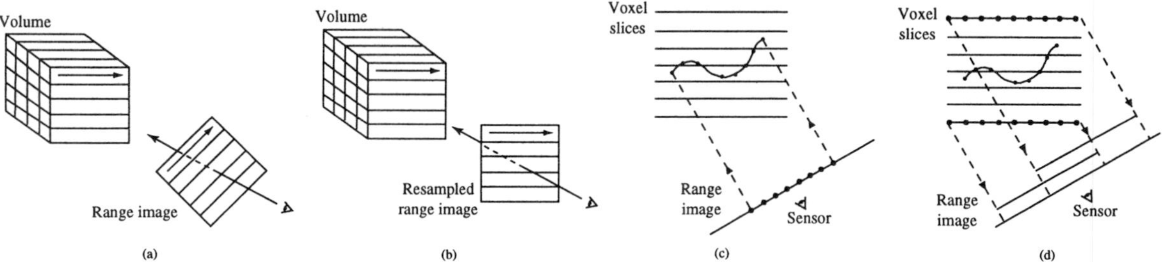

Figure 7. Range image resampling and scanline order voxel updates. (a) Range image scanlines are not in general oriented to allow for coherently streaming through voxel and range scanlines. (b) By resampling the range image, we can obtain the desired range scanline orientation. (c) Casting rays from the pixels on the range image means cutting across scanlines of the voxel grid, resulting in poor memory performance. (d) Instead, we run along scanlines of voxels, mapping them to the correct positions on the resampled range image.

which voxels, if any, are near the range surface. In this way, only relevant pieces of the scanline are processed. In a similar fashion, the space carving steps can be designed to avoid processing voxels that are not seen to be empty for a given range image. The resulting speedups from the binary tree are typically a factor of 15 without carving, and a factor of 5 with carving. We did not implement a brute-force volume update method, however we would expect the overall algorithm described here would be much faster by comparison.

5.2.3 Fast surface extraction

To generate our final surfaces, we employ a Marching Cubes algorithm [20] with a lookup table that resolves ambiguous cases [22]. To reduce computational costs, we only process voxels that have varying data or are at the boundary between empty and unseen.

6 Results

We show results for a number of objects designed to explore the robustness of our algorithm, its ability to fill gaps in the reconstruction, and its attainable level of detail. To explore robustness, we scanned a thin drill bit using the traditional method of optical triangulation. Due to the false edge extensions inherent in data from triangulation scanners [6], this particular object poses a formidable challenge, yet the volumetric method behaves robustly where the zippering method [30] fails catastrophically. The dragon sequence in Figure 11 demonstrates the effectiveness of carving space for hole filling. The use of a backdrop here is particularly effective in filling the gaps in the model. Note that we do not use the backdrop at all times, in part because the range images are much denser and more expensive to process, and also because the backdrop tends to obstruct the path of the object when automatically repositioning it with our motion control platform. Finally, the "Happy Buddha" sequence in Figure 12 shows that our method can be used to generate very detailed, hole-free models suitable for rendering and rapid manufacturing.

Statistics for the reconstruction of the dragon and Buddha models appear in Figure 8. With the optimizations described in the previous section, we were able to reconstruct the observed portions of the surfaces in under an hour on a 250 MHz MIPS R4400 processor. The space carving and hole filling algorithm is not completely optimized, but the execution times are still in the range of 3-5 hours, less than the time spent acquiring and registering the range images. For both models, the RMS distance between points in the original range images and points on the reconstructed surfaces is approximately 0.1 mm. This figure is roughly the same as the accuracy of the scanning technology, indicating a nearly optimal surface reconstruction.

7 Discussion and future work

We have described a new algorithm for volumetric integration of range images, leading to a surface reconstruction without holes. The algorithm has a number of desirable properties, including the representation of directional sensor uncertainty, incremental and order independent updating, robustness in the presence of sensor errors, and the ability to fill gaps in the reconstruction by carving space. Our use of a run-length encoded representation of the voxel grid and synchronized processing of voxel and resampled range image scanlines make the algorithm efficient. This in turn allows us to acquire and integrate a large number of range images. In particular, we demonstrate the ability to integrate up to 70 scans into a high resolution voxel grid to generate million polygon models in a few hours. These models are free of holes, making them suitable for surface fitting, rapid prototyping, and rendering.

There are a number of limitations that prevent us from generating models from an arbitrary object. Some of these limitations arise from the algorithm while others arise from the limitations of the scanning technology. Among the algorithmic limitations, our method has difficulty bridging sharp corners if no scan spans both surfaces meeting at the corner. This is less of a problem when applying our hole-filling algorithm, but we are also exploring methods that will work without hole filling. Thin surfaces are also problematic. As described in section 3, the influences of observed surfaces extend behind their estimated positions for each range image and can interfere with distance functions originating from scans of the opposite side of a thin surface. In this respect, the apexes of sharp corners also behave like thin surfaces. While we have limited this influence as much as possible, it still places a lower limit on the thickness of surface that we can reliably reconstruct without causing artifacts such as thickening of surfaces or rounding of sharp corners. We are currently working to lift this restriction by considering the estimated normals of surfaces.

Other limitations arise from the scanning technologies themselves. Optical methods such as the one we use in this paper can only provide data for external surfaces; internal cavities are not seen. Further, very complicated objects may require an enormous amount of scanning to cover the surface. Optical triangulation scanning has the additional problem that both the laser and the sensor must observe each point on the surface, further restricting the class of objects that can be scanned completely. The reflectance properties of objects are also a factor. Optical methods generally operate by casting light onto an object, but shiny surfaces can deflect this illumination, dark objects can absorb it, and bright surfaces can lead to interreflections. To minimize these effects, we often paint our objects with a flat, gray paint.

Straightforward extensions to our algorithm include improving the execution time of the space carving portion of the algorithm and demonstrating parallelization of the whole algorithm. In addition, more aggressive space carving may be possible by making inferences about sensor lines of sight that return no range data. In the future, we hope to apply our methods to other scanning technologies and to large scale objects such as terrain and architectural scenes.

Model	Scans	Input triangles	Voxel size (mm)	Volume dimensions	Exec. time (min)	Output triangles	Holes
Dragon	61	15 M	0.35	712x501x322	56	1.7 M	324
Dragon + fill	71	24 M	0.35	712x501x322	257	1.8 M	0
Buddha	48	5 M	0.25	407x957x407	47	2.4 M	670
Buddha + fill	58	9 M	0.25	407x957x407	197	2.6 M	0

Figure 8. Statistics for the reconstruction of the dragon and Buddha models, with and without space carving.

Acknowledgments

We would like to thank Phil Lacroute for his many helpful suggestions in designing the volumetric algorithms. Afra Zomorodian wrote the scripting interface for scanning automation. Homan Igehy wrote the fast scan conversion code, which we used for range image resampling. Thanks to Bill Lorensen for his marching cubes tables and mesh decimation software, and for getting the 3D hardcopy made. Matt Pharr did the accessibility shading used to render the color Buddha, and Pat Hanrahan and Julie Dorsey made helpful suggestions for RenderMan tricks and lighting models. Thanks also to David Addleman and George Dabrowski of Cyberware for their help and for the use of their scanner. This work was supported by the National Science Foundation under contract CCR-9157767 and Interval Research Corporation.

References

[1] C.L. Bajaj, F. Bernardini, and G. Xu. Automatic reconstruction of surfaces and scalar fields from 3D scans. In *Proceedings of SIGGRAPH '95 (Los Angeles, CA, Aug. 6-11, 1995)*, pages 109–118. ACM Press, August 1995.

[2] J.-D. Boissonnat. Geometric structures for three-dimensional shape representation. *ACM Transactions on Graphics*, 3(4):266–286, October 1984.

[3] C.H. Chien, Y.B. Sim, and J.K. Aggarwal. Generation of volume/surface octree from range data. In *The Computer Society Conference on Computer Vision and Pattern Recognition*, pages 254–60, June 1988.

[4] C. I. Connolly. Cumulative generation of octree models from range data. In *Proceedings, Intl. Conf. Robotics*, pages 25–32, March 1984.

[5] B. Curless. *Better optical triangulation and volumetric reconstruction of complex models from range images*. PhD thesis, Stanford University, 1996.

[6] B. Curless and M. Levoy. Better optical triangulation through spacetime analysis. In *Proceedings of IEEE International Conference on Computer Vision*, pages 987–994, June 1995.

[7] A. Dolenc. Software tools for rapid prototyping technologies in manufacturing. *Acta Polytechnica Scandinavica: Mathematics and Computer Science Series*, Ma62:1–111, 1993.

[8] D. Eberly, R. Gardner, B. Morse, S. Pizer, and C. Scharlach. Ridges for image analysis. *Journal of Mathematical Imaging and Vision*, 4(4):353–373, Dec 1994.

[9] H. Edelsbrunner and E.P. Mücke. Three-dimensional alpha shapes. In *Workshop on Volume Visualization*, pages 75–105, October 1992.

[10] A. Elfes and L. Matthies. Sensor integration for robot navigation: combining sonar and range data in a grid-based representation. In *Proceedings of the 26th IEEE Conference on Decision and Control*, pages 1802–1807, December 1987.

[11] H. Gagnon, M. Soucy, R. Bergevin, and D. Laurendeau. Registration of multiple range views for automatic 3-D model building. In *Proceedings 1994 IEEE Computer Society Conference on Computer Vision and Pattern Recognition*, pages 581–586, June 1994.

[12] E. Grosso, G. Sandini, and C. Frigato. Extraction of 3D information and volumetric uncertainty from multiple stereo images. In *Proceedings of the 8th European Conference on Artificial Intelligence*, pages 683–688, August 1988.

[13] P. Hebert, D. Laurendeau, and D. Poussart. Scene reconstruction and description: geometric primitive extraction from multiple viewed scattered data. In *Proceedings of IEEE Conference on Computer Vision and Pattern Recognition*, pages 286–292, June 1993.

[14] A. Hilton, A.J. Toddart, J. Illingworth, and T. Windeatt. Reliable surface reconstruction from multiple range images. In *Fourth European Conference on Com-*

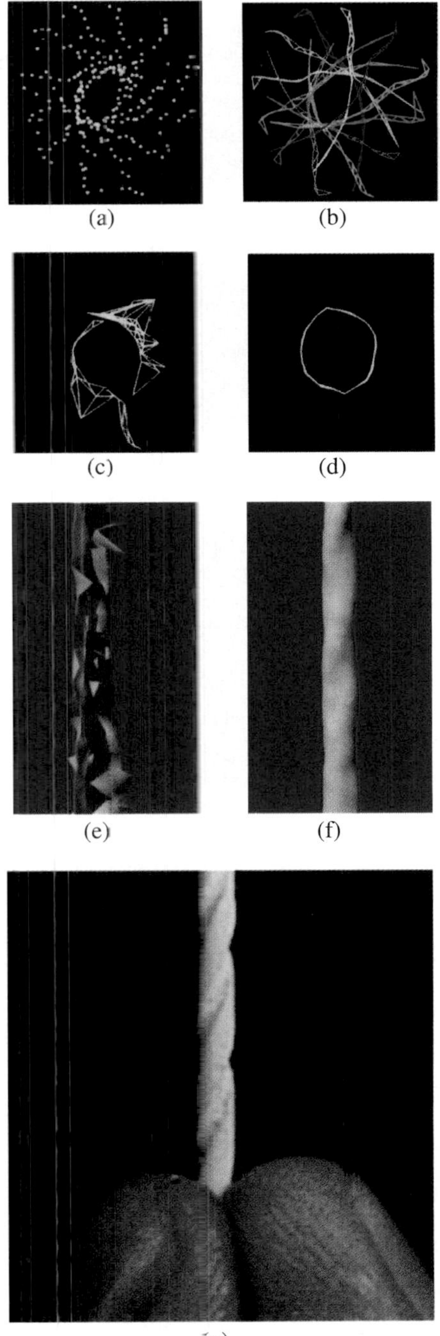

Figure 9. Merging range images of a drill bit. We scanned a 1.6 mm drill bit from 12 orientations at a 30 degree spacing using traditional optical triangulation methods. Illustrations (a) - (d) each show a plan (top) view of a slice taken through the range data and two reconstructions. (a) The range data shown as unorganized points: algorithms that operate on this form of data would likely have difficulty deriving the correct surface. (b) The range data shown as a set of wire frame tessellations of the range data: the false edge extensions pose a challenge to both polygon and volumetric methods. (c) A slice through the reconstructed surface generated by a polygon method: the zippering algorithm of Turk [31]. (d) A slice through the reconstructed surface generated by the volumetric method described in this paper. (e) A rendering of the zippered surface. (f) A rendering of the volumetrically generated surface. Note the catastrophic failure of the zippering algorithm. The volumetric method, however, produces a watertight model. (g) A photograph of the original drill bit. The drill bit was painted white for scanning.

puter Vision, volume I, pages 117–126, April 1996.

[15] Tsai-Hong Hong and M. O. Shneier. Describing a robot's workspace using a sequence of views from a moving camera. *IEEE Transactions on Pattern Analysis and Machine Intelligence*, 7(6):721–726, November 1985.

[16] H. Hoppe, T. DeRose, T. Duchamp, J. McDonald, and W. Stuetzle. Surface reconstruction from unorganized points. In *Computer Graphics (SIGGRAPH '92 Proceedings)*, volume 26, pages 71–78, July 1992.

[17] V. Krishnamurthy and M. Levoy. Fitting smooth surfaces to dense polygon meshes. In these proceedings.

[18] P. Lacroute and M. Levoy. Fast volume rendering using a shear-warp factorization of the viewing transformation. In *Proceedings of SIGGRAPH '94 (Orlando, FL, July 24-29, 1994)*, pages 451–458. ACM Press, July 1994.

[19] A. Li and G. Crebbin. Octree encoding of objects from range images. *Pattern Recognition*, 27(5):727–739, May 1994.

[20] W.E. Lorensen and H. E. Cline. Marching cubes: A high resolution 3D surface construction algorithm. In *Computer Graphics (SIGGRAPH '87 Proceedings)*, volume 21, pages 163–169, July 1987.

[21] W.N. Martin and J.K. Aggarwal. Volumetric descriptions of objects from multiple views. *IEEE Transactions on Pattern Analysis and Machine Intelligence*, 5(2):150–158, March 1983.

[22] C. Montani, R. Scateni, and R. Scopigno. A modified look-up table for implicit disambiguation of marching cubes. *Visual Computer*, 10(6):353–355, 1994.

[23] M. Potmesil. Generating octree models of 3D objects from their silhouettes in a sequence of images. *Computer Vision, Graphics, and Image Processing*, 40(1):1–29, October 1987.

[24] M. Rutishauser, M. Stricker, and M. Trobina. Merging range images of arbitrarily shaped objects. In *Proceedings 1994 IEEE Computer Society Conference on Computer Vision and Pattern Recognition*, pages 573–580, June 1994.

[25] M. Soucy and D. Laurendeau. A general surface approach to the integration of a set of range views. *IEEE Transactions on Pattern Analysis and Machine Intelligence*, 17(4):344–358, April 1995.

[26] G. Succi, G. Sandini, E Grosso, and M. Tistarelli. 3D feature extraction from sequences of range data. In *Robotics Research. Fifth International Symposium*, pages 117–127, August 1990.

[27] R. Szeliski. Rapid octree construction from image sequences. *CVGIP: Image Understanding*, 58(1):23–32, July 1993.

[28] G.H Tarbox and S.N. Gottschlich. IVIS: An integrated volumetric inspection system. In *Proceedings of the 1994 Second CAD-Based Vision Workshop*, pages 220–227, February 1994.

[29] G. Taubin. A signal processing approach to fair surface design. In *Proceedings of SIGGRAPH '95 (Los Angeles, CA, Aug. 6-11, 1995)*, pages 351–358. ACM Press, August 1995.

[30] G. Turk and M. Levoy. Zippered polygon meshes from range images. In *Proceedings of SIGGRAPH '94 (Orlando, FL, July 24-29, 1994)*, pages 311–318. ACM Press, July 1994.

[31] Robert Weinstock. *The Calculus of Variations, with Applications to Physics and Engineering*. Dover Publications, 1974.

A Isosurface as least squares minimizer

It is possible to show that the isosurface of the weighted signed distance function is equivalent to a least squares minimization of squared distances between points on the range surfaces and points on the desired reconstruction. The key assumptions are that the range sensor is orthographic and that the range errors are independently distributed along sensor lines of sight. A full proof is beyond the scope of this paper, but we provide a sketch here. See [5] for details.

Consider a region, R, on the desired surface, f, which is observed by n range images. We define the error between an observed range surface and a possible reconstructed surface as the integral of the weighted squared distances between points on the range surface and the reconstructed surface. These distances are taken along the lines of sight of the sensor, commensurate with the predominant directions of uncertainty (see Figure 10). The total error is the sum of the integrals for the n range images:

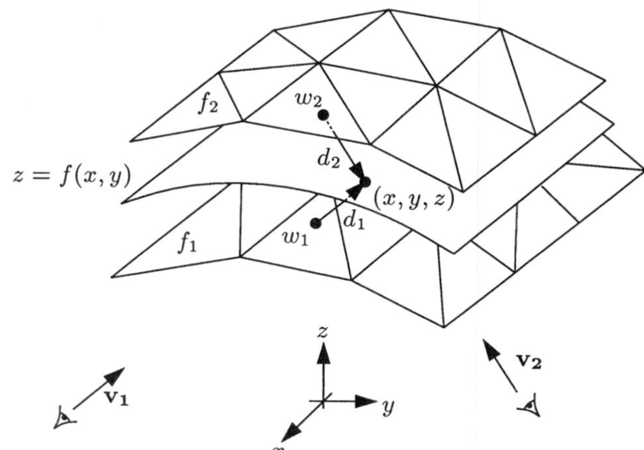

Figure 10. Two range surfaces, f_1 and f_2, are tessellated range images acquired from directions v_1 and v_2. The possible range surface, $z = f(x, y)$, is evaluated in terms of the weighted squared distances to points on the range surfaces taken along the lines of sight to the sensor. A point, (x, y, z), is shown here being evaluated to find its corresponding signed distances, d_1 and d_2, and weights, w_1 and w_2.

$$E(f) = \sum_{i=1}^{n} \iint_{A_i} w_i(s,t,f) d_i(s,t,f)^2 ds dt \tag{6}$$

where each (s, t) corresponds to a particular sensor line of sight for each range image, A_i is the domain of integration for the i'th range image, and $w_i(s, t, f)$ and $d_i(s, t, f)$ are the weights and signed distances taken along the i'th range image's lines of sight.

Now, consider a canonical domain, A, on a parameter plane, (x, y), over which R is a function $z = f(x, y)$. The total error can be rewritten as an integration over the canonical domain:

$$E(z) = \iint_A \sum_{i=1}^{n} \left[w_i(x,y,z) d_i(x,y,z)^2\right] \left[\mathbf{v_i} \cdot (\frac{\partial z}{\partial x}, \frac{\partial z}{\partial y}, -1)\right] dx \tag{7}$$

where $\mathbf{v_i}$ is the sensing direction of the i'th range image, and the weights and distances are evaluated at each point, (x, y, z), by first mapping them to the lines of sight of the corresponding range image. The dot product represents a correction term that relates differential areas in A to differential areas in A_i. Applying the calculus of variations [31], we can construct a partial differential equation for the z that minimizes this integral. Solving this equation we arrive at the following relation:

$$\sum_{i=1}^{n} \partial_{\mathbf{v_i}} [w_i(x,y,z) d_i(x,y,z)^2] = 0 \tag{8}$$

where $\partial_{\mathbf{v_i}}$ is the directional derivative along $\mathbf{v_i}$. Since the weight associated with a line of sight does not vary along that line of sight, and the signed distance has a derivative of unity along the line of sight, we can simplify this equation to:

$$\sum_{i=1}^{n} w_i(x,y,z) d_i(x,y,z) = 0 \tag{9}$$

This weighted sum of signed distances is the same as what we compute in equations 1 and 2, without the division by the sum of the weights. Since the this divisor is always positive, the isosurface we extract in section 3 is exactly the least squares minimizing surface described here.

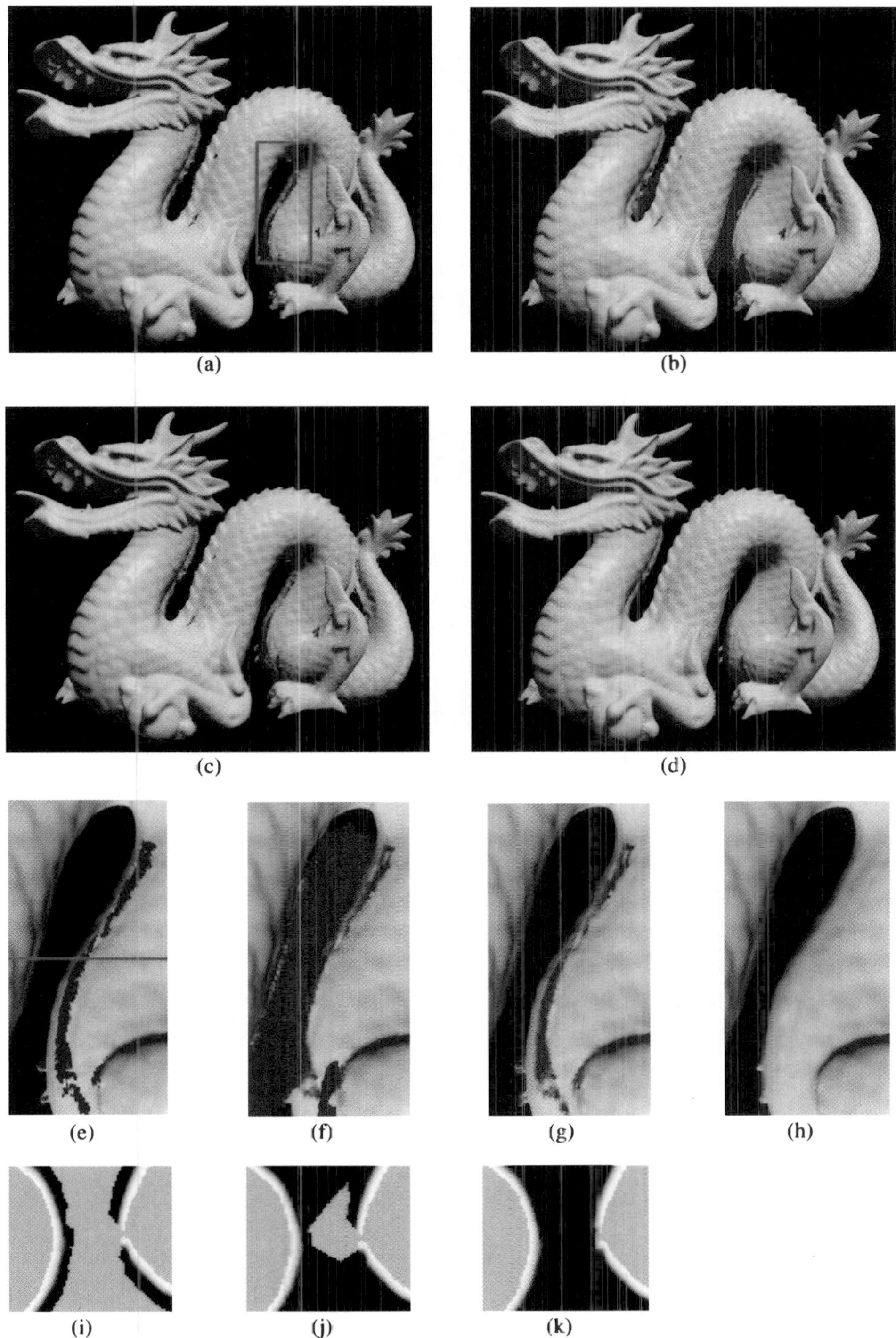

Figure 11. Reconstruction of a dragon. Illustrations (a) - (d) are full views of the dragon. Illustrations (e) - (h) are magnified views of the section highlighted by the green box in (a). Regions shown in red correspond to hole fill triangles. Illustrations (i) - (k) are slices through the corresponding volumetric grids at the level indicated by the green line in (e). (a)(e)(i) Reconstruction from 61 range images without space carving and hole filling. The magnified rendering highlights the holes in the belly. The slice through the volumetric grid shows how the signed distance ramps are maintained close to the surface. The gap in the ramps leads to a hole in the reconstruction. (b)(f)(j) Reconstruction with space carving and hole filling using the same data as in (a). While some holes are filled in a reasonable manner, some large regions of space are left untouched and create extraneous tessellations. The slice through the volumetric grid reveals that the isosurface between the unseen (brown) and empty (black) regions will be connected to the isosurface extracted from the distance ramps, making it part of the connected component of the dragon body and leaving us with a substantial number of false surfaces. (c)(g)(k) Reconstruction with 10 additional range images using "backdrop" surfaces to effect more carving. Notice how the extraneous hole fill triangles nearly vanish. The volumetric slice shows how we have managed to empty out the space near the belly. The bumpiness along the hole fill regions of the belly in (g) corresponds to aliasing artifacts from tessellating over the discontinuous transition between unseen and empty regions. (d)(h) Reconstruction as in (c)(g) with filtering of the hole fill portions of the mesh. The filtering operation blurs out the aliasing artifacts in the hole fill regions while preserving the detail in the rest of the model. Careful examination of (h) reveals a faint ridge in the vicinity of the smoothed hole fill. This ridge is actual geometry present in all of the renderings, (e)-(h). The final model contains 1.8 million polygons and is watertight.

(a) (b) (c) (d) (e)

Figure 12. Reconstruction and 3D hardcopy of the ''Happy Buddha''. The original is a plastic and rosewood statuette that stands 20 cm tall. Note that the camera parameters for each of these images is different, creating a slightly different perspective in each case. (a) Photograph of the original after spray painting it matte gray to simplify scanning. (b) Gouraud–shaded rendering of one range image of the statuette. Scans were acquired using a Cyberware scanner, modified to permit spacetime triangulation [6]. This figure illustrates the limited and fragmentary nature of the information available from a single range image. (c) Gouraud–shaded rendering of the 2.4 million polygon mesh after merging 48 scans, but before hole–filling. Notice that the reconstructed mesh has at least as much detail as the single range image, but is less noisy; this is most apparent around the belly. The hole in the base of the model corresponds to regions that were not observed directly by the range sensor. (d) RenderMan rendering of an 800,000 polygon decimated version of the hole–filled and filtered mesh built from 58 scans. By placing a backdrop behind the model and taking 10 additional scans, we were able to see through the space between the base and the Buddha's garments, allowing us to carve space and fill the holes in the base. (e) Photograph of a hardcopy of the 3D model, manufactured by 3D Systems, Inc., using stereolithography. The computer model was sliced into 500 layers, 150 microns apart, and the hardcopy was built up layer by layer by selectively hardening a liquid resin. The process took about 10 hours. Afterwards, the model was sanded and bead–blasted to remove the stair–step artifacts that arise during layered manufacturing.

Fitting Smooth Surfaces to Dense Polygon Meshes

Venkat Krishnamurthy
Marc Levoy

Computer Science Department
Stanford University

Abstract

Recent progress in acquiring shape from range data permits the acquisition of seamless million-polygon meshes from physical models. In this paper, we present an algorithm and system for converting dense irregular polygon meshes of arbitrary topology into tensor product B-spline surface patches with accompanying displacement maps. This choice of representation yields a coarse but efficient model suitable for animation and a fine but more expensive model suitable for rendering.

The first step in our process consists of interactively painting patch boundaries over a rendering of the mesh. In many applications, interactive placement of patch boundaries is considered part of the creative process and is not amenable to automation. The next step is gridded resampling of each bounded section of the mesh. Our resampling algorithm lays a grid of springs across the polygon mesh, then iterates between relaxing this grid and subdividing it. This grid provides a parameterization for the mesh section, which is initially unparameterized. Finally, we fit a tensor product B-spline surface to the grid. We also output a displacement map for each mesh section, which represents the error between our fitted surface and the spring grid. These displacement maps are images; hence this representation facilitates the use of image processing operators for manipulating the geometric detail of an object. They are also compatible with modern photo-realistic rendering systems.

Our resampling and fitting steps are fast enough to surface a million polygon mesh in under 10 minutes - important for an interactive system.

CR Categories: I.3.5 [Computer Graphics]: Computational Geometry and Object Modeling —curve, surface and object representations; I.3.7[Computer Graphics]:Three-Dimensional Graphics and Realism—texture; J.6[Computer-Aided Engineering]:Computer-Aided Design (CAD); G.1.2[Approximation]:Spline Approximation

Additional Key Words: Surface fitting, Parameterization, Dense polygon meshes, B-spline surfaces, Displacement maps

Authors' Address: Department of Computer Science, Stanford University, Stanford, CA 94305
E-mail: venkat,levoy@cs.stanford.edu
World Wide Web: http://www-graphics.stanford.edu/~venkat, ~levoy

1 Introduction

Advances in range image acquisition and integration allow us to compute geometrical models from complex physical models [9, 36]. The output of these technologies is a dense, seamless (i.e. manifold) irregular polygon mesh of arbitrary topology. For example, the model in figure 12, generated from 75 scans of an action figure using a Cyberware laser range scanner, contains 350,000 polygons. Models like this offer new opportunities to modelers and animators in the CAD and entertainment industries.

Dense polygon meshes are an adequate representation for some applications. Several commercial animation houses employ polygon meshes almost exclusively. However, for reasons of compactness, control, manufacturability, or appearance, many users prefer smooth surface representations. To satisfy these users, techniques are needed for fitting surfaces to dense meshes of arbitrary topology.

A notable property of these new acquisition techniques is their ability to capture fine surface detail. Whatever fitting technique we employ should strive to retain this fine detail. Surprisingly, a unified surface representation may not be the best approach. First, the heavy machinery of most smooth surface representations (for example B-splines) makes them an inefficient way to represent fine geometric detail. Second and perhaps more important, although geometric detail is useful at the rendering stage of an animation pipeline, it may not be of interest to either the modeler or the animator. Moreover, its presence may degrade the time or memory performance of the modeling system. For these reasons, we believe it is advantageous to separate the representations of coarse geometry and fine surface detail.

Within this framework, we may choose from among many representations for these two components. For representing coarse geometry, modelers in the entertainment and CAD industry have long used NURBS [14] and in particular uniform tensor product B-splines. Such models typically consist of control meshes stitched together to the level of continuity desired for an application. In order to address their needs we have chosen uniform tensor product B-splines as our surface representation.

For representing surface detail, we propose using displacement maps. Each pixel in such a map gives an offset from a point on a fitted surface to a point on a gridded resampling of the original polygon mesh. The principal advantage of this representation is that displacement maps are essentially images. As such, they can be processed, retouched, compressed, and otherwise manipulated using simple image processing tools. Some of the effects shown in figures 11 and 12 were achieved using Adobe Photoshop, a commercial photo retouching program.

1.1 System overview

Figure 1 shows the pipeline for our system. We start with a connected polygon mesh. The additional connectivity information offered by a polygonal representation is used to advantage at every stage of our pipeline. Our steps are as follows:

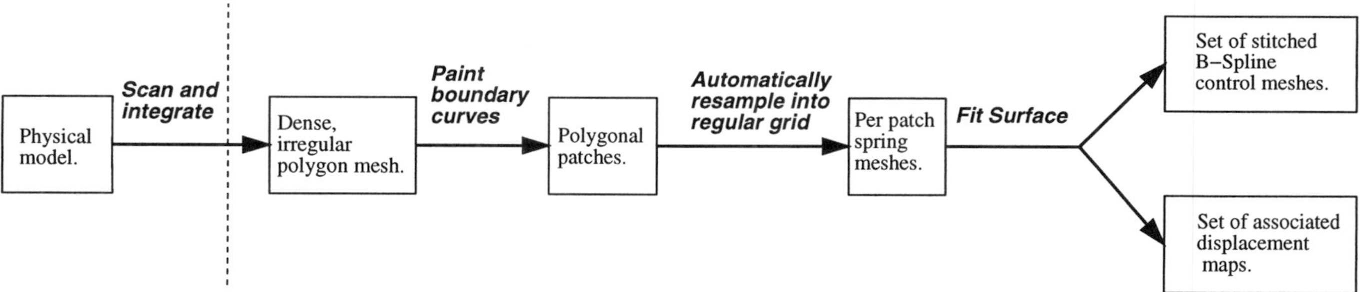

Figure 1. Our surface fitting pipeline: the input to our system is a dense irregular polygon mesh. First, boundary curves for the desired spline patches are painted on the surface of the unparameterized model. The output of this step is a set of bounded mesh regions. We call each such region a polygonal patch. We next perform an automated resampling of this polygonal patch to form a regular grid that lies on the surface of the polygonal patch. We call this regular grid a spring mesh. Finally, we fit surfaces to the spring mesh and output both a B-spline surface representation and a set of associated displacement maps to capture the fine detail.

1. Our first step is an interactive boundary curve painting phase wherein a modeler defines the boundaries of a number of patches. This is accomplished with tools that allow the painting of curves directly on the surface of the unparameterized polygonal model. Here, the connectivity of the polygon mesh allows the use of local graph search algorithms to make curve painting operations rapid. This property is useful when a modeler wishes to experiment with different boundary curve configurations for the same model. Each region of the mesh that a B-spline surface must be fit to is called a *polygonal patch.* Since patch boundaries have been placed for artistic reasons, polygonal patches are not constrained to be height fields. Our only assumptions about them are that each is a rectangularly parameterizable piece of the surface that has no holes.

2. In the next step we generate a gridded resampling for each polygonal patch. This is accomplished by an automatic coarse-to-fine resampling of the patch, producing a regular grid that is constrained to lie on the polygonal surface. We call this grid the *spring mesh.* Its purpose is to establish a parameterization for the unparameterized surface. Our resampling algorithm is a combination of relaxation and subdivision steps that iteratively refine the spring mesh at a given resolution to obtain a better sampling of the underlying polygonal patch. This refinement is explicitly directed by distortion metrics relevant to the spline fit. The output of this step is a fine gridding of each polygonal patch in the model.

3. We now use standard gridded data fitting techniques to fit a B-spline surface to the spring mesh corresponding to each polygonal patch. The output of this step is a set of B-spline patches that represent the coarse geometry of the polygonal model. To represent fine detail, we also compute a displacement map for each patch as a gridded resampling of the difference between the spring mesh and the B-spline surface. This regular sampling can conveniently be represented as a vector (rgb) image which stores a 3-valued displacement at each sample location. Each of these displacements represents a perturbation in the local coordinate frame of the spline surface. This image representation lends itself to a variety of interesting image processing operations such as compositing, painting, edge detection and compression. An issue in our technique, or in any technique for fitting multiple patches to data is ensuring continuity between the patches. We use a combination of knot line matching and a stitching post-process which together give us G^1 continuity everywhere. This solution is widely used in the entertainment industry.

The remainder of this paper is organized as follows. Section 2 reviews relevant previous work. Section 3 describes our techniques for painting boundary curves over polygonal meshes. Section 4 presents our coarse-to-fine, polygonal patch resampling algorithm and the surface fitting process. Section 5 describes our strategy for extracting displacement maps and some interesting applications thereof. Section 6, discusses techniques for dealing with continuity across patch boundaries. Finally, section 7 concludes by discussing future work.

Throughout this paper we will draw on examples from the entertainment industry. However, our techniques are generally applicable.

2 Previous work

There is a large literature on surface fitting techniques in the CAD, computer vision and approximation theory fields. We focus here on only those techniques from these areas that use dense (scanned) data of arbitrary topology to produce smooth surfaces. We can classify such surface fitting techniques as manual, semi-automated and automated.

2.1 Manual techniques

Manual approaches can be divided into two categories. The first category includes all methods for digitizing a physical model directly. For example, using a touch probe, one can acquire only data that is relevant to the final surface model. Catalogues of computer models published by ViewPoint Data Labs and the work of Pixar's animation group [24, 28] exemplify these methods. These methods involve human intervention throughout the data acquisition process and are hence time-consuming, especially if the model is complex or the data set required is large. In contrast, our pipeline employs automatic data acquisition methods [9].

The second category uses scanned data as a template to assist in the model construction process. Point cloud or triangulated data is typically imported into a conventional modeling system. A user then manually projects isolated points to this data as a means of determining the locations of control points (or edit points [15]) for smooth parametric surfaces. These methods require less human intervention than those in the first category but complex models may still require a lot of labour.

2.2 Semi-automated techniques

The approaches in this category take point cloud data sets as input. Examples include commercial systems such as Imageware's Surfacer [33], Delcam's CopyCAD, and some research systems [20, 22]. These approaches begin by identifying a subset of points that are to be approximated. Parameterization of data points is usually accomplished by a user-guided process such as projection of the points to a manually constructed base plane or surface. A constrained, non-linear least squares problem is then solved on this subset of the point cloud to obtain a B-spline surface for the specified region. While point cloud techniques are widely applicable, they fail to exploit topological information already present in the input data. As demonstrated by Curless et al [9] and Turk et al [36], using this additional information can significantly improve quality of reconstruction. In the context of our surface fitting algorithm, working with connected polygonal representations has also facilitated the development of an automatic parameterization scheme.

2.3 Automated surface fitting techniques

Eck et al [12] describe a method for fitting irregular meshes with a number of automatically placed bicubic Bezier patches. For the parameterization step, a piecewise linear approximation to harmonic maps [11] is used, and the number of patches is adjusted to achieve fitting tolerances. While this method produces high quality surfaces, it includes a number of expensive optimization steps, making it too slow for an interactive system. Further, their technique does not separate fine geometric detail from coarse geometry. Particularly for very dense meshes, we find this separation both useful and preferable, as already explained. We compare some other aspects of the parameterization scheme of Eck et al [11] with ours in section 4.10.

We briefly mention some techniques [29, 31] that use hierarchical algorithms to fit parametric surfaces to scanned data sets. While these approaches work well for regular data, they do not address the problem of unparameterized, irregular polygon meshes. Finally, Sclaroff et al [32] demonstrate the use of displacement maps in the context of interpolating data with generalized implicit surfaces. However, this method also works only on regular data sets.

2.4 Relevant work in texture mapping

A key aspect of our method is an automatic parameterization scheme for irregular polygon meshes. As such, there are techniques in the texture mapping literature that address similar problems, notably the work of Bennis et al [6] and that of Maillot et al [21]. Both of these papers present schemes to re-parameterize surfaces for texture mapping. These algorithms work well with regular data sets, such as discretized splines. However, they can exhibit objectionable parametric distortions in general [11]. Pedersen [25] describes a method for texture mapping (and hence parameterizing) implicit surfaces. While the methods work well with implicit surfaces, they rely on smoothness properties of the surface and require the evaluation of global surface derivatives. Irregular polygon meshes in general, are neither smooth nor conducive to the evaluation of global surface derivatives, as discussed by Welch et al [38].

3 Boundary curve specification

Our surface fitting pipeline starts with the user interactively segmenting the polygonal model into a number of regions that are to be approximated by spline patches. A patch is specified by interactively painting its boundary curves. This operation should be fast and provide intuitive feedback to the user. We have found that curves that lie on the surface of the model are easier to specify and manipulate than unconstrained space curves. A polygonal (discrete) geodesic [23] is one possible representation. Unfortunately, this is expensive both to compute and to maintain. We instead represent patch boundaries as sampled geodesics. We call these face-point curves. The steps for painting a boundary curve are shown and described in figure 3.

This painting process yields a piecewise linear face-point curve on the surface through a sequence of picked vertices. We now smooth this face-point curve on the surface using a fitted B-spline

Graph corresponding to polygon mesh	The graph consisting of vertices and edges of the polygon mesh, with edge lengths given by Euclidean distance.
Graph path	A path between two vertices of the above graph.
Polygonal patch	Each bounded region of the polygon mesh, as determined by the painted boundary curves.
Face point	A point that lies on some face of the polygon mesh.
Face-point curve	A list of face points that form a piecewise linear curve.
Spring mesh	A grid of face points that lie on the faces of a polygonal patch.
Force (P2, P1) where P1 and P2 represent points in space	A 3-vector given by P2 − P1.

Figure 2. A glossary of common terms we use through this paper.

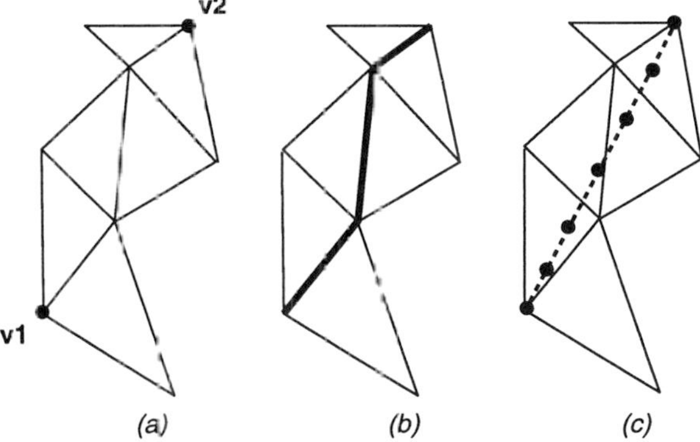

Figure 3. Boundary curve painting. The user picks a sequence of points with a mouse on a 2-D projection (rendering) of the polygon mesh. The program automatically associates the nearest vertex of the mesh to each of these points. Two such vertices (v1 and v2) are shown in (a). Between each successive pair of such vertices from (a), we compute the projection on the surface, of a straight line connecting the two. This is performed in two steps. First, the greedy graph path between these two vertices is computed as shown in (b) (as a thick polyline). This path is then sampled into a face-point curve and smoothed into a straight line as illustrated in (c). Filled circles represent individual face points. The face-point curve now represents a sampling of the projection on the polygonal surface, of a line from v1 to v2.

curve [30]. The resolution of the B-spline for the fit is set interactively by the user. The smoothing operation consists of attracting a face-point curve, which is constrained to lie on the surface of the polygon mesh, to a curve in space. This is a fast technique for obtaining the projection of a space curve to a sampled curve on the polygon mesh. Figure 4 sums up this procedure.

This smoothing process yields a face-point curve that is a sampled representation of the projection of a spline curve on the polygon mesh; the spline determines how much the constructed face-point curve will be smoothed. Since both the painting and smoothing processes use local graph search techniques, they are efficient.

Figures 12b and 12c show two examples of complex sets of curves painted on the object of figure 12a. Each configuration has about 220 curves and took about 2 hours to specify; most of that time was spent actively painting the curves. The next section describes how tensor product B-spline surfaces are fit to each of the delineated patches.

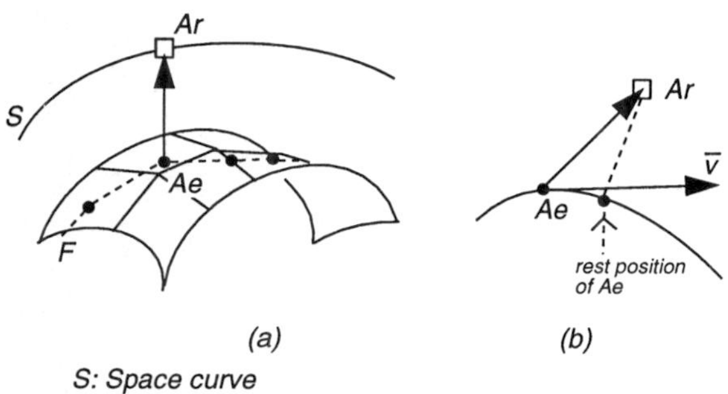

Figure 4. Sliding a face-point curve along a polygon mesh to smooth it. (a) shows an attractor Ar on the space curve and an attractee Ae on the polygon mesh. (b) shows a 1-D version and the rest position of Ae.

4 Fitting B-spline patches

4.1 B-spline fitting theory: overview

In general, parametric curve and surface fitting to irregular data can be formulated as a non-linear least squares problem [10, 30]. The following discussion assumes uniform cubic (order 4) tensor product B-spline surfaces but holds for other kinds of parametric surfaces as well. The equation for a B-spline surface $\vec{P}(u, v)$ can be written as:

$$\vec{P}(u, v) = \sum_{i=0}^{n} \sum_{j=0}^{m} X_{i,j} B_i(u) B_j(v) \quad (1)$$

where $\vec{P}$ is a point in 3-space, u and v are parameter values in the two parametric directions of the surface, $X_{i,j}$'s are control points of the B-spline surface and the B_i are fourth order B-spline basis functions [4].

Given some set of points { $\vec{p_l}$(x, y, z), l=1 ...M} to which a B-spline surface must be fit, we must first make an association of parameter values u and v to each of these data points. Given these associations, an over-constrained system of linear equations can be generated from (1), where the $X_{i,j}$ are unknowns. Each linear equation in this system corresponds to a point $\vec{p_l}$ satisfying (1). Therefore, a least squares solution [19] can be performed to obtain the $X_{i,j}$.

In our application, we are not given parameter associations for our data points. Because the B-spline basis functions are non-linear in the parameter values, the problem of parametric surface fitting requires a non-linear optimization process. This is usually solved by starting with an initial guess for each p_l's u and v values and subsequently iterating between refining these values and re-fitting the surface with the improved parameter associations until some tolerance of fit is achieved [30]. This process is expensive since it requires calculation of spline surface partial derivatives at each of the original data points at every step of the iteration. Furthermore, the convergence of this iteration (and hence the quality of the fitted spline surface) is strongly dependant on the initial parameter values. If these are not good, convergence can be slow and in general is not guaranteed [18, 20].

4.2 Our surface fitting strategy

To avoid the complexity and cost of the non-linear optimization process described above, we first resample each irregular polygonal patch into a regular grid of points (the spring mesh). We can then apply gridded data fitting techniques [29] to this spring mesh to obtain a spline approximation. The advantage of these techniques is that they avoid the parameter re-estimation step described earlier and are hence significantly faster. It is worth pointing out that in our application there is nothing sacrosanct about the original mesh vertices. In particular, the vertices produced by our range image integration method [9] are at a scale that approaches the noise-limited resolution of our sensor. As long as the grid is a reasonably careful sampling of the polygon mesh, surface quality is not compromised. We use a piecewise linear reconstruction for this sampling, which we find to be satisfactory. If in other applications it is required to fit the original mesh vertices, this can be accomplished by first parameterizing the mesh vertices using our regular spring grid and then running the standard non-linear optimization process described above.

The following subsections describe how to perform a gridded resampling of each polygonal patch and discuss some of its advantages and drawbacks. For the discussion, patches are assumed to be four sided; cylindrical, toroidal and triangular patches are all modeled as special cases of four-sided patches.

4.3 Gridded resampling of each polygonal patch

Each polygonal patch can be an arbitrary four-sided region of the polygon mesh. The only constraints are that it must be rectangularly parameterizable and must not have holes. These are reasonable assumptions since the models input to our system are seamless or can easily be made so by acquiring and integrating more scans and by recent hole-filling techniques [9]. Our goal is to generate a uniform grid of points over the polygonal surface that samples the surface well. Finite element literature [34] describes a number of techniques for generating grids over smooth surfaces. Unfortunately, these techniques rely on the existence of higher order global derivatives (i.e. a smooth surface definition already exists). While it is possible to make local approximations to surface curvature for irregular polygonal surfaces [37], there is no scheme to evaluate global derivatives at arbitrary surface positions.

4.4 What is a good gridding of a surface?

Although we cannot utilize the finite element literature directly, it offers useful insight on objective functions one might minimize to produce different surface parameterizations.

Since each polygonal patch is resampled into a regular grid in order to fit a smooth surface, it is important that the grid not lose any geometric detail present in the original data. We have chosen three criteria for our surface grids: (In the following, a grid line along either direction is referred to as an iso-curve; the two directions are called u and v.)

1) *Arc length uniformity*: the grid spacing along a particular iso-curve should be uniform.
2) *Aspect ratio uniformity*: the grid spacing along a u iso-curve should be the same as the grid spacing along a v iso-curve.
3) *Parametric fairness*: Every u and v iso-curve should be of the minimum possible length given the first two criteria.

An obvious criterion we have omitted above is that iso-curves should always lie within the polygonal patch they are supposed to sample.

Our intuitions for the above criteria are based on sampling theory. Since our triangulations come from real models that have been sampled uniformly over their surfaces, our triangle meshes tend to be uniformly dense across different parts of the polygonal model. For a resampling of such a mesh to be faithful, it should give equal importance to equal areas of the surface.

With this intuition in mind, the arc-length criterion accounts for the fact that geometrically interesting detail is equally likely along any given section of an iso-curve on the surface. The aspect-ratio criterion captures the fact that detail is equally likely in either direction of a gridding. Finally, the parametric fairness term, minimizes "wiggles" along the spring iso-curves. This is important since

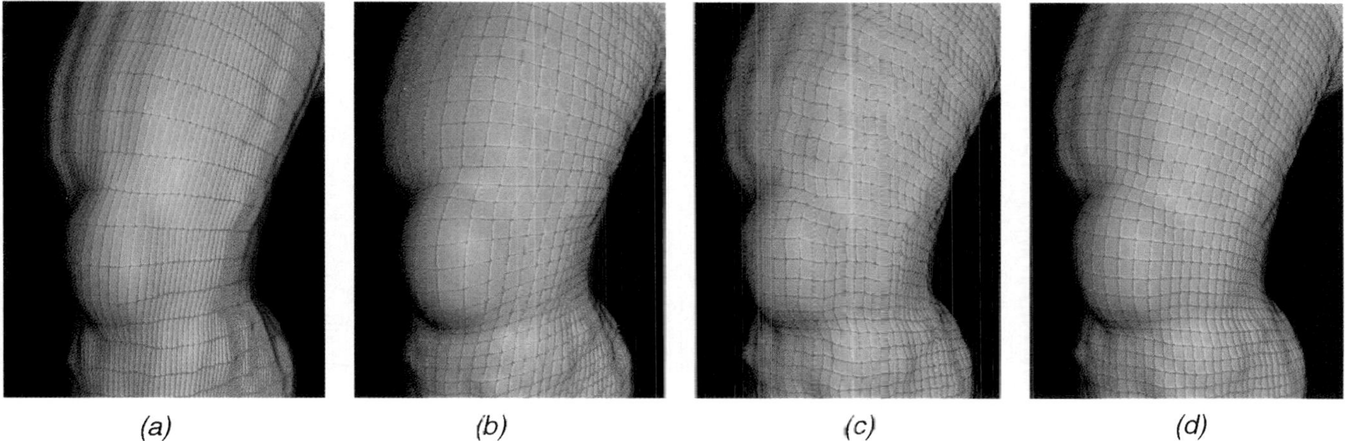

Figure 5. This figure explores the three sampling criteria on part of the right leg of the model in figure 12a. Each of the above images represents a triangulated and smooth shaded spring mesh at a very low resolution. In each case, the number of spring points sampling the polygon mesh was kept the same. The differences arise from their redistribution over the surface. The spring edges are shown in red. (a) shows what happens when the aspect ratio criterion is left out. Notice how a lot of detail is captured in the vertical direction, but not in the horizontal. (b) shows the effect of leaving out the arc length criterion. Notice how the kneecap looks slightly bloated and that detail above and around the knee region is missed. This is because few samples were distributed over the knee resulting in a bad sampling of this region. (c) shows a missing fairness criterion. The iso-curves exhibit many "wiggles". Finally (d) shows the result when all three criteria are met. See figure 8a for the original model and 8e for a full resampling of the leg.

the spline surface follows the spring mesh closely. The fairness criterion thus indirectly minimizes unnecessary wiggles in the spline iso-curves. Note that this term bears some similarities to the idea of fairness in the parametric interpolation literature [16].

4.5 A fast gridding algorithm

Our algorithm is a coarse-to-fine procedure that for each polygonal patch, incrementally builds a successively refined sampling of the patch into a spring mesh. At each subdivision level, the spring mesh points included in the procedure are a subset of face points of the polygonal patch. Here are the steps of the gridding algorithm:

1) Perform a seed fill of the patch. This restricts graph searches to vertices of this patch only.
2) Compute an initial guess for the iso-curves using Dijkstra's shortest-path algorithm, with an appropriate aspect ratio for this patch.
3) Refine the spring mesh using the arc length and fairness criteria.
4) Subdivide the spring mesh.
5) Iterate between steps 3 and 4 until the number of spring mesh points reaches a density close to that of the number of vertices of the polygonal patch.

In our system, the user can stop the resampling at any stage to view incremental results and fit a spline surface to the spring mesh points at the current resolution. We consider some of these steps in detail in the following subsections.

4.6 Initialization of iso-curves

To obtain an initial guess for each u and v iso-curve, we use Dijkstra's single-source, single-destination, shortest-path algorithm [1] to compute a path between corresponding pairs of points along opposing boundary curves. The initial number of iso-curves in each direction are chosen to be proportional to the aspect ratio of the patch. This is computed as the ratio of the longer of the two boundary curves in either direction.

The starting spring mesh points are computed as intersections of these initial iso-curves; the curves must intersect if the patch is rectangularly parameterizable. Dijkstra's algorithm is $O(n\log(n))$ in the number of vertices to be searched. However, since the vertex set is restricted to that of a single patch and we search for only a small set of initial iso-curves, this procedure is rapid. Starting with a large number of iso-curves is both slower and not guaranteed to produce as good a final spring mesh as starting with a small number of iso-curves and using a coarse-to-fine refinement. We return to this point in section 4.10.

4.7 Refining the spring mesh: relaxation

The initial guess for the spring mesh, as obtained above, can be quite poor. The next step in the algorithm is to refine the position of the spring mesh points using a relaxation procedure. In our choice of the number of spring mesh points to place along each boundary curve, we have implemented criteria 2 (section 4.4): aspect ratio uniformity. Subsequent subdivisions are all uniform. During our relaxation procedure, we apply the remaining two criteria of arc length and fairness.

The relaxation procedure works as follows. Let P_{up}, P_{down}, P_{left} and P_{right} represent the positions of the 4 neighboring spring points in the u and v directions of the spring point P. The algorithm computes a resultant force on each of these points and slides it along the surface to a new position.

Minimizing arc length distortion along one of P's iso-curves is achieved by moving P towards whichever neighbor (on the same iso-curve) is farther away from it. Consider the two forces $Force(P_{up}, P)$ and $Force(P_{down}, P)$. We make the direction of the larger of these two the direction of a new force F_{ud}. The magnitude of F_{ud} is set to be the difference of the two magnitudes. We perform a similar computation in the other direction (left-right) as well to get a force F_{lr}. Let us denote the resultant of F_{lr} and F_{ud} by F_{arc}. This resultant becomes one of the two terms in equation (2) below.

Fairness distortion is minimized by moving the point P to a position that minimizes the energy corresponding to the set of springs consisting of P and P's immediate neighbors along both iso-curves.

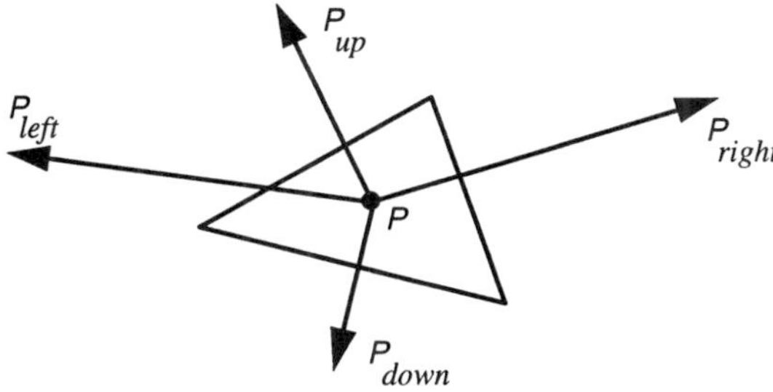

Figure 6. shows the neighbors of a face point P of the spring mesh. The resultant force in a relaxation step is some linear combination of these forces. See the text for details.

This corresponds to computing a force F_{fair} equal to the resultant of the forces acting on P by its four neighbors: *Force*(P_{up}, P), *Force*(P_{down}, P), *Force*(P_{left}, P) and *Force*(P_{right}, P).

The point P is moved according to a force given by a weighted sum of F_{fair} and F_{arc}:

$$F_{result} = \alpha * F_{fair} + \beta * F_{arc} \qquad (2)$$

The relaxation iteration starts with $\alpha = 0$ and $\beta = 1$ and ends with $\alpha = 1, \beta = 0$. This strategy has proved to produce satisfactory results.

Note that we have used Euclidean forces in the previous step, i.e. forces that represent the vector joining two spring points. A relaxation step based on Euclidean forces alone is fast but not guaranteed to generate good results in all cases. Figure 7a shows an example where Euclidean forces alone fail to produce the desired effect.

In contrast to Euclidean forces, geodesic forces are forces along the surface of the mesh. These would produce the correct motion for the spring points in the above case. One approach to solving the problem exemplified by Figure 7a, would be to use geodesic forces, or approximations thereof, as substitutes for Euclidean forces in the relaxation step. However this is an expensive proposition since the fastest algorithm for point to point geodesics is $O(n^2)$ in the size of the patch [7]. Even approximations to geodesics such as local graph searches are $O(n)$ and would be too expensive to perform at every relaxation step.

A solution to the problem is motivated by figure 7b; create a new spring point $P_{mid-point}$ that lies on the surface halfway between $P1$ and $P2$. This point generates new Euclidean forces acting on the original points, moving them towards each other on the surface. We call this process spring mesh subdivision.

4.8 Subdividing the spring mesh

Spring mesh subdivision is based on a graph search and refinement algorithm. Given two spring points $P1$ and $P2$ our algorithm computes a new face point P that is the mid-point of the two spring points and that lies on the graph represented by the patch. The procedure is:

1.) Find the two closest vertices v1 and v2 on $P1$ and $P2$'s faces.
2.) Compute a breadth first graph path from v1 to v2. The midpoint of this path serves as a first approximation to P's location.
3.) Refine this location by letting the forces given by *Force*($P1$, P) and *Force*($P2$, P) act on P, moving it to a new position on the surface. This process is distinct from the relaxation process. It is used only to obtain a better approximation for P.

Subdivision along boundary curves is based on a static resampling of the face point curve representation; these points are never moved during the relaxation and subdivision steps. We terminate

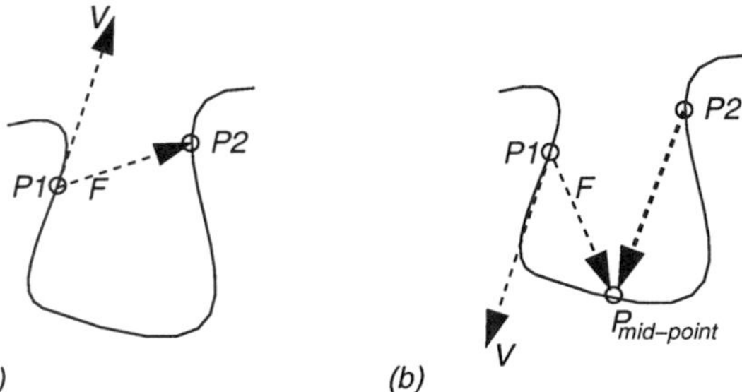

Figure 7. shows a case where relaxation alone fails to move a spring mesh point in the desired direction. In each case F represents the force on $P1$ from its right neighbor and V represents the resulting direction of motion. The desired motion of the point $P1$ is into the cavity. In (a) just the opposite occurs; the points move apart. (b) shows how this case is handled by subdividing the spring mesh along the surface. See the text for details.

subdivision when the number of spring points increases to within a certain range of the polygonal patch's vertices.

4.9 B-spline fitting to gridded data

The techniques described above minimize parametric distortion in the spring mesh. In particular, they enforce minimal distortion with respect to aspect ratio and edge lengths while ensuring parametric fairness. The resulting spring meshes have low area distortion as well, as evidenced by the example shown in figure 5.

The final step in our algorithm is to perform an unconstrained, gridded data fit of a B-spline surface to each spring mesh. As pointed out earlier, fitting to a good resampling of the data does not compromise surface quality. We refer the reader to [29] for an excellent tutorial on the subject of gridded data fitting. Figure 8 summarizes the sampling and fitting processes on a cylindrical patch of the model from figure 12.

4.10 Discussion

Our two-step approach of gridding and then fitting has several desirable characteristics. First, it is fast. This can be understood as follows. At each level of subdivision, each spring mesh point must traverse some fraction of the polygons as it relaxes. The cost of this relaxation thus depends linearly on size of the polygon mesh. It obviously also depends on the size of the spring mesh. If these two were equal, as would occur if we immediately subdivided the spring mesh to the finest level, then the cost of running the relaxation would be $O(n^2)$. If, however, we employ the coarse-to-fine strategy described in the foregoing sections, then at each subdivision level, four times as many spring mesh points move as on the previous (coarser) level, but they move on average half as far. Thus, the cost of relaxation at each subdivision level is linear in the number of spring mesh points, and the total cost due to relaxation is $O(n \log n)$. This argument breaks down if we start with a large initial set of iso-curves. Similar arguments apply to the cost of subdivision.

A second advantage of our overall strategy is that it allows a user to pause the iteration at an intermediate stage and still obtain good quality previews of the model. This is a useful property for an interactive system, specially when dealing with large meshes. In particular, subdivision to higher levels can be postponed until the model designer is satisfied with a patch configuration.

A third advantage of our approach is that once the resampling is done, the spline resolution can be changed interactively, since no further parameter re-estimation is necessary. We have found this to be a useful interactive tool for a modeler, specially when making the tradeoff between explicitly represented geometry and displacement mapped detail as explained in section 5.

As mentioned earlier, there are other schemes that may be used to

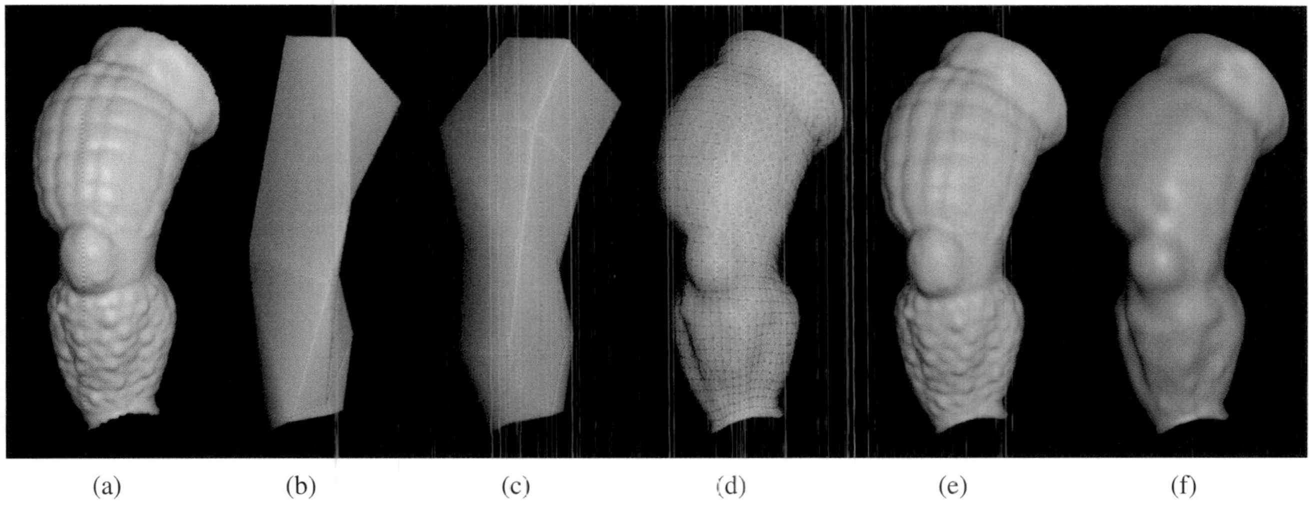

(a) (b) (c) (d) (e) (f)

Figure 8. The above represents a summary of our strategy for resampling a polygonal patch into a regular grid. (a) shows the original polygonal patch (the right leg from the model in figure 12a. This particular patch is cylindrical and has over 25000 vertices. (b), (c), (d) and (e)show a triangulated and smooth shaded reconstruction of the spring mesh at various stages of our re-sampling algorithm. We omit the lines from (e) to prevent clutter. (b) shows the initial guess for u and v iso-curves (under 4 seconds). Notice that the guess is of a poor quality. (c) shows the mesh after the first relaxation step (under 1 second). (d) shows the spring mesh at an intermediate stage, after a few relaxation and subdivision steps (under 3 seconds). (e) shows the final spring mesh without the spring iso-curves. Notice how the fine detail on the leg was accurately captured by the resampled grid. This resampling took 23 seconds. All times are on a 250 Mhz Mips R4400 processor. (f) shows a spline fit that captures the coarse geometry of the patch. This surface has 27x36 control points. It took under 1 second to perform a gridded data fit to the spring mesh of (e).

parameterize irregular polygon meshes. In particular, the harmonic maps of Eck et al[11] produce parameterizations with low edge and aspect ratio distortions. However, the scheme has two main drawbacks for our purposes. First, it can cause excessive area distortions in parameter space. Second, the algorithm employs an $O(n^2)$ iteration to generate final parameter values for vertices of the mesh and no usable intermediate parameterizations are produced. As pointed out in the discussion above, we have found intermediate parameterizations useful in an interactive system.

Our fitting technique is capable of capturing both fine and coarse geometry. However, we typically use it only to capture the coarse geometry. Consider for example the polygonal patch from figure 8a. We find that most of its coarse geometry has been captured by the spline surface of figure 8e. Although the remaining surface detail might be of little use to an animator, it is desirable to retain and use this information as well, if only for rendering.

While there are a variety of multi-resolution techniques that can be applied to capture these details in a unified surface representation [13, 15], for reasons discussed earlier, we represent the fine detail in our models as displacement maps. In the next section we first describe how to extract displacement maps from a polygonal patch and then demonstrate some of the operations that are enabled by this representation.

5 Capturing fine detail with displacement maps

A *displacement map* perturbs the position of a surface based on a displacement function defined over the surface [8]. Displacement maps are usually applied during rendering and are available in a number of commercial renderers. A typical formulation for a bivariate parametric surface, such as a B-spline is: given a point $P(u, v)$ on the surface, a displacement map is a function $\mathbf{d}(u, v)$ giving a perturbation of the point P in space. In general $\mathbf{d}$ can be a vector or a scalar. In the first case, the new position of the point is $P + \vec{\mathbf{d}}$. In the second case, the new position of the point is usually interpreted as $P + \hat{N}\mathbf{d}$, where $\hat{N}$ represents the surface normal at (u, v).

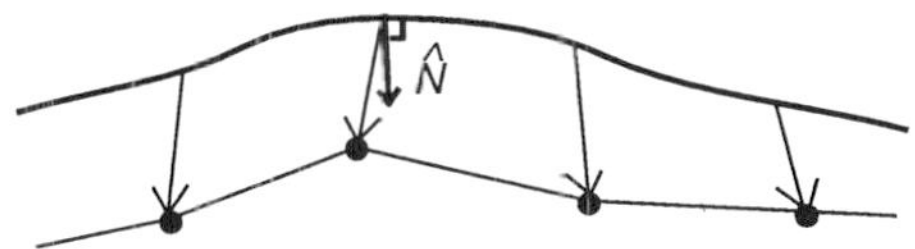

Figure 9 A vector displacement map over a curve. Displacement vectors are shown from an iso-curve S of the spline surface to an iso-curve P of the spring mesh. This map recreates the spring mesh (with a bilinear reconstruction).

5.1 Vector displacement maps

In the context of our fitting system, the obvious displacement function relates points on the spline surface to points on triangles of the original polygon mesh. However, computing such a function requires projecting perpendicularly from the spline surface to the original unparameterized mesh - an expensive operation. Furthermore, our fitting procedure is premised on the assumption that the spring mesh is a faithful representation of the original mesh. Therefore, we define a displacement function that relates points on the spline surface to points on the parameterized spring mesh surface.

Even given this simplification, computing a displacement function using perpendicular projection is difficult. In particular, the method may fail if the spring mesh curves sharply away from the spline surface. We can avoid this difficulty by defining displacements as offsets to vertices of the spring mesh from corresponding points on the spline surface. Recall that there is a natural association of the spring mesh points to parameter values: these are the same parameters that were used for the surface fitting step. We thus obtain a regular grid of displacement vectors at the resolution of the spring mesh. These are represented in the local coordinate frame of the spline surface. For applications that modify the underlying surface (such as animation), this choice of coordinate frame allows the displacements to move and deform relative to the surface. The displacement function $\mathbf{d}(u, v)$ is then given by a reconstruction from this grid of samples. We have used a bilinear filter for the images shown in this paper.

Note that the displacement map is essentially a resampled error function since it represents the difference of the positions of the spring points from the spline surface.

Since the displacement map, as computed, is a regular grid of 3-vectors, it can conveniently be represented as an rgb image. This representation permits the use of a variety of image-processing operations such as painting, compression, scaling and compositing to manipulate fine surface detail. Figure 11 and Figure 13 explore these and other games one can play with displacement maps.

5.2 Scalar displacement maps

While vector displacement maps are useful for a variety of effects, some operations such as (displacement image) painting are more intuitive on grayscale images. There are several methods of arriving at a scalar displacement image. One method is to compute a normal offset from the spline surface to the spring mesh. However, as discussed earlier, this method is both expensive and prone to non-robustness in the presence of high curvature in the spring mesh.

Instead we have used two alternative formulations. The first computes and stores at each sample location (or pixel) the magnitude of the corresponding vector displacement. In this case, modifying the scalar image scales the associated vector displacements along their existing directions. A second alternative, stores at each sample location the component of the displacement vector normal to the spline surface. Modifying the scalar image therfore changes only the normal component of the vector displacement.

Both of these last two options offer different interactions with the displacement map. Figure 11 employs the third option - normal component editing.

5.3 Bump maps

A *bump map* is defined as a function that performs perturbations on the direction of the surface normal before using it in lighting calculations [5]. In general, a bump map is less expensive to render than a displacement map since it does not change the geometry (and occlusion properties) within a scene but instead changes only the shading. Bump maps can achieve visual effects similar to displacement maps except in situations where the cues provided by displaced geometry become evident such as along silhouette edges. We compute and store bump maps using techniques very similar to those used for displacement maps; at each sample location instead of storing the displacement we store the normal of the corresponding spring mesh point. Figures 13d and e show a comparison of a displacement mapped spline and a bump mapped spline, both of which are based on the same underlying spring mesh. Notice how, differences are visible at the silhouette edges.

6 Continuity across patch boundaries

Thus far we have addressed the sampling and fitting issues connected with a single polygonal patch. In the presence of multiple patches, we are faced with the problem of keeping patches continuous across shared boundaries and corners. If displacement maps are used, it is essential to keep the displacement mapped spline surface continuous.

The extent of inter-patch continuity desired in a multi-patch B-spline (or more generally, NURBS) model depends on the domain of application. For example, in the construction of the exterior of a car body, curvature plots and reflection lines [14] are frequently used to verify the quality of surfaces. In this context, even curvature continuous (C^2) surfaces might be inadequate. Furthermore, workers in the automotive industry often use trimmed NURBS and do not necessarily match knot lines at shared patch boundaries during model construction. Therefore it is not always possible to enforce mathematical continuity across patch boundaries. Instead, statistical or visual continuity is enforced based on user specified tolerances for position and normal deviation. These are either enforced as linear constraints to the fitting process [2, 33], or they are achieved through an iterative optimization process [22].

In the animation industry, by contrast, curvature continuity is seldom required and tangent continuity (G^1) usually suffices. To achieve this the number of knots are usually forced to be the same for patches sharing a boundary. This has several advantages. In the first place, control point deformations are easily propagated across patch boundaries. Secondly, there is minimal distortion at boundaries in the process of texture mapping. Finally, the process of maintaining patch continuity during an animation becomes easier; continuity is either made part of the model definition [24] or is re-established on a frame by frame basis using a stitching post-process.

Our system can be adapted to either of the above paradigms (i.e. either statistical or geometric continuity). Since our focus in this paper is on the entertainment industry, we enforce geometrical continuity, and for this purpose we use a stitching post-process. Specifically, we allow an animator to specify the level of continuity required for each boundary curve (C^0 or G^1). Unconstrained, gridded data fitting to each patch leaves us with C^{-1} spline boundaries. We use end-point interpolating, uniform, cubic B-splines. To maintain mathematical continuity we constrain adjacent patches to have the same number of control points along a shared boundary. Following boundary conditions for these surfaces as defined by Barsky [3], C^0 continuity across a shared boundary curve is obtained by averaging end control points between adjacent patches. Alternatively, G^1 continuity can be obtained by modifying the end control points such that the tangent control points (last two rows) "line up" in a fixed ratio over the length of the boundary.

Patch corners pose a harder problem. We refer the reader to [27] for a detailed account of this problem. For the kinds of basis functions we use, projecting the 4 corner control points of each of the patches meeting at that corner to an average plane guarantees G^1 continuity.

For the case of displacement mapped splines, continuity may be defined on the basis of the reconstruction filter used for the displacement maps. Recall that we generate these from the spring meshes and that we use bilinear reconstruction. Displacement mapped splines will therefore exactly recreate the spring mesh. Also adjacent patches can at most be position continuous with a bilinear reconstruction filter. Therefore, if the spring resolutions are the same at a shared boundary of two patches, they will be continuous by virtue of the reconstruction. However, spring mesh resolutions can differ across shared boundaries. This can result in occasional T-joint discontinuities. The problem is solved by averaging bordering rows of displacement maps in adjacent patches. This ensures that there is no cracking at patch boundaries.

Figure 12 shows a case study of the use of our system to fit spline surfaces, with associated displacement maps, to a large and detailed polygonal mesh of an action figure.

7 Conclusions and future work

In conclusion, we have presented fast techniques for fitting smooth parametric surfaces, in particular tensor product B-splines, to dense, irregular polygon meshes. A useful feature of our system is that it allows incremental previewing of large patch configurations. This feature is enabled by our coarse-to-fine gridded resampling scheme and proves invaluable when modelers wish to experiment with different patch configurations of the same model. We also provide a useful method for storing and manipulating fine surface detail in the form of displacement map images. We have found that this representation empowers users to manipulate geometry using tools outside our modeling system.

Our system has several limitations. First, because it relies on surface walking strategies and mesh connectivity to resample polygonal patches, it breaks down in the presence of holes in the polygon mesh. However, new range image integration techniques include methods for filling holes.

Another limitation is that B-spline surface patches, our choice to represent coarse geometry, perform poorly for very complex surfaces such as draped cloth. B-splines have other disadvantages as well, such as the inability to model triangular patches without excessive parametric distortion. Despite these limitations, B-splines (and NURBS in general) are widely used in the modeling industry. This has been our motivation for choosing this over other representations.

There are a number of fruitful directions for future research. Straightforward extensions include developing tools to assist in boundary curve painting and editing, improving robustness in the presence of holes, adding further constraints to the the parameterization process, allowing variable knot density at the fitting stage, implementing other continuity solutions, and using adaptive spring grids for sampling decimated meshes. An example of a boundary painting tool is a "geometry-snapping" brush that attaches curves to features as the user draws on the object. Examples of constraints to the parameterization process include interactively placed curve and point "attractors" within a patch.

An interesting application of the parameterization portion of our system is the interactive texture mapping and texture placement [26] for complex polygonal models. Related to this is the possibility of applying procedural texture analysis/synthesis techniques [17] to create synthetic displacement maps from real ones. Using our techniques such maps can be applied to objects of arbitrary topology.

8 Acknowledgements

We thank Brian Curless for his range image integration software, David Addleman and George Dabrowski of Cyberware for the use of a scanner, Lincoln Hu and Christian Rouet of Industrial Light and Magic for advice on the needs of animators, and Pat Hanrahan, Hans Pederson, Bill Lorensen for numerous useful discussions. We also thank the anonymous reviewers for several useful comments. This work was supported by the National Science Foundation under contract CCR-9157767 and Interval Research Corporation.

References

[1] A.V.Aho and J.D.Ullman. *Data structures and algorithms*. Addison-Wesley, 1979.

[2] L Bardis and M Vafiadou. Ship-hull geometry representation with b-spline surface patches. *Computer Aided Design*, 24(4):217–222, 1992.

[3] Brian A. Barsky. End conditions and boundary conditions for uniform b-spline curve and surface representations. *Computers In Industry*, 3, 1982.

[4] Richard Bartels, John Beatty, and Brian Barsky. *An Introduction to Splines for Use in Computer Graphics and Geometric Modeling*. Morgan Kaufmann Publishers, Palo Alto, CA, 1987.

[5] James F. Blinn. Simulation of wrinkled surfaces. In *Computer Graphics (SIGGRAPH '78 Proceedings)*, volume 12, pages 286–292, 1978.

[6] J. Vezien Chakib Bennis and G. Iglesias. Piecewise surface flattening for non-distorted texture mapping. In *Computer Graphics (SIGGRAPH '91 Proceedings)*, volume 25, pages 237–246, July 1991.

[7] Jindong Chen and Yijie Han. Shortest paths on a polyhedron. In *Proc. 6th Annual ACM Symposium on Computational Geometry*, pages 360–369, June 1990.

[8] Robert L. Cook. Shade trees. In *Computer Graphics (SIGGRAPH '84 Proceedings)*, volume 18, pages 223–231, July 1984.

[9] Brian Curless and Marc Levoy. A volumetric method for building complex models from range images. In *Computer Graphics (SIGGRAPH '96 Proceedings)*, August 1996.

[10] Paul Dierckx. *Curve and Surface Fitting with Splines*. Oxford Science Publications, New York, 1993.

[11] Matthias Eck, Tony DeRose, Tom Duchamp, Hugues Hoppe, Michael Lounsbery, and Werner Stuetzle. Multiresolution analysis of arbitrary meshes. In *Computer Graphics (Proceedings of SIGGRAPH '95)*, pages 173–182, August 1995.

[12] Matthias Eck and Hugues Hoppe. Automatic reconstruction of b-spline surfaces of arbitrary topological type. In *Computer Graphics (Proceedings of SIGGRAPH '96)*, August 1996.

[13] Hugues Hoppe et al. Piecewise smooth surface reconstruction. In *Computer Graphics (Proceedings of SIGGRAPH '94)*, pages 295–302, July 1994.

[14] Gerald Farin. *Curves and Surfaces for Computer Aided Geometric Design*. Academic Press, 1990.

[15] David R. Forsey and Richard H. Bartels. Hierarchical B-spline refinement. In *Computer Graphics (SIGGRAPH '88 Proceedings)*, volume 22, pages 205–212, August 1988.

[16] Mark Halstead, Michael Kass, and Tony DeRose. Efficient, fair interpolation using Catmull-Clark surfaces. In *Computer Graphics (SIGGRAPH '93 Proceedings)*, volume 27, pages 35–44, August 1993.

[17] David Heeger and James R. Bergen. Pyramid-based texture analysis/synthesis. In *Computer Graphics (SIGGRAPH '95 Proceedings)*, pages 229–237, July 1995.

[18] J Hoschek and D Lasser. *Fundamentals of Computer Aided Geometric Design*. AK Peters, Wellesley, 1993.

[19] Charles L. Lawson and Richard J. Hanson. *Solving Least Square Problems*. Prentice-Hall, Englewood Cliffs, New Jersey, 1974.

[20] W. Ma and J P Kruth. Parameterization of randomly measured points for least squares fitting of b-spline curves and surfaces. *Computer Aided Design*, 27(9):663–675, 1995.

[21] Jerome Maillot. Interactive texture mapping. In *Computer Graphics (SIGGRAPH '93 Proceedings)*, volume 27, pages 27–34, July 1993.

[22] M. J. Milroy, C Bradley, G. W. Vickers, and D. J. Weir. G1 continuity of b-spline surface patches in reverse engineering. *Computer-Aided Design*, 27:471–478, 1995.

[23] J. S. B. Mitchell, D. M. Mount, and C. H. Papadimitriou. The discrete geodesic problem. *SIAM J. Comput.*, 16:647–668, 1987.

[24] Eben Ostby. Describing free-form 3d surfaces for animation. In *Workshop on Interactive 3D Graphics*, pages 251–258, 1986.

[25] Hans K. Pedersen. Decorating implicit surfaces. In *Computer Graphics (Proceedings of SIGGRAPH '95)*, pages 291–300, August 1995.

[26] Hans K. Pedersen. A framework for interactive texturing on curved surfaces. In *Computer Graphics (Proceedings of SIGGRAPH '96)*, August 1996.

[27] Jorg Peters. *Fitting smooth parametric surfaces to 3D data*. Ph.d. thesis, Univ. of Wisconsin-Madison, 1990.

[28] William T. Reeves. Simple and complex facial animation: Case studies. In *State Of The Art In Facial Animation, SIGGRAPH course 26*, pages 90–106. 1990.

[29] David R.Forsey and Richard H. Bartels. Surface fitting with hierarchical splines. In *Topics in the Construction, Manipulation, and Assessment of Spline Surfaces, SIGGRAPH course 25*, pages 7–0–7–14. 1991.

[30] D. F. Rogers and N. G. Fog. Constrained b-spline curve and surface fitting. *Computer Aided Geometric Design*, 21:641–648, December 1989.

[31] Francis J. M. Schmitt, Brian A. Barsky, and Wen hui Du. An adaptive subdivision method for surface-fitting from sampled data. In *Computer Graphics (SIGGRAPH '86 Proceedings)*, volume 20, pages 179–188, August 1986.

[32] Stan Sclaroff and Alex Pentland. Generalized implicit functions for computer graphics. In *Computer Graphics (SIGGRAPH '91 Proceedings)*, volume 25, pages 247–250, July 1991.

[33] Sarvajit S. Sinha and Pradeep Seneviratne. Single valuedness, parameterization and approximating 3d surfaces using b-splines. *Geometric Methods in Computer Vision 2*, pages 193–204, 1993.

[34] J. F. Thompson. *The Eagle Papers.* Mississippi State University, P.O. Drawer 6176, Mississippi State, MS 39762.

[35] Greg Turk. Re-tiling polygonal surfaces. In *Computer Graphics (SIGGRAPH '92 Proceedings)*, volume 26, pages 55–64, July 1992.

[36] Greg Turk and Marc Levoy. Zippered polygon meshes from range images. In *Computer Graphics (SIGGRAPH '94 Proceedings)*, pages 311–318, July 1994.

[37] William Welch and Andrew Witkin. Free–Form shape design using triangulated surfaces. In *Computer Graphics (Proceedings of SIGGRAPH '94)*, pages 247–256, July 1994.

[38] William Welch and Andrew Witkin. Free-form shape design using triangulated surfaces. In *Computer Graphics (SIGGRAPH '94 Proceedings)*, volume 28, pages 237–246, July 1994.

Appendix A

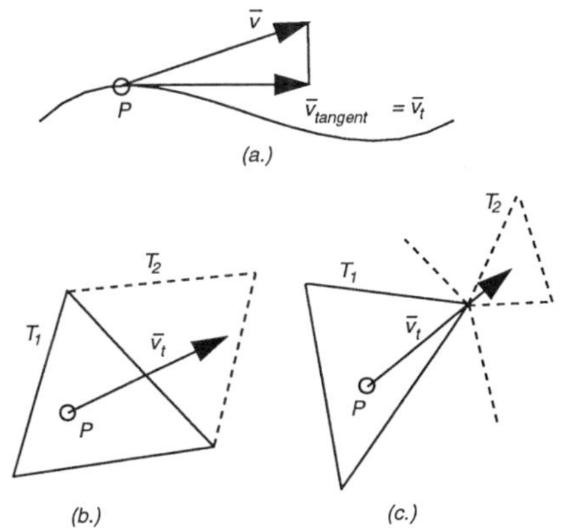

Figure 10. Fig a.) shows a side view of a face point being pulled over the surface. (b) and (c) show a top view of the two cases that arise when P moves: it either intersects an edge or it intersects a vertex.

An operation we use often on face points is sliding them on the surface. We call this procedure *MovePointOnSurface*. There are a number of ways of implementing this on polygonal surfaces. Turk [35] describes a scheme where points first leave the surface and then are re-projected back. We use instead a scheme where points never leave the surface but instead just slide along it. Our algorithm projects the force on a face-point P to P's plane. The point P is moved along the surface, till it either meets an edge or a vertex. In either case we determine the appropriate next triangle to move in to using our adjacency structure (eg: a winged-edge representation).

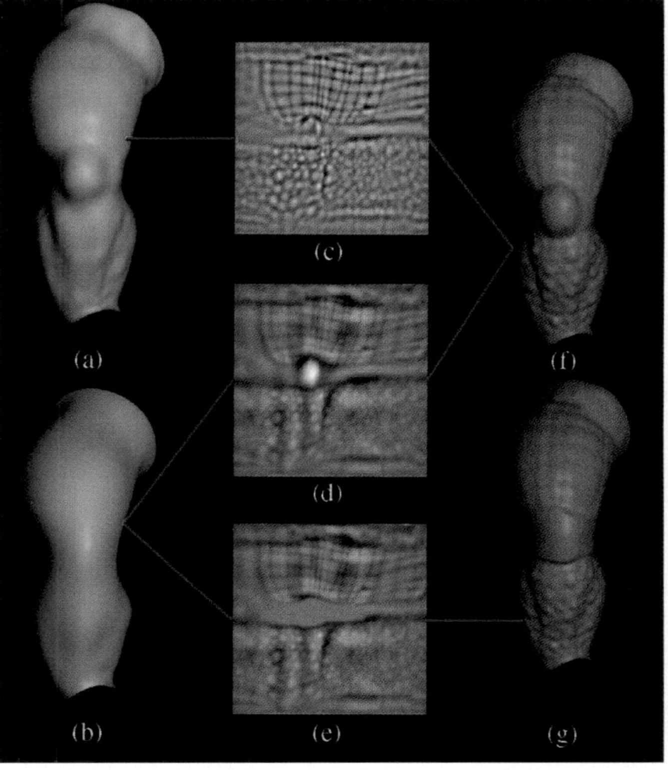

Figure 11. This figure explores the possibility of multi-resolution editing of geometry using multiple displacement map images. All grayscale displacement images in this figure represent the normal component of their corresponding displacement maps. Displacement values are scaled such that a white pixel represents the maximum displacement and black, the minimum displacement. (a) shows a B-spline surface with 24x30 control points that has been fit to the patch from figure 8a. (c) is its corresponding displacement image. (b) shows a B-spline surface with 12x14 control points that was also fit to the same patch. Its displacement image is shown in (d). The combination of spline and displacement map in both cases reconstructs the same surface (i.e. the original spring mesh of figure 8e). This surface is shown in (f). We observe that (c) and (d) encode different frequencies in the original mesh. For example (d) encodes a lot of the coarse geometry of the leg as part of the displacement image (for example the knee), while (c) encodes only the fine geometric detail, such as bumps and creases. As such, the two images allow editing of geometry at different scales. For example, one can edit the geometry of the knee using a simple paint program on (d). In this case, the resulting edited displacement map is shown in (e) and the result of applying this image to the spline of (b) gives us an armour plated knee that is shown in (g). Operations such as these lead us to the issue of whether multiple levels of displacement map can essentially provide a image filter bank for geometry i.e. an alternative multi-resolution surface representation based on images. Note however that the images from (c) and (d) are offsets from different surfaces and the displacements are in different directions, so they cannot be combined using simple arithmetic operations.

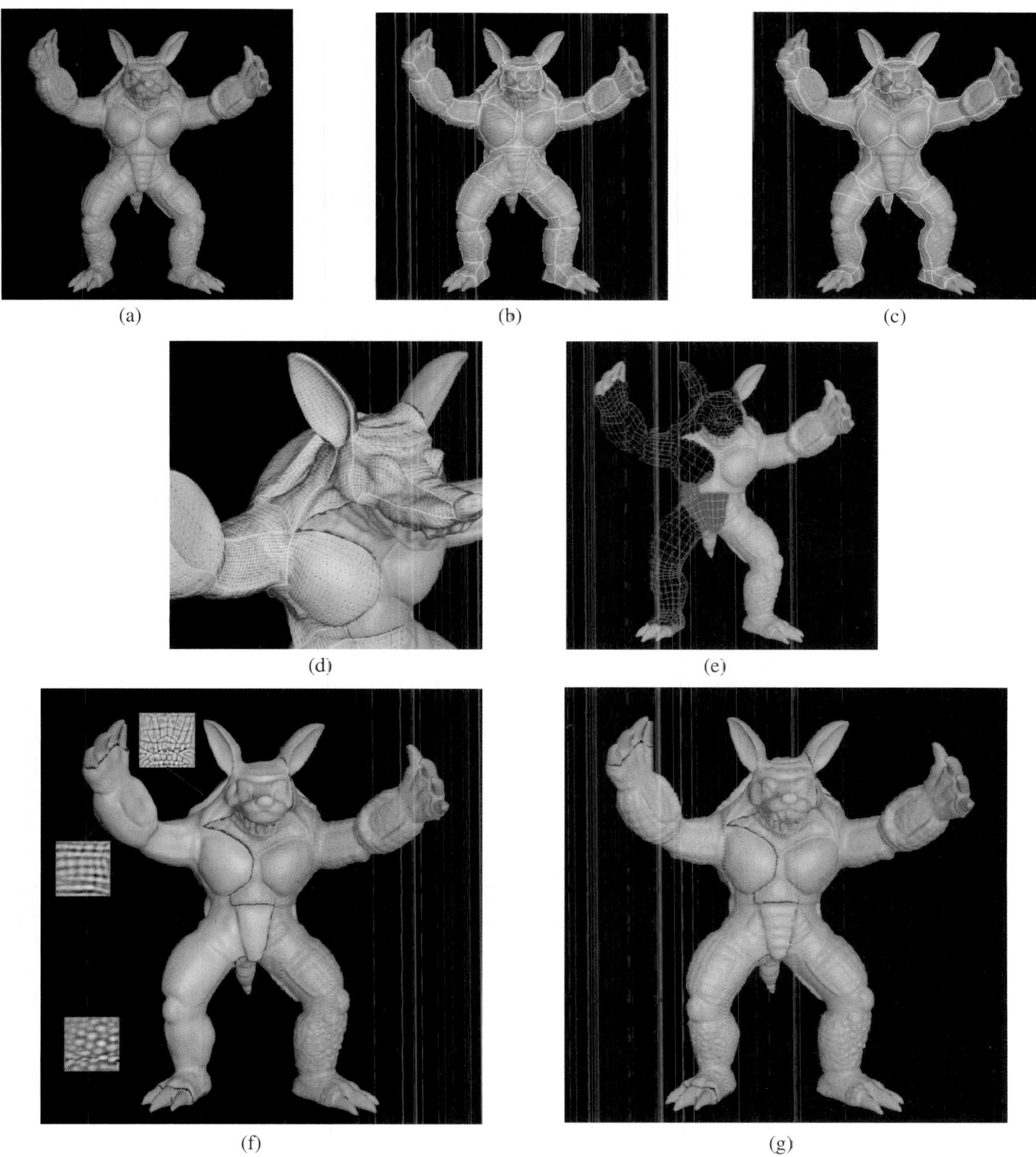

Figure 12. Data fitting to a scanned model. (a) is the polygonal model (over 350,000 polygons, 75 scans). (b) and (c) show two different sets of boundary curves painted on the model. Each was specified interactively in under 2 hours. The patch boundaries for (d), (e), (f) and (g) are taken from (b). (d) is a close up of the results of our gridded resampling algorithm at an intermediate stage. The spring mesh is reconstructed and rendered as triangles and the spring edges are shown as red lines. The right half of the figure is the original polygon mesh. (e) shows u and v iso-curves for all the fitted and stitched spline patches. (The control mesh resolution was chosen to be 8x8 for all the patches.) (f) shows a split view of the B-spline surfaces smooth shaded on the left with the polygon mesh on the right. A few interesting displacement maps are shown alongside their corresponding patches. (g) shows a split view of the displacement mapped spline patches on the left with the polygon mesh on the right. Note that the fingers and toes of the model were not patched. This is because insufficient data was acquired in the crevices of those regions. This can be easily remedied by using extra scans or hole filling techniques [9]. The total number of patches for (b and d through g) were 104 (only the left half have been shown here). The gridding stage took 8 minutes and the gridded fitting with 8x8 control meshes per patch, took under 10 seconds for the entire set of 104 patches. All timings are on a 250 Mhz MIPS R4400 processor.

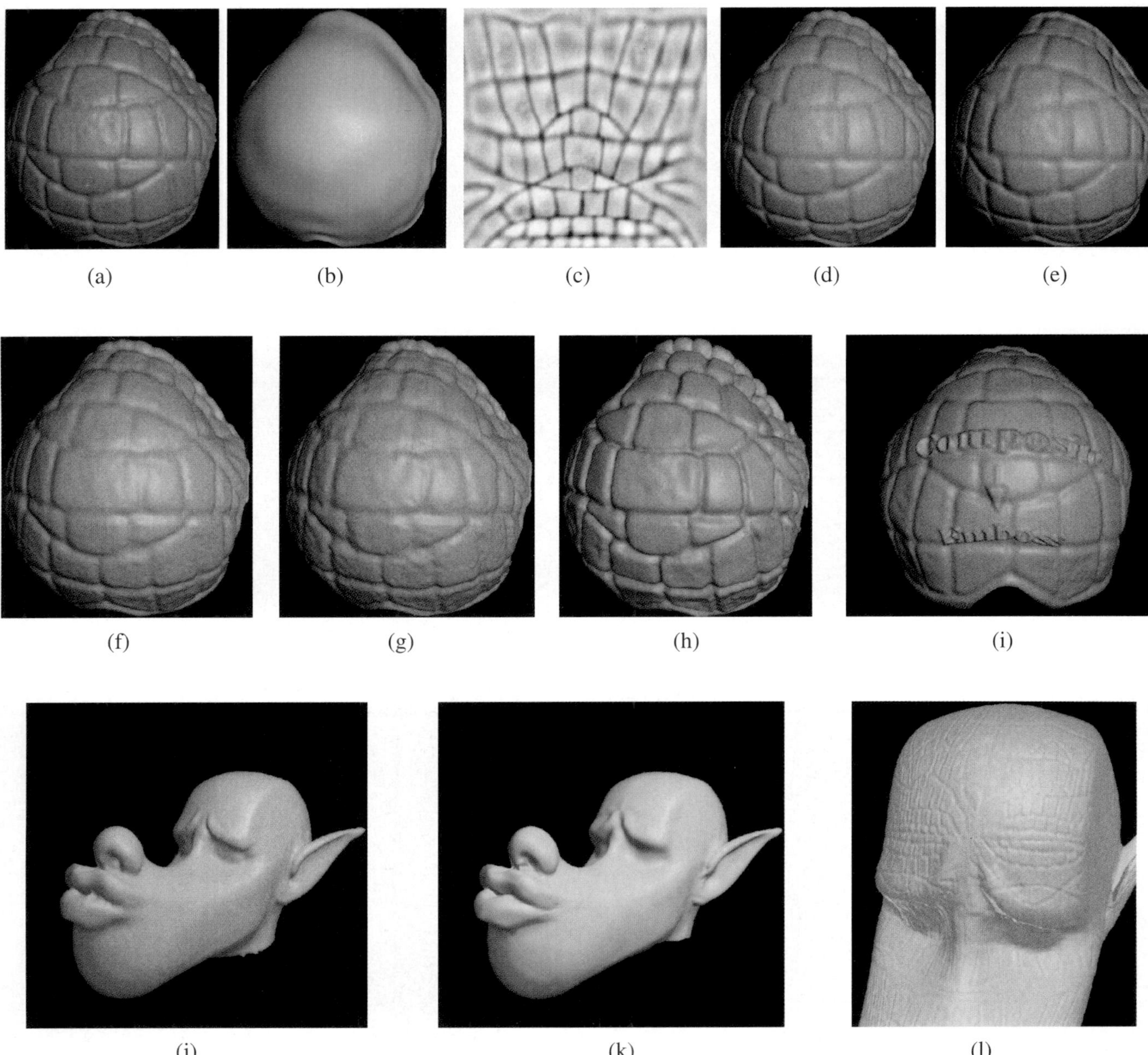

Figure 13. Games one can play with displacement maps: (a) shows a patch from the back of the model in 12a. The patch has over 25,000 vertices. We obtained a spline fit (in 30 seconds) with a 15x20 control mesh, shown in (b) and a corresponding vector displacement map. The normal component of the vector displacement map, is displayed as a grayscale image in (c). (d) and (e) show the corresponding displacement and bump mapped spline surface. The differences between (d) and (e) are evident at the silhouette edges. The second row of images show a selection of image processing games on the displacement map. (f) shows jpeg compression of the displacement image to a factor of 10 and (g) shows compression to a factor of 20. (h) represents a scaling of the displacement image, to enhance bumps. (i) demonstrates a compositing operation, where an image with some words was alpha composited with the displacement map. The result is an embossed effect for the lettering. Finally, the third row of images (j - l) show transferring of displacement maps between different objects. (j) is a relatively small polygonal model of a wolf's head (under 60,000 polygons). It was fit with 54 spline patches in under 4 minutes. The splined model is shown in (k). (l) shows a close up view of a partially splined result, where we have mapped the displacement map from (c) onto each of 4 spline patches around the eyes of the model.

Automatic Reconstruction of B-Spline Surfaces of Arbitrary Topological Type

Matthias Eck
University of Darmstadt

Hugues Hoppe
Microsoft Research

ABSTRACT

Creating freeform surfaces is a challenging task even with advanced geometric modeling systems. Laser range scanners offer a promising alternative for model acquisition—the 3D scanning of existing objects or clay maquettes. The problem of converting the dense point sets produced by laser scanners into useful geometric models is referred to as surface reconstruction.

In this paper, we present a procedure for reconstructing a tensor product B-spline surface from a set of scanned 3D points. Unlike previous work which considers primarily the problem of fitting a single B-spline patch, our goal is to directly reconstruct a surface of arbitrary topological type. We must therefore define the surface as a network of B-spline patches. A key ingredient in our solution is a scheme for automatically constructing both a network of patches and a parametrization of the data points over these patches. In addition, we define the B-spline surface using a *surface spline* construction, and demonstrate that such an approach leads to an efficient procedure for fitting the surface while maintaining tangent plane continuity. We explore adaptive refinement of the patch network in order to satisfy user-specified error tolerances, and demonstrate our method on both synthetic and real data.

CR Categories and Subject Descriptors: I.3.5 [Computer Graphics]: Computational Geometry and Object Modeling - surfaces and object representations; J.6 [Computer-Aided Engineering]: Computer-Aided Design.

Additional Keywords: surface fitting, shape recovery, range data analysis.

1 INTRODUCTION

In the fields of computer graphics and computer-aided design (CAD), advanced modeling systems such as SOFTIMAGE 3D, ALIAS/WAVEFRONT, CATIA, and ICEM SURF have made possible the design of highly detailed models. Even so, it is still difficult with these systems to directly create organic shapes such as human faces and freeform surfaces such as car-body panels.

Email: eck@mathematik.th-darmstadt.de
Email: hhoppe@microsoft.com

The advent of laser range scanners offers an alternative means of acquiring geometric models: the 3D scanning of existing objects. With 3D scanning, modeling systems can import organic or sculptured shapes that would otherwise be difficult to create. For instance, in the automobile industries, many artists prefer to initially sculpt car bodies in clay, as they find that CAD systems lack the tactile and visual advantages of the traditional medium. Similarly, many models used in computer graphics are first created in clay or wood and subsequently scanned into digital forms. In addition, 3D scanning permits *reverse engineering*, allowing existing manufactured parts to be incorporated or modified into new CAD designs.

Laser range scanners produce large collections of points on surfaces of objects. The problem of converting these data points into useful geometric models is referred to as *surface reconstruction*. There is a large body of literature on the reconstruction of surfaces of simple topological type, such as deformed planar regions and spheres (see Section 2). Methods have been developed to reconstruct meshes of arbitrary topological type [3, 13, 34], but the resulting representations are often verbose since many planar faces are required to accurately model curved surfaces (e.g. Figure 9l). For this reason, it is desirable to use a representation with smooth surface primitives. Some recent work addresses the problem of reconstructing smooth surfaces of arbitrary topological type using subdivision surfaces [11] and algebraic surfaces [2, 24]. However, these two smooth surface representations are not commonly supported within current modeling systems. Indeed, for better or worse, the ubiquitous smooth surface primitive is the tensor product B-spline patch. The general class of non-uniform rational B-splines (NURBS) is considered by many the de facto CAD standard.

In this paper we present a procedure for automatically reconstructing a B-spline surface S of arbitrary topological type from an unorganized set of points $P = \{\mathbf{p}_1, \ldots, \mathbf{p}_N\}$. To our knowledge, this reconstruction problem has not been addressed previously. The problem presents two major difficulties:

- Since a single B-spline patch can only represent surfaces of simple topological type (deformed planar regions, cylinders, and tori), a surface of arbitrary topological type must be defined as a network of B-spline patches. Automatically constructing both a network of patches and a parametrization of the data points over these patches is a difficult task.
- The reconstructed B-spline patch network is often expected to be smooth (by which we mean tangent plane continuous or G^1). Enforcing G^1 continuity between adjacent patches while at the same time fitting the patch network to the points is a challenging problem.

Our B-spline reconstruction procedure adapts the previous surface reconstruction work of Hoppe et al. [12, 13], the parametrization work of Eck et al. [6], and the B-spline construction scheme of

Peters [27], as summarized in Sections 3.1, 3.2, and 3.4 respectively. The main contributions of this paper are:

- It presents a combinatorial optimization method for building a quadrilateral domain from a triangular one (Section 3.3), a crucial step in constructing the B-spline patch network. The optimization method makes use of *harmonic maps* to minimize distortion in the resulting reparametrization.
- It presents an efficient method for fitting a G^1 B-spline surface of arbitrary topological type to unorganized points. The fitting method makes use of a surface spline construction to maintain G^1 continuity between patches. As a consequence, fitting the surface to the data involves only a sparse linear least squares problem with a few linear constraints.
- It introduces a scheme for adaptive refinement of the quadrilateral patch network, and demonstrates the use of this refinement strategy in attempting to fit B-spline surfaces within user-specified error tolerances.
- Most importantly, it brings together all these techniques into an effective procedure addressing an important problem in computer graphics and geometric modeling: automatic reconstruction of B-spline surfaces of arbitrary topological type.

In addition to surface reconstruction, our procedure can also be applied to the problem of surface approximation. That is, it can be used to approximate an arbitrary initial surface S_0 with a B-spline surface (e.g. Figures 10j–10l) as shown in Section 4.

2 RELATED WORK

Reconstruction of B-spline surfaces There has been considerable work on fitting B-spline surfaces to 3D points. However, most methods either assume that the surface has simple topological type, or require user intervention in setting up the patch network.

For instance, Dietz [4], Hoschek and Schneider [15], Rogers and Fog [30], and Sarkar and Menq [31] assume that the surface is a single open B-spline patch (a deformed quadrilateral region), possibly with trimmed boundaries. Forsey and Bartels [9] consider fitting a single hierarchical B-spline patch to gridded data. Schmitt et al. [32] assume that the surface is a deformed cylinder and explore adaptive refinement of the B-spline surface in fitting cylindrical range data.

Andersson et al. [1], Fang and Gossard [7], Krishnamurthy and Levoy [17], and Milroy et al. [23] fit B-spline surfaces of arbitrary topological type, but require the user to manually delineate the patch boundaries either by labeling "boundary points" or by drawing boundary curves on an approximating surface. The same is true of current commercial systems such as Imageware's Surfacer [16]. Furthermore, the initial parametrizations of the data points is critical in the fitting process, as demonstrated by Ma and Kruth [22], and these schemes may require additional user intervention to obtain good initial parameter distributions. Krishnamurthy and Levoy [17] develop a hierarchical relaxation procedure for automatically computing these parameter values.

In contrast, our method is able to reconstruct a B-spline surface of arbitrary topological type without user assistance. To our knowledge this has not been done before. Moreover, the surface consists of a network of low-degree, tensor-product B-spline patches that meet with G^1 continuity.

Reconstruction of other smooth surface representations Hoppe et al. [11] reconstruct piecewise smooth surfaces of arbitrary topological type using a subdivision surface representation. Both Bajaj et al. [2] and Moore and Warren [24] reconstruct G^1 piecewise algebraic surfaces of arbitrary topological type. Their surfaces are defined as algebraic patches within 3D (tetrahedral) triangulations of $\mathbf{R}^3$. They consider adaptive refinement of the 3D triangulation based on the quality of fit.

3 ALGORITHM

Our B-spline surface reconstruction algorithm consists of 5 successive steps. We first present a brief overview of these steps and illustrate them with the example in Figure 9. Sections 3.1–3.5 describe the details of the 5 steps.

1. *Constructing an initial parametrization over a dense approximating mesh M_0:*

   Using the previous surface reconstruction work of Hoppe et al. [12, 13], Step 1 constructs from an unorganized set of points $P = \{\mathbf{p}_1, \ldots, \mathbf{p}_N\}$ (Figure 9a) an initial surface approximation in the form of a dense triangular mesh M_0 (Figure 9b). The points P are projected onto M_0 to obtain their initial parametrizations. Our purpose in constructing M_0 is to find a parametric domain of the correct topological type. Of course, this particular domain is unwieldy since it may consist of thousands of faces.

2. *Reparametrizing over a simple triangular base complex $K_\triangle$:*

   Using the parametrization work of Eck et al. [6], Step 2 automatically constructs from the initial mesh M_0 both a simple *base complex* $K_\triangle$ (Figure 9e) and a continuous parametrization $\rho_\triangle : K_\triangle \rightarrow M_0$. As the construction exploits the mathematical framework of harmonic maps, the parametrization $\rho_\triangle$ tends to have low metric distortion. The parametrization of P from Step 1 are mapped through $\rho_\triangle^{-1}$ to obtain new parametrizations over $K_\triangle$.

3. *Reparametrizing over a quadrilateral domain complex $K_\square$:*

   By merging faces of $K_\triangle$ pairwise, Step 3 constructs a new base complex $K_\square$ whose faces consist solely of quadrilaterals (Figure 9f). The merging process is cast as a combinatorial graph optimization problem, whose goals are both to find a maximum pairing and to minimize parametric distortion. We again make use of harmonic maps to find a good reparametrization of the points P from $K_\triangle$ to $K_\square$.

4. *B-spline fitting:*

   Step 4 defines over each face f of $K_\square$ a tensor product B-spline patch $\mathbf{s}_f$ using the surface splines scheme of Peters [27] such that the patches $\mathbf{s}_f$ collectively form a G^1 B-spline surface S. More precisely, this construction consists of two steps. First, a control mesh M_x is defined by topologically subdividing $K_\square$. Second, the control points $\mathbf{d}^f_{r,s}$ of $\mathbf{s}_f$ are defined as affine combinations of the vertices V_x of M_x. Fitting S to the points P is cast as an optimization problem over V_x, and is solved by alternating between a linear least squares fitting step and a parameter correction step. The result of this fitting process is shown in Figures 9g–9i.

5. *Adaptive refinement:*

   In order for P and S to differ by no more than a user-specified error tolerance ϵ, Step 5 adaptively subdivides the faces of $K_\square$ into smaller quadrilateral subfaces based on the fit errors. After each step of subdivision, Step 4 is reinvoked to fit the refined surface. Further subdivisions are performed until the error tolerance ϵ is satisfied. The result is a refined domain complex $K_\boxplus$ (Figure 9j) and a new control mesh (Figure 9k) defining a new B-spline surface S (Figure 9l) within ϵ of P.

3.1 Constructing an initial parametrization over a dense approximating mesh M_0

From an unorganized set of points P, Step 1 constructs an initial surface approximation M_0 and parametrizes the points over this initial domain. This step is performed using the surface reconstruction method of Hoppe et al., which we briefly summarize now.

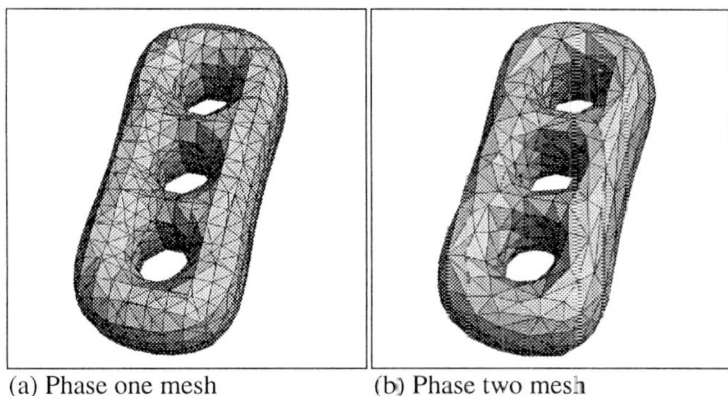

(a) Phase one mesh (b) Phase two mesh

Figure 1: Example of the two-phase surface reconstruction method of Hoppe et al.. (Refer also to Figures 9a and 9b.)

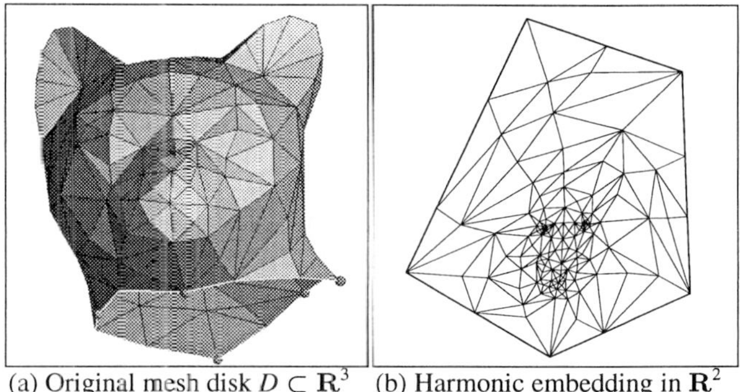

(a) Original mesh disk $D \subset \mathbf{R}^3$ (b) Harmonic embedding in $\mathbf{R}^2$

Figure 2: An example of a harmonic map. (The vertices indicated by small balls are mapped to the vertices of the polygon.)

Summary of surface reconstruction method of Hoppe et al. Hoppe et al. [12, 13] develop a two-phase procedure for reconstructing a mesh (Figure 1b) approximating an unknown surface S_u from a set of unorganized points P (Figure 9a) sampled on or near S_u.

The goal of phase one [12] is to determine the topological type of S_u and to obtain a crude estimate of its geometry, in the form of a dense mesh (Figure 1a). Using P, phase one defines a function $f : \mathbf{R}^3 \to \mathbf{R}$ that estimates the signed geometric distance to S_u, and then uses a contouring algorithm to extract a mesh approximating its zero set, $Z(f) = \{\mathbf{q} \in \mathbf{R}^3 : f(\mathbf{q}) = 0\}$.

The goal of phase two [13] is to reduce the number of faces in the mesh and to improve its fit to the data (Figure 1b). Phase two optimizes over both the connectivity and geometry of the mesh in order to minimize an energy function that explicitly models the trade-offs of conciseness and accuracy.

Our use of the surface reconstruction method For our purpose, we first run phase one to obtain a crude mesh (Figure 1a). We then use the initial fitting procedure of phase two to improve the geometry of this mesh while keeping its connectivity constant, to obtain the mesh M_0 (Figure 9b). The optimization over connectivity performed later in phase two is unnecessary for our use, since Step 2 (described in the next section) provides a faster algorithm for creating a simpler domain and at the same time constructs a low-distortion parametrization of P over that domain.

To obtain an initial parametrization of P, we project the points onto the mesh M_0. For each point $\mathbf{p}_i$, we store the closest face of M_0 and the barycentric coordinates of the projection of $\mathbf{p}_i$ onto that face.

3.2 Reparametrizing over a simple triangular base complex $K_\triangle$

From the initial mesh M_0, Step 2 constructs a simple base complex $K_\triangle$ (Figure 9e) and a map $\rho_\triangle : K_\triangle \to M_0$ allowing the points P to be reparametrized over $K_\triangle$. This step is achieved using the parametrization method of Eck et al. [6], which we briefly summarize. Next we present a minor modification to the method that facilitates the construction of $K_\square$ in Step 3.

Summary of parametrization method of Eck et al. Eck et al. first introduce a method for mapping a (topological) disk $D \subset M$ of a mesh $M \subset \mathbf{R}^3$ to a convex polygonal region $R \subset \mathbf{R}^2$. As an example, the mesh region in Figure 2a is parametrized over the planar polygon in Figure 2b. Their solution, based on the theory of *harmonic maps*, has the property of minimizing metric distortion. They find that the metric distortion energy $E_{harm}[h]$ associated with a piecewise linear map $h : D \to R$ can be interpreted as the energy of a configuration of springs placed on the edges of D:

$$E_{harm}[h] = 1/2 \sum_{\{i,j\} \in \mathrm{Edges}(D)} \kappa_{i,j} \|h(i) - h(j)\|^2 ,$$

where each spring constant $\kappa_{i,j}$ is a simple function of the lengths of nearby edges in the original mesh D. Thus the (piecewise-linear) harmonic map h on D can be computed by solving a sparse linear least-squares problem.

Since the initial mesh M_0 may have arbitrary topological type, it must first be partitioned into a set of disks in order to apply the harmonic map framework. Eck et al. describe a method for partitioning M_0 into well-shaped triangular regions. This partitioning method is based on generalizing the concepts of Voronoi diagrams and Delaunay triangulations to surfaces of arbitrary topological type. The algorithm automatically selects a set of site faces in M_0 and partitions M_0 into a set of Voronoi tiles, such that each tile comprises those faces closest to a given site (Figure 9c). The Voronoi tiles are grown incrementally from their site faces using a multi-source shortest path algorithm. In order for the Voronoi-like partition to be dual to a triangulation, the sites are chosen to satisfy a set of 4 conditions (see [6]). Next, the method makes use of harmonic maps to construct a Delaunay-like triangular partition $T_1, \ldots, T_r$ (Figure 9d) that is dual to the Voronoi-like partition.

Finally, Eck et al. construct a base complex $K_\triangle$ of r faces (Figure 9e) using the connectivity of the Delaunay-like partition, and parametrize M_0 over this domain by computing the harmonic map from each Delaunay triangle T_i to the corresponding face of $K_\triangle$. The result is a global, continuous parametrization $\rho_\triangle : K_\triangle \to M_0$ of the initial mesh over a simple base complex.

Modification to the parametrization method In Step 3 described in the next section, we construct from $K_\triangle$ a new domain $K_\square$ with quadrilateral faces by matching adjacent pairs of faces in $K_\triangle$. To form a complete matching, the face merging process requires $K_\triangle$ to have an even number of faces. This requirement is met by giving the Voronoi partitioning algorithm an additional condition to satisfy: The dual to the Voronoi partition must have an even number of faces. When this condition is not satisfied, an additional site is added at the face farthest from any current site, and the Voronoi region growing algorithm restarts.

Reparametrization After constructing $K_\triangle$ and $\rho_\triangle$, we map the parametrizations of P obtained in Step 1 through $\rho_\triangle^{-1}$ to obtain parametrizations of P over $K_\triangle$. The new parametrization is illustrated in Figure 9e, where a line segment is drawn between each data point $\mathbf{p}_i$ and its parametric location on $K_\triangle$. Note that we do not define a geometric embedding of $K_\triangle$ into $\mathbf{R}^3$ but have created one in Figure 9e for illustration purposes only.

3.3 Reparametrizing over a quadrilateral domain complex $K_\square$

After Step 2, the points P are parametrized over a base complex $K_\triangle$ made up of an even number of triangular faces. Since the B-spline construction scheme in Step 4 expects a domain made up of quadrilateral faces, the goal of Step 3 is to map $K_\triangle$ onto a quadrilateral domain complex $K_\square$ (Figure 9f).

A simple strategy would be to subdivide each triangular face of $K_\triangle$ into 3 quadrilateral faces by introducing vertices at the edge midpoints and the face centroids. Instead, our method is based on merging triangle faces of $K_\triangle$ pairwise. This merging strategy is advantageous because it results in a domain $K_\square$ with one sixth the number of quadrilaterals as would be obtained from subdivision.

We cast face merging as a graph matching problem. We construct the graph $G = (V_G, E_G)$ that is the dual to $K_\triangle$: each vertex in V_G corresponds to a face of $K_\triangle$, and each edge in E_G corresponds to a pair of faces sharing an edge in $K_\triangle$. Finding a maximum pairing of faces in $K_\triangle$ then amounts to finding a maximum cardinality set $E_m \subset E_G$ of vertex-disjoint edges—an instance of the MAXIMUM MATCHING graph problem on G [18], which can be solved efficiently in $O(|V_G||E_G|)$ time [33].

We would like to obtain a *complete matching*: one in which all faces of $K_\triangle$ are paired. Since we have constructed $K_\triangle$ to have an even number of regions, a complete matching is likely to exist. Although counter-examples may be possible, we have not seen them occur in practice. (It would be interesting to prove if such counter-examples can or cannot exist.) If G was to lack a complete matching, we would resort to global subdivision as described above.

The graph G typically has many possible complete matchings. Of those, we would prefer one that minimizes the distortion of the resulting reparametrization. In order to achieve this, we define a heuristic for the distortion associated with the pairing of two adjacent faces F_i and F_j of $K_\triangle$ as follows. We construct the harmonic map $h_{i,j}$ of the region $T_i \cup T_j$ of M_0 onto a unit square, and use the resulting harmonic energy term $E_{harm}[h_{i,j}]$ as our heuristic measure of distortion. We encode these distortion measures into G by assigning to each edge $e = \{i,j\} \in E_G$ the weight $w(e) = -E_{harm}[h_{i,j}]$. The face merging problem is now cast as an instance of the MAX-MIN MATCHING problem—finding a maximum cardinality matching for which the minimum weight of the edges is maximum [18]. A solution to this combinatorial problem corresponds to a complete pairing of faces of $K_\triangle$ for which the maximal distortion of the face pairs is minimized. The MAX-MIN MATCHING problem can be solved in $O(|V_G|^3)$ time [18]. Since our graphs G typically have on the order of a hundred vertices, computing the matching requires only a few seconds.

Once the matching is computed, the parametrizations of the points P are mapped from $K_\triangle$ to $K_\square$ using the same harmonic maps constructed for the graph optimization problem. Specifically, for each edge $\{i,j\} \in E_m$ of the matching solution, we map the points whose parametrizations lie on faces F_i and F_j of $K_\triangle$ through $h_{i,j}$ onto the unit square, and use the resulting coordinates as (bilinear) parametrizations on the new face $F_{i,j}$ in $K_\square$. The parametrizations are illustrated by the line segments in Figure 9f. Again, we have created an embedding for $K_\square$ in $\mathbf{R}^3$ in the figure for illustration purposes only.

There is one final complication. The resulting $K_\square$ may have interior vertices of degree 2, and such vertices are best avoided for Step 4. When such vertices are present, we merge the two quadrilateral faces adjacent to them into larger quadrilateral faces.

3.4 B-spline fitting

General framework In the most general setting, a B-spline surface $S(K_\square, \mathbf{d})$ is defined as a network of tensor product B-spline surface patches

$$\mathbf{s}_f(u,v) = \sum_{r=0}^{n_f} \sum_{s=0}^{m_f} \mathbf{d}^f_{r,s}\, N_{r,k_f}(u)\, N_{s,l_f}(v)$$

over a domain complex $K_\square$, with local coordinates $(u,v) \in [0,1]^2$ on each face $f \in K_\square$. Here $\mathbf{d}^f_{r,s} \in \mathbf{R}^3$ denote the control points, $N_{r,k_f}(u)$ are the univariate B-spline basis functions of order k_f in the u-direction, defined over the knot sequences $U_f = (u_0, u_1, \ldots, u_{n_f+k_f})$, and $N_{s,l_f}(v)$ are defined analogously over the knot vectors V_f in the v-direction. Definitions of the B-spline basis functions and related evaluation algorithms can be found in textbooks on geometric modeling (e.g. [8, 14]).

Surface reconstruction In surface reconstruction we seek to find the control points $\mathbf{d}^f_{r,s}$ of all patches $\mathbf{s}_f$ such that the distance of the data points P to the surface $S(K_\square, \mathbf{d})$ is minimized. More precisely, we minimize the distance functional

$$E_{dist}(S) = \sum_{i=1}^{N} d^2(\mathbf{p}_i, S)\ .$$

Note that the distance of each point $\mathbf{p}_i$ to the surface S is itself the solution of a minimization problem:

$$d(\mathbf{p}_i, S) \;=\; \min_{t_i} \|\mathbf{p}_i - \mathbf{s}(t_i)\|^2 \;=\; \min_{f_i \in K_\square,(u_i,v_i)\in[0,1]^2} \|\mathbf{p}_i - \mathbf{s}_{f_i}(u_i,v_i)\|^2$$

in which $t_i = (f_i, u_i, v_i)$ is the parametrization of the projection of $\mathbf{p}_i$ onto S.

Iterative methods have been developed to solve this type of nested minimization problem in the context of B-spline surface fitting [15, 30]. In these methods, each iteration consists of two steps:

1. *Fitting step:* For fixed parametrizations t_i, the optimal control points $\mathbf{d}$ are found by solving a linear least-squares problem.
2. *Parameter correction step:* For fixed control points $\mathbf{d}$, optimal parametrizations t_i are found by projecting the points onto S.

Usually the fit accuracy is improved considerably after only a few iterations (we typically use 4). (An alternative solution method to this nonlinear problem is the Levenberg–Marquardt optimization method, which has faster convergence rate [31]; however, our simple iterative scheme is sufficient for obtaining reasonable fits.)

Fairness functional One problem with surface fitting is that the resulting surface may have unwanted "wiggles". It is therefore common to augment the energy functional with an additional fairness term [4, 7]:

$$E(\mathbf{d}) = E_{dist}(\mathbf{d}) + \lambda \cdot E_{fair}(\mathbf{d})\ , \quad \lambda \in \mathbf{R}_0^+\ . \qquad (1)$$

The fairness term is often defined to be the *thin plate energy* functional

$$E_{fair}(\mathbf{d}) = \sum_{f\in K_\square} \int_0^1\!\!\int_0^1 \left((\frac{\partial^2}{\partial u^2}\mathbf{s}_f)^2 + 2(\frac{\partial^2}{\partial u\,\partial v}\mathbf{s}_f)^2 + (\frac{\partial^2}{\partial v^2}\mathbf{s}_f)^2 \right) du\,dv$$

(Greiner [10] discusses alternative functionals involving higher-order derivatives.) Note that $E(\mathbf{d})$ can still be minimized with the iterative scheme described previously since $E_{fair}(\mathbf{d})$ is independent of the parameter values t_i and its minimization still gives rise to a linear system.

There remains the problem of finding a reasonable choice for the fairness weight λ. Dietz [4] suggests starting with a relatively large initial weight λ and reducing λ by a factor of 2 after each iteration of parameter correction. In our case, the initial parametrizations obtained in Step 3 are quite good, and we have obtained satisfactory results using simply a small, constant λ.

Continuity Obviously, constraints must be established between adjacent B-spline patches so that they join up seamlessly. To simplify these constraints, most schemes (e.g. [23]) set all patches to have the same knot vectors (i.e. $n = n_f = m_f$ and $U = U_f = V_f$) and the same order $k = k_f = l_f$. Then, simple (G^0) continuity is achieved trivially by sharing control points along the boundaries of adjacent patches. In contrast, tangent plane (G^1) continuity is more difficult since it involves nonlinear constraints on the control points of adjacent patches. There are two main approaches to satisfying these G^1 continuity constraints.

In the first approach [23, 25], the nonlinear G^1 constraints are approximated by introducing an additional penalty term $E_{G^1}(\mathbf{d})$ to minimize. Unfortunately, minimizing $E_{dist}(\mathbf{d}) + E_{fair}(\mathbf{d}) + E_{G^1}(\mathbf{d})$ requires more expensive nonlinear optimization. Moreover, the resulting surface is only approximately tangent-plane smooth, or ϵ-G^1, and the lack of smoothness is often visible in the resulting surfaces (e.g. [23]).

In the second approach, often referred to as *surface splines* or *G-splines* [20, 21, 27, 28, 29], the idea is to construct a network of triangular and/or tensor product Bézier patches from a global control mesh M_x. The control points of these Bézier patches are computed using local combinations of vertices in M_x, and are defined in such a way that the Bézier patches automatically meet with G^1 continuity. Using this approach, the surface is exactly G^1, and the fitting process again involves solving a simple linear system, in which the unknowns are the vertex positions of M_x.

We have opted for the second approach, and have adapted a surface spline scheme of Peters [27]. As described in the next section, we construct over each face of $K_\square$ a single tensor product B-spline patch $\mathbf{s}_f$ with $k = 4$ and $n = 11$. To overcome the problem of fixed n and k, we present in Section 3.5 a refinement scheme that adaptively subdivides $K_\square$ to locally introduce additional degrees of freedom.

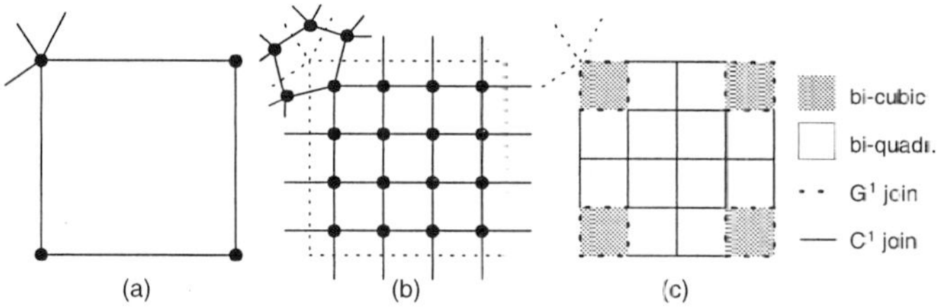

Figure 3: Schematic of the B-spline construction scheme of Peters. (a) one quadrilateral face f of the input mesh M_c; (b) the 4×4 vertices of the refined control mesh M_x associated with f; (c) the 4×4 Bézier patches created from M_x associated with f.

Review of Peters' scheme From a closed mesh M_c of arbitrary topological type, the construction scheme of Peters [27] creates a G^1 B-spline surface S. This construction proceeds in two steps, as illustrated in Figure 3. First, a refined control mesh M_x is created by subdividing M_c using two Doo-Sabin subdivisions [5]. In our application M_c has only quadrilateral faces, and therefore a 4×4 grid of vertices in M_x is associated with each face of M_c as shown in Figure 3b. Note that all vertices of M_x have valence 4 (i.e. 4 adjacent edges) and that M_x consists mainly of 4-sided faces, except for a small number of extraordinary m-sided faces ($m \neq 4$). Also note that the extraordinary faces are isolated, in the sense that each vertex of M_x is adjacent to at most one extraordinary face.

In the second step, a tensor product Bézier patch is constructed centered on each vertex of M_x as shown in Figure 3c. The Bézier patch is defined to be bicubic if the vertex is adjacent to an extraordinary face, otherwise it is defined to be biquadratic. The affine combinations for setting the Bézier control points of these patches as functions of the vertices V_x of M_x are given in the Appendix. Peters [27] proves that the resulting collection of Bézier patches form a G^1 surface, subject to a few linear constraints on V_x near those extraordinary faces for which m is even and greater than 4 (see Appendix). We denote this G^1 surface as $S(V_x)$.

Over each quadrilateral face of M_c, the collection of 4×4 Bézier patches (in general 12 biquadratic and 4 bicubic) can be combined into a single tensor product bicubic B-spline patch (with $k = 4$ and $n = 11$). To satisfy the G^1 and C^1 joins indicated in Figure 3c, the knot sequences in both parameter directions are set to $U_f = V_f = (0, 0, 0, 0, \frac{1}{4}, \frac{1}{4}, \frac{1}{4}, \frac{1}{2}, \frac{1}{2}, \frac{3}{4}, \frac{3}{4}, \frac{3}{4}, 1, 1, 1, 1)$. The B-spline representation requires 15% less storage than storing each Bézier patch separately.

Modified fitting step To apply Peters' scheme to the problem of B-spline fitting, we modify the *fitting step* in the iterative procedure described earlier.

We use the quadrilateral domain complex $K_\square$ as the input mesh M_c to Peters' scheme. Since $K_\square$ does not possess a geometric embedding, only the topological structure K_x of the control mesh M_x can be constructed initially. The vertices V_x of M_x are computed by fitting the B-spline surface $S(V_x)$ to the data points. Specifically, we compute V_x by minimizing the energy functional $E(V_x) = E_{dist}(V_x) + \lambda E_{fair}(V_x)$ for fixed parametrizations $t_i = (f_i, u_i, v_i)$ of the data points $\mathbf{p}_i$.

Since Peters' construction is affine, every point $\mathbf{s}(t)$ on the surface S can be written as an affine combination of V_x. Treating V_x as a matrix whose rows are (x, y, z) coordinates, we can express this affine combination as $\mathbf{s}(t) = \mathbf{y}V_x$ where the entries of the row vector $\mathbf{y}$ are obtained by appropriately composing Bernstein polynomials and the formulas given in the Appendix. We can therefore rewrite E_{dist} as

$$E_{dist}(V_x) = \sum_{i=1}^{N} \|\mathbf{p}_i - \mathbf{y}_i V_x\|^2$$

which is quadratic on V_x. The term E_{fair} can similarly be expressed as a quadratic function over V_x by summing up the thin-plate energies of all Bézier patches and using the formulas given in the Appendix.

Thus, $E(V_x)$ is a quadratic functional on V_x, and therefore its minimization is a linear least squares problem. Moreover, the linear system is sparse because of the locality of the surface construction. As mentioned earlier, some linear constraints on V_x must be satisfied near extraordinary faces for the surface to be G^1. These constraints are introduced into the optimization through the use of *Lagrange multipliers*, making the problem only slightly more difficult (see [19] for details).

Extensions to the basic fitting method We generalize the construction of M_x to allow surface boundaries in $K_\square$. In a construction similar to [26], we add for each boundary edge of $K_\square$ an additional layer of vertices to M_x. To each valence m boundary vertex of $K_\square$ we associate in M_x a $(2m-2)$-sided face if $m \neq 2$ and a 4-sided face if $m = 2$. This process is illustrated in Figure 4. As a result, the boundaries of S are smooth everywhere except at valence 2 boundary vertices of $K_\square$ where surface corners are introduced.

The two Doo-Sabin subdivisions in the first step of Peters' construction serve to isolate the extraordinary faces. With two subdivisions, a 4×4 grid of vertices is introduced on each face of $K_\square$ as shown in Figure 3b. More generally, a construction with $s \times s$ vertices on each face of $K_\square$ still results in a G^1 surface for any

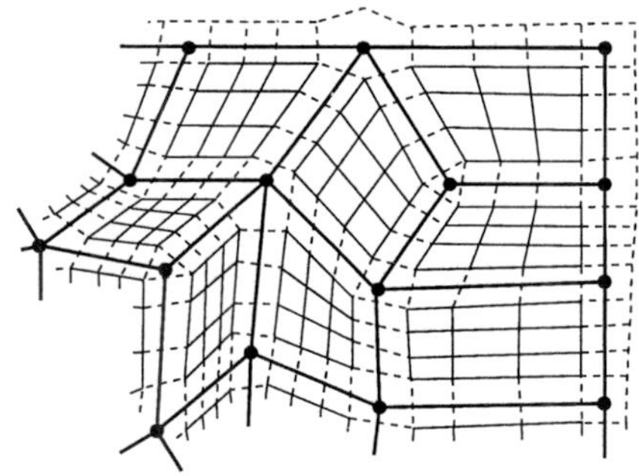

Figure 4: Example of construction of M_x from a domain $K_\square$ containing a boundary.

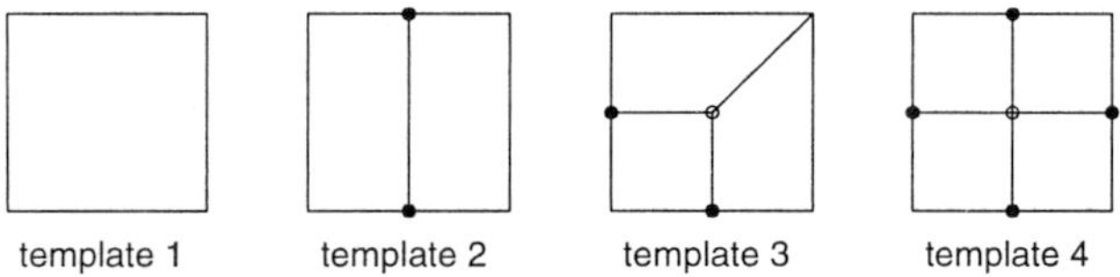

Figure 5: The four face refinement templates.

$s \geq 2$. We have experimented with different values of s in the fitting procedure, but have obtained best visual results with the original setting of $s = 4$.

3.5 Adaptive refinement

The surface fitting algorithm described in Section 3.4 minimizes the total squared distances $\sum_i d(\mathbf{p}_i, S)^2$ of the data points $\mathbf{p}_i$ to the B-spline surface S. It is often desirable to specify a maximum error tolerance for the fit. Step 5 attempts to find a surface S such that $\max_i d(\mathbf{p}_i, S) < \epsilon$ for a user-specified error tolerance ϵ.

To achieve a given tolerance within our least squares optimization framework, it may be necessary to introduce new degrees of freedom into the surface representation. One could achieve this by globally subdividing the domain $K_\square$ (e.g. using template 4 in Figure 5). However, this would introduce degrees of freedom uniformly over the whole surface, even if data points exceed the error tolerance only in isolated neighborhoods.

We instead develop an adaptive refinement scheme. The goal of this refinement scheme is to subdivide any face of $K_\square$ onto which any point $\mathbf{p}_i$ projects with $d(\mathbf{p}_i, S) > \epsilon$, while at the same time ensuring that the resulting subdivided faces still form a valid patch network $K_\boxplus$.

We specify the refinement of $K_\square$ by selecting a subset $E' \subset E$ of edges in $K_\square$. For each edge in E', a new vertex is introduced at its midpoint. (The selection of E' will be discussed shortly.) We then subdivide each face of $K_\square$ using one of the 4 face refinement templates shown in Figure 5, depending on which of its edges are in E'.

Note that constraints exist on valid choices of E', since the face refinement templates can only be applied to faces with 0, 2, or 4 refined edges. To satisfy these constraints, any chosen set E' is augmented with additional edges so that all faces have an even number of refined edges. Our algorithm for achieving this closure is as follows. We place all faces of $K_\square$ onto a stack. In each iteration, we remove the face at the front of the stack. If it has three refined edges, we add the fourth edge to E' and push the neighboring face on the stack. If instead it has one refined edge, we add to E' the next clockwise edge on the face and push the neighboring face on the stack. The algorithm is guaranteed to terminate, since, in the worst case, E' will contain all edges of $K_\square$ (which leads to global refinement). Figure 6 demonstrates a refinement obtained when a single edge is initially placed in E'.

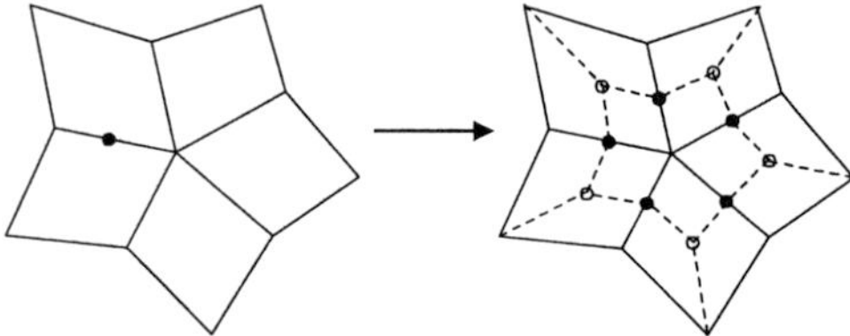

Figure 6: Example of closure of E': on the left E' initially contains only one edge; on the right its computed closure contains 5 edges, resulting in the face refinement indicated by the dashed edges.

We now address the problem of selecting the set E' that determines the refinement. Our algorithm considers all data points with $d(\mathbf{p}_i, S) > \epsilon$ in order of decreasing $d(\mathbf{p}_i, S)$. For each of these data points, if the face onto which it projects is not set to be subdivided (i.e. none of its edges are in E'), then all its edges are added to E', and the closure of the resulting E' is computed.

Having constructed the locally refined domain $K_\boxplus$, we update the parametrizations of the points P. The new vertices introduced in $K_\boxplus$ lie either at the midpoints of edges (coordinates $(0, \frac{1}{2})$, $(1, \frac{1}{2})$, $(\frac{1}{2}, 0)$, $(\frac{1}{2}, 1)$), or at the centroid of faces (coordinates $(\frac{1}{2}, \frac{1}{2})$). Reparametrization on faces created by face refinement templates 1, 2, and 4 proceeds in the obvious way, since there exists a unique piecewise bilinear map between the original face and the quadrilateral subfaces. For a face subdivided by template 3, however, such a bilinear map does not exist on the two trapezoid pieces, so we approximate it by assuming that the original quadrilateral has the geometry of a square.

After adaptive refinement, the fitting method of Step 4 is reinvoked. The resulting surface may still not be within ϵ of all the points, indicating that further refinement is necessary. We repeat the process of refinement and refitting until the error tolerance ϵ is satisfied. Figures 9j– 9l show the resulting surfaces.

4 RESULTS

Figure 9 shows the reconstruction of a B-spline surface from a set of 4000 points; this synthetic data set was obtained by randomly sampling an existing surface. Figures 10a–10c, 10d–10f, and 10g–10i show reconstructions using real data obtained from a laser range scanner (courtesy of Technical Arts Co.).

Figures 10j–10l show the B-spline approximation of a mesh S_0 of 69,473 faces. To approximate S_0, a set P of 30,000 points is sampled randomly from its surface. Step 1 of the procedure is skipped, and S_0 is used directly as the initial mesh M_0.

Table 1: Parameter settings and execution times.

Object	#points	Tolerance	Fairness	Execution times (minutes)				
	N	ϵ	λ	Step 1	Step 2	Step 3	Step 4	Step 5
holes3	4,000	0.6%	0.1	1	1	1	12	134
club	16,585	0.7%	0.1	6	1	1	11	599
foot	20,021	0.3%	0.05	7	13	1	12	228
skidoo	37,974	0.7%	0.1	12	2	1	14	132
bunny	30,000	1.5%	0.1	—	16	1	45	200

As Table 1 indicates, the user-specified parameters are the maximum error tolerance ϵ and the fairness weight λ. (To make these values unitless, we uniformly scale the data points P to fit within a unit cube.) The table also compares the execution times of the 5

Table 2: Surface complexities and B-spline fit errors.

Object	M_0 #faces	$K_\triangle$ #faces	Initial S #patches	fit error rms	fit error max	Refined S #patches	fit error rms	fit error max
holes3	2,080	98	49	0.14%	0.75%	178	0.07%	0.59%
club	5,152	72	35	0.22%	1.36%	285	0.06%	0.41%
foot	10,972	62	29	0.20%	1.20%	156	0.03%	0.27%
skidoo	3,661	30	15	0.23%	3.00%	94	0.03%	0.69%
bunny	69,473	162	72	0.43%	4.64%	153	0.19%	1.44%

successive steps, as obtained on a 105 MHz HP 735 workstation. Table 2 lists for each example the complexities of the initial mesh M_0 and the base complex $K_\triangle$. It also shows the fit errors of both the initial B-spline surface (Step 4) and the adaptively refined B-spline surface (Step 5), giving both rms and maximum errors as percentages of the object diameter.

5 SUMMARY AND FUTURE WORK

We have developed a procedure for constructing a G^1 tensor product B-spline surface of arbitrary topological type from a set of 3D points without user assistance. The procedure makes use of a surface spline construction to obtain G^1 continuity; we show that such an approach leads to an efficient B-spline fitting method. We have introduced an adaptive refinement algorithm. Finally, we have applied our procedure to reconstruct B-spline surfaces within user-specified maximum error tolerances on a number of real data sets.

There exist a number of areas for future research. The procedure should be extended to allow reconstruction of piecewise smooth surfaces that contain discontinuities such as creases and corners [11]. Currently our algorithm has difficulty with such features, as it approximates them by adaptively refining the smooth surface numerous times (e.g. the "club" data set). Identifying these discontinuities as well as other "characteristic" lines on the surface may require some user intervention. Hopefully semi-automated segmentation methods can be developed that do not require complete specification of patch boundaries. Such methods could replace Steps 2 and 3 of our procedure.

In the context of surface approximation, the current procedure provides error bounds $d(\mathbf{p}_i, S)$ between a set of sampled points and the approximating surface; instead a stronger error bound would be the distance $d(S_0, S)$ between the original surface and its approximation.

Some surfaces such as the mesh in Figure 10j contain fine geometric detail that is difficult to approximate with a smooth surface representation. As demonstrated by [17], this detail can be stored conveniently in the form of a displacement map from the underlying smooth surface.

ACKNOWLEDGMENTS

We wish to thank Ken Birdwell of Technical Arts Co. for the laser range data, and Greg Turk and Marc Levoy for the "bunny" mesh.

REFERENCES

[1] Andersson, E., Andersson, R., Boman, M., Elmroth, T., Dahlberg, B., and Johansson, B. Automatic construction of surfaces with prescribed shape. *CAD 20* (1988), 317–324.

[2] Bajaj, C., Bernardini, F., and Xu, G. Automatic reconstruction of surfaces and scalar fields from 3D scans. *Computer Graphics (SIGGRAPH '95 Proceedings)* (1995), 109–118.

[3] Curless, B., and Levoy, M. A volumetric method for building complex models from range images. *Computer Graphics (SIGGRAPH '96 Proceedings)* (1996).

[4] Dietz, U. Erzeugung glatter Flächen aus Meßpunkten. Technical Report 1717, Department of Mathematics, University of Darmstadt, Germany, February 1995.

[5] Doo, D., and Sabin, M. Behaviour of recursive division surfaces near extraordinary points. *CAD 10*, 6 (September 1978), 356–360.

[6] Eck, M., DeRose, T., Duchamp, T., Hoppe, H., Lounsbery, M., and Stuetzle, W. Multiresolution analysis of arbitrary meshes. *Computer Graphics (SIGGRAPH '95 Proceedings)* (1995), 173–182.

[7] Fang, L., and Gossard, D. Reconstruction of smooth parametric surfaces from unorganized data points. In *Curves and Surfaces in Computer Vision and Graphics 3* (1992), J. Warren, Ed., vol. 1830, SPIE, pp. 226–236.

[8] Farin, G. *Curves and Surfaces for Computer Aided Geometric Design*, 3rd ed. Academic Press, 1992.

[9] Forsey, D., and Bartels, R. Surface fitting with hierarchical splines. *ACM Transactions on Graphics 14*, 2 (1995), 134–161.

[10] Greiner, G. Variational design and fairing of spline surfaces. *Computer Graphics Forum 13*, 3 (1994), 143–154.

[11] Hoppe, H., DeRose, T., Duchamp, T., Halstead, M., Jin, H., McDonald, J., Schweitzer, J., and Stuetzle, W. Piecewise smooth surface reconstruction. *Computer Graphics (SIGGRAPH '94 Proceedings)* (1994), 295–302.

[12] Hoppe, H., DeRose, T., Duchamp, T., McDonald, J., and Stuetzle, W. Surface reconstruction from unorganized points. *Computer Graphics (SIGGRAPH '92 Proceedings) 26*, 2 (1992), 71–78.

[13] Hoppe, H., DeRose, T., Duchamp, T., McDonald, J., and Stuetzle, W. Mesh optimization. *Computer Graphics (SIGGRAPH '93 Proceedings)* (1993), 19–26.

[14] Hoschek, J., and Lasser, D. *Fundamentals of Computer Aided Geometric Design.* AK Peters, Wellesley, 1993.

[15] Hoschek, J., Schneider, F.-J., and Wassum, P. Optimal approximate conversion of spline surfaces. *CAGD 6* (1989), 293–306.

[16] Imageware, Corp. Surfacer product information. http://www.iware.com/htmls/surfacer.html.

[17] Krishnamurthy, V., and Levoy, M. Fitting smooth surfaces to dense polygon meshes. *Computer Graphics (SIGGRAPH '96 Proceedings)* (1996).

[18] Lawler, E. L. *Combinatorial optimization: networks and matroids.* Holt, Rinehart, and Winston, 1976.

[19] Lawson, C., and Hanson, R. *Solving Least Squares Problems.* Prentice-Hall, Englewood Cliffs, NJ, 1974.

[20] Lee, S., Tan, H., and Majid, A. Smooth piecewise biquartic surfaces from quadrilateral control polyhedra with isolated n-sided faces. *CAD 27* (1995), 741–758.

[21] Loop, C. Smooth spline surfaces over irregular meshes. *Computer Graphics (SIGGRAPH '94 Proceedings)* (1994), 303–310.

[22] Ma, W., and Kruth, J. Parametrization of randomly measured points for least squares fitting of B-spline curves and surfaces. *CAD 27* (1995), 663–675.

[23] Milroy, M., Bradley, C., Vickers, G., and Weir, D. G^1 continuity of B-spline surface patches in reverse engineering. *CAD 27* (1995), 471–478.

[24] MOORE, D., AND WARREN, J. Approximation of dense scattered data using algebraic surfaces. In *Proc. of the 24th Annual Hawaii Intnl. Conf. on System Sciences, Kauai, HI, USA* (1991), V. Milutinovic and D. Shriver, Eds., IEEE Comp. Soc. Press, pp. 681–690.

[25] MORETON, H., AND SÉQUIN, C. Functional optimization for fair surface design. *Computer Graphics 26*, 3 (July 1992), 167–176.

[26] NASRI, A. H. Boundary-corner control in recursive-subdivision surfaces. *CAD 23*, 6 (1991), 405–410.

[27] PETERS, J. Constructing C^1 surfaces of arbitrary topology using biquadratic and bicubic splines. In *Designing Fair Curves and Surfaces*, N. Sapidis, Ed. SIAM, 1994, pp. 277–293.

[28] PETERS, J. Biquartic C^1-surface splines over irregular meshes. *CAD* (1995). submitted.

[29] REIF, U. Biquadratic G-spline surfaces. *CAGD 12* (1995), 193–205.

[30] ROGERS, D., AND FOG, N. Constrained B-spline curve and surface fitting. *CAD 21* (1989), 641–648.

[31] SARKAR, B., AND MENQ, C.-H. Parameter optimization in approximating curves and surfaces to measurement data. *CAGD 8* (1991), 267–290.

[32] SCHMITT, F., BARSKY, B., AND DU, W. H. An adaptive subdivision method for surface fitting from sampled data. *Computer Graphics (SIGGRAPH '86 Proceedings) 20* (1986), 179–188.

[33] TARJAN, R. Data structures and network algorithms. *CBMS-NSF Regional Conference Series in Applied Mathematics 44* (1983).

[34] TURK, G., AND LEVOY, M. Zippered polygon meshes from range images. *Computer Graphics (SIGGRAPH '94 Proceedings) 28*, 3 (1994), 311–318.

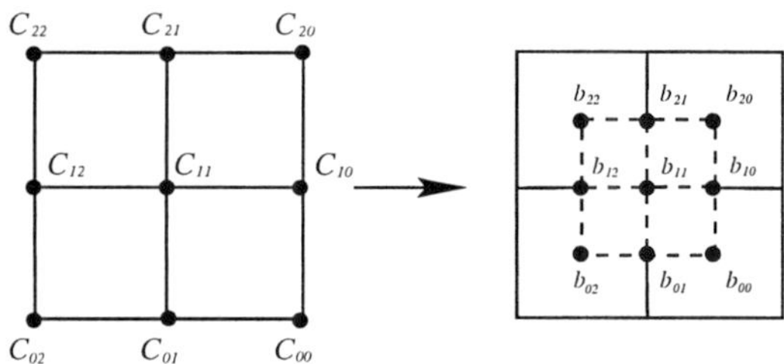

Figure 7: Regular case: neighborhood of vertex $C_{11} \in V_x$ giving rise to a biquadratic patch.

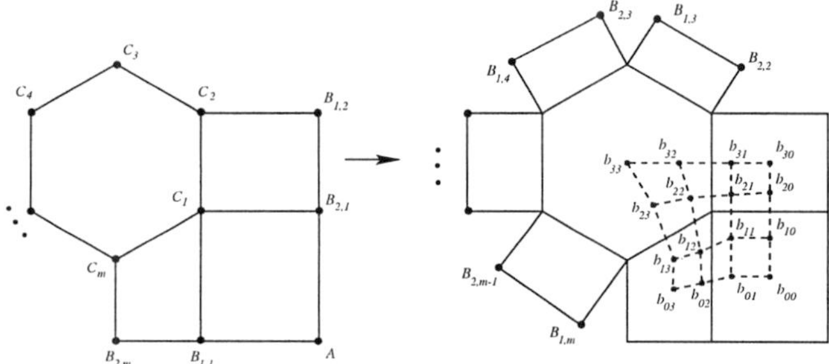

Figure 8: Extraordinary case: neighborhood of vertex $C_1 \in V_x$ giving rise to a bicubic patch

APPENDIX

The purpose of this appendix is to present the formulas expressing the control points of the Bézier patches of S (Figure 3c) as affine combinations of the control mesh vertices V_x (Figure 3b) in Peters' surface spline construction [27].[1] Recall that a Bézier patch is associated with each vertex of M_x.

Regular case Since Peters' surface scheme generalizes biquadratic B-splines, in the regular case of a vertex C_{11} adjacent to four 4-sided faces (Figure 7), a biquadratic Bézier patch is created. The formulas for its Bézier points are obtained trivially:

$$\begin{aligned} b_{00} &= (C_{00} + C_{10} + C_{01} + C_{11})/4 \\ b_{10} &= (C_{11} + C_{10})/2 \\ b_{01} &= (C_{11} + C_{01})/2 \\ b_{11} &= C_{11} \end{aligned}$$

(The remaining Bézier points follow by symmetry.)

Near extraordinary face At a vertex C_1 near an m-sided extraordinary face (Figure 8), a bicubic Bézier patch is created. The formulas for its Bézier points are quite difficult and are derived in [27]:

$$\begin{aligned} b_{00} &= (B_{2,1} + B_{1,1} + C_1 + A)/4 \\ b_{10} &= (5B_{2,1} + B_{1,1} + 5C_1 + A)/12 \\ b_{20} &= (5B_{2,1} + B_{1,2} + 5C_1 + C_2)/12 \\ b_{30} &= (B_{2,1} + B_{1,2} + C_1 + C_2)/4 \\ b_{11} &= (5B_{2,1} + 5B_{1,1} + (25 + 4a)C_1 + (1 - 4a)A)/36 \\ b_{21} &= ((5-10a)B_{2,1} + (1+2a)B_{1,2} + (25+6a)C_1 + (5+2a)C_2)/36 \\ b_{31} &= h_{1,1} \\ b_{22} &= \begin{cases} -\sum_{i=1}^{m}(-1)^i h_{3,i} & \text{if } m \text{ is odd,} \\ -\frac{2}{m}\sum_{i=1}^{m}(-1)^i (m-i)\, h_{3,i} & \text{if } m \text{ is even,} \end{cases} \\ b_{32} &= h_{2,1} \\ b_{33} &= \frac{1}{m}\sum_{i=1}^{m} C_i \end{aligned}$$

where the following abbreviations are used:

$$\begin{aligned} c &= \cos(2\pi/m) \\ a &= c/(1-c) \\ h_{1,i} &= ((1-2a)B_{2,1} + (1-2a)B_{1,2} + (5+2a)C_1 + (5+2a)C_2)/12 \\ h_{2,i} &= \frac{1}{m}\sum_{l=1}^{m} C_l + \frac{2a}{3c}\cos(2\pi l/m)\,(C_{i+l} + C_{i+l+1}) \\ h_{3,i} &= (1 - \frac{2}{3}c)\,h_{2,i} + \frac{2}{3}c\,h_{1,i} \end{aligned}$$

(The remaining Bézier points again follow by symmetry.)

Finally, in the case that the number of sides m of the extraordinary face is even and greater than 4 the following linear condition must hold for G^1 continuity:

$$\sum_{i=1}^{m}\sum_{j=1}^{2}(-1)^{i+j}B_{i,j} = 0$$

[1] Some minor mistakes in the original manuscript have been corrected.

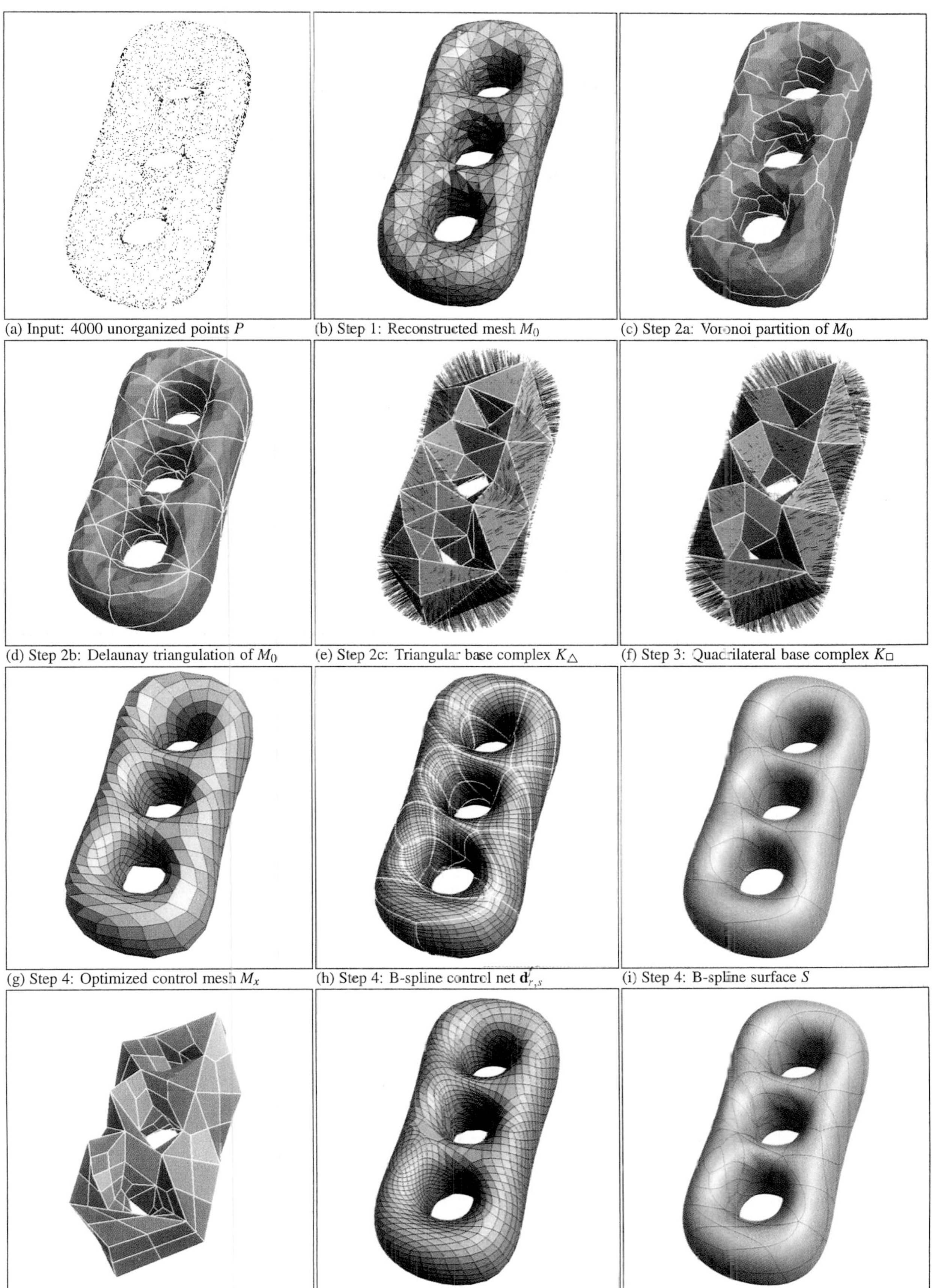

(a) Input: 4000 unorganized points P (b) Step 1: Reconstructed mesh M_0 (c) Step 2a: Voronoi partition of M_0

(d) Step 2b: Delaunay triangulation of M_0 (e) Step 2c: Triangular base complex $K_\triangle$ (f) Step 3: Quadrilateral base complex $K_\square$

(g) Step 4: Optimized control mesh M_x (h) Step 4: B-spline control net $\mathbf{d}^{f}_{r,s}$ (i) Step 4: B-spline surface S

(j) Step 5: Adaptively refined $K_\boxplus$ (k) Step 5: Optimized control mesh M_x (l) Step 5: Final B-spline surface S

Figure 9: Illustration of the B-spline surface reconstruction procedure. From the points P in (a), the procedure automatically creates the G^1 B-spline surface in (l) which deviates from P by no more than 0.59% of the object's diameter.

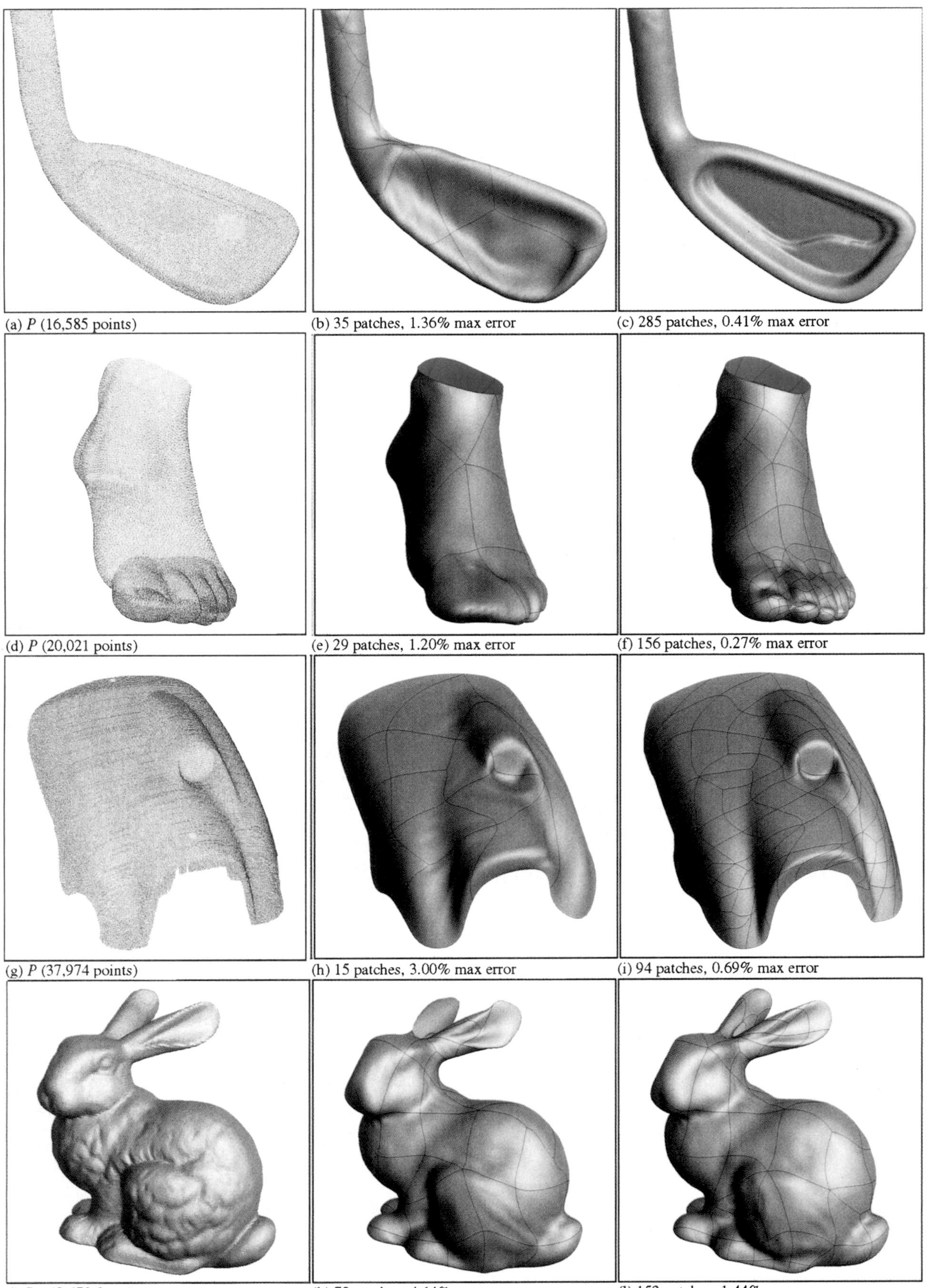

Figure 10: Three more examples of surface reconstruction and one example of surface approximation. The second column shows the initial B-spline surface S (Step 4); the third column shows S after adaptive refinement (Step 5).

Reconstructing Curved Surfaces From Specular Reflection Patterns Using Spline Surface Fitting of Normals

Mark A. Halstead[†‡] Brian A. Barsky[‡§] Stanley A. Klein[§] Robert B. Mandell[§]

University of California at Berkeley

ABSTRACT

We present an algorithm that reconstructs a three-dimensional surface model from an image. The image is generated by illuminating a specularly reflective surface with a pattern of light. We discuss the application of this algorithm to an important problem in biomedicine, namely the measurement of the human cornea, although the algorithm is also applicable elsewhere. The distinction between this reconstruction technique and more traditional techniques that use light patterns is that the image is formed by *specular* reflection. Therefore, the reconstruction algorithm fits a surface to a set of normals rather than to a set of positions. Furthermore, the normals do not have prescribed surface positions. We show that small surface details can be recovered more accurately using this approach. The results of the algorithm are used in an interactive visualization of the cornea.

CR Categories: I.3.5 [Computer Graphics]: Computational Geometry and Object Modeling; J.6 [Computer-Aided Engineering]: Computer-Aided Design.

Keywords: Surface reconstruction, videokeratography, corneal modeling, photogrammetry, normal fitting.

1 INTRODUCTION

A problem of particular interest to the computer graphics community is how to construct accurate computer models of existing objects. One use of these reverse-engineered models is to populate rendered scenes with realistic objects. Another important use is for computer-aided visualization, where the models are displayed in ways that expose information for analysis. An example is medical imaging, in which models of a patient's anatomy are first extracted from measurements made by a variety of scanners (for example MRI or ultrasound [7]). The models are then displayed in various forms for diagnosis. The success of this approach has made medical imaging one of the more important applications of computer graphics and modeling. In addition to displaying the reconstructed models, they can be used to provide a valuable starting point for other operations. For example, in the area of computer-aided design (CAD), an architect can input a model of an existing building, then design and visualize modifications by editing the existing structure. Reverse-engineering is also studied in disciplines other than computer graphics and modeling. For example, in the machine vision community, it appears under the guise of automatic object recognition.

This paper presents a solution to an important reverse-engineering problem in biomedicine: constructing a computer model of the human cornea. The cornea is the outer layer of the eye, and plays the primary role in focusing images on the retina. The algorithm that we have devised to construct a model of the cornea is of interest to the graphics community for the following reasons:

- We derive the surface model by applying backward ray-tracing to simulate reflection at a specular surface and the resulting virtual image.
- We use a variation on the standard B-spline surface representation to increase the efficiency of the backward ray-tracing by at least an order of magnitude.
- We solve a problem of fitting a surface to a set of normals at unprescribed locations.
- The algorithm we present here has significantly advanced the frontier of corneal modeling and visualization.

Building a model of a physical object usually proceeds in two stages: data capture, and construction of the model from the data. Data capture takes many forms. For a survey of techniques, the reader is referred to [6, 14]. A common technique uses correspondences between two or more images of an object taken from different positions [5]. Stereopsis or depth disparity allows the recovery of an approximate depth map for the object. Depth is also recovered by a different class of techniques that use structured light. In this approach, the object is illuminated with a pattern to form an image. The geometric relationship between the light source, the object, and the image recording device is sufficient to determine depth. In some cases, estimates of surface orientation are also provided. Examples include laser rangefinders, slit-ray or grid projectors, and Moiré pattern generators [1, 22, 26].

In most cases, the data is returned as samples of surface position. A model is built by fitting the captured positional data with a surface [8, 11, 12, 20, 21, 23]. Problems faced at this stage include surface discontinuities, and noisy or missing data. Terzopoulos [25] presents a robust algorithm

[†]Apple Computer, 1 Infinite Loop M/S 301-3J, Cupertino, CA 95014.

[‡]Computer Science Division, University of California, Berkeley, CA 94720-1776. www.cs.berkeley.edu/projects/optical/

[§]School of Optometry, University of California, Berkeley, CA 94720-2020.

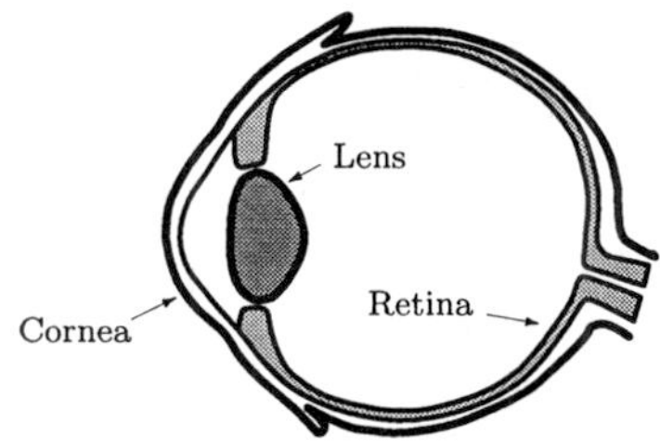

Figure 1: Cross-section of the eye.

which handles these problems using a multigrid approach. In [24], the model is built from implicit algebraic surfaces. The problem of joining positional data taken from different measurements is addressed in [27]. Hoppe [13] discusses an algorithm for recovering surfaces with complex topology from range data.

The important distinction between these fitting problems and the one presented in this paper is that we measure surface *orientation* rather than surface position. This presents a number of interesting challenges and leads to a new approach to surface fitting. The problem differs from those faced by the vision community (such as shape-from-shading [5]) in that we rely on the specular reflection of illumination at the surface in order to reconstruct very small surface features.

As shown in Figure 1, the cornea is the transparent tissue that forms the foremost surface of the eye. Refraction at the air/cornea interface accounts for approximately three-quarters of the focusing power of the eye. Consequently, the exact shape of the cornea is critical to visual acuity. Even subtle deviations of corneal shape can have a significant impact on vision. Measurements must be at the level of submicrons to be meaningful. It is the high precision needed for the measurements that leads us to measure corneal orientation rather than position, and that makes surface reconstruction a challenging problem.

Vision problems arise when the cornea is asymmetric or is too peaked or flat to focus light uniformly on the retina. Eyeglasses and contact lenses address the problem by pre-refracting the light so that the overall effect of the corrective lens plus cornea is more uniform. Recent surgical techniques change the degree of refraction by adjusting the shape of the cornea directly. *Radial keratotomy* (RK) and *astigmatic keratotomy* (AK) reduce the curvature of the cornea by weakening the structure with radial cuts; *photorefractive keratectomy* (PRK) and *laser in-situ keratomileusis* (LASIK) achieve a similar result by ablating corneal material with an excimer laser.

All these procedures benefit from having accurate models of corneal shape. Until recently, however, models used in the optometric community have assumed that the cornea is spherical, ellipsoidal, toric (like a section cut from a torus), or has radial symmetry. On a gross scale, most corneas do have these smooth shapes. However, we wish to measure, and model, deviations from these simple shapes that are on the order of microns and that contribute significantly to the refractive power of the surface.

Ideally, we would like to have an algorithm that, in clinical practice, can scan a patient's cornea and display usable results almost immediately. We have developed an interactive program that presents a good approximation to the shape of a patient's cornea within seconds, and then continues to refine the display until micron accuracy is achieved.

2 MEASURING SURFACE SHAPE

Depth from binocular disparity does not work well for measuring corneal shape, since the surface has no distinctive variation in texture. This makes it difficult to identify correspondences between multiple images. Therefore, we consider measurement techniques in which the surface is illuminated by a pattern of light. The resulting image is recorded by a scanner such as a CCD array. There are two ways to apply this technique, which we will refer to as approach A and approach B.

Applications of approach A are more typical. Often referred to as *raster photogrammetry*, they require a pattern of one or more lines to be projected along a known direction onto a diffuse surface [4, 27, 30]. The projected pattern acts as a secondary diffuse source, which is viewed by the scanner along a direction off-axis to the direction of projection. The observed distortion of the lines indicates the variation in surface distance from the projector, and fully determines the position of a set of sample points. This approach is used, for example, by the Cyberware laser scanner [27]. Lately, interest has focused on fitting the data points with surface models, and combining the results from multiple scans [27].

The approach taken by applications of type Bis for a specular surface, rather than diffuse, near a diffusely emitting source pattern. The scanner captures the virtual image of the pattern caused by specular reflection at the surface. As with approach A, the shape of the surface affects the scanned image. However, the relationship between the shape and the image is harder to define, as it now depends on surface orientation as well as position.

One advantage of approach B is that very small deviations in surface orientation cause large changes in the image. There is no such magnification possible in approach A — a change in orientation has no effect on the scanned image, and a change in position causes changes only of the same magnitude. The accuracy is therefore limited by the resolution of the scanning device. We believe that, with a good reconstruction algorithm, approach B allows submicron level detail to be recovered. This paper describes such a reconstruction algorithm.

2.1 Videokeratography

Fortunately, the cornea in its normal state is covered by a thin layer of tears and presents a specular surface. This means that we can conveniently image the surface using approach B. Over the last few years, simple observation devices based on this approach and used in the optometric community have evolved into the *videokeratograph* [15, 16, 19, 29, 31]. This instrument contains a video camera to capture a digital image which is analyzed by an on-board computer. Although there are variations among systems, a standard arrangement is to have the source pattern painted on the inner surface of a cone. The cone has a hole in its apex through which a system of lenses and a CCD array capture the reflected image (Figure 2). The most common source pattern is alternating black and white concentric rings. Recently, however, we have been experimenting with a prototype source pattern, not commercially available, that resembles a dartboard. We show later how such a pattern allows a more accurate reconstruction.

In preparation for measurement, the patient's line of sight is aligned with the axis of the cone and the image is brought into focus. After capturing an image (Figure 3), the videokeratograph performs a processing step to locate prominent

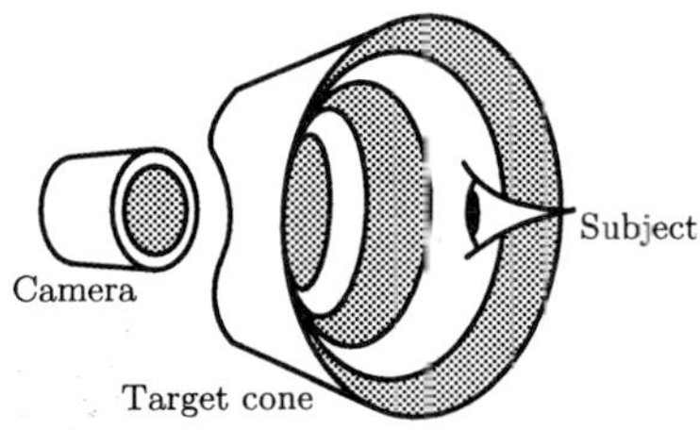

Figure 2: Videokeratograph.

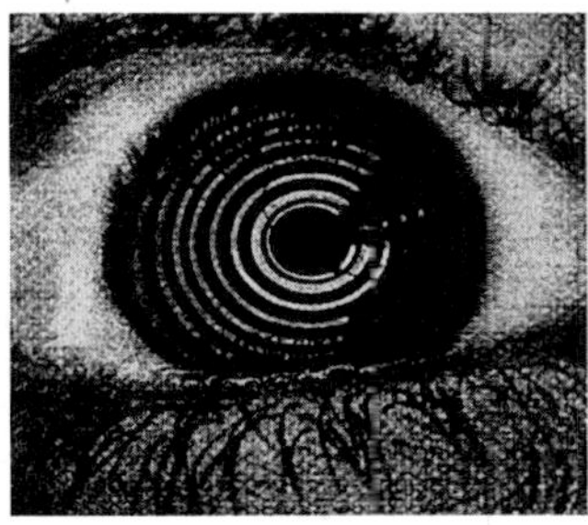

Figure 3: Captured videokeratograph image.

image features. The nature of these features varies between source patterns. For both the concentric ring and the dartboard sources, the feature set includes the edges between regions of black and white in the image. These edges are located with standard image processing techniques and are discretely sampled. For the dartboard source, the crossings created by the junction of four black and white patches form an additional feature set. The aim of our reconstruction algorithm is to generate a model of the corneal surface from the image feature positions and the geometry of the videokeratograph. Previous algorithms have failed to recover continuous, accurate surface models [4, 10, 15, 16, 23, 30]. Our algorithm satisfies these goals.

3 RECONSTRUCTION ALGORITHM

The reconstruction algorithm inputs a set of feature samples from a videokeratograph image. The goal is to find a surface that, if placed in the videokeratograph, would create the same image. With certain assumptions and constraints, we claim that this surface is a good fit to the original cornea.

In order to find the surface, we use a simulation of the videokeratograph. As explained in Section 2.1, light from the source pattern is reflected at the corneal surface and gathered by a system of lenses to form the videokeratograph image. We simulate this process by backward ray-tracing, as illustrated in Figure 4. In the simulation, the system of lenses is replaced by its equivalent nodal point[1], which becomes the center of projection. The video CCD array becomes the image plane, with which we associate the coordinate system (u, v).

In Section 2.1, we noted that image processing techniques are used to extract features such as edges and crossings from the videokeratograph image. The positions of these features in (u, v) are sampled to form the set $\{\mathbf{f}_i : i = 1 \ldots k\}$. Our algorithm relies on the fact that features in the image correspond to features in the source. For example, a sample point taken from an edge in the image is the reflection of some point on an edge in the source. If we trace a ray from the sample point $\mathbf{f}_i$ on the image to the surface (through the nodal point) we can identify a ray that goes from the surface to the "correct" point on the source (that is, some point on the corresponding source feature). In Figure 4, this second ray is shown as a dashed line. These two rays — the incident ray $\hat{\mathbf{i}}_i$ and the modified reflected ray $\hat{\mathbf{r}}_i^*$, where the hat indicates normalization — define a modified surface normal vector:

$$\hat{\mathbf{n}}_i^* = \frac{\hat{\mathbf{r}}_i^* - \hat{\mathbf{i}}_i}{\left|\hat{\mathbf{r}}_i^* - \hat{\mathbf{i}}_i\right|}.$$

[1]For our purposes, the action of a camera with one or more lenses is adequately modeled by a pinhole camera positioned at the nodal point

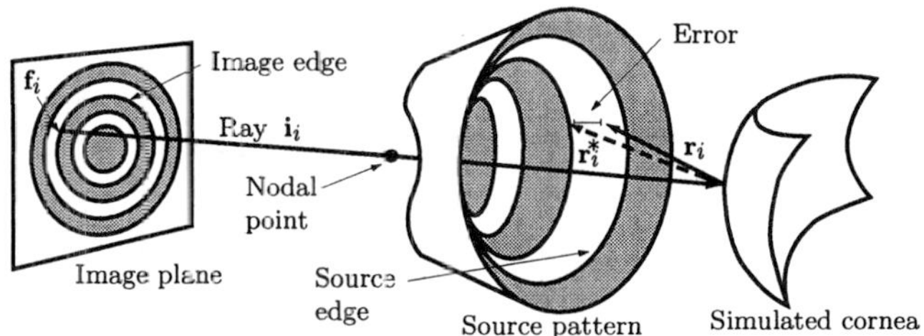

Figure 4: Simulation using ray-tracing.

The modified reflected ray and the modified normal vector may differ from the actual reflected vector $\hat{\mathbf{r}}_i$ and the actual normal vector $\hat{\mathbf{n}}_i$. In this case, we attempt to adjust the surface so that it interpolates the modified normal.

We determine a modified normal vector for each image sample and fit the set of normals with a new surface. Because the backward rays intersect the new surface at new positions, the set of modified normals we just fit is now incorrect, so we must recompute them and repeat the fitting step. This leads to an iterative process which we initialize by taking a guess at the shape of the cornea. Each iteration consists of a *normal fitting* phase and a *refinement phase*. The normal fitting phase determines the set of modified normals using the current surface and fits them with a new surface. The refinement phase adds degrees of freedom to the surface model as needed for a more accurate fit.

3.1 The Normal Fitting Phase

For each sample $\mathbf{f}_i$, we determine the modified normal $\hat{\mathbf{n}}_i^*$ using the current surface. We define the *range* of $\mathbf{f}_i$ to be the set of points in the source pattern that could be imaged to $\mathbf{f}_i$. This set may form a curve, such as the entire source edge in the above example, or it may contain a single point. The latter case arises when the dartboard pattern is used, because crossings can be located exactly in the source.

Using backward ray-tracing from $\mathbf{f}_i$ and the current surface, we find where the reflected ray $\hat{\mathbf{r}}_i$ intersects the source pattern. We then determine which point in the range lies nearest the intersection. The ray from the surface to this point is $\hat{\mathbf{r}}_i^*$.

The set $\{\hat{\mathbf{n}}_i^* : i = 1 \ldots k\}$ is viewed as a set of normal vector constraints which, together with a positional constraint discussed in the next section, is fit with a new surface S^*. The details are given in Section 3.4 after we have described the surface representation scheme.

3.2 Convergence and Uniqueness of Solution

The search process clearly must be iterative, since each normal fitting phase changes not only the normal vectors of the surface but the position, which causes the rays from the image plane to intersect at new locations. We have no formal proof that our search algorithm will always converge, but in all trial runs we have observed rapid and stable convergence to a good solution.

For a given set of features, there may be zero, one, or many surfaces that generate matching images. The result depends on the distribution of image features and the representation chosen for the surface model. Fortunately, we are working in a restricted problem domain, in which we can assume that the cornea has a smooth, regular shape. This assumption is based on the fact that the cornea is a pliable tissue subject to internal pressure. Based on this assumption, we formulate the search process to favor smoothly varying surfaces. With the further assumption that the number of degrees of freedom in the surface model is related to its smoothness, we begin the search with a surface of few degrees of freedom, and incrementally add degrees of freedom until a satisfactory solution is found.

Although this algorithm may not be a rigorous statement of our goal, it has given more than satisfactory results in practice. Note that we use far more features than degrees of freedom, so that the search for a match is overconstrained.

Section 3.5 will discuss efficient methods for adding degrees of freedom to the model using refinement.

To further reduce the number of possible solutions, we impose one or more interpolation constraints. The constraint that we use most often is to fix the position of the apex of the cornea. Some videokeratograph systems have attachments that can directly measure this position. If the information is not directly available, it can be estimated from the image and the known focal length of the camera lens. The algorithm then generates an initial surface that interpolates this point, and maintains the interpolation constraint for the remainder of the search.

3.3 Surface Representation

The representation of S is carefully chosen to allow the efficient execution of the normal fitting phase. At first glance, conventional CAGD wisdom would suggest the use of a parametric polynomial patch scheme — such as tensor product B-splines with control points in $\mathbb{R}^3$ — to define the position of S in (x, y, z). One drawback of this scheme is that numerically expensive algorithms such as root finding are required to compute the ray/surface intersections during the backward ray-tracing stage.

In contrast, we use a representation scheme that allows the point of intersection of a ray to be determined simply by taking a linear combination of scalar control points. Furthermore, the coefficients of the linear combination remain constant throughout the search, and are computed only once, at initialization.

Figure 5 illustrates how the scheme works. By suitably scaling the feature positions $\mathbf{f}_i$, we can assume that the image plane lies at $z = -1$ and that $u \equiv x, v \equiv y$. We define $D(u, v)$ to be the z-coordinate of the point of intersection between the surface and the ray that originates at (u, v) and passes through the nodal point. The coordinates of this point are

$$x = -uD(u, v) \quad (1)$$
$$y = -vD(u, v) \quad (2)$$
$$z = D(u, v). \quad (3)$$

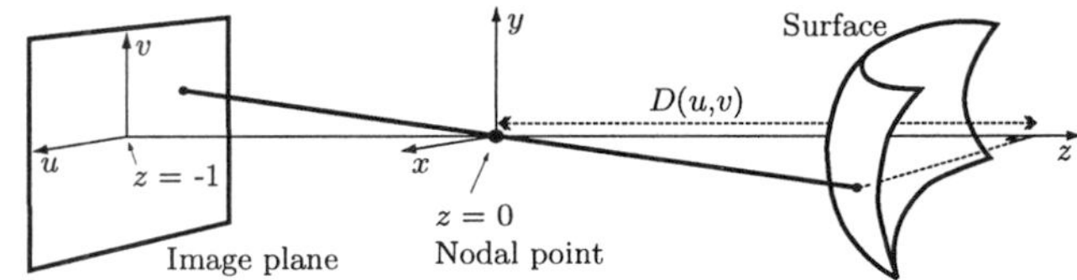

Figure 5: Surface representation scheme.

These equations define the surface S in (x, y, z), parameterized by image plane coordinates (u, v). Furthermore, the representation is ideal for the backward ray-tracing task, since, by definition, the equations directly give the intersection of each ray with S.

In the current implementation, $D(u, v)$ is represented by a set of biquintic tensor product B-spline patches, with uniform knot spacing and no boundary conditions [3]. A surface consisting of $(m-5) \times (n-5)$ patches is defined by an $m \times n$ array of control points $\{P_{1,1}, \ldots, P_{m,n}\}$ in $\mathbb{R}^1$. From the definition of (x, y, z), we find that the x-coordinate patches of S are degree 6 polynomials in u and degree 5 in v; the y-coordinate patches are degree 5 in u and degree 6 in v; and the z-coordinate patches are degree 5 in both u and v. The surface S can be rendered using standard techniques for polynomial patch surfaces.

We have chosen to use biquintic patches rather than a lower degree representation because of the high degree of smoothness exhibited by the cornea. Furthermore, one of our scientific visualization tasks is to display curvature maps of the surface. Since the formula for curvature involves second partial derivatives of surface position, a bicubic representation allows cusps in curvature, whereas a biquintic formulation provides for smoother joins at patch boundaries.

Since the feature positions $\{\mathbf{f}_i : i = 1 \ldots k\}$ are defined by the input image, their (u, v) coordinates, which are used as ray origins for backward ray-tracing, remain fixed throughout the search. For fixed (u, v), the functions x, y, z given by (1)–(3) are linear combinations of the control points $\{P_{1,1}, \ldots, P_{m,n}\}$. This is a consequence of the B-spline function $D(u, v)$ being linear in $\{P_{1,1}, \ldots, P_{m,n}\}$ for fixed (u, v). For each of the k features, we can evaluate the basis functions of $D(u, v)$ at the feature's coordinate and multiply by $-u$ (for x) or $-v$ (for y) to find the coefficients that multiply each of the control points. Collecting these coefficients together in matrix form, we can write

$$\begin{aligned} x &= M_x[P_{1,1}, \ldots, P_{m,n}]^T \\ y &= M_y[P_{1,1}, \ldots, P_{m,n}]^T \\ z &= M_z[P_{1,1}, \ldots, P_{m,n}]^T, \end{aligned}$$

where M_x, M_y and M_z are $k \times mn$ matrices that are precomputed and stored using a sparse matrix representation for efficient evaluation.

Similarly, we derive matrices M_x^u and M_x^v such that $\partial x/\partial u = M_x^u[P_{1,1}, \ldots, P_{m,n}]^T$ and $\partial x/\partial v = M_x^v[P_{1,1}, \ldots, P_{m,n}]^T$. Together with matrices M_y^u, M_y^v, M_z^u, and M_z^v for y and z, these are used to find expressions for the surface tangent vectors in the u and v directions:

$$\begin{aligned} \mathbf{t}_u &= \partial\mathbf{S}(u, v)/\partial u \\ \mathbf{t}_v &= \partial\mathbf{S}(u, v)/\partial v \\ \text{where } \mathbf{S}(u, v) &= [x(u, v), y(u, v), z(u, v)]. \end{aligned}$$

The surface normal required for computing the reflected ray during ray-tracing is given by $\mathbf{t}_u \times \mathbf{t}_v$.

3.4 Solving the Normal Fitting Problem

In Section 3.1, the normal fitting problem was defined as finding the surface S^* that fits the prescribed surface normals $\{\hat{\mathbf{n}}_i^* : i = 1 \ldots k\}$ subject to one or more interpolation constraints.

Let (x_c, y_c, z_c) be a point interpolated by the surface. Using (1)–(3), we find that the constraint is satisfied if

$$D(-x_c/z_c, -y_c/z_c) = z_c.$$

Using the same technique employed to construct the matrix M_z in the previous section, we determine coefficients $\{c_{1,1}, \ldots, c_{m,n}\}$ such that

$$D(-x_c/z_c, -y_c/z_c) = [c_{1,1}, \ldots, c_{m,n}][P_{1,1}, \ldots, P_{m,n}]^T = z_c.$$

This constraint equation is linear in the control points, and some number, say s, of interpolation constraints are expressed in matrix form as

$$C[P_{1,1}, \ldots, P_{m,n}]^T = [z_1, \ldots, z_s]^T,$$

where C is an $s \times mn$ matrix.

Let N be the $mn \times t$ matrix whose columns span the null space of C. Given an input surface S with control points $\{P_{1,1}, \ldots, P_{m,n}\}$ that satisfies the constraints, all other surfaces S^* that satisfy the constraints, and hence are possible solutions to the normal fitting problem, have control points given by

$$[P^*_{1,1}, \ldots, P^*_{m,n}]^T = [P_{1,1}, \ldots, P_{m,n}]^T + N[Q_1, \ldots, Q_t]^T. \quad (4)$$

Now consider a feature $\mathbf{f}_i$ with image plane coordinates (u_i, v_i). The modified surface normal computed for this feature is $\hat{\mathbf{n}}_i^* = (n^*_{i,x}, n^*_{i,y}, n^*_{i,z})$. We can require S^* to have a scalar multiple of this normal by using the pair of constraints

$$\begin{aligned} \hat{\mathbf{n}}_i^*.\mathbf{t}_u|_{u_i,v_i} &= 0, \\ \text{and } \hat{\mathbf{n}}_i^*.\mathbf{t}_v|_{u_i,v_i} &= 0. \end{aligned}$$

Using the matrices from the previous section, and defining $diag(\alpha_1, \ldots, \alpha_j)$ to be the $j \times j$ matrix with $\alpha_1, \ldots, \alpha_j$ on the diagonal and zeroes elsewhere, we write the pairs of constraints for all features as

$$\begin{aligned} \big[diag(n^*_{1,x}, \ldots, n^*_{k,x})M^u_x + diag(n^*_{1,y}, \ldots, n^*_{k,y})M^u_y + \\ diag(n^*_{1,z}, \ldots, n^*_{k,z})M^u_z\big]\,[P^*_{1,1}, \ldots, P^*_{m,n}]^T &= 0 \\ \big[diag(n^*_{1,x}, \ldots, n^*_{k,x})M^v_x + diag(n^*_{1,y}, \ldots, n^*_{k,y})M^v_y + \\ diag(n^*_{1,z}, \ldots, n^*_{k,z})M^v_z\big]\,[P^*_{1,1}, \ldots, P^*_{m,n}]^T &= 0 \end{aligned}$$

These normal constraint equations are combined to form the simpler expression

$$M[P^*_{1,1}, \ldots, P^*_{m,n}]^T = 0. \quad (5)$$

Substituting (4) into (5), we arrive at a system of linear equations which is solved in a least squares sense for $[Q_1, \ldots, Q_t]$:

$$MN[Q_1, \ldots, Q_t]^T = -M[P_{1,1}, \ldots, P_{m,n}]^T. \quad (6)$$

The final control points $[P^*_{1,1}, \ldots, P^*_{m,n}]$ of the new surface S^* are determined by substitution of $[Q_1, \ldots, Q_t]$ into (4).

The $k \times t$ matrix MN in (6) has the same number of rows as there are image features, and the number of columns is no more than the number of surface control points minus one. To ensure a sensible fit to the data, we overconstrain the system by using as many as 20 to 30 times as many features as control points. This is an attempt to smooth out errors in the feature location process. The least squares solution to the resulting rectangular system is found with standard numerical algorithms. In the current implementation, the sparsity of MN is not used to advantage.

3.5 Refinement

The goal of our interactive system is to rapidly display an initial, approximate solution which is then improved incrementally. Therefore, the initial search iterations should execute quickly at the expense of accuracy. Since each iteration is dominated by the solution of (6), this goal is satisfied by performing the initial iterations with a small number of control points and features. Accuracy is improved at the expense of iteration time by increasing the number of control points and features, which is consistent with the algorithm discussed in Section 3.2 in regard to uniqueness of solution.

In our current implementation, which uses biquintic B-spline patches with uniform knot spacing, the number of control points is increased by subdividing each patch into four subpatches. A new knot is inserted at the midpoint of each knot interval in both u and v. The new control points are derived using simple linear combinations of the old, with coefficients given by an application of the Oslo algorithm [3, 9].

The search begins with a single patch model of the surface. Refinement is performed when the mean change in angle between normals at successive iterations falls below a given threshold. The model moves through representations using $(4, 16, 64, \ldots)$ patches until the maximum change in normal falls below a predetermined threshold at a predetermined level of refinement.

A typical feature set contains over 5000 samples. For low subdivision levels, this is more than we need, so a subset of features is used. This subset is chosen so that the image is uniformly sampled.

4 RESULTS

To test the algorithm, we need to run it on surfaces whose shape is accurately known. Unfortunately, it is difficult to manufacture interesting test cases. For this reason, we have tested the algorithm on both data collected from real objects and data generated synthetically. The synthetic data is generated automatically from various surface definitions by a software simulation of the videokeratograph.

Figures 9a-10d show some frames illustrating the progress of the algorithm. The results of the search process are displayed to the user after each iteration. The algorithm is formulated so that a good approximation to the final answer is reached in a few seconds, so the user can start analyzing the results immediately. A more accurate picture evolves over the next few minutes.

In Figure 9, there are four frames showing the patches converging to a solution. The input data is a simple ellipsoid with axis radii of 8mm 9mm, and 10mm. The image data for this example was synthetically generated and is shown in Figure 6. For illustration purposes, we show the exact ellipsoid (lower surface) plus the current solution offset above. However, since the difference in shape is so small, we magnify this difference by a factor of 20 in order to better visualize the progress of the algorithm. The surface colors indicate the logarithm (base 10) of the distance in millimeters between the current solution and the exact ellipsoid. In the final frame, we can see that good convergence has been achieved. We measure the error as the distance in z between the two surfaces, computed at a large number of sample points in the x, y plane. The RMS error for this example was 9.2×10^{-6}mm, which is 0.0092 microns. This extremely high accuracy is typical of all synthetic data sets we have tried.

Figure 10 shows frames from another run of the algorithm. The input data in this example is again synthetically generated, and is shown in Figure 7. The aim here is to simulate *keratoconus*, which is a condition in which the cornea has a local region of high curvature [2, 17, 18]. The surface is generated from a sphere with a rotationally symmetric bump grafted onto it. The bump and the sphere meet with curvature continuity. The curvature at the peak of the bump is significantly greater than the curvature of the sphere. This situation has not been handled very well by existing algorithms. Our algorithm, however, has no difficulty in finding an accurate solution. Note that the bump rises only approximately 20 microns above the sphere. This is a deviation of about 0.2 percent of the radius of the sphere. However, the bump causes large deviations in the image rings (Figure 7), demonstrating that we can record smaller deviations using an image formed by specular reflection than one formed by diffuse reflection.

Rather than color encode the distance between the current solution and the actual surface, in Figure 10 we have color encoded the separation between the current surface and a sphere whose radius is the same as that of the input test surface. This form of rendering illustrates one of our visualization techniques, which is to display the surface separation from a best-fitting ellipsoid. This enhances the deviations so that the bump, which is positionally very close to the sphere, becomes noticeable. In this example, we get extremely high positional accuracy of 0.013 microns.

Figure 8 illustrates the results of the algorithm run on real data taken from a cornea. In this case, we cannot report accuracy information because the true shape is unknown. Nonetheless, we can render it with our in-house scientific visualization software package. Figure 8 shows the surface with pseudo-color representing Gaussian curvature (and the height information in the image is simply the true height of the 3-D surface). The red area on the left depicts a local area of high Gaussian curvature. The vectors correspond to the direction of minimum curvature at each point on the surface. This image demonstrates how effective the use of curvature can be in conveying subtle changes in shape.

We have run the algorithm on real data measured from physical ellipsoids of known radii. In these runs, the final accuracy lies in a range of 0.9-1.5 microns of mean error in z. This is still extremely accurate, but it is significantly larger than the error in the synthetic runs. We conclude that the error is introduced, not by the algorithm, but by the feature extraction algorithm and in the measurements we have made of the physical videokeratograph geometry (such as distance between rings, etc.). We are currently addressing these issues.

In all these runs, the final surface consists of 8×8 patches. This gives adequate accuracy, although there is no reason why we cannot go to the next level of 16×16 patches. Beyond that, we reach the limits of the feature sampling process. In the source patterns we currently use, the features are not uniformly spread across the image but are concentrated along boundaries between areas of black and white rings. This limits how small the patches can be, because if a patch falls between feature clusters it will be unconstrained (except by continuity between adjacent patches).

5 CONCLUSION

We have presented an algorithm that reconstructs the shape of the cornea from a single videokeratograph image. The algorithm is interesting because it fits a surface to a set of normals rather than to a set of positions. Furthermore, the normals are not associated with spatial positions as in standard normal fitting problems. This distinguishes it from more typical surface reconstruction problems. The normal fitting is necessary because the surface imaging technique uses reflection from a specular surface. This improves its ability to detect small variations in surface position because surface orientation is a more sensitive indicator of shape variations than is surface position. This technique can be applied to objects other than the human cornea, and any applications that require high accuracy would be candidates. However, we have made some assumptions about the surface that allow us to proceed with little direct information about the corneal position. For example, we only require a single positional constraint. These assumptions are valid in the case of corneas. For other more general objects where these assumptions could not be made, more positional measurements may be needed to provide additional constraints.

REFERENCES

[1] ALTSCHULER, M., ALTSCHULER, B., AND TABOADA, J. Laser electro-optic system for rapid three-dimensional (3-D) topographic mapping of surfaces. *Optical Engineering 20*, 6 (1981), 953–961.

[2] BARSKY, B. A., MANDELL, R. B., AND KLEIN, S. A. Corneal shape illusion in keratoconus. *Invest Opthalmol Vis Sci 36 Suppl.:5308* (1995).

[3] BARTELS, R. H., BEATTY, J. C., AND BARSKY, B. A. *An Introduction to Splines for Use in Computer Graphics and Geometric Modeling.* Morgan Kaufmann, 1987.

[4] BELIN, M. W., LITOFF, D., AND STRODS, S. J. The PAR technology corneal topography system. *Refract Corneal Surg 8* (1992), 88–96.

[5] BLAKE, A., AND ZISSERMAN, A. *Visual Reconstruction.* MIT Press, 1987.

[6] BOLLE, R., AND VEMURI, B. On three-dimensional surface reconstruction methods. *IEEE Trans. PAMI 11*, 8, 840–858.

[7] BRINKLEY, J. Knowledge-driven ultrasonic three-dimensional organ modeling. *IEEE Trans. PAMI 7*, 4, 431–441.

[8] CHENG, F., AND BARSKY, B. A. Interproximation: Interpolation and approximation using cubic spline curves. *Computer-Aided Design 23*, 10 (1991), 700–706.

[9] COHEN, E., LYCHE, T., AND RIESENFELD, R. Discrete B-splines and subdivision techniques in computer aided geometric design and computer graphics. *Computer Graphics and Image Processing 14* (1980), 87–111.

[10] DOSS, J. D., HUTSON, R. L., ROWSEY, J. J., AND BROWN, D. R. Method for calculation of corneal profile and power distribution. *Arch Ophthalmol 99* (1981), 1261–5.

[11] FAVARDIN, C. *Determination automatique de structures geometriques destinees a la reconstruction de courbes et de surfaces a partir de donnees ponctuelles.* PhD thesis, Universite Paul Sabatier, Toulouse, France, 1993.

[12] GOSHTASBY, A. Surface reconstruction from scattered measurements. *SPIE 1830* (1992), 247–256.

[13] HOPPE, H., DEROSE, T., DUCHAMP, T., HALSTEAD, M., JIN, H., MCDONALD, J., SCHWEITZER, J., AND W., S. Piecewise smooth surface reconstruction. *Computer Graphics (SIGGRAPH '94 Proceedings)* (July 1994), 295–302.

[14] JARVIS. A perspective on range finding techniques for computer vision. *IEEE Trans. PAMI 5*, 2 (1983), 122–139.

[15] KLYCE, S. D. Computer-assisted corneal topography, high-resolution graphic presentation and analysis of keratoscopy. *Invest Ophthalmol Vis Sci 25* (1984), 1426–35.

[16] KOCH, D. D., FOULKS, G. N., AND MORAN, T. The corneal eyesys system: accuracy, analysis and reproducibility of first generation prototype. *Refract Corneal Surg 5* (1989), 424–9.

[17] KRACHMER, J. H., FEDER, R. S., AND BELIN, M. W. Keratoconus and related noninflammatory corneal thinning disorders. *Surv. Ophthalmol 28*, 4 (1984), 293–322.

[18] MAGUIRE, L. J., AND BOURNE, W. D. Corneal topography of early keratoconus. *Am J Ophthalmol 108* (1989), 107–12.

[19] MAMMONE, R. J., GERSTEN, M., GORMLEY, D. J., KOPLIN, R. S., AND LUBKIN, V. L. 3-D corneal modeling system. *IEEE Trans Biomedical Eng 37* (1990), 66–73.

[20] MOORE, D., AND WARREN, J. Approximation of dense scattered data using algebraic surfaces. Tech. rep., TR 90-135, Rice University, 1990.

[21] PRATT, V. Direct least-squares fitting of algebraic surfaces. *SIGGRAPH '87 Conference Proceedings* (1987), 145–152.

[22] SATO, Y., KITAGAWA, H., AND FUJITA, H. Shape measurement of curved objects using multiple slit-ray projections. *IEEE Trans. PAMI 4*, 6 (1982), 641–649.

[23] SCHMITT, F., BARSKY, B. A., AND DU, W.-H. An adaptive subdivision method for surface fitting from sampled data. *SIGGRAPH '86 Conference Proceedings* (1986), 179–188.

[24] TAUBIN, G. An improved algorithm for algebraic curve and surface fitting. In *Proc. 4th International Conf. on Comp. Vision, Berlin* (1993), pp. 658–665.

[25] TERZOPOLOUS, D. Regularization of inverse visual problems involving discontinuities. *IEEE Trans. PAMI 8* (1986), 413–424.

[26] TOPA, L., AND SCHALKOFF, R. An analytical approach to the determination of planar surface orientation using active-passive image pairs. *Computer Vision, Graphics, and Image Processing 35* (1994), 404–418.

[27] TURK, G., AND LEVOY, M. Zippered polygon meshes from range images. *Computer Graphics (SIGGRAPH '94 Proceedings)* (1994), 311–318.

[28] VAN SAARLOOS, P. P., AND CONSTABLE, I. Improved method for calculation of corneal topography for any photokeratoscope geometry. *Optom Vis Sci 68* (1991), 960–6.

[29] WANG, J., RICE, D. A., AND KLYCE, S. D. A new reconstruction algorithm for improvement of corneal topographical analysis. *Refract. Corneal Surg 5* (1989), 379–387.

[30] WARNICKI, J. W., REHKOPF, P. G., AND CURTIN, S. A. Corneal topography using computer analyzed rasterographic images. *Am. J. Opt 27* (1988), 1125–1140.

[31] WILSON, S. E., AND KLYCE, S. D. Advances in the analysis of corneal topography. *Surv. Ophthalmol. 35* (1991), 269–277.

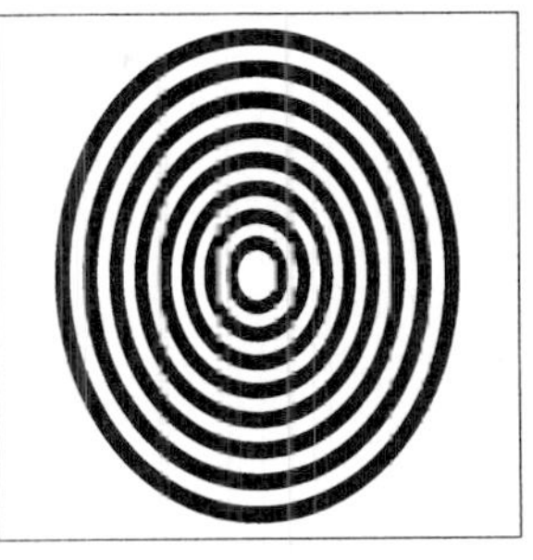

Figure 6: Synthetic ellipsoid image.

Figure 7: Synthetic "bump on sphere" image.

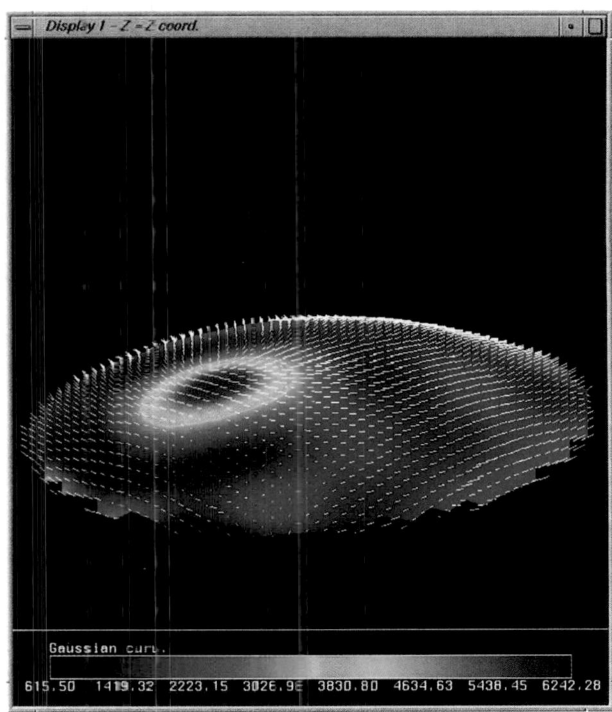

Figure 8: Visualization in 3D of surface recovered from real data.

Figure 9: Steps in recovering the shape of an ellipsoid.

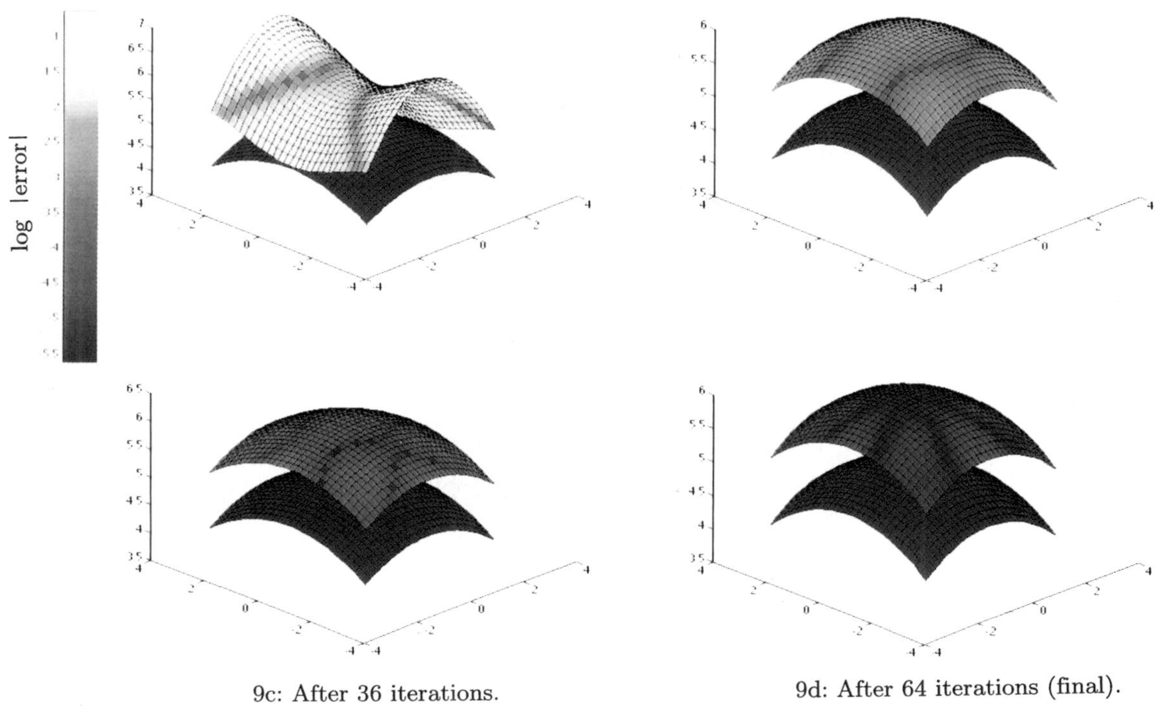

9c: After 36 iterations.

9d: After 64 iterations (final).

Figure 10: Steps in recovering the shape of a "bump on sphere".

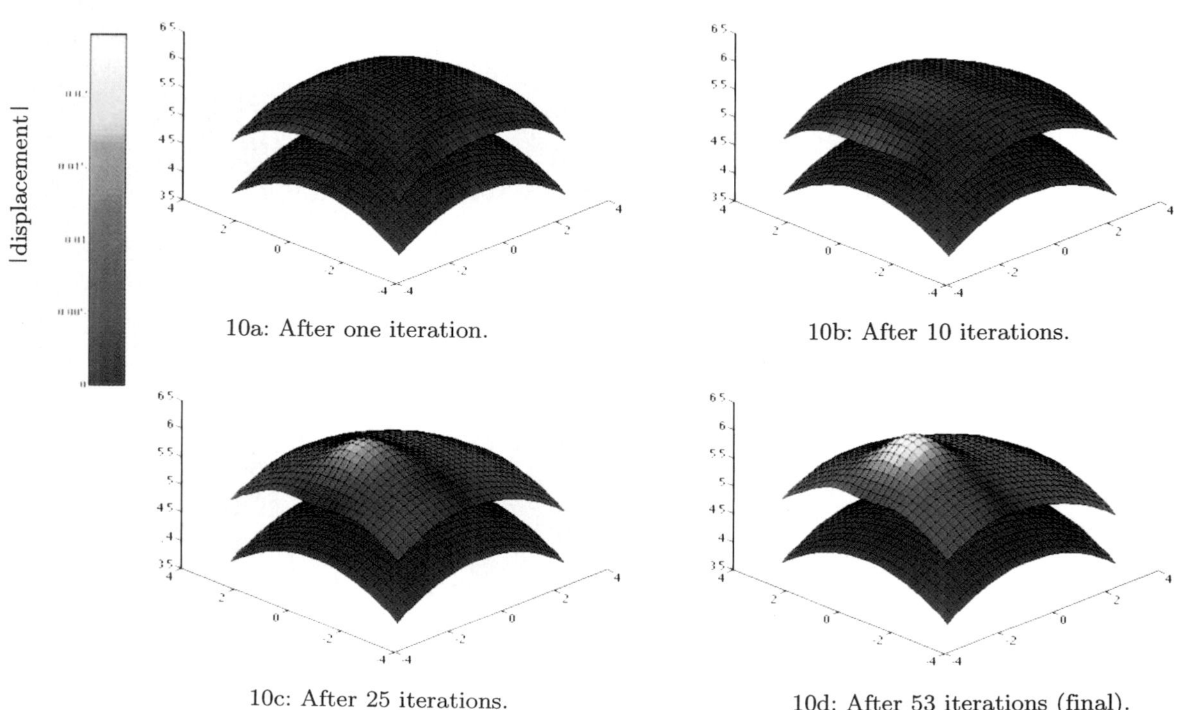

10a: After one iteration.

10b: After 10 iterations.

10c: After 25 iterations.

10d: After 53 iterations (final).

Coarse-Grained Parallelism for Hierarchical Radiosity Using Group Iterative Methods

Thomas A. Funkhouser
Bell Laboratories *

Abstract

This paper describes algorithms that allow multiple hierarchical radiosity solvers to work on the same radiosity solution in parallel. We have developed a system based on a group iterative approach that repeatedly: 1) partitions patches into groups, 2) distributes a copy of each group to a slave processor which updates radiosities for all patches in that group, and 3) merges the updates back into a master solution. The primary advantage of this approach is that separate instantiations of a hierarchical radiosity solver can gather radiosity to patches in separate groups in parallel with very little contention or communication overhead. This feature, along with automatic partitioning and dynamic load balancing algorithms, enables our implemented system to achieve significant speedups running on moderate numbers of workstations connected by a local area network. This system has been used to compute the radiosity solution for a very large model representing a five floor building with furniture.

CR Categories and Subject Descriptors:
D.1.3 [Programming Techniques]: *Concurrent Programming - Distributed Programming*; I.3.7 [Computer Graphics]: *Three-Dimensional Graphics and Realism - Radiosity.*

1 Introduction

An important application of computer graphics is lighting simulation for architectural design. Although radiosity methods are often used for simulating illumination of building interiors, current radiosity algorithms generally are not fast enough or robust enough to handle large architectural models complete with furniture due to their large computational and memory requirements. A plausible approach for accelerating such a large computation is to partition the problem among multiple concurrent processors each of which solves a separate subcomputation. This approach is particularly attractive using a network of loosely connected workstations since this type of "parallel computing resource" is common today in many industrial and research laboratories.

In this paper, we describe a new approach to executing large radiosity computations in parallel. The key innovation is a group iterative algorithm that partitions the patches into groups, and iteratively solves radiosities for patches in each group separately on different processors in parallel, while dynamically merging updated radiosities into a single solution. The primary advantage of this approach is that different group subcomputations update separate subsets of the form factors and radiosities, and therefore they can execute hierarchical radiosity solvers concurrently with little or no contention. This feature, along with dynamic load balancing algorithms, enables our implemented system to achieve significant speedups with moderate numbers of workstations distributed on a local area network. In our implementation, no single process accesses the entire scene database, and thus we are able to compute accurate radiosity solutions for very large models.

The paper is organized as follows. The next section reviews the radiosity method and describes previous work on parallel radiosity systems. Section 3 describes the classical group iterative method and discusses how it can be applied to radiosity problems. An overview of our system organization appears in Section 4, while detailed descriptions of the partitioning and load balancing algorithms are included in Section 5. Section 6 contains results of experiments with our system. Finally, Section 7 contains a brief summary and conclusion.

*Murray Hill, NJ 07974, funk@research.att.com

2 Previous work

Radiosity methods [14] simulate diffuse global illumination by computing the amount of light arriving at each patch by emission or diffuse reflection from other patches. If each patch is composed of elements (i.e., substructured [5]), the method must solve the following linear system of equations:

$$B_i = E_i + \rho_i \sum_{j=1}^{n} B_j F_{ij} \qquad (1)$$

where B_i is the radiosity of element i, E_i is the emission of element i, ρ_i is the diffuse reflectivity of element i, F_{ij} is the fraction of the energy leaving element i that arrives element j, and n is the number of elements in the scene.

The primary challenges in implementing the radiosity method are efficient computation and storage of the form factors. For each form factor, F_{ij}, a visibility calculation must be performed to determine a visibility percentage for elements i and j. This calculation must consider other patches in the scene as potential blockers, and thus accounts for the majority of the computation time in most radiosity systems.

There has been considerable prior work on parallel implementations of the radiosity method. Most of this work has been applied to the progressive radiosity algorithm [6] which has $O(n^2)$ computational complexity when solved to full convergence. Implementations for this algorithm have been described for MIMD computers [2, 3, 16, 19], SIMD computers [8], transputers [9], shared memory multi-processors [1, 7], and networks of workstations [4, 20]. Recently, a few papers have appeared describing work on parallelizing the Monte Carlo Radiosity algorithm [10, 30]. Most current implementations require a complete description of the scene's geometry to be resident in memory on all processors, thus limiting the size of models for which they can be applied.

There has been relatively little work on parallel implementations of the hierarchical radiosity method, which is surprising at first glance since its asymptotic complexity is $O(n)$ [17]. Singh [23] implemented a parallel hierarchical radiosity solver for a shared memory multiprocessor system in which each processor was initially assigned a queue of element-element interactions to process. When a processor subdivided an element, it added new interactions for the element's children to the head of its own queue. Load balancing was achieved by task stealing – idle processors removed and processed interactions from the tail of other processors' queues. Due its communication intensive nature, this approach is not practical for a network of distributed workstations.

Zareski [31] implemented a parallel version of the hierarchical radiosity algorithm on a network of workstations using a master-slave architecture in which each slave performed patch-ray intersection calculations for a separate subset of patches in the scene. For each element-element interaction, the master process constructed a set of rays and distributed them to every slave for parallel calculation of intersections with each slave's subset of the patches. After the slaves returned their hits for each ray, the master computed form factors and updated radiosities. Speedup with this fine-grained approach was thwarted by both master processing bottlenecks and the overhead of inter-process communication, resulting in longer execution times with more processors.

There are several aspects of the hierarchical radiosity algorithm that make parallelization difficult. First, since two patches can interact at any level of their hierarchies, subcomputation times are highly variable making load balancing difficult. Second, since both shooter and receiver patches can be subdivided dynamically, reader/writer locks must be used to enforce concurrency control during updates, and deadlock avoidance/resolution must be considered. The computation required to manage concurrency control and deadlock during access to the element radiosity and mesh hierarchies can significantly reduce speedup results.

In summary, none of the previous parallel systems is fast or robust enough to compute an accurate radiosity solution for a very large building model because they suffer from at least one of the following shortcomings: 1) greater than $O(n)$ computational complexity, 2) replication of the entire model for each processor, 3) inaccuracies due to energy transfer or form factor approximations (e.g., hemi-cube artifacts), 4) limited speedup due to contention during access to shared data, and 5) communication overhead for process control.

In order to scale to very large models, a radiosity system must use an efficient matrix solution method, such as hierarchical radiosity. The algorithm must be partitioned into separate concurrent subcomputations that each access a small subset of the model. In order to scale to many processors, the separate subcomputations must read/write separate regions or copies of the model to avoid slowdowns due to contention. Finally, the granularity of parallelism must be coarse enough to allow execution with minimal overhead for communication between participating processors. The design and implementation of a parallel radiosity system meeting these criteria is the topic of this paper.

3 Group Iterative Methods

The radiosity method must solve a linear system of equations represented by the row-diagonally dominant interaction matrix shown in Figure 1. Group iterative methods partition the B_i variables into groups, and rather than just relaxing one variable at a time, they relax an entire group during a single step [13, 29]. Gauss-Seidel group iteration relaxes each group using current estimates for B_js from other groups, while Jacobi group iteration uses B_js from other groups updated at the end of the previous complete iteration through all groups.

$$\begin{bmatrix} 1-\rho_1 F_{11} & -\rho_1 F_{12} & \cdots & -\rho_1 F_{1n} \\ -\rho_2 F_{21} & 1-\rho_2 F_{22} & \cdots & -\rho_2 F_{2n} \\ \vdots & & & \vdots \\ -\rho_n F_{n1} & -\rho_n F_{n2} & \cdots & 1-\rho_n F_{nn} \end{bmatrix} \begin{bmatrix} B_1 \\ B_2 \\ \vdots \\ B_n \end{bmatrix} = \begin{bmatrix} E_1 \\ E_2 \\ \vdots \\ E_n \end{bmatrix}$$

Figure 1: The radiosity matrix equation.

Application of Jacobi group iteration in the radiosity domain can be interpreted as partitioning elements into groups, and then iteratively "gathering" radiosity to elements using current radiosities from elements in the same group and radiosities from the end of the previous complete iteration for elements in other groups. Elements within the same group bounce energy back and forth to convergence during each iteration, while elements in different groups exchange energy only once per iteration (see Figure 2).

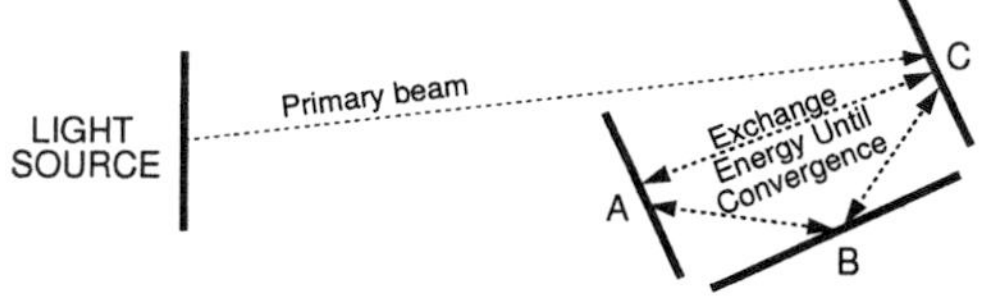

Figure 2: One relaxation step for group "ABC".

There are several advantages to the group iterative approach for large radiosity problems, particularly with regards to parallel processing. First, each group "gathering" step updates radiosities only for the elements in its group, which is advantageous for concurrency control when compared to "shooting" algorithms that update radiosities for all elements in each step [3]. Second, with Jacobi methods, updates to the radiosity values of elements in each group depend only upon radiosity values copied at the end of the previous iteration, and do not require access to current radiosity values for elements in all groups. This property allows multiple radiosity solvers to execute concurrently on different groups, with each solver updating a separate copy of the radiosity values without readers/writers contention. It then becomes practical to use efficient, yet complicated, radiosity algorithms, such as Hierarchical Radiosity [17], to solve each group subproblem. Finally, group methods exhibit better cache coherence than element-by-element methods [13] since links between patches in the same group can be reused several times as the group is solved to convergence. This feature is particularly important for radiosity problems whose form factor matrices do not fit in memory all at once.

In this paper, we describe the design and implementation of a radiosity system based on group iterative techniques that uses multiple concurrent hierarchical radiosity solvers. For each iteration, the system automatically partitions the patches describing a scene into groups and executes hierarchical radiosity solvers to compute converged radiosity solutions for separate groups on separate processors using separate versions of the model in parallel. Throughout the computation, updated versions of the element radiosities are copied into a master scene database for later use by other processors. Since hierarchical substructuring and form factor calculations are performed for different groups in parallel on the separate processors accessing separate copies of the model, we can accelerate overall computation times due to parallelism with little or no contention. Since coordination of processes is performed at a coarse-grained level (groups), relatively little communication is required between processes. As a result, significant speedups are possible for moderate numbers of processors. Furthermore, since each processor must store only the working set for computations for one group at a time, the approach scales to support very large models.

4 System Organization

Our system is organized in a Master-Slave configuration with one master and P slaves running concurrently on separate processors. The slaves are used to execute radiosity computations, while the master performs dynamic load balancing and data distribution. All processes maintain independent (partial) copies of the scene database, and slaves communicate with the master only via TCP messages. This organization allows distribution across loosely-coupled workstations without shared memory, or even shared disks.

4.1 Flow of Control

The flow of control between the master and slave processes is shown in Figure 3. The master iteratively relaxes groups until convergence. For each "master iteration," the master partitions patches of the scene database into groups, and then dynamically distributes the groups to slaves one at a time for group relaxation computations. These automatic partitioning and scheduling algorithms are the focus of this paper, and are described in detail in the following section. This section describes the organization of the system in which these algorithms execute.

The master starts by spawning P slave processes (usually on remote computers) and opens a TCP socket connection to each of them. It uses the `select` UNIX system call to detect messages from multiple slaves. Whenever a slave, S_i, indicates it is ready, the master selects a group, G, from a list of candidate groups waiting to be processed during the current master iteration. Next, it downloads to S_i all patches potentially visible to any patch in group G (i.e., the "working set" for G). After the downloads have completed, the master sends slave S_i a message indicating that it can begin its radiosity computations for group G. While S_i relaxes group G to convergence, the master continues servicing other slaves. After slave S_i finishes its computation, it sends updated radiosity values back to the master for use in the current or future iterations.

Each slave runs asynchronously on a separate processor under the guidance of the master process as shown on the right side of Figure 3. When a slave receives a *download* message from the master, it updates its local copy of the patches it receives, waits for a *compute* message from the master, and then invokes a hierarchical radiosity solver to gather radiosity to all patches in group G until convergence.

The radiosity solver is based on the hierarchical (wavelet) radiosity system described in [15, 17, 27]. Although its de-

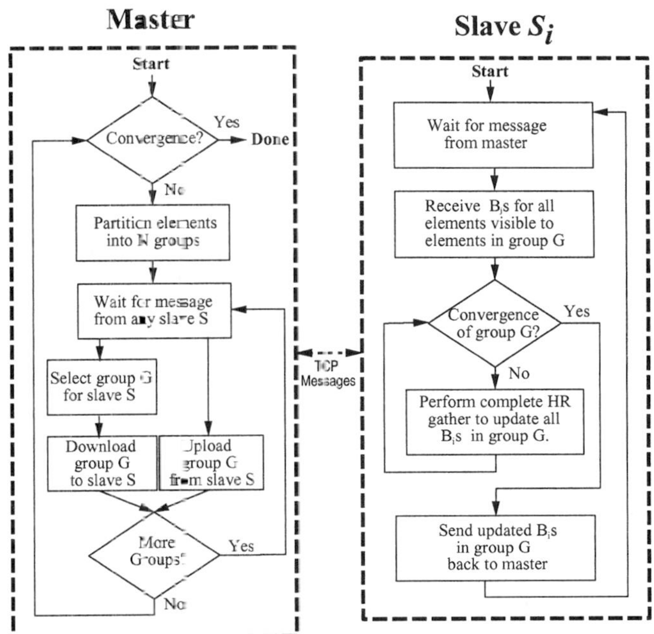

Figure 3: Master-slave flow of execution.

tails are not the focus of this paper, it is important to note that it stores its evolving solution in a disk-resident database and loads into memory only the data required for the current subcomputation. It manages a fixed size, memory-resident, LRU cache to store the most recently used elements and links (form factors) in hopes that they will be used again before they are discarded. As computation of the form factors is the most costly component of the system execution, effective management of this cache is critical to avoiding costly recomputation or re-loading from disk. This feature of the slave solver is advantageous for the group iterative approach. Since gathers are performed multiple times to the elements of the same group in succession, the group algorithms exhibit far greater cache coherency, and in our case, we are often able to re-use links computed for two elements multiple times before they are discarded from the cache. In contrast, effective cache management would be very difficult with classical gather algorithms that make successive sweeps over all patches in the entire database.

After the radiosity computation for group G has been completed, the slave writes into its local cache updated versions of all patches in G, including the refined hierarchical element meshes and radiosities for each patch, and sends to the master an *upload* message containing a packed representation of these patches. This updated version of G is merged into the master scene database and can potentially be downloaded to other slaves for later computations.

Note that communication between master and slave occurs only three times for each group iteration: 1) to download patches to the slave at the beginning of an iteration, 2) to invoke a radiosity computation, and 3) to upload patches from the slave at the end of an iteration. This coarse-grained approach to parallelism is important. Other efforts to parallelize the radiosity method with a master-slave organization have found master processing to be a bottleneck, and communication overhead has diminished speedup results significantly using relatively few slave processors. Our strategy is to design a system in which a master coordinates execution of the slaves, but at a very coarse granularity, with very infrequent communication.

4.2 Data Distribution

The scene description is initially available only to the master. It is stored in a database containing patches represented by quad-trees of elements with diffuse reflectivity, radiosity, and emission attributes. The patches are stored in the scene database arranged in clusters specified by the modeler at scene creation time. The scene database also contains precomputed cluster-to-cluster visibility information. The cluster visibility calculation is performed off-line using the algorithms described in [26] and generates a list for each cluster indicating which other clusters are potentially visible to it – i.e., not occluded by a wall, ceiling, or floor. Although clustering and visibility techniques are an important research area, and essential to the efficient execution of our radiosity system, these topics are not addressed in this paper. See [21, 22, 24, 26] for further information.

Since only the master has access to the complete scene database, it must download portions of the database (i.e., potential working sets) to slaves during execution. We define the potential working set for a group G to be all the patches, including their element meshes and radiosities, that are visible to any patch in G. This definition of the working set is a conservative over-estimate of the set of data the slave may need access to during radiosity gather operations for any group. Since patches in occluded clusters cannot exchange energy directly, we can use the precomputed cluster-to-cluster visibility information of the scene database to compute the potential working set efficiently.

During execution, the master keeps an index of which clusters have already been downloaded to each slave. It traverses the cluster-to-cluster visibility lists for all clusters containing patches in group G, checking whether the potentially visible cluster, C, is already up-to-date on the slave, S_i. If not, it reads from the disk-resident scene database all the data describing patches in C, including the hierarchical mesh of elements with radiosities. It packs this data into a buffer and performs a write to the TCP socket for slave S_i. Finally, it marks slave S_i up-to-date for cluster C in its index, and continues checking for other potentially visible clusters to download. Note that all patches of a cluster are required to be in the same group, making this download processing somewhat more efficient. After all clusters in the working set of G are up-to-date on slave S_i, the master sends a short message indicating which clusters belong to group G, and directing it to gather radiosity to all patches in those clusters to convergence.

After the slave has updated the radiosities for all patches in group G to convergence, it sends an upload message to the master with complete updates for every cluster C in group G. The master writes these updates back to a new version of cluster C in its disk-resident database. It then marks clusters in G out-of-date for all slaves except S_i, causing them to be freshly downloaded for subsequent gather operations for clusters visible to G. With this concurrent "copy-update-replace methodology," our system does not truly execute either the Jacobi group or Gauss-Seidel group iterative method, as it is indeterminate whether the old or updated copies of a group's variables will be used during each group relaxation step. Proof of convergence with this optimization is shown in the following section.

The data distribution features of our system are important for scaling to support computations with very large models. The master stores only the scene database header information in main memory (generally less than 20MB), while the clusters, patches, and elements reside on disk. Each slave receives and stores only the subset of the scene database required for its computation, avoiding full replication of the entire database on any processor as is required by most other parallel radiosity systems.

4.3 Convergence Proof

Proof of convergence of our parallel group iterative method can be shown by comparison to the standard sequential group Jacobi method, which is known to converge [29]. Consider splitting the matrix A (as in $Ax = b$) into $A = D-L-U$ where D has blocks along the diagonal, L has the opposites of element below D, and U has opposites of elements above D. For the radiosity equation, A is monotone (i.e., it has non-negative elements along the diagonal and non-positive elements elsewhere), D is monotone, $L \geq 0$, and $U \geq 0$.

The standard group Jacobi method iterates according to the following equation:

$$x_{k+1} = I_J x_k + D^{-1} b$$
$$where\ I_J = D^{-1}(L+U)$$

whereas our modified group method iterates using some variables updated in the current iteration and some updated in the previous iteration:

$$x_{k+1} = I_M x_k + (D - L_1^k)^{-1} b$$
$$where\ I_M = (D - L_1^k)^{-1}(L_2^k + U),$$
$$L = L_1^k + L_2^k, L_1^k \geq 0,\ and\ L_2^k \geq 0$$

We can show that our modified group method converges if the error is reduced during each iteration. Since

$$\frac{||x_{k+1} - x||}{||x_k - x||} \approx \rho(I_M)$$

where $\frac{||x_{k+1}-x||}{||x_k - x||}$ is a suitable vector norm, and $\rho(I_M)$ is the spectral radius of I_M, convergence is guaranteed if $\rho(I_M) \leq \rho(I_J) < 1$. We prove $\rho(I_M) \leq \rho(I_J)$ using corollary 5.6 on page 125 of Young [29]:

> "Let A be a monotone matrix and let $A = Q_1 - R_1$ and $A = Q_2 - R_2$ be two regular splittings of A. If $R_2 \leq R_1$, then $\rho(Q_2^{-1}R_2) \leq \rho(Q_1^{-1}R_1)$."

A regular splitting of A is one in which $A = Q - R$ where $Q^{-1} \geq 0$ and $R \geq 0$. For the standard group Jacobi iteration method, let $A = Q_1 - R_1$ where $Q_1 = D$ and $R_1 = L + U$. Note that $Q_1^{-1} \geq 0$ since D is monotone and $R_1 \geq 0$ since $L \geq 0$ and $U \geq 0$. For our modified group iteration method, let $A = Q_2 - R_2$ where $Q_2 = D - L_1^k$ and $R_2 = L_2^k + U$. Note that $Q_2^{-1} \geq 0$ since $D - L_1^k$ is monotone. Also note that $R_2 \geq 0$ since $L_2^k \geq 0$ and $U \geq 0$, and $R_2 \leq R_1$ since $L \geq L_2^k$.

Applying corollary 5.6 and convergence of the standard group Jacobi method, we see that $\rho(I_M) < 1$ and the modified group iterative method must converge:

$$\rho(I_M) = \rho(Q_2^{-1}R_2) \leq \rho(Q_1^{-1}R_1) = \rho(I_J) < 1$$

5 Parallel Programming

A general strategy for parallel programming is to decompose a computation into a set of independent subcomputations, and then to distribute the subcomputations for execution in parallel on available processors. The important issues are to find an appropriate decomposition (i.e., partition patches into groups), and to schedule execution of the subcomputations effectively (i.e., load balancing). These issues are addressed in detail in this section.

5.1 Group Partitioning

Goals and Strategies

Based on intuition derived from experimentation with our system, we have developed the following set of guidelines that constrain our automatic partitioning algorithms: 1) the number of groups, N, should be bounded from below so that there are guaranteed to be enough groups to schedule effectively on P slave processors (e.g., $N > 8P$); 2) each group should be large enough that the time required to distribute its computation to a slave is not more than it would have been to perform it locally on the master; and 3) each group should be small enough that the links for radiosity updates to all elements in the group fit in a slave's memory-resident cache so that they may be re-used over and over again without recomputation as the group is solved to convergence. We combine these constraints with the goals of maximizing intra-group form factors while minimizing inter-group form factors to form the basis of our partitioning algorithms.

For practical purposes, we consider only partitionings in which all patches of a cluster are assigned to the same group. This restriction simplifies the partitioning algorithms, and aids execution of the data distribution algorithms during execution of our radiosity system, as described in the previous section.

Conceptually, we address the cluster partitioning problem as a computation on a *form factor graph* in which each node in the graph represents a cluster, and each edge represents an estimate of the form factor between its nodes' clusters (a simple form factor graph is shown in Figure 4). With this formulation, we state the cluster partitioning problem as follows: assign nodes of the form factor graph to groups such that the cumulative weight of edges between nodes in the same group divided by the cumulative weight of all edges is maximal.

Unfortunately, this problem is equivalent to the Graph Bisection Problem [12], which is known to be NP-complete. However, we have developed two automatic algorithms that find approximate and useful solutions in polynomial time. The first algorithm, called the *Merge Algorithm*, starts by assigning each cluster to a separate group and then iteratively merges groups. Conversely, the second algorithm, called the *Split Algorithm*, starts by assigning all clusters to the same group and then recursively splits groups. Either algorithm can be used to construct groups, or the algorithms can be applied successively to iteratively refine groups.

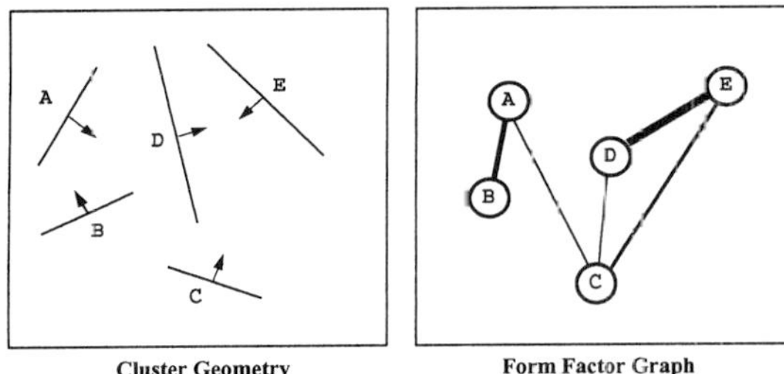

Figure 4: Simple scene (left) with its form factor graph (right). Edge thickness represents form factor magnitude.

Merge Algorithm

The *Merge Algorithm* operates on an augmented version of the form factor graph in which nodes represent groups rather than clusters. In this augmented graph, the edge between two nodes representing groups A and B has weight equal to the sum of the form factors between all combinations of clusters in groups A and B. Initially, a graph is created with one node for each cluster. For the purposes of constructing this graph, an edge weight is set to zero (or the edge is not created at all) if two clusters are known to be occluded from one another (as determined by a lookup in the precomputed cluster-to-cluster visibility information stored in the scene database). Otherwise, the form factor, F_{AB}, from one cluster A to another cluster B is estimated as the solid angle subtended by a disk representing cluster B [28]:

$$F_{AB} = r^2/(d^2 + r^2) \tag{2}$$

where d is the distance between A and B, and r is the radius of a sphere bounding B. This approximation is an over-estimate that does not consider individual patch orientations and assumes that A is entirely visible to B.

Once the form factor graph has been constructed, the Merge Algorithm iteratively merges groups (nodes of the graph) until no further combinations are possible within the following constraints: 1) the number of groups is greater than a user specified minimum, *MinGroups*, and 2) the estimated number of links for any group with more than one cluster is below a user specified maximum, *MaxLinks*. By default, *MaxLinks* is arbitrarily set to be $1.25 * TotalLinks/MinGroups$, where *TotalLinks* is the sum of the link estimates for all groups.

The key challenge for implementation of the Merge Algorithm is selecting two appropriate groups to merge during each step of the algorithm. We take a greedy approach. The pair of groups, A and B, is chosen whose merger causes the greatest increase in the ratio of intra-group edge weights divided by the total of all edge weights. If the merger of these groups meets all constraints, they are combined into one. During the merge operation, edges from A and B to other nodes are replaced by ones to the new merged node. The weight of this new edge is the sum of the weights of the edges it replaces (see Figure 5). The algorithm repeatedly merges groups until it can no longer find any pair of groups to merge legally, or the solution cannot be improved. In the worst case, when all clusters are visible to one another, the algorithm is bounded by $O(N^2 logN)$. However, in situations such as building interiors, where visibility sets are usually of constant size, the average execution time for the merge algorithm is $O(N logN)$.

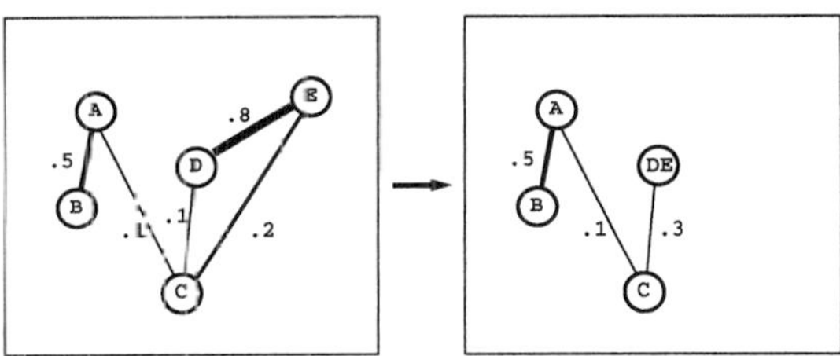

Figure 5: Merge operation for nodes 'D' and 'E'.

Split Algorithm

The *Split Algorithm* uses a strategy that is the converse of the Merge Algorithm. It starts with all clusters assigned to a single group and then recursively splits groups until further splits do not improve the solution. This algorithm can be interpreted as a recursive binary partitioning of the form factor graph.

During each step of the algorithm, our goal is to choose an appropriate partition of one group into two new ones that meet all size constraints and have minimal inter-group form factors. We use geometric split heuristics originally developed for construction of spatial subdivisions for use in visibility determination (e.g., BSP trees [18]). Specifically, we partition the model along planes aligned with "major occluding" polygons of the model (see [25] for details). As the model is split recursively by these planes, clusters are assigned to groups depending on whether their centroid lies above or below the splitting plane (see Figure 6). This process is applied recursively until no groups can be split within minimum group size constraints, or until no further "major occluder" polygons can be found. The algorithm runs in $O(NlogN)$. If split planes are chosen appropriately (i.e., such that the cumulative form factors between clusters on separate sides of the plane are small), it generates a partitioning with little exchange of energy between groups during a radiosity simulation.

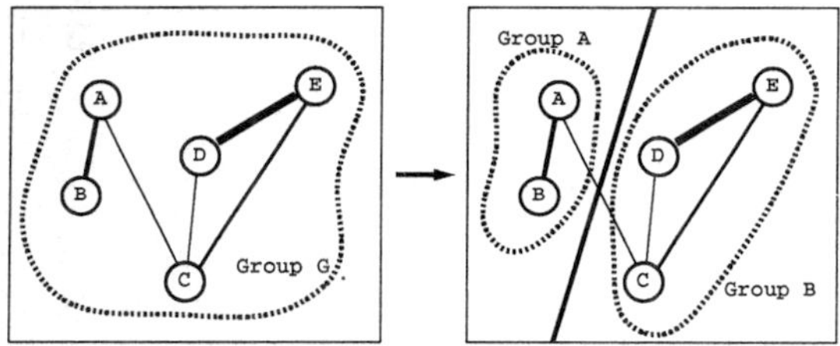

Figure 6: Split operation creating groups 'A' and 'B'.

Figure 7 shows two sets of 16 groups constructed using the Merge and Split algorithms, respectively, for a one floor building model comprising 1667 clusters. (clusters are shaded based upon which group they were assigned). Using the Merge algorithm, groups tend to be formed from clusters that are visible to each other (e.g., offices across hallways), whereas groups tend to be formed from clusters that are nearby each other using the Split algorithm (e.g., neighboring offices).

Merge Algorithm Split Algorithm

Figure 7: Groups formed by the merge and split algorithms.

5.2 Scheduling

Load balancing is a primary concern in any parallel system. Our goal is to schedule group radiosity subcomputations on slaves in a manner that maximizes the rate of convergence to an overall solution. Unfortunately, this *Multi-Processor Scheduling Problem* is NP-Complete since each subcomputation is non-preemptable, task execution times are highly variable, and workstations may have different performance capabilities [11]. In this section, we describe our approximation algorithms for scheduling and load balancing.

First-Fit Decreasing Algorithm

A common scheduling strategy for minimizing the total completion time for a set of tasks run on multiple processors is to select tasks in order of their expected execution times, largest to smallest. This strategy is called the *First Fit Decreasing* (FFD) algorithm [11]. The idea is to schedule the large tasks first so that there is less chance that their execution times will extend beyond the last execution time of any other task.

We have applied this principal in our radiosity system. The difficult challenge is to predict in advance how long a radiosity computation for a group will take. We estimate the relative compute time for a transfer of radiosity from one cluster A to another cluster B by F_{AB}. This estimate is based on the observation that slave compute times are dictated by the number link evaluations (ray-patch intersections), which is determined by the errors in computed element-element form factor estimates, which in turn are roughly correlated to form-factors. In order to estimate the computation time for gathers to a group of clusters, G, we sum estimated computation times for all cluster pairs in which at least one of the two clusters is in G, and the clusters are known to be at least partially visible to one another via the form factor graph.

To execute the FFD algorithm, the master sorts groups according to computation time estimates as they are constructed. Then, groups are simply assigned in FFD order as slaves become available during execution.

Working Set Algorithm

The general principal of minimizing total completion time for a set of independent subcomputations is not enough to guarantee a fast convergence rate for our radiosity system. We must also consider factors affecting data download performance, duplicate calculation, and energy distribution. These issues are particularly important because each slave maintains a local cache of data containing element radiosities and links previously computed. The history of which groups a slave has previously processed affects the download time and the energy distribution rate for the current computation. These issues are likely even more important for a system utilizing bi-directional links (our system creates uni-directional links) in which case re-use of inter-group links could be a significant scheduling consideration.

We have developed a dynamic scheduling algorithm that considers data download factors when scheduling group computations on slaves. The *Working Set* (WS) algorithm uses a heuristic that is designed to assign groups to slaves for which their working set has already been downloaded. Each time a slave S_i becomes available, it considers groups remaining to be processed during this iteration. For each candidate group, G, it computes the percentage of the clusters visible to any cluster in G that are already resident on S_i. It then subtracts from this value the percentage of clusters visible to G that are not resident on S_i, but are resident on some other slave. This latter factor helps to keep the visibility sets of groups assigned to different slaves separated. The difference between these two percentages forms the heuristic that the Working Set algorithm uses to choose the best group for each slave dynamically as the system executes.

Combined Scheduling Algorithm

The methodologies of the FFD and WS algorithms can be combined. We generally use a combined scheduling algorithm (FFD-WS) that dynamically chooses a group as each slave becomes available according to the WS heuristic subject to the constraint that every group must be scheduled within "*delta*" slots of its position in FFD order. This algorithm is equivalent to the FFD algorithm if $delta = 1$, and it is equivalent to the WS algorithm if $delta = \infty$. Otherwise, if $1 < delta < N$, we hope to realize the advantages of both the FFD and WS approaches.

6 Results and Discussion

In order to test the effectiveness of the group iterative approach for solving large radiosity problems in parallel, we executed a series of experiments with our system using different group partitioning and load balancing algorithms. During these experiments, we used up to eight Silicon Graphics slave workstations, each with a 150MHz R4400 processor and at least 80MB of available memory, 32MB of which was available for caching links. The workstations were spread over two separate local area networks and did not share disk files. Unless stated otherwise, the *Merge Algorithm* was used to construct 256 groups, and the *FFD-WS* algorithm was used with $delta = 16$ for dynamic load balancing. In all experiments except the one described in Section 6.1, the master process performed two complete iterations in which a slave gathered to every patch in each group twice with a moderately fine error tolerance. During the initial slave iteration, patches gathered radiosity only from the lights.

Our test model in every experiment was the computation of a radiosity solution for one unfurnished floor of the Soda Hall building model. This test model contained 6,418 patches in 1,667 clusters, 242 of which contained only emissive patches. The total area of all surfaces was 10,425,645 square inches. Although this test model was not particularly complex, it was useful for experimentation. With a larger model, it would have been impractical for us to investigate algorithmic trade-offs by performing many executions of the radiosity solver with different parameters.

6.1 Group Iteration Results

We first compared the performance of the group iterative method to traditional iterative methods (independent of parallel processing) by computing the radiosity solution for our test model using a single processor both with and without grouping of patches. During the first test, patches were not grouped, and 4 traditional Gauss-Seidel iterations were made over all patches. During the second test, patches were partitioned into 256 groups by the Merge algorithm. Then, three Gauss-Seidel group iterations were made over all groups, during which every patch in a group gathered radiosity twice (groups were not solved to full convergence during each step). During the test without grouping, every patch gathered radiosity from every other patch four times. In contrast, during the test with grouping, patches gathered radiosity six times from patches within the same group, but only three times from patches in other groups. Plots of transfer rates measured during these tests are shown in Figure 8. Circles on the plots indicate the end of a compete sweep through all variables in each test.

Even without parallel processing, the group iterative method out-performed the traditional approach during this experiment. The performance difference was mostly due to the fact that the group method more effectively made use of links and patches cached in memory by the solver. As described in Section 4, the solver maintained LRU memory

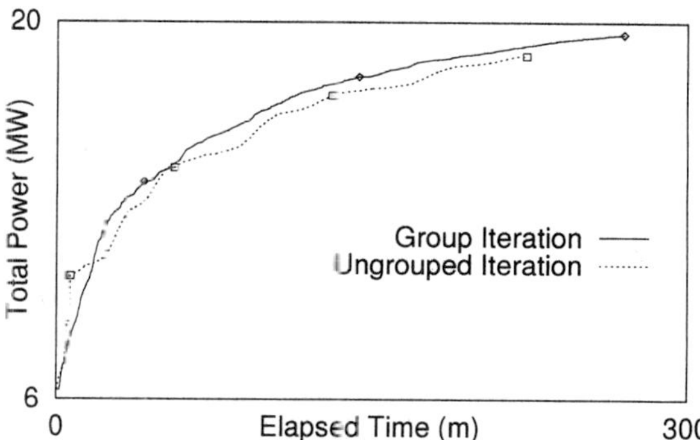

Figure 8: Transfer rates for grouped/ungrouped iteration.

resident caches of links and patches. Patches that did not fit in the cache had to be flushed to disk, while links that did not fit in the cache were discarded and later recomputed. During this experiment, although the total amount of storage required for links exceeded the cache limit (32MB), the maximum working set for any group did not. As a result, since the group method cycled over patches in each group multiple times in succession, it was often able to re-use previously computed links (45% of the time). In contrast, the traditional method executed a worst-case access pattern for the LRU cache, making complete sweeps through all patches in succession, and thus was not able to re-use any links.

6.2 Partitioning Results

We next studied the effects of different group partitioning algorithms by executing a sequence of tests with 8 slaves using the following methods to partition clusters into 256 groups:

- **Merge:** Groups were constructed using the Merge Algorithm with $MinGroups = 256$.
- **Split:** Groups were constructed using the Split Algorithm partitioning on floors, ceilings, and walls of the building model with $MaxGroups = 256$.
- **Region:** Clusters were assigned to groups based on the (x,y) coordinates of their centroids in a 16x16 grid.
- **Random:** Clusters were assigned to groups randomly.

Figure 9 contains plots of transfer rates measured during these tests. The system converged fastest using partitions generated automatically with the Merge and Split Algorithms. This is due to the fact that these algorithms combined clusters into the same group based on estimated form factor and proximity relationships. During every test, each patch gathered radiosity a total of four times – two iterations in a slave for each of two master iterations. This

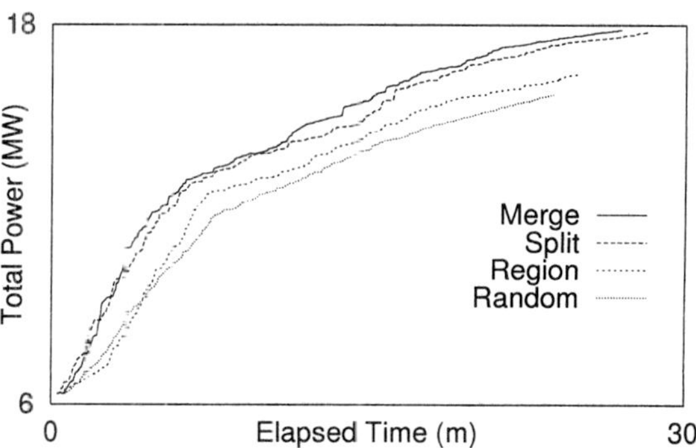

Figure 9: Transfer rates for different partitioning algorithms.

means that energy was distributed with four reflections between clusters in the same group, while only two reflections occurred between clusters in different groups. As expected, the performance of the group iterative approach was better using partitions with larger intra-group form factors.

6.3 Granularity Results

We studied the effects of group granularity by measuring system performance using 8 slaves for tests with groups of different sizes. Using the Merge Algorithm, we executed tests with the clusters partitioned into 32, 128, 256, and 1,425 groups. The test with 1425 groups represents construction of a separate group for each cluster containing at least one reflective patch.

Plots of transfer rates measured in each test appear in Figure 10. We found that the advantage of the group iterative method is reduced if groups are very small since there is little opportunity to re-use links computed for intra-group radiosity transfers. On the other hand, if we used just a few large groups, the data required for all intra-group links exceeded a slave's cache capacity for some groups, reducing the effectiveness of the cache. Also, it was more difficult to schedule a relatively few, large subcomputations across available slave processors in order to achieve the best possible completion times. During our experiments, tests performed best with 256 groups that roughly corresponded to the small, convex regions of the model. This result depends on a variety of factors, including the size of link caches in slaves and the variability of group sizes.

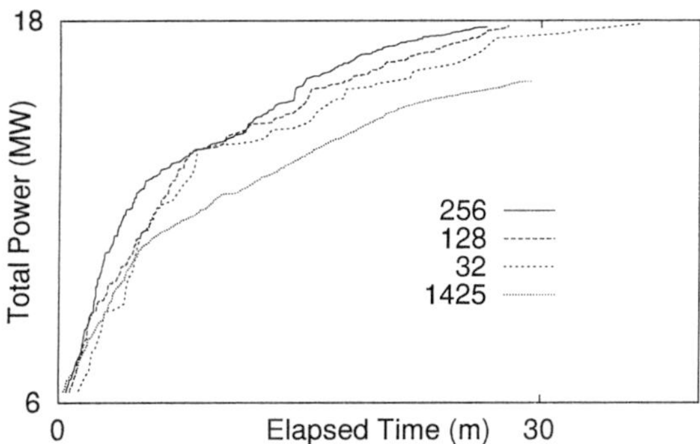

Figure 10: Transfer rates for different group granularities.

6.4 Scheduling Results

We investigated load balancing and scheduling effects by executing a series of tests using 8 slaves with different scheduling algorithms:

- **FFD:** Groups were assigned to slaves in FFD order.
- **WS:** Groups were assigned to available slaves dynamically to minimize the WS heuristic.
- **FFD-WS:** Groups were assigned to slaves dynamically using the FFD-WS algorithm with *delta* = 16.

From statistics measured during these tests, we found that the scheduling factors impacting convergence rates most were: 1) master-slave download times, and 2) slave idle times (particularly at the end of each iteration). As expected, the master spent the least amount of time downloading data to slaves during tests using the WS algorithm (98 seconds). The advantages of the WS approach can be seen in Figure 11, in which all 256 groups are shaded according to which of the 8 slaves they were assigned during tests using the FFD and WS algorithms. The coherence of the working sets assigned to slaves using the WS algorithm allows the system to minimize data downloads and maximize energy transfers.

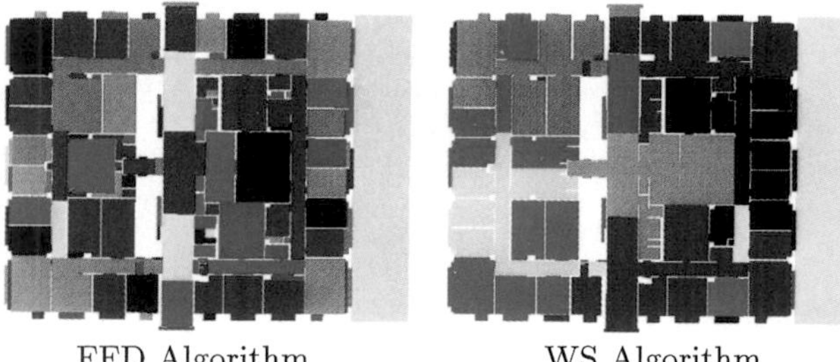

Figure 11: Visualization with groups shaded by slave.

Unfortunately, the test using the WS algorithm also spent the most amount of time waiting for the last slave to finish at the end of each iteration (547 seconds). In particular, one very large group computation was postponed until the very end of the second iteration, causing the master and seven of the slaves to sit idling while the eighth slave finished its computation for that group. In contrast, the FFD algorithm spent a small amount of time waiting for the last slave at the end of each iteration (13 seconds), but it spent the most time downloading data to slaves (248 seconds).

The trade-offs between scheduling to minimize downloads and scheduling to minimize time waiting for the last slave can be seen in Figure 12, which shows a vertical elapsed time-line for each of the 8 slaves during tests with the FFD, WS, and FFD-WS algorithms. Every distinct vertical bar segment represents radiosity computation for one group on one slave. Using the FFD algorithm, the execution time predictor does fairly well, and longer tasks are generally scheduled earlier in each iteration (the first of the two master iterations ends approximately 1/3rd of the way up the time-line). However, because the master spends more time downloading data to slaves (synchronously), there are more frequent and longer periods during which a slave is waiting for the master (blank spaces between vertical bars). Using the WS algorithm, although download times are far less (intra-bar gaps are smaller), the computation for one very large group was scheduled near the end of iteration 2 (on Slave 2) causing the master and all other slaves to wait for it to complete. The combined FFD-WS algorithm seemed to achieve a good combination of download times (191 seconds) and wait times (8 seconds), and thus converged most rapidly.

Figure 12: Slave compute time (solid) vs. wait time (blank).

6.5 Speedup Results

Finally, we executed an experiment to determine how much speedup is possible with our system via parallel processing. During this experiment, we solved the one floor test model four times using 1, 2, 4, and 8 slaves, respectively. A plot of speedup for increasing numbers of slave processes is shown in Figure 13.

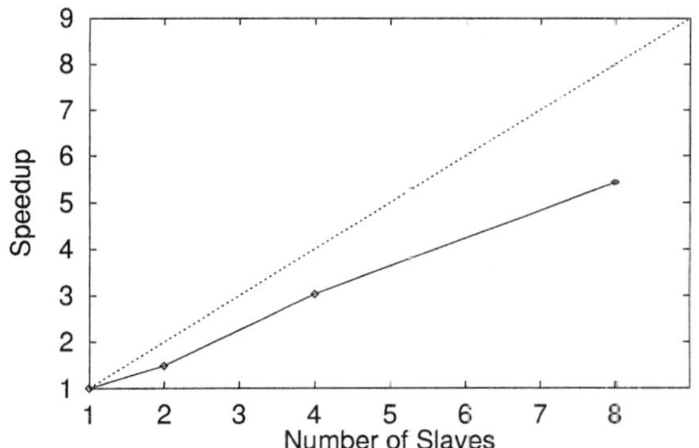

Figure 13: Transfer rate speedup for 1, 2, 4, and 8 slaves.

For up to 8 slave processors, the system maintains a 65-75% speedup. The speedup is less than 100% due to the synchronous master-slave communication model of our system. Although the group iterative approach provides a relatively coarse granularity of parallelism, the master communicates with slaves synchronously in our current implementation – i.e., it can only talk to one slave at a time. As a result, if two slaves finish a subcomputation and become ready for further processing at the same time, one must wait while the master exchanges data with the other. The impact of this effect is determined by the likelihood that a slave will finish a subcomputation while the master is processing data for another slave. Although this likelihood grows with the number of slaves, it is also affected by the relationship of time required for master processing of downloads/uploads versus the time required for slave processing of a group radiosity subcomputation. For solutions in which the slave radiosity subcomputations are longer relative to the data distribution times, speedup results are better.

The speedup bottleneck resulting from our current synchronous communication model with a centralized master can be mitigated somewhat by enhancing the master to use asynchronous I/O protocols or by switching to communication protocols in which slaves transfer data among themselves under master coordination. Based on our preliminary results, we are optimistic that the group iterative approach provides coarse enough granularity that our master-slave system can scale to large numbers of slave processors with the addition of enhanced communication methods. Unfortunately, we have not yet implemented these improvements, and do not currently have access to enough workstations to determine the absolute limits of our current system.

The speedup experiments point out an interesting trade-off of our parallel group iterative approach. On one hand, when more slaves compute concurrently, we are able to evaluate more element interactions in less time. On the other hand, since updated radiosity values are distributed from the master to a slave workstations only after they have been uploaded from other slaves, Gauss-Seidel group iteration is achieved only during tests with one slave. In contrast, if all groups were scheduled simultaneously on different slaves, the system would perform a true Jacobi group iteration. As more slaves are added to the system, the system more closely resembles Jacobi iteration since more and more computations are performed with copies of radiosity values last updated at the end of the previous iteration. Further research is required to investigate the impact of this effect.

6.6 Practical Results

As a final test, we computed a radiosity solution for a very large model using the system described in this paper. The model represents five floors of a large building with approximately 250 rooms containing furniture. It was constructed with 14,234 clusters comprising 280,836 patches, 8,542 of which were emitters and served as the only light sources. The total area of all surfaces was 75,946,664 square inches. Three complete iterations were made through all patches using an average of 4.96 slave processors in 168 hours. The entire computation generated 7,649,958 mesh elements and evaluated 374,845,618 element-to-element links.

During this execution, the master spent 0.8% of its time constructing and scheduling groups, 4.4% downloading data to slaves, 2.5% uploading results from slaves, and 89.0% waiting for slaves. The slaves spent 0.1% of its time downloading data from the master, 0.1% uploading results to the master, 79.1% updating radiosities, and 5.0% waiting for the master. Although it was not practical for us to solve this model using a single processor for comparison, we estimate the speedup due to parallelism as the time spent performing radiosity computations in slaves divided by the elapsed time, which was 3.9 in this case, or 79% of linear speedup.

Figure 14 shows renderings of this large radiosity solution from various viewpoints captured during an interactive walkthrough. Outlines around mesh elements are included in the bottom-right image for detailed inspection. Note the adaptive refinement of elements in areas of partial visibility (e.g., on the floor near the legs of tables and chairs) due to hierarchical radiosity meshing. To the author's knowledge, this model is the most complex for which a radiosity solution has ever been computed.

7 Conclusion

This paper describes a system for computing radiosity solutions for very large polygonal models using multiple concurrent processes. A master process automatically partitions the input model into groups of patches and dynamically schedules slave processes which execute independent hierarchical radiosity solvers to update the radiosities of patches in separate groups. During experiments with this system, uniprocessor group methods out-performed traditional methods due to improved cache coherence, while multi-processor group methods achieved further speedups of 65-75% using up to 8 slave workstations.

We have found that the implementation and analysis of a distributed approach to the radiosity problem requires careful consideration of group partitioning, data distribution, and load balancing issues. Coarse-grained parallel execution using multiple separate copies of a shared database allows multiple processors to execute concurrently with little contention or synchronization overhead. However, since updates to the shared database are executed with coarse granularity, many of the subcomputations may be performed using out-of-date database values, potentially reducing the convergence rate.

The conflicting goals between computing in parallel versus computing with the most up-to-date data results in an

Figure 14: Images captured during an interactive walk through one large radiosity solution.

interesting trade-off whose resolution is affected by a multitude of factors, including the size of workstation memories, the size of working sets, the speed of the network, and so on. We believe that examining issues in parallel execution for large computations distributed over a network is an interesting research area that will become more and more important as networked computing resources become more and more prevalent.

Acknowledgements

The author thanks Roland Freund and Wim Sweldens for developing the convergence proof appearing in this paper. I am also grateful to Pat Hanrahan, Peter Schroder, and Stephen Gortler for their helpful insights and discussion, and to Seth Teller and Celeste Fowler for their efforts building the original radiosity system at Princeton. Finally, special thanks to Carlo Séquin and the UC Berkeley Building Walkthrough Group for building the model of Soda Hall and for getting me started on this research project.

References

[1] Baum, D., and Winget, J. Real Time Radiosity Through Parallel Processing and Hardware Acceleration. Computer Graphics (1990 Symposium on Interactive 3D Graphics), 24, 2, 67-75.

[2] Bouatouch, K., and Priol, T. Data Management Scheme for Parallel Radiosity. Computer-Aided Design, 26, 12, December, 1994, 876-883.

[3] Chalmers, A, and Paddon, D. Parallel Processing of Progressive Refinement Radiosity Methods. Second Eurographics Workshop on Rendering, Barcelona, Spain, May, 1991.

[4] Chen, S.E. A Progressive Radiosity Method and its Implementation in a Distributed Processing Environment. Master's Thesis, Cornell University, 1989.

[5] Cohen, M., Greenberg, D., Immel, D., and Brock, P. An Efficient Radiosity Approach for Realistic Image Synthesis. IEEE Computer Graphics and Applications, 6, 3 (March, 1986), 25-35.

[6] Cohen, M., Chen, S., Wallace, J., and Greenberg, D. A Progressive Refinement Approach to Fast Radiosity Image Generation. Computer Graphics (Proc. SIGGRAPH '88), 22, 4, 75-84.

[7] Drettakis, G., Fiume, E., and Fournier, A. Tightly-Coupled Multi-Processing for a Global Illumination Algorithm. EUROGRAPHICS '90, Montreux, Switzerland, 1990.

[8] Drucker, S., and Schroder, P. Fast Radiosity Using a Data Parallel Architecture. Third Eurographics Workshop on Rendering, 1992.

[9] Feda, M., and Purgathofer, W. Progressive Refinement Radiosity on a Transputer Network. Second Eurographics Workshop on Rendering, 1991, 139-148.

[10] Feda, M., and Purgathofer, W. Progressive Ray Refinement for Monte Carlo Radiosity. Fourth Eurographics Workshop on Rendering, 1993, 15-25.

[11] Garey, M., and Johnson, D. Computers and Intractability: A Guide to the Theory of NP-Completeness. W.H. Freeman and Company, New York, 1979.

[12] Guattery, S., and Miller, G. On the Performance of Spectral Graph Partitioning Methods. 1995 ACM-SIAM Symposium on Discrete Algorithms (SODA), 1995.

[13] Golub, G., and Van Loan, C. Matrix Computations. John Hopkins University Press, Baltimore, MD, 2nd Edition, 1989.

[14] Goral, C., Torrance, K., Greenberg, D., and Battaile, B. Modeling the Interaction of Light Between Diffuse Surfaces. Computer Graphics (Proc. SIGGRAPH '84), 18, 3, 213-222.

[15] Gortler, S., Schroder, P., Cohen, M., and Hanrahan, P. Wavelet Radiosity. Computer Graphics (Proc. SIGGRAPH '93), 221-230.

[16] Guitton, P., Roman, J., and Subrenat, G. Implementation Results and Analysis of a Parallel Progressive Radiosity. In 1995 Parallel Rendering Symposium, Atlanta, Georgia, October, 1995, 31-37.

[17] Hanrahan, P., and Salzman, D. A Rapid Hierarchical Radiosity Algorithm. Computer Graphics (Proc. SIGGRAPH '91), 25, 4, 197-206.

[18] Naylor, B. Constructing Good Partitioning Trees. Graphics Interface '93. Toronto, CA, May, 1993, 181-191.

[19] Paddon, D., and Chalmers, A. Parallel Processing of the Radiosity Method. Computer-Aided Design, 26, 12, December, 1994, 917-927.

[20] Recker, R., George, D., and Greenberg, D. Acceleration Techniques for Progressive Refinement Radiosity. Computer Graphics (1990 Symposium on Interactive 3D Graphics), 24, 2, 59-66.

[21] Rushmeier, H., Patterson, C., and Veerasamy, A. Geometric Simplification for Indirect Illumination Calculations. Graphics Interface '93, May, 1993, 227-236.

[22] Sillion, F. A Unified Hierarchical Algorithm for Global Illumination with Scattering Volumes and Object Clusters. IEEE Transactions on Visualization and Computer Graphics, I, 3, September, 1995.

[23] Singh, J.P., Gupta, A. and Levoy, M. Parallel Visualization Algorithms: Performance and Architectural Implications. IEEE Computer, 27, 7 (July 1994), 45-55.

[24] Smits, B., Arvo, J., and Greenberg, D. A Clustering Algorithm for Radiosity in Complex Environments. Computer Graphics (Proc. SIGGRAPH '94), 435-442.

[25] Teller, S., Visibility Computations in Densely Occluded Polyhedral Environments. Ph.D. thesis, Computer Science Division (EECS), University of California, Berkeley, 1992. Also available as UC Berkeley technical report UCB/CSD-92-708.

[26] Teller, S., and Hanrahan, P. Global Visibility Algorithms for Illumination Computations. Computer Graphics (Proc. SIGGRAPH '93), 239-246.

[27] Teller, S., Fowler, C., Funkhouser, T., and Hanrahan, P. Partitioning and Ordering Large Radiosity Computations. Computer Graphics (Proc. SIGGRAPH '94), 443-450.

[28] Wallace, J., Elmquist, K., Haines, E. A Ray Tracing Algorithm for Progressive Radiosity. Computer Graphics (Proc. SIGGRAPH '89), 23, 3, 315-324.

[29] Young, D.M. Iterative Solution of Large Linear Systems. Computer Science and Applied Mathematics. Academic Press, New York, 1971.

[30] Zareski, D., Wade, B., Hubbard, P. and Shirley, P. Efficient Parallel Global Illumination using Density Estimation. 1995 Parallel Rendering Symposium. Atlanta, Georgia, October, 1995, 47-54.

[31] Zareski, D. Parallel Decomposition of View-Independent Global Illumination Algorithms. Master's thesis, Cornell University, 1996.

Talisman: Commodity Realtime 3D Graphics for the PC

Jay Torborg James T. Kajiya
Microsoft Corporation

ABSTRACT

A new 3D graphics and multimedia hardware architecture, code-named Talisman, is described which exploits both spatial and temporal coherence to reduce the cost of high quality animation. Individually animated objects are rendered into independent image layers which are composited together at video refresh rates to create the final display. During the compositing process, a full affine transformation is applied to the layers to allow translation, rotation, scaling and skew to be used to simulate 3D motion of objects, thus providing a multiplier on 3D rendering performance and exploiting temporal image coherence. Image compression is broadly exploited for textures and image layers to reduce image capacity and bandwidth requirements. Performance rivaling high-end 3D graphics workstations can be achieved at a cost point of two to three hundred dollars.

CR Categories and Subject Descriptors: B.2.1 [Arithmetic and Logic Structures]: Design Styles - Parallel, Pipelined; C.1.2 [Processor Architectures]: Multiprocessors - Parallel processors, Pipelined processors; I.3.1 [Computer Graphics]: Hardware Architecture - Raster display devices; I.3.3 [Computer Graphics]: Picture/Image Generation - Display algorithms.

INTRODUCTION

The central problem we are seeking to solve is that of attaining ubiquity for 3D graphics. Why ubiquity? Traditionally, the purpose of computer graphics has been as a tool. For example, mechanical CAD enhances the designer's ability to imagine complex three dimensional shapes and how they fit together. Scientific visualization seeks to translate complex abstract relationships into perspicuous spatial relationships. Graphics in film-making is as a tool that realizes the vision of a creative imagination. Today, computer graphics has thrived on being the tool of choice for augmenting the human imagination.

However, the effect of ubiquity is to promote 3D graphics from a *tool* to a *medium*. Without ubiquity, graphics will remain as it does today, a tool for those select few whose work justifies investment in exotic and expensive hardware. With ubiquity, graphics can be used as a true medium. As such, graphics can be used to record ideas and experiences, to transmit them across space, and to serve as a technological substrate for people to communicate within and communally experience virtual worlds. But before it can become a successful medium, 3D graphics must be universally available: the breadth and depth of the potential audience must be large enough to sustain interesting and varied content.

jaytor@microsoft.com kajiya@microsoft.com

How can we achieve ubiquity? There are a few criteria: 1) hardware must be so inexpensive that anyone who wants it can afford it, 2) there must be a minimum level of capability and quality to carry a wide range of applications, and 3) the offering must carry compelling content. This paper will treat the first two problems and a novel hardware approach to solving them.

There are two approaches to making inexpensive graphics hardware. One approach is to make an attenuated version of conventional hardware. In the next section we make an analysis of the forces driving the cost of conventional graphics architectures. By mitigating some of these costs, one may obtain cheaper implementations with more modest performance. Over a dozen manufacturers are currently exploring this approach by cutting down on one or another cost factor. The risk of this approach, of course, is that each time one cuts cost, one also cuts performance or quality.

An alternative approach is to look to new architectures that have a fundamentally different character than the conventional graphics pipeline. This is an approach pioneered at the high end by the Pixel Planes project [Fuc89], PixelFlow [Mol92], and various parallel ray tracing machines [Nis83, Pot89]. At the low end, Nvidia [Nvi95] is offering such a different architecture. We present an architecture that very much is in the spirit of this latter path, delivering a high performance, high quality graphics system for a parts cost of $200 to $300.

The second criterion, quality, must be evaluated in terms of the applications and content to be executed by the machine. Here we make a fundamentally different assumption from that underlying the conventional graphics pipeline. We believe that the requirements and metric of performance for a ubiquitous graphics system to be much different than that for a system designed primarily for mechanical CAD. In MCAD the ability to accurately and faithfully display the shape of the part is a strict requirement. The metric of performance is often polygons per second, but ultimate result is frame rate—a low-cost system will display at a much slower rate than a high-performance system, but both will be able to display the shape accurately with the exactly the same image. One of our central assumptions is that in applications and content for ubiquitous graphics this situation is reversed. In a system to be used as a medium, rather than as a tool, the ability to smoothly convey motion, to be synchronized with sound and video, and to achieve low-latency interaction are critical requirements. We believe the fidelity of the shapes, the precise nature of their geometric relationships, and image quality are performance metrics. In our architecture we have striven to make it possible for one to always be able to interact in real-time, at video frame rates (e.g. 72-85 Hz). The difference between high-cost and low-cost systems will be in the fidelity and quality of the images.

FUNDAMENTAL FORCES

A graphics system designer struggles with two fundamental forces: memory bandwidth, and system latency. To achieve low-cost, a third force looms large: memory cost.

Space considerations do not allow us to detail all the bandwidth requirements for a conventional graphics pipeline. The considerations are straightforward: for example, simple multiplication shows display refresh bandwidth for a 75 Hz, 640x480x8 frame buffer requires 23MB per second, while that for 1024x768x24 requires 169 MB per second. If we add the requirements for z-buffering (average depth complexity of 3 with random z-order), texture map reads with various antialiasing schemes (point sample, bilinear, trilinear, anisotropic), and additional factors imposed by anti-aliasing, we obtain the following chart:

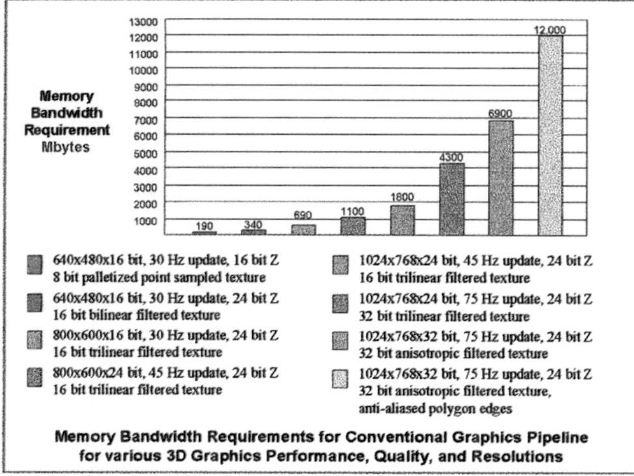

Memory Bandwidth Requirements for Conventional Graphics Pipeline for various 3D Graphics Performance, Quality, and Resolutions

Memory bandwidth is a key indicator of system cost. The left hand two columns indicate where current 3D accelerators for the PC are falling. A full up SGI RE2—a truly impressive machine—boasts a memory bandwidth of well over 10,000 MB per second. Its quite clear that SGI has nothing to fear from evolving PC 3D accelerators, which utilize traditional 3D pipelines, for some time to come.

The second force, system latency, is handled mainly through careful design of the basic algorithms of the architecture, as well as careful pipelining to mask memory latencies.

The third force, memory cost, traditionally has not been of great concern to high-end systems because achieving the aggregate bandwidth has required large amounts of memory. The next chart shows the results of calculating memory requirements for a conventional graphics pipeline with different levels of performance.

Over the last two decades, the drop in price per bit of semiconductor memory has been phenomenal. A look at an early DRAM vs. today's reveals interesting trends.

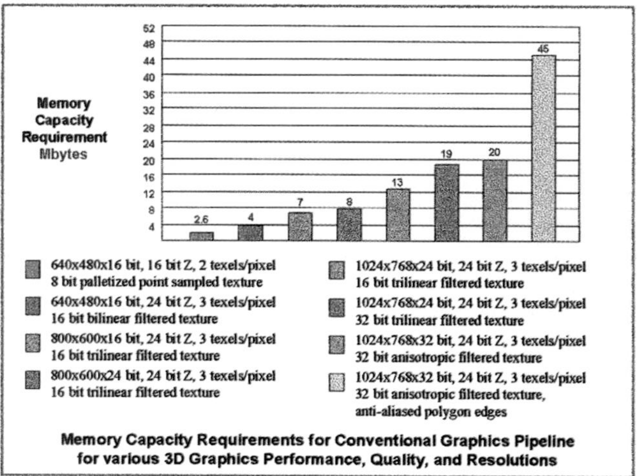

Memory Capacity Requirements for Conventional Graphics Pipeline for various 3D Graphics Performance, Quality, and Resolutions

Note that although capacity has improved tremendously, latency and bandwidth have not made similar improvements. There is every indication that these trends will continue to hold.

These charts suggest that achieving high-quality imagery using the conventional graphics pipeline is an inherently expensive enterprise. Those who maintain that improvements in CPU and VLSI technology are sufficient to produce low-cost hardware or even software systems that we would consider high-performance today, have not carefully analyzed the nature of the fundamental forces at work.

	1976	1995	Change	Change per Year
Access Time	350 ns	50 ns	7X	10%
Bandwidth (per data pin)	2 Mb/sec	22 Mb/sec	11X	12%
Capacity	4 Kbit	16 Mbit	4096X	50%
Cost per MByte	$ 16,500	$ 23	720X	40%

IMAGE PROCESSING AND 3D GRAPHICS

Although the conventional graphics pipeline uses massive amounts of memory bandwidth to do its job, it is equally clear that much of this bandwidth is creating unused, if not unusable, capacity. For example, the conventional pipeline is fully capable of making every frame a display of a completely different geometric model at full performance. The viewpoint may skip about completely at random with no path coherence at all. Every possible pixel pattern may serve as a texture map, even though the vast majority of them are perceptually indistinguishable from random noise. A frame may be completed in any pixel order even though polygons tend to occupy adjacent pixels.

In our architecture we have sought to employ temporal coherence of models, of motion, of viewpoint, and spatial coherence of texture and display. We have found that this approach greatly mitigates the need for large memory bandwidths and capacities for high-quality systems.

A fundamental technique we have used repeatedly is to replace image synthesis with image processing. That image processing and 3D graphics have always had an intimate theoretical relationship, is evident to anyone perusing the contents of a typical SIGGRAPH proceedings. Even in high-quality off-line rendering, image processing and composition has served essential functions for many years. But, with a few exceptions like the Pixar Image Computer [Lev84], Regan's image remapping system [Reg94], and the PixelFlow architecture [Mol92] this relationship has not extended into the physical embodiment of hardware.

In a sense, one can view texture mapping as an example of marrying images and 3d graphics early in the pipeline. Segal, et. al. [Seg92] have shown that texture mapping, especially when considered in context with multiple renderings can simulate many lighting effects. We have adopted this idea for the real-time context, calling it multi-pass rendering.

Image compositing and image morphing have been long used in the utilization of temporal coherence—at least in software systems, [Coo87, Che94, Che95, McM95]. Our architecture extends these ideas into the real-time hardware domain, for the case of affine image transformations.

HARDWARE ARCHITECTURE

There are four major concepts utilized in Talisman, these are:

- Composited image layers with full affine transformations.
- Image compression.
- Chunking.
- Multi-pass rendering.

Composited Image Layers

The Talisman hardware does not incorporate a frame buffer in the traditional sense. Instead, multiple independent *image layers* are composited together at video rates to create the output video signal. These image layers can be rendered into and manipulated independently. The graphics system will generally use an independent image layer for each non-interpenetrating object in the scene. This allows each object to be updated independently so that object update rates can be optimized based on scene priorities. For example, an object that is moving in the distant background may not need to be updated as often, or with as much accuracy, as a foreground object.

Image layers can be of arbitrary size and shape, although the first implementation of the system software uses only rectangular shaped layers. Each pixel in a layer has color and alpha (opacity) information associated with it so that multiple layers can be composited together to create the overall scene.

Several different operations can be performed on these image layers at video rates, including scaling, rotation, subpixel positioning, and skews (i.e., full affine transformations). So, while image layer update rates are variable, image layer transformations (motion, etc.) occur at full video rates (e.g. 72 to 85 Hz), resulting in much more fluid dynamics than can be achieved by a conventional 3D graphics system that has no update rate guarantees.

Many 3D transformations can be simulated by 2D imaging operations. For example, a receding object can be simulated by scaling the size of the image. By utilizing 2D transformations on previously rendered images for intermediate frames, overall processing requirements are significantly reduced, and 3D rendering power can be applied where it is needed to yield the highest quality results. Thus, the system software can employ temporal level of detail management and utilize frame-to-frame temporal coherence.

By using image layer scaling, the level of spatial detail can also be adjusted to match scene priorities. For example, background objects (e.g., cloudy sky) can be rendered into a small image layer (low resolution) which is then scaled to the appropriate size for display. By utilizing high quality filtering, the typical low resolution artifacts are reduced.

A typical 3D graphics application (particularly an interactive game) trades off geometric level of detail to achieve higher animation rates. The use of composited image layers allow the Talisman system to utilize two additional scene parameters—temporal level of detail and spatial level of detail—to optimize the effective performance as seen by the user. Further, the Talisman system software can manage these trade-offs automatically without requiring application support.

Image Compression

Talisman broadly applies image compression technology to solve these problems. Image compression has traditionally not been used in graphics systems because of the computational complexity required for high quality, and because it does not easily fit into a conventional graphics architecture. By using a concept we call chunking (described below), we are able to effectively apply compression to images and textures, achieving a significant improvement in price-performance.

In one respect, graphics systems *have* employed compression to frame buffer memory. High end systems utilize eight bits (or more) for each of three color components, and often also include an eight bit alpha value. Low end systems *compress* these 32 bits per pixel to as few as four bits by discarding information and/or using a color palette to reduce the number of simultaneously displayable colors. This compression results in very noticeable artifacts, does not achieve a significant reduction in data requirements, and forces applications and/or drivers to deal with a broad range of pixel formats.

The compression used in Talisman is much more sophisticated, using an algorithm similar to JPEG which we refer to as TREC to achieve very high image quality yet still provide compression ratios of 10:1 or better. Another benefit of this approach is that a single high quality image format (32 bit true color) can be used for all applications.

Chunking

A traditional 3D graphics system, or any frame buffer for that matter, can be, and usually is, accessed randomly. Arbitrary pixels on the screen can be accessed in random order. Since compression algorithms rely on having access to a fairly large number of neighboring pixels in order to take advantage of spatial coherence, and only after all pixel updates have been made, the random access patterns utilized by conventional graphics algorithms make the application of compression technology to display buffers impractical.

This random access pattern also means that per-pixel hidden surface removal and anti-aliasing algorithms must maintain additional information for every pixel on the screen. This dramatically increases the memory size requirements, and adds another performance bottleneck.

Talisman takes a different approach. Each image layer is divided into pixel regions (32 x 32 pixels in our reference implementation) called *chunks*. The geometry is presorted into bins based on which chunk (or chunks) the geometry will be rendered into. This process is referred to as *chunking*. Geometry that overlaps a chunk boundary is referenced in each chunk it is visible in. As the scene is animated, the data structure is modified to adjust for geometry that moves from one chunk to another.

While chunking adds some upstream overhead, it provides several significant advantages. Since all the geometry in one chunk is rendered before proceeding to the next, the depth buffer need only be as large as a single chunk. With a chunk size of 32 x 32, the depth buffer is implemented directly on the graphics rendering chip. This eliminates a considerable amount of memory, and also allows the depth buffer to be implemented using a specialized memory architecture which can be accessed with very high bandwidth and cleared instantly from one chunk to the next, eliminating the overhead between frames.

Anti-aliasing is also considerably easier since each 32 x 32 chunk can be dealt with independently. Most high-end graphics systems which implement anti-aliasing utilize a great deal of additional memory, and still perform relatively simplistic filtering. By using chunking, the amount of data required is considerably reduced (by a factor of 1000), allowing practical implementation of a much more sophisticated anti-aliasing algorithm.

The final advantage is that chunking enables block oriented image compression. Once each 32 x 32 chunk has been rendered (and anti-aliased), it can then be compressed with the TREC block transform compression algorithm.

Multi-pass Rendering

One of the major attractions of the Talisman architecture is the opportunity for 3D interactive applications to break out of the late 1970's look of CAD graphics systems: boring lambertian Gouraud-shaded polygons with Phong highlights. Texture mapping of color improves this look but imposes another characteristic appearance on applications. In the 1980's, the idea of programmable shaders and procedural texture maps[Coo84, Han90] opened a new versatility to the rendering process. These ideas swept the off-line rendering world to create the high-quality images that we see today in film special effects.

By reducing the bandwidth requirements using the techniques outlined above, Talisman can use a single shared memory system for all memory requirements including compressed texture storage and compressed image layer storage. This architecture allows data created by the rendering process to be fed back through the texture processor to be used as data in the rendering of a new image layer. This feedback allows rendering algorithms which require multiple passes to be implemented.

By coupling multi-pass rendering with a variety of compositing modes, texture mapping techniques [Seg92], and a flexible shading language, Talisman provides a variety of rendering effects that have previously been the domain of off-line software renderers. This includes support of functions such as shadows (including shadows from multiple light sources), environment mapped reflective objects, spot lights, fog, ground fog, lens flare, underwater simulation, waves, clouds, etc.

REFERENCE HARDWARE IMPLEMENTATION

The Talisman architecture supports a broad range of implementations which provide different performance, features, rendering quality, etc. The *reference* implementation is targeted at the high-end of the consumer PC market and is designed to plug into personal computers using the PCI expansion bus. This board replaces functionality that is typically provided by a Windows accelerator board, a 3D accelerator board, an MPEG playback board, a video conferencing board, a sound board, and a modem.

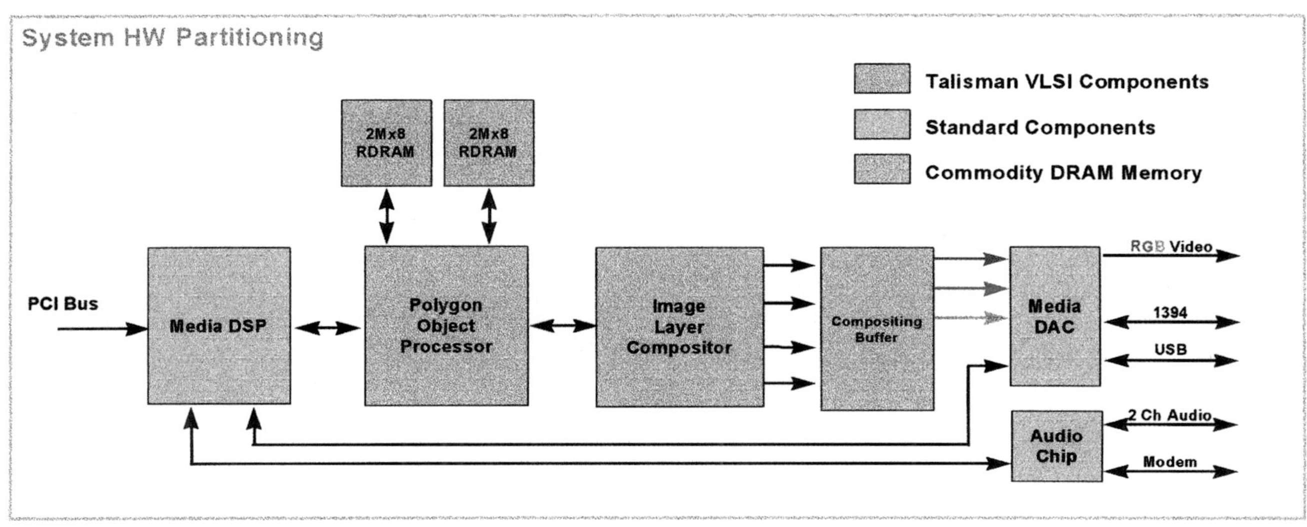

The reference hardware consists of a combination of proprietary VLSI devices and commercially available components. The VLSI components have been developed using a top-down modular design approach allowing various aspects of the reference implementation to be readily used to create derivative designs.

The reference implementation uses 4 Mbytes of shared memory implemented using two 8-bit Rambus channels. The Rambus memory provides higher bandwidth than traditional DRAM at near commodity DRAM pricing. This shared memory is used to store image layers and texture data in compressed form, DSP code and data, and various buffers used to transfer data between processing subsystems. A 2MB configuration is also possible, although such a configuration would have lower display resolution and would have other resource limitations.

The Media DSP Processor is responsible for video codecs, audio processing, and front-end graphics processing (transformations, lighting, etc.). The reference HW implementation uses the Samsung MSP to perform these functions. The DSP combines a RISC processor with a specialized SIMD processor capable of providing high performance floating point and integer processing (>1000 MFLOPS/MOPS). A real-time kernel and resource manager deals with allocating the DSP to the various graphics and multimedia tasks which are performed by this system.

The Polygon Object Processor is a proprietary VLSI chip which performs scan-conversion, shading, texturing, hidden-surface removal, and anti-aliasing. The resulting rendered image layer chunks are stored in compressed form in the shared memory.

The Image Layer Compositor operates at video rates to access the image layer chunk information from the shared memory, decompress the chunks, and process the images to perform general affine transformations (which include scaling, translation with subpixel accuracy, rotation, and skew). The resulting pixels (with alpha) are sent to Compositing Buffer.

Memory Use - Typical Scenario		**Net Memory Requirements**
Image Layer Data Storage		
Display Resolution	*1024 x 768*	
Average Image Layer Size	*128 x 128*	
Average Image Layer Depth Complexity	*1.7*	
Image Layer Data Compression Factor	*5*	
Image Layer Memory Management Overhead	*51 bytes per 32x32 chunk*	
Memory Allocation Overhead	*4 bytes per 128 bytes*	
Total Image Layer Data Storage Requirements		1,171,637 bytes
Display Memory Management	64 bytes per image layer	5,222 bytes
Texture Data Storage		
Number of Texels	*4,000,000 texels*	
Percent Texels with Alpha	*30%*	
Avg. Number of Texture LODs	*6*	
Texture Data Compression Factor	*15*	
Total Texture Data Storage Requirements		1,415,149 bytes
Command Buffers		53,248 bytes
Audio Output Buffer		2,450 bytes
Audio Synthesis Data		32,768 bytes
Wav Table Buffer		524,800 bytes
Media DSP Program and Scratch Mem		524,288 bytes
Total		**3,729,563 bytes**

Image layer chunk data is processed 32 scan lines at a time for display. The Compositing Buffer contains two 32 scan line buffers which are toggled between display and compositing activities. Each chip also contains a 32 scan line alpha buffer which is used to accumulate alpha for each pixel. The Video DAC includes a USB serial channel (for joysticks, etc.), and an IEEE1394 media channel (up to 400 Mbits/sec. for connection to an optional break-out box and external A/V equipment), as well as standard palette DAC features.

A separate chip is used to handle audio digital to analog and analog to digital conversion.

The table above indicates the total memory usage for a typical 3D application scenario. For the same scenario, the memory bandwidth requirements are shown in the following table.

Memory Bandwidth - Typical Scenario	
Pixel Rendering (avg. depth complexity 2.5)	32.4 Mbytes/sec
Display Bandwidth	130.0 Mbytes/sec
Texture Reads	
Texels per Pixel (anisotropic filtering)	*16*
Texture Cache Multiplier (avg. texel reuse)	*2.5*
Texture Read Bandwidth	58 Mbytes/sec
Polygon Command (30,000 polygons/scene)	61.0 Mbytes/sec
Total 3D Pipeline Bandwidth	281.4 Mbytes/sec

POLYGON OBJECT PROCESSOR

The Polygon Object Processor is one of the two primary VLSI chips that are being developed for the reference HW implementation.

Unique Functional Blocks

Many of the functional blocks in the Polygon Object Processor will be recognized as being common in traditional 3D graphics pipelines. Some of the unique blocks are described here. The operation of this chip is provided later in the paper.

Initial Evaluation - Since polygons are processed in 32 x 32 chunks, triangle processing will typically not start at a triangle vertex. This block computes the intersection of the chunk with the triangle and computes the values for color, transparency, depth, and texture coordinates for the starting point of the triangle within the chunk.

Pixel Engine - performs pixel level calculations including compositing, depth buffering, and fragment generation for pixels which are only partially covered. The pixel engine also handles z-comparison operations required for shadows.

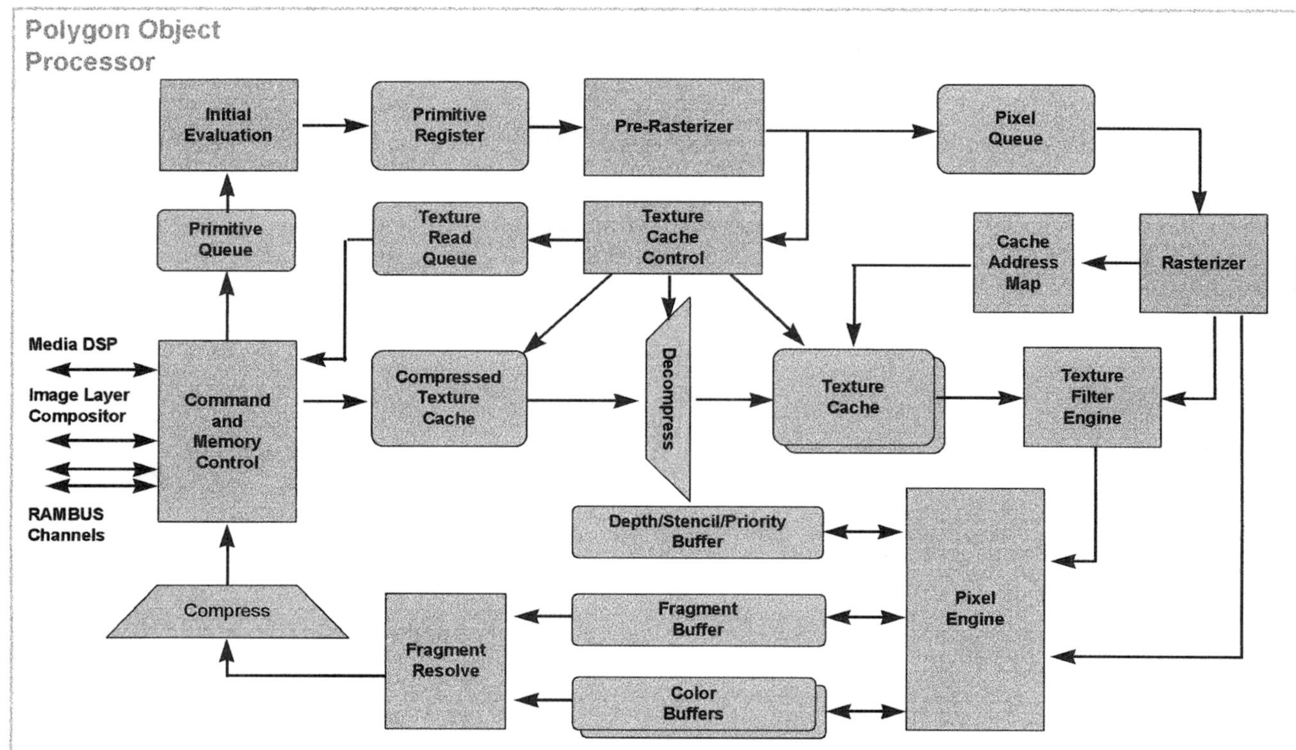

Fragment Resolve - performs the final anti-aliasing step by resolving depth sorted pixel fragments with partial coverage or transparency.

Coping with Latency

One of the most challenging aspects of this design was coping with the long latency to memory for fetching texture data. Not only do we need to cope with a decompression step which takes well over 100 12.5 ns. cycles, but we are also using Rambus memory devices which need to be accessed using large blocks to achieve adequate bandwidth. This results in a total latency of several hundred cycles.

Maintaining the full pixel rendering rate was a high priority in the design, so a mechanism that could ensure that texels were available for the texture filter engine when needed was required. The basic solution to this problem is to have two rasterizers - one calculating texel addresses and making sure that they are available in time, and the other performing color, depth, and pixel address interpolation for rendering. While these rasterizers both calculate information for the same pixels, they are separated by up to several hundred cycles.

Two solutions were considered for this mechanism - one was to duplicate the address calculations in both rasterizers; the other was to pass the texture addresses from the first rasterizer (called the Pre-Rasterizer in the block diagram) to the second rasterizer using a FIFO.

In this case, texture address calculation logic in the rasterizers is fairly complex to deal with perspective divides and anisotropic texture filtering (discussed later). To duplicate this logic in both rasterizers required more silicon area than using the pixel queue, so the latter approach was chosen.

POP Area Calculation			0.35 Micron
Functional Block	**Gates**	**RAM bits**	**Total Area**
RAC Cell			5.17
Memory Interface	4,500	12,288	1.77
Input Logic	10,044	0	1.09
Setup Logic	30,920	0	3.92
Scan Convert	125,510	57,760	18.38
Texture Lookup	83,450	0	8.87
Pixel Logic	86,090	137,216	20.03
Cache Logic	42,000	71,680	10.91
Compression Logic	33,120	32,896	14.62
Decompression Logic	47,000	16,000	6.02
			90.77
Testability Gates	50,000		6.55
Interblock Routing Area			9.73
Core Area			107.05
I/O Cells Area			21.69
Total Area			**128.75**

Die Area and Packaging

The total die area of the Polygon Object Processor is shown in the following table. The die area figures shown here are estimates since the layout of this part was not complete at the time of paper submission.

The Polygon Object Processor is implemented using an advanced 0.35 micron four layer metal 3.3 volt CMOS process. The die is mounted in a 304 pin thermally-enhanced plastic package.

IMAGE LAYER COMPOSITOR

The Image Layer Compositor is the other custom VLSI chip that is being developed for the reference HW implementation. This part is responsible for generating the graphics output from a collection of depth sorted image layers.

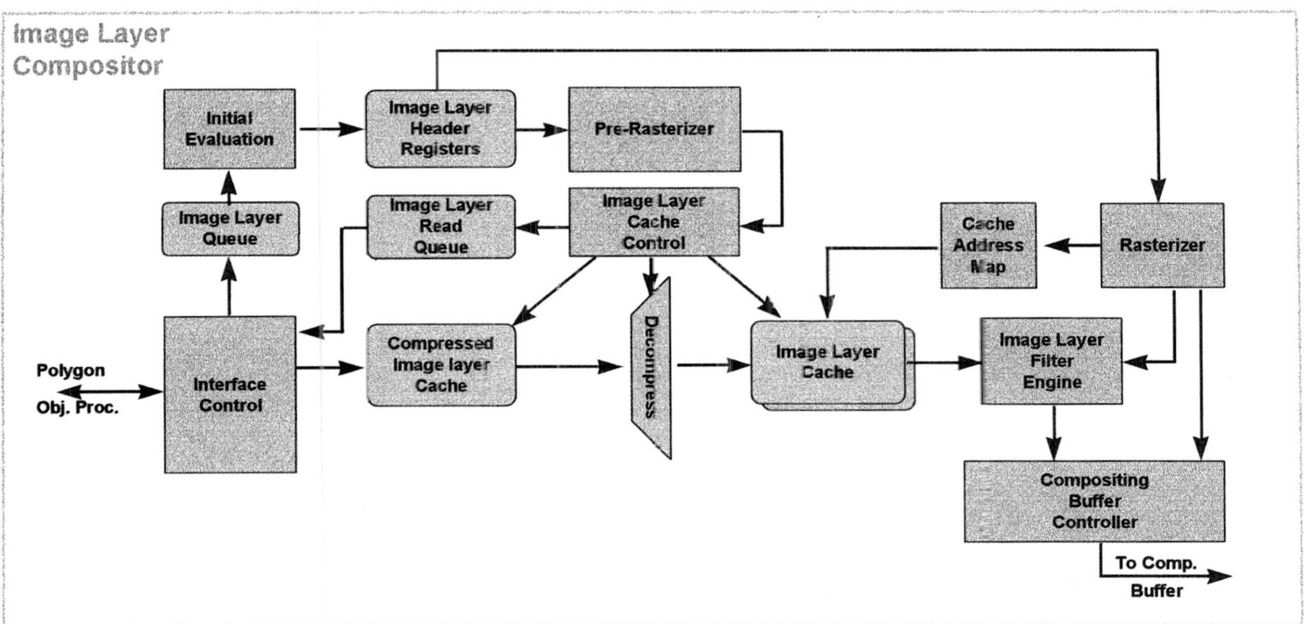

Comparison with Polygon Object Processor

You will notice that this block diagram is similar in many ways to the Polygon Object Processo. In fact, many of the blocks are identical to reduce design time. In many ways, the Image Layer Compositor performs the same operations as triangle rasterization with texture mapping.

In addition to the obvious differences (no depth buffering, anti-aliasing, image compression, etc.) there are a couple of key differences which significantly affect the design:

Rendering Rate - the Image Layer Compositor must composite the images of multiple objects at full video rates with multiple objects overlapping each other. To support this, the rendering rate of the Image Layer Compositor is eight times higher than the Polygon Object Processor.

Texture/Image Processing - the sophistication of the image processing used by the Image Layer Compositor is significantly reduced in order to keep silicon area to a reasonable level. Instead of performing perspective correct anisotropic filtering, this chip performs simple bi-linear filtering and requires only linear address calculations (since perspective transforms are not supported).

These differences significantly affect the approach used to deal with memory latency. The rasterizer in the Image Layer Compositor is significantly simpler due to the simplified image processing, and the higher pixel rate requires the pre-rasterizer to be much further ahead of the rasterizer. As a result, the Image Layer Compositor eliminates the Pixel Queue and simply recalculates all the parameters in the second rasterizer.

Die Area and Packaging

The total die area of the Image Layer Compositor is shown in the following table. The die area figures shown here are estimates since the layout of this part was not complete at the time of paper submission.

ILC Area Estimate			**0.35 Micron**
Functional Block	**Gates**	**RAM bits**	
Interface Controller	2,290	2,048	1.40
Initial Evaluation	10,514	0	1.35
Header Registers	7,550	2,048	1.25
Pre-Rasterizer	21,018	0	2.65
Rasterizer	19,019	0	2.35
Cache Logic	41,350	71,636	18.30
Decompressor	86,000	25,856	21.00
Filter Engine	21,608	0	4.10
Compositing Buffer Controller	1,200	0	0.25
Testability Gates	50,000		6.60
Interblock Routing Area			4.65
Core Area			63.90
I/O Cells Area			16.99
Total Area			**80.89**

The Image Layer Compositor is implemented using an advanced 0.35 micron four layer metal 3.3 volt CMOS process. The die is mounted in a 304 pin thermally-enhanced plastic package.

OPERATION

This section describes the overall operation of the system and discusses some of the key features.

Objects and Image Layers

As in a traditional 3D graphics system, objects are placed in the virtual environment by the application specifying their position, orientation, and scale relative to the coordinate system of the virtual environment. The transform engine uses this information, in conjunction with the viewpoint specification to construct the synthetic scene.

In this system, however, independent objects are rendered into separate image layers which are composited together at video rates to create the displayed image. Independent objects can be described directly by the APIs (in the case of the Windows PC, this is done using DirectDraw and Direct3D [Mic95]), or can be calculated automatically based on object hierarchy and bounding boxes. The latter approach will likely be used for virtual reality environments described using behavior languages where the relative motion of objects can be predicted.

In our implementation, the host processor maintains control of real-time display operation. The object database is maintained in host memory, and primitive descriptions are passed to the graphics system as needed for rendering. Unlike a traditional 3D graphics system, the entire display is not updated at the same time. Each image layer can be updated based on scene priorities.

As previously discussed, an affine image transformation can be applied to each image layer at video rates as it is composited. This affine transformation is used to simulate a 3D transformation of the object. The appropriate affine transform and the geometric and photometric error that results is computed based on a least square error of selected points within the object.

The host software maintains a priority list of image layers to be updated based on perceptible error and object priorities. More error is allowed for objects that are not considered primary, allowing higher quality to be maintained for the important elements in the scene. For those objects that are not updated, the system will always try to produce the best possible result using affine transforms on previously rendered image layers.

Image layer transforms can be processed considerably faster than re-rendering the geometry - typically 10 to 20 times faster. Since the frame to frame changes of animated objects are typically small, an affine transformed image of a 3D object can be used for several frames before incurring enough distortion to require re-rendering. This gives a tremendous performance advantage to the front end of the graphics pipeline; and since the polygon rendering requires significantly more processing resources, the net result is significantly higher price-performance.

Image Layer Chunking

As previously noted, all image layers are processed as 32 x 32 pixel regions known as chunks. Prior to sending graphics rendering primitives to the Talisman hardware, the host processor must sort the geometry for each image layer into these independent regions.

After some experimentation, we determined that it was more efficient to sort into 64 x 64 regions and allow the hardware to process this geometry for each of the four 32 x 32 chunks in the region.

Sorting into these 64 x 64 regions can be accomplished using a variety of algorithms. In the simplest case, a binary sort is performed based on bounding volumes using an algorithm similar to polygon scanline techniques (active lists, etc.). More advanced algorithms utilize incremental algorithms based on the temporal behavior of the environment. We have found that we can achieve full performance using static algorithms on a mid-range personal computer.

Primitive Rendering

The Talisman software provides the capability to render independent triangles, meshed triangles (strips and fans), lines, and points. All of these primitives are converted to triangles for rendering by the Polygon Object Processor. Triangle rendering provides numerous simplifications in the hardware since it is always planar and convex.

All coordinate transformations, clipping, lighting, and initial triangle set-up is handled by the Media DSP using 32 bit IEEE floating point.

During scan conversion, the Polygon Object Processor uses the linear equation parameters generated by the Media DSP to determine if the triangle is visible in the current chunk. The edge equations are also stored in the Primitive Registers until required by the Pre-Rasterizer and Rasterizer.

As previously discussed, rasterization is split into two sections which are separated by several hundred clock cycles. This separation allows the first section (the Pre-Rasterizer) to determine which texture blocks will be required to complete rendering of the triangle. This information is sent to the Texture Cache Controller so that it can fetch the necessary data from the common memory system, decompress it, and move it into the specialized high-speed on-chip memory system used by the texture filtering engine, as described below.

The second section, the Rasterizer, calculates the color, translucency, depth, and coverage information, and passes this to the Pixel Engine where it can be combined with the texture information to determine the output pixel color.

Texture Mapping

Texture data is stored in the common memory system in the TREC compressed image format. 8x8 blocks are grouped together in 32x32 chunks for memory management purposes, although each 8x8 block is individually addressable. The 32x32 chunks are identical in format to the image layer chunks, allowing textures and image layers to be used interchangeably (although textures are generally mip-mapped).

Data is fetched from the common memory in blocks called Memory Allocation Units. Each MAU is 128 bytes, allowing high bandwidth utilization from the Rambus DRAMs to be achieved.

As texture blocks are needed, they are fetched into a compressed texture cache in the Polygon Object Processor. The compressed texture cache holds sixteen MAUs. Holding texture data in compressed form increases the effective size of the compressed texture cache by the compression factor (typically 15 times).

Texture blocks are decompressed as required by the texturing engine and placed in an on-chip decompressed texture cache. A total of sixteen 8x8 texture blocks are cached in RGBα format. The texture cache allows each texel to be used for an average of 2.5 pixel calculations.

A texture filter kernel is generated on the fly for each pixel, depending on the texture resolution, offset, orientation, and Z-slope. The texture processor supports anisotropic filtering with up to 2:1 anisotropy at full pixel rendering rates. Higher anisotropy is supported at lower rendering rates. The resulting filter quality is considerably better than the tri-linear filtering that is commonly used in high-end graphics workstations, and will result in sharper looking images. Tri-linear filtering is also available at full pixel rendering rates.

Hidden Surface Removal

The Polygon Object Processor has an on-chip 32 x 32 pixel depth buffer (with 26 bits per pixel) used to store the depth of the closest primitive to the eye point at each pixel location. The 26 bit depth value uses between 20 and 24 bits for depth with the remaining 2 to 6 bits used for priority and/or stencil. Priority is used to eliminate depth buffering artifacts due to coplanar objects. Priority is tagged per surface, and indicates which surface should be considered as closer to the viewpoint, if the depth of the two surfaces at the specific pixel location are within a certain depth tolerance of each other. The depth tolerance is a fixed value which is based on the overall accuracy of the graphics pipeline with regards to computing pixel depth values.

The Polygon Object Processor also supports translucent triangles, translucent textures, and triangle edge anti-aliasing, all of which fall outside of normal depth buffer operations. To properly compose pixels which are only partially covered, or have an alpha value less than 1.0, the Talisman system has special anti-aliasing hardware, which is described below.

Anti-Aliasing

One of the significant advantages of the chunking architecture used by Talisman is that high quality anti-aliasing can be implemented cost effectively, without the need for large memory systems. The algorithm we have implemented is compatible with depth buffering and translucent surfaces.

The color buffer always stores the pixel value for the front most, fully opaque, fully covered pixel at each pixel location in the 32x32 chunk. Pixels with partial geometric coverage or which are translucent are contained in a fragment buffer (the basic anti-aliasing algorithm is loosely based on the A-Buffer algorithm described by L. Carpenter [Car84]). Each entry in the fragment buffer provides the color, alpha, depth, and geometric coverage information associated with these pixels. Multiple fragment buffer entries can be associated with a single pixel location within the 32x32 chunk. Memory is managed within the fragment buffer using a linked list structure.

To represent the geometric coverage of a pixel by a polygon edge, a coverage mask is used. In the Talisman system, a 4x4 mask is used, which effectively divides each pixel into 16 sub-pixels. The Talisman hardware does not store an individual entry for each sub-pixel, as do many high end graphics systems of this quality, but instead stores a simple coverage mask which tags which virtual sub-pixels the fragment entry would cover. The 4x4 coverage mask is generated using an algorithm similar to the algorithm described by A. Schilling [Sch91] in order to provide improved dynamic results for near horizontal and near vertical edges.

All fragments generated by the scan converter are tested against the 32x32 pixel depth buffer prior to being sent to the fragment buffer. This eliminates storage and subsequent processing of any fragments which are obscured by a nearer fully covered, fully opaque pixel.

To further reduce the number of fragments that are stored and subsequently processed, the Pixel Engine implements a merging operation for complimentary fragments. In many cases, at a single pixel location, sequential fragments are from the mating edges of adjacent polygons which represent a common surface within an object. In these cases, the pixel depth and color are often virtually identical, with the only difference between the two fragments being the coverage masks. The Pixel Engine compares the incoming fragment to the most recently received fragment at that pixel location, and if the depth and color are within predefined limits, combines the fragments by ORing the incoming fragment coverage mask with the stored fragment coverage mask, and stores the result in place of the stored coverage mask. The rest of the incoming fragment data is discarded, eliminating the use of another fragment entry. When this operation occurs, the resulting mask is tested to see if full coverage has been reached. If full coverage is achieved, the pixel is moved out of the fragment buffer and placed in the 32x32 pixel depth buffer, freeing up additional fragment memory.

Once all the polygons for the chunk are rendered, the anti-aliasing engine resolves the remaining pixel coverage values performing front-to-back compositing of each pixel which has one or more fragments associated with it. As a chunk is being resolved, the Rasterizer, Pixel Engine, etc. are rendering the next chunk. As fragments are freed up by the resolve process, they are added to the free fragment list where they can be used by the next chunk being rendered.

Shadows

The Pixel Engine supports a full range of compositing functions which are useful for multipass rendering. One of the most common uses is for the generation of real-time shadows. The Polygon Object Processor implements a shadow buffer algorithm that determines which parts of the object are in shadow from a given light source. This is done in three passes, assuming a single light source.

In the first pass, a *shadow buffer* is generated by rendering the scene from the point of view of the light source [Wil78, Ree87]. The shadow buffer generated from this step is a depth buffer, where each pixel depth location is set to the average depth of the two closest surfaces to the light source. This is done to eliminate the possibility of the front surface casting a shadow on itself due to accuracy errors in the algorithm, and was first described by A. Woo [Woo92]. This shadow buffer is then saved in the common memory system.

In the second pass, the scene is rendered from the eyepoint, generating a normally lit scene from the single light source.

In the third pass, the scene is rendered from the eye point, to generate the shadow contribution to the image. As the scene is rendered, the shadow buffer is accessed using the texture map addressing hardware, and the shadow buffer depth is compared with a projection of the surface depth in the shadow buffer coordinate system. If the surface depth is behind the shadow buffer depth, it is in shadow. For each pixel in the eyepoint scene, a 4x4 or 8x8 set of nearest shadow buffer locations are visited, each producing an *in-front* or *behind* result. A trapezoid weighted filter is multiplied against the results of the shadow depth compares, giving a resulting shadow factor, ranging from 0 to 1.0. The trapezoid filter gives a soft, anti-aliased edge to the shadow in the resulting scene. The shadow factor is used to attenuate the pixel intensity from the scene rendered in pass two.

Display Image Generation

A data structure defining the image layer display list (sorted in depth order) is stored in shared memory and is traversed every frame time to determine how the image layers are displayed. This data structure can be modified by the host at any time to control the temporal behavior of each image layer (and hence each independently rendered object).

Image layer compositing is performed 32 scanlines at a time. The Image Layer Compositor traverses the image layer data structure (sorted in front to back order), performing image transforms on those chunks that are visible in each 32 scanline band.

The Compositing Buffer is a specialty memory device developed for the Talisman architecture. This part has two 32 scanline color buffers (24 bit RGB) and a 32 scanline alpha buffer. One of the color buffers is used for compositing into while the other is being used for streaming the video data out to the monitor. The two buffers ping-pong back and forth so that as one scanline region is being displayed, the next is being composited. The single 32 scanline alpha buffer is used only for compositing and is cleared at the start of each new 32 scanline region.

The Image Layer Compositor (which does the image layer chunk addressing, decompressing, and image processing), passes the color data and alpha data to the Compositing Buffer for each pixel to be composited. Since the sprites are processed in front to back order, the alpha buffer can be used to accumulate opacity for each pixel, allowing proper anti-aliasing and transparency.

FUNCTIONALITY AND PERFORMANCE

The features and major performance goals for the reference implementation are:

- Single PCI board implementation with audio, video, 2D and 3D graphics.
- High resolution display capability - 1344 x 1024 @ 75 Hz.
- 24 bit true-color pixel data at all resolutions for maximum image fidelity.
- Optimized for 3D animation at full refresh rates (75 Hz) using a combination of image layer animation and 3D rendering. Scene complexity of 20,000 to 30,000 rendered polygons or higher can be supported. This is comparable to a 3D graphics workstation capable of 1.5 to 2 million polygons per second.
- Polygon Object Processor pixel rendering rate of 40 Mpixels per second with anisotropic texturing and anti-aliasing. Image Layer Compositor pixel compositing rate of 320 Mpixels/sec.
- Very high quality image generation incorporating anisotropic texture filtering, subpixel-filtered anti-aliasing, translucent surfaces, shadows, blur, fog, and custom shading algorithms.
- Front-end geometry processor to off-load transformations, clipping, lighting, etc.
- Full resolution (720 x 486) MPEG-2 decode, as well as other video codecs. Video can be used as surface textures, and can be combined with graphics animations.
- Base system has two-channel 16-bit audio inputs and outputs with DSP based MIDI synthesis (wave table and other mechanisms supported), 3D spatialization, and digital audio mixing. Other audio processing is also supported.

CONCLUSIONS

The Talisman architecture demonstrates how a fresh look at 3D animation hardware can result in dramatic improvements in price-performance. The system described in this paper has a bill of materials of $200 to $300, yet can achieve performance and quality comparable or superior to high-end image generators and 3D graphics workstations.

The first reference implementation is a high-end PC board level system with adequate functionality to meet a broad range of applications. The goal of the Talisman architecture is to significantly improve the quality, performance, and integration of media technologies on the PC. This first implementation is intended to be a realization of this goal at a price point that is viable for consumer applications, and to be a reference from which derivative designs can be created.

Although the reference implementation or other products based on this technology are not yet on the market, we believe that products based on the architecture described in this paper will have retail street prices of $200 to $500.

The Talisman architecture has been fully simulated and Verilog models are complete. We expect prototype implementations of this hardware by late this year.

ACKNOWLEDGMENTS

The authors would like to thank the entire Talisman research and develop team for their contributions to this program. We would specifically like to thank Jim Blinn, Joe Chauvin, Steve Gabriel, Howard Good, Andrew Glassner, Kent Griffin, Bruce Johnson, Mark Kenworthy, On Lee, Jed Lengyel, Nathan Myhrvold, Larry Ockene, Bill Powell, Rob Scott, John Snyder, Mike Toelle, Jim Veres, and Turner Whitted for their contributions to the HW architecture, algorithms, and demos, although many others also contributed.

REFERENCES

[Ake88] Akeley, K. and T. Jermoluk, "High Performance Polygon Rendering", *Proceedings of SIGGRAPH 1988* (July 1988), p239-246.

[Ake93] Akeley, Kurt, "Reality Engine Graphics", *Proceedings of SIGGRAPH 1993* (July 1993), p109-116.

[Car84] Carpenter, L. "The A-Buffer, an Anti-Aliased Hidden Surface Method", *Proceedings of SIGGRAPH 1984*, (July 1984), p103-108.

[Che94] Shenchang Eric Chen, Lance Williams, View interpolation for image synthesis, *Proceedings of SIGGRAPH 93*, (August 1993), pp. 279-288.

[Che95] Shenchang Eric Chen, QuickTime VR—an image based approach to virtual environment navigation, *Proceedings of SIGGRAPH 95*, (August 1995), pp. 29-38.

[Coo84] Cook, R, "Shade Trees", *Proceedings of SIGGRAPH 1984*, July 1984, p223-231.

[Coo87] Cook, R., L. Carpenter, E. Catmull, "The REYES Image Rendering Architecture, *Proceedings of SIGGRAPH 1987* (July 1987). p95-102

[Fuc89] Fuchs, H., J. Poulton, J. Eyles, T. Greer, J. Goldfeather, D. Ellsworth, S. Molnar, G. Turk, B. Tebbs, L. Isreal, "Pixel Planes 5: A Heterogenous Multiprocessor Graphics System Using Processor-Enhanced Memories", *Proceedings of SIGGRAPH 89*, p79-88.

[Han90] Hanrahan, P. and J. Lawson, "A Language for Shading and Lighting Calculations", *Proceedings of SIGGRAPH 1990*, August 1990, p289-298.

[Lev84] Levinthal, A., T. Porter, "Chap - a SIMD Graphics Processor", *Proceedings of SIGGRAPH 84*, p77-82.

[Mic95] Microsoft, "DirectDraw API Specification" and "Direct3D API Specification", Microsoft Corporation Redmond WA, 1995.

[McM95] Leonard McMillan, Gary Bishop, Plenoptic modeling: an image-based rendering system, *Proceedings of SIGGRAPH 95*, (August 1995), pp. 39-46.

[Mol91] Molnar, S., "Image Composition Architectures for Real-Time Image Generation", *PhD Dissertation*, University of North Carolina, 1991.

[Mol92] Molnar, S., J. Eyles, J. Poulton, "PixelFlow: High Speed Rendering Using Image Composition", *Proceedings of SIGGRAPH 1992* (July 92), p231-240

[Nis83] H. Nishimura, H. Ohno, T. Kawata, LINKS-1: a parallel pieplined multimicrocomputer system for image creation, Proceedings of the 10th Symposium on computer architecture (1983), pp.387-394

[Nvi95] Nvidia, various press releases on the Nvidia NV1 Multimedia Accelerator, Nvidia Corporation, Sunnyvale CA, 1995.

[Pot89] Michael Potmesil and Eric Hoffert, The PixelMachine: a parallel image computer, Proceedings of SIGGRAPH 89, (July 1989), pp. 69-78.

[Reg94] Regan, M. and R. Pose, "Priority Rendering with a Virtual Reality Address Recalculation Pipeline", *Proceedings of SIGGRAPH 1994* (July 94), p. 155-162.

[Ree87] Reeves, W. , D. Salesin, R. Cooke, "Rendering Anti-aliased Shadows with Depth Maps", *Proceedings of SIGGRAPH 87*, p283-291.

[Sch91] Schilling, A. "A New Simple and Efficient Anti-aliasing with Subpixel Masks", *Proceedings of SIGGRAPH 1991* (July 1991), p133-141.

[Seg92] Mark Segal, Carl Korobkin, Rolf van Widenfelt, Jim Foran, Paul Haeberli, Fast shadows and lighting effects using texture mapping, *Proceedings of SIGGRAPH 92*, (July 1992), pp. 249-252.

[Wil78] Williams, L., "Casting Curved Shadows on Curved Surfaces", *Proceedings of SIGGRAPH 78*, p270-274.

[Woo92] Woo, A. in "The Shadow Depth Map Revisited", in *Graphics Gems*, edited by D. Kirk, Academic Press, Boston, 1992, p338-442.

SAMPLE

This sample image, and the one shown on the frontispiece of the 1996 SIGGRAPH Proceedings were generated using a bit and cycle accurate simulator of the Talisman reference hardware. Both of these images are single frames from an animation that will be rendered in realtime on the Talisman hardware.

VC-1: A Scalable Graphics Computer with Virtual Local Frame Buffers

Satoshi Nishimura Tosiyasu L. Kunii

The University of Aizu†

Abstract

The VC-1 is a parallel graphics machine for polygon rendering based on image composition. This paper describes the architecture of the VC-1 along with a parallel polygon rendering algorithm for it. The structure of the VC-1 is a loosely-coupled array of 16 general-purpose processors, each of which is equipped with a local frame buffer. The contents of the local frame buffers are merged in real time for generating the final image. The local frame buffers are virtualized with a demand-paging technique, by which the image memory capacity for each local frame buffer is reduced to one eighth of full-screen capacity. Polygons are rendered in either pixel parallel or polygon parallel depending on the on-screen area of each polygon. The real performance of the VC-1 as well as estimated performance for systems with up to 256 processors is shown.

CR Categories and Subject Descriptors: C.1.2 [Processor Architectures]: Multiprocessors - MIMD, Parallel processors; B.3.2 [Memory Structures]: Design Styles - Virtual memory; I.3.1 [Computer Graphics]: Hardware Architecture - Parallel processing, Raster display devices; I.3.3 [Computer Graphics]: Picture/Image Generation - Display algorithms; I.3.7 [Computer Graphics]: Three-Dimensional Graphics and Realism - Visible line/surface algorithms.

Additional Key Words and Phrases: demand paging, frame buffers, parallel polygon rendering, scalable.

1 Introduction

The increasing demand for real-time generation of high-quality images puts more and more emphasis on the importance of scalability in high-end graphics machines. In mechanical CAD or virtual reality applications, solid models composed of more than one million polygons are often used for generating high-quality images. To display such models at the rate of 30 frames per second, more than 30 million polygons need to be processed in one second, which requires hundreds of processors with current technology. Thus, scalability is the most important issue in order to satisfy such a demand.

The image composition architecture proposed by Molnar [8] is the most promising candidate for future polygon-rendering machines because of its linear scalability. According to Molnar et al. [9], graphics machine architectures can be categorized into three types. The first category, called *sort-first*, performs both geometry calculation and rasterization in pixel parallel, while the second category, named *sort-middle*, executes geometry calculation in object parallel and rasterization in pixel parallel. The sort-middle category, to which most of today's commercial machines including Silicon Graphics RealityEngine [1] belong, has limits on the number of processors since its communication network becomes bottlenecked on a large-scale system when the results of geometry calculation are sent to every rasterization processor. The sort-first category has a similar problem. The last category, called *sort-last*, performs both geometry calculation and rasterization in object parallel, and is possibly scalable since the required bandwidth of its communication network is almost constant against the number of polygons. The sort-last category can be further divided into two classes based on which set of data is transmitted via the communication network. In the first class, each rasterization processor sends only the pixels generated [7]. This class is hard to scale because implementing a scalable communication network for this class is difficult. The second class of the sort-last category is the image composition architecture, in which case each processor outputs all the pixels on the screen. With image composition architecture, a linearly-structured communication network can be used, and therefore, there is no difficulty with increasing the number of processors.

The history of image composition architecture descends from Cohen and Demetrescu's proposal [2]. Various modifications or additions are later applied by many researchers; for example, the integration of a geometry calculation unit in each processor [13], anti-aliasing by generating a depth-sorting list of pixel values [14, 16], anti-aliasing by alpha-blending [15], and the implementation of Phong shading on this architecture [4]. Molnar's architecture differs from these architectures in that each processor can handle plural polygons while the architectures listed above can handle just one polygon per processor.

Figure 1 depicts Molnar's image composition architecture. Each processor has its own full-screen frame buffer, called a local frame buffer, which holds a subimage (including Z-values) generated by the processor. This subimage possibly overlaps with the subimages generated by other processors. The contents of all the local frame buffers are merged periodically by the image merger at the speed of the CRT scan. During merging, depth values are taken into account in order to accomplish hidden surface removal. Palovuori [12] has implemented a system based on this architecture.

One of the problems with this architecture lies in the memory cost for local frame buffers. Since frame buffer bandwidth is one of the critical factors of graphics machines, frame buffer memory should be fast as possible. However, enabling fast memory of full-screen capacity for each processor is impractical if the number of processors is large. Therefore, the use of low-speed memories is imposed, which will degrade the system's performance.

One possible method for overcoming this problem is the region-based approach utilized in the PixelFlow system [10]. In this approach, the screen is divided into several regions, and each local frame buffer holds the pixel information only for one region. To hold pixel information for the entire screen, a global frame buffer is placed between the image merger and the CRT. Prior to rasterization, each processor performs geometry calculations and classifies polygons according to regions using xy-buckets. Then, the polygons are rasterized in multiple passes: for each pass, images for one region are generated on the local frame buffers, and then, the images are merged and stored into the appropriate section on the

†Tsuruga, Ikki-machi, Aizu-Wakamatsu City, Fukushima, 965-80, Japan. Email: nisim@u-aizu.ac.jp, kunii@u-aizu.ac.jp

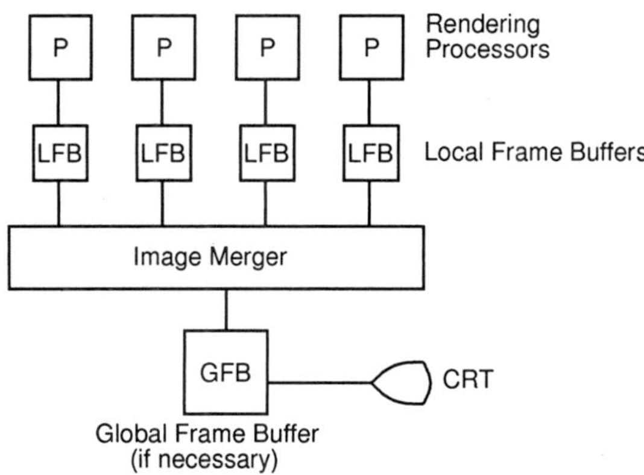

Figure 1: Image composition architecture

global frame buffer. With this method, the memory requirement for the local frame buffer is reduced in inverse proportion to the number of regions. However, it suffers from the following disadvantages:

1. The load balancing problem becomes more difficult.
   In the full-screen approach, it is enough to execute global synchronization once per frame. In the region-based approach, global synchronization is necessary for each pass. Therefore, processor idle time increases since a processor can not start the processing in the next region until all the other processors finish processing the current region.

2. The clipping time increases.
   Polygon clipping occurs not only with the screen boundary but also with region boundaries.

In order to solve these problems, we propose an alternative approach called a *virtual local frame buffer* for reducing the frame buffer memory requirement. Section 2 describes the principle of the virtual local frame buffer. Section 3 presents a prototype machine called the VC-1 developed for justifying the virtual local frame buffer. Section 4 discusses a parallel polygon rendering algorithm suitable for the VC-1 architecture. Section 5 shows the results of performance measurement and compares the virtual frame buffer approach with the region-based approach. Section 6 discusses the scalability of the VC-1 architecture. Section 7 concludes this paper with some suggestions for future research.

2 Virtual Local Frame Buffer

Access to the local frame buffer (LFB) tends to have space locality. In other words, a processor seldom generates an image filling the entire screen. In most cases, only a part of the screen is accessed.

The virtual local frame buffer (VLFB) utilizes this characteristic to reduce the memory requirement. We use a demand-paging technique so that the LFB can virtually hold the pixel information of the entire screen. The screen is divided into small equal-sized rectangular regions called *patches*, and memory units are allocated only to such patches that the processor has accessed (Figure 2). To implement this, two types of memories are used: *image memory* and a *patch table*. Image memory holds pixel information and its capacity is less than full-screen capacity. The patch table maintains the access existence and image memory address of every patch.

In most cases, generated images can be completely stored in image memory. However, when access locality is weak, it is possible that image memory is exhausted. This situation is called a *local frame buffer overflow* (LFB overflow). To handle this, the global frame buffer (GFB) in Figure 1, which is a full-screen frame buffer holding both color and depth information, is necessary. The GFB is cumulative: it stores pixel values only when a new pixel value is closer to the viewer than the one previously stored in the GFB.

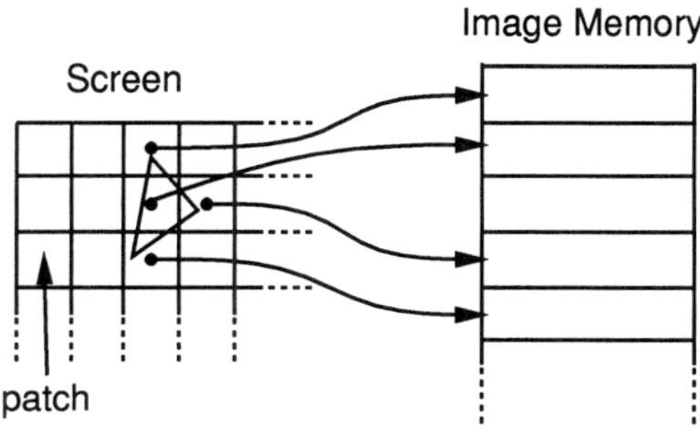

Figure 2: Virtual local frame buffer

When an LFB overflow occurs in a processor, the processor suspends rendering until a certain number of patches in the LFB are transferred to the GFB, and then it continues rendering. Since the GFB is cumulative, the patches can be reused to store a different part of the screen once its contents are transferred to the GFB.

There are two concerns with the VLFB. One is that LFB access time may increase because two memories, the patch table and image memory, are accessed during each access operation. However, by organizing a two-stage pipeline consisting of patch table access and image memory access, the access time increase will be mitigated. The other concern is processor idle time due to LFB overflows. In our implementation, true real-time image generation no longer becomes possible if an LFB overflow occurs in some processor. However, LFB overflows are nearly avoidable with the careful consideration of the image memory capacity as well as a software technique called adaptive parallel rasterization described in Section 4.2.

3 The VC-1

The VC-1 (Figures 3, 10 and 11) is a loosely-coupled multiprocessor with a frame buffer subsystem containing the VLFBs. The primary purposes of the VC-1 are to evaluate our architecture and also to provide an environment for developing parallel software for the architecture. Rendering speed is not a primary design goal; instead, flexibility is maximized. For this reason, the VC-1 has no special hardware accelerators for rasterization.

3.1 Processing Elements

The VC-1 has 16 processing elements, each of which contains the Intel i860 processor operating at 40MHz together with an 8MB local memory. The peak floating-point operation performance of the VC-1 is 1.3 GFLOPS. This high performance makes it possible to apply the VC-1 not only to polygon rendering but also to ray tracing or other numerical applications.

The processing elements are connected by both point-to-point communication links and a broadcast bus. The point-to-point communication links are organized in a modified 2D-torus topology and able to exchange data between any pair of processors or between a processor and the host computer at the speed of 20Mbits/sec. The broadcast bus can transmit data from either the host computer or one of the processors to all the processors. The peak bandwidth of the broadcast bus is 27Mbytes/sec. With polygon rendering, only the broadcast bus is utilized; communication links are reserved for other algorithms.

The sync line is a 1-bit line realizing global synchronization across all the processors. The host computer can optionally participate in the global synchronization.

3.2 The Host Computer

The host computer is an IBM-compatible personal computer equipped with communication interfaces for the VC-1. All the data

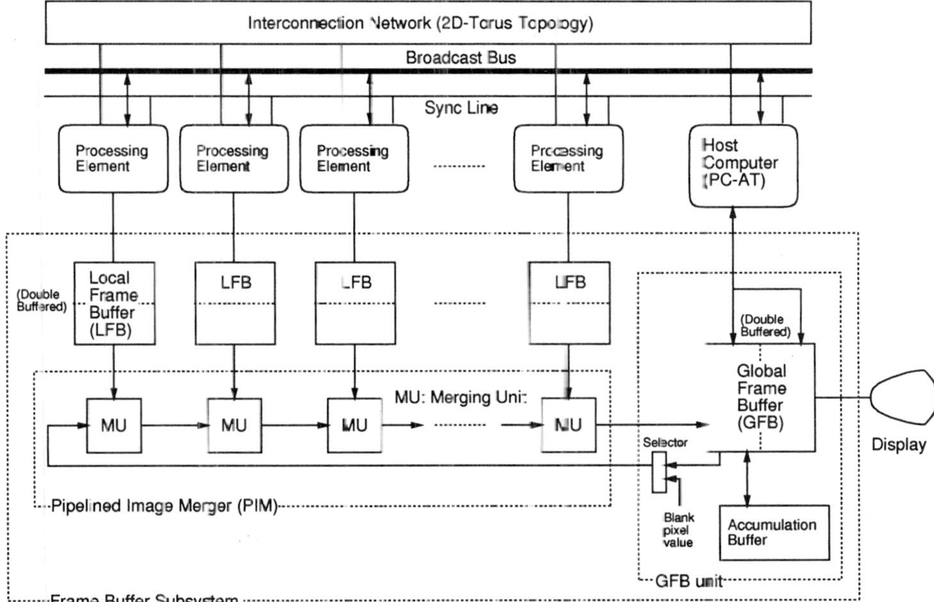

Figure 3: The structure of the VC-1

necessary for calculation, including i860 program codes or polygon data, initially reside in the hard disk of the host computer and are loaded to the local memory of the processors via the broadcast bus.

The host computer has a direct access path to the global frame buffer. This is useful for dumping created images or displaying a cursor on the screen, for example.

3.3 Frame Buffer Subsystem

Local Frame Buffer

The LFB is double-buffered so that the processor can generate the image of the next frame in parallel with the image composition of the previous frame. One buffer is called the front buffer, which is accessed by the processor, and the other is called the back buffer, of which the contents are transmitted to the image merger. These buffers are swapped at the end of each frame generation as well as at the LFB overflow.

Figure 4 shows a block diagram of the LFB unit. The color and depth values are stored in *image memory* consisting of high-speed static RAMs. The image memory capacity for each buffer is 1/4.7 of full-screen capacity. The address space of the image memory is divided into *pages*, each of which has the capacity for storing a patch. Each page is assigned a unique sequential number called a page identifier.

The *patch table* is a high-speed static RAM that maintains the status of every patch. The status consists of a 1-bit field, called a page existence flag, and a 12-bit field, called a page ID field. The page existence flag indicates whether an image memory page is allocated or not. The page ID field contains the identifier of the associated image memory page. Patch size options include 4×4, 8×8, and 16×16 pixels. Usually, the 4×4-pixel configuration yields the best performance. Other patch sizes are designed for evaluation purposes.

The *scan counter* is a free-running counter that controls the transmission from the LFB to the image merger. The counter value advances according to the raster scan order; it starts from the upper-left corner of the screen and ends at the lower-right corner. When it reaches the end, it restarts immediately at the beginning. The clock and reset signals of this counter come from the GFB unit.

The *page ID generator* (PIG) is a counter used for the automatic allocation of a new image memory page. Its value indicates the identifier of the next free page.

The LFB access operations are performed through a two-stage

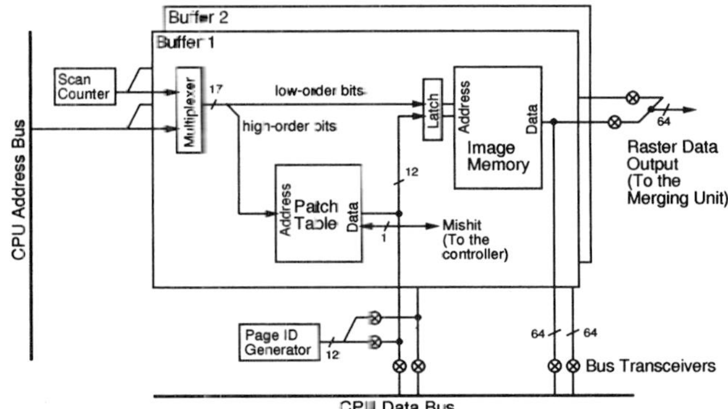

Figure 4: Local frame buffer

pipeline. The first stage reads the patch table and examines the page existence flag. If the flag is false, the first stage also updates the page table entry with the PIG value, sets the page existence flag to true, and increments the PIG. The second stage accesses the image memory. In the first stage, it takes 4 CPU clocks if the page existence flag is false; otherwise, it takes 3 clocks. The second stage always takes 3 clocks. Therefore, LFB access operations can be executed at intervals of 3 or 4 clocks. For more detailed descriptions about LFBs, see [11].

Pipelined Image Merger

The pipelined image merger (PIM) periodically merges the images stored in the LFBs according to the raster scan order. The PIM consists of a linearly-connected array of per-processor elements called merging units (MUs). Each MU receives two pixel values and outputs whichever one has the smallest screen depth. When a corresponding image memory page is not resident on an LFB, the LFB sends a possible maximum depth value to its MU, which makes the MU forward the pixel value from the neighboring unit.

Each MU performs a depth comparison and data selection through a 4-stage pipeline. Therefore, the PIM, as a whole, constructs a $4n$-stage pipeline, where n represents the number of processors. To realize pipeline processing, the scan counter in each

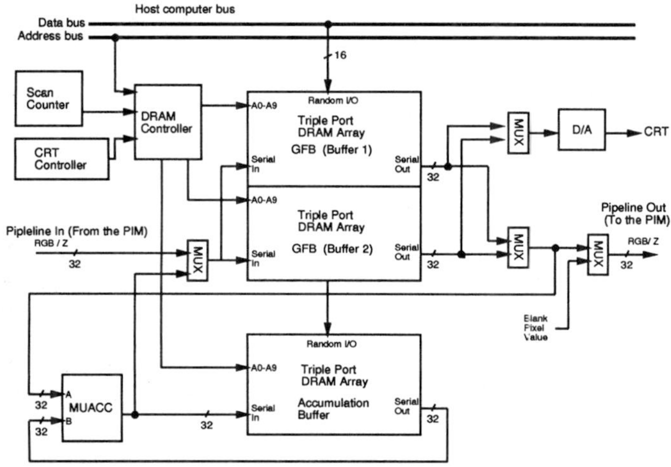

Figure 5: Global frame buffer unit

LFB is advanced by 4 pixels in comparison with the succeeding LFB.

The time needed for merging one full-screen image (denoted by T_m) is equal to $(M + \beta) \cdot N \cdot t + 4 \cdot n \cdot t$, where M and N are respectively horizontal/vertical screen sizes, t is the PIM clock period, and β is the number of PIM clocks required for per-scanline overhead processing in the GFB unit. The first term represents the time for scanning the entire screen, and the second term represents the pipeline delay time. Obviously, T_m should be less than the target frame interval (33.3ms in our case). In the VC-1, those parameters are $M = 640$, $N = 480$, $n = 16$, $\beta = 20$, and $t = 80$ nsec., and therefore, $T_m = 25.3$ msec.

Global Frame Buffer

There are two purposes for inserting the GFB between the PIM and the CRT display:

- to deal with the LFB overflow, and
- to make the PIM raster scan asynchronous with the CRT raster scan.
  This is preferable because the scanning frequency can be set independently to a value convenient for each unit, and also because the image composition can be continued even during the blanking periods of the CRT scan.

Figure 5 shows the structure of the GFB unit. The GFB is double-buffered: one buffer is for CRT refresh, and the other buffer receives images from the PIM. Double-buffering prevents incomplete images from appearing on the CRT. Both of the buffers have full-screen capacity and hold both color and depth information. The roles of these buffers are alternated at the end of image generation.

In addition to the GFBs, there is another full-screen buffer called an *accumulation buffer*, which implements anti-aliasing with multi-pass accumulation [6]. The merging unit for the accumulation buffer (MUACC) is used to accumulate the image stored in one of the GFBs into the accumulation buffer.

The GFBs and accumulation buffer are implemented with triple-port DRAMs. The two serial access ports of the triple-port DRAMs are used for data transmissions with the PIM or to refresh the CRT, while the random access port is utilized for direct access from the host computer.

Fast Screen Clearing

In the VC-1, the LFBs are cleared as follows. The image memory is automatically cleared by hardware while it functions as the back buffer. When the back buffer is read out according to the scan counter, it is cleared immediately after each read operation. As for the patch table, the processor must clear all the patch table entries with software after each LFB swap.

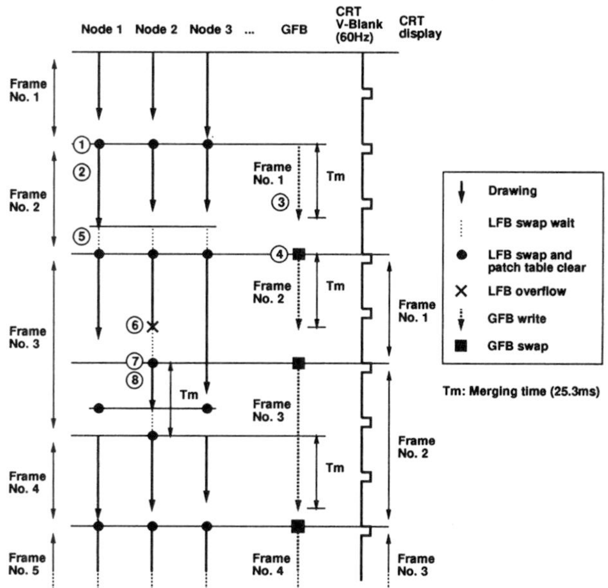

Figure 6: A timing diagram for buffer swapping

Explicit clearance of the GFB is avoided in the following way. During the first round of the image merging scan after the GFB is swapped, blank pixel values are sent to the PIM input (i.e., to the most left MU in Figure 3) so that the old contents of the GFB are replaced. After the first round is completed, the GFB becomes cumulative by sending the old contents of the GFB to the PIM input.

Buffer Swap Control

A timing diagram for buffer swapping is illustrated in Figure 6. When each processor completes image generation, it waits for all of the other processors to complete their tasks using global synchronization, and then it swaps its LFB (①). After this swapping, the processor immediately clears the patch table and starts generating the next frame (②). Parallel with this, the contents of back buffers are merged into the GFB (③). When the merge is completed (i.e., T_m has passed since the last LFB swap), the host computer swaps the GFB after synchronization with the CRT vertical blanking period (④).

When image generation is completed earlier than the GFB swap for the previous frame, the LFB swap is postponed until the completion of the GFB swap (⑤). Without this control, the current frame's image will be mixed with the previous frame's image. An LFB swap on a processor is also blocked if T_m has not passed since the last LFB swap on that processor; otherwise, the unsent contents in the back buffer will be lost.

When an LFB overflow occurs in a particular processor (⑥), an extra LFB swap is executed on that processor (⑦). Like a normal LFB swap, this LFB swap is also postponed until both of the conditions mentioned above are met. Then, the processor clears its patch table and resumes drawing (⑧). A processor's worst-case idle time upon an LFB overflow is 33.3ms. We could reduce this time by utilizing the back buffer's image memory pages immediately after they are sent to the GFB rather than waiting until all the contents in the back buffer are transferred; however, this greatly complicates LFB hardware.

4 Parallel Polygon Rendering on the VC-1

An outline of the rendering routine on the VC-1 is as follows. First, the scene database is transmitted from the host computer to each processor's local memory via the broadcast bus. Polygon data are partitioned into subsets, each of which is loaded to a different processor's local memory. Other database components, such as the eye position or light source information, are duplicated to all of the processors' local memory. Next, the host computer broadcasts a command packet to all the processors, by which each processor starts geometric calculations and rasterization for assigned polygons. When the image generation is completed, frame buffers are swapped as described previously.

In generating animated images, the scene database on each processor's local memory is incrementally modified, i.e., only the inter-frame difference of the database is transmitted between frames rather than retransmitting the whole database. For example, if the eye position has changed between frames, only the viewing matrix is transmitted.

4.1 Polygon Assignment

The mapping of polygons to processors is one of the key factors influencing system performance. Three points have to be considered in relation to this problem: (1) load balancing, (2) the reduction of duplicated polygon vertices among processors, and (3) the minimization of LFB overflows. As for (1), it is not enough for reasonable load balancing only to keep the number of polygons even, since the processing time of a polygon depends on its size and clipping conditions. Problems (1) and (2) have been discussed by some researchers [3, 5]; however, (3) is a new problem specific to our architecture.

The simplest way to achieve load balancing is to allocate independent polygons one by one to the most lightly loaded processor at each moment. If there is more than one choice, the target processor is selected randomly among them. This method is advantageous in (1); however, it is unacceptable with respect to (2) because common vertices shared by neighboring polygons are likely scattered to different processors. Moreover, this method is disadvantageous in (3) because each processor generates a highly discrete image consuming a large number of patches.

A more practical method is to allocate clusters of polygons to the most lightly loaded processor rather than allocating independent ones [5]. The number of polygons in each cluster is called the cluster size (denoted by w). Each cluster contains up to w polygons which are geometrically close to each other. The sequence of polygons specified implicitly by the user through a graphics library tends to have space coherence, i.e., two polygons consecutively indicated by the user have a high probability of being geometrically close. Therefore, it is sufficient when constructing clusters to let the first w polygons in the sequence be the first cluster, let the next w polygons be the second cluster, and so on. With this method, the best balance of the aforementioned three points can be achieved by tuning the value of w.

4.2 Adaptive Parallel Rasterization

The clustering method is not sufficient for reasonable load balancing if some polygons occupy a large area on the screen. For example, the scene shown in Figure 13(c) has one large-sized polygon constructing the table. Such a polygon not only causes load concentration but also increases the LFB overflow. To avoid these problems, we developed a technique called adaptive parallel rasterization (APR).

The APR method rasterizes a polygon in pixel parallel when its estimated size is larger than a predetermined value called the APR threshold; otherwise, the polygon is rasterized in polygon parallel as usual. After geometry calculation, the processors calculate the on-screen area of each polygon. If the area is larger than the APR threshold, the screen coordinates and colors of the vertices of the polygon are broadcast to all the processors using the broadcast bus. When a processor receives the broadcast data, it rasterizes the polygon only for the pixels that are assigned to the processor. Figure 12 illustrates a processor assignment based on APR.

One of the concerns of APR is the overhead due to the area calculation of the polygons. However, on the VC-1 which calculates the area as the vector product of the two edges of a triangle, it is known from experiments that the overhead is less than 3% of the total computation time.

5 Evaluation Results

In this section, the VC-1 architecture and our parallel polygon rendering methods are evaluated using the sample scenes shown in Figure 13. For systems with 16 or less processors, real performance is shown. For systems with 17 to 256 processors, estimated performance is displayed.

Using the VC-1, the rendering time for over 16 processors is estimated. When APR is not performed, the rendering time is estimated using one of the processors and the host computer as follows. Initially, the rendering time for each logical processor of the estimation target system is measured on the physical processor, and then, the system rendering time is calculated as the maximum of the measured rendering times. If APR is active, the rendering time is split into polygon-parallel and pixel-parallel parts, and the estimation is performed in two passes; the first pass determines the polygon-parallel part of the rendering time, and the second pass figures out the complete rendering time. These methods yield exactly the same performance as real performance (See [11] for justification). For a 16-processor system or smaller, it is confirmed from experiments that the performance estimated by this method coincides with real performance.

5.1 Rendering Time

Figure 7 indicates the rendering time for each sample scene varying the number of processors. The rendering time decreases in inverse proportion to the number of processors as long as they do not reach 33.3ms, which is the lower limit determined by the speed of the image merger and the rate of CRT refresh. For scenes composed of many polygons, such as the *ter250* scene (containing 203522 polygons), the excellent scalability of the VC-1 architecture is observed. In fact, a speed 190 times faster is achieved with 256 processors for the *ter250* scene. The maximum rendering performance of the VC-1 calculated from Figure 7 is 514K polygons per second for a 16-processor system and 6.1M polygons per second for a 256-processor system.

Figure 4.2 shows the rendering time as a function of image memory capacity. As the image memory capacity decreases, the rendering time increases because of LFB overflows. In a 16-processor system, it is observed that 1/8 of full-screen capacity is enough to render all the sample scenes without significant performance degradation. Similarly, in a 256-processor system, image memory capacity can be reduced to 1/32 of full-screen capacity.

5.2 The Effect of Adaptive Parallel Rasterization

Figure 9 displays the relationship between the APR threshold and rendering time. As the APR threshold becomes larger (i.e., as the ratio of polygon-parallel rasterization increases), load balancing becomes worse and also LFB overflows increase. Conversely, as the APR threshold becomes smaller, total rasterization time as well as broadcast communication time increase. Therefore, we have a minimum rendering time at some APR threshold. When the *table* scene is rendered with 16 processors, the most appropriate APR threshold is 500, where the rendering time is reduced to 75% of the rendering time without APR (i.e., the rendering time when the APR threshold is infinity).

It becomes clear from further experiments that the main advantageous effect of APR is the reduction of LFB overflows rather than the improvement of load balancing. Without APR, a polygon whose

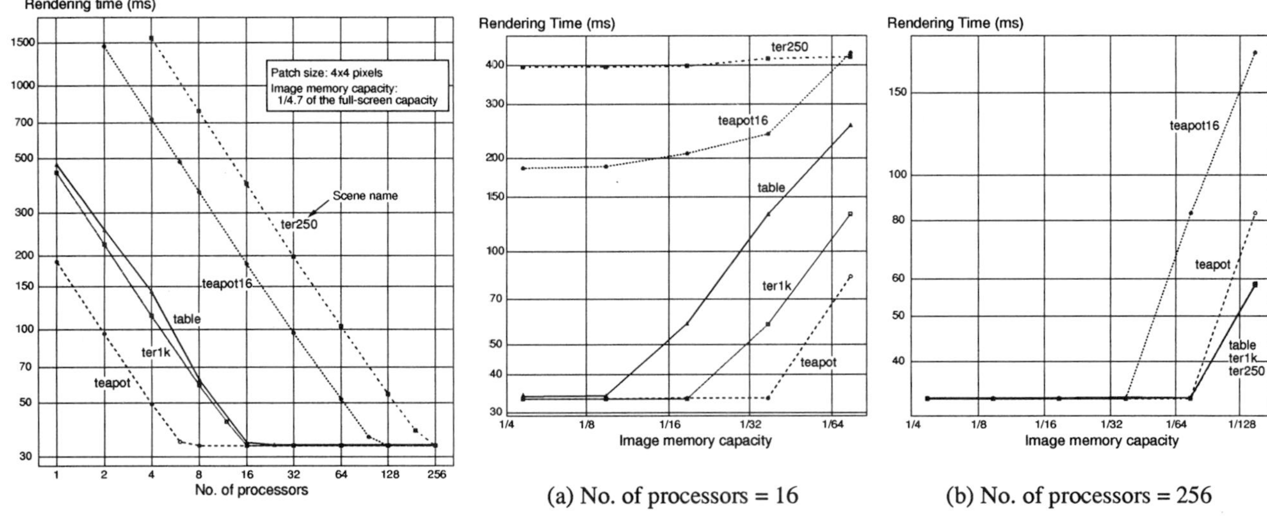

(a) No. of processors = 16

(b) No. of processors = 256

Figure 7: Rendering time versus the number of processors

Figure 8: Rendering time versus image memory capacity

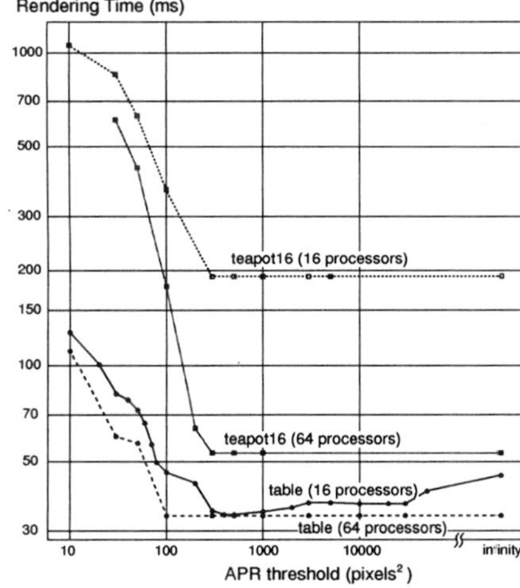

Figure 9: Rendering time versus the APR threshold

image is larger than the image memory capacity would inevitably cause an LFB overflow, which often leads to significant performance degradation. APR avoids LFB overflows by dividing such a large polygon into pieces and effectively making image memory consumption even among processors.

5.3 Comparison with the Region-Based Approach

As described in Section 1, the PixelFlow system reduces image memory capacity by dividing the screen into regions and rasterizing polygons in multiple passes. Each renderer in the PixelFlow system actually has several buffers to improve load balancing. We simulated this memory-saving method on the VC-1 for comparison.

Table 1 contrasts the performances for the two different memory-saving methods when the *ter1k* scene is rendered with 16 processors. We averaged these values over 48 different view angles. The number of buffers indicates the number of independently accessible LFB banks in a processor. For the VLFB, this number is 2 because we use double-buffering. For the region-based approach, this number corresponds to the maximum number of regions which each renderer can hold. The geometry calculation time refers to the total time for transformation, lighting, and region classification. The rasterization time represents the total time for clipping and rasterization. The global synchronization time indicates processor idle time due to load imbalance.

Table 1: Comparison with the region-based approach

Memory-saving method	VLFB	RB 2×2†	RB 4×4†	RB 4×4†
Number of buffers	2	2	2	4
Image memory capacity for each buffer	1/8	1/4	1/16	1/16
Total image memory capacity	1/4	1/2	1/8	1/4
Rendering time	33.4ms	51.0ms	73.5ms	66.9ms
Geometry calculation time	12.3ms	14.1ms	14.1ms	14.1ms
Rasterization time	14.7ms	29.1ms	41.5ms	41.5ms
Global synchronization time	1.4ms	7.3ms	17.3ms	10.7ms

† 'RB $m \times n$' means the region-based approach in which the screen is divided into $m \times n$ regions.

With the VLFB, the *ter1k* scene can be rendered in 33.4ms using an image memory whose total capacity is 1/4 of full-screen capacity. On the other hand, if the region-based approach is taken, the rendering time increases considerably even if the image memory capacity is 1/2. There are two main reasons for this: the increase of rasterization time due to additional clipping tasks for region boundaries and the increase of global synchronization time resulting from the aggravation of load balancing.

It is possible to introduce special hardware for clipping in order to improve the performance for the region-based approach. Nevertheless, this will only lighten the increase in rasterization time. The increase in global synchronization time is essential except for that due to the load imbalance caused by the clipping.

The superiority of the VLFB becomes more remarkable in large-scale systems. In the VLFB, the image memory capacity decreases as the number of processors increases. However, the region-based approach has no such characteristic.

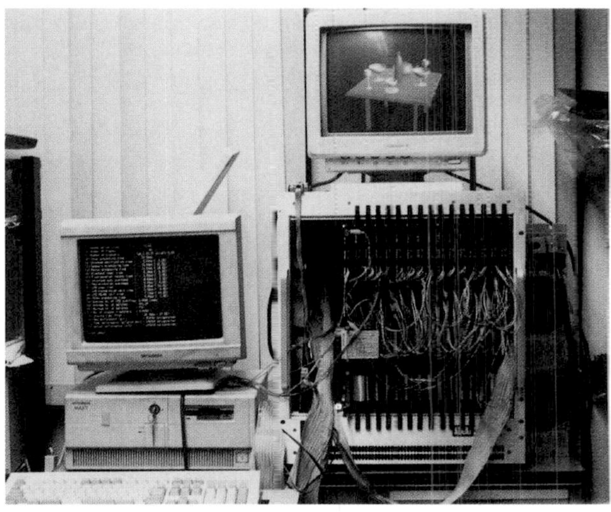

Figure 10: The VC-1

Figure 11: The VC-1 main board

This board contains a CPU, a local memory, communication interfaces, an LFB unit and a merging unit. It is a 6-layer printed circuit board whose size is 356 × 400mm.

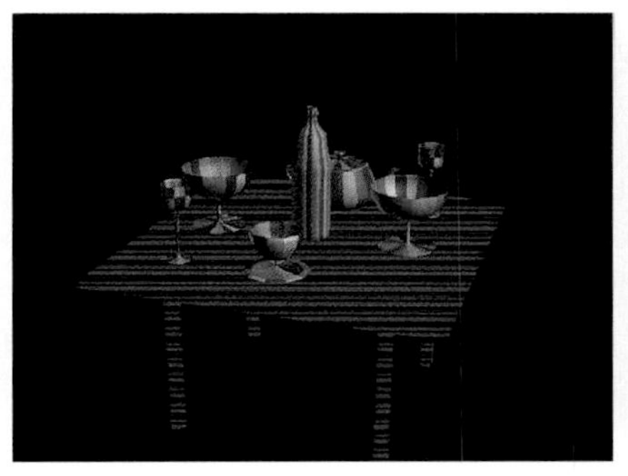

Figure 12: Processor assignment with APR

The color of each polygon identifies the processor to which the polygon is assigned. The large polygons constructing the table are rasterized in pixel parallel with line interleaving.

(a) teapot (No. of polygons = 4096)

(b) teapot16 (No. of polygons = 65536)

Figure 13: Sample scenes

(c) table (No. of polygons = 10224)

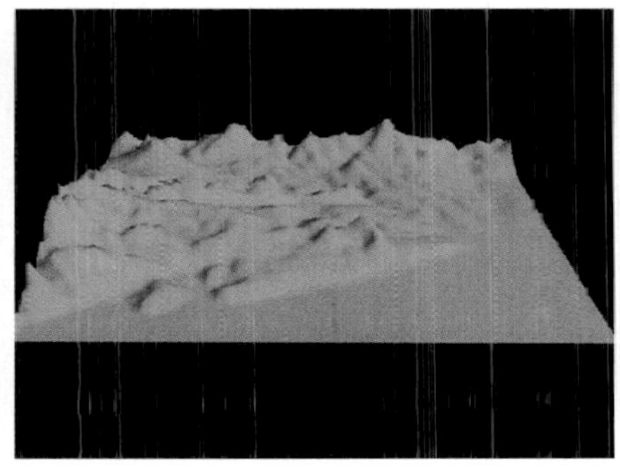

(d) ter1k (No. of polygons = 12482)

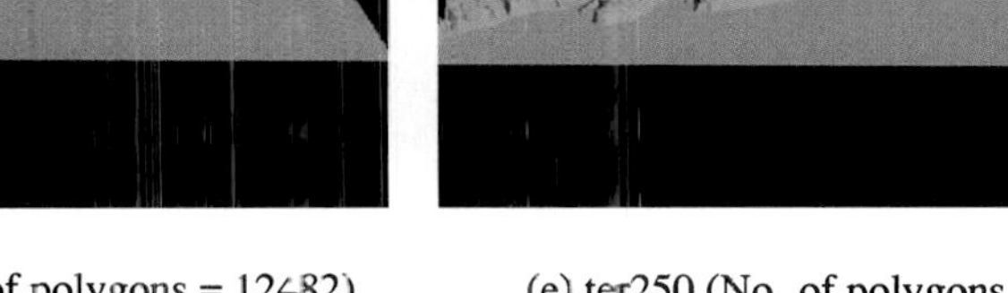

(e) ter250 (No. of polygons = 203522)

Figure 13: Sample scenes (continued)

6 Discussions

As the number of processors increases, the APR threshold should be lowered, since the image memory capacity for each processor decreases. One might think that this limits the system scalability because the number of polygons transmitted via the broadcast bus increases. However, the average size of these polygons tends to become smaller as the number of processors increases, and therefore, we believe that this is not a serious limitation.

To perform anti-aliasing with true real-time image generation or to increase screen resolution, the bandwidth of the image merger must be increased in proportion to the number of samples per pixel or the number of pixels on the screen. As a result, an extremely high bandwidth will be required. This is a major weakness of image composition architecture, although we think that future advancement in device technology will take care of this. As for scalability, this still remains regardless of these extensions.

If special hardware for rasterization is added to our architecture, the number of polygons per processor will increase. This does not necessarily mean an increase in image memory capacity. The image memory capacity is strongly related to the number of pixels accessed in each processor, which is represented as $a \cdot p/n$, where a is the average size of polygons, p is the total number of polygons, and n is the number of processors. Since $a \cdot p$ (i.e., the number of pixels totaled over all the polygons) usually remains constant against changes in the number of polygons, $a \cdot p/n$ is invariable no matter how p/n increases. As for scalability, adding special hardware does not influence this.

VC-1 is designed mainly for retained-mode graphics APIs. It is possible to support immediate-mode APIs if the host computer broadcasts the whole scene database for each frame; however, the system will no longer be scalable because the broadcast bus will be bottlenecked. It seems that there is no way to make a scalable machine with immediate-mode APIs since they enforce the serial traversal of the database in the host computer. Even with the retained-mode APIs, the broadcast bus may be bottlenecked when the coordinates of the polygon vertices are constantly changing. However, this problem can be solved by allowing the node processors to determine the coordinates by solving physical equations or dividing curved surfaces, for example.

7 Conclusions

In this paper, we proposed a novel frame buffer architecture called the *virtual local frame buffer* to reduce the memory requirement in parallel graphics machines based on image composition. To evaluate the architecture, we developed a prototype machine called the VC-1. From experiments on the VC-1, it was observed that the virtual local frame buffer technique reduces the image memory capacity to 1/8 of full-screen capacity in a 16-processor system and to 1/32 in a 256-processor system without sacrificing the system's performance. This reduction enables us to use fast static RAMs for the local frame buffer, by which rendering performance is improved.

The adaptive parallel rasterization method, which selects an appropriate parallelization approach based on a threshold value, is essential to the virtual local frame buffer. Without this technique, the system performance would be degraded considerably due to the exhaustion of the image memory. However, the problem of how to find the optimal threshold, which guarantees the avoidance of this exhaustion, is still open.

In the future, we would like to extend our architecture to support both anti-aliasing and texture mapping. We are also planning to add special hardware for rasterization to this architecture to improve polygon rendering performance.

Acknowledgments

We greatly appreciate the financial support of Kubota Computer, Inc. We are also grateful to the members of the past VC-1 project in the University of Tokyo, Ryo Mukai, Reiji Suda and Yukio Sakagawa for their help in hardware design, and Jun Naito for his assistance in software development. Special thanks go to Hiroyuki Nitta for his help in gathering equipment and materials and providing useful technical information. We would also like to thank Thomas Orr for his thoughtful comments.

References

[1] AKELEY, K. RealityEngine Graphics. *Proceedings of SIGGRAPH '93* (August 1993), 109–116.

[2] COHEN, D., AND DEMETRESCU, S. A VLSI approach to Computer Image Generation. Tech. rep., Information Sciences Institute, University of Southern California, 1979.

[3] COX, M. *Algorithms for Parallel Rendering*. PhD thesis, Dept. of Computer Science, Princeton University, 1995.

[4] DEERING, M., WINNER, S., SCHEDIWY, B., DUFFY, C., AND HUNT, N. The Triangle Processor and Normal Vector Shader: A VLSI System for High Performance Graphics. *ACM Computer Graphics 22*, 4 (August 1988), 21–30.

[5] ELLSWORTH, D., GOOD, H., AND TEBBS, B. Distributing Display Lists on a Multicomputer. *ACM Computer Graphics 24*, 2 (March 1990), 147–154.

[6] HAEBERLI, P., AND AKELEY, K. The Accumulation Buffer: Hardware Support for High-Quality Rendering. *ACM Computer Graphics 24*, 4 (August 1990), 309–318.

[7] KUBOTA COMPUTER INC. TITAN2 Technical Overview, 1993.

[8] MOLNAR, S. Combining Z-buffer Engines for Higher-Speed Rendering. In *Advances in Computer Graphics Hardware III* (1988), Springer Verlag, pp. 171–182.

[9] MOLNAR, S., COX, M., ELLSWORTH, D., AND FUCHS, H. A sorting classification of parallel rendering. *IEEE Computer Graphics and Applications 14*, 4 (July 1994), 23–32.

[10] MOLNAR, S., EYLES, J., AND POULTON, J. PixelFlow: High-Speed Rendering Using Image Composition. *ACM Computer Graphics 26*, 2 (July 1992), 231–240.

[11] NISHIMURA, S. *A Parallel Architecture for Computer Graphics Based on the Conflict-Free Multiport Frame Buffer*. Doctoral dissertation, Dept. of Information Science, Faculty of Science, The University of Tokyo, 1995.

[12] PALOVUORI, K. An Implementation of an Linearly Expandable Graphics Processing Architecture. Tech. Rep. 8-94, Dept. of Electrical Engineering, Tampere University of Technology, Finland, 1994.

[13] ROMAN, G. C., AND KIMURA, T. VLSI perspective of real-time hidden-surface elimination. *Computer-Aided Design 13*, 2 (March 1981), 99–107.

[14] SCHNEIDER, B.-O. A Processor for an Object-Oriented Rendering System. *Computer Graphics Forum 7*, 4 (1988), 301–310.

[15] SHAW, C. D., GREEN, M., AND SCHAEFFER, J. A VLSI Architecture for Image Composition. In *Advances in Computer Graphics Hardware III* (1988), Springer Verlag, pp. 183–199.

[16] WEINBERG, R. Parallel Processing Image Synthesis and Anti-Aliasing. *ACM Computer Graphics 15*, 3 (August 1981), 55–62.

Rendering from Compressed Textures

*Andrew C. Beers, *Maneesh Agrawala, and †Navin Chaddha

* Computer Science Department
Stanford University

†Computer Systems Laboratory
Stanford University

Abstract

We present a simple method for rendering directly from compressed textures in hardware and software rendering systems. Textures are compressed using a vector quantization (VQ) method. The advantage of VQ over other compression techniques is that textures can be decompressed quickly during rendering. The drawback of using lossy compression schemes such as VQ for textures is that such methods introduce errors into the textures. We discuss techniques for controlling these losses. We also describe an extension to the basic VQ technique for compressing mipmaps. We have observed compression rates of up to 35 : 1, with minimal loss in visual quality and a small impact on rendering time. The simplicity of our technique lends itself to an efficient hardware implementation.

CR categories: I.3.7 [Computer Graphics]: 3D Graphics and Realism - Texture; I.4.2 [Image Processing]: Compression - Coding

1 Introduction

Texture mapping is employed on high-end graphics workstations and rendering systems to increase the visual complexity of a scene without increasing its geometric complexity[7]. Texture mapping allows a rendering system to map an image onto simple scene geometry to make objects look much more complex or realistic than the underlying geometry. Recently, texture mapping hardware has become available on lower-end workstations, personal computers, and home game systems.

One of the costs of texture mapping is that the texture images often require a large amount of memory. For a particular scene, the memory required by the textures is dependent on the number of textures and the size of each texture. In some cases, the size of the textures may exceed the size of the scene geometry[3].

In hardware systems supporting real–time texture mapping, textures are generally placed in dedicated memory that can be accessed quickly as pixels are generated. In some hardware systems, textures are replicated in memory to facilitate fast parallel access [1]. Because texture memory is a limited resource in these systems, it can be consumed quickly. Although memory concerns are less severe for software rendering systems since textures are stored in main memory, there are advantages to conserving texture memory. In particular, using less memory for textures may yield caching benefits, especially in cases where the textures do not fit in main memory and cause the machine to swap.

*Gates Hall, Stanford University, Stanford, CA 94305
maneesh@cs.stanford.edu
http://www-graphics.stanford.edu/

One way to alleviate these memory limitations is to store compressed representations of textures in memory. A modified renderer could then render directly from this compressed representation. In this paper we examine the issues involved in rendering from compressed texture maps and propose a scheme for compressing textures using vector quantization (VQ)[4]. We also describe an extension of our basic VQ technique for compressing mipmaps. We show that by using VQ compression, we can achieve compression rates of up to 35 : 1 with little loss in the visual quality of the rendered scene. We observe a 2 to 20 percent impact on rendering time using a software renderer that renders from the compressed format. However, the technique is so simple that incorporating it into hardware should have very little impact on rendering performance.

2 Choosing a Compression Scheme

There are many compression techniques for images, most of which are geared towards compression for storage or transmission. In choosing a compression scheme for texture mapping there are several issues to consider. In this section we discuss these issues and we show how VQ compression addresses each of them.

Decoding Speed. In order to render directly from the compressed representation, an essential feature of the compression scheme is fast decompression so that the time necessary to access a single texture pixel is not severely impacted. With VQ, decompression is performed through table lookups and is very fast. A transform coding scheme such as JPEG[10] is more expensive because extracting the value of a texture pixel would require an expensive inverse Discrete Cosine Transform (DCT) computation.

Random Access. It is difficult to know in advance how a renderer will access a texture. Thus, texture compression schemes must provide fast random access to pixels in the texture. For compression schemes like JPEG or run length coding which produce variable rate codes, extracting a texture pixel might require decompressing a large portion of the texture. Unlike variable rate codes, fixed-rate VQ represents each block of texture pixels with a fixed number of bits. Since the number of bits is known in advance, indexing any particular pixel is fast and easy.

Compression Rate and Visual Quality. While lossless compression schemes, such as Lempel–Ziv compression[12], will perfectly preserve a texture, they achieve much lower compression rates than lossy schemes. However, using a lossy compression scheme introduces errors into the textures. With VQ, there are many parameters that can be used to control these errors. A major difference between images and textures is that images are viewed on their own, while textures are viewed as part of a scene with orientation and size dependent on the mapping from scene surface to texture. Thus, for image compression algorithms, the visual quality of the compressed image is most important, while for texture compression algorithms, the visual quality of the rendered scene, not the texture map, is most important.

Encoding Speed. Experimenting with the compression rate versus visual quality tradeoff can be difficult if encoding is slow. Although optimal VQ encoding can be a time-consuming process, fast sub-optimal encoding algorithms exist. Texture compression, however, is an asymmetric application of compression, since decoding speed is essential while encoding speed is useful but not necessary.

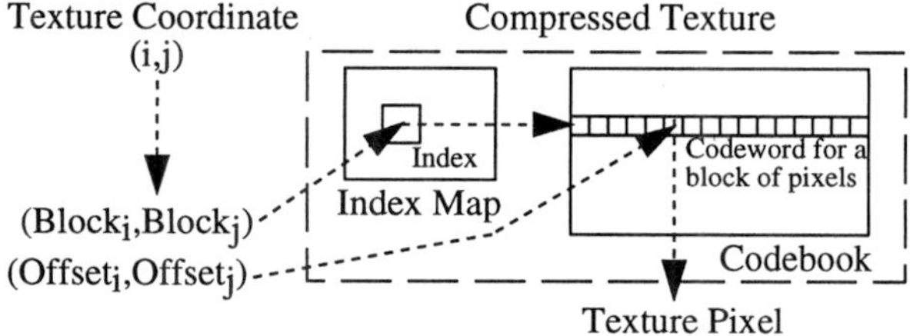

Figure 1: Accessing a pixel from a compressed texture.

3 Rendering

We have chosen VQ as our texture compression algorithm because it addresses all of the issues presented in the previous section, and in particular it supports fast decompression. When using VQ, we consider a texture as a set of pixel blocks. VQ attempts to characterize this set of blocks by a smaller set of representative blocks called a *codebook*. A lossy–compressed version of the original image is represented as a set of indices into this codebook, with one index per block of pixels. This set of indices is called the *index map*. The texture can be decompressed by looking up each block of pixels in the codebook via its index. In [9], such an indexed-lookup technique is used to page in uncompressed textures from disk on demand. Color quantization algorithms such as the Median Cut Algorithm[6] use this same indexed-lookup technique for representing 24 bit images with 8 bits per pixel. A method for compressing 3D volumes using VQ and a fast technique for volume rendering directly from this compressed format is presented in [8]. While we will describe exactly how to encode textures using VQ in section 4, we first show how to render directly from VQ compressed textures.

The rendering algorithm is outlined in the following algorithm. Assuming that the (s, t) texture coordinate has already been converted to an integral (i, j) location within the texture, we:

1. Determine in which block B pixel (i, j) lies, and the offset of pixel (i, j) within that block.
2. Lookup the index associated with block B to determine the corresponding codeword in the codebook.
3. Lookup the pixel (i, j) within this codeword block.

The three step process is shown pictorially in figure 1. Step 1 is easily implemented with fast bit shift and logical operators when texture and block sizes are a power of two. To achieve the highest compression rate we store the index map in a packed representation. Therefore, in step 2, two memory accesses and a few simple bit operations may be required if the size of each index is such that the indices do not fall on word boundaries. However, for word aligned indices, the appropriate index can be determined with a single lookup.

4 Encoding

The most critical part of encoding a texture using VQ is designing the codebook. The Generalized Lloyd Algorithm (GLA)[4] is one technique for generating a codebook. It is an iterative clustering algorithm which yields a locally optimal codebook for a given set of pixel blocks, called the *training set* of vectors.We generally use all the blocks in the original texture as our training set. The algorithm begins by selecting a set of potential codewords from the training set and then iterates on the following steps. Each training vector is grouped with the nearest codeword, based on some distortion measure such as Euclidean distance. The centroids of the groups are chosen as the new set of codewords, and the process repeats until the set of codewords converges.

Although this "Full Search" approach is locally optimal, generating the codebook is computationally expensive. A faster technique for producing the codebook is Tree Structured VQ[4]. This approach designs the codebook recursively, organizing the codebook as a binary tree. The first step is to find the centroid of the set of training vectors, which becomes the root level codeword. To find the children of this root, the centroid and a perturbed centroid are chosen as initial child codewords. The GLA is then used to converge on the locally optimal codewords for this first level in the tree. The training vectors are split into two groups based on these locally optimal codewords and the algorithm recurses on each of these subtrees. Note that once the child codewords have been chosen, the training vectors are permanently grouped with the nearest codeword. Since codewords cannot jump across subtrees, this approach is not guaranteed to produce the locally optimal codebook, but is substantially faster than Full Search VQ [4].

Once the codebook has been generated we encode a texture by mapping each block of pixels to the nearest codeword. With Full Search VQ we exhaustively search for the nearest codeword. With Tree Structured VQ, we can traverse the codebook tree always taking the path with the closest codeword. Thus, both codebook generation and texture encoding are faster with Tree Structured VQ than with Full Search VQ. We use Tree Structured VQ for quick experimentation, and Full Search VQ for generating final codebooks.

5 Texture Encoding Tradeoffs

In generating the VQ encoding for a texture we have control over several parameters that can be used to tradeoff compression rate for the quality of the compressed texture. This tradeoff must be considered carefully when encoding textures for a given scene. In this section we describe some of the parameters in VQ encoding that affect this tradeoff.

We have many choices on how to partition the image data into training vectors when designing a VQ codebook. The size of a vector is dictated by the dimensions of the block of pixels being coded and the number of color channels used to define the color of each pixel. We can either design a codebook for each color channel separately, or treat components of a color as a single value and code them together. We use the latter approach, which results in a higher compression rate since only one codebook and index map is used, instead of one codebook and index map per color channel.

The size of the codebook influences the compression rate in two ways. A larger codebook will lower the compression rate by increasing the size of the compressed representation. A larger codebook also means that the indices into the codebook will require more bits, increasing the size of the index map. However, a larger codebook will contain more of the representative blocks giving us better quality compressed textures. The size of the pixel block used in texture encoding also has a large effect on the overall compression rate. For example, if we use 4×4 blocks when encoding a texture, each RGB pixel block contains $4 \times 4 \times 3 = 48$ bytes. With a 256 entry codebook, we use a 1 byte index to represent each pixel block, yielding a base compression rate of $48 : 1$. The overall compression rate is reduced from the base rate by the storage requirements of the codebook. For example, when encoding a 512×512 image using a 256 entry codebook, the overall compression rate falls to $27.4 : 1$. With 2×2 blocks the base compression rate is only $12 : 1$. However, there are fewer possible 2×2 blocks than 4×4 blocks, and therefore, 2×2 codebooks produce better quality compressed textures than 4×4 codebooks. Similarly we could use larger blocksizes to gain higher compression rates for worse quality.

To achieve additional compression, we can encode three channel RGB textures in the 4:1:1 YUV format, commonly used in video standards. This format stores the color channels U and V decimated by a factor 2 both horizontally and vertically, and the luminance channel Y at full resolution. Converting from this YUV representa-

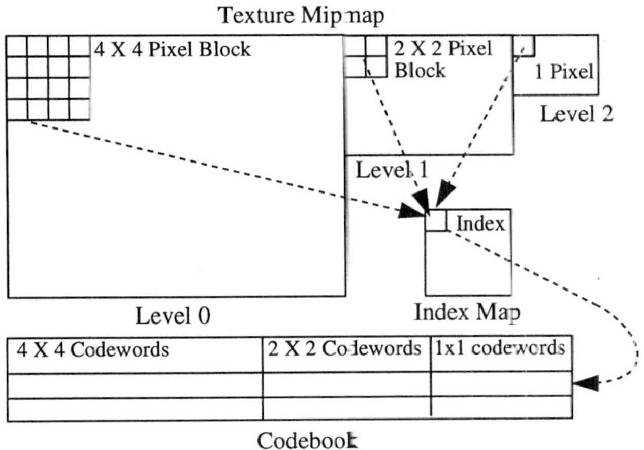

Figure 2: The encoding of three consecutive levels of a mipmap.

tion back to the RGB representation used by most renderers requires only multiplication by a constant 3x3 matrix, which is easily implemented in hardware.

We can also increase the compression rate by amortizing the cost of a larger codebook over several textures. We train a codebook on multiple textures to determine one codebook for all of them. A single codebook may be enough to characterize all of the textures in a scene. If one codebook results in too many compression artifacts, we can group the textures and design one codebook per group.

6 Mipmapping

An effective way to resample textures is by using a mipmap[11]. A mipmap stores a texture as an image pyramid, and is designed to allow efficient filtering of a texture. Each mipmap level stores a filtered version of the texture corresponding to a particular image pixel to texture pixel ratio. To apply a mipmapped texture, we compute texture coordinates (s, t) and an approximation to d, the image pixel to texture pixel ratio. Because these values are not integral in most cases, trilinear interpolation is used to determine the texture value.

One way to compress mipmaps would be to compress each mipmap level individually. However, we can take advantage of the correlation between successive layers of a mipmap by encoding several levels at once, generating one codebook as well as one index map for the group of levels. This allows us to gain higher compression rates in compressing mipmaps.

To compress a mipmap, we begin by compressing the original texture using 4×4 blocks. Given the codebook for this first mipmap level, we can form a codebook for the next level by averaging each 4×4 codeword down to a 2×2 codeword. Similarly, a codebook for the third level of the mipmap can be formed by averaging these 2×2 codewords down to single pixel codewords. Instead of storing three codebooks, we can combine them into one codebook containing extended codewords. Each extended codeword is formed by concatenating the 4×4 codeword with the corresponding subsampled 2×2 and 1×1 codewords. Note that the index maps for the three levels are identical, and therefore can be shared. The encoding of three mipmap levels is shown pictorially in figure 2. The full mipmap can be formed by repeating this process for every group of three levels, creating a separate index map and codebook for every group of three. In practice, once the size of a mipmap level is less than 32×32 pixels, we store it uncompressed.

For the trilinear interpolation, each (s, t, d) mipmap texture coordinate is converted to the eight nearest integral (i, j, L) mipmap locations in two adjacent levels of the mipmap. To access a pixel in a given level L we first determine the group of levels to which L belongs. The texture coordinates are then used to look up the index into the codebook from the index map for that group of levels. The level number determines in which part of the extended codeword the desired pixel is stored. Finally, the block offsets of the pixel are used to address the desired pixel.

Trial		Overall Rate	MSE
RGB Files:	All: 4096, 4 × 4, RGB	11.8:1	12.12
RGB Files:	All: 4096, 4 × 4, YUV	15.3:1	16.17
RGB Files:	Signs, Roads: 256, 2 × 2, YUV Other: 4096, 4 × 4, YUV	12:7:1	11.27
RGB Files:	Signs: 256, 2 × 2, YUV Roads, Other: 256, 4 × 4, YUV	24.5:1	16.19

Table 3: For each of these trials, one channel textures were compressed using 256, 2 × 2 codewords, and RGBA textures were compressed using 256, 2 × 2 codewords.

The drawback of our mipmap encoding approach is that the quality of the compressed level 1 and level 2 mipmaps can not be any better than the quality of the compressed level 0 mipmap, even though smaller sized codewords are used for levels 1 and 2. Interpolative VQ[5] [4] is an alternative technique for compressing image pyramids such as mipmaps. The general approach is to perform VQ on a subsampled image, decompress the image, interpolate it up to the next larger image size and VQ the difference between the interpolated image and the original. The benefits of this approach are that it takes advantage of the correlation between successive levels in the mipmap during encoding, and unlike the scheme we propose, the quality of each compressed mipmap level is somewhat independent of the quality of other mipmap levels. However, Interpolative VQ also requires a separate codebook per mipmap level, and retrieving a pixel from a particular mipmap level requires building up the the pixel value from the most subsampled mipmap level up to the desired level, accessing a codeword from each mipmap level in between. Although we have not performed direct comparisons to our encoding scheme, these two drawbacks make Interpolative VQ unattractive for fast texture mapping applications and we do not to use it in encoding mipmaps.

7 Results

We have evaluated our proposed VQ texture compression method by rendering texture mapped scenes using two different renderers: IRIS Performer and a custom software scan converter. We present the results for two scenes in this section. Since we cannot directly load our compressed format into Performer, we compress and decompress each texture in a preprocessing step that introduces compression errors into the textures. While we cannot directly compare rendering speed we can compare the visual quality of the rendered images. We also use a software scan converter to render textures directly from our compressed format. This allows us to compare both rendering times for, and the visual quality of, images rendered with and without compressed textures. We experiment with several of the VQ encoding parameters discussed in section 5 and report the compression rates for each of the scenes.

The Performer Town is a fully texture mapped virtual environment, containing 85 textures which require a total of 5 MB when uncompressed. Although most of the textures are three channel RGB textures, there are 14 one channel intensity textures and 7 four channel RGBA textures. We compress the intensity textures with a single codebook containing 256 codewords and a blocksize of 2 × 2. We generate a separate codebook for the RGBA textures again using 256 2 × 2 codewords. We vary several parameters in compressing the RGB textures and the overall compression results are given in table 3. The mean squared error (MSE) for a color channel is computed as the sum of squared differences between original frame pixels and corresponding pixels from the compressed texture frame, di-

Texturing used	Filter	Rate	Avg. MSE
Wood,Marble: 128, 4×4 YUV Top: 128, 2×2 YUV	Point	34.7:1	34.7
Wood,Marble: 256, 4×4 YUV Top: 256, 2×2 YUV	Point	28.3:1	19.1
all: 256, 2×2, YUV	Point	11.5:1	37.9
separate: 256, RGB	Mipmap	17.6:1	14.2
separate: 1024, RGB	Mipmap	8.0:1	13.3

Table 4: Compression rates and average MSE for 50 frames of the Topspin animation. As shown in plate 2, the scene contains three textures: Wood, Marble and Top.

Sampling	Textures used	Rendering Time	Increase
Point	Uncompressed	21.0 sec	
	VQ w/8 bit index	21.4 sec	1.7%
	VQ w/12 bit index	23.0 sec	9.6%
Mipmap	Uncompressed	65.4 sec	
	VQ w/8 bit index	69.5 sec	6.3%
	VQ w/12 bit index	78.3 sec	19.7%

Table 5: Rendering time for the Topspin animation for uncompressed and compressed textures using 8 and 12 bit indices. Twenty frames were rendered at 400×400 on a 132MHz MIPS R4600.

vided by the number of pixels in the frame. The MSE results we present are calculated for the frame shown in plate 1 and are averaged across the three RGB color channels.

The first two rows of table 3 present the results of using a single codebook across all the RGB textures. Using 4×4 blocks, certain textures such as signs, billboards and roads contain some noticeable artifacts. Based on this observation we separated the RGB textures into three groups: signs and billboards, roads, and all others, using a separate codebook for each group. This allows us to use smaller 2×2 blocks for the signs and roads, while using 4×4 blocks for the other textures. As shown in table 3, we can achieve slightly higher compression rates with a smaller average MSE using separate codebooks (see rows 1 and 3). Using separate codebooks, even at a compression rate of 24.5:1, the rendered scenes must be examined closely to see the artifacts in the textures, as shown in plate 1.

The Topspin animation contains three texture maps requiring 1.4 MB when uncompressed. We render this animation using a software scan converter. Some compression rates for this animation using point mapped and mipmapped textures are given in table 4. Note that the MSE numbers presented in this table are averaged across the 50 frames in the Topspin animation. We do not vary the codebook blocksize for mipmaps, since this is fixed by our three level codebook architecture. A separate compressed mipmap is generated for each of the three textures in the Topspin animation.

A frame from this animation rendered with point sampled textures is shown in plate 2, while the textures are shown in plate 3. The frame is almost free of artifacts, although there is some blockiness in the foreground Marble texture. The Wood and Marble textures in plate 3 have been cropped and enlarged to make the compression artifacts more visible.

The timing results for the Topspin animation are presented in table 5. Index maps with 12 bit indices take more time to decode than those with 8 bit indices because two lookups and bit manipulations are required to extract each index instead of a single lookup. Although these timing results indicate the computational overhead of rendering from VQ compressed textures in a software renderer, they do not represent a situation in which texture compression would be used. In a software renderer textures would only be compressed if the uncompressed textures surpass the main memory limit and cause the machine to swap. In such a situation, compression would alleviate the swapping, thereby drastically improving rendering times.

In a hardware implementation of this scheme, specialized addressing logic could be built to reduce the the penalty caused by irregular index sizes.

8 Conclusions

We have presented a method for rendering directly from VQ compressed texture maps. The advantage of using VQ over other compression schemes is that it addresses many of the issues involved in choosing a compression scheme for texture mapping. In particular, decompression is inexpensive. Even though VQ compression is lossy, we have been able to achieve compression rates of up to $35 : 1$ with few visible artifacts in the rendered images.

There are several directions in which this work may be extended. Designing codebooks currently requires some experimentation with the various VQ encoding parameters. While an automatic method for designing "optimal" codebooks would be useful, designing a measure of optimality is difficult. There has been some work on designing perceptual distortion measures to minimize such distortions in compressed images [2]. For texture mapping however, distortion in the rendered scene, not the compressed textures, must be minimized, so the distortion measure must use information about how the textures will be mapped into the scene. It may be possible to use a hint driven approach that allows the application designer to provide hints about characteristics like which textures are similar to one another, or which textures are more or less important to preserve perfectly. The VQ compression approach naturally extends to other classes of texture maps such as bump maps, displacement maps and environment maps. Each of these classes of textures has some unique filtering or access issues and although our preliminary results indicate that VQ compression works well for them, we are studying them in more detail.

Using VQ compressed textures in a rendering system is a viable method for reducing the memory overhead of texture mapping. Such compression is ideal for rendering systems that use specialized texture memory and aim for real-time performance. It will allow lower-end systems such as PCs and home game systems to achieve greater graphical realism through the use of more complex textures.

Acknowledgments

Homan Igehy and Gordon Stoll provided the scan converter used to generate timing results. The Performer Town database appears courtesy of Silicon Graphics and Paradigm Simulation.

References

[1] Kurt Akeley. RealityEngine graphics. In *Computer Graphics (SIGGRAPH '93 Proceedings)*, volume 27, pages 109–116, August 1993.

[2] N. Chaddha, P. Chou, and T. Meng. Scalable compression based on tree structured vector quantization of perceptually weighted generic block, lapped and wavelet transforms. *IEEE International Conference on Image Processing*, October 1995.

[3] Lawrence French. Toy story. *Cinefantastique*, 27(2):36–37, 1995.

[4] A. Gersho and R. M. Gray. *Vector Quantization and Signal Compression*. Kluwer Academic Publishers, 1991.

[5] H.-M. Hang and B. Haskell. Interpolative vector quantization of color images. In *TCOM*, pages 465–470, 1987.

[6] Paul S. Heckbert. Color image quantization for frame buffer display. In *Computer Graphics (SIGGRAPH '82 Proceedings)*, volume 16, pages 297–307, July 1982.

[7] Paul S. Heckbert. Survey of texture mapping. In M. Green, editor, *Proceedings of Graphics Interface '86*, pages 207–212, May 1986.

[8] P. Ning and L. Hesselink. Fast volume rendering of compressed data. In G. Nielson and D. Bergeron, editors, *Proc. Visualization '93*, pages 11–18, October 1993.

[9] Darwyn Peachey. Texture on demand. Technical report, Pixar, 1990.

[10] W.B. Pennebaker and J.L. Mitchell. *JPEG Still Image Data Compression Standard*. Van Nostrand Reinhold, 1993.

[11] Lance Williams. Pyramidal parametrics. In *Computer Graphics (SIGGRAPH '83 Proceedings)*, volume 17, pages 1–11, July 1983.

[12] L. Ziv and A. Lempel. A universal algorithm for sequential data compression. *IEEE Trans. Inform.Theory, Vol.IT-23*, (3), May 1977.

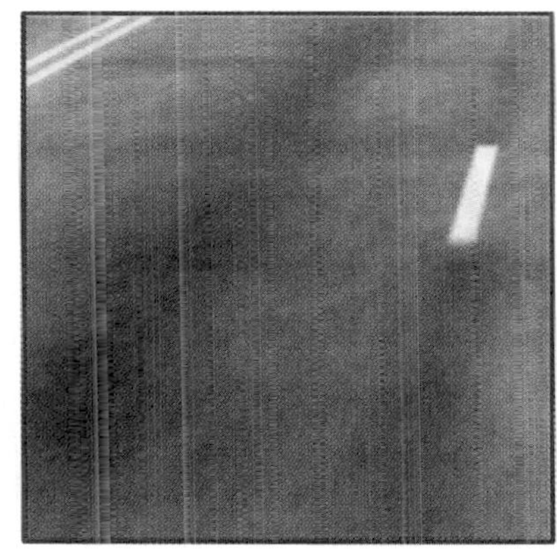

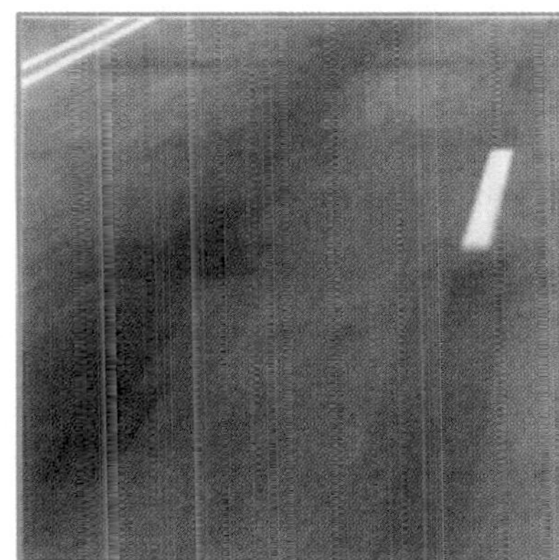

Plate 1: A frame from the Performer Town virtual environment. The frame on the left is rendered with uncompressed textures, while the frame on the right is rendered with textures compressed 24.5:1. The RGB textures were separated into three groups: signs, roads and others, and a separate codebook was generated for each group. The complete parameters for this trial are presented in row 4 of Table 3. The artifacts in the frames are more apparent in the enlargements shown below the rendered frames. The enlargements outlined in red are from the original frame while those outlined in green are from the compressed frame.

Plate 2: A frame from the Topspin animation, rendered with point sampled textures. The frame on the left is rendered with uncompressed textures. The frame on the right is rendered with textures compressed 28.3:1. The MSE between these two frames is 18.46, and the average MSE across the 50 frame animation is 19.10.

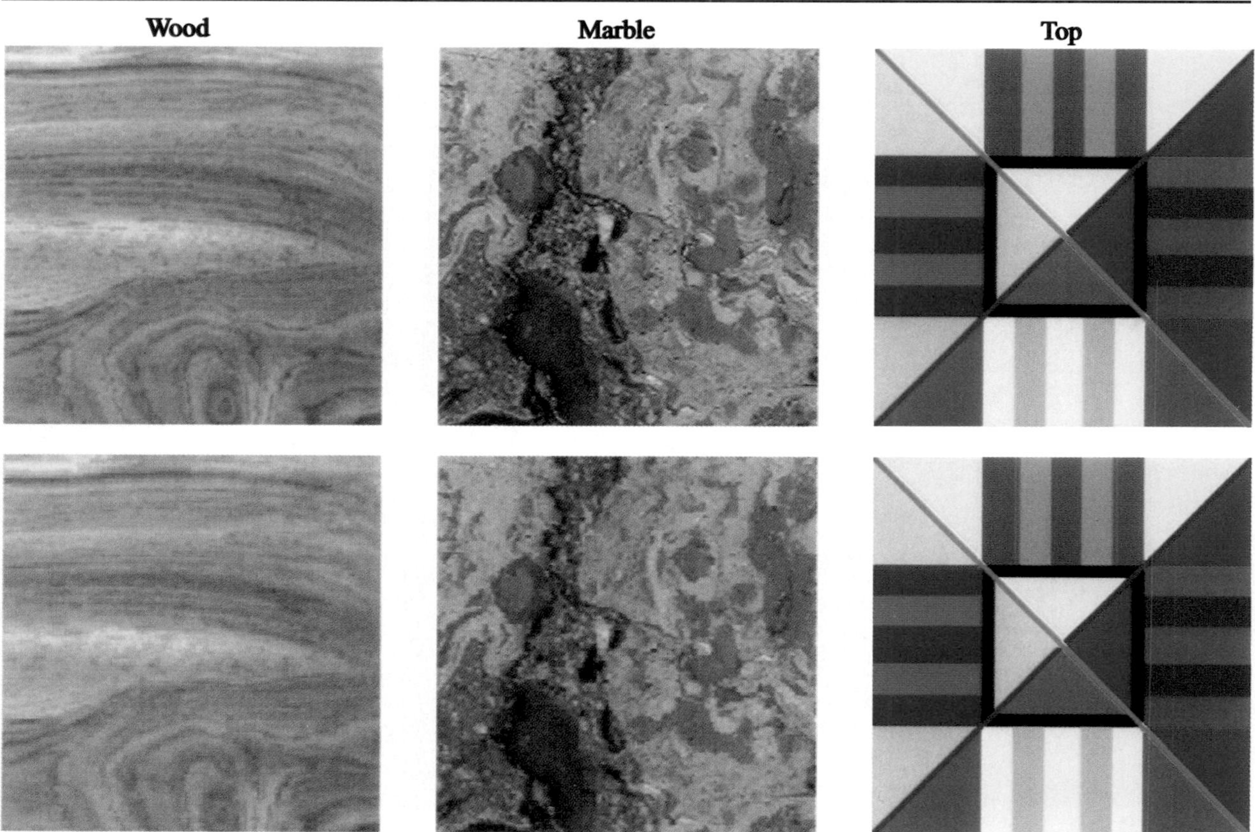

Plate 3: The textures used in the Topspin animation shown in plate 1. The top row contains the original uncompressed textures. The bottom row contains textures compressed in YUV space. The Wood and Marble textures were compressed using a combined codebook containing 256 codewords of 4x4 blocks, giving a compression rate of 38.4:1. The codebook for the Top texture contains 256 codewords of 2x2 blocks, giving a compression rate of 11.0:1. The MSE of the Wood texture is 36.56. The MSE of the Marble texture is 165.60. The MSE of the Top texture is 12.13.

Display of Clouds Taking into Account Multiple Anisotropic Scattering and Sky Light

Tomoyuki Nishita
Fukuyama University
Sanzo, Higashimura-cho, Fukuyama,
729-02 Japan
nis@eml.hiroshima-u.ac.jp

Yoshinori Dobashi
Hiroshima University
1-4-1, kagamiyama, Higashi-hiroshima,
739 Japan
doba@eml.hiroshima-u.ac.jp

Eihachiro Nakamae
Hiroshima Prefectural University
Nanatsuka-cho, Shoubara City,
727 Japan
naka@bus.hiroshima-pu.ac.jp

Abstract

Methods to display realistic clouds are proposed. To display realistic images, a precise shading model is required: two components should be considered. One is multiple scattering due to particles in clouds, and the other factor to be considered is sky light. For the former, the calculation of cloud intensities has been assumed to be complex due to strong forward scattering. However, this paper proposes an efficient calculation method using these scattering characteristics in a positive way. The latter is a very significant factor when sky light is rather stronger than direct sunlight, such as at sunset/sunrise, even though sky light has been ignored in previous methods.

This paper describes an efficient calculation method for light scattering due to clouds taking into account both multiple scattering and sky light, and the modeling of clouds.

CR Categories and Subject Descriptors:
I.3.3 [**Computer Graphics**]: Picture/Image Generation
I.3.7 [**Computer Graphics**]: Three-Dimensional Graphics and Realism
Key Words: Clouds, Multiple scattering, Sky light, Participating Media, Optical Length, Photo-realism, Radiative Transfer

1 INTRODUCTION

Display of natural scenes such as mountains, trees, the earth, the sea, and the waves have been attempted. This paper discusses the display of clouds. The display of clouds is indispensable for the background images of buildings and flight simulators. For displaying clouds, mapping of fractal textures onto ellipsoids is often used. However, we discuss a display method taking account of light scattering due to cloud particles illuminated by sky light. The color of clouds varies according to the relationship between the viewing direction and the position of the sun. The intensity of clouds is dependent on absorption/scattering effects due to clouds particles.

The albedos of clouds are very high: It is well known that for objects with such a high albedo multiple scattering can not be ignored[4]. Clouds are illuminated by both direct sunlight and sky light affected by atmospheric scattering. Their reflected light from the ground (or the sea) also can not be ignored, and we take these effects into account. That is, this paper discusses not only a local illumination model of clouds, but also a global illumination model taking into account the color variation of incident light on them passing through the atmosphere and sky light.

A brief description of our proposed method is as follows. Clouds are defined by density fields, which are modeled by the metaball technique. Shapes of clouds are modeled by applying the fractal technique to metaballs. The particles they consist of have strong forward scattering characteristics. This was considered as one of the difficulties due to the intensity calculation in the previous work. We use this characteristic in a positive way. That is, the space, which should be calculated, is restricted because the scattering direction is very narrow. For the calculation of multiple scattering, the space containing the clouds is subdivided into a number of volume elements (voxels). As a preprocess, a sample space is prepared, which is defined as a parallelepiped consisting of a set of some voxels with the average density of the clouds, the high order of scattering at a specified voxel from the other voxels in the space is calculated and stored, before the calculation of scattering due to every voxel in the total space. By using this pattern which is the contribution ratio at each voxel in the sample space to the specified voxel, the calculation cost for the total space can be reduced. At least the 3rd order of scattering is calculated in our paper. The spectrum and spatial distribution of sky light are precalculated by taking into account Rayleigh scattering and Mie scattering by assuming negligible attenuation due to cloud particles. The intensity of the first order of scattering at each voxel due to sky light (including reflected light from the ground) can be easily calculated by using the optical depths from the cloud surface, stored in a look-up table.

Finally, several examples are demonstrated in order to show the effectiveness of the method proposed here.

2 Previous Work

Density volume display methods such as those of clouds in previous work are divided into two categories, mapping technique and physical model taking into account scattering/absorption due to particles. For the former, Gardner[7] used a mapping technique of fractal textures onto ellipsoids. For the latter, the displaying of the atmosphere(sky color), water color, and particles such as ice has been developed: a) for light scattering from particles in the air, the shafts of light caused by spot lights[18][9], light beams passing through gaps in clouds or through leaves[15], the sky color taking account of atmospheric scattering[14][12], scattered light due to nonuniform density particles such as clouds and smoke[18][24][10][26], the color of the atmosphere viewed from space[20], the effect of the radiosity of a participating medium[23], and multiple anisotropic volume scattering[16][10][1]. b) the display of the color of water affected by particles in the water, such as ponds[11], the color of the sea as viewed from outer space[20] and optical effects such as shafts of light within water[22]. and c) the display of Saturn's rings (reflective ice particles)[2], and subsurface scattering such as skin[8].

In this paper we focus our discussion on multiple scattering. For high albedo particles, multiple scattering should be calculated. On this, Kajiya[10] was first to offer a solution. For multiple scattering the two-pass method[10][16][23] is usually used. The first pass deposits flux from the light source and the light scattered at each cloud voxel. The second pass gathers the scattered light along each viewing ray. Kajiya used spherical harmonics to express the intensity distribution of scattered light at each voxel as a function of direction. As cloud particles have strong forward scattering characteristics (caused by a narrow phase function), a relatively high order of spherical harmonics are required for representation of the distribution of light scattered. In the case of the phase function described in section 3.3, the 20th order of harmonics and more than 400 coefficients at each voxel may be required. Max's approach[16] is to allocate the radiosity leaving each volume element into a collection of M direction bins of constant intensity. This discrete ordinate method also requires many direction bins to express such a narrow scattering beam. Even though the distribution of scattering becomes slightly isotropic after multiple scattering, some error appears in the first order of scattering. Blasi[1] used the Monte Carlo method for determining the scattering direction of photons, but he did not calculate the scattered component in the viewing ray. Therefore, this method can not be considered as one which takes into account anisotropic phase function. Hanrahan[8] proposed a method for subsurface scattering, but this method is limited to layered surfaces such as skin and leaves; this method is not applicable to complex shapes such as clouds. Stam [26] took into account multiple scattering to display gaseous phenomena such as fire. He employed LU-decomposition to solve a matrix equation. He ignored the phase function.

Here, we propose a method which takes into account multiple scattering, sky light effects, and reflection from the ground.

3 Shading Model for Clouds

3.1 Basic Ideas

In order to render the particles in clouds, the following elements should be taken into account: (i) Phase functions should be taken into account; scattering by small particles such as air molecules is called Rayleigh scattering, and scattering by aerosols such as dust is called Mie scattering. The sizes of particles in clouds are relatively large (i.e., 2-40 μm), so the particles have strong forward scattering. (ii) The multiple scattering of light among particles in clouds can not be neglected because their albedos are very high[4][25]: 0.7 - 0.9 for cumulus and stratus. (iii) The clouds are illuminated by both direct sunlight and sky light. And they are also illuminated by the reflected light of direct sunlight and sky light from the ground (i.e., reflected groundlight). (iv) The effects of the atmosphere should be considered. The scattered light at the clouds is attenuated by particles in the atmosphere and reaches the viewpoint. Sunlight is absorbed when light passes through the atmosphere. (v) The density distributions of clouds are not uniform.

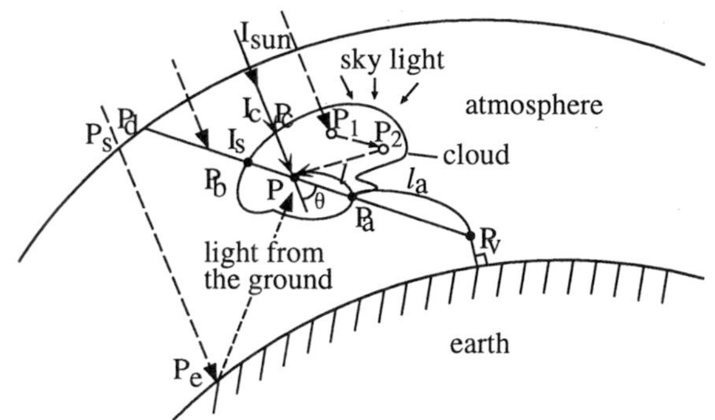

Figure 1: Light paths through clouds.

As shown in Fig.1, the following optical paths or optical effects also should be considered. (1) Particle P in a cloud is illuminated by direct sunlight (I_{sun}), scattered light from the other particles (path P_1P_2P), sky light (or sky radiance), and reflected light from the earth. (2) The light reaching viewpoint is determined by every particle on the viewing ray; the incident light of sky light to the cloud at P_b (I_s), particles in clouds (P_bP_a), and particles in the atmosphere (P_aP_v). The intensity is obtained by integrating all the scattered light due to these particles. The attenuation of light due to these particles is also considered. (3) The sky light consists of light scattered by particles in the air. The spatial and spectrum distribution of sky light depends on the sun position. The atmosphere consists of air molecules and aerosols; their scattering characteristics obey Rayleigh scattering and Mie scattering, respectively. The density distributions of air molecules and aerosols vary exponentially with altitude. (4) The reflected light from the earth consists of the direct sunlight and sky light. The direct sunlight is attenuated by the path P_sP_e and the reflected light is also attenuated by the path P_eP. The scattered light due to particles on these paths are added.

As described above, the optical paths are complicated, we can express these optical effects as the block diagram, as shown in Fig.2.

This paper discusses a rendering algorithm for clouds taking into account at least the 3rd order of multiple scattering.

3.2 Calculation of Light Scattering for Clouds

Let's discuss first the calculation method for single scattering due to cloud particles.

As shown in Fig.1, let's denote the intensity of incident sunlight to a cloud as I_c and the intensity of that behind the cloud (i.e., sky light) as I_s, the intensity of light from the cloud at P_a, I_a, which is the summation of the attenuated light of scattering on P_aP_b of the viewing ray and the attenuated sky light I_s due to the cloud. I_a can be obtained by the following equation:

$$\begin{aligned} I_a(\lambda) &= I_s(\lambda) exp(-\tau(P_aP_b, \lambda)) \\ &+ \int_{P_a}^{P_b} I_p(\lambda)\beta\rho(l)F(\theta)exp(-\tau(PP_a, \lambda))dl, \quad (1) \end{aligned}$$

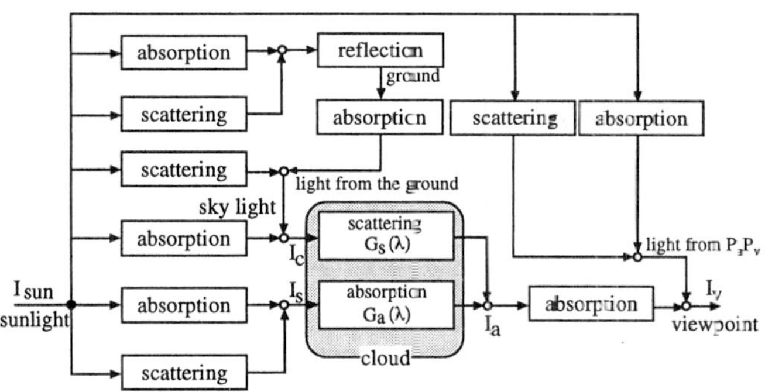

Figure 2: Block diagram for the intensity reaching the viewpoint passing through clouds.

where the first term means the incident light at P_b is attenuated by particles on the path of P_aP_b, and the second the scattered light due to particles on the path. λ is the wavelength of the light, F the scattering phase function indicating the directional characteristics of scattering, θ the scattering angle (see Fig. 1), ρ the density, I_s the intensity of the sky light in the viewing direction, τ the optical length obtained by integrating the attenuation coefficient β along the path, i.e., given by $\tau(S,\lambda) = \int_0^S \beta\rho(s)ds$ (S is path length).

As the incident light at point P has been attenuated due to movement through the cloud (P_cP), the incident intensity at P is obtained by,

$$I_p(\lambda) = I_c(\lambda)exp(-\tau(PP_c,\lambda)), \qquad (2)$$

where I_c is the attenuated light of I_{sun} which is the solar radiation at the top of the atmosphere. Equation (1) is rewritten by using gains G_a and G_s;

$$I_a(\lambda) = I_s(\lambda)G_a(\lambda) + I_c(\lambda)G_s(\lambda). \qquad (3)$$

Therefore, the intensity reaching the viewpoint is represented by the block diagram as shown in Fig. 2. As shown in Figs. 1 and 2, the types of the incident light onto the cloud are the intensity of sky light in the viewing direction, I_s, the attenuated intensity of I_{sun}, sky light I_{sky}, and the reflected light from the ground. See reference [20] for the calculation method for atmospheric scattering. The light reaching viewpoint P_v can be obtained as the remainder after scattering and absorption due to air molecules along the path between P_a and P_v. The calculation methods for multiple scattering and sky light (including reflection from the ground) are described in section 3.4 and 3.5, respectively.

3.3 Phase Function

Scattering of light due to particles (water droplets) in clouds obeys Mie scattering. The characteristics of scattering depend on the size of the particles, and have strong forward scattering. That is, when the scattering angle θ (see Fig. 1) is greater than 10°, the scattering intensity becomes less than 10%, compared to that at angle 0°. As various sizes of particles exist, the phase function is expressed by the linear combination of several phase functions;

$$F(\theta) = \sum_{i=0}^{K} w_i F_i(\theta), \qquad (4)$$

where K is the number of types of functions, and w_i is weight for phase function i. The Henyey-Greenstein function is well known as a phase function. Recently, Cornette[6] improved it, which gives more reasonable physical expression:

$$F(\theta, g) = \frac{3(1-g^2)}{2(2+g^2)} \frac{(1+cos^2\theta)}{(1+g^2-2gcos\theta)^{3/2}}, \qquad (5)$$

where g is an asymmetry factor and is a function (see [20]) which is determined by the cloud condition and the wave length (see references[6] for the parameters of clouds). If $g = 0$, this function is equivalent to Rayleigh scattering. In this paper, two functions, Rayleigh (e.g., 5%) and Mie scattering (the remainder) for cloud particles, are combined.

For scattering due to clouds the spectrum of scattering is not much influenced compared with scattering due to air molecules. Therefore, the color of clouds depends on the spectrum of incident light.

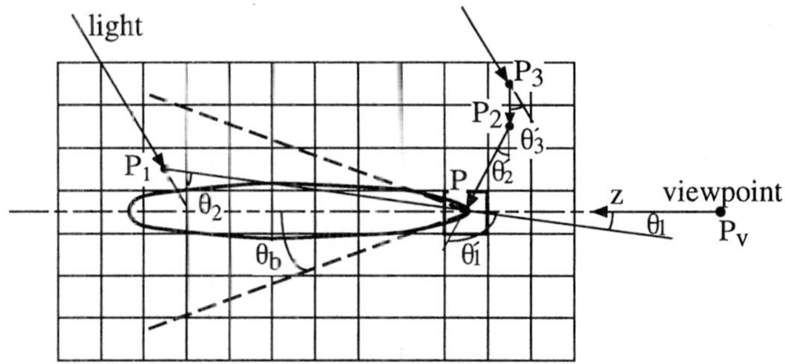

Figure 3: Calculation of multiple scattering and reference pattern.

3.4 Multiple Scattering

For solving multiple scattering phenomena, two methods have been developed; solving integral equations and using the Monte Calro method. This paper combines both of these. The space including some clouds is subdivided into a number of volume elements, and shooting/receiving energy among them is calculated. For calculating its exchanging energy among the elements, a form factor generally used in radiosity methods is useful. Rushmeier[23] introduced the volume/volume form factor: form factor F_{kj} represents the ratio of the total scattered and emitted energy leaving element V_k which is absorbed or scattered by volume element V_j, but her method is limited to isotropic scattering. The phase function is an important factor for energy transport. In our method the form factors are calculated by taking into account the phase function. That is, in the numerical integral for form factors the phase functions having angles between the viewpoint and sub-voxels are multiplied. Let's consider the beam spread which is an angle including most of scattered energy (see θ_b in Fig 3). Every volume element within the beam spread of the phase function is subdivided into smaller sub-voxels compared with the regular voxels.

Let's denote the intensity at point P in direction ω as $I(P,\omega)$, the extinction coefficient per unit length as β, the length of cloud in viewing ray S, the path length from P as s ($s = 0$ at P, P_S ; S from P). Then $I(P,\omega)$ is expressed by

$$I(P,\omega) = I(P_S,\omega)exp(-\tau(PP_S)) + \int_{s=0}^{S}[\beta\rho(s)exp(-\tau(P(s)P))\frac{1}{4\pi}\int_{4\pi}F(\theta)I(P,\omega')d\omega']ds, (6)$$

where θ is phase angle between ω and ω': ω' is angular variable for integration. The problem is that I exists in both sides of the equation. To solve this, this space is subdivided into a number of volume elements. If we denote the number of voxels as N, and the number of the discrete directions as M, then MN matrix equations should be solved.

For a narrow phase function (strong forward scattering), the matrix becomes sparse because even if some volume elements existing outside of the beam spread shoot their energy to the volume element P to be calculated, the energy hardly contribute to the intensity at P in the viewing direction. The form factors for distant pairs of elements are very small. Therefore, we can predict which voxel affects a specified volume element. That is, a sample space is prepared, light scattering in the space is calculated before the calculation of scattering due to every voxel in the whole space. By using the contribution pattern of voxels in the sample space, the calculation cost can be reduced. Fig.3 shows a sample space, the ellipsoid means the scaled phase function when the viewpoint is assumed as a light source. This region tells us which voxels contribute to scattering at point P. The contribution ratio of voxel at P_1 to P is high because it exists within the beam spread.

For a given viewpoint and a light direction, assume the uniform density (average density), and then calculate the voxels which affect a specified voxel. The scattered light in the viewing direction at point P through every path of the 2nd and 3rd orders of scattering are calculated (e.g., P_1P; 2nd order path,P_3P_2P; 3rd order path in Fig.3). These results, the 2nd and 3rd order components, are stored at each voxel and the total scattered intensity at P due to every voxel is calculated. By using these results, each contribution ratio to the total intensity can be obtained. We refer to this contribution-ratio pattern in a look-up table as a *reference pattern (or a template)*. For simplifying, the z-axis of the voxel is assumed to be in line with the viewing ray. That is, the edges of the voxel coincide with the principal axes of the eye coordinates system.

For N voxels, the number of paths for the 2nd order of scattering is $(N-1)$, and the number of paths for the 3rd order of scattering is $(N-1)^2$. In our experiments, when $8 \times 8 \times 16$ voxels are used as a reference pattern, 1,046,529 paths were required for the 3rd order of the scattering, but only 400 paths effectively contribute 90% of the total intensity. The above size of voxels is just an example, we used more large sizes of the reference patterns as described later. For the 3rd order of scattering, it is equivalent to that the intensity is determined by multiplying two form factors and three phase functions of angles of θ_1', θ_2' and θ_3', as shown in Fig.3.

In our examples, the percentages of the 2nd and 3rd order of scattering are roughly 10-40% and 1-3% for small phase angles (less than 10°), 40-70% and 2-10% for large phase angles: these data depend on the conditions such as cloud density. For the large phase angles, the higher order of scattering may be required. But to save the computation time, we truncated more than 4th order of scattering.

In general, as geometric factors, such as form factors and phase angles, are much more effective compared with the density distribution, we assumed that the contribution pattern of voxels taking into account non-uniform density is close to the reference pattern of uniform density. The voxels in the whole space are scanned by the reference pattern; this process is similar to filtering in image processing, in our case the reference pattern being equivalent to a 3-D filter.

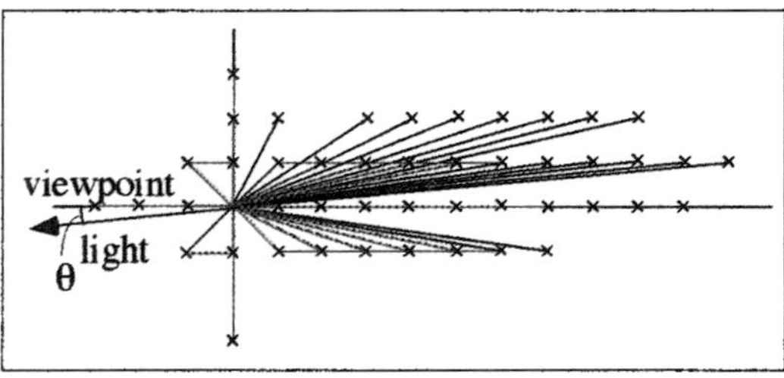

(a) Phase angle 10°

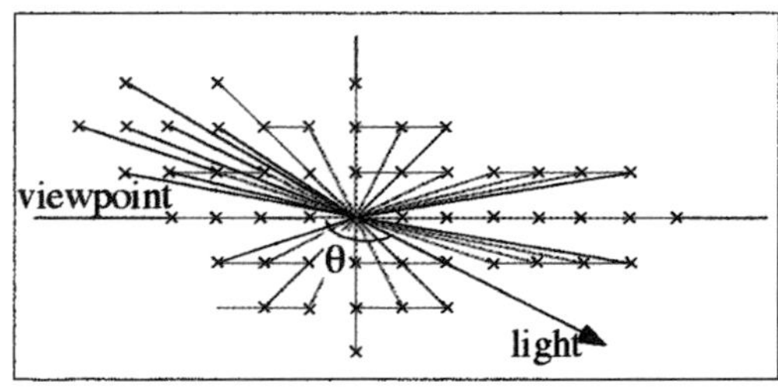

(b) Phase angle 160°

Figure 4: Examples of reference patterns.

The proposed algorithm includes the following steps:

step 1) : The center of the reference pattern is set to voxel P to be calculated, and the intensities of light scattered due to other voxels affecting voxel P are calculated and are accumulated on the strength of the reference pattern; the voxels whose contribution ratios are higher than a given threshold are selected. The form factors between each pair of voxels are stored over the look-up table along with the reference pattern. In our method, the modified form factors are stored as described before: they are obtained by multiplying the values of phase functions.

step 2) : The attenuation ratio (or optical length) for the sunlight at each voxel is stored. Moving the reference pattern, voxel by voxel, over the whole space, the light scattered (the 2nd and 3rd order of scattering) in the viewing direction at each voxel can be stored. The density distribution of the sample space for the reference pattern and the whole space to be calculated are different. So, the attenuation between the voxels should be calculated, even though the stored data in the reference pattern for the form factors and the values of phase functions can be used.

step 3) : For each pixel, the intensity is obtained by line integral: the intensity of the 1st order of scattering at a sampling point on the viewing ray is calculated by using the attenuation ratio stored at each voxel, and the intensities of the 2nd and 3rd order of scattering at the sampling point are interpolated from them stored at voxles.

As examples, Fig.4 shows the distribution of voxels with high contribution ratios in the cases of the phase angle of 10° and 160°, respectively. In the figure, the viewpoint is located on the left side, the black lines show the paths having a high contribution to the 2nd order of scattering (i.e., scattered twice like path P_1P in Fig.3), the green lines show the 1st path with a high contribution to the 3rd order of scattering (i.e., scattered three times), and the pink lines show the 2nd path with the maximum contribution to the voxels with a high contribution to the 3rd order of scattering. Let's consider the 2nd order scattering. As shown in Fig.5, the distribution of voxels which have high contribution ratios (e.g., more than 80%) are categorized into the following two cases.

Case A): light source and viewpoint are located in the opposite sides (Fig.5(a)).

Case B): light source and viewpoint are located in the same side (Fig.5(b)).

In both of these cases, three sub-spaces, R_f, R_b, and R_c, contribute to the light scattered at voxel P in the viewing direction. The 1st order of scattering due to particles in R_f is strong because of the small phase angle, even though the 2nd order of scattering at P is weak because of the large phase angle. Even though the 1st order of scattering in R_b is weak because of a large phase angle, the 2nd order of scattering at P is strong because of the small phase angle. In R_c distances of voxels from P are very close, so the form factors are large even though the phase functions are small. As shown in these figures, the sub-spaces with high contribution ratios depend on the light and viewing directions, and they also depend on the size of voxel, density, and extinction coefficients. Thus the size of the reference pattern is adaptively determined. First, we prepare a large sample space (e.g., $30 \times 30 \times 30$ voxels). And we can get the reasonable size of the reference pattern by the following method. To get the reference pattern, every possible path in a sample space is examined, and the bounding box of voxels having high ratios is selected as the reference pattern.

Even though the computational cost is reduced by this method, it is not sufficient. Therefore, we employ the following additional stochastic method. The voxels to be calculated are selected by using random numbers within the paths with a high contribution ratio. The summed intensity of these paths is corrected by using the ratio of the selected paths: assuming the number of the calculated paths to be n_1, the number of paths with a high contribution rate to be n_2, the summed intensity as I, and the total contribution ratio due to n_2 paths as r, then the intensity can be estimated by Irn_2/n_1. In our experiments, only 10% of the voxels in the reference pattern contribute 50% of the total intensity in a case. To use these voxels with high possibility we can improve the accuracy. We uses the constant density assumption for the sample space. If the sub-space to be calculated has wide range of density, it is solved by increasing ratio r. We set $r = 0.8$ in our examples. In the preprocessing stage (i.e., step 1: obtaining the reference pattern), the paths, whose contribution ratio are higher than r, are selected. Though we have discussed multiple scattering up to the 3rd order, the idea using the reference pattern can be expanded to higher orders.

Applying the method described above, the intensity at each voxel can be obtained and be stored. In the rendering step, the intensities at each sampling point on the viewing ray are integrated. In order to obtain high accuracy, the intensity of the first order scattering is calculated at each sampling point even though tri-linear interpolation is used for the intensity of the higher order of scattering and the attenuation (or optical depths) stored at each voxel.

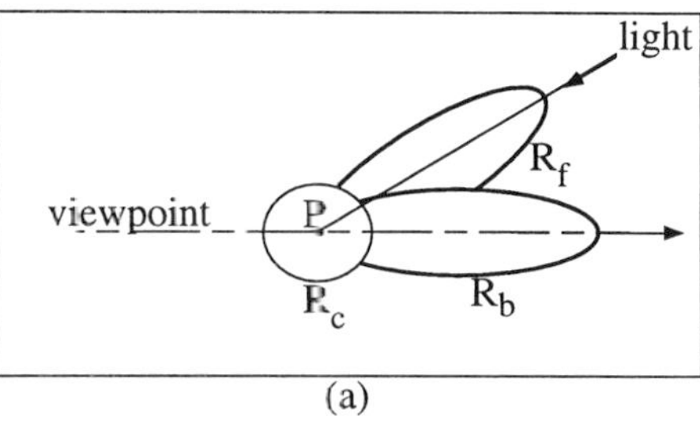

(a)

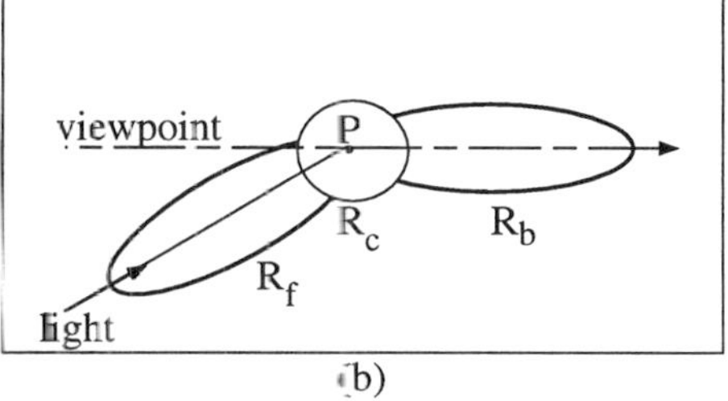

(b)

Figure 5: Sub-spaces with high contribution ratios.

3.5 Atmospheric Effects (Sky Light)

Clouds are visible even if the sun is hidden behind other clouds, after sunset or before sunrise; in other words, the intensity of the sunlight is rather feeble. This implies that sky light can not be ignored.

The intensity of sky light is determined by the scattering and/or absorption of air molecules and aerosols. The former obeys Rayleigh scattering (proportional to the fourth power of the wave length) while the latter obeys Mie scattering. The color of sky light changes depending on the altitude of the sun and the observer's position. Note that the intensity of the sky around the sun is stronger than elsewhere. See reference[20] for the calculation method for sky light. Direct sunlight attenuates when passing through the atmosphere. The incident light to a cloud (see Figs. 1 and 2), I_s, is attenuated sunlight and the light scattered due to particles in the atmosphere.

In meteorology it is well known that the brightness of clouds is affected by the reflected light from the ground. The reflected light from the ground is assumed as upward sky light because of the scattered light due to particles between the cloud and the ground. The reflected light has two components; direct sunlight and sky light. See reference[20] for the calculation method for the reflected light from sky light. Even though the albedo of the ground depends on materials such as soil, trees, sand, we used average albedos (spectrum reflectivity in this case) used in reference[25] which are weighted averages of that of each material.

Single scattering for sky light (and reflected light from the ground) is calculated as follows. Ignoring attenuation by cloud particles, a particle (i.e., voxel) is illuminated by the sky light from every direction: The light scattered in the viewing direction arrives at the viewpoint. Since the sky dome can be considered a hemisphere with a large radius[17], the particle can be considered at the center of the hemisphere. Thus, it is possible to take it for granted that the radiance distribution incident onto each particle in a cloud is identical (assuming the difference in the altitude is small). In the case of the calculation of sky light on the ground, the hemisphere is enough. But clouds exist at a high altitude, so the sky light from the bottom should also be considered: the top hemisphere is due to pure sky light and the bottom hemisphere consists of the light scattered due to particles in the bottom of clouds and the attenuated light of reflected light from the ground. The sky dome is divided into several sky elements, and the intensity of the light scattered in the view direction I_v is obtained by calculating the solid angle of the sky elements and their intensities.

In practice, the incident light onto a particle is attenuated

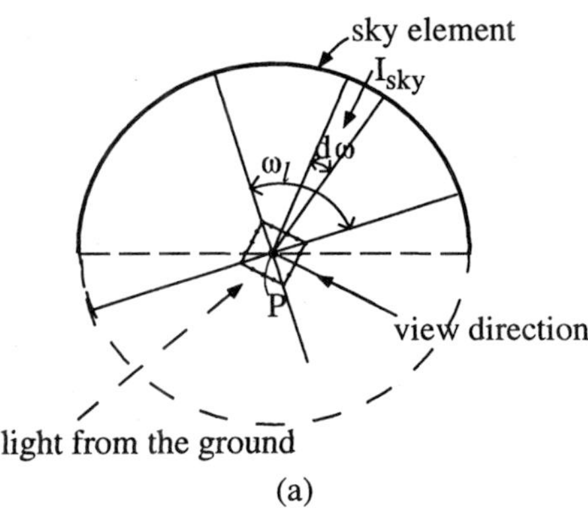

(a)

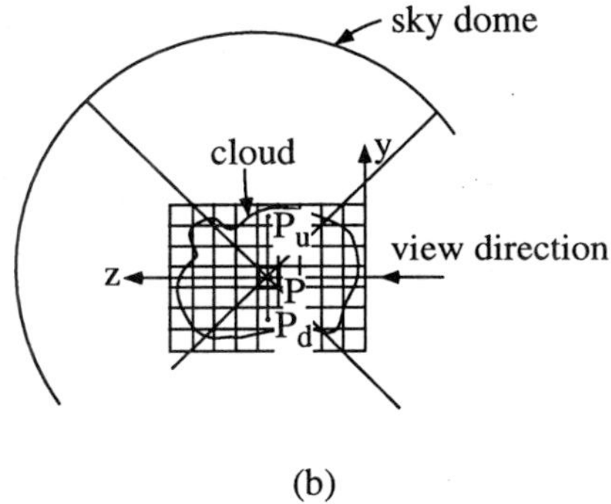

(b)

Figure 6: Calculation of skylight.

by the other particles in the cloud. Therefore, the attenuation factor (transmittance) toward each sky element which is caused by them and which is obtained from its optical length, should be taken into account. Let's denote the number of the sky elements as K, I_v is obtained by

$$I_v(\lambda) = \sum_{l=0}^{K} t_l \int_{\omega_l} F(\theta) I_{sky}(\omega, \lambda) d\omega = \sum_{l=0}^{K} t_l I_l(\lambda), \quad (7)$$

where t_l is the attenuation factor for the direction of sky element l due to cloud particles, w_l is a solid angle of sky element l, F the phase function, and I_{sky} is the intensity of sky element l, and I_l is the integrated intensity for the sky element. In the rendering process, the attenuation factors t_l from each particle on the viewing ray to all sky elements must be calculated. To calculate these efficiently, we use a look-up table. We make use of the fact that it is easy to calculate the optical length in both the principal and diagonal axes of the voxel.

Let's consider the six faces comprising of the voxel as a simple example (see Fig. 6(a)). The incident light of sky light passing through each face can be calculated by setting the eye at the center of the cube. Each face of the cube is divided into small meshes, which is similar to the hemi-cube method[5]. The attenuation factors (or optical depths) in x, y, and z-directions can be used for six sky elements. Thus, if the accumulated attenuations for each axis are calculated once and stored at each voxel, it is sufficient to get the intensity at the viewpoint by multiplying the attenuation coefficient t_l by the intensity at the voxel and make a summation of them. Note that, in the case of the first order scattering, the intensity of the sky in the viewing direction is the most important as the forward scattering is strong. For example, let's consider the attenuation in y direction at voxel P (see Fig. 6(b)). At voxel P, the attenuation, t, between P and P_u was stored. If the attenuation at P_d is t_d, the attenuation between P_d and P is easily calculated as t/t_d. Even though we only describe for six directions, it is possible to increase the accuracy by preparing the attenuations in other directions, such as diagonal. As described above, sky elements around the sun are very significant since the intensity surrounding the sun is much greater. To take this into account, the attenuation in the sun's direction stored at each voxel can be utilized.

In addition to the density, the attenuation in the sun's direction, the attenuation factors in $K/2$ directions, and the intensity of light due to the higher order scattering are stored for each voxel.

4 MODELING OF CLOUDS

For modeling clouds, controlling its shape and density distribution is necessary. In this paper, the density distribution of the cloud is defined by using the meta-ball technique[21] (or blobs[3]). Each meta-ball is defined by its center, radius, and the density at the center of the ball. The field value at any point is defined by distances from the specified points in space. The density distribution of a meta-ball is given by a polynomial function in degree 6 of the distance from its center([21]). The surface of a cloud is defined by the isosurfaces of potential fields defined by the meta-balls.

In the rendering process, the intersection of the isosurface (i.e., cloud surface) with a viewing ray is calculated by ray tracing, which effectively expresses the density distribution on a ray by using Bézier function of degree 6 (see [21]). Bézier Clipping[19] is employed for the calculation of intersections.

First, several meta-balls are arranged to form the basic shape of the cloud. Then, small meta-balls on the surface of the cloud are generated recursively by using the following fractal method to form the subtle fringe of the cloud.

The method of generating new balls on a curved surface is as follows. The isosurface is extracted by the marching-cubes algorithm [13] and triangulated. New balls are then generated within each triangle (their positions and radii are determined randomly). Generating new balls produces a new surface, which is again triangulated. And again new balls are generated. This procedure is repeated. By making the radius smaller the further from the center of the cloud, the smaller balls appear around the fringe.

The bottom of a cloud is sometimes relatively flat, and the top of it is bumpy. To realize this kind of shape, the normal vectors of the generated triangles on the iso-surface can be used. If the normal vector is not downward new balls are created, otherwise the generation of balls is limited. By using this technique we can control the cloud shape, and make possible clouds which grow upwards.

5 EXAMPLES

Fig. 7 shows an example of clouds: the altitude of the sun in Figs.(a), (b), and (c) is 65°, 10° and 5° (sunset), respectively. These examples depict beautiful variations in the color of the clouds and sky. One can see the bright edges of cloud in Fig.(b) because the sun is behind the cloud.

Fig.8 shows examples of cumulonimbus. The atmospheric effect between the clouds and the viewpoint is calculated, so the color of the clouds is bluish (Fig.(a)) or reddish (Fig.(b)).

The number of meta-balls for these clouds for Figs.7 and 8 are 338 and 358, respectively.

This calculation was done on an IRIS Indigo2 (R4400). The computation times for Fig 7 (a), and Fig.8 (a) were 20 minutes, and 31.3 minutes, respectively (image width=500).

In these examples, the size of voxels is 100^3 in average, but if they are sparse, we could save the memory by using the list-structure.

6 CONCLUSION

We have proposed an algorithm for a physical based image synthesis of clouds. As shown in the examples, the proposed method gives us photo-realistic images taking into account anisotropic multiple scattering and sky light. The advantages of the proposed method are as follows:

(1) For anisotropic multiple scattering, the optical paths of the light scattered in the viewing direction are limited because of strong forward scattering (a narrow phase function). Employing the pattern expressing the contribution ratio at each voxel to the specified voxel in the sample space, the calculation cost for the total space can be reduced.

(2) For sky light, the spectrum of the sky light is calculated by taking into account scattering/absorption due to particles in the atmosphere, and the intensity of light scattered at one voxel illuminated by each sky element is stored. The intensity of the first order scattering at every voxel due to sky light can be easily calculated by using the optical depths from the cloud surface stored in a look-up table. The reflected light from the ground can be calculated by treating it as upward sky light.

(3) The clouds can be modeled by using metaballs. The complicated cloud surfaces are generated by a fractal technique applying to metaballs.

Shading models for clouds and snow are basically the same because the intensity from clouds or snow reaching the viewpoint is determined by light scattered and absorbed due to particles in clouds/snow. Even though this paper discussed a display method of clouds, the proposed method can be applied to snow.

Acknowledgment

The authors wish to thank Prof. Yamashita and Kaneda in Hiroshima University for many valuable discussions. The original title of our paper included 'snow'. But it and the part of the paper dealing with snow are removed by following the reviewers' advice. We are going to submit the paper on snow as a separate paper. We would like to acknowledge to the reviewers for their helpful comments.

References

[1] P. Blasi, B.L. Saec, C. Schlics, "A Rendering Algorithm for Discrete Volume Density Objects, " *Proc. of EUROGRAPHICS'93*, Vol.12, No.3 (1993) pp.201-210.

[2] J.F. Blinn, "Light Reflection Functions for Simulation of Clouds and Dusty Surfaces, " *Computer Graphics*, Vol. 16, No. 3 (1982) pp. 21-29.

[3] J.F. Blinn, "A Generalization of Algebraic Surface Drawing," *ACM Tog*, Vol.2, No.3 (1980) pp.235-256.

[4] C.F. Bohren, "Multiple scattering of light and some of its observable consequences, " *Am. J. Phys.* Vol.55, No.6 (1987) pp.524-533.

[5] M.F. Cohen, D.P. Greenberg, "The Hemicube, A Radiosity Solution for Computer Environment,", *Computer Graphics*, Vol.19 No.3 (1985) pp.31-40.

[6] W.M. Cornette, J.G. Shanks, "Physical reasonable analytic expression for the single-scattering phase function," *Applied Optics*, Vol.31, No.16 (1992) pp.3152-3160.

[7] G.Y. Gardener, "Visual Simulation of Clouds," *Computer Graphics*, Vol.19, No.3 (1985) pp.297-303.

[8] P. Hanrahan, W. Krueger, "Reflection from Layered Surfaces due to Subsurface Scattering," *Proc. of SIGGRAPH'93* (1994) pp.165-174.

[9] M. Inakage,"Volume Tracing of Atmospheric Environments," *The Visual Computer*, 7 (1991) pp.104-113.

[10] J.T. Kajiya, B.V. Herzen, "Ray tracing Volume Densities," *Computer Graphics*, Vol.18, No.3 (1984) pp.165-174.

[11] K. Kaneda, G. Yuan, E. Nakamae, T. Nishita, "Photorealistic Visual Simulation of Water Surfaces Taking into account Radiative Transfer," *Proc. of CG & CAD'91*, (China) (1991) pp.25-30.

[12] K. Kaneda, T. Okamoto, E. Nakamae, T. Nishita, "Photorealistic Image Synsesis for Outdoor scenery Under Various Atmospheric Conditions," *The Visual Computer*, Vol.7 (1991) pp.247-258.

[13] W.E. Lorensen, H.E. Cline, "Marching Cubes: a High Resolution 3D Surface Construction Algorithm," *Computer Graphics*, Vol.21, No.4 (1987) pp.163-169.

[14] R.V. Klassen, "Modeling the Effect of the Atmosphere on Light, " *ACM Transaction on Graphics*, Vol. 6, No. 3 (1987) pp. 215-237.

[15] N. Max, "Light Diffusion through Clouds and Haze, " *Graphics and Image Processing*, Vol.33, No.3 (1986) pp.280-292.

[16] N. Max, "Efficient Light Propagation for Multiple Anisotropic Volume Scattering," *Proc. of the Fifth Eurographics Workshop on Rendering* (1994) pp.87-104.

[17] T. Nishita, and E. Nakamae, "Continuous tone Representation of Three-Dimensional Objects Illuminated by Sky Light," *Computer Graphics*, Vol. 20, No. 4 (1986) pp. 125-132.

[18] T. Nishita, Y. Miyawaki, E. Nakamae, "A Shading Model for Atmospheric Scattering Considering Distribution of Light Sources," *Computer Graphics*, Vol. 21, No. 4 (1987) pp. 303-310.

[19] T. Nishita, T.W. Sederberg, M. Kakimoto, "Ray Tracing Rational Trimmed Surface Patches," *Computer Graphics*, Vol.24, No.4 (1990) pp.337-345.

[20] T. Nishita, T. Shirai, K. Tadamura, E. Nakamae, "Display of The Earth Taking into Account Atmospheric Scattering, " *Proc. of SIGGRAPH'93* (1993) pp.175-182.

[21] T. Nishita, E. Nakamae, "A Method for Displaying Metaballs by using Bézier Clipping," *Proc. of EUROGRAPHICS'94*, Vol.13, No.3 (1994) c271-280.

[22] T. Nishita, E. Nakamae, "Method of Displaying Optical Effects within Water using Accumulation Buffer," *Proc. of SIGGRAPH'94* (1994) pp.373-379.

[23] H.E. Rushmeier, K.E. Torrance, "The Zonal Method for Calculating Light Intensities in The Presence of a Participating Medium," *Computer Graphics*, Vol.21, No.4 (1987) pp.293-302.

[24] G. Sakas, M. Gerth, "Sampling and Anti-Aliasing of Discrete 3-D Volume Density Textures," *Proc. of EUROGRAPHICS'91* (1991) pp.87-102.

[25] S. Sekine, "Corrected Color Temperature of Daylight(2) : Characteristics on Clear Sky and Overcast Sky," *J. Illumination Engineering Inst. Japan* , Vol.79, No.11 (1995) pp.621-627.

[26] J. Stam, E. Fiume, "Depicting Fire and Other Gaseous Phenomena Using Diffusion Processes," *Proc. of SIGGRAPH'95* (1995) pp.129-136.

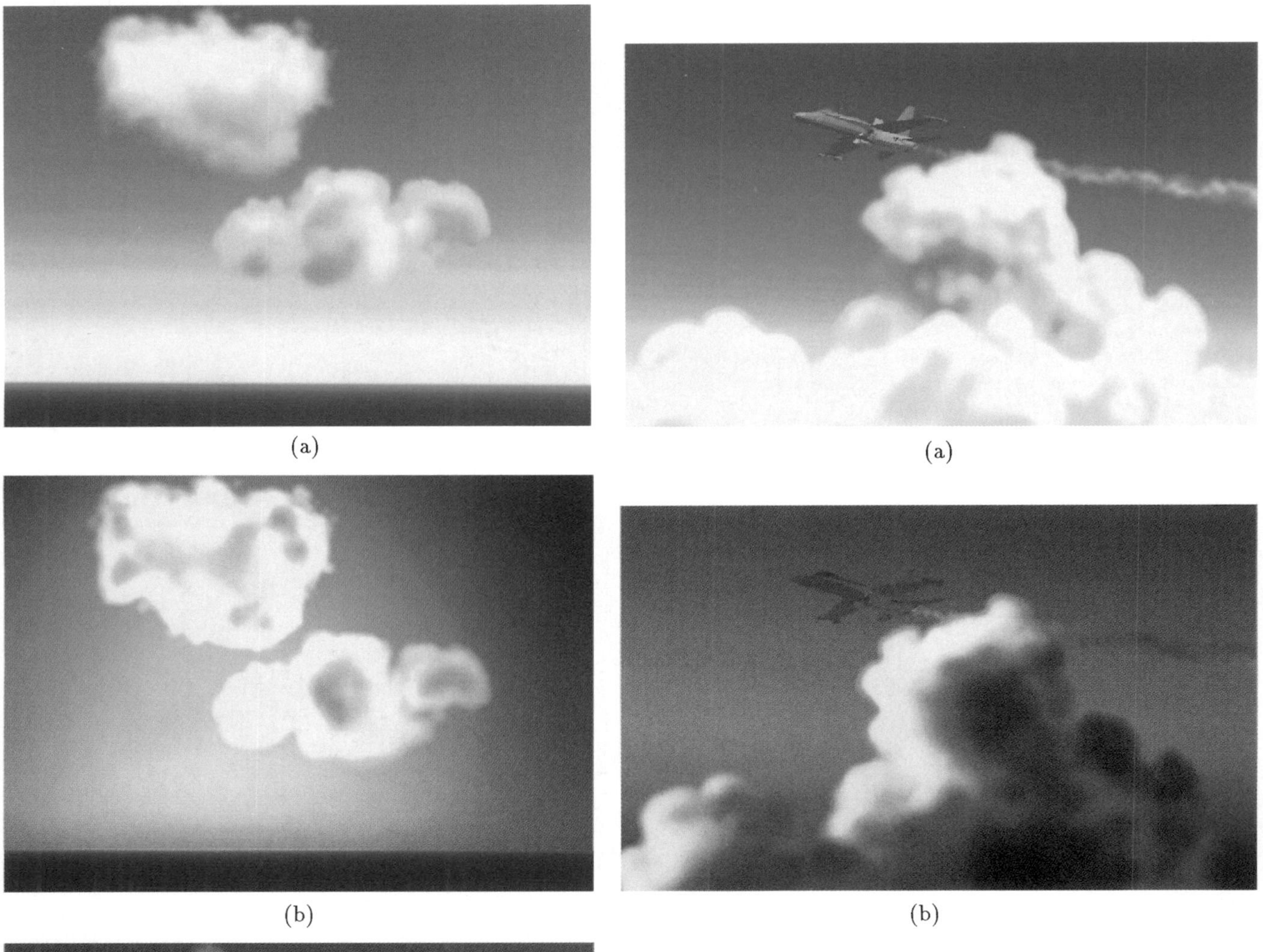

(a)

(b)

(c)

Figure 7: Examples of clouds.

(a)

(b)

Figure 8: Examples of cumulonimbus.

Modeling and Rendering of Metallic Patinas

Julie Dorsey*
Massachusetts Institute of Technology

Pat Hanrahan†
Stanford University

Abstract

An important component that has been missing from image synthesis is the effect of weathering. In this paper, we present an approach for the modeling and rendering of one type of weathering — metallic *patinas*. A patina is a film or incrustation on a surface that is produced by the removal of material, the addition of material, or the chemical alteration of a surface. Oxidation, sulphidization, and painting are examples of phenomena that produce patinas.

We represent a surface as a series of layers. Patinas are simulated with a collection of operators, such as "coat," "erode," and "polish," which are applied to the layered structure. The development of patinas is modulated according to an object's geometry and local environmental factors. We introduce a technique to model the reflectance and transmission of light through the layered structure using the Kubelka-Munk model. This representation yields a model that can simulate many aspects of the time-dependent appearance of metals as they are exposed to the atmosphere or treated chemically. We demonstrate the approach with a collection of copper models.

CR Categories and Subject Descriptors: I.3.7 [Computer Graphics]: Three-Dimensional Graphics and Realism I.3.6 [Computer Graphics]: Methodology and Techniques.

Additional Key Words and Phrases: weathering and appearance, material models, time-dependent phenomena, reflection models.

1 Introduction

All materials have an inherent tendency to change in appearance or composition when exposed to the physical and chemical conditions of the surrounding environment. The rate of change is dependent on the material's characteristics and the degree of its exposure. The deterioration, decay, and change in appearance of materials due to the effects of the surrounding environment are generally termed *weathering*. Specific examples of weathering include the corrosion of metals, efflorescence on stone and brick, fungal attack on organic materials [28], and the wear and tear of everyday life.

Techniques for realistic image synthesis have advanced dramatically in recent years. However, a common criticism of such images is that they look too ideal, and therefore animators and modelers go to great lengths to create a more natural look. An outstanding example of this approach is the techniques to simulate wear and tear in the recent movie *Toy Story* produced at Pixar [9]. Many texture maps per surface were used to model scuffs, dirt, gouges and so on. Unfortunately, this use of texture maps is labor intensive and somewhat ad hoc. Each texture map must be hand-painted and combined using special shaders. It is also very difficult to properly account for certain effects, such as a spill that crosses the boundary between two patches. There is clearly a need for modeling and rendering tools that make it is easier to create naturally worn surfaces.

Figure 1: Example of a real patina.

In addition to its importance in computer graphics, visualization of weathering effects has broad applicability to a variety of additional fields. Moreover, practitioners in other fields have studied weathering effects for many years, and their theories and studies are good sources from which to draw.

- For many applications it is useful to predict how a material will look in the future. For example, in architecture and preservation, it is important to understand how the surfaces of buildings change over time. Since buildings may stand for hundreds of years, much of their final appearance is dominated by weathering effects [22, 24].

- Conversely, there are applications where modeling weathering interactions is applicable to the inverse problem of understanding the history of an object from its current appearance. Restoration fundamentally involves returning a weathered object to its true initial appearance [7].

- Many materials are created pre-weathered. These materials are treated in various ways to simulate the process of weathering. Since such treatments can be highly desirable (from prewashed jeans to fake antiques), modeling them is important [24].

Our long range goal is to develop easily controllable models of weathered materials for computer graphics. This task involves the identification of the basic physical processes underlying changes in appearance and the development of appropriate computer models. Since weathering involves the action of many environmental forces over time, this will require simulating these processes. Such simulations will also give us the ability to visualize changes over time. We expect that different materials may require different modeling effects. For example, stone, wood and metals weather quite differently because their chemistry and material structures are very different. In this paper we consider only the modeling and rendering of metallic patinas as a starting point.

Metals are particularly susceptible to weathering interactions and often develop a characteristic *patina*. The term patination is generally reserved for effects involving the chemical alteration of the

*Room NE43-213, 545 Technology Square, Cambridge, MA 02139. http://graphics.lcs.mit.edu/~dorsey

†370 Gates Computer Science Building 3B, Stanford, CA 94305-4070. http://www-graphics.stanford.edu/~hanrahan

surface resulting in a change in color. It may describe the results of either deliberately applied craft processes or natural corrosion [16].

Metals in general — and the finished metal surface in particular — begin to change under the influence of the atmosphere, or the local chemical environment, as soon as they are exposed. Copper and its alloys are particularly interesting, as they have broad aesthetic as well as practical applications.

1.1 Previous Work

To date, the simulation of weathering effects has been given little explicit attention in the computer graphics literature. Related work exists in three areas: procedural textures and fractal surface growth models, specific weathering models, and layered surface representations.

Procedural textures [6] can be used to build up complex patterns that often resemble natural effects. For example, the "shade tree" concept of Cook [4] allowed arbitrary procedures to define a different shading model for each surface, as well as lighting and atmospheric optics. Perlin [26] described an entire procedural language to define textures and laid the foundation for the stochastically-generated textures that permeate rendering today. Finally, Turk [30] and Witkin and Kass [33] introduced synthetic texture models inspired by biochemical processes. In this paper, we use procedural textures in a new way: to vary parameters of a physically-inspired model of material properties over time. We draw on fractal surface growth models, used mainly in physics and various branches of engineering. These models are concerned with the morphology of various pre-formed interfaces and with the dynamics of how the morphology develops over time [1].

Starting with procedural texture models, several researchers have attempted to simulate related weathering effects. Becket and Badler [2] modeled surface imperfections through texture specification and generation techniques, which are based on fractal subdivision and simple distribution models. Blinn modeled the appearance of dusty surfaces, given the thickness of the dust layer [3]. More recently, Hsu and Wong [15] introduced functions for simulating dust accumulation that attempt to mimic the dust adherence process. In addition, Miller [23] proposed a set of algorithms for local and global accessibility shading; this type of shading yields visual effects that resemble tarnish on surfaces. We take a different approach — focusing in considerable detail on one particular material and its changes in appearance due to weathering.

A particularly promising method for modeling the appearance of materials is to treat a surface as a set of layers. For example, a common application of RenderMan is to develop surface descriptions as a series of layers [31]. Another area of interest is the modeling of reflection and transmission of light through layered surfaces. Hanrahan and Krueger [13] present a model for subsurface scattering in layered surfaces in terms of one-dimensional linear transport theory. This model is useful for rendering common layered materials such as skin, snow, and dust. In this work, we build on such layered representations by developing a set of tools for modeling and rendering surface and subsurface structures as a function of time.

1.2 Overview

We begin by briefly reviewing the physical basis of metallic patinas. We then present a representation of a metal surface as a stack of layers and propose a collection of operators that can be applied to the layered structure to produce a taxonomy of patination effects. We also discuss how patinas can be modulated according to environmental factors and the surface geometry. Next, we offer a method of rendering the layered structure. Last, we demonstrate the approach on several complex models.

2 Physical Basis of Patina Formation

Natural patinas develop primarily as the result of the process of atmospheric corrosion [22, 25]. The atmosphere alters the surface of a metal, causing gradual changes that quickly tarnish it with a thin, but uneven, dark coloring, and may eventually convert the whole surface into crumbly mineral products. In this section, we briefly describe the principal causes of natural patination. Similarly, artificial patinas are deliberately induced through various surface treatments designed to mimic and exaggerate the natural processes.

The corrosion process forms a complicated system of reacting layers consisting of the metal, corrosion products, surface electrolyte, and the atmosphere. The exact nature of the surface chemistry underlying the development of surface coatings and the factors that influence how they form and break down are major foci of current corrosion research. Unfortunately, the experimental data to support a physical simulation that would predict the appearance of a metal is not yet available. Therefore, in this paper we present a phenomenological model for the development of patinas, based on observed physical behavior.

2.1 Composition and Formation of Copper Patinas

In order to study the development of metallic patinas, we chose copper as a representative metal. The patinas of copper and copper alloys are classic examples of layered structures. When viewed in cross-section (see Figure 3 [8]) multiple layers are distinctly visible to the eye. Vernon and Whitby identified the principal chemical constituents of such natural copper patinas in the 1930s [32]. More recently, Franey and Davis [8] and Graedel et al. [11] have carried out a series of investigations, which have provided a detailed picture of the basic composition and formation mechanisms of natural patinas on copper.

Clean copper surfaces exposed to the atmosphere quickly form a thin layer of dull brown tarnish that gradually changes with time to a reddish brown color, which is indicative of copper oxide, or mineral cuprite [8, 22]. Once this layer is in place, subsequent layers grow much more slowly. The primary chemical constituents of the patina on copper and copper alloys include copper oxides, sulphides, and inorganic and organic copper salts. Copper sulphide is very dark brown, and the sulphide coating forms integrally with the underlying metallic crystal structure. Thus, the sulphide layer often appears relatively shiny. The copper salts, consisting mostly of sulphates, chlorates, and nitrates, come in a wide variety of colors. Copper sulphate causes the characteristic green color of aged copper. Figure 2 contains a key showing the approximate color of some of the most important copper minerals.

2.2 Dependence on Physical Environment

Figure 2 is a schematic diagram of the patination process as it can be outlined for three environments based on Graedel's observations [10]. This diagram indicates the varying composition of the patina in the environments and average lengths of time for development.

The left column represents four primary stages of patina growth in a marine environment. The first and second stages, which are common to the other two environments, involve the formation of a layer of tarnish and a layer of cuprite at the copper surface. The third stage is characterized by the formation of several copper minerals, with atacamite and other chlorine-containing substances expected to predominate because of the high chloride concentration near the sea. Small amounts of organic matter are also present within the structure. The final stage of the process augments the patina with similar minerals and binding materials.

On land, a patina of a different composition is produced. Both rural and urban air have moderate to high concentrations of sulfur. Thus, the transition from the second to the third stage involves sulphurization atop the cuprite, with some atacamite being formed as well. The initial form of the sulphur compound is primarily the mineral posnjakite; an organic binder is also present in the patina.

The final stage differs in the two environments. In the rural case, where there are only moderate concentrations of acid and oxidized sulfur in the atmosphere, the formation of sulfates proceeds slowly, and a mixed patina of atacamite and brochantite is typical. In urban areas, there are higher concentrations of sulfur, favoring the formation of the basic sulfate minerals antlerite and brochantite. Organic compounds are also incorporated into the patina as it forms.

In a marine environment, patinas grow in thickness at an average rate of 1μm per year. In a rural environment, the rate is less, about $.5\mu$m per year; in an urban environment the rate is slightly greater, about $1 - 2\mu$m. These rates are highest during the first few years of exposure and approach a lower, almost negligible rate after about 20 years [22]. While the preceding section gives a description of the development of patinas in three different environments, including the constituents of the patina and general growth rates, the development can be further influenced by a specific surrounding environment. Wetness is perhaps the most important factor in the patination process. Patination occurs more rapidly in areas of the surface that retain stagnant water. Thus, horizontal or inclined surfaces patinate more rapidly than vertical surfaces [11]. In addition, exposure to daylight decreases the rate of patination due to evaporation of surface water.

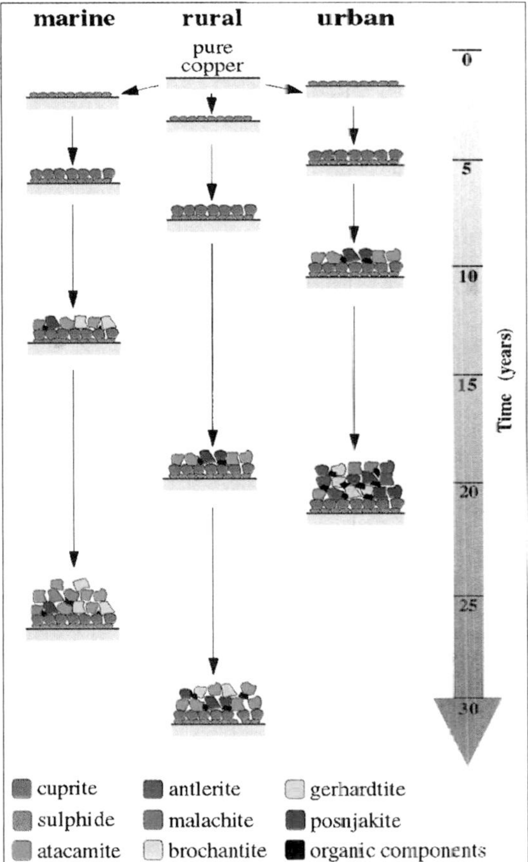

Figure 2: A schematic diagram of the processes involved in the growth of copper patinas in marine, rural, and urban atmospheres.

There are many other factors that affect the corrosion of metals, such as the composition of the electrolyte on the surface and the temperature; variations in surface thickness due to abrasions, polishing, and pitting are also relevant. However, the influence of these factors is not well understood [22], and we do not consider them further in this paper.

3 Modeling

As we observed in the previous section, the development of a metallic patina is a process that proceeds in a complex system of layers. In this section we describe a representation of the structure of a layered material and a set of operators that can be applied to this representation to simulate a variety of effects. By writing a script in terms of these operators, the weathering of the material as a function of time may be simulated.

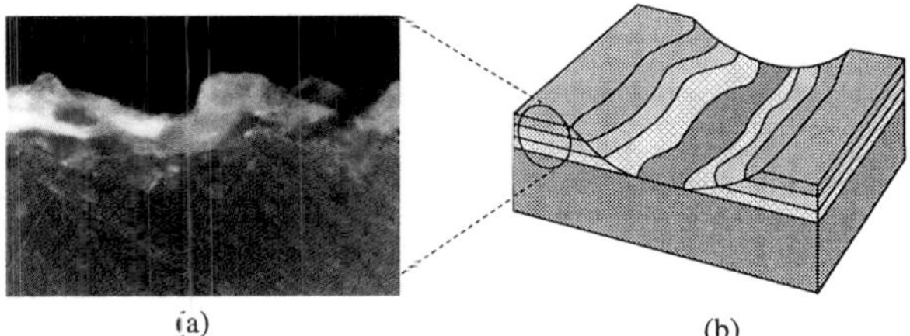

(a) (b)

Figure 3: A surface patina as a stack of layers. (a) Micrograph of a copper surface showing the layers. (b) Our abstraction of the layered structure.

3.1 Layers and Materials

In our representation, a surface contains a stack of n layers (see Figure 3). The "0"-th layer is assumed to be the base material with an essentially infinite thickness. The total thickness of the stack of layers is assumed to be small relative to the area covered by the layer. Each individual layer also has a thickness, although it may be zero at certain points. We have varied only the thickness as a function of position, but other properties could be similarly controlled.

The remainder of the material properties do not depend on position. Each layer consists of a homogeneous material. The surface of each material has the standard set of surface shading parameters such as diffuse and specular colors and an overall roughness or shininess. In addition each material has two volumetric properties that control how light is transmitted and reflected due to subsurface scattering in the layer. The light reflection and transmission properties of layers and the rendering of the layer structure are discussed in Section 4.

3.2 Operators

The development of a patina is implemented as a series of operators on layers. By controlling the sequencing of these operators, a wide variety of effects may be created. Our current implementation includes the following operators:

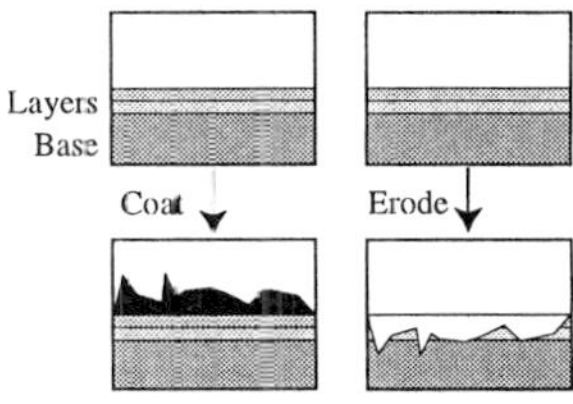

Figure 4: The coat and erode operators.

- **coat *material thickness thickness-map***

  The coat operator adds a new layer of material to a surface. The new layer has a specified maximum thickness that is modulated by the thickness map (see Figure 4).

- **erode *thickness thickness-map***

  The erode operator removes material from a layered surface. The depth of the erosion may be controlled by a thickness map. The erosion operator proceeds through the stack of layers decreasing the thickness of each layer until the desired amount of material has been removed. This provides a means to cut into a material and expose underlying layers. In principle, the amount of an erosion may depend on the hardness of the material in each layer, although our current system does not store hardness as a material attribute (see Figure 4).

- **fill** ***material height height-map***

  The fill operator deposits material up to a given absolute height above the base material. This is somewhat akin to filling all the valleys with water until it reaches a given height. This is a simple way to simulate the deposition of material in cracks and crevices.

- **polish** ***height height-map***

  The polish operator removes material until a given absolute height above the base material is reached. The result is a smoothing effect across a surface. A variation of the operator removes material until a given area of surface is exposed. This version of the operator was motivated by observing profiles and statistics of rough surfaces after they have been polished [29].

- **offset** ***radius***

  The offset operator applies a material to a surface by first applying a thick coat and then removing the part accessible to a sphere of a given radius. The offset surface is computed using techniques described by Miller [23]. (We have implemented both versions of his operator: one computes the largest tangent sphere, the other forms a positive and then a negative offset surface and compares that to the height of the original surface).

We have implemented a simple scripting language to describe the sequential application of different operators. This can be used simply to assemble a layered surface from a set of materials and texture maps. In this case each material and thickness map represents the current characteristics of the layered surface. This makes it possible to give the user control over the ordering of various operators and special effects such as polishing. Alternatively, the operators can be repeatedly applied to simulate the action of the environment on the surface. When used in this way the scripts may be generated by a program that attempts to cycle through various operations occurring through time. In Section 5 we will show several example scripts.

3.3 Texture/Thickness Maps

The operators we have described are able to model a multi-layered patina, but one that is completely uniform and devoid of the variations and richness of detail that any natural process generates. Next, we will explain a few simple, physically plausible methods to modulate these operators across the surface, simulating the detail present in the real aging process. In our system we have used two representations for spatially-varying thickness maps:

1. **Rectangular texture maps.** In this implementation the thickness is controlled by a standard 2D texture map.

2. **Triangulations as texture maps.** This implementation represents thicknesses as values attached to the vertices of a triangulation.

In order to simulate variations in thickness over time, we have implemented a series of fractal surface growth models for use with the layer structure. Many of these approaches are variations of models from the book by Barabási and Stanley [1]. We chose a set of models that deals with the deposition of material and the lateral growth of patches on surfaces. These models are particularly appropriate for modeling the types of patterns that emerge in the corrosion process, as corrosion typically begins with the deposition of water and particulate matter from the atmosphere onto a surface. Patches develop and spread based on the amount of water and other substances on the surface. Our implementation of these models includes several growth rates, such as linear, parabolic, and logarithmic. We provide the following models:

Steady thickening (ST). This model creates a very simple, relatively uniform pattern, which increases in thickness with time. We sample a surface evenly with a small number of points. An initial thickness is assigned to each of these points, and the thickness at intermediate points is interpolated. Over time, the thickness at each sample point is increased by a user-specified growth rate. A small amount of noise is added to the pattern to keep the appearance natural.

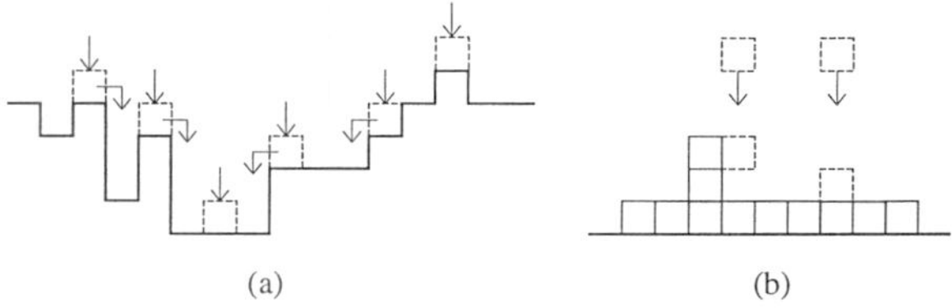

Figure 5: (a) Random deposition; the bent arrows indicate RD with surface relaxation. (b) Ballistic deposition.

Random deposition (RD). Random deposition is the simplest growth model that we utilize. From a randomly chosen position over the surface, a particle falls vertically until it reaches the top of the surface under it, whereupon it is deposited. We implement this model by randomly choosing a position i and increasing its height $h(i,t)$ by one, where t denotes the time step. A variation of this model, random deposition with surface relaxation, allows the deposited particle to diffuse along the surface up to a finite distance, settling when it finds the position with the lowest height (see Figure 5a). Due to the relaxation process, the final interface — or surface of the layer — will be smooth, compared to the model without relaxation, which is extremely rough.

Ballistic deposition (BD). In the Ballistic deposition model, a particle is also released from a randomly chosen position above a surface and follows a straight vertical trajectory until it reaches the surface, whereupon it sticks (see Figure 5b). The height of the interface at that point i is increased to $\max[h(neighboring\_points,t), h(i,t) + 1]$. Growth is defined quantitatively through a simple function that calculates the *mean height* of the surface. If the deposition rate (number of particles arriving at a position) is constant, the mean height increases linearly with time. In addition, the *interface width*, which describes the roughness of the surface, is defined by the rms fluctuation in height. The key difference between the RD and BD models is that the RD interface is uncorrelated — i.e. the thickness at each point on the surface grows independently, since there is no mechanism that can generate correlations along the interface. In BD, the fact that particles are capable of sticking to the edge of neighboring points leads to lateral growth.

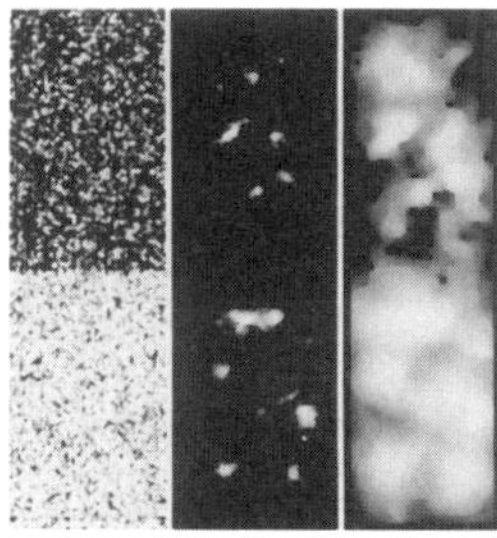

Figure 6: A lattice of blocked and unblocked cells (left), early stage of pattern formation (middle), late stage of pattern formation (right).

Directed percolation depinning (DPD). Starting with a collection of initial patches on a surface, we develop an interface that grows in all directions in two-dimensions and increases in thickness. We begin with a simple 2D lattice and mark a percentage of cells as *blocked* and others as *unblocked*. Over time, patches are much more likely to advance onto an unblocked cell than a blocked cell (the rules for it are much less stringent). In our version of the model, unblocked cells imply concentrations of moisture on the surface and thus stimulate growth.

Figure 6 shows a representative, initial lattice (where black indicates blocked and white indicates unblocked) and a collection of patches at early and mature stages. In this case, the seed patches are 10×10 squares. The patches grow in the direction of their principal neighbors (cardinal directions) based on a simple probability function and according to whether the given cell is blocked. Note that the pattern develops much more readily in the bottom half of the image, reflecting the lower percentage of blocked cells. Over time as the initial patches spread across the surface, the system inserts additional seed patches at unoccupied positions according to a given probability; these patches grow according to the same rules. The above process creates the bottom level or overall pattern. The upper levels (accounting for variations in thickness) are filled in as follows: the probability of a cell appearing in level $l+1$ is proportional to the number of cells in level l that support it. Variations in thickness are denoted by gray levels; white is solid and black is void. Other initial patterns and lattices could be used, and such components could be varied as a function of time.

In our current system the development of the layer structure through time is controlled in two ways. In addition to scripting different operations, specific growth models, as described above, can be used to generate thickness maps through time. These growth models can be controlled by environmental factors and the geometry of the surface. Finally, the layer structure is output as a series of material properties and texture maps, which are passed to the rendering system. This allows additional control over the final appearance of the surface.

The use of development models represents something of a black box in that it is possible to use other procedural models or scanned patterns to generate the thickness maps. In addition to the approaches described above, we also make use of standard procedural texturing approaches, such as noise and turbulence functions [6]. We have found the above models to be especially useful. However, as additional information is learned about the development of patinas, more exact models could be used, without affecting the overall patina modeling framework.

4 Rendering

The appearance of a layered structure is a result of light interacting with the surface and subsurface. Surfaces arise at the interfaces between layers. Light is reflected from the surface depending on the surface roughness and the specular color. The surface reflection gives the layer a glossy appearance. Light is also reflected from and transmitted through the interior depending on the absorption and scattering properties of the material. The subsurface reflection gives the layer a matte or diffuse appearance. The fact that light is also transmitted through the stack of layers causes the colors of different layers to be mixed; it also allows underlying materials to remain partially visible.

4.1 Single Layer

To model reflection and transmission through a single layer we use the Kubelka-Munk (KM) model [21]. The KM model is widely used in the paint, printing, and textile industries to compute diffuse colors due to subsurface scattering [17]. The book by Kortum is an excellent source of information about the KM model [18].

The KM model was recently introduced to computer graphics by Haase and Meyer [12]. In that work the color of a thick layer of paint consisting of several pigments was quantitatively modeled. Given the relative concentrations of several pigments, they were able to predict the final appearance of the paint. The KM model was compared to the standard additive or subtractive color models used in computer graphics and was found to be more accurate. They also used the KM model to estimate the pigment concentrations needed to match a given color. In this work we use the KM model to predict the color effects due to variations in layer thickness and to predict the color of a stack of layers of different pigments.

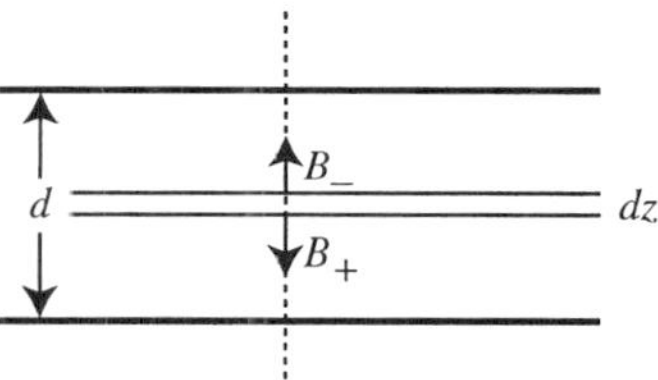

Figure 7: Positive and negative flux density within a layer.

The KM model corresponds roughly to 1-dimensional volume radiosity. Figure 7 shows the transport of light within a layer. The KM model assumes that the light distribution is directionally isotropic, but varies as a function of depth. The light distribution therefore is described by the flux density (energy per unit area), or volume radiosity, in the inward or positive, and outward or negative directions, denoted by B_+ and B_-.

As light propagates through the volume it may be absorbed or scattered, according to the following coupled differential equations

$$\begin{aligned}\frac{\partial B_+}{\partial z} &= -(K+S)B_+ + SB_- \\ \frac{\partial B_-}{\partial z} &= SB_+ - (K+S)B_-\end{aligned}$$

where K is the absorption per unit length, and S is the backscattering per unit length. Backscattering decreases the energy flow in one direction, thereby causing an increase in the opposite direction.

These equations have an analytical solution for a homogeneous layer of thickness d [19]. Given these solutions it is possible to compute the reflectance R and transmittance T through a layer:

$$\begin{aligned}R &= \frac{B_-(0)}{B_+(0)} = \frac{\sinh bSd}{a \sinh bSd + b \cosh bSd} \\ T &= \frac{B_+(d)}{B_+(0)} = \frac{b}{a \sinh bSd + b \cosh bSd}\end{aligned}$$

Here $a = (S+K)/S$ and $b = \sqrt{a^2-1}$. Note that in general K and S are functions of wavelength, hence the calculations involved in the KM model must be performed separately for each color sample.

The major problem in using the KM theory is the determination of the layer parameters K and S. One method is based on the formula for the reflectance of an infinitely thick layer:

$$R_\infty = 1 + \frac{K}{S} + \sqrt{\frac{K}{S}^2 + 2\frac{K}{S}}.$$

This formula can be inverted and the ratio K/S computed from R_∞. Thus, measuring the reflectance of an optically thick sample allows one to compute K/S. Another common method for determining the KM parameters is to measure the reflectance of a thick layer and then the reflectance of a layer of known thickness over a background material of known reflectance. A good discussion of different methods for determining the KM parameters in the context of computer graphics is contained in Haase and Meyer [12].

In our work we have estimated the KM parameters by matching synthesized color samples to physical copper and mineral specimens, as well as photographs, such as those found in Hughes and Rowe [16]. We generally match R_∞ to the sample, determine K/S from the above formula, and assume a value for S. This approach has enough accuracy to capture the range of colors and color effects that we are attempting to model. A more careful study involving detailed comparisons with physical samples under controlled weathering conditions would require more accurate radiometric and colorimetric measurements. However, this is beyond the scope of this study.

4.2 Multiple Layers

Kubelka also extended his model to account for the reflectance and transmittance, including all scattering events, due to a stack of layers [20]. The reflectance and transmittance of two layers may be merged to yield an equivalent reflectance and transmittance:

$$R = R_1 + \frac{T_1^2 R_2}{1 - R_1 R_2}$$

$$T = \frac{T_1 T_2}{1 - R_1 R_2}$$

This compositing process can be repeated, sequentially combining two layers into a single layer, to account for the reflection and transmission through a stack of n layers. We normally do this front to back, although it can be done in any order. Thus it is essentially no more difficult to compute the diffuse reflectance and transmittance, including all possible transport paths, for a stack of n layers than for a single layer. These formulas may also be used to combine a stack of layers with an opaque base layer. (Note that most formulations of the KM model explicitly include composition with a background layer R_g.)

We call this process *subsurface compositing* to differentiate it from the normal compositing operators widely used in computer graphics [27]. Subsurface compositing differs from normal compositing in that visible light is always assumed to be transmitted through each layer twice, which gives rise to a T^2 factor in front of each reflectance. This lowers the visibility of underlying layers. Subsurface compositing also accounts for the effect of multiple scattering which leads to a $1/(1 - R_1 R_2)$ factor which increases the contribution from each layer. These are important effects when viewing a stack of adjoining layers; it differs from the typical case in computer graphics where a set of disjoint partially transparent reflecting surfaces are being viewed. In this case it is incorrect to only consider one-dimensional interreflection, and the light source is not necessarily emanating from the eye.

4.3 BRDF

The above techniques are used during rendering to compute an approximation to the BRDF of each point on the layered surface. We assume the final BRDF consists of a diffuse term and a mixture of glossy terms. The diffuse reflectance of a stack of layers is computed exactly as described above, and needs no further explanation.

Accounting correctly for glossy reflection is more complicated, so we make several assumptions to simplify rendering. Glossiness is caused by light reflection at the interface between layers. Traditionally in computer graphics there is only a single interface between air and the material — the surface itself — and this interface causes the glossy appearance; in a layered structure there are multiple interfaces. In our system we perform the following two steps. First, glossy reflection at each interface is modeled using the standard computer graphics model for shiny surfaces; that is, with a specular color and a microfacet distribution function parameterized by the surface roughness, $C_s(N \cdot H)^{1/r}$. Each interface inherits its properties from the material below it, hence, each interface may have a different roughness and color. Second, to account for attenuation due to absorption and scattering in the layers above the interface, the specular color is multiplied twice by diffuse transmittance of the intervening layers calculated using the KM equations. The output glossy BRDF consists of a set of surface roughnesses and attenuated specular colors. The renderer needs to be modified to sum over this set of microfacet distributions when computing the final glossy reflection component. If the final specular color of one of the glossy terms is 0, that usually implies that it has been covered by an opaque material.

This method of computing glossy reflection is an approximation for several reasons. First, it is not strictly correct to use the diffuse transmittance to attenuate the incoming and outgoing radiance because even with a homogeneous layer the transmittance will be a function of direction. Second, the above model does not account for scattering events in the intervening layers before or after the glossy reflection. In general, accounting for this would require the full solution of the one-dimensional transport equation, as was done in Hanrahan and Krueger [13]. The precise nature of the errors introduced by these approximations needs further study. But our approximations capture quite well all the major visual effects that we hoped to achieve.

Finally, we output the final thickness of the stack of layers by summing the thicknesses of each layer. This final thickness may be used to either perturb the normals or displace the surface during final rendering.

5 Results

To demonstrate the modeling and rendering approaches described in the paper, we show results from several complex simulations.

5.1 Copper Strips

Figure 8 depicts the weathering of copper strips exposed to marine, rural, and urban environments respectively over the course of a thirty year period (in six year increments). This example shows the possibilities for the development of natural patinas in distinct environments. In all cases, the basic development of the patina was derived from the background material presented in Section 2. The patterns used in the layer maps were created though the fractal surface growth models described in Section 3.3; in the scripts below, the models are identified with the algorithm name, growth rate, step number, and total number of steps. Names such as `marine_patina_3` signify mixtures of the substances outlined in Figure 2 and are treated as materials with the various operators; the integer indicates the specific stage in this chart. The development of the patina was simulated using the layer structure and combinations of operators. The leftmost strips represent the appearance of pure copper — the starting point for the simulations.

Marine environment. The top row is a simulation of changes due to a typical marine environment. Here, we used the BD and DPD models to vary the thickness of the layers as a function of time. The BD model yields spotty patterns that are characteristic of marine environments, which often leave uneven coatings of moisture and salts on surfaces. The DPD model provides a patchy but more uniform coating of patina in the latter stages. In the last stage, we erode away a small portion of the top layer. The script for the last strip in the series is the following:

```
new copper;
coat tarnish_1 0.35 texture(BD_linear_1_20);
coat cuprite_2 1.2 texture(DPD_linear_5_40);
coat marine_patina_3 3.0 texture(BD_linear_10_20)
coat marine_patina_4 1.8 texture(DPD_linear_20_40);
erode 0.5 texture(BD_linear_5_20);
render maps;
```

Rural environment. The middle row is a simulation of effects common in a typical rural environment. Note that it takes longer for the green patina to begin to appear here. Patinas in rural environments tend to be quite spatially homogeneous. To capture this quality, we used the ST pattern generator to vary the thickness of the layers in the sequence. The script for the last strip in this series is the following:

```
new copper;
coat tarnish_1 0.25 texture(ST_cubic_1_20);
coat cuprite_2 1.0 texture(ST_cubic_5_20);
coat rural_patina_3 1.0 texture(ST_cubic_10_20);
coat rural_patina_4 1.1 texture(ST_cubic_15_20);
render maps;
```

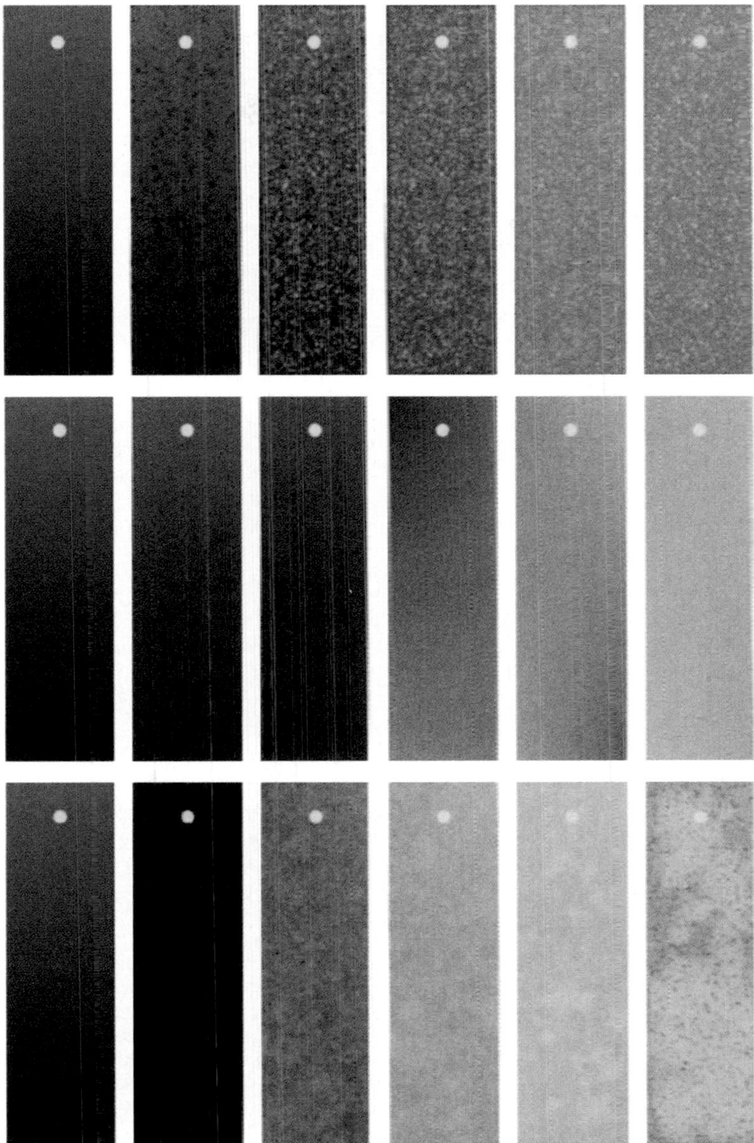

Figure 8: Copper time lines: marine environment (top); rural environment (middle); urban environment (bottom).

Urban environment. The bottom row is representative of changes due to an urban environment. Here, the films are very thick. Note that in this case, the green copper salts begin to appear much earlier in the sequence. Half way into the sequence, the surface is covered with a thick, almost continuous, coating. In this sequence, we used the DPD model to generate the variations in thickness. This model gives rise to fairly continuous patches that grow laterally on the surface. It is common for urban patinas to be very soluble and to develop coatings of soot/dirt. To capture this quality, we erode away some of the patina and add a layer of dirt on the surface using the RD model on the last strip in the sequence. Here is the script for this strip:

```
new copper;
coat tarnish_1 0.55 texture(RD_linear_1_40);
coat cuprite_urban_2 1.0 texture(RD_cubic_10_40);
coat patina_urban_3 4.0 texture(DPD_cubic_5_40);
coat patina_urban_4 3.0 texture(DPD_cubic_10_40);
erode 0.8 texture(DPD_linear_30_40);
coat dirt 1.9 texture(BD_linear_5_20);
render maps;
```

Figure 9 illustrates the layers and the final BRDF parameters for the urban series. Note that the layer structure records the evolution of the strip from bottom to top. The initial development (bottom row) features output from the RD algorithm without surface relaxation. The remaining rows show patterns created with the DPD model. In the top row, the dirt pattern created with the BD model is visible. It is interesting to observe that each layer has constant surface properties; all the variations in color and texture arise from varying the thickness of the different layers.

5.2 Buddha

Figure 11 shows the development of the patina on a small statue of a buddha. The buddha model was created from a Cyberware scan and consists of approximately 60,000 small evenly sized triangles. In these pictures the table and wall are rendered using conventional texturing techniques, and the buddha is rendered using the techniques described in this paper.

In this experiment the various stages of the development of the patina are simulated in the RenderMan shading language. A shader

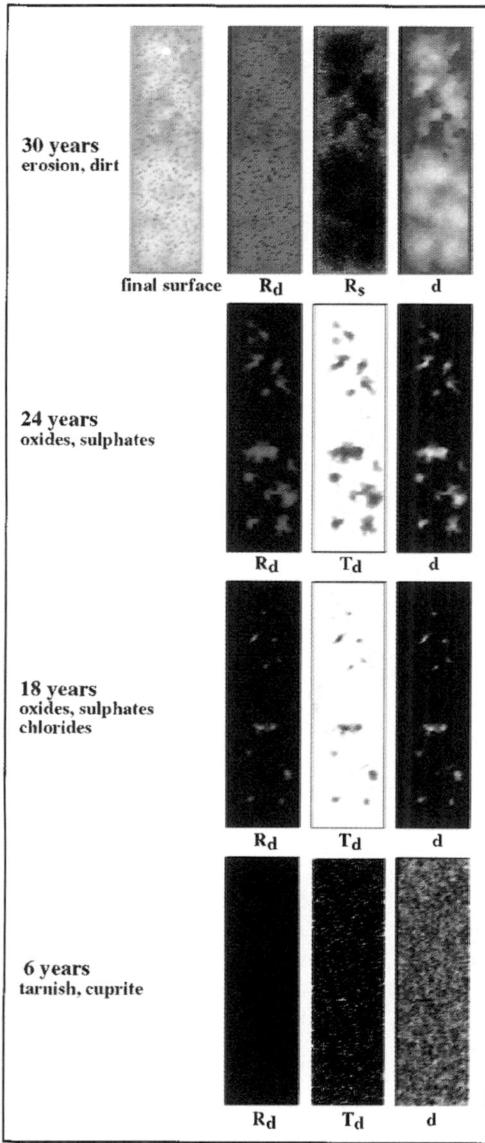

Figure 9: Layer properties and the final BRDF parameters for the urban series.

was written that modeled a three-layered surface: base copper, a tarnished layer, and a green patina. Parameters related to thickness are shown as a function of time in Figure 10. The thickness of different layers also depends on position and other factors as follows:

- The thickness of the tarnish layer was computed using two functions. The first, labeled tarnish in Figure 10, models tarnishing due to atmospheric processes. This parameter does not vary spatially. The second parameter, labeled polish, shows the decrease in tarnish thickness due to polishing the buddha. This parameter does vary spatially as determined by the accessibility map (the accessibility map is computed as a preprocess, and therefore there is a single accessibility value per triangle) [23]. Thus, tarnish appears in cracks and crevices, and shiny copper appears in exposed areas.
- The green patina consists of a steadily thickening layer and a set of steadily growing random patches. The steadily thickening layer depends on the local wetness of the surface; the wetter the surface the thicker the patina. The wetness is controlled by a precomputed exposure map, that gives the average irradiance due to the sun and sky received by that part of the surface, and a simple function that decreases the average wetness of inclined surfaces. Another simple procedure increases the wetness along the base of the statue where water is likely to accumulate; this effect changes through time under control of the base parameter. The patches of the patina are controlled by a random fractal surface growth process. To show the flexibility of the system, the surface growth pattern is computed using the standard noise function in the shading language. The thickness of these various components of the patina change through time as shown in Figure 10. The curve labeled body controls the thickness of the steadily thickening layer, the curve labeled base controls the thickness along the bottom, and the curve labeled bump controls the thickness of the random growth process.

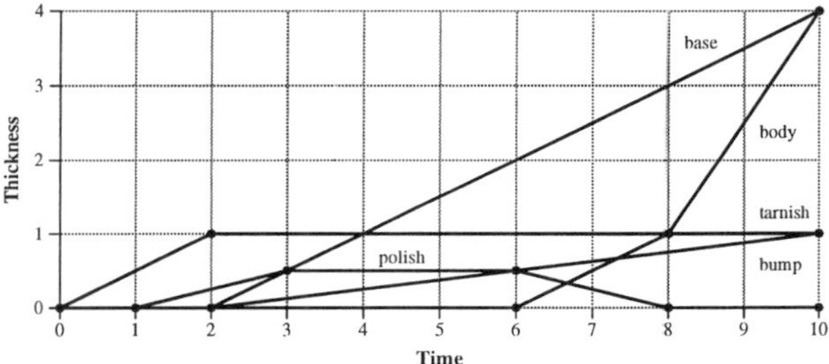

Figure 10: Development of patina on the buddha statue.

5.3 Towers

Figure 12 shows two copper-covered towers of different ages in an urban environment. The tower on the left displays a dark cuprite coating due to a few years of exposure; the tower to the right has a green patina typical of several decades of exposure.

For this simulation, we modulated the appearance of the patina based on several functions. As in the previous example, the wetness is controlled by a precomputed exposure map and a simple function that decreases the average wetness on inclined surfaces. For example, inclined areas that face south have thinner layers of patina, reflecting the fact that they would be dryer. We also used an accessibility map to vary the thickness of the patinas across the surfaces.

The new tower to the left is covered with a thin layer of cuprite. In addition, some simple texture maps were created with a noise function and combined with the layer structure to simulate the staining due to the flow of water over the top of the tower. Modeling such washing and staining effects is the subject of a separate work [5].

In the tower on the right, there is a thin layer of cuprite on the base copper. This is augmented with a fairly uniform layer of patina. We also added a thin layer of dirt, which is common to urban patinas. All layers are varied by simple noise functions.

6 Summary and Discussion

We have presented an approach for the modeling and rendering of one type of weathering — metallic patinas. A surface is represented as a set of layers. This representation resembles the underlying structure of the physical model of a patina. A set of operators was introduced that can simulate a wide variety of weathering effects. We also presented an approach to modeling the reflection and transmission through the layer structure using the Kubelka-Munk model. The modeling and rendering approach is capable of simulating a variety of metallic patinas.

Although we attempted to model the development of patinas on surfaces based on the available physical evidence, our model is still a phenomenological one. We believe that an exact model is not possible at this time, as the more general problem of the atmospheric corrosion of metals is not yet fully understood. However, the new layered model would appear to have great usefulness in computer graphics due to the ease with which it is possible to give the designer

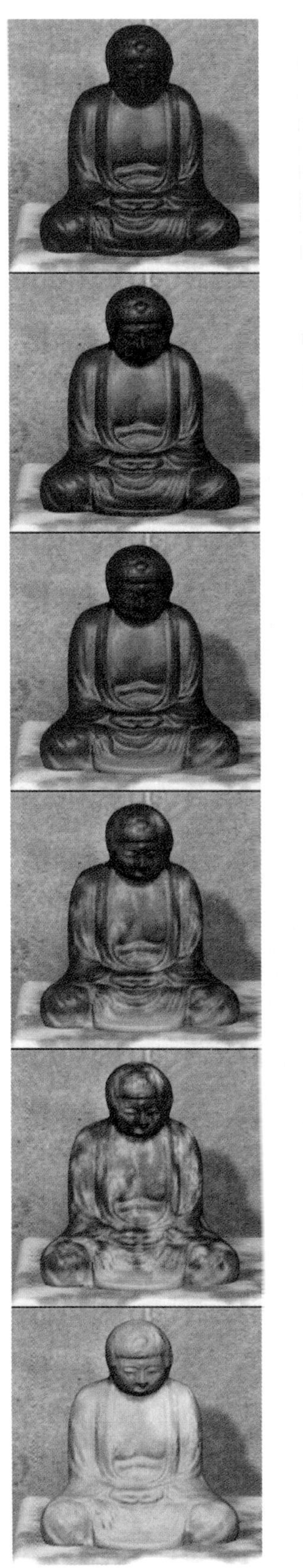

Figure 11: *A sense of time.* On the left is a sequence of images showing the aging of a statuette. Time progresses from top to bottom. The larger image above illustrates the buildup of both the underlying smooth copper sulphide tarnish and the rough green patina.

Figure 12: *Two copper-covered towers.* (Left) After a few years of exposure. (Right) After several decades of exposure.

control over a wide variety of processes important in determining the final appearance of an object.

This representation of a material is significant, as it can accommodate the time-varying nature of a surface and its exposure to a complex class of weathering effects. We believe that this general model will be applicable to other materials as well. The problem of creating physically-based models of real materials, which can incorporate variations over time, is an important topic for computer graphics. This is a difficult problem, as the factors that determine the changes in appearance of materials operate simultaneously and are not completely understood. These difficulties notwithstanding, many interesting research directions remain. One area is in the design of models for other materials, such as wood or plastics. Another topic is the development of more complex operators, which can simulate dynamic processes, such as erosion. Last, we would like to add interactive operators to the system. These would be especially useful for creating patterns due to various brushes used in artificial patination techniques.

Acknowledgements

We would like to thank Jeff Feldgoise for modeling the tower scene and Matt Pharr for help rendering it, Brian Curless for scanning the buddha model, Hans Pedersen for providing a geometry translator, Steve Westin for reviewing an early draft of the paper, Craig Kolb for video assistance, Tom Graedel for the copper micrograph, and the anonymous reviewers for helpful suggestions. This research was supported by research grants from the National Science Foundation (CCR-9207966 and CCR-9624172) and the MIT Cabot and NEC Funds, and by equipment grants from Apple and Silicon Graphics Inc.

References

[1] BARABÁSI, A. L., AND STANLEY, H. E. *Fractal Concepts in Surface Growth.* Cambridge University Press, Cambridge, 1995.

[2] BECKET, W., AND BADLER, N. I. Imperfection for realistic image synthesis. *Journal of Visualization and Computer Animation 1*, 1 (Aug. 1990), 26–32.

[3] BLINN, J. F. Light reflection functions for simulation of clouds and dusty surfaces. *Computer Graphics 16*, 3 (July 1982), 21–29.

[4] COOK, R. L. Shade trees. *Computer Graphics 18*, 3 (July 1984), 223–231.

[5] DORSEY, J., PEDERSEN, H. K., AND HANRAHAN, P. Flow and changes in appearance. In *Computer Graphics Proceedings* (1996), Annual Conference Series, ACM SIGGRAPH.

[6] EBERT, D. S., Ed. *Texturing and Modeling.* Academic Press, New York, 1994.

[7] FLEMING, S. J. *Dating in Archaeology.* St. Martin's Press, New York, 1977.

[8] FRANEY, J. P., AND DAVIS, M. E. Metallographic studies of the copper patina formed in the atmosphere. *Corrosion Science 27*, 7 (1987), 659–688.

[9] FRENCH, L. Toy story. *Cinefantastique 27*, 2 (1995), 36–37.

[10] GRAEDEL, T. E. Copper patinas formed in the atmosphere – a qualitative assessment of mechanisms. *Corrosion Science 27*, 7 (1987), 721–740.

[11] GRAEDEL, T. E., NASSAU, K., AND FRANEY, J. P. Copper patinas formed in the atmosphere. *Corrosion Science 27*, 7 (1987), 639–652.

[12] HAASE, C. S., AND MEYER, G. W. Modeling pigmented materials for realistic image synthesis. *ACM Tran. Graphics 11*, 4 (Oct. 1992), 305–335.

[13] HANRAHAN, P., AND KRUEGER, W. Reflection from layered surfaces due to subsurface scattering. In *Computer Graphics Proceedings* (1993), Annual Conference Series, ACM SIGGRAPH, pp. 165–174.

[14] HANRAHAN, P., AND LAWSON, J. A language for shading and lighting calculations. *Computer Graphics 24*, 4 (Aug. 1990), 289–298.

[15] HSU, S., AND WONG, T. Simulating dust accumulation. *IEEE Computer Graphics and Applications 15*, 1 (Jan. 1995), 18–22.

[16] HUGHES, R., AND ROWE, M. *The Colouring, Bronzing and Patination of Metals.* Watson-Guptill Publications, New York, 1991.

[17] JUDD, D. B., AND WYSZECKI, G. *Color in Business, Science, and Industry.* John Wiley & Sons, New York, 1975.

[18] KORTUM, G. *Reflectance Spectroscopy.* Springer-Verlag, New York, 1969.

[19] KUBELKA, P. New contributions to the optics of intensely light-scattering material, part I. *J. Opt. Soc. Am. 38* (1948), 448.

[20] KUBELKA, P. New contributions to the optics of intensely light-scattering material, part II: Non-homogeneous layers. *J. Opt. Soc. Am. 44* (1954), 330.

[21] KUBELKA, P., AND MUNK, F. Ein beitrag zur optik der farbanstriche. *Z. tech. Physik. 12* (1931), 593.

[22] MATTSSON, E. *Basic Corrosion Technology for Scientists and Engineers.* Ellis Horwood Limited, New York, 1989.

[23] MILLER, G. Efficient algorithms for local and global accessibility shading. In *Computer Graphics Proceedings* (1994), Annual Conference Series, ACM SIGGRAPH, pp. 319–326.

[24] MOSTAFAVI, M., AND LEATHERBARROW, D. *On Weathering: The Life of Buildings in Time.* MIT Press, Cambridge, MA, 1993.

[25] NEWMAN, R. C., AND SIERADZKI, K. Metallic corrosion. *Science 263* (1994), 1708–1709.

[26] PERLIN, K. An image synthesizer. *Computer Graphics 19*, 4 (July 1985), 287–296.

[27] PORTER, T., AND DUFF, T. Compositing digital images. *Computer Graphics 18*, 3 (July 1984), 253–259.

[28] SIMPSON, J. W., AND HORROBIN, P. J. *The Weathering and Performance of Building Materials.* MTP Publishing Co, London, 1970.

[29] THOMAS, T. R., Ed. *Rough Surfaces.* Longman, New York, 1982.

[30] TURK, G. Generating textures for arbitrary surfaces using reaction-diffusion. *Computer Graphics 25*, 4 (July 1991), 289–298.

[31] UPSTILL, S. *The Renderman Companion.* Addison-Wesley, New York, 1990.

[32] VERNON, W. H. J., AND WHITBY, L. The open air corrosion of copper, a chemical surface patina. *Journal Instit. of Metals 42*, 6 (1932), 181–195.

[33] WITKIN, A., AND KASS, M. Reaction-diffusion textures. *Computer Graphics 25*, 4 (July 1991), 299–308.

Visual Models of Plants Interacting with Their Environment

Radomír Měch and Przemyslaw Prusinkiewicz[1]
University of Calgary

ABSTRACT

Interaction with the environment is a key factor affecting the development of plants and plant ecosystems. In this paper we introduce a modeling framework that makes it possible to simulate and visualize a wide range of interactions at the level of plant architecture. This framework extends the formalism of Lindenmayer systems with constructs needed to model bi-directional information exchange between plants and their environment. We illustrate the proposed framework with models and simulations that capture the development of tree branches limited by collisions, the colonizing growth of clonal plants competing for space in favorable areas, the interaction between roots competing for water in the soil, and the competition within and between trees for access to light. Computer animation and visualization techniques make it possible to better understand the modeled processes and lead to realistic images of plants within their environmental context.

CR categories: F.4.2 **[Mathematical Logic and Formal Languages]**: Grammars and Other Rewriting Systems: *Parallel rewriting systems*, I.3.7 **[Computer Graphics]**: Three-Dimensional Graphics and Realism, I.6.3 **[Simulation and Modeling]**: Applications, J.3 **[Life and Medical Sciences]**: Biology.

Keywords: scientific visualization, realistic image synthesis, software design, L-system, modeling, simulation, ecosystem, plant development, clonal plant, root, tree.

1 INTRODUCTION

Computer modeling and visualization of plant development can be traced back to 1962, when Ulam applied cellular automata to simulate the development of branching patterns, thought of as an abstract representation of plants [53]. Subsequently, Cohen presented a more realistic model operating in continuous space [13], Lindenmayer proposed the formalism of L-systems as a general framework for plant modeling [38, 39], and Honda introduced the first computer model of tree structures [32]. From these origins, plant modeling emerged as a vibrant area of interdisciplinary research, attracting the efforts of biologists, applied plant scientists, mathematicians, and computer scientists. Computer graphics, in particular, contributed a wide range of models and methods for synthesizing images of plants. See [18, 48, 54] for recent reviews of the main results.

One aspect of plant structure and behavior neglected by most models is the interaction between plants and their environment (including other plants). Indeed, the incorporation of interactions has been identified as one of the main outstanding problems in the domain of plant modeling [48] (see also [15, 18, 50]). Its solution is needed to construct predictive models suitable for applications ranging from computer-assisted landscape and garden design to the determination of crop and lumber yields in agriculture and forestry.

Using the information flow between a plant and its environment as the classification key, we can distinguish three forms of interaction and the associated models of plant-environment systems devised to date:

1. The plant is affected by global properties of the environment, such as day length controlling the initiation of flowering [23] and daily minimum and maximum temperatures modulating the growth rate [28].

2. The plant is affected by local properties of the environment, such as the presence of obstacles controlling the spread of grass [2] and directing the growth of tree roots [26], geometry of support for climbing plants [2, 25], soil resistance and temperature in various soil layers [16], and predefined geometry of surfaces to which plant branches are pruned [45].

3. The plant interacts with the environment in an information feedback loop, where the environment affects the plant and the plant reciprocally affects the environment. This type of interaction is related to *sighted* [4] or *exogenous* [42] mechanisms controlling plant development, in which parts of a plant influence the development of other parts of the same or a different plant through the space in which they grow. Specific models capture:

   – competition for *space* (including collision detection and access to light) between segments of essentially two-dimensional schematic branching structures [4, 13, 21, 22, 33, 34, 36];

   – competition between root tips for *nutrients* and *water* transported in soil [12, 37] (this mechanism is related to competition between growing branches of corals and sponges for nutrients diffusing in water [34]);

[1]Department of Computer Science, University of Calgary, Calgary, Alberta, Canada T2N 1N4 (mech|pwp@cpsc.ucalgary.ca)

- competition for *light* between three-dimensional shoots of herbaceous plants [25] and branches of trees [9, 10, 11, 15, 33, 35, 52].

Models of exogenous phenomena require a comprehensive representation of both the developing plant and the environment. Consequently, they are the most difficult to formulate, implement, and document. Programs addressed to the biological audience are often limited to narrow groups of plants (for example, poplars [9] or trees in the pine family [21]), and present the results in a rudimentary graphical form. On the other hand, models addressed to the computer graphics audience use more advanced techniques for realistic image synthesis, but put little emphasis on the faithful reproduction of physiological mechanisms characteristic to specific plants.

In this paper we propose a general *framework* (defined as a modeling methodology supported by appropriate software) for modeling, simulating, and visualizing the development of plants that bi-directionally interact with their environment. The usefulness of modeling frameworks for simulation studies of models with complex (emergent) behavior is manifested by previous work in theoretical biology, artificial life, and computer graphics. Examples include cellular automata [51], systems for simulating behavior of cellular structures in discrete [1] and continuous [20] spaces, and L-system-based frameworks for modeling plants [36, 46]. Frameworks may have the form of a general-purpose simulation program that accepts models described in a suitable mini-language as input, *e.g.* [36, 46], or a set of library programs [27]. Compared to special-purpose programs, they offer the following benefits:

- At the conceptual level, they facilitate the design, specification, documentation, and comparison of models.
- At the level of model implementation, they make it possible to develop software that can be reused in various models. Specifically, graphical capabilities needed to visualize the models become a part of the modeling framework, and do not have to be reimplemented.
- Finally, flexible conceptual and software frameworks facilitate interactive experimentation with the models [46, Appendix A].

Our framework is intended both for purpose of image synthesis and as a research and visualization tool for model studies in plant morphogenesis and ecology. These goals are addressed at the levels of the simulation system and the modeling language design. The underlying paradigm of plant-environment interaction is described in Section 2. The resulting design of the simulation software is outlined in Section 3. The language for specifying plant models is presented in Section 4. It extends the concept of environmentally-sensitive L-systems [45] with constructs for bi-directional communication with the environment. The following sections illustrate the proposed framework with concrete models of plants interacting with their environment. The examples include: the development of planar branching systems controlled by the crowding of apices (Section 5), the development of clonal plants controlled by both the crowding of ramets and the quality of terrain (Section 6), the development of roots controlled by the concentration of water transported in the soil (Section 7), and the development of tree crowns affected by the local distribution of light (Section 8) The paper concludes with an evaluation of the results and a list of open problems (Section 9).

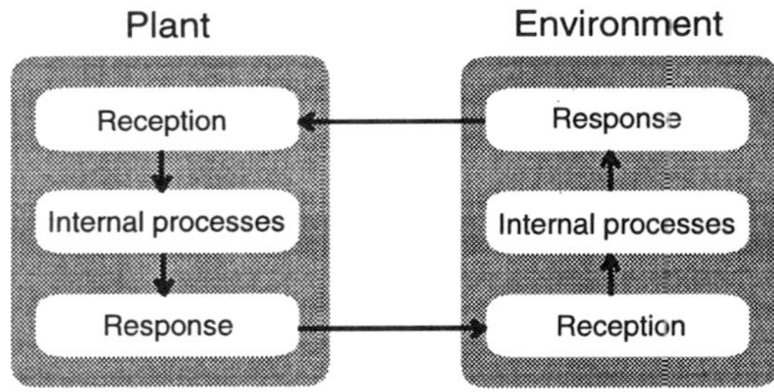

Figure 1: Conceptual model of plant and environment treated as communicating concurrent processes

2 CONCEPTUAL MODEL

As described by Hart [30], every environmentally controlled phenomenon can be considered as a chain of causally linked events. After a stimulus is perceived by the plant, information in some form is transported through the plant body (unless the site of stimulus perception coincides with the site of response), and the plant reacts. This reaction reciprocally affects the environment, causing its modification that in turn affects the plant. For example, roots growing in the soil can absorb or extract water (depending on the water concentration in their vicinity). This initiates a flow of water in the soil towards the depleted areas, which in turn affects further growth of the roots [12, 24].

According to this description, the interaction of a plant with the environment can be conceptualized as two concurrent processes that communicate with each other, thus forming a feedback loop of information flow (Figure 1). The plant process performs the following functions:

- reception of information about the environment in the form of scalar or vector values representing the stimuli perceived by specific organs;
- transport and processing of information inside the plant;
- generation of the response in the form of growth changes (*e.g.* development of new branches) and direct output of information to the environment (*e.g.* uptake and excretion of substances by a root tip).

Similarly, the environmental process includes mechanisms for the:

- perception of the plant's actions;
- simulation of internal processes in the environment (*e.g.* the diffusion of substances or propagation of light);
- presentation of the modified environment in a form perceivable by the plant.

The design of a simulation system based on this conceptual model is presented next.

3 SYSTEM DESIGN

The goal is to create a framework, in which a wide range of plant structures and environments can be easily created, modified, and used for experimentation. This requirement led us to the following design decisions:

- The plant and the environment should be modeled by separate programs and run as two communicating processes. This design is:
  - compatible with the assumed conceptual model of plant-environment interaction (Figure 1)
  - consistent with the principles of structured design (modules with clearly specified functions jointly contribute to the solution of a problem by communicating through a well defined interface; information local to each module is hidden from other modules);
  - appropriate for interactive experimentation with the models; in particular, changes in the plant program can be implemented without affecting the environmental program, and *vice versa*;
  - extensible to distributed computing environments, where different components of a large ecosystem may be simulated using separate computers.
- The user should have control over the type and amount of information exchanged between the processes representing the plant and the environment, so that all the needed but no superfluous information is transferred.
- Plant models should be specified in a language based on L-systems, equipped with constructs for bi-directional communication between the plant and the environment. This decision has the following rationale:
  - A succinct description of the models in an interpreted language facilitates experimentation involving modifications to the models;
  - L-systems capture two fundamental mechanisms that control development, namely flow of information from a mother module to its offspring (cellular descent) and flow of information between coexisting modules (endogenous interaction) [38]. The latter mechanism plays an essential role in transmitting information from the site of stimulus perception to the site of the response. Moreover, L-systems have been extended to allow for input of information from the environment (see Section 4);
  - Modeling of plants using L-systems has reached a relatively advanced state, manifested by models ranging from algae to herbaceous plants and trees [43, 46].
- Given the variety of processes that may take place in the environment, they should be modeled using special-purpose programs.
- Generic aspects of modeling, not specific to particular models, should be supported by the modeling system. This includes:
  - an L-system-based plant modeling program, which interprets L-systems supplied as its input and visualizes the results, and
  - the support for communication and synchronization of processes simulating the modeled plant and the environment.

A system architecture stemming from this design is shown in Figure 2. We will describe it from the perspective of extensions to the formalism of L-systems.

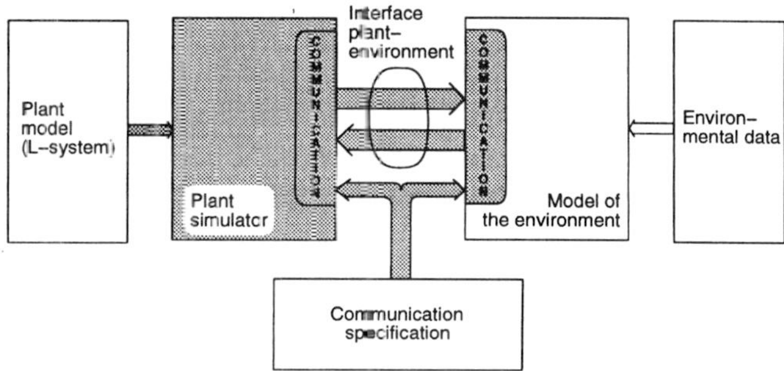

Figure 2: Organization of the software for modeling plants interacting with their environment. Shaded rectangles indicate components of the modeling framework, clear rectangles indicate programs and data that must be created by a user specifying a new model of a plant or environment. Shaded arrows indicate information exchanged in a standardized format.

4 OPEN L-SYSTEMS

Historically, L-systems were conceived as closed cybernetic systems, incapable of simulating any form of communication between the modeled plant and its environment. In the first step towards the inclusion of environmental factors, Rozenberg defined *table L-systems*, which allow for a change in the set of developmental rules (the production set of the L-system) in response to a change in the environment [31, 49]. Table L-systems were applied, for example, to capture the switch from the production of leaves to the production of flowers by the apex of a plant due to a change in day length [23]. *Parametric L-systems* [29, 46], introduced later, made it possible to implement a variant of this technique, with the environment affecting the model in a quantitative rather than qualitative manner. In a case study illustrating this possibility, weather data containing daily minimum and maximum temperatures were used to control the rate of growth in a bean model [28]. *Environmentally-sensitive L-systems* [45] represented the next step in the inclusion of environmental factors, in which local rather than global properties of the environment affected the model. The new concept was the introduction of query symbols, returning current position or orientation of the turtle in the underlying coordinate system. These parameters could be passed as arguments to user-defined functions, returning local properties of the environment at the queried location. Environmentally-sensitive L-systems were illustrated by models of topiary scenes. The environmental functions defined geometric shapes, to which trees were pruned.

Open L-systems, introduced in this paper, augment the functionality of environmentally-sensitive L-systems using a reserved symbol for bilateral communication with the environment. In short, parameters associated with an occurrence of the communication symbol can be set by the environment and transferred to the plant model, or set by the plant model and transferred to the environment. The environment is no longer represented by a simple function, but becomes an active process that may react to the information from the plant. Thus, plants are modeled as open cybernetic systems, sending information to and receiving information from the environment.

In order to describe open L-systems in more detail, we need to recall the rudiments of L-systems with turtle interpretation. Our presentation is reproduced from [45].

An L-system is a parallel rewriting system operating on branching structures represented as *bracketed strings* of symbols with associated numerical parameters, called *modules*. Matching pairs of square brackets enclose branches. Simulation begins with an initial string called the *axiom*, and proceeds in a sequence of discrete *derivation steps*. In each step, *rewriting rules* or *productions* replace all modules in the predecessor string by successor modules. The applicability of a production depends on a predecessor's context (in context-sensitive L-systems), values of parameters (in productions guarded by conditions), and on random factors (in stochastic L-systems). Typically, a production has the format:

$$id : lc < pred > rc : cond \rightarrow succ : prob$$

where id is the production identifier (label), lc, $pred$, and rc are the left context, the strict predecessor, and the right context, $cond$ is the condition, $succ$ is the successor, and $prob$ is the probability of production application. The strict predecessor and the successor are the only mandatory fields. For example, the L-system given below consists of axiom ω and three productions p_1, p_2, and p_3.

ω: A(1)B(3)A(5)
p_1: A(x) →A(x+1) : 0.4
p_2: A(x) →B(x–1) : 0.6
p_3: A(x) < B(y) > A(z) : y < 4 →B(x+z)[A(y)]

The stochastic productions p_1 and p_2 replace module $A(x)$ by either $A(x+1)$ or $B(x-1)$, with probabilities equal to 0.4 and 0.6, respectively. The context-sensitive production p_3 replaces a module $B(y)$ with left context $A(x)$ and right context $A(z)$ by module $B(x+z)$ supporting branch $A(y)$. The application of this production is guarded by condition $y < 4$. Consequently, the first derivation step may have the form:

$$A(1)B(3)A(5) \Rightarrow A(2)B(6)[A(3)]B(4)$$

It was assumed that, as a result of random choice, production p_1 was applied to the module $A(1)$, and production p_2 to the module $A(5)$. Production p_3 was applied to the module $B(3)$, because it occurred with the required left and right context, and the condition $3 < 4$ was true.

In the L-systems presented as examples we also use several additional constructs (*cf.* [29, 44]):

- Productions may include statements assigning values to local variables. These statements are enclosed in curly braces and separated by semicolons.
- The L-systems may also include arrays. References to array elements follow the syntax of C; for example, $MaxLen[order]$.
- The list of productions is ordered. In the deterministic case, the first matching production applies. In the stochastic case, the set of all matching productions is established, and one of them is chosen according to the specified probabilities.

For details of the L-system syntax see [29, 43, 46].

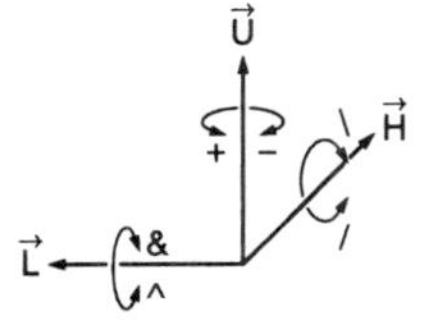

Figure 3: Controlling the turtle in three dimensions

In contrast to the parallel application of productions in each derivation step, the interpretation of the resulting strings proceeds sequentially, with reserved modules acting as commands to a LOGO-style turtle [46]. At any point of the string, the *turtle state* is characterized by a position vector $\vec{P}$ and three mutually perpendicular orientation vectors $\vec{H}$, $\vec{U}$, and $\vec{L}$, indicating the turtle's heading, the up direction, and the direction to the left (Figure 3). Module F causes the turtle to draw a line in the current direction. Modules $+$, $-$, &, $\wedge$, / and \ rotate the turtle around one of the vectors $\vec{H}, \vec{U}$, or $\vec{L}$, as shown in Figure 3. The length of the line and the magnitude of the rotation angle can be given globally or specified as parameters of individual modules. During the interpretation of branches, the opening square bracket pushes the current position and orientation of the turtle on a stack, and the closing bracket restores the turtle to the position and orientation popped from the stack. A special interpretation is reserved for the module %, which cuts a branch by erasing all symbols in the string from the point of its occurrence to the end of the branch [29]. The meaning of many symbols depends on the context in which they occur; for example, $+$ and $-$ denote arithmetic operators as well as modules that rotate the turtle.

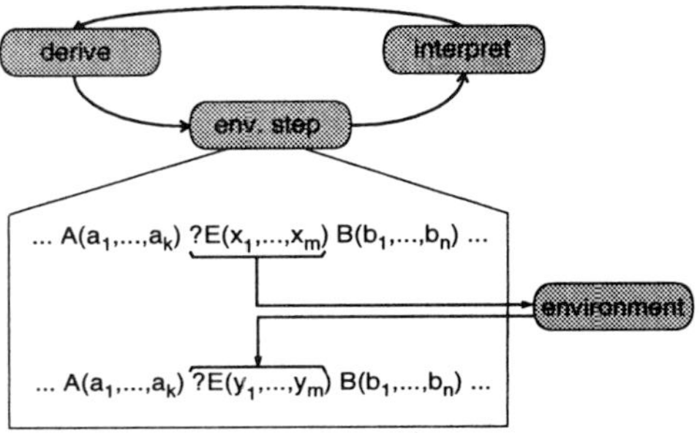

Figure 4: Information flow during the simulation of a plant interacting with the environment, implemented using an open L-system

The turtle interpretation of L-systems described above was designed to visualize models in a postprocessing step, with no effect on the L-system operation. Position and orientation of the turtle are important, however, while considering environmental phenomena, such as collisions with obstacles and exposure to light. The environmentally-sensitive extension of L-systems makes these attributes accessible during the rewriting process [45]. The generated string is interpreted after each derivation step, and turtle attributes found during the interpretation are returned as parameters to reserved *query modules*. Syntactically, the query modules have the form $?X(x, y, z)$, where $X = P, H, U$, or L. Depending on the actual symbol X, the values of parameters x, y, and z represent a position or an orientation vector.

Open L-systems are a generalization of this concept. *Communication modules* of the form $?E(x_1, \ldots, x_m)$ are used both to send and receive environmental information represented by the values of parameters $x_1, \ldots, x_m$ (Figure 4). To this end, the string resulting from a derivation step is scanned from left to right to determine the state of the turtle associated with each symbol. This phase is similar to the graphical interpretation of the string, except that the results need not be visualized. Upon encountering a communication symbol, the plant process creates and sends a message to the environment including all or a part of the following information:

- the address (position in the string) of the communication module (mandatory field needed to identify this module when a reply comes from the environment),
- values of parameters x_i,
- the state of the turtle (coordinates of the position and orientation

vector, as well as some other attributes, such as current line width),

- the type and parameters of the module following the communication module in the string (not used in the examples discussed in this paper).

The exact message format is defined in a *communication specification file*, shared between the programs modeling the plant and the environment (Figure 2). Consequently, it is possible to include only the information needed in a particular model in the messages sent to the environment. Transfer of the last message corresponding to the current scan of the string is signaled by a reserved end-of-transmission message, which may be used by the environmental process to start its operation.

The messages output by the plant modeling program are transferred to the process that simulates the environment using an interprocess communication mechanism provided by the underlying operating system (a pair of UNIX pipes or shared memory with access synchronized using semaphores, for example). The environment processes that information and returns the results to the plant model using messages in the following format:

- the address of the target communication module,
- values of parameters y_i carrying the output from the environment.

The plant process uses the received information to set parameter values in the communication modules (Figure 4). The use of addresses makes it possible to send replies only to selected communication modules. Details of the mapping of messages received by the plant process to the parameters of the communication modules are defined in the communication specification file.

After all replies generated by the environment have been received (a fact indicated by an end-of-transmission message sent by the environment), the resulting string may be interpreted and visualized, and the next derivation step may be performed, initiating another cycle of the simulation.

Note that, by preceding every symbol in the string with a communication module it is possible to pass complete information about the model to the environment. Usually, however, only partial information about the state of a plant is needed as input to the environment. Proper placement of communication modules in the model, combined with careful selection of the information to be exchanged, provide a means for keeping the amount of transferred information at a manageable level.

We will illustrate the operation of open L-systems within the context of complete models of plant-environment interactions, using examples motivated by actual biological problems.

5 A MODEL OF BRANCH TIERS

Background. Apical meristems, located at the endpoints of branches, are engines of plant development. The apices grow, contributing to the elongation of branch segments, and from time to time divide, spawning the development of new branches. If all apices divided periodically, the number of apices and branch segments would increase exponentially. Observations of real branching structures show, however, that the increase in the number of segments is less than exponential [8]. Honda and his collaborators modeled several hypothetical mechanisms that may control the extent of branching in order to prevent overcrowding [7, 33] (see also [4]). One of the models [33], supported by measurements and earlier simulations of the tropical tree *Terminalia catappa* [19], assumes an exogenous interaction mechanism. *Terminalia* branches form horizontal tiers, and the model is limited to a single tier, treated as a two-dimensional structure. In this case, the competition for light effectively amounts to collision detection between the apices and leaf clusters. We reproduce this model as the simplest example illustrating the methodology proposed in this paper.

Communication specification. The plant communicates with the environment using communication modules of the form $?E(x)$. Messages sent to the environment include the turtle position and the value of parameter x, interpreted as the vigor of the corresponding apex. On this basis, the environmental process determines the fate of each apex. A parameter value of $x = 0$ returned to the plant indicates that the development of the corresponding branch will be terminated. A value of $x = 1$ allows for further branching.

The model of the environment. The environmental process considers each apex or non-terminal node of the developing tier as the center of a circular leaf cluster, and maintains a list of all clusters present. New clusters are added in response to messages received from the plant. All clusters have the same radius ρ, specified in the environmental data file (*cf.* Figure 2). In order to determine the fate of the apices, the environment compares apex positions with leaf cluster positions, and authorizes an apex to grow if it does not fall into an existing leaf cluster, or if it falls into a cluster surrounding an apex with a smaller vigor value.

The plant model. The plant model is expressed as an open L-system. The values of constants are taken from [33].

#define r_1 0.94 /* contraction ratio and vigor 1 */
#define r_2 0.87 /* contraction ratio and vigor 2 */
#define α_1 24.4 /* branching angle 1 */
#define α_2 36.9 /* branching angle 2 */
#define φ 138.5 /* divergence angle */
ω: –(90)[F(1)?E(1)A(1)]+(φ)[F(1)/?E(1)A(1)]
+(φ)[F(1)?E(1)A(1)]+(φ)[F(1)/?E(1)A(1)]
+(φ)[F(1)?E(1)A(1)]

p_1: ?E(x) < A(v) : x == 1 $\rightarrow$
[+(α_2)F(v*r_2)?E(r_2)A(v*r_2)] –(α_1)F(v*r_1)/?E(r_1)A(v*r_1)
p_2: ?E(x) $\rightarrow \varepsilon$

The axiom ω specifies the initial structure as a whorl of five branch segments F. The divergence angle φ between consecutive segments is equal to 138.5°. Each segment is terminated by a communication symbol $?E$ followed by an apex A. In addition, two branches include module /, which changes the directions at which subsequent branches will be issued (left *vs.* right) by rotating the apex 180° around the segment axis.

Production p_1 describes the operation of the apices. If the value of parameter x returned by a communication module $?E$ is not 1, the associated apex will remain inactive (do nothing). Otherwise the apex will produce a pair of new branch segments at angles α_1 and α_2 with respect to the mother segment. Constants r_1 and r_2 determine the lengths of the daughter segments as fractions of the length of their mother segment. The values r_1 and r_2 are also passed to the process simulating the environment using communication modules $?E$. Communication modules created in the previous derivation step are no longer needed and are removed by production p_2.

Figure 5: Competition for space between two tiers of branches simulated using the Honda model

Simulation. Figure 5 illustrates the competition for space between two tiers developing next to each other. The extent of branching in each tier is limited by collisions between its apices and its own or the neighbor's leaf clusters. The limited growth of each structure in the direction of its neighbor illustrates the phenomenon of *morphological plasticity*, or adaptation of the form of plants to their environment [17].

6 A MODEL OF FORAGING IN CLONAL PLANTS

Background. Foraging (propagation) patterns in clonal plants provide another excellent example of response to crowding. A clonal plant spreads by means of horizontal stem segments (*spacers*), which form a branching structure that grows along the ground and connects individual plants (*ramets*) [3]. Each ramet consists of a leaf supported by an upright stem and one or more buds, which may give rise to further spacers and ramets. Their gradual death, after a certain amount of time, causes gradual separation of the whole structure (the *clone*) into independent parts.

Following the surface of the soil, clonal plants can be captured using models operating in two dimensions [5], and in that respect resemble *Terminalia* tiers. We propose a model of a hypothetical plant that responds to favorable environmental conditions (high local intensity of light) by more extensive branching and reduced size of leaves (allowing for more dense packing of ramets). It has been inspired by a computer model of clover outlined by Bell [4], the analysis of responses of clonal plants to the environment presented by Dong [17], and the computer models and descriptions of vegetative multiplication of plants involving the death of intervening connections by Room [47].

Communication specification. The plant sends messages to the environment that include turtle position and two parameters associated with the communications symbol, $?E(type, x)$. The first parameter is equal to 0, 1, or 2, and determines the type of exchanged information as follows:

- The message $?E(0, x)$ represents a request for the light intensity (irradiance [14]) at the position of the communication module. The environment responds by setting x to the intensity of incoming light, ranging from 0 (no light) to 1 (full light).
- The message $?E(1, x)$ notifies the environment about the creation of a ramet with a leaf of radius x at the position of the communication module. No output is generated by the environment in response to this message.
- The message $?E(2, x)$ notifies the environment about the death of a ramet with a leaf of radius x at the position of the communication module. Again, no output is generated by the environment.

The model of the environment. The purpose of the environment process is to determine light intensity at the locations requested by the plant. The ground is divided into patches (specified as a raster image using a paint program), with different light intensities assigned to each patch. In the absence of shading, these intensities are returned by the environmental process in response to messages of type 0. To consider shading, the environment keeps track of the set of ramets, adding new ramets in response to a messages of type 1, and deleting dead ramets in response to messages of type 2. If a sampling point falls in an area occupied by a ramet, the returned light intensity is equal to 0 (leaves are assumed to be opaque, and located above the sampling points).

The plant model. The essential features of the plant model are specified by the following open L-system.

```
#define α 45              /* branching angle */
#define MinLight 0.1      /* light intensity threshold */
#define MaxAge 20         /* lifetime of ramets and spacers */
#define Len 2.0           /* length of spacers */
#define Prob_B(x)         (0.12+x*0.42)
#define Prob_R(x)         (0.03+x*0.54)
#define Radius(x)         (sqrt(15–x*5)/π)
ω:  A(1)?E(0,0)

p1:  A(dir) > ?E(0,x) : x >= MinLight
            → R(x)B(x,dir)F(Len,0)A(–dir)?E(0,0)
p2:  A(dir) > ?E(0,x) : x < MinLight  → ε

p3:  B(x,dir) → [+(α*dir)F(Len,0)A(–dir)?E(0,0)] : Prob_B(x)
p4:  B(x,dir) → ε : 1–Prob_B(x)

p5:  R(x) → [@o(Radius(x),0)?E(1,Radius(x))] : Prob_R(x)
p6:  R(x) → ε : 1–Prob_R(x)

p7:  @o(radius,age): age < MaxAge  → @o(radius,age+1)
p8:  @o(radius,age): age == MaxAge  → ?E(2,radius)

p9:  F(len,age): age < MaxAge  → F(len,age+1)
p10: F(len,age): age == MaxAge  → f(len)

p11: ?E(type,x) → ε
```

The initial structure specified by the axiom ω consists of an apex A followed by the communication module $?E$. If the intensity of light x reaching an apex is insufficient (below the threshold $MinLight$), the apex dies (production p_2). Otherwise, the apex creates a ramet initial R (*i.e.*, a module that will yield a ramet), a branch initial B, a spacer F, and a new apex A terminated by communication module $?E$ (production p_1). The parameter dir, valued either 1 or -1, controls the direction of branching. Parameters of the spacer module specify its length and age.

A branch initial B may create a lateral branch with its own apex A and communication module $?E$ (production p_3), or it may die and disappear from the system (production p_4). The probability of survival is an increasing linear function $Prob_B$ of the light intensity x that has reached the mother apex A in the previous derivation step. A similar stochastic mechanism describes the production of a ramet by the ramet initial R (productions p_5 and p_6), with the probability of ramet formation controlled by an increasing linear function $Prob_R$. The ramet is represented as a circle $@o$; its radius is a decreasing function $Radius$ of the light intensity x. As in the case of spacers, the second parameter of a ramet indicates its age, initially set to 0. The environment is notified about the creation of the ramet using a communication module $?E$.

The subsequent productions describe the aging of spacers (p_7) and ramets (p_9). Upon reaching the maximum age $MaxAge$, a ramet is removed from the system and a message notifying the environment about this fact is sent by the plant (p_8). The death of the spacers is simulated by replacing spacer modules F with invisible line segments f of the same length. This replacement maintains the relative position of the remaining elements of the structure. Finally, production p_{11} removes communication modules after they have performed their tasks.

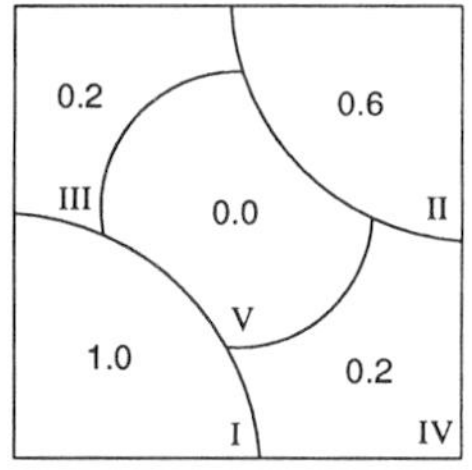

Figure 6: Division of the ground into patches

Simulations. Division of the ground into patches used in the simulations is shown in Figure 6. Arabic numerals indicate the intensity of incoming light, and Roman numerals identify each patch. The development of a clonal plant assuming this division is illustrated in Figure 7. As an extension of the basic model discussed above, the length of the spacers and the magnitude of the branching angle have been varied using random functions with a normal distribution. Ramets have been represented as trifoliate leaves.

The development begins with a single ramet located in relatively good (light intensity 0.6) patch II at the top right corner of the growth area (Figure 7, step 9 of the simulation). The plant propagates through the unfavorable patch III without producing many branches and leaves (step 26), and reaches the best patch I at the bottom left corner (step 39). After quickly spreading over this patch (step 51), the plant searches for further favorable areas (step 62). The first attempt to reach patch II fails (step 82). The plant tries again, and this time succeeds (steps 101 and 116). Light conditions in patch II are not sufficient, however, to sustain the continuous presence of the plant (step 134). The colony disappears (step 153) until the patch is reached again by a new wave of propagation (steps 161 and 182).

The sustained occupation of patch I and the repetitive invasion of patch II represent an emerging behavior of the model, difficult to predict without running simulations. Variants of this model, including other branching architectures, responses to the environment, and layouts of patches in the environment, would make it possible to analyze different foraging strategies of clonal plants. A further extension could replace the empirical assumptions regarding plant responses with a more detailed simulation of plant physiology (for example, including production of photosynthates and their transport and partition between ramets). Such physiological models could provide insight into the extent to which the foraging patterns optimize plants' access to resources [17].

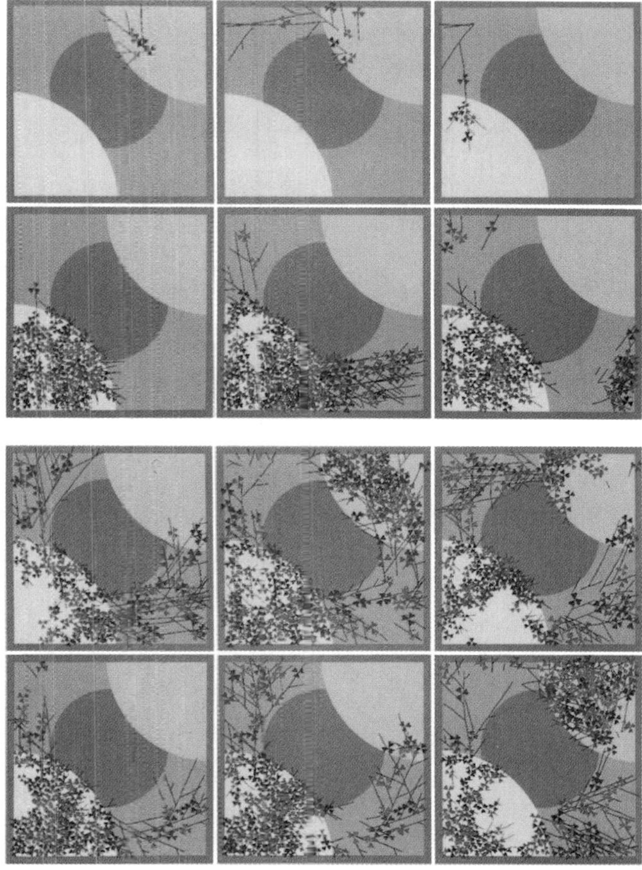

Figure 7: Development of a hypothetical clonal plant simulated using an extension of L-system 3. The individual images represent structures generated in 9, 26, 39, 51, 62, and 82 derivation steps (top), followed by structures generated in 101, 116, 134, 153, 161, and 182 steps (bottom).

7 A MODEL OF ROOT DEVELOPMENT

Background. The development of roots provides many examples of complex interactions with the environment, which involve mechanical properties, chemical reactions, and transport mechanisms in the soil. In particular, the main root and the rootlets absorb water from the soil, locally changing its concentration (volume of water per unit volume of soil) and causing water motion from water-rich to depleted regions [24]. The tips of the roots, in turn, follow the gradient of water concentration [12], thus adapting to the environment modified by their own activities.

Below we present a simplified implementation of the model of root development originally proposed by Clausnitzer and Hopmans [12]. We assume a more rudimentary mechanism of water transport, namely diffusion in a uniform medium, as suggested by Liddell and Hansen [37]. The underlying model of root architecture is similar to that proposed by Diggle [16]. For simplicity, we focus on model operation in two-dimensions.

Communication specification. The plant interacts with the environment using communication modules $?E(c, \theta)$ located at the apices of the root system. A message sent to the environment includes the turtle position $\vec{P}$, the heading vector $\vec{H}$, the value of parameter c representing the requested (optimal) water uptake, and the value of parameter θ representing the tendency of the apex to follow the gradient of water concentration. A message returned to the plant specifies the amount of water actually received by the apex as the value of parameter c, and the angle biasing direction of further growth as the value of θ.

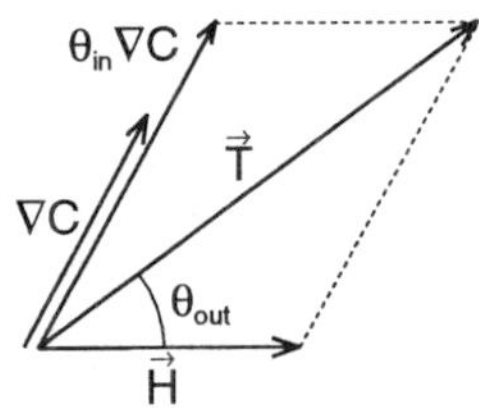

Figure 8: Definition of the biasing angle θ_{out}

The model of the environment. The environment maintains a field C of water concentrations, represented as an array of the amounts of water in square sampling areas. Water is transported by diffusion, simulated numerically using finite differencing [41]. The environment responds to a request for water from an apex located in an area (i, j) by granting the lesser of the values requested and available at that location. The amount of water in the sampled area is then decreased by the amount received by the apex. The environment also calculates a linear combination $\vec{T}$ of the turtle heading vector $\vec{H}$ and the gradient of water concentration ∇C (estimated numerically from the water concentrations in the sampled area and its neighbors), and returns an angle θ between the vectors $\vec{T}$ and $\vec{H}$ (Figure 8). This angle is used by the plant model to bias turtle heading in the direction of high water concentration.

The root model. The open L-system representing the root model makes use of arrays that specify parameters for each branching order (main axis, its daughter axes, *etc.*). The parameter values are loosely based on those reported by Clausnitzer and Hopmans [12].

```
#define N 3                                /* max. branching order + 1 */
Define: { array
Req[N] = {0.1, 0.4, 0.05},                 /* requested nutrient intake */
MinReq[N] = {0.01, 0.06, 0.01},            /* minimum nutrient intake */
ElRate[N] = {0.55, 0.25, 0.55},            /* maximum elongation rate */
MaxLen[N] = {200, 5, 0.8},                 /* maximum branch length */
Sens[N] = {10, 0, 0},                      /* sensitivity to gradient */
Dev[N] = {30, 75, 75},                     /* deviation in heading */
Del[N–1] = {30, 60},                       /* delay in branch growth */
BrAngle[N–1] = {90, 90},                   /* branching angle */
BrSpace[N–1] = {1, 0.5}                    /* distance between branches */
}
ω: A(0,0,0)?E(Req[0],Sens[0])

p1: A(n,s,b) > ?E(c,θ) : (s > MaxLen[n]) || (c < MinReq[n]) → ε
p2: A(n,s,b) > ?E(c,θ) :
        (n >= N–1) || (b < BrSpace[n]) {h=c/Req[n]*ElRate[n];}
        → +(nran(θ,Dev[n]))F(h) A(n,s+h,b+h)?E(Req[n],Sens[n])
p3: A(n,s,b) > ?E(c,θ) :
        (n < N–1) && (b >= BrSpace[n]) {h=c/Req[n]*ElRate[n];}
        → +(nran(θ,Dev[n]))B(n,0)F(h)
          /(180)A(n,s+h,h)?E(Req[n],Sens[n])
p4: B(n,t) : t < Del[n] → B(n,t+1)
p5: B(n,t) : t >= Del[n]
        → [+(BrAngle[n])A(n+1,0,0)?E(Req[n+1],Sens[n+1])]
p6: ?E(c,θ) → ε
```

The development starts with an apex A followed by a communication module $?E$. The parameters of the apex represent the branch order (0 for the main axis, 1 for its daughter axes, *etc.*), current axis length, and distance (along the axis) to the nearest branching point.

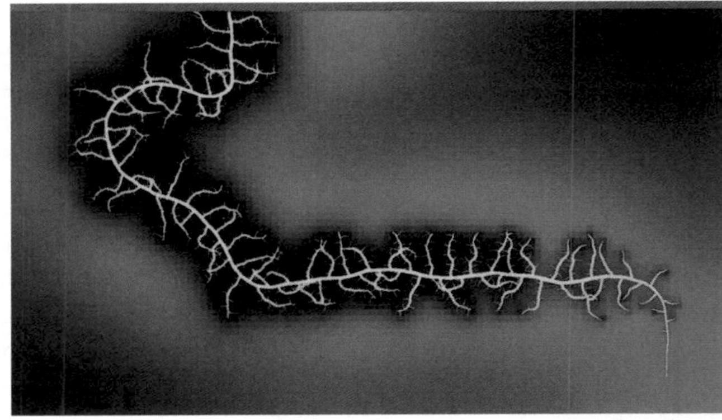

Figure 9: A two-dimensional model of a root interacting with water in soil. Background colors represent concentrations of water diffusing in soil (blue: high, black: low). The initial and boundary values have been set using a paint program.

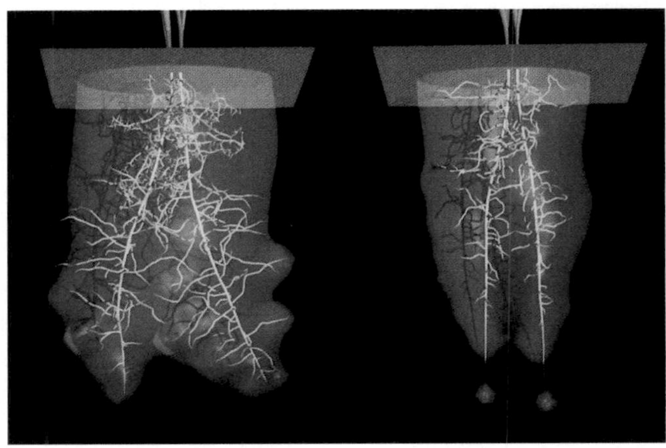

Figure 10: A three-dimensional extension of the root model. Water concentration is visualized by semi-transparent iso-surfaces [55] surrounding the roots. As a result of competition for water, the roots grow away from each other. The divergence between their main axes depends on the spread of the rootlets, which grow faster on the left then on the right.

Productions p_1 to p_3 describe possible fates of the apex as described below.

If the length s of a branch axis exceeds a predefined maximum value $MaxLen[n]$ characteristic to the branch order n, or the amount of water c received by the apex is below the required minimum $MinReq[n]$, the apex dies, terminating the growth of the axis (production p_1).

If the branch order n is equal to the maximum value assumed in the model $(N - 1)$, or the distance b to the closest branching point on the axis is less than the threshold value $BrSpace[n]$, the apex adds a new segment F to the axis (production p_2). The length h of F is the product of the nominal growth increment $ElRate[n]$ and the ratio of the amount of water received by the apex c to the amount requested $Req[n]$. The new segment is rotated with respect to its predecessor by an angle $nran(\theta, Dev[n])$, where $nran$ is a random function with a normal distribution. The mean value θ, returned by the environment, biases the direction of growth towards regions of higher water concentration. The standard deviation $Dev[n]$ characterizes the tendency of the root apex to change direction due to various factors not included explicitly in the model.

If the branch order n is less than the maximum value assumed in the model $(N-1)$, and the distance b to the closest branching point on the axis is equal to or exceeds the threshold value $BrSpace[n]$, the apex creates a new branch initial B (production p_3). Other aspects of apex behavior are the same as those described by production p_2.

After the delay of $Del[n]$ steps (production p_4), the branch initial B is transformed into an apex A followed by the communication module $?E$ (production p_5), giving rise to a new root branch. Production p_6 removes communication modules that are no longer needed.

Simulations. A sample two-dimensional structure obtained using the described model is shown in Figure 9. The apex of the main axis follows the gradient of water concentration, with small deviations due to random factors. The apices of higher-order axes are not sensitive to the gradient and change direction at random, with a larger standard deviation. The absorption of water by the root and the rootlets decreases water concentration in their neighborhood; an effect that is not fully compensated by water diffusion from the water-rich areas. Low water concentration stops the development of some rootlets before they have reached their potential full length.

Figure 10 presents a three-dimensional extension of the previous model. As a result of competition for water, the main axes of the roots diverge from each other (left). If their rootlets grow more slowly, the area of influence of each root system is smaller and the main axes are closer to each other (right). This behavior is an emergent property of interactions between the root modules, mediated by the environment.

8 MODELS OF TREES CONTROLLED BY LIGHT

Background. Light is one of the most important factors affecting the development of plants. In the essentially two-dimensional structures discussed in Section 5, competition for light could be considered in a manner similar to collision detection between leaves and apices. In contrast, competition for light in three-dimensional structures must be viewed as long-range interaction. Specifically, shadows cast by one branch may affect other branches at significant distances.

The first simulations of plant development that take the local light environment into account are due to Greene [25]. He considered the entire sky hemisphere as a source of illumination and computed the amount of light reaching specific points of the structure by casting rays towards a number of points on the hemisphere. Another approach was implemented by Kanamaru *et al.* [35], who computed the amount of light reaching a given sampling point by considering it a center of projection, from which all leaf clusters in a tree were projected on a surrounding hemisphere. The degree to which the hemisphere was covered by the projected clusters indicated the amount of light received by the sampling point. In both cases, the models of plants responded to the amount and the direction of light by simulating heliotropism, which biased the direction of growth towards the vector of the highest intensity of incoming light. Subsequently, Chiba *et al.* extended the models by Kanamaru *et al.* using more involved tree models that included a mechanism simulating the flow of hypothetical endogenous information within the tree [10, 11]. A biologically better justified model, formulated in terms of production and use of photosynthates by a tree, was proposed by Takenaka [52]. The amount of light reaching leaf clusters was calculated by sampling a sky hemisphere, as in the work by Greene. Below we reproduce the main features of the Takenaka's model using the formalism of open L-systems. Depending on the underlying tree architecture, it can be applied to synthesize images of deciduous and coniferous trees. We focus on a deciduous tree, which requires a slightly smaller number of productions.

Communication specification. The plant interacts with the environment using communication modules $?E(r)$. A message sent by the plant includes turtle position $\vec{P}$, which represents the center of a spherical leaf cluster, and the value of parameter r, which represents the cluster's radius. The environment responds by setting r to the flux [14] of light from the sky hemisphere, reaching the cluster.

The model of the environment. Once all messages describing the current distribution of leaves on a tree have been received, the environmental process computes the extent of the tree in the x, y, and z directions, encompasses the tree in a tight grid ($32 \times 32 \times 32$ voxels in our simulations), and allocates leaf clusters to voxels to speed up further computations. The environmental process then estimates the light flux Φ from the sky hemisphere reaching each cluster (shadows cast by the branches are ignored). To this end, the hemisphere is represented by a set of directional light sources S (9 in the simulations). The flux densities (radiosities) B of the sources approximate the non-uniform distribution of light from the sky (*cf.* [52]). For each leaf cluster L_i and each light source S, the environment determines the set of leaf clusters L_j that may shade L_i. This is achieved by casting a ray from the center of L_i in the direction of S and testing for intersections with other clusters (the grid accelerates this process). In order not to miss any clusters that may partially occlude L_i, the radius of each cluster L_j is increased by the maximum value of cluster radius r_{max}.

To calculate the flux reaching cluster L_i, this cluster and all clusters L_j that may shade it according to the described tests are projected on a plane P perpendicular to the direction of light from the source S. The impact of a cluster L_j on the flux Φ reaching cluster L_i is then computed according to the formula:

$$\Phi = (A_i - A_{ij})B + A_{ij}\tau B$$

where A_i is the area of the projection of L_i on P, A_{ij} is the area of the intersection between projections of L_i and L_j, and τ is the light transmittance through leaf cluster L_j (equal to 0.25 in the simulations). If several clusters L_j shade L_i, their influences are multiplied. The total flux reaching cluster L_i is calculated as the sum of the fluxes received from each light source S.

The plant model. In addition to the communication module $?E$, the plant model includes the following types of modules:

- Apex $A(vig, del)$. Parameter vig represents vigor, which determines the length of branch segments (internodes) and the diameter of leaf clusters produced by the apex. Parameter del is used to introduce a delay, needed for propagating products of photosynthesis through the tree structure between consecutive stages of development (years).

- Leaf $L(vig, p, age, del)$. Parameters denote the leaf radius vig, the amount of photosynthates produced in unit time according to the leaf's exposure to light p, the number of years for which a leaf has appeared at a given location age, and the delay del, which plays the same role as in the apices.

- Internode $F(vig)$. Consistent with the turtle interpretation, the parameter vig indicates the internode length.

- Branch width symbol $!(w, p, n)$, also used to carry the endogenous information flow. The parameters determine: the width of the following internode w, the amount of photosynthates reaching the symbol's location p, and the number of terminal branch segments above this location n.

The corresponding L-system is given below.

```
#define φ 137.5        /* divergence angle */
#define α0 5           /* direction change - no branching */
#define α1 20          /* branching angle - main axis */
#define α2 32          /* branching angle - lateral axis */
#define W 0.02         /* initial branch width */
#define VD 0.95        /* apex vigor decrement */
#define Del 30         /* delay */
#define LS 5           /* how long a leaf stays */
#define LP 8           /* full photosynthate production */
#define LM 2           /* leaf maintenance */
#define PB 0.8         /* photosynthates needed for branching */
#define PG 0.4         /* photosynthates needed for growth */
#define BM 0.32        /* branch maintenance coefficient */
#define BE 1.5         /* branch maintenance exponent */
#define Nmin 25        /* threshold for shedding */
Consider: ?E[]!L       /* for context matching */
ω: !(W,1,1)F(2)L(1,LP,0,0)A(1,0)[!(0,0,0)]!(W,0,1)

p1: A(vig,del) : del<Del → A(vig,del+1)
p2: L(vig,p,age,del) : (age<LS)&&(del<Del–1) → L(vig,p,age,del+1)
p3: L(vig,p,age,del) : (age<LS)&&(del==Del–1)
        → L(vig,p,age,del+1)?E(vig*0.5)
p4: L(vig,p,age,del) > ?E(r) : (age<LS) && (r*LP>=LM)
        && (del == Del) → L(vig,LP*r–LM,age+1,0)
p5: L(vig,p,age,del) > ?E(r) : ((age == LS)||(r*LP<=LM))
        && (del == Del) → L(0,0,LS,0)
p6: ?E(r) < A(vig,del) : r*LP–LM>PB {vig=vig*VD;}
        → /(φ)[+(α2)!(W,–PB,1)F(vig)L(vig,LP,0,0)A(vig,0)
              [!(0,0,0)]!(W,0,1)]
          –(α1)!(W,0,1)F(vig)L(vig,LP,0,0)/A(vig,0)
p7: ?E(r) < A(vig,del) : r*LP–LM > PG {vig=vig*VD;}
        → /(φ)–(α0)[!(0,0,0)]
          !(W,–PG,1)F(vig)L(vig,LP,0,0)A(vig,0)
p8: ?E(r) < A(vig,del) : r*LP–LM <= PG → A(vig,0)
p9: ?E(r) → ε
p10: !(w0,p0,n0) > L(vig,pL,age,del) [!(w1,p1,n1)]!(w2,p2,n2) :
        {w=(w1^2+w2^2)^0.5; p=p1+p2+pL–BM*(w/W)^BE;}
        (p>0) || (n1+n2 >=Nmin) → !(w,p,n1+n2)
p11: !(w0,p0,n0) > L(vig,pL,age,del) [!(w1,p1,n1)]!(w2,p2,n2)
        → !(w0,0,0)L%
```

The simulation starts with a structure consisting of a branch segment F, supporting a leaf L and an apex A (axiom ω). The first branch width symbol ! defines the segment width. Two additional symbols ! following the apex create "virtual branches," needed to provide proper context for productions p_{10} and p_{11}. The tree grows in stages, with the delay of $Del + 1$ derivation steps between consecutive stages introduced by production p_1 for the apices and p_2 for the leaves. Immediately before each new growth stage, communication symbols are introduced to inform the environment about the location and size of the leaf clusters (p_3). If the flux r returned by the environment results in the production of photosynthates $r * LP$ exceeding the amount LM needed to maintain a cluster, it remains in the structure (p_4). Otherwise it becomes a liability to the tree and dies (p_5). Another condition to production p_5 prevents a leaf from occupying the same location for more than LS years.

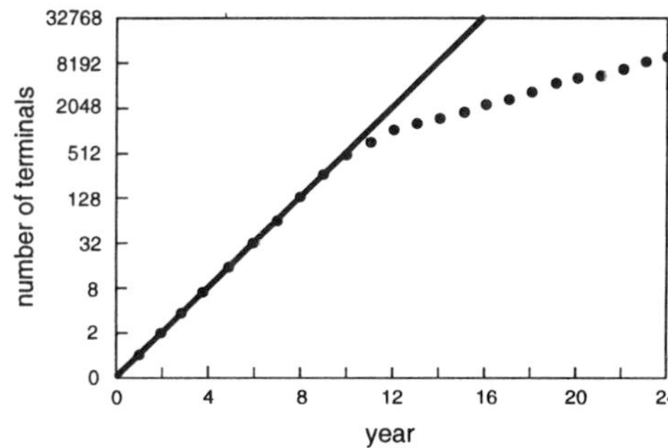

Figure 11: The number of terminal branch segments resulting from unrestricted bifurcation of apices (continuous line), compared to the number of segments generated in a simulation (isolated points)

The flux r also determines the fate of the apex, captured by productions p_6 to p_8. If the amount of photosynthates $r * LP - LM$ transported from the nearby leaf exceeds a threshold value PB, the apex produces two new branches (p_6). The second parameter in the first branch symbol ! is set to $-PB$, to subtract the amount of photosynthates used for branching from the amount that will be transported further down. The length of branch segments vig is reduced with respect to the mother segment by a predefined factor VD, reflecting a gradual decrease in the vigor of apices with age. The branch width modules ! following the first apex A are introduced to provide context required by productions p_{10} and p_{11}, as in the axiom.

If the amount of photosynthates $r * LP - LM$ transported from the leaf is insufficient to produce new branches, but above the threshold PG, the apex adds a new segment F to the current branch axis without creating a lateral branch (p_7). Again, a virtual branch containing the branch width symbol ! is being added to provide context for productions p_{10} and p_{11}.

If the amount of photosynthates is below PG, the apex remains dormant (p_8). Communication modules no longer needed are removed from the structure (p_9).

Production p_{10} captures the endogenous information flow from leaves and terminal branch segments to the base of the tree. First, it determines the radius w of the mother branch segment as a function of the radii w_1 and w_2 of the supported branches:

$$w = \sqrt{w_1^2 + w_2^2}.$$

Thus, a cross section of the mother segment has an area equal to the sum of cross sections of the supported segments, as postulated in the literature [40, 46]. Next, production p_{10} calculates the flow p of photosynthates into the mother segment. It is defined as the sum of the flows p_L, p_1 and p_2 received from the associated leaf L and from both daughter branches, decreased by the amount $BM * (w/W)^{BE}$ representing the cost of maintaining the mother segment. Finally, production p_9 calculates the number of terminal branch segments n supported by the mother segment as the sum of the numbers of terminal segments supported by the daughter branches, n_1 and n_2.

Production p_{10} takes effect if the flow p is positive (the branch is not a liability to the tree), or if the number n of supported terminals is above a threshold N_{min}. If these conditions are not satisfied,

Figure 12: A tree model with branches competing for access to light, shown without the leaves

Figure 13: A climbing plant growing on the tree from the previous figure

production p_{11} removes (sheds) the branch from the tree using the cut symbol %.

Simulations. The competition for light between tree branches is manifested by two phenomena: reduced branching or dormancy of apices in unfavorable local light conditions, and shedding of branches which do not receive enough light to contribute to the whole tree. Both phenomena limit the extent of branching, thus controlling the density of the crown. This property of the model is supported by the simulation results shown in Figure 11. If the growth was unlimited (production p_6 was always chosen over p_7 and p_8), the number of terminal branch segments would double every year. Due to the competition for light, however, the number of terminal segments observed in an actual simulation increases more slowly. For related statistics using a different tree architecture see [52].

Figure 14: A model of deciduous trees competing for light. The trees are shown in the position of growth (top) and moved apart (bottom) to reveal the adaptation of crown geometry to the presence of the neighbor tree.

A tree image synthesized using an extension of the presented model is shown in Figure 12. The key additional feature is a gradual reduction of the branching angle of a young branch whose sister branch has been shed. As the result, the remaining branch assumes the role of the leading shoot, following the general growth direction of its supporting segment. Branch segments are represented as texture-mapped generalized cylinders, smoothly connected at the branching points (*cf.* [6]). The bark texture was created using a paint program.

As an illustration of the flexibility of the modeling framework presented in this paper, Figure 13 shows the effect of seeding a hypothetical climbing plant near the same tree. The plant follows the surface of the tree trunk and branches, and avoids excessively dense colonization of any particular area. Thus, the model integrates several environmentally-controlled phenomena: the competition of tree

Figure 15: A model of coniferous trees competing for light. The trees are shown in the position of growth (top) and moved apart (bottom).

branches for light, the following of surfaces by a climbing plant, and the prevention of crowding as discussed in Section 6. Leaves were modeled using cubic patches (*cf.* [46]).

In the simulations shown in Figure 14 two trees described by the same set of rules (younger specimens of the tree from Figure 12) compete for light from the sky hemisphere. Moving the trees apart after they have grown reveals the adaptation of their crowns to the presence of the neighbor tree. This simulation illustrates both the necessity and the possibility of incorporating the adaptive behavior into tree models used for landscape design purposes.

The same phenomenon applies to coniferous trees, as illustrated in Figure 15. The tree model is similar to the original model by Takenaka [52] and can be viewed as consisting of approximately horizontal tiers (as discussed in Section 5) produced in sequence by the apex of the tree stem. The lower tiers are created first and therefore potentially can spread more widely then the younger tiers higher up (the *phase effect* [46]). This pattern of development is affected by the presence of the neighboring tree: the competition for light prevents the crowns from growing into each other.

The trees in Figure 15 retain branches that do not receive enough light. In contrast, the trees in the stand presented in Figure 16 shed branches that do not contribute photosynthates to the entire tree, using the same mechanism as described for the deciduous trees.

Figure 16: Relationship between tree form and its position in a stand.

The resulting simulation reveals essential differences between the shape of the tree crown in the middle of a stand, at the edge, or at the corner. In particular, the tree in the middle retains only the upper part of its crown. In lumber industry, the loss of lower branches is usually a desirable phenomenon, as it reduces knots in the wood and the amount of cleaning that trees require before transport. Simulations may assist in choosing an optimal distance for planting trees, where self-pruning is maximized, yet there is sufficient space between trees too allow for unimpeded growth of trunks in height and diameter.

9 CONCLUSIONS

In this paper, we introduced a framework for the modeling and visualization of plants interacting with their environment. The essential elements of this framework are:

- a system design, in which the plant and the environment are treated as two separate processes, communicating using a standard interface, and
- the language of open L-systems, used to specify plant models that can exchange information with the environment.

We demonstrated the operation of this framework by implementing models that capture collisions between branches, the propagation of clonal plants, the development of roots in soil, and the development of tree crowns competing for light. We found that the proposed framework makes it possible to easily create and modify models spanning a wide range of plant structures and environmental processes. Simulations of the presented phenomena were fast enough to allow interactive experimentation with the models (Table 1).

There are many research topics that may be addressed using the simulation and visualization capabilities of the proposed framework. They include, for instance:

- Fundamental analysis of the role of different forms of information flow in plant morphogenesis (in particular, the relationship between endogenous and exogenous flow). This is a continuation of the research pioneered by Bell [4] and Honda *et al.* [7, 33].

Fig.	Number of		Derivation		Time[a]	
	branch segments	leaf clusters	steps	yrs	sim.	render.
5	138	140	5	5	1 s	1 s
7	786	229	182	NA	50 s	2 s
9	4194	34[b]	186	NA	67 s	3 s
10	37228	448[b]	301	NA	15 min	70 s
12	22462	19195	744	24	22 min	13 s[c]
15	13502	3448	194	15	4 min	8 s[d]

[a] Simulation and rendering using OpenGL on a 200MHz/64MB Indigo^2 Extreme
[b] active apices
[c] without generalized cylinders and texture mapping
[d] branching structure without needles

Table 1: Numbers of primitives and simulation/rendering times for generating and visualizing selected models

- Development of a comprehensive plant model describing the cycling of nutrients from the soil through the roots and branches to the leaves, then back to the soil in the form of substances released by fallen leaves.

- Development of models of specific plants for research, crop and forest management, and for landscape design purposes. The models may include environmental phenomena not discussed in this paper, such as the global distribution of radiative energy in the tree crowns, which affects the amount of light reaching the leaves and the local temperature of plant organs.

The presented framework itself is also open to further research. To begin, the precise functional specification of the environment, implied by the design of the modeling framework, is suitable for a formal analysis of algorithms that capture various environmental processes. This analysis may highlight tradeoffs between time, memory, and communication complexity, and lead to programs matching the needs of the model to available system resources in an optimal manner.

A deeper understanding of the spectrum of processes taking place in the environment may lead to the design of a mini-language for environment specification. Analogous to the language of L-systems for plant specification, this mini-language would simplify the modeling of various environments, relieving the modeler from the burden of low-level programming in a general-purpose language. Fleischer and Barr's work on the specification of environments supporting collisions and reaction-diffusion processes [20] is an inspiring step in this direction.

Complexity issues are not limited to the environment, but also arise in plant models. They become particularly relevant as the scope of modeling increases from individual plants to groups of plants and, eventually, entire plant communities. This raises the problem of selecting the proper level of abstraction for designing plant models, including careful selection of physiological processes incorporated into the model and the spatial resolution of the resulting structures.

The complexity of the modeling task can be also addressed at the level of system design, by assigning various components of the model (individual plants and aspects of the environment) to different components of a distributed computing system. The communication structure should then be redesigned to accommodate information transfers between numerous processes within the system.

In summary, we believe that the proposed modeling methodology and its extensions will prove useful in many applications of plant modeling, from research in plant development and ecology to landscape design and realistic image synthesis.

Acknowledgements

We would like to thank Johannes Battjes, Campbell Davidson, Art Diggle, Heinjo During, Michael Guzy, Naoyoshi Kanamaru, Bruno Moulia, Zbigniew Prusinkiewicz, Bill Remphrey, David Reid, and Peter Room for discussions and pointers to the literature relevant to this paper. We would also like to thank Bruno Andrieu, Mark Hammel, Jim Hanan, Lynn Mercer, Chris Prusinkiewicz, Peter Room, and the anonymous referees for helpful comments on the manuscript. Most images were rendered using the ray tracer `rayshade` by Craig Kolb. This research was sponsored by grants from the Natural Sciences and Engineering Research Council of Canada.

REFERENCES

[1] AGRAWAL, P. The cell programming language. *Artificial Life 2*, 1 (1995), 37–77.

[2] ARVO, J., AND KIRK, D. Modeling plants with environment-sensitive automata. In *Proceedings of Ausgraph'88* (1988), pp. 27 – 33.

[3] BELL, A. *Plant form: An illustrated guide to flowering plants.* Oxford University Press, Oxford, 1991.

[4] BELL, A. D. The simulation of branching patterns in modular organisms. *Philos. Trans. Royal Society London, Ser. B 313* (1986), 143–169.

[5] BELL, A. D., ROBERTS, D., AND SMITH, A. Branching patterns: the simulation of plant architecture. *Journal of Theoretical Biology 81* (1979), 351–375.

[6] BLOOMENTHAL, J. Modeling the Mighty Maple. Proceedings of SIGGRAPH '85 (San Francisco, California, July 22-26, 1985), in *Computer Graphics*, 19, 3 (July 1985), pages 305–311, ACM SIGGRAPH, New York, 1985.

[7] BORCHERT, R., AND HONDA, H. Control of development in the bifurcating branch system of *Tabebuia rosea*: A computer simulation. *Botanical Gazette 145*, 2 (1984), 184–195.

[8] BORCHERT, R., AND SLADE, N. Bifurcation ratios and the adaptive geometry of trees. *Botanical Gazette 142*, 3 (1981), 394–401.

[9] CHEN, S. G., CEULEMANS, R., AND IMPENS, I. A fractal based *Populus* canopy structure model for the calculation of light interception. *Forest Ecology and Management* (1993).

[10] CHIBA, N., OHKAWA, S., MURAOKA, K., AND MIURA, M. Visual simulation of botanical trees based on virtual heliotropism and dormancy break. *The Journal of Visualization and Computer Animation 5* (1994), 3–15.

[11] CHIBA, N., OHSHIDA, K., MURAOKA, K., MIURA, M., AND SAITO, N. A growth model having the abilities of growth-regulations for simulating visual nature of botanical trees. *Computers and Graphics 18*, 4 (1994), 469–479.

[12] CLAUSNITZER, V., AND HOPMANS, J. Simultaneous modeling of transient three-dimensional root growth and soil water flow. *Plant and Soil 164* (1994), 299–314.

[13] COHEN, D. Computer simulation of biological pattern generation processes. *Nature 216* (October 1967), 246–248.

[14] COHEN, M., AND WALLACE, J. *Radiosity and realistic image synthesis.* Academic Press Professional, Boston, 1993. With a chapter by P. Hanrahan and a foreword by D. Greenberg.

[15] DE REFFYE, P., HOULLIER, F., BLAISE, F., BARTHELEMY, D., DAUZAT, J., AND AUCLAIR, D. A model simulating above- and below-ground tree architecture with agroforestry applications. *Agroforestry Systems 30* (1995), 175–197.

[16] DIGGLE, A. J. ROOTMAP - a model in three-dimensional coordinates of the structure and growth of fibrous root systems. *Plant and Soil 105* (1988), 169–178.

[17] DONG, M. *Foraging through morphological response in clonal herbs.* PhD thesis, Univeristy of Utrecht, October 1994.

[18] FISHER, J. B. How predictive are computer simulations of tree architecture. *International Journal of Plant Sciences 153 (Suppl.)* (1992), 137–146.

[19] FISHER, J. B., AND HONDA, H. Computer simulation of branching pattern and geometry in *Terminalia* (Combretaceae), a tropical tree. *Botanical Gazette 138*, 4 (1977), 377–384.

[20] FLEISCHER, K. W., AND BARR, A. H. A simulation testbed for the study of multicellular development: The multiple mechanisms of morphogenesis. In *Artificial Life III*, C. G. Langton, Ed. Addison-Wesley, Redwood City, 1994, pp. 389–416.

[21] FORD, E. D., AVERY, A., AND FORD, R. Simulation of branch growth in the *Pinaceae*: Interactions of morphology, phenology, foliage productivity, and the requirement for structural support, on the export of carbon. *Journal of Theoretical Biology 146* (1990), 15–36.

[22] FORD, H. Investigating the ecological and evolutionary significance of plant growth form using stochastic simulation. *Annals of Botany 59* (1987), 487–494.

[23] FRIJTERS, D., AND LINDENMAYER, A. A model for the growth and flowering of *Aster novae-angliae* on the basis of table (1,0)L-systems. In *L Systems*, G. Rozenberg and A. Salomaa, Eds., Lecture Notes in Computer Science 15. Springer-Verlag, Berlin, 1974, pp. 24–52.

[24] GARDNER, W. R. Dynamic aspects of water availability to plants. *Soil Science 89*, 2 (1960), 63–73.

[25] GREENE, N. Voxel space automata: Modeling with stochastic growth processes in voxel space. Proceedings of SIGGRAPH '89 (Boston, Mass., July 31–August 4, 1989), in *Computer Graphics* 23, 4 (August 1989), pages 175–184, ACM SIGGRAPH, New York, 1989.

[26] GREENE, N. Detailing tree skeletons with voxel automata. SIGGRAPH '91 Course Notes on Photorealistic Volume Modeling and Rendering Techniques, 1991.

[27] GUZY, M. R. A morphological-mechanistic plant model formalized in an object-oriented parametric L-system. Manuscript, USDA-ARS Salinity Laboratory, Riverside, 1995.

[28] HANAN, J. Virtual plants — Integrating architectural and physiological plant models. In *Proceedings of ModSim 95* (Perth, 1995), P. Binning, H. Bridgman, and B. Williams, Eds., vol. 1, The Modelling and Simulation Society of Australia, pp. 44–50.

[29] HANAN, J. S. *Parametric L-systems and their application to the modelling and visualization of plants.* PhD thesis, University of Regina, June 1992.

[30] HART, J. W. *Plant tropisms and other growth movements.* Unwin Hyman, London, 1990.

[31] HERMAN, G. T., AND ROZENBERG, G. *Developmental systems and languages.* North-Holland, Amsterdam, 1975.

[32] HONDA, H. Description of the form of trees by the parameters of the tree-like body: Effects of the branching angle and the branch length on the shape of the tree-like body. *Journal of Theoretical Biology 31* (1971), 331–338.

[33] HONDA, H., TOMLINSON, P. B., AND FISHER, J. B. Computer simulation of branch interaction and regulation by unequal flow rates in botanical trees. *American Journal of Botany 68* (1981), 569–585.

[34] KAANDORP, J. *Fractal modelling: Growth and form in biology.* Springer-Verlag, Berlin, 1994.

[35] KANAMARU, N., CHIBA, N., TAKAHASHI, K., AND SAITO, N. CG simulation of natural shapes of botanical trees based on heliotropism. *The Transactions of the Institute of Electronics, Information, and Communication Engineers J75-D-II*, 1 (1992), 76–85. In Japanese.

[36] KURTH, W. *Growth grammar interpreter GROGRA 2.4: A software tool for the 3-dimensional interpretation of stochastic, sensitive growth grammars in the context of plant modeling. Introduction and reference manual.* Forschungszentrum Waldökosysteme der Universität Göttingen, Göttingen, 1994.

[37] LIDDELL, C. M., AND HANSEN, D. Visualizing complex biological interactions in the soil ecosystem. *The Journal of Visualization and Computer Animation 4* (1993), 3–12.

[38] LINDENMAYER, A. Mathematical models for cellular interaction in development, Parts I and II. *Journal of Theoretical Biology 18* (1968), 280–315.

[39] LINDENMAYER, A. Developmental systems without cellular interaction, their languages and grammars. *Journal of Theoretical Biology 30* (1971), 455–484.

[40] MACDONALD, N. *Trees and networks in biological models.* J. Wiley & Sons, New York, 1983.

[41] PRESS, W. H., TEUKOLSKY, S. A., VETTERLING, W. T., AND FLANNERY, B. P. *Numerical recipes in C: The art of scientific computing. Second edition.* Cambridge University Press, Cambridge, 1992.

[42] PRUSINKIEWICZ, P. Visual models of morphogenesis. *Artificial Life 1*, 1/2 (1994), 61–74.

[43] PRUSINKIEWICZ, P., HAMMEL, M., HANAN, J., AND MĚCH, R. Visual models of plant development. In *Handbook of formal languages*, G. Rozenberg and A. Salomaa, Eds. Springer-Verlag, Berlin, 1996. To appear.

[44] PRUSINKIEWICZ, P., AND HANAN, J. L-systems: From formalism to programming languages. In *Lindenmayer systems: Impacts on theoretical computer science, computer graphics, and developmental biology*, G. Rozenberg and A. Salomaa, Eds. Springer-Verlag, Berlin, 1992, pp. 193–211.

[45] PRUSINKIEWICZ, P., JAMES, M., AND MĚCH, R. Synthetic topiary. Proceedings of SIGGRAPH '94 (Orlando, Florida, July 24–29, 1994), pages 351–358, ACM SIGGRAPH, New York, 1994.

[46] PRUSINKIEWICZ, P., AND LINDENMAYER, A. *The algorithmic beauty of plants.* Springer-Verlag, New York, 1990. With J. S. Hanan, F. D. Fracchia, D. R. Fowler, M. J. M. de Boer, and L. Mercer.

[47] ROOM, P. M. 'Falling apart' as a lifestyle: the rhizome architecture and population growth of *Salvinia molesta. Journal of Ecology 71* (1983), 349–365.

[48] ROOM, P. M., MAILLETTE, L., AND HANAN, J. Module and metamer dynamics and virtual plants. *Advances in Ecological Research 25* (1994), 105–157.

[49] ROZENBERG, G. T0L systems and languages. *Information and Control 23* (1973), 357–381.

[50] SACHS, T., AND NOVOPLANSKY, A. Tree from: Architectural models do not suffice. *Israel Journal of Plant Sciences 43* (1995), 203–212.

[51] SIPPER, M. Studying artificial life using a simple, general cellular model. *Artificial Life 2*, 1 (1995), 1–35.

[52] TAKENAKA, A. A simulation model of tree architecture development based on growth response to local light environment. *Journal of Plant Research 107* (1994), 321–330.

[53] ULAM, S. On some mathematical properties connected with patterns of growth of figures. In *Proceedings of Symposia on Applied Mathematics* (1962), vol. 14, American Mathematical Society, pp. 215–224.

[54] WEBER, J., AND PENN, J. Creation and rendering of realistic trees. Proceedings of SIGGRAPH '95 (Los Angeles, California, August 6–11, 1995), pages 119–128, ACM SIGGRAPH, New York, 1995.

[55] WYVILL, G., MCPHEETERS, C., AND WYVILL, B. Data structure for soft objects. *The Visual Computer 2*, 4 (February 1986), 227–234.

Flow and Changes in Appearance

Julie Dorsey *
Massachusetts Institute of Technology

Hans Køhling Pedersen†
Stanford University

Pat Hanrahan‡
Stanford University

Abstract

An important, largely unexplored area of computer image generation is the simulation of weathering and its effects on appearance. Weathering results from the interaction of the environment with the materials in the world. The flow of water is one of the most pervasive and important natural forces involved in the weathering of materials, producing a distinctive set of patterns of washes and stains. This paper presents an intuitive phenomenological model for the flow of water over surfaces that is capable of generating such changes in appearance.

We model the flow as a particle system, each particle representing a "drop" of water. The motion of the water particles is controlled by parameters such as gravity, friction, wind, roughness, and constraints that force the particles to maintain contact with the surface. The chemical interaction of the water with the surface materials is governed by a set of coupled differential equations describing both the rate of absorption of water by the surface and the rate of solubility and sedimentation of deposits on the surface. To illustrate the power of this simple model, we show examples of flows over complex geometries made from different materials: the resulting patterns are striking and very difficult to achieve using traditional texturing techniques.

CR Categories and Subject Descriptors: I.3.7 [Computer Graphics]: Three-Dimensional Graphics and Realism I.3.6 [Computer Graphics]: Methodology and Techniques.

Additional Key Words and Phrases: weathering, material models, physically-inspired texturing, particle systems, light reflection models.

1 Introduction

Over time, the natural environment acts upon materials and changes their appearance. These processes and changes are termed *weathering*. Through weathering, objects become tarnished, bleached, stained, eroded, and otherwise modified. Weathering is unavoidable and therefore must be simulated to make realistic pictures of natural environments.

For many years, computer graphics researchers and practitioners have been grappling with the problem of creating surfaces that have a worn appearance. In the production of Pixar's recent computer-generated film *Toy Story*, for example, weathering effects such as scuffs and dirt were added to the surfaces by painting textures and compositing them within a programmable shader [6]. However, this process is very time consuming. Current tools for texturing geometric models made from many surfaces are primitive; for example, it is very difficult to match textures across surface boundaries or account properly for area distortions caused by the parameterization. More fundamentally, the texture mapping approach does not take into account the structure or properties of a given material or the processes in the surrounding environment that account for weathering. Our long range goal is to simulate the effect of the environment on complex material surfaces so that their appearance may be controlled semi-automatically.

The focus of this paper is the modeling of changes in appearance caused by the flow of water over complex surfaces. Figure 1 contains several photographs we have collected showing the weathering of various buildings. Inspection of these photographs reveals that many of the complex patterns on the surfaces are due to the flow of water. Water may wash dirt from some areas and clean them; in other areas dirt and other materials are deposited, creating stains. The patterns produced by this process are visually rich and very difficult to model with current texturing techniques.

Exactly how water travels over surfaces is very complicated and is dependent on a large number of variables. Unfortunately, the workings of complex flows are still not fully understood based on first principles [1]. However, for the purposes of this study, we are concerned with the patterns created by the flow of water on surfaces, not the detailed appearance of the flow itself. We therefore present a phenomenological model, based on particle systems and rate equations governing the absorption of water by the surface and the sedimentation of deposits. This model is simple and robust, and it is capable of generating a wide range of flow effects.

1.1 Related Work

Relevant previous work can be conveniently divided into two major categories: techniques for simulating fluid flow and particle systems. In this section, we discuss our approach in light of these categories.

Flow models. Kass and Miller presented an approach for animating water using a set of partial differential equations [8]. They used a wetness map to simulate the wetting and drying of sand as water passes over it. Miller and Pearce described a model for animating viscous fluids by simulating the forces of particles interacting with one another [12]. The focus of both of these works was on the realistic appearance of the flow itself, both in terms of its motion and rendering. In addition, Musgrave et al. proposed a simple, heuristic erosion model that simulates hydraulic and thermal erosion processes on fractal terrains [14].

Particle systems. Particle systems represent an effective approach to modeling objects whose behavior over time cannot be well-represented in terms of the surface of the objects [17, 18]. In such a system, a collection of particles evolves over time. The

*NE43-213, 545 Technology Square, Cambridge, MA 02139. http://graphics.lcs.mit.edu/~dorsey

†Current address: NE43-218, 545 Technology Square, Cambridge, MA 02139. http://graphics.lcs.mit.edu/~hkp

‡370 Gates Computer Science Building 3B, Stanford, CA 94305-4070. http://www-graphics.stanford.edu/~hanrahan

(a) (b) (c) (d) (e) (f) (g) (h)

Figure 1: A collection of representative flow effects.

evolution is determined by applying certain rules to the particles. Particle motion may follow either deterministic or stochastic laws of motion. Particle systems have been used to model trees, grass, fog, waterfalls, and fire [5, 16, 23].

In a related work, Small described a parallel approach to the problem of modeling watercolor by predicting the actions of pigment and water when applied to paper fibers [19]. This model was cast as a complex cellular automata on the Connection Machine II. Small's model produces nice results, but it is limited to two dimensions and requires excessive processing power.

The specific technical contribution of this paper is to combine particle systems with processes similar to those used to model watercolors. This allows us to simulate the effects of material transport on complex surfaces.

1.2 Overview

The remainder of this paper is structured as follows. We first introduce the basic mechanisms of flow and staining and give examples of typical effects that inspired our work. We then describe our flow model in detail, both the dynamics of particles and the coupled differential equations controlling absorption and sedimentation. Finally, we illustrate the model with examples of flows over complex geometries: a building facade, two statues, and a portion of a Gothic cathedral.

2 Background

Figure 1 features photographs of real scenes that show many effects of the flow of water over surfaces. In this paper, we will demonstrate that a number of these effects can be captured with a simple underlying model. In this section we describe the motivation behind the development of our model with a discussion of the mechanisms of flow and staining including a review of the major factors involved. We then discuss a series of specific representative effects that are associated with this process.

2.1 Exposure and Runoff

The basic factors affecting the rate of flow over a surface are the quantities of incident water, the height, inclination and geometry of the surface, and the absorption of water by the material comprising the surface [1, 4].

One of the major features of the pattern of flows on a building is the arrangement of water sources. From these sources, water flows downward under the influence of gravity. This is often termed *primary flow.* This depends on which parts of the structure receive the most incident water and the effect of geometry on directing the flow. Typically the flow separates into streams, and, in a way similar to rivers, produces patterns that often become self-reinforcing. Figure 1a shows a typical example of flows on a wall of moderate exposure. In particular, the window sills and lintels above the windows serve to concentrate the flow on both sides of the windows.

The absorption of water by the surface is controlled by the *absorptivity*, or rate of water uptake, and the *absorption*, or capacity to absorb water. *Runoff* occurs when the surface is fully saturated (i.e. has no more capacity to absorb water) or non-absorbent (i.e. has a low absorptivity). Figure 2 shows the relationship between incident rain, runoff, and absorption for several materials [2]. Curve A represents a spongy material with high absorptivity and absorption. This material has the capacity to absorb all the incident water over time, hence there is no runoff. Curve B describes a moderately absorbent concrete with high absorptivity but a limited absorption capacity. Initially, from t_0 to t_2, all incident water is absorbed and there is no runoff. However, from t_2 to t_3, because of

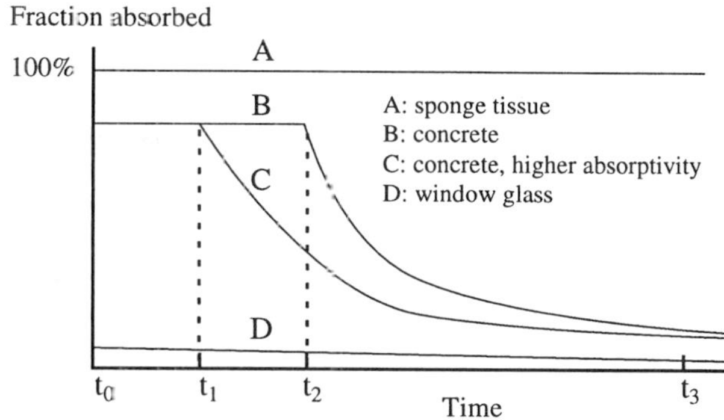

Figure 2: Simplified diagram showing absorption over time for several materials assuming a constant rain.

saturation, the amount absorbed is less than the incident amount; hence, some rain is absorbed but an increasing quantity runs off. In Curve C, which gives the behavior of concrete with a higher absorptivity, runoff starts sooner, because the material becomes saturated more quickly. Finally in Curve D, which describes a very non-absorbent material such as glass, the amount of water that is absorbed is very small and drops off slowly during the time span; thus there is significant runoff.

The exposed parts of a structure become saturated first, so the flow starts there and proceeds onto dryer areas below. These lower surfaces absorb a proportion of the water until they too have a rate of incidence that exceeds the rate of absorption.

Splashback is a phenomenon that occurs where a wall meets the ground. Here, water hits the ground adjacent to the building and causes dirt from the ground to be propelled up and deposited a short distance up the wall. This effect also occurs when water hits horizontal ledges higher up on a building. Figure 1b shows an excellent example of splashback at the base of a building.

2.2 Staining

The washing and staining of surfaces are strongly influenced by external, directional sources of dirt. These sources include a variety of airborne pollutants, such as exhaust from traffic or smoke emissions from industrial plants, loose material on the ground carried against the base of the building by splashback, or dirt of a biological source ranging from bird droppings to plant growth.

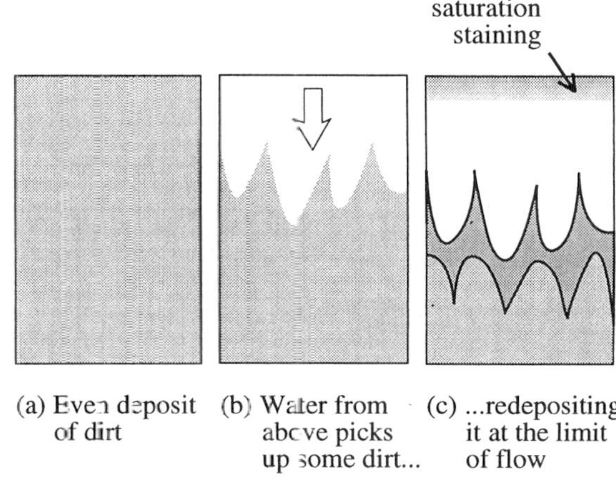

Figure 3: The basic mechanisms of staining.

In Figure 1h, the pattern of dirt on the spindles in the balustrade is due to a directional dirt source. The effect of an external source can also be observed in Figure 1a. The right side of the building curves away from the street, which leads to a reduction in the exposure to dirt caused by street traffic.

Without the effects of rainfall, dirt would be distributed fairly evenly over vertical surfaces, with higher concentrations on horizontal regions such as window sills. Although large quantities of dirt are disfiguring (as is the case with buildings completely blackened by soot), generally an even distribution of dirt due to exposure is not considered staining. However, a different picture emerges when water flows over a surface. Dirt is picked up by water movement and redeposited elsewhere, so that its distribution becomes uneven. The areas that are exposed to a rapid flow of water may be washed clean, whereas those where the dirt is redeposited have a greater accumulation. This basic mechanism is illustrated in Figure 3.

An interesting effect occurs at the locus of points on the surface where the runoff stops; this interface is critical with respect to staining, since this is where any dirt picked up by the runoff water is redeposited [10]. A very similar stain occurs when water evaporates, leaving behind any soluble material. Another interesting effect occurs when a non-absorbent surface is adjacent to a porous surface. In this case, the staining is limited to the porous material. In Figure 1g, the top portion of the bridge is made of a non-absorbent metal, which causes a large portion of the incident water to run onto the porous stone work below, causing significant staining.

Another important effect in staining is *differential flow*, which occurs when water running over one material dissolves small quantities of the material and deposits them as stains elsewhere. A common example, known as the *spilt-milk* effect, can be readily observed in places where runoff from concrete leads to white streaking on brickwork below. Other examples include green stains generated by runoff from copper [3] or rust stains from other corroded metals such as iron. If there are several materials present, even more complex patterns of stains may occur depending on the relative solubilities of the different materials. Figures 1c and 1d depict examples of differential flow. In Figure 1c the circled region shows the spilt-milk effect caused by the deposits from a limestone window sill. In Figure 1d the circled region shows an example where rust from an iron chain has been washed onto the street below.

In areas that are exposed to water for long periods of time, *saturation staining* often occurs. Different materials have a different color response to saturation; most porous materials become darker due to a decrease in the average scattering angle caused by the interaction of the water and the substrate. Figure 1f illustrates saturation staining. Here, water collects on the ridge at the base of the building.

3 Flow Model

In this section, we describe a model that qualitatively captures many of the flow effects described in the previous section. The model has three basic inputs: surface geometry to create structures, materials for the structures and loose deposits, and the environment. Our flow simulator is based on particle systems and rate equations. Particles are used to model water "droplets" both on the surface and in the air. The environment description specifies the initial distribution of water droplets. Equations of motion describe the movement of each water particle over the surface accounting for gravity, friction, contact forces, and the influence of obstacles. The quantity of water in a particle decreases through absorption into the base material of the surface or evaporation. Water droplets may dissolve material, carry it to a different location, and subsequently deposit it there. This model is simple conceptually, is easy to implement, and only requires modest computation.

Surface geometry is represented as a collection of parametric patches. The current system supports two types of patches: polygons and cubic spline patches. The geometric information is augmented with topological information that describes adjacency relationships between all the patches; this is essential because the flow must be continuous across a patch boundary. Each parametric surface also has a set of two-dimensional texture coordinates which is used to index a set of texture maps attached to each surface. For example, the amount of water absorbed by the surface is stored in a *saturation map*.

In addition to water, the system also models other materials. Each patch represents a surface of a solid object made from a base material, which is coated with a mixture of loose deposits. The concentration of each loose deposit is stored in a texture map attached to the surface. Each type of material has an associated set of rendering properties, e.g. diffuse and specular colors, shininess, and a set of physical properties, e.g. roughness, absorptivity, and other rate constants. These properties are summarized in Table 1.

Material Properties		
	Properties	Notation
Material	Diffuse color	C_d
	Specular color	C_s
	Shininess	s
	Roughness	r
	Absorption	a
	Absorptivity	k_a
Deposits	Diffuse color	C_d
	Adhesion rate constant	k_S
	Solubility rate constant	k_D

Table 1: Attributes of the two major classes of materials: base materials and loose deposits. Rate constants (properties beginning with k) are used in the differential equations controlling absorption of water and sedimentation of loose deposits (see Table 3).

3.1 Water Particle Model

In our model water is represented as a collection of water particles. The attributes of each water particle are shown in Table 2; they include the mass or volume of the particle, as well as positional attributes. Particle systems have been used widely in computer graphics and the techniques we use for modeling their motion are well described in the literature [20, 22].

Water Particle Properties	
Attribute	Notation
Mass	m
Position	x
Velocity	v
Soluble material i	S_i

Table 2: Particle attributes.

Water particles are created on the geometric model according to a distribution function for incident rain. This function depends on exposure to the prevailing rain direction. These distribution functions will be discussed in more detail in Section 3.4. The flow of water particles along the surface depends on a set of forces: gravity, friction, self-repulsion, and diffusion. Gravity and friction cause the particles to flow downward; self-repulsion prevents the particles from clumping and causes the motion to be more fluid-like (see Figure 4). Normally the flow of particles is constrained to lie on the surface; this is done by projecting the resulting force vector onto the

Figure 4: Particle simulation on a complex model.

tangent plane of the surface, as described in Turk [20]. Obstacles are detected by comparing the surface normal at subsequent time steps. If the surface normal changes abruptly, a probability distribution function determines whether the particle should continue on its present course, or ricochet away from the obstacle.

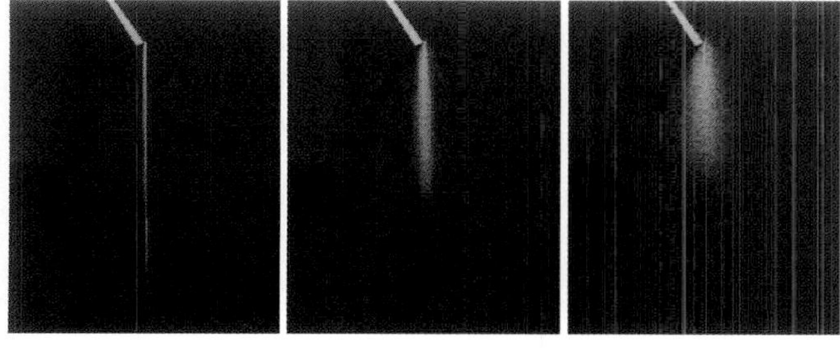

Figure 5: The effects on the flow due to surface roughness. The three figures are generated with different surface roughnesses: the surface on the left is smoothest; the surface on the right is roughest.

In order to create more interesting flows on surfaces that are geometrically smooth, we have experimented with two simple rough surface models. In the first model, a scalar roughness controls a diffusion process. To simulate diffusion, each particle is subjected to a random force in the tangent plane to the surface; the magnitude of the displacement force is proportional to the roughness parameter. Figure 5 shows the effect of roughness on the flow. As can be seen, increasing the roughness causes the particles to disperse, whereas decreasing the roughness causes the flow to be streaky. In the second model, a displacement map is added to a surface. The displacement map is used to perturb the surface normal which in turn defines a perturbed tangent plane. When a displacement map is present, the resulting force is first projected onto the true tangent plane and then reprojected onto the perturbed tangent plane. This simple technique causes the particles to conform to the displacement map — flowing more slowly across a bumpy surface and hence collecting in cavities and cracks, and streaming along cracks and valleys.

To model the effects of secondary flow, particles are allowed to fall off a surface. A particle leaves the surface if the angle between its velocity vector and the surface tangent exceeds a prespecified critical angle. When a particle loses contact with the surface, it falls vertically under the influence of gravity until it hits another surface. Since computing such intersections can be computationally intensive, we pre-compute a table of positions where particles will land when they fall off the surface. This is an important feature, as our models consist of large numbers of patches.

Together, these steps form a model capable of reproducing a sufficiently wide variety of effects to generate interesting weathered appearances. Complex flow patterns arise naturally by constraining particles to remain on the surface, thereby forcing the particles to conform to the geometry. Collisions naturally divert particles around obstacles and allow for non-local interactions between different parts of the model. Roughness and displacement maps change the look of flows on different surfaces. A snapshot of particles flowing over a complex surface is shown in Figure 4.

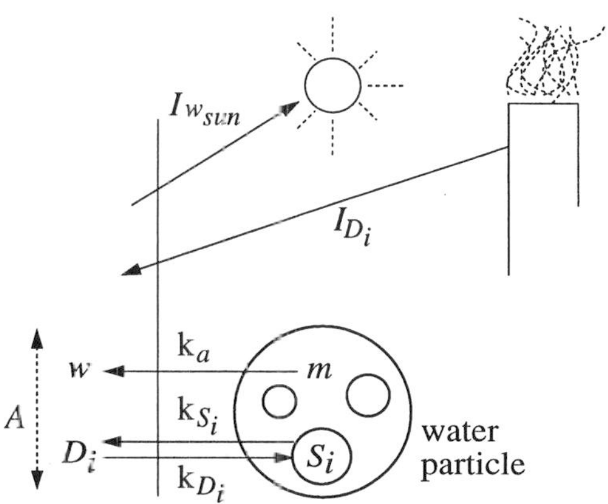

Figure 6: Absorption and deposition model.

3.2 Absorption Model

The absorption of water by a surface depends largely on the properties of void space, or pores, in the material. However, for practical purposes the following model is often adopted [2]: Three parameters control the absorption: *absorption*, *absorptivity*, and *saturation*. Absorption is the maximum amount of water that the surface may hold, whereas absorptivity is the rate that the surface absorbs water. Saturation is the ratio of the actual water absorbed to the capacity of the surface. The amount of water absorbed depends on the absorptivity and the duration of exposure, but it is limited by the absorption. This effect can be modeled by adjusting the absorptivity as a function of the saturation.

The absorption process is shown diagrammatically in Figure 6, and the equations that govern the process are contained in Table 3. As a water particle moves across a porous surface, its mass will decrease due to absorption and evaporation. At each time step, after the position of the particle is updated, its mass is updated by numerically integrating a differential equation controlling absorption and evaporation. When the mass of the particle falls below some threshold, it "dies" and is removed from the simulation.

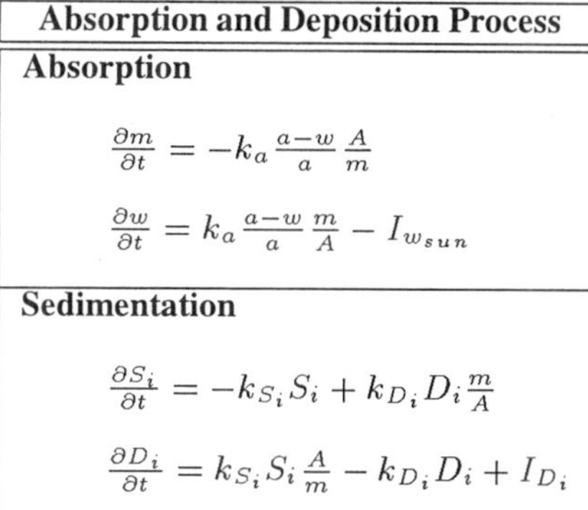

Absorption and Deposition Process

Absorption

$$\frac{\partial m}{\partial t} = -k_a \frac{a-w}{a} \frac{A}{m}$$

$$\frac{\partial w}{\partial t} = k_a \frac{a-w}{a} \frac{m}{A} - I_{w_{sun}}$$

Sedimentation

$$\frac{\partial S_i}{\partial t} = -k_{S_i} S_i + k_{D_i} D_i \frac{m}{A}$$

$$\frac{\partial D_i}{\partial t} = k_{S_i} S_i \frac{A}{m} - k_{D_i} D_i + I_{D_i}$$

Table 3: Sedimentation equations. The top two equations control the absorption of water by the surface; the bottom two equations control the sedimentation of loose deposits. In this last set of equations, the subscript i is used to signify different types of deposits. S_i is the concentration of dissolved material in a water particle, and D_i is the concentration of material deposited on the surface. All other parameters and functions are described in Tables 1 and 2.

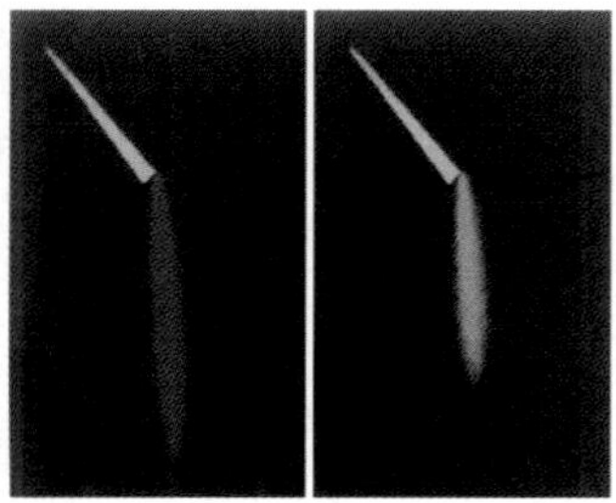

Figure 7: The effects on the flow due to absorption of a porous surface. The two figures show the amount of absorbed water on two surfaces with different absorptions. Because the surface on the left has a lower absorption than the one on the right, it becomes saturated sooner and the water streak is longer. In contrast, the surface on the left absorbs more water limiting the length of the streak. Since more water is inside the streak on the right, the streak is brighter.

Figure 7 illustrates the flow pattern from a pipe across a surface with two different absorptions. To make these images, the quantity of water absorbed at each point by the surface is stored in a saturation map. This saturation map may be used by the rendering system to modulate the appearance of the surface. Unlike this figure, a saturation stain makes the surface appear darker; this point will be discussed in Section 3.5.

3.3 Deposition Model

The last main category of surface attributes controls transport and deposition of various substances such as dirt. In our model, these sedimentation characteristics are captured by two parameters: *solubility*, describing the rate at which water picks up surface deposits, and *adhesion*, specifying the rate of redeposition from water particles on to the surface. These parameters may vary for different materials.

The sedimentation process is shown diagrammatically in Figure 6, and the equations governing the process are shown in Table 3. These coupled differential equations depend on the relative concentrations of the materials in the water particle and on the surface. In the case of a water particle, the concentration is defined to be material per unit mass; in the case of the surface, the concentration is the material per unit area. Note that as a water particle's mass decreases due to evaporation, the concentration of dissolved materials decreases. Thus, the rate of deposition naturally increases during evaporation, causing the dissolved material to be deposited on the underlying surface.

The relative solubility and adhesion of deposits on a surface play a major role in the generation of stains. When water dissolves material from a surface, it has the effect of washing the surface. When water deposits material, it has the effect of staining the surface. The combination of these two effects, when coupled with the flow, can generate complex stain patterns. Even more complex patterns arise if multiple materials with different solubilities are present. More examples of this will be shown in the results.

3.4 Environment Model

Environment attributes	
Attribute	Notation
Rain	$I_{w_{rain}}$
Sunlight	$I_{w_{sun}}$
Deposits	I_{D_i}

Table 4: Environment

The external factors affecting the flow are shown in Table 4. In this section we describe the models we used to generate the images in this paper. Although it should be emphasized that it is very easy to add more complex environmental models to the system.

As described in Section 3.1, the rate and direction of incident rain seeds the particle flow process. We model this by creating rain sources that emit rain drops. In our model, the direction of rain is controlled by the direction of wind. This in turn is given by randomly perturbing the prevailing wind direction. These drops are traced until they intersect the model and are deposited in an exposure map. For efficiency reasons we precompute these exposure maps. During the flow simulation the exposure determines the probability that a water particle will be created at different points on the surface; however, once a particle is created, water sources have no effect on the particle's mass.

The rate of evaporation is very sensitive to the orientation of the surface and whether it is shadowed. This effect may be modeled by computing the total solar irradiance, both due to the sky and the sun itself. In some of the experiments performed in this paper, the evaporation rate is set to be constant.

Finally, the initial distribution of deposits of various types may also be controlled with directional sources, or prestored in a texture map.

3.5 Rendering

To create final renderings, we use simple methods to approximate the diffuse color of the loose deposits and to account for wet surfaces and saturation stains. The color of the deposit layer is computed simply by summing the color of each deposit, weighted by the concentration of that deposit from the appropriate texture map. An alpha value is computed using a similar technique, and this is used to composite the deposit color over the base material. The color of a wet surface is modified to make it look darker. To approximate this effect, we simply modulate the diffuse reflectivity depending upon the saturation of the surface.

4 Results

In this section we show results for four complex models: a building facade, two statues, and a section of a cathedral.

Figure 8: Building facade. Rendering without flow patterns (left). Rendering with flow patterns (right).

4.1 Building Model

Figure 8 shows side-by-side renderings of the building, without (on the left) and with (on the right) the flow effects. Figure 9 shows the changes in appearance due to the flows in more detail. The building was modeled using AutoCAD and consists of approximately 450 polygons. All the flow effects in this series were created in approximately three hours on a Silicon Graphics Reality Engine2 with a 250 Mhz R4400 processor.

In the center section of the building alongside the main window, there are several examples of primary flows that continue until the water reaches the stone work comprising the base of the building. The flow has the effect of washing dirt and soot from the brick and depositing it on the lower parts of the building. Note the difference between the patterns generated by the flows on the yellow brick and grey stone below. This is caused by the greater roughness of the brick surface relative to the smoother stone. On the stone at the base of the building, there are subtle splashback effects making the lower part even dirtier. Notice the underside of the vertical panels that curve outward to the left of the yellow brick section: here there is evidence of saturation staining. There is also staining due to partial flows on the sign below the lamp, in this case simulating a rust stain where the lamp meets the building. Similar staining and accumulation of a patina [3] are shown on the copper rain pipe on the left side of the building. Finally, on the sides of the upper window there is a pattern due to the differential flow of the copper patina.

To compute these images, the simulation results are stored in standard texture maps, and these are input into the rendering system. Each surface has nine texture maps, thus the final rendering uses over 4,000 texture maps (although a fair number of these are very small). In our system, we combine the texture maps using a shading language similar to the one used in RenderMan. In these images, displacement maps are used to vary the height of the surface of bricks and stones; ray tracing is used so that the displacement maps self-shadow the surface which adds to the realism of the pictures.

4.2 Venus de Milo

Figure 10 shows the development of washing and staining patterns due to flows over a statue of *Venus de Milo*, a classic work of art. The model was created from a Cyberware scan and consists of approximately 260,000 small, evenly sized triangles. This data was then used to create 63 bicubic patches, which are input to the flow simulation system. All the flow effects in this sequence were created in a session of approximately twenty minutes in length.

The left image depicts the original, white marble statue prior to the flow simulation. It is pure white, with no imperfections, and is rendered with only diffuse reflection and a single light source.

The right image shows the results of applying a uniform coating of reddish brown dirt across the statue, followed by a flow simulation to wash the surface. There are noticeable streaks in the dirt patterns due to the flow, and a randomness due to the individual nature of each particle. Dirt accumulates in various parts of the statue where the surface is protected from the path of the flow, such as under the left arm. The dirt texture conforms to the folds in the fabric below. For example, the upper surfaces of the convex parts of

Figure 9: Closeups of flow patterns on the building facade.

the folds are clean; the lower surfaces are dirty. The pattern is more uniform on the base of the statue and areas closest to the ground, since less water reached that part of the statue. It is not possible to achieve these effects with simple accessibility [11]. The image was rendered using a diffuse model for the marble, and the dirt layer was composited using the same technique as for the building.

4.3 Gargoyle

Figure 11 shows a scanned model of a gargoyle before and after the application of a simple flow pattern. The model was created from a Cyberware scan and consists of approximately 310,000 triangles. This data was then used to create 30 bicubic patches, which were input to the flow simulation system. The reflection function of the metallic surface was modified to make the surface appear as if it were covered by a thin layer of soot that was partially washed away.

4.4 Cathedral

Figure 12 shows a portion of a Gothic cathedral, which was simulated in our system. The cathedral and its statues and gargoyles were modeled using approximately 100,000 polygons which then had displacement maps applied to them, leading to a geometric complexity of over 6,000,000 polygons. The gutters and drainage system on the cathedral were carefully designed to be similar to those on actual cathedrals: water flows down the upper roof to a gutter below the railing which directs the water down the main columns, and down along the top of the flying buttresses [9]. Water exits the system below the statues of the saints. The gutter above the middle section of the facade was blocked, so that the gutter backed up and the particles spilled over the front of the building. As a result, there was much less flow beneath the statue of the saint on the left than the statue on the right. All flow simulations were performed using the displacement maps, so that the flow conformed to the actual displaced geometry; this is evident in the cracks between the stones.

5 Summary and Discussion

We have described a system for simulating the flow of water over complex surfaces. The flow conforms to the geometry of the shapes, and the water interacts with the surface materials. Specifically, the system is able to simulate the absorption of water by the material and the transport of deposits by dissolving and carrying surface material, and later redepositing it. As a result, a wide range of flow effects may be simulated, yielding complex patterns showing washing and staining.

The system is simple, robust, and practical. By using particle systems a wide range of phenomena are easily programmed. We believe the system can be extended to include additional factors, such as windblown dust and biological growth. Also, by embedding the flow model in an interactive system, the user can control the flows to produce the desired images, which is required if a physical model is to be used for artistic purposes. Finally, the methods we use to describe textures on complex surfaces are fairly general; they could be used as a basis for the creation and design of other complex patterns on these surfaces.

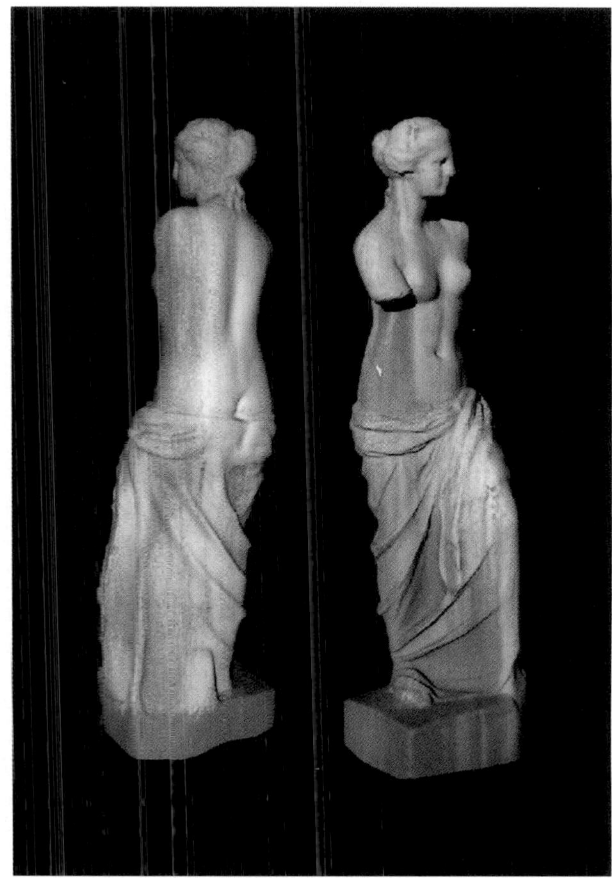

Figure 10: Simulated flows on *Venus de Milo*. Rendering without flow patterns (left). Rendering with flow patterns (right).

Water flows are a major cause of the weathering of outdoor structures and objects and must be simulated to create convincing pictures of such environments. The key to modeling weathering is to simulate the effects of the environment on the materials. Although our pictures have many effects new to computer graphics, it takes only a few minutes studying and comparing the real to the virtual examples to realize that there is still much research to be done. This is a challenging new direction for computer graphics.

Acknowledgements

Thanks to Jeff Feldgoise for modeling the cathedral and building facade, Reid Gershbein for help rendering the gargoyle, Matt Pharr for building much of the rendering system and for help with the final renderings, Craig Kolb for help assembling and printing the final images, Tamara Munzner for video assistance, and the anonymous reviewers for their suggestions. Thanks also to Brian Curless, Venkat Krishnamurthy and Marc Levoy for providing access to the Cyberware scanner and their software for creating complex models; their system was used to scan the statues. This work was supported by research grants from the National Science Foundation (CCR-9207966 and CCR-9624172) and the MIT Cabot and NEC Research Funds, and by equipment grants from Apple and Silicon Graphics Inc.

References

[1] ACHESON, D. J. *Elementary Fluid Dynamics*. Oxford Univerity Press, New York, NY, 1992.

[2] ADDLESON, L., AND RICE, C. *Performance of Materials in Buildings*. Butterworth Heinemann, Boston, MA, 1991.

[3] DORSEY, J., AND HANRAHAN, P. Modeling and rendering of metallic patinas. In *Computer Graphics Proceedings* (1996), Annual Conference Series, ACM SIGGRAPH.

[4] DULLIEN, F. A. L. *Porous Media: Fluid Transport and Pore Structure*, second ed. Academic Press, New York, NY, 1992.

[5] FOURNIER, A., AND REEVES, W. T. A simple model of ocean waves. *Computer Graphics 20*, 4 (Aug. 1986), 75–84.

[6] FRENCH, L. Toy story. *Cinefantastique 27*, 2 (1995), 36–37.

[7] JOHNSON, J. B., HANEEF, S. J., AND HEPBURN, B. J. Laboratory exposure systems to simulate atmospheric degradation of building stone under dry and wet deposition. *Atmospheric Environment 24A*, 10 (Oct 1990), 2785–2792.

[8] KASS, M., AND MILLER, G. Rapid, stable fluid dynamics for computer graphics. *Computer Graphics 24*, 4 (Aug. 1990), 49–57.

[9] LIPPERT, H. G. Systeme zur dachentwasserung bei gotischen kirchenbauten. *Architecture. Zeitschrift fur Geschichte der Baukunst 24*, 1 (1994), 111–128.

[10] MASO, J. C., Ed. *Pore Structure and Moisture Characteristics*. Chapman and Hall, New York, 1987.

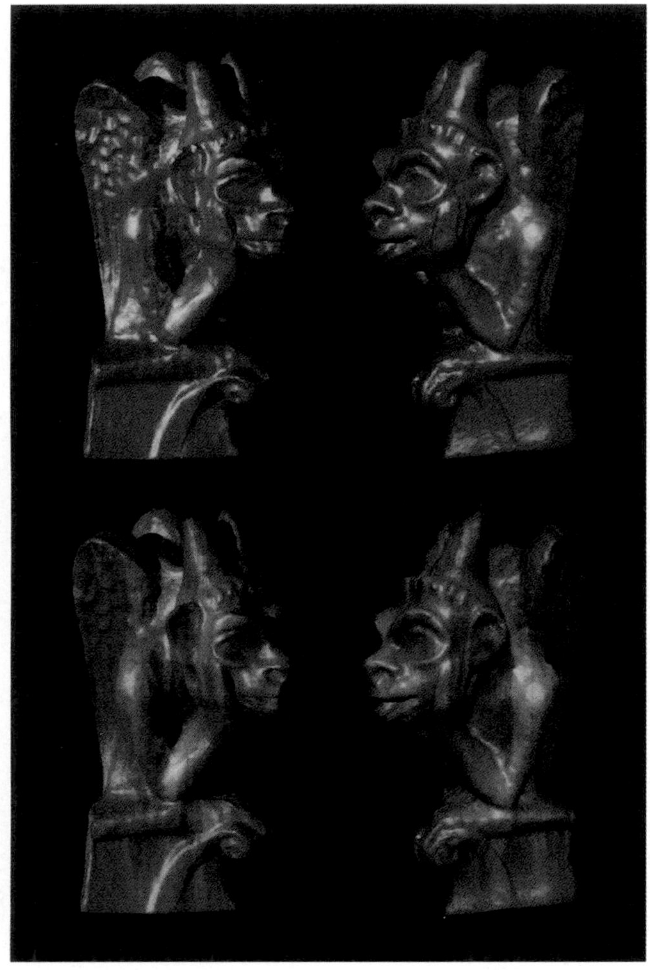

Figure 11: Simulated flows on a gargoyle. Rendering without flow patterns (top). Rendering with flow patterns (bottom).

Figure 12: Simulated flows on a Gothic cathedral.

[11] MILLER, G. Efficient algorithms for local and global accessibility shading. In *Computer Graphics Proceedings* (1994), Annual Conference Series, ACM SIGGRAPH, pp. 319–326.

[12] MILLER, G., AND PEARCE, A. Globular dynamics: A connected particle system for animating viscous fluids. *Computers and Graphics 13*, 3 (1989), 305–309.

[13] MOSTAFAVI, M., AND LEATHERBARROW, D. *On Weathering: The Life of Buildings in Time*. MIT Press, Cambridge, MA, 1993.

[14] MUSGRAVE, F. K., KOLB, C. E., AND MACE, R. S. The synthesis and rendering of eroded fractal terrains. *Computer Graphics 23* (July 1989), 41–50.

[15] PAZ, O. *A Draft of Shadows and Other Poems*. New Directions, New York, NY, 1979.

[16] PEACHEY, D. R. Modeling waves and surf. *Computer Graphics 20*, 4 (Aug. 1986), 65–74.

[17] REEVES, W. T. Particle systems – a technique for modeling a class of fuzzy objects. *ACM Trans. Graphics 2* (Apr. 1983), 91–108.

[18] REEVES, W. T., AND BLAU, R. Approximate and probabilistic algorithms for shading and rendering structured particle systems. *Computer Graphics 19*, 4 (July 1985), 313–322.

[19] SMALL, D. Simulating watercolor by modeling diffusion, pigment, and paper fibers. In *Proceedings of SPIE '91* (Feb. 1991), pp. 70–76.

[20] TURK, G. Generating textures for arbitrary surfaces using reaction-diffusion. *Computer Graphics 25*, 4 (July 1991), 289–298.

[21] WINKLER, E. M. *Stone in Architecture: Properties and Durability*. Springer-Verlag, New York, NY, 1994.

[22] WITKIN, A. P., AND HECKBERT, P. S. Using particles to sample and control implicit surfaces. In *Computer Graphics Proceedings* (1994), Annual Conference Series, ACM SIGGRAPH, pp. 269–278.

[23] YAEGER, L., UPSON, C., AND MYERS, R. Combining physical and visual simulation — creation of the planet Jupiter for the film "2010". *Computer Graphics 20*, 4 (Aug. 1986), 85–93.

[24] YALIN, M. S. *Mechanics of sediment transport*, second ed. Oxford, New York, NY, 1977.

Simulating Facial Surgery Using Finite Element Models

R. M. Koch*, M. H. Gross*, F. R. Carls†
D. F. von Büren*, G. Fankhauser*, Y. I. H. Parish*

*Swiss Federal Institute of Technology (ETH), Zürich
† Dept. of Maxillofacial Surgery, University Hospital, Zürich

ABSTRACT

This paper describes a prototype system for surgical planning and prediction of human facial shape after craniofacial and maxillofacial surgery for patients with facial deformities. For this purpose it combines, unifies, and extends various methods from geometric modeling, finite element analysis, and image processing to render highly realistic 3D images of the post surgical situation. The basic concept of the system is to join advanced geometric modeling and animation systems such as *Alias* with a special purpose finite element model of the human face developed under *AVS*. In contrast to existing facial models we acquire facial surface and soft tissue data both from photogrammetric and CT scans of the individual. After initial data preprocessing, reconstruction, and registration, a finite element model of the facial surface and soft tissue is provided which is based on triangular finite elements. Stiffness parameters of the soft tissue are computed using segmentations of the underlying CT data. All interactive procedures such as bone and soft tissue repositioning are performed under the guidance of the modeling system which feeds the processed geometry into the FEM solver. The resulting shape is generated from minimizing the global energy of the surface under the presence of external forces. Photorealistic pictures are obtained from rendering the facial surface with the advanced animation system on which this prototype is built.

Although we do not claim any of the presented algorithms themselves to be new, the synthesis of several methods offers a new facial model quality. Our concept is a significant extension to existing ones and, due to its versatility, can be employed in different applications such as facial animation, facial reconstruction, or the simulation of aging. We illustrate features of our system with some examples from the Visible Human Data Set.™

CR Descriptors: I.3.5 [**Computational Geometry and Object Modeling**]: Physically Based Modeling; I.3.7 [**Three-Dimensional Graphics and Realism**]; I.4.6 [**Segmentation**]: Edge and Feature Detection - Pixel Classification; I.6.3 [**Applications**];

Additional Keywords and Phrases Finite Element Method, Facial Surgery Simulation, Facial Modeling, Data Reconstruction.

INTRODUCTION

Background and Previous Work

Since the human face plays a key role in interpersonal relationships, prediction of post-surgical morphology and appearance of human faces for patients with facial deformities is a critical issue in facial

*Swiss Federal Institute of Technology, Institute for Information Systems, Department of Computer Science, ETH Zentrum, CH-8092 Zürich, Switzerland. {grossm, koch}@inf.ethz.ch

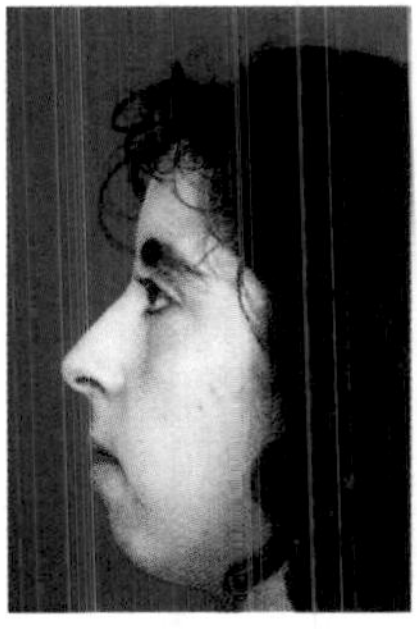
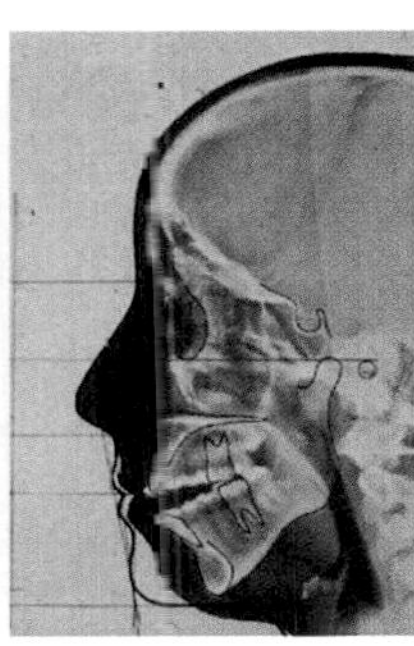
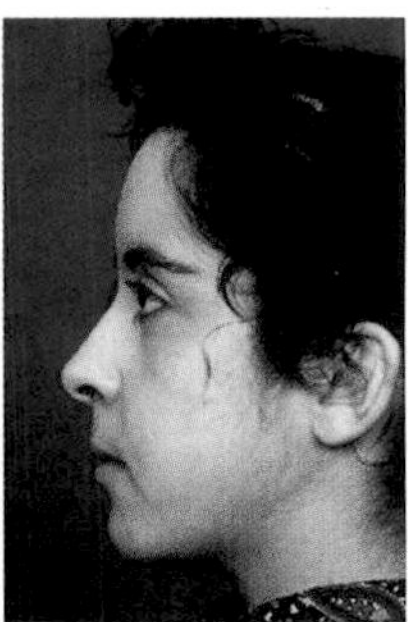

a) b) c)

Figure 1: Example of a facial disharmony resulting from a craniofacial disorder and its correction. a) Presurgical facial shape contour (profile). b) Lateral X-ray image of the skull with actual and planned new soft tissue profiles (2D). c) Postsurgical appearance after maxillofacial procedures. (Data source: Courtesy Prof. H. F. Sailer, Dept. of Maxillofacial Surgery, University Hospital Zürich, Switzerland)

surgery. Even very subtle malformations of facial proportions can strongly affect the appearance of a face and determine on aesthetic aspects such as individual beauty [4]. In addition, many procedures in maxillofacial surgery lead to a change in the facial morphology of the patient, e.g. cutting of the jaw bones (osteotomies) and bringing them into a desired position. Maxillofacial surgery also consists of the resection of malformed parts of the face or tumors and the reconstruction of missing or malformed structures. Furthermore, the treatment of patients with facial fractures influences facial shape and surface. Therefore, surgeons often face the problem of predicting a fair facial surface before the actual surgery is carried out. Figure 1a and 1c illustrate a typical malformation of a young girl's face and its correction by surgery. Typically, the maxillofacial surgeon (sometimes with the help of a medical artist) draws the patients predicted profile to give at least a 2D appearance of the future face. A lateral X-ray with the actual and predicted soft tissue profiles is presented in Figure 1b. It is clear that both surgeons and their patients have a strong demand for a method which enables them to compute highly realistic 3D pictures of the post surgical shape. Any computation should be based on data available, or at least easy to obtain from the patient, e.g. CT scans. More specifically, with the development of advanced range scanners [15] the idea was born to combine both volume and surface data to build a physically based facial model. Obviously, the model has to capture the most important anatomical and mechanical parameters of the face. Furthermore, it should allow interactive manipulations and the prediction of resulting facial shape.

It is straightforward to investigate computer graphics literature where facial modeling has a long tradition. Early works such as [12] restricted themselves to pure geometric deformations, mostly carried out directly on parametric surface models. However, with physically based modeling paradigms, more realistic facial models based on mass spring systems feature a linear approximation of the facial surface. The particle based approach is also used to govern control vertices of parametric B-spline models and thus provides continuous shape descriptions. In particular, the works of Terzopoulos e.a. [10, 16] extend the prior approaches in many significant ways: Anatomy is incorporated and an elaborate model of facial skin layers and muscles is proposed which is essential to compute realistic facial appearance.

In facial animation, computational complexity is a fundamental constraint, and real-time performance is often much more important than a highly accurate facial shape in terms of a still image.

To conclude, the methods mentioned above are based on strategies which exclude them from immediate use in facial surgery:

- In most cases facial models are adapted from a template face instead of generated directly from the underlying data set.
- The elastomechanics of the surface is only approximated by spring-mass systems which can be considered linear and hence C^0-continuous finite elements.
- Unsatisfactory approximations of the patient's skull surface were used which are essential for surgical applications.
- Although [10] proposes a very elaborate and elegant model, the underlying facial tissue is still template based and does not account for individual variations of the different layers and tissue types.

Our Approach

In the following paper we present a human facial model that enables prediction of facial deformations after surgery. In contrast to prior approaches, our goal is to approximate the physics as closely as possible and to accept higher computational costs. Therefore, we extend the models described earlier in 3 ways:

1. We employ a non-linear, globally C^1 continuous finite element model of the facial surface which is based on triangular polynomial shape functions similar to the modeling paradigm proposed by [2]. Increasing the number of finite elements results in a facial surface that tends to be C^3 continuous.
2. We compute the external forces of the model by connecting the surface with nodal springs to the skull. The individual spring stiffnesses are computed by means of 3D line integration through the CT data.
3. We build our model on top of commercially available modeling, visualization, and animation systems which support interactive geometric manipulation and rendering.

We organize our paper as follows: First, we give an overview of the system and describe the general set-up as a combination of commercial tools and individual components. In section 2 we elaborate on the different preprocessing steps to build the facial model. They range from geometry extraction and adaptive surface meshing to the computation of spring stiffnesses. Section 3 reviews the finite element model we employ. Particular emphasis is given to triangular patches. Section 4 illuminates the processing steps necessary to initialize the FEM model and perform computational surgery. Finally, we demonstrate the proposed system with experimental results obtained from the Visible Human Data Set™(VHD) [11].

1 System Overview

This section expands on the different procedures, data processing steps, and general set-up of our simulation system illustrated in the chart of Figure 2.

Our data sources consist of laser range scans, CT data or, for the VHD, photo slices. Our system combines a higher order polynomial FEM surface model with a mesh of springs attached to the skull. In order to generate a model for an individual patient, the following processing steps are necessary:

First of all, an initial facial surface is extracted from the data sources and an adaptive surface mesh computed for further processing. The mesh of springs connecting the surface and the skull requires that the skull has the same mesh topology as the skin. Therefore, we project the skin vertices down to the skull. One of the major advantages of our model is that it derives stiffness from the underlying volume data set, which makes a segmentation procedure necessary. All surgical planning is performed interactively on the precomputed skull model. Further interaction is required to define boundary conditions and the stretching and bending tensors crucial to achieve robust results. The FEM pipeline is comprised of computations for local and global stiffness matrices, preloading, assembling, solving and disassembling to obtain the new shape. Finally, the facial surface is rendered using *Alias*.

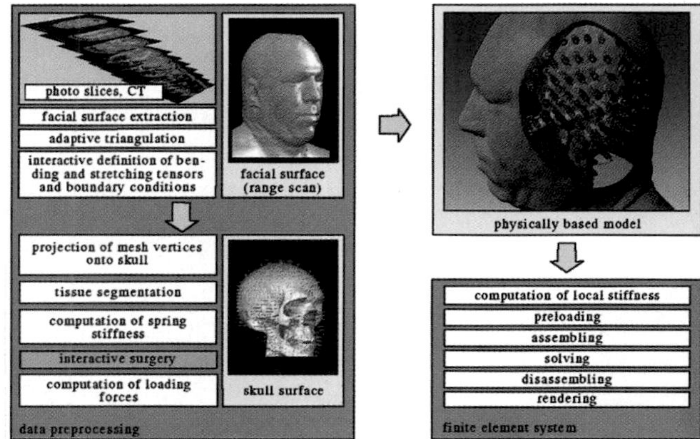

Figure 2: Illustration of data flow, procedures, and system set-up for maxillofacial surgery planning.

2 Data Acquisition and Preprocessing

The following section explains the different preprocessing steps essential for generating an initial facial model of the patient. Once again, most of the methods we employ are part of the standard repertoire of graphics and imaging algorithms, and hence we do not describe them all in detail here.

2.1 Facial Surface and Volume Data

As stated earlier, our system targets facial surgery simulation based on laser range surface data and CT volume data. Typical laser scans are often recorded by Cyberware scanners. Because scanning time is a critical issue due to motion artifacts, faster devices such as the one presented in [15] have been developed. In our experimental set-up we use the VHD as a reference. Figures 3a and 3b show examples of transaxial color photos and CT scans which have been scaled, clipped, and registered with respect to reference points. In order to extract the surface from the photo slices, we simulate a range scan procedure as described below.

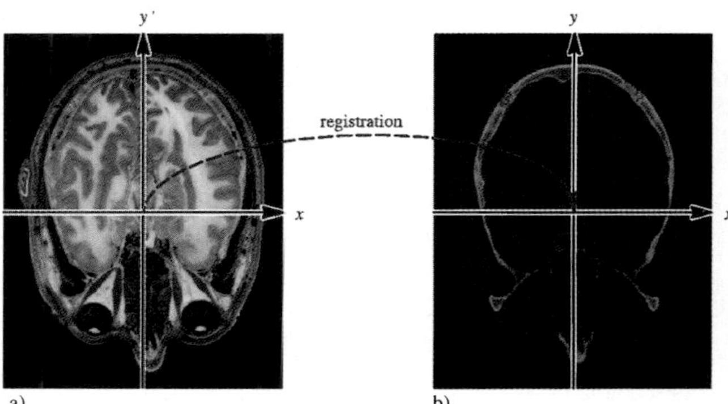

Figure 3: Volume data sets. a) Photo slice of the VHD. b) Corresponding CT slice. (Data source: Visible Human Project, Courtesy National Library of Medicine)

2.2 Extraction of the Facial Surface and Skull

The range scan simulation is accomplished by a two pass procedure, as shown in Figure 4. The first pass, which performs an edge detection using the Canny operator [1], is applied to the red channel of Figure 3a. Figure 4a shows the edge detection results. In the second pass, we intersect the image with rays through the center with a given angular resolution $\Delta\phi$. The respective range value is computed in accordance with the first intersection of the ray with the Canny edges. The result of this procedure is depicted in Figure 4b. It is clear that the surface computed in this way can be transformed into a cylindrical coordinate system without obtaining degenerated triangles. This surface coordinate system is initially applied to define tangential vector orientation used during the FEM processing step and is visualized as a grid mapped onto the surface. The parametric coordinates are denoted by (u, v). The same procedure holds for the extraction of the skull from the CT data set. Bone tissue produces high intensity values in CT data and can be enhanced with windowing operations. The final skull shape is shown in Figure 4c.

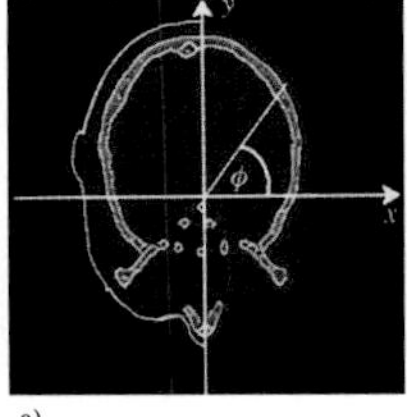
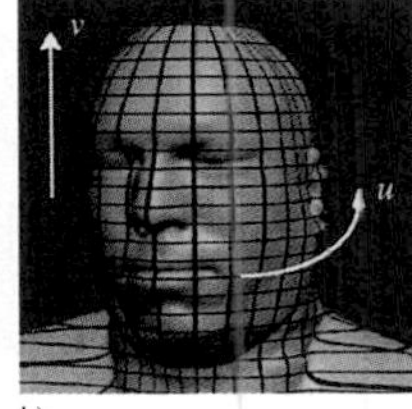
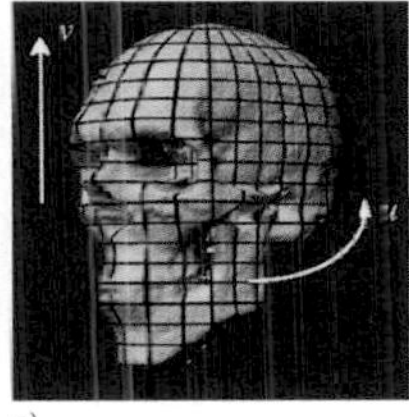

a) b) c)
Figure 4: Facial surface and skull data extraction. a) Edges detected from a CT slice using the Canny edge detector (yellow edges) and simulated range scans for skull (red) and skin (skin-colored). b) Facial surface and underlying (u, v) coordinate system. c) Skull surface sharing the same coordinate system.

The above procedure is vulnerable to some minor artifacts due to self occlusion (e.g. nostrils, ears), but it successfully avoids the generation of non-manifold shapes as an isosurface tool might produce [14]. The resulting skull is sufficiently shaped to perform facial surgery.

2.3 Adaptive Meshing

The surface model is based on a finite element surface defined over an arbitrary triangulation of the parameter domain. Therefore, a trade-off has to be found between computational costs and precision. Since the computing time depends mostly on the number of triangular patches, a good adaptive triangulation of the parameter domain is an essential preprocessing step. There are a wide range of meshing and triangulation schemes available in the literature, like Delaunay, greedy meshing, or wavelets [5]. We decided to use a slightly modified version of the method of [13] for thinning and retiling. The mesh has to follow the 2D parameter domain and additional effort has to be spent at its boundaries. In our case, we start with a given trivial mesh directly obtained from the laser range scan as presented in Figure 5a. It is thinned out up to a given quality threshold, as visualized in Figure 5c. A mesh comparable to Figure 5b is used for all results presented in this paper. The final bust of the VHD was generated from the original data set by subsampling by 2. The initial mesh consisted of 69k triangles and was reduced to 39k.

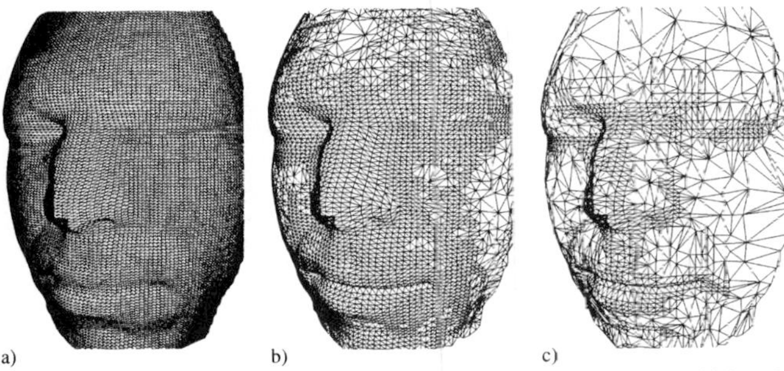

a) b) c)
Figure 5: Adaptive triangular meshes of the facial surface of the VHD. a) Initial mesh generated by an equally spaced subsampling by $2^{0.5}$ (21k triangles). b) Adaptive mesh with 7k triangles after subsampling by 2. c) Adaptive mesh consisting of 2.5k triangles.

In order to remove high frequency spikes resulting from gaps in the Canny edges and from wire ropes in the VHD, additional Gaussian low pass filtering was performed locally.

2.4 Registration and Segmentation

Registration of facial surface and CT data is fundamental to the task of modeling the facial tissue. Although many automatic matching methods have been proposed in the computer vision literature [8], fully automatic techniques are still prone to errors. In the general case of laser range scans and CTs from different sources we carry out the registration manually by setting landmarks [6]. However, in the experimental set-up with the VHD, the facial surface is computed directly on the volume data set (see section 2.2) and registration is accomplished inherently.

In order to compute a 3D physically based model of the individual's facial tissue, it is necessary to provide detailed information on the different tissue types which have different physical parameters. [10] proposes an elaborate 5-layered soft tissue model with biphase springs, but individual compositions of the patient's facial tissue are not considered. For this reason, we base the computation of the spring stiffness on a segmentation of the underlying volume data. In the general case of CT data sets, much work has been done to provide appropriate tissue extraction, but intensity-based methods [3] still do a good job. In this case, the intensity range is segmented into different tissue types which tend to be Gaussian distributed, as shown in Figure 6a. The resulting segmentation is illustrated in Figure 6b. In the special case of photo slices, more elaborate color clustering methods can be applied, such as in Figure 6c.

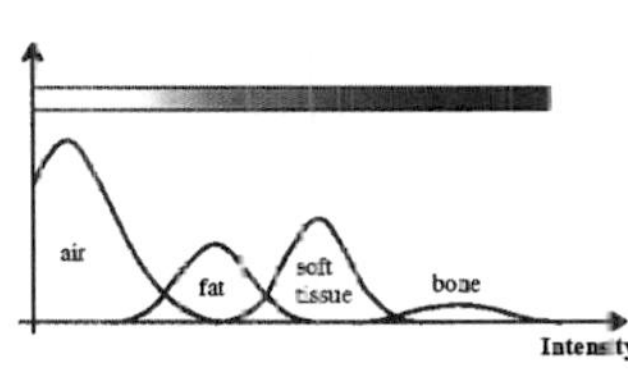

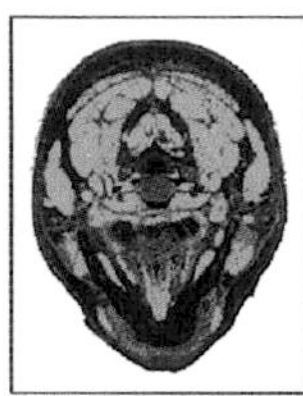

a) b) c)
Figure 6: a) Intensity distribution of different tissue types in CT data. b) Threshold-based segmentation of a CT slice. c) Color-based segmentation of a photo slice.

For all results presented in this paper we have assigned the stiffness values of Table 1 to the different tissue types. These values are proportional to the corresponding spring stiffness values. Only tissue between skin and skull is considered.

Table 1: Spring stiffness parameters.

tissue type	color (red, green, blue)	stiffness
bone	(extracted from CT)	∞
skin	151, 125, 90	200.0
muscle	80, 40, 35	100.0
fat dark	165, 140, 100	10.0
fat bright	190, 160, 110	20.0

2.5 Spring Mesh Topology

Every vertex $\mathbf{x}_s^i$ of the facial surface mesh belongs to a vertex $\mathbf{x}_b^i$ on the skull. This relation enables us to construct a mesh of springs between skin and skull. The attachment point on the skull $\mathbf{x}_b^i$ is computed by tracing the surface normal $\mathbf{n}_i$ of the skin through the tissue in the direction to the skull. $\mathbf{n}_i$ is approximated by averaging the normals of all adjacent triangles. The skull intersection point $\mathbf{x}_b^i$ is found by thresholding the CT data set registered to the facial surface. We distinguish between two types of springs:

Main springs connect the skin vertices $\mathbf{x}_s^i$ with the skull vertices $\mathbf{x}_b^i$ on the bone. They are normal to the skin surface.

Strut springs connect a skin vertex $\mathbf{x}_s^i$ with the neighbors $\mathbf{x}_b^{neighbor(i,j)}$ of the related skull vertex $\mathbf{x}_b^i$.

Figure 7 illustrates this relationship. We do not use biphase springs

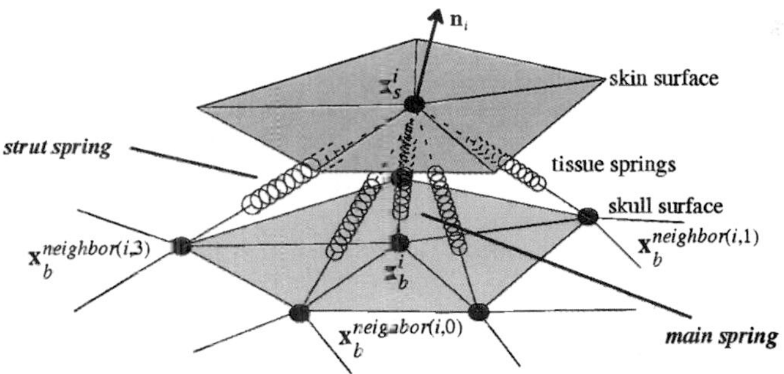

Figure 7: Spring mesh for soft tissue modeling.

since we are interested in the stationary shape, rather than dynamic behavior. Our tissue model assumes the skin directly connected to the underlying bone. There is no sliding between tissue and bone surface and none between different tissue types. Any extension of the model towards sliding and non-sliding tissue parts would require additional segmentations and is a task for future work.

2.6 Computation of the Spring Stiffness from CT

To compute the spring stiffnesses according to the segmentation presented in section 2.4, we have to consider that a spring penetrates different types of facial tissue on its way from the skin surface to the skull attachment point. We cope with this problem by decomposing the spring into a set of smaller springs which are connected in series.

Let $c(\mathbf{x})$ be the tissue stiffness as a function of the spatial parameter $\mathbf{x}$, and let $\mathbf{x}_s^i$ and $\mathbf{x}_b^i$ be the parameter values for the skin and bone attachment points of one individual spring k. The overall stiffness c_k of the resulting spring is computed by line integration from the surface node to the skull attachment point.

$$\frac{1}{c_k} = \int_{\mathbf{x}_s^i}^{\mathbf{x}_b^i} \frac{1}{c(\mathbf{x})} d\mathbf{x} \qquad (1)$$

For a discrete set of L springs with individual lengths $l_k^1, \ldots, l_k^L$ and stiffnesses $c_k^1, \ldots, c_k^L$ connected in series, as in Figures 8a and b, the upper integral collapses to

$$\frac{1}{c_k} = \frac{1}{l_k} \sum_{h=1}^{L} \frac{l_k^h}{c_k^h} \qquad \text{with } l_k = \sum_{h=1}^{L} l_k^h \qquad (2)$$

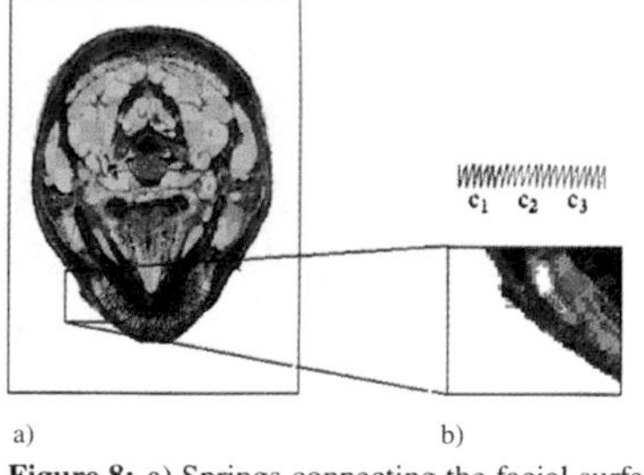

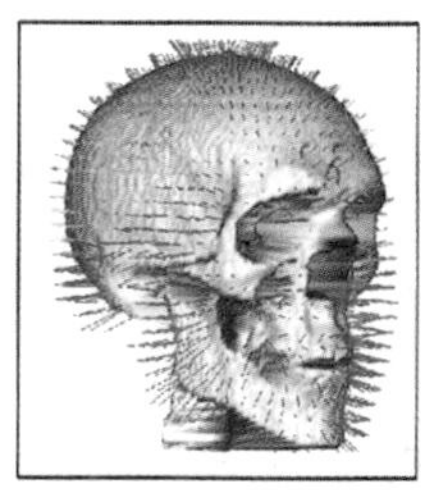

a) b) c)

Figure 8: a) Springs connecting the facial surface nodes with the skull. b) Decomposition into smaller springs connected in series as they penetrate different tissue types. c) Distribution of spring stiffnesses as pseudo-colored vectors.

This summation starts from the skin surface and runs along the surface normal to the skull attachment point. If the normal does not intersect the skull, a maximum distance from the surface is assumed and the spring stiffness is set to zero. The skull attachment points are also used in section 4.4 for calculation of the loading forces after bone repositioning.

As stated earlier, an adaptively triangulated surface mesh is applied. Hence, different springs k are affecting differently sized surface areas Δ_k. It is recommended to solve this problem by additional weighting of either the stiffness value c_k or the resulting force with Δ_k. See also section 4.4.

Figure 8c illustrates the distribution of spring stiffnesses for the VHD using pseudo-colored vectors.

3 The Finite Element Model

This section discusses the finite element surface model we use to represent the facial surface. Finite element modeling is a fundamental engineering method with many different types of elements proposed in the past. We focus on the construction of globally C^1 continuous shape functions over triangles. Global continuity is required for smooth representation and rendering of the facial shape. Furthermore, the triangular approach is topologically more flexible and fixes irregular meshes of the parameter domain. C^1 triangular finite elements have first been proposed by [17] and used by [2] to develop physically based modeling paradigms.

3.1 Variational Surface Modeling

The mathematical description of deformable surface models is well studied and can be considered a variational approach. The resulting shape $\mathbf{w}(u, v)$ is computed by minimizing the overall energy E_{surf} under the presence of external and internal loading forces. The shape's internal deformation energy E_{def} depends on its natural resistance against bending and stretching. α and β denote the respective tensors defining the individual material properties. The surface energy has to be computed over the parameter domain $\mathbf{\Omega}$. For convenience we follow the notation of [17] and [2].

$$E_{def} = \int_{\mathbf{\Omega}} (\alpha \, \mathbf{stretching} + \beta \, \mathbf{bending}) \, d\mathbf{\Omega} \qquad (3)$$

$$\alpha = \begin{bmatrix} \alpha_{11} & \alpha_{12} \\ \alpha_{12} & \alpha_{22} \end{bmatrix}, \quad \beta = \begin{bmatrix} \beta_{11} & & \\ & \beta_{22} & \\ & & \beta_{12} \end{bmatrix}$$

More specifically, let $\mathbf{f}(u, v)$ be the external forces applied to a surface $\mathbf{w}(u, v)$, and let $\mathbf{w}_u, \mathbf{w}_{uu}, \mathbf{w}_v, \mathbf{w}_{vv}$ be the first and second order derivatives in the principal directions. We can reformulate (3) to

$$E_{surf} = \int_{\mathbf{\Omega}} \begin{matrix} \alpha_{11}\mathbf{w}_u^2 + \alpha_{12}\mathbf{w}_u\mathbf{w}_v + \alpha_{22}\mathbf{w}_v^2 + \\ \beta_{11}\mathbf{w}_{uu}^2 + 2\beta_{12}\mathbf{w}_{uv}^2 + \beta_{22}\mathbf{w}_{vv}^2 \end{matrix} - 2\mathbf{fw} \, d\mathbf{\Omega} \qquad (4)$$

The central idea underlying the finite element approach is to compute an approximate solution of the unknown shape $\mathbf{w}(u, v)$ by dividing $\mathbf{w}(u, v)$ into patches $\mathbf{w}_p(u, v)$ and using expansions with weighted sums of bases ϕ_l, which form the *finite elements*:

$$\mathbf{w}_p(u, v) \approx \sum_l \mathbf{a}_l \phi_l \qquad (5)$$

where $(u, v) \in \mathbf{\Omega}_p$ is the local parameter space of a surface patch p.

These bases are defined over a finite domain $\mathbf{\Omega}_p$ provided by the initial discretization of the underlying parameter domain $\mathbf{\Omega}$. Thus, the problem of solving the upper functional is reduced to find appropriate weights $\mathbf{a}_l$. These weights represent the coordinates of the shape function in a functional space spanned by the ϕ_l.

Based on the upper relation, the functional (4) can be rewritten in matrix form so it collapses to

$$\mathbf{Ka} = \mathbf{F} \qquad \begin{matrix} \mathbf{K}\text{: System global stiffness matrix} \\ \mathbf{F}\text{: External load vector} \end{matrix} \qquad (6)$$

This method allows the global stiffness matrix to be composed by assembling all local stiffness matrices of the different finite elements. $\mathbf{K}$ is usually a large, sparse matrix and sophisticated libraries for efficient handling are available [9].

This approach is fundamentally different from the finite difference method where the solution is only provided at discrete shape points.

Many different types of shape functions have been proposed in the past, depending on the job they have been tailored for. We face two essential requirements for our application:

1. Topologically flexible discretization of the parameter domain in terms of irregular triangular meshes.
2. Global C^1 continuity to ensure a smooth shape for further rendering.

This leads directly to C^1 shape functions over barycentric coordinates. Although these types of finite elements can be found in [17], there is no ready-to-use recipe for how to construct them. For this reason, we explain our construction scheme in detail below.

3.2 Globally C^1 Continuous Shape Functions

The globally C^1 continuous shape functions can be derived from the very popular $\mathbf{N}^9$ shape functions. Let r, s, t define a barycentric coordinate system with $r + s + t = 1$. The following 9 DOF polynomial elements $N_1, \ldots, N_9$ independently fix the nodal displacements and derivatives along the triangle edges, according to Figure 9. $N_1, \ldots, N_3$ are given by Hermite type polynomials (7) All other $N_4, \ldots, N_9$ can be computed by cyclic shifting of r, s, and t.

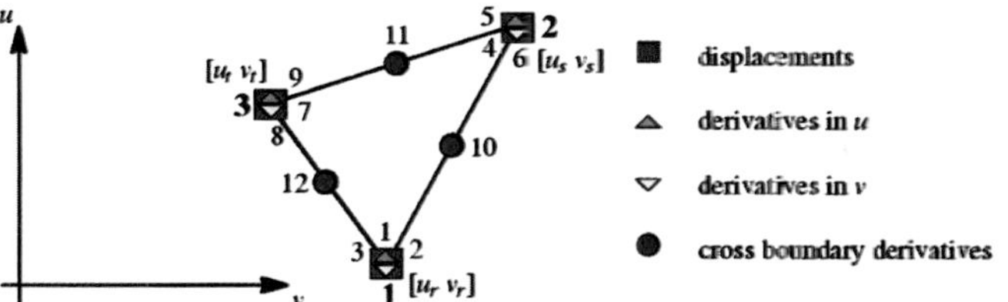

Figure 9: Indices of shape functions which control the nodal displacements and all derivatives.

$$\begin{aligned} N_1 &= r + r^2 s + r^2 t - rs^2 - rt^2 \\ N_2 &= r^2 s + \tfrac{1}{2} rst \\ N_3 &= r^2 t + \tfrac{1}{2} rst \\ N_{10} &= \tfrac{r^2 s^2 t(1+t)}{(r+t)(s+t)} \end{aligned} \tag{7}$$

In order to achieve global C^1-continuity, we have to control the cross boundary derivative of two adjacent triangular patches without influencing the other DOFs. This can be accomplished by extending the initial set of shape functions with the polynomials N_{10}, N_{11}, and N_{12}. They only influence the cross boundary derivative of the respective edge. Figure 10 shows how N_1, N_2, N_3, and N_{10} affect the displacement and boundary derivatives of node r.

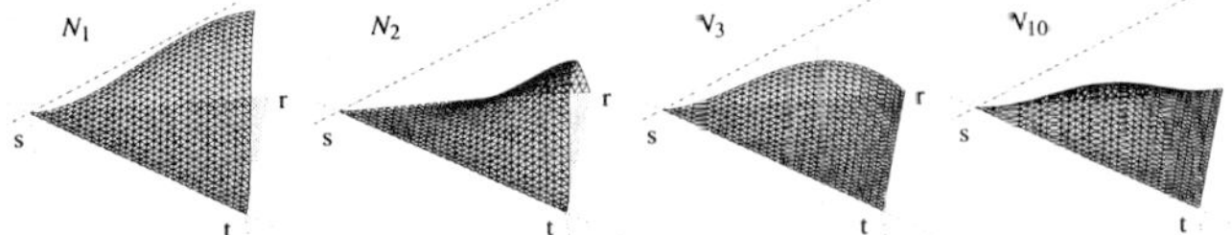

Figure 10: Illustration of the fundamental shape functions N_1, N_2, N_3, and N_{10} to control the displacements and derivatives.

Unfortunately, the cross boundary derivatives of our initial set of C^0 bases do not vanish. Therefore, it is necessary to correct these contributions. This correction is performed by evaluating the derivatives of the $N_1, \ldots, N_9$ shape functions normal to all triangle edges rs, st, and tr in the underlying global (u, v) parameter space. Let m_i^{rs} be the derivative of the shape function N_i normal to edge rs. We can define a modified set of shape functions $\bar{N}_i$ whose cross boundary derivatives vanish. This is done by correcting them with appropriate weighted sums of the functions $N_{10}, \ldots, N_{12}$.

$$\bar{N}_i = N_i - 8\Delta \left(\frac{N_{10} m_i^{rs}}{len_{rs}} + \frac{N_{11} m_i^{st}}{len_{st}} + \frac{N_{12} m_i^{tr}}{len_{tr}} \right) \tag{8}$$

The upper correction term is influenced by twice the triangular area Δ, by the individual lengths of the edges ($len_{rs}, len_{st}, len_{tr}$), and by a factor of 4 which is the inverse of the derivative values of N_{10}, N_{11}, and N_{12} at the edge midpoints.

Additional effort has to be spent to take into account the actual orientation of the triangular patch in the global surface coordinate system. The detailed description of the computation of m_i is beyond the scope of this paper but can be found in [2].

Now the definition of the final set of globally C^1 continuous shape functions ϕ_i is straightforward:

$$\begin{aligned} \phi_1 &= \bar{N}_1 & \phi_7 &= \bar{N}_7 \\ \phi_2 &= (c_3 \bar{N}_2 - c_2 \bar{N}_3) 2\Delta & \phi_8 &= (c_2 \bar{N}_8 - c_1 \bar{N}_9) 2\Delta \\ \phi_3 &= (-b_3 \bar{N}_2 + b_2 \bar{N}_3) 2\Delta & \phi_9 &= (-b_2 \bar{N}_8 + b_1 \bar{N}_9) 2\Delta \\ \phi_4 &= \bar{N}_4 & \phi_{10} &= sig_{rs} \tfrac{r^2 s^2 t(1+t)}{(r+t)(s+t)} \tfrac{2\Delta}{len_{rs}} \\ \phi_5 &= (c_1 \bar{N}_5 - c_3 \bar{N}_6) 2\Delta & \phi_{11} &= sig_{st} \tfrac{s^2 t^2 r(1+r)}{(s+r)(t+r)} \tfrac{2\Delta}{len_{st}} \\ \phi_6 &= (-b_1 \bar{N}_5 - b_3 \bar{N}_6) 2\Delta & \phi_{12} &= sig_{tr} \tfrac{t^2 r^2 s(1+s)}{(t+s)(r+s)} \tfrac{2\Delta}{len_{tr}} \end{aligned} \tag{9}$$

We require

$$\begin{aligned} a_1 &= u_s v_t - u_t v_s \\ b_1 &= v_s - v_t \\ c_1 &= u_t - u_s \end{aligned} \tag{10}$$

and for the sig operator which is incorporated in $\phi_{10}, \ldots, \phi_{12}$

if $(u_r - u_s = 0)$ {
  if $(v_r - v_s > 0)$ $sig_{rs} := 1$; **else** $sig_{rs} := -1$;
}
else {
  if $(u_r - u_s > 0)$ $sig_{rs} := 1$; **else** $sig_{rs} := -1$;
}

and finally get all other a_i, b_i, c_i, sig_{st}, and sig_{tr} by cyclic shift of the indices.

For each edge shared by two triangular patches we have to find a unique definition of the sign of their normal direction. This is necessary for the assembling step in the finite element system and is taken into account during the transformation of the shape function from the local barycentric coordinate system into the global cartesian coordinates.

Now, a global convention for the cross boundary normal $\mathbf{n}$ can be defined via the dot product:

$$\mathbf{n} := \begin{cases} \mathbf{n} & \text{for} \quad \mathbf{n} \cdot \mathbf{v} > 0 \\ \mathbf{u} & \text{for} \quad \mathbf{n} \cdot \mathbf{v} = 0 \\ -\mathbf{n} & \text{else} \end{cases} \tag{11}$$

where $\mathbf{v}$ is the $\mathbf{v}$-axis of the surface coordinate system at the edge midpoint.

Figure 11 shows two adjacent patches e_1 and e_2. In order to keep the C^1 continuity across the common edge, the corresponding cross boundary normals $\mathbf{n}_j$ and $\mathbf{n}_k$ have to point in the same direction.

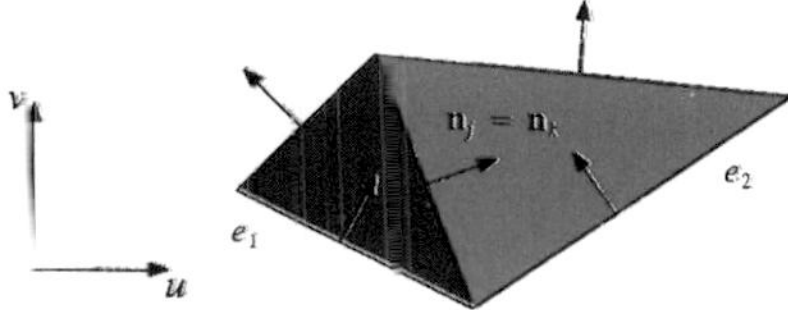

Figure 11: Orientation of cross boundary normals on two adjacent finite elements.

The set of shape functions $\phi_1, \ldots, \phi_{12}$ enables us to construct globally C^1 contiuous shapes over irregular triangular meshes. This is illustrated for a 3-patch surface with its center node displaced in the z-direction in Figures 12a-d for an increasing number of subdivisions. As the number of polygons increases, the approximation converges to a continuous shape.

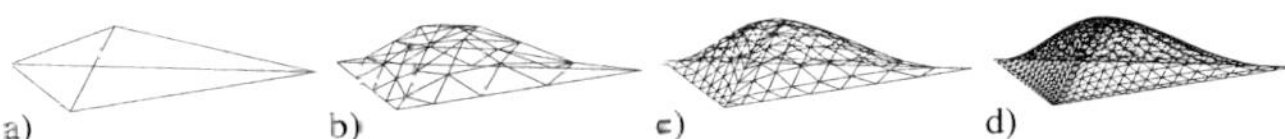

Figure 12: 3 patch element whose center node is displaced. a) Underlying triangular mesh. b), c), d) Approximations using 4, 8, and 16 edge subdivisions.

The final shape is determined by the weighted sum of the $\phi_1, \ldots, \phi_{12}$, as in (5). Due to the parametric approach, an individual ϕ_i has vector-related weights and the resulting weighting vector $\mathbf{a}$ has 36 entries:

$$\mathbf{a} = \left[\mathbf{w}_{\phi_1}, \mathbf{w}_{\phi_2}, \ldots, \mathbf{w}_{\phi_8}, \mathbf{w}_{\phi_9}, \mathbf{w}_{\phi_{10}}, \mathbf{w}_{\phi_{11}}, \mathbf{w}_{\phi_{12}} \right]^T \tag{12}$$

3.3 Computation of Local and Global Stiffness

As explained earlier, the central idea of the finite element approach is to approximate the global solution of the energy functional by piecewise shapes which are represented by linear combinations of the shape functions. Let $\mathbf{a}_e$ be the weight vector of a single finite element e and $\Phi_e = (\phi_1, \ldots, \phi_{12})^T$ be the corresponding vector of the shape functions. We obtain the fractional energy of an individual patch $\mathbf{E}_e$ by

$$\begin{aligned} \mathbf{E}_e = &\int_{\Omega_e} \mathbf{a}_e^T \left(\Phi_{e,str}^T \alpha \Phi_{e,str} + \Phi_{e,ben}^T \beta \Phi_{e,ben} \right) \mathbf{a}_e \, d\Omega_e \\ &- 2 \int_{\Omega_e} \mathbf{f}^T \Phi_e \mathbf{a}_e \, d\Omega_e \end{aligned} \tag{13}$$

Since $\mathbf{a}_e$ is constant over e, we are able to reformulate (13) as

$$\mathbf{E}_e = \mathbf{a}_e^T \mathbf{K}_e \mathbf{a}_e - 2\mathbf{F}_e \mathbf{a}_e \tag{14}$$

where $\mathbf{K}_e$ und $\mathbf{F}_e$ represent the local patch stiffness matrix and the external load vector

$$\mathbf{K}_e = \int_{\Omega_e} \left(\mathbf{\Phi}_{e,str}^T \alpha \mathbf{\Phi}_{e,str} + \mathbf{\Phi}_{e,ben}^T \beta \mathbf{\Phi}_{e,ben} \right) d\Omega_e \tag{15}$$

$$\mathbf{F}_e = \int_{\Omega_e} \mathbf{f}^T \mathbf{\Phi}_e \, d\Omega_e \tag{16}$$

In order to compute $\mathbf{K}_e$, it is neccessary to evaluate the first and second order derivatives $\mathbf{\Phi}_{e,str}$ and $\mathbf{\Phi}_{e,ben}$ of the $\mathbf{\Phi}_e$ related to the barycentric coordinate system. This is accomplished by a set of operators which are explained in [2].

Although it is possible to provide analytic descriptions of these derivatives they end up in very complex expressions. Hence, we use finite differences to approximate them in our current implementation. The outer integral of the stiffness matrix is calculated by Gaussian quadrature.

The last step of the finite element approach is to assemble the local stiffness matrices and force vectors into a global system of equations, according to (6). Therefore, all local matrices and vectors are superimposed in accordance to their topological relations.

4 Computational Surgery

This section explains additional computations, constraints, parameters, and boundary conditions neccessary to accomplish facial surgery simulations. A fundamental precondition is the definition of the boundary conditions of the finite element shape in terms of rigid and non-rigid nodes. Furthermore, we have to assign different stretching and bending tensors for each local finite element to compute the local stiffness matrices. The computation of the initial shape vector itself has to be performed in advance because it can be considered an initial equilibrium state of the shape. Nodal displacement forces applied onto the finite elements are due to the tissue springs attached to the skull.

4.1 Boundary Conditions

For all finite element approximations of differential equations, the boundary conditions are fundamental. Boundary conditions define a unique solution and diminish the overall degree of freedom. Figure 13 illustrates the influence of different boundary conditions on the final shape for a simple 32 patch surface. Although the same external force vector is applied, due to the different boundary conditions at the four boundaries (depicted in red), the resulting shapes are not equal. Note that the boundary conditions are set both for nodal displacements and for all derivatives.

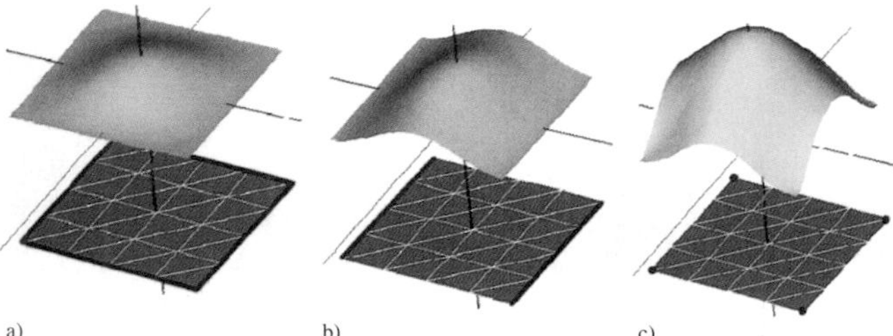

a) b) c)

Figure 13: Different boundary conditions (red) and their influence on a simple shape under the presence of the same external load vector. a) All edges fixed. b) Vertical edges fixed. c) Corner vertices only fixed.

The same situation holds for the facial skin surface. A careful definition of the boundary conditions is critical to a satisfying solution and helps to enhance computational performance by lowering the dimensionality of the global stiffness matrix. Since in facial surgery most procedures affect only parts of the facial shape, we explicitly define displacement conditions. A distinction between *rigid* and *non-rigid* nodes is proposed, i.e. only non-rigid nodes can be displaced during the FEM computation. This is very effective because even in very complicated cases, backside, neck, and hair do not change dramatically in shape.

For users' convenience we define the whole set of boundary conditions in terms of binary texture maps on the facial shape, as shown in Figure 14a. The red regions are non-rigid, the blue ones are rigid. The texture map itself can be generated with an interactive paint program, for instance *Alias Paint*. In Figure 14c a typical deformation of the facial shape is presented in accordance with the boundary conditions set in Figure 14a and the nodal displacement forces indicated as blue lines in Figure 14b.

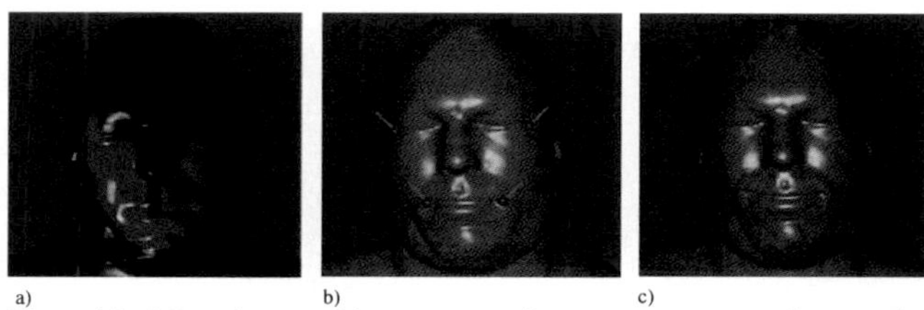

a) b) c)

Figure 14: a) Boundary conditions represented as a texture map onto the range data (blue: rigid nodes, red: non-rigid nodes). b) Interactive definition of nodal forces. c) Deformation of the facial shape in accordance with the boundary conditions on the left.

4.2 Stretching and Bending Parameters

Similar to the spring stiffness, the stretching and bending tensors may change their values for different regions of the face. More specifically, facial skin stiffness is a function of age, sex, weight, and other parameters [4]. Higher values lead to higher internal energy of a deformed surface patch, thus giving rigid parts of the face high α and β values. Changing the stretching and bending parameters influences the size of the deformed facial region and the displacement of individual surface nodes if a loading force is applied.

An interactive paint procedure is also used to assign stretching and bending parameters of different regions of the face. A well-suited facial segmentation algorithm for the automatic setting of facial stretching and bending parameters can be found in [6]. For all computations in this paper, the parameters were set constant over the surface of one triangular patch. Typical settings are $\alpha = 0.01$ for stretching, and $\beta = 0.02$ for the bending factor. Higher values guarantee appropriate deformations of facial regions with underlying cartilage (ears, nose). Figure 15 illustrates the variation of the surface parameters color-coded for the VHD. Darker colors indicate positive deviations and brighter colors negative deviations from the values above.

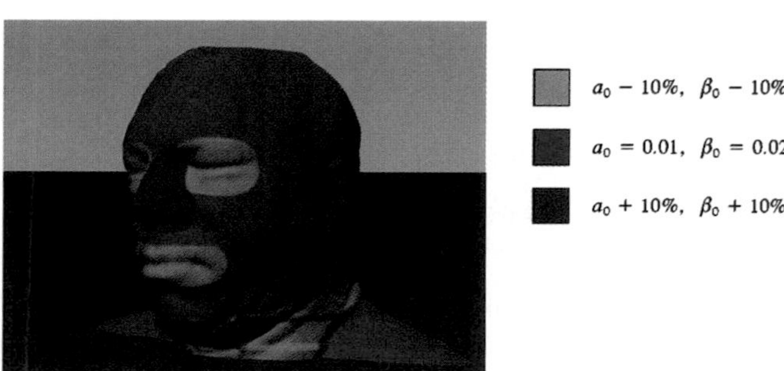

Figure 15: Variation of the stretching and bending tensors as a texture map.

4.3 Initialization

A fundamental task during a FEM modeling step of the kind we propose here is to compute the initial shape of the face from the input data. More specifically, we have to determine the initial weight vector $\mathbf{a}_{init}$ which controls the contribution of each shape function to the overall facial shape based on adaptive triangular meshes like the one in Figure 5. Conversely, once the initial weight vector is derived from the underlying data set, the FEM approach provides us with a set of *virtual nodal preloading vectors* $\mathbf{F}_{init}$, as given in (17). Although this initial preloading is inherent to the approach, it can be considered an external energy which forces the deformable surface into the initial presurgical facial shape.

$$\mathbf{F}_{init} = \mathbf{K}\mathbf{a}_{init} \tag{17}$$

In other words, the initialization of our model is a two pass process:

1. Estimation of the $\mathbf{a}_{init}$ weight vector from the initial facial surface.
2. Computation of the preload vector $\mathbf{F}_{init}$.

The estimation of $\mathbf{a}_{init}$ can be carried out as follows: The displacement vectors $\mathbf{w}_{\phi_1}$, $\mathbf{w}_{\phi_4}$, and $\mathbf{w}_{\phi_7}$ are given immediately from the vertex positions of the triangular mesh. Any nodal derivative vector in (u, v) direction $\mathbf{w}_{\phi_2}$, $\mathbf{w}_{\phi_3}$, $\mathbf{w}_{\phi_5}$, $\mathbf{w}_{\phi_6}$, $\mathbf{w}_{\phi_8}$, and $\mathbf{w}_{\phi_9}$ as well as any cross boundary derivative vector $\mathbf{w}_{\phi_{10}}$, $\mathbf{w}_{\phi_{11}}$, and $\mathbf{w}_{\phi_{12}}$ at the midpoints of the triangle edges are computed using the approximated surface normals $\mathbf{n}_{uv}$ at the coordinates (u, v). $\mathbf{n}_{uv}$ is computed by averaging the normals of adjacent triangles. For a given normal vector $\mathbf{n}_{uv}$, the slope vectors in u and v direction can be approximated as follows:

$$\begin{aligned}\frac{\partial \mathbf{w}(u,v)}{\partial u} &\approx \frac{\mathbf{a}_{cyl} \times \mathbf{n}_{uv}}{\left\|\mathbf{a}_{cyl} \times \mathbf{n}_{uv}\right\|} \\ \frac{\partial \mathbf{w}(u,v)}{\partial v} &\approx \frac{\frac{\partial \mathbf{w}(u,v)}{\partial u} \times \mathbf{n}_{uv}}{\left\|\frac{\partial \mathbf{w}(u,v)}{\partial u} \times \mathbf{n}_{uv}\right\|}\end{aligned} \tag{18}$$

where $\mathbf{a}_{cyl}$ is the rotation axis of the underlying cylindrical coordinate system. The cross boundary slopes at the edge midpoints are derived as (19).

$$\begin{aligned}\mathbf{w}_{\phi_{10}} &\approx sig \frac{\mathbf{e}_{rs} \times \mathbf{n}_{uv}}{\|\mathbf{e}_{rs} \times \mathbf{n}_{uv}\|} \\ \mathbf{w}_{\phi_{11}} &\approx sig \frac{\mathbf{e}_{st} \times \mathbf{n}_{uv}}{\|\mathbf{e}_{st} \times \mathbf{n}_{uv}\|} \\ \mathbf{w}_{\phi_{12}} &\approx sig \frac{\mathbf{e}_{tr} \times \mathbf{n}_{uv}}{\|\mathbf{e}_{tr} \times \mathbf{n}_{uv}\|}\end{aligned} \tag{19}$$

where sig are the respective signs to guarantee condition (11), and $\mathbf{e}_{rs}$, $\mathbf{e}_{st}$, and $\mathbf{e}_{tr}$ are vectors pointing in the edge direction.

Figure 16a illustrates the estimated derivatives encoded as small lines of different colors around the nose and mouth. The resulting FEM shape is presented in Figure 16b, where the shape functions are subdivided by 2.

a) 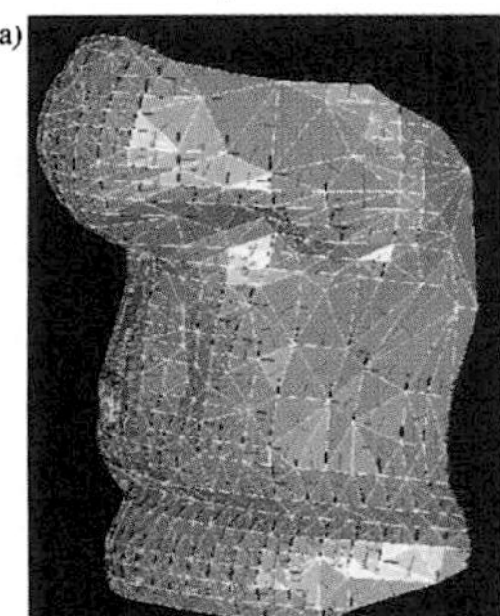 b) 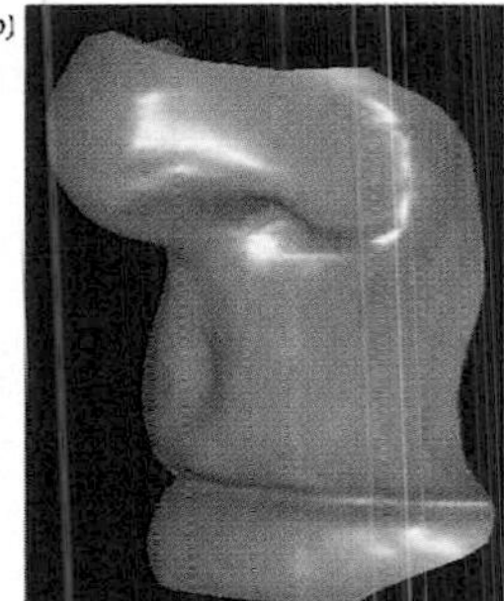

Figure 16: Triangulated part of the facial skin (nose). a) The nodal derivatives in $\mathbf{u}, \mathbf{v}$ direction are represented in red and blue and the cross boundary derivatives are shown in green. b) Initial shape as a result of the precomputation step.

4.4 Repositioning of Bones: Computation of Nodal Loading Forces

We perform any surgical procedure on the skull as a geometric modeling step with *Alias*. The skull used for surgery is shown in Figure 17a. As stated earlier, the initial facial mesh is projected along the normals of every surface vertex onto the skull. This provides a mesh on the skull surface which is topologically identical to the skin mesh, as in Figure 17b. This skull has many artifacts arising from the underlying generation method. The jaw bone is marked in a different color and will be repositioned subsequently.

After surgery on the skull the translations $\mathbf{t}^i$ and $\mathbf{t}^{\text{neighbor}(i)}$ of the spring-related skull attachment points at position $\mathbf{x}_b^i$ and $\mathbf{x}_b^{\text{neighbor}(i)}$ have to be computed. This is performed by matching the affected regions of the skull in Figure 17b with the model in Figure 17c. The result of this procedure is illustrated in Figure 17d.

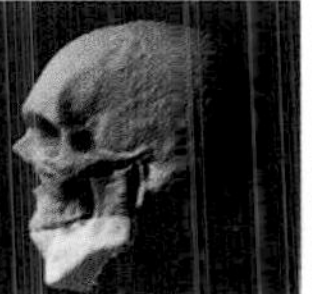  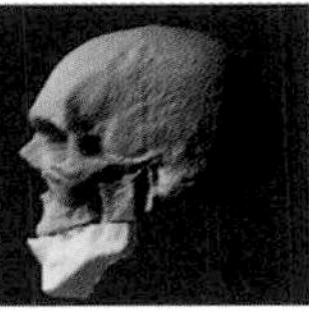 

a) b) c) d)

Figure 17: Maxillofacial surgery on the skull. a) Initial model of the presurgical skull. b) Skin vertices projected onto the skull. c) Final skull after repositioning of the jaw bone. d) Projected vertices for c).

Any deformation of the skull generates a force $\mathbf{f}_{def,i}$ on the surface node $\mathbf{x}_s^i$ which influences the energy equilibrium (13) between the internal energy of the surface and the preloading energy described in the former section. $\mathbf{f}_{def,i}$ is computed as follows:

$$\mathbf{f}_{def,i} = k_c k_i \sum_{j \in S_i} \frac{\mathbf{s}_{ij} - \mathbf{t}^j}{\|\mathbf{s}_{ij} - \mathbf{t}^j\|} c_{ij} \left(\|\mathbf{s}_{ij}\| - \|\mathbf{s}_{ij} - \mathbf{t}^j\| \right) \tag{20}$$

Vertex indices are equal for related skin and skull nodes.

$\mathbf{f}_{def,i}$	Deformation force at skin vertex i as a result of a deformation of the skull.
k_c	Force scaling constant.
k_i	Mesh dependent scaling factor.
S_i	Set of skull nodes for all springs attached at vertex i on the skin.
$\mathbf{s}_{ij}$	Spring connecting skin vertex i at position $\mathbf{x}_s^i$ with skull vertex j at position $\mathbf{x}_b^j$, i.e. $\mathbf{x}_s^i - \mathbf{x}_b^j$.
$\mathbf{t}^j$	Translation vector of the skull vertex j as a result of a surgery on the skull.
c_{ij}	Stiffness of spring $\mathbf{s}_{ij}$.

The mesh dependent scaling factor k_i is defined by

$$k_i = \sum_{j \in P_i} \Delta_j \tag{21}$$

where P_i is the set of all triangles containing node i, and Δ_j the area of the mesh triangle j. Figure 18 illustrates the upper relations for a particular node i.

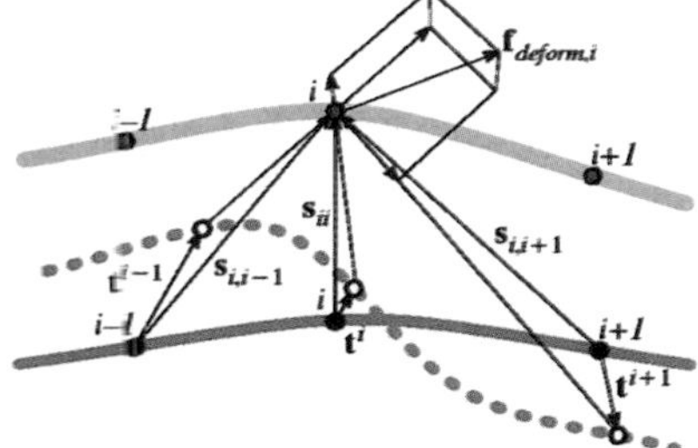

Figure 18: Computation of the nodal loading forces.

The deformation energy of the facial surface is derived from the nodal displacement forces as follows:

$$\mathbf{F}_{def} = \int_{\Omega} \mathbf{f}_{def}^T \boldsymbol{\Phi} \, d\Omega \tag{22}$$

4.5 Solving the Global System

The external energy vector $\mathbf{F}_{ext}$ is computed by superimposing the nodal preloading energy $\mathbf{F}_{init}$ with the deformation energy $\mathbf{F}_{def}$.

The global energy equilibrium can be reformulated for the resulting shape vector $\mathbf{a}_{result}$ by

$$\mathbf{K}\mathbf{a}_{result} = \mathbf{F}_{init} + \mathbf{F}_{def} \tag{23}$$

It is recommended to carry out the simulation in small steps, including the recalculation of the patch stiffnesses of all patches affected in the last step.

5 Results

The goal was to predict the facial shape after standard procedures in craniomaxillo facial surgery. Figures 19a-c show the shapes of the skull and face before and after an osteotomy and advancement of the lower jaw bone. These pictures represent the corresponding deformations of skin in profile and frontal view. Obviously, the surgical procedure strongly affects the appearance of the face. This is even more striking in Figures 19d-f where an osteotomy and advancement of the upper jaw bone is presented. All computations are based on the methods described above. The pictures are rendered with *Alias*.

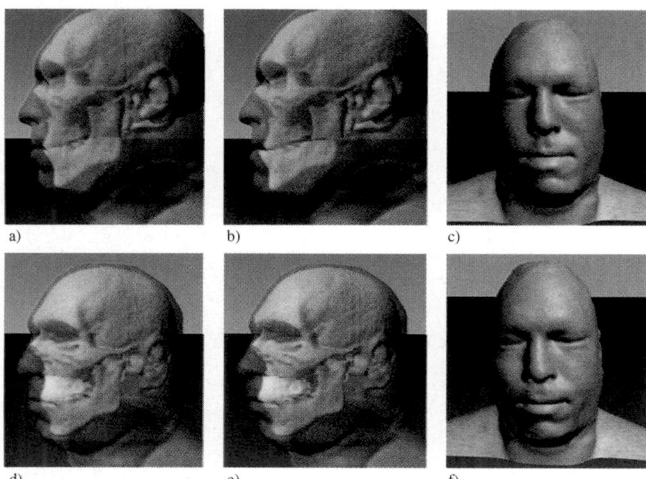

Figure 19: Results on the VHD. a), b), and c) Profiles and frontal view before and after advancement of the lower jaw. d), e), and f) Situation before and after surgery on the upper jaw.

The affected facial region of the first surgical procedure comprises about 3.1k triangles. The computation of the global stiffness matrix took approximately 17 minutes, the solving of the global equation system 11 minutes. The calculations were carried out on a *SGI Indigo*^{2}, R4400, 200MHz, 192MB.

6 Discussion and Future Work

We present a system which enables us to predict deformations of the facial shape after surgical procedures. Our prototype system uses commercial tools for geometric modeling and rendering. In contrast to existing approaches in physically based modeling of facial shapes, our approach is based on non-linear finite elements, and therefore provides a continuous approximation of the facial geometry. We consider our approach to be a significant extension in this field because we build the model on both laser range scans and CT volume data. This enables us to compute individual physical parameters. Some results achieved with our system are demonstrated using the VHD.

We are aware that some processing steps presented here are specific to the underlying data. Usually neither high resolution CT scans comparable to the VHD, nor photo slices are available. With future generations of MR and CT scanners, however, we expect that both facial surface and skull of the patient will be available at sufficient resolutions to make range scans obsolete.

Our future research is directed towards true 3D volume FEM systems based on tetrahedralizations. They would integrate both the current surface and volume spring model and allow incorporation of more anatomic features. In this case, the global C^1 constraint could be relaxed and replaced by local continuity properties. Further effort has to be spent on our current geometric model of skull and skin, which is based on polygons. It is clear that polysets perform worse than NURB representations and do not guarantee lossless data conversions between the FEM system and *Alias*. Other important topics are incompressible finite elements which can cope with the problem of wrinkles. The current rendering quality has to be enhanced with using texture maps and better reflection models for facial skin. Sophisticated models, such as in [7], have to be investigated for suitability. Finally, our goal is to carry out a case study with individual patients of different ages, genders and ethnic origins and to compare the computed results with those achieved by actual surgery. We expect also that an error quantification would help us to improve the model towards better performance.

7 Acknowledgement

The authors would like to thank Caroline Westort for her native-english review of the text.

References

[1] CANNY, J. F. A computational approach to edge detection. *IEEE Transactions on Pattern Analysis and Machine Intelligence 8*, 6 (1986), pp. 679–697.

[2] CELNIKER, G., AND GOSSARD, D. Deformable curve and surface finite elements for free-form shape design. In *Computer Graphics (SIGGRAPH '91 Proceedings)* (July 1991), ACM SIGGRAPH, T. W. Sederberg, Ed., vol. 25, pp. 257–266.

[3] DREBIN, R. A., CARPENTER, L., AND HANRAHAN, P. Volume rendering. In *Computer Graphics (SIGGRAPH '88 Proceedings)* (Aug. 1988), ACM SIGGRAPH, J. Dill, Ed., vol. 22, pp. 65–74.

[4] FARKAS, L. G. *Anthropometry of the Head and Face*, second ed. Raven Press, 1994.

[5] GROSS, M. H., GATTI, R., AND STAADT, O. Fast multiresolution surface meshing. In *Proceedings of IEEE Visualization '95* (1995), IEEE Computer Society Press, pp. 135–142.

[6] GROSS, M. H., AND KOCH, R. Visualization of multidimensional shape and texture features in laser range data using complex-valued Gabor wavelets. *IEEE Transactions on Visualization and Computer Graphics 1*, 1 (Mar. 1995), pp. 44–59. ISSN 1077-2626.

[7] HANRAHAN, P., AND KRUEGER, W. Reflection from layered surfaces due to subsurface scattering. In *Computer Graphics (SIGGRAPH '93 Proceedings)* (Aug. 1993), ACM SIGGRAPH, J. T. Kajiya, Ed., vol. 27, pp. 165–174.

[8] HARALICK, R. M., AND SHAPIRO, L. G. *Computer and Robot Vision*, vol. 1–3. Addison-Wesley, 1992.

[9] KUNDERT, K. S., AND SANGIOVANNI-VINCENTELLI, A. *A Sparse Linear Equation Solver.* Dept. of Electrical Engineering and Computer Sciences, University of California, Berkeley, 1988.

[10] LEE, Y., TERZOPOULOS, D., AND WATERS, K. Realistic face modeling for animation. In *Computer Graphics (SIGGRAPH '95 Proceedings)* (Aug. 1995), ACM SIGGRAPH, R. Cook, Ed., vol. 29, pp. 55–62.

[11] NATIONAL LIBRARY OF MEDICINE. *The Visible Human Project.* http://www.nlm.nih.gov/extramural_research.dir/visible_human.html, 1995.

[12] PARKE, F. I. Parameterized models for facial animation. *IEEE Computer Graphics and Applications 2* (Nov. 1982), pp. 61–68.

[13] SCHROEDER, W. J., ZARGE, J. A., AND LORENSEN, W. E. Decimation of triangle meshes. In *Computer Graphics (SIGGRAPH '92 Proceedings)* (Aug.1992), ACM SIGGRAPH, E. E. Catmull, Ed., pp. 65–70.

[14] VAN GELDER, A., AND WILHELMS, J. Topological considerations in isosurface generation. Tech. Rep. UCSC-CRL-94-31, Baskin Center for Computer Engineering and Information Sciences, University of California, Santa Cruz, 1994.

[15] VANNIER, M. W., PILGRAM, T., BHATIA, G., BRUNSDEN, B., AND COMMEAN, P. Facial surface scanner. *IEEE Computer Graphics and Applications 11*, 6 (Nov. 1991), pp. 72–80.

[16] WATERS, K. A muscle model for animating three-dimensional facial expression. In *Computer Graphics (SIGGRAPH '87 Proceedings)* (July 1987), ACM SIGGRAPH, M. C. Stone, Ed., vol. 21, pp. 17–24.

[17] ZIENKIEWICZ, O. C. *The Finite Element Method*, fourth ed., vol. 1–2. McGraw-Hill, 1994.

Superior Augmented Reality Registration by Integrating Landmark Tracking and Magnetic Tracking

Andrei State, Gentaro Hirota, David T. Chen, William F. Garrett, Mark A. Livingston

Department of Computer Science
University of North Carolina at Chapel Hill

http://www.cs.unc.edu/~us/hybrid.html

ABSTRACT

Accurate registration between real and virtual objects is crucial for augmented reality applications. Existing tracking methods are individually inadequate: magnetic trackers are inaccurate, mechanical trackers are cumbersome, and vision-based trackers are computationally problematic. We present a hybrid tracking method that combines the accuracy of vision-based tracking with the robustness of magnetic tracking without compromising real-time performance or usability. We demonstrate excellent registration in three sample applications.

CR Categories and Subject Descriptors: I.3.7 [Three-Dimensional Graphics and Realism]: *Virtual Reality*, I.3.1: [Hardware Architecture]: *Three-dimensional displays*, I.3.6 [Methodology and Techniques]: *Interaction techniques*.

Additional Keywords and Phrases: Augmented reality, stereo video see-through head-mounted display, frame buffer techniques, registration, calibration.

1 MOTIVATION

While the advent of Head-Mounted Displays (HMDs) and affordable real-time computer graphics engines has given rise to much research in the field of Virtual Reality (VR), comparatively little work has been done in the closely-related field of Augmented Reality (AR). A VR system immerses the user in a totally synthetic, computer-generated environment. An AR system, on the other hand, merges computer-synthesized objects with the user's space in the real world. Synthetic objects enhance the user's interaction with, or his perception of, the real world [Azuma95].

The following are typical requirements for an AR system:

(1) Accurate registration between synthetic and real objects: a virtual object should appear at its proper place in the real world, otherwise the user cannot correctly determine spatial relationships. Dynamic registration is particularly important when the user moves around the environment. The relative position between real and synthetic objects should be constant.

(2) Reasonable image generation rate (10 Hz) and stereopsis: these are important for good depth perception. The lack of kinetic or stereoscopic depth cues greatly reduces the believability of an augmented environment.

(3) Simple initial set up procedure: users of AR applications should not have to be familiar with the specific techniques used in AR systems.

(4) Minimal constraint on user motion: in most applications, the user wants to move without restriction.

(5) Low latency: minimal delay between the user's movement and the display update is required for smooth and effective interaction.

Among these requirements, the accurate registration turns out to be a very difficult problem. Current AR systems cannot convincingly meet this requirement. Typically a virtual object appears to swim about as the user moves, and often does not appear to rest at the same spot when viewed from several different positions.

In current AR systems, most of these registration errors are due to the limitations of the tracking systems [Holloway95] No conventional tracker satisfies all of the above requirements.

2 PREVIOUS WORK

There has been much research in the field of tracking and registration. Most tracking systems used today in fully immersive VR systems have been magnetic. In the field of computer vision there is a wealth of research on motion tracking.

Today's magnetic trackers are subject to large amounts of error and jitter. An uncalibrated system can exhibit errors of 10 cm or more, particularly in the presence of magnetic field disturbances such as metal and electric equipment. Carefully calibrating a magnetic system can reduce position errors to within 2 cm [Livingston95]. Despite their lack of accuracy, magnetic trackers are popular because they are robust and place minimal constraints on user motion.

Other AR systems have used mechanical [Sutherland68] or optical [Ward92, Azuma94] tracking systems. Both of these systems generally have better accuracy than magnetic trackers, but are burdensome. Mechanical systems tether the user and have a limited working volume, and the optical tracker in [Ward92] requires four dedicated tracking cameras mounted on the user's HMD.

In a video see-through AR system [Azuma95], video images of the user's view are always available. Using those images to track the camera's position and orientation should be

CB #3175 Sitterson Hall, Chapel Hill, NC 27599-3175. Tel: +1-919-962-1700.
E-mail: {state, hirota, chen, garrett, livingst}@cs.unc.edu

a reasonable approach, and camera tracking has been extensively investigated in the field of computer vision or photogrammetry. Nevertheless, recovering 3D information from 2D images is not an easy task. An intrinsic problem of computer vision is that an almost infinite number of possibilities must be considered until the images can be interpreted correctly.

Model-based vision assumes a priori knowledge of the 3D geometry of visible objects, reducing the problem from shape recovery to mere camera motion tracking [Lowe87, Lowe92]. Even by simplifying the problem this way, model-based vision methods must still extract object features from images. This typically requires special-purpose image processing hardware to achieve real-time updates. Further acceleration can be achieved through the use of fiducials or landmarks. These artificial "features" of objects simplify image analysis.

The advantage of vision-based tracking when applied to video-see-through AR is that it uses the very same image on which synthetic objects are overlaid. Therefore nearly perfect registration can be achieved under certain conditions [Mellor95, Uenohara95].

The problem of vision-based methods is their instability; to save computation cost, they make numerous assumptions about the working environment and the user's movements, but those assumptions are often impractical. For example, they usually assume temporal coherence of camera movement in order to avoid frequent use of costly search algorithms [Faugeras86, Grimson90] that establish the correspondence between image features and model features. Thus, they usually cannot keep up with quick, abrupt user movements. No vision-based tracker reliably deals with the occlusion of features caused by deformable objects (e.g. hands). Once a vision tracker's assumptions fail, the results can be catastrophic.

Computationally, most vision-based methods use iterative minimization techniques that rely on frame-to-frame coherence. Linearization reduces the problem to a single global solution but requires the vision-based tracker to extract a relatively large amount of information from features or landmarks [Mellor95].

Since image analysis and correspondence finding are costly and error-prone, and because landmarks can be occluded, obscured, or may disappear from the camera's view at any time, it is impractical to attempt to continuously track a large number of features in real time.

3 CONTRIBUTION

We have developed a hybrid tracking scheme which has the registration accuracy of vision-based tracking systems and the robustness of magnetic tracking systems.

We use video tracking of landmarks as the primary method for determining camera position and orientation. This tracking method inherits the accuracy of some vision-based methods, but avoids unnecessary computational cost and reduces the demands on the image analyzer.

Color-coding the landmarks helps the system to quickly identify and distinguish between landmarks. This not only eases system setup and improves performance but also lets the system handle abrupt user movement.

A global non-linear equation solver and a local least square minimizer are used to reduce the burden on the image analyzer. Typically 3 landmarks suffice to determine camera position and orientation. Our formulation gives a universal solution for single and stereo camera cases.

The result of the vision-based tracker is also used for on-the-fly calibration of the magnetic tracker, which assists the rest of the system in four different ways:

Image analysis acceleration: The magnetic tracker helps narrow the landmark search area on images, speeding up the landmark search process.

Selection from multiple solutions: Information from the magnetic tracker is often used to select one of several solutions of a non-linear equation.

Backup tracking: the magnetic tracker acts as the primary tracker if the image analyzer cannot locate enough landmarks. Since the magnetic tracker is *locally calibrated* on-the-fly, we avoid complete loss of registration. If 1 or 2 landmarks (not enough for a unique solution) are detected, several *heuristic methods* are used to minimize registration loss.

Sanity check of the vision-based tracker: As mentioned above, vision-based tracking is sometimes unstable. We avoid catastrophic failure by monitoring the difference between results from the magnetic tracker and the vision-based tracker and discarding corrections that exceed a certain magnitude.

4 SYSTEM HARDWARE

All principal components of our system are commercial, off-the-shelf devices. Our system consists of:

- a Virtual Research VR-4 HMD.
- two Panasonic GP-KS102 CCD video cameras with Cosmicar F1.8 12.5 mm lenses (28° field of view, selected for minimal optical distortion), attached to the HMD.
- an Ascension Flock of Birds™ magnetic tracker with Extended Range Transmitter; the magnetic tracking sensor is attached to the HMD.
- a Silicon Graphics Onyx™ RealityEngine^2™ graphics workstation equipped with a Sirius Video™ real-time video capture device (Sirius), and a Multi-Channel Option™.

The HMD-mounted cameras are 64 mm apart—a typical interpupillary distance for humans—and are oriented with a convergence angle of 4° for sufficient stereo overlap in a tabletop working environment. This angle was chosen for one of our driving applications [State96], which involves manipulation directly in front of the user.

The Sirius captures stereo video images from the head-mounted cameras in real-time and transfers the images to the graphics frame buffer of the RealityEngine^2.

5 SYSTEM OVERVIEW

The hybrid tracker analyzes sensor data from two input streams: real-time video images from the stereo cameras, and tracking reports from the magnetic tracking sensor. The system assumes that the two cameras and the tracking sensor are rigidly interconnected and are rigidly attached to the HMD and the user's head. *Head pose* will refer to the position and orientation of this rigid HMD-cameras-sensor assembly.

We assume that the geometry of this assembly is known and that the transformations between the various coordinate systems (cameras, sensor) have been determined via calibration procedures. We also assume that the world space positions of the landmarks used in the vision-based tracking algorithm are precisely calibrated. All calibration procedures are described in Section 8.

5.1 Operation

For each stereo image pair (i.e. frame), the hybrid tracker attempts to determine the head pose from the landmarks' positions in the images. If this attempt is successful, it determines an error-correcting transformation between the magnetic tracker reading and the head pose computed by the vision-based tracker. We will refer to this transformation as the *magnetic tracker error*.

The magnetic tracker error computed in one frame is used to predict the head pose in the next frame (temporal coherence). This prediction is subsequently used to compute the expected positions of the landmarks in image space. Figure 1 shows the data flow within the hybrid tracker.

At startup, the magnetic tracker error is initialized to zero. The head pose predictor therefore passes the readings from the magnetic tracker unchanged to the landmark predictor, which computes the expected image-space search areas for the landmarks. Using this data as a starting point, the image analyzer searches for landmarks in the video images.

As soon as the first landmark is detected, the head pose is adjusted via a simple heuristic to line up the detected landmark in image space [Bajura95]. The resulting adjusted head pose—in the case of a single landmark only head orientation is adjusted—is fed back to the landmark predictor for re-prediction of landmark search areas. The system uses these improved values to find additional landmarks, thus iteratively refining its knowledge about the head pose. Each time a new landmark is found, an appropriate head pose adjuster or solver is invoked, depending on the total number of landmarks detected.

There are two distinct cases:

(1) If the number of detected landmarks is not sufficient to completely determine the head pose (under-determined cases), the methods used are local, heuristic position and/or orientation adjusters (Section 7.1) such as the single-landmark method mentioned above.

(2) In well-determined and over-determined cases, a global, analytical solver is invoked (Section 7.2). This solver may compute multiple solutions, in which case a solution selector is invoked. The selector attempts to pick a solution by verifying the consistency of all detected landmarks but is not always able to determine a single best solution. In particular, we often encounter situations in which only 3 different landmarks are visible in both cameras. In such cases we use the sensor reading from the magnetic tracker to determine which solution is correct.

In all cases, under-, well- and over-determined, the computed or adjusted head poses are first subjected to sanity checks. Then they are fed back to the landmark predictor to iteratively detect additional landmarks. This continues until a maximum preset number have been found or until all landmarks in the two stereo images have been found.

The solutions resulting from well- or over-determined cases are stabilized by a local least-square optimizer. If the head pose remains under-determined even after exhaustive search for additional landmarks, the partial correction derived by the most recently invoked heuristic adjuster(s) is retained.

The magnetic tracker error (whether computed and optimized or merely partially corrected) is preserved for head pose prediction in the next frame. This constant, 0th order prediction for the magnetic tracker error is adequate given that our system's frame rates rarely exceed 15 Hz in stereo. We use higher-order prediction (linear, combining the magnetic tracker errors from the 2 most recent frames) only if the application and the tracking environment allow higher frame rates (e.g. non-stereo operation). [Azuma94] showed that higher-order prediction works best at high frame rates.

The corrected head pose delivered by the hybrid tracker yields excellent AR registration between real and virtual objects. Figure 2 shows a view within a video-see-through HMD. A tabletop model with cuboids and landmarks is accurately registered with a computer model of the cuboids (white wireframe lines).

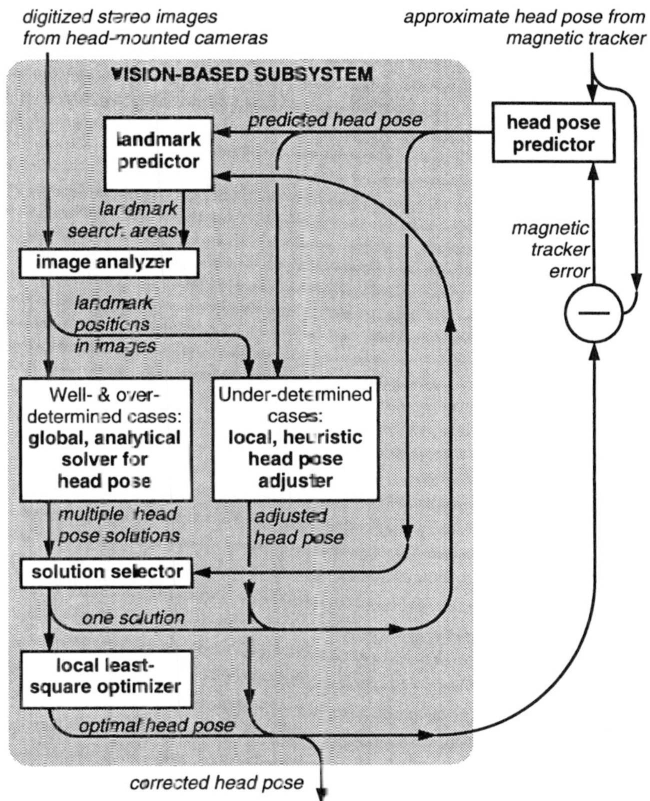

Figure 1. Data flow within the hybrid tracker.

5.2 Vision-only tracking

Vision-only tracking (i.e., without assistance from the magnetic tracker) requires only minor modifications. The predicted head pose delivered to the landmark predictor and to the heuristic adjusters is estimated directly from the head pose in the previous frame(s).

6 LANDMARK TRACKING

The image analyzer detects and tracks landmarks in the video images. Since this is the most time-consuming task in our system, its performance is a primary design concern.

6.1 Landmark shape and color

The landmarks used by the hybrid tracker are two-color concentric circular dots. Eleven such landmarks are visible in Figure 2. Each landmark consists of an inner dot and a surrounding outer ring with a diameter that is 3 times larger than the diameter of the inner dot. We use four different colors (mixed from commercial fluorescent fabric paints), which we label as red, green, blue, and yellow; thus we can create 12 unique combinations which can be recognized and identified by the landmark finder.

Color landmarks are useful in several ways. Multiple colors simplify and accelerate low-level pixel inspection, resulting in quick detection. The concentric layout makes our method very robust. While the search algorithm might be easily fooled if it were simply looking for a uniform spot of a single color (as in earlier versions of our system), the more complex structure of two-color landmarks makes spurious detection much more unlikely (Figure 3).

6.2 Operation

The landmark finding subsystem consists of two main components: the landmark predictor, which predicts where the

Figure 2. View inside the HMD while the user's head is stationary. The axis-aligned search areas accelerate landmark search. Eleven out of the 12 different landmarks created with two-color concentric rings are visible. Note accurately registered computer-generated cuboid outlines (white).

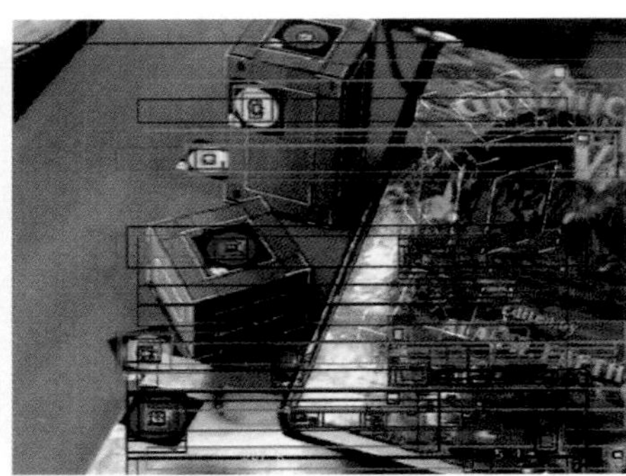

Figure 3. Maintaining registration in the presence of spurious color spots. During landmark search, only specific color and shape signatures are recognized as valid landmarks. Other color areas are inspected but rejected.

Figure 4. Maintaining registration while the user's head is in motion. Some of the landmarks were not contained within their initial search areas, so the search areas were progressively expanded. Note motion blur.

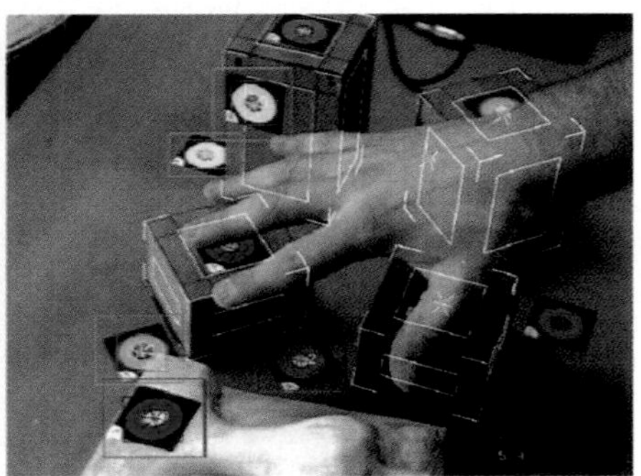

Figure 5. Correct head pose despite landmark occlusion. The landmark tracker is robust enough to handle occlusion. The design of the landmarks makes it possible to detect partial occlusion.

landmarks should be in the video camera image, and the image analyzer, which locates the landmarks in the image.

6.2.1 Landmark predictor

The main task of the landmark predictor is to compute the expected positions and extents of landmarks in image space. For each landmark, a search area is determined based upon the predicted extent. Since the image analyzer operates by exhaustive pixel searches inside search areas, it is important to keep the extents small, i.e., to "tightly" track the landmarks in image space with bounding boxes (Figure 2).

As described above, the hybrid tracker incrementally improves head pose after each newly-found landmark, increasing the accuracy of the predicted positions and predicted extents of the remaining undetected landmarks. As shown in [Bajura95], lining up a single landmark often results in dramatically improved registration. Therefore lining up the first landmark detected often yields accurate search areas for the remaining landmarks, accelerating the subsequent searches. Similar ideas can be found in computer vision literature [Lowe87, Lowe92].

When searching for the first landmark, there are no landmark-derived head pose corrections available, so it is important that the first landmark in each frame be easy to detect. This means the first landmark should have a relatively small search area, and there should be a high probability of actually finding it within that area. To this end, the landmark predictor keeps track of potentially detectable landmarks and sorts them in order of decreasing expected ease of detection. The landmark predictor uses predicted and iteratively improved head poses to compute the expected positions of the landmarks in image space. In addition to this 3D prediction, the landmark predictor performs an internal 2D image space prediction which is not based on input from the magnetic tracker, but only on detected landmarks. For each landmark, the 3D and 2D predictions are compared; if the distance between the two predicted positions is below a preset threshold or if the expected position is far enough from the edge of the image, then the landmark is assigned a high score for ease of detection.

6.2.2 Image analyzer

The second component of the landmark finder is the image analyzer, which starts its search for a landmark by inspecting the search area defined by the landmark predictor.

The first step is pixel marking. Every pixel is classified as belonging to one of the landmark colors or as belonging to no landmark based on the ratios of *RGB* component values. For our specific camera and frame grabber hardware, and under the lighting conditions in our lab, such a simple algorithm can reliably distinguish between only a small number of different colors. We use the four colors mentioned in Section 6.1.

The algorithm looks first for areas whose color matches the color of the outer ring of a concentric landmark and then attempts to locate the inner color dot within the identified area. The marked regions are segmented by horizontal and vertical signature [Haralick93] to determine their centers of mass. If a marked region does not fit inside the bounding box of the search area, the search area is enlarged (Figure 4). For large search areas, a lower sampling density of as little as 1 in 64 (8×8) pixels is used initially; the sampling density is then successively increased as the algorithm reduces the search areas while refining its estimate of the landmark's location.

For all candidate detections consisting of an outer color ring and an inner color dot, two additional tests are performed:

(1) The number of marked pixels in both the inner dot and the outer ring are determined and their ratio is computed. In our case the diameter of the outer ring is 3 times the diameter of the inner dot, so the ratio of marked pixels must be close to 3×3-1=8. If not, the candidate is rejected.

(2) If the centers of mass of the outer and inner regions are not close enough, the landmark may be partially occluded or clipped (explained below). The candidate is rejected.

For accepted candidates, the center of mass of the inner dot is taken as the center of the landmark. Using the center of only the inner dot instead of the average of the centers of the inner and outer areas is advantageous when a landmark becomes partially occluded. In such a case the outer dot will become occluded first, but as long as the landmark passes test (2), the center will be computed correctly. When the occluding object starts approaching the center dot, the center of mass of the outer ring shifts noticeably, and the candidate fails test (2) and is rejected (Figure 5). If we did not reject these landmarks, then the center would drift before the landmark disappears, corrupting the head pose solutions.

7 HEAD POSE DETERMINATION

Three cases arise when determining the head pose from landmarks. The landmarks represent a set of constraints that is under-determined, well-determined, or over-determined.

7.1 Under-determined case

Until the image analyzer detects at least three different landmarks, the head pose cannot be completely determined from landmarks alone. In these cases, the magnetic tracker is the primary source of information about head pose. A static position calibration lookup table and on-the-fly calibration for the magnetic tracker enable us to use an arsenal of heuristic correctors. These rely on the initial head position being reasonably accurate. After a first rough correction via the predicted magnetic tracker error, a local, heuristic adjustment is applied to the head pose. Different heuristic adjustment methods are used depending on the number of landmarks available.

The heuristic adjusters are designed to ensure highest possible head pose and registration accuracy even when very few landmarks have been detected. They bridge the gap between magnetic-only and vision-based operation of our system. The adjusters are designed to improve head pose as smoothly as possible while more and more landmarks are detected. As a result of this, the hybrid tracker is characterized by reluctant degradation in accuracy when landmarks are lost. When landmarks are re-acquired, the system quickly recovers.

A total of six different under-determined cases exist for our stereoscopic system. The following list describes the basic ideas behind the heuristic adjusters in each case:

(1) Camera 1 sees landmark A, camera 2 sees no landmarks. This is the simple case described and used in [Bajura95]. The method does not adjust head position; it corrects only head orientation by lining up landmark A in the view of camera 1. Only two orientation degrees of freedom can be corrected. The remaining, uncorrected orientation degree of freedom is best described as "rotation about A."

(2) Camera 1 sees two landmarks, A and B, camera 2 sees no landmarks. The method lines up both A and B in the view of camera 1 by reorienting the head. This orientation correction is preceded by a small position correction which is computed to minimize the rotation angle of the following orientation correction. In other words, the head is moved to a position from which the landmarks can be lined up by only minimally changing head orientation. In addition to the slight position adjustment, all three orientation degrees of freedom are corrected.

(3) Camera 1 sees landmark A, camera 2 sees landmark B. This case is similar to (2), except that the two landmarks appear in different camera views. The method lines up A and B in their respective camera views by reorienting the head after the initial position correction. All three orientation degrees of freedom can be corrected. Head position is adjusted slightly, similarly to (2).

(4) Camera 1 sees landmark A, camera 2 sees the same landmark A. The method computes the distance a from the head to landmark A via triangulation in the 2 camera images and adjusts head position by moving the head to the nearest point on a sphere of radius a centered at landmark A. In addition to this position adjustment, two out of the three orientation degrees of freedom can be corrected as in (1).

(5) Camera 1 sees landmarks A and B, camera 2 sees landmark A but not landmark B. This is a hybrid of the methods from (3) and (4). The method triangulates landmark A as in (4), thereby determining its distance a from the head. Then a position adjustment to minimize orientation change is applied as in (3), but with the additional constraint that the position be adjusted towards a point on the sphere of radius a, centered at landmark A's world-space position. In addition to this slight position adjustment, all three orientation degrees of freedom can be corrected as in (3).

(6) Camera 1 sees two landmarks, A and B, camera 2 sees the same two landmarks, A and B. Here the triangulation technique from (4) can be applied to both landmarks, yielding two spheres of diameters a and b, which are centered at their respective landmarks' positions in world space. The two spheres intersect in a circle. The head position is adjusted by translating the head to a point on the circle from which the 2 landmarks can be lined up in the two views by only minimally correcting head orientation. In addition to the slight position change, the three orientation degrees of freedom can be adjusted with a method similar to (2).

The above list shows all possible configurations of 1 or 2 landmarks with a binocular system. As soon as a third landmark is detected in one of the camera views, the system switches to the well-determined case described in the next section.

7.2 Well-determined case

In this section we describe the analytical methods used to determine the head pose when necessary and sufficient information is available from the image analyzer. These methods are based on global equation solvers.

7.2.1 Global solution

Let us consider the head as fixed and the world as attached to landmarks that are moving. The actual head motion can be obtained as an inverse transformation of the landmarks' motions.

We need at least 3 positions of non-collinear points to determine a rigid three-space motion. Therefore 3 non-collinear landmarks are essential. If we find 3 landmarks on the two cameras' image planes, that gives us 3 X-Y coordinate pairs. It is not difficult to see that 6 independent values are sufficient information to determine a 6-degree-of-freedom rigid motion for the head.

Figure 6 shows the geometric relationships between two cameras $\vec{C}_1$ and $\vec{C}_2$ and three landmarks $\vec{L}_1$, $\vec{L}_2$ and $\vec{L}_3$. The landmarks $\vec{L}_1$ and $\vec{L}_2$ are detected at $\vec{I}_1$ and $\vec{I}_2$ in the image of $\vec{C}_1$, and the landmark $\vec{L}_3$ is detected at $\vec{I}_3$ in the image of $\vec{C}_2$. The special case in which all three landmarks are detected by one camera can be treated as a case where $\vec{C}_1 = \vec{C}_2$. Therefore we can consider Figure 6 as the general case.

The unit direction vectors $\vec{V}_1$, $\vec{V}_2$ and $\vec{V}_3$ are obtained simply as: $\vec{V}_1 = \frac{\vec{I}_1 - \vec{C}_1}{|\vec{I}_1 - \vec{C}_1|}$, $\vec{V}_2 = \frac{\vec{I}_2 - \vec{C}_1}{|\vec{I}_2 - \vec{C}_1|}$ and $\vec{V}_3 = \frac{\vec{I}_3 - \vec{C}_2}{|\vec{I}_3 - \vec{C}_2|}$.

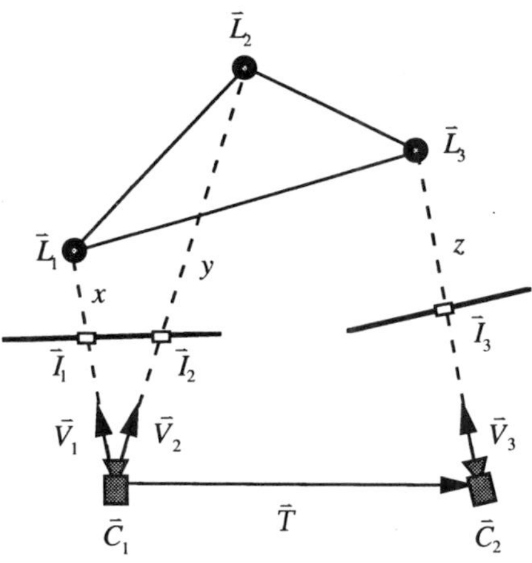

Figure 6. Geometric relationships between three landmarks and the two stereo cameras.

The triangle $\bar{L}_1$-$\bar{L}_2$-$\bar{L}_3$ is undergoing a rigid motion, hence we do not know where it is. But, since we know the positions of $\bar{L}_1$, $\bar{L}_2$ and $\bar{L}_3$ from landmark calibration (Section 8), we can compute the lengths of the 3 edges. They are:

$$L_{12} = |\bar{L}_2 - \bar{L}_1|,\ L_{23} = |\bar{L}_3 - \bar{L}_2| \text{ and } L_{31} = |\bar{L}_1 - \bar{L}_3|.$$

Since both cameras are rigidly mounted on the head set, $\bar{T} = \bar{C}_2 - \bar{C}_1$ is also a constant measured through static calibration (Section 8).

Let x, y and z be $|\bar{L}_1 - \bar{C}_1|$, $|\bar{L}_2 - \bar{C}_1|$ and $|\bar{L}_3 - \bar{C}_2|$ respectively. The result is:

$$L_{12} = |x\bar{V}_1 - y\bar{V}_2| \qquad L_{31} = |(\bar{T} + z\bar{V}_3) - x\bar{V}_1| \qquad (1)$$
$$L_{23} = |y\bar{V}_2 - (\bar{T} + z\bar{V}_3)|$$

Taking the square of both sides of (1) results in:

$$\begin{aligned} a \quad &+ b\cdot x\cdot y + x^2 + y^2 = 0 \\ c + d\cdot y + e\cdot z &+ f\cdot y\cdot z + y^2 + z^2 = 0 \\ g + h\cdot x + e\cdot z &+ j\cdot x\cdot z + x^2 + z^2 = 0 \end{aligned} \qquad (2)$$

where $a \ldots j$ are constants given by:

$$a = -L_{12}^2 \qquad d = -2\bar{T}\cdot\bar{V}_2 \qquad g = \|\bar{T}\|^2 - L_{31}^2$$
$$b = -2\bar{V}_1\cdot\bar{V}_2 \qquad e = 2\bar{T}\cdot\bar{V}_3 \qquad h = -2\bar{T}\cdot\bar{V}_1$$
$$c = \|\bar{T}\|^2 - L_{23}^2 \qquad f = -2\bar{V}_2\cdot\bar{V}_3 \qquad j = -2\bar{V}_1\cdot\bar{V}_3$$

This is a system of equations consisting of 3 quadratic equations with 3 variables and a total degree of 2x2x2=8. The solutions of this system can be thought of as the intersection of three ellipsoidal cylinders with infinite extents in the x, y and z directions respectively.

If there is only one camera, i.e. $\bar{T} = 0$, then d, e and h vanish. In this special case, the following substitution reduces (2) into a system with 2 quadratic equations:

$x' = x/z$ and $y' = y/z$ [Fischler81].

For the general case the solution is more complicated. We use a robust global equation solver that utilizes resultants and polynomial matrices to reduce the system to an eigenvalue problem [Manocha94]. First we eliminate x and y from the system via Dixon's resultant [Dixon08]. The resultant is a determinant of a 6x6 matrix where each element is up to degree 3 in terms of z. The matrix can be written as a matrix polynomial:

$$\mathbf{M}(z) = \mathbf{M}_3 z^3 + \mathbf{M}_2 z^2 + \mathbf{M}_1 z + \mathbf{M}_0 \qquad (3)$$

Since $\mathbf{M}_3$ is singular, by substituting $z' = 1/z$ into (3), we get:

$$\mathbf{M}'(z') = \mathbf{M}_0 z'^3 + \mathbf{M}_1 z'^2 + \mathbf{M}_2 z' + \mathbf{M}_3$$

We want z' such that $\det \mathbf{M}'(z') = 0$. We can find solutions for z' as eigenvalues of the companion matrix of $\mathbf{M}'(z')$:

Once we have z', $z = 1/z'$ is plugged into (2), and an (x, y) solution pair that satisfies the three equations can be found.

7.2.2 Selecting one solution

There are eight solutions to our system of equations, so we have to find the most sound one among them. In general, imaginary solutions are trivially rejected, and the physics of the cameras tell us to discard all negative solutions. We typically find two positive solutions. Then the problem is how to disambiguate between these two.

If the image analyzer has detected additional landmarks (that is, in addition to the ones used to solve the equations), we can use these landmarks for disambiguation. Using each remaining candidate solution of the camera, we project the additional landmarks onto the image planes and check how closely the projections match the detected positions. This matching error method works most of the time, but, as shown in [Fischler81], there are degenerate cases in which two or more extra landmarks project to exactly the same position in the image. In addition, errors in landmark detection prevent us from rejecting solutions with small matching errors. However, the most problematic case occurs when we do not have any redundant landmarks, i.e. when we have already used all three available landmarks for equation solving.

In such cases we resort to the aid of the magnetic tracker. Unless the two solutions are very close to each other, we can disambiguate by selecting the solution that best matches the magnetic tracker's readings.

7.3 Over-determined case

Since the equation solver uses only the minimum necessary number of landmarks, it is sensitive to landmark tracking error. Least square error minimization allows us to find an optimum solution using all the detected landmarks. This process neutralizes fluctuations in landmark tracking and significantly stabilizes the final head pose, thereby yielding superior frame-to-frame coherence in registration.

The optimization process is local and depends on the availability of a good initial guess. In any case, the optimizer will converge towards a single solution. It is therefore not advisable to use the optimizer in underdetermined cases, due to the infinite number of solutions. Similarly, in well-determined cases, the number of solutions is finite, but invoking the optimizer would result in convergence towards a single solution. This would preclude inspecting the multiple solutions with the goal of selecting the best one. We therefore invoke the optimizer only when we are confident that a good approximate solution has been found via the methods described in Section 7.2.

The mathematical relationships between the user's head, the head-mounted camera, a landmark and the projected image of the landmark as seen by the camera are:

$$\begin{bmatrix} I_x \\ I_y \end{bmatrix} = \begin{bmatrix} I'_x/I'_z \\ I'_y/I'_z \end{bmatrix} \qquad (4)$$

$$\begin{bmatrix} I'_x \\ I'_y \\ I'_z \end{bmatrix} = \begin{bmatrix} 1 & 0 & 0 \\ 0 & 1 & 0 \\ 0 & 0 & \frac{1}{f} \end{bmatrix} \begin{bmatrix} \mathbf{R_c} & -\mathrm{R}_c\vec{T}_c \end{bmatrix} \begin{bmatrix} \mathbf{R_h} & -\mathbf{R}_h\vec{T}_h \\ 0\ 0\ 0 & 1 \end{bmatrix} \begin{bmatrix} L_x \\ L_y \\ L_z \\ 1 \end{bmatrix} \quad (5)$$

In the above equations,

$\vec{T}_h$ is a 3D vector representing the position of the head in the world space.

$\mathbf{R}_h$ is a 3x3 rotation matrix representing the orientation of the head in world space.

$\vec{T}_c$ is a 3D vector representing the position of the camera in the head coordinate system

$\mathbf{R}_c$ is a 3x3 rotation matrix representing the orientation of the camera in the head coordinate system.

f is the focal length.

(L_x, L_y, L_z) is the position of a landmark in world space.

(I_x, I_y) is the projected position of the landmark in image space.

(I'_x, I'_y, I'_z) is the projected position of the landmark in homogeneous image space.

I'_x, I'_y and I'_z of (4) can be eliminated using (5). Then (4) can be written simply as

$$F_x = I_x - P_x(L_x, L_y, L_z) = 0$$
$$F_y = I_y - P_y(L_x, L_y, L_z) = 0$$

where P_x and P_y are a combined transformation function that maps a world coordinate to a 2D image coordinate. All values except for $\vec{T}_h$ and $\mathbf{R}_h$ are given, therefore F_x and F_y are functions of $\vec{T}_h$ and $\mathbf{R}_h$;

$$F_x(\vec{T}_h, \mathbf{R}_h) = 0 \text{ and } F_y(\vec{T}_h, \mathbf{R}_h) = 0 \quad (6)$$

Let (t_x, t_y, t_z) be the three components of $\vec{T}_h$. $\mathbf{R}_h$ has 9 elements, but a rotation has only 3 real degrees of freedom. This means we can express $\mathbf{R}_h$ as simple rational functions of 3 variables, u, v and w. In our implementation, these parameters are defined as follows. First the initial orientation is converted to a quaternion, then a hyperplane is defined such that it is tangential to the unit hypersphere at the point corresponding to this initial quaternion. Finally u, v and w. are defined as a 3D coordinate system in the hyperplane. Hence (6) can also be written as:

$$F_x(t_x, t_y, t_z, u, v, w) = 0. \text{ and } F_y(t_x, t_y, t_z, u, v, w) = 0 \quad (7)$$

If we find **n** landmark-projection pairs, using (7) we can set up a system of **2n** equations with 6 variables.

Since I_x and I_y are measured values, F_x and F_y may not vanish. Instead, they should be considered measurement errors in image space.

If the total number of distinct landmarks detected by the two cameras is at least 3, and the total number of landmark-projection pairs detected is at least 4, then this system is overdetermined. In this case we must be able to solve the system as a non-linear, least-square minimization problem using iterative methods. To this end, we incorporated an implementation of the Levenberg-Marquardt algorithm [More80, Fletcher87] into the system. Since a good initial guess is provided by the previously described analytical methods, an optimized solution is computed in only a few milliseconds.

7.4 Non-stereo operation

The hybrid tracker can also operate with a single camera (non-stereo). In that case, none of the binocular solution methods are applied. This means that only heuristic adjusters (1) and (2) from Section 7.1 are used, and only the simplified monocular global three-landmark solver is used. Local optimization is performed using only landmarks visible in one camera.

8 STATIC CALIBRATION

The initial calibration of the system determines numerous static parameters that are required by the tracking procedures described in Sections 5-7. The following list describes the static calibration procedures.

(1) Camera-to-magnetic-sensor transformation: The transformation between a camera and the magnetic tracker's sensor is calculated using an iterative procedure proposed in [Bajura95].

(2) Intrinsic camera parameters: The camera lenses were selected for their low distortion characteristics—well below 1% barrel distortion in the corners of the image. This allows us to keep the mathematical camera model in our system very simple: it is a pin-hole model (no distortion, no skew, 1:1 aspect ratio). This model has only three intrinsic degrees of freedom, which we define as the 3D coordinates of the center of projection with respect to the CCD camera's pixel array. Note that the focal length is in fact equal to one of the three coordinates. We calibrate these coordinates for each camera individually using the vision-based tracker. First we position each camera to see as many landmarks as possible. Then we execute the landmark tracking procedure described in previous sections. The residual error of the least square optimization is an indicator for the accuracy of the estimated intrinsic parameters. An optimization method is then applied to find values for the intrinsic parameters that minimize the residual error. We do not dynamically calibrate the intrinsic camera parameters, because producing reliable results would require tracking considerably more landmarks than our system can identify [Tsai87].

(3) Interocular Transformation: To calculate the transformation between the left and right cameras, we first calibrate the intrinsic parameters as described above. Then we operate the hybrid tracker in dual-mono mode, i.e., by tracking and correcting each camera individually, as described in Section 7.4. In this mode, the transformation between the cameras is not used in the tracking algorithms. It can be computed as the transformation between the cameras' coordinate systems as they are determined by the vision-based tracker. For accurate results, each of the two cameras should see at least three, but preferably more landmarks. We average the data acquired over 10 frames to reduce the effect of landmark tracking errors This interocular calibration procedure is fast enough for real time execution if desired.

(4) Landmark centers: The world space positions of all the landmark centers are acquired using a precise mechanical arm (FARO Metrecom IND-1).

The FARO mechanical arm is an auxiliary tracker in our system. It is also used to acquire accurate models for real-world objects (for example, the computer model of the cuboids in Figures 2-5). The coordinate system of the mechanical arm must be calibrated to the coordinate system of the magnetic system. To this end, we measure a reference system with both trackers. The reference is a lab-mounted wooden box.

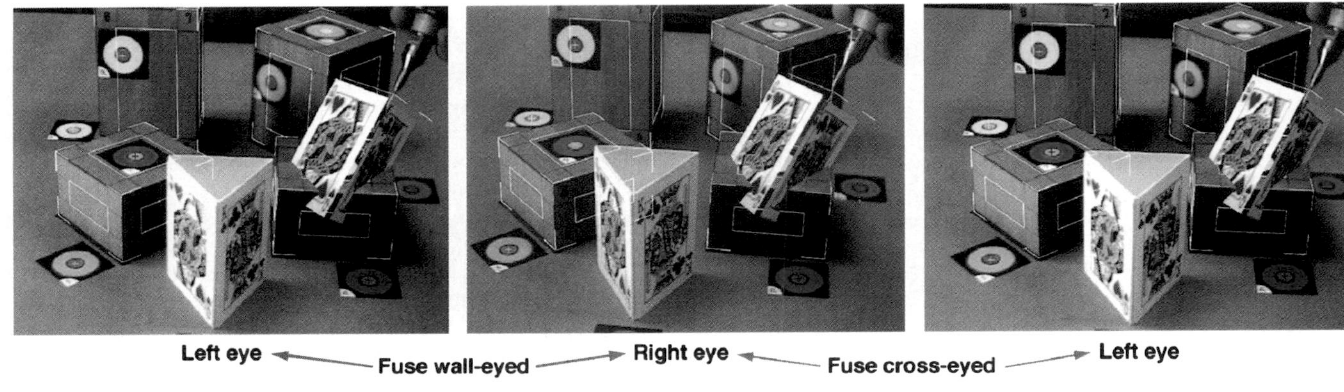

Left eye ← Fuse wall-eyed → Right eye ← Fuse cross-eyed → Left eye

Figure 7. Virtual and real card prisms. Accurate registration makes it possible to acquire an object's texture by projecting the video image onto a precisely registered polygonal model of the object. Notice accurate interpenetration of the virtual card prism and the (real) gray cuboids. The computer-generated white outlines on the cuboids in the background also illustrate the precise registration. Note 3D coordinate axes at the tip of the mechanical arm (top right) used to move the virtual card prism.

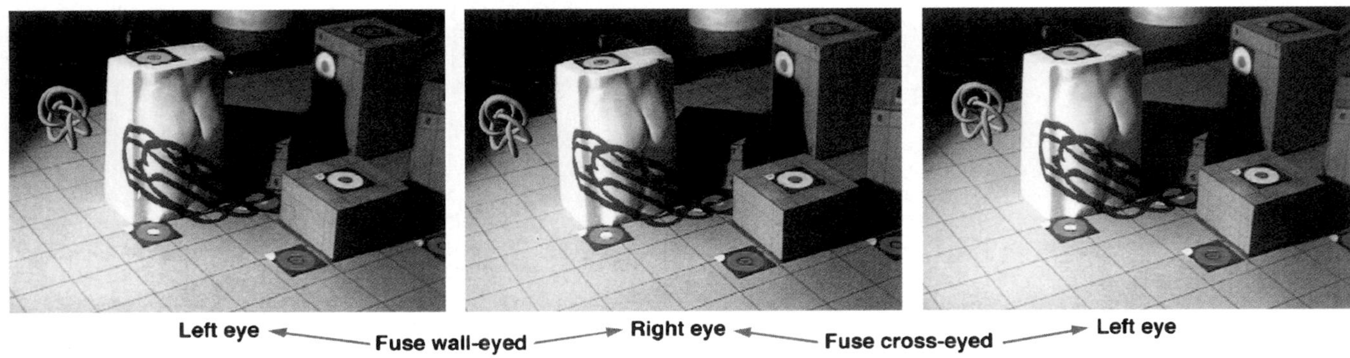

Left eye ← Fuse wall-eyed → Right eye ← Fuse cross-eyed → Left eye

Figure 8. Virtual shadow into the real environment. A polygonal model of the sculpture is registered to the real sculpture. The virtual knot floating beside it casts a shadow onto the sculpture and the ground plane. A tracked light source moves real and virtual shadows in sync.

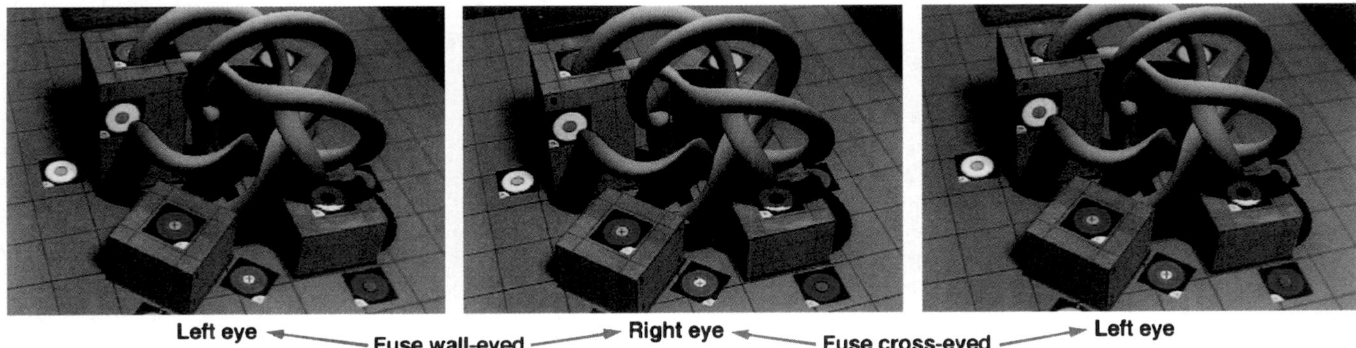

Left eye ← Fuse wall-eyed → Right eye ← Fuse cross-eyed → Left eye

Figure 9. Another example of accurate interpenetration: the virtual knot penetrates into the gray cuboids and also casts virtual shadows into the scene. The landmarks that are occluded by the virtual knot are still used for tracking.

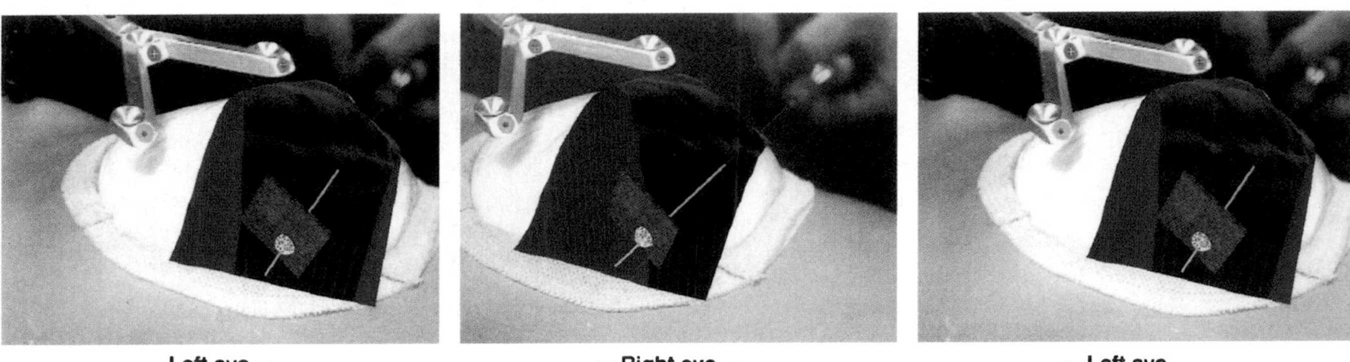

Left eye ← Fuse wall-eyed → Right eye ← Fuse cross-eyed → Left eye

Figure 10. Experimental AR system for ultrasound-guided needle biopsy of the breast. A mechanically tracked needle (marked by a red line) is inserted into a training phantom of a human breast. An ultrasound image positioned within the breast is enhanced with a yellow sphere which marks the targeted lesion. Precise stereoscopic registration between the real needle and its virtual extension (green), used for aiming, is essential. The Y-shaped object at the top holds three color landmarks used by an older version of the hybrid tracker.

9 RESULTS AND DISCUSSION

To evaluate the registration performance of our system, we built the tabletop scene shown in Figures 2-5 and 7-9. We register the real world cuboids to computer models. The registration errors are represented by the distances between computer-generated edges and the corresponding real world edges. Typically these errors are below 1 pixel.

We demonstrate the registration accuracy of our method in three experimental AR systems. Figure 7 demonstrates a 3D copy and paste operation in which a virtual copy is made of a real object. The user manipulates the virtual copy of the card prism. Notice that the virtual prism intersects with the real cuboids in a convincing manner. For the 3D copy operation, the real card prism is measured with the mechanical arm. After each face is defined by digitizing its vertices, a texture is extracted from the camera image and is applied to the face.

Figure 8 demonstrates a virtual object, a knot, casting a shadow on a real object, a sculpture. The geometry of the sculpture was digitized with the mechanical arm and placed in the scene. The (real) light source is tracked (by the mechanical arm), and the shadow map is calculated in real-time [Segal92]. Figure 9 shows a similar scene. The knot intersects the real objects, emphasizing the accurate registration of the synthetic imagery (the knot and its shadow) with the real cuboids.

We have also used hybrid tracking in an experimental system designed ultimately to aid physicians in performing ultrasound-guided needle biopsies [State96]. In such a procedure the physician may be attempting to pierce a suspicious lump in a patient's breast. Traditionally ultrasound echography images are used to locate the lump and aim the needle. Our experimental system creates a virtual display of the lump and the needle. The ultrasound image slice which also contains a computer-enhanced display of the target lump, appears to lie within the patient, correctly registered in space. Figure 10 shows images from this system. A mechanically tracked needle is being inserted into a training phantom of a human breast. This system uses an early version of our hybrid tracker that did not use two-color concentric landmarks.

It is difficult to quantitatively determine the final camera position and orientation error in an AR system. It is nearly impossible to evaluate the accuracy of the intrinsic camera parameter calibration and of the interocular transformation calibration procedures. This is due to the fact that ground truth values are unavailable. We have therefore implemented a simulator for the camera video images. The simulator generates synthetic stereo images, complete with landmarks. The intrinsic parameters for the (simulated) cameras are user-settable, as are landmark calibration errors, landmark tracking errors, and magnetic tracker errors. Using the simulator, we determined that the intrinsic parameter calibration is very sensitive to landmark tracking errors and landmark calibration errors. We also determined that intrinsic parameter errors affect interocular calibration accuracy.

The system's final camera position and orientation errors when used in the tabletop cuboids environment are generally below 2 mm and 0.2° (simulator data). This assumes very accurate landmark calibration and image analysis. In practice, camera pose errors are larger but seldom exceed 1 cm and 1 degree in overdetermined cases. It is important to note that in this system—as opposed to AR systems in general [Holloway95]—the effects of position and orientation errors are not cumulative. Instead, they neutralize each other's influence on registration accuracy in the region of space containing landmarks. It follows that our system's registration accuracy is in large part due to the design decision to track landmarks in the target images.

10 FUTURE WORK

Our system is not without limitations. The most important of these is suboptimal performance due to the lack of synchronization between the magnetic tracker and the vision-based subsystem. The magnetic tracker's readings lag behind the camera video images, which makes the magnetic tracker error grow beyond reasonable values if the head moves quickly. Since the landmark predictor does not compute useful landmark search areas in such cases, this leads to full-screen searches and thus to noticeable glitches. The obvious way to reduce the influence of lag is by using a faster head tracker [Mine93a] and sophisticated prediction algorithms [Azuma94]. Delaying the video images [Bajura95] is also possible but undesirable since it increases overall system latency.

Additional though less severe synchronization problems are due to sequential scanout in the video cameras [Mine93b]. Our system does not account for the 17-msec time difference between the top and the bottom scanlines of the video images. Nor does it compensate for the latency difference between the left and right camera video images. The effects of such latency differences could be reduced by time-stamping detected landmarks and by reformulating the head pose correctors and solvers to exploit the time stamps.

Under even lighting conditions (Figure 7), the image analyzer can easily recognize our fluorescent landmarks. But despite the use of adaptive brightness evaluation for each landmark, harsh or changing lighting conditions (Figure 8) noticeably diminish the analyzer's performance. Landmark recognition reliability and tracking accuracy could be improved by building constant-intensity landmarks, such as active (for example back-lit) fiducials, or by using retro-reflective materials in combination with an HMD-mounted light source.

A more realistic camera model incorporating optical distortion should make the system usable with wide-angle lenses, thus providing a wide field of view and large stereo overlap. To determine the image-space landmark centers more accurately in wide-angle views, perspective correction should be performed on the centers' coordinates.

Finally, our wish list also includes: attaching landmarks to moving objects (in order to track object motion simultaneously with camera position and orientation), using the system at a different scale (for example, in a room-sized environment), and real-time tracking of visually unobtrusive natural features.

ACKNOWLEDGMENTS

We wish to express our gratitude to Ronald T. Azuma, Michael Bajura, David C. Banks, Gary Bishop, Stephen and Clara Chen, D'nardo Colucci, Henry Fuchs, Arthur Gregory, Stefan Gottschalk, David Harrison, Marco Jacobs, Fred Jordan, Kurtis Keller, Amy Kreiling, Shankar Krishnan, Alan Liu, Dinesh Manocha, Mark McCarthy, Michael North, Stephen M. Pizer, Scott Pritchett, Russell M. Taylor II, Bruce Scher, Chris Tector, John Thomas, Greg Turk, Peggy Wetzel, Mary C. Whitton, Scott Williams, Steve Work, and Silicon Graphics, Inc.

We thank the anonymous reviewers for their comments and criticism.

This work was supported in part by ARPA DABT63-93-C-0048 ("Enabling Technologies and Application Demonstrations for Synthetic Environments"). Approved by ARPA for Public Release—Distribution Unlimited. Additional partial support was provided by the National Science Foundation Science and Technology Center for Computer Graphics and Scientific Visualization (NSF prime contract 8920219).

REFERENCES

AZUMA, R. A Survey of Augmented Reality. *SIGGRAPH 1995 Course Notes #9* (Developing Advanced Virtual Reality Applications).

AZUMA, R., BISHOP, G. Improved Static and Dynamic Registration in an Optical See-through HMD. Proceedings of SIGGRAPH 94 (Orlando, FL, July 24-29, 1994). In *Computer Graphics* Proceedings, Annual Conference Series, 1994, ACM SIGGRAPH, pp. 197-203.

BAJURA, M., NEUMANN, U. Dynamic Registration Correction in Video-Based Augmented Reality Systems. *IEEE Computer Graphics and Applications* (September 1995), pp. 52-60.

DIXON, A.L. The Elimination of Three Quantics in Two Independent Variables. *Proceedings of the London Mathematical Society*, 6 (1908), 49-69, pp. 209-236.

DRASCIC, D. ARGOS: A Display System for Augmenting Reality. *ACM SIGGRAPH Technical Video Review, Volume 88: InterCHI 1993 Conference on Human Factors in Computing Systems* (1993).

FAUGERAS, O.D., HEBERT, M. The Representation, Recognition and Locating of 3-D Objects. *Int. J. Robotics Res.*, 5:3 (1986), pp. 27-52.

FISCHLER, M.A., BOLLES, R.C. Random Sample Consensus: A Paradigm for Model Fitting with Applications to Image Analysis and Automated Cartography. *Communications of the ACM*, 24:6 (1981), pp. 381-395.

FLETCHER, R. *Practical Methods of Optimization.* John Wiley and Sons, Inc., New York (1987).

GRIMSON, W.E.L. *Object Recognition by Computer: The Role of Geometric Constraints.* MIT Press, Cambridge (1990).

HARALICK, R.M., SHAPIRO, L.G. *Computer and Robot Vision, Volume I*, Addison-Wesley (1993), p. 48.

HOLLOWAY, R. *Registration Errors in Augmented Reality Systems.* Ph.D. dissertation, University of North Carolina at Chapel Hill (1995).

JANIN, A., ZIKAN, K., MIZELL, D., BANNER, M., SOWIZRAL, H. A videometric tracker for augmented reality applications. *Proceedings of SPIE,* November 1994 (Boston).

KANCHERLA, A.R., ROLLAND, J.P., WRIGHT, D.L., BURDEA, G. A Novel Virtual Reality Tool for Teaching Dynamic 3D Anatomy. *Proceedings of CVRMed '95* (Nice, France, April 3-5, 1995) pp. 163-169.

LIVINGSTON, M., STATE, A. Improved Registration for Augmented Reality Systems via Magnetic Tracker Calibration. *University of North Carolina at Chapel Hill Technical Report TR95-037* (1995).

LOWE, D.G. Three-Dimensional Object Recognition from Single Two-Dimensional Images. *Artificial Intelligence*, 31 (1987), pp. 355-395.

LOWE, D.G. Robust Model-based Motion Tracking Through the Integration of Search and Estimation. *International Journal of Computer Vision*, 8:2 (1992), pp. 113-122.

MANOCHA, D. Solving Systems of Polynomial Equations. *IEEE Computer Graphics and Applications* (March 1994), pp. 46-55.

MELLOR, J.P. Realtime Camera Calibration for Enhanced Reality Visualization. *Proceedings of CVRMed '95* (Nice, France April 3-5, 1995), pp. 471-475.

MINE, M.R. Characterization of End-to-End Delays in Head-Mounted Display Systems. *University of North Carolina at Chapel Hill Technical Report TR93-001* (1993a).

MINE, M.R., BISHOP, G. Just-In-Time Pixels. *University of North Carolina at Chapel Hill Technical Report TR93-005* (1993b).

MORE, J.J., GARBOW, B.S. HILLSTROM, K.E. User Guide for MINPACK-1. *Argonne National Laboratory Report ANL-80-74* (1980).

SEGAL, M., KOROBKIN, C., VAN WIDENFELT, R., FORAN, J., HAEBERLI, P. Fast Shadows and Lighting Effects Using Texture Mapping. Proceedings of SIGGRAPH '92 (Chicago, IL, July 26-31, 1992). In *Computer Graphics*, 26, 2 (July 1992), ACM SIGGRAPH, New York, 1992, pp. 249-252.

SILICON GRAPHICS, INC. *Sirius Video Technical Report.* Silicon Graphics, Inc., Mountain View, CA (1994).

STATE, A., LIVINGSTON, M., GARRETT, W.F., HIROTA, G., WHITTON, M.C., PISANO, E.D.(MD), FUCHS, H.. Technologies for Augmented-Reality Systems: Realizing Ultrasound-Guided Needle Biopsies. Proceedings of SIGGRAPH '96 (New Orleans, LA, August 4-9, 1996). In *Computer Graphics* Proceedings, Annual Conference Series, 1996, ACM SIGGRAPH.

SUTHERLAND, I.E. A Head-Mounted Three Dimensional Display. *Fall Joint Computer Conference* (1968), pp. 757-764.

TSAI, R. Y. A Versatile Camera Calibration Technique for High-Accuracy 3D Machine Vision Metrology Using Off-the-Shelf TV Cameras and Lenses. *IEEE Journal of Robotics and Automation*, RA-3:4 (August 1987), pp. 323-344.

TUCERYAN, M., GREER, D.S., WHITAKER, R.T., BREEN, D.E., CRAMPTON, C., ROSE, E., AHLERS, K.H. Calibration Requirements and Procedures for a Monitor-Based Augmented Reality System. *IEEE Transactions on Visualizations and Computer Graphics,* 1:3 (September 1995), pp. 255-273.

UENOHARA, M., KANADE, T. Vision-Based Object Registration for Real-Time Image Overlay. 1995 Conference on Computer Vision, Virtual Reality and Robotics in Medicine (Nice, France, April 1995), pp. 13-22.

WANG, L.-L., TSAI, W.-H. Computing Camera Parameters using Vanishing-Line Information from a Rectangular Parallelepiped. *Machine Vision and Applications,* 3 (1990), pp. 129-141.

WARD, M., AZUMA, R., BENNETT, R., GOTTSCALK, S., FUCHS, H. A Demonstrated Optical Tracker with Scalable Work Area for Head-Mounted Display Systems. *Proceedings of the 1992 Symposium on Interactive 3D Graphics* (Boston, MA, March 1-April 1, 1992), pp. 43-52.

YOO, T.S., OLANO, T.M. Instant Hole (Windows into Reality). *University of North Carolina at Chapel Hill Technical Report TR93-027* (1993).

Technologies for Augmented Reality Systems: Realizing Ultrasound-Guided Needle Biopsies

Andrei State, Mark A. Livingston, William F. Garrett, Gentaro Hirota, Mary C. Whitton, Etta D. Pisano, MD*
and
Henry Fuchs

Departments of Computer Science and *Radiology
University of North Carolina at Chapel Hill

http://www.cs.unc.edu/~us/

ABSTRACT

We present a real-time stereoscopic video-see-through augmented reality (AR) system applied to the medical procedure known as ultrasound-guided needle biopsy of the breast. The AR system was used by a physician during procedures on breast models and during non-invasive examinations of human subjects. The system merges rendered live ultrasound data and geometric elements with stereo images of the patient acquired through head-mounted video cameras and presents these merged images to the physician in a head-mounted display. The physician sees a volume visualization of the ultrasound data directly under the ultrasound probe, properly registered within the patient and with the biopsy needle. Using this system, a physician successfully guided a needle into an artificial tumor within a training phantom of a human breast.

We discuss the construction of the AR system and the issues and decisions which led to the system architecture and the design of the video see-through head-mounted display. We designed methods to properly resolve occlusion of the real and synthetic image elements. We developed techniques for real-time volume visualization of time- and position-varying ultrasound data. We devised a hybrid tracking system which achieves improved registration of synthetic and real imagery and we improved on previous techniques for calibration of a magnetic tracker.

CR Categories and Subject Descriptors: I.3.7 [Three-Dimensional Graphics and Realism]: *Virtual Reality,* I.3.1: [Hardware Architecture]: *Three-dimensional displays,* I.3.6 [Methodology and Techniques]: *Interaction techniques,* J.3 [Life and Medical Sciences]: *Medical information systems.*

Additional Keywords and Phrases: Augmented reality, stereo video see-through head-mounted display, ultrasound echography, 3D medical imaging, BSP tree, calibration, registration.

CB #3175 Sitterson Hall, Chapel Hill, NC 27599-3175. Tel: +1-919-962-1700. E-mail: {state, livingst, garrett, hirota, whitton, fuchs}@cs.unc.edu

*Department of Radiology, 503 Old Infirmary 226, CB #7510, Chapel Hill, NC 27599-7510. Tel: +1-919-966-6957. E-mail: pisano@rad.unc.edu

1 INTRODUCTION

Since the early days of computer graphics, people have wanted to merge synthetic imagery with their view of the surroundings to create an enhanced view of reality. The range of applications that can potentially benefit from augmented reality (AR) technology includes architecture, mechanical repair, circuit wiring, and health care. Due to a few key technical problems—the quality of merged display systems, occlusion conflicts between real and synthetic objects, real-time image generation, and registration of real and synthetic objects—very few AR systems have been placed in users' hands.

We made advances on the above issues while building an AR system designed to assist a physician with ultrasound-guided needle biopsy of the breast or with cyst aspiration. Figure 1 shows the stereo view displayed in the head-mounted display (HMD) worn by the physician during the AR-guided insertion procedure. With conventional methods the physician has only a non-registered two-dimensional ultrasound image (and perhaps pre-scan 2D medical imagery such as X-ray images) to assist her in the inherently three-dimensional task of guiding a needle to a biopsy target. Our system displays a synthetic opening, or *pit*, into the patient and one or more ultrasound *slices* that are emitted by the tracked hand-held ultrasound probe. We hope that presenting such imagery in the proper context of patient anatomy will make these widely-practiced needle biopsies easier to perform both in the breast and, eventually, also in other, less accessible parts of the body. Figure 2 shows the physician examining a patient in our lab and Figure 3 shows the image she sees in her HMD.

This paper describes the hardware and software of the AR system used by the physician during experiments with training models and human subjects. Section 2 briefly summarizes previous work in AR, and Section 3 discusses some of the issues in building such systems. We present our system in detail in Section 4. Section 5 focuses on issues related to the AR HMD. Section 6 describes how we achieve proper occlusion relationships. Section 7 presents our new real-time volume visualization technique for ultrasound data. Section 8 discusses techniques used to improve registration. We discuss what we have learned from the development and the operation of our system in Section 9. We conclude with a discussion of likely future work in Section 10.

2 PREVIOUS WORK

AR is not a new concept. Ivan Sutherland's original HMD allowed the user to see both the real world and virtual objects [Sutherland68]. The VCASS system [Furness86] used an optical see-through HMD to superimpose flight and target data onto a pilot's view. The Boeing Company has a group working

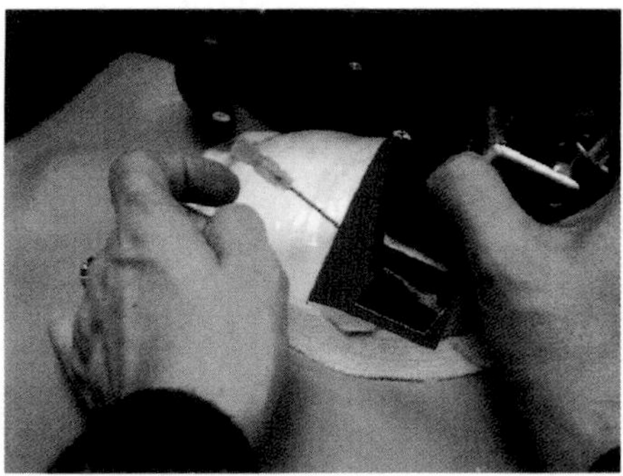
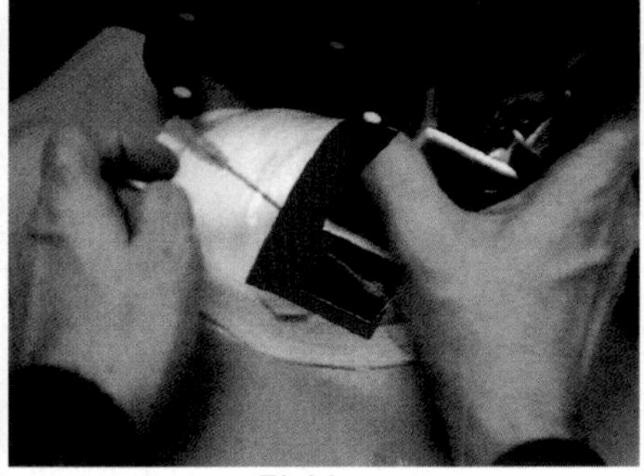
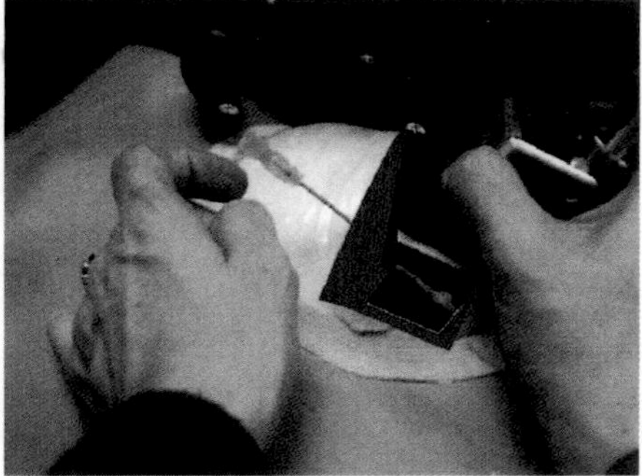

Left eye ← Fuse wall-eyed → Right eye ← Fuse cross-eyed → Left eye

Figure 1. Real-time stereo HMD views from AR system in use during ultrasound-guided needle insertion into phantom training breast. Both the needle and the target lesion are visible in the live ultrasound slice attached to the tracked hand-held probe. Note synthetic opening into the breast and accurate registration between the needle and its image in the ultrasound slice.

on an AR system to guide a technician in building a wiring harness for an airplane electrical system [Sims94]. A similar system places text labels of engine parts in the user's view when he points at the real object [Rose94].

Medical applications of AR include visualization and training for surgical interventions. Such systems have been demonstrated by groups at the MIT AI Lab [Mellor95], at Brigham & Women's Hospital [Lorensen93], and elsewhere. These systems use MRI or CT data that is collected before the procedure, then registered to the patient during the procedure. Previous systems built in our lab have demonstrated AR ultrasound visualization [Bajura92, State95, State94]. These earlier systems were limited to non-invasive procedures such as exploratory visualization of a fetus in the womb.

3 AR SYSTEM DESIGN

To a computer graphics veteran, building our AR system may appear straightforward or even simple. It appears that all we must do is add a real-time rendering of ultrasound data to a live video background. However, realizing a working system requires addressing the technical problems of stereo AR, real-time volume rendering of time- and position-varying ultrasound data, and precise registration of real and synthetic image elements. In this section, we describe and justify our choice of technologies for various system components.

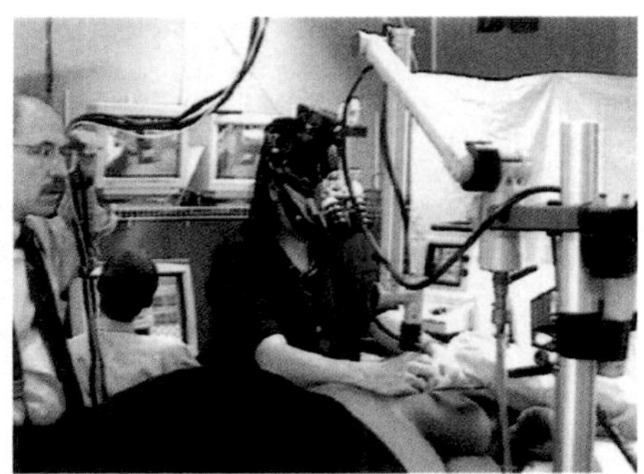

Figure 2. Physician wearing AR HMD with stereo cameras examines patient in preparation for biopsy. The ultrasound probe is attached to a mechanical tracking arm.

3.1 Merging real and synthetic imagery

By definition, an AR system must allow the user to see the real world. There are two common technologies for AR HMDs: *optical see-through* and *video see-through.* In the former, beam splitters (e. g., half-silvered mirrors) optically combine light from the environment with computer-generated display elements. In the latter, video cameras mounted on the HMD acquire images of the real world which are then electronically combined with computer-generated imagery. This can be accomplished via analog technology (e.g. luminance keying or chroma keying) or via real-time digital video capture and digital compositing, as in our current system. The combined video images are then displayed in the (conventional, "opaque") HMD. More details about these technologies can be found in [Azuma95].

For our system, we chose video see-through (a decision which dates back to [Bajura92]). The four key advantages of video see-through over optical see-through which led to this decision are:

(1) support for proper occlusion relationships between real and virtual objects (provided that depth of real objects is known or can be determined) [Wloka95].

(2) ability to balance the brightness of synthetic and real imagery on a pixel-by-pixel basis.

(3) ability to match the latencies (delays) of synthetic and

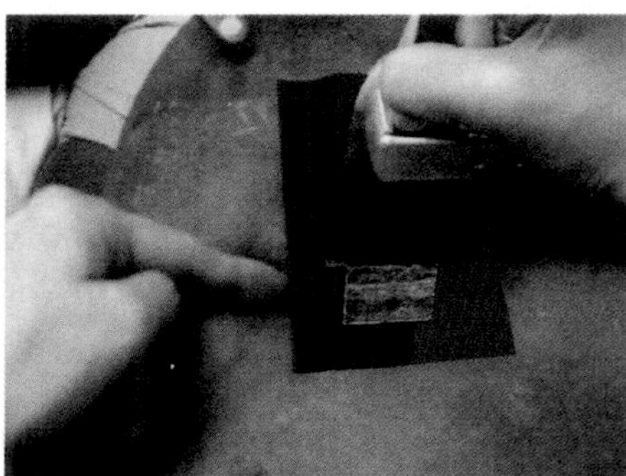

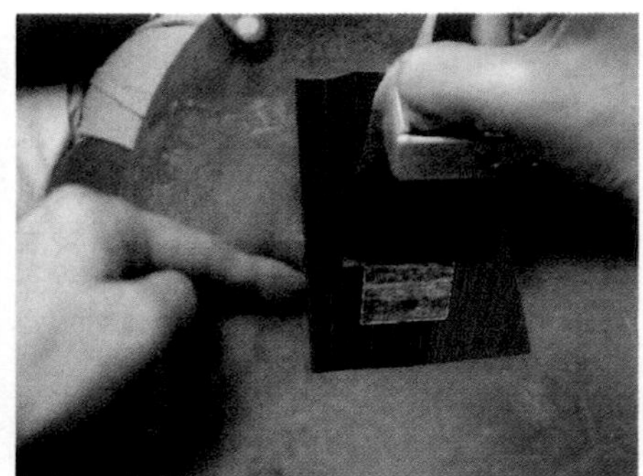

Left eye ← Fuse wall-eyed → Right eye ← Fuse cross-eyed → Left eye

Figure 3. Real-time stereo HMD view during patient examination (Figure 2) showing a single ultrasound slice properly positioned within the patient's breast. The physician's left index finger points towards the cyst (visible as a dark spot in the ultrasound slice).

real imagery [Bajura95].

(4) ability to use vision-based registration strategies, such as video tracking of landmarks—provided that the video image is digitized and available for image processing.

The above items are critical to the design of our system. We accept, for now, the drawbacks of video see-through technology: low resolution for the real-world imagery and the spatial offset between the user's eyes and the locations of the HMD-mounted cameras used to acquire the real world images. These problems will be solved in future HMDs [Colucci95].

In video see-through, the cameras introduce several issues not present in optical see-through. The field of view and angle of convergence (and thus the amount of stereo overlap) of the cameras should match those of the HMD in order for the synthetic imagery to have the same alignment and perspective as the real world imagery. This requires measuring the intrinsic parameters of the cameras.

3.2 Tracking

Accurate tracking is crucial for precise registration of real and synthetic imagery, especially in a medical application where surgical intervention is to be performed under AR guidance. In our system we must track the physician's head and the hand-held ultrasound probe.

In selecting a head tracking system, we wanted to avoid encumbering the physician, so we chose a magnetic tracker. Unfortunately, the metallic structures in our lab interfere with its accuracy. To overcome this, we combine magnetic tracking with vision-based landmark tracking for improved registration.

Tracking of the ultrasound probe must be extremely precise for correct registration of ultrasound slices (both slice-to-slice and slice-to-patient). The probe is usually positioned over a confined area of the patient's body and gathers data only when in contact with the patient, so it has a small working and tracking volume. Furthermore, the probe is already tethered to the ultrasound machine. We therefore elected to accurately track the probe with a 6-degree-of-freedom mechanical tracker even though it hinders probe motion to a certain extent.

3.3 Image generation platform

The success of [Cullip93, Cabral94] and the availability of fast hardware for rendering texture-mapped polygons led us to choose hardware texture mapping for ultrasound data visualization. Our system requires an image generation platform that supports real-time video acquisition for three channels: one ultrasound video stream and two camera video streams. The latter are inspected by vision-based registration algorithms. On the output side, the system must be able to generate two video output streams for the HMD as well as a user interface screen.

4 SYSTEM DESCRIPTION

4.1 System Configuration

The principal hardware platform of our system is a Silicon Graphics Onyx™ Reality Engine²™ graphics workstation (Onyx) equipped with a Sirius Video™ real-time video capture device (Sirius) and a Multi-Channel Option™ (MCO) that outputs multiple video streams that can be used for the left and right eye displays. The Sirius simultaneously acquires video signals from a PIE Medical Scanner 200 ultrasound machine (PIE) and from two Panasonic GP-KS102 head-mounted CCD video cameras equipped with Cosmicar F1.8 12.5 mm lenses (28° field of view, selected for minimal optical distortion). Through its serial ports, the Onyx acquires tracking data from two trackers: a FARO Metrecom IND-1 mechanical arm (FARO), which tracks the ultrasound probe, and an Ascension Flock of Birds™ magnetic tracker for the user's head. The Onyx generates stereo video signals to be displayed within the Virtual Research VR-4 HMD (VR-4). PIE, VR-4 with cameras and Flock sensor, and FARO are all visible in Figure 2.

4.1.1 Video Input

The Sirius allows simultaneous acquisition and digital processing of two video streams. This constraint required us to combine the video streams from the two head-mounted cameras into a single stream for the purpose of acquisition (and to devise a software method to split them again after capture for the purpose of stereo output). A commercial analog multiplexer (QD Technology QD-1110) combines the camera video signals into a single analog signal by selecting odd video fields from one camera and even fields from the other.

The Sirius has two digital video inputs but only one analog video input. Both the ultrasound machine and the multiplexer produce analog video streams. Hence, one of these two streams had to be converted into digital format. Since we were willing, at the time, to compromise the ultrasound imaging subsystem but not the overall "AR feel," and since the PIE's video had to be time-base corrected, we opted to convert the ultrasound video to digital format. The time-base correction and the conversion to digital format both introduce lag into this video stream.

The constraints imposed by our system and by the hardware platform are summarized in the following list:

(1) The Sirius can capture and process only two video streams simultaneously.

(2) Video streams captured by the Sirius can be routed to main memory, texture memory, or the frame buffer. The frame buffer and texture memory, however, cannot be used as destinations at the same time. Hence main memory must be one of the destinations for our two streams, while the other can be either frame buffer or texture memory.

(3) Separation of a field-multiplexed video stream is best done if the stream is captured into the frame buffer (fast). It can also be done if captured into main memory (albeit slow), but it is virtually impossible if captured into texture memory.

(4) The camera video contains landmarks which must be detected; therefore it cannot be captured into texture memory. If it is captured into main memory (convenient for inspection), it will have to be copied to the frame buffer for display. If it goes into the frame buffer, it will have to be copied into main memory for landmark search (moderately slow, since in practice only the areas of the image containing landmarks need to be transferred and inspected).

(5) The Sirius captures video into texture memory only in a 512×1024×24-bit format, severely limiting the number of frames that can be held at any one time. This is unacceptable since we want to be able to simultaneously display multiple textured ultrasound slices. However, the ultrasound video images are monochrome and could easily fit into 256×256×8 bits of texture memory each (with downsampling). Therefore ultrasound video cannot be captured directly into texture memory, although it must eventually be loaded into texture memory so that we can take advantage of the hardware texturing capability.

(6) We had only one Sirius unit and one graphics pipeline.

From this (over-determined) set of constraints it follows that the (digital) ultrasound video signal must be captured into main memory, where it is resampled (by the CPU) into the 256×256×8-bit format, and then transferred into texture memory. The combined (analog) camera video signal is captured by the Sirius into the frame buffer.

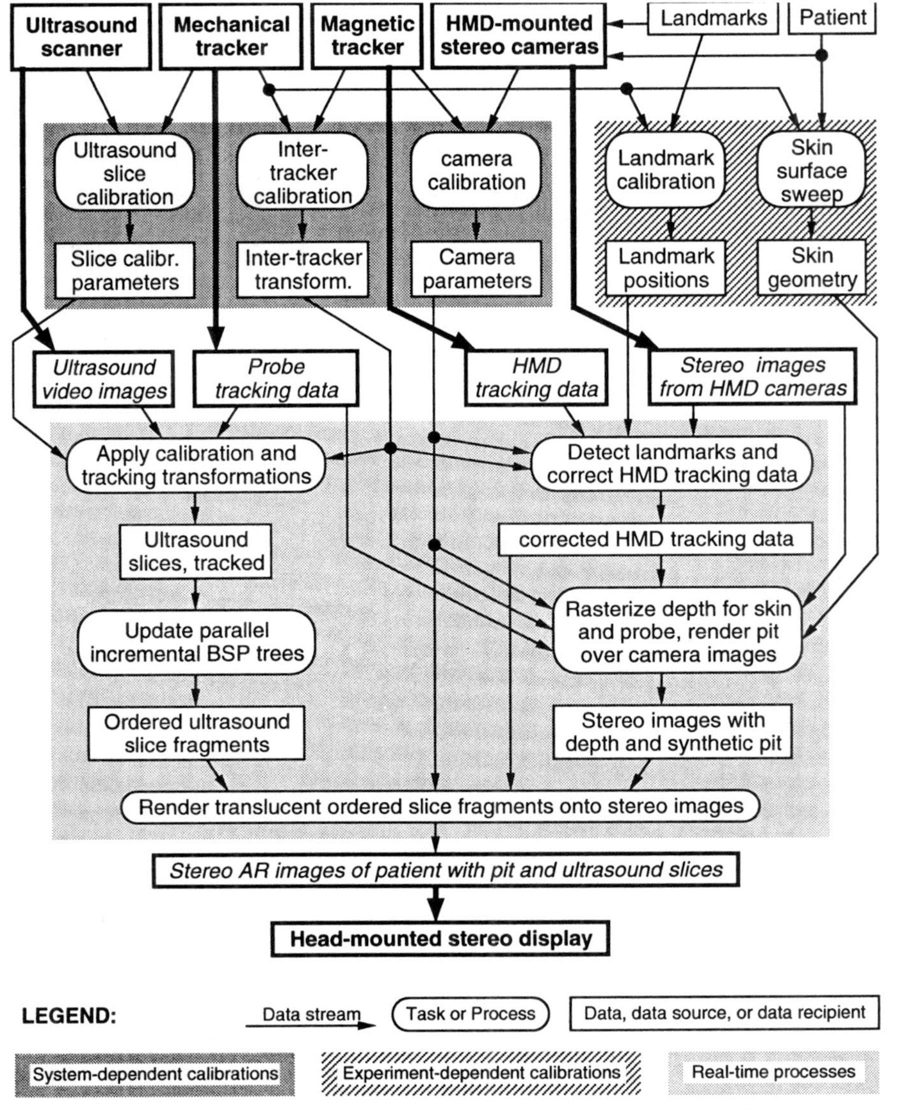

Figure 4. Data flow within stereo AR system for ultrasound visualization

4.1.2 *Tracking Input*

The Flock magnetic tracker and the FARO mechanical tracker are attached to the Onyx via two dedicated 38,400 baud serial lines. The FARO operates at a maximum rate of 27 Hz, the Flock at 103 Hz (both, however, are read asynchronously within the main loop software on the Onyx). The ultrasound probe is mounted on the FARO arm with a custom-built mount. The Flock receiver is mounted on a plastic arm which is rigidly attached to the stereo camera rig on the VR-4 HMD.

4.1.3 *Video Output*

We selected an MCO configuration that simultaneously transmits a 1280×1024 high-resolution image and two 640×480 VGA images. The high-resolution image is used for the user interface. The two VGA images contain the viewports for camera image capture and hence for the AR imagery. The VGA signals are fed via commercial VGA-to-S-Video scan converters (Extron Super Emotia) into the left and right eye displays of the VR-4. We also carry these two signals to standard VGA monitors in the lab so that people other than the HMD wearer can observe. The monitors for all three output signals are visible in Figure 2.

4.2 System Operation

Figure 4 shows the data flow within the system. Across the top are the input sources. The system captures input data from four different sources that "sample" the real world—two video streams (camera, ultrasound) and two tracking data streams (head, probe). These four streams are processed into the stereoscopic AR HMD display that is the system's output (bottom of the diagram). The upper third of the diagram shows the calibration procedures that must be performed before system operation; the lower two thirds depicts the data flow required to produce a stereo image pair.

4.2.1 *Calibration*

The first set of calibration procedures are system-dependent calibrations of the input video streams and tracking streams. The ultrasound machine is calibrated to determine a transformation between pixels in the ultrasound video stream and the local coordinate system of the tracked ultrasound probe (a plane equation and scale factors for the ultrasound slice). The procedure also calibrates the area of the ultrasound video image that contains scanned data (a polygonal outline for the ultrasound slice) [State94]. During system operation, this area is resampled into the 256×256×8 format to be loaded into texture memory.

A calibration procedure similar to [Bajura95] is performed on the camera-sensor rig to determine the transformation between the head tracking sensor and the cameras' local coordinate systems. The cameras' intrinsic parameters (location of the center of projection, field of view) are also determined, albeit with limited accuracy [State96]. Finally, a transformation between the coordinate systems of the magnetic and mechanical trackers is determined by calibrating each to a reference coordinate system (a lab-mounted wooden frame).

The second set of calibrations are experiment-dependent calibrations. First, we sweep the patient's skin with the mechanical tracker and acquire 3D points on the surface. Section 6 describes how we use this surface to generate proper occlusion cues. Second, we record the precise location of the landmarks used by the hybrid head tracking algorithm (described in Section 8).

4.2.2 *Real-time processing*

The bottom two thirds of Figure 4 shows the real-time processes implemented on the Onyx. For each (stereo) frame to be generated, the software captures one frame from the ultrasound video stream, one frame from the multiplexed camera image stream, and readings from each of the two trackers.

The ultrasound video defines a texture for the ultrasound slice polygon to be displayed. The slice's position and orientation is determined by the probe tracking data together with the off-line calibration parameters. The slice polygon is processed by a dual BSP tree algorithm described in Section 7.

The multiplexed stereo camera video frame is captured into the frame buffer and split into the left and right eye images (odd fields into the left eye image, even fields into the right). Each scan line is duplicated in order to preserve aspect ratio. The left and right eye areas of the frame buffer correspond to the output regions of the MCO's two VGA channels.

The Flock report is used to estimate the locations of the landmarks visible in the camera images. The landmarks' actual positions in the video images are then determined by image analysis, and corrected position and orientation data is computed for each camera. Based on this data, the pit and other geometric elements are rendered on top of the video image background, as described in Section 6. Finally, the ultrasound slices are rendered using the dual BSP tree. The rendering stages are executed twice, once for each eye.

5 STEREO VIDEO-SEE-THROUGH HMD

Without stereo depth cues, the physician user of our system cannot assess the distance to the patient or the depth of a lesion within the breast. The construction of a stereo video-see-through HMD (visible in Figure 2) was key to physician acceptance of our system and to the start of patient trials.

5.1 Head-mounted cameras

We mounted cameras on the front of the HMD on top of the housing for the LCD displays. In this arrangement, the camera's centers of projection are located approximately 5 cm above and 8 cm in front of the wearer's eyes, who must learn to compensate for this constant eye offset. Even after accommodation training, we expect the user's performance to be impaired [Rolland95].

For the mount, we used an interpupillary distance of 64 mm and chose a fixed convergence angle of 4°. The horizontal field of view of the lenses is 28°, producing a stereo overlap of roughly 80% at a working distance of 50 cm. The 4° convergence is a compromise; we could achieve 100% overlap with a larger convergence angle (about 7.4°), but then viewing the images inside the HMD would cause eye strain since the display convergence angle does not match the camera convergence angle. (The convergence angle of 4° also makes the stereograms in this paper slightly difficult to fuse.)

The limited light sensitivity of our cameras causes problems for the image analysis technique mentioned in Section 8.2. In order to get enough light for good image quality and landmark tracking, the iris of the cameras must be opened to the point that the depth of field is less than the depth extent of the working volume in our application. We therefore manually adjust the focus on the cameras as necessary.

5.2 Head-mounted display

The VR-4 weighs over 2 pounds before the 1.5 pounds of camera and fixtures are added. Most of this weight is concentrated around the user's eyes, making the device very front-heavy. A counterweight provides balance, but nearly doubles the weight of the HMD.

The horizontal field of view in the VR-4 is approximately 40° for each eye, compared to 28° in each camera. This mismatch leads to a "telephoto" viewing experience similar to that of using binoculars. The VR-4 displays can be set to a convergence angle of either zero or three degrees.

The stereo images acquired by the Sirius have a resolution of 646×243 for each eye (due to left-right field multiplexing). The complete AR views generated by the system have a final resolution of 640×480 for each eye. However, the resolution of the VR-4 is only roughly 250×230. Within those pixels we map the 256×256 ultrasound data slice (downsampled from the original 512×512) to a small fraction of the screen—about 40×40 for the image in Figure 1. In Figure 1, a 3 mm breast lesion would image on approximately 3×3 VR4 HMD pixels,

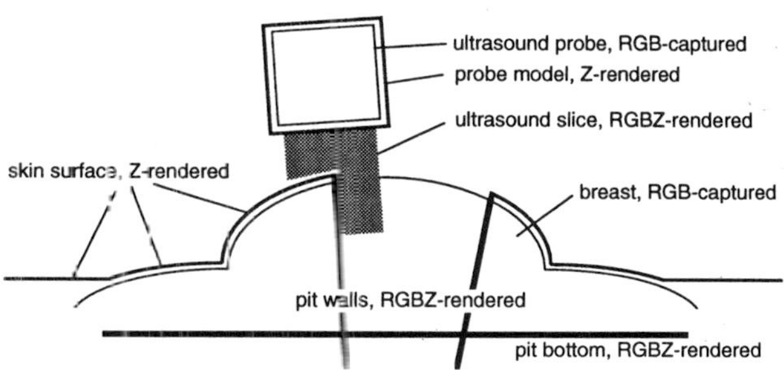

Figure 5. Geometric elements for the synthesis of occlusion cues

and a 22-gauge needle would appear 0.7 pixels thick. The HMD resolution is hence adequate for training phantom experiments—where thicker needles can be used—but insufficient for human subject trials.

6 OCCLUSION

To present correct occlusion cues in our visualization, we must enhance the pure *RGB* color information acquired by the HMD-mounted cameras with proper depth (or *z*) values. We use a set of geometric elements that are rendered in depth (*z*) only (and not in *RGB*). The top edges of the pit must be spatially aligned with the patient's skin, otherwise the pit and the rendering of the ultrasound data will appear pasted on or swimming across the patient's skin, rather than appearing (and staying) properly positioned with respect to the patient (Figure 5).

For both correct occlusion and correct registration of the pit, we must know the location and shape of the patient's skin in 3D lab space. To acquire this information, we sweep the tip of the FARO over the patient's skin and collect (unordered) 3D points from the surface. (This assumes that the patient will not move during or after the procedure.) The collection procedure is one of the experiment-specific calibrations in Section 4.2.1.

To resolve occlusion, the unordered set of points must be converted into a polygonal surface. Techniques such as Delaunay triangulation can be applied only to 2D arrays of points; we therefore exploit the shape of the human body and convert the points into cylindrical coordinates using a horizontal cylinder axis that is roughly aligned with the patient's spinal column. Delaunay triangulation is then applied in the cylinder's height-angle domain, under the assumption that the surface to be constructed is a radius field—i. e., that it can be expressed as a function *radius* = *radius(height, angle)*, similar to Cyberware™ scans. We then resample the mesh output from the Delaunay triangulation into a regular grid in the height and angle dimensions.

The regular grid of the resampled triangles, together with the cylindrical coordinate system in which it is defined, is then used to create a polygonal model of the patient's skin surface, as well as a polygonal model of the pit, which is embedded within the skin surface model. Z-rendering of the surface model minus the pit opening results in a correct *z*-buffer for the patient surface. *RGBZ*-rendering of the pit model results in a colored and *z*-buffered pit; As a result of this process, synthetic elements such as the ultrasound slice attached to the transducer can now penetrate into or disappear below the skin of the patient, except within the pit, where they remain visible.

In addition, we *z*-render a polygonal model for the (FARO-tracked) ultrasound probe, which enables the probe to occlude synthetic image elements if it passes in front of them. For example, if the probe is positioned between the HMD cameras and the pit, the probe obscures the pit (Figures 1, 3). We do not track other real world elements such as the physician's hands, which hold the probe and may also pass between the

Frame	Scene 1	Tree 1	Scene 2	Tree 2
1				
2				
3				
4				
5				
6				
7				
8				

	new	active	expired
Ultrasound slices:			
BSP tree fragments:			

Figure 6. Dual parallel BSP tree for $n = 3$. The shaded areas represent the tree selected for rendering. Both trees are updated.

HMD cameras and the patient's breast, so we cannot eliminate all depth conflicts from the user's field of view. Nevertheless, the implementation of depth images for certain components of the real world has significantly enhanced our visualization.

7 REAL-TIME INCREMENTAL VOLUME VISUALIZATION

The AR system must produce stereo visualizations in near real-time (at least 10 stereo frames per second) from a dynamic volumetric target (for example, a cyst within the breast plus a moving needle). While the dataset is a 3D volume, the data is acquired as a sequence of 2D slices. We have implemented a dynamic volumetric display that maintains a set of such slices in the system. During the generation of each output frame, as a new frame is acquired from the ultrasound video stream, one new slice is added to the set and the oldest slice is removed from it. Thus the system always displays the n most recent slices. Volume reconstruction (even incremental reconstruction [Ohbuchi92]) of a set of slices into a regular grid is computationally too expensive. Instead, we use the Onyx' texturing hardware to visualize the slices as polygons with translucent textures. The shape of the polygon is determined as part of the calibrations described in Section 4.2.1. The texture for the polygon comes from the ultrasound video frame.

Rendering of the volume is accomplished by rendering the collection of (possibly intersecting) translucent textured polygons. Due to its hardware texturing capability and large texture memory, the Onyx is well-suited for this kind of volume visualization. The translucent polygons must be presented to the graphics pipeline in back-to-front order. We use a binary space partition (BSP) tree to establish the order [Fuchs80].

The set of n polygons contained in the BSP tree constantly changes. We delete a polygonal slice from the BSP tree as each new slice is added. Unfortunately deletion of a polygon from a BSP tree is more expensive than insertion, particularly if polygon fragmentation and the associated decrease in efficiency are to be avoided. Leaving expired polygons in the tree while tagging them as expired (so that they are not rendered) is also problematic when new slices are being added at each frame: the size of the tree can grow as the square of the number of insertions [Fuchs80].

We solve the BSP tree update problem by constructing and maintaining two BSP trees, out of phase in time, in the following manner: Let n be the number of ultrasound slices the user wants displayed (Figure 6). As the first n slices arrive during frames 1 through n, they are added to only the first tree. When slice n+1 arrives, it is inserted into the first BSP tree, slice 1 is marked "expired" (but is not removed) from the tree, and the second BSP tree is started with this single slice, n+1. With slices n+2 through 2n, the new slice is inserted into both trees, the appropriate old slice in the first tree is marked "expired," and the first tree continues to be rendered. After processing slice 2n, the second tree contains (exactly) the most recent n slices and no "expired" slices and unnecessary fragments to slow down the traversal and rendering. The rendering is now switched to the second tree, the first tree is deleted (to be initialized next with slice 2n+1). The procedure continues in this way, always rendering from the older tree until the newer one contains n slice images.

The HMD view in Figure 7 shows a volume visualization of a lesion within a breast training phantom penetrated by a needle.

8 IMPROVING REGISTRATION

The breast biopsy task requires very high precision. The physician may be required to place a thin needle – for example, 22 gauge (0.7 mm diameter) for cyst aspiration, 14 gauge (2.1 mm diameter) for biopsy – into a 3 mm cyst. Of the trackers we have tried, none have the accuracy and precision required for this medical application. We therefore combine a mechanical tracker (FARO), a magnetic tracker (Flock) corrected by a lookup table, and vision-based tracking to

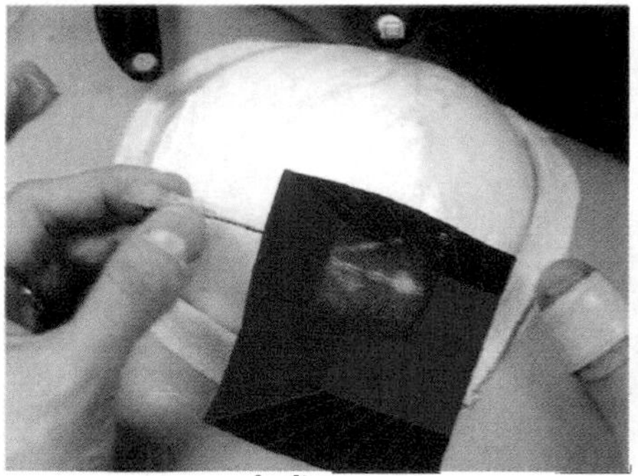

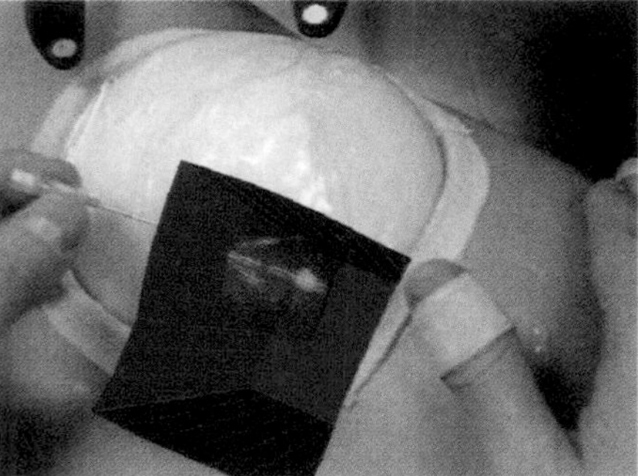

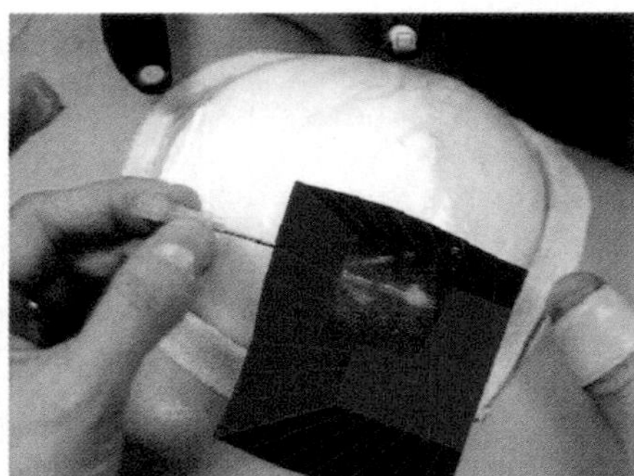

Figure 7. Real-time stereo HMD view with ultrasound volume display. A needle has been inserted into the breast phantom; the inside of the phantom has been imaged with the probe, resulting in a volume representation of the inside of the breast. The needle is registered with its image inside the ultrasound volume. The phantom also contains needle traces from previous insertion attempts.

achieve improved registration of real imagery (patient, ultrasound probe, biopsy needle) and synthetic imagery (ultrasound slices, rendered visual and occlusion cues).

8.1 Correction table for magnetic tracker

The Flock is the primary head tracker. Since our lab has metal in the floor, ceiling, and light fixtures, and since we use metal objects and electric fields within the work environment (FARO, PIE), there is a significant amount of static distortion of the magnetic field. Distortion is one of the possible sources for the Flock's tracking errors of up to 10 cm in position and up to 10° in orientation within our tracking area. Removing the sources of distortion is often not desirable (in the case of FARO and PIE) or not possible (floor, ceiling, lights). Expanding upon the work of others [Bryson92, Ghazisaedy95], we therefore statically calibrated the Flock.

For the calibration procedure, we affix the Flock sensor to the FARO (buffered by plastic) and collect sample points at thousands of arbitrary locations in the work environment. We then determine the error in the Flock reports by comparing Flock and FARO readings. We then resample these error values into a rectilinear look-up table.

The calibrated Flock performs quite well for position, with errors by 80 percent, down to an average post-correction error of 0.5 cm. The calibration does not enjoy such success for orientation correction, however. It reduces orientation error by only 40 percent, down to 1.4 degrees on average. Further details can be found in [Livingston95].

8.2 Vision-based tracking

Even after table-based correction, the Flock is not sufficiently accurate for the application's registration requirements. We therefore use a hybrid head tracking algorithm and image landmarks to obtain higher accuracy. Our landmarks are fluorescent discs positioned in view of the HMD-mounted cameras, typically close to the sterile field (visible in Figure 1.). The positions of the landmarks in world space are known; they are calibrated with the FARO as part of the experiment-specific calibrations outlined in Section 4.2.1.

Landmark tracking is performed by the Onyx CPU, using the stereo images captured into the frame buffer by the Sirius. The software attempts to predict expected landmark positions. This minimizes the size of the pixel arrays that must be transferred from the frame buffer into main memory and searched for landmarks. If a single landmark is detected, two out of three degrees of freedom of the camera's orientation can be corrected under simplifying assumptions [Bajura95]. With two landmarks, orientation can be corrected fully, again under the same assumptions. With three landmarks, camera position and orientation can be determined completely to within a sign. With knowledge of the transformation between the camera coordinate systems of the stereo cameras—a system-dependent calibration not mentioned in Section 4.2.1—the system can even correct both cameras with landmarks detected in only one of the cameras. Furthermore, the system stores the correction and applies it to the raw Flock reading even if no landmarks are visible. However, the quality of the correction degrades rapidly in such cases and the HMD wearer is required to keep the landmarks in view. An improved version of our hybrid tracking system is described in [State96].

9 SUMMARY AND CONCLUSIONS

Using the AR system described here, a physician successfully guided a biopsy needle into an artificial tumor within a life-sized breast model. The system is sufficiently robust and accurate for the physician to report that the procedure on the breast model was easy. The key efforts that led to this milestone were the construction of a stereo input and stereo output video see-through head-mounted display, methods for properly resolving occlusion between real and synthetic objects, a new real-time volume visualization method using parallel BSP trees, a closed-loop vision-based head tracking algorithm, and judiciously applied calibration techniques for all input data streams (cameras, trackers, ultrasound probe).

An AR visualization viewed by an "over-the-shoulder" observer during two patient case studies demonstrated some of the remaining problems with the AR system. The resolution of the HMD is insufficient for good visualization of the ultrasound image. The HMD with stereo cameras is too heavy. The image landmarks are difficult to keep in view and unoccluded for the physician. Finally, the data captured in real-time from the four input streams is not synchronized. While we have significantly improved spatial registration, temporal registration (synchronization) remains a problem.

10 FUTURE WORK

We envision the introduction of a system such as ours into the operating room, but advances in several areas are required before this goal can be realized. First, the HMD should be considerably lighter and feature higher-quality image acquisition (cameras) as well as higher-resolution displays. In future video-see-through HMDs the optical paths of camera and user's eye should be aligned, in order to eliminate the eye offset problem. This can be accomplished by folding the camera's optical path with mirrors. Second, head tracking should be more accurate and less dependent on (or even completely independent of) landmarks. We are investigating a better orientation calibration for the magnetic tracker and are considering alternatives such as optical trackers, to be used alone or as part of a hybrid tracking technique.

The input streams must be synchronized (temporally registered). Data from these is currently captured asynchronously, at discrete intervals, from the four input devices. Ideally, all four signals should sample the real world at the same moment in time, thus ensuring that the stereo AR display shows a consistent enhanced view of the real world, albeit delayed with respect to the real world by the time it took to synthesize the view. In practice, each of the streams has a certain amount of lag associated with it. Precise knowledge about the lag in each stream holds the potential for eliminating or compensating for lag differences between streams. We have begun to devise experiments and software organization strategies for this purpose.

An operative system should address a number of additional problems. The noisy quality of ultrasound images of human tissue makes targets such as cysts or tumors difficult to recognize and even more challenging to visualize volumetrically. (The image in Figure 7 was acquired in a training phantom.) It is therefore necessary to explore techniques for improved real-time identification (segmentation) and visualization of cysts and lesions in human breast tissue. Finally, methods to track the skin surface and its deformations in real time are required.

ACKNOWLEDGMENTS

It takes many people to realize a complex system like the one described here. We wish to express our gratitude to John Airey, Ronald T. Azuma, Michael Bajura, Andrew Brandt, Gary Bishop, David T. Chen, D'nardo Colucci, Darlene Freedman, Arthur Gregory, Stefan Gottschalk, David Harrison, Linda A. Houseman, Marco Jacobs, Fred Jordan, Kurtis Keller, Amy Kreiling, Shankar Krishnan, Dinesh Manocha, Mark McCarthy, Michael North, Ryutarou Ohbuchi, Stephen M.

Pizer, Scott Pritchett, Russell M. Taylor II, Chris Tector, Kathy Tesh, John Thomas, Greg Turk, Peggy Wetzel, Steve Work, the anonymous patients, the Geometry Center at the University of Minnesota, PIE Medical Equipment B.V., Silicon Graphics, Inc., and the UNC Medical Image Program Project (NCI P01 CA47982).

We thank the anonymous reviewers for their comments and criticism.

This work was supported in part by ARPA DABT63-93-C-0048 ("Enabling Technologies and Application Demonstrations for Synthetic Environments"). Approved by ARPA for Public Release—Distribution Unlimited. Additional support was provided by the National Science Foundation Science and Technology Center for Computer Graphics and Scientific Visualization (NSF prime contract 8920219).

REFERENCES

AZUMA, R. A Survey of Augmented Reality. SIGGRAPH 1995 Course Notes #9 (Developing Advanced Virtual Reality Applications), pp. 20-1 through 20-38.

AZUMA, R., BISHOP, G. Improving Static and Dynamic Registration in an Optical See-through HMD. Proceedings of SIGGRAPH 94 (Orlando, Florida, July 24-29, 1994). In *Computer Graphics* Proceedings, Annual Conference Series, 1994, ACM SIGGRAPH, pp. 197-204.

BAJURA, M., FUCHS, H., OHBUCHI, R. Merging Virtual Objects with the Real World. Proceedings of SIGGRAPH '92 (Chicago, Illinois, July 26-31, 1992). In *Computer Graphics* 26, 2 (July 1992), ACM SIGGRAPH, New York, 1992, pp. 203-210.

BAJURA, M., NEUMANN, U. Dynamic Registration Correction in Video-Based Augmented Reality Systems. *IEEE Computer Graphics and Applications* (September, 1995), pp. 52-60.

BARBER, C.B., DOBKIN, D.P., HUHDANPAA, H. The Quickhull Algorithm for Convex Hull. *Geometry Center Technical Report GCG53,* 1993.

BRYSON, S. Measurement and Calibration of Static Distortion of Position Data from 3D Trackers. *SPIE Stereoscopic Displays and Applications III*, 1992, pp. 244-255.

CABRAL, B., CAM, N., FORAN, J. Accelerated Volume Rendering and Tomographic Reconstruction Using Texture Mapping Hardware. *Proceedings of the 1994 Symposium on Volume Visualization* (Washington, D. C., October 1994), pp. 91-97, 131, back cover.

COLUCCI, D., CHI, V. Computer Glasses: A Compact, Lightweight, and Cost-effective Display for Monocular and Tiled Wide Field-of-View Systems. *Proceedings of SPIE*, Vol. 2537, pp. 61-70 (1995).

CULLIP, T.J., NEUMANN, U. Accelerating Volume Reconstruction With 3D Texture Hardware. *University of North Carolina Department of Computer Science Technical Report* TR93-027.

FUCHS, H., ABRAM, G., GRANT, E. Near Real-time Shaded Display of Rigid Objects. Proceedings of SIGGRAPH '83 (July 1983). In *Computer Graphics*; 17, 3 (July 1983), ACM SIGGRAPH, New York, 1983, pp. 65-72.

FUCHS, H., KEDEM, Z., NAYLOR, B. On Visible Surface Generation by a Priori Tree Structures. Proceedings of SIGGRAPH '80 (July 1980). In *Computer Graphics*; 14, 3 (July 1980), ACM SIGGRAPH, New York, 1980, pp. 124-133.

FURNESS, T. The super cockpit and its human factors challenges. *Proceedings of the Human Factors Society*, 30, 1968, pp. 48-52.

GARRETT, W.F., FUCHS, H., STATE, A., WHITTON, M.C. Real-Time Incremental Visualization of Dynamic Ultrasound Volumes Using Parallel BSP Trees. *University of North Carolina Department of Computer Science Technical Report TR96-018.*

GHAZISAEDY, M., ADAMCZYK, D., SANDIN, D., KENYON, R., DEFANTI, T. Ultrasonic Calibration of a Magnetic Tracker in a Virtual Reality Space. *Proceedings of the Virtual Reality Annual International Symposium '95*, IEEE Computer Society, Los Alamitos, CA, 1995, pp. 179-188.

LALOUCHE, R.C., BICKMORE, D., TESSLER, F., MANKOVICH, H.K., KANGARALOO, H. Three-dimensional reconstruction of ultrasound images. *SPIE'89, Medical Imaging*, SPIE, 1989, pp. 59-66.

LIVINGSTON, M.A., STATE, A. Magnetic Tracker Calibration for Improved Registration in Augmented Reality Systems. *University of North Carolina Department of Computer Science Technical Report TR95-037.*

LORENSEN, W., CLINE, H., NAFIS, C., KIKINIS, R., ALTOBELLI, D., GLEASON, L. Enhancing reality in the operating room. *Proceedings of Visualization 1993* (Los Alamitos, CA, October 1993), pp. 410-415.

MELLOR, J.P. Enhanced Reality Visualization in a Surgical Environment. MS Thesis, MIT Department of Electrical Engineering, 1995.

NAYLOR, B., AMANATIDES, J., THIBAULT, W. Merging BSP Tree Yields Polyhedral Set Operations. Proceedings of SIGGRAPH '90 (Dallas, Texas, August 1990). In *Computer Graphics*; 24, 4 (August 1990), pp. 115-124.

NELSON, T., ELVINS, T. Visualization of 3D Ultrasound Data. *IEEE Computer Graphics and Applications*, (November, 1993), pp. 50-57.

OHBUCHI, R., CHEN, D.T., FUCHS, H. Incremental Volume Reconstruction and Rendering for 3D Ultrasound Imaging. *University of North Carolina Department of Computer Science Technical Report TR92-037.*

ROBINETT, W., ROLLAND, J.P. A Computational Model for the Stereoscopic Optics of a Head-Mounted Display. *Presence,* Vol. 1, No. 1 (Winter 1992), pp. 45-62.

ROLLAND, J.P., BIOCCA, F., BARLOW, T., KANCHERLA, A.R. Quantification of Adaptation to Virtual-Eye Location in See-Thru Head-Mounted Displays. *Proceedings of the Virtual Reality: Annual International Symposium '95*, IEEE Computer Society, Los Alamitos, CA, 1995, pp. 56-66.

ROSE, E., BREEN, D., AHLERS, K., CRAMPTON, C., TUCERYAN, M., WHITAKER, R., GREER, D. Annotating Real-World Objects Using Augmented Reality. *Proceedings of Computer Graphics International 1995* (Leeds, UK, June, 25-30, 1995), pp. 357-370.

SIMS, D. New Realities in Aircraft Design and Manufacture. *IEEE Computer Graphics and Applications*, (March, 1994), p. 91.

STATE, A., CHEN, D.T., TECTOR, C., BRANDT, A., CHEN, H., OHBUCHI, R., BAJURA, M., FUCHS, H. Case Study: Observing a Volume-Rendered Fetus within a Pregnant Patient. *Proceedings of IEEE Visualization '94,* October 1994, pp. 364-368, CP-41.

STATE, A., HIROTA, G., CHEN, D.T., GARRETT, W.F., LIVINGSTON, M.A. Superior Augmented Reality Registration by Integrating Landmark Tracking and Magnetic Tracking. Proceedings of SIGGRAPH '96 (New Orleans, LA, August 4-9, 1996). In *Computer Graphics* Proceedings, Annual Conference Series, 1996, ACM SIGGRAPH.

STATE, A., MCALLISTER, J., NEUMANN, U., CHEN, H., CULLIP, T.J., CHEN, D.T., FUCHS, H. Interactive Volume Visualization on a Heterogeneous Message-Passing Multicomputer. *Proceedings of the 1995 Symposium on Interactive 3D Graphics* (Monterey, CA, April 1995), pp. 69-74, 208, front cover.

SUTHERLAND, I. A head-mounted three dimensional display. *Proceedings of the Fall Joint Computer Conference*, 1968.

WLOKA, M.M., ANDERSON, B.G. Resolving Occlusion in Augmented Reality. *Proceedings of the 1995 Symposium on Interactive 3D Graphics* (Monterey, CA, April 1995), pp. 5-12.

Adding Force Feedback to Graphics Systems: Issues and Solutions

William R. Mark[1] Scott C. Randolph[2] Mark Finch[3] James M. Van Verth[4] Russell M. Taylor II[5]

Department of Computer Science*
University of North Carolina at Chapel Hill

ABSTRACT

Integrating force feedback with a complete real-time virtual environment system presents problems which are more difficult than those encountered in building simpler force-feedback systems. In particular, lengthy computations for graphics or simulation require a decoupling of the haptic servo loop from the main application loop if high-quality forces are to be produced. We present some approaches to these problems and describe our force-feedback software library which implements these techniques and provides other benefits including haptic-textured surfaces, device independence, distributed operation and easy enhancement.

CR Descriptors: H.1.2 [Models and Principles]: User/Machine Systems; C.3 [Special-Purpose and Application-Based Systems]: Real-time systems; I.3.7 [Computer Graphics]: Three-Dimensional Graphics and Realism – *Virtual Reality*; I.6.8 [Simulation and Modeling]: Types of Simulation – *Distributed*.

Additional Keywords: haptic, force feedback, friction model, intermediate surface representation, scientific visualization, interactive graphics, virtual environment, virtual world.

1. INTRODUCTION

As designers of interactive computer systems work to increase the information flow between the computer and the user, sensory modalities other than vision become increasingly important. One such modality is force feedback. The sensing of forces is closely coupled to both the visual system and one's sense of three-dimensional space; the eyes and hands work in concert to explore and manipulate objects.

* CB #3175, Sitterson Hall; Chapel Hill, NC 27599. Tel. +1.919.962.1700
Authors' current organizations and contact information:
1 UNC-CH; markw@cs.unc.edu; www.cs.unc.edu/~markw
2 Spectrum Holobyte; randolph@holobyte.com; www.holobyte.com
3 Numerical Design, Ltd.; mf@ndl.com; www.ndl.com/ndl
4 Virtus Corp.; jim.van.verth@virtus.com; www.cs.unc.edu/~vanverth
5 UNC-CH; taylorr@cs.unc.edu; www.cs.unc.edu/~taylorr

Force feedback usefully enhances the capabilities of virtual environment systems; [17] showed that force feedback increases productivity in solving rigid-body placement problems and [8] demonstrated an atomic-surface modification system which would not have been feasible with graphics alone.

Virtual environment force displays use models and algorithms described in the robotics and teleoperation literature for low-level control—see for example [9][22][23]. When combining a computer graphics engine, a simulation, and a force-feedback device into one system, there are several areas of concern in addition to that of low-level control. The force-feedback component of such a system should:

- Maintain a high update rate in the force servo loop.
- Present high quality forces without detectable artifacts.
- Transparently support different force-feedback devices.
- Interface easily and cleanly with the rest of the system.

We discuss some approaches to these problems and present the Armlib force-feedback library [13] as one solution.

2. PROBLEMS AND SOLUTIONS

It has been clearly shown that it is necessary to run the simulation and graphics loops of virtual environment (VE) systems asynchronously in order to maintain reasonable display update rates (around 20 Hz) in the presence of long simulation computations. [11][20]

Such a decoupling is even more critical for force display, where update rates of several hundred Hz are required to produce high-quality forces. The necessary rate depends somewhat on the characteristics of the force-feedback device and control algorithm, but, for example, [1] required an update rate of 500 Hz for their system. If the update rate falls below the required minimum, the user begins to notice high-frequency discontinuities and hard surfaces become either soft or unstable.

We can decouple the simulation and haptic loops on a single machine by using either multiple processors or *very* frequent context switches. However, it is often more practical to dedicate one real-time machine to the haptic servo loop, and use other machine(s) for the rest of the virtual environment tasks (simulation, high-performance graphics, etc.). This strategy allows each machine to be well matched to its task. It also allows for flexible system configuration, which is particularly useful in a research environment.

The general case of such a split system connects the force-feedback device directly to a *force server*. This server tracks the *probe* of the force-feedback device (held in the user's hand) and executes the force-feedback servo loop. The application connects to this force server through some communication channel, retrieving position information from the server and sending descriptions of forces or force fields to it. We currently use a TCP/IP Ethernet communications channel because we must connect to existing graphics and research equipment; a low-latency, high-bandwidth channel such as shared memory would be superior.

Kim et al. [12] did the first work in this area, showing that teleoperation systems benefit from a decoupling of low-level force servo loops from higher-level control. Adachi et al. [1] were the first to apply the technique to virtual environment force-feedback systems. Rather than simply supplying a single force vector to the force-feedback controller, they supply an *intermediate representation* (their term, which we adopt) for a force model. This representation is updated infrequently by the application code, but is evaluated at a high update rate by the force-feedback controller.

Gomez et al. [10] demonstrate a system which takes almost the opposite approach. Their main simulation runs on the force-feedback machine and sends state updates to a graphics machine.

2.1 Intermediate representations

The kind of intermediate representation that is most useful depends on the application. A molecular modeling system might use spheres of contact. An immersive design system could send a representation of nearby surfaces. A simulation meant to teach understanding of physics force fields [3] might send equations to the server that describe the field.

Mitsuishi et al. [16] demonstrate a remote milling system which uses an intermediate representation of average tool force.

We describe two general intermediate representations, *plane and probe* and *point-to-point spring*, and our extensions to these types.

Plane and probe

In the *plane and probe* model, the force server keeps models of a plane which the probe can contact. [1] When the probe penetrates the plane, a restorative spring force that depends on the depth of the penetration is applied. The result is a surface with controllable sponginess against which the user can push (see Figure 1).

Using this model, the application computes a local planar approximation to the surface at the user's hand location each time through its main loop. The user feels a firm plane (forces updated at ~1 kHz by the force server), while the plane's position is updated more slowly (at ~20 Hz) by the application. The increase in local force update rate from 20 Hz to 1 kHz dramatically increases the maximum firmness of the surface while maintaining a stable system.

Figure 2 shows how this this technique works in one application, the Nanomanipulator, which allows the user to control the motion of a microscopic tip as it travels over a surface. [8] The initial implementation of the Nanomanipulator system performed its force computations on the graphics host, using Armlib only to read positions and send forces to the force-feedback device. This method restricted the force updates to at most the system loop update rate, which was around 20 Hz. The result was either a soft surface with sluggish response or an unusably unstable surface. Decoupling the application and force servo loops using our plane and probe model resulted in a much more stable and stiff surface.

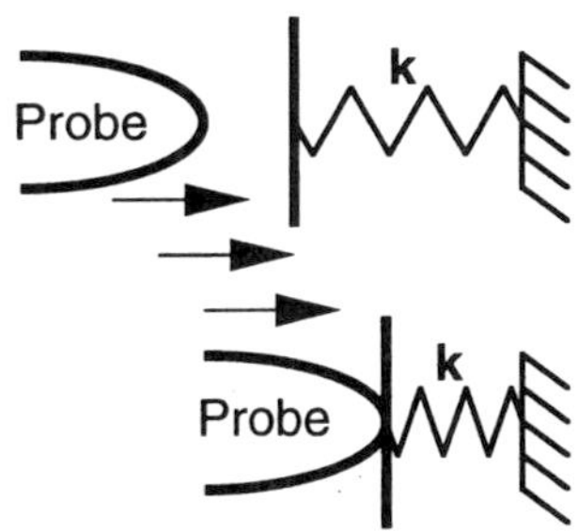

Figure 1: *A hard surface is approximated by a plane connected to a spring. When the probe encounters the plane, a spring force with spring constant* ***k*** *is applied. Very high values of* ***k*** *produce a surface that feels hard. The force is normal to the plane.*

Surface friction and texture

The surface model just described produces forces which are always perpendicular to the surface. The resulting surfaces feel like oiled glass, with the probe tending to slip off convex surface areas and into concave ones.

Previous researchers have demonstrated the importance of surface friction models in allowing the user to explore a surface without slipping. Several researchers [5][18][19] investigated models that combine static friction (which holds the probe at a fixed spot) with kinetic friction (which slows the probe's movement once it breaks free of the static friction). Adachi et al. [1] model only kinetic friction, using a velocity-based term.

Minsky et al. [15] model haptic surface textures using a friction-like technique. Rather than directly representing variations in surface height, they represent these variations using a 2D lateral force field. This field is proportional to the gradient of the surface height function. Because their force-feedback device has only two degrees of freedom, lateral forces are not proportional to the normal force, as is typical for a friction model.

We have implemented a friction model that includes both static and kinetic components and can represent simple surface textures. Adjustment of the parameters produces surfaces that feel like concrete, sand, rubber, skin, or cloth. The model is rapidly computable, allowing a high update rate. Figure 3 shows the parameters of our model graphically; an explanation follows.

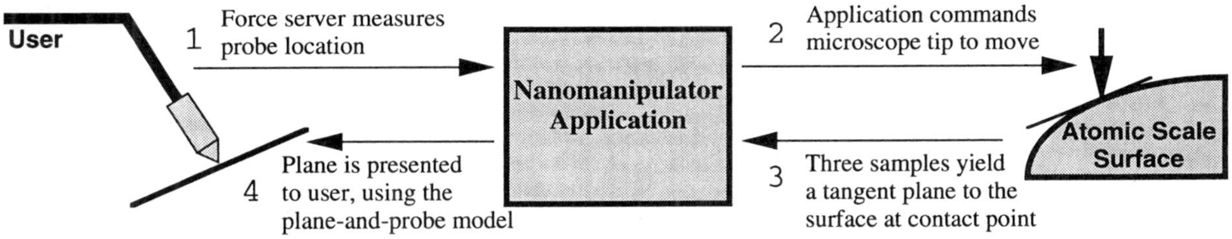

Force-Feedback Device

Atomic Force Microscope

User

1 Force server measures probe location

Nanomanipulator Application

2 Application commands microscope tip to move

Atomic Scale Surface

3 Three samples yield a tangent plane to the surface at contact point

4 Plane is presented to user, using the plane-and-probe model

Figure 2: *The Nanomanipulator application uses surface height readings from the microscope tip to determine a local plane approximation which is sent to the force server.*

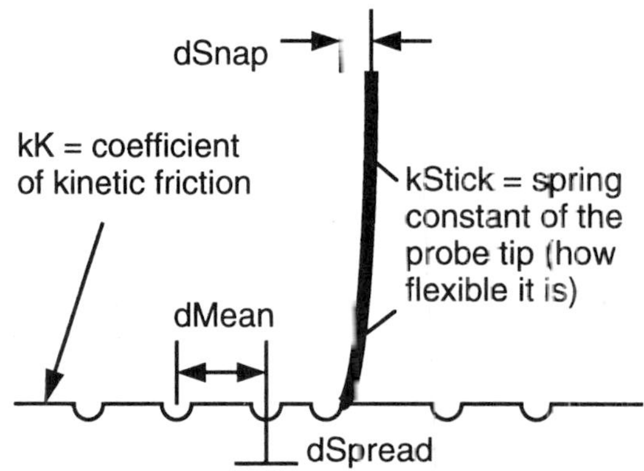

***Figure 3:** Surface friction model. The tip slides across the surface against kinetic friction **kK** until it hits a snag. Snags populate the surface with mean distance **dMean** between them, uniformly distributed within **dSpread**. The tip sticks in the snag, bending with spring constant **kStick** until moved more than **dSnap**, then it jumps free.*

Our friction model is that of a surface populated by snags being probed by a flexible tip. When the tip is not stuck in a snag, it moves across the surface opposed by a friction force that is proportional to the normal force (with coefficient of kinetic friction *kK*). When the probe encounters a snag, it sticks there until the probe moves more than *dSnap* units away from the sticking point, in any tangent direction. While it is snagged, a force tangent to the surface pulls the tip towards the center of the snag. This force is proportional to both the normal force and to the distance from the snag center (with spring constant *kStick)*.

The snags tend to hold the probe in place on the surface. This tendency provides a natural "station keeping" on surfaces with high snag density (such as sandpaper).

The snags are placed around the surface with a mean distance between snags of *dMean*, uniformly distributed within *dSpread*. In fact, we populate the surface with snags dynamically. After leaving a snag, the tip will encounter another placed with uniform probability between *dMean-dSpread/2* and *dMean+dSpread/2* units away from the first snag, regardless of the tangent direction traveled. Additionally, if the forward motion of the tip (movement away from the previous snag) ceases, it is considered to have encountered a snag at the point where forward motion stopped. Although actual surfaces could be measured to determine parameters for our model, in practice we have explored the parameter space interactively in order to produce different surfaces.

This parameterized snag distribution, which controls the transition from kinetic to static friction, is what sets our friction model apart from previous static/kinetic friction models. Salcudean and Vlaar [18] based their kinetic-to-static transition entirely on probe velocity. Salisbury et. al. [19] transitioned immediately, without providing steady-state kinetic friction. Our technique allows simulation of simple surface textures in addition to modeling standard friction. It provides these benefits while using only simple computations that allow us to maintain a high update rate.

Multiple planes

One plane often suffices to model a smooth surface, as it can be continually positioned in the correct orientation to provide the normal to the surface at the point of contact. However, a model of an object with a sharp inner edge (such as the inside corner of a box) requires multiple planes to constrain probe motion in several directions at once. Armlib extends [1] by providing this multi-plane capability, although as [24] points out, this technique can result in errors when the planes are not at right angles to each other.

Multiple probes

It is sometimes necessary to simulate a probe that is larger than a single point. An application that allows users to feel around in a virtual room with their hand is an example of such a system. One virtual probe is created for each finger on the hand and one for the palm, allowing the user to feel multiple contacts between the world and the hand (for example, resting the hand flat on a virtual desktop). Since the points might be contacting different objects, each has its own local surface with which it can collide. For example, when pulling out a chair, the thumb may rest on top of the chair while the index finger pulls it away from the table. Since the force-feedback device has only one physical probe, the user experiences the sum of the virtual probe forces; the effect is similar to sticking a single finger in a very stiff glove.

Point-to-point springs

Some applications allow the user to pick and drag objects which are subject to complex forces. Examples of such objects include rigid bodies participating in a many-body simulation and atoms in a protein, which are subject to forces determined by a molecular dynamics simulation. Often the calculation of the forces acting on the object is so complex that it can only be performed once or twice a second. Furthermore, there is usually no rapidly-computable local approximation to these forces which will remain valid for the entire interval between full calculations.

We approach this problem by implementing a compliant connection between the application loop and the force-feedback servo loop. The technique uses a simulated spring to connect the probe endpoint to the appropriate body in the simulation, as shown in Figure 4. The user experiences forces which are both reasonable and stable.

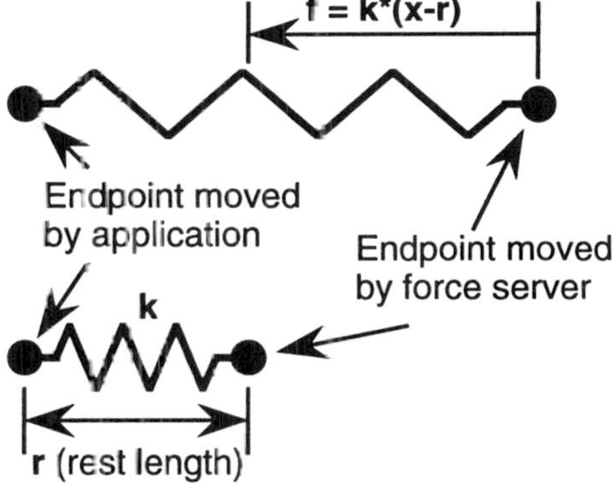

***Figure 4:** Point-to-point spring, which couples one point moved by the application (at ~1 Hz) to another moved by the force server (at ~1 kHz). The spring constant is **k**.*

The method is based on that used in [21] for mouse-based interaction. Another member of our lab, Yunshan Zhu, implemented it for a force-feedback device using two asychronous loops on the graphics host. That success led us to integrate the technique into Armlib's force server.

In this method, the application controls the motion of one endpoint of the spring at its slower update rate, while the other endpoint follows the probe motion at the force update rate. The spring applies force both to the probe (pulling the user's hand towards the point of contact) and to the application (typically adding forces into the simulation). Adjustment of the spring constant controls the tightness of the coupling between application and probe; a weaker spring produces small forces in the application while a tighter spring causes more discontinuity in the force when the application endpoint moves.

In order to prevent the user from moving the probe too rapidly, we may in the future add adjustable viscosity to the force-server loop. Viscosity would tend to keep the probe from moving large distances (and thus adding large forces) between simulation time steps.

Multiple springs

Using a single point of contact between the application and the force server, it is only possible to specify forces, not torques. This restriction is overcome by attaching springs to multiple application points and multiple virtual probes. Acting together, multiple springs can specify a force and general torque on the probe and the application model (see Figure 5).

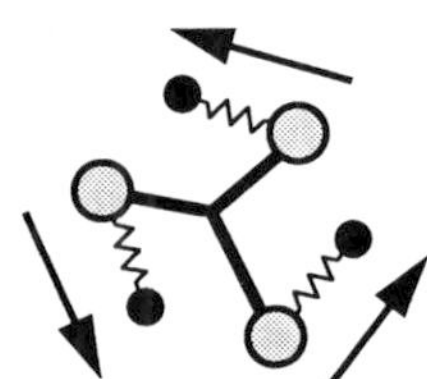

Figure 5: *Torque from multiple springs.*

2.2 Preventing force discontinuity artifacts

As pointed out in [1], the plane-and-probe model works well only when the plane equation is updated frequently compared to the lateral speed of probe motion. As shown in Figure 6, this restriction is most severe on sharply-curving surfaces. A sharp discontinuity occurs in the force model when the probe is allowed to move large distances before the new surface approximation is computed. If the discontinuity leaves the probe outside the surface, the probe drops suddenly onto the new level. Worse, if the probe is embedded in the new surface, it is violently accelerated until it leaves the surface (and sometimes the user's hand).

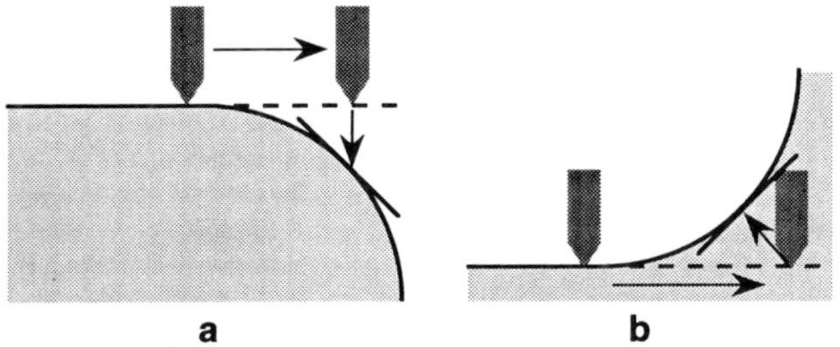

Figure 6: *Probe motion that is rapid compared to the surface curvature causes a sharp discontinuity when the new plane equation arrives. Case* ***a*** *shows the free-fall that occurs for convex surfaces. The more severe case* ***b*** *shows the sudden force caused by being deeply embedded in the surface.*

To solve the problem of extreme forces when the probe is embedded in the new surface, we have developed a *recovery time* method. This method is applied during the time immediately after new surface parameters arrive. If the probe is outside the surface at the time the parameters change, the system works as described above, dropping suddenly to the surface. If the probe is within the surface, then the normal direction for the force remains as above but the force magnitude is reduced so as to bring the tip out of the surface over a period of time, rather than instantaneously. This period of time is adjustable, and serves to move the probe out of the surface gently, while still maintaining proper direction for the force at all times. Figure 7 illustrates this algorithm.

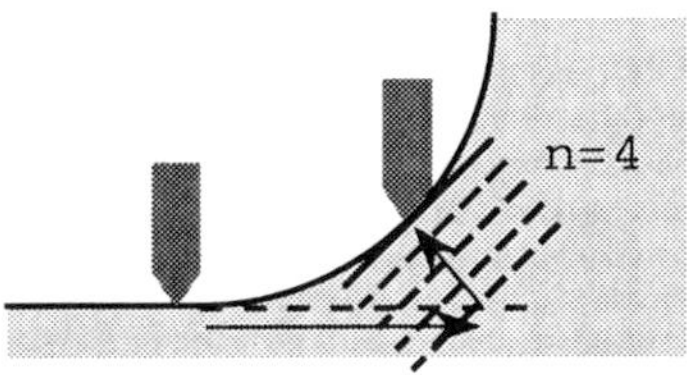

Figure 7: *When a new plane equation would cause the probe to be embedded in the surface, the recovery time algorithm artificially lowers the plane to the probe position then raises it linearly to the correct position over* ***n*** *force loop cycles.*

This method allows the presentation of much stiffer-feeling surfaces (higher spring constant) without noticeable discontinuities. By using recovery times of up to 0.05 second, the Nanomanipulator application was able to increase the surface spring constant by a factor of 10.

A recovery-time algorithm is also required in the point-to-point spring model. When the only adjustable parameter is the spring constant, there is a trade-off between how tightly the probe is tied to the application endpoint (higher **k** is better) and how smooth the transition is when the application moves its endpoint (lower **k** is better). We avoid this tradeoff by allowing the application to specify the rate of motion for its endpoint after an endpoint update. When the application sets a new position for its endpoint (or a new rest length for the spring), the point smoothly moves from its current location to the new location over the specified number of server loop iterations.

2.3 Flexibility and extensibility

Our force-feedback software has evolved from application-specific device-driver routines [4], through a device-specific but application-independent library controlling our Argonne-III Remote Manipulator, to the current device-independent remote-access library, Armlib.

Armlib provides connectivity to widely-used graphics engines (SGI, HP and Sun workstations) over commonly-used networks (Ethernet and other TCP/IP). It supports commercially-available force displays (several varieties of SensAble Devices PHANToM [14], and Sarcos Research Corporation Dexterous Master), as well as our Argonne-III Remote Manipulator from Argonne National Laboratories. Armlib supports the simultaneous use of multiple force-feedback devices, for multi-user or multi-hand applications. The application selects the device(s) it needs to use at runtime.

Armlib structure

Armlib provides device independence at the API level by using a cartesian coordinate system with an origin at the center of the device's working volume. Forces and positions can be automatically scaled so that software will work unchanged with devices of different sizes.

The device independence extends to Armlib's internal structure (Figure 8). Device-dependencies are compartmentalized in a set of simple low-level "device-driver" routines, which handle the reading of joint positions, the writing of joint forces, and the serializing of the robot link configuration. Higher levels of the library, including the intermediate representation servo loops, function in cartesian space. The conversion from joint space to cartesian space and back is handled by a common set of routines which utilize a Denavit-Hartenberg based description of each device to compute the forward kinematics and Jacobian matrix at runtime (see e.g. [9]). These routines effectively discard most torque information for three DOF devices such as the standard PHANToM.

The compartmentalization of device dependencies facilitates the addition of both new device types and new library capabilities. Because code for intermediate representations uses only cartesian space, this code works automatically for all devices. The ease of making changes is illustrated by the fact that it took only two days to add support for the PHANToM device to our library, and less than two days to add the code for our spring-based intermediate representation.

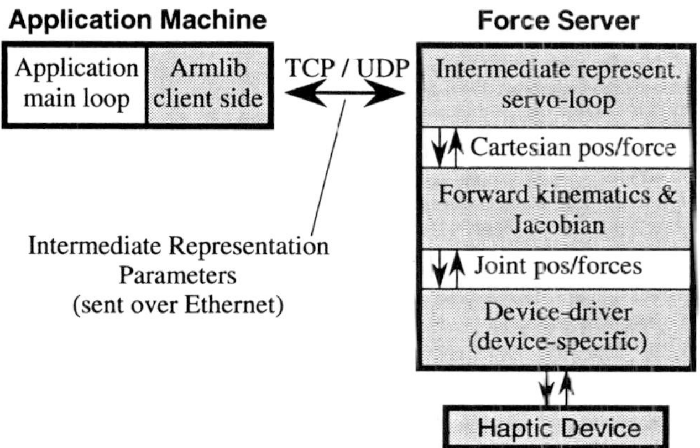

Figure 8: *Armlib's structure. Intermediate representation parameters pass between the client (application & API) and the force server over the Ethernet. The intermediate representation servo loop functions entirely in cartesian space. Device-dependencies are contained in the joint-space device-driver.*

Client/Server communications

There are two types of information passed between the application and the force server. Commands affecting system state (starting, stopping, initiating local force computation) must be delivered intact and not lost. In contrast, position reports and updates to intermediate representation parameters are sent frequently, so a lost packet can be ignored since a new one will arrive shortly. (In fact, ignoring these lost packets is the correct approach; retransmission is time consuming). We decided to use two channels between the client and server, the *command* and *data* channels. We currently use a TCP stream connection for the command channel (reliable, high overhead) and use UDP datagrams (unreliable, low overhead) for the data channel. Our client-server communications routines are well-compartmentalized, so the substitution of different protocols would be simple.

Armlib provides an asychronous *continual report* mode, in which the server sends position reports at regular intervals (using the data channel), rather than on request. This mode avoids the wait for a round-trip network message which is required by standard requests. The application can poll for these continual reports or block for them. Armlib also provides the application with a file descriptor indicating report arrival which can be `select()`'d by event-driven applications such as those written under X-Windows.

Performance

All of the intermediate representation features (plane-vs.-probe, multiple probes, recovery time, friction, and point-to-point springs) are orthogonal, and can be used singly or in combination. These tools produce a rich interaction environment at high update rates. We achieve 1 kHz on a 133 MHz Pentium processor for our custom six sense-DOF, three force-DOF PHANToM. The rate is even higher on a standard PHANToM. When we use a recovery time with our plane-and-probe model, we achieve stable hard surface stiffnesses of 2100 N/m on our custom PHANToM.

3. RESULTS AND SIGNIFICANCE

We have presented a system-based approach to solving the problems encountered when integrating force feedback into real-time computer graphics applications. Armlib combines and extends earlier work in intermediate representation of surfaces and in surface friction. It:

- Extends the intermediate representation of [1] by adding multiple surfaces.
- Introduces point-to-point springs as a form of intermediate representation on a force server.
- Extends previous work on surface friction by adding to the friction model the capability to produce simple haptic textures at high update rates.

Armlib also provides new functions and features. It:

- Presents a recovery-time algorithm to reduce sudden forces due to changes in the intermediate representation, both for local planes and point-to-point springs.
- Provides device independence, a simple interface, and easy extensibility through a compartmentalized and multi-layered design.
- Provides a fully-functional system running on readily-available networks and commercial hardware. Several groups outside our lab are already using our system.

4. FUTURE DIRECTIONS

The development of Armlib is driven by the needs of particular applications in our lab; we add capabilities as they become necessary. Use of existing library features to explore new areas is already underway. The Nanomanipulator project is working to adjust the friction parameters based on characteristics of the surface under the microscope.

One useful intermediate representation we would like to add is a 3-D linear approximation to the nearby force field; i.e. a first order Taylor series expansion of the force field about the most recent position. Such a representation would be useful for smoothly varying force fields.

Some applications might benefit from an enhancement of our plane-and-probe model to allow for half-planes, or even general convex planar polygons. This capability would allow several plane-and-probe constraints to be used simultaneously at convex points of intersection, such as the *outside* of a box. But this approach can also produce problems of its own; Zilles and Salisbury [24] provide a good discussion of some of these issues and discuss a technique to attack them.

It might be worthwhile in some applications to support simple curved surfaces as an intermediate representation type.

The implementation of the force servo loop for our plane and probe model is relatively simple. Work by Colgate and Brown [6] provides guidance on how to do better in attacking this "virtual wall" problem. Doing so would require providing our library with information about the dynamic behavior of each supported force-feedback device. We would also like to add a braking pulse like that described by Salcudean and Vlaar [18] to our virtual wall.

Armlib works with very simple intermediate representations. There is a continual temptation to add progressively more complex intermediate representations and associated calculations. There is of course a tradeoff in doing so—more complex representations take longer to evaluate, thus reducing the force update rate. A possible solution is to add another layer to our system. Such a layer might be in charge of object-level contacts and dynamics, and the calculation of the plane equations for our intermediate representation. It could address the fact that under some circumstances multiple simultaneous contacts should not be treated independently [7]. This layer would still run faster than the application main loop, but would be more complex (and thus slower) than the force server's intermediate representation servo loop.

5. AVAILABILITY

The latest information on Armlib is available from our haptics research web page, http://www.cs.unc.edu/Research/graphics/force. The Armlib source code and documentation are available by FTP at ftp://ftp.cs.unc.edu/pub/packages/GRIP/armlib/. A SIGGRAPH course this year [2] presents some additional tutorial information about Armlib.

ACKNOWLEDGEMENTS

Support for this work was provided by grant number RR02170 from the National Institutes of Health National Center for Research Resources. Our SARCOS arm was provided by DARPA. The Argonne Remote Manipulator is on loan from Argonne National Laboratories.

We would like to thank other contributors to our work. Frederick P. Brooks, Jr. and William V. Wright, the investigators for our NIH grant, provided support and ideas. Other students, in particular Yunshan Zhu, Kimberly Passarella-Jones, and Chris Dimattia contributed to Armlib and the ideas presented here. John Hughes attended to our force-feedback hardware. Finally, the anonymous reviewers (and one in particular) made some very helpful suggestions.

REFERENCES

[1] ADACHI, Y., KUMANO, T., OGINO, K. Intermediate Representation for Stiff Virtual Objects. *Proc. IEEE Virtual Reality Annual Intl. Symposium '95* (Research Triangle Park, N. Carolina, March 11-15), pp. 203-210.

[2] BAILEY, M., JOHNSON, D., KRAMER, J. MASSIE, T., TAYLOR, R. So Real I Can Almost Touch It: The Use of Touch as an I/O Device for Graphics and Visualization. *SIGGRAPH 96 Course Notes #37* (New Orleans, Louisiana, August 1996).

[3] BATTER, J. J., BROOKS, F. P. JR. GROPE-I: A computer display to the sense of feel. *Proc. Intl. Federation of Information Processing Congress '71* (Ljubljana, Yugosolavia, Aug. 23-28). *Information Processing '71*, vol. 1, pp. 759-763.

[4] BROOKS, F. P. JR., OUH-YOUNG, M., BATTER, J. J., KILPATRICK, P. J. Project GROPE—Haptic displays for scientific visualization. *Proc. SIGGRAPH 90* (Dallas, Texas, Aug. 6-10, 1990). In Computer Graphics 24, 4 (August 1990), pp. 177-185.

[5] BUTTOLO, P., KUNG, D., HANNAFORD, B. Manipulation in Real, Virtual and Remote Environments. *Proc. IEEE Conf. on Systems, Man and Cybernetics* (Vancouver, BC, Oct. 1995), vol. 5, pp. 4656-4661.

[6] COLGATE, J. E., BROWN, J. M. Factors Affecting the Z-Width of a Haptic Display. *Proc. IEEE Intl. Conf. on Robotics and Automation* (San Diego, Calif., May 8-13, 1994), vol. 4, pp. 3205-3210.

[7] COLGATE, J. E., STANLEY, M. C., BROWN, J. M. Issues in the Haptic Display of Tool Use. ASME Haptic Interfaces for Virtual Environment and Teleoperator Systems 1994, In *Dynamic Systems and Control 1994* (Chicago, Illinois, Nov. 6-11), vol. 1, pp. 140-144.

[8] FINCH, M., CHI, V., TAYLOR, R. M. II, FALVO, M., WASHBURN, S., SUPERFINE, R. Surface Modification Tools in a Virtual Environment Interface to a Scanning Probe Microscope. *Proc. 1995 Symposium on Interactive 3D Graphics* (Monterey, CA, April 9-12, 1995), pp. 13-18.

[9] FU, K. S., GONZALEZ R. C., LEE, C. S. G. *Robotics control, sensing, vision and intelligence*. McGraw-Hill, New York, 1987.

[10] GOMEZ, D., BURDEA, G., LANGRANA, N. Integration of the Rutgers Master II in a Virtual Reality Simulation. *Proc. IEEE Virtual Reality Annual Intl. Symposium '95* (Research Triangle Park, N. Carolina, March 11-15), pp. 199-202.

[11] GOSSWEILER, R., LONG, C., KOGA, S., PAUSCH, R. DIVER: A Distributed Virtual Environment Research Platform. *Proc. IEEE 1993 Symposium on Research Frontiers in Virtual Reality* (San Jose, Calif., Oct. 25-26, 1993), pp. 10-15.

[12] KIM, W. S., HANNAFORD, B., BEJCZY, A. K. Force-Reflection and Shared Compliant Control in Operating Telemanipulators with Time Delay. *IEEE Transactions on Robotics and Automation*, April 1992, pp. 176-185.

[13] MARK, W. R., RANDOLPH, S. C., FINCH, M., VAN VERTH, J. M. UNC-CH Force-Feedback Library, Revision C. University of North Carolina at Chapel Hill, Computer Science Technical Report #TR96-012, Jan. 30, 1996. [Available at http://www.cs.unc.edu]; Also: *ibid*, Revision C.2. May 10, 1996. [Not a TR. Available at ftp://ftp.cs.unc.edu/pub/packages/GRIP/armlib]

[14] MASSIE, T. M., SALISBURY, J. K. The PHANToM Haptic Interface: A Device for Probing Virtual Objects. ASME Haptic Interfaces for Virtual Environment and Teleoperator Systems 1994, In *Dynamic Systems and Control 1994* (Chicago, Illinois, Nov. 6-11), vol. 1, pp. 295-301.

[15] MINSKY M., OUH-YOUNG, M., STEELE, M., BROOKS, F. P. JR., BEHENSKY, M. Feeling and Seeing: Issues in Force Display. *Proc. 1990 Symposium on Interactive 3D Graphics* (Snowbird, Utah, March 25-28, 1990). In Computer Graphics 24, 2, pp 235-243.

[16] MITSUISHI, M., HORI, T., HATAMURA, Y., NAGAO, T., KRAMER, B. Operational environment transmission for manufacturing globalization. *Proc. 1994 Japan-U.S.A. Symposium on Flexible Automation* (Kobe, Japan, July 11-18, 1994), vol. 1, pp. 379-382.

[17] OUH-YOUNG, M., *Force Display In Molecular Docking*. Ph. D. Dissertation, University of North Carolina at Chapel Hill, UNC-CH Computer Science TR90-004, February, 1990.

[18] SALCUDEAN, S. E., VLAAR, T. D. On the Emulation of Stiff Walls and Static Friction with a Magnetically Levitated Input/Output Device. ASME Haptic Interfaces for Virtual Environment and Teleoperator Systems 1994, In *Dynamic Systems and Control 1994* (Chicago, Illinois, Nov. 6-11), vol. 1, pp. 303-309.

[19] SALISBURY, K., BROCK, D., MASSIE, T., SWARUP, N., ZILLES, C. Haptic Rendering: Programming Touch Interaction with Virtual Objects. *Proc. 1995 Symposium on Interactive 3D Graphics* (April 9-12, Monterey, Calif.), pp. 123-130.

[20] SHAW, C., LIANG, J, GREEN, M., SUN, Y. The decoupled simulation model for VR systems. *Proc. 1992 Conf. on Human Factors in Computer Systems (CHI '92)* (Monterey, Calif., May 3-7, 1992), pp. 321-328.

[21] SURLES, M. C. An Algorithm With Linear Complexity For Interactive, Physically-based Modeling of Large Proteins. *Proc. SIGGRAPH 92* (Chicago, Illinois, July 26-31, 1992). In Computer Graphics, 26, 2 (July 1992), pp. 221-230.

[22] SHERIDAN, T. B. *Telerobotics, Automation, and Supervisory Control.* MIT Press, Cambridge, Mass., 1992.

[23] SNYDER, W. E. *Industrial Robots: Computer Interfacing and Control.* Prentice-Hall, Englewood Cliffs, New Jersey, 1985.

[24] ZILLES, C. B., SALISBURY, J. K. A Constraint-based God-object Method for Haptic Display. ASME Haptic Interfaces for Virtual Environment and Teleoperator Systems 1994, In *Dynamic Systems and Control 1994* (Chicago, Illinois, Nov. 6-11), vol. 1, pp. 146-150.

Image-Guided Streamline Placement

Greg Turk, University of North Carolina at Chapel Hill
David Banks, Mississippi State University

Abstract

Accurate control of streamline density is key to producing several effective forms of visualization of two-dimensional vector fields. We introduce a technique that uses an energy function to guide the placement of streamlines at a specified density. This energy function uses a low-pass filtered version of the image to measure the difference between the current image and the desired visual density. We reduce the energy (and thereby improve the placement of streamlines) by (1) changing the positions and lengths of streamlines, (2) joining streamlines that nearly abut, and (3) creating new streamlines to fill sufficiently large gaps. The entire process is iterated to produce streamlines that are neither too crowded nor too sparse. The resulting streamlines manifest a more hand-placed appearance than do regularly- or randomly-placed streamlines. Arrows can be added to the streamlines to disambiguate flow direction, and flow magnitude can be represented by the thickness, density, or intensity of the lines.

CR Categories: I.3.3 [Computer Graphics]: Picture/Image generation; I.4.3 [Image Processing]: Enhancement.

Additional Key Words: Vector field visualization, flow visualization, streamline, random optimization, random descent.

1 Introduction

The need to visualize vector fields is common in many scientific and engineering disciplines. Examples of vector fields include velocities of wind and ocean currents (*e.g.*, for weather forecasting), results of fluid dynamics simulation (*e.g.*, for calculating drag over a body), magnetic fields, blood flow, components of stress and strain in materials, and cell migration during embryo development. Existing techniques for vector field visualization differ in how well they represent such attributes of the vector field as magnitude, direction, and critical points.

This work was motivated by two recent innovations for displaying vector fields: spot noise [van Wijk 91] and line-integral convolution (LIC) [Cabral & Leedom 93]. We wondered how to compare the results of the techniques. What is the gauge that measures how well a certain method depicts a vector field? Evidently the placement of the graphical elements is tremendously important. The graphical elements (e.g. coherent streaks) should follow the flow direction, but they should not be spaced too close together or too far apart. Both spot noise and LIC can produce images where stream-aligned streaks are evenly distributed, but that is more an indirect result than a guiding principle in the algorithms. How can the streamlines be positioned to explicitly satisfy a desired distribution?

The elegant hand-designed streamline drawings in physics texts (for example in Figure 1a) provide ample inspiration for vector field illustrations. The streamlines in such illustrations are placed so that no region is devoid of streamlines and no region is overpopulated with them. The eye is drawn to regions where the density of ink in one place differs greatly from that of the surrounding region. When the density of the streamlines is allowed to vary in such illustrations, it is usually to represent field magnitude, where denser line spacing shows greater field strength.

Bertin shows another effective hand-designed representation of flow where the direction of ocean current is represented by chains of arrows that are laid out end-to-end so that the eye connects arrows into streamlines and thus gets a stronger sense of flow orientation [Bertin 83]. The success of this representation depends on having chosen proper endpoints for these chains so that nowhere does the image become cluttered. The techniques presented in our paper will permit designers of vector-field visualizations to control streamline-spacing automatically in order to achieve results that mimic hand-drawn figures.

2 Previous Work

A *streamline* is an integral curve that is everywhere tangent to a given vector field (see, for example, [Kundu 90]). Many researchers have examined how to effectively and accurately *integrate* streamline paths through both regular and irregular meshes. To our

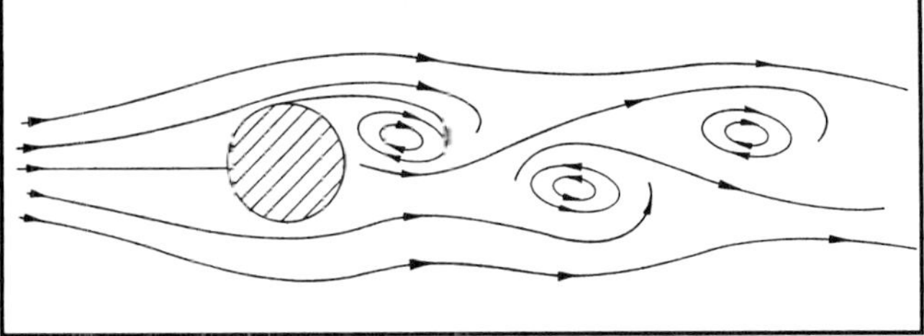

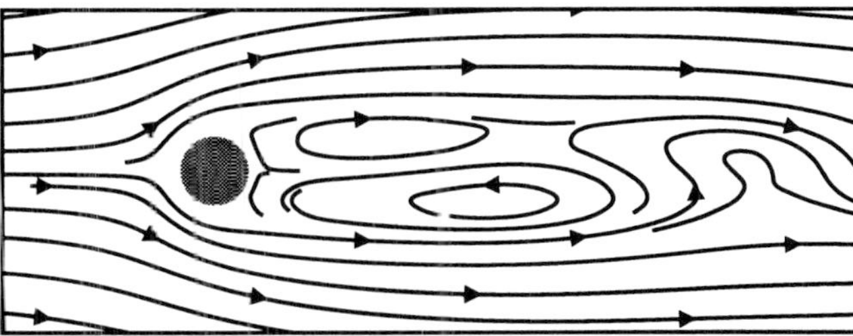

Figure 1: (a) Hand-designed illustration of flow around a cylinder, taken from [Feynman 64] and used with permission from the California Institute of Technology. (b) Automatically generated flow lines using streamline optimization. Data is from fluid flow simulation.

surprise, however, discussions of how best to *place* streamlines are almost nonexistent in the visualization literature. We are aware of three techniques that are used to "seed" streamlines within a vector field: regular grids, random sampling, and user-specified seed points for initiation of streamlines. Our knowledge of random and regular grid seeding of streamlines is almost entirely limited to private communications with visualization researchers. The one published technique that we have found uses particle traces on a 3D surface that are terminated when they come too close to the paths of other particles [Max *et al.* 94]. The virtual wind tunnel (a 3D immersive display system for flow visualization) allows users to initiate streamlines singly or in bundles [Bryson & Levit 91].

Recently there have been several exciting developments in displaying vector fields using texture synthesis. Line integral convolution is a procedure that stretches a given image along paths that are dictated by a vector field [Cabral & Leedom 93] [Forsell 94] [Stalling & Hege 95]. Spot noise is a method of creating noise-like texture by compositing many replicas of a shape [van Wijk 91] [de Leeuw & van Wijk 95]. When the shapes that create spot noise textures are stretched according to a given vector field, the resulting images illustrate the vector field's direction. Both line integral convolution and spot noise are well-suited to depicting the fine detail of flow *orientation*. They are somewhat less successful (in a single, static image) at showing the flow *magnitude*; moreover, the local flow direction is ambiguous in the sense that it can be interpreted to be either of two directions that are 180 degrees apart.

A very different method of illustrating vector field data is to show the important *topological* features of the flow. In general, streamlines that lie in a small neighborhood follow nearly-parallel paths. The exceptions (in a continuously differentiable vector field) occur in neighborhoods of points with zero-valued vectors. Several researchers have developed techniques to identify these critical points (sources, sinks, spirals, centers, and saddles) and the streamlines that issue from them in eigen-directions [Globus *et al.* 91] [Helman & Hesselink 91]. These particular points and curves partition a vector field into simpler regions where a texture-based method suffices to display details of the vector field [Delmarcelle & Hesselink 94].

The remainder of this paper is organized as follows. In Section 3 we present a key concept in our work– a visual quality measure for flow illustrations– and show how this measure can create visually pleasing illustrations containing short arrows. In Section 4 we demonstrate the creation of illustrations that contain well-placed long streamlines. Section 5 discusses how these streamlines can be enhanced to produce a final illustration. We conclude by discussing other applications that might use optimization based on a visual quality measure.

3 Placement of Streamlets

Hedgehog illustrations (sometimes called vector plots) are perhaps the most commonly used method of illustrating a two-dimensional vector field. These are short field-aligned segments or arrows whose base points lie on a regular grid (see Figure 2). The lengths of the segments are often varied according to the field magnitude. The popularity of hedgehog illustrations is almost surely due to their ease of implementation. The resulting images can be slightly enhanced by using short streamlines (streamlets) that curve with the flow instead of using straight lines. We use such streamlets in our figures 2, 3, and 4.

Two artifacts are often present in hedgehog plots. First, the human eye often picks out runs of adjacent arrows and groups them together visually, despite the fact that these groups are an artifact of the underlying grid pattern and not related to the vector field being

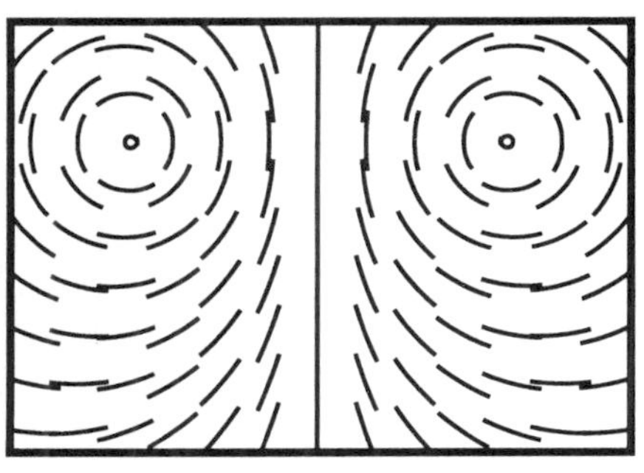

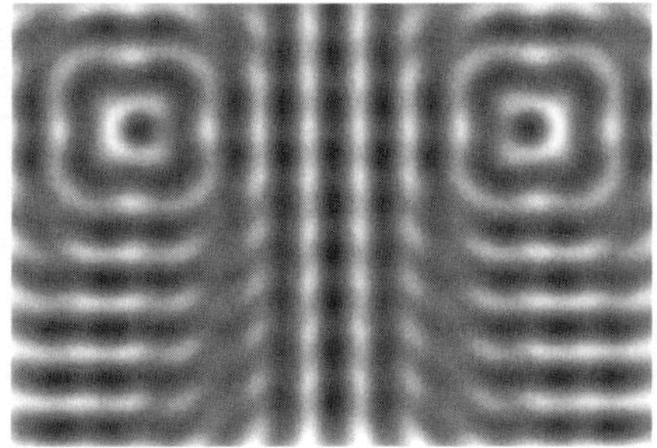

Figure 2: (a) Short streamlines with centers placed on a regular grid (top); (b) filtered version of same (bottom).

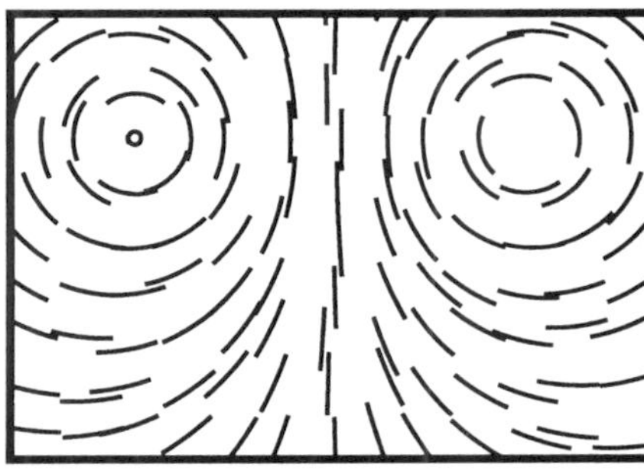

Figure 3: (a) Short streamlines with centers placed on a jittered grid (top); (b) filtered version showing bright and dark regions (bottom).

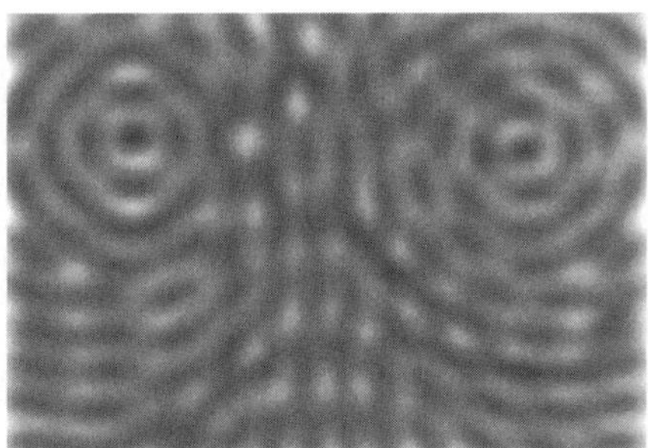

Figure 4: (a) Short streamlines placed by optimization (top); (b) filtered version showing fairly even gray value (bottom).

illustrated. This effect can be seen in Figure 2a where three vertical columns of streamlets erroneously suggest the presence of three parallel field lines. One way to lessen this problem is to oversample the seed points that produce the short segments. The drawback with oversampling is that the resulting image becomes so filled with streamlets that the eye can no longer discern individual elements. A better solution to the sampling problem is to introduce noise, slightly jittering the positions of the arrows to make their regularity less noticeable [Crawfis & Max 92] [Dovey 95]. This strategy is illustrated in Figure 3a.

The second problem with hedgehogs is that as streamlets are placed close together, portions of neighboring arrows come very close to one another and may even overlap. Jittering the streamlets may in fact make the overlaps more frequent (compare Figures 2a and 3a). The twin problems of overlapped streamlets and grid regularity both distract the viewer from the data being visualized; we would like to reduce such distractions. We achieve this goal by using an energy measure to guide streamlet placement and thus improve the quality of the final image.

3.1 Optimization of Streamlet Positions

In the discussion that follows, S represents a collection of streamlets s_n for a given vector field V. The elements of S are idealized zero-width curves, distinct from the geometric primitives (*e.g.*, line segments or anti-aliased curves) employed to render them. We denote by $I(x,y)$ the idealized two-dimensional image of the streamlets in S, with $I(x,y) = 0$ except along streamlines in S where it behaves like the Dirac delta function.

Our method creates hedgehog plots by incrementally improving an initial collection of streamlets. The initial collection can be created by placing the streamlets either on a regular grid or in some random fashion, and the final results appear to be independent of which initialization method is chosen. An image may be improved by selecting one streamlet at random and moving it a small amount in a random direction. If the resulting image has a lower energy measure (lower energy means better quality) then that change is accepted. This process is repeated many times, terminating when the energy reaches a threshold or when acceptance of random changes become rare. Such a process is sometimes referred to as random optimization or random descent. Figure 4a shows the result of this algorithm applied to the same vector field as in Figures 2 and 3. Notice how the streamlets of Figure 4 are more evenly spaced than in Figures 2 and 3.

The energy measure that guides the optimization is based on a low-pass-filtered (blurred) version of the image of S which is compared against a uniform gray-level. Let $L * I$ represent a low-pass-filtered version of the image I, where L is a given filter function. If t is the target gray-scale value, then we define the energy measure E as the squared error integrated over the domain:

$$E(I) = \int_x \int_y [(L * I)(x,y) - t]^2 \, dx \, dy$$

The motivation for this energy measure is that the eye is drawn to regions of an illustration where the density of ink is uneven, and in a hedgehog plot we do not want to draw the eye to any inadvertently bright or dim places. The streamlets should be evenly placed across the image instead of being crowded in any one location. A blurred image contains high values where the streamlets are too close together and low values in regions that are devoid of streamlets. Salisbury and his co-workers made similar used of low-pass filtering to decide whether or not to lay down strokes for pen-and-ink illustrations [Salisbury *et al.* 94]. Figure 2b and 3b show low-pass-filtered versions of Figures 2a and 3a. Locations where two streamlets crowd together in Figures 2a and 3a appear as a high intensity (black) spot in Figures 2b and 3b. Figure 4a and 4b show the corresponding images after the optimization routine has been run. The intensity level in Figure 4b is more uniform than in Figures 2b and 3b.

When the optimization process is animated it looks as though each streamlet is pushing away other nearby streamlets, reminiscent of methods that use repulsion between points to evenly distribute samples on a surface [Turk 91] [Witkin & Heckbert 94]. This similarity should come as no surprise, since both methods are designed to minimize an energy term by making small changes in the position of graphical elements. In fact, we too have implemented streamlet-repulsion as a method for creating hedgehog plots. The visual results of the repulsion method are very similar to the results of random optimization, and the running times are also similar. We pursued the random-descent technique rather than the repulsion method because we expected random descent to be easily extensible to the more complicated task of placing longer streamlines within V (Section 4).

3.2 Implementation of Low-Pass Filter

This section describes the implementation details for efficiently computing the energy term for a given set S of streamlets. There are three components to this computation: the representation of the blurred image, the low-pass filter used to perform the blur, and the manner in which we apply the filter to calculate this blurred image.

It would be computationally prohibitive to calculate the energy term E by actually filtering an entire image each time we consider a random change to some streamlet s_n. Instead, we associate with s_n certain information about how it affects the low-pass-filtered image. The blurred image B contains pixel values for an image of S. A streamlet maintains a list of pixels that it affects in B, together with the values that it contributes to each of those pixels. To test whether moving s_n would improve the value of E, we first remove the contribution of s_n from its list of pixels in B and correct the value of E based on the changes. Next, we add in the pixel contributions for the new position of s_n and recalculate E. We retain the change to s_n if the new value of E is better; otherwise we revert to the old position for s_n. The (un-blurred) image I is purely a conceptual aid, and at no time during optimization do we generate an actual representation of I.

Two criteria influence the choice of a filter to create the blurred image B. First, the filter kernel should have compact support so that filtering operations are fast to compute. Second, the point-spread function should fall off smoothly so that the quality measure changes smoothly with small changes in streamline position. This allows the optimization to detect changes in E even for small changes in the image.

We use the following circularly symmetric filter kernel (from a basis function of cubic Hermite interpolation) to blur the image:

$$K(x, y) = 2r^3 - 3r^2 + 1, \qquad r < 1$$

$$K(x, y) = 0, \qquad r >= 1$$

where $r = \mathrm{sqrt}(x^2 + y^2) / R$.

This function has a similar shape to a two-dimensional Gaussian filter, but it falls off to zero at a distance R away from its center. The ideal density for a set of streamlines may be varied across the image by stretching or shrinking the radius R of the filter.

We sample a streamlet s_n at a finite number of points, resulting in a piecewise-linear curve composed of zero-width line segments. We calculate the filtered image of each segment by considering those pixels in the filtered image that are within a distance R of the segment. The contribution of the line segment to a particular pixel in the filtered image can quickly be computed by a variant of the technique used by Feibush for polygon anti-aliasing [Feibush *et al.* 80]. The line segment is rotated about the pixel center so that it lies horizontally, and then two table-lookups based on the segment's endpoints are used to determine the kernel-weighted contribution to the pixel. We have found that a very coarse low-pass filtered image suffices to guide the placement of streamlines. Typically we use a filter kernel that extends just two or three pixels in radius. The filtered images in Figures 2, 3 and 4 were computed at a much higher resolution than this for expository purposes.

4 Long Streamlines

This section describes how the optimization technique from Section 3 can be extended to create images containing long, evenly-distributed streamlines. One goal of this procedure is to enable fine control over the distance between adjacent streamlines, whether that target spacing be constant-valued or position-dependent. A second goal is to avoid interrupting the streamlines. Since each endpoint of a streamline distracts from the visual flow of the image, our images should favor fewer, longer streamlines over numerous, shorter streamlets. It is not always possible to satisfy the two goals of uniform streamline separation and infrequent streamline breaks. In places where the vector field converges (*e.g.* near a sink) these two goals are at odds with one another. Our solution to the dilemma is to let the energy function be the arbiter between uniform spacing and long streamlines.

The optimization procedure for creating a hedgehog plot consists of repeatedly considering small changes to the positions of the streamlets, accepting only the changes that improve the measure E. The procedure for creating a set of longer streamlines s_n is similar. We improve a set S of streamlines by considering several kinds of changes to the streamlines. In addition to changes in a streamline's position, the algorithm also allows the operations of streamline insertion/deletion, lengthening/shortening of streamlines, and combination of two streamlines, end-to-end, into a single streamline. We use the same quality measure E to determine which changes will be accepted. In pseudo-code, the process for creating the collection S of long streamlines is as follows.

```
S ← null { S begins as an empty set of streamlines }

{ find an initial group of streamlets }
foreach position (x,y) on a grid
  insert streamlet s at (x,y) into S to produce S'
  if E(S') < E(S) then
    S ← S'

{ improve the collection of streamlines in S }
repeat until accepted changes are rare
  choose an operation
  apply operation to random element(s) of S to produce S'
  if E(S') < E(S) then
    S ← S'
```

Figure 5b shows a collection of streamlines created with the above optimization procedure. The streamlines are evenly spaced and their endpoints are generally located where the vector field diverges or converges. For comparison, Figure 5a shows long streamlines whose seed points lie on a regular grid so that streamline density varies greatly.

Figure 5: (a) Long streamlines with centers regularly placed on a grid (top); (b) Streamlines placed by density-based optimization (bottom). This data is a randomly generated vector field.

4.1 The Allowable Operations

The primitive streamline operations that we employ to improve the quality of an image are described in more detail below.

Move: Change the position of the seed point of the streamline. Each streamline is defined in terms of this seed point and a length to travel forward and backward through the flow.

Insert: Create a new streamlet.

Delete: Remove a streamline entirely from S.

Lengthen: Add a positive value to the length of the streamline (relative to the seed point) in the forward or backward direction.

Shorten: Subtract from the length of the streamline (relative to the seed point) in the forward or backward direction.

Combine: Connect two streamlines whose endpoints are sufficiently close to one another. The location of the join is a weighted average of the two endpoints based on the relative lengths of the streamlines. The length of the new streamline is the sum of the lengths of the two parent streamlines.

Why do we allow so many kinds of changes during the optimization process? Presumably we could create any possible collection of streamlines using only **insert** and **delete** operations if we allow newly-inserted streamlines to assume any length and position. However, an actual implementation of the optimization process using such a restricted set of operations would be prohibitively slow to converge. We use the larger complement of operations so that the optimization procedure can move smoothly through the space of all collections of streamlines. For example, suppose that joining two particular streamlines would greatly improve the measure E. The optimization routine could choose at random to remove each of these streamlines and, also at random, create another streamline that fills the void left by the two that were removed. It is very unlikely that these three independent events would happen by chance. Explicitly providing a **combine** operation makes this small change in visual appearance much more likely to occur.

We find candidate pairs of streamlines for the **combine** operation by querying a data structure that maintains the positions of streamline endpoints and can return pairs of endpoints whose distance is less than a given tolerance. There are several ways in which we can favor joining together streamlines. We could add a term to the energy function that gives a higher energy to those images that contain more streamlines. Instead of this approach, however, we choose to accept **combine** operations if they result in a new value of E that is no greater than the old energy value plus a tolerance.

We can animate the optimization process by displaying the collection of streamlines every time a favorable change occurs. An animation of the optimization indicates the role of each operation. First, streamlets are inserted throughout the image. After this initial phase is finished the result looks much like a hedgehog plot using a jittered grid, reminiscent of a Poisson-disk distribution of points. Next, many of the streamlines gradually lengthen. As streamline endpoints approach one another, pairs of streamlines combine to form longer streamlines. This dual process of lengthening and joining creates many longer streamlines that typically follow nearly-parallel trajectories. Gradually the changes in the image become minor, and many of the changes at this stage are streamlines moving a small distance, evening the spacing between neighbors. Changes are accepted with decreasing frequency, and the process is terminated when accepted changes become sufficiently rare.

4.2 Acceleration Using an Oracle

The stochastic optimization produces good results, but it spends considerable time entertaining changes that are unlikely to improve the image. The method can be accelerated by using an *oracle* that suggests changes that are likely to decrease the energy function E. An oracle is only effective if it can be consulted quickly and its answers are generally reliable. The oracle described in this section typically speeds up the convergence of the optimization by a factor of three to five.

There are two systematic ways for an oracle to select changes to propose: an *image-based* approach, and a *streamline-based* approach. Our oracle uses a combination of the two. The image-based approach examines the blurred image B to identify places where the streamlines are too sparse. The oracle makes **insert** suggestions in these places. The streamline-based approach examines the neighborhood of each individual streamline to decide if an operation applied to the streamline is likely to improve the image. The oracle uses information gathered from around a streamline to decide whether to suggest a **lengthen**, **shorten** or **move** operation. More precisely, the oracle keeps a running measure of how "energetic" a given streamline is, and it maintains a priority queue that orders the streamlines based on their individual level of energy. When consulted, the oracle returns one of the most energetic streamlines, along with a suggestion of how to lessen its measure of energy.

The energy of a streamline is the sum on three factors: "desire" to lengthen, "desire" to shorten, and "desire" to move. Each of these factors is calculated by sampling the image B at a small number of positions near the streamline. The desire to lengthen is computed by comparing the target gray level t with the image values a short distance beyond the endpoints of the streamline. The lower these values are with respect to t, the greater the streamline desires to grow into this empty region. The desire to shorten is found by sampling B on either side of the streamline endpoints. If these values are too high, the streamline desires to shrink. The desire to move is computed by comparing the image values on one side of the streamline with the values on the other side. The greater the difference between these two values, the more the streamline desires to change its position. We typically consult 20 samples of the image B to determine each of the three factors that determine a streamline's energy. This sampling is an inexpensive task in comparison to creating the entire path of a streamline and then low-pass-filtering the resulting curve.

The oracle need not bother suggesting that a streamline be deleted. Every time the optimization routine attempts to modify a streamline it can easily check whether entirely removing the streamline improves the total energy measure E of the image. This is done by evaluating E after the contribution of the streamline to the image B is removed and before the altered streamline's effect is added to B.

The oracle is important for improving efficiency, but it is the energy measure E that drives the optimization. The oracle is used purely as a source of suggestions for how to reduce E, not as a source of directives that are applied blindly. The oracle's suggestions are only accepted if the change improves the image quality. We have found it effective for the oracle to propose 50% of the changes, and for the other changes to be chosen completely at random. Thus *any* change to the collection of streamlines is possible, which makes it unlikely that the optimization will overlook a worthwhile improvement arising from any systematic bias of the oracle.

4.3 Intensity Tapering at Streamline Ends

Some streamlines must terminate within a region of converging flow or else the target density of the image cannot be preserved there.

Figure 6: Field magnitude has been redundantly mapped onto streamline density and width. Large magnitude is indicated by dense, thin curves.

The resulting break of the streamline is visually jarring if it is rendered as a rectangular end cap. We make the termination less abrupt by gradually decreasing the width or intensity of the streamline near its endpoint. We can gently fade a streamline by allowing yet another operation, namely streamline *tapering*. Each streamline carries with it (in addition to its center and length) two positions along its length that indicate where to begin linearly fading to the background color at either endpoint. This intensity tapering is used to weight the contribution of the streamline to the filtered image B. Streamline tapering allows the optimization to find an even closer match to the ideal gray-scale value in regions near the streamline ends. In practice we have found it most effective to let intensity tapering be a separate optimization phase, after the streamlines have settled into their final position. In this final phase each streamline is allowed to perform only two operations: 1) changes in length, and 2) changes in the locations at which to begin intensity tapering. Performing the intensity tapering after long streamlines have been formed avoids the possibility that the optimization will produce many short, intensity-tapered streamlines to satisfy the target density. Figures 6 and 8 are rendered using the tapering information to modulate streamline width and intensity, respectively.

Saito and Takahashi have demonstrated a similar tapering effect for drawing contour lines of a scalar field [Saito & Takahashi 90]. They use information about the gradient of the scalar field to guide the fading out of the contour lines. Their technique can also be used for drawing streamlines of vector fields where the divergence is zero everywhere, but it has no obvious generalization when the divergence is non-zero (*e.g.* fields with sources and sinks).

4.4 Optimization Issues

Two recent techniques in computer graphics provided inspiration for the optimization approach described here. The first of these is the work by Andrew Witkin and Paul Heckbert for distributing particles over an implicit surface [Witkin & Heckbert 94]. In their constrained optimization method, they let a small number of seed particles repel one another in order to distribute themselves evenly over a surface. They found that it is helpful to allow the initial particles to grow, split, shrink or die to accommodate any change in surface area when the surface geometry is being edited. Their operations on particles are analogous to our operations on streamlines.

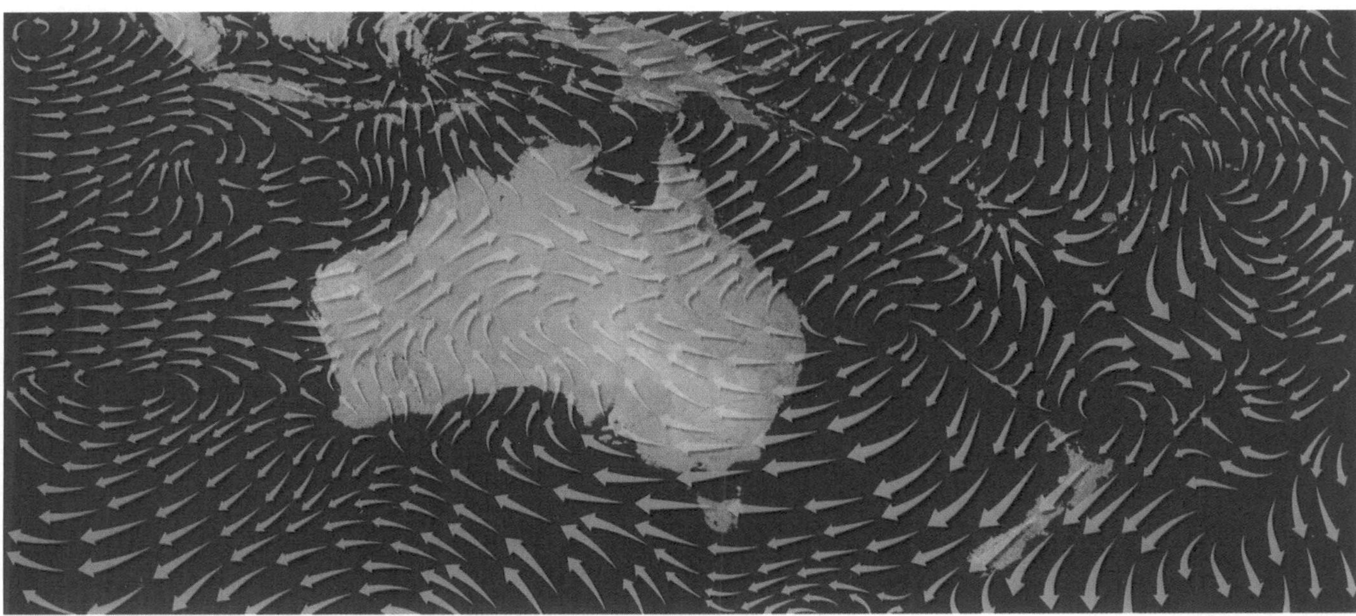

Figure 7: Chains of arrows indicate wind direction and magnitude over Australia. The arrows were deposited along streamlines created by streamline optimization. Higher velocity is indicated by larger arrows. The vector field data was calculated using a numerical weather model.

A second source of inspiration was the mesh optimization work by Hugues Hoppe and co-workers [Hoppe *et al.* 93]. Their technique uses three fundamental operations to automatically simplify a polygonal mesh: edge split, edge collapse, and edge swap. They used an energy measure to guide the optimization by random descent. The high quality of the results produced by this method encouraged us to try random descent in streamline optimization.

One frequently-voiced concern about optimization techniques is that the behavior of the system is highly sensitive to the values of many parameters. An example of such a parameter for streamline optimization is the maximum distance a streamline can move. The fear is that the system may require a large amount of "parameter tweaking." Happily, we have found it unnecessary to change our parameter settings between datasets. The single parameter that we specify for an illustration is the desired distance between neighboring streamlines (which can even be position-dependent). Other parameters are derived from this target-distance. We believe that researchers who implement the techniques described here will not have difficulty replicating our results. To relieve the burden of re-implementing our technique, we are making our source code publicly available at http://www.cs.msstate.edu/~banks/IGSP.

5 Binding Visual Attributes to Streamlines

There is an important distinction between a streamline (a zero-width integral curve) and the geometric elements associated with its display. A simple approach for displaying a streamline is to draw an anti-aliased curve that connects vertices sampled along the streamline, but such a constant-width, constant-intensity curve is not necessarily the best way to visualize the flow. For example, the curves are unchanged if all the vectors reverse direction in the underlying vector field; that is, the sense of flow direction is ambiguous in a simple streamline display. Arrows can be inserted into the image to disambiguate the flow direction. We apply two different techniques to bind arrow-shaped glyphs to streamlines. The first technique is to traverse the streamlines and deposit an arrow whenever the integrated arc-length along a streamline is sufficient to accommodate the arrow's length. Such an object-order traversal is appropriate for binding a long chain of glyphs onto a streamline. The second approach is to distribute arrow-glyphs uniformly throughout the image and then snap them to the nearest point on a streamline. Such an image-order traversal is appropriate for images with only a few scattered arrows serving as reminders of the flow direction.

Often some important scalar quantity is associated with a vector field. The scalar value might be the temperature or density in a fluid flow, or it might be the magnitude of the vector field at each point. We would like to bind visual attributes to display such a scalar quantity along with the streamlines. The thickness and the grayscale-intensity of a streamline offer two convenient visual attributes to convey a scalar quantity. Figure 6 shows a vector field whose magnitude is bound to the width of the streamlines and where the streamlines themselves have been placed so that the scalar field determines the distance between neighboring streamlines.

6 Results

In this section we show some examples of images constructed using the optimization method for positioning long streamlines. The first example is Figure 1b, which illustrates a numerical simulation of flow around a cylinder. The arrowheads in this figure disambiguate flow orientation in the eddies. Figure 7 shows computed wind velocity in the vicinity of Australia. First, the long streamline optimization method placed streamlines through the image. Then

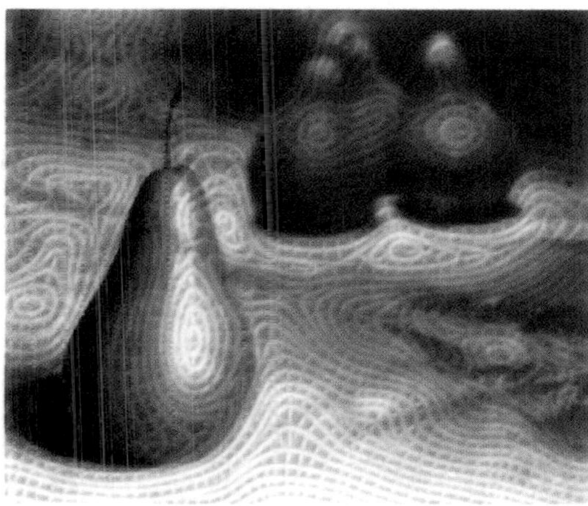

Figure 8: "Pears." The texture in this image was created by combining streamlines in two directions: along the gradient of the blurred intensity and at 90 degrees to the gradient. Original photograph courtesy of Herb Stokes.

arrows were bound to these streamlines. The size of the arrow indicates the wind magnitude. The arrows line up head-to-tail so that the eye can easily follow from one to the next, as is favored by illustrators [Bertin 83]. Human-subject studies have shown that if a graphical stroke varies in width from large to small, people have a strong sense that the direction is towards the larger end [Fowler & Ware 89]. This guided our choice of tapered arrows in Figure 7.

Another application of the streamline-placement technique is to create iso-intensity contours that are evenly spaced. Consider the effect of highlighting several discrete intensity levels in a gray-scale image: even if the intensity-values are chosen in equal increments, the resulting contours are likely to clump together in some regions and spread apart in others. Our optimization technique provides a convenient way to adaptively sample the intensity values so that the curves are uniformly distributed in the image. Figure 8 shows how the technique can be applied to a color photograph. We converted the image to monochrome, blurred it, and then calculated its gradient vector field. We ran the optimization on the gradient vector field and on a vector field orthogonal to it (and thus aligned with the iso-value lines). The two sets of streamlines that resulted were combined and used as a mask to apply the original color values to the grayscale image. The effect is akin to weaving, with constant-intensity thread being used along the contours.

Our streamline optimization program was written in C++, and the calculations for the figures herein were performed on a Silicon Graphics Indigo2 with an R4400 processor operating at 250 MHz. Figures 4 (a) and 5 (b) were created in under one minute, and the streamlines for Figures 6, 7 and 8 required roughly 15 minutes each. We expect that fine-tuning the code would improve the speed by a factor of two to four.

7 Conclusion and Future Work

There are several logical extensions to the streamline optimization method presented in this paper. This same process can be used to create streamlines on curved surfaces by running the optimization in the parametric space of the surface and correcting for mapping distortions. The technique could also be used to create streamlines in three dimensions, although computational efficiency will probably become an issue. The density of 3D streamlines could be made dependent on additional properties of the vector field, such as proximity to vortex cores. Another research area is in creating illustrations that reveal different levels of detail when the viewer is at various distances.

We expect that the notion of guiding the placement of graphical elements by a visual measure of quality will have applications beyond vector field visualization. For instance, a similar optimization method might prove useful in placing graphical elements in a texture. Another potential use for such techniques is for computer generation of illustrations that have a hand-drawn appearance [Saito & Takahashi 90] [Winkenbach & Salesin 94].

8 Acknowledgments

We thank Glenn Wightwick of IBM Australia and Lloyd Treinish of the IBM T. J. Watson Research Center for the Australia wind data. Earth image is courtesy of Geosphere, Inc. The fluid flow data of Figure 1 was provided courtesy of David Rudy, NASA Langley Research Center. We thank Peggy Wetzel and Mary Whitton for help in making video of this work. Funding for this work was provided in part by the NSF Science and Technology Center for Computer Graphics and Scientific Visualization. Travel support was provided by ICASE and the NSF Engineering Research Center at MSU.

9 Bibliography

[Bertin 83] Bertin, Jacques, *Semiology of Graphics*, translated from French, The University of Wisconsin Press 1983.

[Bryson &Levit 91] Bryson, Steve and Creon Levit, "The Virtual Wind Tunnel: An Environment for the Exploration of Three-Dimensional Unsteady Flows," *Proceedings Visualization '91*, San Diego, California, October 22–25, pp. 17–24.

[Cabral & Leedom 93] Cabral, Brian and Leith (Casey) Leedom, "Imaging Vector Fields Using Line Integral Convolution," *Computer Graphics Proceedings*, Annual Conference Series (SIGGRAPH '93), pp. 263–270.

[Crawfis & Max 92] Crawfis, Roger and Nelson Max, "Direct Volume Visualization of Three Dimensional Vector Fields," *Proceedings of the 1992 Workshop on Volume Visualization*, pp. 55–60.

[de Leeuw & van Wijk 95] de Leeuw, Willem C., and Jarke van Wijk, "Enhanced Spot Noise for Vector Field Visualization," *Proceedings Visualization '95*, Atlanta, Georgia, Oct. 29 – Nov. 3, pp. 233–239.

[Delmarcelle & Hesselink 94] Delmarcelle, Thierry and Lambertus Hesselink, "The Topology of Symmetric, Second-Order Tensor Fields," *Proceedings Visualization '94*, Washington, D.C., October 17–21, pp. 140–147.

[Dovey 95] Dovey, Don, "Vector Plots for Irregular Grids," *Proceedings Visualization '95*, Atlanta, Georgia, Oct. 29 – Nov. 3, pp. 248–253.

[Feibush *et al.* 80] Feibush, Eliot, Marc Levoy and Robert Cook, "Synthetic Texturing Using Digital Filters," *Computer Graphics Proceedings*, Annual Conference Series (SIGGRAPH '80), pp. 294–301.

[Feynman 64] Feynman, Richard P., Robert B. Leighton and Matthew Sands, *The Feynman Lectures on Physics*, Addison-Wesley, Reading, Massachusetts, 1964.

[Forssell 94] Forsell, Lisa K., "Visualizing Flow over Curvalinear Grid Surfaces Using Line Integral Convolution," *Proceedings Visualization '94*, Washington, D.C., October 17–21, pp. 240–247.

[Fowler & Ware 89] Fowler, David and Colin Ware, "Strokes for Representing Univariate Vector Field Maps," *Graphics Interface '89*, London, Ontario, June 19–23, 1989, pp. 249–253.

[Globus *et al.* 91] Globus, A., C. Levit and T. Lasinski, "A Tool for Visualizing the Topology of Three-Dimensional Vector Fields," *Proceedings Visualization '91*, San Diego, California, October 22–25, pp. 33–40.

[Helman & Hesselink 91] Helman, J. L. and L. Hesselink, "Visualization of Vector Field Topology in Fluid Flows," *IEEE Computer Graphics and Applications*, Vol. 11, No. 3, pp. 36–46.

[Hoppe *et al.* 93] Hoppe, Hugues, Tony DeRose, Tom Duchamp, John McDonald and Werner Stuetzel, "Mesh Optimization," *Computer Graphics Proceedings*, Annual Conference Series (SIGGRAPH '93), pp. 19–26.

[Kundu 90] Kundu, Pijush K., *Fluid Mechanics*, Academic Press, Inc., San Diego, 1990.

[Max *et al.* 94] Max, Nelson, Roger Crawfis and Charles Grant, "Visualizing 3D Velocity Fields Near Contour Surfaces," *Proceedings Visualization '94*, Washington, D.C., October 17–21, pp. 248–255.

[Saito & Takahashi 90] Saito, Takafumi and Tokiichiro Takahashi, "Comprehensible Rendering of 3-D Shapes," Computer Graphics, Vol. 24, No. 4 (SIGGRAPH '90), pp. 197–206.

[Salisbury *et al.* 94] Salisbury, Michael P., Sean E. Anderson, Ronen Barzel and David H. Salesin, "Interactive Pen-and-Ink Illustration', *Computer Graphics Proceedings*, Annual Conference Series (SIGGRAPH '94), pp. 101–108.

[Stalling & Hege 95] Stalling, Detlev and Hans-Christian Hege, "Fast and Resolution Independent Line Integral Convolution," *Computer Graphics Proceedings*, Annual Conference Series (SIGGRAPH '95), pp. 249–256.

[Turk 91] Turk, Greg, "Generating Textures on Arbitrary Surfaces Using Reaction-Diffusion," *Computer Graphics*, Vol. 25, No. 4 (SIGGRAPH '91), pp. 289–298.

[van Wijk 91] van Wijk, Jarke J., "Spot Noise: Texture Synthesis for Data Visualization," *Computer Graphics*, Vol. 25, No. 4 (SIGGRAPH '91), pp. 309–318.

[Winkenbach & Salesin 94] Winkenbach, Georges and David H. Salesin, "Computer-Generated Pen-and-Ink Illustrations," *Computer Graphics Proceedings*, Annual Conference Series (SIGGRAPH '94), pp. 91–98.

[Witkin & Heckbert 94] Witkin, Andrew and Paul Heckbert, "Using Particles to Sample and Control Implicit Surfaces," *Computer Graphics Proceedings*, Annual Conference Series (SIGGRAPH 94), pp. 269–277.

Scale-Dependent Reproduction of Pen-and-Ink Illustrations

Mike Salisbury *Corin Anderson* *Dani Lischinski* *David H. Salesin*

Department of Computer Science and Engineering
University of Washington

Abstract

This paper describes a representation for pen-and-ink illustrations that allows the creation of high-fidelity illustrations at any scale or resolution. We represent a pen-and-ink illustration as a low-resolution grey-scale image, augmented by a set of discontinuity segments, along with a stroke texture. To render an illustration at a particular scale, we first rescale the grey-scale image to the desired size and then hatch the resulting image with pen-and-ink strokes. The main technical contribution of the paper is a new reconstruction algorithm that magnifies the low-resolution image while keeping the resulting image sharp along discontinuities.

CR Categories and Subject Descriptors: I.3.3 [Computer Graphics]: Picture/Image Generation — Display algorithms; I.3.6 [Computer Graphics]: Methodology and Techniques — Device independence; I.4.3 [Image Processing]: Enhancement — Filtering.

Additional Key Words: discontinuity edges, image magnification, image resampling, non-photorealistic rendering, scale-dependent rendering, stroke textures.

1 Introduction

The medium of pen and ink offers many advantages for visually communicating ideas. Pen-and-ink illustrations can be easily printed alongside text, using the same ink on the same paper, without degradation. Moreover, good reproduction quality can be obtained on commonplace 300 or 600 dot-per-inch laser printers as well as on lower-resolution monochrome displays. Although pen-and-ink illustrations allow only monochromatic strokes of the pen, the resulting illustrations are often striking in their beauty and simplicity [11, 24].

While the areas of photorealistic rendering and paint systems have received considerable attention in the literature, creating pen-and-ink illustrations on a computer is a relatively new area. Recently, Winkenbach and Salesin [28] described an automated rendering system that produces pen-and-ink illustrations from 3D polyhedral architectural models. This system can render an illustration of a model at different scales and resolutions by applying procedural stroke textures to an analytic representation of the image. Concurrently, Salisbury *et al.* [23] proposed an interactive system that allows the user to "paint" an image with prioritized stroke textures. This system is particularly useful for applying stroke textures to a scanned or synthetic image, effectively creating an "artistically-halftoned" monochrome version of the original. The user creates the pen-and-ink illustration on the screen, and the illustration is saved as a long list of Bézier strokes. One problem with this straightforward WYSIWYG approach is that illustrations represented in this manner cannot be reproduced at different scales or resolutions without significantly changing their overall appearance.

University of Washington, Box 352350, Seattle WA 98195-2350
{ salisbur | corin | danix | salesin }@cs.washington.edu

By way of example, consider the three illustrations shown in Figure 1. Figure 1(b) shows the original illustration at the size for which it was designed by the artist. If we wish to double the size of the illustration, we cannot merely scale it by a factor of two; such a scaling lightens the tone by spreading the same number of strokes over a larger area, as demonstrated by Figure 1(c). While this effect could be mitigated by thickening the strokes in the scaled-up version, the character of the illustration would be considerably altered. Conversely, scaling the illustration down darkens the tone as the density of strokes increases (Figure 1(a)). We would instead like our computer-generated illustrations to maintain both the thickness and density of their strokes when they are rescaled. Changing resolutions could also produce unwanted effects. For instance, all three illustrations in Figure 1 would look darker on a 300 dot-per-inch printer as they use strokes that are too thin for that resolution.

Another problem with storing illustrations as Bézier strokes is that the sheer number of strokes can make such a representation expensive to store, slow to transmit, and cumbersome to include in electronic documents. For example, the size of each illustration in Figure 1 is about one megabyte in PostScript [1].

In this paper, we extend the work of Salisbury *et al.* by proposing an alternative representation for pen-and-ink illustrations that is scale- and resolution-independent as well as compact. Instead of storing each of the individual strokes comprising an illustration, we keep an underlying grey-scale image for each stroke texture in the illustration along with a pointer to the stroke texture itself. To render the illustration at a particular scale and resolution, the grey-scale images are first rescaled and then hatched with strokes.

The proposed image-based representation is quite simple; however, maintaining true scale- and resolution-independence also requires solving an interesting related problem whose solution is not so straightforward. Since pen-and-ink illustrations hatch an image with strokes, they tend to be insensitive to fine texture detail. Thus it is often sufficient for the underlying grey-scale image to have a relatively low resolution. However, magnifying a low-resolution image for reproducing a large illustration on a high-resolution output device typically results in undesirable blurring of the hard edges, or *discontinuities*, in the image.

The question, then, is how to resample images while preserving certain discontinuity edges. In order to be able to produce crisp edges in illustrations at all possible output scales and resolutions, we need to maintain information about discontinuity edges in the underlying image and explicitly take these edges into account in the resampling process. In this paper, we describe a new resampling algo-

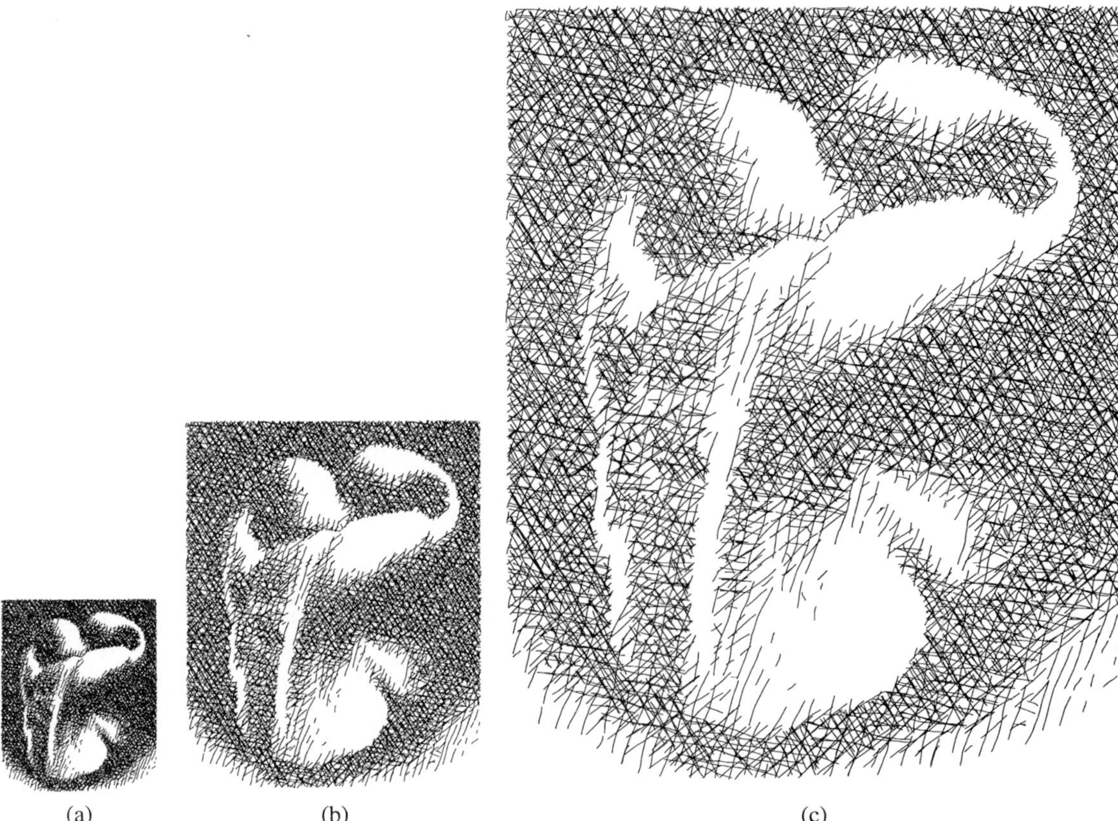

Figure 1 The same illustration at three different scales: (b) is the original; (a) and (c) demonstrate that naive rescaling changes tone and character.

rithm to implement this process. This algorithm, which is essentially a discontinuity-sensitive reconstruction filter, is the main technical contribution of the paper.

1.1 Related work

Line-art illustration has been explored previously by a number of authors. Elber [9], Saito and Takahashi [21], Winkenbach and Salesin [28], Strothotte *et al.* [25], and Lansdown and Schofield [14] all use 3D models to generate illustrations. Pneuli and Bruckstein [20] and Salisbury *et al.* [23] both generate illustrations starting from grey-scale images. However, neither of these last two works addresses the problem of rescaling such illustrations.

There are several paint systems that offer a measure of resolution-independence. Paint By Numbers [12] stores images as collections of resolution-independent strokes, Live Picture [16] represents the operations on images as a resolution-independent history, and Live-Paint [19] provides resolution-independent procedural ink. However, none of these approaches provides any means of magnifying scanned images beyond their original resolution while preserving discontinuities. The resampling algorithm described in this paper could conceivably be used for this purpose in any of these systems.

The idea of making explicit use of discontinuities in functions, surfaces, and images is not new. Discontinuities have been used to construct good meshes for radiosity [13, 15] and to fit piecewise-cubic interpolants for radiance functions [22]. Franke and Nielson described several methods for surface reconstruction from scattered data with known discontinuities [10]. Zhong and Mallat [31] pioneered work in image compression by storing edges detected at multiple scales. Yomdin and Elichai [30] also describe an image compression algorithm that locates and utilizes various types of edges in images to obtain a lossy compression scheme that avoids reconstruction artifacts in the vicinity of edges.

1.2 Overview

In the next section we describe in more detail our proposed representation scheme for pen-and-ink illustrations, and we present a new algorithm for image rescaling that preserves the discontinuities of the original image. Section 3 describes how pen-and-ink illustrations are created and reproduced in our illustration system. Section 4 presents several examples of illustrations and describes our experience with the proposed technique. We conclude and offer directions for further research in Section 5.

2 Reconstructing images with discontinuities

This section describes the core of our pen-and-ink illustration system: an image-based representation for illustrations, and a new reconstruction algorithm for resampling images with discontinuities.

We have two major requirements of our representation. First, it should allow us to produce pen-and-ink illustrations at any scale and resolution without changing the tone or character of the illustration. Second, the resulting illustrations must keep "sharp features" sharp and "smooth features" smooth. By "sharp features" we mean abrupt changes in intensity along certain prescribed boundaries of the image, which we refer to as *discontinuities*. While we want our illustrations to exhibit crisp edges along discontinuities, we would like the tone to change smoothly everywhere else. In particular, it is important that the rescaling algorithm not introduce any spurious discontinuities.

One could imagine several possible representations that would meet our requirements. For example, we could maintain a history of all the operations performed on an image, along the lines of Live Picture [16], and then simply replay the history at the desired resolution when rendering the output. Although this approach is simple and basically sound, it has two main disadvantages. First, the representation's size and rendering time grow with the number of editing operations, and not necessarily with the complexity of the image. Second, this approach does not allow scanned or rendered images to be magnified beyond their original sizes without blurring their sharp features.

Another alternative is to use a collection of polynomial patches in order to construct an explicit image function that interpolates the image sample values. One difficulty with this representation is the problem of handling discontinuities, since it is not obvious how to modify a smooth patch representation to incorporate arbitrary arrangements of discontinuities. Another difficulty is the problem of determining control points so that the surface accurately approximates an arbitrary target image without introducing ringing artifacts from maintaining the smoothness constraints.

For our representation, we have chosen to use a combination of uniformly-spaced image samples and piecewise-linear discontinuity curves called *discontinuity edges*. Any arrangement of discontinuity edges is allowed, provided they intersect only at their endpoints. Thus, discontinuity edges are not constrained to form closed regions. Instead, we allow "open" discontinuities that have dangling edges not connected to any other. We would like the tone to change smoothly around the open end of such a discontinuity but change sharply across the discontinuity edge. It is crucial to allow open discontinuities, as they frequently arise in images, especially when discontinuity edges are obtained by performing edge detection on a scanned image (see Figure 6(b)).

In the rest of this section, we'll describe the algorithm we use to produce an image of arbitrary scale and resolution from our representation.

2.1 Problem statement

The problem that we would like to solve can be stated formally as follows:

Given: A set of uniformly-spaced discrete sample (pixel) locations $\{x_i\}$, a set of corresponding intensity values $\{f_i\}$, and a set of line segments $\{\ell_i\}$ (the discontinuity edges);

Find: A function $f(x)$ that is smooth everywhere except across the discontinuity edges, such that $f(x)$ interpolates the values f_i.

The reconstructed function $f(x)$ can then be resampled at a higher rate than the original image, resulting in a magnified version of the image, or it can be resampled at a lower rate after band-limiting, yielding a minified version of the image.

2.2 Reconstruction algorithm

Reconstruction of a continuous signal $f(x)$ from uniformly-spaced discrete samples $\{(x_i, f_i)\}$ may be performed by convolving with a reconstruction kernel $k(x)$, whose weights at the sample points sum to one:

$$f(x) = \sum f_i\, k(x - x_i). \tag{1}$$

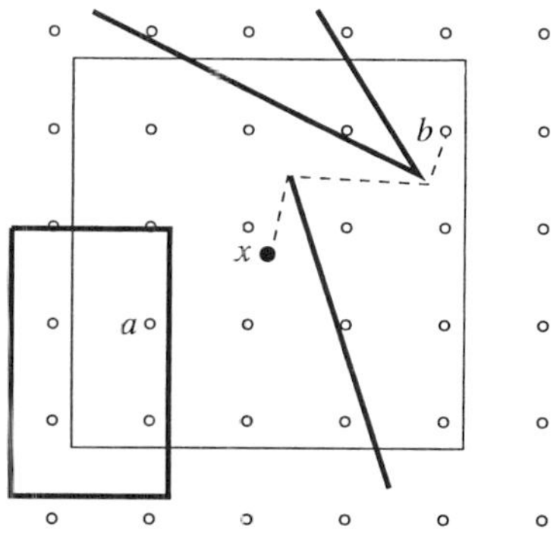

Figure 2 Several discontinuity edges (shown as thick lines) intersect the support of a 4×4 kernel centered at x. The dashed line indicates the shortest unobstructed path from x to b.

A variety of reconstruction kernels is available, including several interpolation kernels that effectively fit interpolants of various degrees to the input samples [29]. In this section, we describe a modification to the standard convolution framework that will cause the reconstructed function to be discontinuous across the discontinuity edges while preserving smoothness everywhere else.

In order to reconstruct the value at point x, we first check whether there are any discontinuity edges that cross the support of the kernel centered at x. If no such discontinuities exist, the reconstructed value $f(x)$ is given by equation (1).

Things become more interesting when one or more image samples under the kernel's support are separated from x by a discontinuity edge. Consider, for example, the situation in Figure 2. The thick solid lines indicate discontinuity edges that intersect the square support of the kernel centered at x (marked by a black dot). Input samples such as a cannot be reached from x without crossing a discontinuity edge. Clearly such samples should not have any effect on the value of $f(x)$. Input samples such as b cannot be "seen" directly from x; however, they can be reached by going around the discontinuities. To ensure that $f(x)$ changes smoothly as x moves around these discontinuities, the sample b should have some effect on the value $f(x)$. Intuitively, this effect should be commensurate with the "ease" of reaching b from x without crossing discontinuities.

Thus, in order to preserve discontinuities in the reconstructed function $f(x)$, we replace the reconstruction kernel k with a modified kernel $\tilde{k}$, which attenuates k's entries according to each entry's reachability. To describe our new kernel, we must first define some terms.

Let $d(x, x_i)$ be the Euclidean distance between x and x_i, and let $sp(x, x_i)$ be the length of the shortest unobstructed path between the two points (see Figure 2). We define the *detour cost* between x and x_i as:

$$detour(x, x_i) = sp(x, x_i) - d(x, x_i) \tag{2}$$

Our modified kernel $\tilde{k}$ thus attenuates k:

$$\tilde{k}(x - x_i) = \alpha(x, x_i)\, k(x - x_i) \tag{3}$$

where the attenuating function $\alpha(x, x_i)$ is defined as:

$$\alpha(x, x_i) = \begin{cases} 1 & \text{if } detour(x, x_i) = 0 \\ & \quad \text{(i.e., if } x_i \text{ is visible from } x\text{)} \\ 0 & \text{if } detour(x, x_i) \geq r \\ & \quad \text{(i.e., if } x_i \text{ is too "far")} \\ 1 - 3t^2 + 2t^3 & \text{if } detour(x, x_i) < r, \\ & \quad \text{where } t = detour(x, x_i)/r \end{cases} \tag{4}$$

The constant r above is the detour cost beyond which a sample has no effect on x. We have found that a value of $r = 1$ works well for

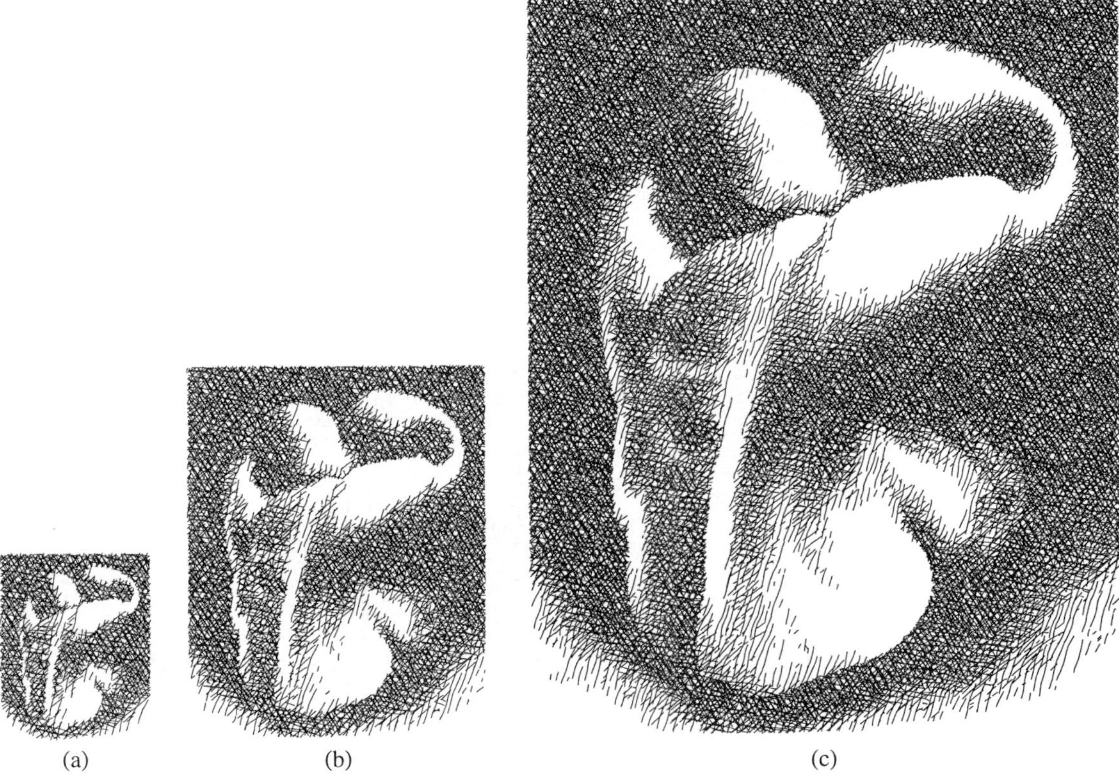

Figure 3 A pepper at three different scales. Original photograph by Edward Weston [27].

our 4 × 4 filter. The cubic polynomial in the third case above was chosen in order to ensure that $\alpha(x, x_i)$ is C^1 continuous.

Note that the modified kernel $\tilde{k}$ no longer has the property that its weights at the sample points sum to one. To compensate, we turn the convolution in equation (1) into a *weighted-average* convolution:

$$f(x) = \frac{\sum f_i\, \alpha(x, x_i)\, k(x - x_i)}{\sum \alpha(x, x_i)\, k(x - x_i)} \tag{5}$$

This form of convolution has been used previously for filtering non-uniform samples [7, 8, 18].

The kernel modification described above is applicable to any reconstruction kernel. In our implementation, we chose the cubic convolution kernel described by Wolberg [29]. This kernel has negative lobes, as do most interpolating kernels. This property introduces a slight complication into our reconstruction algorithm, as it is possible for the magnitude of the sum in the denominator of equation (5) to become very small. Dividing by small numbers magnifies any noise in the calculation, causing visible bright "speckles" in the reconstructed image. To overcome this difficulty, we switch to the entirely non-negative B-spline kernel [29] whenever the denominator in equation (5) falls below a certain threshold. To avoid introducing a discontinuity at places where the switch occurs, we smoothly blend between the two kernels as the denominator approaches zero. A precise definition of these two kernels is given in Appendix A.

Our resampling algorithm resembles the "distance penalty fault" method described by Franke and Nielson for surface reconstruction from scattered data with known discontinuities [10]. However, our algorithm is specialized to uniform grid data, and by using the general notion of detour cost it can handle arbitrary arrangements of discontinuity edges. Another difference is that, unlike Franke and Nielson's algorithm, ours is not restricted to positive weighting functions, allowing better frequency response.

Computing shortest paths

To complete the description of our reconstruction algorithm, it remains to explain how we compute the length of the shortest path between two points. We will refer to an endpoint of a discontinuity edge as a *discontinuity vertex.* If a discontinuity vertex is in the middle of a chain of discontinuity edges and is thus reachable from multiple sides, we consider each side of the vertex to be a distinct discontinuity vertex for the purposes of this minimum distance algorithm. As a preprocessing step, we compute the distance between all pairs of discontinuity vertices using Dijkstra's all-pairs shortest paths algorithm [2]. Then, during reconstruction, to compute the shortest path between two particular points x_1 and x_2 that cannot "see" each other, we find the sets V_1 and V_2 of discontinuity vertices directly visible to x_1 and x_2, respectively, within a certain ellipse that surrounds them both. This ellipse has foci at x_1 and x_2 and contains all points x such that

$$d(x, x_1) + d(x, x_2) \le d(x_1, x_2) + r \tag{6}$$

Any discontinuity vertex beyond this distance would make the detour cost larger than the maximum detour cost r, thereby forcing the sample's attenuation $\alpha(x, x_i)$ to zero.

Given the sets V_1 and V_2, the length of the shortest path between points x_1 and x_2 is simply

$$sp(x_1, x_2) = \min_{v_1 \in V_1, v_2 \in V_2} \{d(x_1, v_1) + sp(v_1, v_2) + d(v_2, x_2)\} \tag{7}$$

In order to rapidly determine the set V for any point x we first construct a constrained Delaunay triangulation (CDT) [6] containing

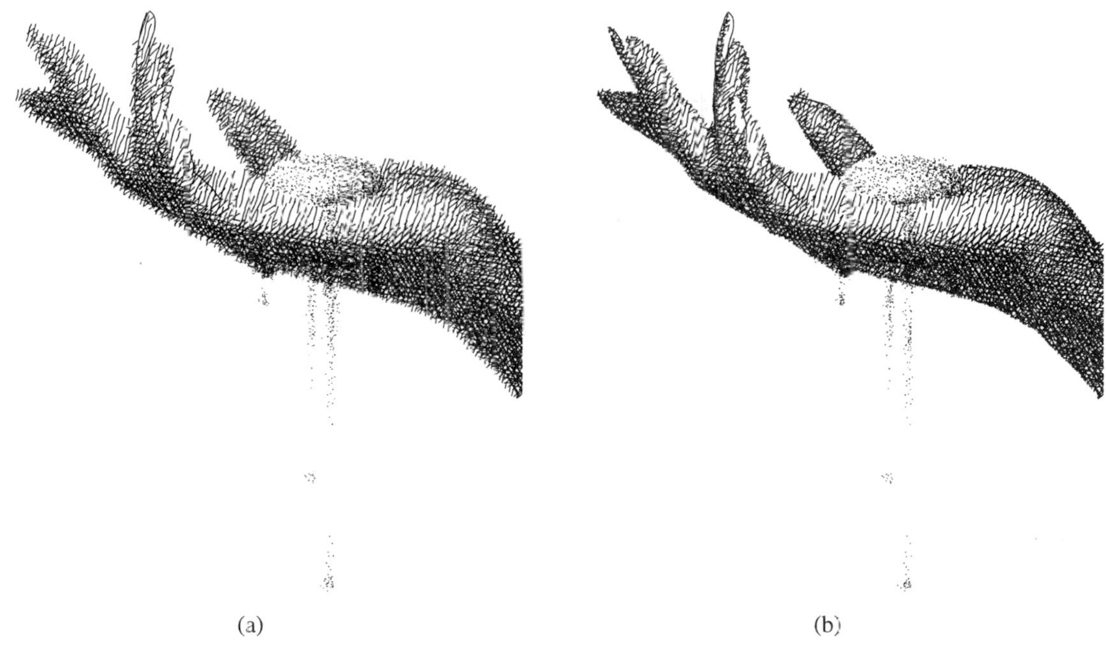

(a) (b)

Figure 4 An illustration with standard filtering (a) and with our algorithm (b). Both illustrations were produced from images of the same resolution. Original photograph by Walter Swarthout [26].

all of the discontinuity edges in the image as a preprocessing step. Then, given the point x we locate the CDT face containing x. Starting from this face, we recursively visit all nearby faces that are reachable without crossing discontinuity edges. The vertices of all visited faces are tested to see if they are visible from x. To test the visibility of vertex v, we march from x towards v in the CDT and stop either when a discontinuity edge is crossed (in which case v is not directly visible), or when v is reached (in which case it is visible).

It costs $O(n^3)$ to compute the shortest paths between all pairs of n discontinuity edge vertices. The CDT can be constructed in $O(n \log n)$ time. Both of these computations are performed only once, in the preprocessing stage. For each point x at which the function is reconstructed (i.e., for each pixel location in the resampled image), we need to compute the detour cost for as many as sixteen pixels in the original image, as described above. The cost of this computation is at worst quadratic in the number of discontinuity vertices within the kernel's support, but this number is typically small.

3 Creating and reproducing illustrations

Our illustration representation consists of a list of discontinuity edges and a grid of grey-scale sample values.

To create an illustration, we start from a grey-scale image. This image can be generated by rendering, digitally painting, or scanning in a printed image. We find discontinuity edges using Canny's edge detector [5]. Then we compute one sample value at each pixel center. For most pixels, the source image pixel value is a good approximation to the sample value. However, for pixels containing discontinuities, the pixel value typically corresponds to an average of the image function on both sides of the discontinuity and is thus unsuitable as a sample value. In this case we extrapolate the sample value from nearby "uncontaminated" samples that are reachable without crossing discontinuities.

Once this process is completed, we reduce the resolution of the sample grid as much as possible while maintaining enough detail to create a satisfactory result. If too few samples remain, some areas bounded by discontinuities may not contain any reachable sample values. In this situation we must allow the reconstruction filter to cross discontinuities. Thus, reducing the resolution too much may have the effect of blurring or eliminating small features altogether, even if their edges are part of the representation. Determining the appropriate reduction factor automatically is an interesting problem for future work.

Once the image has been reduced, we assign to it a stroke texture along with an optional set of *outline strokes* used to surround selected regions of the image. The outline strokes can be chosen from the set of discontinuity edges. To make use of multiple stroke textures, the image can be separated into grey-scale overlays, each of which is associated with its own stroke texture.

In order to view or print an illustration, we first produce a grey-scale image of the desired size with the algorithm described in Section 2. Since we want to avoid unnaturally sharp edges in the final illustration, we only magnify the image to one half of the desired size with our reconstruction algorithm. We then expand the image by an additional factor of two using a standard separable reconstruction filter, which can be applied much more quickly in a separate stage. This technique generates just enough blurring along the edges to give the illustrations a hand-drawn feel.

We finally re-render the illustration with a stroke texture in an automatic process called *blasting*. The blasting algorithm takes a grey-scale image and a stroke texture as input and creates an illustration with strokes, which, when taken together, produce the same tone as was present in the underlying image. We use the same approach as Salisbury *et al.* [23] for producing strokes and placing them into an illustration. This approach consists of repeatedly selecting a stroke from the stroke texture and computing the tone in the vicinity of the stroke that would result if it were added. The stroke is rejected if it makes the illustration darker than the tone of the underlying image anywhere along its length. Whereas the system of Salisbury *et al.* generates candidate strokes only underneath the user's brush, we automatically place strokes that cover the entire illustration.

Figure 5 Keys. Original photograph by Randy Miller [17].

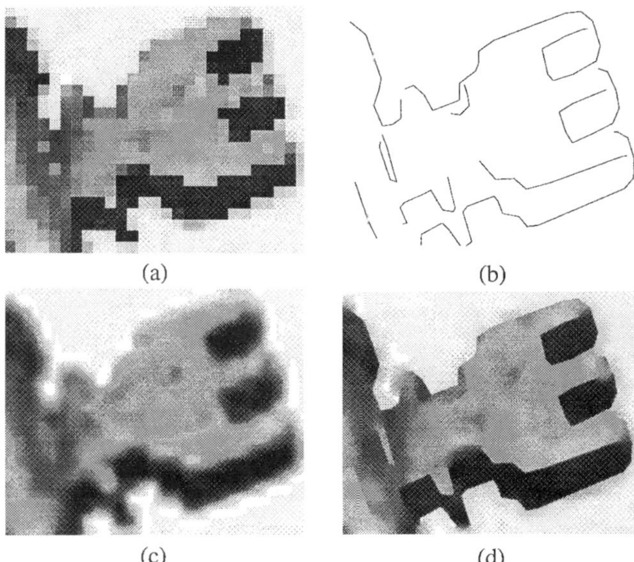

Figure 6 Close-ups of Figure 5: (a) the underlying low-resolution grey-scale image; (b) the discontinuity edges used; (c) the grey-scale image produced using standard magnification; and (d) the image produced by our resampling algorithm.

4 Results

We present several illustrations that demonstrate the various capabilities of our representation.

Figure 3 shows an illustration rendered at three scales. Each of these scales maintains the correct tone and gives the same overall texture effect. Note that different collections of actual strokes were used to generate the illustration at the various sizes. Compare these illustrations to those in Figure 1, where the same set of strokes was used for each scale, resulting in undesirable alterations in tone and overall effect.

Figure 4 demonstrates the advantage of maintaining and respecting discontinuities. Figure 4(a) is an illustration produced by blasting an image that was rescaled without maintaining discontinuities. The illustration in 4(b) is the same as 4(a) except that it was rescaled using our magnification algorithm. Notice that the outline edges do not align with the edges of the fingers in illustration 4(a). Also of interest is the use of multiple textures in both Figures 4 and 5.

The illustrations in Figures 6 and 7 are close-ups of the lower-right-hand corner of Figure 5 and show the potential for using our representation to generate poster-sized illustrations. Figure 6(a) shows the pixel values stored by the representation, which along with the discontinuity edges in 6(b) can be used to generate 6(d) and, in turn, 7(b). The images in 6(c) and 6(d) are the grey-scale images that were used to blast the illustrations in 7(a) and 7(b). All of the edges in these and the other illustrations we present were found automatically with our edge detector.

Notice in Figure 6(b) that the key is not completely surrounded by edges. In places where no discontinuity edges are present, our reconstruction produces smooth changes in grey-scale, even in the vicinity of discontinuity endpoints.

Table 1 gives the storage requirements and reconstruction times required for the illustrations in this paper. The REPRESENTATION column gives the number of pixels stored on disk, the number of discontinuities used, and the total size of both in kilobytes. The OUTPUT column gives the size of the reconstructed grey-scale image that was used for blasting, and the size, in megabytes, of the PostScript file used for printing. Finally, the TIME column gives the time required to pre-process, enlarge, and blast the image with strokes. These times were measured on a Silicon Graphics workstation with a 250MHz R4400 processor. To summarize the table, our representation reduces the storage requirements of these illustrations by a factor of 100–1000, and it takes from 1–7 minutes to render them.

5 Future work

Our experience with the proposed technique suggests several areas for future research:

- *PostScript renderer.* The reduced size of our representation currently offers no practical advantage in transmission to printers or web browsers because they do not recognize our representation. One solution is to write rendering code in the languages that these devices do understand. For example, a PostScript printer could be sent illustration rendering code written in PostScript along with several standard stroke textures. This code could then generate an illustration at any requested scale and resolution directly on the output device. Similar programs could be written in Java or Acrobat to allow web browsers to render illustrations.
- *Scalable textures.* Currently our stroke textures are applied at a single scale: if the illustration is magnified, the texture shrinks relative to the image. While this effect is acceptable for uniform textures, it could be objectionable for textures with recognizable patterns. It might be better to have a multiresolution stroke texture that could change scale with the illustration. Then, as the scale of the texture increased, finer resolution strokes could automatically be added to the illustration.
- *Combining with multiresolution images.* Our representation and resampling algorithm are currently limited to traditional uniresolution images. We would like to extend our technique to handle multiresolution image representations, such as the one described by Berman *et al.* [4]. In this case, we would also want to develop

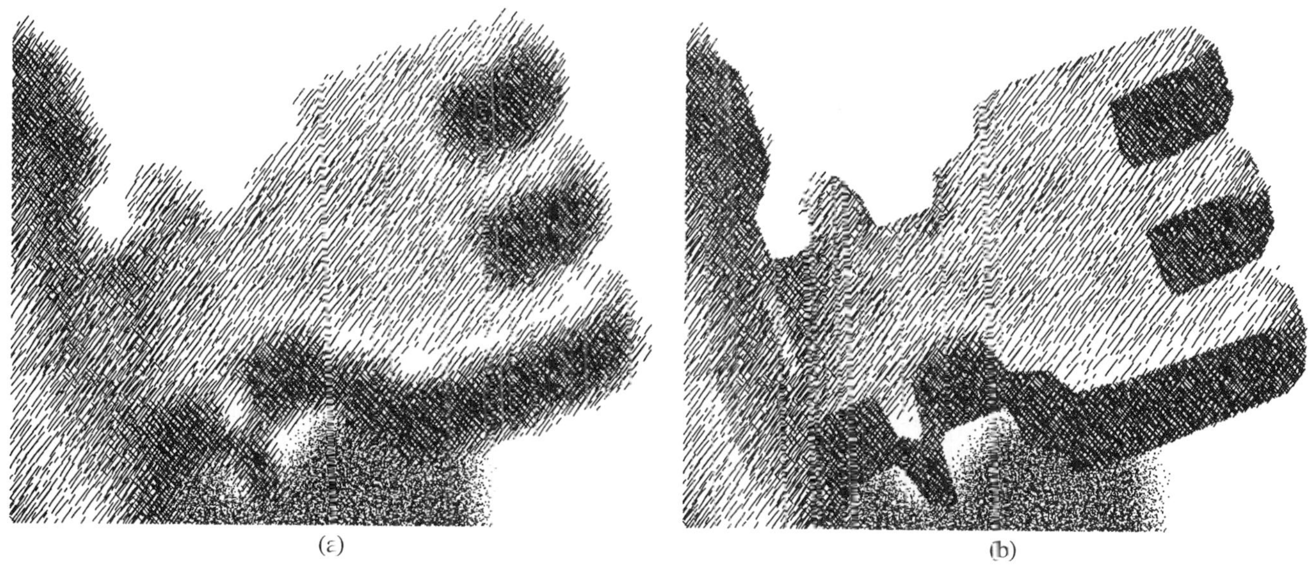

(a) (b)

Figure 7 Illustrations produced from Figures 6(c) and 6(d).

		REPRESENTATION			OUTPUT		TIME		
Fig	Content	ImgSize (pixels)	# Edges	Storage (KB)	ImgSize (pixels)	PS Size (MB)	PrePro (sec)	Enlarge (sec)	Blast (sec)
3a	Pepper	102×128	270	10.5	204×256	0.2	39	3	5
3b	Pepper	102×128	270	10.5	408×512	1.0	39	35	11
3c	Pepper	102×128	270	10.5	816×1024	3.8	39	108	35
4a	Hand	64×64	—	1.2	1024×1024	1.0	—	3	45
"	Egg	128×128	—	1.4	1024×1024	1.0	—	4	128
4b	Hand	64×64	237	2.3	1024×1024	1.0	19	130	41
"	Egg	128×128	143	1.9	1024×1024	1.0	8	41	134
5	Keys	128×128	504	7.9	1024×1024	2.4	220	142	43
"	Shadow	64×64	111	1.5	1024×1024	2.4	3	100	120
7a	Key closeup	27×22	—	0.7	864×704	1.9	—	2	29
"	Shadow	27×22	—	0.2	864×704	1.9	—	2	88
7b	Key closeup	27×22	107	1.0	864×704	2.0	8	195	27
"	Shadow	27×22	6	0.3	864×704	2.0	1	30	84
8	Billiard	71×61	326	5.4	568×488	1.3	47	81	19

Table 1 Illustration sizes and speeds.

a multiresolution discontinuity representation in which different discontinuities could be present at different scales.

- *Image compression.* Given our algorithm's ability to reproduce large images from a compact representation, it is natural to consider the possibility of using it as a more general image compression mechanism. One complication with such an approach may be the lack of texture detail in the reconstructed images.

Acknowledgments

We would like to thank Sean Anderson for his help early in the project.

This work was supported by an Alfred P. Sloan Research Fellowship (BR-3495), an NSF Postdoctoral Research Associates in Experimental Sciences award (CDA-9404959), an NSF Presidential Faculty Fellow award (CCR-9553199), an ONR Young Investigator award (N00014-95-1-0728), a grant from the Washington Technology Center, and industrial gifts from Interval, Microsoft, and Xerox.

References

[1] Adobe Systems Incorporated. *PostScript Language Reference Manual.* Addison Wesley, Reading, Massachusetts, 2nd edition, 1994.

[2] Alfred V. Aho, John E. Hopcroft, and Jeffrey D. Ullman. *Data Structures and Algorithms.* Addison-Wesley, Reading, Massachusetts, 1987.

[3] Arthur Beck. Photograph. In *Photographis 81, The International Annual of Advertising and Editorial Photography*, p. 151. Graphis Press Corp., 1981.

[4] Deborah F. Berman, Jason T. Bartell, and David H. Salesin. Multiresolution painting and compositing. In *Computer Graphics* Proceedings, Annual Conference Series, pp. 85–90. ACM Press, July 1994.

[5] John Canny. A computational approach to edge detection. *IEEE Transactions on Pattern Analysis and Machine Intelligence*, 8(6):679–698, November 1986.

[6] L. Paul Chew. Constrained delaunay triangulations. *Algorithmica*, 4:97–108, 1989.

[7] Robert L. Cook. Stochastic sampling in computer graphics. *Transactions on Graphics*, 5(1):51–72, January 1986.

[8] Mark A. Z. Dippé and Erling Henry Wold. Antialiasing through stochastic sampling. *Computer Graphics*, 19(3):69–78, July 1985.

[9] Gershon Elber. Line art rendering via a coverage of isoparametric curves. *IEEE Transactions on Visualization and Computer Graphics*, 1(3):231–239, September 1995.

[10] Richard Franke and Gregory M. Nielson. Surface approximation with imposed conditions. In R. E. Barnhill and W. Boehm, editors, *Surfaces in CAGD*, pp. 135–146. North-Holland Publishing Company, 1983.

[11] Arthur L. Guptill. *Rendering in Pen and Ink*. Watson-Guptill Publications, New York, 1976.

[12] Paul E. Haeberli. Paint by numbers: Abstract image representations. *Computer Graphics*, 24(4):207–214, August 1990.

[13] Paul Heckbert. Discontinuity meshing for radiosity. In *Third Eurographics Workshop on Rendering*, pp. 203–226, Bristol, UK, May 1992.

[14] John Lansdown and Simon Schofield. Expressive rendering: A review of nonphotorealistic techniques. *IEEE Computer Graphics and Applications*, 15(3):29–37, May 1995.

[15] Dani Lischinski, Filippo Tampieri, and Donald P. Greenberg. Discontinuity meshing for accurate radiosity. *IEEE Computer Graphics and Applications*, 12(6):25–39, November 1992.

[16] T. Marshall. Lively pictures (Power Mac image editing). *BYTE*, 20(1):171–172, January 95.

[17] Randy Miller. Photograph. In *Photographis 77, The International Annual of Advertising and Editorial Photography*, p. 72. Graphis Press Corp., 1977.

[18] Don P. Mitchell. Generating antialiased images at low sampling densities. *Computer Graphics*, 21(4):65–72, July 1987.

[19] Ken Perlin and Luiz Velho. Live Paint: painting with procedural multiscale textures. In *Computer Graphics* Proceedings, Annual Conference Series, pp. 153–160. ACM Press, August 1995.

[20] Yachin Pnueli and Alfred M. Bruckstein. **Dig$^{\mathbf{i}}$**$_D$*ürer* — a digital engraving system. *The Visual Computer*, 10(5):277–292, 1994.

[21] Takafumi Saito and Tokiichiro Takahashi. NC machining with G-buffer method. *Computer Graphics*, 25(4):207–216, July 1991.

[22] David Salesin, Daniel Lischinski, and Tony DeRose. Reconstructing illumination functions with selected discontinuities. In *Third Eurographics Workshop on Rendering*, pp. 99–112, Bristol, UK, May 1992.

[23] Michael P. Salisbury, Sean E. Anderson, Ronen Barzel, and David H. Salesin. Interactive pen-and-ink illustration. In *Computer Graphics* Proceedings, Annual Conference Series, pp. 101–108. ACM Press, July 1994.

[24] Gary Simmons. *The Technical Pen*. Watson-Guptill Publications, New York, 1992.

[25] Thomas Strothotte, Bernhard Preim, Andreas Raab, Jutta Schumann, and David R. Forsey. How to render frames and influence people. *Computer Graphics Forum*, 13(3):455–466, 1994. Eurographics '94 Conference issue.

[26] Walter Swarthout. Photograph. In *Photographis 75, The International Annual of Advertising, Editorial, and Television Photography*, p. 133. Graphis Press Corp., 1975.

[27] Edward Weston. *Aperture Masters of Photography, Number Seven*, p. 29. Aperture Foundation, Inc., New York, 1988.

[28] Georges Winkenbach and David H. Salesin. Computer-generated pen-and-ink illustration. In *Computer Graphics* Proceedings, Annual Conference Series, pp. 91–100. ACM Press, July 1994.

[29] George Wolberg. *Digital Image Warping*. IEEE Computer Society Press, Los Alamitos, California, 1990.

[30] Y. Yomdin and Y. Elichai. Normal forms representation: a technology for image compression. In *Image and Video Processing*, volume 1903 of *Proceedings of the SPIE — The International Society for Optical Engineering*, pp. 204–214. SPIE, February 1993.

[31] S. Zhong and S. Mallat. Compact image representation from multiscale edges. In *Proceedings. Third International Conference on Computer Vision*, pp. 522–525. IEEE Computing Society Press, December 1990.

Figure 8 Billiard balls. Original photograph by Arthur Beck [3].

Appendix A: Kernel definitions

The cubic convolution kernel we used is a member of the following family of kernels [29]:

$$k(x) = \begin{cases} (a+2)|x|^3 - (a+3)|x|^2 + 1 & 0 \le |x| < 1 \\ a|x|^3 - 5a|x|^2 + 8a|x| - 4a & 1 \le |x| < 2 \\ 0 & 2 \le |x| \end{cases} \quad (8)$$

We chose the value $a = -0.5$, which makes the Taylor series approximation of the reconstructed function agree in as many terms as possible with the original signal.

The non-negative B-spline kernel we used is defined as follows:

$$k(x) = \frac{1}{6} \begin{cases} 3|x|^3 - 6|x|^2 + 4 & 0 \le |x| < 1 \\ -|x|^3 + 6|x|^2 - 12|x| + 8 & 1 \le |x| < 2 \\ 0 & 2 \le |x| \end{cases} \quad (9)$$

This kernel is called the *Parzen window*.

Rendering Parametric Surfaces in Pen and Ink

Georges Winkenbach *David H. Salesin*

Department of Computer Science and Engineering
University of Washington
Seattle, Washington 98195

Abstract

This paper presents new algorithms and techniques for rendering parametric free-form surfaces in pen and ink. In particular, we introduce the idea of "controlled-density hatching" for conveying tone, texture, and shape. The fine control over tone this method provides allows the use of traditional texture mapping techniques for specifying the tone of pen-and-ink illustrations. We also show how a planar map, a data structure central to our rendering algorithm, can be constructed from parametric surfaces, and used for clipping strokes and generating outlines. Finally, we show how curved shadows can be cast onto curved objects for this style of illustration.

CR Categories and Subject Descriptors: I.3.3 [Computer Graphics]: Picture/Image Generation; I.3.6 [Computer Graphics]: Methodology and Techniques.

Additional Key Words: non-photorealistic rendering, comprehensible rendering, pen-and-ink rendering, resolution-dependent rendering, stroke textures, controlled-density hatching, outlining, shadow algorithms.

1 Introduction

In many applications—from architectural design, to medical texts, to industrial maintenance and repair manuals—a stylized illustration is often more effective than photorealism. Illustrations convey information better, consume less storage, are more easily reproduced, are more capable of conveying information at various levels of detail, and are in many respects more attractive than photorealistic images.

In a previous paper [22], we introduced a system for automatically generating pen-and-ink illustrations of three-dimensional architectural models. In that paper, we showed how many of the principles of traditional pen-and-ink rendering, such as achieving tones through texture, could be simulated algorithmically. In particular, we introduced the concept of a "prioritized stroke texture", which is used to reproduce arbitrary tones and convey textures simultaneously.

However, this earlier work was limited to polyhedral models. With curved surfaces, a number of the fundamental assumptions we used break down. Most notably, in this earlier work we assumed flat-shaded surfaces, and we used BSP trees both for creating a planar map data structure and for clipping individual strokes quickly.

In this paper, we generalize our previous work to handle curved surfaces formulated parametrically, such as B-splines surfaces, NURBS, and surfaces of revolution. We introduce a mechanism for creating "controlled-density hatching," which allows strokes to gradually disappear in light areas of a surface or in areas where too many strokes converge together, and allows new strokes to gradually come into existence in dark areas or areas in which the existing strokes begin to diverge too much. With controlled-density hatching, we are able to exert fine-grain control over the tone depicted in various areas of a pen-and-ink image. We use this newly acquired ability, together with traditional (image-based) texture mapping techniques, to extend considerably the repertoire of effects that can be achieved with stroke textures. We demonstrate these effects with texture maps used for surface detail, bump mapping, and environment ("reflection") mapping. In addition, we show how a planar map can be created and strokes efficiently clipped without the use of BSP trees. Finally, we describe a simple method to handle the casting of curved shadows onto curved objects.

1.1 Related work

A few authors have addressed similar goals in their published work.

Dooley and Cohen proposed a system to enhance a traditional shaded images with illustration techniques [3, 4]. They showed how line and surface qualities could be customized by the user to create more effective images.

Saito and Takahashi [18] used "G-buffers" and image processing techniques to enhance ray-traced images with illustration features. Their system handles outlining, hatching, and shadows. However, the use of strokes that we propose allows perhaps more expressiveness and extends the range of illustrations that can be created automatically.

Leister presented a technique to emulate copper-plate rendering [12], an engraving technique used for old styles of printing. A ray-tracing approach is used to render curves on free-form objects. These curves lie at the intersection of parallel planes with the 3D object being rendered. An advantage of this approach is that it easily handles reflections and shadowing.

The Piranesi system proposed by Lansdown and Schofield [11] also uses non-photorealistic techniques to create illustrations from 3D models. Piranesi uses a standard graphics pipeline to create a 2D reference image akin to a G-buffer. The user is then allowed to select specific regions of the image and apply textures that emulate natural media interactively or automatically.

Elber [5] described an algorithm to cover NURBS surfaces with isoparametric curves, thus emulating a form of line-art rendering. However, his approach does not address a number of the issues in pen-and-ink illustration considered in this paper, such as building tone with stroke textures, outlining objects only when necessary, and rendering shadows.

1.2 Overview

The rest of this paper is organized as follows. Section 2 gives a brief review of some of the key principles of pen-and-ink illustration, and summarizes the system architecture used for creating illustrations of polyhedral models. Section 3 describes the various algorithms that lie at the heart of our system. Section 4 describes the particular stroke textures we used for the figures in this paper, and gives statistics for these results. Finally, Section 5 suggests some areas for future work.

2 Background

In this section, we briefly review some of the principles of pen-and-ink illustration; much more detailed studies can be found in a number of texts [9, 13, 17]. We then describe some of the key architectural features of the pen-and-ink illustration system we introduced in our previous work, upon which the results in this paper are based.

2.1 Principles of pen-and-ink illustration

Some of the key principles of pen-and-ink illustration include:

- *Strokes.* Strokes are the fundamental building-blocks of pen-and-ink illustration. The thickness and density of the strokes is varied to achieve subtle shading effects. In addition, strokes should also have some variation in thickness and waviness so as not to appear too "mechanical."
- *Texture.* Texture results from a large number of pen strokes placed in juxtaposition. The character of the strokes is important for conveying texture—for example, crisp, straight lines are good for "glass," whereas rough, sketchy lines are good for "old" materials.
- *Tone.* The perceived grey level or "tone" is a function of the density of the strokes in a particular region of the illustration. The same strokes that are used to convey texture must also be used to achieve the desired tone.
- *Outline.* Outlining play an essential role in illustration; indeed, outlining is one of the key features that differentiates illustration from photorealistic imagery. Outlines are generally introduced only where they are required to disambiguate regions of similar tone. The quality of the outline stroke must also be varied to convey texture.

2.2 System architecture for polyhedral models

The system for automatically producing pen-and-ink illustrations of polyhedral models, upon which the results in this paper are based, is not very different from a traditional photorealistic renderer. The input to the system consists of a 3D polyhedral model, one or more light sources, and a camera specification. The output is an illustration in the style of pen and ink.

To render a scene, the polyhedral renderer begins by computing the visible surfaces and the shadow polygons, using 3D BSP trees for both operations [1, 7]. The outcome is a set of convex polygons that can be ordered in depth with respect to the view point. The renderer uses these polygons to build both a 2D BSP tree and a planar map representations of the visible surfaces in the scene. It then renders each region in the planar map using a procedural stroke texture. The collection of strokes required to render each flat-shaded surface is generated without considering occlusions. Each stroke is then clipped against the visible portions of the surface using the 2D BSP tree. Finally, the outline strokes are drawn by considering all the edges of the planar map, and rendering only those edges necessary for the illustration, according to the outlining principles.

3 Algorithms

The pen-and-ink rendering system that we describe in this paper utilizes the same basic architecture as the polygonal renderer we introduced in our earlier work. It also uses the same procedural stroke texture idea, and relies on a planar map for generating outlines and clipping strokes. However, in the presence of free-form surfaces, many of the techniques used in the polygonal renderer no longer work. In this section, we present our solutions to these problems.

3.1 Controlled-density hatching

To produce pen-and-ink illustrations from parametric surfaces, the most fundamental change from a polyhedral renderer is in the generation of the stroke textures.

Curved surfaces require a much more sophisticated approach than flat-shaded polygonal surfaces, which can be hatched in a uniform fashion. First, we will need a way of orienting the hatching strokes along a surface. Second, we will need some mechanism for allowing strokes to gradually disappear in light areas of a surface or in areas where too many strokes converge together. Conversely, we will also need to allow new strokes to gradually appear in dark areas or areas in which the existing strokes begin to diverge too much. We will call such a mechanism *controlled-density hatching.*[1]

To solve the first problem, that of choosing an orientation for the hatching strokes, we simply use a grid of lines in the *parameter domain* (u, v). The grid consists of parallel lines running in one or more user-specified directions. For most illustrations, we simply use isoparametric curves, which run parallel to u and/or v.

We now turn to the second problem, that of achieving controlled-density hatching. Achieving a given tone by hatching an arbitrary parametric surface is a non-trivial problem. Figure 1 illustrates the difficulty, even for the case of a simple two-dimensional transformation. In this case, rendering isoparametric curves with constant thickness results in an image with varying tones. Our solution is to adjust the thickness of the strokes in order to keep the "apparent tone" constant. Figure 2 illustrates the same concept, but in this case, for a perspective view of a sphere.

In order to solve this problem formally, we begin by defining a *stroke* γ as a pair of functions $(\lambda(t), \theta(t))$, where $\lambda(t)$ is a line in the parameter domain (u, v), and $\theta(t)$ is a *thickness function*, which describes the *thickness* used in rendering the stroke at every parameter value t. Furthermore, we define the *apparent tone* of an image in the neighborhood of a given point in *image space* (x, y) to be the ratio of the amount of ink deposited in that neighborhood to its area. If the point (x, y) happens to lie on a stroke, the apparent tone can also be expressed as the ratio θ/d, where θ is the thickness of the stroke and d is its image-space separation from adjacent strokes.

With these definitions, the controlled-density hatching problem can be formally stated as follows.

Given:

- *A parametric surface* $\sigma : (u, v) \mapsto (x_w, y_w, z_w)$*, which maps points in the parameter domain* (u, v) *to points in* world space (x_w, y_w, z_w)*;*
- *a perspective viewing transformation* $\mathcal{V} : (x_w, y_w, z_w) \mapsto (x, y)$*, which maps (visible) points in world space to points in image space* (x, y)*;*
- *a hatching direction* $\mathbf{h} = (h_u, h_v)$ *in the parameter domain; and*
- *a target tone function* $T(x, y)$*.*

Find: *A set of strokes* $\gamma_i = (\lambda_i, \theta_i)$*, with lines* λ_i *in the parameter domain running parallel to the hatching direction* $\mathbf{h}$*, such that the apparent tone of mapping the strokes through* $\mathcal{M} = \mathcal{V} \circ \sigma$ *is* $T(x, y)$*.*

[1] For this work, we consider only surfaces with a global parameterization, such as B-spline surfaces, NURBS, and surfaces of revolution. Ideas for generalizing to a broader class of surfaces, such as patch-based surfaces and smoothly-shaded polygonal meshes, are discussed in Section 5.

Figure 1 Controlled-density hatching for a simple 2-dimensional transformation $\mathcal{M} : (u, v) \mapsto (u, v + v \cdot \exp(\sin(u)))$. Rendering isoparametric curves with constant thickness results in an image with varying tones (left). We adjust the thickness of the strokes in order to keep the "apparent tone" constant (right).

The key step in solving this problem will be to determine exactly how the images of two parallel lines in the parameter domain converge and diverge when seen in image space.[2] In particular, let $\lambda_i(t)$ and $\lambda_{i+1}(s)$ be two parallel lines that are d units apart in the parameter domain, and let $\lambda_i'(t)$ and $\lambda_{i+1}'(s)$ be their images, under $\mathcal{M}$, in image space. We would like to know the distance d' between the two image-space curves as a function of t. Once we have this distance function $d'(t)$, we can use it to adjust the thickness and spacing of the strokes to compensate for any spreading or compression.

A simple closed-form expression for the distance between the two curves $\lambda_i'(t)$ and $\lambda_{i+1}'(s)$ does not exist in general, so we seek to approximate it. We begin by writing the mapping $\mathcal{M}$ as two scalar-valued functions

$$\mathcal{M}(u, v) \equiv (X(u, v), Y(u, v))$$

To approximate the behavior of $\mathcal{M}$ in a small neighborhood about (u, v) we consider the Jacobian matrix

$$J(u, v) = \begin{bmatrix} X_u & X_v \\ Y_u & Y_v \end{bmatrix}$$

where X_u, X_v and Y_u, Y_v are the partial derivatives of X and Y with respect to u and v respectively. The Jacobian matrix J is a linear transformation, which can be thought of as a Taylor expansion of $\mathcal{M}$ in the neighborhood of (u, v) truncated to the first-order terms. Under J, the two parallel lines λ_i and λ_{i+1} in parameter space map to parallel lines, denoted by $J(\lambda_i)$ and $J(\lambda_{i+1})$, in image space.

To estimate how much the curves λ_i' and λ_{i+1}' diverge, we look at the ratio ρ_i of the distance d_i' between the lines $J(\lambda_i)$ and $J(\lambda_{i+1})$ in image space, and the distance d_i between the lines λ_i and λ_{i+1} in the parameter domain. If the line λ_i is given by the implicit-form coefficients $\langle a, b, c\rangle$, then the ratio ρ_i is given by (see Appendix A):

$$\rho_i = \frac{d_i'}{d_i} = \sqrt{\frac{(X_u Y_v - X_v Y_u)^2 \, (a^2 + b^2)}{(aY_v - bY_u)^2 + (bX_u - aX_v)^2}} \qquad (1)$$

The ratio $\rho_i(t)$ is a scalar-valued function that approximates how the distance between strokes is altered by the mapping $\mathcal{M}$. We call ρ_i the *stretching factor* of $\mathcal{M}$. When ρ_i is large, the lines spread apart; when ρ_i is small, they compress together. The *maximum stretching factor* $\overline{\rho}_i = \sup_t(\rho_i(t))$ taken along the line λ_i plays a special role: given two lines λ_i and λ_{i+1} offset by the distance d, it allows us to evaluate the maximum spacing $\overline{d_i}' = \overline{\rho}_i d$ between the two corresponding strokes.

[2] Note that the degree to which strokes in image space converge or diverge is dictated not only by the parametric surface, but also by the final projection to image space.

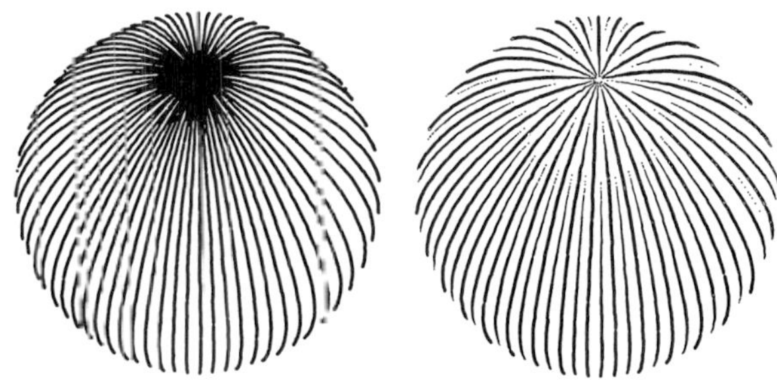

Figure 2 Controlled-density hatching for a perspective view of a sphere. Again, rendering isoparametric curves with constant thickness results in an image with varying tones (left). Using varying stroke thicknesses keeps the "apparent tone" constant (right).

We are now ready to generate strokes so as to achieve the target tone $T(x, y)$. We will do this in four steps.

First, we must decide what the maximum distance $\overline{d}'$ between two strokes in the image should be. This value is dictated by the maximum (or darkest) tone $\overline{T}$ that must be achieved anywhere on the surface, and the *maximum stroke thickness* $\overline{\theta}$ set by the user. To guarantee that $\overline{T}$ can be achieved, given $\overline{\theta}$, the strokes need to be spaced by no more than $\overline{d}' = \overline{\theta}/\overline{T}$ on the image plane.

Second, we note that because the stretching factor ρ_i is derived from a first-order approximation of $\mathcal{M}$, it is accurate only for very small steps in parameter space. In practice, however, the strokes must be spread apart by a comparatively large distance. To work around this problem, we use a stepping technique. To spread two strokes by a distance $\overline{d}'$, we take a series of small step of size δ in parameter space, updating the stretching factor after each step. Stepping starts from the line λ_i, and proceeds until the accumulated image-space distance, given by $\sum_j \overline{\rho}_j \delta$, equals or exceeds $\overline{d}'$. In our implementation, δ is set to $0.01\overline{d}'/\overline{\rho}_i$.

Third, we must modulate the thickness of the strokes to accurately render the tone $T(x, y)$. Two factors influence the thickness of the stroke $\lambda_i'(t)$ the actual image-space distance $d'(t)$ between the strokes, and the tone to be achieved. The stepping algorithm devised in the first step guarantees that two adjacent strokes are spread by at most $\overline{d}'$. However, the actual spacing $d'(t)$ can be smaller. To compensate for this variation, the thickness of stroke λ_i' must be scaled by the ratio $d'(t)/\overline{d}' \approx \rho_i(t)/\overline{\rho}_i$. Finally, to take into account the varying tone, we also scale the stroke thickness by the ratio $T(t)/\overline{T}$. In summary, the thickness of $\lambda_i'(t)$ is given by

$$\theta_i(t) = \frac{T(t)}{\overline{T}} \frac{\rho_i(t)}{\overline{\rho}_i} \overline{\theta}$$

Finally, we introduce an additional feature to create more interesting hatching. Although the strokes generated by the method above accurately render the target tone, the thicknesses of all the strokes vary simultaneously. A more appealing effect is achieved when short and long strokes are interspersed, as depicted on the right side of Figure 1. This effect is created by introducing an additional *spreading* factor σ, set by the user. The initial strokes are spread by the distance $\sigma\overline{d}'$ instead of $\overline{d}'$. The extra gaps created are then recursively filled with additional *filler* strokes.

The expression for the thickness $\theta_i(t)$ of a filler stroke γ_i at level ℓ of recursion is slightly more complicated. To derive it, we first note that the image-space distance between two adjacent strokes at level ℓ of recursion is given by

$$d'_\ell(t) = \frac{\sigma \overline{d}}{2^\ell}\frac{\rho_i(t)}{\overline{\rho}_i} = \frac{\sigma\overline{\theta}}{2^\ell \overline{T}}\frac{\rho_i(t)}{\overline{\rho}_i} \qquad (2)$$

With this style of recursive hatching, we would like to achieve the target tone by using the thickest possible strokes, before introducing a filler stroke at level ℓ. Consequently, if $\theta_i(t) > 0$ for some t, then the thickness of the neighboring strokes at recursion level $\ell - 1$ is $\overline{\theta}$. The contribution to the tone from these strokes is $T_{\ell-1} = \overline{\theta}/d'_{\ell-1}$, while stroke γ_i contributes $T_\ell = \theta_i(t)/d'_\ell$. Finally, the overall target tone to achieve is $T(t) = T_{\ell-1} + T_\ell = \overline{\theta}/d'_{\ell-1} + \theta/d_\ell$. Substituting for $d'_{\ell-1}$ and d'_ℓ using equation (2), and noting that $\theta_i(t)$ cannot exceed $\overline{\theta}$, yields

$$\theta_i(t) = \min\left\{\overline{\theta}, \left(\frac{\sigma T(t)}{2^\ell \overline{T}}\frac{\rho_i(t)}{\overline{\rho}_i} - \frac{1}{2}\right)\overline{\theta}\right\}$$

The recursion stops when $\theta_i(t) \leq 0$ everywhere along the stroke. The minimum thickness of a stroke is dictated either by the pixel size, or by a constant set by the user. However, "visually thinner" sizes can still be obtained by using dashed strokes.

The hatching textures of all the figures shown in this paper were generated using this recursive algorithm. Typically, σ ranges between 2 and 8.

3.2 The planar map

As discussed in Section 1.2, a key data structure of the pen-and-ink illustration system for polyhedral models was a planar map of all the visible surfaces and shadow polygons. This planar map was constructed with the help of 2D and 3D BSP trees [22]. Recent results introduced by Naylor and Rogers [15] show how to build 2D BSP trees with Bézier curves. However, it is not clear how this work can be generalized to handle scenes containing parametrically defined curved surfaces. It is also not clear how Chin and Feiner's BSP-tree-based shadow algorithm can be generalized in the presence of curved surfaces. For these reasons, we devised a method for computing the planar map and the shadows that does not rely on BSP trees.

3.2.1 Constructing the planar map

The planar map data structure partitions the image plane into homogeneous regions so that each region corresponds to a single visible object in the scene. In our new algorithm, the planar map is constructed in three main phases.

In the first phase, we tessellate every object in the scene into a polygonal mesh. The resolution of the tessellation is chosen so as to yield a reasonably-accurate approximation to the object. Our implementation uses a fixed resolution set by the user, although a flatness criterion could also be used.

In the second phase, we compute higher-resolution piecewise-linear approximations for all the silhouette curves of the meshed objects. This step is required to obtain smooth and accurate silhouettes without requiring an unduly fine tessellation. Our technique is very similar to the one developed for hidden-curve removal by Elber and Cohen [6], only it operates on a polygonal mesh, rather than on a parametric surface directly. To find the silhouette curves, we first identify the mesh edges that span the silhouette. To do this, we examine the normal vectors at the two endpoints of every edge. If the projections of the normals on the viewing direction are in opposite directions, then the edge spans the silhouette. In this case, the two mesh faces adjoining the edge are subdivided, and the process is repeated. Our implementation performs a fixed number of subdivisions in this manner. Finally, the silhouette curve is further refined, using a root-finding method to evaluate a more precise silhouette point along each remaining mesh edge that spans the silhouette. A piecewise-linear silhouette curve is then constructed by connecting all of the silhouette points in the mesh.

In the third and final phase, we construct the planar map itself. Initially, the planar map consists of a single region corresponding to the entire display area. Each mesh face is then inserted into the planar map in turn. First, the face is projected onto the view plane, and its edges are merged with those of the planar map. Next, we resolve occlusions between the new face and the existing faces in the planar map that are covered by the new face. Our implementation currently assumes non-intersecting objects; thus, for each existing face in the planar map, we merely need to determine whether the existing face or the face being inserted is closer to the viewer. We do this by summing up the distance from the view point to the 3D point corresponding to each edge midpoint. Whichever face yields the smallest sum is considered to be closer to the viewer. If the face being inserted is closer, the planar map region is updated to reflect the new information.

Once all objects have been inserted into the planar map, each resulting region corresponds to a single visible 3D face in the mesh decomposition. In our implementation, we maintain a link from each region to its 3D face. In turn, each 3D mesh maintains a link to its original object. These links are used by the procedural stroke textures to compute a variety of information, as described in Section 3.3.

3.2.2 Robustness issues

A common problem in geometric algorithms, and one to which our planar map construction algorithm is certainly not immune, is that it is not always easy to maintain consistency between the topological and geometric information in the data structure when imprecise computations like floating-point arithmetic are used [10, 19]. To build the planar map robustly, we use a method inspired by the work of Gangnet *et al.* [8]. Notably, we restrict all the line endpoints to

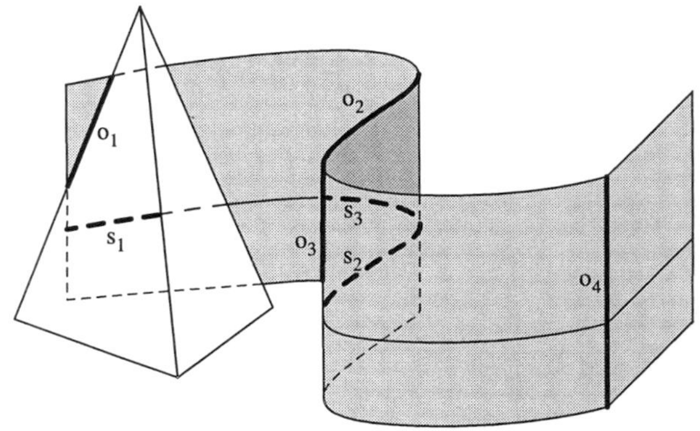

Figure 3 Several cases must be considered when tracing outlines (edges labeled o_1 to o_4), and clipping strokes (edges labeled s_1 to s_3).

Figure 4 Creating a pen-and-ink illustration. The steps involved are not so different from those required to create an attractive photorealistic rendering. From left to right: constant-density hatching; smooth shading with rough strokes, using a single light source; smooth shading with straighter, longer strokes adjusted to depict glass; introducing environment mapping; and, finally, the same image after adjusting the reflection coefficients, shown at full size in Figure 5.

lie on an integer lattice, and we use infinite-precision rational arithmetic to compute all intersections exactly. Because the planar map stores only line segments, the number of bits required for the intermediate computations is bounded. In particular, we use 14-bit integers to represent the lattice points, which allows all intersections to be stored using 32-bit rational integer numbers. This choice limits us to a resolution of about 800 dots per inch over a 10 × 10-inch image-space area. (See Winkenbach [21] for more details.)

3.3 Using the planar map

As in the original polyhedral renderer, the planar map is used for rendering outline edges. In this work, the planar map is additionally used for clipping individual strokes to visible regions. Here we consider how these two processes can be implemented for curved surfaces.

3.3.1 Outlining

Object outlines are constructed from edges of the planar map. With curved surfaces, four types of planar map edges can give rise to an outline edge (see Figure 3):

- Case o_1: an edge that bounds two regions belonging to different objects. The texture for such an outline edge is taken from the object closest to the view point. In the case of two abutting surfaces, this choice is arbitrary.
- Case o_2: an edge that bounds two regions belonging to the same object, but whose corresponding 3D mesh faces have opposite orientations.
- Case o_3: an edge that bounds two regions belonging to the same object and having the same orientation, but at different depths.
- Case o_4: an edge that arises from a C^1 discontinuity on the surface.

An outline path is assembled by appending as many adjacent outline edges as possible. The darkness of the stroke along an outline edge is affected by two factors:

- *The tone value on the surface* — letting an outline edge fade away in regions of highlight reinforces the quality of the shading.
- *The contrast between two adjoining surfaces* — if the tone difference between the two adjacent surfaces is small, a darker outline is required to mark the boundary.

The degree to which these criteria affect the outline is selectable by the user.

3.3.2 Generating stroke paths

Both outline and texture strokes are initially constructed as 3D polyline curves, called *stroke paths*. Each stroke path vertex stores several items of information, including the parametric coordinate, the corresponding 3D position, and the tone evaluated on the surface at that point. The number of vertices in the path is adjusted using a subdivision algorithm, with the goal of accurately capturing not only the shape of the stroke, but also any variation in tone. The latter is particularly important when texture, bump, or environment maps with small features are present.

3.3.3 Clipping stroke paths

Using the planar map, we generate strokes for all surfaces that are at least partially visible. However, these strokes can potentially extend into invisible regions. To clip the strokes in the presence of curved surfaces, we break each stroke at the silhouette points, yielding segments that either face toward or away from the view point. Each of these segments is then projected onto the planar map and clipped. (If the object being rendered is a solid, then back-facing stroke segments can be rejected immediately.) The clipping process starts by locating the planar map region in which the stroke's first vertex lies. The visibility of the stroke is then tested for every planar map edge that the stroke crosses. When the visibility changes, a root-finding method is used to find the intersection between the path and the planar map edge. The intersection point is then added to the path, breaking it into smaller segments.

Several tests are used to determine the visibility of a stroke segment within a face of the planar map. They are, in order of application (see Figure 3):

1. *Same object* — the planar map face must be linked to the same 3D object that the stroke is covering (eliminates s_1).
2. *Same orientation* — the planar map face must be linked to a 3D mesh face that has the same orientation (back-facing or front-facing) with respect to the view point as the 3D surface point along the stroke path (eliminates s_2).
3. *Same depth* — the 3D location of the path vertex must be close to the corresponding 3D location of the 3D mesh face. This last test is required since, with free-form surfaces, several different points on the same surface can project to the same 2D point (eliminates s_3).

If all three tests succeed, the segment is visible and marked as such. Only the visible segments of each stroke are drawn.

Figure 5 Glass bottle. An environment map is used to give the illusion of a reflected surrounding.

Figure 6 Wooden bucket. The bucket is modeled as a single surface of revolution. The planks are created by a prioritized stroke texture.

3.4 Shadows

In the polygonal version of the renderer, polygons were split along shadow boundaries before being inserted into the 2D BSP tree. Hence, the different partitions in the BSP-tree would distinguish between regions that were in and out of shadow. The shadows were then rendered with strokes clipped to the shadow regions. Unfortunately, with curved surfaces, shadow boundaries are much more difficult to generate. Thus, we decided to use a simpler two-pass clipping approach inspired by Williams [20] instead.

Shadow strokes are generated for all the visible surfaces. To clip these strokes, we build an additional *shadow planar map* with respect to the light source, in addition to the *view planar map*. Each shadow stroke is first clipped against the view planar map, just like all other strokes. In a second pass, the remaining visible shadow strokes are clipped against the shadow planar map; this time, however, just the portions of the strokes that are *not* visible from the light source (and therefore in shadow) are preserved and rendered.

Note that the view planar map and the shadow planar map lie in distinct 2D spaces. Therefore, each visible stroke left after the first clipping pass must be re-mapped to the shadow planar map space before the second clipping pass can take place.

4 Results

In this section, we demonstrate the rendering algorithms with several examples. The rendering times for these figures can be found in Table 1.

All of the examples in this paper were created using an iterative design process, not unlike the procedure typically used in creating an attractive photorealistic rendering. First, we generally set up one or more light sources, then adjust the quality of the strokes, then add any texture maps, and finally adjust the various reflection-model parameters until an appealing illustration is achieved. Figure 4 illustrates this process for the glass bottle, shown at full size in Figure 5.

4.1 Texture mapping

Controlled-density hatching allows "fine grain" control over the tone of a pen-and-ink illustration. With this new capability, we can use traditional texture mapping techniques to vary the tone on the surface of an object. For example, Figure 5 uses an environment map to enhance the illusion of the glass material. Figure 6 uses a bump map to perturb the shading on the wooden planks. Figure 7 uses an ordinary texture map to create the geometric pattern on the bowl; it also uses a bump map to emboss the word "MILK" and create a slightly irregular surface on the jug.

4.2 Other texture styles

The basic hatching algorithm described in this paper can be used to generate many other texture styles:

- *Wood.* The wood texture shown in Figure 6 uses a variety of strokes, much like the prioritized stroke texture for wood used in the polygonal version of the renderer. Thin wavy strokes are used to convey wood grain, while longer strokes of varying thickness delineate the gaps between the wood boards.
- *Stippling.* Figures 7 and 8 show the use of stippling to build tone values. To create the stipples, we generate hatching strokes as described previously. However, the resulting stroke paths are not rendered directly; instead, they serve as curves along which the stipples are drawn. The spacing between the stipple marks along the stroke path is randomized. In addition, the stipple marks are also offset from the path by a small random distance.
- *Crosshatching.* Figure 7 also shows the use of crosshatching — using more than one hatching direction — to create dark shadow tones. Crosshatching is also used on the cane in Figure 8 .

Figure 7 Ceramic jug and bowl. A traditional (image-based) texture map is used to model the details on the bowl as well as the stains on the table. A bump map is used to emboss the word "MILK" on the jug, and to give some irregular variation to its surface.

Fig	*Model*	*Planar map*	*Rendering*
5	*Glass bottle*	*74*	*46*
6	*Wooden bucket*	*21*	*44*
7	*Jug and bowl*	*126*	*128*
8	*Hat and cane*	*230*	*120*

Table 1 Rendering times for various illustrations presented in this paper. All times are in seconds, and were measured on a Power Mac 7100/80.

5 Conclusion and future work

In this paper, we have introduced the concept of controlled-density hatching, which allows strokes to be generated so as to simultaneously convey tone, texture, and shape for parametric surfaces. Because controlled-density hatching provides "fine grain" control of the tone of an illustration, we were also able to use traditional texture mapping techniques to extend the range of effects that can be achieved with pen-and-ink rendering. We have also described an algorithm to construct a planar map from parametric surfaces, and we have shown how this planar map can be used for outlining and stroke clipping, in addition to resolving occlusions. Finally, we have described a simple method to render shadows with strokes.

Perhaps the biggest limitation of this work is that it deals only with surfaces possessing a global parameterization. Unfortunately, many commonly used surface representations, such as patch-based surfaces, implicit surfaces, subdivision surfaces, and smoothly-shaded polygonal meshes, do not have this property. One possible solution is to parameterize such surfaces, using for example the methods of Maillot *et al.* [14] or Pedersen [16]. Another alternative is to do away with the parameterization altogether, and to instead generate strokes along directions that are more intrinsic to the geometry of the surface — for example, along directions of principal curvature [2]. This approach may also be suitable for mapping stroke textures on polygonal meshes, since surface curvature can still be approximated in this case [14].

Acknowledgments

We would like to thank Jorge Stolfi for many useful discussions during the early phase of this project.

This work was supported by an Alfred P. Sloan Research Fellowship (BR-3495), an NSF Presidential Faculty Fellow award (CCR-9553199), an ONR Young Investigator award (N00014-95-1-0728), and industrial gifts from Interval, Microsoft, and Xerox.

References

[1] Norman Chin and Steven Feiner. Near real-time shadow generation using BSP trees. *Computer Graphics*, 23(3):99–106, 1989.

[2] Manfredo P. do Carmo. *Differential Geometry of Curves and Surfaces*. Prentice-Hall, Inc., Englewood Cliffs, New Jersey, 1976.

[3] Debra Dooley and Michael F. Cohen. Automatic illustration of 3D geometric models: Lines. *Computer Graphics*, 24(2):77–82, March 1990.

[4] Debra Dooley and Michael F. Cohen. Automatic illustration of 3D geometric models: Surfaces. In *Proceedings of Visualization '90*, pages 307–314, October 1990.

[5] Gershon Elber. Line art rendering via a coverage of isoparametric curves. *IEEE Transaction on Visualization and Computer Graphics*, 1(3):231–239, September 1995.

[6] Gershon Elber and Elaine Cohen. Hidden curve removal for free form surfaces. *Computer Graphics*, 24(4):95–104, August 1990.

[7] H. Fuchs, Z. M. Kedem, and B. F. Naylor. On visible surface generation by a priori tree structures. *Computer Graphics*, 14(3):124–133, July 1980.

[8] Michel Gangnet, Jean-Claude Hervé, Thierry Pudet, and Jean-Manuel Van Thong. Incremental computation of planar maps. *Computer Graphics*, 23(3):345–354, July 1989.

[9] Arthur Leighton Guptill. *Rendering in Pen and Ink*. Watson-Guptill Publications, New York, 1976.

Figure 8 Hat and cane. Both the hat and the cane are modeled with B-spline surfaces. The ribbon is modeled as a separate B-spline surface. Note the curved shadow that the hat projects on its rim, and the use of crosshatching on the curved portion of the cane.

[10] Christoph Hoffman. The problems of accuracy and robustness in geometric computation. *Computer*, 22:31–42, 1989.

[11] John Lansdown and Simon Schofield. Expressive rendering: A review of nonphotorealistic techniques. *IEEE Computer Graphics and Applications*, 15(3):29–37, May 1995.

[12] Wolfgang Leister. Computer generated copper plates. *Computer Graphics Forum*, 13(1):69–77, 1994.

[13] Frank Lohan. *Pen and Ink Techniques*. Contemporary Books, Inc., Chicago, 1978.

[14] Jérôme Maillot, Hussein Yahia, and Anne Verrout. Interactive texture mapping. Proceedings of SIGGRAPH 93 (Anaheim, California, August 1-6, 1993). In *Computer Graphics*, Annual Conference Series, 1993.

[15] Bruce Naylor and Lois Rogers. Constructing partitioning trees from Bézier-curves for efficient intersection and visibility. In *Proceedings of Graphics Interface '95*, pages 44–55, 1995.

[16] Hans Køhling Pedersen. Decorating implicit surfaces. Proceedings of SIGGRAPH 95 (Los Angeles, California, July 6-11, 1995). In *Computer Graphics*, Annual Conference Series, 1995.

[17] Tom Porter and Sue Goodman. *Manual of Graphic Techniques 4*. Charles Scribner's Sons, New York, 1985.

[18] Takafumi Saito and Tokiichiro Takahashi. Comprehensible rendering of 3D shapes. *Computer Graphics*, 24(4):197–206, August 1990.

[19] David H. Salesin. *Epsilon Geometry: Building Robust Algorithms from Imprecise Computations*. PhD thesis, Stanford University, March 1991. Available as Stanford Report number STAN-CS-91-1398.

[20] Lance Williams. Casting curved shadows on curved surfaces. *Computer Graphics*, 12(3):270–274, August 1978.

[21] Georges Winkenbach. *Computer-Generated Pen-and-Ink Illustration*. PhD thesis, University of Washington, May 1996.

[22] Georges Winkenbach and David H. Salesin. Computer-generated pen-and-ink illustration. Proceedings of SIGGRAPH 94 (Orlando, Florida, July 24-29, 1994). In *Computer Graphics*, Annual Conference Series, 1994.

A Deriving the stretching factor

To derive the expression for the stretching factor ρ_i, given in equation (1), we first note that the linear transformation J maps points (u, v) in parameter space to points (x, y) in image space by

$$J \begin{bmatrix} u \\ v \end{bmatrix} = \begin{bmatrix} x \\ y \end{bmatrix} \tag{3}$$

Next, we write the implicit equations for line λ_i and its image $J(\lambda_i)$, using the implicit-form coefficients $\langle a, b, c \rangle$ for λ_i, and $\langle a', b', c' \rangle$ for $J(\lambda_i)$:

$$[a \; b] \begin{bmatrix} u \\ v \end{bmatrix} + c = [a' \; b'] \begin{bmatrix} x \\ y \end{bmatrix} + c' = 0 \tag{4}$$

Combining equations (3) and (4), we readily establish that

$$\begin{aligned} [a' \; b'] &= [a \; b] J^{-1} \\ c' &= c \end{aligned} \tag{5}$$

The distance d between two parallel lines with implicit-form coefficients $\langle a, b, c \rangle$ and $\langle a, b, c + \epsilon \rangle$ is $d = \epsilon / \sqrt{a^2 + b^2}$. The stretching factor ρ_i is given by the inverse ratio of the distance d_i between the lines λ_i and λ_{i+1}, and the distance d_i' between their images $J(\lambda_i)$ and $J(\lambda_{i+1})$:

$$\begin{aligned} \rho_i &= \frac{d_i'}{d_i} = \frac{\epsilon / \sqrt{(a')^2 + (b')^2}}{\epsilon / \sqrt{a^2 + b^2}} \\ &= \sqrt{\frac{(X_u Y_v - X_v Y_u)^2 \, (a^2 + b^2)}{(aY_v - bY_u)^2 + (bX_u - aX_v)^2}} \end{aligned}$$

Painterly Rendering for Animation

Barbara J. Meier
Walt Disney Feature Animation

Abstract

We present a technique for rendering animations in a painterly style. The difficulty in using existing still frame methods for animation is getting the paint to "stick" to surfaces rather than randomly change with each frame, while still retaining a hand-crafted look. We extend the still frame method to animation by solving two major specific problems of previous techniques. First our method eliminates the "shower door" effect in which an animation appears as if it were being viewed through textured glass because brush strokes stick to the viewplane not to the animating surfaces. Second, our technique provides for frame-to-frame coherence in animations so that the resulting frames do not randomly change every frame. To maintain coherence, we model surfaces as 3d particle sets which are rendered as 2d paint brush strokes in screen space much like an artist lays down brush strokes on a canvas. We use geometric and lighting properties of the surfaces to control the appearance of brush strokes. This powerful combination of using 3d particles, surface lighting information, and rendering 2d brush strokes in screen space gives us the painterly style we desire and forces the brush strokes to stick to animating surfaces. By varying lighting and choosing brush stroke parameters we can create many varied painterly styles. We illustrate the method with images and animated sequences and present specific technical and creative suggestions for achieving different looks.

CR Categories and Subject Descriptors: I.3.3 [Computer Graphics]: Picture/Image Generation; I.3.5 [Computer Graphics]: Three-Dimensional Graphics and Realism – Color, Shading, Shadowing, and Texture.

Key Words: painterly rendering, non-photorealistic rendering, particle systems, painting, abstract images.

Author's current affiliation: Hammerhead Productions.
email: bjm@gg.caltech.edu or barb@hammerhead.com

1 Introduction

A painting reduces a subject to its essence. The process of painting is an artist's interpretation of the world, real or imagined, to a two-dimensional canvas. By not depicting every detail, the painter allows the viewer to complete the picture, to share in the interpretative process. Of course the process begins with the painter who, by abstracting a scene, can direct the viewer's eye to the area of interest by simplifying unimportant details. A painter can exaggerate the effect of light to create a wide tonal range that creates richness and drama at the center of interest. By using the largest brush stroke possible to represent small forms and textures, the painter creates a shorthand for conveying details. The character of brush strokes define the character of a surface and how light is reflected from it; surfaces that are well-blended imply smoothness or softness while direct, unblended strokes imply stronger lighting or more pronounced surface texture. Painters use varying edge definition, edges that are distinct in one place and lose themselves in another, to add rhythm to a composition. Letting brush strokes cross edge boundaries can also help unify an entire composition. By varying brush stroke texture, size, and direction, the artist can not only define forms, but also provide rhythm and energy that help direct the viewer's eye. Larger, smoother brush strokes tend to recede in depth while small, textured strokes depict foreground detail. A painter can even use brush strokes to represent light and atmosphere. Whatever the painting style, a certain amount of abstraction, or economy of description, strengthens the composition and provides focus [5, 6, 13].

Computer rendering provides an easy, automated way to render everything in a scene with fine detail. This creates static images that do not invite the viewer into the process. In particular, when creating images for animation, focus and simplification are essential to showing action in a clear way since the temporal nature of the image gives the viewer much less time to let their eyes wander about the scene [16]. Certainly focus and simplicity can be achieved with computer rendering tools by carefully controlling lighting and surface attributes and unnecessary detail can be obscured using hierarchical modeling, but it is still difficult to obtain the level of abstraction that is evident in a good painting. Even the brush strokes of a painting contribute to the abstraction of its subject and add another dimension to which a viewer can respond. One could not imagine looking at a Van Gogh painting without experiencing the energy of his brush strokes. Hand-drawn and hand-painted animations have an energetic quality that is lacking in most computer-rendered animation. Often when computer methods try to mimic the wavering quality of hand-drawn animation, too much randomness creeps in and makes the animation noisy. A human artist drawing each frame is better able to control frame-to-frame coherence, while maintaining a hand-crafted look.

Figure 1: **Frames from a painterly rendered animation.** The painterly renderer is particularly well-suited for abstracting natural textures like the cloudy sky, hay, and plowed ground in this example. Note that the haystack texture does not exhibit the problems of traditional texture-mapping in which the gift-wrapped texture gets dense near silhouette edges. The overlapping brush strokes on the plowed ground imply volume rather than flat, painted texture as the view animates, even though the surface is planar. We use the largest brush strokes to paint the sky, using brush texture and random hue variation to create clouds that do not exist in the color reference picture. The original haystack geometry is simply a cone resting on a cylinder. We represent the hay with a brush stroke shorthand that eliminates the need to model and color every piece of hay.

We want to take advantage of the benefits of a painterly look on computer-rendered animating geometry. Aesthetically, a still frame should have the characteristics of an oil or pastel painting: details should be abstracted by shorthand brush strokes, the roundness of forms should be defined by brush stroke directions, color should break the boundaries of surfaces to create rhythm in the composition, brush stroke size and texture should be varied according to the kind of surface being depicted, and the effects of light should be exaggerated to help provide focus, all as if an artist had painted on a physical canvas. Technically, the rendered images should maintain coherence in animated sequences and should not change in a random way every frame. Images should not have the gift-wrapped look of painted textures that are mapped onto the geometry using traditional methods. Our goal is not to eliminate the need for observational understanding and artistic vision, but rather to provide a tool that automates the drawing of brush strokes, but leaves the artistic decisions about lighting, color, and brush stroke characteristics to the user.

The focus of most rendering research in the last two decades has been on the creation of photorealistic imagery. These methods are quite sophisticated, but tend to create imagery that is mechanical-looking because detail is represented very accurately. Recently there has been a movement toward more creative and expressive imagery in computer graphics but few techniques that provide ways to achieve different looks, especially for animation. Some computer painting tools can mimic successfully the hand-drawn line quality, painterly look, and energy of traditional media, but these tools typically work only for still frames. These tools and related work are discussed in section 2.

Our solution, presented in section 3, is to generate a set of particles that describe a surface, depth-sort the particles in camera space, and render them as 2d brush strokes in screen space using a painter's algorithm [7]. The look of the 2d brush strokes, including color, size, and orientation, is derived from the geometry, surface attributes, and lighting characteristics of the surface. These attributes are designed by the user and either associated directly with the particles or encoded in rendered images of the geometry, called reference pictures. We illustrate our work with images and animations that have been successfully rendered to achieve a painterly look using this algorithm (Figures 1, 5, and 7), and in section 4 we discuss the images. Finally, in section 5, we present aesthetic techniques and technical considerations for creating various image styles.

2 Related Work

Our work combines core ideas from two areas of previous work: 1) painterly rendering of still images from reference pictures and 2) particle rendering. From the first research area, our work was most directly inspired by [4]. Haeberli described a system for creating painterly images from a collection of brush strokes that obtain

```
create particles to represent geometry
for each frame of animation
    create reference pictures using geometry, surface
        attributes, and lighting
    transform particles based on animation parameters
    sort particles by distance from viewpoint
    for each particle, starting with furthest from viewpoint
        transform particle to screen space
        determine brush stroke attributes from
            reference pictures or particles and randomly
            perturb them based on user-selected parameters
        composite brush stroke into paint buffer
    end (for each particle)
end (for each frame)
```

Figure 2: Painterly rendering algorithm.

their attributes, such as position, color, size, and orientation, from synthetically rendered or photographic reference pictures. Several commercial systems, such as [3] and [8], have incorporated the idea of reference pictures, and Saito and Takahashi use a similar concept, the G-buffer, to create simplified illustration-type images [11]. Our system also uses reference pictures to obtain brush stroke attributes.

In Haeberli's system brush stroke positions are randomly distributed, so successive frames of an animation would change randomly. Alternatively, the positions and sizes of brush strokes could remain constant over the animation, but this creates the "shower door" effect, because brush strokes are effectively stuck to the view-plane not to the animating surfaces. The University of Washington illustration systems [12, 17] provide methods for rendering images in a pen-and-ink style, but again, the randomness that is employed to achieve the hand-drawn look would cause successive frames to change randomly.

We solve the temporal randomness problem by using particle rendering methods. If we treat brush strokes as particles that are stuck to surfaces, we eliminate both the "shower door" effect and random temporal noisiness. Reeves first presented an algorithm for rendering particles without using traditional 3D models to represent them, instead drawing them as circles and motion-blurred line segments in screen space [10]. We also render particles in screen space, but use 2d brush stroke shapes instead of circles and line segments.

Rendering 2d shapes in screen space is one of the core concepts of our work. Fleischer et al. [2] described a similar method, except they place *3d* geometric elements on surfaces in *model* space, which are then rendered traditionally as geometric textures such as scales, feathers, and thorns. The appearance of their 3d shapes compared to our 2d brush strokes is quite different.

Finally, Strassmann presented a technique for modeling brush strokes as splines for Sumi-E style painting, a Japanese brush-and-ink technique [14]. This system is designed primarily for still images, but does provide a simple method for animation. The user specifies key frames for each brush stroke that are interpolated over time. Our approach is different in that we provide a rendering technique rather than an interactive system and we are emulating a more impressionistic style of painting with short paint dabs rather than long graceful strokes.

3 Painterly Rendering

In this section, we describe our painterly rendering algorithm as shown in Figure 2.

We begin by creating a particle set that represents geometry such as a surface. The particles are transformed to screen space and sorted in order of their distance from the viewpoint. We use a painter's algorithm to render particles as 2d brush strokes starting with the particles furthest from the viewpoint, and continuing until all particles are exhausted. Each brush stroke renders one particle. The look of the rendered brush strokes, including color, shape, size, texture, and orientation, is specified by a set of reference pictures or by data that is stored with the particles. Reference pictures are rendered pictures of the underlying geometry that use lighting and surface attributes to achieve different looks. The attributes for a particle are looked up in the reference pictures in the same screen space location at which a particle will be rendered finally. Figure 3 illustrates the painterly rendering pipeline.

In the following sections, we begin by discussing particle placement. Next we explain brush stroke attributes, how they are applied, and how the reference pictures that encode the attributes are created. Finally, we present various ways of manipulating the brush stroke attributes to produce painterly images.

3.1 Generating Particles

There are many methods of populating a surface with particles, such as those described in [15] and [18]. We employ a simple method that starts with a parametric surface and a desired number of particles. We tessellate the surface into triangles that approximate the surface. Then, for each triangle, we compute its surface area and randomly distribute particles within it. The number of particles for a triangle is determined by the ratio of its surface area to the surface area of the entire surface. The particle placer may store additional information with the particles such as color, size, and orientation. After the initial particle placement, these additional attributes or the particles' positions may be modified by performing various functions on them. Alternatively, the entire particle set can be generated from a particle system simulation [9].

3.2 Specifying and Applying Brush Attributes

In order to render a brush stroke, we need the following attributes: **image, color, orientation, size,** and **position.**

The brush **image** is a color image with alpha. The image may be solid or it may contain texture as shown in Figure 4. A single image may be used as is or it may be used to cut a shape from a random position in a sheet of texture, providing each brush stroke with unique texture. Although the brush can be a full color image, we typically use monochrome images that are the same in all channels so that the brush itself does not impart color, just texture.

Orientation, color, and **size** are either stored with the individual particles or obtained from reference pictures. If these attributes are associated with the particles, then they are used directly by the renderer; otherwise, the attributes are sampled from reference pictures which encode information about surface geometry and lighting characteristics by screen space location. Reference pictures can be generated in several ways, but typically are rendered images of the particle set or surface. After a particle's position is transformed to screen space, we use the 2d transformed position to look up color, orientation, and size information in the same 2d location in the appropriate reference pictures. Example reference pictures for these attributes are shown in Figure 3.

The reference picture used for **color** information is typically a smooth-shaded rendered image of the surface with appropriate color attributes and lighting. Texture maps are generally not necessary except to describe broad color changes across the surface. The painterly rendering will provide texture and high frequency variations in color.

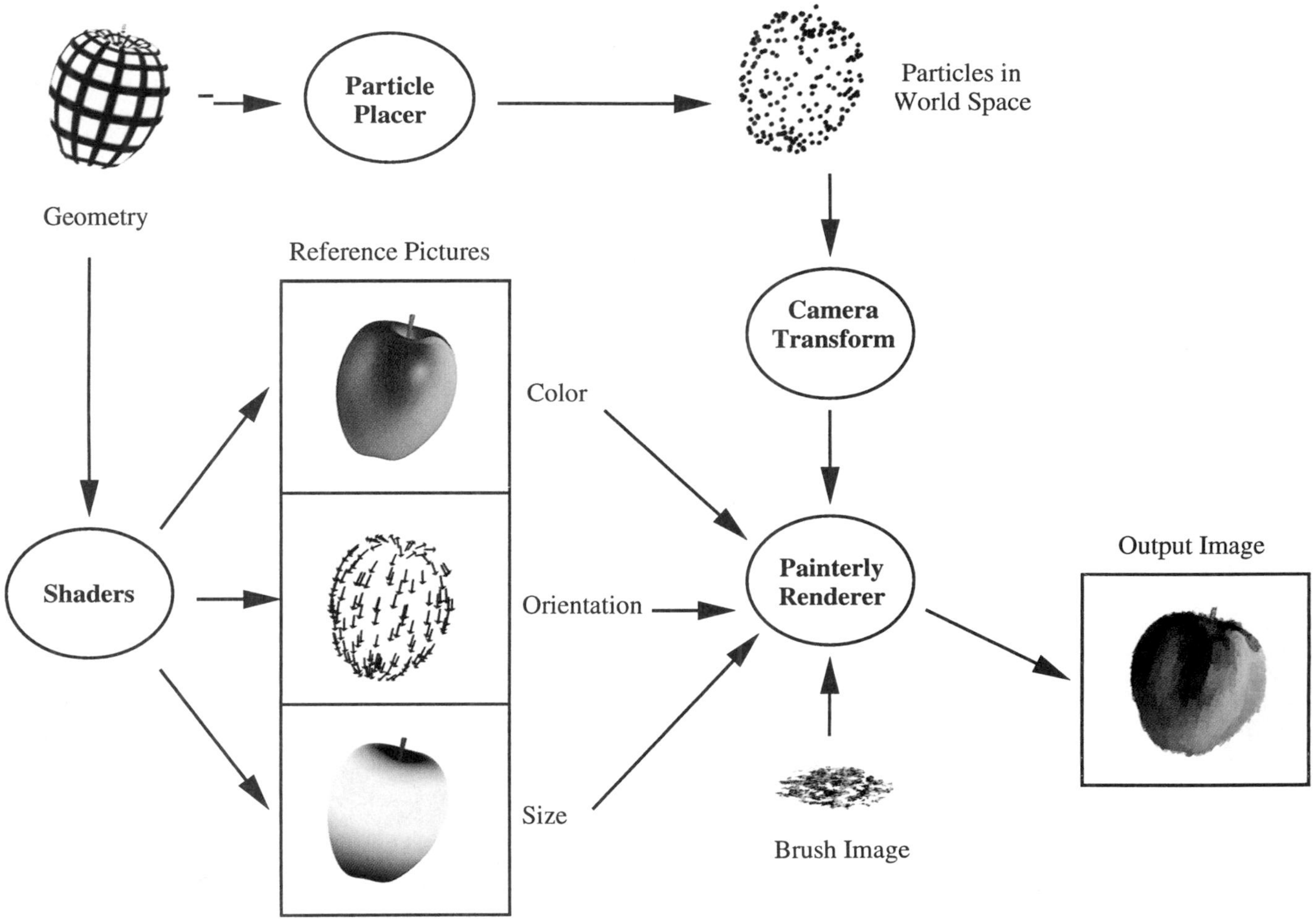

Geometry

Particle Placer

Particles in World Space

Reference Pictures

Camera Transform

Shaders

Color

Orientation

Size

Painterly Renderer

Output Image

Brush Image

Figure 3: An example of the painterly rendering pipeline. The *particle placer* populates a surface with particles. The surface geometry is rendered using various *shaders* to create brush stroke attribute reference pictures. Note that the arrows in the orientation image are representational in this diagram; the orientations are actually encoded in the color channels of the image. The particles, which are transformed into screen space, the reference pictures, and the brush image are input to the *painterly renderer*. The renderer looks up brush stroke attributes in the reference pictures at the screen space location given by each particle's position and renders brush strokes that are composited into the final rendered image.

The reference picture that encodes **orientation** information is an image made with a specialized shader that encodes surface normals in the resulting image. This surface normal shader projects the 3d surface normals into two dimensions along the view vector or another specified vector. Alternatively, we may constrain orientations to line up with the direction of a surface parameter or texture coordinate.

Finally, the brush **size** reference picture is a scalar image that encodes x and y scaling information. We linearly map the range of values in the image to the range of user-specified sizes so that the areas with small values are painted with the smallest brushes and the areas with high values are painted with the largest brushes. Again, we can use lighting, texture maps, or specialized shaders to achieve the desired look.

Brush stroke **position** comes from the particle's position in screen space. Position may be modified by a function such as moving it in the direction of a velocity vector or adding noise.

To apply the attributes, the brush image is either used directly or cut from a sheet of texture, multiplied by the color and alpha, scaled by the size, and rotated to the orientation, each as specified in the corresponding reference picture or by data stored with the particle.

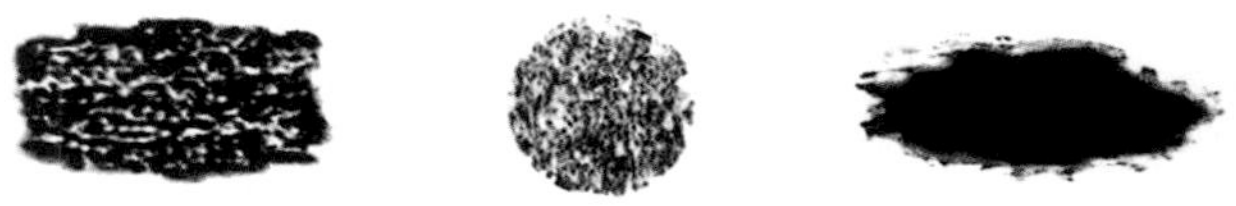

Figure 4: Some brush images used to create the paintings in this paper.

Once attributes are applied, brush strokes are composited into the final rendered image at the position specified by the particle.

3.3 Animating Parameters and Randomness

It is possible to animate brush stroke attributes by animating characteristics of the reference pictures, but it is necessary for the reference

Figure 5: **Four styles of painterly rendered fruit.** By choosing different brush images and painting parameters, we have created four different looks from the same set of reference pictures. The upper left image has the soft, blended quality of a pastel painting. The pointillistic version, in the upper right, remaps the original saturations and values from the color reference picture to a new range. A squiggle brush image and increased hue variation were used to create marker-style strokes in the lower left image. The brush used to create the lower right contained some opaque black that helps to create a woodcut print style.

pictures to change smoothly over time so that the final rendered images are not temporally noisy.

Using randomness is important in achieving a hand-crafted look; therefore, we can randomly perturb the brush stroke attributes based on user-selected parameters. Figure 6 illustrates the lack of richness and texture that results when randomness is not used.

To maintain coherence, a seed is stored with each particle so that the same random perturbations will be used for a particular particle throughout an animation. The user specifies the amount of randomness by choosing a range about the given attribute. For example, we may specify that brush rotations be determined by an orientation reference picture, but to eliminate the mechanical look of the brushes lining up perfectly, we specify that we are willing to have brush orientations fall within the range of -10 to +20 degrees from the orientation given in the reference picture. The resulting slightly random orientations give the strokes a more hand-crafted look.

Figure 6: **Applying randomness to brush stroke attributes.** This image was rendered without color, orientation, or scale variation. Compare it to the images in Figure 1 which were painted with all of those attributes jittered. Note how the painterly texture of the sky and mountains is dependent on random color variations. In the haystacks, orientation and scale changes make them look less mechanical in the jittered version.

4 Results

Figures 1, 5, and 7 are images rendered using our algorithm that show a variety of different painterly looks. In Figure 1, we show frames from a Monet-style haystack animation. The still frames look like oil paintings and the brush strokes animate smoothly throughout the animation. The painterly renderer is particularly well-suited to the impressionist style because it composes a painting with many small brush strokes. In this example, we are not concerned with defining exact boundaries and instead let the overlapping brush strokes create a rhythm that unifies the composition. Large brush strokes tend to extend beyond the silhouette edge, cre-

Figure 7: **Beach ball animation frames.** In this example the beach ball is bouncing, squashing, and stretching from frame to frame. Our technique works as well for animating objects as for the haystack example where only the camera position is animating.

ating a semi-transparent look that is most apparent when surfaces are animated. We believe this adds to the painterly look. Using smaller, denser, or more opaque strokes near the edges would create a more opaque, solid look. We have used the painterly technique of abstraction to depict many of the surfaces in this animation. For example, in the sky we used the brush texture and color variation to abstractly depict sweeping clouds. The hay is captured with a brush stroke texture that shows an appropriate amount of detail. Finally because our technique uses overlapping 2d brush strokes, we have avoided the gift-wrapped look of a smooth-edged, texture-mapped surface.

In Figure 5, we show a plate of fruit rendered in four styles. The reference pictures used to create the images were the same for all four, with the exception of the orientation image for the lower right image. The different looks were achieved by varying the brush image, the amount of jittering, and the brush size. Of course even more looks could be created by changing the reference pictures, but one of the strengths of the painterly renderer is the richness of the user-selectable parameter set. For example the upper right image was brightened and desaturated by mapping colors in the color reference picture to new saturation and value ranges. Conversely, the colors in the lower right image are richer because the brush image contained some opaque black. In this painting, the brush strokes become the dominant subject of the painting.

Finally, in Figure 7, we show three frames from an animated bouncing ball sequence. Our technique works equally well for an animating, deforming object like the squashing and stretching ball in this example, as for an animated camera as shown in the haystacks example. Large brush strokes give the ball an imprecise boundary which gives the ball animation a hand-drawn look quite different from the mechanical look that a traditionally-rendered version would have.

5 Discussion and Techniques

As with any image creation process, it takes some experimentation to get the desired image. In this section, we describe some of the techniques that we've discovered. We begin with our strategies for achieving creative images and then present some technical discussion on how we achieve them.

5.1 Creative Techniques

We have discovered many techniques for rendering aesthetically pleasing images. Chief among these is separately rendering subsets of the particle set and compositing these layers into a finished image. We find that our most successful images are created using traditional painting methods such as creating a rough value underpainting with large brush strokes, adding layers of color to define the form, and then adding small brush strokes where we want more detail. Our implementation provides a skip operation that allows us to render every *n*th particle. We typically render the surface in two or three layers using image processing techniques to shrink the silhouette edge toward the center of the object. The outside layers are painted sparsely, while the inside layers are painted thickly. We also use image processing techniques to isolate highlight and shadow areas to be rendered separately. Building up layers of semi-transparent textured brush strokes, perhaps even rendering the same particle multiple times with different brush stroke characteristics, is important in achieving the painterly look. In the haystacks example, the haystacks consist of four layers: a rough dark blue underpainting, an overall orange layer, a yellow detail layer, and a sparse white highlight layer. These layers and how they contribute to the final image are shown in Figure 8.

We also usually render the objects in a scene as separate layers. In the haystack example, we painted the sky, mountains, field, each haystack, and each haystack shadow as a separate layer. This allowed us to use very large brush strokes on the sky and not worry about them creeping too far into the mountains. By rendering these layers separately, we were better able to use the painting parameters most appropriate for each layer. The fruit images in Figure 5 were rendered in three layers: the wall, the table, and the plate of fruit. In this case, because the brush stroke characteristics of each fruit were similar, we wanted the brushes strokes to interact as much as possible to enhance the painterly look.

We typically use only one light source to maintain focus in the composition. We use exaggerated hue as well as value variations to distinguish light and shadow areas. For example, the sunset light on the haystacks is emphasized through exaggerated use of orange and blue. Shadows may be rendered by compositing a shadow element onto the color reference picture and rendering the surface and the shadow at the same time, or shadows may be painted as a separate layer and composited, giving the user more creative control.

We use many traditional painting techniques such as using background color in shadow areas to help them recede and juxtaposing complementary colors, such as the orange and blue of the haystacks, to create a shimmering light effect. We repeat brush stroke color, size, and texture in different areas of the scene, as shown in the fruit example, to marry the various elements into a unified composition. Users of the painterly renderer are encouraged to examine the numerous existing texts on traditional painting techniques for more possibilities.

5.2 Technical Considerations

If reference pictures are used, it is often helpful to "grow" the reference image outward using image processing techniques, so that when we look up particular screen locations we don't fall off the edge of the surface onto anti-aliased or unrendered parts of the image. This is applicable only if we are rendering layers separately and then compositing them afterwards. To ensure that individual

Figure 8: Compositing a haystack from several layers. Each layer of the haystack is shown by itself on the left while its contribution to the composited image is shown on the right. We used image processing techniques on the color reference picture to isolate the shadow and highlight areas to be painted separately. Following traditional painting techniques, we created a dark blue underpainting of the shadow areas as shown in the top row. The next layer provides most of the color and texture of the haystack, but allows some of the blue underpainting to show through. The bottom two rows show two separate detailed highlight layers and a final shadow layer that helps integrate the haystack with the field. For each layer, we changed the brush size and the amount of color variation.

brush strokes do not jitter in size and orientation slightly with every frame, it is also useful to blur the orientation and size images slightly. Perfect particle placement and sub-pixel sampling would eliminate the need for these steps, but we have found that these techniques work well in practice.

The simple surface normal shader that we described previously provides surface normal information based on a particular orientation of the surface after it has been through a camera transformation. But as a surface animates, so does its orientation with respect to the camera. This gives a particular look, but we prefer to have brush strokes oriented with respect to the surface and not change as the surface animates. To achieve this, we have specified our desired orientations with respect to the (u, v) surface parameters in texture maps. A special shader looks up values in the maps and then applies the camera transformation to them to obtain the screen space orientation that is output to the reference picture.

Brush stroke attributes may be stored with the particles or encoded in reference pictures. An advantage to storing attributes with the particles is that we avoid aliasing errors looking up values in reference pictures. An advantage to using reference pictures is that they are usually quickly rendered and thus easily changed and can encode more complex lighting information. Storing attributes with particles is better for those that are unlikely to change because rerunning the particle placement or simulation may be costly. In practice, a mixture of the two methods works well.

At first glance, one might suggest we not render back-facing particles, but this is very important in animation since particles will pop on and off as they become visible and invisible if we cull the back-facing ones. If we always render them, however, they will be revealed gradually as they become visible. Front-Facing brush strokes must be dense enough to obscure back-facing particles, unless a translucent effect is desired. In practice, we find that we do not always want to render a completely opaque object if we are building up textured layers of paint, but we also do not want to see through to the back-facing brush strokes if they are animating. In this case, we do cull back-facing particles, letting them fade in as they get close to front-facing to eliminate the popping effect as particles come into view. This was necessary in the haystack example so that as the view animates, we do not see the back side of each sparse layer through the front.

One should also note that because particles are sorted by distance from the viewpoint at each frame, there will be some popping of brush strokes in front or behind one another as particles animate, but with some attention to brush stroke size and translucency, this effect is not visually problematic and can add to the painterly effect.

6 Future Directions

Although our use of the renderer thus far has been to create images that are entirely painted, we can imagine incorporating this look with traditional rendering methods. For example, when artists depict foliage, they don't paint every leaf. Instead, they use brush strokes to abstractly represent the leaves. Certainly particle rendering methods have been used for this purpose before [10], but we believe our technique can eliminate complex modeling issues such as generating realistic tree models made of particles, and that the level of control we provide for achieving different looks will prove to be a more powerful but easier-to-use tool. We foresee using this method to render surfaces that are difficult to model and render using traditional geometry and texture maps. This class of objects, which includes many of those found in nature, must be abstracted when rendered because of their high complexity.

Our renderer does not handle changing object sizes in an automated way. We can address this issue with staging or by animating the brush size reference picture; however, it would be helpful if the renderer could automate brush stroke size based on the screen surface covered, and then change the size smoothly as the object changes size using multi-resolution techniques such as those used by [1].

We would like to use a better particle placement method that covers both the geometric surface and screen space more evenly. While we can address this situation with the layer rendering technique described above, this is not always satisfactory and also requires active intervention by the user. Metric tensor techniques [18] could be used to specify particle density for surfaces that do not radically change their orientation with respect to the viewpoint within an animation, but other multi-resolution methods might be required for those surfaces that do change orientation.

Finally, although we are unlimited in brush stroke shape, we find a rectangular or oval shape works best to show changes in orientation, but these shapes stick out along the edges of curved surfaces. We would like to implement longer, deformable brushes than can follow curves on a surface.

7 Conclusions

We have presented a new technique for rendering animations in a painterly style. Our work has brought together two previous rendering methods: using reference pictures to define 2d brush stroke attributes and using particles to define the locations where brush strokes will be rendered. Our algorithm solves the two major problems of rendering animations with previous painterly techniques. First, images created by our renderer are coherent over time and do not exhibit random frame-by-frame changes. Second, brush strokes stick to animating surfaces, not to the viewplane, thus eliminating the "shower door" effect. We have illustrated our algorithm with images that have painterly qualities such as exaggerated use of light, broken silhouette edges that create rhythm, brush stroke textures and sizes that describe surface qualities, and abstracting the subject to strengthen and unify the composition.

8 Acknowledgments

Many thanks to Ken Hahn, Scott Johnston, Jason Herschaft, and Craig Thayer for turning the painterly renderer prototype into a production program, contributing many new ideas and features along the way. Ken Hahn also wrote the particle placer and went beyond the call of duty to make many last minute bug fixes. Thanks to Dave Mullins and Andrea Losch for modeling and rendering support, Craig Thayer and Scott Johnston for valuable comments on early drafts of the paper, and Nancy Smith for video production support. We are grateful to Al Barr and Scott Fraser of Caltech and to Hammerhead Productions for providing production facilities. Finally, many thanks to David Laidlaw for technical discussions about the painterly renderer, extensive paper reviews, diagrams, many hours of paper production support, and help coping with my pregnancy madness.

References

[1] Deborah F. Berman, Jason T. Bartell, and David H. Salesin. Multiresolution painting and compositing. In *Proceedings of SIGGRAPH '94 (Orlando, Florida, July 24–29, 1994)*, Computer Graphics Proceedings, Annual Conference Series, pages 85–90. ACM SIGGRAPH, ACM Press, July 1994.

[2] Kurt W. Fleischer, David H. Laidlaw, Bena L. Currin, and Alan H. Barr. Cellular texture generation. In *SIGGRAPH 95 Conference Proceedings*, Annual Conference Series, pages 239–248. ACM SIGGRAPH, Addison Wesley, August 1995.

[3] Fractal Design Corporation. *Fractal Design Sketcher*. Aptos, California, 1993.

[4] Paul E. Haeberli. Paint by numbers: Abstract image representations. In *Computer Graphics (SIGGRAPH '90 Proceedings)*, volume 24, pages 207–214, August 1990.

[5] Carole Katchen. *Creative Painting with Pastel*. North Light Books, 1990.

[6] Gregg Kreutz. *Problem Solving for Oil Painters*. Watson-Guptill Publications, 1986.

[7] Martin E. Newell, R. G. Newell, and T. L. Sancha. A solution to the hidden surface problem. In *Proc. ACM Nat. Mtg.* 1972.

[8] Parallax Software Limited. *Matador Paint System*. London, 1995.

[9] W. T. Reeves. Particle systems – a technique for modeling a class of fuzzy objects. *ACM Trans. Graphics*, 2:91–108, April 1983.

[10] William T. Reeves and Ricki Blau. Approximate and probabilistic algorithms for shading and rendering structured particle systems. In *Computer Graphics (SIGGRAPH '85 Proceedings)*, volume 19, pages 313–322, July 1985.

[11] Takafumi Saito and Tokiichiro Takahashi. Comprehensible rendering of 3-D shapes. In *Computer Graphics (SIGGRAPH '90 Proceedings)*, volume 24, pages 197–206, August 1990.

[12] Michael P. Salisbury, Sean E. Anderson, Ronen Barzel, and David H. Salesin. Interactive pen–and–ink illustration. In *Proceedings of SIGGRAPH '94 (Orlando, Florida, July 24–29, 1994)*, Computer Graphics Proceedings, Annual Conference Series, pages 101–108. ACM SIGGRAPH, ACM Press, July 1994.

[13] S. Allyn Schaeffer. *The Big Book of Painting Nature in Oil*. Watson-Guptill Publications, 1991.

[14] Steve Strassmann. Hairy brushes. In *Computer Graphics (SIGGRAPH '86 Proceedings)*, volume 20, pages 225–232, August 1986.

[15] Richard Szeliski and David Tonnesen. Surface modeling with oriented particle systems. In *Computer Graphics (SIGGRAPH '92 Proceedings)*, volume 26, pages 185–194, July 1992.

[16] Frank Thomas and Ollie Johnston. *Disney Animation–The Illusion of Life*. Abbeville Press, 1981.

[17] Georges Winkenbach and David H. Salesin. Computer–generated pen–and–ink illustration. In *Proceedings of SIGGRAPH '94 (Orlando, Florida, July 24–29, 1994)*, Computer Graphics Proceedings, Annual Conference Series, pages 91–100. ACM SIGGRAPH, ACM Press, July 1994.

[18] Andrew P. Witkin and Paul S. Heckbert. Using particles to sample and control implicit surfaces. In *Proceedings of SIGGRAPH '94 (Orlando, Florida, July 24–29, 1994)*, Computer Graphics Proceedings, Annual Conference Series, pages 269–278. ACM SIGGRAPH, ACM Press, July 1994.

The Future of Virtual Reality: Head Mounted Displays Versus Spatially Immersive Displays

Organizer: Ed Lantz, Spitz, Inc.
Panelists:
Steve Bryson, MRJ/NASA Ames Research Center
David Zeltzer, Sensory Communication Group, MIT Research Lab of Electronics
Mark T. Bolas, Fakespace
Bertrand de La Chapelle, VIRTOOLS
David Bennett, Alternate Realities Corporation

Introduction

Since its inception, the field of virtual reality (VR) has revolved around the head-mounted display (HMD) as the essential visual display device. VR futurists depicted VR as a personal experience wherein the user interacts with a virtual environment (VE) in a manner synonymous with reality: looking, pointing, walking, physics, etc. Early on, some even declared the classic HMD with data glove to be the only true VR. However, our concept of VR continues to broaden.

An emerging alternative to the HMD is the (walk-in) spatially immersive display (SID). These displays physically surround the viewer with a panorama of imagery, typically produced by video projection. The first application of a SID to VR systems is the CAVE, developed at the University of Illinois at Chicago [Cruz-Neira 93]. More advanced SIDs are now in development utilizing domed video projection technology, which could eventually replace the rectilinear CAVE configuration [Bennett 95, McCutchen 91]. Domed SIDs have been used for many years in military flight simulators [Reno 89]. SIDs offer advantages over HMDs, including group viewing and interaction, wide field of view, high resolution, no cumbersome headgear, and low user fatigue. Also, angular viewing is accomplished without head rotation tracking and its associated response time requirements. Stereoscopic displays are also possible using eye-sequential glasses.

A number of technical challenges remain in the development of both HMDs and SIDs. Currently, VR researchers are consumed with refining the HMD. Advances are being made in wide field-of-view, high resolution HMD technology. Very little research is currently underway on SID implementations. This panel compares the ultimate utility of HMDs versus SIDs in emerging VR applications, such as entertainment, education, computer-aided design, simulators, scientific visualization, 3D animation production, biomedicine, and other potential markets. Important issues include cost, size, user mobility, single and multi-user interactivity, stereoscopic viewing, applicability to augmented reality, special hardware/software requirements, physiological concerns, visual quality, and sense of presence.

Steve Bryson
Let the Task Determine the Display

As the field of VR matures, there has appeared an almost bewildering variety of display technologies that support the VR effect. While there are common measures of display quality, such as resolution, field of view, pixel spacing and so forth, there are other considerations that are very difficult to compare from display to display. These other considerations include comfort, mobility, privacy, opacity, and immersiveness. Rather than try to find the unique "best" display in this very high-dimensional space, I feel that one should analyze the task for which the display is being used. Some tasks, such as an architectural walkthrough, require medium resolution wide field immersive displays with a high degree of mobility. Other tasks, such as information or CAD visualization, may require a collaborative, less immersive high-resolution display that several people can see at once. I will propose a task analysis framework which aids in the selection of a display for a particular task.

David Zeltzer
Specifying a Visual Display System

The visual display system is one element of the human/machine interface to any computer system, and the requirements of the display subsystems – visual, auditory and haptic – are strongly dependent on the application for which they are intended.

So-called "immersive" displays are not always the best strategy. For example, we have shown in our lab that well-designed 2D presentations consistently lead to better performance than stereoscopic displays of 3D scenes for certain air traffic control tasks [Jasek 95]. But if "immersion" is important for a particular application, careful task analysis and requirements engineering can help system designers to formulate specifications for the display systems, as well as to understand the engineering tradeoffs and human factors issues involved.

At MIT we have developed a number of VE systems and applications since the late 1980s. Each of these systems has had differing display requirements. Multimodal displays and "immersive" presentations were often called for; but for some VE applications a workstation CRT was sufficient.

We have implemented "immersive" presentations using different techniques, including

- a head-coupled, stereoscopic HDTV system;
- various HMDs; as well as the walk-in
- CAVE system.

In this presentation, I will briefly describe several of these applications and the display systems that were used, and I will discuss the methodology we employ for specifying a display for a given application.

Mark T. Bolas
Alternative Displays

While the head-mounted display serves as a visual icon of VR, alternative immersive technologies have taken root and grown in industries utilizing 3D computer graphics. Having spearheaded alternative immersive peripherals for more than seven years, I will focus my presentation on the lessons learned and the viewpoints formed by working with hundreds of different users and applications. The presentation will concentrate on the following three areas.

The first is to question what constitutes an immersive display to begin with. Is it a strong feeling of immersion? Is it a First Person Point of View? What sparked the original interest in HMDs, and why are we so eager to abandon it? Is this panel simply full of lazy panelists who are shying away from the hard problems of cutting edge immersive displays to move toward the relative utility and security found in projection based and other alternative displays?

The second area concerns mature media and technologies to help make predictions for the media and technologies we are discussing here. Will HMDs follow the same price drop over time as flat panel displays? If the HMD is similar to a pair of audio headphones, are projection systems analogous to audio speakers? How does content development compare?

Finally, a look toward applications and examples is in order. Starting from a clean slate and armed with all the technology SIGGRAPH has to offer, what is the best solution for a small set of example applications? Is there a best flavor of VR? Is there a best flavor of Ice Cream? What does it take to make both the display technology and the content work together to form a seamless immersive experience?

Bertrand de La Chapelle
Considering the Manufacturing and Engineering End-User

VIRTOOLS is pioneering the implementation of Shared Virtual Workspaces for concurrent engineering, collaborative design, and scene layout for the aerospace, automotive, and nuclear power industries. Based on the experience gathered at VIRTOOLS with manufacturing and engineering clients and on extensive contacts with other potential end-users, we strongly believe in the potential of SIDs for such professional applications. Two aspects will be put forward.

1) HMDs are globally ill-adapted for day-to-day professional applications. A key founding component of the VR concept, HMDs have surely become less cumbersome, less expensive and have increased performance. But:

- even if high resolutions and wide field of view (required for professional applications) ultimately appear, price/performance ratio is mostly driven by games; therefore, price will decrease faster than performance improves.
- weight, eye, and neck fatigue prevent use over several hours; this is not likely to change even with greatly improved performances.
- psychological factors are an important limitation: engineers and decision-makers are very reluctant to use such apparatus, considered game gear.
- HMDs isolate users from one another; collaborative work in the same room requires the creation of sophisticated clones, and people can bump into one another.

The main obstacle for HMDs will not be performance, but seclusion. Therefore, they will prosper in applications where people work in isolation for short periods of time and really need to look around them as if they were in a static real environment. Apart from games, the best applications include training and some maintenance assessment. In most other individual uses, devices like the BOOM™ or the Push™ from Fakespace seem more appropriate, offering high resolution, wide field of view, and less fatigue.

2) SIDs offer the best potential for collaborative applications. They still suffer major drawbacks: underdeveloped, very expensive, requiring much more space and hardware (three channels for the CAVE), they are not yet fully industrialized or standardized. But:

- they provide a better sense of presence through a very large field of view (up to 180x for the ARC Dome) and a high resolution (2000 x 2000 and up).
- they allow prolonged work through reduced fatigue, including in stereoscopy.
- they allow the presence of multiple users in the same environment, who can communicate naturally together.
- large models can be displayed (cars, plane segments, plant sections) at once, whereas you need to turn your head around with an HMD.
- they are very well adapted for applications in which the user interacts strongly with the environment through Virtual Tools (3D widgets) and a 3D interface.

As VR applications evolve from simple walkthroughs towards virtual working environments, SIDs might become the new paradigm for professional use. Key developments in graphics hardware (new generation SGIs) and projection devices (mono-lens high power light valve or future micromirrors) will create a range of standard systems, from individual large screen displays to full-fledged multi-participant domed environments. Present prices will go down, thanks to entertainment applications (including immersive prerecorded rides), and such environments are the key to implementation of full concurrent engineering in manufacturing.

David Bennett
Dome and Shared Spaces

We are on the threshold of new methodologies in visualizing and interacting with information. The emphasis here is on why spatial immersion and, in particular, dome projection provides a better solution than other alternatives for groups of people. The primary focus is on teams of people experiencing 3D information space, and experiencing both immersion and interaction as groups rather than as individuals. The focus is also changing from what is acceptable to a "techie" to what is required by mainstream users. Business people, scientists, moms and dads – all need to feel that VE's are not complex and unusable, but rather as simple to interact with as television.

There is a unique characteristic of domes that makes it ideal for groups, particularly for training and education. Within reasonable constraints, the viewpoint or perspective is the same for everyone. This means that an instructor can be assured that the student is seeing exactly what the instructor sees. Equally important is the sense of presence created with a 180-degree field of view onto a hemisphere, and in a way that is both comfortable and consistent with a real-world experience. The downside of domes is the computational expense of doing distortion correction, limited individual tracking ability, and the space requirements for setting up a dome at your facility. There is as yet no perceived cybersickness; however, motion sickness is still present, just as in any other environment, including the real world.

As we move these technologies forward into everyday life, it is important to focus on simplicity, affordability, portability, and comfort. We have found that acceptance of domes for VR is greater than for HMD's, since it does not require wearing any restrictive devices and "feels" more like what is expected of VR.

References

[Bennett 95] David Bennett, "Providing Solutions Using Virtual Reality," Press Release, Alternate Realities Corp., Research Triangle Park, NC, e-mail `davidb@arc.tda.com`, `http://www.arc.com/ARC.html`

[Cruz-Neira 93] Carolina Cruz-Neira, Daniel J. Sandin, and Thomas A. DeFanti, "Surround-Screen Projection-Based Virtual Reality: The Design and Implementation of the CAVE," Computer Graphics, Annual Conference Proceedings Series, 1993.

[Jasek 95] Jasek, M., N. Pioch and D. Zeltzer, "Effects of Enhanced Visual Displays on Collision Prediction for Air Traffic Control," Proc. 6th IFAC/IFIP/IFORS/IEA Symposium on Analysis, Design and Evaluation of Man-Machine Systems, Cambridge MA. (1995).

[McCutchen 91] David McCutchen, Method and Apparatus for Dodecahedral Imaging System, U.S. Patent #5,023,725, June 11, 1991.

[Reno 89] Capt. Brian A. Reno, "Full Field of View Dome Display System," Proceedings of AIAA/FSTC, pp. 390-394, 1989.

Art on the Web, the Web as Art

Organizer:
Annette Weintraub, The City College of New York
Panelists:
Remo Campopiano, ArtNetWeb
Nan Goggin, University of Illinois at Urbana-Champaign
John F. Simon, Jr., Independent artist
Sharleen Smith, USA Network

Web-specific art work and art sites on the Web are fostering a seamless environment in which the boundary between the artwork itself and the "space" it inhabits is vanishing. The Web offers the promise of a direct and intimate connection between artist and audience, and requires a shift in aesthetics and approaches to storytelling, narrative and interaction. This panel explores this interface of art and art space and the dynamic qualities of art created for the Web.

Roundtable Overview

For many artists, the World Wide Web is no longer merely a means for viewing or distributing art, but has become an art medium in itself with its own distinct characteristics. The shift from making art work available on the Web to utilizing the Web as a dynamic artform has been dramatic, as the "gallery" metaphor is replaced by a variety of approaches that exploit the inherent characteristics of Web-based communication.

The Web has become one of the fastest-growing venues for new art, and an active laboratory for the developmental of graphics and media integration. The evolving environment of the Web provides a unique challenge to artists to explore conjunctions of text and image, narrative and storytelling, and strategies for participation and interaction in real-time – all with direct audience input. The speed of development, the constant changes in the development environment, and the interaction among fine art and commercial site developers and their audience are also important factors in this synergy.

This roundtable will examine some of the kinds of art being developed for the Web. The speakers will offer their perspectives on the components of successful Web-based artwork. Each will present the work of one or more artists making Web-based work, and will focus on sites that integrate Web art works into an aggregate art space. The roundtable will also address the impact of the growing integration of moving images, virtual reality, 3D modeling, interactivity and sound in real time on the Web. Panelists will explore aesthetics, content, interface, and interaction in current work and will examine their implications for future development of art on the Web.

This roundtable includes artists doing Web-based art, developers of art Web sites, and the designer of a commercial Web site with a strong art component. A particular focus of the roundtable is to explore the exchange of ideas and energy between commercial and fine arts sites, and the integration of works of art created for the Web within a particular Web site. The panel of will address these core issues from a variety of distinct perspectives, and will provide an overview of some of the most interesting art work and art sites on the Web. The roundtable will address the question of what differentiates Web-based artwork from other interactive art, consider the interaction of aesthetics and technology, and describe the potential evolution of this form.

Remo Campopiano will present his ideas about the Web as live organism and speak about the development of ArtNetWeb.

Before I found myself tumbling head over heels down the rabbit hole of cyberspace, I was creating installation art. More specifically, I created environments for live animals to act out metaphor for human phenomena. ArtNetWeb grew out of an art project called Virtual Real Estate. Simply put, the idea was to create a digital environment for artists to explore this new medium.

It quickly became evident that we were part of a much bigger phenomenon. "Artnets" were popping up all over the world. When you look at this phenomenon from a global/naturalist perspective; it felt like the living earth was developing a nervous system through telecommunications. Add to this revolutionary breakthroughs in Complexity Theory (Chaos), and you have a unique and provocative view of cyberspace. From this perspective, the telecommunications revolution is not just a new tool, but a living force that seeks to maximize its potential by existing on the edge of chaos...the place of pure creativity.

ArtNetWeb is made up of a group of artists, all exploring the same issues, who are trying to determine what constitutes a Web-based artform, and what the role of the artist is in the telecommunications revolution. As a member of this panel, I will introduce my own ideas on the Web as a dynamic art environment, as well as present work by the group of artists that make up ArtNetWeb.

Nan Goggin will represent the ad319 site, a collaborative art research group based at the University of Illinois. ad319's projects include a spectrum of activity related to digital tools and their impact on making, viewing, and distributing art. These concerns led to the development of one of the first "curated" WorldWideWeb electronic art galleries, the "@art gallery".

In creating the @art gallery we had several goals: 1) creating a moderated virtual gallery space on the Internet; 2) focusing on work created specifically for the medium; and 3) as an experiment to evaluate whether experiencing art on the Internet is emotionally and intellectually fulfilling. In September 1994, when the @art gallery went on-line, web-based art work was very early in gestation. Today, it is just learning to crawl. Partially, we are simply limited by bandwidth; video, sound, and even picture files can still be unwieldy. But more importantly, artists are still becoming acquainted with the medium. What are the inherent and most conceptually profound characteristics of this medium? Is it appropriate to look at models from print media for form, such as book or magazine; or does this medium require completely new forms?

One thing we have learned is that there are no absolutes. While there are forms yet to be created as the tools continue to evolve at an incredible pace, there is also value in emphasizing distribution as a key characteristic of the medium. Several of our exhibitions have acted as virtual exhibition catalogs for their physical counterparts. To address the unanticipated dilemma of so few artists equipped with the html programming skills, an extended goal is to develop a residency program for artists. The University of Illinois at Urbana-Champaign is a fertile environment for web-based development, and there is frequent interdisciplinary activity between the arts and sciences.

If we begin to think of art on the net as an experience and not an object, questions about copyright and ownership can parallel other media. Just as we pay for specific cable channels on TV or subscribe to magazines, there will be similar mechanisms in place on the net in the not too distant future (See the January 1996 issue of Popular Mechanics magazine for a review of the state of "digital dollars"). For me personally, the jury is still out on the experience of art on the net. I have seen very little that I find emotionally and intellectually compelling, but I look to the future with great anticipation.

John F. Simon Jr. will present the work of artists using the Web as a mechanism for real-time participation and speak about the design of adaweb.

Mechanisms for creating art online are continually invented, exploited, and then quickly reinvented. How can Web-based creative projects be understood in the context of art? For example, what distinguishes a Web-based gallery from a gallery stored on CD-ROM? Categorizing the underlying mechanisms of Web-based art helps to understand the work's unique presence.

Art projects can use the Web for more than delivering hyperlinked media, because the Web is structured as millions of "real-time" interconnections. The feedback loop between client and server may be exploited through mechanisms such as creating original content through submission of information, initiating and documenting ongoing dialog both on and off the Web, and creating images and new links based on navigational decisions.

Three projects in particular at adaweb (`http://adaweb.com`) have explored this kind of participatory work. The most popular section of Jenny Holzer's project, Please Change Beliefs, was based on her Truisms work from the 1980s. The "Change" section was a Web-based adaptation of a project that involved photographing truism posters on city walls as they accumulated graffiti. One such photograph is used to open the Web project. Turning to the Web as a new kind of public thoroughfare, the project allows visitors to choose and then modify or rewrite a truism. The altered version of the truism is presented in the style of the original truism poster (alphabetized, all caps) on a page with other people's modified truisms. Several thousand modified truisms were collected within the first few months of the project.

Ben Kinmont's art is based on sharing common tasks and exchanging items with individuals. He often initiates exchange with these people in the street or the space where his work is installed. We Both Belong, extends his work by considering the Web as a kind of public space. Visitors to the site are invited to write to Ben, via the Web, stating a desire to participate in his art project. Ben asks the participants to photograph themselves washing dishes and to mail him the photograph. As a record of the interaction, the letters, the photograph, and other items created in the course of making the project are shown together as an archive both inside and outside the Web. This project highlights an overlap of online and offline spaces by extending Ben's previous artwork into the Web and drawing connections made with people through the Web into Ben's space.

John F. Simon, Jr. worked with Web-based interaction as an experiment in Web viewing in his Alter Stats project. Described as a self-modifying Web self-visualization, the project uses the statistics of the visits (hits) to the project to create images for visualizing those statistics. Each visit to the project further modifies the database of hits to the page and therefore modifies the images created. No visit is identical to any other visit and each visit effects future images. This accumulation of statistics happens at every site, leaving traces of activity. Alter Stats is situated to use the activity of viewing pages as the input for creating images.

Sharleen Smith will comment on the interchange of influence and ideas among commercial and fine-arts sites from her perspective as the art director and developer of "The Dominion" on the Sci-Fi Channel.

Although purists and academicians have decried the commercialization of the Internet, this "gentrification" by corporate America has, in fact, served both to inspire mass culture and to educate artists in the pursuit of their own vision.

Current trends suggest a need for collaboration between the artist and this growing commercial presence. With source code readily accessible to the curious and brave everywhere, it is the commercial sites which push the envelope every day. Why? Because this new medium demands creative thinking and problem solving. Because our metaphors are shifting, and our interfaces must to keep up with them. Communication is evolving... and as business understands all too well, evolution is about the survival of the fittest.

For now, corporate America is in a unique leadership position. Given the rising complexity and cost associated with development of compelling Web sites, it is perhaps unsurprising that commercial sites have become the essential point of reference for the cutting-edge and vanguard of the World Wide Web.

Bracque once described his relationship with Picasso as that of two mountain climbers. One supporting the other in turn to advance to new heights and vistas. It is my belief that only through such synergy of the commercial and artistic can the Web truly evolve.

URLs

@art gallery:
`http://gertrude.art.uiuc.edu/@art/gallery.html`

Electronic Culture and the Training of the 21st Century Artist:
`http://gertrude.art.uiuc.edu/ad319/paper1.html`

adaweb:
`http://adaweb.com`

artnetweb:
`http://artnetweb.com`

The Brown Moo Bird:
`http://moobird.com`

Blast Conversional Archive:
`http://artnetweb.com/projects/blast/home.html`

The Electronic Chronicles:
`http://artnetweb.com/projects/ahneed/first.html`

G.H. Hovagimyan Home Page:
`http://artnetweb.com/gh`

Iola:
`http://artnetweb.com/iola/home.html`

Realms:
`http://artnetweb.com/projects/realms/notes.html`

Betalab:
`http://www.jodi.org/betalab`

Getty AHIP:
`http://www.ahip.getty.edu/ahip/`

Ellipsis Publishing:
`http://www.gold.net/ellipsis/`

Heath Bunting:
`http://www.irational.org/`

Pseudo Online Radio:
`http://pon.pseudo.com`

CICV - Centre de Recherche Pierre Schaeffer:
`http://www.cicv.fr`

USA Networks | Sci-Fi Channel:
`http://www.scifi.com`

VRML: Prelude and Future

Organizer:
Don Brutzman, Naval Postgraduate School
Panelists:
Mark Pesce, Author, VRML List Moderator
Gavin Bell, Silicon Graphics Inc., VRML 2.0 Co-Architect
Andries van Dam, Brown University
Salim AbiEzzi, Microsoft ActiveX Animation

Don Brutzman
brutzman@nps.navy.mil

The meteoric development of the Virtual Reality Modeling Language (VRML) is one of the most important standards developments in graphics and internetworking. An informal, intense, open, and collaborative design process has worked. VRML version one defined a concise and workable scene description language. Version two refined this language to incorporate behavioral animation mechanisms compatible with the current World Wide Web. Networked interoperable interactive 3D graphics are now feasible for everyone's computer We examine lessons learned over the past two years, where VRML is going, and how VRML is triggering fundamental changes in the economics, mindset, and membership of the graphics community.

Although networking has been considered "different" than computer graphics, network considerations are integral to large-scale interactive 3D graphics. Graphics and networks are now two interlocking halves of a greater whole: distributed virtual environments. New capabilities, new applications, and new ideas abound in this rich intersection. Our ultimate goal is to use networked interactive 3D graphics to take full advantage of all computation, content, and people resources available on the Internet.

Realizing the lofty ambitions of VRML has required hands-on attention to myriad technical and people challenges. How do you specify a 3D scene both concisely and compatibly, given a plethora of other formats? How are working (i.e. successful) relationships built among individuals, academia, and companies of all sizes? What is a "networked behavior?" How do we sustainably capture both the specification and the standards process? Does VRML = graphics + the Web + networking + behaviors + everything in the world? In other words, where (or does) VRML stop? Which steps are next?

Graphics, networking, and interoperability breakthroughs repeatedly remove bottlenecks and provide new opportunities. A pattern appears as we attempt to scale up in capability and capacity without limit: every old bottleneck broken reveals another. Understanding bottlenecks, corresponding solutions, and potential upper bounds to growth permits us to develop effective networked graphics. Technically and socially, SIGGRAPH has crossed a threshold in capability. As we overcome current bottlenecks, "effectively networked graphics" will simply mean "applications."

Mark Pesce
mpesce@netcom.com

Perhaps the most singular aspects of the VRML "movement" are its out-of-control nature and its persistent strength in the face of well-organized opposition. From the very beginning–when Tony Parisi and I began to share our work with Tim Berners-Lee and others–we practiced a politic of inclusion, keeping the door open to relationships which could be leveraged into successes for VRML. This speaks more of a process of social engineering than software engineering, and articulates the heart of the difference between VRML and any of its potential competitors (ActiveVRML, OpenFlight, WIRL, etc.). Because VRML has remained open in deed as well as word, because anyone can become a member of the community and contribute, VRML has garnered the support of communities across the graphics and networking industries. In fact, despite the persistent lobbying of many large companies—including Netscape, Silicon Graphics, and Microsoft—the consensus process which brought us both VRML 1.0 and VRML 2.0 has proved resistant to tampering by press release or marketing hype. That's one of the real lessons of VRML: the social fabric of the VRML community is the real key to its success. It's my belief that this lesson has wide application outside the limited domain of VRML; wherever virtual communities are to spring up and flourish, the same conditions must apply.

Gavin Bell
gavin@sgi.com

VRML 2.0 is an incredibly rich file format for creating interactive 3Dmultimedia experiences that are distributed across the Internet. It isalso a solid foundation for solutions to the next hard problem: multi-userworlds.

VRML is a success because it hasn't tried to solve all of the problems of computer graphics, simulation, and networking all at once. When creating something to meet the needs of a very large group of people, it is difficult to balance the limitless number of features requested against the limited amount of design and implementation time available. Rough agreement on both constraints and goals is the key to getting anything accomplished.

Its design is both solid and practical, in part because the Internet gives system designers an invaluable tool: direct feedback from knowledgeable users. We had to convince users that our proposal would solve their problems or they would take their business elsewhere (i.e. vote for another proposal). Giving concrete answers to the stream of "can I do this..." questions ensured that we were solving relevant problems and constantly testing the design.

What's next? Tackling the multi-user problem will first require agreement on exactly which problem should be solved: multi-user "chat" is a mucheasier problem than general multi-user collaboration in a shared virtual world. Solving the more general problem will require additions to both VRML and the infrastructure of the World Wide Web.

Andries van Dam
avd@cs.brown.edu

One of the cliches about standards is that standards bodies produce camels, horses designed by committee. (This cynical comment ignores the clear utility of camels in the desert environment.) Whether they are de facto industry standards promulgated by a leading company or industrial consortium, or de jure official standards promulgated by standards bodies such as the IEEE, the ANSI, and ISO, standards reflect both the strengths and the weaknesses of a technopolitical consensus process that favors compromise.

Recently new standards processes specific to the Internet have emerged, aiming for both greater speed and greater democratic input, e.g. the Internet Engineering Task Force (IETF). The design and adoption of VRML 1.0 and more recently of VRML 2.0 via the VRML list and the ad hoc, self-selected VRML Architecture Group (VAG) is a prime example of an even more rapid process. Both the process and the specification should be of great interest to the graphics community. In particular, I believe that this successful process should force ANSI/ISO to redesign its heavy-weight, overly lengthy standards process. They should now consider a light-weight, fast-track process to review both VRML 2.0 and its legitimate competitors for a net-based multimedia standard. This standard should support various visions of cyberspace: multiple participants distributed virtual environments that contain autonomous objects whose behavioral interactions with participants and each other must be simulated in real time, etc.

I hope that the pressure of various companies to simply ratify the evolving VRML 2.0 spec (or its competitors) will be resisted, and that an open, technically sound, extensible standard will be designed to last us well into the next century. VRML 2.0 should certainly be considered as a baseline for the future standard. Needless to say, if the standards process is not ultra-fast (12-18 months), VRML 2.0 WILL become the de facto standard, with all the advantages and disadvantages that implies. Then the official standard, if it is not VRML 2.0 (or any other solution) will only displace VRML 2.0 if is demonstrably superior, using the Darwinian Web-virus competition model that many Web enthusiasts believe is the dominant force for change on the Web. In summary, I believe that it is important to reexamine the good work the VRML community has done and to take into account other models, and to do that with all deliberate speed.

Salim AbiEzzi
salimabi@microsoft.com

Graphics and multimedia for the Internet are needed for both interactive illustrations embedded in Web pages, and for distributed immersive shared spaces. On the one hand, the majority of Internet users can benefit greatly from added life to Web pages through interactive illustrations, which could be used for advertising, information, and artistic and entertainment purposes. On the other hand, advanced users are interested in shared spaces and their potential for spectacular applications in group entertainment, collaborative engineering, and other far-reaching experiential applications of the Internet.

The VRML community has been focused on 3D spaces and models primarily; for example, the present VRML 2.0 is not designed for sprite animation, hot spots, and synthetic audio, which could be building blocks as essential for interactive illustrations as 3D might be. Furthermore, in order for large 3D spaces to become viable for the majority of Internet users, much faster 3D texturing, higher-bandwidth networking, and more reliable low-latency communication are required It is going to be quite some time before these capabilities become common aspects of the infrastructure.

As VRML 2.0 is considered for standardization by formal organizations, it is important to carefully consider broader Internet needs in the area of graphics and multimedia. I believe that either VRML 2.0 needs to be extended to better support the broader needs, especially in the area of illustrations, or the situation calls for other, possibly complementary, standards.

ActiveX Animation (formerly ActiveVRML) is a product out of Microsoft. It includes a modeling language and a run-time environment that primarily targets Web-interactive illustrations. It provides a novel approach for modeling rich behaviors, media integration, interaction, and events. ActiveX Animation facilitates multimedia coordination and rich media composition. It is suitable for sprite animation, just as it is for 3D and the interplay between the two. I will contrast it with VRML 2.0 and highlight its value for Web-interactive illustrations.

This panel statement can be found online at:
http://www.stl.nps.navy.mil/~brutzman/vrml/siggraph96panel.html

Breaking the Myth: One Picture is NOT (Always) Worth a Thousand Words

Organizer:
Nahum D. Gershon, The MITRE Corporation
Panelists:
Robert Braham, IEEE Spectrum, New York, NY
David Fracchia, Simon Fraser University, Vancouver, Canada
Andrew Glassner, Microsoft Corporation, Redmond, WA
Barbara Mones-Hattal, George Mason University, Fairfax, VA
Russ Rose, Office of Research and Development, Washington, DC

Summary

We need to understand well both the power and frailty of images (e.g., compared to words) to be able to use effectively new visualization and computer graphics technologies in science, education, entertainment, and life, and most importantly in the Internet's World Wide Web. The panel and the audience will discuss and debate the weaknesses of images and the difficulty in representing information clearly; the dependency of visual and information perception on past memories, experiences, beliefs, and culture; the difficulty in making effective use of color; and what could be learned from art and design.

"One picture is worth a thousand words" – Fred R. Barnard

"But words are words" – Shakespeare, Much Ado About Nothing

"... words are images of thought refin'd" – John Keats, O Solitude!

Recent developments of computer visual display hardware on one hand and computer graphics and visualization methods and software on the other have generated new interest in images and visual representations. It is now possible with a "flip of a button" to generate visual depictions of data and information or to take existing images and modify them at ease. This renaissance of visual representation has highlighted the notion of the power of images.

"One picture is worth a 1,000 words," goes the popular saying. People in the graphics and visualization community have perceived it to mean not only that images could portray anything that words can, but that images could do it better than words. However, images may have some disadvantages, and words are sometimes more effective (or powerful) than pictures. To use images effectively, we need to understand when they are equivalent to words, when they are more appropriate than words, and when they are not. This issue has become extremely important with the spread of the World Wide Web (WWW), where many document authors do not know when to use an image and when to express an idea with words.

One problem is that computers representing abstract (e.g., non-numerical) information, and visual computing and display are both new media. The understanding of the characteristics, advantages, and disadvantages of these new media is crucial to their optimal and effective use. This will take some time, however.

Similarly, we need to stop relating to the new medium of visual computing and display as if it were a replica of paper. This new technology allows us go beyond what is possible with paper, and we need to understand the differences between traditional and computer generated images.

This panel and the audience will discuss and debate situations where images (both traditional and computer-generated) do and do not convey information effectively or correctly and where images and words could complement each other.

Nahum Gershon
A Picture is Not a Picture is Not a Picture...: A Picture Could be Worth a 1,000, 1/1,000, or -1,000 Words

The difficulty in representing information clearly, the dependency of visual and information perception on past memories, experiences, beliefs, and culture, and the difficulty in making effective use of color are some examples illustrating the frailty of image representations. To make full and correct use of what display, graphics, and visualization technologies can offer us, we need to take these considerations into account when generating images or when viewing them. It is true, however, that for certain purposes, images do not need to portray reality exactly. But in these cases, we must be sure the viewers are aware of this fact deep in their minds. Otherwise, we might create pictures that are worth 1/1,000 (Hanson, 1970) of a word or even -1,000 words.

We need to make sure people understand that not everything could effectively be put in a visual form. An example is the term text visualization." People usually imply that images could always represent effectively all the information contained within a collection of text documents, and that it is much easier to get this information from images than from words. Is this really possible? If yes, why was language created, why did silent movies contain textual information, and why was sound introduced to film?

Robert Braham – The Shibboleths of Pictorial Elites

The shibboleth, in its original meaning, was nothing more than a single graphical sign (a word in Hebrew) used as a military password/ "passgraph." An enemy user of that graphical sign was caught when even though interpreting its place in the graphical system rationally, he lacked a crucial bit of knowledge about the ambiguities of the graphics known only to the other side — the pictorial elite.

Pictorial elites, even if more well meaning, are now springing up with alarming rapidity, aided by the tools of computer graphics. Basics of semiotic analysis, such as the ramifications of symbolic, indexical and iconic signs, were developed decades ago in linguistic theory, but are powerful concepts for understanding graphics and their power to shape and be shaped by graphic communities.

Using these and other analytical tools, we would do well to compare the graphical/cognitive turning points we are now going through with those that parallel them in earlier times in the West. In the following cases, oral communities – word users – confronted radically new graphics technology: the composition of epic poetry, the Renaissance "rebirth" of 3-D projection, the change from scroll to pamphlet to book, medieval memory technique, and early scientific diagramming, including animation. The history of the earliest notations for Western music, devised for plainchant – an oral communicative system par excellence – holds a particularly interesting position in this light.

David Fracchia
Towards Image Understanding

The phrase "One picture is worth a thousand words" has become cliche in our vernacular. Part of the reason we say it is because we assume that, to quote another cliché, "seeing is believing." That is, as we look around our world, we perceive it at face value as reality. In contrast, while we may acknowledge that words, particularly poetry, may bring to mind multiple images, it is not commonplace to claim that a phrase is worth a thousand pictures. The ambiguity of multiple personal images that arises from verbal communication means that we as a culture do not automatically believe words.

To compensate, our educational system focuses on verbal literacy, allowing us to express ourselves precisely as in mathematics or evocatively as in poetry. In fact, without verbal ambiguity we would lose much of our humor and pleasure in language. Unfortunately, there is no parallel education in visual literacy. While this may not have been a critical issue in the past, now with the advent of advertising, trick photography, and computer graphics we have the potential for creating visual ambiguity. This puts our whole culture at high risk of being fooled by what they see.

As disturbing as this may sound, the extension of humans' propensity to introduce ambiguity into visual images is a healthy indication of the maturity of visual languages as a communication medium. In fact, we revel in being able to create visual forgeries. What is needed now is to parallel the development of visual language with the exploration of visual literacy.

If we simultaneously want to be able to generate images for our amusement and for information dissemination, we need to understand how pictorial ambiguity arises. We know from work by people such as Bertin, Goodman, Laursen, Tufte, and Ware, that these problems can arise in most aspects of visual representation. It has been suggested that before we can disambiguate images, we need to discover the basic components of visual language. However, exactly what these would be is unclear, particularly in the case of computer images. It is possible that our real clues will come from graphic design and/or perceptual psychology.

Andrew Glassner
Different Media Means Different Messages

Words and images speak to different parts of our experience. Both can be primal or abstract, direct or vague. But novels and paintings are not interchangeable; a poem is not a child's finger-painting. These media are complementary, and neither identical nor antagonistic. Artists can combine these languages to produce interesting and meaningful work, but this composite is yet a third form, and does not subsume or replace the others. Words often fail to describe images, but images just as often fail to capture what can be said by words.

Barbara Mones-Hattal
A Picture May Be (Or May Not Be) Worth A Thousand Words: Lessons From The WWW?

A picture may be worth a thousand words, but those words may not be the same from one person to the next. It has always been a challenge for the artist to design with simplicity, subtlety, and sensitivity. The integration of text and image is not new to the artist. The emergence of the World Wide Web, however, has made for unusual and distinctive design issues. A certain urgency has emerged in order to further refine these relationships as on-line design becomes big business. As the WWW becomes a more effective design multimedia tool, it becomes even more important for us to realize when to use text or graphics, or a combination of the two, in order more successfully utilize this new venue.

Studying the WWW affords us new opportunities to gather enormous amounts of information about successful and less successful design strategies. The design and implementation of icons, the use and overuse/misuse of backgrounds, the potential for audio, 3D and interactive 3D have led to both unique and creative spaces and confusing and/or boring ones. An initial concern about bland and limited design options has replaced itself with new and potentially more exciting ones. However, it becomes important to start to discuss and identify what "successful" Web design might mean, so that we may be more able to both recognize and utilize these spaces with greater confidence.

Russ Rose
P1000: A Picture is Worth 1000 Words

In this era of the information explosion, there exists the need to take advantage of the power provided by the human's visual processing system. Visual exploitation will help in understanding the content of the vast uncharted mountains of information, as well facilitate meaningful analyses of that information. Hence, visual representation of the information can be a powerful enabling force relative to improved understanding.

A picture is worth 1000 words; that is, in 1/1000 the time, a visual image can be processed and analyzed, rather than being represented and processed as words. If represented as words, it would often require more than 1000 words, would take 1000 times as long to understand, and would still not communicate the content as comprehensively as a visual image can. The visual representation of the information, however, must be based on a comprehensive and information rich structure. If not, it will easily not be worth a single word, let alone the 1000 words (we all have set through tiring briefings centered around charts cluttered with information-free clip art that provides no more than visual noise).

Progress must continue, and be accelerated, in the area of visual representation of information. This progress will only be made through significant commitment of resources, as well as the focus of intellectual energies for the long term.

Afterword

We need to understand well both the advantages and disadvantages of using words, images, or their combinations. This is essential to the effective use of new visualization and computer graphics technologies in science, education, entertainment, and life, and most importantly in the Internet's World Wide Web. We also need to understand better the new media of visual computing and display, and we must take advantage of the experiences and insights of the art and design communities.

References

Berger, J., *Ways of Seeing*, British Broadcasting Corporation and Penguin Books, 1977.

Gregory, R.L., *Eye and Brain, The Psychology of Seeing*, Princeton University Press, 1990.

Hanson, N.R., in *The Nature and Function of Scientific Theories*, R.G. Colodny (ed.), University of Pittsburgh Press, 1970.

Digital Stunt Doubles: Safety Through Numbers

Organizer:
Jeff Kleiser, Kleiser-Walczak Construction Co.
Panelists:
Frank Vitz, Kleiser-Walczak Construction Co.
Jeff Light, Industrial Light and Magic
Shahril Ibrahim, Boss Films
Richard Chuang Pacific Data Images

Our company has been researching the creation of computer-generated actors, or Synthespians (TM) as we call them, since 1985. Diana Walczak, a partner in the company, sculpted human figures and faces that were digitized and animated for several experimental films shown at SIGGRAPH: SEXTONE FOR PRESIDENT (1988) and DON'T TOUCH ME (1989). As rendering algorithms relentlessly approach photo-realism, the ability to create life-like characters becomes a realistic and cost-effective prospect. The level of detail required to create a convincingly realistic person varies directly as a function of the distance of the person to the camera; a distant figure can be made to look realistic with a fraction of the effort required to render a convincing close-up. "Acting," in the pure sense of the word, requires the camera to be at least in the proximity of a two-shot, and the industry is on the verge of this capability, although it is extremely complex and costly to produce. An interim application of computer-generated characters lies in the representation of distant humans performing motion that is inconvenient or impossible to perform by a live stunt person. Digital Stunt Doubles have recently been used in a variety of applications to substitute for stunt people in the interest of safety, cost, or simply because the stunt would be impossible to accomplish with a live human being.

This panel session is intended to give four industry experts an opportunity to show some of the applications they have found for this technology in recent feature films, and to discuss the timetable for computer graphics as an industry to move up to the next level: from life-like digital stunt doubles to lifelike digital actors.

Frank Vitz

At Kleiser Walczak Construction Company we have been working in the area of computer generated actors for many years. We coined the term "Synthespian" to describe these synthetic actors. We have created a variety of Synthespians... some human, some exotic, some realistic, some fantastic. But it is only relatively recently that our technology has improved to the point where we can now create Synthespians at feature film resolution that are indistinguishable in certain cases from real human actors... Synthespians that can act as Digital Stunt Doubles. The movie "Judge Dredd," starring Sylvester Stallone, was one project that provided us with an opportunity to develop the realistic character animation techniques necessary for Digital Stunt Doubles. The screenplay called for a large number of digital effects shots, including realistic vehicles, explosions, weapons effects, and most exciting: an extended aerial chase sequence through the streets of a futuristic city on flying motorcycles! The Lawmaster Sequence, as it was called, would involve impossibly fast flybys, aerial maneuvers, and stunts . . . all to be seamlessly matted into model city backgrounds. This was a perfect place to use Digital Stunt Doubles. The sequence was divided into two types of shots, Live Actor and Digital Stunt Double shots. The live shots were typically those that involved closeups of the actors speaking, while the Stunt Double shots had difficult camera angles, extreme action, explosions, and so forth. We created digital stunt double versions of two actors, faithfully reproducing their facial features, body proportions, and costumes. We created CGI versions of the Lawmaster Motorcycles that matched the live stunt bikes. We choreographed the motion of the digital bikes to fit into model photography of Mega City. We animated the Stunt Doubles to move realistically on their bikes. We added a variety of additional digital effects, such as explosions, smoke, lens flares, and motion blur to make the illusion more convincing.

In this panel discussion I hope to share some of the details of what we went through during the creation of these Digital Stunt Doubles for "Judge Dredd." We learned a lot during the process, and have some new ideas as a result... ideas that are finding expression in our current projects. The future of computer-generated actors is wide open. I am looking forward to sharing with the other panel members some speculation about where we might be headed.

Jeff Light

As film effects are driven to dizzying heights of more intense action and to create more amazing fantasy, the pressure to create convincing digital stunt doubles is increasing, and the technology to make it possible is becoming more readily available. The use of puppets, dummies, or stunt-persons as stunt doubles has been practiced since the beginning of movie making. Digital stunt doubles are simply the logical extension of this idea.

The need for digital stunt doubles is driven by a number of factors. The performance may be too dangerous or impossible for an actor. A shot that requires thousands of extras may be too expensive to shoot with modern financial constraints. Some scenes may already be composed of sufficiently complex synthetic imagery, such that it is simply *easier* to composite a digital character interacting with other elements in a scene. There are daunting obstacles to overcome in the process of creating a digital stunt double. Primarily, it should not call attention to the fact that it's an effect. The modeling, animation, and rendering must blend seamlessly with surrounding shots. Often, the switch between live action and the CG double will happen *during* the shot, when the audience is focusing their full attention on the character that is being switched! Modeling and rendering hair, skin, and cloth remain difficult obstacles to imitating the look of the original performer. Animating the subtleties of *real* human or animal motion is highly complex. Motion capture or procedural animation approaches may provide partial answers, but are not a panacea.

Since the drive to create an increasing amount of a performance with a digital character is inexorable, the implications of not simply supplanting but actually replacing actors, living or dead, raises important artistic and ethical issues, which I hope we can approach with wisdom.

Shahril Ibrahim

Digital doubles are perhaps the first use of virtual actors. They can be utilized in dangerous and risky situations, and can be used in short segments. The short amount of screen time reduces the complexity of modelling/animating and rendering of a complete human. Digital doubles also allow plasticity of the actor to achieve shots that would be otherwise impossible, for example facial and body morphs. Currently these doubles are produced by either imaging real humans and manipulating the digital information, or by painstakingly animating the humans with a combination of kinematics and dynamics. A hybrid approach is the use of motion capture to drive animated characters. It would be interesting if these animated characters could mimic their physical counterparts to achieve nuances and subtlety of motion.

As technology progresses and our understanding of human motions and behavior increases, these digital stunt doubles may move out of being just a double to being the star character. Some of this has already happened, as in the movie "Species."

Richard Chuang

In 1995, eight of the ten top box office grossing films were dominated by digital visual effects. Audiences flock to these special effects extravaganzas, and directors are increasingly willing to embrace digital techniques to enhance or replace traditional effects. One of the latest techniques to be explored in Hollywood is the use of digital stunt doubles in difficult or dangerous stunt sequences.

What is the difference between replacing a highly-paid actor with a stunt double, and having a performer's data captured digitally and used to create a digital stunt double? In both instances, production creatives are hoping to match the performance qualities of a principal actor without subjecting them to physically challenging or dangerous scenes. Digital stunt doubles provide certain advantages over human stunt doubles.

The digital stunt double can provide a greater degree of flexibility when shooting on a model or miniature set. It is time-consuming to track "witness points" for integration of live actors into model and miniature plates. A digital stunt double provides greater control over scale, motion, and lighting, and is more easily matched to the set.

Concurrently with the demand for action-heavy effects films, stunts are becoming increasingly dangerous and spectacular. Using a digital stunt double is advantageous when a particularly complex or dangerous stunt is required. Rather than placing talent in a dangerous situation, a stunt double can perform a set of movements that match the shot in a safe, controlled environment. The motion data is captured digitally and applied to a computer-generated model, which is based on the physical qualities of the principal actor. Once the raw motion is captured and applied to the model, it is refined to create a scene that would have been unsafe or impossible to shoot practically.

Digital stunt doubles offer directors greater flexibility in changing camera angles, lighting, timing, and even location without having to re-shoot the live action scene. However, a digital stunt double is only as good as the original data captured from human performance and the artistry of the CG animators who translate raw data into finished animation. In most cases, computer animation is not yet suited to creating realistic motion, complete with nuances of expression and gesture that are inherent in human performance. The amount of work it currently takes to perfect a digital character without motion capture data precludes many creative budgets. On the other hand, motion capture data is raw, and must be refined with hand-animation techniques to convey the unique qualities of an individual actor's performance. By combining motion capture data and computer animation, it is possible to get the best of both worlds: a realistic performance, plus the flexibility of being able to modify and adjust the scene in post.

Global Multi-User Virtual Environments

Organizer:
Wolfgang Felger, Fraunhofer Institute for Computer Graphics
Panelists:
Lennart E. Fahlen, Swedish Institute of Computer Science
R. Bowen Loftin, NASA Johnson Space Center & University of Houston
Michael R. Macedonia, Fraunhofer Center for Research in Computer Graphics
Gurminder Singh, National University of Singapore

Summary: Wolfgang Felger

Research and development activities are facing a continuing globalization. Networks are getting more important than companies or institutes. Main reasons for this trend are:

- (Faster) access to new knowledge and technology and its improved transfer.
- Economic reasons.
- Use the particular advantages of multicultural work environments.

Together with a steadily improving technology, the global information society is not far away. In particular, the networking and virtual environment technologies are making much progress and are ready to enable shared, distributed, cooperative activities.

This panel addresses network infrastructure, systems, and applications related to multi-user virtual environments, especially the global (intercontinental/international) aspects of these issues. The panelists will summarize their "lessons learned," will highlight latest activities, and share with the audience their short/mid-term vision on global, multi-user virtual environments.

The panelists intend to enrich their presentations with (multicontinental) live demonstrations. Furthermore, specific applications are showcased at "Digital Bayou" (Where No Man Has Gone Before).

Lennart E. Fahlen

The objective of this panel is to discuss the long term development of future large-scale social electronic spaces. In this time and age, this means networked computer systems that exploit the idea of a place inhabited by users who communicate with one another using the natural and informal means appropriate to a range of social situations (e.g. work, family, leisure, etc.). Ideally, such systems should support many thousands of users engaged in real time interaction with one another.

Below are a number notions relevant to the above goals:

- Users as inhabitants of electronic spaces. Users should experience a sense of immersion within a computer system, as opposed to only interacting with it.
- Infrastructures need to support real-time events similar in scale to gatherings of people in the physical world (e.g. on the scale of today's largest sports and entertainment events). The construction of such large scale electronic spaces introduces critical problems of scale. Some issues to be considered are network-, processing- and perceptual scaleability and the unavoidable latencies caused by the geographical separation of users and nodes.
- The network and software infrastructure required to deliver such applications to the general citizen. Today the WWW provides for large scale multimedia information access and distribution. But seen from the perspective of "users being social beings inhabiting an electronic space," the Web carries severe shortcomings: asymmetry between information provision and consumption, the environment is strangely uninhabited, users are only visible through the information they provide or through a number-of-visitors statistic, there is no provision for real-time interaction and feedback, etc.
- Interaction metaphors and techniques which seamlessly combine information visualization, and access with social interaction. How should socially inhabited electronic spaces be structured, and what tools are needed to construct them? Furthermore, how should people be supported in exploring and navigating such spaces, and how might the structure afford possibilities for social interaction?
- Spatial metaphors seem to present solutions to some technical issues such as access to computational resources, as well as to other people. These alternatives are more promising than traditional solutions (i.e. password protection, passing of tokens etc.).
- How to provide a sense of personal presence and awareness, both direct and peripherally, with other people within an electronic space, and how to achieve this through user embodiment and other representation techniques. A number of social studies show the importance of mutual and peripheral awareness phenomena to the coordination of social interaction. Most current systems have major difficulties conveying presence of other users, awareness of what these other users are doing, and providing mechanisms to represent a user as an embodiment within a single application.
- Techniques for integrating electronic spaces with physical spaces, including notions of shared augmented reality and shared augmented virtuality.
- Intelligent agents as inhabitants of social computing environments (i.e. in the presence of many humans and other agents).
- To see such real and virtual information spaces as inhabited social environments, capable of supporting participation in many different activities and social relations. Also, one should not forget that such environments must be expressive, aesthetic, dramatic, motivational, and inherently enjoyable to use and inhabit.

In summary my position is very much defined by terms such as "inhabited," "social interaction," "awareness," "spatial metaphors," and "mass participation." Furthermore, it has very little to do with "photo realistic rendering," and concerns itself much more with a paradigm shift that views virtual reality and related technologies as providing inhabited social spaces and by conceiving of users as citizens and social beings both at work and play.

R. Bowen Loftin

Opportunities to exploit shared virtual environments abound. Collaborations in art, business, education, engineering, and science could all benefit from the ability of collaborators to share the same environments and the same experiences while directly interacting with information displayed in useful ways. Endeavors in all these spheres of activity are increasingly global in scope, challenging the ability of communications technologies and display/interaction metaphors to enable the sharing of complex environments in real-time. This panel presentation will describe a successful demonstration of a shared virtual environment for training an international astronaut team, and will conclude with an overview of current applications in computational chemistry and science education.

Historically, NASA has trained teams of astronauts by bringing them to the Johnson Space Center in Houston to undergo generic training followed by mission-specific training. The latter begins after a crew has been selected for a mission, often as much as two years before launch.

While some Space Shuttle flights have included an astronaut from a foreign country, the International Space Station will be consistently crewed by teams of astronauts from two or more of the partner nations. Not surprisingly, the international partners in the Space Station program would prefer to significantly reduce the need for their citizen astronauts to travel to and remain in Houston for training.

As a means of demonstrating the feasibility of using shared virtual environments to support the training of international astronaut teams, an experiment was conducted on September 20, 1995. Astronaut Bernard Harris (physically located at the Johnson Space Center in Houston) entered a virtual environment with Astronaut Ulf Merbold (physically located at the Fraunhofer Institute for Computer Graphics in Darmstadt, Germany). Their shared environment consisted of models of the Space Shuttle payload bay and the Hubble Space Telescope (HST). The two astronauts spent over thirty minutes performing the major activities associated with the changeout of the HST's Solar Array Drive Electronics (SADE). Their work included the real-time hand-off of the replacement SADE in exchange for the original SADE. At the conclusion of the task the two astronauts shook hands and waved good-bye.

The positive reaction of both astronauts to this experiment, has led to plans for the development of applications in support of future international missions, and an increase from two to three sites. Before the end of this century, efforts will be made to support shared environment between the ground-based installations and Low Earth Orbit for both "just-in-time" training and performance support for maintenance, science, and emergency medical services.

Applications are also under development that will support the training of multi–service military teams assigned to Operations Other Than War (such as the current peacekeeping operations in Bosnia, or humanitarian relief). Finally, this same technology is being explored as a means of allowing students from widely–separated geographical locations to jointly perform experiments and observations in simulated environments.

The computer graphics community must not believe that the only barriers to the effective use of shared virtual environments are bandwidth and rendering performance. A multitude of psychological, cultural, and human-computer interaction problems must also be successfully solved. The task of creating the technological infrastructure for sharing virtual environments on a global scale is surpassed only by the task of understanding how best to utilize applications built within the context of this infrastructure.

Michael R. Macedonia

This presentation will describe the infrastructure required to support VR in a global environment. Moreover, it will discuss a project that CRCG is participating in to develop that infrastructure – the MAY project.

CRCG has focused its research efforts toward determining how computer networks can be made to transform the workplace into a shared environment, allowing real-time interaction among people and processes without regard to their location. It is this illusion that allows the use of VR and telepresence for applications like distance learning, distributed interactive simulation, and group entertainment.

Emerging international broadband networks will enable the use of VR for applications that span the globe. These tools will support communication among multiple users in order to bridge long distances and different times. Common research, and business and social contacts across continents will become as simple as meetings between partners in one room. For example, the goal of manufacturing enterprises will be able to design, develop, prototype, and test new products in a seamless virtual environment with engineers in Detroit, designers in Munich, and managers in Milan. This is one of the goals of the MAY project.

The MAY project will test emerging communication facilities between research and industrial sites in Germany and the United States of America. The communication makes use of advanced collaboration tools like BERKOM, GroupX and Mbone over a high-speed intercontinental ATM link.

MAY comprises several different goals:

- MAY is intended to gain experience with multimegabit communication facilities bridging large geographical distances and grossly different time zones. The usefulness of group applications for research and industrial activities under the above circumstances will be evaluated.
- MAY shall provide solutions for problems that occur using long distance links like echo in headset-free environments, and the small working time overlap in "continuous development around the clock" scenarios.
- Data load patterns of the link will be monitored to gain knowledge about the resource allocation requirements for these advanced high speed applications.

Gurminder Singh

Nearly half the world's computers are idle at any given time. But at the same time, people face serious deficiency of computing and network resources when it comes to running large scale multi-user virtual worlds. We have been developing architectures to support large numbers of concurrent virtual world users on off-the-shelf PCs and Internet. The first system we developed, called WorldNet, is currently being used to develop several commercial products.

Based on the WorldNet experience, we are currently developing an architecture, named NetEffect, to support and run large scale multi-user virtual worlds that span across continents. The idea is to utilize idle computers located around the world to facilitate communication among virtual worlds. Our architecture is based on using distributed cooperating servers that are able to migrate from one workstation to another.

People around the world are able to volunteer their workstations to act as servers when they are not using them. For example, a person in Vancouver, Canada can volunteer his workstation from 7PM to 7AM every day; this is the time slot when he does not use his machine and is happy if it can be put a better use. We run a collection of master servers around the world on fixed Internet addresses which know about the availability of volunteered machines. The master servers ensure that when a particular server workstation's free time is up, the server is migrated to another available machine; all virtual world clients connected to that server are also migrated to the new server. The client virtual worlds, during their session keep moving around from one server to another without being affected in any significant way.

Based on the above architecture, we are developing interactive discovery learning applications for children. These applications enable children to learn new, useful information through interaction with a game-like interface, and through collaboration with other children on the network. Collaboration among children is supported by enabling and encouraging them to share objects and information with one another.

How Can SIGGRAPH be More Effective in Promoting Computer Graphics?

Organizer:
Nahum D. Gershon, The MITRE Corporation
Panelists:
Alain Chesnais, Alias Wavefront, Paris, France
Bob Ellis, Fountain Hills, AZ
Jose Encarnação, Fraunhofer Institute for Computer Graphics, Darmstadt, Germany
Donald P. Greenberg, Cornell University, Ithaca, NY

Summary

In spite of its glorious past and present, computer graphics is not always appropriately recognized by funding agencies, academia, and industry. The panel members will discuss and debate how SIGGRAPH can or should foster a vigorous agenda for improving the stature of computer graphics research, development, and applications. SIGGRAPH has the potential to affect all walks of life, industry, and academia by actively addressing the right issues. We hope this panel will lead to a working group within the SIGGRAPH Public Policy Task Group to address these issues, formulate recommendations to SIGGRAPH, and carry out activities with the goal of promoting computer graphics.

How Can SIGGRAPH be More Effective in Promoting Computer Graphics?

"If SIGGRAPH does not do it, either somebody will do it or computer graphics will lose importance and weight or recognition over time." Jose Luis Encarnação, acceptance speech of SIGGRAPH's Steven A. Coons Award, 1995

Computer graphics (CG) has a distinguished record of achievements over the past 30 years, and SIGGRAPH has played a large part in this success. Computer graphics is the enabling technology of important areas such as multimedia, visualization and the Internet's World Wide Web. Application areas such as 3D medical imaging, entertainment (film and TV), education, information visualization, pharmaceutical research, weather modeling, automotive and computer industries, and science and engineering have benefited from computer graphics as well.

In spite of CG's impressive influence, the situation today is somewhat different. Computer graphics is not always as well recognized as it should be, and funding agencies do not have programs designated particularly for computer graphics. Few academic computer science departments perceive computer graphics to have basic research value. Few foster (or encourage) research careers in CG for their junior staff members. As a result, there are few graduate programs in computer graphics.

The panel and the audience will discuss the problems facing computer graphics as a discipline, suggest solutions, and explore areas where SIGGRAPH could take action. We hope the panel will inspire a group to work with the SIGGRAPH Public Policy Task Force on these issues to formulate recommendations to SIGGRAPH on how to improve the standing of computer graphics.

Central questions of this panel include:

- How can computer graphics get the proper recognition for its achievements and impact on society?
- How can we increase the level of funding given to computer graphics basic research and R&D?
- How can the academic stature of computer graphics be improved?
- How can we encourage careers in computer graphics?

The above issues raise more specific key issues related to SIGGRAPH. The panel and the audience will discuss these specific key issues for developing an increased effectiveness of CG which include:

- Should SIGGRAPH promote increasing the levels of funding and investments from government agencies and industry? If yes, how?
- How to increase the credibility and support in academia? Would an increased level of funding be sufficient?
- How can SIGGRAPH speak for its members? Options include (informal) lobbying, writing papers in leading magazines, sending representatives to other organizations (e.g., international), polling members and incorporating their recommendations, and providing education to the public, industry's program managers, and policy makers relative to public policy issues.
- SIGGRAPH is a scientific educational organization: Is it appropriate for an educational organization to take positions on social issues?
- Due to change in times: Should SIGGRAPH broaden its charter to go beyond an educational organization – an organization that promotes research and development in computer graphics, its application and implementation across industry, governments, and education? What are the limits on our activities (ACM policies, budget, volunteer time, etc.)?
- How to increase the international involvement of SIGGRAPH and support from international sources?

Alain Chesnais
SIGGRAPH Needs to Define its Public Policy Strategy and its Role in Coming Years

SIGGRAPH as an organization needs to define its public policy strategy, taking the needs of its members into account. A large portion of our member base comes from academia, and SIGGRAPH could play a substantial role in raising the awareness of decision makers concerning their policy regarding computer graphics research and education.

Is this desirable? Could we do it in a manner that respects the various situations presented in the different countries that our members come from? Is academic research and education the only identifiable member community that would want SIGGRAPH to take active measures on their behalf? These are questions that we need to address as SIGGRAPH considers its role in coming years.

Bob Ellis
What are Appropriate Public Policy Activities for SIGGRAPH?

At SIGGRAPH's 1994 Snowbird strategic planning meeting, attendees called for SIGGRAPH to take an increased role in public policy, and this was determined to be one of the seven focus areas for consideration in SIGGRAPH strategic planning. Suggested activities included increased involvement with the public, fostering a social conscience, taking leadership on legal issues, providing accessibility to the technologically disadvantaged, and playing an increased role in political and social issues.

Since that time, working meetings have been held at the annual conferences in 1994 and 1995, and an open meeting was held at the 1995 conference. These meetings have attracted an increasing number of interested participants with a diversity of backgrounds and interests. Key issues that have come from the meetings include the need to inform political policy makers and program managers about computer graphics, and the need to impact the funding for computer graphics research and education.

To many people, public policy activity means taking positions on issues and advocating those positions to members of government and the public. I personally believe that SIGGRAPH's public policy activities, as part of a scientific, educational society, should be limited to providing education on the implications of alternatives for others who do advocate policy positions. This activity serves our members who I believe joined SIGGRAPH primarily for technical reasons. Two projects were started before I became Chair of SIGGRAPH's Public Policy Task Force, and I support them fully: a report on the role of graphics in the Global Information Infrastructure, which has received funding from the SIGGRAPH Special Projects committee, and a white paper identifying significant computer graphics research topics, which has been formally endorsed by the SIGGRAPH Executive Committee.

Jose Luis Encarnação
Promote the Role of Computer Graphics as Enabling Technology and as Technical Professor

ACM SIGGRAPH is extremely successful in being an association for publishing scientists' results, promoting in this way research in Computer Graphics and therefore also by setting trends. ACM SIGGRAPH has also been extremely successful in supporting educational activities in Computer Graphics.

Computer Graphics has evolved to a very high level of importance as a technical discipline and as a key enabling tool for a large spectrum of technologies and applications. I can see a new role for ACM SIGGRAPH in the area of building relationships and synergies between academia, R&D institutions, and industry for the reinforcement of applied and market-oriented research in Computer Graphics. I see another role in supporting the speeding-up of the technology transfer process from academic results into applications and products. An additional role should be to advise policy makers, industry leaders, and program managers at funding agencies on the strategic and technological importance of Computer Graphics. The objective here is to lobby for the entire field of Computer Graphics. For these purposes, ACM SIGGRAPH should assume a strong position of technological, scientific, and trend-setting leadership by extending its profile to also include the role of a professional association.

One way of ACM SIGGRAPH implementing these roles could be to establish a high-ranking forum with executives from policy and industry (suppliers and users) with the task of developing a series of "SIGGRAPH Strategic Workshops" on specific topics, which are important to promote the role of Computer Graphics as an accepted enabling technology and as a technical profession.

Nahum Gershon
Taking a More Active Role

In his acceptance speech of SIGGRAPH's Steven A. Coons Award, 1995, Jose Encarnação, posed the rhetorical question "Is there is a more pro-active role for ACM SIGGRAPH to play?" The answer is yes. SIGGRAPH needs to take a role of a professional organization pursuing the interests of the computer graphics field, as well as the public interest. Governments and industry need to recognize the constructive contribution of CG to many areas and to society in general. Funding must increase, as well as the recognition of academic institutions. This could be achieved by rethinking the roles of SIGGRAPH and adjusting them to the times. We also need to strengthen the tie between academic and applied research crossing over international boundaries. An effective and assertive public policy agenda is the key for achieving the well deserved-support and recognition of computer graphics, and its contribution to society and technology.

Don Greenberg
"The Area is Perceived as Not Having Basic Research Values"

One of my biggest concerns is that a number of the most basic research issues have not been addressed. The "what you see is what you get" (WYSIWYG) paradigm has existed for too long. Although this situation may be acceptable to the entertainment and gaming industries, it is not satisfactory for computer simulations, such as pilot training or architectural design, scientific visualizations, or the medical profession, to name a few.

Perhaps the cause of this might even be the success of SIGGRAPH; images that are created are so visually impressive and plausible that they are accepted as the real thing. But it is now time for change! The computer graphics field is maturing. SIGGRAPH is entering its 23rd year. Processing power is now available, and specialized hardware accelerators are now commonplace. But the same incremental algorithms, developed without a real scientific basis in the late 1960s and early 1970's, are still in use.

Such issues as computational complexity, perceptual thresholds, and metrics for evaluating user interfaces have not been given much attention. Even worse, the feedback loop, the hypothesis, testing, and experimental verification, so prevalent in most scientific disciplines, is almost ignored in computer graphics. With the exponential growth in processing power and bandwidth, we need to set a research agenda to achieve a better foundation for the next generation of computer graphics.

To achieve these goals, it will be necessary to have a multi-disciplinary approach. Computer graphics, at least the rendering portion, has fundamental research issues in the fields of optics, physics, geometry, color science, the software/hardware engineering fields, and a large number of scientific areas normally falling within the domain of computer science or electrical engineering. Maybe this is why the subject does not neatly fall within a computer science department or graduate field, but it is not a sufficient reason for the scarcity of graduate programs (note: this paragraph relates to the paucity of graduate computer graphics programs in the United States).

Afterword

ACM SIGGRAPH, as a society, has the "clout" to influence changes in universities, government, and funding agencies. How and when should this clout be used? Should SIGGRAPH, a professional, educational society try to influence public policy? For those who say, "SIGGRAPH should ...", who is SIGGRAPH? We hope the panel will inspire a group working with SIGGRAPH Public Policy Task Group on these issues to form recommendations to SIGGRAPH on how to improve the standing of computer graphics.

References

1. Ellis, Bob, "SIGGRAPH Public Policy," Computer Graphics, Vol. 30, No. 1, Feb. 1996, pp. 45-46.

2. Encarnação, Jose Luis, acceptance speech of SIGGRAPH's Steven A. Coons Award, Proceedings of SIGGRAPH 95 (Los Angeles, CA, August 6–1, 1995). In *Computer Graphics* Proceedings, Annual Conference Series, 1995, ACM SIGGRAPH, pp. 7–9.

Webbed Spaces: Between Exhibition and Network

Organizers:
Perry Hoberman, Telepresence Research
Victoria Vesna, University of California at Santa Barbara
Panelists:
Ken Feingold, School of Visual Arts
Stelarc, Artist, Sydney, Australia
Lorne Falk, Consultant, Los Angeles
Laura Kurgan, University of Pennsylvania

Artists, curators and theorists, each using the Internet in their own practice, will discuss works that emphasize public installation and multi-user approaches, using these works points of departure to begin a critical discussion of the Internet and its implications for artmaking, representation, and interactivity.

Panel Overview

The Internet (and in particular the World Wide Web) has seen unprecedented growth in the last several years. What started as a mode of communication linking remote sites has become a new public arena. As the Internet continues to mushroom, it is continuously accruing new technological capabilities, such as VRML, Java, graphical MOOs and MUDs, CU-SeeMe and the Mbone. As a result, a variety of cultural entities are beginning to gravitate towards it, including galleries, artists, and public institutions. Because the explosion of the Internet has been so sudden, and because its growth has been accompanied by a huge measure of real excitement as well as calculated hype, there has been little critical discussion of emerging cultural practices in this new realm.

By bringing together artists, curators and theorists, each of whom is actively engaged with the Internet, "Webbed Spaces" will focus on the ramifications of the newly-expanded Internet for artmaking practices, addressing the following issues:

• How can two very different "publics" – one physically present, the other tele-present – be brought into relation to one another? What characteristics distinguish one public from the other? What kinds of interaction become possible between them?

• Is the way the Internet serves to connect geographically distant individuals at the same time that it de-emphasizes physical contact an inevitable consequence of online communication? Does "wired intimacy" go hand in hand with "wired isolation?" What are the ramifications of being wired?

• To what extent is the Internet creating new forms and forums for artmaking, and to what extent is it altering (or merely replacing) existing ones? Should we consider the Internet a new medium? If so, what are its specific characteristics? What is the critical language that can be used to represent it?

• What are the implications of webbed and hybrid work for visual representation, experience, and interactivity?

• How can the Internet be used to extend the fixed space of galleries and other exhibition venues?

• The rhetoric of the Internet often makes the assumption that everything is instantly accessible everywhere to everyone. What are the ramifications of this assumption, especially for the incubation and dissemination of new work? And, despite this rhetoric, what things, places, and people remain excluded, and why?

Lorne Falk
Brave New Audience

The audience for this presentation involves real people living in telepresent neighborhoods, live buildings, and hot rooms. Wired and unwired people in digital niches – a brave new audience. I want to map some of the attributes of this brave new audience in a way that subjectively maps the desires of the people who comprise it.

A keyword is symbiosis. There is a new kind of symbiosis – in the broadest terms, how real and artificial organisms live attached to one another (or one is a tenant of the other) and contribute to each other's support. As an attribute of the brave new audience, symbiosis doesn't negatively contrast different kinds of presence. It recognizes the interrelations between the physical and digital as something mutually beneficial and natural to do. This is both adventurous and consequential – hence, brave.

Physical and digital audiences are, for example, able to interact with one another as a consequence of the (creative) environments they find themselves in. They also eagerly interact with these environments. They have a powerful motivation: the concept of the original, which has dominated aesthetics for most of the twentieth century, is no longer relevant. Instead, the aspiration is to create (spaces) whose identities are infinitely malleable and fully shared with the audience. The brave new audience is encouraged to construct new rules for social conduct, revise concepts of social integration, and even imagine an aesthetics of community unlike what we're used to. In other words, there is an ethical dimension to their behavior. What happens when a creative space is unable to let go of the notion of the original enough to allow the audience to reform or transform, if not the whole space, at least some significant aspect of it?

Ken Feingold
Shared Virtual Environments as/and Art Spaces

This presentation will discuss the evolution of Shared Virtual Environments on the Internet as social environments, spaces for artmaking, and their intersection with actual shared environments. I will assert that it is not information which drives the social and aesthetic experience of using the 'Net, but rather communication with others, the ability to experience extended powers in the physical world, and a suspension of normal formations of "identity;" and that the underlying goal of many works created for the 'Net is not in their widespread distribution, but rather their ability to create linked spaces which are inhabited simultaneously by people in diverse physical locations, and their ability to bridge physical spaces and virtual spaces. I will discuss and develop the idea of such uses of the 'Net as liminal spaces, and discuss notions of personal agency, fantasy, and magic in these spaces, as grounding ideas upon which some recent works of art are being created.

I will discuss the development from text-based MOOs and MUDs and early artists' experiments in their uses as public performance spaces, to my recent experiments using the Mbone to create hybrid actual/virtual spaces in which remote participants meet as telerobotically controlled puppets. I will discuss the social and expressive limits of "uninhabited spaces," such as "publishing" on the 'Web, CGI-driven "interaction," and VRML 1.x, contrasting these with emerging forms such as VRML 2.0 and "The Palace," in which virtual environments are inhabited simultaneously by communicating participants. Further, I will explore the possibility that art is fundamentally related to the human body and physical space, and discuss the relevance of this notion to the topic.

Laura Kurgan
You Are Here: The World Wide Web

As it exists now, the Web gives us a lot to think about in the way of architecture's relation to interface, networks, and data flows. As an environment, the Web incorporates many and diverse spaces within its own very specific limitations. It can be used to illustrate examples of utopian spaces where people can exchange identities, morph their bodies, or form communities; or it can be used by local transportation authorities to upload information from traffic surveillance camera sites on freeways to visualize traffic flows, so that a commuter can see where the traffic jams are located. The interfaces are as diverse as the spaces implied by them.

Whatever the scenario, the Web has become obsessed with mapping itself – from corporate sponsors trying to get profiles and numbers of their users (and a site can capture quite a lot about the user instantly), in order to decide whether this is truly a profitable environment, to speculative mappers of self-organizing systems trying to visualize the constantly changing environments of the links in their home pages, to sites which try to locate the geographical position of their users on a map, to events which are designed to construct a map of those providing input to the site.

What's interesting (precisely because it's so unsatisfying) about most of these representations is their imposition of conventional architectures, and the conventional language of maps, to orient and draw familiar pictures of such an unfamiliar space. Why does it make a difference at what longitude and latitude the server is located? Although they often produce interesting superimpositions of different representational grids, these projects – like so many of Web maps – seem strangely unconscious of their own condition: the map of the Web is on the Web. Their limit is, simply, the inability to find an outside in Web space. In the end, no matter how totalizing the representation of the site wants to be, it's just another address on the Web. No one site dominates another... not just because the Web is decentralized, but because of the paradoxical spatial structure implied: inside and outside are no longer separated by anything like a solid boundary, or a wall.

Stelarc
Fractal Flesh

Consider a body of FRACTAL FLESH, a body whose agency can be electronically extruded on the Net – from one body to another body elsewhere. Not a kind of Cyber-Voodoo. Not of remote control, but of DISPLACING MOTIONS from one physical body to another physical body Net-connected. Such a body's awareness would neither be "all-here" nor "all-there." Awareness and action would slide and shift between bodies. Agency could be shared in the one body or in a multiplicity of bodies in an ELECTRONIC SPACE OF DISTRIBUTED INTELLIGENCE...

Imagine a body directly wired into the Net – a body that moves not because of its internal stimulation, a body that moves not because of being remotely guided by another (or a cluster of remote agents), BUT A BODY THAT QUIVERS AND OSCILLATES TO THE EBB AND FLOW OF NET ACTIVITY. A body that manifests the statistical and collective data flow. A body whose proprioception responds not to its internal nervous system, but to the external stimulation of globally connected computer networks.

THE INTERNET IS AWASH WITH OUTMODED METAPHYSICAL YEARNINGS AND FAR-FETCHED FANTASIES OF DISEMBODIMENT. THE NET IS NOT "MIND TO MIND"-RATHER, IT IS AT PRESENT MERELY A MODE OF TEXTUAL COMMUNICATION, A REDUCTIVE VISUALITY DEPRIVED OF THE COMPLEXITY OF PHYSICAL ACTION & KINESTHETIC POSITION AND ORIENTATION. BODIES ELECTRONICALLY CONNECTED AND ACTUATED TRANSFORM THE NET FROM A MEANS OF INFORMATION TRANSMISSION TO A MODE OF TRANSDUCTION – OF EFFECTING ACTION IN OTHER BODIES AND BITS OF BODIES IN OTHER PLACES.

Advanced Television For The United States: Status and Issues

Organizer:
Gary Demos, DemoGraFX
Panelists:
Alvy Ray Smith, Microsoft
Craig Birkmaier, Pcube Labs
Mark Richer, Advanced Television Systems Committee
Glenn Reitmeier, Sarnoff Labs

The Federal Communications Commission is about to select a standard for Advanced Television for the United States to replace our existing NTSC television system. An advisory commission on advanced television service, "ACATS," appointed by the FCC, is recommending that we deploy a new television system which includes interlace, 59.94 and 60 Hz, and non-square pixel spacing.These parameters are fundamentally incompatible with modern computer graphics displays, which do not use interlace and which operate at display rates exceeding 70 Hz.

Those involved in developing the ACATS do not feel a need to restrict their proposed formats to those that are compatible with computer displays. They further are asserting that the cost and quality loss associated with converting interlaced 60 Hz video to 70+ Hz non-interlaced (progressive scan) pictures is acceptable. However, under their scenario, responsibility to de-interlace and frame rate convert these proposed formats for every computer display would fall upon the computer industry.

Other problematic issues include interlace and 59.94/60Hz, lack of a robust data capacity, non-square pixel spacing in some formats, lack of defined overlay planes, a controversial "16:9" image aspect ratio, overscan issues, and limited colorimetry. It is also proposed that receiving devices decode each of 18 different image formats, spanning a 6:1 range in resolution and data rate.

ACATS proposes that format problems be solved by a later migration strategy away from admittedly obsolete techniques, such as interlaced scanning. However, no scenario is suggested for accomplishing this after deployment of a new television infrastructure, after which some it may be impossible to replace the interlaced portions of the system.

The deployment of a new national television infrastructure is an opportunity to leave behind the obsolete NTSC television system. Since the primary distribution media for computer graphics are film and video, the introduction of new video formats will affect the work of digital production facilities.

Gary Demos

ACATS claims that their proposal is an appropriate compromise, containing some non-interlaced, and some interlaced formats. ACATS is aware that the computer industry needs display rates exceeding 70 Hz for large and bright screens containing computer information. However, they assert that interlace and 59.94 and 60 Hz are needed more than non-interlace 70+ Hz by the existing NTSC broadcast infrastructure and by existing television manufacturers. This panel offers an opportunity to challenge these assertions.

Motion picture film runs at 24 frames per second. The display rate of 72 Hz is naturally suggested since 72 is three times 24. This would satisfy the need of computer displays to exceed 70 Hz. The frame rate of 36 would also form a new natural image motion rate for 72 Hz display.

Image layering represents a powerful alternative to the ACATS proposal. ACATS proposes selection among numerous widely-differing formats. Layering provides a single layered format providing multiple layers of quality in resolution and frame rate within a common data format that would be used by all. The data layer within the ACATS proposal is also not a true layer, since its error rate is not sufficient to carry the multitude of data and code types that will be useful.

ACATS proponents have asserted that 60 Hz and interlace are required because wide screen 72 Hz non-interlace images of a thousand lines cannot fit within the broadcast television channel's capacity of 19 mbits/second. ACATS has further asserted that resolution layering is not feasible. However, it has now been demonstrated that these assumptions are incorrect. Layered images running at 72 frames per second have been demonstrated at 2k x 1k for the highest resolution layer, and 1k x 512 for the base resolution layer, all fitting within 18.5 mbits/second. Movies at 24 frames per second can fit within even less data. The data layer could also be made to be sufficiently error-free to allow carriage of highly desirable multimedia code and data types.

It is therefore unnecessary to continue to debate obsolete image format parameters. The ACATS proposal, which includes interlace, 59.94 and 60 Hz should be rejected, and should be replaced by a layered system operating at 72 Hz. No new interlaced formats should be deployed, since the obsolete interlace technique forms a fundamental barrier of computer display incompatibility. Adoption of the ACATS proposal would most likely prevent the realization of a National Information Infrastructure.

Alvy Ray Smith

What if the Internet, a well-known digital communications channel, had been "standardized" five years ago to carry only video data in a compressed form that subsequently became obsolete due to technological advances. This example is not unlike the standardization of the digital broadcast spectrum that recently was proposed quite seriously. It is simply a digitization of old analog thought, rather than an exploitation of new digital concepts. The largest possible view of broadcast television is as a collection of digital channels that can carry any kind of digital information, not just video. Any standardization that prohibits the full ramifications of this view will appear ridiculous in a very few years.

The Internet is an example of a non-broadcast digital communications medium that was standardized at a very fundamental level only. Atop this minimum protocol standardization, free enterprise is busily constructing numerous useful and exciting businesses. I believe the digital broadcast television spectrum should likewise be minimally standardized, and then allowed to develop with full digital cleverness.

One goal is complete interoperability between broadcast TV and home computers. Digital technology is now sufficiently developed to actually implement the "digital convergence" between the two. There is no reason, other than insufficiently well thought-out infrastructure, for this not to happen now. Key to television and computer interoperability is data sharing, not merely display of television images on a computer screen.

Of the several strictly technical issues concerning the use of the digital spectrum for video data, the most important is this: Interlaced scanning should no longer be supported. If video were being created today, interlace would not be suggested as a new standard. There are far superior ways available to utilize the same bandwidth. We fully expect there to be even better ways in the future. Furthermore, a frame rate of at least 70 Hz should be supported, non-square pixel spacing should be disallowed, an aspect ratio amenable to film should be used, and a true family of resolutions should be defined. All of these issues, however, pale in comparison to the overriding importance of the definition of a digital broadcast data transmission standard.

Craig Birkmaier

A properly conceived digital television system for local, regional, national, and international distribution of digital media will provide a solid foundation for the distribution of all forms of digital media.

The digital television system proposed by the Grand Alliance and the Advanced Television Systems Committee (ATSC) was conceived as a higher resolution "clone" of our existing television system. It carries significant excess baggage for compatibility with existing broadcast practices. This shortsighted approach will limit the opportunity for broadcasters to compete with every other infrastructure provider and programming service.

Nearly a year ago, I submitted the following observations to the ATSC.

The Challenge

1. To develop enabling standards for a digital television system interoperable with all digital communications infrastructures, backward compatibility with existing analog and digital video program archives, and a migration strategy which allows digital television to be delivered using existing NTSC and ITU-Rec-601 acquisition and receiver infrastructures.

2. To stimulate a rapid migration to artifact-free high-resolution video acquisition and display systems, and rapid voluntary replacement of analog NTSC receivers.

The Opportunity

1. To influence and manage the evolution of digital communications systems.
2. To provide a framework within which all effected industries and stakeholders can participate in rapidly developing digital communication system standards and extending them in the future.

3. To ensure that these standards be developed by industry-led initiatives, rather than by government-imposed standards.

4. To ensure the ability to interoperate and rapidly evolve with underlying technology.

The Solution

1. Develop enabling standards for digital television based on a layered, open architecture, which will provide artifact free imagery at multiple quality of service (QOS) levels, to interoperable information appliances.

2. Establish minimum and maximum performance limits for each QOS level rather than rigid point standards.

3. Establish a modular framework.

4. Allow the marketplace to drive the evolution process.

5. The process of maintaining and extending DTV standards and recommended practices should rest with national and international standards organizations.

Mark Richer

The ATSC Digital Television Standard is the result of an eight year long open process. Hundreds of people contributed thousands of hours of effort to create a digital television standard for the United States. The result of this process is a system that utilizes a layered architecture and is compliant with the MPEG-2 international standard for video compression and transport. The ATSC standard provides a flexible system that offers the user a variety of options. The system includes multiple options for video input and compression. The two HDTV formats (1920 x 1080 and 1280 x 720) result in square pixels. The system supports use of both progressive and interlaced scan.

The issue of interoperability is one that has been central in the choice of ATV system parameters. The goal was to provide interoperability with a variety of media including existing NTSC program material and consumer receivers, film, existing HDTV production formats, and computers. There is no consensus on a single approach to achieve interoperability across all media. However, the inherent flexibility of the technology provides options to both service providers and consumers:

- The choice of progressive or interlace scan source material will be made by the program producer.

- The choice of progressive or interlace for transmission will be made by the program service provider.

- The choice of progressive or interlace scan display is an independent choice that will be made by the consumer.

The ATSC digital television standard is the only existing standard in the world that offers the option of progressive scan and square pixels for both standard definition and high definition television. On the other hand, the DBS and cable industries are in the midst of rapidly deploying digital systems that do not incorporate progressive scan and square pixels. For this reason, the ATSC Digital Television Standard should be adopted immediately.

Glenn Reitmeier

The adoption of the Advanced Television Systems Committee's Digital Television Standard and the recommendation of the Advisory Committee on Advanced Television Service that the FCC approve it as a national standard for terrestrial HDTV broadcasting are landmark developments in the convergence of computing and television.

The ATSC Advanced Television (ATV) standard is the most flexible, most computer friendly, most broadly interoperable television system ever developed. It provides powerful interoperability by using:

- A layered digital system architecture that conforms to international data communications models

- Header/descriptors that allow a flexible system today and extensibility for future improvements

- Multiple video formats and frame rates with a heavy emphasis on progressive scan and square pixel formats that facilitate easy computer interoperability

- MPEG-2 video compression that conforms to draft international standards, and that will likely form the basis for most computer multimedia use of motion video

- MPEG-2 transport (packet) format that meets the needs of broadcasting while being designed to be easily interoperable with ATM networks.

In developing the technical basis for the ATSC standard, the Grand Alliance carefully balanced diverse and often conflicting needs from film and television post-production (including computer generated images), broadcasting, cable television, consumer electronics, computing and telecommunications industries. Of course, interoperability must be balanced against other design goals such as HDTV picture quality, restricted-power simulcasting and low cost. Because no rigid single approach could simultaneously meed such a broad spectrum of needs, the result is a standard that is flexible and inclusive.

The ATV standard recommended to the FCC represents the consensus of over 100 companies that participated in the open ACATS process over an eight-year period. Delay in idealistic pursuit of perfection by an interest group can only result in the destruction of consensus and a giant step backwards for television and computer interoperability. After huge investments, failure to promptly commercialize ATV technology will result in the only option being a European or Japanese system - one that has ONLY interlaced scanning and non-square pixels.

The Soul of the Machine: The Search for Spirituality in Cyberspace

Organizers:
Celia Pearce
Erik Davis, Author/Journalist
Panelists:
Mark Pesce, VRML Guru/Author
Paul Godwin, Composer/Musician
Char Davies, Artist
Rita Addison, Artist

"If the work of the city is the remaking or translating of man into a more suitable form than his nomadic ancestors achieved, then might not our current translation of our entire lives into the spiritual form of information seem to make of the entire globe, and of the human family, a single consciousness?" – Marshall McLuhan, Understanding Media

In 1964, Marshall McLuhan first identified the rise of the "information age" and introduced the concept of "The Global Village," an electronic universe of information, ideas and images that could be shared by all. Although his ideas were precipitated by television, the telephone, and the embryonic computer, McLuhan anticipated that all of this would grow together into a new form of collective consciousness.

Today, McLuhan's prophesy is being realized beyond even his wildest imaginings. The astronomical rise of the Internet as a mass medium, continuing advances in immersive virtual reality, and the dramatic shift of media from analog to digital are all leading us to a new level of consciousness, understanding and connection. From Virtual Reality, to electronic music, to the Internet, "The Soul in the Machine: The Search for Spirituality in Cyberspace," brings together a group of esteemed artists, producers, inventors, and authors who are actively investigating, exploring and creating spiritual experiences in the digisphere.

Celia Pearce

Perspective

Celia Pearce's work as both a producer and writer/lecturer has been dedicated to creating and supporting alternatives to the highly visceral content which has dominated commercial interactive multimedia. She is very concerned with the psychological, sociological, and cultural implications of interactive media, and as such has written, taught, and lectured on such topics and interactive art, nonlinear storytelling, alternative VR, and fundamentals of game structure. Her concerns about the human side of technological content led to the idea of proposing a panel on the topic of spirituality in cyberspace. As panel organizer, Celia's emphasis will be to provide an irreverent, entertaining and informed philosophical overview of the subject matter.

Position

Quoting from Marshall McLuhan, Aldus Huxley, and others, I want to introduce the topic in a lively way. My vision of the panel is that it will be more about questions than answers, more about waking people up to issues than giving them information. I want to engage people and challenge them to address issues which might otherwise be taboo. To many, any discussion of spirituality seems antithetical to the computer. But nothing could be further from the truth. As people begin to use cyberspace as a gathering place on a mass level, the result is everything from on-line romance to terrorism. The inevitable "digitization of everything" has profound implications on a spiritual level. Aldus Huxley defines "The Perennial Philosophy" as the divine unity of all things. By converting all media into a single form, we have created a new paradigm for such unity. It is also important to me that the panel not limit itself to pundits pontificating on the possibilities, but that it represent creative individuals who are making real work that addresses some of these issues. This, combined with my own philosophical overview and Erik Davis' closing historical and cultural views, will allow us to deal with this issues at a variety of levels of resolution.

Mark Pesce

Perspective

The development of VRML, the authoring language for creating 3D environments on the Internet, was one of the lead stories in computer technology of 1995. Mark Pesce's contribution to making on-line cyberspace a reality at the exact moment when the Internet has become a mass medium is destined to revolutionize the world. This is clearly Mark's intention. Mark, who was featured on the cover of Wired magazine for its "Techno-Pagans" issue, makes no bones about his commitment to the spiritual applications of computer technology. He will provide his unique perspective on the transcendent qualities of cyberspace as a means to self-awareness through collective consciousness.

Position

Cyberspace is the realm where communication occurs, at the boundary between self and other. In a world which is entirely self-created with the single exception of this boundary between the self and the other, the other assumes the role of the agent of divine novelty, preserving us from the boredom of our own reflection, and acting as the agent of initiation, presenting us with that which removes us from ourselves and places us into a new understanding. Reading from sections of my soon-to-be published Self/Sacred: Body and Being in Cyberspace, I will discuss the nature of the other, the divine, and the essence of communication as the encounter with the sacred self.

Paul Godwin

Perspective

As a composer and musician, Paul has a great deal of experience in musical collaboration, both in composition and performance. His interest in improvisation has led him to create a number of collaborate virtual music spaces that allow people to participate in virtual "jam" sessions. Paul will discuss the process of simulating live jams in cyberspace, and the idea of creating a collective consciousness through real-time, remote collaboration.

Position

I believe that Cyberspace is a vessel for the transmission of human consciousness. The species is literally investing itself into the digital noosphere. The World Wide Web parallels the "real world" in many ways through commerce, education, entertainment, information, and social interaction. But where does the spiritual aspect of human life fall in the entire spectrum of digital activity? How do we feel each other's presence in a consensual, digital world? How do we harness the psychic biological energy fields that resonate in a "brainstorming" or "jam" session?

To address these questions, I will present some of my work in this area, including:

- The Worldsong Project, created in collaboration with Mark Pesce and Dr. Bill Martens, is a distributed network project using VRML to navigate a stratified matrix of the world's audio material. Presented at The Doors of Perception, Amsterdam.

- Ritual Ground Zero, YORB-TV, (Time-Warner Cable TV, NYC) developed with interactive designer Amee Evans, is a live "jamspace" on Interactive Television is controllable by four separate callers, who trigger Gamelan music samples using their telephone's touch-tone buttons. The "physical" jamspace was rendered using SGI Alias and is in full operation each Thursday night on NYC Cable Television.

- SOLACE, or Sacred On-Line Active Communal Environment, is a generic term for a type of space that can be shared spiritually on the Net. One example is an on-line Zendo or vocal meditation space. Here, participants sing or tone into microphones on remote workstations; they hear the other members of their group singing along; as their voices reach unison, the visual interface reflects that unity (a 1-5 point visual mandala generator is employed) and a space for attunement is created.

Char Davies

Perspective

Char Davies' seminal work OSMOSE has been described as a digital meditation space. In contrast with the other projects, all of which emphasize communal consciousness in remote or shared physical spaces, Char's work is based on full-body solitary immersion. OSMOSE is a place for quiet self-discovery and reflection. The visual aesthetic and sounds of OSMOSE are evocative and ambiguous: the user interface is based on intuitive biofeedback of breathing and balance. Together these tend to create a euphoric sense of being unbounded, while simultaneously grounding the experience in the body-core. Quite often, immersion in OSMOSE appears to induce a shift of awareness in participants, in which conceptual boundaries between inner/outer, self/world dissolve, and desire for control and speed is replaced by a serene and contemplative free-fall. Drawing on insights gained from her experience with OSMOSE, Char will discuss the potential of immersive virtual space as a medium for exploring the perception of consciousness.

Position

My work in cyberspace is focused on immersive virtual space – as a spatial-temporal arena for exploring "being-in-the-world." I am somewhat wary of the trend towards collectivity and mind in cyberspace: such a realm, in which the subjective body is denied, may in fact prove to be the epitome of Cartesian desire, symptomatic of an almost pathological denial of our mortality and our materiality, seducing us to turn away even further from the earthly environment in which we, as incarnate beings, are embedded.

My goal is to use the technology to suggest an alternative, re-affirming the role of the body in cyberspace, approaching this space as a medium for stripping away habitual assumptions and re-configuring how we experience ourselves as embodied consciousness enveloped by the world. Forty years ago, the philosopher Gaston Bachelard wrote in ‹La Poetique de l'espace› "...by changing space, by leaving the space of one's usual sensibilities, one enters into communication with a space that is psychically innovating. For we do not change place, we change our Nature."

OSMOSE is such a space.

Rita Addison

Perspective

Rita Addison's work is profound on several levels. In her landmark work "DETOUR: Brain Deconstruction Ahead," Rita created an immersive experience simulating the perceptual damage that she underwent as a result of her 1992 automobile accident. This type of experience cannot be effectively expressed in any other medium than immersive Virtual Reality. The emotional impact of this is immense; one can literally live in another's mind and see the world from their perspective. Unlike most VR, which emphasizes imagination and fantasy, Rita's work is concerned with simulating "real" shifts in perception as a mode of creative expression. Though highly personal, Rita's work is also collaborative in nature, putting people together in a shared space to experience these perceptual shifts as a group. "Synesthesia" has the feeling of an audio-visual jam session in which participants combined biofeedback triggers movement in the environment.

Rita's work is also a testimony to her courage in taking a tragic experience and transforming it into an expression of understanding and enlightenment to be shared with others. As such, her personal journey is the ultimate expression of the resilience of the human spirit.

Position: Authoring Your Own Virtual Environment Journey

I'm keenly interested in discovering new interfaces that will enable us all to more freely create and explore virtual environments. One of the paths I'm exploring is the potential for biosignals to function as not only a "joystick," i.e., as a control, but also as a bridge over which emerging, real-time neurophysiological data can travel to a computer which serves much as a launching pad and returns the data to the observer in a different way than which it was first perceived. I certainly do not have any answers. Rather, I will share what I've learned so far on my exploration with bio-sensing interfaces, including my recent experience producing and showing "Synesthesia" at SuperComputing '95.

Erik Davis

Perspective

Erik Davis is an author and journalist who has devoted his work to the study of digital culture. He has emerged as one of the leaders in discussions of techno-spirituality and has written on this topic for both the technological and theological communities. Erik's background and knowledge of religious traditions and his diligent research into history and trends in digital culture bring a broad scholarly perspective to the subject matter. Erik's presentation will also include a glimpse into the darker side of cyberspace. Just as the opening statement provides an overview to set the stage for work-specific presentations, Erik's closing remarks will bring the topic back into the larger perspective, touching on the past, present, and future of techno-spirituality.

Position

In my brief concluding talk, I will put the other panelists' discussions about spirituality in cyberspace into a larger cultural context, focusing in particular on the role of the religious or spiritual imagination in navigating and responding to the dizzying possibilities and dangers of the telecommunications revolution. I will discuss a few concrete examples of the crossover of spirituality and high technology, and explore what these visions tell us about the cultural and cognitive potentials of computers in general, and the Internet in particular. But while I am encouraged by the magical and utopian strains of thought that have accompanied the massive spread of digital technology into our lives, I also believe we have as much to gain by looking at the dark and paranoid mythologies that have also grown up around the new machines. In our faith in virtual light, we believe our monitors to be windows onto a new world, but we should also consider that we are still seeing through a glass, darkly.

Issues in Networking for Entertainment, Graphics, and Data

Organizer:
Marke Clinger, FORE Systems, Inc.
Panelists:
Robert Amen, Cinesite, Inc.
Ray Feeny, RFX, Inc.
Chuck Garsha, Paramount Studios
Jim McCabe, Full Spectrum Networks
Mark Valenti, Sextant Group

This panel will not only discuss the state-of-the-art in networking graphics, video, audio, voice, and data, but will use the latest technologies to create a virtual panel. An audience at MIT in Boston, MA will be linked via a country wide Asynchronous Transfer Mode (ATM) network to the New Orleans Convention Center to participate "virtually" in this panel. Two way video and graphics will be transported over the ATM network to allow for full participation by the remote audience. That same ATM network will extend to Paramount Studios in Los Angeles, CA to allow a panelist to participate "virtually." This panelist will deliver his presentation from LA using an integrated platform to transport high quality graphics over the same infrastructure as the two-way full motion video.

During the panel the video-to-ATM equipment will be changed, providing the audience and panelists an opportunity to experience the different technologies.

The panelists are from different parts of the industry, but all are using advanced networking techniques and technologies to build the networks that transport multimedia. In addition to delivery of traditional data sets, these networks are built to deliver video, audio, and massive graphics files in real time. One of the networks that will be described was built to allow several auditoriums full of students to observe brain surgery and interact with the surgeon during the surgery. It now delivers traditional data and voice services too. Another network is changing the way a user will look at a network connection. When a studio space is rented to do filming, the production company will rent a network connection providing them connectivity and software services they need while on-site. The computers used can either be rented along with the network, or the customers can bring their own.

The latest video-to-ATM devices will be installed at the three locations. Equipment from several different vendors will be used to give the participants an idea of the quality and capabilities of different types of products. All equipment will support 30 frames per second video transported over ATM. Some of the equipment will also support integrated graphics and video support.

Panelists will present one of their projects that combines state-of-the-art networking with one or more of the following technologies:

- Computer Graphics
- Video
- Audio
- Voice (as in telephony)

The presentations will consist of an overview of the business drivers behind the project, the technical details, and the issues that arose during or after the implementation.

At SIGGRAPH 95, Eastern Carolina University used GraphicsNet 95's country wide ATM network to deliver two video streams and multiple data channels from their university to the LA Convention Center. Using the high quality video link, conference attendees were able to consult with doctors and specialists in North Carolina on health issues. A nurse at the convention center used stethoscopes and thermometers that were attached to the data network so that the remote doctor could view the results. With the high quality video connection and the data flow, a doctor could diagnose a patent remotely; however, these doctors are not licensed in California, therefore they could only offer advice. This is a good example of where technology has surpassed our laws that govern the way society interacts.

What other issues do people deploying advanced networking technologies run into? In local area networking, what are the concerns of the networking specialist? How well are non-technology savvy users adapting to the technology? Are the goals behind the deployment of the technology being realized? What type of functionality is missing? How easy is it to integrate graphics, voice, video, etc. into a network? What issues arose when doing this integration?

In local area networking bandwidth is considered free. The cost to run a fiber optic cable through the building is a relatively cheap one-time charge, so users tend to waste bandwidth. In the wide area network, bandwidth must be purchased, and it is very expensive. New technologies on the market are bringing down the cost to the service providers of this bandwidth. Is this bringing a reduction in the price to the user? What are the issues that need to be considered when connecting to a phone company? What technologies have the panelists employed? Which were successful? What problems did they run into with the different technologies?

During the course of the panelist presentations and the follow-on interactive discussion these questions and issues will be explored.

Graphics PCs will put Workstation Graphics in the Smithsonian

Organizer:
Sam Uselton, MRJ, Inc.
Panelists:
Michael Cox, S3, Inc.
Michael Deering, Sun Microsystems
Jay Torborg, Microsoft
Kurt Akeley, Silicon Graphics

Graphics accelerators for Personal Computers are becoming more powerful and cheaper very rapidly. The panelists will argue whether this development spells the end of graphics workstations as we have known them. Calligraphic displays were supplanted by raster frame buffers; workstations with internal graphics replaced minicomputers with attached frame buffers. Has the next transition arrived? What are the implications? Should we fight the tide or hail the conquerors? Are there other options?

Note: The esteemed panelists have been promised immunity from prosecution and/or persecution based on any statements, positions, posing, or posturing that may occur in the course of this debate, to free them from any concerns of propriety, modesty, self-incrimination, and image maintenance. Their employers have been promised plausible deniability.

First affirmative: Michael Cox

PC graphics will drive workstations (WS) into Chapter 11. At the top of the market pyramid are the few users who need astronomical performance at astronomical prices. At the bottom are the PC masses. PCs will ultimately take the whole pyramid because of unyielding forces: business model, technical requirements, and volume.

1. The WS business model makes workstation graphics conservative by necessity. The PC business model requires innovation. PC graphics will get better and faster, FASTER than WS graphics. WS advances are limited by silicon advances (more gates, more possible). WS customers and ISVs are conservative. Legacy applications drive WS graphics. WS product cycles are 2.5 years. SW and HW development are tightly coupled. Innovation is THE source of value-added in PC graphics; advances will come both with silicon and with changes in the fundamental algorithms and HW/SW partitioning. There are no legacy applications, and interfaces on PCs are fluid anyway. PC product cycles are 1 year. SW and HW development are independent.

2. Technical requirements in the PC market are richer, and will drive solutions to be better and faster. PC graphics are today "playback" graphics, requiring guaranteed real-time rates; WS are "authoring," requiring only interactive rates. As PCs match WS quality, frame rates will be higher. Playback requires much more integrated MEDIA support than authoring. New, richer applications will happen first on PCs. Price insensitivity has driven WS graphics down an evolutionary dead-end (e.g. 2 Gbytes of redundant texture memory, with no solution for the texture download bottleneck); PC price sensitivity will drive superior technical solutions (e.g. UMA instead).

3. More PC volume means more opportunity, more start-ups, more projects, more people, more innovation, greater investment in technology development, better technology. Expect a "brain drain" (who's at Microsoft?). More PC volume also means lower part cost. Even with the same algorithms, PCs win.

New technologies develop in three phases: games, retrofit, innovation. First, toys. Second, the new technology replaces the old. Third, new applications are invented. PCs obviously will dominate the toys. Over time PCs will replace WSs. Where will new applications be developed? First (and perhaps only) on PCs, because of market opportunity, richer media platform, and because that's where most people will be working!

WSs will keep the top of the pyramid for a while. Once, "big iron" ruled. As the smaller, more numerous, more nimble workstations evolved, "big iron" disappeared. Sure, there are today still die-hard applications that need "big iron." Cray, CDC, and Thinking Machines are still in business, but would you want to be one of these companies?

First negative: Michael Deering

3D graphics hardware for PCs have finally found their killer app: home games. Such entertainment cards have become successful by no longer trying to compete with workstation 3D graphics hardware for industrial applications. In multi-billion dollar aerospace and automotive design efforts, time to market is more important than cutting a few percent off the overall design budget. Modern 3D graphics workstations are just that: well integrated computing and rendering engines designed from scratch as a single system, both hardware and software. Such systems now, and for the foreseeable future, deliver system graphical throughput well above anything available on commodity PC platforms. 3D graphics workstations also pay attention to quality: high resolution, "crack" free surface rendering, stable numeric algorithms, high quality anti-aliased lines, and adherence to standards also differentiate most 3D workstations from most 3D PC graphics. Indeed, the most successful PC vendors are busily dumping their half-hearted attempts to achieve such "workstation" quality in an effort to shave a little cost off to be more price competitive in the cutthroat 3D home game market, where such features are not yet needed.

Second affirmative: Jay Torborg

Personal computers have rapidly become a ubiquitous tool for a broad range of applications ranging from games to financial modeling to video servers to computer aided design. Applications that were previously the domain of expensive specialty computer systems are migrating to the PC every day. The significant investment this ubiquity affords has allowed the PC to rapidly close the gap in performance and provide dramatic advantages in price-performance, relative to workstations and other specialized systems.

One significant area near and dear to our hearts in which the PC has yet to catch up is 3D graphics – at least as far as functionality and performance are concerned. There are actually more 3D applications (measured in units) running on PCs now than on the entire installed base of workstations; most of these happen to be games. But the PC is catching up quickly. This significant market is supporting significant investment in this area. In the next few years, tens of millions of HW 3D graphics accelerators will be sold for the PC, many of them far outstripping the 3D performance of a typical workstation today.

The PC has several key advantages over workstations that will allow it to dominate in this area. The CAD market, which has driven the 3D workstation architectures we know today, has very different 3D graphics requirements than the immersive animate environments I expect will dominate PC applications. Since the PC does not have the huge 3D graphics legacy carried by the workstation, we can afford to explore new architectural approaches that leverage current technology to create 3D systems that deliver significant price performance advantages for interactive animate environments. The huge volume potential in the PC market allows aggressive use of advanced semiconductor processes, an alternative that is not economically feasible for low-volume workstations. And the huge base of application developers will insure the availability of compelling content.

These key advantages, which are unique to the PC platform, will allow the PC to rapidly become the 3D graphics platform of choice.

Second negative: Kurt Akeley

3D graphics are increasingly central to interactive computing. Soon all interactive systems will include hardware support for 3D graphics, and will be optimized for interactive 3D rendering. When all PCs and workstations support 3D graphics, it will be true that most graphics applications are PC based, and that PCs command most of the market share for 3D graphics. That this will be true, however, no more implies that PCs will be the 3D graphics platform of choice than the current situation, in which PCs dominate the general-purpose computation market, implies that PCs are the platform of choice for computing. There will always be demand for systems that are faster and more capable than commodity machines, and this market demand will continue to be met by computer vendors. PC graphics will flourish, and workstation graphics will continue to lead the way.

Cognition, Perception and Experience in the Virtual Environment: Do You See What I See?

Organizer:
Linda Jacobson, Silicon Graphics, Inc.
Panelists:
Charlotte Davies, SoftImage
Brenda Laurel, Interval Research
Dr. Creve Maples, Muse Technologies
Mark D. Pesce, Big Book
Dr. Mark Schlager, SRI International
Rob Tow, Interval Research

Description

Virtual reality is real. "We will see high-resolution, low-lag systems doing serious applications within three years," predicted Frederick Brooks, Jr. at SIGGRAPH 94. And indeed we have.

We now possess the algorithms, architecture and hardware. We know the techniques: we understand how to define geometries and assign object behaviors, and we map textures, incorporate collision detection and implement level-of-detail switching. We adopt psychological depth cues from the field of 3D design, implementing linear perspective, motion parallax and occlusion to impart the illusion of three-dimensional space. In giving virtual objects their attributes, we consider the participant's relationship to those objects.

Nonetheless, as various SIGGRAPH 95 panelists pointed out, "Little is understood about how to usefully interact in three dimensions in ways that really help perform tasks" and "There has been a surprising lack of real-world applications in the virtual world...We are unfamiliar with this new medium, unable to utilize its power and to compensate for its limitations."

That is because the primary difficulties facing application developers are not technological, but conceptual.We know the language but we don't know the grammar. We haven't defined the stylistic guidelines. We know how to apply real-time, immersive, interactive techniques using virtual reality technologies, but we don't take a uniform approach to applying our knowledge of how these inputs affect us, and as a result have not developed a consistent UI.

Through virtual reality, we move beyond cognitive computing into the realm of experiential computing. To build useful applications, we must understand how and why experiential computing is fundamentally different from cognitive computing, and how it lets us tap into human capabilities in a way no interface and no form of computer graphics has done before.

This is especially important when we consider that today's successful commercial virtual reality applications are used for training in cognitive tasks and design of products we use everyday. Previous SIGGRAPH panels wondered how to work effectively within immersive environments and explored the state of aesthetics in the virtual environment. If we want to discover how to work effectively and implement aesthetics within immersive environments, we must discover how we learn in those environments and establish a set of guidelines outlining our discoveries. We must bring a greater degree of involvement of cognitive psychology and human-perception experts into the mix of those developing VR technologies and applications.To move into experiential computing, we must be able to communicate how and where humans operate cognitively, perceptually, and experientially. We must create the cyberspatial equivalent of Strunk & White's Elements of Style.

Some issues to be aired during this panel include: how humans perceive information visually, auditorially and proprioceptively; how the mind works when seeking known or unknown information; imagery and associative memory techniques and how they relate to virtual environments; perceptual and cognitive constancy when updating displays.

This panel aims to launch discussion in the SIGGRAPH community of how we see in cyberspace...and to integrate into our understanding of virtual reality's potential these facts registered by Diane Ackerman in her Natural History of the Senses: "The body edits and prunes experience before sending it to the brain for contemplation or action. Not every vagary of sunlight registers on the retina. Not everything we feel is felt powerfully enough to send a message to the brain...[m]uch is lost in translation, or is censored, and in any case our nerves don't fire all at once. Some of them remain silent, while others respond.

> "Our senses also crave novelty. Any change alerts them, and they send a signal to the brain. If there's no change, no novelty, they doze and register little or nothing....A constant state—even of excitement—in time becomes tedious, fades into the background, because our senses have evolved to report changes, what's new, something startling that has to be appraised, a morsel to eat, a sudden danger... The body's quest isn't for truth, it's for survival!"

Panel Format

This is an "issue" panel, in which each panelist will provide a brief statement describing his or her perspective of cognition/perception/experience relative to virtual reality, followed by a lively discussion in which it is expected that the panelists will in some cases disagree with each other, and in others, elaborate upon each other's statements.

It is the goal of the panel organizer to provide a summation of the points made through the Silicon Graphics Web site at `http://www.sgi.com/`.

Charlotte Davies

Conventional design for virtual reality tends to reflect our cultural world-view, resulting in virtual environments filled with static, solid, hard-edged objects in empty space. Similarly, most user interaction tends to be based on metaphors for manipulating machines. Such approaches, ignoring how we subjectively experience being-in-the-world, limit the expressive potential of the medium. There are, however, alternatives.

OSMOSE, the immersive virtual environment that I created with my team at Softimage last year, is an example: photo-realism, linear perspective and Cartesian notions of space have been abandoned for an aesthetic based on transparency, tonal subtlety and spatial ambiguity, for the goal is to evoke multiple meaningful associations rather than merely illustrate. The sound in OSMOSE also seeks to achieve this, further emotionally involving the participant within the space. Directly manipulative interface methods, such as joystick or glove, have been replaced by bodily processes of breathing and balance. Whereas the former methods tend to reduce participation to disembodied eye and controlling hand, these far more intuitive techniques ground the immersive experience in the participant's own body, creating a calming and centering effect and leading to heightened awareness and receptivity.

Several thousand people have been immersed in OSMOSE in the past year. Their responses have confirmed the author's belief that immersive virtual space, when approached with a certain sensibility, has intriguing potential as an educational medium.

Brenda Laurel

Style is a very sticky wicket. The purpose that a work is intended to serve, its form or genre, the materials it encompasses, and the maker's skills, beliefs, and values all influence style strongly. Although Aristotle did not discuss style directly in the Poetics, some twentieth-century structuralists would say that style is the point of articulation between the conceptual elements of a form and the sensible aspects of its unfolding. This provides a neat analytical springboard for examining the root assumptions about the powers of the medium and its fundamental forms. From there we should be able to see ideas embedded in the medium that illuminate the relationships among senses, emotions, thought and reason, and action in virtual environments. These relationships, variously worked out, are the elements of style.

Dr. Creve Maples

Richard Hamming said, "The purpose of computing is insight, not numbers." Today, as the Information Age moves forward, computers touch all aspects of our lives. Far from achieving "insight," however, there is often a feeling that we are slowly sinking under the enormous volumes of data. Helping people to explore, question, and understand complex information is an important criterion for future computational environments. Highly interactive human-computer environments can allow practical solutions to some problems far more rapidly than either human or computer operating independently. User interaction with synthetic, immersive environments presents an exciting and relatively uncharted area.

The human mind is capable of absorbing and processing large volumes of information. Most of this processing, however, occurs at a precognitive level, the results of which serve to alert the cognitive mind to areas of potential interest. Toward that end, and in concert with the idea of a humanistically organized software environment, five areas of human-computer interaction have been defined and investigated: Exploration, Navigation, Presentation, Interaction, and Examination. These five areas serve to define a functional arena for interactive environments and provide the foundation for device and model independent tools.

Mark D. Pesce

We're all taught how to read and write – how many of us are taught to sculpt, or to design a building? Although we all experience the immediacy of space, we're not trained in the canons of architecture. How then, can we expect to develop any interface of immediacy, when we're functionally ignorant of the processes which underlie this experience?

The ideal – an interface which disappears into a "virtual" reality – has seen its realization in only a few works, such as PLACEHOLDER (by Brenda Laurel, Rachel Strickland and Rob Tow) and OSMOSE (by Char Davies), in part because researchers are unable to leave their own thought processes behind and design transparently. In looking to the real, we find a design guide for the virtual; in looking inside ourselves, we find ontology as interface, being as doing.

Dr. Mark Schlager

Virtual environment technology allows developers great freedom in designing spaces, objects, and systems and the perceptual mechanisms through which users interact with them and each other. Steps can be taken to ensure that resulting designs support cognitive aspects of learning activities. Developing virtual environments that support learning requires an understanding of the relationships between the cognitive capacities of the learner, the environment and activities being modeled, and the technical affordances of VR that support information encoding, development of knowledge structures, and performance. For example, input modality and display perspective (e.g., position, ground, and field of view) can be used to enhance information encoding and retrieval. The model of the world represented by the VR designer can support the formation or enhancement of the user's own mental representation by simplifying a complex system and revealing patterns that are difficult to discern. My hope is that the VR research and VR development communities can begin to establish a common language for discussing these issues and jointly formulate a set of design guidelines.

Rob Tow

Twelve percent of women are heterozygous for anomalous color vision, and are tetrachromatic – they see subtle colors that men never will, because men have only one X chromosome, and can at best be trichromatic. People who grow up in Western architectures, with sharp right angles and many vertical and horizontal edges, have more cortical detectors for vertical and horizontal lines than do people who grow up in societies which are uncarpentered and agrarian; they see media such as halftoned pictures with forty-five degree angled screens subtly differently. Kamala and Amala, the famous "wolf-girls" of Bengal, never learned language after they were found in the wild and taken into an English family.

We are all different; from our various genetics, and from the differing interactions of our growing bodies with the external world, both physical and social. Our brains and our bodies gain much of their structure from interacting with the world in the realm of the senses; the structure of the external world is reflected within our own structure – and just as cats raised in an environment with no vertical components don't build cortical detectors for vertical shapes, we have not built cognitive structures for the worlds in which our children will develop – VR will change the very nature of the human mind and soul as it changes the sensory and social worlds in which we live and act. Our children will grow up immersed in this Novum Organum, and we will stand at the edge of the flow that separates them from us, unable to follow them because we literally will not see what they see. Unlike Moses' promised land, this New Atlantis will be of our own making, created as we exteriorize our minds and culture into Turing complete agencies.

Virtual Reality and Mental Disorders

Organizer:
Dorothy Strickland
Panelists:
Larry F. Hodges
Suzanne Weghorst
Nat Durlach

This panel discusses the use of virtual reality and augmented reality treatment for individuals with a variety of mental disorders, including phobias, autism, and Parkinson's Disease. Panelists will describe their actual case studies and the insights and concerns they discovered in their research. The psychologists and computer scientists on the panel will address the ethical, psychological, and social questions. as well as the technical issues which arise from such applications. They will discuss ideas and suggestions for future directions in using virtual reality with mental disorders, and describe what is needed from the graphics community to refine and extend this work.

Despite enthusiasm from the press and media, the virtual reality worlds experienced in a headset are generally disappointing. There are a great many things we can not do well in VR. Visually, virtual environments are still cartoonish and lacking in realism. The combination of current tracker technology and the graphics pipeline guarantee a lag between head movement and response of the visual image. The spaces we can track are small, and tracker accuracy is poor. Haptic cues in virtual environments are usually nonexistent or very limited. As a result, examples of VR applications that offer sufficient value beyond that available from less exotic technologies are still rare.

To create successful applications with today's VR technology, we must begin by asking: what are we good at? Despite all the obvious technical limitations, psychological studies are showing that VR provides a convincing illusion of actually inhabiting a computer-generated space. VR creates and controls sensory stimulation in formerly unattainable ways. Augmented reality allows an overlay of a "real" world with an imaginary world. Both VR and augmented reality can add, delete, or emphasize details to better help mental patients perform basic functions. These unique features can provide the mental patient with specialized, safer treatment techniques for problems that previously were expensive or impossible to treat in traditional training and therapy.

Larry F. Hodges

Virtual reality offers a new human-computer interaction paradigm in which users no longer are simply external observers of images on a computer screen, but are active participants within a computer-generated three-dimensional virtual world. Exposure therapy involves exposing the subject to anxiety-producing stimuli while allowing the anxiety to attenuate. These stimuli are traditionally generated through a variety of modalities including imaginal (subject generates stimulus via imagination) and in vivo (subject is exposed to real situations). Virtual Reality Exposure (VRE) Therapy involves exposing the patient to a virtual environment containing the feared stimulus in place of taking the patient into a real environment or having the patient imagine the stimulus. In a controlled study, VRE Therapy has been shown to be very effective in reducing acrophobic patient anxiety and avoidance of heights. VRE has also been shown in case studies to be successful in treating fear of flying.

VRE Therapy has several advantages, as compared to more traditional exposure modalities. Many stimuli for exposure are difficult to arrange or control, and when exposure is conducted outside of the therapist's office, it becomes more expensive in terms of time and money. The ability to conduct exposures of virtual airplanes for flying phobics or virtual highways for driving phobics, for example, without leaving the therapist's office, would make better treatment available to more sufferers at a lower cost.

In addition to cost reduction, VRE Therapy offers innovative treatment alternatives for patients. Like in vivo therapy, VRE Therapy can provide stimuli for patients who can not imagine well. Unlike therapist-assisted in vivo techniques VRE Therapy will be performed within the confines of a room, thus avoiding public embarrassment and violation of patient confidentiality. Virtual environments have the added advantage of giving the therapist greater control over multiple stimulus parameters, as well as the ability to isolate the particular parameters that are most essential in generating the phobic response. VRE Therapy could also be used as an intermediate step in preparing patients for maintenance therapy involving self-directed in vivo exposure.

Virtual reality exposure therapy is also appropriate for networked delivery of clinical psychology and psychiatry services to remote locations. Since the patient is receiving therapy within a virtual environment, the clinician conducting the therapy session could be present physically or participate via computer networks from a remote location.

Dorothy Strickland

Another potential application for VR is in treating autism. Autism is a pervasive developmental disorder characterized by severe impairment in social, communicative, cognitive, and behavioral functioning. Approximately half of individuals with autism never gain useful communicative speech. Serious difficulties exist with generalization. For example, if an individual learns to identify a wooden chair in one room, the word chair may be limited to that example in that identical setting. Because normal input can be overpowering, individuals with autism may not respond to real environments.

VR affords control of the environment in ways previously unattainable. Regulation of visual and auditory stimulation allows forced attention and focused directions. Input stimuli can be reduced to an individually acceptable level. Distortions in size and character of the components of reality allow matches to the user's expectations or abilities. Distracting visual complexity, sounds, and touch can be removed and introduced in a slow, regulated manner. Minimal modifications across similar scenes may allow generalization to another scene if differences are reduced until the similarities are recognizable. The measurement of user motion response to the environment permits dynamic scene modification and learning emphasis based on response, rather than speech. Two case studies with non-high functioning children with autism indicated that they could be taught the beginning steps necessary to learn how to independently cross a virtual street, an example of using VR to provide a less hazardous and more forgiving environment for developing skills associated with activities of daily living.

VR with autism might provide safe, customized training for situations which would be difficult, if not impossible, to learn from real world exposure. The technology needs are different from general graphic applications. High-speed rendering of complex scene generation is not required. Only limited color ranges recognized by the user are needed. Sound was removed in our study, because the children with autism found processing of vision alone preferable. Larger field of view may be necessary to provide the sense of immersion. Since patients may not be able to indicate if a problem exists in the helmet, judging of safety factors becomes more critical. Standard user input controls need to be simplified. Vestibular mismatch from latency may actually provide a treatment tool with autism where the vestibular system appears to differ from normal systems

The social and ethical issues are more complex. Individuals with autism are often already isolated within their own worlds. To create an artificial computer reality that only extends this isolation may be a disservice to them. Any use of VR should involve limited exposures, with the goal of integrating the artificial setting into its real equivalent.

Suzanne Weghorst

Traditional psychotherapy has focused on modifying behavior by changing the client's internal processes, be they perceptions, interpretations, articulations, contingency associations, or deeper psychoanalytic processes. The goal of therapy, from these perspectives, is to change the client to better fit reality. Augmented reality, or the merging of artificial and natural stimuli, affords the possibility of modifying behavior by altering the client's sensory inputs, in essence changing reality to better fit the client. This approach may be quite effective for certain disorders, particularly those due to specific neurological dysfunction, and may provide an alternative to pharmacological treatment.

I anticipate at least two broad applications of AR in psychotherapy: (1) as a tool to enhance face-to-face therapeutic techniques, and (2) as a "perceptual prosthesis" for everyday use by the client. A candidate example of the former might be in directing the client's attention to the therapist or to some object of discourse. This application would benefit from a collaborative form of augmented reality, termed "shared space."

One fortuitous application of the second approach to AR therapy has been demonstrated in the treatment of Parkinson's Disease. Capitalizing on a well-known but little used visual cueing phenomenon (kinesia paradoxa), appropriate artificial cues can enable walking in akinetic patients and reduce the severity of dyskinesia resulting from long-term drug treatment. Ancillary positive effects on affect and cognitive functioning have also been observed.

Augmented reality technology is currently in its infancy, and its practical applications are somewhat limited. In particular, current visual display methods suffer from restricted field of view, relatively poor spatial resolution, and insufficient brightness in competition with normal ambient light levels. Solutions to these technological problems are in sight, however, and long-term prospects for AR therapy are intriguing.

Nat Durlach

NEEDED RESEARCH ON VR-ASSISTED THERAPY: During the last three years, a number of individuals have begun to explore the use of VR technology in psychotherapy. Most studies to date have focused on behavioral therapy (exposure and desensitization) for phobias such as fear of heights. Although the results of these preliminary efforts appear promising, much work needs to be done in order to determine the ways in which, and the extent to which, VR technology can be truly useful (i.e., cost effective) in this area. In this presentation, we outline briefly some of the R & D issues that we believe require attention.

Research On VR-Assisted Behavioral Therapy For Anxiety Disorders: Previous work in this area needs to be extended by (a) developing improved, less expensive, and easier-to-use VR facilities, (b) systematically evaluating the usefulness of VR by comparing VR-assisted therapy to therapy without VR on various types of clinical populations, and (c) extending the use of VR to a wider variety of anxiety disorders.

Other Types Of Therapeutic Applications: Efforts are also emerging to conceptualize and probe the use of VR for other types of psychotherapeutic interventions and other types of disorders. In addition to the use of VR for expressive purposes, and in addition to the work discussed above concerning autism and Parkinson's Disease, consideration is now being given to its use for treating individuals with distorted body images associated with eating disorders.

Relevant Technical Issues: Among the relevant technical issues that are being considered (apart from those associated with general power, flexibility, ease-of-use, and cost) are those concerned with (a) providing an improved sense of presence for the patient, (b) incorporating appropriate virtual actors in the therapeutic process, (c) designing appropriate VR stations for both the patient and the therapist, as well as the communication channels between them, (d) integrating physiological-response monitoring equipment with traditional VR equipment in an appropriate manner for the patient's VR station, and (e) exploring the potential of haptic interfaces for psychotherapy.

Simplified Systems For Increased Cost-Effectiveness- The Search For The Effective Stimulus: It is easy to envision ideal VR systems that are likely to be useful in psychotherapy. However, realization of these ideal systems lies far in the future. In the meantime, we have to determine which dimensions of the VR experience are most crucial to the success of therapy and focus on the development of systems that perform well along these dimensions.

Potential Hazards: Despite the enthusiasm for VR-assisted therapy among technologists, patients, and some therapists, there are a variety of potential hazards. One class of such hazards relates to sensorimotor and perceptual phenomena such as eye strain, simulator sickness, and distorted perceptual fields. A second class concerns possible psychological damage to the patient resulting from unwanted and unexpected effects of VR on the patient's sense of identity, ability to distinguish between reality and fantasy, etc. A third class concerns psychosocial issues related to societal values about such issues as sex. A fourth class, which has not yet received much attention but probably will in the not-too-distant future, concerns the extent to which VR systems, particularly when augmented by physiological sensors (or displays), constitute ideal systems for "brain washing." Clearly, it makes sense to consider these potential hazards, as well as the potential benefits of VR when making plans for the future.

Building Compelling VRML Worlds

Organizer:
Delle Maxwell
Panelists:
Clay Graham, Silicon Graphics
David Blair, Artist
Delle Maxwell, Independent Designer
James Waldrop, Construct

This panel proposes to explore and compare several different directions in large-scale sites built using VRML that show what 3D on the Web can offer: multimedia, and responsive, changeable, and expandable worlds. Being "large-scale" is not necessarily correlated with the heft of the files; if anything, a better goal is a balance between ideas, visual design, and navigability. With this balance in mind, each panelist is exploring a different domain: the formation of a vocabulary for "virtual architecture," the reconstruction of a lost archaeological site, the exploration of hybrid narrative and the creation of a "procedural cinema," and the creation of a VRML-based web site business. The panelists will present the ideas behind their work, and will as address issues they all have in common: how one weaves motion, lighting, architecture, sound, animation, history, navigation, and narrative into a fabric of interactive experience.

A panel is the most suitable format for this kind of discussion, as it allows the participants to show their most up-to-date work. This is an important consideration in a field that is so fast-moving that "three months make up a Web Year." [1] With that it mind, we expect features like animation, behaviors, sound, and real-time interaction to be integrated into the work that will be shown in August. And in an effort to strike an important balance between the artistic and the technical, we have included panelists that represent both these aspects.

Clay Graham

Clay Graham, a Virtual Architect, will present examples and ideas about a new type of architecture, which is less about physicality and shelter than it is about "Space, Place, Symbol and Sign." [2] His statement is a short synopsis of the book he is currently writing on the subject.

Introduction

VRML holds unknown potential, allowing ordinary people to create unique places and share them with the world. With this democratization of creation comes some responsibility. Just as the artist uses the language of symbolism to communicate the stirrings of the soul, the new architect or designer will communicate through a sculptural and architectural language.

Space

The architectural metaphor serves as a natural point of reference from which the user can read the data. The "space" articulates the domain in which a particular query has taken place. All data extracted from the query resides within the architectural domain. This domain should be constructed with spatial archetypes that are an extension of the way we already see the world. In this way the archetypal elements of wall, floor, datum and column guide the user through the data intuitively without coercion by a modal interface.

Perspective also infers that there is a human scale and texture, and it creates the need to assist the explorer in seeing the spatial domain of optimum interaction. Not only does a space have form, it also has context, or an organizing principle. The question "Where am I?" alludes to the need to define context. This leads to the discussion of Morphology and Topology: the criteria of how are things organized and how are they represented. To represent and organize information with meaning, the designer must look at how the individual elements will interact to become a collective. They will also need to break the information out of its original context to be reorganized dynamically. This leads into the discussion of construction and de-construction, and how the architectural metaphor deals with the creation and reorganization of context. Finally, once one has determined the relations that will create the space, it is necessary to apply construction techniques to create the most interactive and optimum performing space possible.

Place

A place is created by the interaction of objects, the space, and the user. By combining the context or theme for the application with objects that run as "applets," a complex and dynamic relationship develops. These relationships can be refined into a set of guidelines for creating virtual architectures. By determining the type of place, the designer can determine the best model for user interaction and object behavior.

For this reason the world of behaviors relates to the issue of place, because it will be the method whereby interaction is determined. Right now these behaviors are being implemented in scripting languages, such as Java, with the scripts creating events for the behaviors. An interesting problem is recognizing archetypes of behaviors and determining how to incorporate them into successful spaces.

Symbol

Meaning comes not just out of concepts themselves, but through their interrelation and context. Thought is not a thousand islands separated by an ocean, but a complex ambiguous rule system derived from the cross reference and overlap between those elements. This is the primary thesis behind the concept of symbolic arrays.

Art, religion, and culture depend on this overlap to communicate meaning. The cathedral, temple, and masterpiece are not representations of static sign, but rich and complex symbolic systems meant to communicate an ambiguous concept or concepts greater than the sum of their identities.

Sign

Sometimes a designer may wish to create an index to what an object is, or to what it contains explicitly. Signs can be used to create a direct connection to an object or space so that it can be identified easily. Signs act as the direct indexes either to what the object is or to what it contains.

David Blair

Though video hasn't easily yet dropped onto the public digital networks, 3-D (e.g. VRML) does offer a time-based element that qualifies as a procedural cinema. Working from an interest in the instantiation of a unified narrative across multiple media, I am currently designing my next feature in parallel with a 3-D based network site. The beginning crossovers are easy to understand – models for the film become procedural "movies" on the site; these "movies" can return to the film itself as moving images. The potential technical plasticity of this convergence interacts with the strangeness of storymaking; I focus my interest at this point.

Delle Maxwell

I will present a reconstruction of the Aztec ceremonial precinct of Tenochtitlan, the capital of the Aztec/Mexica empire. It is built in collaboration with the Inventor/VRML team at Silicon Graphics. The purpose of this site is educational, as well as experimental: we wish to create a site where exploration of a model can be done in conjunction with readings about its history and meaning in a way that allows one to get a fuller sense of the subject.

The Aztecs were the most powerful civilization of the New World, alternately amazing and horrifying to the Spanish colonizers of the 16th century. The original temples' site was almost completely destroyed by Hernan Cortez and the conquistadors by 1521, and even the location was lost until 1978, when work on Mexico City's subway system uncovered their remains. Archaeologists have since been excavating this site in the heart of present-day Mexico City in hopes of gaining more insight into Aztec culture.

In this case, VRML is used to recreate a place that has, in reality, been lost, except for some building fragments, statuary, offerings, and historical and archaeological texts. The model [4] is connected with this information about the Aztecs and their lives, mythology, and history. Writings on the confrontation of the two cultures, with views from both sides of the same events, are also included. From these fragments we can begin to reconstruct what the environment of Aztecs of over 450 years ago might have been like.

James Waldrop

James and his colleagues at Construct are in the enviable position of building a business that lets them experiment with the kind of web site building referred to as "fun projects" – often collaborations with artists, designers, and architects. Declaring itself an "Internet Design Company," Construct has positioned itself at the forefront of 3D interface design. [5] Making use of tools such as VRML and Java, Construct has created virtual environments that range from the highly realistic – the VRML ArcGallery (for the Interactive Media Festival) – to the abstractly hyperspatial – a network visualization of Tierra. James Waldrop, Construct's Technical Director, will present some of Construct's latest and most interesting projects, including a real-time visualization of the Internet, a completely virtual technology expo, and a 3D asynchronous conferencing interface. Discussion of these projects will include extensive detail surrounding both the design and implementation of interactive, networked 3D spaces.

Notes

[1] Attributed to Mike McCue, founder of Paper, Inc.

[2] Clay's homepage is available for perusal at:
`http://reality.sgi.com/employees/clay/`

[3] "Waxweb" can be accessed via
`http://bug.village.virginia.edu/`
"Jews In Space" is still under construction and not yet available for general viewing. The web address will be available at SIGGRAPH.

[4] This model is based on the original reconstruction in the Museum of Anthropology in Mexico City, by Ignacio Marquina. Thanks to Bob Galbraith for his interpretation and model, which I then rebuilt and augmented for interactive performance. Since this web site is still under major construction, it is not yet available as a URL to the public. The web address will be available at SIGGRAPH.

[5] Check out `http://www.construct.net/` for information on Construct.

Springing into the Fifth Decade of Computer Graphics – Where We've Been and Where We're Going!

Organizer:
Carl Machover, Machover Associates Corp.
Panelists:
Dr. Frederick P. "Fred" Brooks, Jr., University of North Carolina
Dr. Edwin E. "Ed" Catmull, Pixar
Sylvan "Chase" Chasen, Investment Advisor
Robert M. "Bob" Dunn, Enterprise Solutions International
Dr. Bertram "Bert" Herzog, University of Michigan
Dr. Andries "Andy" van Dam, Brown University,
and NSF Science and Technology Center for Graphics and Visualization

It's been a helluva ride for the past 40 years!

In the 50s... computer graphics was a cure for no known disease... a solution in search of a problem. Now, computer graphics has become a cure for EVERY known disease.

How did this happen, and where is it going? A "blue-ribbon" panel of computer graphics pioneers/innovators/practitioners will discuss their successes and foibles of the past and their vision for the future with each making a brief statement about their CG recollections and anecdotes, and making succinct comments about what they see coming up. The following are brief comments that each of the panelists prepared about their expected presentation.

Carl Machover

Machover has been involved in computer graphics for almost four decades as a consultant, entrepreneur, academic, author, and marketeer and was the first SIGGRAPH panels chair. He will discuss the evolution of computer graphics from being a "cure for no know disease" to being a "cure for every known disease."

Early users were "risk takers" since there was little available application software and the user, without really having ROI experience, elected to make significant hardware investments in the hope that the investment would pay off by saving time, saving money, improving decision making, or doing something that couldn't be done any other way. By the early 70s, users in such applications as process control and CAD were reporting ROIs that were attractive to industrial companies in spite of the substantial capital investments required. And by the late 80s and 90s, cost of entry became low enough that the technology took its place beside telephones, typewriters, answering machines, copiers, faxes, and other common office machines, and were acquired just to stay competitive.

Dr. Frederick P. "Fred" Brooks, Jr.

Dr. Brooks is an ACM Newell Award winner, widely read and respected author, and computer graphics pioneer and innovator with particular interest in man-machine interfaces. He will talk about the future of synthetic environments, sometimes called "artificial reality."

Faster graphics engines promise to be able to render 10-20 million polygons/second. This allows a great increase in the complexity of the world models we can move about in real time. John Poulton points out that with screen resolution of about a million pixels and frame update rates on the order of 20 frames/second average, polygon size becomes the scene depth complexity, approaching a few pixels/polygon. The whole purpose of polygons in the first place was to save computation by allowing full computation on vertices and interpolation between. As polygon size becomes less than three, there is no saving. We might as well compute pixels directly.

The first such approach to be explored is image-based rendering, with 2-D image warping interpolating between frames of full 3-D rendering. Just as frame buffers decoupled frame update from image refresh, so this technique promises to decouple world-model change from viewpoint change, to the great relaxing of urgency for 3-D rendering.

Dr. Edwin E. "Ed" Catmull

SIGGRAPH Coons Award recipient Dr. Catmull has led pioneering efforts in animation and rendering for the last twenty years. As a student at the University of Utah he developed texture mapping, Z-buffers, and techniques for displaying curved surfaces. These techniques have become standard in the industry. While a graduate student, he also created one of the first computer-generated effects for films – a computer generated animation of a hand, which was used in the movie "Futureworld." He was the first Director of the Computer Graphics Laboratory at the New York Institute of Technology in 1974. In 1979, Dr. Catmull joined Lucasfilm, managing the Computer Division with the charter to bring high technology into the film industry. In early 1986, when the Computer Division split off from Lucasfilm, he became president of the newly formed company, Pixar.

Between 1986 and 1989, Pixar produced a series of short films, two of which were nominated for Academy Awards, and one, "Tin Toy," received an Oscar in 1987. Dr. Catmull recently was executive producer of the wildly successful "Toy Story," the first full-length computer graphics film.

He will discuss the pursuit of illusions.

Sylvan "Chase" Chasen

"Chase" Chasen pioneered in the use of computer graphics for design and manufacture. Chase was responsible for some of the first production CAD/CAM applications in engineering and design. He was an active contributor to CAD/CAM education and received an SME "Distinguished Contributor" award.

In 1963, officials of Lockheed-Georgia Aircraft Company's newly formed Research Lab, the chief engineer, and other members of management visited MIT to witness and to evaluate Ivan Sutherland's PhD project, "Sketchpad." It was clear that picture-based man-computer communications would give the computer field an added dimension, but would be moderately expensive with little or no apparent short term benefit. A leap of faith was required.

To document our justification, I wrote over 50 pages entitled "Prospectus on Computer Aided Design."

Early in 1964, we formed a dedicated team of people with complementary technical expertise. In early January 1965, we asked management for permission to establish a team of potential CAD/CAM users to study alternative application possibilities, and to select one that would demonstrate cost-benefit potential by the end of the year. By mid-November, we had demonstrated both the creation of a 3D (actually 2 1/2 D) prototype part and the path, converted to a machine-driven tape, for the numerically controlled milling machine to manufacture the part.

This is believed to be the first production-oriented CAD/CAM application of any kind – not just N/C. By the spring of 1966, this led to a fully operational three station time-shared CAD/CAM computer graphic N/C system. Concurrent with the General Motors DAC-1 system (Design Augmented by computers directed by Don Hart), this is believed to be the first multi-station computer graphics system for production usage.

During 1965, Lockheed-California began full scale development of CADAM, and at the 1995 Fall Joint Computer conference, we presented a paper entitled "The Introduction of Man-Computer Graphics into the Aerospace Industry." This was done to document Lockheed's role in the historical beginnings of CAD/CAM and interactive computer graphics.

It is usually easier to start something than to finish it. Therefore, the challenge of today is greater than for the pioneers, Today we have to determine how we can most efficiently link the "islands of automation," make relevant data easy to locate, store and retrieve myriad documents electronically, and standardize the many interfaces among many concerns. Most importantly, how do we train both computer professionals and the lay public to know what question to ask, and to seek answers without intimidation of hosts of complex, bewildering alternatives?

Robert M. "Bob" Dunn

About 20 years ago, Bob Dunn, together with Bert Herzog and under the auspices of SIGGRAPH, chaired the committee that produced one of the first device-independent computer graphic standards, CORE. Bob was SIGGRAPH chair 1973-1975, and together with Jon Meads and Jim Foley, launched the SIGGRAPH Conferences and Exhibitions in the early 70s. After promoting the use of computer graphics in the Army, Bob moved into several responsible industrial positions. Today, he is focused on IT Industry international corporate development.

My Occam's Razor for technology is the position taken by Lord Alfred North Whitehead about 100 years ago, which is "Civilization advances by virtue of the number of operations it can do without thinking about them."

Each time the technology of computing has entered a new setting in which to be of value, the technologies of depiction, representation, portrayal, and illusion (i.e. ?computer graphics?) have faced new challenges. Thinkers, users, and producers face new challenges.

My Occam's Razor for the use of technology are the personal judgements each user makes about whether the cost and effort to adopt and deploy a technology is offset by the gains/pleasure/?pain? from its use. For the researcher, to have devised the more elegant/correct/robust theory/technology/design is the impetus to inquiry and the pursuit of research grants. For the early adopter, to have made it work first and gain bragging rights is justification enough. For those embroiled in hard, real-world problems, getting a solution where one was not possible before is to remove a barrier to success. And for the rest of us mainstream users of technology, if it shows up naturally, installs easily, and can be used directly through our GUI controls, we are willing to be amazed and grateful to the gods of technology for having made the world wonderful.

For Computer Graphics, it still takes too long to do some things that we wish to be ordinary.

Dr. Bertram "Bert" Herzog

As both an academic and an industrialist, Bert Herzog has contributed to, and maintained close contacts with, both worlds. Initially, he was a structural engineer who got interested in analog computers at Case Institute of Technology, and subsequently worked with digital computers while teaching at the University of Michigan. In 1963 he joined Ford Motor Company, where he became involved in modern computer graphics. He returned to the University of Michigan (where he originated some of the first CG short courses), then to the University of Colorado, back to industry, and then back to the University of Michigan. Herzog is EIC of the IEEE publication, Computer Graphics and Applications, co-chair of ACM's 50th Anniversary Celebration, as well as SIGGRAPH Awards chair.

He will ask: How long does it take a vision to reach fruition? There is evidence obtained from now-older but early visionaries that the answer is: Twenty years or more! On the other hand, recent events associated with the Internet and World Wide Web would lead us to believe that instant gratification is, at last, possible. What is wrong with this picture? Does memory play tricks? Can the visionary's optimistic expectations be realized now?

Dr. Andries "Andy" van Dam

Andy was a founder of SIGGRAPH 30 years ago, and has remained a computer graphics innovator and educator. With Dr. Jim Foley, he authored "Fundamentals of Computer Graphics," and with Foley, Feiner, and Hughes, the expanded version "Computer Graphics Principles and Practice." Both are *the* standard references in the field. Dr. van Dam was a recipient of the SIGGRAPH Coons award, and is a member of the National Acadamy of Engineering. He will discuss pre-WIMP, WIMP, and post-WIMP user interfaces, the impact that next-generation graphics and multimedia hardware and software will have on the evolution of user interfaces, and why the user interface is increasingly important in society's use of computers.

References

Brooks,Jr., Frederick P., "The Mythical Man-Month," Addison-Wesley Publishing Co., Inc., 1975.

Chasen, S. H., "Historical Highlights of Interactive Computer Graphics," Mechanical Engineering, November 1981, pp. 32-41.

Chasen, S. H. "The Introduction of Man-Computer Graphics into the Aerospace Industry," FJCC, 1965.

Chasen, S. H. and Dow, J. W., "The Guide for the Evaluation and Implementation of CAD/CAM Systems," CAD/CAM Decisions, 1983.

Foley, van Dam, Feiner, Hughes,"Computer Graphics Principles and Practice (2nd Edition in C)," Addison-Wesley Publishing Company, Inc., 1995.

Machover, Carl, "A Brief, Personal History of Computer Graphics," IEEE Computer, November 1978, pp 38-45.

Machover, Carl, "Four Decades of Computer Graphics." IEEE Computer Graphics and Applications, November, 1994, pp 14-19.

Machover, Carl, "The CAD/CAM Handbook," McGraw-Hill, 1996.

"Retrospectives 1: The early Years in Computer Graphics at MIT, Lincoln Lab and Harvard," Computer Graphics (SIGGRAPH Panel Proceedings) Vol. 23, No. 5, 1989 , pp 1 – 38.

Siders, R. A. et al, "Computer Graphics – A revolution in Design", American Management Association, New York, 1966.

"World-Wide State-of-the-Art" Special Issue, SIGGRAPH Computer Graphics Quarterly , May 1996.

Live Computer Animation

Organizer:
Tim Heidmann
Panelists:
Ken Fuhrman
Tim Heidmann
Chuck Molyneaux

The array of general purpose graphics workstations typically used for computer aided design, scientific computation, visual simulation, and film special effects have become so sophisticated in their ability to generate high-quality, real-time computer animation that they can be used for live creation of graphics and effects for television broadcast. Although the field typically is dominated by special-purpose video processing hardware, these machines are beginning to show up in a variety of innovative applications.

This panel will present some of those innovative applications, talk about the advantages and difficulties of using general-purpose computers for television, discuss their views of the technical and business issues in these applications, and prognosticate about future directions in the art. Undoubtedly, numerous disagreements will arise as to what is and is not an effective and valuable use of this technology. Attendees will be invited to ask questions and share their own views of the industry.

Ken Fuhrman

Broadcasters have just begun to examine the benefits of switching to general purpose graphics workstations from the "black box" solutions currently in use. Computers offer increased flexibility in the look and behavior of the graphics, the ability to network several graphics workstations together, and the opportunity to share one piece of computer graphics hardware between many different graphics applications. Along with these benefits are questions such as how to maintain the high quality standards of the look of the graphics required for network broadcast, how to manage using external data feeds to automatically generate text and images, and how to manage the creation of graphics and put these powerful and complex new tools into the hands of artists.

Developers of new graphics applications are continually facing the inertia of industry "standards." Broadcasters have a set of tools and production methods which are understood and widely available. Unions and the availability of artists with specific skills impose other limits on how graphics can be created. However, broadcasters are beginning to see the possibilities and benefits of using computers, and are starting to bite the bullet and undertake the challenges of using the new technologies.

An important benefit of using computers is the ability to exchange data between a wide range of applications and platforms. EVT has put considerable effort into being able to easily import imagery from several sources, computers as well as video equipment and tools, and from different graphics standards such as EPS. This effort matches the growth of demand for networked systems.

A new question raised by the use of graphics workstations is how to manage what can be done in real time at 60 fps. The typical piece of black box video equipment has a narrow range of capabilities, but can always be relied upon to do its work without dropping fields. Computers offer an unlimited amount of flexibility, but as the complexity increases, so does the calculation time. In traditional non-realtime computer animation this is not a problem, since the computation of each frame just takes a little longer, but in broadcast applications, exceeding the 1/60 second mark has serious implications on the look. There is no simple formula for understanding the limits of a particular computer's capabilities, and the use of tools to monitor performance and detect problems appears to be an unavoidable part of the design process. This is an important part of the education process for broadcasters trying to understand the implications of using the new tools.

The increasing pace of education and raised expectations of broadcasters, combined with the continuing pace of improvements in technology and price, will make this an area of explosive growth over the next few years.

Chuck Molyneaux

There are real day-to-day benefits to be gained by the use of live computer graphics in broadcast. For example, election coverage has always been limited by how quickly changing information could be collected, assembled, and presented. Computers allow much of the process to be done by one device and automated, while at the same time providing flexibility in how the data are to be presented.

Among the difficulties in making use of computers is the technical expertise currently required. To gain real acceptance, these systems must be usable by the artists who currently operate the paint boxes and character generators. Even the process of turning on and logging in to a graphics computer can be daunting. Also, it is necessary to address the special support, repair, and training issues which arise as well.

We are in a period where producers are looking for novelty value, using graphics animation for its "gee-whiz" impact. They are also being driven by fear of falling behind, of being perceived to be outclassed by competing stations. The effect is that producers are making huge leaps to implement complex new systems without the opportunity to evolve into them—to understand their use and value, and to gradually introduce viewers to new concepts and to have a chance to react to the responses of viewers. Many things are making it to air before the question of "is this useful?" has had a chance to be answered.

There is a danger that the quantity and complexity of graphics may overwhelm viewers. Most network news and sports shows are already hugely complex in the number and type of elements used; computers make it easy to generate even more. At what point does it become too much, and begin to diminish the value of the information conveyed to the home?

Virtual sets are currently generating great interest and excitement. The emphasis is on multimillion dollar systems with extensive effects and full virtual worlds. In time, however the excitement will wear off, and Virtual Sets will need to justify their existence on mostly economic reasons. There are many ways parts of this technology can improve a wide range of shows – live out-the-window imagery inserted into stage shows, for example – and the technology has the possibility of becoming yet another tool in the producer's shop.

Use of computers in broadcast is poised for a real breakthrough in the next few years, brought on by:

- The advent of a low cost computer capable of broadcast-quality graphics and video processing.
- The existence of a range of easy-to-use applications that all can run together on a shared machine.
- The evolution of the business model – distribution, training, and support – to enable widespread use.

As this happens, use of computers to generate graphics will become an economic necessity for every television presenter – local, cable, and network – and a core piece of the production process, not just a novelty for the privileged few.

Tim Heidmann

We have begun to see excitement from broadcasters in having graphics computers fill the traditional roles of "black boxes" – character generators, compositors, video effects generators, and in a few very specific applications, such as Virtual Sets. The excitement is growing, because broadcasters are starting to see the benefits of using general purpose workstations:

- The flexibility of applications in news, sports, and entertainment is virtually unlimited.
- Complex data can be gathered automatically and presented visually.
- One piece of hardware can be used for several applications simply with the acquisition of additional software.
- The amount of computer and graphics power and its configuration can grow modularly with the choice of different machines or by adding more machines to the network.
- Several people can be working simultaneously on one graphic or animation, each on their own workstation connected by a network and tied into databases or communication lines.

All these features have tremendous impact on such traditional uses of television graphics as character generation and creation of moving graphics, but we have only begun to explore the possibilities of how graphics can be used in conjunction with live video.

Computer animation is a valuable educational tool. It can be used to illustrate news events, such as plane crashes or developments in a civil war, for which video is unavailable or impossible. In sports, football plays or sailing maneuvers can be illustrated from any point of view. The ability to create the animation quickly, with high quality, and to present it live is necessary for this tool to be usable in a live broadcast environment.

We have also begun to see the possibilities of how computers can be used live to enhance the video presentation. FoxTrax uses a very simple highlight to make it easier for a hockey viewer to follow a tiny black puck as it speeds over the white ice. The data collection, communication, and calculation necessary to achieve that result in real time are substantial, but the graphic itself must be subtle or risk obscuring or distracting from the live action. The inclusion of a virtual athlete in a foot race – a simple marker or a synthetic image of a person – running at the world-record pace can make a race in which the lead runner is far ahead interesting by allowing the broadcaster to concentrate on the real story: how close the athlete is to breaking the record.

The current trend in graphics is to present more information more often, since more data and statistics are available. By making the information visual in the form of a picture, its possible to present more data which can be understood more easily by the viewer, actually simplifying the process.

Live animated graphics, if done well, can also have great entertainment value. Arresting visuals and complex motion can be a great complement to the video alone, can make a show more fun to watch, and can set it apart from its competition.

The biggest problems facing the use of live graphics in broadcast are in helping the broadcaster understand the opportunities and limitations of the technology, and in getting the tools into the hands of the artists in a way that gives them the freedom to independently explore new things. The current approach to making a system usable is to present the operator with a monolithic application, which prevents them from getting into trouble, but which also places severe limits on flexibility and creativity. The tools must continue to evolve to be more open, simple, and powerful.

Imaging Features of Advanced Graphics Architectures

Organizer:
Bob Murphy, Silicon Graphics
Panelists:
Randy Crane, Hewlett-Packard
Kurt Akeley, Silicon Graphics
Steve Howell, Sun Microsystems
Arie Kaufman, SUNY Stonybrook

Why have HP, Sun and SGI focused so heavily on imaging and volume rendering in their latest graphics systems and software interfaces? The various design approaches of HP's image processing accelerator, OpenGL's visualization extensions, and Sun's Visualization Instructions Set (VIS) will be presented, followed by an alternative approach from academia. Panel members will identify the problems each design tried to address, and will discuss both commonalties and differences in design approaches. The panel will conclude with a discussion on where interactive computer graphics systems design is going, and how much impact non-polygonal rendering will have in the future.

The panel will be moderated by Dr. Henry Fuchs, Professor of Computer Science and Radiation Oncology at the University of North Carolina at Chapel Hill. Dr. Fuchs has been working in computer graphics since 1969, and is currently focusing research on interactive 3D medical imaging, virtual environments, and scalable interactive computer graphics architectures.

The three industrial panelists will present their respective product goals and designs for 15 minutes, then the university participant will present alternate approaches. A 20-minute discussion on opportunities for applying the capabilities of these systems will conclude the panel.

Randy Crane

The landscape of the medical imaging market has changed dramatically over the last few years. It is transitioning from custom hardware-based solutions to off-the-shelf workstation and PC-based solutions. Given the increasing cost sensitivity of the market, HP decided to build a low-cost image processing accelerator.

Based on customer feedback, we concluded that the current market needs are primarily 2D and are characterized by filtering, resampling, and window leveling (data mapping). HP sees 3D volumetric rendering as becoming very important in the near future.

To achieve our goal of low cost, we decided to pursue a single chip architecture. As a result of this decision, we focused only on the most common 2D operations. While this solution does not provide the functionality available from a complete texture mapping implementation, it allowed us to meet the project cost goals.

OpenGL was the standard API we chose to expose the capabilities of our hardware. Most of the functionality was already available in the 2D pipeline definition. We merely defined a few extensions that added scaling, translation, and rotation with either bilinear or bicubic interpolation methods. The enhanced 2D pipeline provided our customers with a simplified programming model to access our acceleration technology. The result is a product that met cost goals, provided high performance, and satisfied the needs of our customers.

Kurt Akeley

Demands for interactive photo-realistic image generation driven by applications varying from broadcast television virtual sets, image exploitation in the intelligence community, virtual prototyping in manufacturing industries, and volume rendering in medicine and geophysical sciences have outstripped the abilities of traditional polygonal-based 3-D graphics systems.

At Silicon Graphics, interactive image processing is not a separate discipline. Instead, image processing is just one component of the larger discipline of interactive visualization, which merges 2D graphics, 3D graphics, and n-dimension image processing using the shared technology of texture mapping. Each SGI workstation product accelerates 2D and 3D texture-mapped graphics and image processing operations (such as convolution, histogram computation, and color table substitution) using a single hardware subsystem. The implementations of these visualization subsystems differ radically across the workstation product line (accelerated to their greatest extent in the Indigo Impact and Onyx Infinite Reality combined geometry and imaging pipelines), but all share the single architecture and programming interface defined by the OpenGL specification and its extensions.

There are many advantages to the OpenGL visualization architecture. Graphics and image processing techniques can be combined in single rendering algorithms, effectively solving such problems as rendering embedded polygonal objects in volumetric data, or the reduction of geometry to depth-buffered images in complex geometric scenes. Seemingly disparate problems, such as distortion correction, shadow projection, and volume rendering, all may be implemented using the common, easily accelerated mechanism of texture mapping. Because OpenGL is both orthogonal and procedural, its many mechanisms can be combined in an endless variety of creative ways, enabling applications that its designers had no intention of addressing.

While OpenGL is widely accepted and implemented as a high-performance graphics interface, Silicon Graphics is unique in its commitment to OpenGL as its high-performance visualization architecture.

Steve Howell

The Visual Instruction Set (VIS) extensions to the SPARC architecture provide a powerful imaging and multimedia engine without the need for additional expensive, special-purpose hardware. VIS can perform up to eight integer operations per cycle, making it ideal for compute-intensive tasks such as image processing, video compression and decompression, and volume rendering. VIS can be applied to both memory and display operations. Putting the acceleration in the processor has several advantages over specialized hardware. It allows image data to be treated like any other data: free of any virtual memory or caching restrictions. Also, VIS is scalable, both with processor speed and number of processors. There will always be applications that require additional processing speed, and as SPARC processors get faster, VIS will be able to provide that processing power.

Dr. Arie Kaufman

The high computational requirements of traditional computer graphics led to the development of special-purpose graphics engines, primarily for polygon rendering. Similarly, the special needs of volume rendering, where an image must be computed rapidly and repeatedly from a volume dataset, lends itself to the development of special-purpose volume rendering architectures. A dedicated accelerator, which separates volume rendering from general-purpose computing, seems to be best suited to provide true real-time volume rendering on standard deskside or desktop computers. Volume rendering hardware may also be used to directly view changes of the 3D data over time for 4D (spatial-temporal) visualization, such as in real-time 3D ultrasonography, micro-tomography, or confocal microscopy. This may lead to the direct integration of volume visualization hardware with real-time acquisition devices, in much the same way as fast signal processing hardware became part of today's scanning devices.

Cube-4 is a scalable architecture for true real-time ray-casting of large volumetric datasets. The unique features of Cube-4 are a high bandwidth skewed memory organization, localized and near-neighbor datapaths, and multiple, parallel rendering-pipelines with simple processing units. System performance scales linearly with the number of rendering pipelines, limited only by memory access speed. Cube-4 performs arbitrary parallel and perspective projections of high-resolution datasets at true real-time frame rates. The performance is data- and classification-independent, and can be achieved at a fraction of the cost of a multiprocessor computer. Cube-4 uses accurate 3D interpolation and high-quality surface normal estimation without any pre-computation or data duplication. Consequently, Cube-4 is also appropriate for 4D visualization as an embedded volume visualization hardware system in emerging real-time acquisition devices. Possible hardware implementations of Cube-4 for 30-frames-per-second rates range from an inexpensive PCI board accelerator for 256x256x256datasets, to a workstation accelerator board for 512x512x512 datasets, to a visualization server for 1024x1024x1024 or higher resolutions. The cost-performance of Cube-4 is several orders of magnitude better than existing solutions.

The choice of whether one adopts a general-purpose or a special-purpose solution to volume rendering depends upon the circumstances. If maximum flexibility is required, general-purpose appears to be the best way to proceed. However, an important feature of graphics accelerators is that they are integrated into a much larger environment, where software can shape the form of input and output data, thereby providing the additional flexibility that is needed. A good example is the relationship between the needs of conventional computer graphics and special-purpose graphics hardware. Nobody would dispute the necessity for polygon graphics acceleration, despite its obvious limitations. We are making the exact same argument for volume rendering architectures.

SIGGRAPH 96 COMMITTEE

SIGGRAPH 96 Conference Chair
John Fujii
Hewlett-Packard Company

Conference Coordinator
Molly Morgan

Assistant Conference Coordinator
Robin Myran

Accounting
Smith, Bucklin & Associates, Inc.

Applications Chair
Warren Waggenspack
Louisiana State University

Audio/Visual Support
AVW Audio Visual, Inc.

The Bridge: SIGGRAPH 96 Art Show Chair
Jean Ippolito
Savannah College of Art and Design

Computer Animation Festival Chair
Linda Branagan
Light Source, Inc.

Conference Management
Smith, Bucklin & Associates, Inc.

Copy Coordination
Smith, Bucklin & Associates, Inc.

Courses Chair
Scott Senften
Landmark Graphics Corporation

Digital Bayou Co-Chairs
Clark Dodsworth
Osage Associates

Brian Blau
Intervista Software, Inc.

Educators Program Chair
Rosalee Wolfe
DePaul University

Electronic Support Chair
David Spoelstra
MediaMachine

Exhibition Management
Hall-Erickson, Inc.

Exhibits Chair
Tom Appolloni
US Air Force Academy

Graphic Design/Editing
Q LTD

International Chair
Carolina Cruz-Neira
Iowa State University

Marketing and Media
Smith, Bucklin & Associates, Inc.

Networking/Teleconferencing Chair
Jeff Jortner
Sandia National Laboratories

Online Publications and Promotion Chair
Lyn Bartram
Simon Fraser University

Organization Development
Raoul Buron
Center for Creative Leadership

Panels Chair
Theresa-Marie Rhyne
Lockheed Martin Technical Services
US EPA Scientific Visualization Center

Papers Chair
Holly Rushmeier
IBM T.J. Watson Research Center

Registration
Smith, Bucklin & Associates, inc.

Sketches Chair
F. Kenton Musgrave
The George Washington University

SIGGRAPH 95 Conference Co-Chairs
Brian Herzog
Sun Microsystems Computer Company

Peter Meechan
Alias/Wavefront

SIGGRAPH 95 Conference Coordinator
Betsy Johnsmiller

SIGGRAPH 97 Conference Chair
G. Scott Owen
Georgia State University

SIGGRAPH 98 Conference Chair
Walt Bransford
Thrillistic, LLC

Service Contractor
GES Exposition Services

SIGGRAPH Director for Conferences
Adele Newton
Newton Associates

SIGGRAPH Director for Publications
Stephen Spencer
The Ohio State University

Student Volunteers
Hank Driskill
Digital Domain

Travel Agent
FLYING COLORS

Conference Planning Committee Chair
Adele Newton
Newton Associates

SIGGRAPH 95 Conference Co-Chairs
Brian Herzog
Sun Microsystems Computer Company

Peter Meechan
Alias/Wavefront

SIGGRAPH 95 Conference Coordinator
Betsy Johnsmiller

SIGGRAPH 96 Conference Chair
John Fujii
Hewlett-Packard Company

SIGGRAPH 96 Conference Coordinator
Molly Morgan

SIGGRAPH 97 Conference Chair
G. Scott Owen
Georgia State University

SIGGRAPH 98 Conference Chair
Walt Bransford
Thrillistic LLC

SIGGRAPH 97-99 Chief Staff Executive
Dino Schweitzer
Capstone Management Group, Inc.

SIGGRAPH EXECUTIVE COMMITTEE

Chair
Steve Cunningham
California State University Stanislaus

Vice Chair
Alain Chesnais
Alias/Wavefront

Director for Conferences
Adele Newton
Newton Associates

Director for Communications
Alyce Kaprow
The New Studio

Director for Education
Judith Brown
University of Iowa

Director for Professional Chapters
Scott Lang
United Nations International School

Director for Publications
Stephen Spencer
The Ohio State University

Treasurer
Nan Schaller
Rochester Institute of Technology

Past Chair
Mary C. Whitton
University of North Carolina at Chapel Hill

Directors-at-Large
John C. Hart
Washington State University

Bonnie Mitchell
Syracuse University

PAPERS COMMITTEE

Chair
Holly Rushmeier
IBM T. J. Watson Research Center

Committee
Jules Bloomenthal
Microsoft Corporation

Fred Brooks
University of North Carolina

Tom Calvert
Simon Fraser University

Ed Catmull
Pixar Animation Studios

Tony DeRose
Pixar Animation Studios

Steven Feiner
Columbia University

Eugene Fiume
University of Toronto

Kurt Fleischer
Pixar Animation Studios

A. R. Forrest
University of East Anglia

Pat Hanrahan
Stanford University

Jessica Hodgins
Georgia Institute of Technology

David Kirk
Crystal Dynamics

R. Victor Klassen
Xerox Corporation

Marc Levoy
Stanford University

Bill Lorensen
General Electric Company

Nelson Max
Lawrence Livermore National Laboratory

Gary Meyer
University of Oregon

Richard Parent
The Ohio State University

David Salesin
University of Washington

H. P. Seidel
Universität Erlangen

François Sillion
iMAGIS/IMAG

Richard Szeliski
Microsoft Corporation

Greg Ward
Lawrence Berkeley National Laboratory

Turner Whitted
Numerical Design Limited

PANELS COMMITTEE

Chair
Theresa-Marie Rhyne
Lockheed Martin
US EPA Scientific Visualization Center

Administrator
Dave Taylor
Southwest Point Computing

Committee
Wes Bethel
Lawrence Berkeley National Laboratory

Leo Hourvitz
Pixar Animation Studios

Dorothy Simpson Krause
Massachusetts College of Art

Bill Kroyer
Warner Brothers Feature Animation

Barbara Mones-Hattal
George Mason University

Mary Whitton
University of North Carolina at Chapel Hill

COURSES COMMITTEE

Chair
Scott Senften
Landmark Graphics Corporation

Administrative Assistant
Brenda Hash

Committee
Wayne Carlson
The Ohio State University

Greg Passmore
Consultant

David S. Ebert
University of Maryland Baltimore County

Barb Helfer
The Ohio State University

Nan C. Schaller
Rochester Institute of Technology

Harry F. Smith
University of North Carolina at Wilmington

PAPER REVIEWERS

Greg Abram
Bernard Dov Adelstein
Kurt Akeley
Daniel Aliaga
Bruce Anderson
Tony Apodaca
Didier Arques
Jim Arvo
Ian Ashdown
Daniel Asimov
Ricardo Avila
Norman Badler
Chandrajit Bajaj
Harlyn Baker
Cindy Ball
Tom Banchoff
David Banks
David Baraff
Christina Burbeck
Al Barr
John Barrus
Brian Barsky
R.H. Bartels
Ronen Barzel
Shawn Becker
Andrew Beers
David John Benson
Marshall Bern
Fausto Bernardini
Eric Bier
Rama Bindiganavale
Timothy Binkley
Gary Bishop
Avi Bleiweiss
Jim Blinn
Mark Bloomenthal
Bruce Blumberg
Rod G. Bogart
Harold Boll
Silviu Borac
Kadi Bouatouch
David Brainard
Eric Brechner
Chris Bremser
Jack Bresenham
Duncan Brinsmead
Armin Bruderlin
Martin Buehler
Grigore C. Burdea
Brian Cabral
A.T. Campbell
Loren Carpenter
Navin Chadda
Elaine Chen
Eric Chen
Jim X. Chen
Alain Chesnais
Lillian Chu
Richard Chuang
Michael Clifton
Elaine Cohen
Michael F. Cohen
James M. Coggins
Joao Comba
Rob Cook
Sabine Coquillart
William Cowan
Ingemar Cox
Roger Crawfis
James Cremer
Frank Crow
Brian Curless
Cassidy Curtis
Roger Dannenberg
Trevor Darrell
Mark de Berg
Midori DeLeon
Kalyanmoy Deb
Michael Deering
Thomas A. DeFanti
Leila deFloriani
Venkat Devarajan
Paul Diefenbach
David Dobkin
Julie Dorsey
George Drettakis
Steven Drucker
Tom Duchamp
Tom Duff
Charles Dyer
Dave Ebert
Matthias Eck
Herbert Edelsbrunner
Gershon Elber
Conal Elliott
David Ellsworth
Eric Enderton
Nick England
Erik Erikson
T. Ertl
Reiner Eschbach
Brian Evans
Norberto Ezquerra
Dan Fain
Bart Farell
Gerald Farin
Elliot Feibush
Dieter W. Fellner
Xian-fan Feng
Keith Ferguson
Paulo J.S.G. Ferreira
James A. Ferwerda
Adam Finkelstein
Alain Fournier
Geoffrey C. Fox
David Fracchia
Richard Franke
Bjorn N. Freeman-Benson
Henry Fuchs
Don Fussell
Tinsley Galyean
Geoff Gardner
Jean-Dominique Gascuel
Marie-Paule Gascuel
Reid Gershbein
Nahum Gershon
Andrew Glassner
Michael Gleicher
Luis Goncalves
Steven Gortler
Masataka Goto
Craig Gotsman
Mark Green
Philip Green
Ned Greene
G. Greiner
Cindy Grimm
Georges G. Grinstein
Larry Gritz
Radek Grzeszczuk
Brian Guenter
Leo Guibas
Qingjian Guo
Paul Haeberli
James Hahn
Eric Haines
Roy Hall
Mark Halstead
Mark Hammel
Blake Hannaford
Charles D. Hansen
Andy Hanson
Steven Harrington
John Hart
Martial Hebert
Paul Heckbert
David Heeger
Hans-Christian Hege
Roger D. Hersch
Debby Hindus
Larry F. Hodges
Karl Heinz Höhne
John M. Hollerbach
Mike Hollick
Matthew Holton
Hugues Hoppe
James Hourihan
Donald House
Siu Chi Hsu
Philip Hubbard
John Hughes
Katsushi Ikeuchi
Adam Janin
F.W. Jansen
Fran Januck
Bert Juettler
Chris Johnson
Michael B. Johnson
Peter Jones
Zoran Kačić-Alesić
Florian Kainz
Jim Kajiya
Michael Kallay
Deven Kalra
Takeo Kanade
Kazufumi Kaneda
Sing Bing Kang
D. Karron
Michael Kass
Arie Kaufman
Timothy L. Kay
Michael Kelley
Jim Kent
Isaac V. Kerlow
Ron Kikinis
Chris King
Reinhard Klein
Stanley Klein
Gudrun Klinker
Hyeongseok Ko
Richard Koch
Jeff Koechling
R. Kraft
Axel Kramer
Tosiyasu Kunii
David Kurlander
Phil Lacroute
Eric Lafortune
David Laidlaw
James Landay
David Lane
Jintae Lee
Yuencheng Lee
Wolfgang Leister
Jed Lengyel
Raph Levien
Haim Levkowitz
Jacques Levy-Vehel
J.P. Lewis
Ming Lin
Jim Lipscomb
Dani Lischinski
Peter Litwinowicz
Charles Loop
Tom Lyche
Rob Mace

Blair MacIntyre
Jock Mackinlay
Sang Mah
Dinesh Manocha
Marilyn Mantei
Steve Marchner
Lee Markosian
Joe Marks
Dan McCabe
Michael McCool
Mike McKenna
Leonard McMillan
Radomír Měch
Barbara Meier
Jai Menon
Gavin Miller
Mark Mine
Rosane Minghim
Brian Mirtich
Don Mitchell
Martin Moeck
Steve Molnar
John Montrym
Robin Morris
Eric Mortensen
J. Michael Moshell
H. Mueller
Ken Musgrave
Karol Myszkowski
Ahmad H. Nasri
Bruce Naylor
Shawn Neely
Ulrich Neumann
Tom Ngo
Gregory Nielson
Jeff Nimeroff
Paul Ning
Tomoyuki Nishita
James F. O'Brien
Eben Ostby
Dinesh K. Pai
Jamie Painter
Randy Pausch
Darwyn Peachey
Alex Pentland
Ken Perlin
Jorg Peters
Cary B. Phillips
Robert Phillips
L.A. Piegl
Steve Pieper
Mike Pique
Tom Porter
Frits Post
Helmut Pottmann
Joanna Power
H. Prautzsch
Glenn M. Preminger
Przemyslaw Prusinkiewicz
Claude Puech
David Pugh
Ari Rappoport
Richard Redner
Mathew Regan
Barry Reich
Karl Reinig
G. Renner
Shriram Revankar
Henry Rich
George Robertson
Philip K. Robertson
Doug Roble
Jon Rokne
David Rosenthal
Jarek Rossignac
Holly Rushmeier
Malcolm Sabin
Takafumi Saito
Mike Salisbury
John Salmon
D. Saupe
Stefan Schaal
Ferdi Scheepers
Daniel Schikore
Christophe Schlick
William Schroeder
Tom Sederberg
Doree Seligmann
Carlo Sequin
Jonathan Shade
Rob Shakespeare
Michael Shantzis
Chris Shaw
Mikio Shinya
Peter Shirley
Ken Shoemake
Deborah Silver
David Simon
Eero Simoncelli
Karl Sims
Karan Singh
Kenneth Sloan
Philipp Slusallek
David Small
Alvy Ray Smith
Brian Smith
Brian Smits
Doug Smythe
John Snyder
Lisa Sobierajski
Robert F. Sproull
Jos Stam
Bart Stander
Cliff Stein
Werner Stuetzle
James Stewart
Eric Stollnitz
Maureen Stone
Steve Strassmann
Catherine Stringfellow
Wim Sweldens
Gabriel Taubin
Russell M. Taylor II
Russell Taylor
Seth Teller
Demetri Terzopoulos
Daniel Thalmann
Nadia Thalmann
Bond-Jay Ting
Carlo Tomasi
Jay Torborg
Takashi Totsuka
Joan Truckenbrod
Greg Turk
Matthew Turk
Sam Uselton
Allen Van Gelder
Kees van Overveld
Jarke van Wijk
Michiel van de Panne
Mark VandeWettering
Michael W. Vannier
Amitabh Varshney
Eric Veach
Luiz Velho
Brian Von Herzen
Douglas Voorhies
John Wallace
Dan Wallach
Colin Ware
Joe Warren
Keith Waters
Val Watson
Lloyd Watts
Peter Wavish
Jason Weber
Kevin Weiler
William Welch
Ruediger Westermann
Stephen Westin
Lee Westover
Ross T. Whitaker
Scott Whitman
Richard Wildes
Jane Wilhelms
John Williams
Lance Williams
Reg Willson
Georges Winkenbach
Andrew Witkin
Andrew Woo
Adam Wood-Gaines
Wayne Wooten
Xiaolin Wu
Charles Wüthrich
Brian Wyvill
Roni Yagel
Yanover Yanover
Chris Yessios
Jeffery Yost
Robert Zeleznik
David Zeltzer
Mark Zimmer
Mike Zyda

Exhibitors

(as of 30 April 1996)

3D Construction Company
3D/Eye, c/o Blue Sky Events
3Dfx Interactive
3Dlabs, Inc.
3Name3D/Yglesias Wallock Divekar Inc.
3rd Dimension Technologies, Inc.
4D Vision
5D Ltd.
5DT
A K Peters, Ltd.
ABC News Videosource
Academic Press
Accom, Inc.
Acuris Incorporated
Adaptive Optics Associates, Inc., a United Technologies Company
Addison-Wesley Publishing Company
Adobe Systems Inc.
Advanced Imaging
Advanced Media Production Center
Advanced Visual Systems Inc.
Alias/Wavefront
Alien Skin Software
Anacapa Micro Products, Inc.
Analogus Labs
AniCom Inc.
Animation Magazine
AP Professional
Apple Computer, Inc.
Apunix Computer Services
(Art)n Laboratory
Artbeats Software, Inc.
Ascension Technology Corporation
AT&T
AtLightSpeed, Inc.
auto.des.sys, Inc.
Autodesk, Inc.
Autologic Information International
Autometric Inc.
AV Video/Multimedia Producer
AVID Technology Inc.
B&L Engineering/Oxford Metrics, Ltd.
Balboa Capital
BARCO, Inc.
BioVision
Bit 3 Computer Corporation
Bushey Virtual Construction
CAD Institute
CalComp
Caligari Corporation
Cambridge Animation Systems
Camera Di Commercio di Milano-D.I.M.I.
Canon U.S.A., Inc.
CBS News Archives
CELCO
CGSD Corporation
Charles River Media
Chromatek Inc.
Chyron Corporation
Ciprico Inc.
CIRAD - Unite de modelisation des plantes
Cirrus Logic, Inc.
Cisco Systems
Cogswell College
Computer Graphics World
Consan Incorporated
Coryphaeus Software, Inc.
Creative Digital Research
Crystal River Engineering
CST Entertainment
CTX Opto, Inc.
Cyberware
Data Translation
Denim Software
DeskStation Technology
Desktop Engineering Magazine
Desktop Images
Diamond Multimedia Systems, Inc.
Diaquest, Inc.
Digimation, Inc.
Digital Compositing Systems, Inc.
Digital Equipment Corporation
Digital Equipment Corporation-Semiconductor
Digital Processing Systems Inc.
Digital Video Magazine
Digits 'n Art Software, Inc.
Dimension X
Division, Inc.
EarthLink Network
Eastman Kodak Company
Electric Image, Inc.
ElectroGIG, Inc.
Elsa, Inc.
ENCAD, Inc.
ENEL S.P.A.
Engineering Animation, Inc.
Ensemble Designs
Epson America, Inc.
Eurographics
Evans & Sutherland Computer Corporation
Extron Electronics
Falcon Systems
FARO Technologies Inc.
Fast Electronic U.S., Inc.
Film & Video Magazine
Folsom Research
Fractal Design Corporation
Fujitsu Microelectronics, Inc.
FWB, Inc.
General Reality Company
G.E.V.T., Inc.
GW Hannaway & Associates
Hash Inc.
Herstal Automation
Hewlett-Packard Company
IBM Corporation
I.D. Magazine
IEEE Computer Society
Illustra Information Technologies, Inc.
Image Technology (ND3D: 3D Hard Copies)
IMAGICA Corporation of America
IMAGINA-INA
Immersion Corporation
in:sync corporation
Integrated Computing Engines, Inc. (ICE)
Integrated Research
Interactive Effects
Intergraph Corporation
International Memory Products of Illinois, Inc.
Intrek Systems
IRIS Graphics
Jackrabbit Productions
James Grunder & Associates, Inc.
John Wiley & Sons, Inc.
Kingston Technology Corporation
Laser InSpeck, Inc.
LaserMaster Corporation
LegaSys International, Inc.
Leitch Incorporated
Lightscape Technologies, Inc.
Lightwave Communications, Inc.
Lightwork Design Ltd.
Linker Systems, Inc.
Lockheed Martin c/o Mediatech
Logitech
Macmillan Computer Publishing
Macromedia
Management Graphics, Inc.
Matrox Electronic Systems
Maximum Strategy, Inc.
Mediascape Corporation
MegaDrive Systems, Inc.
MetaTools, Inc.
Micropolis Corporation
Miller Freeman Inc.
Millimeter Magazine
Minicomputer Exchange
Minolta Corporation
Miranda Technologies Inc.
Mirus Industries Corporation
Mitsubishi Electronics America, Inc.
MMS GmbH
Montpellier Languedoc-Roussillon Technopole
Morgan Kaufmann Publishers
Motion Analysis Corporation
MultiGen Inc.
Muse Technologies
Mutoh America Inc.
NEC Electronics Inc.
NewMedia Magazine
NewTek, Inc.
NHK-HDTV Group
Nichimen Graphics, Inc.
NICOGRAPH Association
Nio Software
Northern Digital Inc.
Numerical Algorithms Group, Inc.
NVision, Inc.
O'Reilly & Associates Inc
Odyssey Productions
Omniview
On Production
Onyx Computing, Inc.
Orphan Technologies
Oxberry
P.E. Photron (Precision Equipment Photron)
Pacific Data Images (PDI)
Paradigm Simulation, Inc.
Paragraph International
Parallax Graphics, Inc.
Parity Systems Inc.
PC Video Conversion
PCI-Silicon Graphics World
Pixar
Pixibox
Play Incorporated
Polhemus
Portable Graphics, Inc.
Positron Publishing
Pre/Folio Magazine
Professional Marketing Services
Proxima Corporation
PWS Publishing/ITP
Quantel, Inc.
Questar Productions
QuVIS Inc
Radiance Software
Radius Inc
Red Dog Media
REM Infografica S.A.
The Republic Group, Inc.
Research Triangle Institute
RGB Spectrum
Rhythm & Hues Studios
Ron Scott Inc.
S-MOS Systems, Inc.
Savannah College of Art and Design
Scala, Inc.
Scientific & Computing Animation
Scitex Digital Video, Inc.
Screen Actors Guild
Seiko Instruments USA Inc.
SensAble Devices Inc.
Sense8 Corporation
Side Effects
Sierra Design Labs
Sigma Electronics, Inc.
Silicon Graphics, Inc.
Society of Motion Picture and Television Engineers (SMPTE)
Softimage/Microsoft
Sony Pictures High Definition Center
Springer-Verlag
Sprint c/o Pepper Associates
Square L.A.
StereoGraphics Corporation
Stim
Storage Concepts
Strata, Inc
Sun Microsystems Computer Company
Supercomputing '96
Superscape
Syndesis Corporation
Synthetic Images, Inc.
Tech-Source Inc.
Tektronix Inc.
Template Graphics Software, Inc.
Texas Memory Systems, Inc.
Thomson Broadcast, Inc.
Toon Boom Technology Inc.
Transoft Technology
Vangard Technology, Inc.
Van Nostrand Reinhold
ViaGrafix
Video Systems Magazine
Videomedia, Inc.
Viewpoint DataLabs International Inc.
Viewsonic
Virtuality, Inc.
Wacom Technology
The Walt Disney Company
Western Scientific, Inc.
Westwood Studios
Winsted Corporation
Wired Magazine
Xaos Tools
Yamaha Systems

Cover Image Credits

Front Cover

"Haystacks at Sunset"

In this impressionist image from an animation of Monet-style haystacks, we demonstrate our rendering algorithm which creates painterly style images and is suitable for animation. Geometric 3D surface models have been populated with particles which are rendered in screen space as individual brush strokes. The color, orientation, and size of brush strokes are determined from reference pictures which are traditionally rendered images of the underlying geometry. This technique improves on previous methods by maintaining frame-to-frame coherence for animations.

The painterly renderer is particularly well-suited for abstracting natural textures like the cloudy sky, hay, and plowed ground in this example because it creates texture by composing the image with many semi-transparent textured brush strokes that vary randomly in position, color, orientation, and size based on user-selectable parameters. We have used many traditional painting techniques such as building up layers of paint, allowing silhouette edges to be broken by brush strokes, and letting the brush strokes define the detailed texture of objects to create the painterly look.

Ken Hahn, Scott Johnston, Jason Herschaft, and Craig Thayer wrote parts of the painterly renderer. Many thanks to Dave Mullins and Andrea Losch for modeling and rendering and to David Laidlaw who provided many hours of production support. We are grateful to Al Barr and Scott Fraser of Caltech and to Hammerhead Productions for providing production facilities.

Reference: "Painterly Rendering for Animation," Barbara J. Meier, pp. 477–484.

Frontispiece

"Talisman-rendered Farm Scene"

This image was rendered using a hardware simulator of the Talisman graphics architecture. The actual hardware will render animations of scenes with this quality at 60 frames per second and higher. Scene design courtesy of Andrew Glassner; modelling and animation courtesy of the Microsoft Blender group.

Reference: "Talisman: Commodity Realtime 3D Graphics for the PC," Jay Torborg and Jim Kajiya, pp. 353–364.

Back Cover, left

"Multiresolution Views of the Julia Set"

This figure shows several frames from a multiresolution video sequence of a fractal pattern known as a Julia set. The multiresolution video representation allows a viewer to zoom in and out in both space and time. The top cell shows an entire frame from the animation. The next two cells show zooming in on the lower-left vortex of this fiery beast. The bottom three cells show motion-blurred frames from "zooming out" temporally on the video sequence.

Reference: "Multiresolution Video," Adam Finkelstein, Charles E. Jacobs, David H. Salesin, pp. 281–290.

Back Cover, center top

"Blue Screen Boots"

The goblet and boots on the left are two image objects, or sprites, extracted automatically from shots (not shown) against a pure blue backing and then against a black backing. The sprites are then recomposited with a new background on the right. This shows that an appropriate alpha channel has been created for each sprite to convey its transparency information. The technique is a new one called triangulation matting. Blue screen matting is notoriously difficult, especially for blue or cyan objects, and is not algorithmic as practiced. The triangulation technique is algorithmic but works only for objects that don't move, such as these. Triangulation does not require constant color backings nor the ideal conditions of this example. It requires only that the two backings be completely different, pixel by pixel.

Reference: "Blue Screen Matting," Alvy Ray Smith and James F. Blinn, pp. 259–268.

Back Cover, center middle

"Reconstruction of a prosthetic foot"

These three images demonstrate our automatic procedure for reconstructing a B-spline surface model from a set of 3D points. The first image shows a set of 20,021 3D points obtained by laser scanning the surface of a prosthetic foot. The second image shows an initial reconstructed surface consisting of 29 (bicubic) B-spline patches. Both the network of patches and the parametrizations of the data points over these patches are determined without user assistance. The use of a surface spline construction permits an efficient algorithm for fitting the surface while maintaining tangent plane continuity between patches. The third image shows a surface of 156 B-spline patches obtained after adaptive refinement and refitting. This surface deviates from the points by no more than 0.27% of the object diameter.

The prosthetic foot, courtesy of Moeller Design and Development Inc. (Seattle, WA), was created for Flex-Foot Inc. (Laguna, CA). It was scanned by Ken Birdwell of Technical Arts Co. (Bellevue, WA), using a 3-axis line laser digitizer. The object was mounted on a glass table over a mirrored surface, allowing the entire surface to be scanned without repositioning the object.

Reference: "Automatic Reconstruction of B-Spline Surfaces of Arbitrary Topological Type," Matthias Eck and Hugues Hoppe, pp. 325–334.

Back Cover, center bottom

"Wind over Australia"

This is a visualization of wind velocity over Australia that is based on data from a numerical weather model. Higher velocity wind is represented by larger arrows. The arrows were deposited along streamlines in an end-to-end fashion so that the eye follows the chains of arrows. The streamlines underlying this image were placed by an optimization procedure that uses an energy function that penalizes overly dense or sparse regions of streamline.

Wind simulation data is courtesy of Glenn Wightwick of IBM Australia, and the earth image is courtesy of Geosphere, Inc. We thank Lloyd Treinish of the IBM T.J. Watson Research Center for his extensive aid with this data.

Reference: "Image-Guided Streamline Placement," Greg Turk and David C. Banks, pp. 453–460.

Back Cover, right

"A Sense of Time"

This image shows frames from an animation of the development of a metallic patina on a small copper statue of a buddha. The buddha model was created from a Cyberware scan and consists of approximately 60,000 small, evenly sized triangles. The various stages of the development of the patina were simulated in the RenderMan shading language. A shader was written that modeled a three-layered surface: base copper, a tarnish layer, and a green patina. The thickness of different layers was varied as a function of time according to position and other factors, using devices such as exposure and accessibility maps. Thanks to Brian Curless for scanning the statue and Matt Pharr for computing the accessibility map.

Reference: "Modeling and Rendering of Metallic Patinas," Julie Dorsey and Pat Hanrahan, pp. 387–396.

SIGGRAPH Professional Chapters

Brazil

Sao Paulo ACM SIGGRAPH
Sergio Martinelli
Rua Bairi 294
SP-05059
Sao Paulo
Brazil
Sao_Paulo_Chapter@siggraph.org

Bulgaria

Sofia ACM SIGGRAPH
Stoyan Maleshkov
Technical Univ. of Sofia
Dept of Prog & Computer Appl
Sofia 1756
Bulgaria
Sofia_Chapter@siggraph.org

Canada

Vancouver B.C. ACM SIGGRAPH
Tom Berryhill
PO Box 29147
1996 W. Broadway
Vancouver BC
Canada
Vancouver_BC_Chapter@siggraph.org

France

Paris ACM SIGGRAPH
Thierry Frey
c/o SUPINFOCOM - Terita 3000
2, rue Henri Matisse
59300 Aulnoye-lez-Valenciennes
France
Paris_Chapter@siggraph.org

Israel

Central Israel ACM SIGGRAPH
Craig Gotsman
Dept of Computer Science
Technion-Israel Inst of Tech
Haifa
Israel
Central_Israel_Chapter@siggraph.org

Mexico

Mexico City ACM SIGGRAPH
Arnulfo Zepeda
Mineria 15-401
Col. Escandon
Mexico D.F. 11800
Mexico
Mexico_City_Chapter@siggraph.org

United Kingdom

London ACM SIGGRAPH
Len Breen
31 Old Gloucester St
Bloomsbury
London,
UK
London_Chapter@siggraph.org

United States

California

Los Angeles ACM SIGGRAPH
Aliza Corson
PO Box 90698
Worldway Postal Center
Los Angeles, CA 90009-0698
Los_Angeles_Chapter@siggraph.org

San Francisco ACM SIGGRAPH
Connie Siu
1201 Park Ave Suite 203A
Emeryville, CA 94608
San_Francisco_Chapter@siggraph.org

Silicon Valley ACM SIGGRAPH
Fran Zandonella
PO Box 1205
Mountain View, CA 94042-1205
Silicon_Valley_Chapter@siggraph.org

Colorado

Denver/Boulder ACM SIGGRAPH
Mike McCarthy
PO Box 61402
Cherry Creek Station
Denver, CO 80206-8402
Denver-Boulder_Chapter@siggraph.org

Florida

Ft. Lauderdale ACM SIGGRAPH
Garry M. Paxinos
Metro Link Inc
4711 N. Powerline Road
Fort Lauderdale, FL 33309
Fort_Lauderdale_Chapter@siggraph.org

Orlando ACM SIGGRAPH
Colleen Cleary
PO Box 2208
Winter Park, FL 32790-2208
Orlando_Chapter@siggraph.org

Tampa Bay ACM SIGGRAPH
Steve Pidgeon
PO Box 20782
Tampa, FL 33622
Tampa_Bay_Chapter@siggraph.org

SIGGRAPH Professional Chapters

Georgia

Atlanta ACM SIGGRAPH
D. Alan Stewart
PO Box 250382
Atlanta, GA 30325
Atlanta_Chapter@siggraph.org

Massachusetts

New England ACM SIGGRAPH
Michael Silton
PO Box 194
Bedford, MA 01730
New_England_Chapter@siggraph.org

Minnesota

Minneapolis/St. Paul ACM SIGGRAPH
Stan Bissinger
School of Communication Arts
2526 27th Ave South
Minneapolis, MN 55406
Minneapolis-StPaul_Chapter@siggraph.org

New Jersey

Princeton ACM SIGGRAPH
Douglas Dixon
P.O. Box 1324
Princeton, NJ 08542
Princeton_Chapter@siggraph.org

New Mexico

Rio Grande ACM SIGGRAPH
David Callahan
P.O. Box 8352
Albuquerque, NM 87108-8352
Rio_Grande_Chapter@siggraph.org

New York

New York City ACM SIGGRAPH
Debra Herschmann
SIGMA Imaging
622 3rd Ave, 30th Floor
New York, NY 10017
New_York_Chapter@siggraph.org

North Carolina

NC Research Triangle ACM SIGGRAPH
Randy Brown
SAS Campus Drive RA 459
Cary, NC 27513
Research_Triangle_Chapter@siggraph.org

Texas

Dallas Area ACM SIGGRAPH
Aaron Hightower
Paradigm Simulation Inc.
14900 Landmark Suite 400
Dallas, TX 75240
Dallas_Area_Chapter@siggraph.org

Houston Area ACM SIGGRAPH
Tom Ledoux
2501 Tanglewilde #203
Houston, TX 77063
Houston_Chapter@siggraph.org

Washington

Tri-Cities Washington ACM SIGGRAPH
Donald R. Jones
Pacific Northwest Lab
MS K1-96
PO Box 999
Richland, WA 99352
Tri-Cities_Chapter@siggraph.org

Professional Chapters Committee

Scott Lang, SIGGRAPH Director for Professional Chapters
United Nations International School
24-50 FDR Drive
New York, NY 10010
Phone: +1 (212) 684-7400, Ext. 3270
FAX: +1 (212) 889 - 8959
lang@siggraph.org

Garry Paxinos, Professional Chapters Webmaster
Metro Link Inc
4711 N. Powerline Road
Fort Lauderdale, FL 33309
Phone: +1 (305) 938-0283 Ext. 414
FAX: +1 (305) 938-1982
pax@siggraph.org

Colleen Cleary
Professional Chapters Editor, Computer Graphics
Orange County Sheriff's Office
55 West Pineloch Avenue
Orlando, FL 32806
Phone: +1 (407) 836-4602
FAX: +1 (407) 858-4798
cleary@magicnet.net

Index

(Pages marked with * contain panel summaries)

Index